W9-BXE-585

CHIEF CONTEMPORARY DRAMATISTS

Third Series

TWENTY PLAYS FROM THE RECENT DRAMA OF THE
UNITED STATES, GREAT BRITAIN, GERMANY, AUSTRIA
FRANCE, ITALY, SPAIN, RUSSIA, HUNGARY, CZECHOSLO-
VAKIA, THE YIDDISH THEATRE, AND SCANDINAVIA

SELECTED AND EDITED BY

THOMAS H. DICKINSON

EDITOR, CHIEF CONTEMPORARY DRAMATISTS, FIRST AND SECOND SERIES, ETC.
AUTHOR, AN OUTLINE OF CONTEMPORARY DRAMA, CONTEMPORARY DRAMA
OF ENGLAND, THE CASE OF AMERICAN DRAMA, ETC.

HOUGHTON MIFFLIN COMPANY

The Riverside Press Cambridge

The Riverside Press
CAMBRIDGE · MASSACHUSETTS
PRINTED IN THE U.S.A.

CONTENTS

INTRODUCTION

THIS volume is the third in the series of collections of contemporary plays published under the general title of "Chief Contemporary Dramatists," of which the first was issued in 1915 and the second in 1921. The first volume of the series contained twenty plays, the second volume eighteen plays, the third volume now published again contains twenty plays, making a total in the three volumes published to date of fifty-eight plays from the contemporary drama of England, Ireland, the United States, Germany, France, Russia, Italy, Spain, Belgium, Austria, Hungary, Czechoslovakia, Norway, Sweden, Denmark, Iceland and the Yiddish theater.

We have, then, in these books a single conspectus of the state of dramatic authorship in Europe and North America in our own times. Any attempt to interpret the deeper movements of this period, as these are displayed in the evolving forms of dramatic art, and in the substance, attitudes and world outlook of the plays themselves, is outside the purpose of the present introductory note as it is probably beyond the powers of any one now writing. For this purpose the plays speak for themselves, and they will continue to speak an ever-varying language as time has its way with them. Merely from the external point of view, as evidencing the changing interests of succeeding epochs of the same era and the shifting of dramatic activity here and there across the face of the western world, the plays included in this volume offer abundant material for comment and speculation.

In the first volume of the series, which constituted also the first attempt to survey selectively the modern movement of the theater in mass, it was considered desirable to define the term "contemporary" rather liberally. This was for the reason that it was necessary to include not only a representation of the playwriting of the moment of publication, but as well of those orders of playwriting which in themselves contained the root sources of the contemporary movement. In this volume, then, there were included plays composed at periods as widely separated as 1883 for *Beyond Human Power* and 1910 for *The Madras House* and *The Scarecrow*. While Ibsen was omitted from representation, the entire volume was in fact a tribute to the Ibsen influence. The majority of the plays in the volume were the products of radical and recently liberated thought movements, superimposed upon the dramaturgy of a period in which it had hardly been the function of the theater to think at all.

The second volume covered a narrower scope of years. Though some of the plays included were written as early as the beginning Nineties, the majority belonged to the early years of the Twentieth Century. It was a period of great activity, which nevertheless for sheer dynamics of dramatic imagination did not compare with the last decade of the last century. Much was made of a demand for emancipation from the forms of the well-made play, but this demand had not yet eventuated in new forms. And in the hands of the men of the second generation the old radicalisms began to sound a little hollow. In avoiding the formulas of the well-made play, dramatists as a rule had no better recourse than to turn back to comedy of manners and to romance.

With the Third Series we come to an independent epoch of dramatic history set within narrow limits of time. As certainly as the first period was dominated by the technical and intellectual pressure of the genius of Ibsen, this new era is dominated by the interests, attitudes, mental complexes and revolutionary form valuations of the period appertaining to the war. Not all of the plays in this volume trace directly to the war. But few of them would be completely understandable save in the light of the social and individual psychology that the war produced. The earliest play included in this Third Series is Wedekind's *Such is Life*, a play which, though written more than ten years before the outbreak of the war, may still be read as an illumination of some of the war's aspects. Many of the plays were written after the war by young men whose youth itself was dominated by the approaching catastrophe, young men to whom the revolt of Ibsen is as far away and historic as is the revolt of the French romanticists now just a century ago.

Let us now inquire as to what we may learn from the distribution of the plays included in these three volumes. In the first volume Great Britain was represented by eight plays, the United States by four plays, Germany and France by two apiece, Belguim, Norway, Sweden and Russia by one each. This was the period in which the drama of radical ideas still dominated the theater of Europe and America. As this drama had found active expression in England, moreover as the Irish theater had been one of the most vigorous of the enterprises of the turning century, it was appropriate enough that the playwriting of England should be well represented in a book designed for English speaking readers. In the second volume the situation had changed. The English and Irish representation had sunk to five; that of the United States to three. In comparison with Great Britain the drama of the United States was moving forward; in comparison with the continent the British drama was slipping backward. But the best plays on the continent were not appearing in the old familiar places. The drama of Germany and France was marking time; the drama of Scandinavia was receding from the world stage after the heroic interlude of Ibsen, Bjornson and Strindberg. The real advance in this transition period was taking place in centers off the main road of theatrical history hitherto, in Moscow, Vienna, Rome and Madrid.

When we come to consider the geographical distribution of dramatic movements as represented in the Third Series, we notice first the even more marked decrease in the representation given to the drama of the English speaking world, and the transfer of the United States from second place to a leading position in that category. The decline in comparative representation of English and Continental drama is partly to be explained by an unquestioned slump in creativeness in the British theater during the recent period; also by a no less marked increase in fecundity in several focal points on the continent. Most of the playwrights of first rank in England have either laid down their pens or are doing nothing to enhance their fame. J. M. Barrie is silent; Granville-Barker has turned to making translations of foreign plays. Galsworthy, Drinkwater, Maugham, Ervine continue to compose but offer nothing on the level with their early work. Notable is the scarcity of younger writers in positions of high rank. The Irish theater affords only one playwright, Sean O'Casey, who can compare in gusto with the earlier makers of this theater. Shaw does indeed continue in his sixties and seventies an imaginative fecundity that rounds out one of the most remarkable careers of our times. But Shaw has no followers. His influence has been tonic in the reform of our social structure and in the freshening of our private thinking. He has not created a school of drama nor has he distributed his influence among young playwrights in his own and other lands. Unfortunately we are not yet permitted to include a copy of one of Shaw's plays in the series.

If the English speaking theater tends at present to decline, such is not the case with the theater of America. Yesterday colonial, the American theater has in its best works cut entirely the bonds that tied it alike to the mother country and to the continent. In seeking to make things new, to treat American themes in American ways, the new playwrights have naturally paid the price of experiment. Some of their work shows the prentice hand, but it is an apprenticeship to their own standards and not to any external cult. Even the crudeness occasionally to be found in the American theater is to be preferred to the neatly tailored, factitious work fashioned by the old-line playwrights in England for American consumption. Innovation does not imply merit; on the other hand neither does convention, and in the theater of our times the presumption is on the side of the man who dares. One could mention a dozen plays written in America in as many years in which the objective has been beyond the powers of the dramatist. The American theater is the better because the experiments were made.

Paralleling the comparative decline in the British theater there has been a like decline in the French theater. Yesterday the drama of France either directly or indirectly dominated the theater of Europe. The prestige of this domination lasted after the fact itself was no more. The two most vital dramatists of the last generation in France were Rostand and Brieux. Neither one of these represented the characteristic French dramatic formula of the time; both were distinguished for individual rather than representative qualities. The French theater has not gone the way of either. It has refined its subtilities into mysticism and sharpened its technique until it is capable only of treating little themes.

If in the volume before us it is noticed that a smaller place must be given to the drama of nations formerly held to be leaders in the world stage, it will be remarked as well that an increased representation is given to those countries and races which were before not represented at all or by only a single play. The break-up of the Central Powers, Germany and Austria-Hungary, had two important results in theatrical history. It encouraged an increased productiveness on the part of the dramatists of hitherto submerged groups, and it provided for these the facilities for breaking through onto the world stage. Molnar had been writing successful plays since 1907, but it was not until he stood forth as the Hungarian dramatist *par excellence* that he took his place definitely in the fore-front of European drama. There has been a Bohemian drama on the Ibsen model for many years; the elevation of Czechoslovakia to nationality was followed in due order by the appearance of a characteristic native drama which had the vitality immediately to make its way to international recognition. The Yiddish drama of the submerged races of Western Russia had found an outlet among transplanted peoples in New York City. It was not until the Russian Revolution and the freeing of Poland that the crowning dramatic masterpiece of the Yiddish theater found its way to the stages of Europe and America.

The force that finally decreed the end of the old drama and the advent of the new was that epoch-making convulsion of psychologies of which the physical manifestation was the war. Contrary to common belief, this force began to operate long before the outbreak of hostilities. Turning sometimes in the direction of anarchy and innovation, it was, in the theater at any rate, quite as likely to express itself in the form of reaction away from the Twentieth Century back to earlier forms of theatric expression. The revival of interest in the *commedia dell'arte*, in the mediæval drama, in masks and marionettes is an example of this. So also is the return to the formal restraints of poetic drama so beautifully illustrated in Hofmannsthal's *Electra* and Sem Benelli's *The Love of the Three Kings*. The drama of the Quinteros and of Sierra in Spain with its persistent note of mid-century humanitarianism, its stratified classes, its sense of sin and salvation; the drama of Sigurjónsson, which traces back to a primitive Teutonic communal strain, are as thoroughly in reaction against the age of Ibsen as is the work of the futurists in Italy and the expressionists in Germany.

But the characteristic note of the modern revolt is not found in nostalgia and return. There is not space here to refer to the various types of innovation represented in this book. These may well speak for themselves. But it may be interesting to note the kinds of plays that are not represented. There are here no problem plays as such, no comedies of manners, no romantic plays. There are no villains, heroes, raisonneurs, courtship scenes, seductions, confession or repentance scenes. There are no "ideals" in the derogatory sense in which Ibsen and Shaw use the word. Far away are the times when a facile program of "liberation," social or individual, seemed to hold the key to Utopia. Some features of the drama represented in this book are undoubtedly to be ascribed to a passing phase of the psychology of fatigue. Such is the fashion, not uncommon in the post-war drama, of "playing with life," of treating the theater as a form of sport, of shunning all integrations and savoring the bitter-sweet of disillusion. Other features trace back to profounder factors in our new inquisitiveness, to our increasing interest in the psychologies of primitive races, and to our newly awakened concern with all that lies below the levels of consciousness.

Here are twenty plays selected out of the hundreds and thousands of plays written and produced in our era. The questions inevitably will arise, "Why these plays? Why not other plays?" To these questions the simplest answer will be the best. These plays are presented because they seem to the editor best to combine merit in themselves and representative character in a group. The editor would have been glad to include many other plays. Some he excluded with great reluctance. But at the end the decision was finally simplified by the posing of another question, "If different plays were to be used, which of these should be excluded?"

It may now be well to say a few words about the real limitations that condition a work of this kind. Contrary to the views of some, these do not derive largely from copyright restrictions. These considerations have been so slight in the making of this book as to be negligible. The real limitations are those inherent in the principle of perspective. Probably few scholars who are supremely interested in the drama of any nation will be satisfied that the drama of that nation is here adequately represented. And they may be right. No attempt has been made to represent the various national dramas of Europe and America. The purpose has been to present a typical picture of the drama of western civilization as this manifests itself in various national centers. This is a very different, and, in the mind of the editor, a more important thing to do. In the former case we would get a wide expanse of lowland which would teach us little of the whole. In the latter we see as from a distance only the high hills and mountain peaks. There exists a very useful and sufficiently valid test of vitality for contemporary works of the imagination. This test consists in the power of the work to break its way through national boundaries into international understanding and use. The idea that foreign nations serve as a contemporary posterity in the judgment of works of the imagination is not a new one. But it is assuming greater validity day by day as the movements of inter-communication and inter-dependence fuse the western world into something approaching solidarity. In this respect the beginnings of selection were already made for the editor. With very few exceptions all the plays in this book have demonstrated their power not only in the narrow field of the homeland but on a world stage.

Even with this assistance there was left an ample discretion in choice. With the exception always of the kindly services which have been rendered by colleagues and friends, and within the limits imposed by occasional flat negatives from holders of rights, the collection here offered represents as nearly as possible the editor's own responsibility and choice. It would be impossible to name the many who have placed the editor under obligations for courtesies and helpfulness. Among those whom a peculiar sense of indebtedness requires me to mention are Mr. H. G. Alsberg, Miss Teresa Carbonara, Mr. B. H. Clark, Mr. Louis How, Mr. Arthur Livingston, Mr. John Garrett Underhill, all of New York City; Mr. S. A. Eliot, Jr., of Northampton, Mass.; Mr. G. R. Noyes of Berkeley, California; Mr. Francesco Monotti of Genoa, Italy, and Mr. Otakar Vočadlo of Prague, Czechoslovakia.

THOMAS H. DICKINSON

THE EMPEROR JONES
By EUGENE O'NEILL

CHARACTERS

BRUTUS JONES, *Emperor*

HENRY SMITHERS, *A Cockney Trader*

AN OLD NATIVE WOMAN

LEM, *A Native Chief*

SOLDIERS, *Adherents of Lem*

THE LITTLE FORMLESS FEARS

JEFF

THE NEGRO CONVICTS

THE PRISON GUARD

THE PLANTERS

THE AUCTIONEER

THE SLAVES

THE CONGO WITCH-DOCTOR

THE CROCODILE GOD.

The action of the play takes place on an island in the West Indies as yet not self-determined by White Marines. The form of native government is, for the time being, an Empire.

SCENES

THE EMPEROR JONES

SCENE I

The audience chamber in the palace of the Emperor — a spacious, high-ceilinged room with bare, whitewashed walls. The floor is of white tiles. In the rear, to the left of center, a wide archway giving out on a portico with white pillars. The palace is evidently situated on high ground for beyond the portico nothing can be seen but a vista of distant hills, their summits crowned with thick groves of palm trees. In the right wall, center, a smaller arched doorway leading to the living quarters of the palace. The room is bare of furniture with the exception of one huge chair made of uncut wood which stands at center, its back to rear. This is very apparently the Emperor's throne. It is painted a dazzling, eye-smiting scarlet. There is a brilliant orange cushion on the seat and another smaller one is placed on the floor to serve as a footstool. Strips of matting, dyed scarlet, lead from the foot of the throne to the two entrances.

It is late afternoon but the sunlight still blazes yellowly beyond the portico and there is an oppressive burden of exhausting heat in the air.

As the curtain rises, a native Negro woman sneaks in cautiously from the entrance on the right. She is very old, dressed in cheap calico, barefooted, a red bandana handkerchief covering all but a few stray wisps of white hair. A bundle bound in colored cloth is carried over her shoulder on the end of a stick. She hesitates beside the doorway, peering back as if in extreme dread of being discovered. Then she begins to glide noiselessly, a step at a time, toward the doorway in the rear. At this moment, SMITHERS appears beneath the portico.

SMITHERS is a tall, stoop-shouldered man about forty. His bald head, perched on a long neck with an enormous Adam's apple, looks like an egg. The tropics have tanned his naturally pasty face with its small, sharp features to a sickly yellow, and native rum has painted his pointed nose to a startling red. His little, washy-blue eyes are red-rimmed and dart about him like a ferret's. His expression is one of unscrupulous meanness, cowardly and dangerous. He is dressed in a worn riding suit of dirty white drill, puttees, spurs, and wears a white cork helmet. A cartridge belt with an automatic revolver is around his waist. He carries a riding whip in his hand. He sees the woman and stops to watch her suspiciously. Then, making up his mind, he steps quickly on tiptoe into the room. The woman, looking back over her shoulder continually, does not see him until it is too late. When she does SMITHERS springs forward and grabs her firmly by the shoulder. She struggles to get away, fiercely but silently.

SMITHERS [*tightening his grasp — roughly*]. Easy! None o' that, me birdie. You can't wriggle out, now I got me 'ooks on yer.

WOMAN [*seeing the uselessness of struggling, gives way to frantic terror, and sinks to the ground, embracing his knees supplicatingly*]. No tell him! No tell him, Mister!

SMITHERS [*with great curiosity*]. Tell 'im? [*Then scornfully.*] Oh, you mean 'is bloomin' Majesty. What's the game, any'ow? What are you sneakin' away for? Been stealin' a bit, I s'pose.

[*He taps her bundle with his riding whip significantly.*]

WOMAN [*shaking her head vehemently*]. No, me no steal.

SMITHERS. Bloody liar! But tell me what's up. There's somethin' funny goin' on. I smelled it in the air first thing I got up this mornin'. You blacks are up to some devilment. This palace of 'is is like a bleedin' tomb. Where's all the 'ands? [*The woman keeps sullenly silent. SMITH-*

ERS raises his whip threateningly.] Ow, yer won't, won't yer? I'll show yer what's what.

WOMAN [coweringly]. I tell, Mister. You no hit. They go — all go.

[She makes a sweeping gesture toward the hills in the distance.]

SMITHERS. Run away — to the 'ills?

WOMAN. Yes, Mister. Him Emperor — Great Father. [She touches her forehead to the floor with a quick mechanical jerk.] Him sleep after eat. Then they go — all go. Me old woman. Me left only. Now me go too.

SMITHERS [his astonishment giving way to an immense, mean satisfaction]. Ow! So that's the ticket! Well, I know bloody well wot's in the air — when they runs orf to the 'ills. The tom-tom'll be thumping out there bloomin' soon. [With extreme vindictiveness.] And I'm bloody glad of it, for one! Serve 'im right! Puttin' on airs, the stinkin' nigger! 'Is Majesty! Gawd blimey! I only 'opes I'm there when they takes 'im out to shoot 'im. [Suddenly.] 'E's still 'ere all right, ain't 'e?

WOMAN. Him sleep.

SMITHERS. 'E's bound to find out soon as 'e wakes up. 'E's cunnin' enough to know when 'is time's come. [He goes to the doorway on right and whistles shrilly with his fingers in his mouth. The old woman springs to her feet and runs out of the doorway, rear. SMITHERS goes after her, reaching for his revolver.] Stop or I'll shoot! [Then stopping — indifferently.] Pop orf then, if yer like, yer black cow.

[He stands in the doorway, looking after her.]

[JONES enters from the right. He is a tall, powerfully-built, full-blooded Negro of middle age. His features are typically negroid, yet there is something decidedly distinctive about his face — an underlying strength of will, a hardy, self-reliant confidence in himself that inspires respect. His eyes are alive with a keen, cunning intelligence. In manner he is shrewd, suspicious, evasive. He wears a light blue uniform coat, sprayed with brass buttons, heavy gold chevrons on his shoulders, gold braid on the collar, cuffs, etc. His pants are bright red with a light blue stripe down the side. Patent leather laced boots with brass spurs, and a belt with a long-barreled, pearl-handled revolver in a holster complete his make up. Yet there is something not altogether ridiculous about his grandeur. He has a way of carrying it off.]

JONES [not seeing any one — greatly irritated and blinking sleepily — shouts]. Who dare whistle dat way in my palace? Who dare wake up de Emperor? I'll git de hide frayled off some o' you niggers sho'!

SMITHERS [showing himself — in a manner half-afraid and half-defiant]. It was me whistled to yer. [As JONES frowns angrily.] I got news for yer.

JONES [putting on his suavest manner, which fails to cover up his contempt for the white man]. Oh, it's you, Mister Smithers. [He sits down on his throne with easy dignity.] What news you got to tell me?

SMITHERS [coming close to enjoy his discomfiture]. Don't yer notice nothin' funny to-day?

JONES [coldly]. Funny? No. I ain't perceived nothin' of de kind!

SMITHERS. Then yer ain't so foxy as I thought yer was. Where's all your court? — [sarcastically] — the Generals and the Cabinet Ministers and all?

JONES [imperturbably]. Where dey mostly runs to minute I closes my eyes — drinkin' rum and talkin' big down in de town. [Sarcastically.] How come you don't know dat? Ain't you sousin' with 'em most every day?

SMITHERS [stung, but pretending indifference — with a wink]. That's part of the day's work. I got ter — ain't I — in my business?

JONES [contemptuously]. Yo' business!

SMITHERS [imprudently enraged]. Gawd blimey, you was glad enough for me ter take yer in on it when you landed here first. You didn't 'ave no 'igh and mighty airs in them days!

JONES [his hand going to his revolver like a flash — menacingly]. Talk polite, white man! Talk polite, you heah me! I'm boss heah now, is you fergettin'?

[*The Cockney seems about to challenge this last statement with the facts but something in the other's eyes holds and cows him.*]

SMITHERS [*in a cowardly whine*]. No 'arm meant, old top.

JONES [*condescendingly*]. I accepts yo' apology. [*Lets his hand fall from his revolver.*] No use'n you rakin' up ole times. What I was den is one thing. What I is now's another. You didn't let me in on yo' crooked work out o' no kind feelin's dat time. I done de dirty work fo' you — and most o' de brain work, too, fo' dat matter — and I was wu'th money to you, dat's de reason.

SMITHERS. Well, blimey, I give yer a start, didn't I? — when no one else would. I wasn't afraid to 'ire you like the rest was — 'count of the story about your breakin' jail back in the States.

JONES. No, you didn't have no s'cuse to look down on me fo' dat. You been in jail you'self mure'n once.

SMITHERS [*furiously*]. It's a lie! [*Then trying to pass it off by an attempt at scorn.*] Garn! Who told yer that fairy tale?

JONES. Dey's some tings I ain't got to be tole. I kin see 'em in folk's eyes. [*Then after a pause — meditatively.*] Yes, you sho' give me a start. And it didn't take long from dat time to git dese fool, woods' niggers right where I wanted dem. [*With pride.*] From stowaway to Emperor in two years! Dat's goin' some!

SMITHERS [*with curiosity*]. And I bet you got yer pile o' money 'id safe some place.

JONES [*with satisfaction*]. I sho' has! And it's in a foreign bank where no pusson don't ever git it out but me no matter what come. You didn't s'pose I was holdin' down dis Emperor job for de glory in it, did you? Sho'! De fuss and glory part of it, dat's only to turn de heads o' de low-flung, bush niggers dat's here. Dey wants de big circus show for deir money. I gives it to 'em an' I gits de money. [*With a grin.*] De long green, dat's me every time! [*Then rebukingly.*] But you ain't got no

kick agin me, Smithers. I'se paid you back all you done for me many times. Ain't I pertected you and winked at all de crooked tradin' you been doin' right out in de broad day? Sho' I has — and me makin' laws to stop it at de same time!

[*He chuckles.*]

SMITHERS [*grinning*]. But, meanin' no 'arm, you been grabbin' right and left yourself, ain't yer? Look at the taxes you've put on 'em! Blimey! You've squeezed 'em dry!

JONES [*chuckling*]. No, dey ain't *all* dry yet. I'se still heah, ain't I?

SMITHERS [*smiling at his secret thought*]. They're dry right now, you'll find out. [*Changing the subject abruptly.*] And as for me breakin' laws, you've broke 'em all yerself just as fast as yer made 'em.

JONES. Ain't I de Emperor? De laws don't go for him. [*Judicially.*] You heah what I tells you, Smithers. Dere's little stealin' like you does, and dere's big stealin' like I does. For de little stealin' dey gits you in jail soon or late. For de big stealin' dey makes you Emperor and puts you in de Hall o' Fame when you croaks. [*Reminiscently.*] If dey's one thing I learns in ten years on de Pullman ca's listenin' to de white quality talk, it's dat same fact. And when I gits a chance to use it I winds up Emperor in two years.

SMITHERS [*unable to repress the genuine admiration of the small fry for the large*]. Yes, yer turned the bleedin' trick, all right. Blimey, I never seen a bloke 'as 'ad the bloomin' luck you 'as.

JONES [*severely*]. Luck? What you mean — luck?

SMITHERS. I suppose you'll say as that swank about the silver bullet ain't luck — and that was what first got the fool blacks on yer side the time of the revolution, wasn't it?

JONES [*with a laugh*]. Oh, dat silver bullet! Sho' was luck! But I makes dat luck, you heah? I loads de dice! Yessuh! When dat murderin' nigger ole Lem hired to kill me takes aim ten feet away and his gun misses fire and I shoots him dead, what you heah me say?

SMITHERS. You said yer'd got a charm so's no lead bullet'd kill yer. You was so strong only a silver bullet could kill yer, you told 'em. Blimey, wasn't that swank for yer — and plain, fat-'eaded luck?

JONES [proudly]. I got brains and I uses 'em quick. Dat ain't luck.

SMITHERS. Yer know they wasn't 'ardly liable to get no silver bullets. And it was luck 'e didn't 'it you that time.

JONES [laughing]. And dere all dem fool bush niggers was kneelin' down and bumpin' deir heads on de ground like I was a miracle out o' de Bible. Oh Lawd, from dat time on I has dem all eatin' out of my hand. I cracks de whip and dey jumps through.

SMITHERS [with a sniff]. Yankee bluff done it.

JONES. Ain't a man's talkin' big what makes him big — long as he makes folks believe it? Sho', I talks large when I ain't got nothin' to back it up, but I ain't talkin' wild just de same. I knows I kin fool 'em — I knows it — and dat's backin' enough fo' my game. And ain't I got to learn deir lingo and teach some of dem English befo' I kin talk to 'em? Ain't dat wuk? You ain't never learned ary word er it, Smithers, in de ten years you been heah, dough you knows it's money in you' pocket tradin' wid 'em if you does. But you'se too shiftless to take de trouble.

SMITHERS [flushing]. Never mind about me. What's this I've 'eard about yer really 'avin' a silver bullet moulded for yourself?

JONES. It's playin' out my bluff. I has de silver bullet moulded and I tells 'em when de time comes I kills myself wid it. I tells 'em dat's 'cause I'm de on'y man in de world big enuff to git me. No use'n deir tryin'. And dey falls down and bumps deir heads. [He laughs.] I does dat so's I kin take a walk in peace widout no jealous nigger gunnin' at me from behind de trees.

SMITHERS [astonished]. Then you 'ad it made — 'onest?

JONES. Sho' did. Heah she be. [He takes out his revolver, breaks it, and takes the silver bullet out of one chamber.] Five lead

an' dis silver baby at de last. Don't she shine pretty?

[He holds it in his hand, looking at it admiringly, as if strangely fascinated.]

SMITHERS. Let me see.

[Reaches out his hand for it.]

JONES [harshly]. Keep yo' hands whar dey b'long, white man.

[He replaces it in the chamber and puts the revolver back on his hip.]

SMITHERS [snarling]. Gawd blimey! Think I'm a bleedin' thief, you would.

JONES. No, 'tain't dat. I knows you'se scared to steal from me. On'y I ain't 'lowin' nary body to touch dis baby. She's my rabbit's foot.

SMITHERS [sneering]. A bloomin' charm, wot? [Venomously.] Well, you'll need all the bloody charms you 'as before long, s' 'elp me!

JONES [judicially]. Oh, I'se good for six months yit 'fore dey gits sick o' my game. Den, when I sees trouble comin', I makes my getaway.

SMITHERS. Ho! You got it all planned, ain't yer?

JONES. I ain't no fool. I knows dis Emperor's time is sho't. Dat why I make hay when de sun shine. Was you thinkin' I'se aimin' to hold down dis job for life? No, suh! What good is gittin' money if you stays back in dis raggedy country? I wants action when I spends. And when I sees dese niggers gittin' up deir nerve to tu'n me out, and I'se got all de money in sight, I resigns on de spot and beats it quick.

SMITHERS. Where to?

JONES. None o' yo' business.

SMITHERS. Not back to the bloody States, I'll lay my oath.

JONES [suspiciously]. Why don't I? [Then with an easy laugh.] You mean 'count of dat story 'bout me breakin' from jail back dere? Dat's all talk.

SMITHERS [skeptically]. Ho, yes!

JONES [sharply]. You ain't 'sinuatin' I'se a liar, is you?

SMITHERS [hastily]. No, Gawd strike me! I was only thinkin' o' the bloody lies you told the blacks 'ere about killin' white men in the States.

JONES [angered]. How come dey're lies?

SMITHERS. You'd 'ave been in jail if you 'ad, wouldn't yer then? [With venom.] And from what I've 'eard, it ain't 'ealthy for a black to kill a white man in the States. They burns 'em in oil, don't they?

JONES [with cool deadliness]. You mean lynchin' 'd scare me? Well, I tells you, Smithers, maybe I does kill one white man back dere. Maybe I does. And maybe I kills another right heah 'fore long if he don't look out.

SMITHERS [trying to force a laugh]. I was on'y spoofin' yer. Can't yer take a joke? And you was just sayin' you'd never been in jail.

JONES [in the same tone — slightly boastful]. Maybe I goes to jail dere for gettin' in an argument wid razors ovah a crap game. Maybe I gits twenty years when dat colored man die. Maybe I gits in 'nother argument wid de prison guard was overseer ovah us when we're wukin' de road. Maybe he hits me wid a whip and I splits his head wid a shovel and runs away and files de chain off my leg and gits away safe. Maybe I does all dat an' maybe I don't. It's a story I tells you so's you knows I'se de kind of man dat if you evah repeats one word of it, I ends yo' stealin' on dis yearth mighty damn quick!

SMITHERS [terrified]. Think I'd peach on yer? Not me! Ain't I always been yer friend?

JONES [suddenly relaxing]. Sho' you has — and you better be.

SMITHERS [recovering his composure — and with it his malice]. And just to show yer I'm yer friend, I'll tell yer that bit o' news I was goin' to.

JONES. Go ahead! Shoot de piece. Must be bad news from de happy way you look.

SMITHERS [warningly]. Maybe it's gettin' time for you to resign — with that bloomin' silver bullet, wot?

[He finishes with a mocking grin.]

JONES [puzzled]. What's dat you say? Talk plain.

SMITHERS. Ain't noticed any of the guards or servants about the place to-day, I 'aven't.

JONES [carelessly]. Dey're all out in de garden sleepin' under de trees. When I sleeps, dey sneaks a sleep, too, and I pretends I never suspicions it. All I got to do is to ring de bell and dey come flyin', makin' a bluff dey was wukin' all de time.

SMITHERS [in the same mocking tone]. Ring the bell now an' you'll bloody well see what I means.

JONES [startled to alertness, but preserving the same careless tone]. Sho' I rings.

[He reaches below the throne and pulls out a big, common dinner bell which is painted the same vivid scarlet as the throne. He rings this vigorously — then stops to listen. Then he goes to both doors, rings again, and looks out.]

SMITHERS [watching him with malicious satisfaction, after a pause — mockingly]. The bloody ship is sinkin' an' the bleedin' rats 'as slung their 'ooks.

JONES [in a sudden fit of anger flings the bell clattering into a corner]. Low-flung, woods' niggers! [Then catching SMITHERS' eye on him, he controls himself and suddenly bursts into a low chuckling laugh.] Reckon I overplays my hand dis once! A man can't take de pot on a bob-tailed flush all de time. Was I sayin' I'd sit in six months mo'? Well, I'se changed my mind den. I cashes in and resigns de job of Emperor right dis minute.

SMITHERS [with real admiration]. Blimey, but you're a cool bird, and no mistake.

JONES. No use'n fussin'. When I knows de game's up I kisses it good-by widout no long waits. Dey've all run off to de hills, ain't dey?

SMITHERS. Yes — every bleedin' man jack of 'em.

JONES. Den de revolution is at de post. And de Emperor better git his feet smokin' up de trail.

[He starts for the door in rear.]

SMITHERS. Goin' out to look for your 'orse? Yer won't find any. They steals the 'orses first thing. Mine was gone when I went for 'im this mornin'. That's wot first give me a suspicion of wot was up.

JONES [*alarmed for a second, scratches his head, then philosophically*]. Well, den I hoofs it. Feet, do yo' duty! [*He pulls out a gold watch and looks at it.*] Three-thuty. Sundown's at six-thuty or dereabouts. [*Puts his watch back — with cool confidence.*] I got plenty o' time to make it easy.

SMITHERS. Don't be so bloomin' sure of it. They'll be after you 'ot and 'eavy. Ole Lem is at the bottom o' this business an' 'e 'ates you like 'ell. 'E'd rather do for you than eat 'is dinner, 'e would!

JONES [*scornfully*]. Dat fool no-count nigger! Does you think I'se scared o' him? I stands him on his thick head more'n once befo' dis, and I does it again if he comes in my way —— [*Fiercely.*] And dis time I leave him a dead nigger fo' sho'!

SMITHERS. You'll 'ave to cut through the big forest — an' these blacks 'ere can sniff and follow a trail in the dark like 'ounds. You'd 'ave to 'ustle to get through that forest in twelve hours even if you knew all the bloomin' trails like a native.

JONES [*with indignant scorn*]. Look-a-heah, white man! Does you think I'se a natural bo'n fool? Give me credit fo' havin' some sense, fo' Lawd's sake! Don't you s'pose I'se looked ahead and made sho' of all de chances? I'se gone out in dat big forest, pretendin' to hunt, so many times dat I knows it high an' low like a book. I could go through on dem trails wid my eyes shut. [*With great contempt.*] Think dese ign'rent bush niggers dat ain't got brains enuff to know deir own names even can catch Brutus Jones? Huh, I s'pects not! Not on yo' life! Why, man, de white men went after me wid bloodhounds where I come from an' I jes' laughs at em. It's a shame to fool dese black trash around heah, dey're so easy. You watch me, man I'll make dem look sick, I will. I'll be 'cross de plain to de edge of de forest by time dark comes. Once in de woods in de night, dey got a swell chance o' findin' dis baby! Dawn tomorrow I'll be out at de oder side and on de coast whar dat French gunboat is stayin'. She picks me up, takes me to Martinique when she

go dar, and dere I is safe wid a mighty big bankroll in my jeans. It's easy as rollin' off a log.

SMITHERS [*maliciously*]. But s'posin' somethin' 'appens wrong an' they do nab yer?

JONES [*decisively*]. Dey don't — dat's de answer.

SMITHERS. But, just for argyment's sake — what'd you do?

JONES [*frowning*]. I'se got five lead bullets in dis gun good enuff fo' common bush niggers — and after dat I got de silver bullet left to cheat 'em out o' gittin' me.

SMITHERS [*jeeringly*]. Ho, I was fergettin' that silver bullet. You'll bump yourself orf in style, won't yer? Blimey!

JONES [*gloomily*]. You kin bet yo' whole roll on one thing, white man. Dis baby plays out his string to de end and when he quits, he quits wid a bang de way he ought. Silver bullet ain't none too good for him when he go, dat's a fac'! [*Then shaking off his nervousness — with a confident laugh.*] Sho'! What is I talkin' about? Ain't come to dat yit and I never will — not wid trash niggers like dese yere. [*Boastfully.*] Silver bullet bring me luck anyway. I kin outguess, outrun, outfight, an' outplay whole lot o' dem all ovah de board any time o' de day er night! You watch me!

[*From the distant hills comes the faint, steady thump of a tom-tom, low and vibrating. It starts at a rate exactly corresponding to normal pulse beat — 72 to the minute — and continues at a gradually accelerating rate from this point uninterruptedly to the very end of the play.*]

JONES [*starts at the sound. A strange look of apprehension creeps into his face for a moment as he listens. Then he asks, with an attempt to regain his most casual manner*]. What's dat drum beatin' fo'?

SMITHERS [*with a mean grin*]. For you. That means the bleedin' ceremony 'as started. I've 'eard it before and I knows.

JONES. Cer'mony? What cer'mony?

SMITHERS. The blacks is 'oldin' a bloody meetin', 'avin' a war dance, gettin' their courage worked up b'fore they starts after you.

JONES. Let dem! Dey'll sho' need it!

SMITHERS. And they're there 'oldin' their 'eathen religious service — makin' no end of devil spells and charms to 'elp 'em against your silver bullet. [*He guffaws loudly.*] Blimey, but they're balmy as 'ell!

JONES [*a tiny bit awed and shaken in spite of himself*]. Huh! Takes more'n dat to scare dis chicken!

SMITHERS [*scenting the other's feeling — maliciously*]. Ternight when it's pitch black in the forest, they'll 'ave their pet devils and ghosts 'oundin' after you. You'll find yer bloody 'air 'll be standin' on end before termorrow mornin'. [*Seriously.*] It's a bleedin' queer place, that stinkin' forest, even in daylight. Yer don't know what might 'appen in there, it's that rotten still. Always sends the cold shivers down my back minute I gets in it.

JONES [*with a contemptuous sniff*]. I ain't no chicken-liver like you is. Trees an' me, we'se friends, and dar's a full moon comin' bring me light. And let dem po' niggers make all de fool spells dey'se a min' to. Does yo' s'pect I'se silly enuff to b'lieve in ghosts an' ha'nts an' all dat ole woman's talk? G'long, white man! You ain't talkin' to me. [*With a chuckle.*] Doesn't you know dey's got to do wid a man was member in good standin' o' de Baptist Church? Sho' I was dat when I was porter on de Pullmans, befo' I gits into my little trouble. Let dem try deir heathen tricks. De Baptist Church done pertect me and land dem all in hell. [*Then with more confident satisfaction.*] And I'se got little silver bullet o' my own, don't forgit!

SMITHERS. Ho! You 'aven't give much 'eed to your Baptist Church since you been down 'ere. I've 'eard myself you 'ad turned yer coat an' was takin' up with their blarsted witch-doctors, or whatever the 'ell yer calls the swine.

JONES [*vehemently*]. I pretends to! Sho' I pretends! Dat's part o' my game from de fust. If I finds out dem niggers

believes dat black is white, den I yells it out louder 'n deir loudest. It don't git me nothin' to do missionary work for de Baptist Church. I'se after de coin, an' I lays my Jesus on de shelf for de time bein'. [*Stops abruptly to look at his watch — alertly.*] But I ain't got de time to waste on no more fool talk wid you. I'se gwine away from heah dis secon'. [*He reaches in under the throne and pulls out an expensive Panama hat with a bright multi-colored band and sets it jauntily on his head.*] So long, white man! [*With a grin.*] See you in jail sometime, maybe!

SMITHERS. Not me, you won't. Well, I wouldn't be in yer bloody boots for no bloomin' money, but 'ere's wishin' yer luck just the same.

JONES [*contemptuously*]. You're de frightenedest man evah I see! I tells you I'se safe's 'f I was in New York City. It takes dem niggers from now to dark to git up de nerve to start somethin'. By dat time, I'se got a head start dey never kotch up wid.

SMITHERS [*maliciously*]. Give my regards to any ghosts yer meets up with.

JONES [*grinning*]. If dat ghost got money, I'll tell him never ha'nt you less'n he wants to lose it.

SMITHERS [*flattered*]. Garn! [*Then curiously.*] Ain't yer takin' no luggage with yer?

JONES. I travels light when I wants to move fast. And I got tinned grub buried on de edge o' de forest. [*Boastfully.*] Now say dat I don't look ahead an' use my brains! [*With a wide, liberal gesture.*] I will all dat's left in de palace to you — and you better grab all you kin sneak away wid befo' dey gits here.

SMITHERS [*gratefully*]. Righto — and thanks ter yer. [*As JONES walks toward the door in rear — cautioningly.*] Say! Look 'ere, you ain't goin' out that way, are yer?

JONES. Does you think I'd slink out de back door like a common nigger? I'se Emperor yit, ain't I? And de Emperor Jones leaves de way he comes, and dat black trash don't dare stop him — not yit, leastways. [*He stops for a moment in the doorway, listening to the far-off but insistent beat of the tom-tom.*] Listen to dat roll-call, will you? Must be mighty big drum carry dat far. [*Then with a laugh.*] Well, if dey ain't no whole brass band to see me off, I sho' got de drum part of it. So long, white man.

[*He puts his hands in his pockets and with studied carelessness, whistling a tune, he saunters out of the doorway and off to the left.*]

SMITHERS [*looks after him with a puzzled admiration*]. 'E's got 'is bloomin' nerve with 'im, s'elp me! [*Then angrily.*] Ho — the bleedin' nigger — puttin' on 'is bloody airs! I 'opes they nabs 'im an' gives 'im what's what!

CURTAIN

SCENE II

The end of the plain where the Great Forest begins. The foreground is sandy, level ground dotted by a few stones and clumps of stunted bushes covering close against the earth to escape the buffeting of the trade wind. In the rear the forest is a wall of darkness dividing the world. Only when the eye becomes accustomed to the gloom can the outlines of separate trunks of the nearest trees be made out, enormous pillars of deeper blackness. A somber monotone of wind lost in the leaves moans in the air. Yet this sound serves but to intensify the impression of the forest's relentless immobility, to form a background throwing into relief its brooding, implacable silence.

JONES *enters from the left, walking rapidly. He stops as he nears the edge of the forest, looks around him quickly, peering into the dark as if searching for some familiar landmark. Then, apparently satisfied that he is where he ought to be, he throws himself on the ground, dog-tired.*]

Well, heah I is. In de nick o' time, too! Little mo' an' it'd be blacker'n de ace of spades heahabouts. [*He pulls a bandana handkerchief from his hip pocket and mops off his perspiring face.*] Sho'! Gimme air!

I'se tuckered out sho' 'nuff. Dat soft Emperor job ain't no trainin' fo' a long hike ovah dat plain in de brilin' sun. [*Then with a chuckle.*] Cheer up, nigger, de worst is yet to come. [*He lifts his head and stares at the forest. His chuckle peters out abruptly. In a tone of awe.*] My goodness, look at dem woods, will you? Dat no-count Smithers said dey'd be black an' he sho' called de turn. [*Turning away from them quickly and looking down at his feet, he snatches at a chance to change the subject — solicitously.*] Feet, you is holdin' up yo' end fine an' I sutinly hopes you ain't blisterin' none. It's time you git a rest. [*He takes off his shoes, his eyes studiously avoiding the forest. He feels of the soles of his feet gingerly.*] You is still in de pink — on'y a little mite feverish. Cool yo'selfs. Remember you done got a long journey yit befo' you. [*He sits in a weary attitude, listening to the rhythmic beating of the tom-tom. He grumbles in a loud tone to cover up a growing uneasiness.*] Bush niggers! Wonder dey wouldn't git sick o' beatin' dat drum. Sound louder, seem like. I wonder if dey's startin' after me? [*He scrambles to his feet, looking back across the plain.*] Couldn't see dem now, nohow, if dey was hundred feet away. [*Then shaking himself like a wet dog to get rid of these depressing thoughts.*] Sho', dey's miles an' miles behind. What you gittin' fidgety about? [*But he sits down and begins to lace up his shoes in great haste, all the time muttering reassuringly.*] You know what? Yo' belly is empty, dat's what's de matter wid you. Come time to eat! Wid nothin' but wind on yo' stumach, o' course you feels jiggedy. Well, we eats right heah an' now soon's I gits dese pesky shoes laced up. [*He finishes lacing up his shoes.*] Dere! Now le's see! [*Gets on his hands and knees and searches the ground around him with his eyes.*] White stone, white stone, where is you? [*He sees the first white stone and crawls to it — with satisfaction.*] Heah you is! I knowed dis was de right place. Box of grub, come to me. [*He turns over the stone and feels in under it — in a tone of dismay.*] Ain't heah! Gorry, is I in de right place or isn't

I? Dere's 'nother stone. Guess dat's it. [*He scrambles to the next stone and turns it over.*] Ain't heah, neither! Grub, whar is you? Ain't heah. Gorry, has I got to go hungry into dem woods — all de night? [*While he is talking he scrambles from one stone to another, turning them over in frantic haste. Finally, he jumps to his feet excitedly.*] Is I lost de place? Must have! But how dat happen when I was followin' de trail across de plain in broad daylight? [*Almost plaintively.*] I'se hungry, I is! I gotta git my feed. Whar's my strength gonna come from if I doesn't? Gorry, I gotta find dat grub high an' low somehow! Why it come dark so quick like dat? Can't see nothin'. [*He scratches a match on his trousers and peers about him. The rate of the beat of the far-off tom-tom increases perceptibly as he does so. He mutters in a bewildered voice.*] How come all dese white stones come heah when I only remembers one? [*Suddenly, with a frightened gasp, he flings the match on the ground and stamps on it.*] Nigger, is you gone crazy mad? Is you lightin' matches to show dem whar you is? Fo' Lawd's sake, use yo' haid. Gorry, I'se got to be careful! [*He stares at the plain behind him apprehensively, his hand on his revolver.*] But how come all dese white stones? And whar's dat tin box o' grub I hid all wrapped up in oilcloth?

[*While his back is turned, the* LITTLE FORMLESS FEARS *creep out from the deeper blackness of the forest. They are black, shapeless, only their glittering little eyes can be seen. If they have any describable form at all it is that of a grubworm about the size of a creeping child. They move noiselessly, but with deliberate, painful effort, striving to raise themselves on end, failing and sinking prone again.* JONES *turns about to face the forest. He stares up at the trees, seeking vainly to discover his whereabouts by their conformation.*] Can't tell nothin' from dem trees! Gorry, nothin' 'round heah looks like I evah seed it befo'. I'se done lost de place sho' 'nuff! [*With mournful foreboding.*] It's mighty queer! It's mighty queer! [*With sudden forced defiance — in

an angry tone.*] Woods, is you tryin' to put somethin' ovah on me?

[*From the formless creatures on the ground in front of him comes a tiny gale of low mocking laughter like a rustling of leaves. They squirm upward toward him in twisted attitudes.* JONES *looks down, leaps backward with a yell of terror, yanking out his revolver as he does so — in a quavering voice.*] What's dat? Who's dar? What is you? Git away from me befo' I shoots you up! You don't? ——

[*He fires. There is a flash, a loud report, then silence broken only by the far-off, quickened throb of the tom-tom. The formless creatures have scurried back into the forest.* JONES *remains fixed in his position, listening intently. The sound of the shot, the reassuring feel of the revolver in his hand, have somewhat restored his shaken nerve. He addresses himself with renewed confidence.*] Dey're gone. Dat shot fix 'em. Dey was only little animals — little wild pigs, I reckon. Dey've maybe rooted out yo' grub an' eat it. Sho', you fool nigger, what you think dey is — ha'nts? [*Excitedly.*] Gorry, you give de game away when you fire dat shot. Dem niggers heah dat fo' su'tin! Time you beat it in de woods widout no long waits. [*He starts for the forest — hesitates before the plunge — then urging himself in with manful resolution.*] Git in, nigger! What you skeered at? Ain't nothin' dere but de trees! Git in! [*He plunges boldly into the forest.*]

SCENE III

In the forest. The moon has just risen. Its beams, drifting through the canopy of leaves, make a barely perceptible, suffused, eerie glow. A dense low wall of underbrush and creepers is in the nearer foreground, fencing in a small triangular clearing. Beyond this is the massed blackness of the forest like an encompassing barrier. A path is dimly discerned leading down to the clearing from left, rear, and winding away from it again toward the right. As the scene opens nothing can be distinctly made out. Except for the beating of the tom-tom, which is a trifle louder and quicker than at the close of the previous scene, there is silence, broken every few seconds by a queer, clicking sound. Then gradually the figure of the Negro, JEFF, can be discerned crouching on his haunches at the rear of the triangle. He is middle-aged, thin, brown in color, is dressed in a Pullman porter's uniform and cap. He is throwing a pair of dice on the ground before him, picking them up, shaking them, casting them out with the regular, rigid, mechanical movements of an automaton. The heavy, plodding footsteps of some one approaching along the trail from the left are heard and JONES' voice, pitched on a slightly higher key and strained in a cheery effort to overcome its own tremors.

De moon's rizen. Does you heah dat, nigger? You gits more light from dis out. No mo' buttin' yo' fool head agin' de trunks an' scratchin' de hide off yo' legs in de bushes. Now you sees whar yo'se gwine. So cheer up! From now on you has a snap. [*He steps just to the rear of the triangular clearing and mops off his face on his sleeve. He has lost his Panama hat. His face is scratched, his brilliant uniform shows several large rents.*] What time's it gittin' to be, I wonder? I dassent light no match to find out. Phoo'. It's wa'm an' dat's a fac'! [*Wearily.*] How long I been makin' tracks in dese woods? Must be hours an' hours. Seems like fo'evah! Yit can't be, when de moon's jes' riz. Dis am a long night fo' yo', yo' Majesty! [*With a mournful chuckle.*] Majesty! Der ain't much majesty 'bout dis baby now. [*With attempted cheerfulness.*] Never min'. It's all part o' de game. Dis night come to an end like everything else. And when you gits dar safe and has dat bankroll in yo' hands you laughs at all dis. [*He starts to whistle but checks himself abruptly.*] What yo' whistlin' for, you po' dope! Want all de worl' to heah you? [*He stops talking to listen.*] Heah dat ole drum! Sho' gits nearer from de sound. Dey's packin' it along wid 'em. Time fo' me to move. [*He takes a step forward, then stops — worriedly.*] What's dat odder

queer clickety sound I heah? Dere it is! Sound close! Sound like — sound like — Fo' God sake, sound like some nigger was shootin' crap! [*Frightenedly.*] I better beat it quick when I gits dem notions. [*He walks quickly into the clear space — then stands transfixed as he sees JEFF — in a terrified gasp.*] Who dar? Who dat? Is dat you, Jeff? [*Starting toward the other, forgetful for a moment of his surroundings and really believing it is a living man that he sees — in a tone of happy relief.*] Jeff! I'se sho' mighty glad to see you! Dey tol' me you done died from dat razor cut I gives you. [*Stopping suddenly, bewilderedly.*] But how you come to be heah, nigger? [*He stares fascinatedly at the other who continues his mechanical play with the dice. JONES' eyes begin to roll wildly. He stutters.*] Ain't you gwine — look up — can't you speak to me? Is you — is you — a ha'nt? [*He jerks out his revolver in a frenzy of terrified rage.*] Nigger, I kills you dead once. Has I got to kill you ag'in? You take it den. [*He fires. When the smoke clears away, JEFF has disappeared. JONES stands trembling — then with a certain reassurance.*] He's gone, anyway. Ha'nt or not ha'nt, dat shot fix him. [*The beat of the far-off tom-tom is perceptibly louder and more rapid. JONES becomes conscious of it — with a start, looking back over his shoulder.*] Dey's gittin' near! Dey's comin' fast! And heah I is shootin' shots to let 'em know jes' whar I is! Oh, Gorry, I'se got to run.

[*Forgetting the path he plunges wildly into the underbrush in the rear and disappears in the shadow.*]

SCENE IV

In the forest. A wide dirt road runs diagonally from right, front, to left, rear. Rising sheer on both sides the forest walls it in. The moon is now up. Under its light the road glimmers ghastly and unreal. It is as if the forest had stood aside momentarily to let the road pass through and accomplish its veiled purpose. This done, the forest will fold in upon itself again and the road will be no more.

[JONES *stumbles in from the forest on the right. His uniform is ragged and torn. He looks about him with numbed surprise when he sees the road, his eyes blinking in the bright moonlight. He flops down exhaustedly and pants heavily for a while. Then with sudden anger.*]

I'm meltin' wid heat! Runnin' an' runnin' an' runnin'! Damn dis heah coat! Like a straitjacket! [*He tears off his coat and flings it away from him, revealing himself stripped to the waist.*] Dere! Dat's better! Now I kin breathe! [*Looking down at his feet, the spurs catch his eye.*] And to hell wid dese high-fangled spurs. Dey're what's been a-trippin' me up an' breakin' my neck. [*He unstraps them and flings them away disgustedly.*] Dere! I gits rid o' dem frippety Emperor trappin's an' I travels lighter. Lawd! I'se tired! [*After a pause, listening to the insistent beat of the tom-tom in the distance.*] I must 'a' put some distance between myself an' dem — runnin' like dat — and yit — dat damn drum sounds jes' de same — nearer, even. Well, I guess I a'most holds my lead anyhow. Dey won't never catch up. [*With a sigh.*] If on'y my fool legs stands up. Oh, I'se sorry I evah went in for dis. Dat Emperor job is sho' hard to shake. [*He looks around him suspiciously.*] How'd dis road evah git heah? Good level road, too. I never remembers seein' it befo'. [*Shaking his head apprehensively.*] Dese woods is sho' full o' de queerest things at night. [*With a sudden terror.*] Lawd God, don't let me see no more o' dem ha'nts! Dey gits my goat! [*Then trying to talk himself into confidence.*] Ha'nts! You fool nigger, dey ain't no such things! Don't de Baptist parson tell you dat many time? Is you civilized, or is you like dese ign'rent black niggers heah? Sho'! Dat was all in yo' own head. Wasn't nothin' dere. Wasn't no Jeff! Know what? You jus' get seein' dem things 'cause yo' belly's empty and you's sick wid hunger inside. Hunger 'fects yo' head and yo' eyes. Any fool know dat. [*Then pleading fervently.*] But bless God, I don't come across no more o' dem, whatever dey is! [*Then cautiously.*] Rest! Don't talk! Rest! You needs it. Den you gits on yo' way again. [*Looking at the moon.*] Night's half gone a'most. You hits de coast in de mawning! Den you's all safe.

[*From the right forward a small gang of Negroes enter. They are dressed in striped convict suits, their heads are shaven, one leg drags limpingly, shackled to a heavy ball and chain. Some carry picks, the others shovels. They are followed by a white man dressed in the uniform of a prison guard. A Winchester rifle is slung across his shoulders and he carries a heavy whip. At a signal from the* GUARD *they stop on the road opposite where* JONES *is sitting.* JONES, *who has been staring up at the sky, unmindful of their noiseless approach, suddenly looks down and sees them. His eyes pop out, he tries to get to his feet and fly, but sinks back, too numbed by fright to move. His voice catches in a choking prayer.*]

Lawd Jesus!

[*The* PRISON GUARD *cracks his whip — noiselessly — and at that signal all the convicts start to work on the road. They swing their picks, they shovel, but not a sound comes from their labor. Their movements, like those of* JEFF *in the preceding scene, are those of automatons — rigid, slow, and mechanical. The* PRISON GUARD *points sternly at* JONES *with his whip, motions him to take his place among the other shovelers.* JONES *gets to his feet in a hypnotized stupor. He mumbles subserviently.*]

Yes, suh! Yes, suh! I'se comin'.

[*As he shuffles, dragging one foot, over to his place, he curses under his breath with rage and hatred.*]

God damn yo' soul, I gits even wid you yit, some time.

[*As if there were a shovel in his hands he goes through weary, mechanical gestures of digging up dirt, and throwing it to the roadside. Suddenly the* GUARD *approaches him angrily, threateningly. He raises his whip and lashes* JONES

viciously across the shoulders with it.
JONES *winces with pain and cowers
abjectly. The* GUARD *turns his back on
him and walks away contemptuously.
Instantly* JONES *straightens up. With
arms upraised as if his shovel were a
club in his hands, he springs murder-
ously at the unsuspecting* GUARD. *In
the act of crashing down his shovel on
the white man's skull,* JONES *suddenly
becomes aware that his hands are empty.
He cries despairingly.*]
Whar's my shovel? Gimme my shovel
'til I splits his damn head! [*Appealing to
his fellow convicts.*] Gimme a shovel, one
o' you, fo' God's sake!
[*They stand fixed in motionless attitudes, their eyes on the ground. The*
GUARD *seems to wait expectantly, his
back turned to the attacker.* JONES
*bellows with baffled, terrified rage, tug-
ging frantically at his revolver.*]
I kills you, you white debil, if it's de
last thing I evah does! Ghost or debil,
I kill you agin!
[*He frees the revolver and fires point-
blank at the* GUARD'S *back. Instantly
the walls of the forest close in from both
sides, the road and the figures of the
convict gang are blotted out in an en-
shrouding darkness. The only sounds
are a crashing in the underbrush as*
JONES *leaps away in mad flight and the
throbbing of the tom-tom, still far distant, but increased in volume of sound
and rapidity of beat.*]

SCENE V

*A large circular clearing, enclosed by
the serried ranks of gigantic trunks of tall
trees whose tops are lost to view. In the
center is a big dead stump worn by time into
a curious resemblance to an auction block.
The moon floods the clearing with a clear
light.* JONES *forces his way in through the
forest on the left. He looks wildly about the
clearing with hunted, fearful glances. His
pants are in tatters, his shoes cut and mis-
shapen, flapping about his feet. He slinks
cautiously to the stump in the center and sits
down in a tense position, ready for instant*
*flight. Then he holds his head in his hands
and rocks back and forth, moaning to himself
miserably.*

Oh Lawd, Lawd! Oh Lawd, Lawd!
[*Suddenly he throws himself on his knees and
raises his clasped hands to the sky — in a
voice of agonized pleading.*] Lawd Jesus,
heah my. prayer! I'se a po' sinner, a po'
sinner! I knows I done wrong, I knows it!
When I cotches Jeff cheatin' wid loaded
dice my anger overcomes me and I kills
him dead! Lawd, I done wrong! When
dat guard hits me wid de whip, my anger
overcomes me, and I kills him dead.
Lawd, I done wrong! And down heah
whar dese fool bush niggers raises me up to
the seat o' de mighty, I steals all I could
grab. Lawd, I done wrong! I knows it!
I'se sorry! Forgive me, Lawd! Forgive
dis po' sinner! [*Then beseeching terrifiedly.*]
And keep dem away, Lawd! Keep dem
away from me! And stop dat drum
soundin' in my ears! Dat begin to sound
ha'nted, too. [*He gets to his feet, evidently
slightly reassured by his prayer — with attempted confidence.*] De Lawd'll preserve
me from dem ha'nts after dis. [*Sits down
on the stump again.*] I ain't skeered o' real
men. Let dem come. But dem odders
—— [*He shudders — then looks down at
his feet, working his toes inside the shoes —
with a groan.*] Oh, my po' feet! Dem
shoes ain't no use no more 'ceptin' to hurt.
I'se better off widout dem. [*He unlaces
them and pulls them off — holds the wrecks of
the shoes in his hands and regards them
mournfully.*] You was real, A-one patin'
leather, too. Look at you now. Emperor,
you'se gittin' mighty low!
[*He sighs dejectedly and remains with
bowed shoulders, staring down at the
shoes in his hands as if reluctant to
throw them away. While his attention
is thus occupied, a crowd of figures
silently enter the clearing from all sides.
All are dressed in Southern costumes of
the period of the fifties of the last century.
There are middle-aged men who are
evidently well-to-do planters. There is
one spruce, authoritative individual —
the* AUCTIONEER. *There is a crowd of*

*curious spectators, chiefly young belles
and dandies who have come to the slave-
market for diversion. All exchange
courtly greetings in dumb show and chat
silently together. There is something
stiff, rigid, unreal, marionettish about
their movements. They group themselves about the stump. Finally a
batch of slaves is led in from the left by
an attendant — three men of different
ages, two women, one with a baby in her
arms, nursing. They are placed to the
left of the stump, beside* JONES.

*The white planters look them over
appraisingly as if they were cattle, and
exchange judgments on each. The
dandies point with their fingers and
make witty remarks. The belles titter
bewitchingly. All this in silence save
for the ominous throb of the tom-tom.
The* AUCTIONEER *holds up his hand,
taking his place at the stump. The
groups strain forward attentively. He
touches* JONES *on the shoulder peremptorily, motioning for him to stand on the
stump — the auction block.*

JONES *looks up, sees the figures on all
sides, looks wildly for some opening to
escape, sees none, screams and leaps
madly to the top of the stump to get as
far away from them as possible. He
stands there, cowering, paralyzed with
horror. The* AUCTIONEER *begins his
silent spiel. He points to* JONES, *ap-
peals to the planters to see for themselves.
Here is a good field hand, sound in wind
and limb as they can see. Very strong
still in spite of his being middle-aged.
Look at that back. Look at those shoulders. Look at the muscles in his arms
and his sturdy legs. Capable of any
amount of hard labor. Moreover, of a
good disposition, intelligent and tractable. Will any gentleman start the
bidding? The* PLANTERS *raise their
fingers, make their bids. They are
apparently all eager to possess* JONES.
*The bidding is lively, the crowd inter-
ested. While this has been going on,*
JONES *has been seized by the courage of
desperation. He dares to look down and
around him. Over his face abject terror*

*gives way to mystification, to gradual
realization — stutteringly.]*
What you all doin', white folks? What's
all dis? What you all lookin' at me fo'?
What you doin' wid me, anyhow? [*Suddenly convulsed with raging hatred and fear.*]
Is dis a auction? Is you sellin' me like dey
uster befo' de war? [*Jerking out his revolver just as the* AUCTIONEER *knocks him down
to one of the planters — glaring from him to
the purchaser.*] And *you* sells me? And
you buys me? I shows you I'se a free nigger, damn yo' souls!

[*He fires at the* AUCTIONEER *and at
the* PLANTER *with such rapidity that
the two shots are almost simultaneous.
As if this were a signal the walls of the
forest fold in. Only blackness remains
and silence broken by* JONES *as he
rushes off, crying with fear — and by
the quickened, ever louder beat of the
tom-tom.*]

SCENE VI

*A cleared space in the forest. The limbs of
the trees meet over it forming a low ceiling
about five feet from the ground. The inter-
locked ropes of creepers reaching upward to
entwine the tree trunks give an arched appearance to the sides. The space thus enclosed
is like the dark, noisome hold of some ancient
vessel. The moonlight is almost completely
shut out and only a vague wan light filters
through. There is the noise of someone approaching from the left, stumbling and crawling through the undergrowth.* JONES' *voice
is heard between chattering moans*

Oh, Lawd, what I gwine do now? Ain't
got no bullet left on'y de silver one. If mo'
o' dem ha'nts come after me, how I gwine
skeer dem away? Oh, Lawd, on'y de
silver one left — an' I gotta save dat fo'
luck. If I shoots dat one I'm a goner sho'!
Lawd, it's black heah! Whar's de moon?
Oh, Lawd, don't dis night evah come to an
end! [*By the sounds, he is feeling his way
cautiously forward.*] Dere! Dis feels like
a clear space. I gotta lie down an' rest. I
don't care if dem niggers does cotch me
I gotta rest.

[*He is well forward now where his figure can be dimly made out. His pants have been so torn away that what is left of them is no better than a breech cloth. He flings himself full length, face downward on the ground, panting with exhaustion. Gradually it seems to grow lighter in the enclosed space and two rows of seated figures can be seen behind* JONES. *They are sitting in crumpled, despairing attitudes, hunched, facing one another with their backs touching the forest walls as if they were shackled to them. All are Negroes, naked save for loin cloths. At first they are silent and motionless. Then they begin to sway slowly forward toward each and back again in unison, as if they were laxly letting themselves follow the long roll of a ship at sea. At the same time, a low, melancholy murmur rises among them, increasing gradually by rhythmic degrees which seem to be directed and controlled by the throb of the tom-tom in the distance, to a long, tremulous wail of despair that reaches a certain pitch, unbearably acute, then falls by slow gradations of tone into silence and is taken up again.* JONES *starts, looks up, sees the figures, and throws himself down again to shut out the sight. A shudder of terror shakes his whole body as the wail rises up about him again. But the next time, his voice, as if under some uncanny compulsion, starts with the others. As their chorus lifts he rises to a sitting posture similar to the others, swaying back and forth. His voice reaches the highest pitch of sorrow, of desolation. The light fades out, the other voices cease, and only darkness is left.* JONES *can be heard scrambling to his feet and running off, his voice sinking down the scale and receding as he moves farther and farther away in the forest. The tom-tom beats louder, quicker, with a more insistent, triumphant pulsation.*]

SCENE VII

The foot of a gigantic tree by the edge of a reat river. A rough structure of boulders, like an altar, is by the tree. The raised river bank is in the nearer background. Beyond this the surface of the river spreads out, brilliant and unruffled in the moonlight, blotted out and merged into a veil of bluish mist in the distance. JONES' *voice is heard from the left rising and falling in the long, despairing wail of the chained slaves, to the rhythmic beat of the tom-tom. As his voice sinks into silence, he enters the open space. The expression of his face is fixed and stony, his eyes have an obsessed glare, he moves with a strange deliberation like a sleep-walker or one in a trance. He looks around at the tree, the rough stone altar, the moonlit surface of the river beyond, and passes his hand over his head with a vague gesture of puzzled bewilderment. Then, as if in obedience to some obscure impulse, he sinks into a kneeling, devotional posture before the altar. Then he seems to come to himself partly, to have an uncertain realization of what he is doing, for he straightens up and stares about him horrifiedly — in an incoherent mumble.*

What — what is I doin'? What is — dis place? Seems like I know dat tree — an' dem stones — an' de river. I remember — seems like I been heah befo'. [*Tremblingly.*] Oh, Gorry, I'se skeered in dis place! I'se skeered. Oh, Lawd, pertect dis sinner!

[*Crawling away from the altar, he cowers close to the ground, his face hidden, his shoulders heaving with sobs of hysterical fright. From behind the trunk of the tree, as if he had sprung out of it, the figure of the* CONGO WITCH-DOCTOR *appears. He is wizened and old, naked except for the fur of some small animal tied about his waist, its bushy tail hanging down in front. His body is stained all over a bright red. Antelope horns are on each side of his head, branching upward. In one hand he carries a bone rattle, in the other a charm stick with a bunch of white cockatoo feathers tied to the end. A great number of glass beads and bone ornaments are about his neck, ears, wrists, and ankles. He struts noiselessly with a queer prancing step to a position in the clear ground between* JONES *and the altar. Then with a preliminary, summoning stamp of his foot on the earth, he begins to dance and to chant. As if in response to his summons the beating of the tom-tom grows to a fierce, exultant boom whose throbs seem to fill the air with vibrating rhythm.* JONES *looks up, starts to spring to his feet, reaches a half-kneeling, half-squatting position and remains rigidly fixed there, paralyzed with awed fascination by this new apparition. The* WITCH-DOCTOR *sways, stamping with his foot, his bone rattle clicking the time. His voice rises and falls in a weird, monotonous croon, without articulate word divisions. Gradually his dance becomes clearly one of a narrative in pantomime, his croon is an incantation, a charm to allay the fierceness of some implacable deity demanding sacrifice. He flees, he is pursued by devils, he hides, he flees again. Ever wilder and wilder becomes his flight, nearer and nearer draws the pursuing evil, more and more the spirit of terror gains possession of him. His croon, rising to intensity, is punctuated by shrill cries.* JONES *has become completely hypnotised. His voice joins in the incantation, in the cries, he beats time with his hands and sways his body to and fro from the waist. The whole spirit and meaning of the dance has entered into him, has become his spirit. Finally the theme of the pantomime halts on a howl of despair, and is taken up again in a note of savage hope. There is a salvation. The forces of evil demand sacrifice. They must be appeased. The* WITCH-DOCTOR *points with his wand to the sacred tree, to the river beyond, to the altar, and finally to* JONES *with a ferocious command.* JONES *seems to sense the meaning of this. It is he who must offer himself for sacrifice. He beats his forehead abjectly to the ground, moaning hysterically.*]

Mercy, Oh Lawd! Mercy! Mercy on dis po' sinner.

[*The* WITCH-DOCTOR *springs to the*

river bank. He stretches out his arms and calls to some God within its depths. Then he starts backward slowly, his arms remaining out. A huge head of a crocodile appears over the bank and its eyes, glittering greenly, fasten upon JONES. *He stares into them fascinatedly. The* WITCH-DOCTOR *prances up to him, touches him with his wand, motions with hideous command toward the waiting monster.* JONES *squirms on his belly nearer and nearer, moaning continually.*]

Mercy, Lawd! Mercy!

[*The crocodile heaves more of his enormous hulk onto the land.* JONES *squirms toward him. The* WITCH-DOCTOR'S *voice shrills out in furious exultation, the tom-tom beats madly.* JONES *cries out in a fierce, exhausted spasm of anguished pleading.*]

Lawd, save me! Lawd Jesus, heah my prayer!

[*Immediately, in answer to his prayer, comes the thought of the one bullet left him. He snatches at his hip, shouting defiantly.*]

De silver bullet! You don't git me yit!

[*He fires at the green eyes in front of him. The head of the crocodile sinks back behind the river bank, the* WITCH-DOCTOR *springs behind the sacred tree and disappears.* JONES *lies with his face to the ground, his arms outstretched, whimpering with fear as the throb of the tom-tom fills the silence about him with a somber pulsation, a baffled but revengeful power.*]

SCENE VIII

Dawn. Same as Scene Two, the dividing line of forest and plain. The nearest tree trunks are dimly revealed but the forest behind them is still a mass of glooming shadow. The tom-tom seems on the very spot, so loud and continuously vibrating are its beats.

LEM *enters from the left, followed by a small squad of his soldiers, and by the Cockney trader,* SMITHERS. *LEM is a heavy-set, ape-faced old savage of the extreme*

African type, dressed only in a loin-cloth. A revolver and cartridge belt are about his waist. His soldiers are in different degrees of rag-concealed naked-ness. All wear broad palm-lèaf hats. Each one carries a rifle. SMITHERS is the same as in Scene One. One of the soldiers, evidently a tracker, is peering about keenly on the ground. He points to the spot where JONES entered the forest. LEM and SMITHERS come to look.

SMITHERS [*after a glance, turns away in disgust*]. That's where 'e went in right enough. Much good it'll do yer. 'E's miles orf by this an' safe to the Coast, damn 's ide! I tole yer yer'd lose 'im, didn't I? — wastin' the 'ole bloomin' night beatin' yer bloody drum and castin' yer silly spells! Gawd blimey, wot a pack!

LEM [*gutturally*]. We cotch him. [*He makes a motion to his soldiers who squat down on their haunches in a semi-circle.*]

SMITHERS [*exasperatedly*]. Well, ain't yer goin' in an' 'unt 'im in the woods? What the 'ell's the good of waitin'?

LEM [*imperturbably — squatting down himself*]. We cotch him.

SMITHERS [*turning away from him contemptuously*]. Aw! Garn! 'E's a better man than the lot o' you put together. I 'ates the sight o' 'im but I'll say that for 'im.

[*A sound comes from the forest. The soldiers jump to their feet, cocking their rifles alertly. LEM remains sitting with an imperturbable expression, but listening intently. He makes a quick signal with his hand. His followers creep quickly into the forest, scattering so that each enters at a different spot.*]

SMITHERS. You ain't thinkin' that would be 'im, I 'ope?

LEM [*calmly*]. We cotch him.

SMITHERS. Blarsted fat 'eads! [*Then after a second's thought — wonderingly.*] Still an' all, it might 'appen. If 'e lost 'is bloody way in these stinkin' woods 'e'd likely turn in a circle without 'is knowin' it.

LEM [*peremptorily*]. Sssh! [*The reports of several rifles sound from the forest, followed a second later by savage, exultant yells. The beating of the tom-tom abruptly ceases. LEM looks up at the white man with a grin of satisfaction.*] We cotch him. Him dead.

SMITHERS [*with a snarl*]. 'Ow d'yer know it's 'im an' 'ow d'yer know 'e's dead?

LEM. My mens dey got um silver bullets. Lead bullet no kill him. He got um strong charm. I cook um money, make um silver bullet, make um strong charm, too.

SMITHERS [*astonished*]. So that's wot you was up to all night, wot? You was scared to put after 'im till you'd moulded silver bullets, eh?

LEM [*simply stating a fact*]. Yes. Him got strong charm. Lead no good.

SMITHERS [*slapping his thigh and guffaw-ing*]. Haw-haw! If yer don't beat all 'ell! [*Then recovering himself — scorn-fully.*] I'll bet yer it ain't 'im they shot at all, yer bleedin' looney!

LEM [*calmly*]. Dey come bring him now.
[*The soldiers come out of the forest, carrying JONES' limp body. He is dead. They carry him to LEM, who examines his body with great satisfaction.*]

SMITHERS [*leans over his shoulder — in a tone of frightened awe*]. Well, they did for yer right enough, Jonsey, me lad! Dead as a 'erring! [*Mockingly.*] Where's yer 'igh an' mighty airs now, yer bloomin' Majesty? [*Then with a grin.*] Silver bullets! Gawd blimey, but yer died in the 'eighth o' style, any'ow!

CURTAIN

IN ABRAHAM'S BOSOM
THE BIOGRAPHY OF A NEGRO
IN SEVEN SCENES
By PAUL GREEN

SCENES

CHARACTERS

ABRAHAM McCRANIE — *a Negro*

GOLDIE McALLISTER — *his sweetheart and later his wife*

MUH MACK — *his aunt*

BUD GASKINS
LIJE HUNNEYCUTT } *Turpentine hands for the Colonel*
PUNY AVERY

DOUGLASS McCRANIE — *Abraham's son*

EDDIE WILLIAMS
LANIE HORTON } *Students to Abe*
NEILLY McNEILL

COLONEL McCRANIE — *a Southern gentleman, once the owner of slaves*

LONNIE McCRANIE — *his son*

NOTE: The final *d*'s and *g*'s have been retained in most cases throughout the play as an aid to reading only. In actual conversation the characters drop them, and often the final *t* likewise. Exceptions are usually where these consonants precede stressed words beginning with vowels.

IN ABRAHAM'S BOSOM

SCENE I

In the turpentine woods of eastern North Carolina, forty years ago, near a spring at the foot of a hill. The immediate foreground is open and clear save for a spongy growth of grass and sickly ground creepers. In the rear a wide-spreading tangle of reeds, briars, and alder bushes shuts around the spring in a semi-circle. At the right front the great body of a pine, gashed and barked by the turpentine farmer's axe, lifts straight from the earth. To the left a log lies rotting in the embrace of wild ivy. Maples, bays, dogwoods and other small trees overrun by tenacious vines raise their leafy tops to shade the spot. Through interstices in the undergrowth one can see the pine forest stretching away until the eye is lost in a colonnade of trees. The newly scraped blazes on the pines show through the brush like the downward spreading beards of old men, suggestive of the ancient gnomes of the woods, mysterious and forever watchful.

At the left front four tin dinner pails hang on a limby bush. The sound of axes against the trees, accompanied by the rhythmically guttural "han—n—h! han—n—n—h!" of the cutters comes from the distance. One of the laborers breaks into a high mournful song —

Oh, my foots wuh wet — wid de sunrise dew,
De morning star — wuh a witness too.
'Way, 'way up in de Rock of Ages,
In God's bosom gwine be my villah.

Presently there is a loud halloo near at hand, and another voice yodels and cries, Dinner time—m-m—c! Git yo' peas, ev'ybody! *Voices are heard nearer, a loud burst of laughter, and then three full-blooded Negroes shuffle in carrying long thin-bladed axes, which they lean against the pine at the right. They are dressed in nondescript clothes, ragged and covered with the glaze of raw turpentine. As they move up to the spring they* take off their battered hats, fan themselves, and wipe the streaming sweat from their brows. Two of them are well-built and burly, one stout and past middle age with some pretension to a thin scraggly mustache, the second tall and muscled, and the third wiry, nervous and bandy-legged. They punctuate their conversation with great breaths of cool air.

YOUNG NEGRO. Monkey walking in dis woods.

OLDER NEGRO. Yah, Jaboh procuring round and 'bout um.

LITTLE NEGRO. While us res' he roos' high in pine tree.

YOUNG NEGRO. Fall on Puny's back 'bout th'ee o'clock, git um down. Hee—hee.

PUNY. Ain't no monkey kin ride me, tell you.

[They stand fanning themselves.]
OLDER NEGRO. Dat nigger tough, ain't you, Puny?

PUNY. Tough as whitleather, tough 'y God! *[He gets down on his belly at the spring.]* Mouf 'bout to crack, kin drink dis heah spring dry.

OLDER NEGRO *[slouching his heavy body towards the pool]*. Hunh, me too. Dat axe take water same lak a sawmill.

[He lies down flat and drinks with the other. The water can be heard gluking over the cataract of their Adam's apples. The YOUNGER NEGRO *opens his torn and sleeveless undershirt and stands raking the sweat from his powerful chest with curved hand.]*

YOUNG NEGRO *[after a moment]*. Heigh, Puny, you'n Lije pull yo' guts out'n dat mud-hole and let de engineer take a drink.

[With a sudden thought of devilment he steps quickly forward and cracks their heads together. PUNY *starts and falls*

face foremost in the spring. LIJE, *slow and stolid, saves himself, crawls slowly upon his haunches and sits smiling good-naturedly, smacking his lips and sucking the water from the slender tails of his mustache.*]

LIJE [*cleaning his muddy hands with a bunch of leaves*]. Nunh—unh, not dis time, my boy.

YOUNG NEGRO [*scrambling to his feet, strangling and sputtering*]. Damn yo' soul, why you push me, Bud Gaskins?

BUD [*a threatening note slipping into his laugh*]. Hyuh, hyuh, don't you cuss at me, bo.

PUNY. Why'n't you 'pose on somebody yo' size? Bedder try Lije dere.

BUD *gets down and begins drinking.*

LIJE [*drawling*]. Don't keer 'f 'e do. Ducking good foh you dis hot weather.

PUNY [*helplessly*]. Allus picking at me. Wisht, wisht —

BUD. Heah I is lying down. Come on do whut you wisht. [PUNY *makes no reply but turns off, wiping his face on his shirt sleeve, and staring morosely at the ground.* BUD *gets to his feet.*] Yah, reckon you sail on me and I jam yo' haid in dat spring lak a fence post and drownd you.

PUNY [*his anger smouldering*]. Talk is cheap, black man, cheap!

[*Suddenly afraid of his boldness in replying, he turns and looks at* BUD *in a weak pleading defiance.*]

BUD [*making a frightening movement towards him*]. Mess wid me a-jowing and I knock yo' teef th'ough yo' skull.

LIJE. Hyuh, Bud, you let Puny 'lone.

[*He moves over to his bucket, gets it and sits down on the log at the left.*]

BUD [*turning for his bucket with a movement of disgust*]. Sho' I ain't gwine hurt him — po' pitiful bow-legs.

[PUNY *clenches his hands as if stung to the quick, and then beaten and forlorn reaches for his bucket, the weak member of the herd. He throws off his overall jacket, revealing himself stripped to the waist, and sits down at the pine tree.*]

LIJE [*laying out his food and singing*].

'Way, 'way up in de Rock of Ages,
In God's bosom gwine be my pillah.

BUD [*looking at* PUNY'S *bony bust*]. Uhp, showing off dat 'oman's breas' o' yo'n, is you? Haw-haw.

PUNY [*in sheer ineffectuality now answering him blandly*]. Gwine cool myse'f.

LIJE. Me too, peoples. [*He loosens his belt, pulls out his shirt-tails, undoes his shirt, and pats his belly.*] Lawd, Bud, you sho' led us a race dis mawning on dem dere boxes. Musta sweat a peck er mo'.

BUD [*taking his bucket and sitting on the ground near the center*]. Race? Hunh, wait till fo' o'clock dis evening, you gwine call foh de ca'f rope, sho' 'nough. [*Tickled at the tribute to his powers.*] And po' Puny, de monkey have rid him to deaf.

PUNY. Ain't no monkey rid me, I tells you. Little but loud. Be raght dere when de hawn blows.

BUD. Mought, and you slubbering yo' work. I cawners my boxes lak de Colonel calls foh. You des' gi' 'em a lick and a promise. Ain't it so, Lije?

LIJE [*swallowing a hunk of bread*]. Dunno, dunno. He do all right, reckon.

PUNY. Putt us in de cotton patch, and I kin kill you off de way a king snake do a lizard.

BUD. Picking cotton! Dat 'oman and chillun's job. No reg'lar man mess wid dat. [*Waving his hand at the woods behind him.*] Turpentiming's de stuff.

[*They fall to eating heartily, peas, side-meat, molasses poured in the top of the bucket-lid from a bottle, bread and collards. The axe of a fourth hand is heard still thudding in the forest.*]

LIJE [*jerking his bread-filled hand behind him*]. Whyn't Abe come on? Time he eating.

BUD. Let him rair. 'On't hurt hisse'f a-cutting. Gitting to be de no 'countest hand I ever see.

LIJE. Useter could cut boxes lak a house afiah.

PUNY. And hack! Lawd, dat nigger could hack.

LIJE. De champeen o' de woods and de swamps.

PUNY. Bedder'n Bud, bedder'n all. Knowed him to dip eight barrels many day.

BUD. Cain't he'p whut has been. Ain't

wuth my ol' hat now.   Colonel Mack say so too.   And I heahd Mr. Lonnie talking rough to him over at de weaving house day 'fo' yistiddy 'bout his gitting trifling heah lately.

PUNY. Been gitting no' count since two yeah' 'go.   De time when de white folks hang dat Charlie Sampson on a telegram pole — him whut 'tacked a white 'oman, and dey shoot him full o' holes, ayh Lawd!

BUD. Dey did.   And dat Abe gut his neck stretched hadn't been foh de Colonel. Fool went down dere in de night and cut dat nigger down and bury 'im hese'f.

LIJE [looking around him].   'Twon't do to mess wid white folks and dey r'iled up.

BUD. You said it, bruvver.

PUNY [looking around him].   Won't do. Keep to yo' work, da's all.

BUD. Yeh, work, work foh 'em.   Git yo' money and yo' meat, push on th'ough, axe no questions, no sass, keep to yo' work.

LIJE. Nigger keep mouf shet, let white man do talking.   He safe den.

BUD. Safe!   You done said.   No telegram poles, no shooting, no fiah burn um.

PUNY. Safe is best.

[They lapse into silence under the touch of worry, something undefinable, something not to be thought upon.   They swallow their food heavily.   Presently LIJE stops and looks at the ground.]

LIJE. Abe ain't safe.

BUD. Eyh?

LIJE [gesturing vaguely behind him].   Abe talk too much.

BUD [nodding].   He do, talk too much to white folks.

PUNY. Cain't he'p it, I bet.

BUD. Kin too.   Didn't talk much 'fore dat boy wuh hung.   Worked hard den and say nothing.

LIJE. Sump'n on he mind.   Sump'n deep, worry 'im, trouble —

BUD. Trouble 'bout de nigger, wanter rise him up wid eddication — fact!

PUNY. Hunh, rise him up to git a rope roun' his neck.   Git buried in he own graveyard, don't mind out.   Nigger's place down de bottom.

BUD. Raght on de bottom wid deir hand and legs, muscle power, backbone, down wid de rocks and de shovels and de digging, dat's de nigger.   White man on top.

LIJE. You's talking gospel.

PUNY. Abe say he gwine climb.   I heah him tell de Colonel dat.

BUD. Fo' God!   Whut Colonel say?

PUNY. He ain't say nothing, des' look at 'im.

LIJE. Abe is bad mixed up all down inside.

BUD. White and black make bad mixtry.

LIJE. Do dat.   [Thumping on his chest.] Nigger down heah.   [Thumping his head.] White mens up heah.   Heart say do one thing, head say 'nudder.   Bad, bad.

PUNY. De white blood in him coming to de top.   Dat make him want-a climb up and be sump'n.   Nigger gwine hol' him down dough.   Part of him take adder de Colonel, part adder his muh, 'vision and misery inside.

LIJE. Ssh!

PUNY [starting and looking around].   Colonel Mack he daddy, everybody knows. Lak as two peas, see de favor.

BUD [bitingly].   Talk too much!   Little bird carry news to de Colonel and he fall on you and scrush you.   Ain't nigger, ain't white whut ail him.   Dem damn books he gut to studying last yeah or two.   Cain't go to de woods widdout 'em.   Look up dere on his bucket, foh Christ sake.   [He points to the remaining tin bucket in the bush.   A small book is lying on the top under the handle.   Snorting.]   'Rifmatic I bet.   Give a nigger a book and des' well shoot him. All de white folks tell you dat.

PUNY [pouring molasses on his bread].   He sma't dough, in his haid.   Dat nigger gut sense.

LIJE. Hus dat.   Gitting so he kin cipher raght up wid de Colonel.

PUNY [looking at BUD].   Bet some day Colonel Mack put him woods boss over us.

BUD. Ain't no nigger gwine boss me, hoss-cake.   Split his haid open wid my axe.

LIJE [leaning back and emitting a halloo]. Heighp, you Abe!   Dinner!   Gwine cut all day?

BUD. Gi' him de full title and he'll heah you.

LIJE [*grinning*]. Aberham, Aberham McCranie!

PUNY. Yeh, you, Aberham Lincoln, whut drapped de nigger he freedom from de balloon, you better git yo' grub!

[*An answering shout comes out of the forest.*]

BUD. Trying to cut past time, mebbe us'll think he sma't.

PUNY. Don't keer whut you think, Bud, gitting so he look down on you and de rest of us.

BUD. Damn yo' runty soul, whut you know 'bout it? Ain't no nigger living kin look down on me and git by wid it. Do, and I make 'em smell o' dat.

[*He clenches his heavy fist and raises it to heaven.*]

PUNY. Jesus! Dat Abe take you up in one hand and frail yo' behime to a blister.

LIJE. Whut make you two black-gyard so much?

BUD [*to* PUNY]. Keep on, keep on, little man. Some dese days you gwine come missing.

[*He crams a handful of cornbread into his mouth.*]

LIJE [*drawling*]. Try a little fist and skull and work de bile out'n yo' systems. [*Looking off and singing.*]

Dark was de night and cold de ground. . . .

BUD [*spitting in scorn*]. Ain't gwine bruise my fistes on his old skull. Don't 'spec' to notice him no mo'. [*He falls to eating in huge mouthfuls.*] But he bedder quit th'owing dat Abe in my face, I tells him dat.

PUNY. Don't see why dat make you mad.

BUD. It do dough. I don't lak him and his uppity ways, I don't.

PUNY. Hunh, and you was one o' de fust to brag on him foh goin' on sho't rations so de Colonel buy him books and learn 'im to teach school.

BUD. Sho't rations. Ain't no sho't rations, and dat Goldie gal bringing him pies and stuff eve'y day. Be here wid a bucket in a few minutes, I betcha. Fool love de ve'y ground he squat on! And he look down on her caze her ign'ant. And teach school! Been heahing dat school teaching

business de whole yeah. He ain't gwine teach no school. Niggers 'on't send to him, dey 'on't. Niggers don't want no schooling.

PUNY. Mought. Abe tol' me dis mornin' dat de Colonel gwine fix it wid de 'missioners or something in town to-day. I know whut de matter wid you, Bud. Hee-hee.

BUD. Whut?

PUNY [*hesitating*]. Abe come riding by in de two-hoss coach. Us'll be bowing and a-scraping. Us'll pull off'n our hats and be "Howdy, Mister Aberham." [BUD *turns and looks at him with infinite scorn, saying nothing.*] And Bud? [BUD *makes no answer.*] Bud?

BUD. Whut?

PUNY. Dat Goldie business whut worrying you, hee-hee. She love Abe and—

BUD [*bounding up and kicking* PUNY'S *bucket and food into the bushes*]. Damn yo' lousy soul, minner mind stomp you in de dirt!

[*He towers over the terrified* PUNY, *who lies flat on his back whimpering.*]

PUNY. Don't hit me, Bud. Foh Gohd's sake! I des' joking.

LIJE. Go at it, fight it out.

[*Singing as he watches them.*

De bones in de grave cried Ca'vary
De night King Jesus died.

BUD [*kicking dirt at* PUNY *and going back to his bucket*]. Done told him now. Ain't gwine say no mo'! Next time be my fist rammed down his th'oat, and turn him wrong side out'ards.

[ABE *comes in at the right, carrying his axe. He is a young Negro, with a touch of the mulatto in him, of twenty-five or six, tall and powerfully built, dressed much like the others in cap and turpentine-glazed clothes. He puts his axe by the pine at the right, pulls off his cap and fans himself, while he pinches his sweaty shirt loose from his skin. His shaggy head, forehead and jaw are marked with will and intelligence. But his wide nostril and a slumbrous flash in his eye that now and then shows itself suggest a passionate and dangerous person when aroused. From the change in the actions of the others when he enters it is evident that they respect and even fear him.*]

ABE. What's de trouble 'tween you and Puny, Bud?

BUD [*sullenly*]. Ain't no trouble.

PUNY [*crawling around on the ground and collecting his spilled food*]. Ain't nothing, Abe, I des' spilled my rations.

[ABE *gets his book down and seats himself in the shade at the left. He begins working problems, using a stub of a pencil and a sheet of crumpled paper.*]

LIJE. Puny, I got some bread left you kin have.

[*He pulls a harp from his pocket and begins to blow softly.*]

PUNY [*straightening out his mashed bucket and closing it*]. I don't want nothing else, Lije. Et all I kin hold. [*After a moment.*] Putt yo' bucket up foh you.

[*He gets* LIJE'S *bucket and hangs it along with his own in the limby bush. BUD eats in silence, puts up his bucket, gets a drink from the spring, and resumes his seat, hanging his head between his knees.* PUNY *goes to the spring and drinks.*]

BUD [*pouring snuff into his lip*]. Don't fall in an' git drownded, Puny.

PUNY. Want some water, Lije?

[*He goes to the log, curls himself up in the shade beside it and prepares to sleep.*]

LIJE [*stirring lazily*]. Believe I does.

[*He goes to the spring and drinks, returns to the pine tree and sits down.*]

PUNY. Ain't you g'in' eat no dinner, Abe?

[ABE *makes no reply.*]

LIJE. Call him again. [*Touching his head with his finger.*] Deep, deep up dere.

PUNY. Heigh, Abe, bedder eat yo' grub.

ABE [*starting*]. You call me?

PUNY. You so deep stud'in' didn't heah me. Bedder eat yo' dinner. Git full o' ants settin' up dere.

ABE. I goin' to eat later.

BUD. Yeh, when Goldie come.

ABE. Hunh!

BUD. You heahd me.

ABE [*irritably*]. Don't let me heah no mo'.

BUD. Hunh?

ABE. You heahd me. [PUNY *snickers from his log with audible delight.* LIJE *waits a moment and then lies down.* BUD *reaches out and tears a bush from the ground and casts it angrily from him.*] I'll eat my dinner when it please me, you gentlemens allowing. [*There is a touch of anger in his voice which he apparently regrets on second thought, for he goes on more kindly.*] Goldie said she goin' to fetch me sump'n t' eat today. I got to work dis problem. Been on it two days now. Cain't git it out'n my head. Ain't been able to sleep two nights. [BUD *sits staring and spitting straight before him. Presently* LIJE *begins to snore, then* PUNY *follows.* ABE *goes on with his figuring.* BUD *turns over on the ground and goes to sleep.* ABE *becomes more and more absorbed in the problem he is working. He mutters to himself.*] How many sheep? How many sheep? [*He clutches at his hair, gnaws his pencil, and turns to the back of his book.*] Answer say fifteen. Cain't make it come out fifteen, cain't, seem lak, to save me. Man must have answer wrong. Six go into fo'teen, three, no, two times and — two over. [*His voice dies away as he becomes lost in his work. Presently his face begins to light up. He figures faster. Suddenly he slaps his knee.*] Dere whah I been missing it all de time. I carried two 'stid o' one. Blame fool I is. [*He hits the side of his head with his knuckle. In his excitement he calls out.*] Puny, I gitting dat answer. [*But* PUNY *is snoring away. In a moment he throws down his book with beaming face.*] I got it, folkses, I got it. Fifteen! Dat white man know whut he doing, he all time git dem answer right. [*He turns expectantly towards* LIJE.] I got it, Lije. [LIJE *makes no answer. He turns towards* PUNY *again, starts to speak but sees he is asleep.*] BUD! [*But* BUD *makes no answer. The heavy breathing of the sleepers falls regularly upon his ears. His face sinks into a sort of hopeless brooding.*] Yeh, sleep, sleep yo' life away. I figger foh you, foh me, foh all de black in de world to lead 'em up out'n ignorance. Dey don't listen, dey don't heah me, dey in de wilderness, don't wanta be led. Dey sleep, sleep in bondage. [*He bows his head between his knees.] Sleep in sin. [*Presently.*] Time me to eat.

[*He reaches for his bucket and is about to open it when* PUNY *springs high into the air with a squeak of terror, and begins rolling over and over in the leaves and briars.*]

PUNY. Come heah, folkses, come heah git dis thing off'n me.

[*He clutches at his breeches.* LIJE *and* BUD *start up out of their sleep.*]

LIJE. Who dat run-mad man?

BUD. Dat damn Puny, sump'n in he britches!

ABE. Be still, Puny, I git it out. [*He goes up to the frightened* PUNY, *reaches down his trousers and pulls out a mouse.*] Nothing but a little bitty old field mice.

[*He throws the mouse into the thicket.* LIJE *and* BUD *break into roaring laughter.* PUNY *sits down exhausted, fanning himself angrily.*]

PUNY. Laugh, laugh, all o' you. Dat thing bite same as mud turkle. Yeh, funny, funny, lak hell to you.

[*He snaps his mouth closed and fans himself the more furiously. A loud shout comes from off the left.*]

ABE. Stop yo' laughing, I heah somebody hollering.

[*A second halloo comes down the hill.*]

PUNY. Dat de Colonel and Mr. Lonnie!

BUD. Sound lak 'em. Da's who 'tis.

ABE [*going off at the left*]. Heah we is, Colonel Mack, at de spring eating dinner! [*He comes back.*] Colonel Mack and Mr. Lonnie coming on down heah.

PUNY. Co'se. Gut to see how many boxes us cleaned up dis mawning.

ABE. He tell me 'bout de school now. [*He stirs around him in his excitement.*] Mebbe dat his main business heah in de middle o' de day.

BUD. Hunh, mebbe. Gut some special work want done. Wanter hurry us to it, dat's whut.

[*The sound of voices is heard approaching from the left, and almost immediately the* COLONEL *and his son* LONNIE *come in. The* COLONEL *carries a riding whip. He is a stout, run-down old Southerner with all the signs of moral and intellectual decadence upon him. Lechery, whiskey, and levity of living have taken their toll of him, and yet he has retained a kind of native good-naturedness. His shirt front and once pointed beard are stained with the drippings of tobacco juice. There is something in his bearing and in the contour of his face that resembles* ABE. *His son, a heavyish florid young man of twenty-three or four, walks behind him.*]

COLONEL [*in a high jerky voice*]. Snoozing, hanh?

ABE. Just finishing our dinner, suh.

PUNY. Us 'bout to wuk over-time to-day, Colonel.

COLONEL. Not likely, I reckon. Say, I want you fellows, all four of you, to get over to the swamp piece on Dry Creek. Boxes there are running over, two quarts in 'em apiece, prime virgin. [*They begin to move to their feet.*] No, I don't mean to go right now. Gabe's coming by on the big road here [*jerking his whip towards the rear*] with a load of barrels and the dippers in about a half-hour. Meet him out there.

LONNIE. Yeh, we want to git the wagons off to Fayetteville to-night.

COLONEL. How you get on cornering this morning, Bud?

BUD. Purty good, suh. Us fo' done 'bout all dat pastuh piece, suh.

COLONEL. Fine, fine. That's the way. Puny and Lije stay with you?

BUD. Raght dere eve'y jump.

LIJE. Yessuh, yessuh!

PUNY. When he gi' de call we gi' 'im de 'sponse eve'y time, suh. Yes, suh, us kept 'im crowded.

COLONEL. We got to git on, Lonnie. Want to see how the scrape's coming over on Uncle Joe's Branch. Be up on the road there in half a' hour.

LONNIE [*stopping as they go out*]. Got so you doing any better work lately, Abe?

ABE [*starting*]. Suh!

LONNIE. You heard me.

ABE. I didn't understand you, Mr. Lonnie.

LONNIE. You understood me all right. [*Pointing to the book on the ground.*] Let them damned books worry you still?

COLONEL. Come on, Lonnie.

ABE [*stammering*]. I dunno — I ——

COLONEL. Still holding out on short rations, ain't you, Abe?

[*There is the least hint of pride in the* COLONEL'S *voice.*]

ABE [*somewhat confused*]. I studying whut I kin, slow go, slow go.

COLONEL. Stick to it. You the first nigger I ever see so determined. But then you're uncommon! [*The* COLONEL *moves on.*] Come on, Lonnie.

ABE [*following somewhat timidly after him*]. Colonel Mack, did di— you — what'd dey say over dere 'bout that little school business?

COLONEL. Bless my soul, 'bout to forgit it. I talked it over with the board and most of 'em think maybe we'd better not try it yet.

ABE [*his face falling*]. When dey say it might be a good time? I gitting right 'long wid dat 'rithmetic and spelling and reading. I kin teach de colored boys and gals a whole heap right now, and I'll keep studying.

COLONEL [*impatiently*]. Oh, I dunno. Time'll come mebbe. Mebbe time won't come. Folks is quare things y' know.

[*He moves on.*]

ABE. Cain't you git 'em to let me try it awhile? Reckon ——

COLONEL. I don't know, I tell you. Got my business on my mind now.

LONNIE. He's done told you two or three times, can't you hear?

ABE [*his eyes flashing and his voice shaking with sudden uncontrollable anger*]. Yeh, yeh, I hear 'im. Dem white folks don't keer — dey

LONNIE [*stepping before him*]. Look out! none of your sass. Pa's already done more for you than you deserve. He even stood up for you and they laughing at him there in town.

ABE [*trembling*]. Yeh, yeh, I knows. But dem white folks don't think — I going to show 'em, I ——

LONNIE [*pushing himself before him*]. Dry up. Not another word.

ABE [*his voice breaking almost into a sob*]. Don't talk to me lak dat, Mr. Lonnie.

Stop him, Colonel Mack, 'fore I hurt him.

[*The other Negroes draw off into a knot by the pine tree, mumbling in excitement and fear.*]

COLONEL. Stop, Lonnie! Abe, don't you talk to my son like that.

LONNIE. By God, I'm going to take some of the airs off'n him right now. You've gone around here, sorry, worthless — worse every day for the last year. What you need is a good beating, and I'm gonna give it to you.

[*He steps backwards and snatches the whip from his father's hand.*]

COLONEL. Stop that, Lonnie!

LONNIE. Keep out of this yourself. [*He comes towards* ABE.] I'll beat his black hide off'n him.

ABE. Keep 'im back dere, Colonel Mack. I mought kill him! Keep 'im off.

LONNIE. Kill him! All right, do it, damn you!

[*He strikes* ABE *across the face with his whip. With a snarl* ABE *springs upon him, tears the whip from his hands and hurls him headlong into the thicket of briars and bushes. Then he stands with his hands and head hanging down, his body shaking like one with the palsy.*]

PUNY [*screaming*]. You done kilt Mr. Lonnie! Oh, Lawdy, Lawdy!

COLONEL [*running to* LONNIE *who is crawling up out of the mud with his clothes and skin torn. He is sobbing and cursing.*] Are you hurt? How bad are you hurt?

LONNIE. Let me git at that son of a bitch and I'll kill him dead. [*Moaning.*] Oh, I'll beat his brains out with one o' them axes.

COLONEL. If you ain't dead, you'd better keep your hands off'n him. I'll fix him. [*He reaches down and picks up the whip — thundering.*] Git down on your knees, Abe! Git down, you slave! I'm gonna beat you.

[ABE *jerks his head up in defiance, but before the stern face of the* COLONEL *his strength goes out of him. He puts his hands up in supplication.*]

ABE. Don't beat me, Colonel Mack, don't beat me wid dat whip!

COLONEL. Git down on your knees!

I've beat many a slave, and I'll show you how it feels.

[*He strikes him several blows.*]

ABE [*falling on his knees*]. Oh, Lawd, have muhcy upon me!

[*The* COLONEL *begins to beat him blow upon blow.* PUNY, BUD *and* LIJE *stand near the pine in breathless anxiety.*]

PUNY. De Colonel'll kill 'im!

BUD [*seizing his arm*]. Shet dat mouf, nigger!

COLONEL [*as he brings the whip down*]. Let this be a lesson to you to the end of your life!

ABE [*his back twitching under the whip, his voice broken*]. Muhcy, Colonel Mack, muhcy!

COLONEL. You struck a white man, you struck my son

ABE [*raising his tear-stained face*]. I yo' son too, you my daddy.

[*He throws himself down before him, embracing his feet. The* COLONEL *lowers the whip, then drops it behind him.*]

LONNIE [*his voice husky with rage*]. You hear what he say? Hear what he called you?

[*He seizes the whip and in a blind rage strikes the prostrate* ABE *again and again.*]

COLONEL [*stepping between them*]. Stop it! Give me that whip. [LONNIE *nervelessly hesitates and then reluctantly hands him the whip.*] Go on back out to the road and wait for me. Trot! [LONNIE *in disgust and rage finally goes off at the left nursing his face in his arms.*] Get up, Abe. Get up, I say.

[ABE *sits up, hugging his face between his hands. The* COLONEL *wets his handkerchief in the spring, and with his hands on* ABE'S *head bathes the bruises on his neck and shoulders.*]

ABE [*in a voice grown strangely dignified and quiet*]. Thank 'ee, thank 'ee, Colonel Mack.

COLONEL [*breathing heavily*]. Thanky nothing. I had to beat you, Abe, had to. Think no more about it. Dangerous thing, hitting a white man. But this is the end of it. Won't be no law, nothing but this. Put some tar and honey on yourself to-night and you'll be all right to-morrow. [*The bushes are suddenly parted at the rear and a tall sinuous young mulatto woman bounds through. She carries a bucket in her hand. At the sight of the* COLONEL *bathing* ABE'S *head and neck she rushes forward with a low cry. The* COLONEL *turns towards her.*] Now, Goldie, ain't no use cutting up. Abe been in a little trouble. Nothing much.

GOLDIE [*moaning*]. I heahd de racket and I 'fraid somebody being kilt. Is you hurt bad, Abe, honey babe? [*She bends tenderly over him, her hand running over his hair.*] Who huht you, honey, who huht you?

COLONEL [*handing* GOLDIE *his handkerchief*]. Look after him, Goldie. [*He goes out at the left calling.*] Wait a minute, Lonnie!

GOLDIE. Whut dey do to you, Abe? Who huht you? [*All the time she is rubbing his neck, dabbing his shoulders with the handchief, and cooing over him.*] Why'n you kill dem white mens if dey hurt you? You kin do it, break 'em lak broomstraws.

ABE [*standing up*]. Ain't nobody hurt me. I crazy dat's whut, crazy in de haid. Ain't nobody hurt me.

GOLDIE [*clinging to him*]. You is hurt, hurt bad. Look at yo' po' neck and shoulders. Look at 'em beat wid great whales on 'em!

ABE [*growling*]. Ain't nobody hurt me, I tell you.

GOLDIE. Lay yo'se'f down heah and let me smoove off yo' forehead and put some cold water on dat mark crost yo' face. Please'm, Abe.

ABE [*suddenly crying out in a loud voice*]. I ain't nothing, nothing. Dat white man beat me, beat me like a dawg. [*His voice rising into a wail.*] He flail me lak a suck-egg dawg! [*He rocks his head from side to side in a frenzy of wrath.*] Lemme git to him! [*He falls on his knees searching in the leaves and finds a stone.* GOLDIE *stands wringing her hands and moaning. He jumps to his feet, raising the stone high above his head.*] Lemme git to him, I scrush his God-damn head lak a eggshell!

[*He moves to the left to follow the*
COLONEL. GOLDIE *throws her arms
around his neck.*]

GOLDIE. No, no, you ain't gwine out
dere, Abe, Abe!

PUNY [*crying out*]. Stop him, Bud!
Lije, keep him back!

LIJE [*coming from the pine tree*]. Hyuh,
now you, Abe, stop dat.

BUD [*moving quickly before him and
blocking his path*]. Stop dat, fool. You
gwine fix it to git yo'se'f hung up on a telegram pole. Body be so full o' holes, sift
sand.

GOLDIE [*sobbing*]. Don't do it, Abe, sugar babe. [*Throws herself upon his breast.*]

BUD [*reaching toward her*]. Seem lak you
take yo'se'f off'n dat man!

ABE [*pulling her arms from around him*].
Lemme loose, lemme loose. [*After a moment he throws the stone down.*] I ain't going do nothing.

[*He sits down on the log at the left,
holding his head in his hands.*]

GOLDIE [*bringing her bucket*]. Hyuh, eat
sump'n, Abe, you feel better. I gut some
pie and some cake in heah foh you.

PUNY [*stepping back and forth in senseless
excitement*]. Somebody gwine git kilt at dis
mess, somebody ——

ABE [*pushing GOLDIE away*]. I ain't
want nothing t' eat, ain't hongry.

LIJE. Bedder eat, Abe. Git yo' stren'th
back.

ABE [*savagely*]. Ain't hongry, I keep
telling you.

[GOLDIE *drops on her knees beside
him and laying her head in his lap
clasps her arms around him.*]

GOLDIE [*sobbing softly*]. Oh, boy, boy,
why dey beat you up so? Whut you do to
'em?

ABE. Fool, fool I is. Crazy, dat's it.

BUD [*sharply*]. He g'in Mr. Lonnie and
de Colonel back talk. Cain't sass white
mens and git 'way wid it. Abe orter know
better.

[LIJE *wanders over to the right blowing
his harp softly and forlornly.*]

PUNY [*sitting down on the ground*].
Cain't be done, Abe. Cain't.

BUD [*stripping leaves from a bush and

watching GOLDIE *as she carries on over* ABE].
Hyuh, 'oman, stop dat rairing. [*Muttering
to himself.*] Nevah see two bigger fools.

[ABE *puts his hands mechanically on*
GOLDIE'S *shoulders and begins stroking
her.*]

ABE. Stop it, baby. Ain't no use to cry.

[PUNY *sits with his mouth open in
astonishment watching them.* LIJE *lays
himself back on the ground and blows his
harp, apparently no longer interested.*]

BUD [*jealousy rising within him*]. Heigh,
Goldie, git up from dat man's lap. He
ain't keer nothing foh you. [GOLDIE'S *sobs
die away and she is quiet.*] He say you
foolish many time. He look down on you.

GOLDIE [*raising her tear-stained face*].
How you know? You jealous, Bud Gaskins. He better man dan you. Wuth
whole town of you. [*Catching* ABE *by the
hand and picking up her bucket.*] Come on,
come on, honey, le's go off dere in de woods
and eat our dinner by ourse'ves!

BUD [*coming up to her*]. Hyuh, you stay
out'n dat woods wid him, nigger.

ABE [*standing up*]. Yeh, yeh, I come
wid you.

[*He moves as one in a dream, and
reaches out and pushes* BUD *behind him.*]

GOLDIE [*her face alight, a sort of reckless
and unreal abandonment upon her*]. I
knows where dere's a cool place under a big
tree. And dey's cool green moss dere and
soft leaves. Le's go dere, boy. I gwine
tend to you and feed you. [*She moves
across towards the right, leading* ABE *like a
child.*] We make us a bed dere, honey.
[LIJE *sits up watching them.*] Us forgit de
'membrance o' all dis trouble. [*A kind of
ecstasy breaking in her voice.*] Dere de
birds sing and we hear de little branch
running over de rocks. Cool dere, sweet
dere, you kin sleep, honey, rest dere, baby.
Yo' mammy, yo' chile gwine love you,
make you fohgit.

ABE [*moved out of himself*]. Yeh, yeh, I
come wid you. I don't keer foh nothing,
not nothing no mo'. You, des' you'n me.

GOLDIE. Ain't no worl', ain't no Lije and
Bud, nobody. Us gwine make us a 'biding
place and a pillah under dat green tree.
[*In sweet oblivion.*] Feel yo' arms around

me, my lips on yo'n. We go singing up to heaben, honey, togedder — togedder.

[*They go off, her voice gradually dying away like a nun's chant.*]

BUD [*breaking a sapling in his grasp*]. Gwine off, gwine off in de woods togedder dere lak hawgs.

PUNY [*bounding up, his body shaking in lascivious delight*]. I gwine watch 'em — hee-hee — I gwine watch 'em.

LIJE [*knocking him back*]. Bedder stay out'n dat woods. Abe kill you.

PUNY [*standing up by the pine tree*]. Kin see 'em, her still a-leading 'im.

LIJE [*standing up and peering off to the right*]. Dere on de cool moss and de sof' green leaves.

BUD [*stripping the limbs from the top of the broken sapling*]. Ain't gwine look. Dey fools, bofe fools. [*Raging out.*] Dere she go playing de hawg. Didn't know she lak dat. [*He sucks in his breath with the sound of eating something.*] Wisht to Gohd I knowed she lak dat. I de man foh her. Bud Gaskins. I tame her, Gohd damn her, I tame her down and take dat speerit out'n her.

[*He crowds out his chest and walks up and down.*]

PUNY [*grasping* LIJE'S *arm*]. Cain't hardly see 'em no mo', kin you?

LIJE. Kin hardly.

BUD [*his anger and jealousy disappearing in physical emotion and vulgar curiosity*]. Whah dey now?

LIJE [*pointing*]. Dere, dere, dey crossing de branch now.

PUNY [*breathlessly*]. I see 'em. I see 'em. He arm 'round her now, her head on he shoulder. [*He capers in his excitement.*] Lawd! Lawd!

BUD [*with a loud brutal laugh as he slaps* LIJE *on the back*]. On de sof' green moss.

LIJE [*laughing back and dragging his harp across his mouth*]. Whah de leaves is cool.

PUNY. Cain't see 'em no mo'. [*He whirls about and turns a handspring.*] Whoopee, folkses! Gwine run away wid myse'f!

BUD [*his eyes shining*]. Down whah de branch water run.

[*He shuffles a jig among the leaves.*]

LIJE [*blowing upon his harp*]. Singing raght up to heaben!

[*He plays more wildly as they all drop into a barbaric dance that gradually mounts into a dionysiac frenzy.*]

PUNY. Heaben!

BUD. Jesus, Lawd, Fadder and Son!

LIJE [*singing loudly as they dance, the music running into a quick thumping rhythm*].

My feets wuh wet wid de sunrise dew,
De mawning stah wuh a witness too.
'Way, 'way up in de Rock of Ages,
In God's bosom gwine be my pillow.

[*They gambol, turn and twist, run on all fours, rear themselves up on their haunches, cavort like goats.*]

PUNY. In God's bosom — hanh!

BUD. In who bosom?

LIJE. In who bosom, bubber!

[*A loud halloo comes down from the hill in the rear, unnoticed by them.*]

PUNY. In Goldie's bosom. Hee-hee-hee.

BUD and LIJE. Haw-haw-haw! Hee-hee-hee! In God's bosom gwine be my pillah.

[*The halloo is repeated.*]

LIJE. Hyuh, dere dat Gabe calling us. Better git, or de Colonel have dat stick on our back.

[*They gather up their buckets and axes.* PUNY *clambers up the pine a few feet and drops to the ground.*]

BUD. Kin see?

PUNY. See nothing. Hee-hee!

LIJE. Gut to leave 'em now. Abe ketch it 'gin don't mind out. He not coming wid us.

BUD. He done foh now. Dat gal gut him hard and fast. [*Snorting scornfully.*] Books, books! Rise 'em up, lak hell!

LIJE. I done told you. Heart say dis, head say dat. Bad mixtry. Bad. Crazy!

PUNY [*shouting*]. Heigh, you Gabe! Coming!

[*They move out at the rear up the hill, singing, laughing and jostling each other.*]

'Way, 'way down by de sweet branch water
In her bosom gwine be he pillah!

Hee-hee — haw — haw —!

[*Their loud brutally mocking laughter
floats back behind them.*]

SCENE II

A spring day about three years later, in
ABRAHAM MCCRANIE'S *two-room cabin. The
room is roughly built of framed material and
unceiled. To the right front is a fireplace
with a green oakwood fire going. A wood
box is to the right of the chimney. To the
left rear of the room is a bed, and at the left
center rear a door leads out to the porch. To
the right of the door a window gives a view
of wide-stretched cotton fields. Below the
window close to the wall is a rough home-
made chest with several books on it, and hanging between it and the door is a sort of calendar, with the illustration of a slave leaving his
chains behind and walking up a hill towards
the sunrise. There is a caption at the top of
the print in large letters — "*WE ARE RISING.*"
Several old dresses, bonnets, and coats hang
on the nails in the joists in the right rear.
A door in the right center leads into the
kitchen. At the left front is a dilapidated old
bureau, small pieces of wood taking the
place of lost casters. The top drawer is open,
sagging down like a wide lip, with stray bits
of clothing hanging over the edge. A bucket
of water and a pan are on the bureau. There
are several splint-bottomed chairs and a
rocker in the room.*

When the curtain rises MUH MACK *is
sitting by the fire rocking a bundle in her
arms. She is a chocolate-colored Negress of
near sixty, dressed in a long dirty wrapper,
and barefooted. Her graying hair is wrapped
in pigtails and stands around her head
Medusa-like. A long snuff-stick protrudes
from her mouth, and now and then the fire
sputters with a frying noise as she spits into
it.* GOLDIE'S *long gaunt form lies stretched
on the bed at the left partly covered by a sheet,
her head hanging off on her arm. She is
constantly raising in her languid hand a
stick with a paper tied to it to shoo away the
flies.* MUH MACK *rocks and sings.*

MUH MACK.

*Oohm — oohm — hoonh — oohm — oohm —
Dis heah baby de pu'tiest baby,*

*Pu'tiest baby in de lan'.
He gwine grow up champeen sojer,
Mammy's honey, onlies' man.
Oohm — oohm — hoonh — oohm — oohm —*

GOLDIE [*in a tired voice*]. How he coming now?

MUH MACK [*shaking her finger and wag-
ging her head at the bundle*]. Done seen um
grow. Look at me lak he know me.

GOLDIE [*with a long sigh*]. I so tiahed,
tiahed. Seem lak I kin sleep forever.

MUH MACK. Lie and sleep, sleep. Git
yo' stren'th.

GOLDIE. I tiahed but cain't sleep. [*She
lapses into silence. The old woman rocks
and sings. Presently* GOLDIE *raises her
head.*] Whut day to-day?

MUH MACK. Sa'd'y.

GOLDIE. Seem lak I cain't 'member
nothing. Whut day he come?

MUH MACK. He come a-Chuesday.

GOLDIE. Dat make him — le's see, how
old?

MUH MACK. Fo' day now.

GOLDIE [*suddenly sitting up with a gasp*].
Dem udder two die, one th'ee days,
udder'n fo'.

MUH MACK. Nanh — nanh, lie back
down. Dis heah baby live be a hundred.
He strong, he muscled. Dem udder po'
little 'uns puny, bawn to die. De mark
was on 'em f'om de fust.

GOLDIE [*bending her head between her
knees and weeping softly*]. Dey was so pitiful and liddle. I cain't fohgit how dey
feel and fumble foh me wid deir liddle
hands and dey hongry.

MUH MACK [*irritably*]. Bless Gohd,
crying adder dem, and gut dis fine 'un
heah. Lay yo'se'f down on dat bed and res'.

GOLDIE. Cain't fohgit 'em, cain't.

MUH MACK. Hunh, mought as well and
dey done plowed in de ground.

GOLDIE [*her tears beginning to flow again*].
Yeh, yeh, dey is! Abe didn't try to keep
Mr. Lonnie f'om cutting down dem plum
bushes and plowing up dat hedgerow. I
hold it 'gin him long as I live.

MUH MACK. Why foh? De dead's de
dead. Let de earf hab 'em. Let cotton
grow over 'um. No use mo'ning. Think
on de living.

GOLDIE. Po' Abe, 'on't his fault dough. He proud, stand by see white mens plow over 'em, say nothin', 'on't beg foh his babies.

MUH MACK. Cain't blame 'im! He stiff neck. God break his spirit. Gi' 'im two dead 'uns to fetch 'im down. He bedder humble now. [*Talking half to herself.*] He talk proud lak, gwine raise up big sons, leader 'mong men. Fust 'un come thin, liddle lak a rat. He hate 'im. He die. God call 'im. Second come, Ol' Moster keep him liddle, thin. He die too. Abe gitting down to sackcloff and ashes in he mind, mebbe. God see him down crying foh muhcy, He send dis 'un, strong. Israel man. He gwine flourish, he gwine wax.

GOLDIE [*stretching herself out on the bed*]. Abe say dis 'un gwine die too, same lak de udders. He don't look at 'im, pay no 'tention.

MUH MACK. Hunh, he will dough when he see 'im fleshen up wid he sucking.

GOLDIE. Whah he?

MUH MACK. Went down in de new ground planting cawn. Won't make nothing dough and it de light o' de moon. He be heah directly foh he dinner.

GOLDIE. Po' Abe wuk too hard.

MUH MACK [*snorting*]. Wuk too hahd de mischief! Ain't wuk whut ail him. He studyin' ol' books and mess too much. Crap shows it.

GOLDIE. He don't look well, neiver.

MUH MACK. Cain't look well and worry all time. [*A step is heard on the porch.*] Dere he now. Take dis baby. Gut to put dinner on de table.

[*She takes the baby over to* GOLDIE, *lays it by her side, goes out at the right, and is heard rattling dishes and pans in the kitchen.*]

GOLDIE [*crooning over her baby*]. Now you go sleep, res' yo'se'f, git strong and grow gre't big.

[ABE *comes in at the rear carrying a hoe and a file. He is barefooted and dressed in overalls, ragged shirt and weather-stained straw hat. Sitting down near the center of the room, he begins filing his hoe.*]

ABE [*without looking around*]. How you come on?

GOLDIE. Better, I reckon. [*With a sharp gasp.*] Hyuh, why you fetch dat hoe in de house?

ABE [*paying no attention to her query*]. Baby still living, hunh?

GOLDIE. Abe, take dat hoe out'n dis house. Mought bring bad luck on you. [*Raising herself up in bed.*] Mought bring sump'n on de baby.

ABE. Cain't swub dem new-ground bushes wid no dull hoe.

GOLDIE [*pleading*]. Take it out'n de house, I say.

ABE. When I damn ready.

GOLDIE [*calling*]. Muh Mack! Muh Mack!

MUH MACK [*coming to the door at the right*]. What ails you? [*She sees* ABE *filing his hoe.*] Lawd he'p us! Throw dat thing out, throw it out! Ain't gut no sense. Goldie too weak to be worried up.

ABE. Aw right den. I finish wid it now. Set o' fools. Eve'ything got a sign 'tached to it. Ign'ant, bline!

[*He throws the hoe out through the rear door and gets a book from the chest and begins reading.*]

MUH MACK. Back at dem books, Lawd, never see sich.

[*She goes scornfully back to the kitchen.*]

ABE [*half growling*]. Says heah niggers gut to git out'n dem 'spicions and being 'fraid. Ain't no signs wid evil and good in 'em. I read dat last night. [*Reading and halting over the words.*] "The Negro is a superstitious person. There are signs and wonders in the weather, some fraught with evil, some with good. He plants his crops according to the moon, works and labors under the eye of some evil spirit of his own imagining." [*Closing the book with a bang.*] Heah dat?

GOLDIE. I heah but don't mind it. Mean nothing. White man wrote it, and he don't know.

ABE. Dat's jest it; he do know. Nigger one don't know. Dat book wrote foh you, Muh, and all de rest of de bline.

GOLDIE. Put up dem ol' books. Seem

lak you keer mo' foh 'em dan you do dis heah baby, and he a fine boy chile.

ABE [throwing the book back on the chest]. What he nohow? Ain't 'rested in 'im. Ain't no use being. He be dead in week. God done cuss me and my household. No luck at nothing. Cain't raise chillun, cain't raise crap, nothing. Ain't dry weather, wet. Ain't wet, dry. Heah May month and cold 'nough foh freeze. [He stretches his feet to the fire.] De damn crows down dere on de creek pulling up my cawn faster'n I kin plant it. [He rocks his head.] Jesus!

GOLDIE [pleading]. Abe, honey, don't git down. Things coming better now. Dis boy gwine make you feel better. Heah he lie now des' smiling lak he onderstand me. [Bending over the baby.] Yeh you is gwine grow up and take trouble off'n yo' po' daddy. Yeh, you is.

ABE [holding his head in his arms]. Listen to dat talk, listen dere. [Bitterly.] 'Oman know. She know. Heah I am wid no money to buy me shoes. [Holding up his dust-stained foot.] Dere you is, foot, cut wid glass, full o' b'rars, wo' out stumping de roots and snags, and I cain't buy nothing to kiver you wid.

GOLDIE. De Colonel give you shoes, you ax him.

ABE. Ain't gwine ax him nothing, not nothing. [Suddenly clenching his fist and hitting his thigh.] Dat man beat me, beat me at de spring th'ee yeah ago, I ain't fohgit. [He gets up and strides over to the bed and looks down at the suckling infant.] Dere you lie drinking yo' grub in. What you keer? Nothing.

[He lays his hand roughly on the baby and pinches him. The child lets out a high thin wail.]

GOLDIE [beating his hand off]. Quit dat pinching dat baby. Quit it!

ABE [laughing brutally as he walks up and down the floor]. Yeh, you fight over 'im now and he be plowed in de ground lak de udders in a month. Hee-hee! Ain't dis a hell of a mess! It sho' God is. And us ain't got 'nough to feed a cat. You'n Muh cook and slay and waste fast I make it. Note at de sto' done tuck up, crap done all mortgaged up 'head o' time. Cain't make ends meet, cain't. [Throwing his hands out hopelessly.] Ayh God! [Stopping.] He cain't heah me.

GOLDIE [wretchedly]. Oh, Abe, we git on somehow, us will. And Muh'n me don't waste. I be up wid you in de fields by de middle o' de week. Po' chile, you need sleep, need rest.

ABE. Make no difference. Wuk our guts out do no good. I tell you, gal, de nigger is down, down. De white man up dere high, setting up wid God, up dere in his favor. He git eve'ything, nigger git de scraps, leavings. [Flaring out.] Ain't no God foh de nigger, dat's white man's God. Dat come to me down in de new ground.

[He sits down again, tapping his feet on the floor.]

GOLDIE [wiping her eyes]. Honey, you gut to stop talking lak dat. Cain't be bad luck allus. I'se 'feared when you talk dat wild talk. God heah it he do. [MUH MACK comes and stands in the door.] He mought be doing all dis to make us good, make us humble down befo' him.

ABE. Humble down, hell! Look at de udder niggers den. Dey shout and carry on in de church, pray and pay de preachers in deir blindness. Dey humble. What do God do? Starve 'em to deaf. Kill 'em off lak flies wid consumption. Dey dying 'long de river same as de chillun in de wilderness.

MUH MACK. You blaspheaming, da's whut you doing. No wonder Gohd take yo' babies 'way, no wonder he make yo' mule die, blast down yo' plans and send de crows and cold weather and root lice to destroy yo' craps. [Her eyes flashing.] You gut to change yo' ways. Some day he gwine re'ch down from de clouds and grab you by de scruff o' de neck and break you cross he knee. He gi'n you fine baby chile, you don't thank him. You gut to fall down, pray, git low, git humble. [Her voice rises into a semi-chant.] You dere, Jesus, heah my prayer. Dis heah sinner, he weeked, he blaspheam. Save him and save dis po' liddle baby.

GOLDIE [weeping over the child]. Do, Lawd, heah our prayer.

[ABE *sits down in his chair and stares moodily into the fire.*]

MUH MACK [*crying out*]. Dem dere ol' books cause it, da's whut. Burn um up, burn um wid fiah. Yo' wild talk gwine make de Upper Powers drap lightning on dis house, gwine destroy all of us. [*She wraps her arms before her, mumbling and swaying from side to side. Suddenly she raises her head and striding over to the chest shakes her fist at the books and kicks them.*] You de trouble. I hates de sight o' you, and I wish dere wa'n't nary one o' you in de worl'.

ABE [*throwing her back*]. Look out, 'oman! Don't you tech my books!

MUH MACK. You mash my arm!

[*With a wail she goes out at the right and is heard sobbing in the kitchen.*]

GOLDIE. Oh, you struck huh! Abe — Abe ——

[*She sits up in the bed rocking the baby and quieting him. A heavy step sounds on the porch. ABE sits before the fire smoothing out the leaves of a book, as a voice calls from the outside.*]

VOICE. Heigh, you, Abe!

GOLDIE [*quickly*]. Dat de Colonel out dere, Abe.

ABE [*going to the door*]. Yes, suh, dat you, Colonel Mack?

COLONEL [*coming in*]. Yes. How you come on, all of you? [*He looks around the room and at the bed. Three years have worked a great change in him. He is stouter, his face mottled, and he walks with difficulty, propped on a stick.*] Been wanting to see that fine baby, Abe.

ABE [*quietly*]. Yes, suh, yes, suh.

MUH MACK [*coming in*]. And he sho' is a fine 'un. [*Standing near the COLONEL.*] Fine and strong same lak Abe when he wuh bawn.

COLONEL. What's the matter, Goldie? Ain't been fighting, have you all? Who was that making a racket in here?

GOLDIE [*keeping her head lowered*]. I all right, Colonel Mack.

MUH MACK [*wiping her eyes*]. Ain't no row, Colonel. Want you to 'suade dat Abe git rid o' dem ol' books. 'Nough trouble come on us 'count of um.

COLONEL [*laughing*]. The devil, let him keep his books. He's the only nigger in the whole country worth a durn. Let me see the baby. [GOLDIE *shows the baby.*] That's a fine un, Abe. He'll live. Let me feel him. [*Holding him up.*] Heavy, gracious!

[MUH MACK *looks at him intently and there is the vaguest touch of malice in her voice as she speaks.*]

MUH MACK. Lawd, it all comes to me ag'in. Jest sech a day as dis thirty yeah ago you come down heah and hold Abe up dat-a-way.

COLONEL [*looking through the window a long while*]. Time hurries on, it goes by in a hurry. [ABE *looks before him with an indefinable expression on his face. A constrained silence comes over them and the* COLONEL *takes a sort of refuge in gazing intently at the child. Once or twice he clears his throat.*] Yes, Callie, we're getting old.

[*For an instant all differences are passed away and they are four human beings aware of the strangeness of their lives, conscious of what queer relationships have fastened them together.*]

MUH MACK [*starting*]. Yes, suh, w' ain't gut much longer.

[*The baby begins to cry and the* COLONEL *smiles.*]

COLONEL. Here, take him, Goldie. Favors Muh Mack, don't favor you, Abe.

ABE. Yes, suh.

COLONEL [*drawing a heavy, folded paper from his pocket slowly and with weighty dignity*]. I got a little surprise for you'n Goldie, Abe. [*He puts on his spectacles, opens the paper and starts to read.*] "Whereas" — [*He stops as if convulsed with pain, and presently goes on*] "I devise to Abraham McCranie a house and tract of land containing twenty-five acres and formerly known as the 'Howington place,' to him and his heirs forever." [*Hesitating a moment and folding the paper together.*] Then follows a description of the place in course and distance, Abe, which I won't read. It's all signed up and recorded in the court-house.

[*He feels around him heavily for his stick.*]

ABE [*incredulously*]. Whut dat? Dat foh me?

COLONEL. Yes, for you. A deed to this house and twenty-five acres of land, yours.

[*He holds out the paper to* ABE.]

ABE [*taking it with trembling hands*]. Lawd, Colonel Mack, whut I gwine say?

COLONEL. Say nothing. Say thanky if you want to.

ABE [*overcome*]. Thanky, suh, thanky, suh.

COLONEL. Shake hands on it, Abe.

ABE [*wiping his hand on his shirt*]. Thanky, suh.

[*The* COLONEL *looks at his bent head with strange intentness, and then drops* ABE'S *hand.*]

GOLDIE. Oh, Colonel Mack!

[*Her eyes are shining with thankfulness.*]

MUH MACK. Abe, you's gut land, boy, you owns you a piece o' land, Glory!

[*She runs up to the* COLONEL *and covers his hands with kisses.*]

COLONEL [*waving her off*]. Nothing, nothing to do for him. He deserves it. [*Looking straight at* ABE.] You do, boy. I want to see you go forward now. You had a hard time the last three years.

GOLDIE. He has, po' boy. He had it hard since de day he married me.

COLONEL. Hunh. He couldn't a done better nowhere. I know. [*The* COLONEL *picks up his stick which he has laid across the bed.*] Well, I got to move on. [*He stops near the door.*] And, Abe, how's your book business coming on?

ABE. I — I studying and reading now and den. Most too tiahed every night dough to do much.

COLONEL. Don't give up like Lonnie. Sent him to school, and sent him to school, even tried him at the university, won't stay. He ain't worth a damn, that's what. [*Turning toward the door and stopping again.*] Well, I've got another little surprise for you in celebration of that fine boy. [*He looks down and taps on the floor.*]

ABE [*excitedly*]. Whut is it, Colonel Mack, suh?

COLONEL. How'd you like to try your hand at teaching a little school next fall?

[MUH MACK *throws up her hands.*]

GOLDIE [*breathlessly*]. Oh, me!

ABE [*in confusion*]. Teach school? Yessuh, I ——

COLONEL. I'm going to have that old Quillie house fixed up and put some benches in it and a blackboard. I'll get two Negroes to serve with me on the school board and we'll try you out. [*Smiling queerly.*] I been reading your books, too, Abe.

ABE [*with a great breath*]. I gwine teach school — at last!

COLONEL [*going shakily out at the door*]. Yes, at last. Now don't forget your crop, Abe, and study yourself to death.

ABE [*following him*]. Colonel Mack, you, you — I — I ——

COLONEL. Take care of that baby. Raise him up right. And, Abe, don't forget you ain't gonna have no easy time. I'll get a lot of cussing for this, well as you. Go on eat your dinner. [*He stops on the porch and calls.*] Here, Goldie, take this fifty cents and buy the boy a stick of candy. [*He steps to the door and throws the coin on the bed.*] Take care of him and don't kill him on collards and beans.

[*He goes off.*]

ABE [*calling after him*]. I ain't, Colonel, I gwine raise him. I gwine make a man —— [*He stops and stands watching the old man going in the lane. Then he turns and stumbles into the room with shining face.*] I — I fohgives him all. I don't 'member dat beating by de spring no mo'.

GOLDIE [*reaching out from the bed and grasping his hand*]. Oh, honey babe, our troubles's ended. We gwine — we gwine have 'nough t'eat and you gwine be happy.

[*She turns over in the bed and begins to cry softly.*]

ABE [*patting her shoulders*]. Dere, dere, don't you cry, chile. [*He wipes his eyes with his sleeve.*] I been mean man. [*In a husky voice.*] I treat my gal mean, blaspheam 'gin de Lawd. I gwine do better, I —— [*A sob chokes in his throat.*]

MUH MACK [*coming up to him and clasping her arms around him*]. Bless de Lawd, you gwine do bedder now.

[*She sits down in a chair and bows her head in her lap.*]

GOLDIE. He good man, de Colonel. He too good to us. Raise us up, help us.

ABE [*vaguely*]. Up! Lift me up! Up! Up tow'd de sun! [*He glances at the calendar.*] Dat whup don't hurt no mo'. De 'membrance is passed away. [*Thumping on his breast.*] Ain't no mo' bitter gall in heah. Peace. It come all suddent over me. [*He suddenly falls on his knees by the bed in a sobbing burst of prayer.*] O God, God of de po' and of de sinful!

MUH MACK [*whispering*]. Yea, our God.

ABE. De black man's God, de white man's God, de one and only God, heah me, heah my prayer.

MUH MACK [*swaying and moaning*]. Heah 'im, Jesus!

GOLDIE [*softly*]. We dy chillun, Lawd.

ABE. Dy little chillun, and you pow'ful. You de Almighty, us de dust in dy hand. Us po' and weak, us nothing. Lak de grasshopper, lak de po' fee-lark, swept away in de storm. Man gut no stren'th in um, no muscle kin raise him, 'cepting yo' power. He walk in de wind, de wind take 'im away. Let dere be fiah, and de fiah burn um. It devour 'im. Same lak de broomstraw he fall befo' it. Man cain't stand. He lost, lost. Shet in de grave, shet till de judgment.

MUH MACK. Jesus! Jesus!

GOLDIE [*piteously*]. Jesus!

ABE. He fall in de winter. He lie down in de summer. De spring come and find him gone.

MUH MACK. Ha' muhcy, our Fadder.

GOLDIE [*whispering*]. Jesus, fohgive 'im.

ABE [*his voice rising into a chant*]. De dirt stop up his po' mouf. Peace come to him in de ground. And de friends do cry, dey wail and beat deir breas'. Dey call foh deir love' ones, and dey don't answer. Deir tongue make no mo' speech, from de graveyard, from de deep grave.

MUH MACK. Yea, Lawd!

ABE. Dey gone at de planting, gone at de harvest. De hoe dull wid rust, de harness wait on de peg, de bridle break, de collar hang dere useless. Dey ain't no mo' hoeing, ain't no mo' plowing, no shoe track in de furrow. Man gone, same lak a whisper, hushed in de graveyard, in de deep grave.

MUH MACK. Oh, ha' muhcy 'pon us.

GOLDIE. Muhcy!

ABE [*raising his head up, his eyes closed*]. Heah us, heah us, heah me dis day, heah my po' prayer. Fohgive me my sins, my blaspheamy. Wipe out de evil o' my weeked days. Purify, make clean, fohgit de 'membrance o' my transgression. Now heah I do humble down, I do cohnfess. Lift me, raise me, up, up!

MUH MACK. Hallelujah!

GOLDIE. Amen.

ABE [*bowing his head in a storm of grief*]. Re'ch down yo' hand and gimme stren'th. Now I draw nigh, I feel yo' sperit. Save me, save me now! [*MUH MACK and GOLDIE pray and moan aloud. Presently ABE stands up and cries out exultantly.*] He save me, he done save me! He done fohgive me!

MUH MACK [*clapping her hands wildly*]. Bless de Lawd, bless um!

GOLDIE [*faintly*]. Thank Jesus, save my baby and my husban'.

[*ABE is silent a moment, his face working with emotion. He turns and bends down over the bed.*]

ABE. Po' little fellow, he sleep and rest. [*He puts his arms around GOLDIE and she clings to him.*] Honey chile, I changed I gwine take new holt. From dis day I begins. I sorry foh all de past. [*He loosens her arms from around his neck and stands up, a strange set look on his face.*] I gwine keep heart now, look up, rise. I gwine lead. [*Looking down at the baby.*] I gwine raise him up a light unto peoples. He be a new Moses, he bring de chillun out of bondage, out'n sin and ign'ance.

[*He turns suddenly and goes to the bucket at the left, pours some water out in a pan and sets it on the bed. Then he bends down and lifts the baby in his hand. MUH MACK looks up, drying her eyes.*]

GOLDIE. Whut dat, Abe? Whut dat you doing?

ABE [*dipping his hand in the water and holding the child aloft, his face lighted up in a beatific smile*]. On dis day I names you Douglass. You gwine be same lak him. Yeh, better. You gwine be a light in darkness, a mighty man. [*He dips his hand into the water and sprinkles the child.*] I baptize you and consecrate you to de salvation ob my people dis day! Amen!

[*The women stare at him transfixed, caught out of themselves. He bends his head and stands with the child stretched before him as if making an offering to some god.*]

SCENE III

Winter of the same year. The old Quillie house, a Negro cabin of one bare room, now fitted up as a school-house. At the left center is a squat rusty cast-iron stove, the pipe of which reels up a few feet and then topples over into an elbow to run through the wall. A box of pine knots rests on the floor by it. Four or five rough pine benches, worn slick by restless students, stretch nearly the length of the room, ending towards a small blackboard nailed to the wall in the rear center. Between the benches and the blackboard is the teacher's rickety table with a splint-bottomed chair behind it. To the right rear is a small window, giving a glimpse of brown broomsedge stretching up a gentle hill, and beyond, a ragged field of stripped cornstalks, gray now and falling down in the rot of winter rains. To the left rear is a door opening to the outside.

The curtain rises on the empty room. Presently ABRAHAM MCCRANIE *comes in, carrying a tin lunch bucket and two or three books. He is wearing an old overcoat and a derby hat, both making some claims to a threadbare decency. He sets the bucket and books on the table and hangs his coat and hat on a nail in the wall at the right; then comes back to the stove, revealing himself dressed in baggy trousers, worn slick with too much ironing, heavy short coat, cheap shirt, and a celluloid collar with no tie. With his pocket-knife he whittles some shavings from a pine knot and starts a fire in the stove. He looks at his watch, beats his hands together from cold, and stirs about the room, his brow wrinkled in thought and apparent* worry. *Again and again he goes to the door and stares out expectantly. Looking at his watch the second or third time, he goes and rings a farm bell, the cord of which hangs down by the door outside.*

ABE [*shouting toward the empty fields as the bell booms*]. Books! Books! Come in to books! [*He returns and sits down by the stove.*] No scholars in sight. [*With a sigh he goes to the board and writes laboriously across the top:* "January 21. An idle brain is the devil's workshop." *While he is writing, three Negro students come in carrying a bucket and a book or two each — a lazy slumbrous girl of eighteen or twenty, a stout thick-lipped youth about the same age, and a little serious-faced ragged boy of ten.* ABE'S *face brightens at the sight of them.*] Good morning, chillun. Late. Everybody a little late.

STUDENTS [*standing uncertainly around the stove*]. Good morning, Mr. Mack.

ABE [*finishing his writing*]. This will be our motto foh to-day. [ABE'S *speech has improved somewhat. When he speaks with conscious deliberation he substitutes "this" for "dis," "that" for "dat," and so on. But when in a hurry or excited he drops back into his old methods. He addresses the little boy.*] Read it, Eddie, out loud.

EDDIE [*eagerly*]. I kin read it, Mr. Mack. [*In a slow and halting voice he reads.*] "A' idle brain is the devul's wukshop."

ABE. Good, fine. Kin you read it, Neilly?

NEILLY [*boldly*]. Yeh, suh, read it raght off.

ABE. And how 'bout you, Lanie?

LANIE [*dropping her heavy-lidded eyes*]. I kin too.

[*She and* NEILLY *look at each other with a fleeting smile over some secret between them.* EDDIE *gazes up at them, his lips moving silently as if over something to be told which he dare not utter.*]

ABE [*pulling out his watch*]. Twenty minutes to nine. Whah the other scholars? [*No one answers.* NEILLY *gives the girl a quick look and turns deftly on his heel and kicks the stove, sticking up his lips in a low whistle.*] You see the Ragland chillun on the road, Lanie?

LANIE [*enigmatically*]. Yessuh, I see 'em.

[ABE *goes to the door and rings the bell again.*]

ABE. Books! Books! Come in to books. [*He turns back into the room and stands pondering.*] How 'bout the Maffis chillun?

NEILLY. Ain't coming!

ABE. Dey say so?

NEILLY. Yessuh.

ABE [*shortly*]. Take yo' seats. We'll go on wid our lessons if nobody else don't come. [*He goes to his table.*]

EDDIE [*pulling excitedly at* LANIE'S *dress*]. G'won, ax him whut he gwine do.

LANIE [*snatching herself loose from him*]. Shet up. Ain't my business.

ABE. Put yo' buckets up and take yo' seats and listen to the roll-call. All the late ones ketch it on the woodpile and sweeping up the school-yard. [*Eyeing them.*] I said take yo' seat.

[EDDIE *hurries to his seat.*]

NEILLY. Ain't gwine have no school, is we?

ABE. Hunh?

NEILLY. Ain't gwine be no mo' school.

[LANIE *giggles.*]

ABE [*with a worried note in his voice*]. Going have school same as usual. Seem lak all of 'em late dough. Take yo' seats, time foh the spelling lesson. Won't have de scripture reading dis mawning.

NEILLY. De rest of 'em done quit school.

[LANIE *giggles again.*]

ABE. Stop dat giggling and go to yo' seat. [*She moves to her seat sulkily.*]

EDDIE [*in a high frightened quaver*]. Mr. Mack, dey all say de school ain't gwine run no mo' and dey ain't coming.

ABE. How dey hear it? I ain't heard it. [*No one answers.*] Whah'd you folks get all dis news, Neilly?

NEILLY. Dey was all talking it down de road. We wouldn't a-come eiver, but Eddie dah beg me and Lanie so hard to come wid 'im. Ain't no mo' folks coming dough.

ABE [*hitting the table with his fist*]. Sump'n' up. Dey got to show me fo' I

quits, dey got to show me. Putt up yo' buckets and things, we going have school. [*They reluctantly set down their buckets near the wall and stand waiting.*] Take yo' seats, I say, and listen to yo' name. [*He pulls out a cheap arm-and-hammer memorandum book and begins calling the roll.*] Lanie Horton.

LANIE. Presunt.

[*She looks around at the bare seats and gives her senseless giggle.*]

ABE. Vanderbilt Jones, absent; 'Ona May Jordan, absent; Jane Matthews, absent; Sister Matthews, absent; Jennie McAhlister, absent; Neilly McNeill.

NEILLY. Present. [*He smiles at* LANIE.]

ABE. Arthur Ragland, absent. Didn't 'spect him back nohow. Dora Ragland, absent; Nora Ragland, absent; Eddie Williams.

EDDIE. Prizzunt.

[ABE *sits drumming on the table and staring before him. The students twist about on their seats in embarrassment.*]

ABE [*roughly*]. Spelling lesson! [*The three move out and stand in a line before him.*] How many of you been over it at least fo' times? [EDDIE *raises his hand.*]

EDDIE. I been over it nine times fo'w'd and six back'ards.

ABE. You, Neilly?

NEILLY. I been over it onct and part twict, Mr. Mack.

ABE. Lanie?

LANIE. I dunno hardly.

ABE. Have you studied it any?

LANIE [*pouting*]. I done lost my book somewhah.

ABE. And you wuh supposed to be head to-day. You'n Neilly kin clean up the paper and sweep 'round the well at recess. Le's see yo' book, Eddie. [EDDIE *hands him his book.*] Eddie you got a head-mark yistiddy; so you foot to-day. [*Opening the book.*] The first word is "chew," chew, lak vittles, Lanie, "chew."

LANIE. C-c. C-u, "chew."

ABE. One mo' trial.

LANIE [*pondering a long while*]. I cain't spell dat.

ABE. Yes, you kin. Try it.

LANIE. C-h-u, "chew."

ABE. Next.

NEILLY [*smiling ruefully*]. Too hahd foh me. Des' well pass on.

ABE [*working his jaws up and down*]. Watch me wuk my jaws. That's chew, chewing. Spell at it, Neilly, "chew."

NEILLY [*scratching his head and nervously boring the floor with the toe of his shoe*]. Cain't do it, cain't fohm no letters in my head.

ABE. I'll have to pass it den.

NEILLY [*taking a hopeless shot at it*]. S-s. S-u, "chew." No, dat wrong. I seed dat word on de page, but cain't remember it now. I cain't spell it. Gi' it to Eddie, he kin.

ABE. All right, Eddie.

EDDIE. C-h-e-w — "chew."

[*He darts around* NEILLY *and* LANIE *and stands triumphantly at the head of the class.*]

ABE. I goin' send you back to yo' seats to study twenty minutes. Then come back heah and don't you make no such mess of it. I'll put the writing lesson up while you study. [*They go to their seats.*] Lanie, you look wid Eddie in his book. [*He turns to the board and begins to write down the copy models. As he writes, the students mumble over their words in a drone.* NEILLY *and* LANIE *begin talking to each other in low whispers.* EDDIE *is lost in his book.* LANIE *suddenly giggles out loud, and* ABE *turns quickly from his board.*] Heigh you, Lanie, stand up in dat corner over thah. School isn't out yit.

LANIE. I ain't done nothing. [*Half audibly.*] "Isn't!"

ABE. Don't talk back. Stand in de corner wid yo' face to de wall. Hyuh, Eddie, you read in dis reader and let her have yo' book.

[LANIE *creeps over to the corner and mouths over her lesson.* ABE *finishes his apothegm,* "A wise man will rise with the sun, or before it." *He is finishing another,* "Wise children will imitate the manners of polite people," *when there is a stir at the door and* PUNY AVERY *comes in, swallowed up in a teamster's coat and carrying a long blacksnake whip in his hand.*]

PUNY. Good mawning.

ABE. Good morning, Mr. Avery.

[*At the appellation of "Mister,"* PUNY *stuffs his cap against his mouth to hide a grin.*]

PUNY. How you come on, Mr. Mc-Cranie? Kin I warm my hands a minute? Freezing col' setting on dat waggin seat.

[*He moves up to the stove and stretches his hands above it.*]

ABE. Help yo'se'f. Be a snow fo' night, I believe.

PUNY. Yeh, or — look lak it.

[*He warms himself, and* ABE *sits at the table watching him questioningly. Now and then his gaze drops upon the whip.*]

ABE. Hauling lumber over the river?

PUNY. Is dat. [*Looking at* LANIE *in the corner.*] Whut she do?

ABE. Misbehaved.

PUNY. Seem lak yo' school kinda thin. [ABE *says nothing.*] Been gittin thinner ev'y since de Colonel died last fall, ain't it?

ABE. Been dropping off some since then.

PUNY. Whah all de rest o' de scholars?

ABE. Haven't showed up yet.

PUNY. Uhm.

ABE. Why you want to know, might I ask.

PUNY [*authoritatively*]. Already know. And foh yo' own good I come by to tell you and to bring you a message.

ABE [*looking at him intently and then waving his hand at the three students*]. You chillun kin go out and have recess now. Mr. Avery wants to see me on a little business. [LANIE *and* NEILLY *get their coats and walk out.* EDDIE *remains crouched in his seat, unconscious of his surroundings.*] What message you got foh me?

PUNY. You des' well quit de school business raght heah and now. Dey ain't gwine send to you no mo'.

ABE. What's the trouble?

PUNY. Trouble! You gone and done it, you has, when you beat Will Ragland's boy yistiddy. Will so mad he kin kill you.

ABE [*anger rising in his voice*]. Needn't think I'm skeahed of him.

PUNY. I knows you ain't. But you wants to keep on teaching, don't you?

ABE. Yeh, and I'm going to.

PUNY. Nunh-unh, you ain't neiver. Will went 'round last night and gut everybody to say dey won't gwine send to you no mo'. Dey ain't gwine stand foh no nigger beating deir young 'uns.

ABE [angrily]. I had a right to beat him. I couldn't make him work no other way, and 'sides he told a lie to me. Said he didn't eat up po' little Sis Maffis' dinner. Several of 'em seen him do it.

PUNY. Cain't he'p it. You beat 'im so dey had to have a doctor foh him, and Will done gone to de sher'ff to git out papers foh you.

ABE [starting out of his chair]. Gwine have me 'rested?

PUNY. He is dat. And mo', I reckon. And my advice to you is to git f'om heah. As a member of de school boa'd I say, bedder leave.

ABE. He think he kin run me 'way?

PUNY. Don't know what he think. Know I wouldn't lak to lie in no white man's jail-house, dat's me.

ABE. De otheh members of the boa'd know 'bout it?

PUNY. Us had a meeting last night.

ABE. What dey say?

PUNY [fumbling in his pockets]. Dey all side wid Will, 'count o' de beating and 'count o' dat speech you made in chu'ch last Sunday.

ABE. Wuh Mr. Lonnie dere?

PUNY. He dere and he send dis heah writing to you.

[He pulls a note from his pocket and hands it to ABE, who opens it excitedly.]

ABE [clenching his fist]. Dat man say heah — God- ——— He say de boa'd done all 'cided de school got to stop. [He tears the note to pieces and throws it on the floor.] He say dere he know a good job in Raleigh at public wuk he kin git me. [Bitterly.] Say I do better at dat dan farming or school. [Pacing the floor, he throws his hand above his head.] Nanh, anh — suh, I sets a oaf on high, I ain't going let 'em run me off. Dey cain't skeah me. Dey cain't run me off lak I stole sump'n'. [He turns on PUNY with blazing eyes and EDDIE now watches him terrified.] Why you all vote dat way? Whyn't you stand up and vote foh me? You know I trying do right. You weak, coward, no backbone.

PUNY [backing toward the door]. I ain't gut nothing 'gin you, Abe. Why you 'buse me?

ABE. Git out o' heah. All o' you down on me. Dat speech was so. It was right. Dat beating was right. [Crying out.] I ain't gwine give in. Dey cain't run me. You cain't run me. I fight 'em. I stay heah. Let 'em putt me in de jail, I last till de jail rot down. [He moves menacingly toward PUNY, who flees through the door and slams it after him.] I come through deir bars, deir iron won't hold me. I'll git dere, I'll come. My flesh will be as tough as deir iron! [He goes to the table and picks up his books. He opens the Bible and stands thinking. Dropping into his chair, he sits with his elbow on the table and his chin in his hand, gazing into the distance. The anger and bitterness gradually pass from his face.] Dat man's talk, proud. Cain't push through 'thout help — [putting his hand on the Bible] — 'thout help from up there. [He bows his head on the table. EDDIE begins to sob and, leaving his seat timidly, approaches ABE's bent form, gulping and wiping his nose and eyes with his sleeve. ABE looks up and puts his arm around him.] Son, this heah's the last of this school. But we cain't stop, we got to keep on. [EDDIE leans his head against him, his sobs increasing.] Got to keep studying, got to keep climbing. [After a moment he stands up and writes across the board, "This School is stopped for a while." LANIE and NEILLY come inquiringly in.] Chillun, ain't goin' to be no mo' school till mebbe next yeah. You kin go home. [LANIE giggles and NEILLY looks at him with familiar condescension.] But I wants to dismiss with a word of prayer. [At a sign from him, EDDIE falls on his knees by the table. He gets down at his chair.] Our Father, where two or three is gathered ——— [NEILLY and LANIE look at him, pick up their buckets and scurry out giggling and laughing. ABE springs to his feet, his face

*blank with astonishment.   He calls after
them furiously.*]   Heigh, heigh, you!
   [*They are heard going off, their sharp
   laughter softening in the distance.*]
NEILLY. 'Fo' Gohd, he down on his
knees!
LANIE [*her voice growing faint*].   Yeh,
and he 'bout kilt Arth yistiddy.
NEILLY. Haw — haw — haw.
LANIE. Hee — hee — hee.
                   [*Their voices die away.*]

SCENE IV

*Fifteen years later.   A room in the pov-
erty-stricken Negro section of Durham,
North Carolina, as it was then.   When the
curtain rises,* GOLDIE *is washing at a tub
placed on a goods-box at the left of the room.*
MUH MACK *is seated at the fireplace at the
right, bent under a slat bonnet and dozing.
Pots and pans are piled around the hearth
and a kettle is singing on the fire.   Several
garments are hanging on chairs before the
fire drying.*
   *To the left rear is a bed with a pile of
rough-dried clothes on it.   A door at the
center rear leads into another room.   To the
right of the door is a low chest with books and
dishes set upon it.   At the right front by the
chimney is a small window letting in the
sickly light of a dying winter day.   In the
center of the room is a small eating-table
covered with a greasy, spotted oil-cloth.*
   *For several minutes neither of the women
says anything.* GOLDIE *washes heavily at
the tub, her body bent and disfigured with the
years of toil and poverty and the violence of
childbirth.   She wrings out a garment and
takes it to the fireplace.*

GOLDIE [*lifelessly*].   Move yo'se'f, Muh.
Lemme hang up dis shirt.
MUH MACK [*testily as she moves her chair
with her body*].   Lemme 'lone.   Cain't
sleep, rest — nothing.
   [GOLDIE *drags up a chair, hangs the
   shirt on it and returns to her washing.
   Her movements are slow, ox-like, and in
   her eyes now and then comes a sort of
   vacant look as if some deadening disease
   has had its way within her brain, or as*

*if trouble and worry have hardened her
beyond the possibility of enthusiasm
or grief any more.   Between her eyes a
deep line has furrowed itself, a line
often found on the foreheads of those who
think a great deal or those who are forgetting how to think at all.   And her
mouth has long ago fastened itself into
a drawn anguished questioning that
has no easeful answer in the world.
She washes away at the tub, the garment
making a kind of flopping sound
against the board.   After a moment
she calls to* MUH MACK.]
GOLDIE. Gitting neah 'bout day-down,
Muh.   Time to start supper.
MUH MACK [*whom age and poverty have
made meaner than before*].   Yeh, yeh, it is,
and I gut to git it, I reckon.
GOLDIE [*making an effort to hurry*].
Yeh, Mis' Duke got to have her clothes to-
morrow, I done said.
MUH MACK [*getting slowly to her feet*].
Oh, me my!   My leg done gone to sleep!
[*She fumbles among the pans on the hearth.*]
Yo' water hyuh all gwine bile 'way.
GOLDIE. Gimme hyuh!
   [*She takes the kettle and pours the
   water into the tub and then goes on
   scrubbing the clothes.*]
MUH MACK. Whut I gwine cook?
GOLDIE. Make some cawn bread, and
dey's a little piece o' Baltimo' meat in de
chist.
   [MUH MACK *arranges her pan on the
   fire with much grumbling and growling
   and goes over to the chest.*]
MUH MACK [*knocking the pile of books off
with a bang*].   Heah dem ol' books of
Abe's piled right hyuh in de way.   Minner
mind to burn 'em up.   Allus whah dey ain't
gut no business.
GOLDIE [*abstractedly*].   Yeh, yeh.   Always minner mind to burn 'em.
   [MUH MACK *opens the chest and
   pulls out a small piece of white
   meat.*]
MUH MACK. Hunh, look at dis, will you?
Ain't mo'n 'nough to fill my old hollow toof.
I et dat old meat and cawn bread till it
makes me heave to look at it.
GOLDIE. Dat all dey is.

MUH MACK. Dat won't make a mou'ful foh Abe. Whut we gwine eat?

GOLDIE. Abe won't eat it nohow, and I don't want nothing. You'n Douglass kin eat it.

MUH MACK. Bofe of you gwine die if you don't eat. Dat Abe been living off'n cawfee and bread two weeks now. No wonder he look lak a shadow and cain't ha'f do his work.

GOLDIE. Cain't eat when you ain't gut it.

MUH MACK. Well, starving ain't gwine give you stren'th to git no mo'. How you gwine keep washing foh folks and you don't eat?

GOLDIE [bowing her head in weariness over the tub, her voice rising with sudden shrillness]. Oh, Lawd Gohd in heaven, I don't know.

MUH MACK. Calling on Gohd ain't gwine he'p you git no supper eiver. [Throwing the meat back into the chest and slamming the lid.] Well, I ain't gwine cook dat old mess. I'll set right heah by dis fiah and starve wid you and Abe.

GOLDIE [drying her hands on her apron]. I gut des' one mo' fifty-cent piece in dat pocketbook. I'll git it and run out and buy some liver den. Po' Abe gut to live somehow. [She goes out at the rear and returns immediately holding an empty ragged purse in her hand.] Whah my ha'f dollar! Whah is it?

MUH MACK [dropping into a chair by the fire]. Hunh, needn't ax me. Ain't seed it.

GOLDIE [sitting down and rocking back and forth]. Somebody stole it. [Turning upon MUH MACK.] You done gin it to dat Douglass.

MUH MACK. Ain't.

GOLDIE. Yeh, you has, you has.

MUH MACK [beating the floor with her foot]. Ain't, I tell you.

GOLDIE [staggering to her feet]. And he off somewhah's spending it foh ice-cream and mess.

MUH MACK. Don't keer 'f I did. Po' boy do widdout all de time.

GOLDIE [falling on the tub with renewed vigor]. Cain't cry now!

MUH MACK. G'won down dere and git dat man to let you have sump'n' on a credit. You can pay 'im to-morrow when Mis' Duke pay you.

GOLDIE. He done said he ain't gwine let us have no mo' widdout de money.

MUH MACK. Mebbe Abe fetch sump'n' when he come.

GOLDIE. How kin he and dey don't pay 'im off till to-morrow evening?

MUH MACK [suddenly crying out with a whimper]. Look lak us gwine starve spite of all. I wants to go back home. I wants to go back to home. Mr. Lonnie won't let us do widdout.

GOLDIE. I been wanting to go back foh fifteen yeah, but Abe's gwine die fo' he go back.

MUH MACK [beating her hands together in her lap]. Crazy, crazy! He de biggest fool in de whole world.

GOLDIE. Needn't keep talking 'bout Abe. [Bravely and hopelessly.] He doing de best he kin.

MUH MACK [her anger rising]. Dere you set, Goldie McCranie, and say dat, after he done drug you f'om pillar to post foh fifteen yeah. Doing de best he kin! He ain't nothing, des' wuss'n nothing! He des' a plumb fool. But he mammy wuh a fool befo' 'im. Da's how come he in dis worl'.

GOLDIE. Stop dat. He sick, been sick a long time, po' fellow, and he keep trying.

MUH MACK. Sick! He wa'n't sick back dere when he got into co't and lost all his land trying to git dem lawyers to keep 'im out'n jail, and he beat dat Will Ragland's boy ha'f to death. [GOLDIE bows her head in her hands, swaying from side to side.] De devil in him! Dat's what.

GOLDIE [wretchedly]. You done sot dere by dat fiah and told me dat same tale time and ag'in, day in, day out. I don't want to heah it no mo'.

MUH MACK. Unh-unh. And I reckon you will dough. Wuh he sick, and he cutting up a rust in Raleigh and de niggers and white folks runnin' him out'n dere? It was old Scratch in him dere too. I tells you.

GOLDIE. Dey didn't treat 'im right over dere.

MUH MACK. Hunh. No, dey didn't. And dey didn't treat him raght in Greensboro, did dey? Same old tale dere, gitting in a row wid somebody and ha' to leave. He's mean, mean lak sump'n' mad at de world.

GOLDIE [tossing her head about her]. I dunno. I dunno. He orter nevah married me and gut tied down. Seem lak things all go wrong, crosswise foh him.

MUH MACK [staring at her]. Hunh. Things'll be crosswise wid 'im tell dey straighten 'im out in de grave. Dem's my words. [Blowing her nose in her skirt and half weeping.] If all dat shooting and killing in Wilmington wouldn't make 'im do better, nothing in de Gohd's world kin.

GOLDIE [moaning]. Stop dat talking. I cain't beah it.

MUH MACK. Dat's des' whut you orter stop doing, stop beahing it. Gather up yo' duds and take me'n Douglass and whop off'n leave 'im, dat's what you orter do.

GOLDIE [beating herself with her fists]. I ain't. I ain't. I gwine stay by 'im.

MUH MACK Co'se you gwine stay by 'im — and starve too. Foh dat's whut you'll do. Whut he don't spend on medicine he do on dem old lodges and sich and books and newspapers. And gits turned out'n eve'y one of 'em foh his speeches and wild talk, he do. [With grim satisfaction.] Shoveling dat coal down at de power house reckon'll hold him down foh a while. [With an afterthought.] Hold 'im down till somebody crack his haid wid a shovel and tu'n 'im off. [Stirring the fire and then folding her hands.] I done said my say-so now. Do no good, 'caze you so wropped up in de fool.

GOLDIE [flaring out]. No, it won't do no good. I gwine stick by him. [Rising and turning to her work again.] Dey ain't never done 'im right. Dey all been down on him f'om de fust.

MUH MACK [shrilly]. And 'll be till de last. Otheh niggers makes a living foh deir fambly. Why don't he? Allus gut his eyes on sump'n' else.

GOLDIE. He gwine be a big man yit. Dem udder niggehs do de dirty work and take whut dey kin git. Dey de low-down trash. [Her voice trembling.] He gwine git him a big school some dese days.

MUH MACK [laughing scornfully]. Heehee — hee. Listen at him. He cain't teach nothing. De niggeh school teachers round hyuh know mo'n a minute dan Abe do in a week. Dey been to college at Raleigh and Greensboro and no telling whah. And dey gut some sense 'sides deir learning. Dat li'l Eddie Williams has. He done gone th'ough dat Shaw school in Raleigh and is off doing big wuk. Why couldn't Abe do sump'n' lak dat!

GOLDIE [her voice breaking]. Shet up, I tell you.

MUH MACK [sulkily]. Aw right den, but dat talk don't fill yo' stomach. [Pulling a walking stick from the chimney corner.] I gwine go down to Liza's and ax her to gi' me some supper.

[She groans and creaks to her feet.]

GOLDIE. You been down to Liza's till she's tiahed o' feeding you.

MUH MACK [waving her stick in the air]. Well, you feed me den.

GOLDIE. Wait'll Douglass come f'om school and I'll git him to go down to de cawner and try to git some meat f'om dat man.

MUH MACK. Done past time foh Douglass to be heah. Mought not come till late.

GOLDIE [drying her hands again and patting her hair]. I'll go den. You putt de kittle on foh some cawfee and set de table and I'll be right back. [Fur off a muffled whistle blows.] Dere's de power house whistle. Abe be heah soon. Light de lamp and putt on de table. [She goes out.]

MUH MACK [somewhat mollified, calling after her]. Aw raght.

[She puts her stick back in the corner, fills the kettle and stirs stiffly about her, bringing plates to the table and laying out the knives and forks. She hobbles into the room at the rear and returns with a lamp without any chimney, which she lights at the fireplace and places on the table. While she is engaged in making coffee over the fire, DOUGLASS strolls in. He is a young Negro in short trousers, fifteen or sixteen years old, black as MUH MACK and *with something of a wild and worthless spirit already beginning to show in his face. He carries two ragged books under his arm.*]

DOUGLASS [*dropping the books by the door and kicking them toward the chest*]. Heigh!

MUH MACK [*jumping*]. Who? — hee — hee, you skeahed me, honey. [*She stands up and looks at him indulgently*]. Whah you been so late?

DOUGLASS. Oh, round and about. Stopped by de hot dawg stand awhile chewing de rag wid some fellows.

MUH MACK. How many dem sa'sage things you eat?

DOUGLASS. Dunno. Sev'al.

MUH MACK [*leaning forward, her eyes shining with anticipation*]. Whut you fotch me to eat?

DOUGLASS. I wanted to bring you sump'n', but ——

MUH MACK. You mean you ain't bought me nothing wid dat fifty cents?

DOUGLASS. I fool-lak matched wid some ub'm down dere and had to set 'em up.

MUH MACK. And I so hongry I cain't see straight!

DOUGLASS [*nonchalantly*]. I cain't he'p it.

MUH MACK [*threateningly*]. I gwine tell yo' daddy on you.

DOUGLASS [*looking at her*]. Hunh, you better not. Do and I won't play nary piece foh you in — in two weeks mebbe.

MUH MACK [*turning to her cooking*]. Yo' muh know 'bout it.

DOUGLASS. Why you tell her?

MUH MACK. She guessed at it. She knowed you tuck dat money soon's she found it gone.

DOUGLASS [*alarmed*]. Pap don't know, do he?

MUH MACK. Not yit. He ain't come f'om wuk. [*He turns back into the room at the rear and reappears with a guitar. Sitting down wonderfully at ease, he begins strumming.*] Lawd, Lawd, honey, gi' us a piece 'fo' yo' daddy comes. [*He falls to playing and MUH MACK begins to pat the floor and skip happily now and then as she moves about the fireplace.*] Hee-hee — dat bedder'n eating.

DOUGLASS [*hugging up the "box" and throwing back his head in abandon*]. Hee-hee — ain't it dough! [*He turns and scowls at the books lying on the floor, and begins singing to them.*] Dem old books — [*Strum, strum*] lying in de corner, [*Strum, strum.*] Dem old books — [*Strum, strum*] lying in de corner — [*Strum, strum.*] Lie dere, babies, lie dere! Hee-hee — Muh Mack, I kin make music raght out'n my haid. [*He goes on throwing his fingers across the strings.*]

MUH MACK. You kin, honey, you sho'ly kin.

[*She sits listening happily. He wraps himself over the guitar, his fingers popping up and down the neck of the instrument with marvelous dexterity. His bowed head begins to weave about him rhythmically as he bursts into snatches of song.*]

DOUGLASS [*singing*].

Look down, look down dat lonesome road,
De hacks all dead in line.
Some give a nickel, some give a dime
To bury dis po' body o' mine.

MUH MACK [*staring at him*]. I declah! I declah! Listen at dat chile.

DOUGLASS. Ne'h mind, ne'h min' me. [*Modulating with amazing swiftness from key to key.*] And dere was po' Brady. Po' old Brady.

MUH MACK. Yeh, Brady, dey laid him down to die.

DOUGLASS [*singing*].

Oh, Brady, Brady, you know you done me wrong,
You come in when de game was a-goin' on!
And dey laid po' Brady down.

Wimmens in Gawgy dey heard de news
Walking 'bout in deir little red shoes,
Dey glad, dey glad po' Brady dead.

When I close my eyes to ketch a liddle sleep,
Po' old Brady about my bed do creep,
One mo', des' one mo' rounder gone.

[*While he is singing and playing, ABE come suddenly in at the rear dragging a heavy wooden box in one hand and carrying a dinner-pail in the other. He is dirty and begrimed with coal dust.*]

ABE [*shouting*]. Put up dat box! [DOUGLASS *bounds out of his chair as if shot and backs away from him.*] Putt down dat damn guitah, you good-foh-nothing!

[ABE *hangs his cap and dinner-pail on a nail by the door and comes heavily across to the fire. His face is haggard and old and his shoulders have grown humped with the going of time.* DOUGLASS *slips out with his guitar and presently creeps in and sits stealthily on the chest.* ABE *lays the goods box on the floor and breaks it up and places pieces of it on the fire. Then he sits down and stretches out his feet and stares moodily before him.* MUH MACK *hurries around making bread, frying the hated side meat, and arranging the table.*]

MUH MACK [*tremulously*]. How you feeling? You come quick adder de whistle ——

ABE. Ah, feel lak I'll stifle in heah. [*He strikes his breast once and then follows it with a fury of savage blows.*] Cain't git no wind down in dat b'iler house. [*He drags his hand wearily across his brow and shakes his head as if clearing his eyes of a fog.*] Whah Goldie?

MUH MACK. Gone out to de cawner to git some meat. Time she back.

ABE. How long fo' supper?

MUH MACK. Soon's she gits back and we kin cook de meat.

ABE [*pulling off his shoes and setting them in the corner*]. I' going to lie down a minute till my head clears up. Feel lak it'll blow off at de top. [*Grasping his chair, he staggers to his feet and goes across the room. At the door he stops and looks down at* DOUGLASS.] I' going to tend to you in a little bit.

[DOUGLASS *quails before him.* ABE *goes out and slams the door.*]

MUH MACK. Whut de name o' Gohd ail him now? Wus'n ever.

DOUGLASS [*whimpering*]. He gwine beat me! He'll kill me.

[*The bed is heard creaking in the rear room as* ABE *lies down.*]

MUH MACK. Whut'n de world foh?

[*She stands tapping her hands together helplessly.*]

DOUGLASS. He done heahed sump'n' on me. Oh, he gwine beat me to deaf.

[ABE *is heard turning in his bed again, and he immediately appears in the door.*]

ABE. Shet up dat whimpering. Git over dere and start washing on dem clothes foh yo' po' mammy. [DOUGLASS *darts over and begins rubbing at the board and sniffling.*] Dry up, I tell you.

[ABE *turns back to his bed.*]

MUH MACK [*sitting to the fire and rocking back and forth in her anxiety*]. Oh, Lawd — Lawd!

[*She hides her head in her skirt grumbling and moaning. Presently* GOLDIE *comes in.*]

GOLDIE [*coming over to the tub*]. Look out, son, lemme git at 'em.

[*She falls to washing feverishly.*]

MUH MACK [*looking up*]. Whah dat meat, Goldie?

GOLDIE. Dat man look at me and laugh, dat's whut. [*Turning angrily toward* DOUGLASS.] You went and ——

MUH MACK [*throwing out her hand in alarm*]. Nanh, nanh, Goldie. [*Lowering her voice and nodding to the rear.*] Abe in dere. He find out 'bout dat, he kill de boy. Done say he gwine beat 'im foh sump'n' 'nother.

GOLDIE. When he come?

MUH MACK. He des' dis minute gut heah.

GOLDIE [*in alarm*]. He wuss off, I bet. [*She hurries into the room and is heard talking softly and kindly to* ABE. *He answers her with indistinct growls. In a moment* GOLDIE *returns.*] Putt whut you gut on de table and le's eat. [*She goes on with her washing.*] Abe ain't feeling well. Hadder eat whut he kin, I reckon.

[MUH MACK *puts the bread, coffee and meat on the table.*]

MUH MACK. Come on, you all.

GOLDIE. Come on in, Abe. [ABE *enters in his undershirt and trousers.*] G'won and eat, I don't want nothing.

ABE [*almost falling in his chair*]. Come on and set whedder you can or not. [GOLDIE *takes her place at the table.*] Come on, Douglass.

DOUGLASS. I don't want nothing eiver.

[MUH MACK *draws up her chair.*]

ABE. Don't make no difference. I said come on. [DOUGLASS *gets a chair and takes his place.* ABE *surveys the fare before him.*] Dis all you got foh a working man and he sick?

GOLDIE. I didn' have no money and ——
[*She turns away her head to hide her tears.*]

ABE [*kindly as he reaches out and touches her shoulders*]. Neveh mind, honey chile. [*He closes his eyes with weariness and sits brooding. Presently he raises his head.*] Well, neveh you mind, I ain't hungry. [*Looking at her sadly.*] But you must be plumb wore out wid all dat washing and all. [*Dropping his head.*] Le's have de blessing. Oh, Lawd, we thank Thee foh what we have befo' us. Make us truly thankful foh all Thy gifts and save us at last, we humbly beg, foh Christ's sake, Amen! [*After the blessing is over* GOLDIE *still keeps her head bowed, her shoulders heaving with sobs.* MUH MACK *pours out the coffee and hands it round.* ABE *calls to* GOLDIE.] Come on eat sump'n', Goldie, you feel better, you git yo' stren'th back. Drink some dis coffee. [GOLDIE, *bursting into wild sobs, goes and sits by the fire.*] What's de matter, chile?

MUH MACK. She done wukked to deaf and nothing to wuk on, dat's whut.

ABE [*drinking down a cup of steaming coffee at a gulp*]. Po' me some mo' of dat! [GOLDIE's *sobs gradually die away.*] Come on, honey, don't cry no mo'.

[GOLDIE *stands up and looks toward the table with anguished face.*]

GOLDIE. Abe, Abe honey babe, whut us gwine do?

[*She buries her face in her hands.*]

ABE. You done heahed sump'n', ain't you?

GOLDIE. Yeh, yeh, Liza told me. Jim done come f'om de power house and told her.

ABE [*dully*]. Neveh mind. Come on drink some coffee. We talk 'bout dat directly. I got sump'n' else to tell you, too.

MUH MACK [*staring at him in fear*]. Whut dat happen at de power house?

ABE. I tell you when I git good and ready. Come on, Goldie, chile. [GOLDIE *wipes her eyes and returns to the table to drink her coffee.*] Befo' we gits on what happened wid me, I got a question to ax dis young gentleman. [*Looking across at* DOUGLASS.] Why don't you eat?

DOUGLASS [*falteringly*]. I ain't hongry.

ABE. Try and see do you want anything.

DOUGLASS. I cain't eat nothing.

ABE. How come?

DOUGLASS. I des' don't want nothing.

ABE [*bitterly*]. I reckon I know how come. Dis evening I pass on the other side of de street and see you down dere at dat drink stand settin up dem wuthless niggers wid yo' mammy's good money. [*Savagely.*] Oh, yeh, I know dat's whah you got it. I see you last night watching her putt it away.

GOLDIE. Please don't have no mo' row, Abe.

ABE. I ain't gwine beat 'im foh dat, nunh-unh. Sump'n' else he's goin' to ketch it foh. [*Raging out.*] De teacher stop me on de street and tell me you doing wuss'n ever in yo' books and she done had to putt you back in third reader. [*Swallowing his third cup of coffee down with a hunk of bread, he stands up and stares into the distance.*] Heah we done labor and sweat foh you, fix foh you to rise up and be sump'n'. Eight yeah you been going to school and you won't work, you won't learn. [*He strikes the table with his fist, and the lamp flickers and almost goes out.*] You ain't no good. Onct I thought you gwine go on, climb, rise high and lead.

[*He seizes him by the collar and, lifting him from the floor, shakes him like a rag.*]

DOUGLASS [*sputtering and choking*]. Pap, papa!

MUH MACK [*whining in terror*]. Stop dat! You kill him!

ABE. I teach you to fool wid dem low niggers! I git you out'n dem trifling ways or I'll break yo' back in two. [*He sits down and jerks the boy across his knee and begins beating him blindly.*] I name you foh a great man, a man what stand high lak de sun, and you turn out to be de lowest of de low! Change yo' name, dat's what you better do. [*With a cuff he hurls him across the room, where he falls sobbing and wailing on the floor.*] Shet dat fuss up! [DOUGLASS' *sobs gradually cease.* GOLDIE *starts toward him, but* ABE *jerks her back.*] Let 'im lie dere, de skunk and coward.

[GOLDIE *turns despairingly to her washing again.* ABE *moves to the fire and sits down, pulling a wrinkled newspaper out of his pockets, while* MUH MACK *rocks and slobbers and moans.*]

MUH MACK. You need de law on you, Abe McCranie. You beat dat po' baby ——

ABE. Shet up! You what gwine ruin him. He takes adder you and yo' trifling.

MUH MACK. Oh, I gwine leave heah, find me 'nudder place to stay.

ABE. We all got to git another place to stay.

GOLDIE. Le's go back home, Abe! Le's go back.

MUH MACK. Ha' we gut to leave 'caze whut you done down at de power house? [*Wringing her hands.*] Whut you do down dere? Oh, Lawd!

ABE. Ain't no use waking up de neighborhood wid yo' yelling. I didn't do nothing but stand up foh my rights. A white man sass me and I sass back at him. And a crowd of 'em run me off. Won't be able to git no other job in dis town, God damn it! [*Standing up and shaking his fist.*] God damn de people in dis town! Dem wid deir 'bacco warehouses, and cotton mills, and money in de bank, you couldn't handle wid a shovel! Yeh, dey mortgage up God's great world and shet out de po'!

MUH MACK. Le's go back home. De Colonel fix it in his will so us could have a place to come back to. Mr. Lonnie'll rent us some land.

GOLDIE [*coming over to* ABE'S *chair and dropping on her knees beside him*]. Abe, Abe, le's go back. Please do. Le's go back whah we growed up. Ain't no home

foh us in no town. We gut to git back to de country. Dat's whah we belong.

[*She lays her head in his lap.*] ABE [*looking down at her in sudden tenderness*]. Yeh, yeh, honey. We is gwine back. Adder all dese yeahs I knows now de town ain't no place foh us. Fifteen yeah we been trying to make it and couldn't. Dat's what I was going to tell you. All de signs been ag'in us. I orter knowed it after three or fo' yeahs. Back home de place foh us. Back in our own country. [*Staring before him and a smile suddenly sweetening the hardness of his face.*] We go back dere and take a new start. We going to build up on a new foundation. Took all dese yeahs to show me. [*His voice rising in a sort of nervous exultation.*] Dere's whah my work is cut out to be. It come to me dis evening while I walked on de lonesome street. [*Standing up.*] Seem lak sump'n' spoke to me and said go back down on de Cape Fair River. I heard it plain lak a voice talking. "Dese streets and dese peoples ain't yo' peoples. Yo'n is de kind what works and labors wid de earf and de sun. Dem who knows de earth and de fullness thereof. Dere's whah yo' harvest is to be." And den when I come face to face wid de ruining of my boy, in my anger I see de way clear. We going back, we going back. And dere at last I knows I'm going to build up and lead! And my boy going to be a man. [*Looking at* DOUGLASS *with a hint of pleadingness.*] Ain't it so?

[*But* DOUGLASS *only stares at him coldly and afraid.*]

GOLDIE [*smiling up at him*]. I knows you will. I feel it des' de way you do. I keep telling Muh Mack some day you gwine git dere.

ABE [*gazing down at her*]. Dese yeahs all been sent foh our trial, ain't dey, honey?

GOLDIE. Yeh, yeh, we been tried all foh a purpose.

ABE. And now we ready, ain't we, honey?

GOLDIE. We ready to go back and start all over.

MUH MACK [*repeating uncertainly*]. To start all over.

ABE. To build us a monument from generation unto generation.

GOLDIE [*softly, the tears pouring from her eyes*]. Yeh, yeh.

ABE. And all dis sin and tribulation and sorrow will be forgot, passed away, wiped out till de judgment, won't it, chile?

GOLDIE. It will, oh, I knows it will. We done suffered our share and Old Moster gwine be good to us now.

ABE. Good! Yeh, good!

[*He sits with bowed head.*]

SCENE V

Three years later. The same as Scene Two, in ABE'S *cabin on the McCranie farm. The room shows some sign of improvement over its former state. There is a lambrequin of crêpe paper on the mantel, a wooden clock, and at the right a home-fashioned bookcase with books and magazines. On the rear wall is the same colored print with the caption of the rising slave.*

ABE *is seated at a table near the front writing by a lighted lamp. He is better dressed and more alert than formerly. Further back and to the left of the fireplace sits* MUH MACK *dozing and quarreling in her rocking chair. Her head and face are hid under the same slat-bonnet, and a dirty pink "fascinator" is draped over her bony shoulders. Her huge snuff brush protrudes from her lips and now and then describes a sort of waving motion when she moves her jaws in sleep. Between her knees she clasps her walking-stick.*

Through the window at the rear come bright streaks from the orange afterglow of the west. The November sun has set and the sky near the horizon is fading into a deep gloom under an approaching cloudiness. In the oaks outside the sparrows going to roost pour out a flooding medley of sharp calls resembling the heavy dripping of rain from eaves. For a moment ABE *continues his writing and then lays down his pencil and replenishes the fire. He returns to his chair and sits drumming absently on the table.*

ABE. When Goldie coming back, Muh?

[*His speech is gentle and more cultivated.*]

MUH MACK [*starting out of her sleep*]. Whut you say?

ABE. When Goldie coming back from Mr. Lonnie's?

MUH MACK. When she git done o' dat washing and arning, po' thing.

ABE. Seem like it's time she was back.

MUH MACK. Whut you keer 'bout her and you setting dere all day wuking at dat old speech mess.

ABE. You going to cook any supper?

MUH MACK. Supper! You ax dat and know I cain't git out'n my chaih wid de stiffness and misery. You'll hadder eat cold.

ABE. I've done looked. Ain't nothing cold.

MUH MACK. Den you'll hadder wait till she come. Po', po' thing, wid all her trouble wonder she able to cook or work or do anything.

[*She turns to her snoozing and* ABE *picks up his pencil again and gnaws at it as he works on his speech. Soon he stops and begins tapping on the table.*]

ABE. What trouble she got now?

MUH MACK [*astounded*]. You ax dat and you fixing to bring mo' trouble on us wid yo' schooling and mess. And wid Mr. Lonnie down on you 'bout de crap ag'in. Lawd, Lawd! And who dat won't let his po' boy putt foot in de home? Keep 'im driv' off lak a homeless dawg.

[*She wipes her eyes with a dirty rag.*]

ABE. You talk, but this time they won't be no failing. The school is going through. Then I can talk to Mr. Lonnie. Six men done already promised a thousand dollars. Cain't fail this time, nosuh.

MUH MACK. You don't 'serve nothing, and won't let po' Douglass come back to see his mammy. [*Brightly.*] Dem men mebbe ain't promised. Dey talking.

ABE [*sharply*]. I know. . . . You needn't say another word about it. [*Concerned with the speech.*] I won't let Douglass darken my door.

[MUH MACK *stirs from her doze and sniffles into her rag, wiping the rheumy tears from her eyes.* ABE *turns to his writing. He writes more and more rapidly as he nears the end. Presently he throws down his pencil and stretches his arms back of his head with a weary, happy yawn. He looks towards* MUH MACK *and speaks exultantly.*]

ABE. That's the best I've ever done. They can't go against that, they can't this time.

MUH MACK [*sleepily, rubbing her eyes and speaking coldly*]. Thank God you's finished yo' speech and'll soon be outen my sight and I kin git a liddle nap.

ABE [*not noticing her*]. That crowd's going to listen to me to-night.

MUH MACK. Mebbe dey will, but you's talked yo' life away, and it hain't come to nothing.

ABE [*looking at the speech*]. I've done my best this time. All I got from books and experience is there, and the truth's in it. [*He gathers the closely written sheets together.*] I tell 'em —— [*He turns to his speech and begins to read as he rises from his chair.*] I say, ladies and gentlemen [*he takes no notice of* MUH MACK'S *disgust, as she turns away from him*], this night is going to mean much in the lives of each and every one of us, big and little.

MUH MACK. Hit won't ef dey treats dey chil'en lak you treats yo' one.

ABE [*hurrying on*]. It marks the founding of the Cape Fair Training School, an institution that will one day be a light to other institutions around about. It is to be our aim here, with the few teachers and facilities we can provide, to offer education to the colored children amongst us and offer it cheap. [*He turns toward* MUH MACK *and speaks with more spirit, as if his audience were directly before him. But she turns her back to him and blinks in the fire.*] Looking over the country, ladies and gentlemen, we see eight million souls striving in slavery, yea, slavery, brethren, the slavery of ignorance. And ignorance means being oppressed, both by yourselves and by others — hewers of wood and drawers of water.

[*He picks up his pencil and crosses out a word.*]

MUH MACK [*sarcastically*]. Dey hain't nobody been in slavery since de surrenduh. Ef dey is, how come? And I reckon de hewers o' woods and de drawers o' water is 'bout free as anybody.

ABE [*continuing his speech without noticing her*]. Ignorance means sin, and sin means destruction, destruction before the law and destruction in a man's own heart. The Negro will rise when his chareckter is of the nature to cause him to rise — for on that the future of the race depends, and that chareckter is mostly to be built by education, for it cannot exist in ignorance. Let me repeat again, ladies and gentlemen. We want our children and our grandchildren to march on towards full lives and noble chareckters, and that has got to come, I say, by education. We have no other way. We got to live and learn — and think, that's it. [*He strides in front of the old woman, who has dozed off again under his eloquence. She raises her head with a jerk when he thunders at her.*] A little over forty years ago the white man's power covered us like the night. Through war and destruction we was freed. But it was freedom of the body and not freedom of the mind. And what is freedom of the body without freedom of the mind? It means nothing. It don't exist. [*Throwing his arm out in a long gesture.*] What we need is thinking people, people who will not let the body rule the head. And again I cry out, education. I been accused of wanting to make the Negro the equal of the white man. Been run from pillar to post, living in poverty because of that belief. But it is false. I never preached that doctrine. I don't say that the colored ought to be made equal to the white in society, now. We are not ready for it yet. But I do say that we have equal rights to educating and free thought and living our lives. With that all the rest will come. [*Pointing to the bookcase.*] Them books there show it. [*Caught up in the dreams of his life, he pours out a roll of words and beats the air with his fists.*] Ladies and gentlemen, what's to hinder us from starting a great center of learning here, putting our time and our hope and money and labor into it and not into the much foolishness of this life. What little education I got was by light 'ood knots, and after reading and studying all these years, I am just a little ways along. We must give the children of the future a better chance than we have had. With this one school-building we can make a good start. Then we can get more teachers later on, more equipment, and some day a library where the boys and girls can read about men that have done something for the world. And before many years pass we will be giving instruction in how to farm, how to be carpenters, how to preach, how to teach, how to do anything. [*Forgetful of his written page, he shouts.*] And what will stop us in the end from growing into a great Negro college, a university, a light on a hill, a place the pride of both black and white. [*He stands a moment, lost in thought. Turning through the leaves of his speech, he looks towards* MUH MACK, *who sits hid under her bonnet.*] Ain't that the truth, Muh Mack? Ain't it? [*Anxiously.*] They can't stand out against that, can they? Ain't that a speech equal to the best of the white, ain't it?

[*He coughs.*]

MUH MACK. Lawd Jesus! You's enough to wake de daid. And you brung on yo' cough ag'in.

ABE [*fiercely*]. I tell you it's going through. I believe the people here are with me this time.

MUH MACK. Sounds like de same old tale. [*Bitterly.*] You's made dem dere speeches from Wilmington and Greensboro to I don' know where. It's foolishness, and you knows it. [ABE *arranges the leaves of his speech without listening to her.*] Time you's learning dat white is white and black is black, and Gohd made de white to allus be bedder'n de black. It was so intended from de beginning.

ABE [*staring at her and speaking half aloud*]. We been taught and kept believing that for two hundred years. [*Blazing out.*] But it's a lie, a lie, and the truth ain't in it.

MUH MACK [*going on in her whining, irritating voice*]. Yeh, all yo' life you's hollered Lawd and followed Devil, and look whut it's brung you to. Ef you'd a putt as much time on picking cotton lately as you has on dat speech, you wouldn't have

Mr. Lonnie down on you de way he is. De truf's in dat all right.

ABE [*trying to control his nervousness and anger*]. I ain't a farmer. My business is with schools. [*Hotly.*] Can't you learn nothing? You dribbling old ——, here for twenty years you've heard me talk the gospel and it ain't made no impression on you. [*He turns away, realizing the vanity of his words to her. He speaks to himself and the shadows of the room.*] That speech is so! It's so, and I got to speak it that-away. [*He looks about him with burning eyes and pleads as if with an unseen power.*] The truth's there. Can't you see it? [*His nostrils quiver and he goes on in a kind of sob, calling to the unbeliever hiding within the dark.*] God A'mighty knows they ain't no difference at the bottom. Color hadn't ought to count. It's the man, it's the man that lasts. [*Brokenly.*] Give us the truth! Give us the truth!

[*He coughs slightly, and a queer baffled look creeps over his face. For the moment he seems to sense ultimate defeat before a hidden, unreachable enemy.*]

MUH MACK [*looking at the clock and snapping*]. Thought you's bound to be at de Quillie house by six o'clock. It's done near 'bout time. Git on. I wants my nap.

[*She pours snuff into her lip and turns to her snoozing again. With a hurried look at the clock, ABE crams his speech into his pocket, gets a plug hat from the desk, and blows out the lamp. The room is filled with great leaping shadows from the darting flames of the fireplace.*]

ABE [*at the door*]. You remember what I said about Douglass.

MUH MACK. Git on, git on. [*Whining sarcastically.*] Sho' you'll be a light on de hill and de pride o' de land — and you won't even let a po' old woman see her boy.

ABE [*turning back*]. Damn him! If he puts his foot in this house he'd better not let me get hold of him. They ain't no man, flesh of my flesh or not, going to lie rotten with liquor and crooks around me. That's what I been talking against for twenty years. I drove him off for it and I'd do it again. Just because a little time's passed ain't no reason I've changed.

MUH MACK. He mought a changed and want to do bedder.

ABE [coming back into the room]. Changed enough so he like to got arrested in town yesterday and it his first day back.

MUH MACK [pleading in a high quavering voice]. But I gut to see him. He's been gone two yeah.

ABE. Let him come if he dares. You ruint him with your tales and wuthless guitar playing and I don't want nothing more to do with him.

MUH MACK [mumbling to herself]. I's gwine see him 'fo' he goes 'way back yander ef I has to crawl slam over de river.

ABE [with brightening eye]. You heard me. He ain't no longer mine, and that's the end of it.

MUH MACK [bursting into a rage]. And yo' ain't none o' mine. You's gut all de high notions of old Colonel Mack and de white folks and don't keer nothing foh yo' own. Git on. [He stands looking at the floor, hesitating over something.] Whut you skeered of, de dark?

ABE [shuddering and going across the room and getting an old overcoat from a nail]. Yes, I'm afraid of it. You're right, I'm none of yours, nor my own mother either. You know what I am — no, I dunno whut I am. Sometime I think that's de trouble. [Sharply.] No, no, de trouble out there, around me, everywhere around me. [The despondent look comes back to his face and he speaks more calmly.] I'll cut across the fields the near way. And tell Goldie not to worry. I'll be back by ten with the school good as started. [At the door he turns back again and calls to the old woman earnestly.] Muh Mack, don't let her worry, don't. [But the old woman is asleep.] Let ner sleep, let us all sleep.

[He goes out softly, closing the door behind him.]

SCENE VI

An hour later the same evening. A sandy country road twists out of the gloom of scrubby oaks and bushes at the rear and divides into a fork, one branch turning sharply to the left and the other to the right. The moon has risen low in the east, casting a sickly drunken light over the landscape through the flying clouds. To the left in a field of small loblolly pines the dim outline of a barn can be seen. The tops and the branches of the larger trees move like a vast tangle of restless arms, and the small bushes and grasses hug the earth under the wind's blustering. Down the road in the distance come the sounds of running footsteps. And further off, almost out of hearing, the halloo as of some one pursuing. The footsteps thump nearer, and presently ABE staggers up out of the darkness and falls panting in the edge of the bushes at the right. His hat is gone and his clothes torn. The shouts sound fainter in the night and gradually die away.

ABE crawls to his knees and stares back at the road, his breath coming in great gasps. His learning and pitiful efforts at cultural speech have dropped away like a worn-out garment and left him a criminal.

ABE. Reckon, reckon dey leave me 'lone now, de damn cutth'oats! [Holding his sides with his hands and rocking his head in pain.] Oh, my breast feel lak it'll bust. Yeh, I outrun you, you po' white trash. [Clambering wildly to his feet and staring up the road.] But you done fix me now. You done got all de underholt and lay me on de bottom. [Looking up at the sky and raising his fist above his head.] Dere dat moon looking on it all so peaceful lak. It don't know, it can't feel what dey done to me. [Bursting out with a loud oath.] God damn 'em to hell! Dem white sons of bitches! Dey don't gi' me no chance. Dey stop every crack, nail up every do' and shet me in. Dey stomp on me, squash me, mash me in de ground lak a worm. [His voice breaking into a sob.] Dey ain't no place foh me. I lost, ain't no home, no 'biding place. [He throws himself down on the ground and lays his cheek to the earth. Unseen by him, a light begins to twinkle at the barn. He sits up and looks intently at the ground.] Seem lak dis earf feel sweet to me. It warm me lak it feel sorry.

[*Laying his hand on it as if it were a being.*] Ground, you is my last and only friend. You take me in, you keep me safe from trouble. Wisht I could dig me a hole now and cover me up and sleep till de great judgment day, and nobody never know whah I gone.

[LONNIE McCRANIE, *stout and middle-aged, comes in at left with a lantern.*]

LONNIE. Heigh there!

ABE [*bounding up*]. Keep back, whoever you is. Stay back dere, white man.

LONNIE [*peering forward*]. Who's that cutting up crazy here in the night?

ABE. Ain't nobody, nobody.

LONNIE. Well, by God, Abe, what's the matter?

ABE. That you, Mr. Lonnie?

LONNIE. Yeh. What'n the world's the matter? I was out there at the barn and heard the awfulest racket. Somebody talking like they was crazy.

ABE. Trouble, Mr. Lonnie, trouble.

LONNIE. Trouble, what sort of trouble? [*Coming closer and holding up his light before* ABE.] Great goodness, you're wet as water.

ABE [*straightening up*]. I all right now. Got to go on.

[*He makes a drunken step on the road toward the right.* LONNIE *gets quickly before him.*]

LONNIE. Where you going?

ABE. I going to leave heah, going clean away.

LONNIE. No, you're not. Tell me what's the matter.

ABE. Dem white men run me away from the Quillie house.

LONNIE. That's what the shouting was about, was it?

ABE. Mebbe so, suh.

LONNIE. Uh-huh. You were down there 'bout your school business, anh?

ABE. I wa'n't doing no harm. I was going to talk to 'em 'bout our school foh next year, and when I got there dey was a crowd of low-down white men dere ——

LONNIE. Look out, mind how you talk.

ABE. I minding all right. When I got there, they done run them lazy niggers off

and told me I had to go. [*Grimly.*] Dey couldn't skeer me, though. I went on in de house and started my speech. And den —— [*Throwing out his arms wildly.*] Mr. Lonnie, help me git back at 'em. Help me git de law on 'em.

LONNIE. What'd they do?

ABE. Dey fell on me and beat me and told me I got to git out of de country. And dey run me off. But I reckon some of 'em got dey heads cracked. [*His body swaying with weakness.*] What I going to do? I don't know what?

LONNIE. Go on home and behave yourself.

ABE [*his voice almost cracking*]. I ain't done nothing. I tell you.

LONNIE [*roughly*]. Serves you right. I've told you time and again to quit that messing about and look after your crop and keep in your place. But you won't, you won't. I reckon you'll stay quiet now awhile.

ABE [*pleading with him*]. But I done right. I ain't done nothing to be beat foh.

LONNIE. The devil you ain't! I've been off to-day all around the country trying to get hands to pick out your cotton. It's falling out and rotting in the fields.

ABE. But I ain't lost no time from the cotton patch, 'cepting two or three days and I was sick den. I been sick all to-day.

LONNIE. You needn't talk back to me. If you're sick, what are you doing out to-night and getting yourself beat half to death? Yeh, I reckon I know such tales as that. And you needn't fool with the crop no more. I done levied on it and am going to have it housed myself.

ABE [*moving toward him*]. You mean you tuck my crop away from me?

LONNIE. Don't talk to me like that, I tell you. [*A fit of coughing seizes* ABE.] Call it taking away from you if you want to. I'm done of you. Next year you can hunt another place.

ABE [*his face working in uncontrollable rage*]. Den you's a damn thief, white man.

LONNIE [*yelling*]. Stop that!

ABE [*moving toward him*]. Now I'm

going to pay somebody back. I going to git even.

LONNIE. Stop! I'll bust yo' head open with this lantern.

ABE [*with a loud laugh*]. Yeh, yeh, hit me. Yo' time done come.

[*He makes a movement toward LON-NIE, who swings his lantern aloft and brings it crashing down on his head. The light goes out and the two rocking forms are seen gripping each other's throats under the moon.*]

LONNIE. Let go — let go ——

[ABE *gradually crushes him down to the ground, choking him.*]

ABE [*gnashing his teeth and snarling like a wild animal*]. I choke you, I choke yo' guts out'n yo' mouf. [*He finally throws* LONNIE'S *limp body from him, and then falls upon it, beating and trampling the upturned face.*] Dere you lie now. Dead! [*His voice trails high into a croon.*] I wipe out some de suffering of dis world now! [*Standing up and drawing away from the body.*] I — I — git even, I pay 'em back. [*He begins wiping his hands feverishly upon his trousers.*] Blood! Blood, de white man's blood all over me. [*Screaming out in sudden fear.*] I done kilt somebody! Oh, Lawd, Mr. Lonnie! Mr. Lonnie! [*He falls on his knees by the body.*] What's de matter? Wake up, wake up! . . . Pshaw, he's asleep, fooling. [*Springing to his feet.*] He's dead, dead. [*The wind groans through the trees like the deep note of some enormous fiddle and then dies away with a muffled boom across the open fields.* ABE *stands frozen with horror*] Listen at dat wind, will you! Mercy, dat his spirit riding it and crying! [*He falls prone upon the earth moaning and rocking. In a moment he sits up and holds his head tightly in his hands.*] O — oh, seem lak my head done turnt to a piece o' wood, lak cold as ice. [*He slaps his forehead queerly with his open palms.*] De whole world done seem turnt upside down, everything going round me lak a wheel. [*As he stares wonderingly around and gropes before him like one dreaming, the branches of the trees seem to change their characteristics and become a wild seething of mocking, menacing hands

stretched forth from all sides at him. He snatches up a piece of broken fence rail and snarls at them.*] Don't tech me, I kill you! [*He stands in an attitude of defense and the branches seem to regain their normal appearance. Stupefied, he lets the rail fall to the ground and then wraps his arms spasmodically across his face.*] O Lawd, I going crazy, dat's what! [*He bends over jerking and shivering. Presently from the left he sees appear a shadowy cortège of raggle-taggle country gentry, men and boys carrying muskets, sticks and stones. Their faces, illumined by the moon, are set and frozen in the distortion of hate and revenge. In the midst of them is a young Negro being dragged along with a rope around his neck.* ABE *starts back with a gasp.*] What's dis? Whah am I? [*Suddenly terrified.*] Lawd, dat's a lynching! . . . It's de night o' dat lynching. And dat dere's Charlie — Charlie Sampson. [*Seizing the rail.*] What you white mens doing? [*Crying out.*] Dat you, Charlie! I come save you! [*The group appear to pass silently down the road at the rear, the prisoner throwing out his arms and clawing the air as he is dragged onward.* ABE *springs forward at them and swings his rail through the air. It lands on the ground with a thud. He shrieks.*] Ghosts! Dey's ha'nts! Dey ain't no peoples! [*He stands rooted in his tracks as they disappear down the road. After a moment out of the underbrush at the left steal two shadowy figures dressed in the fashion of the late fifties. One is a young good-looking Negress of twenty, the other a dandified young white man about thirty. As they move across the scene at the rear, the man looks guiltily around him as if in fear of being surprised. The woman stops and points to the thicket at the right. He nods and motions her to move on.* ABE *looks up and sees them stealing away. He leaps to his feet and stares at them in stupefaction.*] Who dat 'oman and white man? [*With a joyous cry he rushes forward.*] Mammy! Mammy! Dat you! Dis heah's Abe, yo' boy! Mammy! [*The figures begin entering the thicket.*] Mammy! Dat you, Colonel Mack? Whah you going? Stay heah, help me, I —— [*The man and the woman *disappear in the bushes.* ABE *stands with his mouth open, staring after them.*] Whut's all dis? Must be anudder dream — a dream. Sump'n' quare. [*He moves cautiously forward and parts the bushes and starts back with a loud oath.*] God damn 'em! Dey dere lak hawgs! [*The fearful truth breaks upon him and he shrieks.*] Stop it! Stop dat, Mammy, Colonel Mack! [*Rushing toward the bushes again and stopping as if spellbound.*] Stop dat, I tell you, dat's me! Dat's me!

[*He stumbles backward over the body of* LONNIE MCCRANIE *and, shrieking, rushes down the road at the left.*]

SCENE VII

Thirty minutes later. DOUGLASS *has arrived and with* MUH MACK *before the fire is giving an account of his travels. He is now about nineteen years old, and has developed into a reckless dissipated youth, dressed in the cheap flashy clothes of a sport.*

DOUGLASS [*turning toward* MUH MACK *with a bitter smile*]. Yeh, I says it and I says it ag'in. Let dem dere Norveners putt Pap in print foh what he's trying to do foh de niggers. Ef dey could see him now down a po' dirt fahmer dey'd not think he's such a sma't man. Let him read his books and git new ide's. Dey won't change de nigger in him, not by a damn sight. He's raght down working a tenant and dat's where he belongs. Git me? Ah, him off to-night making his speeches. I bet to Christ dis heah's his last 'un.

MUH MACK. Foh God's sake don' carry on so. Come on and tell me some mo' 'bout de places you been since you left heah. [*He sits looking in the fire.*] Whut — whut's de matter? You hain't been usual so ficey-lak wid yo' pap. You been drinking?

DOUGLASS [*laughing sweetly*]. Yeh, I been drinking. And I gut cause to cuss de whole works out. [*Looking at her fiercely.*] Listen heah. Let dis slip in yo' yur, foh you'd heah it soon enough. You never has swung a' eight-pound

hammer, steel driving day adder day in the br'iling sun, has you? And you hain't never done it wid a ball and chain on you ca'se you is marked dang'us, has you? and dat foh a whole yeah long? Well, I has.

MUH MACK [*in astonishment*]. You been on de roads since you left?

DOUGLASS [*recklessly*]. I has dat and wo' de convict clo'es des' ca'se in my drunkenness I 'gun to preach some o' his doctrines 'bout dere being no difference 'twixt de cullud and de white. I knowed bedder. But I was drunk and had hearn so many o' his speeches. De judge said he'd des' stop my mouf foh a month. And I gut a knife one day and stobbed a gyard to de hollow. And dey gin me twelve months foh dat.

MUH MACK [*admiring his prowess*]. You allus was one whut fou't at de drap o' de hat.

DOUGLASS [*disgustedly*]. Yeh, a damn fool, and I ain't fohgit how he run me off'n heah and beat me! [*Bursting out with shining eyes.*] Hain't I gut cause to hate him and want to git him down?

MUH MACK. Gittin' on de roads ain't much, Douglass.

DOUGLASS. No, it ain't much to lie in de jug, is it? You do it and you ain't never gwine have no more peace. De cops is allus watching you. You gits de look and dey knows you. Dey tried to 'rest me yistiddy over dere, and I hadn't done nothing. And de old man was knowing to it too. But I's learnt what he'll never learn and it's dis — dat we belongs down wid de pick and de sludge hammer and de tee-arn and de steam shovel, and de heavy things — at de bottom doing de dirty work foh de white man, dat's it. And he ain't gwine stand foh us to be educated out'n it nuther. He's gwine keep us dere. It pays him to. I sees it. And adder all dese yeahs Pap keeps on trying to teach dat men is men. Some white man's gwine shoot his lights out one dese days, see ef dee don't. [*With a reckless forgetfulness.*] And so I says gimme a fast time, a liddle gin to drown down all my troubles in, and den —— [*He goes over to the door and gets his guitar.*] A liddle music to top it off wid. How about it, Muh Mack?

MUH MACK [*straining her eyes through the shadows*]. Whut you gut dere? [*Jubilantly.*] Lawd, Lawd! Ef you ain't brung yo' box wid you! And I ain't heerd nothing but dem sporrers by de do' and dat old rain crow in de hollow since you left two yeah back. Play her, boy, play her.

[*By this time he has sat down by the fire strumming.*]

DOUGLASS [*tuning up while* MUH MACK *sits in a quiver of excitement*]. Lemme play yo' old piece. My 'oman in Rocky Mount said 'twas de onliest chune.

MUH MACK. Dat's it! Dat's it! Lawd, gimme de "Band." I useter be put in de middle every time foh dat step. Dance all day, dance all night, des' so I's home by de broad daylight. Chile, I c'd natch'ly knock de wool off'n 'em.

[*As* DOUGLASS *plays she chuckles and whines with delight and almost rises from her seat. He starts in a quiet manner gradually working up to a paroxysm of pantomime and song.* MUH MACK *begins doing the Jonah's Band Party step with her heels and toes while sitting.* DOUGLASS *spreads his wriggling feet apart, leans forward with closed eyes, and commences the "call," with the old woman's quavery slobbering voice giving the "sponse."*]

CALL. Sech a kicking up san'!
SPONSE. Jonah's ban'!

[*This is repeated; then comes the command to change steps.*]

Hands up, sixteen, and circle to de right,
We's gwine git big eatings heah to-night.

Sech a kicking up san'! *Jonah's Ban'!*
Sech a kicking up san'! *Jonah's Ban'!*

Raise yo' right foot, kick it up high,
Knock dat Mobile buck in de eye.

Sech a kicking up san'! *Jonah's Ban'!*
Sech a kicking up san'! *Jonah's Ban'!*

Stan' up, flat-foot. Jump dem bars.
Karo backwards lak a train o' cyars.

Sech a kicking up san'! *Jonah's Ban'!*
Sech a kicking up san'! *Jonah's Ban'!*

Dance roun', 'oman, show 'em de p'int,
Dem yudder coons don'ter how to coonj'int.

[*By this time* DOUGLASS *is playing a tattoo on the wood of his box and carrying on the tune at the same time.* MUH MACK *has risen from her chair. With her dress to her knees, defying her years, she cuts several of the well-remembered steps. At sight of her bare and thin dry shanks the delirious* DOUGLASS *bursts into loud mocking guffaws and only plays faster.*

The door opens at the right and GOLDIE *comes timidly in. Her face is worn and haggard, and the strained vacant look in her eyes has deepened.* MUH MACK *stops and creeps guiltily to her chair.* DOUGLASS *tapers off his music and stops. For a moment* GOLDIE *stands astonished in the door, holding a bulky tow-sack in her hand. She drops the sack and hurries over to* DOUGLASS.]

GOLDIE. Muhey me! I knowed 'twas you soon's I heard de guitar. And sech carrying-ons!

DOUGLASS [*rising confusedly as she comes up to him*]. How you, Mam?

[*She puts her hand shyly on his arm and then clings convulsively to him, her shoulders heaving with restrained sobs. He lays one arm around her and stands looking tenderly and somewhat foolishly down at her. It is evident that in his way he cares for her. She suddenly raises her head, dries her eyes with her apron, and fetches wood from the box.*]

GOLDIE [*punching the fire*]. Whyn't you let me know Douglass'd come, Muh Mack?

MUH MACK. He des' come.

DOUGLASS [*laying his box on the bed*]. Mam, you set in dis char. You must be cold.

[*She sits down wearily, and he stands with his back to the fire.* MUH MACK *picks up her snuff-brush and slyly begins to dip from her tin box.*]

GOLDIE [*with a sudden start of terror*]. You hain't seed yo' pap, has you?

DOUGLASS. No'm, I ain't seed 'im. I

found out he done gone to de Quillie house
'fo' I come. I slipped in heah and found
Muh Mack asleep. Lawd, I skeahed her
wid a fiah coal.

GOLDIE [*suddenly reaching out and clutch-
ing his hand to her face*]. Don't you and yo'
pap have no trouble. Don't agg him on.
He — he — ain't well and might rile easy.
We — we kin see one 'nother off.

DOUGLASS. Oh, I'se gwine be partickler.
Now don't worry no mo'. It's awright.

GOLDIE [*slowly getting up*]. You all set
while I fix you some supper. I got something good foh Abe and de rest of us.
Lemme show you. [*She brings the bag, sits
down in the chair and takes out a big meaty
ham-bone.* MUH MACK *eyes it hungrily.
Naïvely.*] Ain't dat de finest dough? And
I gut a hawg haid, too, and collards and
cracklings.

DOUGLASS [*angrily*]. Dat's de way wid
dem damn — wid dem white folks. Dey
works you to death and den shoves dey old
skippery meat off on you foh pay.

GOLDIE [*a worried look coming over her
face*]. You hadn't ort to say dat, Douglass.
Mr. Lonnie gi'n me it — all of it. And he
paid me cash foh my work. Abe'll have
a new bottle o' medicine Monday. [*She
fingers the food childishly, and* DOUGLASS
*turns away with a smothered oath. Putting
the food back into the bag, she stands up.*]
Now I'll git you some supper.

DOUGLASS. I cain't stay foh no supper.
I promised to eat down de road wid Joe
Day. Le's set and talk, ca'se we don't
have much time and you can cook adder
I'm gone.

GOLDIE [*hesitating*]. Well — lemme put
dese heah in de kitchen den.
          [*She goes out at the right.*]

DOUGLASS [*turning sharply to* MUH
MACK]. What's de matter wid Mam?

MUH MACK. Won't we des' a-having of
a time when she broke in?

DOUGLASS. Cut out de damn jowing.
What makes Mam act so quare?

MUH MACK [*surprised*]. Do how? She
acts awright.

DOUGLASS. She don't. She acts sort o'
lost lak — wropped up in something.
          [*He scratches his head perplexed.*]

MUH MACK. Ef dey's anything wrong
wid her, it's 'count o' trouble, I reckin.

DOUGLASS. De hell-fi'ed fool! He's
drug her to death wid his wildishness.

MUH MACK. And ef it's trouble dat ails
her, I reckins as how you's done yo' shur in
bringing it on.

          [*He swallows his reply as* GOLDIE
          *comes in. She lights the lamp, then sits
          down and begins staring in the fire.*]

DOUGLASS [*after turning from one side to
the other*]. Mammy, whut's de matter wid
you?

GOLDIE [*brushing her hand across her face
and looking up as she wipes the tears from
her eyes*]. Lawd bless you, chile, dey ain't
nothing. I's des' happy to be wid you.

          [*She catches his hand and holds it a
          moment, then drops it and begins to
          look in the fire again.* DOUGLASS
          *watches her intently a moment and then
          turns away as if somewhat awed by her
          manner. There is a noise of some one's
          coming up on the porch.*]

MUH MACK [*crying out in fear*]. Dat's
him, Douglass! I knows his step. Dat's
yo' pap.

          [GOLDIE *stands up, wringing her
          hands and crying silently as* DOUGLASS
          *gets his guitar and hurries into the
          kitchen. The door at the left opens and
          ABE enters.*]

GOLDIE [*leaning forward and rousing the
fire*]. Did everything turn out —— [MUH
MACK *suddenly screams.* GOLDIE *looks
up and cries out.*] Oh!

          [ABE *comes toward the fire. His
          face is bruised, his clothes torn to shreds,
          and he sways as he walks.*]

MUH MACK [*rising from her chair*]. Dey's
been adder him! Dey's been adder
him!

ABE [*snarling at her*]. Shet up yo' damn
yowling, will you? and don't be rousing de
neighborhood. I'm not dying yit.

          [GOLDIE *stands a moment terror-
          stricken and then runs up to him.*]

GOLDIE. You's hurt, hurt bad, Abe, po'
baby!

ABE [*pushing her back*]. Ain't hurt much.
No time to doctor me now. [*He stands
before the fire.* MUH MACK *collapses in her*

chair. He is no longer the reformer and educator, but a criminal, beaten and hunted.] I come to tell you to git away — [*Panting.*] to — to leave, leave!

GOLDIE [*sobbing and burying her face in her hands*]. Whut's happened! Whut's happened!

MUH MACK [*swaying in her chair and crying to herself*]. Lawdy-a-muhcy on us! Lawd-a-muhcy!

[*For a moment he stands before the women silent, with closed eyes.*]

ABE [*looking at the motto on the wall and repeating the words dully*]. We are rising! [*Echoing.*] We are rising! — He didn't kuow what he said, he didn't. [*He staggers and grips the mantel and stands listening as if to far-away sounds. He turns desperately to the cowering women.*] Git your clothes and leave. You got to go, I tell you everything's finished at de end.

GOLDIE [*wailing*]. What happened at de schoolhouse?

ABE [*pushing his bruised hand across his forehead*]. I cain't, cain't quite think — yeh, they was a crowd of white men at de door with dough-faces on. Said wa'n't going to be no meeting. Dey beat me, run me off. And dey give me till to-morrow to git outen de country. You got to git away, foh it's worse'n dat — oh, it is! [*Calmly and without bitterness.*] Who you reckon set 'em on me? Who you think it was told 'em about de trouble I been in before? Yeh, and he made it out terribler'n it was. Douglass told 'em... He done it. My own flesh and blood. No! No! he was but ain't no more! [*Gloomily.*] But I don't blame him — dey ain't no blaming nobody no longer.

GOLDIE [*fiercely*]. He didn't — he wouldn't turn ag'in' his own pa.

ABE [*sternly*]. Hush! He did though. But it don't matter to-night. And you got to leave. [*Half screaming and tearing at the mantel.*] Now! Now, I tell you.

GOLDIE [*between her sobs*]. Did you — who hurt you?

ABE. I tell you I've done murder, and dey coming for me.

[MUH MACK *sits doubled up with fear, her head between her arms. With*

a sharp gasp GOLDIE *ceases weeping and sits strangely silent.*]

MUH MACK. Murder! Oh, Lawd-a-muhcy! [*She mumbles and sobs in her rag.*]

ABE. Dey drove me away from de meeting. I come back by the road mad. [*He gasps.*] Every white man's hand ag'in' me to de last. And Mr. Lonnie come out to de road when I passed his house and begun to abuse me about de crop. He struck at me, and I went blind all of a sudden and hit him wid my fist. Den we fou't. [*His voice growing shrill.*] And I hit him and hit him. I beat his head in. I killed him dead, dead! I beat on and on until all de madness went out of me and de dark was everywhere. Den I seed a sight —— [*He stops, aghast at the remembrance.*] I left him dere in de night dead on de ground. Dey done found 'im — I heah 'em crying up dere in de night. Dey's coming to git me. [*He holds out his bruised hands.*] His blood's still shining on dem hands. [*He turns his head away in fear.*]

MUH MACK [*in a high whine of terror*]. My God a-mighty! You kilt yo' own flesh!

ABE [*turning wrathfully upon her*]. Yeh, yeh, some bitch went a-coupling wid a white man! And I seed it — seed it! [*He drops his hands helplessly. A sort of terror comes upon him.*] Oh, Lawd God! I'm anudder Cain. I tell you I — I scrushed his head in and beat it till I put out de stars wid blood. Mercy! Mercy! [*With his hands still held before him, he stands with bowed head. After a moment he looks up and speaks calmly, almost resignedly, his dignity coming back to him.*] This is the way it was meant to be, and I'm glad it's ended. [*He stands with his fists to his temples, and then flings out his arms in a wide gesture.*] Oh, but damn 'em! Don't dey know I want to do all for de best. [*Shaking his fist at the shadows.*] I tell you, I tell you I wanted — I've tried to make it come right. [*Lowering his head.*] And now it's come to dis.

[DOUGLASS *comes in from the kitchen and stands away before him, his face filled with shame and fear.* ABE *looks at him without interest.*]

DOUGLASS. Befo' God, Pap, I — I

didn't mean no sech happenings. I never thought —— ABE [*eyeing him coldly*]. Who you? [*More loudly.*] A leader, a king among men! [*To the women.*] Here's Douglass and you can go wid him.

[DOUGLASS *turns back into the kitchen and instantly runs out. His eyes are staring with fear.*]

DOUGLASS [*in a throaty whisper*]. Come on, Mam! [*Twisting his cap in terror.*] Dey's coming. I heerd 'em from de kitchen do'. Dey's coming. Run, Pap! God have muhcy!

[MUH MACK *hobbles to him and tries to pull him through the door at the right. He looks back towards his mother.*]

MUH MACK. Come on! Come on!

DOUGLASS. Mam, Mam, don't stay heah!

ABE [*raising* GOLDIE *from her chair*]. Go on wid him. You ain't to blame foh nothing.

[*He pushes her toward* DOUGLASS. *But she turns and throws her arms around him, clinging silently to his breast.*]

MUH MACK [*pulling* DOUGLASS]. I heahs 'em. Dat's dem coming.

[*With an anxious look at* GOLDIE, DOUGLASS *hurries with* MUH MACK *through the door and into the fields.* ABE *places* GOLDIE *back in her chair and stands looking at her. He catches her by the shoulders and shakes her.*]

ABE. Tell me, what is it, Goldie! What ails you, gal? [*She sits looking dumbly at him and he draws away from her. Presently there is a sound of stamping feet outside, and voices slip in like the whispering of leaves. A stone is thrown against the house, then another and another. One crashes through the window and strikes the lamp. The room is left in semi-darkness.* ABE *with a sob of overwhelming terror falls upon his knees. Twisting his great hands together, he casts up his eyes and cries in a loud voice.*] God, God, where is you now! Where is you, God! [*He begins half sobbing and chanting.*] You has helped befo', help me now. Is you up dere? Heah my voice! [*Fear takes possession of him.*] Blast me, Lawd,

in yo' thunder and lightning, if it is yo' will! Ketch me away in de whirlwind, foh I'm a sinner. Yo' will, yo' will, not mine. Let fiah and brimstone burn me to ashes and scatter me on de earf. [*Gasping.*] I've tried, I've tried to walk de path, but I'm po' and sinful.... Give me peace, rest — rest in yo' bosom — if it is dy will. Save me, Jesus, save me!

[*He falls sobbing to the floor.*]

VOICE [*outside*]. Come out of there, you dirty nigger! [*A shudder runs through him, and his sobs grow less violent.*] Come out! Come out!

[*Another stone crashes through the room. As if ashamed of his weakness,* ABE *rises from the floor. He speaks firmly to the shadows.*]

ABE. In the end it was so intended. [*Looking around him.*] And I end here where I begun. [*He bursts out in a loud voice.*] Yet they're asleep, asleep, and I can't wake 'em!

VOICES.

He's in there.

I hear him talking.

He's done talking now, goddam him!

We'll show him the law all right.

He's got a gun!

Shoot him like a dog.

ABE [*wiping his brow and again speaking in the rôle of the educator trying to convince his everlastingly silent hearers*]. But they'll wake, they'll wake — a crack of thunder and deep divided from deep — a light! A light, and it will be! [GOLDIE *still sits hunched over in her chair. As he speaks he goes to the door at the left.*] We got to be free, freedom of the soul and of the mind. Ignorance means sin and sin means destruction. [*Shouting.*] Freedom! Freedom! [*Lifting up his voice.*] Yea, yea, it was writ, "Man that is born of woman is of few days and full of trouble...." Lak de wind wid no home. Ayh, ayh, nigger man, nigger man —— [*He opens the door.*] I go talk to 'em, I go meet 'em ——

VOICE. Hell! Look out! There he is!

ABE. Yea, guns and killings is in vain. [*He steps out on the porch.*] What we need is to — to — [*His words are cut short by a*

*roar from several guns.   He staggers and falls
with his head in the doorway*] — and we
must have — have ——

[*At the sound of the guns,* GOLDIE
*springs to her feet.   For an instant
everything is still.   Then several shots
are fired into* ABE's *body.*]

VOICE.   Quit the shooting.   He's dead
as a damned door!   Now everybody get
away from here — no talking, no talking.
Keep quiet — quiet.

[*There is the sound of shuffling footsteps and men leaping the fence.   Voices
come back into the room.*]

VOICES.
Yeh, mum's it.
He won't raise no more disturbances!

[*The voices grow more faint.*]

What a bloody murder he done!
He's still now, by God!
It's the only way to have peace, peace.
Peace, by God!

[GOLDIE *moves toward the door
where* ABE *lies.   Halfway across the
room she stops and screams and then
drops down beside his body.*

*The wind blows through the house
setting the sparks flying.*]

THE SILVER CORD
A COMEDY IN THREE ACTS
By SIDNEY HOWARD

TO MY WIFE

Demon — with the highest respect for you — behold your work!

George Sampson to Mrs. R. W.

CHARACTERS

MRS. PHELPS
DAVID, *her son*
ROBERT, *her younger son*
CHRISTINA, *David's wife*
HESTER, *Robert's fiancée*
MAID (*Mute*)

THE SCENES

The action occurs in the present day in Mrs. Phelps's house, which is situated in one of the more mature residential developments of an eastern American city.

First in the living-room on Sunday afternoon.

Then in the living-room again, early that same evening.

Then in David's bedroom, later that same evening.

Then in the living-room, the Monday morning after.

THE SILVER CORD

ACT I

A living-room, built and decorated in the best manner of 1905, and cluttered with the souvenirs of maternal love, European travel, and an orthodox enthusiasm for the arts. There is a vast quantity of Braun Clement and Arundel Society reproduction of the Renaissance Italian masters. The piano features Grieg, Sibelius and MacDowell. A door gives on a spacious hallway. Windows look out over a snow-covered garden.

[*The rise of the curtain discloses* HESTER *lost in the rotogravure sections of the Sunday papers. She is a lovely, frail phantom of a girl with a look of recent illness about her. She wears the simplest and most charming of house frocks. The doorbell rings. There is the least sound of commotion in the hall.* HESTER *looks up. In a moment, the doors open and* DAVID *enters. He is a personable young man, well enough dressed, and a gentleman. He belongs to the somewhat stolid or unimaginative type which is generally characterized, in this country, as "steady." His smile is slow and wide, his speech slow and to the point. His principal quality is a rare and most charming amiability, but he is clearly lacking in many of the more sophisticated perceptions and he is clearly of a conventional bent in his attitude toward life. The door, as he leaves it open, shows* CHRISTINA, *in the act of shedding her fur coat with the assistance of the maid. She, as* DAVID'S *wife, presents something of a contrast to her husband. She is tall, slender, grave, honest, shy, intelligent, most trusting and, when need be, courageous. She has a scientist's detachment and curiosity and these serve oddly to emphasize a very individual womanliness which is far removed from the accepted feminine. One suspects that, where* DAVID *is stubborn, she is open-minded, where he is blind, she is amazingly clear-sighted. That is the difference which makes one the complement of the other. The com-mon quality which brought them together in the holy bonds of matrimony is their mutual candor.* DAVID *is incapable of subtlety;* CHRISTINA *will not bother with it. The result is congeniality. So much for* DAVID *and* CHRISTINA. HESTER *rises.*]

HESTER. Hello!

DAVID. Eh? ... Oh, I beg your pardon! The maid said there wasn't anybody home.

HESTER. You're David, aren't you? [*She advances to meet him.*] I'm Hester.

DAVID. You're *not!* [*He goes quickly toward her and shakes hands as* CHRISTINA *enters.*] Well! [*He turns; smiling broadly to* CHRISTINA.] Look, Chris! Here's Hester who's going to marry my brother Rob.

CHRISTINA [*with the most charming warmth*]. Isn't she lovely!

HESTER. Oh, I think you're dears, both of you! [*The two women kiss.*] Aren't you hours ahead of time?

CHRISTINA. We caught the one o'clock instead of whatever the other was.

DAVID. Where are Mother and Rob?

HESTER. Your mother's drinking tea at ... Aren't there some people named Donohue?

DAVID. Great friends of Mother's. Why aren't you there?

HESTER. Not allowed. I'm having a breakdown.

CHRISTINA. Why don't you telephone her, Dave? She'll want to know that you're here.

DAVID. She'll find out soon enough. Where's Rob?

HESTER. Gone skating.

DAVID [*turns to the window*]. On the pond? No. There's no one on the pond.

HESTER. Somewhere else, then.

CHRISTINA [*hovering over the fire*]. Dave,

do you suppose I could get some tea? I'm half frozen.

DAVID. Of course you can. I'll order it. [*To* HESTER.] What's the maid's name?

HESTER. Delia.

DAVID. Delia. It used to be Hannah and before that it was Stacia who got married to our old coachman, Fred. Well, it's not so bad to be home again!

[ROBERT *enters, very much dressed for skating, and carrying his skates.* ROBERT *only faintly suggests his brother. He is more volatile and stammers slightly.*]

ROBERT. [*A shout.*] Dave!

DAVID. Hello, Robert! [*They shake hands vigorously.*] We were just wondering when you'd come in and Hester said . . .

HESTER [*speaking at the same time*]. Wasn't it lucky I was here to receive them?

ROBERT [*as he shakes* CHRISTINA'S *hand*]. I think this is simply magnificent! [*As he strips off his skating things.*] How did you get here so soon? We weren't expecting you for . . .

DAVID. We caught the one o'clock.

CHRISTINA. Just.

DAVID. We thought it would be fun to surprise you.

ROBERT. Mother'll drop dead in her tracks.

DAVID. How *is* she?

ROBERT. Oh, she's in fine form . . . [*To* CHRISTINA.] You'll adore her.

CHRISTINA. I'm sure I shall.

ROBERT. She *is* marvelous, isn't she, Hester?

HESTER. She is indeed. . . . Perfectly marvelous!

DAVID. Mother's immense. And I'm glad, for Chris's sake, that things worked out this way. First Chris sees the old house. Then she meets Hester. Then Rob comes breezing in, full of health. And, last of all, Mother comes.

ROBERT. It's like a play. I always want things to be like a play. Don't you, Hester?

HESTER. I dunno. Why?

ROBERT. Don't you, Christina? [*But he does not wait for an answer — a habit with him in his better humored moments.*] You

have to tell us you like this old house, you know. Mother and I wouldn't change it for the world.

CHRISTINA [*smiling as she looks around her*]. How about that tea, Dave?

DAVID. Excuse me, Chris! I forgot. . . .

CHRISTINA [*to* ROBERT]. I've been here three minutes and I'm ordering food already!

ROBERT. Well, let me "do the honors."

DAVID. Honors, hell! Isn't Julia still in the kitchen?

ROBERT. Sure she is.

DAVID. Well, I *must* see Julia! [*He goes.*]

ROBERT [*to* CHRISTINA]. Julia'll drop dead, too. I expect half the town'll be dropping dead. Dave's always been the Greek god around this place, you know.

HESTER. He should be.

ROBERT. I can remember the time I didn't think so.

[*A door slams. In the hall,* MRS. PHELPS *is heard talking, excitedly.*]

MRS. PHELPS. Those bags! Have they come, Delia?

HESTER. Here's your mother now.

CHRISTINA. So soon? How nice!

[MRS. PHELPS *enters. She is pretty, distinguished, stoutish, soft, disarming and, in short, has everything one could possibly ask including a real gift for looking years younger than her age, which is well past fifty. She boasts a reasonable amount of conventional culture, no great amount of intellect, a superabundant vitality, perfect health and a prattling spirit. At the moment she is still wearing her hat and furs and she looks wildly about her.*]

MRS. PHELPS. Dave! Dave, boy! Where are you, Dave? Where are you? It's Mother, Dave! [*She does not see him in the room and she is already turning back to the hall without a word or a look for anybody else.*] Where are you, Dave? Come here this minute! Don't you hear me, Dave? It's Mother! [*Then* DAVID *appears in the hall.*] Oh, Dave!

DAVID [*a little abashed by the vigor of this welcome*]. Hello, Mother.

MRS. PHELPS. Dave, is it really you?

DAVID. Guess it must be, Mother.

MRS. PHELPS. Dave, dear!

[*She envelops as much of him as she can possibly reach.*]

DAVID [*prying loose*]. Well! Glad to see us, Mother?

MRS. PHELPS. Glad!

DAVID. You certainly seem to be glad. ... But you haven't spoken to ...

[CHRISTINA, *at his look, steps forward.*]

MRS. PHELPS [*still not seeing her*]. To think I wasn't here!

DAVID. We're ahead of time, you know. Christina ...

MRS. PHELPS. I must have known somehow. Something just made me put down my cup and rush home. But you're not looking badly. You *are* well, aren't you? I do believe you've put on weight. You must be careful, though, not to take cold this weather. Was the crossing awfully rough? Were you seasick? You haven't been working too hard, have you, Dave, boy?

CHRISTINA [*unable to stand on one foot any longer*]. He hasn't been working at all. Not for weeks!

MRS. PHELPS. [*She turns at the sound of the strange voice.*] Eh? Oh!

DAVID. I've been trying to make you take notice of Christina, Mother.

MRS. PHELPS [*with the utmost warmth*]. Oh, my dear Christina, I *am* sorry! [*She kisses* CHRISTINA *on both cheeks.*] Seeing this big boy again quite took me off my feet. Let me look at *you*, now. Why, Dave, she's splendid. Perfectly splendid! I always knew Dave would choose only the best. Didn't I always say so, Dave, boy? [*Which takes her back to* DAVID.] Dave, you *have* been working too hard. I don't like those circles under your eyes.

DAVID. Nonsense, Mother!

CHRISTINA. I think he looks pretty well.

MRS. PHELPS. But only pretty well. I can't help worrying about these big boys of mine. [*Her emotion stops her. She turns gallantly to* ROBERT.] Did you skate, Rob?

ROBERT. As a matter of fact, I couldn't.

They've been cutting ice on the pond and it's full of holes.

MRS. PHELPS. I must have signs put up to-morrow. Remember that, everybody. If any of you do go out in this freezing cold, don't take the short cut across the pond. ... Dave, boy, this is too good to be true. After two whole years away and five, nearly six months married.

[*The maid brings tea.*]

DAVID. Here's tea.

MRS. PHELPS. Sit down here beside me, dear, dear Christina. And, Dave, boy, sit over there where I can see you. Just take my furs, Delia, so I can do my duty in comfort. My boy, my boy, you don't know ... you don't know how happy I am to have you home again! Just hand me my salts, will you, Robin? This excitement has laid me out. Christina, my dear, how do you take your tea?

[*She sits at the table.* ROBIN *has fetched her bottle of "Crown Lavender" from somewhere. She motions him to put it down and proceeds to pour tea.*]

CHRISTINA. Just tea, please. As it comes and nothing in it.

MRS. PHELPS. A real tea drinker! I hope my tea stands the test. [*She passes* CHRISTINA *her cup and ceases to take any notice of her whatsoever.*] Tea, Dave, boy?

DAVID. Please, Mother.

MRS. PHELPS. The same old way?

DAVID. Yes.

MRS. PHELPS. Tea, Robin? [*She hands* DAVID *his cup.*]

ROBERT [*busy passing sandwiches and such*]. As usual, please.

MRS. PHELPS [*very absent-minded about the salts*]. Who do you suppose was asking after you yesterday, Dave, boy? Old George, the doorman, down at the bank. You remember old George? He's so thrilled about your coming back! And Mrs. Donohue's so thrilled! Such a sweet woman! You know, I'm afraid he's drinking again. You must run right over early to-morrow morning and let her have a look at you. I must have some people in to meet you. Some very nice new people who've come here since you went away. Named Clay. He used to be a publisher in

Boston, but he gave it up because he says nobody really cares about good books any more. Of course, this house has been a real godsend to him. I must give a big dinner for you, Dave, and ask all our old friends. I do need your cool head, too, on my business. Robin does his best, but he isn't really a business man. You remember the American Telephone I bought? Mr. Curtin, at the bank, advises me to sell and take my profit, but I don't think so. What do you think, Dave, boy?

HESTER. May I have a cup, please, Mrs. Phelps?

MRS. PHELPS. Hester, my dear, how forgetful of me! How will you have it?

HESTER. As usual.

MRS. PHELPS. Let me see, that's cream and sugar?

HESTER. Only cream. No sugar.

MRS. PHELPS. Of course. Robin, will you give Hester her tea?

ROBERT [as he gives HESTER the cup]. You see, we have to take a back seat now.

MRS. PHELPS. A back seat, Robin?

ROBERT. I'm only warning Hester. She's got to know what to expect in this family when Dave's around.

DAVID. Oh, shut up, Rob!

MRS. PHELPS [smiling]. My two beaux! My two jealous beaux!

ROBERT. Oh, well! Dave's out in the great world now and I'm still the same old homebody I always was. Look at him, Mother!

MRS. PHELPS [looking]. Oh, my boy, my boy, if you knew what it means to me to see all my plans and hopes for you fulfilled. I've dreamed of your being an architect ever since... ever since...

ROBERT. Ever since he first showed an interest in his blocks.

MRS. PHELPS. I have those blocks still, Dave. Do you remember them?

DAVID. Do I remember those blocks!

MRS. PHELPS [solemnly]. You must never forget them, because it's quite true what Robin says and, some day, when you have children of your own, I shall show them the foundation stones of their father's great career. If I have one gift it's the ability to see what people have in them and

to bring it out. I saw what David had in him, even then. And I brought it out.

[She smiles benignly. There is a brief pause. A quizzical frown contracts CHRISTINA's brow.]

CHRISTINA. It seems a risky business.

MRS. PHELPS [turning with that same start which CHRISTINA's voice caused before]. What seems a risky business?

CHRISTINA. The way families have of doing that.

MRS. PHELPS [setting her tea-cup down a little too deliberately]. What could be more natural?

HESTER [coming to CHRISTINA's rescue from an abyss of boredom]. I see what Christina means. From blocks to architecture is a long guess. You might very easily have guessed wrong, you know. I had some rabbits, once, and I loved 'em. Suppose my family had seen what I had in me, then, and brought me up to be a lion tamer?

MRS. PHELPS [offended]. Really, Hester!

HESTER. Isn't that just what happens to most of us? Christina's job doesn't sound like the kind parents usually pick out for a girl, though.

ROBERT. I'll say it doesn't.

CHRISTINA. My parents did pick it out, though. I'm just like the rest.

HESTER. Well, it only goes to prove what I was saying. Christina might have been a homebody instead of a scientist. I might have been a lion tamer. If only our parents hadn't had ideas about us!

DAVID. One guess is as good as another. I daresay I wanted to be a fireman. What do little girls want to be?

HESTER. Queens.

CHRISTINA. Wouldn't it be a pleasant world with nothing but queens and firemen in it!

ROBERT. I guess Mother knew. She always does know.

HESTER. What I say about children is this: Have 'em. Love 'em. And then leave 'em be.

CHRISTINA [amused]. I'm not sure that isn't a very profound remark.

MRS. PHELPS. [She makes up her mind to investigate this daughter-in-law more closely *and, with sudden briskness, takes back the conversation.*] Why don't you two great things take the bags upstairs out of the hall?

DAVID. That's an idea.

MRS. PHELPS. Dear Christina's in the little front room, and Dave, you're in the back in your old room.

DAVID [*surprised*]. I say, Mother... can't we...

HESTER. Don't they want to be together, Mrs. Phelps? Let me move out of the guest room and then...

MRS. PHELPS. Indeed, I'll do nothing of the sort. Hester's here for a rest and I won't upset her. Dave can be perfectly comfortable in his old room and so can Christina in front and it won't hurt them a bit.

CHRISTINA. Of course not....

HESTER. But, Mrs. Phelps...

MRS. PHELPS. Not another word, my dear. [*To* CHRISTINA.] This child has danced herself into a decline and she's got to be taken care of.

DAVE. Right!

ROBERT. Come along, Dave.

MRS. PHELPS. Go and supervise, Hester, and leave me to... to visit with my new daughter.

[DAVE *and* ROB *go*. HESTER *following*.]

HESTER [*as she goes*]. But really, David, I might just as well move. I didn't think. And if you and Christina...

MRS. PHELPS [*a broad smile to* CHRISTINA]. Now, my dear, let me give you another cup of tea.

CHRISTINA. Thank you.

MRS. PHELPS. And take your hat off so that I can really see you. I've never seen a lady scientist before.

CHRISTINA. I hope I'm not so very different from other women.

MRS. PHELPS. I've quite got over being afraid of you.

CHRISTINA. Afraid of me, Mrs. Phelps?

MRS. PHELPS. Can't you understand that? My big boy sends me a curt cable to say that he's marrying a charming and talented research geologist.

CHRISTINA. Biologist.

MRS. PHELPS. Biologist. It did sound just the least bit in the world improbable.

CHRISTINA. Yes.... I can see that.

MRS. PHELPS. Now that I know you, though, I'm very proud to have you for a daughter. Every woman wants a daughter, you know!

CHRISTINA. You're being very nice to me, Mrs. Phelps.

MRS. PHELPS. It isn't at all hard to be nice to you, my dear. Tell me about your tour. You went to Sicily?

CHRISTINA. We did, indeed.

MRS. PHELPS. Sicily, the home of... [*She gives herself up to Sicilian emotion*]... of all those great ancient... poets and... poets. To think of your taking my boy to Sicily where I'd always planned to take him! I've never been, you see. How many opportunities we miss! That's what we're always saying of dead people, isn't it? Though, of course, I shouldn't think of calling David dead merely because he's got married. I do hope you read "Glorious Apollo" before you went to Venice. When I read it, I felt that I had made a new friend. I always make such close friends of my books and, you know, there's no friend like a really good book. And there's nothing like a good historical novel to make a city vivid and interesting. They do bring things back to one. "Glorious Apollo"! What a despicable character that man Byron was! Though I daresay he couldn't have been as bad as he was painted. People do exaggerate so. Especially writers. Do you know "The Little Flowers of St. Francis"?

CHRISTINA. I'm afraid not. Are they exaggerated?

MRS. PHELPS. Well, of course, they're really fairy tales. Only to one with a profoundly religious point of view... and, if there's one thing I pride myself on it *is* my profoundly religious point of view... I always keep the "Little Flowers" on the table beside my bed. And read *in* them, you know? I quite brought Robin up on them. Dave never took to them. Though Dave loved his regular fairy tales. His Grimm and his Hans Christian. You read, I hope?

CHRISTINA. I can. I sometimes have to.

MRS. PHELPS. Oh, my dear, I only meant that I think it's so important, for David's happiness, that you should be what *I* call "a reader." Both my boys learned their classics at their mother's knee. Their Scott and their Thackeray. *And* their Dickens. Lighter things too, of course. "Treasure Island" and "Little Lord Fauntleroy." And you went to Prague, too. Dave wrote me from Prague. Such interesting letters, Dave writes! I wondered why you stayed so long in Prague.

CHRISTINA. It's a charming city, and an architect's paradise. Dave and I thought he ought to look at something besides cathedrals and temples.... There *is* domestic architecture, you know.

MRS. PHELPS. Yes. I suppose there is.

CHRISTINA. People *do* want houses. I'm inclined to think houses are more interesting than churches nowadays.

MRS. PHELPS. Oh, nowadays! I'm afraid I've very little use for nowadays. I've always thought it a pity that Dave and Rob couldn't have grown up in Italy in the Renaissance and known such men as... well, as Cellini.

CHRISTINA. I'm not sure Cellini would have been the ideal companion for a growing boy.

MRS. PHELPS. No? Well, perhaps not. I must certainly take in Prague my next trip abroad. It's really been very hard for me to stay home these last two years. But I said to myself: Dave must have his fling. I don't like mothers who keep their sons tied to their apron strings. I said: Dave will come home to me a complete man. Though I didn't actually look for his bringing you with him, my dear, and coming home a married man. Still... So I stayed home with Robin. And I was glad to. I'm not sure I haven't sometimes neglected Robin for David. Given myself too much to the one, not enough to the other. The first born, you know. We mothers are human, however much we may try not to be. Tell me, Christina, you think David *is* well, don't you?

CHRISTINA. Yes, perfectly.

MRS. PHELPS. He didn't seem quite himself just now.

CHRISTINA. Perhaps he was embarrassed.

MRS. PHELPS. With me? His own mother?

CHRISTINA. Wouldn't I have accounted for it?

MRS. PHELPS. How silly of me not to remember that! Tell me what your plans are — if you have any plans, which I hope you haven't, because I've been making so many for you and such perfect ones.

CHRISTINA. Well, as a matter of fact, we haven't many, but what we have are pretty definite.

MRS. PHELPS. Really! Are they really? What are they?

CHRISTINA. Well, we're going to live in New York, of course.

MRS. PHELPS. Why "New York of course"? It seems to me that you might choose a pleasanter place to live than New York.

CHRISTINA. No doubt of that, Mrs. Phelps. But it does seem a good place for Dave to work and...

MRS. PHELPS. Oh, I can't agree with you!

CHRISTINA. I shouldn't have thought there could be two ways about New York for Dave any more than for me.

MRS. PHELPS. For you?

CHRISTINA. It's where my appointment is.

MRS. PHELPS. Your appointment?

CHRISTINA. At the Rockefeller Institute.

MRS. PHELPS. So that's what takes Dave and you to New York? Your geology.

CHRISTINA. Partly. Only it isn't geology. It's biology.

MRS. PHELPS. Of course. Geology's about rocks, isn't it?

CHRISTINA. Largely.

MRS. PHELPS. And biology?

CHRISTINA. Well — about Life.

MRS. PHELPS [*getting it clear*]. So you're a student of Life, my dear. I do wish David had called you that instead of the other.

CHRISTINA. I understand how you felt, Mrs. Phelps. I hope you don't hold my job against me.

MRS. PHELPS [*with deep feeling*]. My dearest Christina, I don't! Oh, if you thought that, I should be heart-broken. You've made my darling David happy, my dear, and for that I'm prepared to love everything about you. Even your job. Do you smoke?

CHRISTINA. Yes, thank you. May I?

MRS. PHELPS. Please. And I shall, too.... [*They light cigarettes.*] Don't you like my lighter?

CHRISTINA. It's sweet. And very handy, I should think.

MRS. PHELPS. A friend sent it me from London. Let me give it to you.

CHRISTINA. Oh, no.

MRS. PHELPS. Please? I've not had a chance yet to give my new daughter anything. My dearest Christina.... please?

CHRISTINA. Thank you. I shall always keep it and use it.

MRS. PHELPS. I like the little ceremonial gift.... Now, about your job...

CHRISTINA. My job?

MRS. PHELPS. As you call it. I don't like to say "profession" because that has such a sinister sound for a woman. And then science is hardly a profession, is it? Rather more of a hobby. You're planning to continue?

CHRISTINA. With my job? Oh, yes.

MRS. PHELPS. Just as though you hadn't married, I mean?

CHRISTINA. I have to, don't I? To earn my right to call myself a biologist...

MRS. PHELPS. Do people call you that?

CHRISTINA. I guess they call me "doctor."

MRS. PHELPS. You're *not* a doctor?

CHRISTINA. Technically, I am.

MRS. PHELPS. Oh, I can never agree with you that women make good doctors!

CHRISTINA. We shan't have to argue that point. I've no intention of practicing.

MRS. PHELPS. Not at all? Above all, not on David?

CHRISTINA. I shouldn't think of it.

MRS. PHELPS. I remember hearing that doctors never do practice on their own families. I remember that when our doctor here had a baby ... of course, his wife had the baby ... he called in quite an outsider to deliver the child. I remember how that struck me at the time. Tell me more about yourself, my dear. When Dave cabled me about meeting you and marrying you so suddenly...

CHRISTINA. It wasn't so sudden, Mrs. Phelps. I spent a good six or seven months turning him down flat.

MRS. PHELPS [*offended*]. Indeed?

CHRISTINA. Dave and I met in Rome last winter. Then he came to Heidelberg where I was working and I accepted him. ... I'd never given him the least encouragement before.

MRS. PHELPS [*as before*]. Indeed?

CHRISTINA. We were married straight off ... and went to Sicily.

MRS. PHELPS. I didn't know about the preliminaries. Dave never told me. And now you're taking him off to New York!

CHRISTINA. Please don't put it that way.

MRS. PHELPS. I'm stating a fact, my dear girl. After all, you *have* got your — [*She gets it right this time*] — biology to think of.

CHRISTINA. You can't blame me for that, dear Mrs. Phelps, so long as I think of Dave's work, too.

MRS. PHELPS. No.... So long as you do that.... How did you come to select your career?

CHRISTINA. My father was a doctor I grew up in his hospital. Everything followed quite naturally.

MRS. PHELPS. Your father — is he living?

CHRISTINA. He died two years ago. Tragically, but rather splendidly.

MRS. PHELPS. How?

CHRISTINA. He'd been experimenting for years on infantile paralysis and...

MRS. PHELPS. And he died of that? [CHRISTINA *nods rather solemnly.*] Is your mother living?

CHRISTINA. Oh, yes; at home.

MRS. PHELPS. At home?

CHRISTINA. In Omaha.

MRS. PHELPS [*meditatively*]. Omaha...

CHRISTINA. Yes.

MRS. PHELPS. Hm... And you'll go on with your father's experiments?

CHRISTINA. Oh, no! That's not at all in my line.

MRS. PHELPS. What *is* your line?

CHRISTINA. It's hard to say. I did some rather hard work this last year at Heidelberg on the embryos of chickens. In the egg, you know.

MRS. PHELPS. For heaven's sake, what for?

CHRISTINA. Trying to find out something about what makes growth stop.

MRS. PHELPS. Why...?

CHRISTINA. Curiosity, I guess. Now I'm admitting what low people we scientists are. I think that curiosity's all we have. And a little training.

MRS. PHELPS. Does David follow your work?

CHRISTINA. No. And I don't expect him to.

MRS. PHELPS. Quite right. David wouldn't be appealed to by rotten eggs.... Not that he couldn't understand them if they did appeal to him.

CHRISTINA. Of course.

MRS. PHELPS. Isn't the Rockefeller Institute one of those places where they practice vivisection?

CHRISTINA. One of many. Yes....

MRS. PHELPS. Have you...

CHRISTINA. What?

MRS. PHELPS. Experimented on animals?

CHRISTINA. Isn't it a part of my job? Dave understands that. You must try to understand it.

MRS. PHELPS. Very well, I shall try, my dear. Now you must listen to me and try to understand me.... Look at me. What do you see? Simply — David's mother. I can't say of you that you're simply David's wife, because, clearly, you're many things beside that. But I am simply his mother.... I think, as I talk to you, that I belong to a dead age. I wonder if you think that? In my day, we considered a girl immensely courageous and independent who taught school or gave music lessons. Nowadays, girls sell real estate and become scientists and think nothing of it. Give us our due, Christina. We weren't entirely bustles and smelling salts, we girls who did not go into the world. We made a great profession which I fear may be in some danger of vanishing from the face of the earth. We made a profession of motherhood. That may sound old-fashioned to you. Believe me, it had its value. I was trained to be a wife that I might become a mother. [CHRISTINA *is about to protest*. MRS. PHELPS *stops her*.] Your father died of his investigations of a dangerous disease. You called that splendid of him, didn't you? Would you say less of us who gave our lives to being mothers? Mothers of sons, particularly. Listen to me, Christina. David was five, Rob only a little baby, when my husband died. I'd been married six years, not so very happily. I was pretty, as a girl, too. Very pretty. [*This thought holds her for a second*.] For twenty-four years, since my husband died, I've given all my life, all my strength to Dave and Rob. They've been my life and my job. They've taken the place of husband and friends both, for me. Where do I stand, now? Rob is marrying. Dave is married already. This is the end of my life and my job.... Oh, I'm not asking for credit or praise. I'm asking for something more substantial. I'm asking you, my dear, dear Christina, not to take all my boy's heart. Leave me, I beg you, a little, little part of it. I've earned that much. I'm not sure I couldn't say that you owe me that much — as David's mother. I believe I've deserved it. Don't you think I have?

CHRISTINA [*deeply moved*]. My dear, dear Mrs. Phelps!

MRS. PHELPS. It's agreed then, isn't it, that I'm not to be shut out?

CHRISTINA. Of course you're not!

MRS. PHELPS. Not by you, Christina. Nor by your work?

CHRISTINA. No! No!

MRS. PHELPS. Nor by anything?

CHRISTINA. You must know that I should never come between a mother and her son. You must know that I appreciate what you've done for Dave and all you've always been and meant to him. You *must* know that!

MRS. PHELPS. Christina, my dear,

you're a very disarming person. You are indeed. I've known you ten minutes and unloaded my whole heart to you.

CHRISTINA. I'm proud that you trust me.

MRS. PHELPS [*patting her hand*]. Thank you, my dear. And now ... now that you know how I feel ... now you won't go to New York, will you? You won't take Dave to New York?

CHRISTINA [*drawing back in alarm*]. But, Mrs. Phelps!

MRS. PHELPS. Because that *would* be coming between mother and son as you just now said. That could mean only one thing — crowding me out, setting me aside, robbing me....

CHRISTINA [*completely baffled*]. You're quite mistaken, Mrs. Phelps! You've no reason to think any such thing!

MRS. PHELPS. Well, it's nice of you to reassure me, and we don't have to worry about it for some time yet. You'll have plenty of time to see how carefully I've worked everything out for David — and for you, too, my dear. You've a nice, long visit ahead and ...

CHRISTINA. I only wish we *had* a nice long visit, Mrs. Phelps.

MRS. PHELPS. What do you mean?

CHRISTINA. I start work at the Institute a week from to-morrow.

MRS. PHELPS [*staggered*]. What *are* you saying, child?

CHRISTINA. We didn't even bring our trunks up, you know.

MRS. PHELPS [*recovering herself*]. I'll not hear of it! A week of David after two years without him? What *are* you thinking of? Don't you realize that David has practically been my sole companion for nearly twenty-five years?

CHRISTINA. You've had Robert, too.

MRS. PHELPS. I'm not thinking so much of Robert, now. He isn't threatened as David is.

CHRISTINA. Threatened, Mrs. Phelps?

MRS. PHELPS. I don't want to see David's career sacrificed.

CHRISTINA. But, I'm not planning to sacrifice it.

MRS. PHELPS. You make the word sound disagreeable. I admire your work, Christina, but I am very clearly of the impression that it may easily obliterate David's work.

CHRISTINA. I don't see any conflict.

MRS. PHELPS. Aren't you taking him to New York, which he simply loathes? To live in a stuffy tenement ... well, an apartment. ... They're the same thing. .. Without proper heat or sunshine or food? I told you I'd made plans. I've arranged everything for David's best interest. I can't believe that a girl of your intelligence won't realize how good my arrangements are. I happen to own a very large tract of land here. A very beautiful tract, most desirable for residences. To the north of the Country Club just beside the links. Hilly and wooded. You can see it, off there to the left of the pond. I've had many offers for it, most advantageous offers. But I've held on to it, ever since Dave chose his profession. Pleasant Valley, it's called. I shall change the name to Phelps Manor and open it. David will have charge. David will lay out the streets, design the gateways, build the houses and make his fortune, his reputation and his place in the world out of it.

CHRISTINA [*pause, then*]. Don't you mean his place in this part of the world, Mrs. Phelps?

MRS. PHELPS [*positively*]. As well this as any. With me to back him, he's certain of a proper start here, and there can't be any doubt about the outcome. His success is assured here and his happiness and prosperity with it. And yours, too. Don't you see that?

CHRISTINA. It certainly sounds safe enough.

MRS. PHELPS. I knew you'd see. Furthermore, he's never happy in New York.

CHRISTINA. Happiness is very important. Only different people have different ideas of it.

MRS. PHELPS. David's always had my ideas. And they're very sound ones.

CHRISTINA [*politely*]. I'm sure of it. But perhaps they aren't sound for David. I mean, from what I know of him....

MRS. PHELPS. I'm David's mother, my dear. I know him better than you do.

CHRISTINA. I wonder!

MRS. PHELPS. Oh, I do! And I know how little New York has to offer. I know the competition there. I know what the struggle would be. Look at the choice. On the one hand obscurity, a desk in some other man's office, years of hack work and discouragement. On the other, immediate prominence, unquestionable success...

CHRISTINA. With his mother behind him.

MRS. PHELPS. Who better?

CHRISTINA. Oh, I see the difference!

MRS. PHELPS. Yes, don't you! And as to your work, my dear, I'm sure we can keep you busy and contented.

CHRISTINA [smiling in spite of herself]. How will you do that?

MRS. PHELPS. Well, it's hard to say, offhand. But if we really set our minds to it.... I know! I'm the chairman of our hospital here, and I have a great deal of influence with the doctors. We've a beautiful laboratory. You couldn't ask for anything nicer or cleaner or more comfortable than that laboratory. You do your work in a laboratory, I suppose?

CHRISTINA. Usually.

MRS. PHELPS. I'll take you down in the morning and introduce you to Dr. McClintock, homeopathic, but very agreeable, and he'll show you our laboratory. We've just got in a new microscope, too. Oh, a very fine one! One the High School didn't want any more. You'll simply love our laboratory. Oh, you will! It has a splendid new sink with hot and cold running water and quite a good gas stove because it's also the nurses' washroom and diet kitchen. And you'll be allowed to putter around as much as you like whenever it isn't in use by the nurses or the real doctors. I can arrange everything perfectly, my dear. I'm certain that, when you see our laboratory, you'll sit right down and write to Mr. Rockefeller, who, I'm told, is a very kind old man at heart, and won't misunderstand in the least, that you've found an opening here that's ever so much more desirable than his old Institute, where you won't be obliged to cut up cats and dogs. You will think it over, won't you? Going to New York, I mean. Taking Dave to New York and ruining all his prospects?

CHRISTINA [after a pause, in all sincere kindliness]. Mrs. Phelps, the third time I refused Dave, he asked me for a reason. I told him I couldn't throw myself away on a big frog in a small puddle.

MRS. PHELPS. You don't mean that you want him to be a small frog, a mere polliwog, in a great ocean like New York?

CHRISTINA. I'm afraid that's just what I do mean. And when he came back at me three months later with some real sketches and a great deal more humility and with a real job in a real architect's office...

MRS. PHELPS. Has David a job? In New York?

CHRISTINA. A chance anyway. With Michaels.

MRS. PHELPS. Michaels?

CHRISTINA. He's a big man. And he's interested in Dave.

MRS. PHELPS. I don't approve at all. I think it's madness.

CHRISTINA. You may be right. But, isn't it best left to Dave and me?

MRS. PHELPS [deeply hurt at the implication]. My dear Christina, if you think I'm trying to interfere, you're quite mistaken. You're very unfair.... Only tell me what makes you so sure Dave can succeed in New York.

CHRISTINA. I haven't given a thought to whether he'll succeed or not. That depends on his own talent, doesn't it? As to how much he makes, or how we get on, at first, I don't think that matters either... so long as Dave stands really on his own feet.

MRS. PHELPS. Oh, Christina, be honest with yourself. You are sacrificing David!

CHRISTINA. How?

MRS. PHELPS. By thinking only of yourself, of course.

CHRISTINA. Won't you believe that I'm thinking of both of us?

MRS. PHELPS. How can I? It's too bad of you, really. It means — [In despair.] — It means that it's all been for nothing!

CHRISTINA. What has?

MRS. PHELPS [*crescendo, as she walks about*]. All, all that I've done for David and given up for him and meant to him!

CHRISTINA. How can you say that?

MRS. PHELPS. I did so want to be friendly with David's wife. If you knew how I've wished and dreamt and prayed for that!

CHRISTINA [*rising herself*]. But can't we be friends?

MRS. PHELPS. Some day you'll have a child of your own and then you may know what I mean, if . . .

CHRISTINA. If what?

MRS. PHELPS [*the last volley*] If you don't sacrifice your child, too, to this work of yours.

CHRISTINA [*deeply distressed*]. Mrs. Phelps, I wish you wouldn't feel that. It makes me feel that I've got off on a very wrong foot here.

[ROBERT *enters.*]

ROBERT. Christina!

CHRISTINA. Yes?

ROBERT. Dave says, if you want a bath before dinner, you'd better be quick about it.

CHRISTINA. I didn't know it was so late. Thanks. [*She goes to* MRS. PHELPS.] You'll see that I do understand, dear Mrs. Phelps. You'll see that it all comes straight somehow and turns out for the best. Life takes care of such things. All we have to do is to keep out of life's way and make the best of things as *healthily* as possible.

MRS. PHELPS. You think I'm selfish.

CHRISTINA. Oh, no! I don't think anything of the sort!

MRS. PHELPS. Because if there's one thing I pride myself on, I may have many faults, but I am not selfish. I haven't a selfish hair in my head.

CHRISTINA. I tell you, I understand.

[*She kisses her quickly and goes out.*]

ROBERT [*looking curiously after* CHRISTINA]. Mother!

MRS. PHELPS [*wildly*]. Oh, Robin! I'm so lonely! So lonely!

ROBERT [*startled*]. Mother!

MRS. PHELPS. I'm afraid I'm a dreadful coward!

ROBERT. *You*, Mother?

MRS. PHELPS. I ought to have been prepared to lose my two great, splendid sons. I've told myself over and over again that the time would come, and now that it *has* come, I can't face it! She's taking Dave away to New York, away from me, away from all the wonderful plans I've made for him here!

ROBERT. Well, if Dave's fool enough to go!

MRS. PHELPS. I shouldn't do to any woman on earth what she's doing to me!

ROBERT. Of course you wouldn't. But then, Christina isn't your sort, is she?

MRS. PHELPS. You've noticed that, too?

ROBERT. Who *is* your sort, Mother? . . . Oh, it's a wonderful gift you've given us.

MRS. PHELPS. What's that, Robin?

ROBERT. A wonderful ideal of womanhood. You know what I mean.

MRS. PHELPS. No. What?

ROBERT. Your own marvelous self, Mother!

MRS. PHELPS. Dave didn't stop to think of any such ideal, did he?

ROBERT. Oh, Dave!

MRS. PHELPS. Perhaps I shouldn't be hurt. But you can't know what it is to be a mother. I nearly died when Dave was born. Hours and hours I suffered for him, trapped in agony. He was a twelve-pound baby, you know. If I could be sure of his happiness!

ROBERT. You mustn't ask too much.

MRS. PHELPS. You're right. No mother should expect any woman to love her son as she loves him.

ROBERT. Your sons don't expect any woman to love them as you do.

MRS. PHELPS. Oh, Robin! Is that how you feel?

ROBERT. I think it must be. [*She looks at him, watching him think it all out.*] It's a funny business, isn't it? After a woman like you has suffered the tortures of the damned bringing us into the world, and worked like a slave to help us grow up in it, we can't wait to cut loose and give up the one thing we can be sure of! And for what? To run every known risk of disillusion and disappointment.

MRS. PHELPS [struck by this]. What is the one thing you can be sure of, Robin?

ROBERT. You are. Don't you know that? Why can't we leave well enough alone?

MRS. PHELPS. Presently you'll be going too, Rob.

ROBERT. Yes... I know I shall.... But nothing will ever come between us, Mother.

MRS. PHELPS. Come over here by the fire, Robin, and let's forget all these unpleasant things. [She goes to sit by the fire.] Let's have a real old-time talk about nothing at all. Sit down. [He sits as directed on a stool at her feet.] Head in my lap! [He obeys.] So! This has shown me something I've always suspected. That you are my son. David takes after his father.

ROBERT. Mother!

MRS. PHELPS. Tell me, Robin, what you meant just now when you said that about the one thing you can be sure of. Did you mean that you've had dark thoughts about your future?

ROBERT. I must have meant something of the sort.

MRS. PHELPS. Hm.... It was dear of you, my great Robin, to say what you did about my being your ideal. You know my dream has always been to see my two boys married and settled down. But happily! Happily! Has Hester come to any decision about where she wants to spend her honeymoon?

ROBERT. Abroad.

MRS. PHELPS. Nothing more definite than just "abroad"?

ROBERT. No. She doesn't care where we go.

MRS. PHELPS. That seems very odd to me. I took such an interest in my honeymoon. Why, your father and I had every day of it planned, weeks before we were married.... Hester hasn't picked out her flat silver yet, either, has she?

ROBERT. I don't think so.

MRS. PHELPS. I can't understand it!

ROBERT. What?

MRS. PHELPS. Her indifference. It rather shocks me. [She notices that ROBERT is shocked, too.] But I suppose I'm old-fashioned. Like this room. You must give me a little of your time and taste, Robin, before you're married, and advise me about doing this room over.

ROBERT [eagerly]. Have you come to that at last?

MRS. PHELPS. I'm afraid so. How's Hester planning to do your new home?

ROBERT [his spirits subsiding at once]. Oh, I don't know.

MRS. PHELPS. You don't mean to say she hasn't made any plans?

ROBERT. I've been trying to get her interested in house-hunting.

MRS. PHELPS. And she doesn't care about that either?

ROBERT. She says anything will suit her.

MRS. PHELPS. Does she, indeed! Most girls... most normal girls, that is, look forward so to having their homes to receive their friends in.

ROBERT. She leaves it all to me. She says I know much more about such things than she does.

MRS. PHELPS. How little she understands my poor Robin who ought never to be bothered!

ROBERT. Oh, well!

MRS. PHELPS. Do you happen to know if Hester has many friends? I mean, many men friends? Did she have lots of suitors beside you?

ROBERT. I daresay she had loads.

MRS. PHELPS. Do you know that she had?

ROBERT. She never told me so. Why?

MRS. PHELPS. I was wondering. She's been out two years. One does wonder how much a girl has been sought after. But, then, why should she have bothered with others when she thought she could land you? You are rather a catch, you know.

ROBERT. I, Mother?

MRS. PHELPS. Any girl would set her cap for you.

ROBERT. I don't believe Hester did that.

MRS. PHELPS. My dear, I wasn't saying that she did! But why shouldn't she? Only...

ROBERT. Only what?

MRS. PHELPS. I can't help wondering if Hester's feeling for you is as strong as you think it is. [ROBERT wonders, too.] I've been wondering for some time, Robin. I've hesitated to speak to you about it. But after what you've just told me...

ROBERT. Well, it's too late to worry now.

MRS. PHELPS. I can't help worrying, though. Marriage is such an important step and you're such a sensitive, shrinking character. It would be too terrible if you had to go through what you were just speaking of — the disillusionment and disappointment.... I'm only trying to find out what it is that's come between you two young people.

ROBERT. Nothing has, Mother Hester isn't you, that's all!

MRS. PHELPS. Nonsense, Robin!... It isn't that awful woman I was so worried about when you were at Harvard?

ROBERT. I'm not raising a second crop of wild oats.

MRS. PHELPS. Then it *must* be that risk you were speaking of! Oh, why do boys run that risk! Why will they break away!

ROBERT. I wish I knew!

MRS. PHELPS. Perhaps your trouble is that — [*A pause. Then, very low*] — that you don't love Hester.

ROBERT. Oh, love! I must love her or I wouldn't have asked her to marry me. I guess she loves me in her way. Is her way enough? I'll find that out in time. A man ought to marry.

MRS. PHELPS [*a little more positively*]. You *don't* love Hester, and it isn't fair to her!

ROBERT. Yes, I do love her! Only I wonder if I'm the marrying kind. Failing the possibility of marrying you. I mean your double.

MRS. PHELPS [*always increasing*]. You don't love Hester.

ROBERT. I do, I tell you! Who could help loving her? I mean ... Good God, what do I mean?

MRS. PHELPS. Either you don't love Hester or Hester doesn't love you.

ROBERT. She does love me.

MRS. PHELPS. She may say she does, but I haven't seen her showing it.

ROBERT. Mother!

MRS. PHELPS. You don't love Hester and Hester doesn't love you. It's as simple as that, Robin, and you're making a very grave mistake to go on with this. These things may be painful, but they're better faced before than after. Children come after, Robin, and then it's too late! Think, Robin! Think before it's too late! And remember, the happiness of three people is at stake!

ROBERT. Hester's and mine and...

MRS. PHELPS. And mine! And mine! ... Only, I was wrong to say that! You must put my fate out of your mind just as Dave has done. Let Dave find out for himself what he's done. She won't be able to hold him. She won't have time for a home and children. She won't take any more interest in him than Hester takes in you. But you, Robin, *you* can still be saved! I want to save you from throwing yourself away as Dave has. You will face the facts, won't you?

ROBERT. You mean... I'm to... to break with Hester?

MRS. PHELPS. You will be a man?

ROBERT [*pause, then*]. Well ... I'll ... I'll try, Mother.

MRS. PHELPS [*pause, then*]. When?

ROBERT. Well ... the ... the first chance I get.

MRS. PHELPS [*trying not to appear eager*]. To-night? ... You'll have your chance to-night, Robin. I'll see that you get it. Promise me to take it?

ROBERT [*pause*]. All right.... If you think I'd better.... All right....

MRS. PHELPS. Oh, thank God for this confidence between us! Thank God I've saved my boy one more tumble! You'll see it won't be so bad to put up with your mother a little longer! You'll see I've still plenty to give you and to do for you!

ROBERT. My blessed, blessed mother!

MRS. PHELPS [*unable to repress her triumph*]. And I won't have to be lonely now! I won't have to be lonely!

ROBERT. No, Mother! No!

[*He takes her in his arms.*]

MRS. PHELPS. Kiss me.

[*He does; on the lips, fervently. DAVID comes in, dressed for dinner.*]

DAVID. Hello! That's a pretty picture! ... Chris'll be down in a minute.

ROBERT. Where's Hester?

DAVID. In Chris's room. I heard them giggling in there. Isn't it grand they've hit it off so well?

ROBERT [*meeting his mother's eyes*]. Isn't it? I'll make a cocktail. [*He goes.*]

DAVID. You like Christina, don't you, Mother?

MRS. PHELPS. Didn't you know I should?

DAVID. Sure I did! After all, I couldn't have gone far wrong on a wife, could I? I mean, having you for a mother would make most girls look pretty cheesey. I waited a long time. And all the time I was waiting for Chris! You'll see how wonderful Chris is. Why, she gets better every day. I don't know how I ever pulled it off. I swear I don't. I certainly had luck.

MRS. PHELPS. You're happy?

DAVID. You bet I'm happy!

MRS. PHELPS. You're not going to let your happiness crowd me out entirely, are you, Dave, boy?

DAVID [*amiably irritated*]. Oh, Mother! Lay off!

[ROBERT *returns with shaker and cocktail glasses.*]

ROBERT. This is just a preliminary, Mother. We both need it, before we dress.

MRS. PHELPS. Perhaps we do.

DAVID. Shan't we call Chris and Hester?

MRS. PHELPS. No! Just we three!

ROBERT. It'll never be we three any more. I heard them coming as I crossed the hall.

[*He pours the cocktail into the glasses and goes about passing them.*]

MRS. PHELPS. My two boys! My big one and my little one!

DAVID [*calls out*]. Hurry up, Chris!

MRS. PHELPS. If I can keep the little corner Christina doesn't need, Dave... that's all I ask....

DAVID. Don't you worry, Mother. [CHRISTINA *and* HESTER *enter. They are both dressed appropriately for the evening.* CHRISTINA *is particularly lovely.*] Here we are!

CHRISTINA. Thank you, Robert.

[*They sip their cocktails.*]

DAVID. Chris!

CHRISTINA. Yes?

DAVID. Let's tell Mother.

CHRISTINA. Now? In front of everybody?

DAVID. It won't hurt 'em to hear.

CHRISTINA. I don't mind, if they don't.

ROBERT. Mind what?

DAVID. It'll make Mother so happy.

MRS. PHELPS. What will?

DAVID. A surprise Chris and I have got to spring on you!

MRS. PHELPS. How nice! What is it?

CHRISTINA [*a smiling pause — then*]. In about four months I'm going to have a baby.

HESTER. Oh, Christina, how wonderful!

ROBERT. Are you really!

DAVID. Isn't that a grand surprise, Mother?

MRS. PHELPS [*recovering as from a body blow*]. Of course... David. I'm very glad, my dear. Very glad.... Have you a napkin there, Robin? I've spilled my cocktail all over my dress.

CURTAIN

ACT II

SCENE I

The living-room again. It is the same evening, after supper. The lamps are lighted. MRS. PHELPS, HESTER, CHRISTINA, DAVID *and* ROB *are all present.* CHRISTINA, HESTER *and* DAVID *are dressed as we saw them at the end of the first act.* ROB *wears his dinner coat and his mother has changed to a simple evening dress. They have only just finished their coffee and* MRS. PHELPS *is busily showing a collection of photographs which she has in a great Indian basket beside her chair.*

CHRISTINA. What were you doing in the sailor suit, Dave?

DAVID. Dancing the hornpipe, I believe.

MRS. PHELPS [*fondly*]. That was at Miss Briggs's dancing school. Do you remember Miss Briggs, David?

DAVID. Do I! The hornpipe must have been something special, Mother.

MRS. PHELPS. I see that I've marked it "Masonic Temple, April 6th, 1904."

DAVID. It must have been special. They don't usually dance hornpipes in Masonic Temples.

CHRISTINA. Did Miss Briggs teach you to be graceful, Dave?

DAVID. She did indeed. As a boy I was a gazelle. But I got over it.

CHRISTINA. I'm just as glad. I've known one or two adult gazelles.

MRS. PHELPS. Both David and Robin danced beautifully.

DAVID. I haven't thought of Miss Briggs for years. I remember her so well. She seemed so old to me. She must have been old, too. A good deal older than God. She looked it, in spite of her red hair and her castanets. Spain, she used to say, is the land of the dance.

MRS. PHELPS. She had all the nicest children.

DAVID. Castanets and Spanish shawls ... and a police whistle. She blew the whistle at the boys for running and sliding. God knows what dances she taught us. Very different from the steps you indulge in, Hester, with your low modern tastes.

HESTER. Running and sliding sounds very pleasant.

DAVID. We thought that up for ourselves.

MRS. PHELPS. How long ago that all seems! [She shows another photograph.] This is David when he was ten weeks old.

CHRISTINA. Oh, David!

HESTER. Let me see. [CHRISTINA shows her.] What a darling baby! Did they always sit them in shells in those days?

MRS. PHELPS [just a little coldly]. It was a fashion like any other.

CHRISTINA. David on the half shell!

HESTER. Have you ever noticed how much all babies look like Chief Justice Taft?

MRS. PHELPS. [She takes the photographs back in ill-concealed irritation.] David was a beautiful child.

DAVID. I didn't always sit in shells. Mother's got one of me on a white fur rug.

MRS. PHELPS. It hangs over my bed to this day.

CHRISTINA. In the nude?

DAVID. No. In an undershirt.
[HESTER giggles.]

MRS. PHELPS. Fashions change.

CHRISTINA. I suppose they must. David wouldn't think of being photographed in his undershirt, now. Let me see the picture again, Mrs. Phelps.

MRS. PHELPS. I think that's enough for this evening.
[She rises, in great dignity, to put the photographs aside.]

CHRISTINA. Dear Mrs. Phelps, please don't be angry. We were only teasing David. They're awfully interesting pictures.

MRS. PHELPS. Only interesting to me, I'm afraid.

CHRISTINA. Not at all. I loved them. Do show me some more, Mrs. Phelps. Are there many more?

MRS. PHELPS [still stern about them]. Dave and Robin were photographed twice every month until they were twelve years old.

HESTER [calculating rapidly]. Good Lord! That makes over two hundred and fifty of each!

MRS. PHELPS. I never counted. I used to study their photographs, month by month, just as I did their weight. I wasn't satisfied to watch only their bodies grow. I wanted a record of the development of their little minds and souls as well. I could compare the expression of Dave's eyes, for instance, at nine, with their expression at eight and a half, and see the increased depth. And I was never disappointed.

HESTER. I knew a mother once who called her son "her beautiful black swan."

MRS. PHELPS. I should never have called either of my sons by such a name!

ROBERT. I can remember when you used to call us your Arab steeds!

MRS. PHELPS [furious]. Only in fun. Will you put them away, Robin?
[ROBERT takes the photographs.]

ROBERT. Sure you don't want to go through the rest, Mother?

MRS. PHELPS. I'm afraid of boring Christina. Christina has other interests, of course. Higher interests than her husband. Higher even than children, I suspect.

[*There is an abashed, awful pause, at this.* CHRISTINA *looks hurt and baffled.* HESTER *is horrified.* DAVID, *puzzled, rises and goes to the window.* ROBERT *smiles to himself as he stows the photographs away.*]

HESTER [*breaking out*]. Well, of all the . . .

[CHRISTINA, *catching her eye, stops her.*]

MRS. PHELPS [*polite, but dangerous*]. What was it you were about to say, Hester?

HESTER [*recovering herself none too expertly*]. I was just looking at Christina's dress. I was just going to say: "Well of all the lovely dresses I ever saw, that's the loveliest."

CHRISTINA. It *is* nice, isn't it? I got it in Paris. From Poiret. Dave made me.

MRS. PHELPS [*as she studies the dress*]. I've a little woman right here in town who does well enough for me. I know who that dress *would* look well on! Dave, you remember Clara Judd? Such an exquisite figure, Clara had, and such distinction! That dress *wants* distinction and a figure. You might wear it, too, Hester.

[*There is another painful pause.* CHRISTINA *is really crushed.*]

DAVID [*desperately snatching for a change of subject*]. Look, Chris! The moon's up. You can see the kids coasting down the long hill.

CHRISTINA [*joining him at the window gratefully*]. If I weren't all dressed up, I'd join them!

HESTER. Don't you love coasting?

CHRISTINA [*she nods*]. Once last winter we had a big snowfall at Heidelberg. I'd been all day in the laboratory, I remember, straining my eyes out at a scarlet fever culture for our bacteriology man. Krauss, his name was. They called him "The Demon of the Neckar." The theory was that he used to walk along the river bank, thinking up cruel things to say to his students. I never knew such a terrifying

man. . . . Well, this day I'm talking about, I came out of Krauss's laboratory into the snow. Into Grimm's fairy tales, as Dave knows, because Dave's seen Heidelberg. Another bacteriologist, a dear boy from Marburg, came with me. We looked at the snow and we wanted to coast. . . . We found a small boy with a very large sled and we rented it, *with* the boy, who wouldn't trust us not to steal it. We certainly coasted. We got so ardent, we took the funicular up the Schlossberg and coasted down from there. The lights came out along the Neckar and the snow turned the colors and colors snow *can* turn and still we coasted. . . . Presently, we had an accident. A bob turned over in front of us with an old man on it. We couldn't stop and so we just hit the bob and the old man and you know how that is when you're going fast! . . . We picked ourselves up — or, rather, dug ourselves out — and went to see if we'd hurt the old fellow and, God save us, it was Krauss himself! . . . I don't mind telling you our hearts sank. We stood there petrified. But we needn't have worried. Krauss didn't mind. He smiled the sweetest smile — you'd *never* have suspected he had it in him! — and touched his cap like a little boy and apologized for his clumsiness. "My age hasn't improved my skill," he said. . . . I could have kissed him. I wasn't quite sure how he'd have taken that, so, instead, I asked him to join us. He was delighted. We kept it up for another hour, we two students and the great god Krauss. "Jugend ist Trunkenheit ohne Wein!" he said. I daresay he was quoting a poem. . . . He couldn't have been a day under seventy. Three months later, he died of an inoperable internal tumor. In his notes, they found an observation he had written on his condition that very day we coasted. Think of a man who could write observations on his approaching death and then go off to coast afterwards! It's what life can be and should be. It's the difference between life and self.

MRS. PHELPS. Hm! . . .

HESTER. I think that's the most marvelous story I've ever heard!

ROBERT. Isn't it marvelous?

HESTER. I wish I'd known such a man!

CHRISTINA. Do you remember the night *we* coasted in Heidelberg, Dave?

DAVID. Do I? [*To his mother.*] Chris means the night she accepted me!

MRS. PHELPS. Does she really?

DAVID [*dashed and giving it up*]. Yeah. ... Let's go outside and watch the kids, Chris. It'll do us good.

CHRISTINA [*seeing his point*]. Right! I'd love to!

[*They go.*]

MRS. PHELPS. I'm beginning to wonder if Christina's studies at Heidelberg haven't made her just the least little bit in the world pro-German.

HESTER. Mrs. Phelps, how *can* you say such a thing! [HESTER *looks from* ROBERT *to his mother in amazement.* MRS. PHELPS *sits down at the piano and begins to play the easier portions of one of Chopin's nocturnes.*] I think that was simply inspiring!

MRS. PHELPS. I can't play Chopin if you interrupt me, Hester.

HESTER. I'm sorry. I simply can't get Christina out of my mind.

MRS. PHELPS. What do you mean?

HESTER. I mean that I think she's the most perfect person I've ever seen.

MRS. PHELPS. Do you really? Which way did they go, Robin?

ROBERT [*at the window*]. Down the front.

MRS. PHELPS. Can you see them?

ROBERT. They're just standing in the road. Now they're moving down under the trees.

MRS. PHELPS. But they can't even see the long hill from the trees.

ROBERT. They're not looking at the long hill.

MRS. PHELPS. What *are* they looking at?

ROBERT. Each other. It's quite a romantic picture. Now she's put her head on his shoulder. His arm is around her waist. . . .

MRS. PHELPS. Faugh! Call them in!

[*Her irritation produces a discord in the nocturne.* ROBERT *moves to go.*]

HESTER. Oh, don't, Rob! It's the first chance they've had to be alone together.

MRS. PHELPS. They can be alone without David's catching pneumonia, can't they? She drags him out of doors at night in freezing weather to spoon in the road like a couple of mill hands! I should think she might have some consideration for her husband's health, let alone for my feelings.

HESTER [*a little hotly*]. In the first place, it was David who dragged *her* out. In the second, they *are* in love and *do* want to be alone. In the third, I don't see any reason for worrying over the health of any man who looks as husky as David does. And in the fourth, if there *is* any worrying to be done, let me remind you that it's Christina and *not* David who is going to have a baby. [MRS. PHELPS *breaks off her playing in the middle of a phrase.*] I'm sorry if I've shocked you, but the truth is, you've both shocked me.

ROBERT. How have we shocked you?

HESTER. By not being a great deal more thrilled over Christina's baby. When I drank my cocktail to it before dinner, neither of you drank yours. When I wanted to talk about it during dinner, you both changed the subject. You haven't mentioned that baby since dinner, except once, and that was catty! You've known about that baby for over two hours and you aren't excited about it yet! Not what *I* call excited.

MRS. PHELPS. If you'll forgive my saying so, Hester, I'm not sure that an unborn baby is quite the most suitable subject for . . .

HESTER. I'm blessed if I see anything bad form about a baby!

ROBERT. No more does Mother — after it's born.

HESTER. I can't wait for that. I *love* thinking about them. And wondering what they're going to be — I mean, boy or girl. Why, we had bets up on my sister's baby for months before he was born.

MRS. PHELPS. I'm not ashamed to be old-fashioned.

HESTER. You ought to be. This is going to be a very remarkable baby. There aren't many born with such parents. And I intend to go right on talking about it with anyone who'll listen to me. Christina doesn't mind. She's just as interested as I am. I've already made her promise to have my sister's obstetrician.

MRS. PHELPS. Really, Hester!

HESTER. I'd go to the ends of the earth for that man. Christina's baby has put me in a very maternal frame of mind.

MRS. PHELPS. Maternal!

HESTER. What I say is: I'm as good as married. I might as well make the best of my opportunities to get used to the idea. Because I intend to have as many babies as possible.

MRS. PHELPS [glancing at ROBERT]. Is that why you're marrying Rob, Hester?

HESTER. What better reason could I have? I'm sorry if I've shocked you, but, as I said before, you've shocked me and that's that.

[Coolly, MRS. PHELPS goes for the coffee tray. Her eyes meet ROBERT's and there is no mistaking the intention of the look they give him. Then, without a word, she leaves ROBERT and HESTER alone together.]

ROBERT [starting after her]. Mother!... Hester didn't mean.... Oh.... [He turns back to HESTER.] Hester, how could you?

HESTER. I don't know.... But I don't care if I did!

ROBERT. It doesn't make things any easier for me.

HESTER. Oh, Rob, dear, I am sorry!

ROBERT. You've got Mother all ruffled and upset. Now we'll have to smooth her down and have all kinds of explanations and everything. Really, it was too bad of you.

HESTER. I know. I lost my temper.... You understand, don't you?

ROBERT. I understand that you're a guest in Mother's house.

HESTER. Is that all you understand? Oh, Rob!

ROBERT. I'm sorry, Hester. But, for the moment, I'm thinking of Mother.

HESTER. I see.... I'll apologize.

ROBERT. That's up to you.

HESTER. I suppose she'll never forgive me. It isn't this, though.

ROBERT. This?

HESTER. The scene I made.

ROBERT. What do you mean?

HESTER. I don't know.... Some mothers like the girls their sons marry.

ROBERT. Doesn't that depend on the girls?

HESTER. Not entirely.

ROBERT. You mustn't be unjust to Mother.

HESTER. Rob, I'm a little tired of hearing about your mother.... [Suddenly penitent again.] Oh, I didn't mean to say that! I didn't mean it a bit! I'm sorry, Rob.... Now I'm apologizing to you. Don't you hear me?

ROBERT. Yes, I hear you. What then?

HESTER. Oh, what difference does it make? I'm not marrying your mother. I'm marrying you. And I love you, Rob! I love you!

ROBERT. Yes, my dear.

HESTER. I'll never be bad again.

ROBERT. I'm willing to take your word for it.

HESTER. You'd better be. Oh, you are angry with me, Rob!

ROBERT. No. I'm not.

HESTER. You're a queer one.

ROBERT. Think so? How?

HESTER. As a lover. I've never seen another like you.

ROBERT. Haven't you? [A thought strikes him.] Tell me something, Hester.

HESTER. What?

ROBERT. Have you had many?

HESTER. Many what?

ROBERT. Lovers.

HESTER. Oh, Robert, what a thing to say to a lady!

ROBERT. You know what I mean.

HESTER. I'm not quite sure I want to answer.

ROBERT. I'm not asking for their names.

HESTER. Oh, I shouldn't mind that.. the truth is ... I don't know ...

ROBERT. You must.

HESTER. I don't really. I used to think ... oh, quite often ... that one of my beaux was coming to the point ... but..

ROBERT. Yes?

HESTER. But none of them ever did.

ROBERT. That surprises me. Why not

HESTER. I don't think it was entirel lack of allure, Rob.

ROBERT. Of course it wasn't!

HESTER. *I* think it was because I always laughed.

ROBERT. You didn't laugh at me.

HESTER. You looked foolish enough, now that I think of it.

ROBERT. Yes. I daresay.... So I *was* the only one.

HESTER. Say the only one I didn't laugh at, please. You make me sound so undesirable.

ROBERT. I didn't mean to. Tell me, Hester...

HESTER. Anything.

ROBERT. Have you thought what it will mean to be my wife?

HESTER. A very pleasant life.

ROBERT. For you?

HESTER. I certainly hope so.

ROBERT. I don't know that I quite share your enthusiasm for children.

HESTER. You will.

ROBERT. They don't exactly help a career, you know.

HESTER. Have you got a career?

ROBERT. I fully intend to have one.

HESTER. I'm glad to hear it.

ROBERT. I've got just as much talent as Dave has.

HESTER. What kind of talent?

ROBERT. I haven't decided. I can draw pretty well. I'm not a bad musician. I might decide to compose. I might even write. I've often thought of it. And children, you see...

HESTER. I don't know much about careers, but Lincoln had children and adored 'em, and if you can do half as well as he did...

ROBERT. Then my preferences aren't to be considered?

HESTER. You just leave things to me. If we're poor, I'll cook and scrub floors. I'll bring up our children. I'll take care of you whether we live in New York or Kamchatka. This business is up to me, Rob. Don't let it worry you.

ROBERT [*crushed*]. I only wanted to make sure you understood my point of view.

HESTER. If I don't, I shall, so let's cut this short. [*She goes a little huffily to the window,* ROBERT *watching her uneasily.*] Hello!

ROBERT. What is it?

HESTER. There goes your mother down the road.

ROBERT. [*He joins her.*] So it is! What can she be doing?

HESTER. She's fetching her darling David in out of the cold. I knew she would.

ROBERT. Hester, would you mind not speaking that way of Mother?

HESTER. Can't she leave them alone for a minute?

ROBERT. She's the worrying kind.

HESTER. Oh, rot!

ROBERT. Evidently you're bent on making things as difficult as possible for me.

HESTER. I'm sorry you feel that.
[*A long irritable pause, then.*]

ROBERT. Hester?

HESTER. Yes?

ROBERT. Have you thought any more about our honeymoon?

HESTER. Didn't we decide to go abroad?

ROBERT. Abroad's a pretty general term. You were to think *where* you wanted to be taken.

HESTER. I left that to you.

ROBERT. You said you "didn't care."

HESTER. I don't.

ROBERT. Nor where we live after... nor how.

HESTER. I don't... I don't... I want to live with *you.* [*Suddenly warming.*] What's the use of this, Rob?

ROBERT. We've never talked seriously about our marriage before.

HESTER. What is there to say about it?

ROBERT. A great deal.

HESTER. I don't agree. Marriages are things of feeling. They'd better *not* be talked about.

ROBERT. Real marriages can stand discussion!

HESTER. Rob!

ROBERT. What?

HESTER. That wasn't nice.

ROBERT. Wasn't it?

HESTER [*suddenly frightened*]. What's the matter, Rob? I'll talk as seriously as you please. Do I love you? Yes. Am

I going to make you a good wife? I hope so, though I *am* only twenty and may make mistakes. Are you going to be happy with me? I hope that, too, but you'll have to answer it for yourself.

ROBERT. I can't answer it.

HESTER. Why can't you?

ROBERT. Because I'm not sure of it.

HESTER. Aren't you, Rob?

ROBERT. These things are better faced before than after.

HESTER. What is it you're trying to say?

ROBERT. If only we could be sure!

HESTER [*stunned*]. So that's it!

ROBERT. Are you so sure you want to marry me?

HESTER. How can I be — now?

ROBERT. Marriage is such a serious thing. You don't realize how serious.

HESTER. Don't I?

ROBERT. No.... I hope you won't think harshly of me.... And, mind you, I haven't said I wanted to break things off.... I only want...

HESTER. Please, Rob!

ROBERT. No. You've got to hear me out.

HESTER. I've heard enough, thank you!

ROBERT. I'm only trying to look at this thing...

HESTER. Seriously.... I know....

ROBERT. Because, after all, the happiness of three people is affected by it.

HESTER. Three?

ROBERT. As Mother said, before dinner.

HESTER. So you talked this over with your mother?

ROBERT. Isn't that natural?

HESTER. Is your mother the third?

ROBERT. Wouldn't she be?

HESTER. Yes, I suppose she would.... I think you might tell me what else she had to say.

ROBERT. It was all wise and kind. You may be as hard as you like on me, but you mustn't be hard on poor splendid lonely Mother.

HESTER [*savage — under her breath*]. So she's lonely, too!

ROBERT. You *will* twist my meaning!

HESTER. You *said* "lonely."

ROBERT. Perhaps I did. But Mother didn't. You know, she never talks about herself.

HESTER. I see. What else did she say about us?

ROBERT. Well, you haven't been very interested in planning our future. She notices such things.

HESTER. What else?

ROBERT. She sees through people, you know.

HESTER. Through me?

ROBERT. She thought, as I must say I do, that we didn't love each other quite enough to... At least, she thought we ought to think very carefully before we...

HESTER. [*Gripping his two arms with all her strength, she stops him.*] If you really want to be free... if you really want that, Rob, it's all right. It's perfectly all right. ... I'll set you free.... Don't worry.... Only you've got to say so. You've *got* to.... Answer me, Rob. *Do* you want to... do you want to be rid of me? [*There is a pause.* ROBERT *cannot hold her gaze and his eyes fall. She takes the blow.*] I guess that's answer enough. [*She draws a little back from him and pulls the engagement ring from her finger.*] Here's your ring.

ROBERT. Hester! Don't do anything you'll be sorry for afterwards! Don't, please! I can't take it yet!

HESTER. [*Without any sign of emotion, she drops it on a table.*] I shall have an easier time of it, if you keep away from me. I want to save my face... if I can.

ROBERT. Hester, please!

HESTER. All right, if you won't go, I will.

ROBERT. I'm sorry. Of course I'll go.

HESTER. And take your ring with you.

[*He goes to the table, picks up the ring, pockets it and has just got to the door when* HESTER *breaks into furious, hysterical sobbing. Her sobs rack her and seem, at the same time, to strike* ROBERT *like the blows of a whip.*]

ROBERT. For God's sake, Hester.... [*She drops into a chair and sits, staring straight before her, shaken by her sobs of outraged fury and wretchedness.*] Mother! Christina! Come here! Hester... [CHRISTINA *appears in the door.* MRS. PHELPS *follows her.* DAVID *appears.* ROBERT *returns to* HESTER.] Can't you pull yourself together? [*She motions him away.*]

CHRISTINA. What's the matter?

ROBERT. It's Hester. Can't you stop her?

MRS. PHELPS. Good heavens, Robin! What's wrong with the child?

ROBERT. She's... upset... you see, I was just... you know...

MRS. PHELPS. I see!... She's taking it badly.

[HESTER'S *sobs only increase.*]

CHRISTINA. Hester, stop it!

HESTER. I'm all right.... I can't... I ... Christina... please...

CHRISTINA. Open a window, Dave.... Haven't you any smelling salts in the house, Mrs. Phelps?

[MRS. PHELPS *goes for them where she left them at teatime.*]

HESTER. Tell Rob to go away! Tell Rob to go away!

CHRISTINA. Never mind Rob!... Get me some aromatic spirits, one of you! Hurry up!

[ROBERT *goes.*]

MRS. PHELPS. Here are my salts.

CHRISTINA [*peremptorily*]. Hester! [*She holds the salts for* HESTER *to smell.*] Now, stop it! Stop it, do you hear me?

HESTER. I'm trying to stop. If you'd only send these awful people out! Take me away, Christina! Take me back to New York! I've got to get away from here. I can't face them! I can't! I can't!

CHRISTINA. Now, *stop* it!

DAVID [*comes forward from a window*]. Here's some snow in my handkerchief. Rub it on her wrists and temples.

CHRISTINA. Thanks, Dave.

[*She applies it.* HESTER, *by dint of great effort, gradually overcomes her sobs.* ROBERT *returns with a tumbler partly filled with a milky solution of aromatic spirits.*]

MRS. PHELPS [*speaking at the same time, in unfeigned wonderment to* DAVID]. Really, I do wonder at what happens to girls nowadays! When I was Hester's age I danced less and saved a little of my strength for self-control.

ROBERT [*speaking through*]. Here, Dave. Take this.

[DAVID *takes it.* ROBERT *goes again.*]

DAVID *gives the tumbler to* CHRISTINA.]

CHRISTINA. Good! Can you drink this now, Hester?

HESTER. Thank you, Christina. I'm all right now. It was only...

CHRISTINA. Never mind what it was. Drink this. [HESTER *drinks it.*] There, now. That's better. Just sit still and relax.

DAVID. What on earth brought it on?

MRS. PHELPS [*shrugging her shoulders*]. Rob and she must have had a falling out.

DAVID. No ordinary one.... Rob! He's gone.... That's funny.

MRS. PHELPS. He'd naturally be distressed.

HESTER. I'm really all right, now, Christina... and frightfully ashamed....

MRS. PHELPS. You'd better see how Rob is, Dave. His nerves are none too stout. Such scenes aren't good for him.

HESTER [*in a high, strained voice*]. No, isn't that so, Mrs. Phelps?

MRS. PHELPS. Did you speak to me, Hester?

HESTER. Take the smelling salts to Rob with my love.... Oh God, Christina!

CHRISTINA. Now, never *mind*, Hester. You'll go to pieces again.

HESTER. But I've got to mind! And I'm all right! It won't hurt me.... I wish you'd go, David.

CHRISTINA. Yes, Dave, do. I'll come up in a jiffy.

MRS. PHELPS. When Hester's quieted down. [*To* DAVID.] We'd better both go and see how Rob is.

[*She is just going.*]

HESTER. Mrs. Phelps. There's something I want to ask you before we part.

MRS. PHELPS. To-morrow, my dear girl....

HESTER. There isn't going to be any to-morrow.

MRS. PHELPS. What?

HESTER. Rob has just broken our engagement.

MRS. PHELPS. Not really!

CHRISTINA [*staggered*]. Hester, what do you mean?

HESTER. I mean what I say. Rob's just broken our engagement.

[CHRISTINA *motions to* DAVE *to go. He obeys.*]

MRS. PHELPS. I'm immensely distressed, of course.

HESTER [*shaking her head doggedly*]. He talked it all over with you before dinner. He told me that much, so it won't do you the least bit of good to pretend to be surprised.

MRS. PHELPS. Aren't you forgetting yourself, Hester?

HESTER. You made him do it. Why did you make him do it, Mrs. Phelps?

[CHRISTINA, *amazed, draws back to observe the pair of them.*]

MRS. PHELPS [*perfect dignity*]. I don't intend to stand here, Hester, and allow any hysterical girl to be rude to me.

HESTER [*driving on querulously*]. I'm not being rude! All I want to know is why you talked Rob into jilting me. Will you answer me, please?

MRS. PHELPS. Such things may be painful, my dear girl, but they're far less painful before than after.

HESTER. He quoted that much.

CHRISTINA. What's the good of this, Hester?

HESTER. I'm only trying to make her tell me why she did it.

MRS. PHELPS. But, Hester! Really! This is absurd!

HESTER. You've got to! You've got to explain!

MRS. PHELPS. I had nothing to do with Robin's change of heart.

HESTER. You must have had, Mrs. Phelps, and I'm demanding an explanation of why you talked Rob into...

MRS. PHELPS. Isn't it enough that he found out in time that you weren't the wife for him?

HESTER. That isn't the truth!

CHRISTINA. Hester, darling!

HESTER. Can you tell me what he meant when he said that the happiness of *three* people was at stake?

MRS. PHELPS. He must have been thinking of your happiness as well as his own and mine.

HESTER. What about your loneliness?

MRS. PHELPS. This *is* contemptible of you!

CHRISTINA. Really, Hester, this *can't* do any good!

HESTER. I'm going to make her admit that she made Rob...

MRS. PHELPS [*exploding*]. Very well, then, since you insist! I did advise my son to break with you. Do you want to know why?

HESTER. Yes!

MRS. PHELPS. Because of your indifference....

HESTER. Oh!

MRS. PHELPS. Because he came to me to say that you neither love him nor make any pretense of loving him...

HESTER. Rob said that?

MRS. PHELPS. He even said that you must have misconstrued his friendship and that he never wanted to marry you...

HESTER. No!

MRS. PHELPS. And I told him to risk anything... anything, rather than such an appalling marriage...

HESTER. I don't believe a word of it!

MRS. PHELPS. You may believe it or not!

CHRISTINA. Mrs. Phelps, you had really better let me handle this.

MRS. PHELPS. Willingly.

HESTER. Do you believe I took advantage of Rob, Christina?

CHRISTINA. Of course not!

MRS. PHELPS. So you take her side, Christina!

CHRISTINA. I don't believe *that*, Mrs. Phelps.

MRS. PHELPS. [*She realizes that she has gone too far.*] No? Well, perhaps...

CHRISTINA. Whatever Robert may think, I can't believe that he said...

MRS. PHELPS [*frightened*]. Perhaps he didn't say quite that, in so many words... but he certainly meant...

HESTER. I'm going. I'm going now. Right this minute.

MRS. PHELPS. There's a train at nine in the morning. It gets you to New York at twelve. I shall have the car for you at eight-thirty.

HESTER. May I have the car now, please, Mrs. Phelps?

MRS. PHELPS. There's no train to-night.

HESTER. It doesn't matter. I won't stay here. Not another minute. I'll go to the hotel in town.

MRS. PHELPS. You'll do nothing of the sort!

HESTER. You see if I don't!

MRS. PHELPS. You've got to think of appearances!

HESTER. Appearances are your concern. Yours and Rob's. I'm going to the hotel. I don't care what people say! I don't care about anything. I won't stay here!

MRS. PHELPS. Can't you talk to her, Christina? Surely you see... for all our sakes!

HESTER. If you won't let me have the car, I'll call a taxi....

[She plunges towards the telephone.]

MRS. PHELPS. I forbid you!

HESTER [seizing the instrument]. I want a taxi... a taxi.... What is the number?... Well, give it to me.... Locust 4000? Give me Locust 4000!

[MRS. PHELPS hesitates an instant, then, with terrible coolness, steps forward and jerks the telephone cord from the wall. Except for a startled exclamation, very low, from CHRISTINA, there is not a sound. HESTER hangs up the receiver and sets down the dead instrument.]

MRS. PHELPS [after an interminable silence]. You are the only person in the world who has ever forced me to do an undignified thing. I shall not forget it.

[She goes nobly.]

HESTER [weakly, turning to CHRISTINA]. Christina, it isn't true what she said.... He did.... He did want to marry me! Really, he did! He did!

CHRISTINA. Of course he did, darling!

HESTER. I won't stay! I won't stay under that woman's roof!

CHRISTINA. Hester, darling!

HESTER. I'll walk to town!

CHRISTINA. Don't, Hester!

HESTER. That wasn't true, what she said!

CHRISTINA. Of course not!

HESTER. I still love him.... Let me go, Christina, I'll walk...

CHRISTINA. You can't, at this time of night! It wouldn't be safe!

HESTER. I don't care! I won't stay!

CHRISTINA. There! There! You'll come to bed now, won't you!

HESTER. No! No! I can't! I'd rather die! I'll walk to town.

CHRISTINA. You'll force me to come with you, Hester. I can't let you go alone.

HESTER. I won't stay another minute!

CHRISTINA. Do you want to make me walk with you? Think, Hester! Think what I told you before dinner! Do you want to make me walk all that way in the cold?

HESTER [awed by this]. Oh, your baby! I didn't mean to forget your baby! Oh, Christina, you mustn't stay, either! This is a dreadful house! You've got to get your baby away from this house, Christina! Awful things happen here!

CHRISTINA. Hester, darling! Won't you please be sensible and come up to bed?

HESTER [speaking at the same time as her nerves begin to go again]. Awful things, Christina.... You'll see if you don't come away! You'll see!... She'll do the same thing to you that she's done to me. You'll see! You'll see!

CURTAIN

SCENE II

The curtain rises again, as soon as possible, upon DAVID's little bedroom, untouched since the day when DAVID went away to Harvard and scorned to take his prep school trophies and souvenirs with him. The furniture is rather more than simple. The bed is single. There is a dresser. There are only a couple of chairs. The curtains at the single window have been freshly laundered and put back in their old state by MRS. PHELPS in a spirit of maternal archeology. Insignificant loving cups, won at tennis, stand about the dresser. No pennants, no banners. There might be some tennis racquets, golf sticks, crossed skis, a pair of snowshoes, class photographs and framed diplo-

mas. There must also be a fairly important reproduction of Velasquez' Don Balthazar Carlos on horseback, selected by MRS. PHELPS *as* DAVID'S *favorite Old Master. A final touch is* DAVID'S *baby pillow.*

[DAVID *stands in his pajamas and socks, about to enter upon the last stages of his preparations to retire for the night. The room has been strewn with clothing during the preliminary stages. Now he is in the ambulatory state of mind. A series of crosses and circumnavigations produces several empty packs of cigarettes from several pockets, corners of the suitcase, etc. This frustration brings on baffled scratchings of the head and legs. Then he gives up the cigarette problem, turns again to the suitcase, spills out several dirty shirts and finally, apparently from the very bottom, extracts a dressing-gown, a pair of slippers, a tooth-brush and some tooth-paste. He sheds the socks, dons the slippers and dressing-gown and sallies forth with brush and paste to do up his teeth in the bathroom. He goes by the door which gives on the hall at the head of the stairs.*

After he has been gone a few seconds, a tiny scratching sound is heard on the other side of the other door to the room and that is opened from without. We see the scratcher at work conveying the impression that a wee mousie wants to come in. The wee mousie is none other than MRS. PHELPS, *all smiles in her best negligée, the most effective garment she wears in the course of the entire play, carrying the largest eiderdown comfort ever seen on any stage.*

The smile fades a little when she discovers that the room is empty. Then its untidiness catches her eye and she shakes her head reprovingly, as who should say: "What creatures these big boys are!" She goes to work at once, true mother that she is, to pick things up. She loves her work and puts her whole heart into it. The trousers are neatly hung over the back of the chair, the coat and waistcoat hung over them. The shirts, socks and underwear are folded and laid chastely on the seat. One or two of the garments receive devout maternal kisses and hugs. Then she goes to the bed, lifts off the suitcase, pushes it underneath, adjusts the eiderdown, smooths the pillow and kisses that. Last, all smiles

again, she sits, carefully disposing her laces and ribbons, to await DAVID'S *return. She yearns for it and she has not long to wait.*

DAVID *returns. His mother's beaming smile, as he opens the door, arouses his usual distaste for filial sentimentality. It is intensified, now — and very ill-concealed — by the hour, his costume and recent events. He hesitates in the doorway.*]

MRS. PHELPS. Why do you look so startled? It's only Mother!

DAVID [*laconic*]. Hello, Mother!

MRS. PHELPS. I came in to ask if you needed anything and...

DAVID. Not a thing, thanks.

MRS. PHELPS. And to warn you against opening the window in this weather. Oh, and I brought you that extra cover. I've been picking up after you, too!

DAVID [*looking gloomily about*]. You needn't have troubled.

MRS. PHELPS. It took me back to the old days when I used to tuck you up in that same little bed...

DAVID [*a strong hint*]. Yeah.... I'm just turning in, Mother.

MRS. PHELPS [*regardless*].... And then sit in this very chair and talk over all my problems with you. I feel that I must talk to my big boy to-night.... I must get acquainted with my Dave again.

DAVID [*an even stronger hint*]. We're not exactly strangers, are we? And besides, it's getting late.

MRS. PHELPS [*even more persistent*]. It was always in these late hours that we had our talks in the old days when we were still comrades. Oh, are those days gone forever? Don't you remember how we used to play that we had an imaginary kingdom where we were king and queen?

DAVID [*moribund*]. Did we? I wish Chris 'ud come up.

MRS. PHELPS [*a frown and she speaks quickly*]. Have you noticed, Dave, boy, that your room is just as you left it? I've made a little shrine of it. The same curtains, the same...

DAVID [*breaking in*]. I suppose Chris is still trying to get Hester quiet?

MRS. PHELPS. I suppose so.... And

every day I dusted in here myself and every night I prayed in here for...

DAVID [*a little too dryly for good manners*]. Thanks.

MRS. PHELPS [*reproachfully*]. Oh, David, you can't get that horrid scene downstairs out of your mind!

DAVID. No.

MRS. PHELPS. Try! I need my big boy so! Because I'm facing the gravest problem of my life, Dave. And you've got to help me.

DAVID. What is it?

MRS. PHELPS. Is it true that I'm of no more use to my two sons?

DAVID. Whatever put such an idea in your head?

MRS. PHELPS. You did.

DAVID [*shocked*]. I?

MRS. PHELPS [*nodding*]. You weren't really glad to see me this afternoon.

DAVID [*in all sincerity*]. I was.... I was delighted!

MRS. PHELPS [*bravely stopping him*]. Not glad as I was to see you. I noticed, Dave!... And that made me wonder whether this scientific age — because it is a scientific age, Dave — isn't making more than one boy forget that the bond between mother and son is the strongest bond on earth....

DAVID [*not quite sure of the superlative*]. Well, it's certainly strong.

MRS. PHELPS. Do you realize how sinful any boy would be to want to loosen it?

DAVID. Sure I realize that!

MRS. PHELPS. I see so many poor mothers, no less deserving of love and loyalty than I, neglected and discarded by their children, set aside for other interests.

DAVID. What interests?

MRS. PHELPS. All kinds of things.... Wives....

DAVID [*shying*]. Nonsense, Mother!

MRS. PHELPS. The Chinese never set any relationship above their filial piety. They'd be the greatest people on earth if only they'd stop smoking opium.

DAVID. You haven't any kick, have you? I mean: Rob and I haven't let you down?

MRS. PHELPS. Not yet, Dave. But, you know the old saying?

DAVID. What old saying?

MRS. PHELPS. That a boy's mother is his best friend.

DAVID. Oh! Bet I do!

MRS. PHELPS. Do you think of *your* mother as *your* best friend?

DAVID. None better, certainly.

MRS. PHELPS. None better! Hm! You *can* say, though, that you haven't entirely outgrown me?

DAVID. Of course I haven't! Why, I'd hate to have you think that just because I'm a grown man, I...

MRS. PHELPS. No son is ever a grown man to his mother! [*A knock at the door.*] Who can that be at this hour?

DAVID. I hope it's Chris.

[*He starts for the door.*]

MRS. PHELPS [*freezing suddenly as she rises*]. Dave!

DAVID [*turning*]. What?

MRS. PHELPS. Wait.... I mustn't intrude.... Good-night....

DAVID [*calling out*]. Just a minute! [*To his mother, politely.*] You wouldn't be intruding!

MRS. PHELPS. Not on you, I know. But...

DAVID. Not on Chris either!

MRS. PHELPS. I know best. Kiss me good-night.

DAVID. Good-night, Mother.

[*He kisses her cheek.*]

MRS. PHELPS [*a quick hug*]. God bless my big boy!

[*She goes as she came. DAVID's look, as he watches her door close behind her, is baffled. He goes quickly to the other door. ROBERT is standing outside.*]

DAVID. For Pete's sake, Rob! I thought it was Chris!... Why didn't you walk in?

ROBERT. I thought Mother was in here.

DAVID. She was. She just went to bed.

ROBERT [*entering*]. She must have thought it was Chris, too!

DAVID. How do you mean?

ROBERT. I shouldn't rush things if I were you.

DAVID. Maybe you're right. Women are too deep for me.

ROBERT. I came in for a smoke. I had

to talk to you. I've been sitting in my room wondering what you think of all this.

DAVID [*cigarette business*]. I don't think much and that's the truth!

ROBERT. Good God, Dave, can't you be a little easier on me? Didn't you ever feel any doubts when you were engaged? Were you always so sure of Christina that you...

DAVID. The first time I asked Chris to marry me, she made it perfectly clear that, as far as she was concerned, I was to consider myself dripping wet. After that I was too damn scared I wouldn't get her to think whether she loved me or not.

ROBERT [*darkly*]. And I never had one comfortable moment from the time Hester accepted me.

DAVID. Oh, being in love's like everything else. You've got to put some guts in it.

ROBERT [*bitter anger*]. You think I haven't got any guts. You want to make me look like a callous cad! All right, I'll *be* a cad. I don't care what people think about me! But I'll tell you one thing! I'm damned if I'm going to let you turn Mother against me!

DAVID. Do *what?*

ROBERT. You heard me!

DAVID. My God, haven't you outgrown that old stuff yet?

ROBERT. I know from experience what to expect when you and Mother get together. I used to listen at that door, night after night, night after night, while you and Mother sat in here and talked me over. Then I'd watch for the change in her next morning at breakfast when I hadn't slept a wink all night. The way you used to own the earth at those breakfasts! Well, if you try any of that old stuff to-night, I'll lose the only prop I've got left.

DAVID. Isn't it about time you let go of Mother's apron-strings?

ROBERT. You would say that! You don't realize that I'm desperate.

DAVID. Desperate, hell! You're crazy! Mother's gone to bed and... [*The wee mousie scratches at the door again.*] What's that?

MRS. PHELPS [*entering*]. It's only Mother. Are my two beaux quarreling? Jealous, jealous Robin! What's the matter?

DAVID. Nothing.

MRS. PHELPS. A fine man is a frank man, David! Do you think I didn't hear every word you said? Surely you must know that Hester wasn't worthy of your brother?

DAVID. Wasn't she? Well, let's not talk any more about it.

MRS. PHELPS. Oh, but we must. For all our sakes, we must clear the air. *I* have always taken the stand that my boys could do absolutely no wrong and that is the proper stand for a mother to take. Didn't I always side with you in your school scrapes? Even against the masters? Even when you were clearly in the wrong? Of course, I did! And I shall not permit one word of criticism against your brother now. Loyalty, Dave! Loyalty! Come, now! Tell Mother all about it!

DAVID. But if you overheard every word we said!

MRS. PHELPS. "Overheard," David? Am I given to eavesdropping?

DAVID. I didn't say so.

MRS. PHELPS. I simply want to make sure I didn't miss anything while I was in my bath.

DAVID. I don't misunderstand him. I'm sorry for Hester, that's all.

ROBERT. We're all sorry for Hester.

DAVID. I don't think it's your place to be too sorry.

ROBERT. Let's drop it, Mother.

MRS. PHELPS. No. I've got to know what's on Dave's mind. My whole life may hang on it. What is it, Dave? [*Carefully sounding.*] If Robin's not to blame, perhaps I am?

ROBERT [*horrified*]. Mother!

DAVID. What's the use of getting so worked up over nothing?

MRS. PHELPS. Nothing! Can you say "nothing" after what *we* were talking about a few minutes ago?

DAVID [*cornered*]. I only think...

MRS. PHELPS. What?

DAVID. Well, that you've both handed

Hester a somewhat dirty deal. And Chris must think so, too!

MRS. PHELPS [*wary*]. Indeed! And how, please?

DAVID. Well, it comes of what Chris calls "mythologizing."

MRS. PHELPS [*frightened*]. Does Christina discuss our family affairs already?

DAVID. No. It's one of her old ideas about people in general. You mythologize Rob into a little tin god. Rob thinks he is a little tin god. Along comes Hester and falls in love with the real Rob. She never heard of your little tin god Rob. She doesn't deliver the incense and tom-toms. That makes you and Rob sore and the whole works goes to hell. That's mythologizing. Believe me, it can make plenty of trouble.

MRS. PHELPS [*relieved that the criticism is so general*]. If that's all I'm to blame for, I don't know that I can object. Expecting the best of everyone is, at least, a worthy fault. Still, if I may venture an older woman's opinion on one of Christina's ideas?

DAVID. I wish to God I hadn't started this.

MRS. PHELPS. So do I. But perhaps you'll tell me what Christina would say to the true reason for Robin's break with Hester?

DAVID. What is the true reason?

MRS. PHELPS. Do you want to tell him, Robin?

ROBERT [*inspired*]. I broke with Hester because of an ideal, the ideal of womankind Mother gave us both by being the great woman that she is. *I* knew *I* couldn't be happy with any woman who fell short of her.

MRS. PHELPS. What becomes of your "dirty deal" now, David?

DAVID. But I'm not going against that ideal, Mother. That's another thing.

ROBERT. You couldn't have troubled much about it when you married!

MRS. PHELPS. You shouldn't have said that, Robin. I haven't had Christina's advantages. I wasn't given a German education.

DAVID. Now, don't take this out on Chris, Mother.

MRS. PHELPS. I think I know a little of a mother's duty toward her daughter-in-law. Good-night, Robin. I must talk with your brother alone, now. And before you quarrel again, stop to think that you are all I have, you two, and try to consider me. It isn't much to ask and it won't be for long. You both know what the doctors think about my heart! Dr. McClintock tells me I may go at any moment. [*Pause, then.*] Good-night, Robin.

ROBERT [*frightened*]. Good-night, Mother.

MRS. PHELPS. You may come into my room later, if you like. I may need you to comfort me after... [*She waves her hand. He leaves. She has never taken her eyes off* DAVID. *When the door closes behind* ROBERT, *she speaks.*] David, in this moment, when your brother and I most needed your loyalty, you have hurt me more than I have ever been hurt in my life before, even by your father.

DAVID. I never meant to hurt you.

MRS. PHELPS [*working it up*]. You have been wicked, David! Wicked! Wicked!

DAVID. How?

MRS. PHELPS. You have shown me too clearly that what I most dreaded has already come to pass!

DAVID. What, Mother?

MRS. PHELPS. You *have* loosened the bond between us. You *have* discarded me.

DAVID [*horrified*]. But I haven't done any such thing!

MRS. PHELPS. Don't say any more! Act upon your treachery, if you will, but don't, please, don't say another thing. Remember!

The brave man does it with a sword,
The coward with a word!

[*And she sweeps out, slamming her door after her.*]

DAVID [*speaking through her door*]. But I didn't mean anything.... Won't you let me explain?... I didn't know what I was talking about!

[*There is no answer. He rattles the door. It is locked. He comes away, swearing softly under his breath. Then, manfully, he takes refuge in sulks. He kicks off his slippers and throws his dressing-gown aside. He lights a cigarette and flounces into bed, snatching up a book or magazine en route. Just as he is settled, his mother's door opens again very slowly.* MRS. PHELPS *presents a tear-stained face to view and comes in.*]

MRS. PHELPS. Smoking in bed, Dave, boy?

DAVID [*starting up*]. Eh?

MRS. PHELPS. It's only Mother.... No, don't get up.... Let me sit here as I used to in the old days.

DAVID [*sitting up*]. Mother, I didn't mean...

MRS. PHELPS. Never mind. I was wrong to be hurt.

DAVID. But you had me all wrong. I mean... You and I... We're just the same as we always were.... Believe me, we are. ... Why, if anything came to spoil things between us...

MRS. PHELPS [*the first objective conquered*]. That's what I wanted you to say! Now talk to me about Christina.

DAVID [*taken aback without knowing why*]. Huh?

MRS. PHELPS. Give me your hand in mine and tell me all about her.

DAVID [*obeying rather reluctantly*]. What is there to tell?

MRS. PHELPS. Well, for one thing, tell me you think she's going to like me!

DAVID [*warmly*]. She does already!

MRS. PHELPS. Doesn't think I'm an old-fashioned frump?

DAVID. I should say not! How could she?

MRS. PHELPS. She's such a modern young lady. So lovely, but so very up-to-date. You must tell me everything I can do to win her to me. And I'll do it. Though I'm afraid of her, Dave.

DAVID [*amused*]. Afraid of Chris? Why?

MRS. PHELPS. She's so much cleverer than I am. She makes me realize that I'm just a timid old lady of the old school.

DAVID [*nice indignation*]. You old!

MRS. PHELPS [*archly so brave about it*]. Yes, I am!

DAVID. Well, you and Chris are going to be the best friends ever.

MRS. PHELPS. You *are* happy, aren't you?

DAVID. You bet I am!

MRS. PHELPS. Really happy?

DAVID. Couldn't be happier!

MRS. PHELPS. I'm so glad! And I thank God that when your hour struck it didn't strike falsely as it did for Robin. Because any one can see the difference between Christina and Hester. Of course, that's a little the difference between you and Rob. You know what I've always said. You are *my* son. Robert takes after his father. But you mustn't be impatient with Christina if she seems, at first, a little slow, a little resentful of our family. We've always been so close, we three. She's bound to feel a little out of it, at first. A little jealous....

DAVID. Not Chris!

MRS. PHELPS. Oh, come now, Dave! I'm sure she's perfect, but you mustn't try to tell me she isn't human. Young wives are sure to be a little bit possessive and exacting and... selfish at first.

DAVID. We needn't worry about that.

MRS. PHELPS. No.... At first I thought Christina was going to be hard and cold. I didn't expect her to have our sense of humor and I don't believe she has much of that. But we've more than we need already. If only she will learn to care for me as I care for her, we can be so happy, all four of us together, can't we?

DAVID. You bet we can!

MRS. PHELPS [*dreamily*]. Building our houses in Phelps Manor.... Deciding to put an Italian Villa here and a little bungalow there.... [*As* DAVID *grows restive.*] But the important thing for you, Dave, boy, is a sense of proportion about your marriage. I'm going to lecture you, now, for your own good. If, at first, Christina does seem a little exacting or unreasonable, particularly about us, remember that she has to adjust herself to a whole new world here, a very different world from her friends in Omaha. And you must never be impatient with her. Because, if you are, I shall take her side against you.

DAVID. You *are* a great woman, Mother!

MRS. PHELPS. You're the great one!

How many boys of your age let their wives undermine all their old associations and loosen all their old ties!

DAVID. Chris wouldn't try that!

MRS. PHELPS. She might not *want* to. But jealous girls think things that aren't so and say things that aren't true. Morbid things.

DAVID. Morbid things? Chris?

MRS. PHELPS. Only you won't pay too much attention or take her too seriously. I know that, because you would no more let anyone strike at me than I would let anyone strike at you.

DAVID. But Chris wouldn't...

MRS. PHELPS. As I said to Christina this afternoon: "Christina," I said, "I cannot allow you to sacrifice David!"

DAVID. Chris sacrifice me! How?

MRS. PHELPS. Why, by taking you away from your magnificent opportunity here.

DAVID. Oh!

MRS. PHELPS. Be master in your own house. Meet her selfishness with firmness, her jealousy with fairness and her... her exaggerations with a grain of salt....

DAVID. What exaggerations?

MRS. PHELPS. Well, you know... a girl ... a young wife, like Christina... *might* possibly make the mistake of... well, of taking sides... in what happened downstairs, for instance... and without fully understanding.... You can see how fatal *that* would be.... But, if you face the facts always, Dave, boy, and nothing *but* the facts, your marriage will be a happy one. And, when you want advice, come to your mother always.

DAVID. Thanks.

MRS. PHELPS. Now, isn't your mother your best friend?

DAVID. You bet you are, Mummy!

MRS. PHELPS. How long it is since you've called me that! Bless you, my dear, dear boy!

[*She leans over to seal her triumph with a kiss.* CHRISTINA'S *entrance follows so closely upon her knock that the picture is still undisturbed for her to see. She has changed her dress for a very simple negligée. Her mood is dangerous.*]

CHRISTINA. Oh, I beg your pardon!

MRS. PHELPS [*so sweetly, after the very briefest pause*]. Come in, Christina. I was only saying good-night to Dave. Nothing private! You're one of the family now. You must feel free to come and go as you like in the house.

CHRISTINA. Thank you.

MRS. PHELPS. We can accustom ourselves to it, can't we, Dave?

DAVID. Yeah....

CHRISTINA. Dave and I have got so used to sharing the same room, I came in here quite naturally and...

MRS. PHELPS. Here's your dressing-gown, Dave, boy. We won't look while you slip it on.

[*Confusedly* DAVE *gets out of bed and robes himself.* CHRISTINA'S *eyes meet his mother's.* CHRISTINA'S *eyes have the least flash of scorn in them,* MRS. PHELPS' *the least quaver of fear. In that glance, the two women agree on undying enmity.*]

DAVID. You can... you can look now.

CHRISTINA. Are you quite sure *I* may, Mrs. Phelps?

MRS. PHELPS. Whatever else you may have taken from me, Christina, you can*not* take from me the joy of feeling my son here, once more, in his old room, beside me.

CHRISTINA [*marking up the first score*]. I haven't meant to take anything from you, Mrs. Phelps.

MRS. PHELPS [*so sweetly again*]. You know I was only joking. [*She is routed, though.*] Good-night. [*The two women kiss.*] Don't keep Dave up too late. He's very tired. [*She pats* DAVE, *as she passes him on her way to her door.*] You must be tired, too, Christina. How *is* Hester, now?

CHRISTINA. Quite all right, thank you.

MRS. PHELPS. Thank *you!*

[*She blows a kiss to* DAVID *from the door and goes.* CHRISTINA *stands motionless.* DAVID *reaches for a cigarette.*]

DAVID. You look pretty stern, Chris.

CHRISTINA. Do I?

DAVID. You've been a brick.

CHRISTINA. Thanks.

DAVID. Hester *is* all right, isn't she?

CHRISTINA. Yes, poor youngster! I

shouldn't be surprised if she were really in luck, Dave.

DAVID. You may be right. But it isn't exactly up to me to say so, is it?

[*He lights his cigarette. Her eyes burn him up.*]

CHRISTINA. Dave....

DAVID. Yes?

CHRISTINA. Whom do you love?

DAVID. You. Why?

CHRISTINA. I wondered, that's all. I want to be kissed.

DAVID. That's easy.

[*He takes her in his arms.*]

CHRISTINA. Such a tired girl, Dave.... I want to be held on to and made much of. ... I want to feel all safe and warm.... I want you to tell me that you're in love with me and that you enjoy being in love with me. Because just loving isn't enough and it's being in love that really matters.... Will you tell me all that, please, Dave?

DAVID [*hugging her*]. Darling!

CHRISTINA. You haven't kissed me yet.

DAVID [*complying, a trifle absent-mindedly*]. There!

CHRISTINA [*as she draws back from him*]. That isn't what I call making love in a big way.

DAVID [*repeating the kiss with more energy*]. Is that better?

CHRISTINA. There's still something lacking.... What's the matter? There's nobody watching us.

DAVID. That's a funny thing to say.

CHRISTINA. You take me right back to my first beau in Germany. He never got very far, either. All the English he knew was "water closet."

DAVID. Chris! Shame on you!

CHRISTINA. Shame on *you*, making me take to low jokes to amuse you.... I love you.

DAVID. Darling, darling, Chris!

CHRISTINA. I love you! I love you! [*For a moment she clings to him wildly.*] I hate being so far from you to-night, Dave. 'Way off there at the other end of the hall!

DAVID. I'm none too pleased myself. It's just one of Mother's fool ideas.

[*He lowers his voice whenever he mentions his mother.*]

CHRISTINA. She naturally wanted you near *her!*

DAVID. That's it. [*His eyes fall beneath her steady gaze.*] We mustn't talk so loud. We'll keep Mother awake. She can hear every sound we make.

CHRISTINA. Let her hear! It'll do her good!

DAVID. That's no way to talk, Chris!

CHRISTINA. Excuse me. I didn't mean to snap. I've been fearfully shaken up to-night.

DAVID. I know you have.

CHRISTINA. And I'm awfully tired.

DAVID. Poor girl!

CHRISTINA. Poor Hester!... I don't feel like going to bed yet. I want to talk. Do you mind?

DAVID. Go to it.

CHRISTINA. I've never come up against anything like this before, I've heard of it, but I've never met it. I don't know what to do about it. And it scares me.

DAVID. What does?

CHRISTINA. I don't know how to tell you. [*Then with sudden force.*] But I've got to tell you, Dave. I've got to tell you. There are no two ways about that.

DAVID. What are you driving at?

CHRISTINA. Well... [*But she changes her mind.*] May I ask you a question? Rather an intimate one?

DAVID. If you must!

CHRISTINA. Being your wife, I thought I might.

DAVID. Shoot!

CHRISTINA. Do you look on me as apart from all other women? I mean, do you think of all the women in the world and then think of me quite, quite differently? Do you, Dave?

DAVID. I'll bite. Do I?

CHRISTINA. Please answer me. It's awfully important to me just now.

DAVID. Of course I do.... Why is it so important just now?

CHRISTINA. Because that's how I feel about you and all the other men in the world. Because that's what being in love must mean and being properly and happily married. Two people, a man and a woman, together by themselves, miles and miles from everybody, from *everybody* else, glancing around, now and then, at all the rest of mankind, at *all* the rest, Dave, and saying: "Are you still there? And getting along all right? Sure there's nothing we can do to help?"

DAVID. Only we do help, don't we?

CHRISTINA. Only really if we feel that way about one another. Only *by* feeling that way.

DAVID. That's pretty deep! You do go off on the damnedest tacks!

CHRISTINA. Don't you see how that feeling between a man and a woman is what keeps life going?

DAVID. Is it?

CHRISTINA. What else could be strong enough?

DAVID. Perhaps you're right. [*Then, unaccountably, he shies.*] But what's the idea in getting so worked up about it?

CHRISTINA. Because it matters so much, Dave... just now... that you and I feel that way about each other and that we go on feeling that way and exclude everybody, *everybody* else. Tell me you think so, too?

DAVID. Sure, I think so.... [*Then, again, he shies from her inner meaning.*] You're getting the worst habit of working yourself up over nothing!

CHRISTINA. Do you realize, Dave, that the blackest sinner on earth is the man... or woman... who breaks in on that feeling? Or tampers with it in any way? Or perverts it?

DAVID. If you say so, I'll say he is.

CHRISTINA. Ha!

DAVID. Huh?

CHRISTINA. Never mind.... Your brother didn't feel that way about poor Hester, did he?

DAVID. Rob always was a funny egg.

CHRISTINA. Your mother calls him Robin! "Tweet! Tweet! What does the Birdie say?"

DAVID. From all I can gather, Hester didn't feel much of *any* way about him.

CHRISTINA. I know better than that.... I've had that child on my hands for the past hour. I've learned an awful lot, Dave. About her, and *from* her.

DAVID. Look here, Chris.... Don't you get mixed up in this business, will you?

CHRISTINA. I wonder if I'm not mixed up in it already.

DAVID. Well, don't "take sides."

CHRISTINA. I wonder if I can help taking sides.

DAVID. It's none of our business.

CHRISTINA. I wish I were sure of that. [*Baffled, she again shifts her approach.*] Poor little Hester goes to-morrow morning. How long are we staying?

DAVID. Oh, I dunno.

CHRISTINA. A week?

DAVID. We can't do less, can we?

CHRISTINA. Can't we?

DAVID. Don't you want to? [*There is another pause before* CHRISTINA *shakes her head.* DAVID *frowns.*] You see what comes of taking things so hard? I'm just as distressed over what's happened as you are. Maybe more. But I certainly don't want to run away. It wouldn't be right. Mother'd never understand. I'd feel like a bum going off and leaving her in the lurch after this. Think what Rob's put her through to-day and what she'll have to go through with Hester's family and all her friends and everybody else before she's done!

CHRISTINA. She seems to be bearing up.

DAVID. You can't be sure with Mother.

CHRISTINA. Can't you?

DAVID. She's so damned game.

CHRISTINA. Is she?

DAVID. Can't you see that? And, anyway, I've got to look around.

CHRISTINA. What at? The houses in Phelps Manor?

DAVID. I know how you feel, Chris, about Mother's helping hand. But I can't be *throwing* away opportunities, now, can I? With the baby coming?

CHRISTINA [*gravely*]. No, Dave. Of course, you can't. Neither can I.

DAVID. How do you mean?

CHRISTINA. Forgotten all about *my* opportunities, haven't you?

DAVID. What opportunities?

CHRISTINA. My appointment.

DAVID. Didn't Mother say she could scare up something for you here?

CHRISTINA. She thought she might "scare up" a place where I could "putter around" and keep myself "happy and contented" when the "real doctors" weren't working.

DAVID. She didn't mean anything unkind, Chris. Just give Mother a chance and... What are you crying for?

CHRISTINA [hotly untruthful]. I'm not crying.

DAVID. You are!

CHRISTINA. I can't help it....

DAVID. But what's the matter?

CHRISTINA. It doesn't look as if I'm to have much of a show for my eight years of hard work, does it?

DAVID. Mother and I'll dope out something. I couldn't leave her now. You know that. And anyway, I've got to stay till I get my shirts washed. I've only got two left.

CHRISTINA. Then we stay, of course.

DAVID. And I must say, Chris, that I don't think you're quite playing ball to judge my home and my family entirely on what you've seen to-night. Besides, the whole purpose of this visit was to bring you and Mother together and to show Mother that a lady scientist mayn't be as bad as she sounds. Because you and Mother have just got to hit it off, you know.

CHRISTINA. Have we?

DAVID. You're apt to be impatient, Chris, and I'm afraid you're intolerant.

CHRISTINA. Those are bad faults in a scientist.

DAVID. They're bad faults in anybody. ... Now, you just give me time and you'll see how things straighten out.

CHRISTINA. Aren't you satisfied with the way our meeting has come off?

DAVID. There's no use pretending it was ideal. I believe in facing the facts always. But don't you worry. Mother gets on *my* nerves sometimes. You just have to remember what a hard life she's had.

CHRISTINA. How has it been hard?

DAVID. Oh, lots of ways. My father wasn't much, you know.

CHRISTINA. I didn't know. You've never mentioned him.

DAVID. He died when I was five.

CHRISTINA. What was the matter with him? Women or drink?

DAVID. Nothing like that. He just didn't amount to much.

CHRISTINA. Made a lot of money, didn't he?

DAVID. Lots.

CHRISTINA. And left your mother rich. What other troubles has she had?

DAVID. Well, her health.

CHRISTINA. It doesn't seem so bad.

DAVID. It is, though. Heart. And I wish I could tell you half of what she's gone through for Rob and me.

CHRISTINA. Go on and tell me. I'd like to hear.

DAVID. I've heard her say she was born without a selfish hair in her head.

CHRISTINA. No!

DAVID. And that's about true. Why, I've seen her nurse Rob through one thing after another when she'd admit to me that she was twice as sick as he was. I've seen her come in here from taking care of him and she'd be half fainting with her bad heart, but there'd be nothing doing when I'd beg her to get him a nurse. She said we were her job and she just wouldn't give in. And the way she always took interest in everything we did. Why, when she used to come up to school, all the boys went just crazy about her.

CHRISTINA. I'm sure they did. [But she turns the inquiry into more significant channels.] How did your girl friends get on with her?

DAVID. Oh, they loved her, too! Mother used to give us dances here.

CHRISTINA. Did she invite the girls you were in love with?

DAVID. I never fell in love! Not really. Not till I met you.

CHRISTINA. Darling! [She smiles rather absently.] What was the name of the one your mother thought could wear my dress?

DAVID. Clara Judd?

CHRISTINA. Weren't you sweet on Clara?

DAVID. I dunno. What made you ask that?

CHRISTINA. Just something in the way your mother spoke of her this evening. It came back to me. Weren't you?

DAVID. Mother thought so.

CHRISTINA. Used to pester you about Clara, didn't she?

DAVID. She was afraid I was going to marry Clara.

CHRISTINA. I see. Anything wrong with her?

DAVID. With Clara? No. Damn nice girl. You'll meet her.

CHRISTINA. Then why didn't your mother want you to marry her?

DAVID. Thought I was too young.

CHRISTINA. When was it?

DAVID. Summer after the war.

CHRISTINA. You weren't so young, were you?

DAVID. You know Mother.

CHRISTINA. How about your brother? Did he use to fall in love a great deal?

DAVID. I don't know that I'd call it "in love."

CHRISTINA. Why not?

DAVID. It's the family skeleton. She was a chorus girl, my dear. She cost Mother twelve thousand berries.

CHRISTINA. That must have been jolly! Was she the only one or were there others?

DAVID. There were plenty of others. Only they didn't have lawyers.

CHRISTINA. And then Hester?

DAVID. Right.

CHRISTINA. Well, that's all very interesting.

DAVID. What are you trying to prove?

CHRISTINA. An idea this affair of Hester's put into my head. And I must say, it fits in rather extraordinarily.

DAVID. What does?

CHRISTINA. Your being too young to marry after the war and Robert's taking to wild women.... And you had to be three thousand miles from home to fall in love with me! Never mind.... That's enough of that! Now let me tell *you* something. Only you must promise not to get mad.

DAVID. I won't get mad.

CHRISTINA. Promise?

DAVID. Promise.

CHRISTINA. [*A deep breath, then.*] Shirts or no shirts, we've got to get out of here to-morrow.

DAVID [*as though she had stuck him with a pin*]. Now, Chris! Haven't we been over all that?

CHRISTINA. Yes. But not to the bottom of it.

DAVID. What more is there to say?

CHRISTINA [*with sudden violence*]. That a defenseless, trusting, little girl has been cruelly treated! We've got to "take sides" with her, Dave!

DAVID. What's the matter with Hester's own family? This is their business, not ours!

CHRISTINA. We owe it to ourselves to *make* it our business.

DAVID. I don't see it.

CHRISTINA. Why don't you see it? What have you put over your eyes that keeps you from seeing it? Do you dare answer that?

DAVID. Dare? What do you mean?

CHRISTINA. "Face the facts," Dave! "Face the facts!"

DAVID. Rot! You're making a mountain out of a mole-hill!

CHRISTINA. Cruelty to children isn't a mole-hill!

DAVID. You're exaggerating! Hester's engagement isn't the first that was ever broken.

CHRISTINA. Think how it was broken and by whom!

DAVID. You just said she was in luck to be rid of Rob. I'll grant you that. I haven't any more use for Rob than you have.

CHRISTINA. Who stands behind Rob?

DAVID. I don't know what you mean.

CHRISTINA. Don't you?

DAVID. No.

CHRISTINA. All right, I'll tell you.

DAVID [*quickly*]. You needn't.... Are you trying to pick a fight with me?

CHRISTINA. On the contrary. I'm asking you to stand by me.

[*Her eyes corner him.*]

DAVID. I won't go away and leave Mother in the lurch.

CHRISTINA. You see? You do know what I mean!

DAVID. I don't! I'm just telling you I won't let Mother down.

CHRISTINA. You'd rather stand by your

mother than by the right, wouldn't you?

DAVID. Oh, the right?

CHRISTINA. Isn't Hester the right?

DAVID [cornered again]. I can't help it if she is. I won't let Mother down.

CHRISTINA. You'll let me down.

DAVID. Oh, Chris! It's late. Come on. Let's turn in.

CHRISTINA. You'd rather stand by your mother than by me, wouldn't you?

DAVID. No, I wouldn't. I tell you Hester's none of our business.

CHRISTINA. You'll admit this is?

DAVID. What is?

CHRISTINA. This!... Who comes first with you? Your mother or me?

DAVID. Now what's the good of putting things that way?

CHRISTINA. That's what things come to! If your mother and I ever quarreled about anything, if it ever came up to you to choose between sticking by me and sticking by her, which would you stick by?

DAVID. I'd... I'd try to do the right thing....

CHRISTINA. That isn't an answer. That's another evasion.

DAVID. But why ask such a question?

CHRISTINA. Because I love you. Because I've got to find out if you love me. And I'm afraid... I'm afraid....

DAVID. Why?

CHRISTINA. Because you won't see the facts behind all this. I'm trying to tell you what they are and you won't listen. You can't even hear me.

DAVID. I can hear you. And a worse line of hooey I've never listened to in my life.

CHRISTINA [gravely, but with steadily increasing fervor]. Have you ever thought what it would be like to be trapped in a submarine in an accident? I've learned to-night what that kind of panic would be like. I'm in that kind of a panic now, this minute. I've been through the most awful experience of my life to-night. And I've been through it alone. I'm still going through it alone. It's pretty awful to have to face such things alone.... No, don't interrupt me. I've got to get this off my chest. Ever since we've been married I've been coming across queer rifts in your feeling for me, like arid places in your heart. Such vast ones, too! I mean, you'll be my perfect lover one day and the next, I'll find myself floundering in sand, and alone, and you nowhere to be seen. We've never been really married, Dave. Only now and then, for a little while at a time, between your retirements into your arid places.... I used to wonder what you did there. At first, I thought you did your work there. But you don't. Your work's in my part of your heart, what there is of my part. Then I decided the other was just No-Man's Land. And I thought: little by little, I'll encroach upon it and pour my love upon it, like water on the western desert, and make it flower here and bear fruit there. I thought: then he'll be all alive, all free and all himself; not partly dead and tied and blind; not partly some one else — or nothing. You see, our marriage and your architecture were suffering from the same thing. They only worked a little of the time. I meant them both to work all the time. I meant you to work all the time and to win your way, all your way, Dave, to complete manhood. And that's a good deal farther than you've got so far.... Then we came here and this happened with Hester and your brother and you just stepped aside and did nothing about it! You went to bed. You did worse than that. You retired into your private wastes and sat tight.... I've shown you what you should do and you won't see it. I've called to you to come out to me, and you won't come. So now I've discovered what keeps you. Your mother keeps you. It isn't No-Man's Land at all. It's your mother's land. Arid, sterile, and your mother's! You won't let me get in there. Worse than that, you won't let life get in there! Or she won't!... That's what I'm afraid of, Dave: your mother's hold on you. And that's what's kept me from getting anywhere with you, all these months. I've seen what she can do with Robert. And what she's done to Hester. I can't help wondering what she may not do with you and to me and to the baby. That's why I'm asking you to take a stand on this business of Hester's, Dave. You'll never find the right any clearer than it is here. It's a kind of test case for me. Don't you see? What you decide about this is what you may, eventually, be expected to decide about... about our marriage.

DAVID [*a pause, then, with sullen violence*]. No! I'm damned if I see!

CHRISTINA [*breaking*]. Then I can't hope for much, can I?... I feel awfully like a lost soul, right now.... Oh, my God, what am I going to do! What am I going to do!

DAVID. I hope you're going to behave. You ought to be ashamed. Just as I was bringing Mother around to you and...

CHRISTINA [*violently*]. You'd better think a little about bringing me around to your mother!

DAVID. Chris!

CHRISTINA. Why should your mother and I get on?

DAVID. Because you should, that's why. Because she's an older woman and my mother. And you know, just as well as I do...

CHRISTINA. I know a great deal better than you that your mother dislikes me fully as much as I dislike her. You're wasting your time trying to bring your mother and me together, because we won't be brought. You say you believe in facing the facts. Well, let's see you face that one!

DAVID. I've never heard anything so outrageous. When you know what Mother means to me and what...

CHRISTINA [*desperate*]. Your mother! Your mother! Always your mother! She's got you back! Dave, her big boy, who ran off and got married! She's got you back!

DAVID. I won't stand for any more of this. A man's mother is his mother.

CHRISTINA [*crescendo*]. And what's his wife, may I ask? Or doesn't she count?

DAVID. This is morbid rot! She warned me you'd be jealous of her!

CHRISTINA. Did she?

DAVID. But I never expected anything like this!

CHRISTINA. What's going to become of me?

DAVID. I won't stand for any more....

CHRISTINA. Hester's escaped, but I'm caught! I can't go back and be the old Christina again. She's done for. And Christina, your wife, doesn't even exist! That's the fact I've got to face! I'm going to have a baby by a man who belongs to another woman!

DAVID. Damn it, Chris! Do you want Mother to hear you?

CHRISTINA. Do I not!

[MRS. PHELPS *stands in her door, white, but steady.*]

DAVID [*turning, sees her*]. Oh... You *did* hear!

MRS. PHELPS. How could I help hearing every word that Christina said?

DAVID. Oh, this is awful!

MRS. PHELPS. We know, now, where we stand, all three of us.

DAVID. Chris, can't you tell her you didn't mean it?

MRS. PHELPS [*heroic sarcasm*]. Christina isn't one to say things she doesn't mean. And I have no intention of defending myself.

DAVID. Mother, please!... Chris, you'd better beat it.

MRS. PHELPS. I ask her to stay. She has made me afraid ever to be alone with you again. She must have made you afraid to be alone with me.

DAVID. Nonsense, Mother! She hasn't done anything of the sort. You'd better go, Chris. It's the least you can do after what you've said.

CHRISTINA. The very least. I belong with Hester now. [*She goes quickly.*]

DAVID [*turning wildly to his mother*]. I'll straighten everything out in the morning. I swear I will!

MRS. PHELPS [*a very different, very noble tone*]. This is an old story, Dave, boy, and I'm on Christina's side just as I said I should be.

DAVID. I can't have you talking like that, Mother!

MRS. PHELPS. I accept my fate. You have your own life to live with the woman you have chosen. No boy could have given me back the love I gave you. Go to Christina! Make your life with her! No bond binds you to me any longer.

DAVID. That isn't true!

MRS. PHELPS. I'm not complaining. I'm only sorry for one thing. I'm only sorry to see you throw away your chance here, your great chance!

DAVID. But I haven't thrown it away. I'll stay here and work for you, if you want me to.

MRS. PHELPS. Christina won't let you. You know that!

DAVID. She's my wife, isn't she?

MRS. PHELPS. Think what that means, Dave! Think what that means!

DAVID. And you're my mother. I'm thinking what that means, too!

MRS. PHELPS. Then it *isn't* good-bye? Then I've still got my big boy, after all?

DAVID. You bet you've got him!

MRS. PHELPS [*triumph*]. Oh, Dave! Dave! Dave!

DAVID. Now, Mummy! [*But a sound downstairs distracts him.*] Hello! What's that? [*She listens, too.*]

MRS. PHELPS. Heavens, it isn't a fire, is it?

DAVID. Wait... I'll see....

[*He opens the door into the hall and stands listening.*]

CHRISTINA [*off-stage and below*]. I went into her room and she wasn't there and then I looked for her and I found the dining-room window open.

ROBERT [*off-stage and below*]. What do you think has happened?

CHRISTINA [*off-stage and below*]. I don't like to imagine things, but...

ROBERT [*off-stage and below*]. Hester, where are you?

CHRISTINA [*off-stage and below*]. She's got away! I tell you, she's got away! I shouldn't have left her....

DAVID [*speaking during the above*]. What?

MRS. PHELPS. It's Christina and Robert.

DAVID. Something's happened to Hester.

MRS. PHELPS. No!

DAVID. Chris! What's going on?

ROBERT [*off-stage*]. Hester! Where are you, Hester?

CHRISTINA [*appearing in the hall*]. Hester's got away, Dave. Out by the dining-room window. You'll have to get dressed

and find her. She can't get to town to-night in this cold.

DAVID. All right. We'll have a look.

MRS. PHELPS. The little fool! Let her go, Dave!

CHRISTINA. But, Mrs. Phelps, she isn't properly dressed. She didn't even take her coat....

ROBERT [*still calling off-stage and below*]. Hester! Where are you, Hester? Hester! ... Oh, my God!

[CHRISTINA *has walked to the window to look out. She utters an inarticulate scream.*]

DAVID. What is it, Chris?

MRS. PHELPS. Good heavens:

CHRISTINA [*strangled with horror*]. It's the pond! The holes in the pond! Quick, Dave, for heaven's sake!

DAVID. What?... Oh!...

[*He runs out as* CHRISTINA *opens the window.*]

MRS. PHELPS. Dave!... [*To* CHRISTINA.] What is it you say?

ROBERT [*off-stage and below*]. Dave! For God's sake! Hold on, Hester! Don't struggle! [DAVID'S *shouts join his.*]

CHRISTINA [*as she collapses on the bed*]. The pond!... I can't look....

MRS. PHELPS. Oh, I've no patience with people who have hysterics!

CHRISTINA. Mrs. Phelps, the girl's drowning!

MRS. PHELPS. Oh, no!... Not that! [*She, too, goes to the window, but recoils in horror from what she sees.*] They'll save her, won't they? They must... they must save her.... If only... [*Then a new fear overwhelms her.*] If only those two boys don't catch pneumonia! [*And she leaps to the window to call after her sons as they race, shouting, across the snow.*] Robin, you're not dressed! Dave, get your coat! Are you crazy? Do you *want* to catch pneumonia?

CURTAIN

ACT III

The living-room again, and the next morning. MRS. PHELPS *is wearing a simple house dress and busily fixing a great many flowers which she takes from boxes strewn about the stage. After she has been so occupied for a few seconds,* ROBERT *enters.*

ROBERT. The doctor's gone.

MRS. PHELPS [*surprised*]. Without seeing me?

ROBERT. It seems so.

MRS. PHELPS. Doesn't that seem very strange to you, Robin? Of course, I thought it best not to go up to Hester's room with him. In view of the perfectly unreasonable attitude she's taken toward me. But, I should have supposed, naturally, that he'd have made his report to me.

ROBERT. He says she may as well go to-day. He says traveling won't be as bad for her as staying here.

MRS. PHELPS. Did he say that to you?

ROBERT. I couldn't face him. *They* told him the whole story.

MRS. PHELPS. Christina and Hester? [ROBERT *nods*.] I might have known they would.... And he listened to them and never so much as asked for me?

ROBERT. What of it!

MRS. PHELPS. He'll never enter this house again!

ROBERT. So *he* said! He also said there's nothing the matter with your heart and never has been anything the matter with it. He said it would take a stick of dynamite to kill you.

MRS. PHELPS. Damned homeopath!

ROBERT. And that isn't the worst.

MRS. PHELPS. What more?

ROBERT. He said that I'd always been a rotter.

MRS. PHELPS. Oh?

ROBERT. And that I couldn't have been anything else — with such a mother.

[*There is venom in this last.* MRS. PHELPS's *lips stiffen under it.*]

MRS. PHELPS. I think you might have spared me that, Robin.

ROBERT. I didn't mean to be nasty.

MRS. PHELPS. No. Still, there are things one doesn't repeat to sensitive people. [*But a dark foreboding will not be downed.*] Somehow, though, I can't help feeling that...

[*She does not say what she sees in the future.*]

ROBERT. Neither can I.

[*She looks at him in quick fear. Then she returns to her flowers with a shrug.*]

MRS. PHELPS. Oh, well! There can't have been much wrong with the girl if she's able to go this morning.

ROBERT. Thank God for that. [*Then with level-eyed cruelty.*] It might have been serious, though, after what you did to the telephone. Because we couldn't have reached a soul, you know. And without Christina in the house...

MRS. PHELPS. How was I to know the little fool wanted to drown herself?

ROBERT [*shuddering*]. For heaven's sake, don't put it that way!

MRS. PHELPS. How do *you* put it?

ROBERT. She tried to get away, that's all. And she got lost in the dark and...

MRS. PHELPS. I tell you, she tried to kill herself. I've always suspected there was insanity in her family. She had a brother who was an aviator in the war. Everybody knows that aviators are lunatics. Her own conduct has never been what I should call normal. Everything points to insanity. That's another reason why you shouldn't have married her. Because we've never had any of that in our family. Except your father's Bright's Disease. I shall certainly tell everyone that Hester is insane.

ROBERT. Perhaps that *will* make things simpler.

MRS. PHELPS. As to the telephone, it's the only thing I've ever done to be ashamed of, and I said as much when I did it. She made me angry with her wanton attacks on you.

ROBERT. I didn't hear any wanton attacks.

MRS. PHELPS. Where were you?

ROBERT. Out there in the hall.

MRS. PHELPS. You couldn't have heard the things she muttered under her breath.

ROBERT [*an incredulous sneer*]. No! [*There is a pause, sullen on his part, troubled on hers.*] We're just like Macbeth and Lady Macbeth, aren't we?

MRS. PHELPS. For heaven's sakes, how?

ROBERT. We've got into a mess we can't ever get out of. We'll have to get in deeper and deeper until *we* go mad and...

MRS. PHELPS. Don't be ridiculous.

ROBERT. I'm sorry, Mother, but I can't help regretting.

MRS. PHELPS. Regretting what?

ROBERT [*low*]. Hester.

MRS. PHELPS. Nonsense, Robin! I tell you...

ROBERT. What do you know about it? Do you understand me any better than Hester did?

MRS. PHELPS. How *can* you, Robin? I not understand you? Haven't I always told you that however David may take after his father, you are *my* son?

ROBERT. What's that got to do with it?

MRS. PHELPS. Robin!

ROBERT. If I wasn't sure that I *loved* Hester, how on earth can I be sure that I *didn't* love her? I don't know this minute whether I loved her or not. I only know that I'll regret losing her all my life long. [*A movement of exasperation from his mother stops him. Then he concludes.*] Maybe Dave's right about me. Maybe I *am* too weak to love any one.

MRS. PHELPS [*frightened — to herself*]. Dave didn't say *that!*

ROBERT. He said I hadn't any guts.

MRS. PHELPS. Ugh! That horrible word! No, Robin. You must put all such thoughts aside.

ROBERT. I suppose I'll have to take your word for it. [*Then with sudden, cold fury.*] But I won't next time!

MRS. PHELPS. Robin! You're not holding *me* responsible?

ROBERT. Who put the idea in my head? Who persuaded me? Who made me promise?

MRS. PHELPS. Are you implying that *I* came between you?

ROBERT. Well, if you didn't, who did?

MRS. PHELPS. Robin! You ought to be ashamed!

ROBERT. Think so?

MRS. PHELPS. That *you* should turn on me! Some day you'll regret this. It won't be Hester, but *this* that you'll regret. ... When it's too late.

[*And from force of habit her hand steals to her heart.*]

ROBERT. I dare say I've got a life full of regrets ahead of me.

[*He walks sullenly to the window.*]

MRS. PHELPS. You frighten me, Robin! I don't know you like this.

ROBERT. Don't you?

[*There is a pause.* MRS. PHELPS *stares at him in growing horror. He looks out of the window.*]

MRS. PHELPS. No.

ROBERT [*looking out, his back to her*]. That's too bad.... There's Dave putting up danger signs all around the pond! Isn't that like him! After it's too late. [*She turns away from him and dully goes on with her flowers, carrying a bowl of them over to the piano.* ROBERT *watches her coldly. Then a sudden frown contracts his brow and he moves toward her.*] Mother!

MRS. PHELPS. What?

ROBERT. Don't put those flowers there! They're too low!

MRS. PHELPS. Fix them yourself.

ROBERT [*changing them with a jar of something else*]. Isn't that better?

MRS. PHELPS. Much. What an eye you have!

ROBERT. Perhaps I'll develop it some day.

MRS. PHELPS. Would you like to?

ROBERT. I've got to do something.

MRS. PHELPS [*darkly*]. I quite agree. Every young man should have some profession.

[*Then, suddenly and involuntarily, the boy reverts and is a child again.*]

ROBERT. What are we going to do, Mother?

MRS. PHELPS [*low*]. Do?

ROBERT. What are we going to do, you and I? We're in the same boat, you know.

MRS. PHELPS [*lower*]. I don't know what you mean.

ROBERT. Well, what am I going to do, then? I can't stay here and face people after this!

MRS. PHELPS. What will there be to face?

ROBERT [*crescendo*]. You know as well as I do. This story'll be all over this damn town. And Hester's people aren't going to keep quiet in New York. Her brothers go everywhere I go. My friends will begin cutting me in the street.

MRS. PHELPS. If we say she's insane?

ROBERT. What difference will that make?

MRS. PHELPS [*very low*]. The *Paris* sails on Saturday.

ROBERT [*pause, then, tremulously*]. What of it?

MRS. PHELPS. We might go to Washington to hurry our passports.

ROBERT. Could we get passage, though?

MRS. PHELPS [*slowly*]. I've already wired for it. This morning.

ROBERT. I see.... Then we're to sneak away like two guilty fugitives!

MRS. PHELPS [*avoiding his eye*]. Sh! Don't say such things!

[DAVID *enters, his cheeks stung crimson by the cold.*]

DAVID. Phew, it's cold. The pond'll be frozen again by to-morrow if this keeps up. What's the doc say about Hester?

ROBERT. She's leaving us to-day.

DAVID. I'm glad she's well enough.

MRS. PHELPS. There never was anything the matter with her.

DAVID. It's easy to see, Mother, that you don't often bathe in that pond in zero weather.

MRS. PHELPS. I hope I have more self-control. Robin, will you see, please, that the car is ready for Hester?

ROBERT. Yes. [*He goes.*]

DAVID. Anybody seen Chris?

MRS. PHELPS. Not I.

DAVID. No. I suppose not.... What's the idea in the floral display?

MRS. PHELPS. I felt I had to have flowers about me.

DAVID. That sounds pretty Green Hattish.... It has a festive look, too. I don't see what there is to celebrate.

MRS. PHELPS [*noble tragedienne that she is*]. Last night, at a single blow, beauty was stricken out of my life. I can't live without beauty, Dave. You must know

that. So I went to the florist this morning and bought these. They comfort me... a little.

DAVID [*that worried look again*]. I've been thinking, Mother, that maybe, all things considered, after last night, it will be as well for me to take Chris away on Wednesday, say.

MRS. PHELPS. If you like.

DAVID. We can come back later. After things have cooled down.

MRS. PHELPS. Later, I hope, and often.

DAVID. Time does make things easier, doesn't it?

MRS. PHELPS. They say so.

DAVID. When scientists get these wild ideas and fly off the handle, they're just as embarrassed afterwards as any one else would be.

MRS. PHELPS. Naturally.

DAVID. And then Hester's running away and the telephone being busted and all....

MRS. PHELPS. I quite understand.

DAVID. I knew you would.

MRS. PHELPS. [*The boxes and papers all stowed away, she sits down to business.*] What I'm wondering now, though, is what I'm to do with Robin? And I'm afraid you've got to help me with him.

DAVID. I'll do anything I can.

MRS. PHELPS. If I were well and able to stand the things I used to stand before my heart went back on me — because it *has* gone back on me — and before my blood pressure got so high... I shouldn't trouble you. But as I am, and with Robin on the verge of a complete breakdown...

DAVID. But Rob isn't...

MRS. PHELPS. Oh, yes, he is, Dave! He said things to me before you came in that no son of mine would dream of saying unless he had something the matter with him. I've got to get him away.

DAVID. Send him abroad.

MRS. PHELPS. I don't think he ought to go alone. He can't face things alone. He's like his father, in that. You're *my* son, you know. That's why I always turn to you.

DAVID. Why not go with him?

MRS. PHELPS. Because I'm really not well enough in case anything should hap-

pen.... And I don't know what to do.
Oh, Dave, boy, do you think...

DAVID. What?

MRS. PHELPS. That Christina could
spare you for a little? Just a few weeks?
Just long enough to get Rob and me settled
in some restful place? Do you think she
would?

DAVID. There's no need of that!

MRS. PHELPS. Of course, I'd love to
have Christina, too. Only I'm afraid that
would be asking too much. I mean, making her put off her work when she's so set
on it.

DAVID. But Rob isn't going to give you
any trouble.

MRS. PHELPS. Do you think I'd ask
such a sacrifice of you... and Christina, if
I weren't sure that it's absolutely necessary? Oh, I'm not thinking of myself.
I no longer matter. Except that I
shouldn't want to die abroad with only
Robin there, in his present condition.

DAVID. Don't talk that way, Mother!

MRS. PHELPS. Why not? I'm not asking you to be sorry for me. It's Robin I'm
thinking of. Because we haven't done all
that we should for Robin. And now that
I'm old... and sick... dying...
[*She breaks down.*]

DAVID. You're not, Mother!

MRS. PHELPS [*weeping hysterically*]. I
can't cope with him. He'll slip back again
to drinking and fast women...

DAVID. Get hold of yourself, Mother!

MRS. PHELPS [*more hysterical*]. And
when I think of what I might have done
for him and realize that it's too late, that
I haven't any more time... only a few
months... or weeks... I don't know...
I... [*She really becomes quite faint.*]

DAVID [*snatching her hand in terror*].
Mother, what's the matter? Are you ill?

MRS. PHELPS [*recovering by inches as she
gasps for breath*]. No! It's nothing... I...
Just give me a minute... Don't call any
one... I'll be all right.... There!... That's
better!

DAVID. You scared me to death.

MRS. PHELPS. I scare myself sometimes.
You see I do need *somebody's* help.

DAVID. Yes, I see you do.

MRS. PHELPS. And so I thought: well,
since Dave *is* going to build my houses in
Phelps Manor.... You're not going to dis-
appoint me there, I hope?

DAVID. Oh, no!

MRS. PHELPS. Well, then you won't
want to start in that New York office.

DAVID. Why not?

MRS. PHELPS. When you'll be leaving so
soon to begin here? They wouldn't want
you.

DAVID. I hadn't thought of that.

MRS. PHELPS. And so I thought: Well,
he can't begin here until April anyway and
that leaves him with two idle months on
his hands when he might be drawing plans
and getting ideas abroad. Think it over,
Dave, boy.

DAVID. You certainly are a great plan-
ner, Mother.

MRS. PHELPS. I make such good plans!

DAVID. When would you be sailing?

MRS. PHELPS. Well, I... I *had* thought
... vaguely... of sailing on the *Paris*...
Saturday...

DAVID. Good Lord! Give a man time
to think! I want to do the right thing,
but I couldn't leave Chris.... Not with the
baby coming, you know.

MRS. PHELPS. But you'll be home in
plenty of time for that.

DAVID. That may all be, but, just the
same, I wouldn't feel right to leave her.
[*ROBERT returns.*]

MRS. PHELPS. I've just been telling
Dave about our wonderful plans, Robin,
and he's so enthusiastic! I shouldn't
wonder if he came along with us.
[*A sign to DAVID to play up.*]

ROBERT. What *are* the plans?

MRS. PHELPS. Why, your going abroad
to study interior decorating, of course.
[*ROBERT looks surprised.*]

DAVID. Oh, is Rob going to do that?

ROBERT. Any objections?

DAVID. I think it's just the job for you.
Painting rosebuds on bath-tubs.

ROBERT. I can make your houses look
like something after you've finished with
them.

MRS. PHELPS [*ecstatically*]. My two boys
in partnership! Oh, that's always been my

dream! Oh, how simply things come straight when people are willing to co-operate and make little sacrifices! If there's one thing I pride myself on, it's my willingness to make little sacrifices. Here we are, we three, a moment ago all at odds with life and with each other; now united and of a single mind...

DAVID. This is all very fine. But don't you forget that I've got to talk to Christina...

[*But* CHRISTINA *has opened the door upon his very words. She is dressed as she was when she first came to the house. She wears her hat and her fur coat and carries her bag in her hand.*]

CHRISTINA [*speaking as she enters*]. Well, now's your chance, Dave. What have you got to talk to me about?

DAVID [*staring at her*]. What's the idea, Chris?

CHRISTINA [*setting the bag down by the door*]. I'm going away with Hester. Are you coming, too?

DAVID [*staggered*]. Now?

CHRISTINA. In a few minutes. I came down ahead. No, don't go, Mrs. Phelps. And won't you stay, too, Robert? I think it's best that we should thrash this question out together, here and now, for good and all.

MRS. PHELPS. What question, Christina?

CHRISTINA. The David question, Mrs. Phelps. Whether David is going on from this point as your son or as my husband.

ROBERT. What?

CHRISTINA. Isn't that the issue?

[*She asks the question less of* DAVID *than of* MRS. PHELPS, *who turns to her sons in terror.*]

MRS. PHELPS. I can't go through this a second time!

DAVID [*quieting her with a gesture*]. No one expects you to.... [*To* CHRISTINA, *pleading almost pathetically.*] You're not going to begin all that again, Chris?

CHRISTINA. I'm afraid I am.

DAVID. But, just as I was getting everything all straightened out...

CHRISTINA. Were you doing that?

DAVID. If only you'll leave things be,

they'll be all right. You may believe it or not...

CHRISTINA. I can't believe it and I can't leave things be. Oh, I'd walk out without a word, even loving you as I do, if I thought this state of affairs made any one of you happy.

ROBERT. What state of affairs?

CHRISTINA. The state of affairs you've all been living in and suffering from, for so long.

MRS. PHELPS. You might let us judge our own happiness.

CHRISTINA. I might, if you had any. But you haven't.

ROBERT. You're quite sure of that?

CHRISTINA. Quite, Robert. You're all of you perfectly miserable! Am I wrong?

MRS. PHELPS. Christina! Please!

ROBERT. Thank you for being sorry for us!

CHRISTINA. You give me such good reason, Robert. Such awfully good reason! Because you're not really bad people, you know. You're just wrong, all wrong, terribly, pitifully, all of you, and you're trapped...

MRS. PHELPS. What we say in anger, we sometimes regret, Christina....

CHRISTINA. Oh, I'm not angry. I was, but I've got over it. I rather fancy myself, now, as a sort of scientific Nemesis. I mean to strip this house and to show it up for what it really is. I mean to show you up, Mrs. Phelps. Then Dave can use his own judgment.

MRS. PHELPS [*blank terror at this attack*]. Oh! Dave, I...

DAVID. Now, Mother! Chris! Haven't you any consideration for our feelings? Are they nothing to you?

CHRISTINA. I'm trying to save my love, my home, my husband and my baby's father. Are they nothing to you?

DAVID. But surely I can be both a good son and a good husband!

CHRISTINA. Not if your mother knows it, you can't!

MRS. PHELPS [*a last desperate snatch at dignity*]. If you'll excuse me, I'd rather not stay to be insulted again.

[*She is going.*]

CHRISTINA. You'll probably lose him if you don't stay, Mrs. Phelps! [MRS. PHELPS *stays.* CHRISTINA *turns to* DAVID.] No, Dave. There's no good in any more pretending. Your mother won't allow you to divide your affections and I refuse to go on living with you on any basis she will allow.

MRS. PHELPS. I cannot see that this is necessary.

CHRISTINA. It's a question a great many young wives leave unsettled, Mrs. Phelps. I'm not going to make that mistake. [*Back to* DAVE *again.*] You see, Dave, I'm not beating about the bush. I'm not persuading you or wasting any time on tact. Do you want your chance or don't you? Because, if you don't, I'll have to get over being in love with you as best I can and...

DAVID. I wish you wouldn't talk this way, Chris!

CHRISTINA. Are you coming with me? On the understanding that, for the present, until your affections are definitely settled on your wife and child, you avoid your mother's society entirely. Well? What do you say?

DAVID. I don't know what to say.

CHRISTINA. You never do, Dave darling.

DAVID. I'm too shocked. I've never been so shocked in my life.

CHRISTINA [*a glance at her wrist watch*]. Just take your time and think before you speak.

DAVID. I don't mean that I don't know what to say about taking my chance, as you call it. I can answer that by reminding you of your duty to me. I can answer that by calling all this what I called it last night. Morbid rot! But I *am* shocked at your talking this way about my mother and to her face, too!

CHRISTINA. Is that your answer?

DAVID. No, it isn't! But a man's mother *is* his mother.

CHRISTINA. So you said last night. I'm not impressed. An embryological accident is no grounds for honor. Neither is a painful confinement, for I understand, Mrs. Phelps, that you're very proud of the way you bore your children. I know all about

the legend of yourself as a great woman that you've built up these thirty years for your sons to worship. It hasn't taken me long to see that you're not fit to be any one's mother.

DAVID. Chris!

ROBERT [*speaking at the same time*]. See here, now!

MRS. PHELPS. Let her go on! Let her go on! She will explain that or retract it!

CHRISTINA. I'm only too glad to explain. It's just what I've been leading up to. And I'll begin by saying that if my baby ever feels about me as your sons feel about you, I hope that somebody will take a little enameled pistol and shoot me, because I'll deserve it.

MRS. PHELPS [*going again*]. I've been insulted once too often.

CHRISTINA. I don't mean to insult you. I'm being as scientific and impersonal as possible.

ROBERT. Good God!

CHRISTINA [*regardless*]. Speaking of insults, though, what explanation can *you* offer *me* for your rudeness to me as a guest in your house?

MRS. PHELPS. I have not been rude to you.

CHRISTINA. You have been appallingly rude. Second question: Why do you resent the fact that I am going to have a baby?

MRS. PHELPS. I don't resent it.

CHRISTINA. Then why are you so churlish about it?

MRS. PHELPS. Your indelicacy about it would have...

CHRISTINA. That's another evasion. You're afraid that baby will give me another and stronger hold on David and you mean to separate David and me if it's humanly possible.

MRS. PHELPS. I do not! I do not!

CHRISTINA. Did you or did you not bend every effort to separate Hester and Robert?

MRS. PHELPS. I most certainly did not!

CHRISTINA. Then how do you account for the deliberate and brutal lies you told Hester about Robert? Because she did lie to Hester about you, Robert. She told

Hester that you never wanted to marry her.

ROBERT [aghast]. Mother, you didn't!

MRS. PHELPS. Of course, I didn't!

CHRISTINA [Joan of Arc raising the siege of Orleans]. I heard her. And I heard her call both of you back, last night, when you ran out to save Hester from drowning. I heard her call you back from saving a drowning girl for fear of your catching cold. I heard her. I heard her.

DAVID [shaken]. You shouldn't have called us, Mother!

CHRISTINA. Can she deny that her one idea is to keep her sons, dependent on her? Can she deny that she opposes any move that either one of you makes toward independence? Can she deny that she is outraged by your natural impulses toward other women?

MRS. PHELPS [furious]. I deny all of it!

CHRISTINA. You may deny it until you're black in the face; every accusation I make is true! You belong to a type that's very common in this country, Mrs. Phelps — a type of self-centered, self-pitying, son-devouring tigress, with unmentionable proclivities suppressed on the side.

DAVID. Chris!

CHRISTINA. I'm not at all sure it wouldn't be a good idea, just as an example to the rest of the tribe, to hang one of your kind every now and then!

ROBERT. Really!

CHRISTINA. Oh, there are normal mothers around; mothers who want their children to be men and women and take care of themselves; mothers who are people, too, and don't have to be afraid of loneliness after they've outlived their motherhood; mothers who can look on their children as people and enjoy them as people and not be forever holding on to them and pawing them and fussing about their health and singing them lullabies and tucking them up as though they were everlasting babies. But you're not one of the normal ones, Mrs. Phelps! Look at your sons, if you don't believe me. You've destroyed Robert. You've swallowed him up until there's nothing left of him but

an effete make-believe. Now he's gone melancholy mad and disgraced himself. And Dave! Poor Dave! The best he can do is dodge the most desperate kinds of unhappiness by pretending! How he survived at all is beyond me. If you're choking a bit on David, now, that's my fault because you'd have swallowed him up, too, if I hadn't come along to save him! Talk about cannibals! You and your kind beat any cannibals I've ever heard of! And what makes you doubly deadly and dangerous is that people admire you and your kind. They actually admire you! You professional mothers! .... You see, I'm taking this differently from that poor child upstairs. She's luckier than I am, too. She isn't married to one of your sons. Do you remember what she said about children yesterday? "Have 'em. Love 'em. And leave 'em be."

MRS. PHELPS. You are entitled to your opinions, Christina, just as I am to mine and David is to his. I only hope that he sees the kind of woman he's married. I hope he sees the sordidness, the hardness, the nastiness she offers him for his life.

CHRISTINA [an involuntary cry of pain]. I'm not nasty! I'm not!

MRS. PHELPS. What have you to offer David?

CHRISTINA. A hard time. A chance to work on his own. A chance to be on his own. Very little money on which to share with me the burden of raising his child. The pleasure of my society. The solace of my love. The enjoyment of my body. To which I have reason to believe he is not indifferent.

MRS. PHELPS [revolted]. Ugh!

CHRISTINA. Can you offer so much?

MRS. PHELPS. I offer a mother's love. Or perhaps you scoff at that?

CHRISTINA. Not if it's kept within bounds. I hope my baby loves me. I'm practically certain I'm going to love my baby. But within bounds.

MRS. PHELPS. And what do you mean by within bounds?

CHRISTINA. To love my baby with as much and as deep respect as I hope my baby will feel for me if I deserve its respect. To love my baby unpossessively; above all, unromantically.

MRS. PHELPS. I suppose that's biology! You don't know the difference between good and evil!

CHRISTINA. As a biologist, though, I do know the difference between life and death. And I know sterility when I see it. I doubt if evil is any more than a fancy name for sterility. And sterility, of course, is what you offer Dave. Sterility for his mind as well as for his body. That's your professional mother's stock in trade. Only we've been over that, haven't we? Well, Dave! How about it?

ROBERT. I think this has gone far enough!

MRS. PHELPS. No! This woman has got to answer me one question.

CHRISTINA. Willingly. What is it?

MRS. PHELPS. How old were you when you married?

CHRISTINA. The same age I am now. Twenty-nine.

MRS. PHELPS. I was twenty.

CHRISTINA. Just Hester's age.

MRS. PHELPS [riding over her]. I was twenty and my husband was fifteen years older than I. Oh, thirty-five isn't old, but he was a widower, too, and an invalid. Everyone told me I'd made a great match. And I thought I had. But before we'd been married a week, I saw my illusions shattered. I knew at the end of a week how miserable and empty my marriage was. He was good to me. He made very few demands on me. But he never dreamed of bringing the least atom of happiness into my life. Or of romance. ... Only a woman who has lived without romance knows how to value it.... That isn't true of my life either. I didn't live without romance. I found it ... and I'm proud to have found it where you say it doesn't belong... in motherhood. I found it in my two babies. In Dave first and in Robin four years later. I found it in doing for them myself all those things which, nowadays, nurses and governesses are hired to do. To spare mothers! I never asked to be spared.... Their father died.

The night he died, Robin had croup and I had to make the final choice between my duties. I stayed with Robin. You, with your modern ideas and your science, Christina, would you have chosen differently? I knew the difference between life and death that night. And I've known it for every step of the way I battled for Robin's health, every step as I taught Dave his gentleness and his generosity. ... If I made my mistakes, and I'm only human... I'm sorry for them. But I can point to my two sons and say that my mistakes could not have been serious ones. ... Think! I was a widow, rich and very pretty, at twenty-five. Think what that means! But I had found my duty and I never swerved from it.... There was one man in particular. A fine man. But I resisted. I knew that second marriage was not for me. Not when I had my sons. I put them first, always.... I shall not stoop to answer any of the foulnesses you have charged me with. They are beneath my dignity as a woman and my contempt as a mother. No, there is one I cannot leave unanswered. That word "sterility." Sterility is what I offer David, you say. I wonder, is sterility David's word for all he has had of me these thirty years? Let him answer that for himself. All my life I have saved to launch my two boys on their careers, saved in vision as well as in money. I don't offer my sons a love half dedicated to selfish, personal ambition. I don't offer them careers limited by the demands of other careers. I offer David a clear field ahead and a complete love to sustain him, a mother's love, until a real marriage, a suitable marriage may be possible for him. And I do not deny that I would cut off my right hand and burn the sight out of my eyes to rid my son of you! ... That is how I answer your impersonal science, Christina.

CHRISTINA [before either of the boys can speak]. I see!... Well.... It's a very plausible and effective answer. And I'm sure you mean it and I believe it's sincere. But it is the answer of a woman whose husband let her down pretty hard and who turned for satisfaction to her sons.... I'm almost sorry I can't say more for it, but I can't.... [*She turns from* MRS. PHELPS *to the two sons.*] It's a pity she didn't marry again. Things would have been so much better for both of you if she had. [*Then, with an increasing force, to* DAVID.] But the fact remains, Dave, that she did separate you and me last night and that she separated us because she couldn't bear the thought of our sleeping together. [*They flinch at this, but she downs them.*] And she couldn't bear that because she refuses to believe that you're a grown man and capable of desiring a woman. And that's because, grown man that you are, down, down in the depths of her, she still wants to suckle you at her breast!

DAVID [*a cry of horror*]. Chris!

ROBERT [*at the same time*]. Good God!

MRS. PHELPS [*at the same time*]. No!

CHRISTINA. You find that picture revolting, do you? Well, so it is.... I can't wait any longer for your answer, Dave.

DAVID. I don't think you've any sense of decency left in you. Of all the filthy, vile...

CHRISTINA. I'm sorry you feel that way.

DAVID. How else *can* I feel?

CHRISTINA. Is that your answer?

DAVID. I want to do the right thing, but...

CHRISTINA. Remember me, won't you, on Mother's Day! [*Then she calls out.*] Are you ready, Hester?

DAVID. You make things mighty hard, Chris, for a man who knows what fair play is and gratitude and all those other things I naturally feel for my mother.

CHRISTINA. Do I?

DAVID. What do you expect me to say?

CHRISTINA. I don't know. I've never known. That's been the thrill of it. [HESTER, *dressed for her journey, appears in the door and stands beside* CHRISTINA. CHRISTINA's *arm encircles the younger girl's shoulders.*] It's time, Hester.

HESTER. Isn't David coming with us?

CHRISTINA. I'm afraid not.

HESTER. Oh, Christina!

CHRISTINA. Sssh! Never mind. It can't be helped.

ROBERT [*breaking out*]. Hester! Hester! Couldn't we try again? Couldn't you...

HESTER. What?

ROBERT. I mean... what are you going to do... now?

HESTER. I don't know. [*Then a smile comes through.*] Yes, I do, too, know. I'm going to marry an orphan.

CHRISTINA [*a long look at* DAVID]. Good-bye, Dave.

DAVID [*desperately pleading*]. Chris, you can't! It isn't fair to me!

CHRISTINA [*still looking at him*]. I'm sorry it's come to this.... It might easily have been so...

[*Her voice chokes with crying. She picks up her bag where she put it down beside the door and goes quickly out.* HESTER, *with a reproachful glance at* DAVID, *follows her.* DAVID *stands rigid.* MRS. PHELPS *watches him.* ROBERT *covers his face with his hands. Then the front door slams and* DAVID *comes suddenly to life.*]

DAVID [*a frantic cry*]. Chris! [*He turns excitedly to his mother.*] I'm sorry, Mother, but I guess I'll have to go.

MRS. PHELPS [*reeling*]. No, Dave! No! No!

DAVID. I guess she's right.

MRS. PHELPS. Oh, no!! You mustn't say that! You mustn't say that!

DAVID [*holding her off from him*]. I can't help it. She said we were trapped. We *are* trapped. I'm trapped.

MRS. PHELPS [*absolutely beyond herself*]. No! No! She isn't right! She can't be right! I won't believe it!

DAVID [*breaking loose from her*]. I can't help that!

MRS. PHELPS [*speaking at the same time*]. For God's sake, Dave, don't go with her! Not with that awful woman, Dave! That wicked woman! For God's sake don't leave me for her, Dave! [*She turns wildly to* ROBERT.] You know it isn't true, Robin! You know it was vile, what she said! Tell him! Tell him! [*But he is gone.*] Dave! My boy! My boy! My boy! Oh, my God! Dave! She isn't right! She isn't, Dave! Dave! Dave!

[*The front door slams a second time. An awful pause, then.*] He's gone.

ROBERT [*uncovering his face*]. Who? Dave?

MRS. PHELPS. Can you see them from the window?

ROBERT [*looking out*]. Yes.... They're talking.... Now he's kissed her and taken the suitcase.... Now he's helping Hester ... Hester into the car.... Now he's getting in.... Now they're starting.

MRS. PHELPS. I loved him too much. I've been too happy.   Troubles had to come. I must be brave. I must bear my troubles bravely.

ROBERT [*turning to her*].   Poor Mother!

MRS. PHELPS. I must remember that I still have one of my great sons. I must keep my mind on that.

ROBERT [*a step or two toward her*]. That's right, Mother.

MRS. PHELPS. And we'll go abroad, my great Robin and I, and stay as long as ever we please.

ROBERT [*as he kneels beside her*]. Yes, Mother.

MRS. PHELPS [*her voice growing stronger as that deeply religious point of view of hers comes to her rescue*].   And you must remember that David, in his blindness, has forgotten.   That mother love suffereth long and is kind; envieth not, is not puffed up, is not easily provoked; beareth all things; believeth all things; hopeth all things; endureth all things.... At least, I think *my* love does?

ROBERT [*engulfed forever*].   Yes, Mother.

CURTAIN

THE DOVER ROAD
AN ABSURD COMEDY IN THREE ACTS
By A. A. MILNE

PEOPLE OF THE PLAY

THE HOUSE

Dominic

The Staff

Mr. Latimer

THE GUESTS

Leonard

Anne

Eustasia

Nicholas

Act I. *Evening.*

Act II. *Next morning.*

Act III. *Three days later. Evening.*

The Scene is the Reception-Room of Mr. Latimer's house, a little way off the Dover Road.

THE DOVER ROAD

ACT I

What Mr. Latimer *prefers to call the reception-room of his house is really the hall. You come straight into it through the heavy oak front door. But this door is so well built, so well protected by a thick purple curtain, and the room so well warmed by central heating, that none of the usual disadvantages of a hall on a November night attach to it. Just now, of course, all the curtains are drawn, so that the whole of this side of the hall is purple-hung. In the middle of the room, a little to the right is a mahogany table, clothless, laid for three. A beautiful blue bowl, filled with purple anemones, helps, with the silver and the old cut-glass, to decorate it. Over the whole room there is something of an Arabian-night-adventure air; Dulac might have had a hand in the designing of it. Three large alabaster bowls filled with fruit hang from ceiling on purple cords. These bowls are electrically fitted. In the day-time, perhaps, it is an ordinary hall, furnished a trifle freakishly, but in the night-time one wonders what is going to happen next.*

[*The Scene opens in darkness, except for firelight. Then all lights are switched up to full, including those in the bowls of flowers, and* Dominic, *tall, stout and grave, the major-domo of the house, in a butler's old-fashioned evening dress, draws centre curtains apart and comes in. He stands down* L.C., *looking at the room to see that all is as it should be. He turns round and waits a moment. The* Staff *comes in — in other words, two* Footmen *and two* Chambermaids. *The* Men *come from the* R., *the* Women *from the* L. *Over their clothes, too,* Mr. Latimer *has been a little freakish. The* Women *come down* L. *The* Men *down* R. *(up and down stage) as* Dominic *crosses to* C.]

Dominic. The blue room in the east wing is ready?

The Men. Yes, Mr. Dominic.

Dominic. The white room in the west wing is ready?

The Women. Yes, Mr. Dominic.

Dominic [*taking out his watch and looking at it*]. The procedure will be as before.

The Four. Yes, Mr. Dominic.

Dominic. See to it that I have no fault to find. That will do.

[*They turn militarily and go out up* C. — Women L., Men R.]

[Dominic *moves towards fireplace* L. *As the front-door chime is heard he goes to the front door and opens it. The top bolt, chain and key only are used.* Leonard, *in fur-coat and hat, is seen standing outside. He is a big, well-made man of about thirty-five — dark, with a little black tooth-brush moustache. When the door opens he gets his first sight of the interior of the room and is evidently taken by surprise.* Dominic *stands* R. *of opening.*]

Leonard. Oh — er — is this — er — an hotel? My chauffeur said — we've had an accident, been delayed on the way — he said that we could put up here. [*He turns round and calls*] Here, Saunders! This can't be the place. [*To* Dominic.] Perhaps you could tell me ——

Anne [*from outside, invisible*]. Saunders has gone, Leonard!

Leonard [*turning round*]. Gone! What the devil ——

Dominic. Saunders was perfectly correct, my lord. This *is* a sort of hotel.

Anne [*getting out of the car, but still invisible*]. He went off as soon as you got out of the car. Leonard, did you sur ——

[*She comes into the light; he is holding her arm. She is young, tall, pretty; cool and self-confident in the ordinary way, but a little upset by the happenings of the night.*]

DOMINIC [to LEONARD]. Saunders was perfectly correct, my lord. This *is* a sort of hotel.

LEONARD [*puzzled and upset*]. What the devil's happened to him?

[*He looks out into the darkness.*]

DOMINIC. Doubtless he has gone round to the garage to get the doors open. Won't your lordship —— [DOMINIC *comes down* R.C.]

LEONARD. You can put us up? Just for to-night. My — er — wife and myself ——

DOMINIC. If your lordship and her ladyship will come in.

[*He waits for them.*]

LEONARD [*to* ANNE, *coming down a step or two.*] It's the best we can do, dear. I'm frightfully sorry about it, but, after all, what difference ——

ANNE [*giving him a look which means "Don't talk like this in front of hotel servants," comes down to* L.]. I dare say it will be quite comfortable. [*As if that were all he was apologizing for.*] It's only for one night.

[LEONARD *crosses up stage to* R.C.]

DOMINIC. Thank you — my lady.

[*He shuts and bolts the door, puts key in his waistcoat pocket. There is an air of finality about it. Noise of bolt turns both round to look. They are locked in now for good.*]

LEONARD [*his eye on the supper-table, is saying to himself*]. Dashed rummy sort of hotel. [*He moves slowly down to* R.]

DOMINIC [*comes to her* L.]. Allow me, my lady.

[*She gives him her cloak and gloves, and crosses* R.C. *to* LEONARD, *who starts — then hands him his hat, and* DOMINIC *helps him off with his coat.*]

LEONARD. You can give us something to eat?

ANNE. I don't want anything, Leonard.

LEONARD [*crosses* L. *to her*]. Nonsense, dear.

DOMINIC. Supper will be served in five minutes, my lord.

ANNE [*coming down a step. Suddenly*]. Do you know who we are?

DOMINIC. I have not that pleasure, my lady.

ANNE. Then why do you call me "my lady"?

LEONARD [*disliking a scene*]. My dear!

ANNE [*waving back* LEONARD's *protesting arm*]. No, Leonard. [*Crosses* C. *to* DOMINIC]. Well?

DOMINIC. His lordship mentioned that your ladyship was his wife.

ANNE. Y-yes.... Then you know *him* by sight?

LEONARD [*complacently*]. Well, my dear, that need not surprise you.

DOMINIC. I knew his lordship's rank, my lady. Not his lordship's name.

LEONARD [*surprised. Crosses* C. *to* DOMINIC]. My rank? How the devil——?

DOMINIC. Supper will be served in five minutes, my lady.

[DOMINIC *goes up* R. WOMAN SERVANT *appears* L., MAN R., *and* DOMINIC *gives them the clothes.*]

[*They turn and exit, followed* R. *by* DOMINIC.] [*There is silence for a little. They look at the table, at the room, at each other. Then* LEONARD *says it aloud.*]

LEONARD. Dashed rummy sort of hotel!

ANNE. Leonard, I don't like it.

LEONARD [*goes to her,* L.C.]. Pooh! Nonsense, dear.

ANNE. It almost seems as though they had expected us.

LEONARD [*laughing. Crosses to fireplace*]. My dear child, how could they? In the ordinary way, we should have been at Dover — why, almost at Calais by this time.

ANNE. I know. [*In distress.*] Why aren't we? [*Goes towards him.*]

LEONARD. The car — Saunders, a fool of a chauffeur — a series of unfortunate accidents ——

ANNE. Do you often have these unfortunate accidents, Leonard?

LEONARD. My dear Anne, you aren't suggesting that I've done this on purpose.

ANNE. No, no. [*Sits in settee* L.C.] But why to-night of all nights?

LEONARD. Of course, it's damned annoying missing the boat, but we can get it to-morrow morning. We shall be in Paris to-morrow night.

ANNE. To-morrow night — but that makes such a difference. I hate every *hour* we spend together like this in England.

LEONARD. Well, really, I don't see why.

ANNE. You must take it that I do, Leonard. I told you from the first that it was run-away or nothing with me; there was going to be no intrigue, no lies and pretences and evasions. And, somehow, it seems less — less sordid, if we begin our new life together in a new country. [*With a little smile, turns to front.*] Perhaps the French for what we are doing is not quite so crude as the English.

[*He turns to fire.*] Yes, I know it's absurd of me, but there it is!

LEONARD [*with a shrug*]. Oh, well! [*Taking out his case.*] Do you mind a cigarette?

ANNE [*violently. Rises and goes* c.]. Oh, why do men *always* want to smoke, even up to the moment when they're going to eat? Can't you breathe naturally for five minutes?

LEONARD [*sulkily — putting his case back*]. I beg your pardon.

ANNE [*down to* L. *of table* R.C.]. No. I beg yours.

LEONARD. You're all to bits.

ANNE. Nerves, I suppose.

LEONARD. Nonsense! My Anne with nerves? [*Bitterly.*] Now, if it had been Eustasia —— [*Turns to front.*]

ANNE [*coldly*]. Really, Leonard, I think we had better leave your wife out of the conversation.

LEONARD. I beg your pardon.

[*Turns to her.*] ANNE [*to herself*]. Perhaps you're right. In a crisis we are all alike, we women.

LEONARD [*going* c. *to her*]. No, damn it, I won't have that. It's — it's blasphemy. Anne, my darling —— [*He takes her hands.*]

ANNE [*her hands on his chest*]. Oh!... I am different, aren't I?

LEONARD. Darling!

ANNE. I'm not a bit like — like any-body else, am I, not even when I'm cross?

LEONARD. Darling!

ANNE. And you do love me, don't you?

LEONARD. Darling!

[*He wants to kiss her, but she stops him.*]

ANNE. Now you're going to smoke.

[DOMINIC *enters. She takes cigarette from his case, and puts it in his mouth.*]

Now sit down here. [*Puts him in settee.*] I'll light it for you. Matches? [*She holds out her hand for them.*]

DOMINIC [*who has come in noiselessly*]. Match, my lady.

[*Strikes match and holds it to his cigarette —* ANNE *starts back to* c. *They are both rather confused.*]

[DOMINIC *puts down match-box on table* L.C. *and exit* DOMINIC.]

LEONARD [*starts up and watches him off*]. Damn that fellow!

[*Puts cigarette on ash-tray on mantel.*]

ANNE [*smiling*]. After all, darling, he thinks I'm your wife... or don't wives light their husband's cigarettes?

LEONARD. I believe you're right, Anne. There is something odd about this place.

ANNE [*moves to him.* So *you* feel it, too, now? [*Looks round.*]

LEONARD. What did he mean by saying he knew my rank, but not my name?

ANNE [*lightly, moving step back*]. Perhaps he looked inside your hat — like Sherlock Holmes — and saw the embroidered coronet.

LEONARD. How do you mean? There's nothing inside my hat.

ANNE. No, darling. That was a joke.

LEONARD [*crosses* R.C., *looking at the table*]. And the table laid. [*Looks round.*] Only one table.

ANNE [*both are now* c.]. Yes, but it's for three. They didn't expect *us*.

LEONARD [*relieved*]. Three, yes.... It's probably a new idea in hotels — some new stunt of Harrod's — or what's the fellow's name? — Lyons. A country-house hotel.

[DOMINIC *comes in.*]

By the way, Anne, what are you going to drink?

DOMINIC. Bollinger '06, my lord.

[*Both start back.*]

Mr. Latimer will be down in two minutes, my lady. He asks you to forgive him for not being here to receive you.

LEONARD. Mr. Latimer? Who on earth is Mr. Latimer?

DOMINIC [*looks disdainfully at him and turns to* ANNE]. If you would wish to be shown your room, my lady ——

ANNE [*who has not taken her eyes off him*]. No, thank you.

LEONARD [*stepping towards him*]. Look here, my man, is this an hotel, or have we come to a private house by mistake?

DOMINIC. A sort of hotel, my lord. I assure your lordship there is no mistake. Thank you, my lady.

[*Finger and thumb holding right corner of his coat — a favourite trick of his.*]

[*Exit* DOMINIC R. *up stage.*]

ANNE [*laughing half-hysterically as she sits in chair down* L.]. Very original man, Harrod. Or is it Lyons?

LEONARD. Look here, I'm going to get to the bottom of this.

[*He starts after* DOMINIC.]

ANNE. Why bother? Mr. Latimer will be here in two minutes.

LEONARD [*turning back down* C.]. Yes, but who the devil's Mr. Latimer?

ANNE [*with interest, rising*]. Leonard, do you always arrange something fascinating like this when you elope? I think it's so romantic of you. [*Kneels with one knee on settee.*] But don't you think that the mere running away is enough just at first? Leaving the fogs and the frets of England, the weariness and the coldness of it, and escaping together to the warm, blue, sun-filled South — isn't that romantic enough? Why drag in a mysterious and impossible inn, a mysterious and impossible Mr. Latimer? You should have kept that for afterwards [*moves towards fireplace*], for the time when the poetry was wearing out, and we were beginning to get used to each other.

LEONARD [*coming down to her*]. My dear girl, what *are* you driving at? I say again — do you really think that I *arranged* all this?

ANNE [*with a shrug*]. Well, somebody did.

[*Enter* DOMINIC, *who comes to the back of table* R.C.]

DOMINIC. Mr. Latimer.

[*The two* FOOTMEN *and the two* CHAMBERMAIDS *come in and take up positions on each side of* C. *opening.* LEONARD *goes* R.]

[MR. LATIMER *comes in.*]

LATIMER [*comes down to* ANNE L.]. Good evening! [*Crosses* R. *to* LEONARD.] Good evening!

[DOMINIC *signs to the* STAFF, *who retire.*]

[*He bows with an air. A middle-aged gentleman, dressed rather fantastically as regards his tie and his dinner jacket. He carries a flower in his hand.*]

LEONARD. Good evening! Er ——

[LATIMER *turns and follows* DOMINIC *off up* R., *sniffing his flower, and then returns.*]

LATIMER. You will forgive me for being announced in my own house, but I find that it saves a good deal of trouble. If I had just come in and said, "I am Mr. Latimer," then *you* would have had to say, "And I am — er — So-and-so, and this is — er ——" Exactly. I mean, we can get on so much better without names. But, of course ——

LEONARD. You will excuse me, sir, but ——

LATIMER [*going happily on*]. But, of course, as you were just going to say, we must call each other *something*. [*Thoughtfully.*] I think I shall call you Leonard.

[*They start.*]

There is something about you — forgive the liberty — something Leonardish. [*With a very sweet smile to* ANNE.] I am sure you agree with me.

ANNE [*smiling*]. I am wondering whether this is really happening, or whether I am dreaming it.

[LEONARD *taps his head significantly.*]

LATIMER [*his back to* LEONARD]. And Leonard isn't wondering at all; he is just tapping his forehead with a great deal of expression.

[*Putting flower in his buttonhole.*]

[LEONARD, *who was doing this, stops in some confusion.*]

LEONARD [*coldly*]. I think we have had enough of this, Mr. Latimer. I was giving you the benefit of the doubt. If you are not mad, then I will ask you for some other explanation of all this nonsense.

LATIMER [*to himself, sniffing the flower in his buttonhole*]. An impetuous character, Leonard. It must be so obvious to everybody else in the room that an explanation will be forthcoming. But why not a friendly explanation following a friendly supper.

ANNE. Are we your guests?

LATIMER. Please.

ANNE. Thank you. [*Curtsies.*]

LATIMER. But there is still this question of names. Now we agreed about Leonard ——

ANNE [*looking at LATIMER fearlessly*]. My name is Anne.

LATIMER. Thank you, *Miss* Anne.

LEONARD [*awkwardly*]. Er — my wife.

LATIMER. Then I am tempted to leave out the "Miss."

LEONARD [*going to him* C.]. Look here ——

LATIMER [*turning to him*.] But there is nothing to look at if I do, Leonard.

[DOMINIC *enters, followed by the* STAFF.]

Ah, supper. [*Goes to top of table.*]

ANNE. May I take off my hat?

LATIMER. If you please.

[*She puts it on table* L.C.]

Will you sit here, Anne?

[*She crosses him. He indicates the chair on the right of him.*]

And you here, Leonard?

[*The chair on the left.*]

[LEONARD *goes reluctantly and sits.* DOMINIC *behind his chair.*]

That's right. [LATIMER *sits down.*]

[DOMINIC *and the* STAFF *serve the supper. Five of them, so things go quickly.*]

A little fish, a bird, a little sweet.
Enough to drink, but not too much to eat.

I composed that in my bath this morning. There was a pretty little air attached to it.

[*Hums "The King."*] Some trifling flowing tune which has escaped me for the moment. The wine has been waiting for you since 1906. How different from the turbot — 'twas but yesterday it scarce had heard the name of Le-o-nard.

[*They are all served with fish — and the wine has been poured out.*]

Dominic, dismiss the staff. We would be alone.

[STAFF *exit, followed by* DOMINIC.]

[*He rises, glass in hand.*] My friends, I will give you a toast. [*He raises his glass.*] A Happy Ending! [*He drinks.*]

ANNE [*they clink glasses*]. A Happy Ending!

LATIMER. You do not drink, Leonard.

[*He drinks.*]

You would have the adventure end unhappily, as is the way of the modern novel?

LEONARD. I don't understand the beginning of it, Mr. Latimer. I don't — if you will forgive my saying so — I don't see how *you* come in. Who are you?

ANNE. Our host, Leonard.

LEONARD. So it seems, my dear. But, in that case, how did we come here? My chauffeur told us that this was an hotel — your man assured me, when I asked him, that it *was* an hotel — a sort of hotel. And now it seems that we are in a private house. Moreover, we seem to have been expected. And then again — if you will forgive me — it appears to be an unusual kind of house. I tell you frankly that I don't understand it.

LATIMER [*his mouth full of fish*]. I see your difficulty, Leonard.

LEONARD [*stiffly*]. Nor am I accustomed to being called Leonard by a perfect stranger.

LATIMER. What you are saying to yourself is, "Who is this man, Latimer? Is he *known?* Is he in the Stud Book? — I mean, Debrett. Is he, perhaps, one of the Hammersmith Latimers, or does he belong to the Ealing Branch?"

ANNE [*eating calmly*]. What does it matter?

LATIMER. Yes, but then, *you* like the fish; Leonard doesn't.

LEONARD. I have no fault to find with the fish. You have an excellent cook.

LATIMER [*rises, gravely bowing*]. I beg your pardon. I thank you.

[DOMINIC *comes in.*]

Dominic, his lordship likes the fish.

DOMINIC. Thank you, sir. I will inform the cook.

[LATIMER *sits.*   *Exit* DOMINIC L.]

ANNE. Mr. Latimer, when you are giving us your [*pause*], explanations after supper, I wish you would add just one more to them.

LATIMER. But, of course.

[DOMINIC *enters.*]

ANNE. Your Mr. Dominic's appearances are so apt. How is it done?

LATIMER [*pulling down his cuff*]. Yes, I'll make a note of that. [*He writes on it.*] "Dominic, apt appearance of." Admit the bird, Dominic.   [DOMINIC *exits.*]

LEONARD [*rising stiffly*]. I'm afraid we shall have to be getting on now, Mr. Latimer. . . . Anne, dear. . . we are much obliged for your hospitality, but — er — I imagine we are not far from Dover ——

[DOMINIC *and* SERVANTS *enter.*]

LATIMER. On the Dover Road, certainly.

LEONARD. Exactly. So if you would — er — have instructions given to my chauffeur — er ——

[*He hesitates as* WOMEN *go to sideboard and serve the bird — the* MEN *stand up* R.]

LATIMER. Dominic, his lordship's glass is empty. He wishes to drink my health.

DOMINIC. I beg your pardon, my lord.

[DOMINIC *fills the glass.*]

LATIMER. And while he is up, just find his lordship a more comfortable chair. He has been a little uneasy on that one all through the fish.

[DOMINIC *replenishes* LATIMER'S *glass.* DOMINIC *comes* L.C., *motions to* MANSERVANT, *who removes his chair up to* R.]

DOMINIC. I beg your pardon, my lord.

[*The other* MANSERVANT *approaches with another one from up* L.]

LATIMER [*rising with his glass, and drinking to* LEONARD]. Your happiness!

[*He sits down, and motions to* LEONARD, *who mechanically sits down, too.*]

Now, for the bird. [*To* ANNE.] I like these little ceremonies in between the courses — don't you?

ANNE. I'm liking my supper.

[WOMEN *go round with plates of chicken.*]

LATIMER. I am so glad. [*As* ANNE *is helped.*] I shot this bird, myself. [*He looks at it through his glass.*] What is it, Dominic?

DOMINIC. *Poulet en casserole* with mushrooms, sir.

LATIMER. *Poulet en casserole* with mushrooms. I shot the mushrooms.

[DOMINIC *motions to* STAFF — *they exit; he follows.*]

[*To* LEONARD.] Let me introduce your chicken to you, Leonard, one of the Buff-Orpingtons. I dare say you know the family. His mother was a Wyandotte. He was just about to contract an alliance with one of the Rock girls, the Plymouth Rocks, when the accident happened.

[*They are alone again now, plates and glasses well filled.*]

[LEONARD *jumps up.*]

Dear me! Not a *third* chair, surely?

LEONARD. Look here, Mr. Latimer, this has gone on long enough. I do not propose to sit through a whole meal without some further explanation. Either we have that explanation now, or else — Anne, dear — or else we'll be getting on our way.

LATIMER [*thoughtfully*]. Ah, but which is your way?

LEONARD. Dover. My chauffeur seems to have got off the track a little, but if you can put us on the Dover Road ——

LATIMER [*to himself*]. The Dover Road! The Dover Road! A dangerous road, my friends. And you're travelling in the dark.

LEONARD. Really. Mr. Latimer, that needn't frighten us.

ANNE [*putting out her hand*]. What do you mean?

LATIMER. A strange road, Anne, for *you*; a new untravelled road.

LEONARD. Nonsense! She's often been this way before. Haven't you, dear?

ANNE [*shaking her head*]. No.... But I'm not frightened, Mr. Latimer.

[*There is silence for a little. Then* DOMINIC *appears noiselessly, followed by* STAFF.]

LATIMER. Dominic, supper is over. [*He finishes his champagne, and with it his seriousness.*] His lordship loved the chicken — too well to eat it, and adored the mushrooms — in silence. Inform the cook.

DOMINIC. Yes, sir.

LATIMER. Shall we —— ?

[*All rise —* ANNE *crosses to* L.]

LATIMER [*offering his case to* ANNE]. A cigarette?

ANNE. No, thank you.

LATIMER. You permit it?

ANNE. Of course.

LATIMER. Thank you. [*Offers cigarette to* LEONARD.] Leonard!

LEONARD. No, thank you.

DOMINIC [*to* LEONARD]. Cigar, my lord?

[*Brings cigar-box and matches from table* L.C. LEONARD *declines, but on noticing the brand, relents.*]

LEONARD [C.] Er — thanks.

[*The* STAFF *clear the table and retire.*]

LATIMER. Which chair would you like, Anne? There? [ANNE *sits in settee.*] That's right. Now then, Leonard [*goes to him* C.] we want something especially comfortable for you. You are a little finnicky about chairs, if you don't mind my saying so.... What about *that* one? Just try it and see how you like it.

[LEONARD *falls into the chair down* L., *up to the neck almost.*]

Yes, I think you will be happy there. And I shall sit here.

[*Sits on down-stage arm of settee.*]

[DOMINIC *turns chair* C. *into table — turns and bows to* LATIMER *and exits.*]

LEONARD [*with as much dignity as is possible from that sort of chair*]. I am waiting, Mr. Latimer.

LATIMER. I am waiting, Leonard, for your questions.

ANNE. Let me begin with one.

[LATIMER *turns to* ANNE.]

Your table was laid for three. For whom were the other two places intended?

LATIMER. For yourself and Leonard.

ANNE. You expected us?

LATIMER. Yes.

ANNE. How did you know we were coming?

LATIMER. Saunders had instructions to bring you.

LEONARD [*starting up from his chair — or trying to, legs in air*]. Saunders! My chauffeur! Do you mean to say ——

LATIMER [*rises and goes to him*]. Let me help you, Leonard. You have the wrong chair again. It is difficult to be properly indignant in that one.

[*He helps him into a sitting posture.*]

That's better. [*Goes and draws arm-chair up* L. *to settee and sits.*] You were saying ——

LEONARD. Do you mean to tell me that you had the audacity to bribe my chauffeur?

LATIMER. No, no, Leonard. What I mean is, that you had the foolhardiness to bribe my friend Saunders to be your chauffeur.

LEONARD. Upon my word ——

ANNE. Who is Saunders?

LATIMER. Saunders? He's Joseph's brother. Joseph was the gentleman in yellow, who helped you to wine.

LEONARD [*out of the chair at last. Crosses* C.]. How dare you interfere in my concerns in this way, sir?

ANNE. Before you explain how you dare, Mr. Latimer, I should like to know *why* you are so interested in us. Who are you?

LATIMER. No more than Mr. Latimer. It is a purely impersonal interest which I take — and I take it just because you are going the Dover Road, my dear, and it is a dangerous road for a young girl to travel.

ANNE [*very cool, very proud, rises*]. I don't think I asked you to be interested in me.

LATIMER. Nobody does, my dear. But I am very interested in all my fellow-travellers. It is my hobby.

LEONARD. Anne!

[*He means "let's get out of this." He makes a movement to the front door.* ANNE *following.*]

LATIMER. The door is locked, Leonard.

LEONARD [*crosses to* LATIMER L., *bending over him and putting his face very close to* LATIMER'S]. Ah! Then 'I will give you one minute in which to open it, Mr. Latimer.

[DOMINIC *has come in up* L. *door below columns. The two* FOOTMEN *enter up* R. *with coffee set.*]

LATIMER. Dominic, his lordship's face is just a little too close to mine. Could you? ... Thank you.

[LEONARD *has started back on noticing* DOMINIC, *turns to face* C. *and is confronted by the two* MEN *with trays.*]

Coffee? Excellent.

LEONARD. No, thanks.

[*They offer it to* ANNE.]

ANNE. No, thank you.

[*They turn to* LATIMER.]

LATIMER. No, thank you.

[*They exit.*]

By the way, Dominic, did you go round to the hospital this afternoon?

[LEONARD *up* C.]

DOMINIC. Yes, sir. The young gentleman is getting on nicely. He was able to take a little bread-and-milk this morning.

LATIMER. Ah, I'm glad. Nothing solid yet?

DOMINIC. No, sir. The jaw is still very tender.

[DOMINIC *walks toward* LEONARD *threateningly — and turns up and exits* C. *to* R.]

LATIMER [*to* LEONARD *who moves down* R.]. He bumped it against my knuckles last week. An impetuous young fellow. He was running away with — dear me, I forget her name — I always forget names. I think he called her "Pussy." She had several children. [*Unconsciously he has shot his cuff, and sees suddenly the note he has made.*] What's this? "Dominic, apt appearance of."

[ANNE *moves to settee eagerly.*]

Oh yes. [*He turns to* ANNE.] It's very simple. A little fad of mine. There are bells everywhere in this room: in every chair, on the table, in the floor; wherever I am I can press a bell for Dominic. He is always just outside the door on reception evenings. Yes.

ANNE [*looks at* LEONARD]. That was a little warning you were giving just now?

LATIMER [*apologetically*]. Yes. I thought it better. Leonard is so impetuous. Joseph and Jacob were both amateur champions in their day; Dominic is a very heavy faller. He never has to fall on a man twice.

[LEONARD *sits.*]

If all this is quite understood at the beginning, it makes it so much easier.

ANNE. Mr. Latimer, I assure you that this is not a sudden freak of fancy, and that I know my own mind. I ask you, as a gentleman, to open the door.

LATIMER [*shaking his head*]. I am afraid it is impossible, Anne.

[ANNE *shrugs her shoulders and sits down* L. *of table* R.C.]

LEONARD [*calm for the moment*]. So we are kept here by force, Mr. Latimer?

LATIMER. Need we insist upon it? Let us rather say that you have postponed your visit to France in order to spend a few days with a friend.

LEONARD. I prefer to say force.

LATIMER [*with a bow*]. I do not dictate your words to you. Your movements for the moment — yes. So let us say "force."

LEONARD. We are prisoners, in fact?

LATIMER. Within the limits of my house.

LEONARD. And if my — my wife chose to walk out of your front door to-morrow morning, your — your fellow-conspirators would lay hands on her and stop her?

LATIMER [*rises, crosses to settee, sits on arm of it*]. My dear Leonard! Why should your — your wife want to walk out of the front door to-morrow? What would she want to do in the garden in November? Do be reasonable!

LEONARD. Suppose she wished to walk to the nearest police-station?

LATIMER [*to* ANNE]. Do you?

ANNE [*with a smile*]. Could I?

LATIMER. If you stood on Leonard's shoulders you might just reach the top of the wall.... Dominic tells me that they have lost the key of the gates. Very careless of them!

LEONARD [*springs up*]. Well, I ——
[*She motions to him and he sits again.*]
It's monstrous!

ANNE. Yes, but we can't keep on saying that. Here we are apparently, and here we have to stay. But I still want to know very much *why* Mr. Latimer has this great desire for our company.

LEONARD [*rises*]. You have the advantage of me now, sir, but you will not always have it. The time will come when I shall demand satisfaction for this insult. [*Sits.*]

LATIMER [*with an air, rising and bowing*]. My lord! Letters addressed to me at the Charing Cross Post Office will always be forwarded. [*Sits.*]

LEONARD [*slightly upset. Rises*]. This gross insult to myself and — er — my wife. [*Sits.*]

LATIMER [*shaking his head*]. No, no. Not your wife.

LEONARD [*rises*]. How dare you!

LATIMER [*in alarm*]. Surely I haven't made a mistake. [*To* ANNE.] You and he are running away together, aren't you?

LEONARD [*a step nearer*]. Look here, sir ——

ANNE [*rises*]. Oh, Leonard, what's the good? We aren't ashamed of it, are we? Yes, Mr. Latimer, we are running away together.

LATIMER. Of course! Why not? Leonard, *you* aren't ashamed of it, are you?

LEONARD. I object to this interference in my private affairs by a ——

LATIMER. Yes, yes, but you've said all that. It's interfering of me, damnably interfering. But I am doing it because I want you both to be happy.

LEONARD. I can look after my own happiness, thank you!

LATIMER [*rising*]. And this lady's?

LEONARD. She is good enough to believe it. [*Taking her hand.*]

ANNE [*going to* LATIMER, L.C.]. I am not a child. Do you think I haven't thought? — the scandal, the good name I am going to lose, the position of that other woman. I have thought of all these things.

LATIMER. There is one thing of which you haven't thought, Anne.

ANNE. I am afraid you are old-fashioned,

Mr. Latimer. You are going to talk to me of morality.

LATIMER [*smiling*]. Oh no, I wasn't.

ANNE [*not heeding him*]. Living alone here, a bachelor, within these high walls — [*moves up and round, arms up*] — which keep the world out, you believe what the fairy-books tell us, that once two people are married they live happy ever after.

LATIMER. Oh no, I don't.

ANNE [*comes down* R. *to* LEONARD]. I am the wicked woman coming between the happy husband and wife, breaking up the happy home. Is that it, Mr. Latimer?

LEONARD. Rubbish! The happy home! Why, this is my first real chance of happiness.   [*Takes her hand.*]

LATIMER. His first real chance of happiness! As he said when he proposed to Eustasia. [*Goes* L. *to fireplace.*]

LEONARD [*upset*]. What's that?

LATIMER [*to* ANNE]. May I ask *you* some questions now?

ANNE. Yes.

LATIMER. Eustasia will divorce him?

LEONARD. We shall not defend the suit.

LATIMER. And then you will marry Anne?

LEONARD. Another insult, Mr. Latimer. I shall not forget it.

LATIMER. I beg your pardon. I simply wanted an answer.

ANNE. He will marry me.
                [*Takes* LEONARD'S *arm.*]

LATIMER. I see. And *then*, as the fairy-books tell us, you will live happy ever after?   [*ANNE* is silent.]

LEONARD. I need hardly say that I shall do my best to — er ——

LATIMER [*goes* C.]. And then, as the fairy-books tell us, you will live happy ever after? I live within my high walls which keep the world out: I am old-fashioned, Anne. You are modern, you know the world. You don't believe the fairy-books, and yet — you are going to live happy ever after?

LEONARD [*crosses to hat*]. I don't see what you're driving at.

LATIMER. Anne does.

ANNE [*raising her eyes to him*]. I take the risk, Mr. Latimer.

[LATIMER *goes to* ANNE R.C., LEONARD *moves down* L.C.]

LATIMER. But a big risk.... Oh, believe me, I am not so much out of the world as you think. Should I have known all about you, should I have brought you here, if I were? I know the world; I know the risks of marriage. Marriage is an art — well, it's a profession in itself. [*Sharply.*] And what are you doing? Marrying a man whose only qualification for the profession is that he has tried it once, and made a damned hash of it.

LEONARD. Well, really, sir!

[ANNE *sits* L. *of table.*]

LATIMER. Isn't it true? [*Goes to him.*]

LEONARD. Well — er — I admit my marriage has not been a happy one, but I venture to say — well, I don't wish to say anything against Eustasia ——

LATIMER. Please go on. Life is too short for us to be gentlemen all the time.

LEONARD [*explosively*]. Well, then, I say that not even Saint Michael and all his angels could have made a success of it. I mean, not even Saint Michael.

LATIMER. Yet you chose her.

[LEONARD *is silent — goes to chair* L., *sits.*]

[*After a pause.*] Miss Anne, I am not being moral. You see, I am a very rich man, and we have it on good authority that it is difficult for a very rich man to be a very good man. But, being a very rich man, I try to spend my money so that it makes somebody else happy besides myself. It's the only happy way of spending money, isn't it? And it is my hobby to prevent people — to try if I can prevent people — making unhappy marriages.... It's wonderful what power money gives you. Nobody realizes it, because nobody ever spends it save in the obvious ways.... You may say that I should have prevented Leonard from marrying Eustasia in the first place. I have done that sometimes. I have asked two young people here — oh, properly chaperoned — and guests, not prisoners as you are — two young people who thought that they were in love, and I have tried to show each to the other in the most unromantic light. Sometimes the

engagement has been broken off. Sometimes they have married — and lived happy ever after... but mostly, it is my hobby to concentrate on those second marriages into which people plunge — with no parents now to restrain them — so much more hastily even than they plunged into their first adventure. Yet how much more carefully they should be considered, seeing that one, at least, of the parties has already shown an utter ignorance of the art of marriage?... And so, my dear friends, when I hear — and a rich man has many means of hearing — when I hear that two people are taking the Dover Road, as you were taking it to-night, I venture to stop them, and say — in the words of the fairy-book — "Are you sure you are going to live happy ever after?"

LEONARD [*after a pause*]. Your intentions may be good, but I can only repeat that your interference is utterly unwarranted. And you are entirely mistaken as to the power and authority which your money gives you.

LATIMER. Authority, none. But power? [*He laughs.*] Why, my dear Leonard, if I offered you a hundred thousand pounds to go back to your wife to-night, this lady would never see you again.

LEONARD [*rises*]. Well, of all the damnable things to say!...

LATIMER. How damnable the truth is! Think it over to-night. You are a poor man for your position... think of all the things you could do with a hundred thousand pounds. Turn it over in your mind... and then over and over again. A hundred thousand pounds.

[LEONARD *is beginning to turn it.*]

ANNE [*scornfully*]. Is this part of the treatment? Am I being shown my lover when he is mercenary?

LATIMER [*with a laugh*]. Oh no! If that were part of my treatment, there would be no marriages at all. Oh no, it isn't a genuine offer. [*To* LEONARD.] It's off, Leonard.

[LEONARD *wakes up suddenly, a poor man, drops his cigar.*]

You needn't think it out any more. Besides, you misunderstand me. I don't want to separate you by force — I have no right to.

ANNE. But how modest suddenly!

LATIMER [*with a bow and a smile*]. Madam, I admire your spirit.

ANNE. Leonard, I am receiving the attentions of another man. Beware of jealousy ——

[LEONARD *sits* L.]

All part of the treatment, Mr. Latimer?

LATIMER. You're splendid. [*Seriously.*] But I meant what I said just now. I am not preventing you from going the Dover Road, I am only asking you to wait a few days and see how you get on. It may be that you two are the perfect soul-mates; that your union has already been decreed in Heaven and will be watched over by the angels. If so, nobody will rejoice in your happiness more than I. I shall not say "You have no right to be happy together. Leonard must remain with his lawfully-wedded Eustasia." Believe me, I do not waste my money, my time, my breath in upholding the sanctity of an unhappy marriage. I was brought up in the sanctity of an unhappy marriage; even as a child, I knew all about it. [*Less seriously.*] But oh, my dear Anne, let us have a little common sense before we adventure marriage with a man who is always making a mess of it. We know what Leonard is — how perfectly hopeless as a husband.

ANNE. I don't think that is quite fair.

LATIMER. Well, as far as we can tell, you've never made a happy marriage yet, have you, Leonard?

LEONARD [*sulkily*]. I don't want to say anything against Eustasia ——

LATIMER. Good God, man, aren't you shouting it all the time? Why else are you here? But don't try to pretend that it's all Eustasia's fault.

LEONARD [*doubtfully*]. Well ——

LATIMER. Or that it will be all Anne's fault *next* year.

LEONARD. What do you mean, next year?

LATIMER. I beg your pardon. I should have said, the year after next.

[LEONARD *struggles out of chair. There is a little silence.*]

ANNE [*rises*]. I think I will go to bed. How long do you want us to wait, Mr. Latimer?

LATIMER. Could you spare a week? You, with so many years in front of you.

ANNE. I have a father. I left him a note to say what I was doing. We don't see much of each other, but I thought it polite. Does that interfere with your plans at all?

LATIMER [*smiling*]. Not at all. There was a little mistake about the delivery of that note. Your father is under the impression that you are staying with friends — in Kent . . . a great power — money.

ANNE. I congratulate you on the perfection of your methods. Good night, Mr. Latimer.

[DOMINIC *enters* C., *followed by* MAID.]

LATIMER [*to* DOMINIC]. Dominic, her ladyship will retire.

DOMINIC. Yes, sir.

[MAID *takes* ANNE'S *hat from table* L.C. *and moves to door* L.]

LATIMER. Good night, Miss Anne.

ANNE [*holding out her hand suddenly*]. Without prejudice.

LATIMER [*bending over it gallantly*]. Ah, but you are prejudicing me entirely.

MAID. This way, my lady.

[MAID *leads the way to a door up* L. *and* ANNE *follows her. Exeunt* MAID *and* ANNE L., DOMINIC C.]

LATIMER [*sits on end of table* R.C., *laughs*]. And did *you* leave a note for *your* father, Leonard?

LEONARD. You ought to know. You appear to have conspirators everywhere: Saunders — and I suppose Anne's maid — and God knows who else.

LATIMER. Money, Leonard, money. A pity you refused that hundred thousand pounds

[MANSERVANT *enters* C. *with salver of whisky, soda and glasses — puts it on table* L.C. *and exits.*]

You could have bribed the Archbishop of Canterbury to curse me. . . . Well, a week here won't do either of you any harm. Have a whisky and soda?

LEONARD. I am not at all sure that I ought to drink in your house.

LATIMER. You will be thirsty before you go.

LEONARD [*hesitating*]. Well ——

LATIMER. That's right. Help yourself, won't you? [*He does so.*]

LEONARD [*helping himself*]. Please understand that I do this, as I do everything else in your house, under protest. [*Raises glass.*]

LATIMER. Your protest is noted — a strong one.

[LEONARD *comes down* L., *leaving cigar on ash-tray on table.*]

LEONARD. And, as I have already said, your conduct is perfectly outrageous.

[*He sinks into the depths of arm-chair* L.]

LATIMER. And, as I have already said, you can't do moral indignation from that chair. Remember what happened to you last time.

LEONARD. Perfectly outrageous. [*He drinks.*]

LATIMER. Have another cigar?

LEONARD. I shall go to bed as soon as I have drunk this. [*He drinks.*]

LATIMER. You wouldn't care for a game of billiards first?

LEONARD. I am not in the mood for billiards.

LATIMER. By the way, we have another runaway couple here. But their week of probation is just over. They expect to leave to-morrow.

LEONARD. I am not interested in your earlier crimes.

LATIMER. I think you would be interested in *this* couple, Leonard.

LEONARD. I assure you I am not.

LATIMER. Ah! [*Picking up a review and settling himself in settee.*] Very good article this month by Sidney Webb. You ought to read it.

LEONARD. I am not interested in Sidney Webb.

LATIMER. Breakfast is at ten o'clock in here.

LEONARD [*struggling out of his chair*]. I shall eat it — under protest.

[*Puts glass on mantelshelf — goes* C.]

LATIMER. You're off? Then I'll say good night.

[*The two* FOOTMEN, JOSEPH *and* JACOB, *have come in, one to* R.C. — *one to door* L. DOMINIC *follows and stands up stage* C.]

LEONARD [*stiffly*]. Good night.

[LEONARD *walks up to the door* L. JACOB *is in front of it.* LEONARD *is pulled up at sight of him.*]

DOMINIC [*indicating the opening* R.]. This way, my lord.

LEONARD [*looking from one to the other*]. Er — er — thanks.

[*He goes across and turns, to find* JOSEPH *immediately behind him.* LEONARD, *hands in pockets, whistles and exits* R. JACOB *exits* C.]

[MR. LATIMER *is left alone with* "*Sidney Webb.*" DOMINIC *comes down* C., *glances at him — finger and thumb holding corner of coat — then goes up and exit* C., *closing curtains.*]

CURTAIN

ACT II

TIME. *It is the next morning.*

[EUSTASIA, LEONARD'S *wife, who should be sitting patiently at home wondering when he will return, is having breakfast with an attractive young man called* NICHOLAS. *She is what people who talk like that, call "a nice little thing"; near enough to thirty to wish it were twenty. At present she is making a good deal of fuss over this dear boy,* NICHOLAS. *Breakfast is practically over.* NICHOLAS, *in fact, is wiping his mouth.*]

EUSTASIA [*seated behind table* R. C.]. Finished, darling?

NICHOLAS [R. *of table*]. Yes, thank you, Eustasia.

EUSTASIA. A little more toast?

NICHOLAS. No, thank you, Eustasia.

EUSTASIA. Just a little tiny teeny-weeny bit if his Eustasia butters it for him?

NICHOLAS. No, thank you. I've really finished.

EUSTASIA. Another cup of coffee?

NICHOLAS [*with a sigh*]. No, thank you, Eustasia.

EUSTASIA. Just a little bit of a cup if his Eustasia pours it out for her own Nicholas, and puts the sugar in with her own ickle fingers?

NICHOLAS. No more coffee, thank you.

EUSTASIA. Then he shall sit in a more comfy chair while he smokes his nasty, horrid pipe, which he loves so much better than his Eustasia. [*He rises and crosses* c.] He doesn't really love it better?
[*Rising, goes to him.*]

NICHOLAS [*laughing uneasily*]. Of course, he doesn't.

EUSTASIA. Then kiss her to show that he doesn't.

NICHOLAS. You baby.
[*He kisses her cheek.*]

EUSTASIA. And now give me your pipe.
[*He gives it her reluctantly. She kisses it and gives it back to him, making a face.*]
There! And she doesn't really think it's a nasty, horrid pipe, and she's ever so sorry she said so.... [*He goes up* L., *sits.*] Oh!
[*She sees a dish of apples on table* L.C. *suddenly.*]

NICHOLAS. What is it?

EUSTASIA. Nicholas never had an apple!

NICHOLAS. Oh no, thanks. I don't want one.

EUSTASIA. Oh, but he must have an apple! It's so good for him. [*Takes apple.*] An apple a day keeps the doctor away. You *must* keep the doctor away, darling, else poor Eustasia will be miserable.

NICHOLAS [*with an effort*]. I've finished my breakfast.

EUSTASIA [*goes up* R.C. *toward sideboard*]. Not even if his Eustasia peels it for him?

NICHOLAS. No, thank you. I assure you that I have had all I want.

EUSTASIA. Sure? [*Replaces apple.*]

NICHOLAS. Quite sure, thank you. Where are you going to sit?
[*She goes to him, takes his hands and puts him in settee and sits beside him — he* R. — *she* L.]

EUSTASIA [*indicating the settee*]. Nicholas sit there and Eustasia sit next to him.

NICHOLAS [*without much enthusiasm*]. Right.

EUSTASIA [*snatches pouch*]. Eustasia fill his pipe for him?

NICHOLAS [*he takes it back*]. No, thanks. It is filled, thank you. [*He lights his pipe.*]
[*They are silent for a little and at last he speaks, a little uncomfortably.*]
Er — Eustasia.

EUSTASIA. Yes, darling.

NICHOLAS. We've been here a week.

EUSTASIA. Yes, darling. A wonderful, wonderful week. And now to-day we leave this dear house where we have been so happy together, and go out into the world together ——
[*Takes match from him and puts it on ash-tray on mantel.*]

NICHOLAS [*who has not been listening to her*]. A week. Except for the first day, we have had all our meals alone together.

EUSTASIA [*sentimentally*]. Alone, Nicholas.

NICHOLAS. Four meals a day. That's twenty-four meals.

EUSTASIA. Twenty-four!

NICHOLAS. And at every one of those meals you have asked me at least four times to have something more, when I had already said that I didn't want anything more; or, in other words, you have forced me to say "No, thank you, Eustasia," ninety-six times when there was absolutely no need for it.

EUSTASIA [*hurt*]. Nicholas!

NICHOLAS [*inexorably*]. We are both young. I am twenty-six, you are ——

EUSTASIA [*quickly*]. Twenty-five.

NICHOLAS [*looking at her and then away again*]. You are twenty-five. If all goes well — [*sighs*] — we may look to have fifty years more together. Say two thousand five hundred weeks. Multiply that by a hundred, and we see that, in the course of our joint lives, you will, at the present rate, force me to say "No, thank you, Eustasia" two hundred and fifty thousand times more than is necessary.

EUSTASIA [*pathetically*]. Nicholas!

NICHOLAS [*pipe in mouth*]. I wondered

if we couldn't come to some arrangement about it, that's all.

EUSTASIA [*in tears*].   You're cruel! Cruel!

> [*She sobs piteously, snatching his handkerchief.*]

NICHOLAS [*doggedly*].   I just wondered if we couldn't come to some arrangement.

EUSTASIA [*completely overcome*].   Oh! Oh! Nicholas! My darling!

> [*Sobs on end of couch.*]
> [NICHOLAS, *his hands clenched, looks grimly in front of him. He winces now and then at her sobs. He tries desperately hard not to give way, but in the end they are too much for him.*]

NICHOLAS. Darling! Don't!

> [*She goes on sobbing.*]

There! There! I'm sorry. Nicholas is sorry. I oughtn't to have said it. Forgive me, darling.   [*Her sobs get less.*]

EUSTASIA [*sitting up*].   It's only because I love you so much, and w-want you to be well, and you m-must eat. [*Weeps again.*]

NICHOLAS. Yes, yes, Eustasia, I know. It is dear of you.

EUSTASIA. Ask any doctor. He would say you m-must eat.   [*Weeps.*]

NICHOLAS. Yes, darling.

EUSTASIA. You m-must eat.   [*Weeps.*]

NICHOLAS [*resigned*].   Yes, darling.

EUSTASIA [*sitting up and wiping her eyes*]. What's a wife for, if it isn't to look after her husband when he's ill, and to see that he eats?

NICHOLAS. All right, dear, we won't say anything more about it.

EUSTASIA. And when you had that horrid cold and were so ill, the first day after we came here, I did look after you, didn't I, Nicholas, and take care of you and make you well again?

NICHOLAS. You did, dear. Don't think I am not grateful. You were very kind. [*Wincing at the recollection.*] Too kind.

EUSTASIA. Not too kind, darling. I love looking after you, and taking care of you!   [*Replaces handkerchief in his pocket. Thoughtfully, to herself.*]   Leonard was never ill.

NICHOLAS. Leonard?

EUSTASIA. My husband.

NICHOLAS. Oh!... I'd never thought of him as Leonard — I prefer not to think about him. I've never seen him, and I don't want to talk about him.

EUSTASIA. No, darling.   *I* don't want to, either.

NICHOLAS. We've taken the plunge and — [*bravely*] — and we're not going back on it.

EUSTASIA [*surprised*].   Darling!

NICHOLAS. As a man of honour, I —— Besides, you can't go back now — I mean, I took you away and — well, here we are [*bravely*] — here we are.

EUSTASIA [*amazed*].   Darling, you aren't regretting?

NICHOLAS [*hastily*].   No, no!

> [*She again snatches his handkerchief.*]

No, no, no!

EUSTASIA. Oh, yes, you are.

> [*Again sobs on end of couch.*]

NICHOLAS. *No! No!* [*He is almost shouting.*]   Eustasia, listen! I love you! I'm *not* regretting! I've never been so happy!   [*She is sobbing tumultuously.*] So HAPPY, EUSTASIA! I... HAVE... NEVER ... BEEN ... SO ... HAPPY! Can't you hear?

> [*Her sobs cease.*]

EUSTASIA [*throwing her arms round his neck — he subsides*].   Darling!

NICHOLAS [*comforting her*].   There, there, there, there, there!

EUSTASIA [*drying her eyes*].   Oh, Nicholas, you frightened me so. Just for a moment I was afraid you were regretting.

NICHOLAS. No, no!

EUSTASIA [*pause*].   How right Mr. Latimer was!

> [*She is leaning affectionately on him.*]

NICHOLAS [*with conviction*].   He was, indeed.

EUSTASIA. How little we really knew of each other when you asked me to come away with you!

NICHOLAS. How little!

EUSTASIA. But this week has shown us to each other as we really are.

NICHOLAS. It has.

EUSTASIA. And now I feel absolutely safe. We are ready to face the world together, Nicholas.

[*She sighs and leans back happily in his arms.*]

NICHOLAS. Ready to face the world together.

[*He has his pipe in his left hand, which is round her waist. Her eyes are closed, her right hand encircling his neck. He tries to bend his head down so as to get hold of his pipe with his teeth. Several times he tries and just misses it. Each time he pulls her a little closer to him, and she sighs happily. At last he gets hold of it. He leans back with a sigh of relief — she also lies back.*]

[MR. LATIMER *comes in down* R. — *to behind couch.*]

LATIMER. Good morning, my friends, good morning.

NICHOLAS. Oh, good morning.

[*Rising — moves to end of couch.*]

EUSTASIA. Good morning.

LATIMER. So you are leaving me this morning and going on your way?

NICHOLAS [*without enthusiasm*]. Yes.

EUSTASIA. But we shall never forget this week, dear Mr. Latimer.

LATIMER. You have forgiven me for asking you to wait a little so as to make sure?

EUSTASIA. Oh, but you were so right! I was just saying so to Nicholas. Wasn't I, Nicholas?

NICHOLAS. Yes. About a minute ago. [*Looks at wrist watch.*] About two minutes ago.

LATIMER. And so now you are sure of yourselves?

EUSTASIA. Oh, so sure, so very sure. Aren't we, Nicholas?

NICHOLAS. Absolutely sure.

LATIMER. That's right. [*Looking at his watch.*] Well, I don't want to hurry you, but if you have any little things to do, the car will be here in half an hour, and ——

EUSTASIA [*rises and goes up to* L.C.]. Half an hour? Oh, I must fly. [*She begins.*]

NICHOLAS [*not moving*]. Yes, we must fly.

LATIMER [*going to the door with* EUSTASIA]. By the way, you will be interested to hear that I had two other visitors last night.

EUSTASIA [*stopping excitedly*]. Mr. Latimer! You don't mean another — couple?

LATIMER. Yes, another romantic couple.

EUSTASIA. Oh, if I could but see them before I go! Just for a moment! Just to reconcile them to this week of probation! To tell them what a wonderful week it can be!

LATIMER [*goes to open door* L.]. You shall. I promise you that you shall.

EUSTASIA. Oh, thank you, dear Mr. Latimer. [*Exit* EUSTASIA L.]

[LATIMER *comes down* R.C.]

NICHOLAS [L.C.]. I say.

LATIMER. Yes?

NICHOLAS [*slowly*]. I say, what would you — I mean, supposing — because you see — I mean, it isn't as if —— Of course, now —— [*He looks at his watch and finishes up sadly.*] Half an hour. Well, I suppose I must be getting ready.

[*He goes towards the opening* R.]

LATIMER [*as he gets there*]. Er — Nicholas.

NICHOLAS [*turning round*]. Yes?

LATIMER. Just a moment.

NICHOLAS [*coming back to him*]. Yes?

[LATIMER *takes* NICHOLAS *by the arm, and looks round the room to see that they are alone.*]

LATIMER [*in a whisper*]. Cheer up!

NICHOLAS [*excitedly*]. What!

[LATIMER *has let go of his arm and moved away, whistling "Wedding March." The light dies out of* NICHOLAS' *eyes, and he shrugs his shoulders despairingly.*]

[*Without any hope.*] Well, I'll go and get ready. [*Exit* NICHOLAS, R.]

[DOMINIC *enters with newspaper — followed by the four* SERVANTS, *who proceed to clear away the old breakfast dishes, etc., and lay afresh. Exeunt.*]

LATIMER. Ah, good morning, Dominic.

DOMINIC. Good morning, sir. A nicish morning, it seems to be, sir.

LATIMER [*sits in settee*]. A very nicish morning. I have great hopes of the world to-day.

DOMINIC. I am very glad to hear it, sir.

LATIMER. We must all do what we can, Dominic.

DOMINIC. That's the only way, isn't it, sir?

LATIMER. Great hopes, great hopes.

DOMINIC [*handing him "The Times"*]. The paper, sir.

LATIMER. Thank you. [*He looks at the first page.*] Any one married this morning? Dear me, quite a lot. One, two, three, four, five, six, seven, eight, nine — ten. [*Sung to tune of "Wedding March."*] Ten! Twenty happy people, Dominic!

DOMINIC. Let us hope so, sir.

LATIMER. Let us hope so.... By the way, how was his lordship this morning?

DOMINIC. A little depressed, sir.

LATIMER. Ah!

DOMINIC. There seems to have been some misunderstanding about his luggage. A little carelessness on the part of somebody, I imagine, sir.

LATIMER. Dear me! Didn't it come with him?

DOMINIC. I'm afraid not, sir.

LATIMER. Tut, tut, how careless of somebody! Can't we lend him anything?

DOMINIC. Joseph offered to lend him a comb, sir — his own comb — a birthday present last year, Joseph tells me. His lordship decided not to avail himself of the offer.

LATIMER. Very generous of Joseph, seeing that it was a birthday present.

[*The two* MAIDS *re-enter with replenished coffee-pot, milk, and toastrack.*]

DOMINIC. Yes, sir. Unfortunately, Joseph had come down to the last blade of his safety-razor this morning. His lordship is rather upset about the whole business, sir. [*Exeunt* MAIDS.]

LATIMER. Well, well, I dare say a little breakfast will do him good.

DOMINIC. Yes, sir; let us hope so, sir. Are you ready for breakfast now, sir?

[ANNE *comes in* L.]

LATIMER [*getting up and going to her up* L.]. Good morning, Miss Anne. May I hope that you slept well?

[DOMINIC *puts finishing touches to table.*]

ANNE. Very well, thank you.

LATIMER. I am so glad.... All right, Dominic.

DOMINIC. Thank you, sir.

[*Exit* DOMINIC *up* C. *to* L.]

LATIMER. Are you ready for breakfast?

ANNE [*goes to table*]. Quite ready, Mr. Latimer. But what about Leonard?

LATIMER. Leonard? [*Brings chair from up* C. *down to* L. *of table.*]

ANNE. I made sure that I was to have a practice breakfast with Leonard this morning. I have been thinking of a few things to say up in my room.

LATIMER [*smiling*]. Say them to me instead.

ANNE. They are very wifely.

LATIMER. But think what good practice.

ANNE [*smiling*]. Very well. [*At the cups.*] Tea or coffee, darling?

LATIMER. Oh no, that will never do. You know by now that I always have coffee — half milk and three lumps of sugar. [*Goes up to sideboard* R.]

ANNE. Of course. How silly of me!

[*She pours out the coffee.*]

LATIMER [*taking the covers off the dishes*]. Omelette — fish — kidney and bacon?

ANNE. Now *you're* forgetting.

LATIMER [*putting back the covers*]. No, I'm remembering. Toast and marmalade — isn't that right?

ANNE. Quite right, dear.

LATIMER [*to himself*]. I knew she would like marmalade. No wonder that Leonard ran away with her.

[*He puts the toast and marmalade close to her.*]

ANNE. Your coffee, darling.

LATIMER. Thank you, my love....

[*She laughs.*]

"My love" is very connubial, I think.

[*Sits* L. *of table.*]

ANNE. Delightfully so. Do go on.

LATIMER. Er — I am sorry to see in the paper this morning — which I glanced at, my precious, before you came down —— How do you like "my precious"?

ANNE. Wonderfully life-like. Are you sure *you* haven't been married before?

LATIMER. Only once. Eustasia. You had not forgotten Eustasia?

ANNE. I am afraid I had. In fact, I had forgotten for the moment that you were being Leonard.

LATIMER [*bowing*]. Thank you. I could wish no better compliment.

ANNE [*laughing, in spite of herself*]. Oh, you're too absurd!

LATIMER [*in* LEONARD'S *manner*]. Of course, I don't wish to say anything against Eustasia....

ANNE. My dear Leonard, I — I really think we might leave your first wife out of the conversation.

LATIMER. Yes, you want to get that off pat. You'll have to say that a good deal, I expect. Well, to resume. I am sorry to see in the paper this morning that Beelzebub, upon whom I laid my shirt for the 2.30 race at Newmarket yesterday — and incidentally your shirt, too, darling — came in last, some five minutes after the others had finished the course.... Tut, tut, how annoying!

ANNE. Oh, my poor darling!

LATIMER. The word "poor" is well chosen. We are ruined.

ANNE. At least, let me share your ruin with you.

LATIMER. No, we are not ruined. Pass the toast. I can always refuse to pay my gambling debts.

ANNE. Oh, my love. I thought you were a man of honour!

LATIMER. So I am. Then I shall write my autobiography instead.

ANNE. You know what I *want* you to do, Leonard?

LATIMER. No. I have forgotten.

ANNE [*seriously*]. I should like to see you in the House of Lords, taking your rightful place as a leader of men, making great speeches.

LATIMER [*imitates* LEONARD'S *voice*]. My dear Anne, I may be a peer, but I am not a dashed politician — what!

ANNE [*wistfully*]. I wish you were.

LATIMER [*himself*]. I will be anything *you* like, Anne.

[LATIMER *leans towards her, half-serious, half-mocking.*]

ANNE [*with a little laugh*]. How absurd you are! Some more coffee?

LATIMER [*passing his cup*]. To which I answer, "A little more milk." Do you realize that this goes on for fifty years?

ANNE. Well, and why not?

LATIMER. Fifty years. A solemn thought. But let it not mar our pleasure in the meal that we are having together now. Let us continue to talk gaily together. Tell me of any interesting dream you may have had last night — any little adventure that befell you in the bath — any bright thought that occurred to you as you were dressing.

ANNE [*thoughtfully*]. I had a very odd dream last night.

LATIMER. I am longing to hear it, my love.

ANNE. I dreamt that you and I were running away together, Leonard, and that we lost our way and came to what we thought was an hotel. But it was not an hotel. It was a very mysterious house, kept by a very mysterious man called Latimer.

LATIMER. How very odd! Latimer? Latimer? No, I don't seem to have heard of the fellow.

ANNE. He told us that we were his prisoners. That we must stay in his house a week before we went on our way again. That all the doors were locked, that there were high walls round the garden, that the gates of the garden were locked, so that we could not escape, and that we must wait a week together in his house to see if we were really suited to each other.

LATIMER. What an extraordinary dream!

ANNE. It was only a dream, wasn't it?

LATIMER. Of course! What is there mysterious about the house? [*He throws a hand round the room.*] What is there mysterious about this — dear me — I always forget names.

ANNE. Latimer.

LATIMER. Mr. Latimer? And as for any one being kept prisoner — here — in this respectable England — why!

ANNE. It is absurd, isn't it?

LATIMER. Quite ridiculous.

ANNE [*getting up*]. I thought it was. [*She goes to the front door and opens it.*] You see, I thought it was. [*She steps out into the garden.*] You see, the gates are open, too! [*She comes back.*] What an absurd dream to have had! [*She sits down again.*]

LATIMER. There's no accounting for dreams. I had an absurd one, too, last night.

ANNE. What was it?

LATIMER. A lonely house. Father and daughter living together. Father, old, selfish, absorbed in his work. [*She drinks.*] Daughter, left to herself; her only companion, books; knowing nothing of the world. A man comes into her life; the first. He makes much of her. It is a new experience for the daughter. She is grateful to him, so grateful; so very proud that she means anything to him. He tells her when it is too late that he is married; talks of an impossible wife; tells her that she is his real mate. Let her come with him and see something of the world which she has never known. She comes.... Dear me, what silly things one dreams!

ANNE. Absurd things. [*Rises.*] When can we have the car?

LATIMER. The car?

ANNE. Leonard's car.

LATIMER. You wish to continue the adventure?

ANNE. Why not?

LATIMER. Dear, dear! What a pity! [*Looking at his watch.*] In twenty-five minutes!

ANNE. That will do nicely, thank you.

LATIMER [*rises*]. We must let Leonard have a little breakfast first, if he is to cross the Channel to-day. In twenty-five minutes, then.

ANNE [*half-holding out her hand*]. I shall see you again?

LATIMER [*shakes her hand*]. If only to wish you God-speed.

[ANNE *looks at him for a moment, and then goes out,* L.]

[LATIMER *looks after her for a little, then picks up his paper, goes up* C. *to window* L., *whistling the "Wedding March."* LEONARD *sneezes, off* R., *and comes in. Sneezes again. He is in a dirty, rather disreputable, once white, bath gown. His hair is unbrushed, his cheeks — the cheeks of a dark man —*

unshaved and blue. *He has a horrible pair of bedroom slippers on his feet, above which, not only his socks, but almost a hint of pantaloons may be seen on the way to the dressing-gown. He comes in nervously, and is greatly relieved to find that the breakfast-table is empty. He does not notice* MR. LATIMER. *On his way to the table he stops at a mirror on the wall* R., *and, standing in front of it, tries to persuade himself that his chin is not so bad, after all. He then goes up* R., *helps himself to a kipper, and brings it down to* R. *of table. Then he pours himself out some coffee, and falls to ravenously, sitting* R. *of table.*]

LATIMER. Ah, good morning, Leonard.

LEONARD [*starting violently and turning round*]. Good Lord! I didn't know you were there.

LATIMER [*sits at back of table*]. You were so hungry. . . . I trust you slept well.

LEONARD. Slept well! Of all the damned draughty rooms.... Yes, and what about my luggage?

LATIMER [*surprised*]. Your luggage?

LEONARD. Yes, never put on the car — your fellow, what's-'is-name — Joseph says.

LATIMER. Dear me! We must inquire into this. Lost your luggage? Dear me! That's a very unfortunate start for a honeymoon. That means bad luck, Leonard.

[DOMINIC *comes in,* C.]

Dominic, what's this about his lordship's luggage?

DOMINIC. Yes, sir! Joseph tells me there must have been some misunderstanding about it, sir. A little carelessness on the part of somebody, I imagine, sir.

LATIMER. Dear me! Didn't it come with him?

DOMINIC. I'm afraid not, sir.

LATIMER. Tut, tut, how careless of somebody! Thank you, Dominic.

DOMINIC. Thank you, sir.

[*Exit* DOMINIC C.]

LATIMER. Lost your luggage. How excessively annoying! [*Anxiously.*] My dear Leonard, what is it?

LEONARD [*whose face has been shaping for it for some seconds*]. A-*tish*-oo!

LATIMER. At any rate, I can lend you a handkerchief.

[*He does so.* LEONARD *takes it just in time and sneezes violently again.*]

LEONARD. Thank you.

LATIMER. Not at all. That's a very nasty cold you've got. How wise of you to have kept on a dressing-gown.

LEONARD. The only thing I could find to put on.

LATIMER. But surely you were travelling in a suit yesterday? I seem to remember a brown suit.

LEONARD. That fool of a man of yours ——

LATIMER [*distressed*]. You don't mean to tell me ——

[DOMINIC *comes in* C.]

Dominic, what's this about his lordship's brown suit?

DOMINIC. Yes, sir! Owing to a regrettable misunderstanding, sir, his lordship's luggage ——

LATIMER. Yes, but I'm not talking about his twenty-five other suits; I mean the nice brown suit that he was wearing yesterday. It must be somewhere. I remember noticing it. I remember —— [*He holds up his hand.*] Just a moment, Dominic....

LEONARD. A-*tish*-oo!

LATIMER. I remember saying to myself, "What a nice brown suit Leonard is wearing!" Well, where is it, Dominic?

DOMINIC. Yes, sir. I seem to remember the suit to which you are referring. I'm afraid that Joseph had an unfortunate accident with it.

LEONARD [*growling*]. Damned carelessness!

DOMINIC. Joseph was bringing back the clothes after brushing them, sir, and happened to have them in his arms while bending over the bath in order to test the temperature of the water for his lordship. A little surprised at the unexpected heat of the water, Joseph relinquished the clothes for a moment, and precipitated them into the bath.

LATIMER. Dear me! How extremely careless of Joseph!

DOMINIC. Yes, sir, I have already reprimanded him.

LEONARD. That fellow ought to be shot.

LATIMER. You're quite right, Leonard. Dominic, shoot Joseph this morning.

DOMINIC. Yes, sir.

LATIMER. And see that his lordship's suit is dried as soon as possible.

DOMINIC. Yes, sir. It is being dried now, sir.

LATIMER. But it must be dried thoroughly, Dominic. His lordship has a nasty cold, and ——

LEONARD. A-*tish*-oo!

LATIMER. A very nasty cold. I'm afraid you are subject to colds, Leonard?

LEONARD. The first one I've ever had in my life. [*He sniffs.*]

LATIMER. Do you hear that, Dominic? The first one his lordship has ever had in his life.

DOMINIC. Yes, sir. If you remember, sir, Mr. Nicholas and one or two other gentlemen who slept there, caught a very nasty cold. Almost looks as if there must be something the matter with the room.

LEONARD. Damned draughtiest room....

LATIMER. Dear me! You should have told me of this before, Dominic. We must have the room seen to at once. And be sure that his lordship has a different room to-night.

DOMINIC. Yes, sir. Thank you, sir.

[*Exit* DOMINIC C.]

LATIMER [*rises, goes to sideboard — brings down two omelette dishes. Sympathetically*]. My dear fellow, I am distressed beyond words, but you know the saying, "Feed a cold; starve a fever." You must eat, you must eat. We must be firm with this cold. We must suffocate it. How wise of you not to shave this morning. The protection offered by the beard, though small, is salutary. But I was forgetting — perhaps you lost your razor, too!

LEONARD. Damned careless fellows!

LATIMER. I must lend you mine.

LEONARD [*feeling his chin*]. I say, I wish you would.

LATIMER. I'll get it at once. Meanwhile, eat. No half measures with this cold of yours. [LEONARD *sneezes.*] My poor fellow! My poor fellow!

[LATIMER *reluctantly exits* R. LEONARD *gets busy with his breakfast.*]

[*Enter* ANNE, L.]

ANNE [*hurrying in*]. Leonard, my dear! [*She observes him more thoroughly.*] My *dear* Leonard!

LEONARD [*his mouth full*]. G'morning, Anne. [*Goes to her up* C.]

ANNE [*coldly*]. Good morning.

LEONARD [*napkin in hand*]. How are you this morning? [*Wiping his mouth.*]

ANNE. No, please go on with your breakfast. [*In alarm.*] What is it?

[*His face assumes an agonized expression. He sneezes* — ANNE *shudders.*]

LEONARD. Got a nasty cold. Can't understand it. First one I've ever had in my life.

ANNE. Do you sneeze like that much?

LEONARD. Off and on.

ANNE. Oh!... Hadn't you better get on with your breakfast?

LEONARD. Well, I will, if you don't mind. Good thing for a cold, isn't it? Eat a lot.

ANNE. I really know very little about colds.... Do get on with your breakfast.

LEONARD [*going back*]. Well, I will, if you don't mind. You had yours?

ANNE. Yes.

LEONARD [*sits*]. That's right. [*Resuming it.*] Did you have one of these kippers?

ANNE. No.

LEONARD. Ah! A pity. I will say that for Latimer's cook, she knows how to do a kipper. Much more difficult than people think. [*Eats.*]

ANNE. I really know very little about kippers.

LEONARD. I have often wondered why somebody doesn't invent one without bones. [*He takes a mouthful.*] Seeing what science can do nowadays ——

[*He stops.* ANNE'S *eye is on him. He says nothing, but waves his hand for her to look the other way.*]

ANNE. What is it?

[*He frowns fiercely and continues to wave.*]

[*She says coldly.*] I beg your pardon.

[*She turns away, goes to fireplace* L. *He removes a mouthful of bones.*]

LEONARD [*cheerfully*]. Right-oh, darling. ... After all, what do they *want* all these bones for? Other fish .manage without them. [*He continues his kipper.*]

ANNE [*after a pause*]. Leonard, when you can spare me a moment I should like to speak to you.

LEONARD [*eating*]. My darling, all my time is yours.

ANNE. I should like your undivided attention if I can have it.

LEONARD. Fire away, darling. I'm listening.

ANNE [*going to him*]. Have you finished your — kipper?

LEONARD. Yes, thank you.

ANNE [*she takes the plate away*]. What are you going to have next?

[*Brings plate, knife and fork from sideboard.*]

LEONARD. Well, what do you recommend? [*He sniffs violently.*]

ANNE [*taking off a cover*]. Omelette? I don't think it has any bones.

LEONARD. What's in that other dish? [*She takes off the cover.*] Kidneys? What are the kidneys like?

ANNE [*coldly*]. Well, you can see what they *look* like.

LEONARD. I mean, did you try one?

ANNE [*impatiently*]. Oh, they're delightful. I tried several.

[*Helps himself in three goes.*] There! Got the toast? Butter? [*She gives it him.*] Salt?

[*He looks for something.*] Now, what is it?

LEONARD. Pepper.

ANNE. Pepper — there. Now have you got everything?

LEONARD. Yes, thank you, my dear.

[*He picks up his knife and fork.*]

ANNE. Then, before you actually begin, I have something I want to say to you.

LEONARD. You're very mysterious. What is it?

ANNE. There is nothing mysterious about it at all. It's perfectly plain and obvious. Only I do want you to grasp it.

LEONARD. Well?

[*Sneezes.* ANNE *waits for him to finish.*]

Well?

[*He is still flourishing his handkerchief.* ANNE *waits patiently. He puts it back in his pocket.*]

Well?

ANNE. The car will be here in a quarter of an hour.

LEONARD. The car?

ANNE. The automobile.

LEONARD. But whose car?

ANNE. Ours. More accurately, yours.

LEONARD. But what for?

ANNE [*patiently. Her face down to his*]. We are running away together, dear. You and I. It had slipped your memory, perhaps, but I assure you it is a fact. The car will take us to Dover, and the boat will take us to Calais, and the train will take us to the South of France. You and I, dear — when you've finished your breakfast.

LEONARD. But what about Latimer?

ANNE. Just you and I, dear. Two of us only. The usual number. We shall not take Mr. Latimer.

LEONARD. My dear Anne, you seem quite to have forgotten that this confounded fellow, Latimer, has got us prisoners here until he chooses to let us go. [*With dignity.*] I have not forgotten. I eat his kidneys now, but he shall hear from me afterwards. Damned interference!

ANNE. Have you been dreaming, Leonard? *Before* all those kippers and kidneys and things?

LEONARD. Dreaming?

ANNE. The car will be here in a quarter of an hour. Why not? It is *your* car. This is England, this is the twentieth century. We missed the boat and spent the night here. We go on our way this morning. Why not?

LEONARD. Well, you know; I said last night it was perfectly ridiculous for Latimer to talk that way. I mean, what has it got to do with *him?* Just a bit of leg-pulling — that's what I felt all the time.... Stupid joke! [*Picking up his knife and fork.*] Bad taste, too.

ANNE [*moves to* c.]. You did hear what I said, didn't you? The car will be here in

a quarter of an hour. I don't know how long it takes you to — [*she glances him over*] — to shave — and — and dress properly, and — and brush your hair, but I fancy you ought to be thinking about it quite seriously. You can have some more kidneys another time.

LEONARD. B-but I can't possibly go like this.

ANNE. No, that's what I say.

[*Hitting her hand.*]

LEONARD. I mean, I haven't got any luggage, for one thing... and with a cold like this, I'm not at all sure —

ANNE. You've lost your luggage?

[*Leans over table.*]

LEONARD. Apparently it was left behind by ——

ANNE [*with anger*]. You let yourself be tricked and humiliated by this Mr. Latimer, you let me be humiliated; and then when I say that, whatever happens, I *won't* be humiliated, you — you lost your luggage! [*Goes* c.]

LEONARD. *I* didn't lose it. It just happens to *be* lost.

ANNE. And you catch a cold!

LEONARD. *I* didn't catch it. It caught *me.*

ANNE. The — the humiliation of it!... And now what do you propose to do?

LEONARD. As soon as my luggage turns up, and if I am well enough to travel ——

ANNE [*flings her hand out*]. Meanwhile, you accept this man's hospitality....

LEONARD. Under protest. [*Helping himself from the dish.*] I shall keep a careful account of everything that we have here.

ANNE. Well, that's your third kidney; you'd better make a note of it.

LEONARD [*with dignity*]. As it happens, I was helping myself to a trifle more bacon. ... As I say, I shall keep a careful account, and send him a cheque for our board and lodging, as soon as we have left his roof.

ANNE. Well... [*going* L.] I had some coffee and one slice of toast and a little marmalade. About a spoonful. And a cup of tea and two thin slices of bread and butter upstairs. Oh, and I've had two baths. They're extra, aren't they? A hot one last night and a cold one this morning. I think that's all. Except supper last night, and you would'nt let me finish that, so I expect there'll be a reduction.... You want a note-book with one of those little pencils in it.

[*Comes to chair c. and then up stage.*]

LEONARD [*reproachfully*]. I say, Anne, look here ——

ANNE. Do go on with your breakfast.

LEONARD. You're being awfully unfair. How can we possibly go now? Why, I haven't even got a pair of trousers to put on.

ANNE [*comes to table again*]. You're not going to say you've lost those, too!

LEONARD [*sulkily*]. It's not my fault. That fellow — what's-his-name....

ANNE [*steps back to c. up stage*]. What made you even *think* that you could take anybody to the South of France? Without any practice, at all?... [*Comes down L.C.*] If you had been taking an aunt to Hammersmith... well, you might have lost a bus or two... and your hat might have blown off ... and you would probably have found yourselves at Hampstead the first two or three times... and your aunt would have stood up the whole way... but still, you might have got there eventually. I mean, it would be worth trying — if your aunt was very anxious to get to Hammersmith. [*Goes to chair c.*] But the South of France! My dear Leonard, it's so audacious of you!

LEONARD [*annoyed*]. Now, look here, Anne ——

[MR. LATIMER *comes in cheerily, with shaving-pot, brush, safety-razor and towel, puts them on cabinet down* R. *and the towel round* LEONARD'S *shoulders.*]

LATIMER. Now then, Leonard, we'll soon have you all right. [*He puts the things down.*] Ah, Anne, you don't mind waiting while Leonard has a shave? [*Goes to her,* c.] He wanted to grow a special beard for the Continent, but I persuaded him not to. The French accent will be quite enough. [*Picking up the razor. Goes to* R. *of* LEONARD.] Do you mind Wednesday's blade? I used Tuesday's myself, this morning.

ANNE. Oh, Mr. Latimer, I find that we shall not want the car, after all.

LATIMER. No? [*Comes to her,* c.]

ANNE. No. Poor Leonard is hardly well enough to travel. I hope that by to-morrow, perhaps — but I am afraid that we must trespass on your hospitality until then. I am so sorry.

LATIMER. But I am charmed to have you. Let me tell your maid to unpack.

ANNE. Don't trouble, thanks. I've got to take my hat off. [*Very sweetly for* LATIMER'S *benefit.*] I shan't be a moment, Leonard darling. [ANNE *goes out.*]

LATIMER [*comes down* c.]. Now then, Leonard darling, to work.

[LEONARD *reluctantly lays down knife and fork, picks up the tray and moves to opening* R.]

But where are you going?

LEONARD. Upstairs, of course.

LATIMER. Is that wise — with a cold like yours?

LEONARD. Dammit, I can't shave down here!

LATIMER. Oh, come, we mustn't stand on ceremony when your life is at stake. You were complaining only five minutes ago of the draught in your room. Now, here we have a nice even temperature...

LEONARD. Well, there's something in that.

LATIMER. There's everything in it. Of course, you've never had a cold before, so you don't know; but any doctor will tell you how important it is to stay in one room with a nice even temperature. You mustn't dream of going upstairs.

LEONARD [*surrendering*]. Well ——

LATIMER. That's right. Got everything you want? There are plenty of mirrors. Which period do you prefer? Queen Anne?

LEONARD. This is all right, thanks.

LATIMER. Good! Then I'll leave you to it. [*Exit* LATIMER.

[LEONARD *butters a piece of toast, and takes it with him to a glass on the wall he applies the soap. His cheeks are just getting beautifully creamy when the* SERVANTS *enter to clear the table* ~

LEONARD *goes* C., *watches them — and eats his last bit of toast on their exit — and goes* R. *as* NICHOLAS *enters.*]

NICHOLAS [C.]. Hallo!

LEONARD [*looking round*]. Hallo!

NICHOLAS. Shaving?

LEONARD [*exasperated*]. Well, what the devil did you think I was doing?

NICHOLAS. Shaving. [*Cross* L.C.]
[LEONARD *goes on with the good work.*]

LEONARD. A-*tish*-oo!

NICHOLAS. Got a cold? [*Sitting on settee.*]

LEONARD. Obviously.

NICHOLAS [*sympathetically*]. Horrid, sneezing when you're all covered with soap.

LEONARD [*a step toward him*]. Look here, I didn't ask for your company, and I don't want your comments.

NICHOLAS. Well, if it comes to that, I was here first, and I didn't ask *you* to shave in the hall.

LEONARD [*with dignity*]. There are reasons which make it necessary for me to shave in the hall.

NICHOLAS. Don't bother to tell me. I know 'em.

LEONARD. What do you mean?

NICHOLAS. You're the couple that arrived last night?

LEONARD [*looking at him thoughtfully*]. And you're the couple that is leaving this morning?

NICHOLAS. Exactly.

LEONARD. Yes, but I don't see ——

NICHOLAS. You haven't tumbled to it yet?

LEONARD [*not understanding*]. Tumbled to what? [*Again faces mirror.*]

Nicholas. The fact that a week ago there were reasons why it was necessary for me to shave in the hall.

LEONARD. You — you don't mean ——

NICHOLAS. Yes, I do.

LEONARD. You lost your luggage?

NICHOLAS. Yes.

LEONARD. You woke up with a nasty cold?

NICHOLAS. Yes... horrid, sneezing when you're all covered with soap.

LEONARD [*excitedly*]. I say, that fellow

— what's-his-name — didn't drop *your* clothes in the bath?

NICHOLAS. Oh, rather.... Damned smart chap, Latimer!

LEONARD. Damned scoundrel!

NICHOLAS. Oh no. He's quite right. One learns a lot down here.

LEONARD. I shall leave this house at once — as soon as I have shaved.
[*Goes* R., *continues shaving.*]

NICHOLAS. You still want to?
[*Turns to him.* LEONARD *looks at him in surprise.*]
Oh, well, you've hardly been here long enough, I suppose.

LEONARD. What do you mean? Don't *you* want to any more?

NICHOLAS. Latimer's quite right, you know. One learns a lot down here.

LEONARD [*grunts, shaving*]. What about the lady?

NICHOLAS. That's the devil of it.

LEONARD. My dear fellow, as a man of honour you're bound to go on.

NICHOLAS. As a man of honour, ought I ever to have started?

LEONARD. Naturally, I can't give an opinion on that.

NICHOLAS. No.... You want to be careful with that glass. The light isn't too good. I should go over it all again.

LEONARD [*stiffly*]. I am accustomed to shaving myself, thank you.

NICHOLAS. I was just offering a little expert advice. You needn't take it.

LEONARD [*surveying himself doubtfully*]. H'm, perhaps you're right. [*He lathers himself again. In the middle of it he stops and says.*] Curious creatures, women.

NICHOLAS. Amazing.

LEONARD. It's a life's work in itself trying to understand 'em. And then you're no further.

NICHOLAS. A week told *me* all I wanted to know.

LEONARD. They're so unexpected.

NICHOLAS. So unreasonable.

LEONARD. What was it the poet said about them?

NICHOLAS. What didn't he say?

LEONARD. No. *You* know the one I

mean. How does it begin?... "O woman, in our hours of ease ——"

NICHOLAS. "Uncertain, coy and hard to please."

LEONARD. That's it. Well, I grant you *that* ——

NICHOLAS. Grant it me! I should think you do! They *throw* it at you with both hands.

LEONARD. But in the next two lines he misses the point altogether. When — what is it? — "When pain and anguish wring the brow ——"

NICHOLAS [*with feeling*]. "A ministering angel thou."

LEONARD. Yes, and it's a lie. It's simply a lie.

NICHOLAS. My dear fellow, it's the truest thing anybody ever said. Only — only one gets too much of it.

LEONARD. True? Nonsense!

NICHOLAS. Evidently you don't know anything about women.

LEONARD [*steps toward him. Indignantly*]. *I* don't know anything about women?

NICHOLAS. Well, you said yourself just now that you didn't.

LEONARD. I never said — What I said ——

NICHOLAS. If you did know anything about 'em, you'd know that there's nothing they like more than doing the ministering angel business.

LEONARD. Ministering angel!

NICHOLAS. "Won't you have a little more of this, and won't you have a little more of that, and how is the poor cold to-day — and ——?"

LEONARD. You really think that women talk like that?

NICHOLAS. How else do you think they talk?

LEONARD. My dear fellow!... Why, I mean, just take my own case as an example. [*Goes to L. end of table as* LATIMER *enters* R.] Here am I, with a very nasty cold, the first I've ever had in my life. I sit down to a bit of breakfast — not wanting it particularly, but feeling that, for the sake of my health, I ought to try and eat something. And what happens?

[LATIMER *has entered during this speech. He stops and listens to it, standing beside* LEONARD *down* R.C.]

LATIMER [*trying to guess the answer*]. You eat too much.

LEONARD [*turning round angrily*]. Ah, so it's you! You have come just in time, Mr. Latimer. I propose to leave your house at once.

LATIMER [*surprised*]. Not like that? Not with a little bit of soap just behind the ear? [LEONARD *hastily wipes it.*] The other ear. [LEONARD *wipes that one.*] That's right.

LEONARD. At once, sir.

NICHOLAS. You'd better come with us. We're just going.

LEONARD. Thank you.

LATIMER. Four of you. A nice little party.

[LATIMER *goes up* R. *and to* C., *laughing — followed by* LEONARD. ANNE *comes in* L.]

LEONARD. Anne, my dear, we are leaving the house at once. Are you ready?

ANNE [*looking from one to the other in surprise*]. But I've just taken off my hat. Besides, you can't go like that?

[NICHOLAS *rises and goes* L. LEONARD *hastily wipes his ear again.*]

LATIMER. No, no. She means the costume this time.

LEONARD. Mr. Latimer, I insist on having my clothes restored to me.

LATIMER. Wet or dry, you shall have them.

EUSTASIA [*from outside* L.]. Nich-o-las!

[LEONARD *looks up in astonishment.*]

NICHOLAS [*down* L., *gloomily*]. Hallo!

EUSTASIA. Where — are — you?

NICHOLAS. Here!

[EUSTASIA *comes in* L.]

EUSTASIA. Are you ready, darling?

[LEONARD *moves to opening* R. *She stops on seeing them all and looks from one to the other. She sees her husband.*] Leonard!

NICHOLAS [*understanding*]. Leonard!

LEONARD. Eustasia!

ANNE [*understanding*]. Eustasia!

[*They stare at each other open-*

mouthed — *all but* MR. LATIMER. *His
eyes on the ceiling, sings the "Wedding
March" tune to himself.*]
ANNE [*impatiently*]. Oh, isn't anybody
going to say anything? Mr. Latimer, while
Leonard is thinking of something, you
might introduce me to his wife.
LATIMER. I beg your pardon. Eustasia,
this is Anne.
ANNE. How do you do?
EUSTASIA. How do you do?
LATIMER. Leonard, this is Nicholas.
NICHOLAS [*nodding*]. We've met, quite
old friends.
LEONARD. I repudiate the friendship.
We met — under false pretences. I — I
— well, upon my word, I don't know *what*
to say. [*Goes down* R.]
NICHOLAS. Then don't say it, old boy.
Here we all are, and we've got to make the
best of it.
LEONARD. I — I — a-*tish*-oo!
EUSTASIA [*alarmed. Crosses to him down
R.*]. Leonard, you have a cold?
NICHOLAS. A very nasty cold.
ANNE [*coldly*]. It will be better when he
has finished his breakfast.
LEONARD [*hurt*]. I *have* finished my
breakfast. A long time ago.
ANNE. I beg your pardon. [*She indi-
cates the towel round his neck.*] I misunder-
stood.
LEONARD [*pulling it away, throws it on
cabinet* R.]. I've been shaving.
EUSTASIA. But, Leonard dear, I don't
understand. I've never known you ill
before.
LEONARD. I never have been ill before.
But I *am* ill now. Very ill. And nobody
minds. Nobody minds, at all. This fellow, Latimer, invaygles me here ——
LATIMER. Inveegles.
LEONARD. I shall pronounce it how I
like. It is quite time I asserted myself. I
have been too patient. You invaygle me
here ——
LATIMER. I still think inveegle is better.
LEONARD. — and purposely give me a
cold. You [*pointing accusingly to* ANNE]
are entirely unmoved by my sufferings,
instead of which you make fun of the
very simple breakfast which I had forced

myself to eat. You [*to* NICHOLAS] run
away with my wife, at a time when I am
ill and unable to protect her, and you [*to*
EUSTASIA]... well, all I can say is, that
you surprise me, Eustasia, you surprise
me; I didn't think you had it in you.
LATIMER. A masterly summing-up of the
case. Well, I hope you're all ashamed of
yourselves.
EUSTASIA. But, Leonard, how rash of
you to *think* of running away with a cold
like this. [*She goes up and comforts him.*]
You must take care of yourself — Eustasia
will take care of you, and get you well.
Poor boy! He had a nasty, nasty cold, and
nobody looked after him. Mr. Latimer, I
shall want some mustard, and hot water,
and eucalyptus ——

[*Enter* DOMINIC C.]

LATIMER. But, of course!
[LEONARD *up stage* R.C. EUSTASIA R.]
LEONARD [*goes to* ANNE]. There you
are! As soon as somebody who really
understands illness comes on the scene, you
see what happens. Mustard, hot water,
eucalyptus — she has it all at her fingers'
ends.
DOMINIC [C.]. Yes, sir?
LATIMER [*down* L.C.]. A small mustard
and water for his lordship.
EUSTASIA. It's to put his feet in, not to
drink.
LATIMER. A large mustard and water.
DOMINIC. Yes, sir.
EUSTASIA. Hot water.
DOMINIC. Yes, my lady.
EUSTASIA. And if you have any euca-
lyptus ——
DOMINIC. Yes, my lady, we got some
in specially for his lordship.
LATIMER. Did Mr. Nicholas absorb all
the last bottle?
DOMINIC. Yes, sir.
NICHOLAS [L. *with feeling*]. I fairly lived
on it.
DOMINIC [*to* EUSTASIA]. Is there any-
thing else his lordship will require?
NICHOLAS. What about a mustard-
plaster?
LEONARD. You kindly mind your own
business.

EUSTASIA. No, I don't think there's anything else, thank you.

NICHOLAS. Well, I call it very unfair. I had one.

LEONARD. Oh, did you? Well, in that case, Eustasia, I certainly don't see why ——

LATIMER [to DOMINIC]. Two mustard plasters. We mustn't grudge his lordship anything.

DOMINIC. Yes, sir. [DOMINIC retires.]

[EUSTASIA and LEONARD cross to L. down stage.]

EUSTASIA [to LEONARD]. Now, come over here, darling, near the fire. Lean on me.

ANNE. Surely one can walk with a cold in the head!

NICHOLAS. No, it's very dangerous.

[Goes up L.]

LATIMER. Nicholas speaks as an expert.

EUSTASIA [settling LEONARD]. There! Is that comfy?

LEONARD. Thank you, Eustasia.

EUSTASIA. We'll soon have you all right, dear.

LEONARD [pressing her hand]. Thank you.

LATIMER [after a little silence]. Well, as Nicholas said just now, "Here we all are, and we've got to make the best of it." What are we all going to do?

ANNE. Please leave me out of it. I can make my own arrangements.

[She gives them a cool, little bow as she crosses L. NICHOLAS opens door for her.]

If you will excuse me. [She goes out.]

[DOMINIC comes in with a clinical thermometer on a tray, C.]

DOMINIC. I thought that her ladyship might require a thermometer for his lordship's temperature.

EUSTASIA [coming to him, C.]. Thank you. I think it would be safe just to take it. And I wondered if we couldn't just put this screen round his lordship's chair.

DOMINIC. Certainly, my lady. One can't be too careful.

[DOMINIC goes to get screen up L. NICHOLAS is attempting to get it, but

DOMINIC snaps it together and comes down L. with it.]

EUSTASIA. Yes, that's right.

[LATIMER to NICHOLAS, who crosses to him up R.C.]

LATIMER. Did you have the screen?

NICHOLAS. Oh, rather.

LATIMER. And the thermometer?

NICHOLAS. Yes... funny thing was, I liked it just at first. I don't mean the actual thermometer. I mean all the fussing.

LATIMER. It's a wonderful invention, a cold in the head. It finds you out. There's nothing like it, Nicholas, nothing.

EUSTASIA [to DOMINIC]. Thank you. And you're bringing the other things?

DOMINIC [crosses C. and up]. Yes, my lady, as soon as ready.

[DOMINIC goes out C.]

EUSTASIA. Thank you. [To LEONARD.] Now, dear. Under the tongue.

[He puts it in his mouth.]

LEONARD [mumbling]. I don't think I ever ——

EUSTASIA. No, dear, don't try to talk.

NICHOLAS [coming close to LATIMER, who has dropped to table R.]. I say ——

LATIMER. Well?

NICHOLAS [indicating the screen]. I say — not too loud.

LATIMER [in a whisper]. Well?

NICHOLAS. Well, what about it?

LATIMER. What about what?

NICHOLAS. I mean, where do I come in?

[NICHOLAS takes LATIMER up R.]

As a man of honour, oughtn't I to — er — you see what I mean? Of course, I want to do the right thing.

LATIMER. Naturally, my dear Nicholas. It's what one expected of you.

[NICHOLAS brings LATIMER down to table R. again.]

NICHOLAS. I thought that if I slipped away now, unostentatiously ——

LATIMER. With just a parting word of farewell ——

NICHOLAS. Well, that was what I was wondering. Would anything in the nature of a farewell be in good taste?

LATIMER. I see your point.

NICHOLAS. Don't think that I'm not just as devoted to Eustasia as ever I was.

LATIMER. But you feel that in the circumstances you could worship her from afar with more propriety.

NICHOLAS [waving a hand at the screen]. Yes. You see, I had no idea that they were so devoted.

LATIMER. But their devotion may not last for ever.

NICHOLAS. Exactly! That's why I thought I'd slip away now.

LATIMER. Oh, Nicholas! Oh, Nicholas!

NICHOLAS [a little offended]. Of course, I don't want to say anything against Eustasia ——

LATIMER. But the whole house is full of people who don't want to say anything against Eustasia. [Goes to c.]

NICHOLAS. But, you see —— Look out, here's Miss Anne.

[ANNE comes in, L.]

LATIMER. Anne, you're just in time. Nicholas wants your advice.

NICHOLAS. I say, shut up! We can't very well ——

ANNE. Mr. Latimer, I went upstairs to get my things and find my way to the nearest railway station. But — but there is a reason why I am not going, after all, just yet. I thought I'd better tell you.

LATIMER. Were you really thinking of going? [She nods.] I'm so glad you've changed your mind.

ANNE [with a smile]. There are reasons why I had to.

LATIMER. Bless them... Nicholas, I believe she stayed just so that she might help you.

ANNE. What does Mr. Nicholas want?
[Cross to NICHOLAS up R.]

NICHOLAS. I say, it's awfully good of you and all that, but this is rather — I mean, it's a question that a fellow ought to settle for himself.

LATIMER. What he means is, ought he to get his things and find his way to the nearest railway station?

ANNE [dismayed]. Oh no!

LATIMER. There you are, Nicholas!

NICHOLAS [rather flattered]. Oh, well —

well —— [He looks at her admiringly.] Well, perhaps you're right.

EUSTASIA [the three minutes up]. There!
[She takes the thermometer out and comes from behind the screen to c.]

LATIMER. His temperature! An exciting moment in the history of the House of Lords. [He comes down to EUSTASIA.]

NICHOLAS [to ANNE]. I say, do you really think I ought to stay?

ANNE. Please, Mr. Nicholas, I want you to stay.

NICHOLAS. Right-oh — then I'll stay.

LATIMER [over EUSTASIA'S shoulder]. A hundred and nine.

LEONARD [putting his head round the screen]. I say, what ought it to be?

NICHOLAS [coming down R.C.]. Ninety-eight.

LEONARD. Good Lord, I'm dying!

EUSTASIA. Just ninety-nine. A little over normal, Leonard, but nothing to matter.

LATIMER. Ninety-nine — so it is. I should never have forgiven myself if it had been a hundred and nine.

NICHOLAS [coming up to LATIMER]. It's all right, I'm going to.

EUSTASIA [surprised]. Going to? Going to what?

NICHOLAS [confused]. Oh, nothing.

LATIMER. What he means is, that he is going to be firm. He thinks we all ought to have a little talk about things. Just to see where we are.

EUSTASIA. Well, things aren't quite as they were, are they? If I'd known that Leonard was ill — but I've seen so little of him lately. And he's never been ill before.

NICHOLAS. Of course, we ought to know where we are.

LATIMER. Yes. At present, Leonard is behind that screen, which makes it difficult to discuss things properly. Leonard, could you ——

EUSTASIA. Oh, we mustn't take any risks. I think I might just move the screen back for a moment.

[Does so and arranges hood of gown over LEONARD'S head and goes and sits in settee.]

LATIMER. Delightful!

NICHOLAS. Sit here, Miss Anne, won't you?

[*They arrange themselves.* ANNE R. *of table,* LATIMER C. *of table.* LATIMER *indicates the other chair to* NICHOLAS, *who moves into it.*]

LATIMER [*behind table*]. There! Now, are we all here?... We are. Then with your permission, ladies and gentlemen, I will open the proceedings with a short speech.

NICHOLAS. Oh, I say, must you?

LATIMER. Certainly.

EUSTASIA [*to* LEONARD]. Hush, dear.

LEONARD. I didn't say anything.

EUSTASIA. No, but you were just going to.

LATIMER [*severely*]. Seeing that I refrained from making my speech when Leonard had the thermometer in his mouth, the least he can do now is to listen in silence.

LEONARD. Well, I'm ——

[*Attempts to rise.* EUSTASIA *stops him with a gesture.*]

LATIMER. I resume. [*Sits.*] By a fortunate concatenation of circumstances, ladies and gentlemen — or, as more illiterate men would say, by a bit of luck — two runaway couples have met under my roof. No need to mention names. You can all guess for yourselves. But I call now — this is the end of my speech, Leonard — I call upon my noble friend over there to tell us just why he left the devoted wife by his side in order to travel upon the Continent.

LEONARD. Well, really ——

LATIMER. Naturally, Leonard does not wish to say anything against Eustasia. Very creditable to him. But can it be that the devoted wife by his side wishes to say anything against Leonard?

EUSTASIA. You neglected me, Leonard, you know you did. And when I was so ill ——

LEONARD. My dear, you were *always* ill. That was the trouble.

LATIMER. And you were never ill, Leonard. *That* was the trouble... you heartless ruffian!

EUSTASIA [*to* LEONARD]. Hush, dear.

LATIMER. Why couldn't you have had a cold sometimes? Why couldn't you have come home with a broken leg, or lost all your money, or made a rotten speech in the House of Lords? If she could never be sorry for *you,* for whom else could she be sorry except herself? [*To* EUSTASIA.] I don't suppose he even lost his umbrella, did he?

ANNE. Oh, he must have lost that.

LATIMER. Eustasia, ladies and gentlemen, is one of those dear women, one of those sweet women, one of those delightful women — [*aside to* ANNE] — stop me if I'm overdoing it — one of those adorable women who must always cosset or be cossetted. She couldn't cosset Leonard! Leonard wouldn't cosset her. Hence — the Dover Road.

EUSTASIA. How well you understand, Mr. Latimer!

LATIMER. Enter, then, my friend Nicholas —— [*Shaking his head at* NICHOLAS.] Oh, Nicholas! Oh, Nicholas! Oh, Nicholas! [*Face in hands.*]

NICHOLAS [*uneasily*]. What's all that about?

LATIMER. Anything you say will be used in evidence against you. Proceed, my young friend.

NICHOLAS. Well — well — well, I mean, there she was.

LATIMER. Lonely.

NICHOLAS. Exactly.

LATIMER. Neglected by her brute of a husband. [*As* LEONARD *opens his mouth.*] Fingers crossed, Leonard — who spent day and night rioting in the House of Lords while his poor little wife cried at home.

NICHOLAS. Well ——

LATIMER. Then out spake bold Sir Nicholas —— [*Aside to* ANNE.] This was also composed in my bath —

> Then out spake bold Sir Nicholas,
> An Oxford man was he:
> "Lo, I will write a note to-night
> And ask her out to tea."

NICHOLAS. Well, you see ——

LATIMER. I see, Nicholas... and so here we all are.

ANNE. Except me.

LATIMER. I guessed at you, Anne. You remember? Did I guess right?

ANNE. Yes.

LATIMER. And so here we all are... and what are we all going to do? My house is at your disposal for as long as you wish. The doors are open for those who wish to go... Eustasia?

EUSTASIA. My duty is to stay here — to look after my husband.

LATIMER. Well, that settles Eustasia... Anne?

ANNE. Of necessity, I must stay here — for the present.

LATIMER. Well, that settles Anne... Nicholas?

NICHOLAS. I stay here, too — [looking at ANNE] — from choice.

LATIMER. Well, that settles Nicholas... Leonard?

[DOMINIC, followed by ALL THE STAFF, men first, comes in C., together with a collection of mustard bath, plasters, eucalyptus, etc., etc.]

LATIMER [looking round at the interrupters]. Ah!... And this will settle Leonard.

[The bath and towel are laid at LEONARD'S feet. EUSTASIA takes one tray and NICHOLAS the other, which they deposit also as STAFF continue up L. and exit C.]

CURTAIN

ACT III

Three days later and evening again.

[ANNE is standing busy with some coins and a pencil and paper, an A.B.C. and her purse.]

ANNE. Three and fourpence ha'penny.

[Sits. She is trying to work out how much it costs to go home, and subtracting three and fourpence ha'penny from it. Having done this, she puts the paper, pencil and the purse in her bag.]

[Rises.] One pound two shillings and sixpence. [She goes toward the opening R. One gathers that she has come to a decision. Calling.] Nich-o-las!

NICHOLAS [from outside]. Hallo!

ANNE. Where — are — you?

NICHOLAS. Coming.

[Enter NICHOLAS. She goes C.]

Just went upstairs to get a pipe. [Putting his hand to his pocket.] And now I've forgotten it.

ANNE. Oh, Nicholas, how silly you are.
[She sits down in settee.]

NICHOLAS [sitting on arm of settee.] I don't want to smoke, you know.

ANNE. I thought men always did.

NICHOLAS. Well, it depends what they're doing.

[There is no doubt what HE is doing. He is making love to ANNE, the dog, and ANNE is encouraging him.]

ANNE [looking away]. Oh!

NICHOLAS. I say, it has been rather jolly here the last three days, don't you think?

ANNE [looking out front]. It has been rather nice.

NICHOLAS. We've sort of got friendly.

ANNE. We have, haven't we?

NICHOLAS. You've been awful nice to me.

ANNE [looks at him]. You've been nice to me.

NICHOLAS. I should have gone, you know, if it hadn't been for you.

ANNE [looking front]. I don't know what I should have done if you had gone.

NICHOLAS. You did ask me to stay, didn't you?

ANNE [looks at him]. Yes. I couldn't let you go.

NICHOLAS. Do you know what you said? You said, "Please, Mr. Nicholas, I want you to stay." [Her eyes drop.] I shall always remember that [lovingly to himself.] "Please, Mr. Nicholas, I want you to stay." I wonder what made you think of saying that. [Leaning over her.]

ANNE. I wanted us to be friends. I wanted to get to know you, to make you think of me as — as your friend.

NICHOLAS. We are friends, Anne, aren't we?

ANNE. I think we are now, Nicholas.

NICHOLAS [with a sentimental air]. Friends!

[ANNE, *wondering if she shall risk it, summons up her courage and takes the plunge.*]

ANNE. Nicholas!

NICHOLAS. Yes?

ANNE [*timidly*]. I — I want you to do something for me.

NICHOLAS. Anything, Anne, anything.

ANNE. I don't know whether I ought to ask you ——

NICHOLAS. Of course, you ought!

ANNE. But you see, we *are* friends — [*looks at him*] — almost like brother and sister ——

NICHOLAS [*disappointed*]. Well, I shouldn't put it quite like that ——

ANNE. And I thought I might ask you ——

NICHOLAS. Of course, Anne. You know I would do anything for you.

ANNE. Yes... Well — well — [*in a rush*] — well, then, will you lend me one pound two shillings and sixpence till next Monday? [*Hands clenched and pushed forward.*]

NICHOLAS [*flabbergasted*]. Lend you ——!

ANNE. To-day's Friday. I'll send you the money off on Sunday, I promise. Of course, I know one oughtn't to borrow money from men, but you're different. Almost like a brother. I knew you would understand.

NICHOLAS [*rises, turns away from her*]. But — but — I *don't* understand.

ANNE [*ashamed*]. You see, I — I only have three and fourpence ha'penny, and it costs one pound five and tenpence to get home. [*Indignantly.*] Oh, it is a shame the way men always pay for us, and then when we really want money we haven't got any.... [*Turns to him.*] But I *will* pay you back on Sunday. I have some money at home; I meant to have brought it.

NICHOLAS. But — but why do you suddenly ——

ANNE [*draws back*]. Suddenly? I've been wanting it ever since that first morning. I went upstairs to get my hat, meaning to walk straight out of the house — and then I looked in my purse and found — [*pathetically*] — three and fourpence ha'penny. What was I to do?

NICHOLAS. Any one would have lent you anything.

ANNE [*coldly*]. Leonard, for instance?

NICHOLAS [*thoughtfully*]. Well — no.... No. You couldn't very well have touched Leonard. But, Latimer ——

ANNE [*scornfully*]. Mr. Latimer! The man who had brought us here, locked us up here, and started playing Providence to us — I was to go on my knees to *him* and say, "Please, dear Mr. Latimer, would you lend me one pound two shillings and sixpence, so that I may run away from your horrid house." Really!

NICHOLAS. Well, you seem to have been pretty friendly with him these three days.

ANNE. Naturally, I am polite to a man when I am staying in his house. That's different.

NICHOLAS. As a matter of fact, Latimer has been jolly decent. Anyway, he has saved us both from making silly asses of ourselves.

ANNE [*scornfully*]. And you think I am grateful to him for *that*?... Doesn't *any* man understand *any* woman?

NICHOLAS [*annoyed*]. Are you suggesting that *I* don't understand women?

ANNE. I'm suggesting that you should lend me one pound two shillings and sixpence.

NICHOLAS [*sulkily, feeling in his pockets. Turning away*]. Of course, if you're in such a confounded hurry to get away from here — do you mind all silver?

ANNE [*eagerly*]. Not at all.

NICHOLAS. In such a confounded hurry to get away from here ——

[*He counts the money.*]

ANNE. Why ever should I want to stay?

NICHOLAS. Well — Well —— [*With a despairing shrug.*] Oh, lord! Ten shillings — fourteen and six — why should she want to stay. [*To* ANNE.] Why do you think *I'm* staying?

ANNE [*unkindly*]. Because you're so fond of Mr. Latimer. He's so jolly decent.

NICHOLAS [*looking at the money in his hand*]. One pound two shillings and sixpence. I suppose, if I told you what I really thought about it all, you'd get on your high horse again and refuse the

money from *me*.... So I won't tell you.
Here you are.

ANNE [*gently*]. You didn't think I was
in love with you, Nicholas?

[NICHOLAS *looks uncomfortable.*]
In three days? Oh, Nicholas!

NICHOLAS. Well — well, I don't see ——
[*Holding out the money.*] Here you are.

ANNE. From a friend?

NICHOLAS. From a friend.

ANNE. Lent to a friend?

NICHOLAS. Lent to a friend.

ANNE [*rises. Grabs money*]. Thank
you, Nicholas. [*She runs to the door* L.,
exit, and comes in again.] Thank you very
much, Nicholas. [*Exit* ANNE.]

NICHOLAS. Well, I'm damned!

[*He sits in settee gloomily, his legs
stretched out and regards his shoes.
As far as we can tell, he goes on saying:
"Well, I'm damned" to himself.*
EUSTASIA *and* LEONARD *come in* C.
from L. — *she* R. *of him. He is properly dressed now, but still under*
EUSTASIA'S *care, and she has his arm, as
if he were attempting a very difficult feat
in walking across the hall.*]

NICHOLAS [*looking round*]. Hallo!
[*Getting up.*] Do you want to come here?

LEONARD [*hastily*]. Don't go, old boy,
don't go. Plenty of room for us all.

EUSTASIA [*puts* LEONARD *in settee. To*
NICHOLAS]. Thank you so much. Leonard is not very strong yet. His temperature is up again to-day. [*To* LEONARD.]
You will be better on the sofa, darling.
[*To* NICHOLAS.] I'm so sorry to trouble
you.

NICHOLAS. Not at all. I was just going,
anyhow. [*Feeling in his pockets.*] Got to
get my pipe. Left it upstairs, like an
ass.

LEONARD [*taking out his case*]. Have a
cigarette instead?

NICHOLAS. Rather have a pipe, thanks.
[*He makes for the opening* R.]

LEONARD [*anxiously*]. But you'll come
back? [*She crosses to* L. *of* LEONARD.]

NICHOLAS [*unwillingly*]. Oh — er —
right-oh. [*Exit* NICHOLAS.]

LEONARD. Come and keep us company.
To EUSTASIA, *who is piling cushions behind*

him.] Thanks, Eustasia, thanks. That's
quite all right.

EUSTASIA. Another cushion for your
back, darling?

LEONARD. No, thanks.

EUSTASIA. Quite sure?

LEONARD. Quite sure, thanks.

EUSTASIA. I can easily get it for you.

LEONARD [*weakly*]. Oh, very well.

EUSTASIA. That's right. [*Getting the
cushion from chair* L.] You *must* be comfortable. Now, are you sure *that's* all right?

LEONARD. Quite all right, thank you.

EUSTASIA. Sure, darling? Anything else
you want, I can get it for you at once. A
rug over your knees?

LEONARD. No, thank you, Eustasia.

EUSTASIA. You wouldn't like a hot-water
bottle?

LEONARD [*with a sigh*]. No, thank you,
Eustasia.

EUSTASIA. You've only got to say, you
know. Now shall we talk, or would you
like me to read to you?

LEONARD [*choosing the lesser evil*]. I
think read — no, I mean talk — no, read
to me.

EUSTASIA [*rising*]. It's for you to say,
darling.

LEONARD [*his eyes closed*]. Read to me,
Eustasia.

EUSTASIA [*gets book from table behind
settee. Opening her book*]. We'll go on
from where we left off. We didn't get very
far — I marked the place... [*Sits.*] Yes,
here we are — "...the sandy desert of
Arabia and Africa, 4." And then there's a
little footnote at the bottom; that's how I
remember it. [*Reading the footnote.*]
"Tacit. Annal. 1. ii. Dion Cassius 1. lvi, p.
833, and the speech of Augustus himself."
That doesn't seem to mean much. "It
receives great light from the learned notes
of his French translator M. Spanheim."
Well, that's a good thing. Spanheim —
sounds more like a German, doesn't it?
Now, are you sure you're quite comfortable,
dear? [*Hitting cushion, which disturbs him.*]

LEONARD [*his eyes closed*]. Yes, thank
you, Eustasia.

EUSTASIA. Then I'll begin. [*In her
reading-aloud voice.*] "Happily for the

repose of mankind, the moderate system recommended by the wisdom of Augustus, was adopted by the fears and vices of his immediate successors. Engaged in the pursuit of pleasure or the exercise of tyranny, the first Cæsars seldom showed themselves to the armies, or to the provinces; nor were they disposed to suffer that those triumphs which their indolence neglected should be usurped by the conduct and valour of their lieutenants. [*Speeding up.*] The military fame of a subject was considered as an insolent invasion of the Imperial prerogative; and it became the duty as well as interest of every Roman general to guard the frontiers entrusted to his care — [*recklessly*] — without aspiring to conquests which might have proved no less fatal to himself than to the vanquished barbarians." ... And then there's another footnote. Perhaps it would be better if I read all the footnotes afterwards — what do you think, darling? Or shall we take them as they come?

LEONARD [*without opening his eyes*]. Yes, dear.

EUSTASIA. Very well. This is footnote 5. "Germanicus, Suetonius Paulinus and Agril — and Agriloca" — [*she stumbles over the name*] — "were checked and recalled in the course of their victories. Corbulo was put to death." Oh, poor Corbulo, what a shame! "Military merit, as it is admirably expressed by Tacitus, was, in the strictest sense of the word ——" Well, there are *two* words, and they are both in Latin. I suppose Tacitus wrote in Latin. But it doesn't really matter, because it's only a footnote. [*Anxiously.*] Are you liking the book, darling?

LEONARD. Very much, dear.

EUSTASIA. It's nicely written, but I don't think it's very exciting. I don't think Mr. Latimer has a very good taste in books. I asked him to recommend me something *really* interesting to read aloud, and he said that the two most interesting books he knew were Carlyle's *French Revolution* and — and — [*looking at the cover*] — Gibbon's *Roman Empire....* Fancy, there are four volumes of it and six hundred pages in a volume. We're at

page four now. [*She reads a line or two to herself.*] Oh, now this *is* rather interesting, because it's all about *us.* "The only accession which the Roman Empire received during the first century of the Christian Era was the province of Britain." Fancy! "The proximity of its situation to the coast of Gaul seemed to invite their arms; the pleasing, though doubtful intelligence, of a pearl fishery, attracted their avarice." And then there's another little footnote — I suppose that's to say it was Whitstable. [*Getting to it.*] Oh no. "The British pearls proved, however, little value, on account of their dark and livid colour." How horrid. "Tacitus observes ——" Well, then Tacitus says something again... I *wish* he would write in English. Now, where was I? Something about the pearls. Oh yes. "After a war of about forty years" — good gracious! — "undertaken by the most stupid, maintained by the most dissolute, and ——"

[NICHOLAS *returns with his pipe,* R.]

NICHOLAS. Oh, sorry; I'm interrupting.

LEONARD [*waking up*]. No, no; Eustasia was just reading to me. [*To* EUSTASIA.] You mustn't tire yourself, dear. [*To* NICHOLAS.] Stay and talk.

NICHOLAS [*comes* C.]. What's the book? Carlyle's *French Revolution?*

EUSTASIA [*primly*]. Certainly not. [*Looking at the title again.*] Gibbon's *Roman Empire.*

NICHOLAS. Any good?

EUSTASIA. Fascinating. Isn't it, Leonard?

LEONARD. Very.

NICHOLAS. You ought to try Carlyle, old chap.

LEONARD. Is *he* good?

NICHOLAS [*who has had eight pages read aloud to him by* EUSTASIA]. Oh, topping.

EUSTASIA [*looking at his wrist watch*]. Good gracious! I ought to be dressing.

LEONARD [*looking at his watch*]. Yes, it is about time.   [*Attempts to rise*

NICHOLAS. Yes.

EUSTASIA. Now, Leonard darling, don't think it would be safe for you to change. Not to-night. To-morrow if you like.

LEONARD. I say, look here, you said that last night.

EUSTASIA. Ah, but your temperature has gone up again.

NICHOLAS. I expect that's only because the book was so exciting.

LEONARD. Yes, that's right.

EUSTASIA. But I took his temperature *before* I began reading.

NICHOLAS. Perhaps yesterday's instalment was still hanging about a bit.

EUSTASIA [*to* LEONARD]. No, darling, not to-night. Just to please Eustasia.

LEONARD [*sulkily*]. Oh, all right.

EUSTASIA. That's a good boy. Now stay here, and perhaps if he's very good and his Eustasia dresses very quickly, he shall have just a little more of that nice book before dinner.

[*She walks to the door* L., NICHOLAS *going with her to open it. He crosses as if to exit* R.]

LEONARD. I say, don't go, old chap. You can change in five minutes.

NICHOLAS. Right-oh.

[*Comes down and sits on table* R.C. *There is silence for a little.*]

LEONARD. I say.

NICHOLAS. Yes?

LEONARD [*thinking better of it*]. Oh, nothing.

NICHOLAS [*after a pause*]. Curious creatures, women.

LEONARD. Amazing.

NICHOLAS. They're so unexpected.

LEONARD. So unreasonable.

NICHOLAS. Yes...

LEONARD [*suddenly throwing cushions from behind him*]. I *hate* England at this time of year.

NICHOLAS. So do I.

LEONARD. Do you go South, as a rule?

NICHOLAS. As a rule.

LEONARD. Monte?

NICHOLAS. Sometimes. We had thought — I half thought of Nice this year.

LEONARD. Not bad. We were — I think I prefer Cannes, myself.

NICHOLAS. There's not much in it.

LEONARD. No.... [*After a pause.*] Between ourselves, you know — quite between ourselves — I'm about fed up with women.

NICHOLAS. Absolutely.

LEONARD. You are, too.

NICHOLAS. Rather. I should think so.

LEONARD. They're so dashed unreasonable.

NICHOLAS. So unexpected....

LEONARD [*pause, then suddenly*]. Had you booked your rooms?

NICHOLAS. At Nice? Yes.

LEONARD. So had I.

NICHOLAS. At Cannes?

LEONARD. Yes.... [*An idea comes to him — rises and goes* C., *beckoning* NICHOLAS.] I say, what about it?

[*He waves a hand at the door.*]

NICHOLAS. Do you mean ——?

LEONARD. Yes.

NICHOLAS. Evaporating?

LEONARD. Yes. Quite quietly, you know.

NICHOLAS. Without ostentation.

LEONARD. That's it.

NICHOLAS. It's rather a scheme. And then we shouldn't waste the rooms. At least, only one set of them. I'll tell you what. I'll toss you whether we go to Nice or Cannes.

LEONARD. Right.

[*He takes out a coin and tosses.*]

NICHOLAS. Tails.

LEONARD [*uncovering the coin*]. Heads! Do you mind coming to Cannes?

NICHOLAS. Just as soon, really. When shall we go? To-morrow?

LEONARD. Mightn't get a chance to-morrow. Why not to-night? It seems a pity to waste the opportunity.

NICHOLAS. You mean while she's dressing?

LEONARD. The opportunity. We can sleep the night at Dover and cross to-morrow morning.

NICHOLAS. She'll be after us.

LEONARD. Nonsense!

NICHOLAS. My dear chap, you don't know Eustasia.

LEONARD. I don't know Eustasia? Well!

NICHOLAS [*with conviction*]. She'll be after you like a bird. You've never seen Eustasia when she has got somebody ill to look after.

LEONARD. I've never seen Eustasia? Well!

NICHOLAS. My dear chap, you've only had three days of her; I had six.... Lord! ... Look here, we shall have to ——

[*Enter* LATIMER, R.]

LATIMER. What, Leonard, all alone?

NICHOLAS [*turns to him*]. I say, you're the very man we want.

LEONARD [*frowning*]. S'sh!

[*Hits* NICHOLAS *and crosses* L.C.]

LATIMER [*comes* C.]. Leonard, don't shish Nicholas when he wants to speak to me.

NICHOLAS [*to* LEONARD]. It's all right, old chap. Latimer is a sportsman.

LATIMER [*to* LEONARD]. There! You see the sort of reputation I have in the West End. [*To* NICHOLAS.] What is it you want to do? Run away?

LEONARD. Well — er ——

NICHOLAS. I say, however did you guess?

LATIMER. Leonard's car has had steam up for the last twenty-four hours, waiting for a word from its owner.

LEONARD [*seeing the South of France*]. By Jove!

LATIMER. And you are going with him, Nicholas?

NICHOLAS. Yes. Thought I might as well be getting on. Very grateful and all that, but can't stay here for ever.

LATIMER [*wondering what has happened between* NICHOLAS *and* ANNE]. So you are going, too. I thought —— Well! [*He is obviously a little excited by the realization that* NICHOLAS *means nothing to* ANNE.] Nicholas is going, too!

LEONARD. I say, you do understand — I mean about — [*indicates* EUSTASIA] — I mean, when I'm quite well again — start afresh and all that. Cosset *her* a bit. But when you're ill — or supposed to be ill — well, I mean, ask Nicholas.

NICHOLAS. Oh, rather.

LATIMER. My dear Leonard, why all these explanations? Who am I to interfere in other people's matrimonial affairs? You and Nicholas are going away — good-bye!

[*He holds out his hand.*]

NICHOLAS. Yes, but what about Eustasia? She's not going to miss the chance of cossetting Leonard just when she is getting into it. She'll be after him like a bird.

LATIMER. I see. So you want me to keep her here?

NICHOLAS. That's the idea; if you could.

LATIMER. How can I keep her here if she doesn't want to stay?

LEONARD. Well, how do you keep *any*body here?

LATIMER. Really, Leonard, I am surprised at you. By the charm of my old-world courtesy and hospitality, of course.

LEONARD. Oh! Well, I doubt if that keeps Eustasia.

LATIMER [*shaking his head sadly*]. I am afraid that that is only too true. In fact, the more I think of it, the more I realize that there is only one thing which will keep this devoted wife from her afflicted and suffering husband.

LEONARD *and* NICHOLAS. What?

[DOMINIC *comes in* C.]

LATIMER. Dominic, his lordship and Mr. Nicholas are leaving at once. His lordship's car will wait for them outside the gates. See that a bag is packed for them.

DOMINIC. Yes, sir.

LATIMER. And come back when you've seen about that.

DOMINIC. Yes, sir. [DOMINIC *exit*, R.]

LATIMER. The car can return here for the rest of your luggage, and take it over in the morning.

NICHOLAS. Good!

LEONARD. Er — thanks. [*Anxiously.*] What were you going to say about the only way of — er ——

LATIMER. The only way of keeping this devoted wife from her afflicted and suffering husband?

LEONARD. Yes. What is it?

LATIMER. Somebody else must have a temperature. Somebody else must be ill. Eustasia must have somebody else to cosset.

NICHOLAS. I say, how awfully sporting of you!

LATIMER. Sporting?

NICHOLAS. To sacrifice yourself like that

LATIMER. I? You don't think *I* am going to sacrifice myself, do you? No, no, it's Dominic.

[DOMINIC *coming in*, R.]

DOMINIC. Yes, sir.   [LATIMER *goes* L.]

LATIMER. Dominic, are you ever ill?

DOMINIC. Never, sir, barring a slight shortness of the breath!

LATIMER [*to the others*]. That's awkward. I don't think you can cosset a shortness of the breath.

NICHOLAS [*to* DOMINIC]. I say, you could pretend to be ill, couldn't you?

DOMINIC. With what object, sir?

NICHOLAS [*awkwardly*]. Well — er ——

LEONARD. You see ——

[DOMINIC *turns his eyes on him*.]

Oh!

LATIMER. Her ladyship is training to be a nurse. She has already cured two very obstinate cases of nasal catarrh, accompanied by debility and a fluctuating temperature. If she brings one more case off successfully, she not only earns the diploma but the gold medal of the Royal Therapeutical Society.

NICHOLAS. The Royal Thera ——

DOMINIC. — peutical, sir.

NICHOLAS. That's right.

LEONARD. Yes, that's right.

DOMINIC. And you would wish me to be that third case, sir?

LEONARD. That's the idea.

DOMINIC. And be cosseted back to health again by her ladyship.

LATIMER. Such would be your inestimable privilege.

DOMINIC. I am sorry, sir; I must beg respectfully to decline.

NICHOLAS. I say, be a sport.

LEONARD [*awkwardly*]. Of course, we should — naturally, you would not — er — ose anything by — er ——

LATIMER. His lordship wishes to imply that, not only would your mental horizon be widened during the period of convalescence, but that material blessings would also flow. Isn't that right, Leonard?

LEONARD. Yes, that's it!

NICHOLAS. A commission on the gold medal. Naturally.

DOMINIC. I am sorry, sir; I am afraid I cannot see my way.

NICHOLAS *and* LEONARD. I say ——

LATIMER. Thank you, Dominic.

DOMINIC. Thank you, sir.

[*Exit* DOMINIC C.]

[LATIMER *goes up* L.   NICHOLAS *moves to* R.]

NICHOLAS. Well, that's torn it.   [*To* LATIMER.] If you're quite sure that *you* wouldn't like to have a go? It's the chance of a lifetime to learn all about the French Revolution.

LATIMER [*comes down* C.]. Well, well! [*He realizes that if* EUSTASIA *goes*, ANNE *goes*.] Something must be done. [*He smiles suddenly*.] After all, why not?

LEONARD [*eagerly*]. You will?

LATIMER. I will.

NICHOLAS. I say ——

LATIMER [*waving them off*]. No, no. Don't wait. Fly!

LEONARD. Yes, we'd better be moving. Come on!   [*Runs to opening* R.]

NICHOLAS [*turning to* LATIMER]. There's an awfully good bit in the second chapter ——

LATIMER [*holding up a finger*]. Listen! I hear her coming.

LEONARD. Good Lord!   [*They fly*, R.]

[LATIMER, *left alone, gives himself up to thought. He goes* L.   DOMINIC *comes in*, C.]

LATIMER. Oh, Dominic, in consequence of your obstinate good health, I am going to sacrifice myself for — I mean I myself am going to embrace this great opportunity of mental and spiritual development.

DOMINIC. Yes, sir. Very good of you, I'm sure, sir.

LATIMER. What sort of illness would you recommend?

DOMINIC. How about a nice sprained ankle, sir?

LATIMER. You think that would go well?

DOMINIC. It would avoid any interference with the customary habits at mealtimes, sir. That's a sort of monotony about bread-and-milk; no inspiration about it, sir, whether treated as a beverage or as a comestible.

LATIMER. I hadn't thought about bread-and-milk.

DOMINIC. You'll find that you will have little else to think about, sir, if you attempt anything stomachic. Of course, you could have the usual nasty cold, sir.

LATIMER. No, no, not that. Let us be original....

DOMINIC. How about Xerostomia, sir? Spelt with an X.

LATIMER. Is that good?

DOMINIC. Joseph tells me that his father has had it for some years.

LATIMER. Oh! then perhaps we oughtn't to deprive him of it.

DOMINIC. I looked it up in the dictionary one Sunday afternoon, sir. They describe it there as "an abnormal dryness of the mouth."

[*The four* SERVANTS *enter and lay table as at opening of play.*]

LATIMER. I said I wanted to be original, Dominic.

DOMINIC. Quite so, sir.

LATIMER. It's a difficult problem.

DOMINIC. Very difficult, sir — very knotty, if I may say so.

LATIMER. Perhaps it would be better if I left it to the inspiration of the moment.

DOMINIC. Yes, sir.

EUSTASIA [*off*]. Leonard — Leonard.

DOMINIC. This appears to be the moment, sir.

LATIMER. But the inspiration tarries. Just go to her ladyship, Dominic — while I — while I — think.

DOMINIC. Yes, sir.

LATIMER. Any little delaying observation you could make to her about the weather or the political situation ——

DOMINIC. Leave it to me, sir.

LATIMER. Just to keep her attention while I assume a recumbent position.

[*He arranges cushions in settee. Exit* DOMINIC C. *to* R., *followed by* SERVANTS, *who go* L.]

[LATIMER *lies down at full length on the sofa and begins to groan; putting a hand first on his stomach, then on his elbow, then on his head. He looks up cautiously; the room is empty.*]

LATIMER [*disappointedly*]. Throwing it away! [*He hears footsteps and settles down again.*]

[ANNE *comes in* L., *hat on, bag in hand. She is* C. *when a groan reaches her. She stops. Another groan comes. She comes toward the sofa with an "Oh!" of anxiety.*]

ANNE [*alarmed*]. What is it? [*She kneels by him.*]

LATIMER [*cheerfully*]. Hallo, Anne, is it you? [*He sits up.*]

ANNE [*she gets up*]. Yes, what is it?

LATIMER [*bravely*]. Oh, nothing, nothing. A touch of neuralgia.

ANNE. Oh ... you frightened me.

LATIMER [*much more pleased about this than he ought to be*]. Did I, Anne? I'm sorry.

ANNE. You were groaning so, I thought — I didn't know *what* had happened.... [*Sympathetically.*] Is it very bad?

LATIMER. Not so bad as it sounded, Anne.

ANNE. I know how bad it can be; father has it sometimes. Then I have to send it away. May I try?

[*Behind couch, pulls him back.*]

LATIMER [*remorsefully*]. Anne!

[*She leans over from the back of him, and begins to stroke his forehead with the tips of her fingers. He looks up at her.*]

ANNE. Close your eyes.

LATIMER. Ah, but that's so difficult now.

ANNE. It will go soon.

LATIMER. Not too soon....

ANNE. Aren't faces funny when they're upside down?

LATIMER. You have the absurdest little upside-down face that ever I saw, Anne.

ANNE [*laughing a little*]. Have I?

LATIMER. Why do you wear a hat on your chin? [*She laughs.*]

LATIMER. Why do you wear a hat?

ANNE. I was going away.

LATIMER. Without saying good-bye?

ANNE [*ashamed*]. I — I think so.

LATIMER. Oh, Anne!

ANNE [*hastily*]. I should have written.

LATIMER. A post-card.

ANNE. A letter.

LATIMER. With many thanks for your kind hospitality. Yours sincerely.

ANNE. Yours *very* sincerely.

LATIMER. P.S. I shall never see you again.

ANNE. P.S. I shall never forget.

LATIMER. Ah, but you *must* forget....

ANNE [*after a pause*]. Is it better?

LATIMER. No. [*Lazily.*] It is just the same. It will always be the same. It is unthinkable that anything different should ever happen. In a hundred years' time we shall still be like this. You will be a little tired, perhaps; your fingers will ache; but I shall be lying here, quite, quite happy.

ANNE. You shall have another minute — no more.

LATIMER. Then I shall go straight to the nearest chemist and ask for threepenny-worth of Anne's fingers, please.

[*They are silent for a little. Then she stops and listens, hearing LEONARD and NICHOLAS whisper, off R.*]

What is it?

ANNE. I thought I heard something. Whispers.

[*He takes her hand and pulls her round to end of settee.*]

LATIMER. Don't look round.

[LEONARD *and* NICHOLAS, *in hats and coats, creep cautiously in. Very noise-lessly, fingers to lips, they open the front door and creep out.*]

ANNE. What was it? Was it ——?

LATIMER. Yes, an episode in your life. Over, buried, forgotten....

ANNE. It never really happened, did it?

LATIMER. Never. We must have read about it somewhere; or was it in a play?

ANNE. Yes, that was it — we were in a box together.

LATIMER. Munching chocolates. Such a child she was. Do you remember how she made us laugh with her little grown-up ways?

DOMINIC *comes in* C. *from* L. *and stops suddenly on seeing them.*]

DOMINIC. I beg your pardon, sir.

[ANNE *goes down* R.C.]

LATIMER. Go on, Anne. [*Happily.*] I was having neuralgia, Dominic.

DOMINIC [C.]. A stubborn complaint, as I have heard, sir.

LATIMER. Miss Anne is making me well. ... What did you want, Dominic?

DOMINIC. Her ladyship says, will you please excuse her if she is not down to-night.

LATIMER [*to* ANNE]. Shall we excuse her if she is not down to-night?

DOMINIC. The fact is, sir, that Joseph is taken suddenly ill, sir, and ——

LATIMER [*to himself*]. I never thought of Joseph! [*Rises, goes down* L.]

ANNE. Oh, poor Joseph! What is it?

DOMINIC. A trifling affection of the throat, but necessitating careful attention, her ladyship says.

LATIMER [*goes toward* ANNE]. Please tell her ladyship how very much I thank her for looking after Joseph... and tell Joseph how very sorry I am for him.

DOMINIC. Yes, sir. [*He goes out* C.]

LATIMER. You can't go now, Anne. You will have to stay and chaperon Eustasia and me.

[*She laughs and shakes her head.*]

ANNE. No.

LATIMER. Must you go?

ANNE. Yes.

LATIMER. Back to your father?

ANNE. Yes.

LATIMER. Then — let us say good-bye now. There is a magic in your fingers which goes to my head and makes me think ridiculous things. Let us say good-bye now.

ANNE [*taking his hand*]. Good-bye. I wish *you* had been my father. [*Exit* L.]

[MR. LATIMER *stands there, wondering how he likes this. He walks across to a mirror,* L., *to have a look at himself. While he is there,* DOMINIC *comes in.*]

LATIMER [*at the mirror*]. Dominic, how old would you say I was?

DOMINIC. More than that, sir.

LATIMER [*with a sigh*]. Yes, I'm afraid I am. And yet I look very young. Sometimes I think I look too young.

DOMINIC. Yes, sir.

LATIMER. Miss Anne has just asked me to be her father.

DOMINIC. Very considerate of her, I'm sure, sir.

LATIMER. Yes ... to prevent similar mistakes in the future, I think I shall wear a long white beard.

DOMINIC. Yes, sir. Shall I order one from the Stores?

LATIMER. Please.

DOMINIC. Thank you, sir. Is Miss Anne leaving to-night, sir?

LATIMER. Yes.... Don't overdo the length, Dominic, and I like the crinkly sort.

DOMINIC. Yes, sir.... One of our most successful weeks, on the whole, if I may say so, sir. [*Finger and thumb holding coat.*]

LATIMER [*thoughtfully*]. Yes... yes....

Well, well, we must all do what we can, Dominic.

DOMINIC. That's the only way, isn't it, sir?

[*Doorbell rings as* LATIMER *and* DOMINIC *face audience, smiling.* LATIMER *exit,* R.]

[DOMINIC *goes up* C. *and opens the big front door. A* LADY *and* GENTLEMAN, *in motoring costume, enter.*]

A VOICE. Oh — er — is this — er — an hotel?

DOMINIC. A sort of hotel, your Grace.

A VOICE. My chauffeur said — we've had an accident, been delayed on the way — he said that ——

[*And in the middle of this the curtain comes down.*]

JUNO AND THE PAYCOCK
A TRAGEDY IN THREE ACTS
By SEAN O'CASEY

THE CHARACTERS IN THE PLAY

"CAPTAIN" JACK BOYLE

JUNO BOYLE, *his wife*

JOHNNY BOYLE } *their children*

MARY BOYLE

"JOXER" DALY   *Residents in the Tenement*

MRS. MAISIE MADIGAN

"NEEDLE" NUGENT, *a tailor*

MRS. TANCRED

JERRY DEVINE

CHARLIE BENTHAM, *a school teacher*

AN IRREGULAR MOBILIZER

TWO IRREGULARS

A COAL-BLOCK VENDOR

A SEWING MACHINE MAN

TWO FURNITURE REMOVAL MEN

TWO NEIGHBOURS

SCENE

A few days elapse between Acts I and II, and two months between Acts II and III. During Act III the curtain is lowered for a few minutes to denote the lapse of one hour. Period of the play, 1922.

JUNO AND THE PAYCOCK

ACT I

The living room of a two-room tenancy occupied by the BOYLE *family in a tenement house in Dublin. Left, a door leading to another part of the house; left of door a window looking into the street; at back a dresser; farther to right at back, a window looking into the back of the house. Between the window and the dresser is a picture of the Virgin; below the picture, on a bracket, is a crimson bowl in which a floating votive light is burning. Farther to the right is a small bed partly concealed by cretonne hangings strung on a twine. To the right is the fireplace; near the fireplace is a door leading to the other room. Beside the fireplace is a box containing coal. On the mantelshelf is an alarm clock lying on its face. In a corner near the window looking into the back is a galvanized bath. A table and some chairs. On the table are breakfast things for one. A teapot is on the hob and a frying-pan stands inside the fender. There are a few books on the dresser and one on the table. Leaning against the dresser is a long-handled shovel — the kind invariably used by labourers when turning concrete or mixing mortar.* JOHNNY BOYLE *is sitting crouched beside the fire.* MARY *with her jumper off — it is lying on the back of a chair — is arranging her hair before a tiny mirror perched on the table. Beside the mirror is stretched out the morning paper, which she looks at when she isn't gazing into the mirror. She is a well-made and good-looking girl of twenty-two. Two forces are working in her mind — one, through the circumstances of her life, pulling her back, the other, through the influence of books she has read, pushing her forward. The opposing forces are apparent in her speech and her manners, both of which are degraded by her environment, and improved by her acquaintance — slight though it be — with literature. The time is early forenoon.*

MARY [*looking at the paper*]. On a little bye-road, out beyant Finglas, he was found.

[MRS. BOYLE *enters by door on right; she has been shopping and carries a small parcel in her hand. She is forty-five years of age, and twenty years ago she must have been a pretty woman; but her face has now assumed that look which ultimately settles down upon the faces of the women of the working-class: a look of listless monotony and harassed anxiety, blending with an expression of mechanical resistance. Were circumstances favourable, she would probably be a handsome, active and clever woman.*]

MRS. BOYLE. Isn't he come in yet?

MARY. No, mother.

MRS. BOYLE. Oh, he'll come in when he likes; struttin' about the town like a paycock with Joxer, I suppose. I hear all about Mrs. Tancred's son is in this mornin's paper.

MARY. The full details are in it this mornin'; seven wounds he had — one enthcrin' the neck, with an exit wound beneath the left shoulder-blade; another in the left breast penethratin' the heart, an'...

JOHNNY [*springing up from the fire*]. Oh, quit that readin', for God's sake! Are yous losin' all your feelin's? It'll soon be that none of yous'll read anythin' that's not about butcherin'!

[*He goes quickly into the room on left.*]

MARY. He's gettin' very sensitive, all of a sudden!

MRS. BOYLE. I'll read it myself, Mary, by an' by, when I come home. Everybody's sayin' that he was a die-hard — thanks be to God that Johnny had nothin' to do with him this long time.... [*Opening the parcel and taking out some sausages, which she places on a plate.*] Ah, then, if

that father o' yours doesn't come in soon
for his breakfast, he may go without any;
I'll not wait much longer for him.

MARY. Can't you let him get it himself
when he comes in?

MRS. BOYLE. Yes, an' let him bring in
Joxer Daly along with him? Ay, that's
what he'd like, an' that's what he's waitin'
for — till he thinks I'm gone to work, an'
then sail in with the boul' Joxer, to burn all
the coal an' dhrink all the tea in the place,
to show them what a good Samaritan he is!
But I'll stop here till he comes in, if I have
to wait till to-morrow mornin'.

VOICE OF JOHNNY INSIDE. Mother!

MRS. BOYLE. Yis?

VOICE OF JOHNNY. Brings us in a dhrink
o' wather.

MRS. BOYLE. Bring in that fella a
dhrink o' wather, for God's sake, Mary.

MARY. Isn't he big an' able enough to
come out an' get it himself?

MRS. BOYLE. If you weren't well yourself you'd like somebody to bring you in a
dhrink o' wather.

[*She brings in drink and returns.*]

MRS. BOYLE. Isn't it terrible to have to
be waitin' this way! You'd think he was
bringin' twenty poun's a week into the
house the way he's going on. He wore out
the Health Insurance long ago, he's afther
wearin' out the unemployment dole, an',
now, he's thryin' to wear out me! An'
constantly singin', no less, when he ought
always to be on his knees offerin' up a
Novena for a job!

MARY [*tying a ribbon, fillet-wise around
her head*]. I don't like this ribbon, ma; I
think I'll wear the green — it looks betther
than the blue.

MRS. BOYLE. Ah, wear whatever ribbon
you like, girl, only don't be botherin' me.
I don't know what a girl on strike wants to
be wearin' a ribbon round her head for or
silk stockin's on her legs either; it's wearin'
them things that make the employers
think they're givin' yous too much money.

MARY. The hour is past now when we'll
ask the employers' permission to wear
what we like.

MRS. BOYLE. I don't know why you
wanted to walk out for Jennie Claffey; up

to this you never had a good word for
her.

MARY. What's the use of belongin' to a
Trades Union if you won't stand up for
your principles? Why did they sack her?
It was a clear case of victimization. We
couldn't let her walk the streets, could we?

MRS. BOYLE. No, of course yous
couldn't — yous wanted to keep her company. Wan victim wasn't enough. When
the employers sacrifice wan victim, the
Trades Unions go wan betther be sacrificin'
a hundred.

MARY. It doesn't matther what you say,
ma — a principle's a principle.

MRS. BOYLE. Yis; an' when I go into oul'
Murphy's to-morrow, an' he gets to know
that, instead o' payin' all, I'm goin' to
borry more, what'll he say when I tell him
a principle's a principle? What'll we do if
he refuses to give us any more on tick?

MARY. He daren't refuse — if he does,
can't you tell him he's paid?

MRS. BOYLE. It's lookin' as if he was
paid, whether he refuses or no.

[JOHNNY *appears at the door on left. He
can be plainly seen now; he is a thin
delicate fellow, something younger than*
MARY. *He has evidently gone through
a rough time. His face is pale and
drawn; there is a tremulous look of
indefinite fear in his eyes. The left
sleeve of his coat is empty, and he walks
with a slight halt.*]

JOHNNY. I was lyin' down; I thought
yous were gone. Oul' Simon Mackay is
thrampin' about like a horse over me head,
an' I can't sleep with him — they're like
thunder-claps in me brain! The curse o' —
God forgive me for goin' to curse!

MRS. BOYLE. There, now; go back an' lie
down agan, an' I'll bring you in a nice cup
o' tay.

JOHNNY. Tay, tay, tay! You're always
thinkin' o' tay. If a man was dyin', you'd
thry to make him swally a cup o' tay!

[*He goes back.*]

MRS. BOYLE. I don't know what's goin'
to be done with him. The bullet he got in
the hip in Easter Week was bad enough, but
the bomb that shatthered his arm in the

fight in O'Connell Street put the finishin' touch on him. I knew he was makin' a fool of himself. God knows I went down on me bended knees to him not to go agen the Free State.

MARY. He stuck to his principles, an', no matther how you may argue, ma, a principle's a principle.

VOICE OF JOHNNY. Is Mary goin' to stay here?

MARY. No, I'm not goin' to stay here; you can't expect me to be always at your beck an' call, can you?

VOICE OF JOHNNY. I won't stop here be meself!

MRS. BOYLE. Amn't I nicely handicapped with the whole o' yous! I don't know what any o' yous ud do without your ma. [To JOHNNY.] Your father'll be here in a minute, an' if you want anythin', he'll get it for you.

JOHNNY. I hate assin' him for anythin'.... He hates to be assed to stir.... Is the light lightin' before the picture o' the Virgin?

MRS. BOYLE. Yis, yis! The wan inside to St. Anthony isn't enough, but he must have another wan to the Virgin here!

[JERRY DEVINE enters hastily. He is about twenty-five, well set, active and earnest. He is a type, becoming very common now in the Labour Movement, of a mind knowing enough to make the mass of his associates, who know less, a power, and too little to broaden that power for the benefit of all. MARY seizes her jumper and runs hastily into room left.]

JERRY [breathless]. Where's the Captain, Mrs. Boyle; where's the Captain?

MRS. BOYLE. You may well ass a body that: he's wherever Joxer Daly is — dhrinkin' in some snug or another.

JERRY. Father Farrell is just afther stoppin' to tell me to run up an' get him to go to the new job that's goin' on in Rathmines; his cousin is foreman o' the job, an' Father Farrell was speakin' to him about poor Johnny an' his father bein' idle so long, an' the foreman told Father Farrell to send the Captain up an' he'd give

him a start — I wondher where I'd find him?

MRS. BOYLE. You'll find he's ayther in Ryan's or Foley's.

JERRY. I'll run round to Ryan's — I know it's a great house o' Joxer's.

[He rushes out.]

MRS. BOYLE [piteously]. There now, he'll miss that job, or I know for what! If he gets win' o' the word, he'll not come back till evenin', so that it'll be too late. There'll never be any good got out o' him so long as he goes with that shouldhershruggin' Joxer. I killin' meself workin', an' he sthruttin' about from mornin' till night like a paycock!

[The steps of two persons are heard coming up a flight of stairs. They are the footsteps of CAPTAIN BOYLE and JOXER. CAPTAIN BOYLE is singing in a deep, sonorous, self-honouring voice.]

THE CAPTAIN. Sweet Spirit, hear me prayer! Hear... oh... hear... me prayer ... hear, oh, hear... Oh, he... ar... oh, ho... ar... me... pray... er!

JOXER [outside]. Ah, that's a darlin' song, a daaarlin' song!

MRS. BOYLE [viciously]. Sweet spirit hear his prayer! Ah, then, I'll take me solemn affeydavey, it's not for a job he's prayin'!

[She sits down on the bed so that the cretonne hangings hide her from the view of those entering.]

[THE CAPTAIN comes slowly in. He is a man of about sixty; stout, grey-haired and stocky. His neck is short, and his head looks like a stone ball that one sometimes sees on top of a gate-post. His cheeks, reddish-purple, are puffed out, as if he were always repressing an almost irrepressible ejaculation. On his upper lip is a crisp, tightly cropped moustache; he carries himself with the upper part of his body slightly thrown back, and his stomach slightly thrust forward. His walk is a slow, consequential strut. His clothes are dingy, and he wears a faded seaman's cap with a glazed peak.]

BOYLE [*to* JOXER, *who is still outside*]. Come on, come on in, Joxer, she's gone out long ago, man. If there's nothing else to be got, we'll furrage out a cup o' tay, anyway. It's the only bit I get in comfort when she's away. 'Tisn't Juno should be her pet name at all, but Deirdre of the Sorras, for she's always grousin'.

[JOXER *steps cautiously into the room. He may be younger than* THE CAPTAIN *but he looks a lot older. His face is like a bundle of crinkled paper; his eyes have a cunning twinkle; he is spare and loosely built; he has a habit of constantly shrugging his shoulders with a peculiar twitching movement, meant to be ingratiating. His face is invariably ornamented with a grin.*]

JOXER. It's a terrible thing to be tied to a woman that's always grousin'. I don't know how you stick it — it ud put years on me. It's a good job she has to be so often away, for [*with a shrug*] when the cat's away, the mice can play!

BOYLE [*with a commanding and complacent gesture*]. Pull over to the fire, Joxer, an' we'll have a cup o' tay in a minute.

JOXER. Ah, a cup o' tay's a darlin' thing, a daaarlin' thing — the cup that cheers but doesn't...

[JOXER'S *rhapsody is cut short by the sight of* JUNO *coming forward and confronting the two cronies. Both are stupefied.*]

MRS. BOYLE [*with sweet irony — poking the fire, and turning her head to glare at* JOXER]. Pull over to the fire, Joxer Daly, an' we'll have a cup o' tay in a minute! Are you sure, now, you wouldn't like an egg?

JOXER. I can't stop, Mrs. Boyle; I'm in a desperate hurry, a desperate hurry.

MRS. BOYLE. Pull over to the fire, Joxer Daly; people is always far more comfortabler here than they are in their own place.

[JOXER *makes hastily for the door.* BOYLE *stirs to follow him; thinks of something to relieve the situation — stops, and says suddenly.*]

Joxer!

JOXER [*at door ready to bolt*]. Yis?

BOYLE. You know the foreman o' that job that's goin' on down in Killesther, don't you, Joxer?

JOXER [*puzzled*]. Foreman — Killesther?

BOYLE [*with a meaning look*]. He's a butty o' yours, isn't he?

JOXER [*the truth dawning on him*]. The foreman at Killesther — oh yis, yis. He's an oul' butty o' mine — oh, he's a darlin' man, a daarlin' man.

BOYLE. Oh, then, it's a sure thing. It's a pity we didn't go down at breakfast first thing this mornin' — we might ha' been working now; but you didn't know it then.

JOXER [*with a shrug*]. It's betther late than never.

BOYLE. It's nearly time we got a start, anyhow; I'm fed up knockin' round, doin' nothin'. He promised you — gave you the straight tip?

JOXER. Yis. "Come down on the blow o' dinner," says he, "an' I'll start you, an' any friend you like to brin' with you." Ah, says I, you're a darlin' man, a daaarlin' man.

BOYLE. Well, it couldn't come at a betther time — we're a long time waitin' for it.

JOXER. Indeed we were; but it's a long lane that has no turnin'.

BOYLE. The blow up for dinner is at one — wait till I see what time it 'tis.

[*He goes over to the mantelpiece, and gingerly lifts the clock.*]

MRS. BOYLE. Min' now, how you go on fiddlin' with that clock — you know the least little thing sets it asthray.

BOYLE. The job couldn't come at a betther time; I'm feelin' in great fettle, Joxer. I'd hardly believe I ever had a pain in me legs, an' last week I was nearly crippled with them.

JOXER. That's betther an betther; ah, God never shut wan door but he opened another!

BOYLE. It's only eleven o'clock; we've lashins o' time. I'll slip on me oul' moleskins afther breakfast, an' we can saunther down at our ayse. [*Putting his hand on the shovel.*] I think, Joxer, we'd betther bring our shovels?

JOXER. Yis, Captain, yis; it's betther to go fully prepared an' ready for all eventualities. You bring your long-tailed shovel, an' I'll bring me navvy. We mighten' want them, an', then agen, we might: for want of a nail the shoe was lost, for want of a shoe the horse was lost, an' for want of a horse the man was lost — aw, that's a darlin' proverb, a daarlin'...

[As JOXER *is finishing his sentence*, MRS. BOYLE *approaches the door and* JOXER *retreats hurriedly. She shuts the door with a bang.*]

BOYLE [*suggestively*]. We won't be long pullin' ourselves together agen when I'm working for a few weeks.

[MRS. BOYLE *takes no notice.*]

BOYLE. The foreman on the job is an oul' butty o' Joxer's; I have an idea that I know him meself. [*Silence.*]... There's a button off the back o' me moleskin trousers.... If you leave out a needle an' thread I'll sew it on meself.... Thanks be to God, the pains in me legs is gone, anyhow!

MRS. BOYLE [*with a burst*]. Look here, Mr. Jacky Boyle, them yarns won't go down with Juno. I know you an' Joxer Daly of an oul' date, an', if you think you're able to come it over me with them fairy tales, you're in the wrong shop.

BOYLE [*coughing subduedly to relieve the tenseness of the situation*]. U-u-u-ugh.

MRS. BOYLE. Butty o' Joxer's! Oh, you'll do a lot o' good as long as you continue to be a butty o' Joxer's!

BOYLE. U-u-u-ugh.

MRS. BOYLE. Shovel! Ah, then, me boyo, you'd do far more work with a knife an' fork than ever you'll do with a shovel! If there was e'er a genuine job goin' you'd be dh'other way about — not able to lift your arms with the pains in your legs! Your poor wife slavin' to keep the bit in your mouth, an' you gallivantin' about all the day like a paycock!

BOYLE. It ud be betther for a man to be dead, betther for a man to be dead.

MRS. BOYLE [*ignoring the interruption*]. Everybody callin' you "Captain," an' you only wanst on the wather, in an oul' collier from here to Liverpool, when anybody, to listen or look at you, ud take you for a second Christo For Columbus!

BOYLE. Are you never goin' to give us a rest?

MRS. BOYLE. Oh, you're never tired o' lookin' for a rest.

BOYLE. D'ye want to dhrive me out o' the house?

MRS. BOYLE. It ud be easier to dhrive you out o' the house than to dhrive you into a job. Here, sit down an' take your breakfast — it may be the last you'll get, for I don't know where the next is goin' to come from.

BOYLE. If I get this job we'll be all right.

MRS. BOYLE. Did ye see Jerry Devine?

BOYLE [*testily*]. No, I didn't see him.

MRS. BOYLE. No, but you seen Joxer. Well, he was here lookin' for you.

BOYLE. Well, let him look!

MRS. BOYLE. Oh, indeed, he may well look, for it ud be hard for him to see you, an' you stuck in Ryan's snug.

BOYLE. I wasn't in Ryan's snug — I don't go into Ryan's.

MRS. BOYLE. Oh, is there a mad dog there? Well, if you weren't in Ryan's you were in Foley's.

BOYLE. I'm telling you for the last three weeks I haven't tasted a dhrop of intoxicatin' liquor. I wasn't in ayther wan snug or dh'other — I could swear that on a prayer-book — I'm as innocent as the child unborn!

MRS. BOYLE. Well, if you'd been in for your breakfast you'd ha' seen him.

BOYLE [*suspiciously*]. What does he want me for?

MRS. BOYLE. He'll be back any minute an' then you'll soon know.

BOYLE. I'll dhrop out an' see if I can meet him.

MRS. BOYLE. You'll sit down an' take your breakfast, an' let me go to me work, for I'm an hour late already waitin' for you.

BOYLE. You needn't ha' waited, for I'll take no breakfast — I've a little spirit left in me still!

MRS. BOYLE. Are you goin' to have your breakfast — yes or no?

BOYLE [*too proud to yield*]. I'll have no

breakfast — yous can keep your breakfast. [*Plaintively.*] I'll knock out a bit somewhere, never fear.

MRS. BOYLE. Nobody's goin' to coax you — don't think that.

[*She vigorously replaces the pan and the sausages in the press.*]

BOYLE. I've a little spirit left in me still.

[JERRY DEVINE *enters hastily.*]

JERRY. Oh, here you are at last! I've been searchin' for you everywhere. The foreman in Foley's told me you hadn't left the snug with Joxer ten minutes before I went in.

MRS. BOYLE. An' he swearin' on the holy prayer-book that he wasn't in no snug!

BOYLE [*to* JERRY]. What business is it o' yours whether I was in a snug or no? What do you want to be gallopin' about afther me for? Is a man not to be allowed to leave his house for a minute without havin' a pack o' spies, pimps an' informers cantherin' at his heels?

JERRY. Oh, you're takin' a wrong view of it, Mr. Boyle; I simply was anxious to do you a good turn. I have a message for you from Father Farrell: he says that if you go to the job that's on in Rathmines, an' ask for Foreman Mangan, you'll get a start.

BOYLE. That's all right, but I don't want the motions of me body to be watched the way an asthronomer ud watch a star. If you're folleyin' Mary aself, you've no pereeogative to be folleyin' me. [*Suddenly catching his thigh.*] U-ugh, I'm afther gettin' a terrible twinge in me right leg!

MRS. BOYLE. Oh, it won't be very long now till it travels into your left wan. It's miraculous that whenever he scents a job in front of him, his legs begin to fail him! Then, me bucko, if you lose this chance, you may go an' furrage for yourself!

JERRY. This job'll last for some time too, Captain, an' as soon as the foundations are in, it'll be cushy enough.

BOYLE. Won't it be a climbin' job? How d'ye expect me to be able to go up a ladder with these legs? An', if I get up aself, how am I goin' to get down agen?

MRS. BOYLE [*viciously*]. Get wan o' the labourers to carry you down in a hod!

You can't climb a laddher, but you can skip like a goat into a snug!

JERRY. I wouldn't let meself be let down that easy, Mr. Boyle; a little exercise, now, might do you all the good in the world.

BOYLE. It's a docthor you should have been, Devine — maybe you know more about the pains in me legs than meself that has them?

JERRY [*irritated*]. Oh, I know nothin' about the pains in your legs; I've brought the message that Father Farrell gave me, an' that's all I can do.

MRS. BOYLE. Here, sit down an' take your breakfast, an' go an' get ready; an' don't be actin' as if you couldn't pull a wing out of a dead bee.

BOYLE. I want no breakfast, I tell you; it ud choke me afther all that's been said. I've a little spirit left in me still.

MRS. BOYLE. Well, let's see your spirit, then, an' go in at wanst an' put on your moleskin trousers!

BOYLE [*moving towards the door on left*]. It ud be betther for a man to be dead! U-ugh! There's another twinge in me other leg! Nobody but meself knows the sufferin' I'm goin' through with the pains in these legs o' mine!

[*He goes into the room on left as* MARY *comes out with her hat in her hand.*]

MRS. BOYLE. I'll have to push off now, for I'm terrible late already, but I was determined to stay an' hunt that Joxer this time. [*She goes off.*]

JERRY. Are you going out, Mary?

MARY. It looks like it when I'm putting on my hat, doesn't it?

JERRY. The bitther word agen, Mary.

MARY. You won't allow me to be friendly with you; if I thry, you deliberately misundherstand it.

JERRY. I didn't always misundherstand it; you were ofen delighted to have the arms of Jerry around you.

MARY. If you go on talkin' like this, Jerry Devine, you'll make me hate you!

JERRY. Well, let it be either a weddin' or a wake! Listen, Mary, I'm standin' for the Secretaryship of our Union. There's only one opposin' me; I'm popular with all the men, an' a good speaker — all are sayin' that I'll get elected.

MARY. Well?

JERRY. The job's worth three hundred an' fifty pounds a year, Mary. You an' I could live nice an' cosily on that; it would lift you out o' this place an'...

MARY. I haven't time to listen to you now — I have to go.

[*She is going out when* JERRY *bars the way.*]

JERRY [*appealingly*]. Mary, what's come over you with me for the last few weeks? You hardly speak to me, an' then only a word with a face o' bitterness on it. Have you forgotten, Mary, all the happy evenin's that were as sweet as the scented hawthorn that sheltered the sides o' the road as we sauntered through the country?

MARY. That's all over now. When you get your new job, Jerry, you won't be long findin' a girl far betther than I am for your sweetheart.

JERRY. Never, never, Mary! No matther what happens you'll always be the same to me.

MARY. I must be off; please let me go, Jerry.

JERRY. I'll go a bit o' the way with you.

MARY. You needn't, thanks; I want to be by meself.

JERRY [*catching her arm*]. You're goin' to meet another fella; you've clicked with some one else, me lady!

MARY. That's no concern o' yours, Jerry Devine; let me go!

JERRY. I saw yous comin' out o' the Cornflower Dance Class, an' you hangin' on his arm — a thin, lanky strip of a Micky Dazzler, with a walkin'-stick an' gloves!

VOICE OF JOHNNY [*loudly*]. What are you doin' there — pullin' about everything!

VOICE OF BOYLE [*loudly and viciously*]. I'm puttin' on me moleskin trousers!

MARY. You're hurtin' me arm! Let me go, or I'll scream, an' then you'll have the oul' fella out on top of us!

JERRY. Don't be so hard on a fella, Mary, don't be so hard.

BOYLE [*appearing at the door*]. What's the meanin' of all this hillabaloo?

MARY. Let me go, let me go!

BOYLE. D'ye hear me — what's all this hillabaloo about?

JERRY [*plaintively*]. Will you not give us one kind word, one kind word, Mary?

BOYLE. D'ye hear me talkin' to yous? What's all this hillabaloo for?

JERRY. Let me kiss your hand, your little, tiny, white hand!

BOYLE. Your little, tiny, white hand — are you takin' leave o' your senses, man?

[MARY *breaks away and rushes out.*]

BOYLE. This is nice goin's on in front of her father!

JERRY. Ah, dhry up, for God's sake!

[*He follows* MARY.]

BOYLE. Chiselurs don't care a damn now about their parents, they're bringin' their fathers' grey hairs down with sorra to the grave, an' laughin' at it, laughin' at it. Ah, I suppose it's just the same everywhere — the whole worl's in a state o' chassis! [*He sits by the fire.*] Breakfast! Well, they can keep their breakfast for me. Not if they went down on their bended knees would I take it — I'll show them I've a little spirit left in me still! [*He goes over to the press, takes out a plate and looks at it.*] Sassige! Well, let her keep her sassige. [*He returns to the fire, takes up the teapot and gives it a gentle shake.*] The tea's wet right enough.

[*A pause; he rises, goes to the press, takes out the sausage, puts it on the pan, and puts both on the fire. He attends the sausage with a fork.*]

BOYLE [*singing*].

When the robins nest agen,
And the flowers are in bloom,
When the Springtime's sunny smile seems to
    banish all sorrow an' gloom;
Then me bonny blue-ey'd lad, if me heart be true
    till then —
He's promised he'll come back to me,
When the robins nest agen!

[*He lifts his head at the high note, and then drops his eyes to the pan.*]

BOYLE [*singing*]. When the...

[*Steps are heard approaching; he whips the pan off the fire and puts it under the bed, then sits down at the fire. The door opens and a bearded man looking in says:*]

You don't happen to want a sewin' machine?

BOYLE [*furiously*]. No, I don't want e'er a sewin' machine!

[*He returns the pan to the fire, and commences to sing again.*]

BOYLE [*singing*].

When the robins nest agen,
And the flowers they are in bloom,
He's . . .

[*A thundering knock is heard at the street door.*]

BOYLE. There's a terrible tatheraraa — that's a stranger — that's nobody belongin' to the house. [*Another loud knock.*]

JOXER [*sticking his head in at the door*]. Did ye hear them tatherarahs?

BOYLE. Well, Joxer, I'm not deaf.

JOHNNY [*appearing in his shirt and trousers at the door on left; his face is anxious and his voice is tremulous*]. Who's that at the door; who's that at the door? Who gave that knock — d'ye yous hear me — are yous deaf or dhrunk or what?

BOYLE [*to* JOHNNY]. How the hell do I know who 'tis? Joxer, stick your head out o' the window an' see.

JOXER. An' mebbe get a bullet in the kisser? Ah, none o' them thricks for Joxer! It's betther to be a coward than a corpse!

BOYLE [*looking cautiously out of the window*]. It's a fella in a thrench coat.

JOHNNY. Holy Mary, Mother o' God, I. . .

BOYLE. He's goin' away — he must ha' got tired knockin'.

[JOHNNY *returns to the room on left.*]

BOYLE. Sit down an' have a cup o' tay, Joxer.

JOXER. I'm afraid the missus ud pop in on us agen before we'd know where we are. Somethin's tellin' me to go at wanst.

BOYLE. Don't be superstitious, man; we're Dublin men, an' not boyos that's only afther comin' up from the bog o' Allen — though if she did come in, right enough, we'd be caught like rats in a thrap.

JOXER. An' you know the sort she is —

she wouldn't listen to reason — an' wanse bitten twice shy.

BOYLE [*going over to the window at back*]. If the worst came to the worst, you could dart out here, Joxer; it's only a dhrop of a few feet to the roof of the return room, an' the first minute she goes into dh'other room, I'll give you the bend, an' you can slip in an' away.

JOXER [*yielding to the temptation*]. Ah, I won't stop very long anyhow. [*Picking up a book from the table.*] Whose is the buk?

BOYLE. Aw, one o' Mary's; she's always readin' lately — nothin' but thrash, too. There's one I was lookin' at dh'other day: three stories, The Doll's House, Ghosts, an' The Wild Duck — buks only fit for chiselurs!

JOXER. Didja ever rade *Elizabeth, or Th' Exile o' Sibayria*. . . ah, it's a darlin' story, a daarlin' story!

BOYLE. You eat your sassige, an' never min' *Th' Exile o' Sibayria*.

[*Both sit down;* BOYLE *fills out tea, pours gravy on* JOXER'S *plate, and keeps the sausage for himself.*]

JOXER. What are you wearin' your moleskin trousers for?

BOYLE. I have to go to a job, Joxer. Just afther you'd gone, Devine kem runnin' in to tell us that Father Farrell said if I went down to the job that's goin' on in Rathmines I'd get a start.

JOXER. Be the holy, that's good news!

BOYLE. How is it good news? I wondher if you were in my condition, wculd you call it good news?

JOXER. I thought. . .

BOYLE. You thought! You think too sudden sometimes, Joxer. D'ye know, I'm hardly able to crawl with the pains in me legs!

JOXER. Yis, yis; I forgot the pains in your legs. I know you can do nothin' while they're at you.

BOYLE. You forgot; I don't think any of yous realize the state I'm in with the pains in me legs. What ud happen if I had to carry a bag o' cement?

JOXER. Ah, any man havin' the like of them pains id be down an' out, down an' out.

BOYLE. I wouldn't mind if he had said it to meself; but, no, oh no, he rushes in an' shouts it out in front o' Juno, an' you know what Juno is, Joxer. We all know Devine knows a little more than the rest of us, but he doesn't act as if he did; he's a good boy, sober, able to talk an' all that, but still...

JOXER. Oh ay; able to argufy, but still..

BOYLE. If he's runnin' afther Mary aself, he's not goin' to be runnin' afther me. Captain Boyle's able to take care of himself. Afther all, I'm not gettin' brought up on Virol. I never heard him usin' a curse; I don't believe he was ever dhrunk in his life — sure he's not like a Christian at all!

JOXER. You're afther takin' the word out o' me mouth — afther all, a Christian's natural, but he's unnatural.

BOYLE. His oul' fella was just the same — a Wicklow man.

JOXER. A Wicklow man! That explains the whole thing. I've met many a Wicklow man in me time, but I never met wan that was any good.

BOYLE. "Father Farrell," says he, "sent me down to tell you." Father Farrell!... D'ye know, Joxer, I never like to be beholden to any o' the clergy.

JOXER. It's dangerous, right enough.

BOYLE. If they do anything for you, they'd want you to be livin' in the Chapel. ... I'm goin' to tell you somethin', Joxer, that I wouldn't tell to anybody else — the clergy always had too much power over the people in this unfortunate country.

JOXER. You could sing that if you had an air to it!

BOYLE [becoming enthusiastic]. Didn't they prevent the people in '47 from seizin' the corn, an' they starvin'; didn't they down Parnell; didn't they say that hell wasn't hot enough nor eternity long enough to punish the Fenians? We don't forget, we don't forget them things, Joxer. If they've taken everything else from us, Joxer, they've left us our memory.

JOXER [emotionally]. For mem'ry's the only friend that grief can call its own, that grief... can... call... its own!

BOYLE. Father Farrell's beginnin' to take a great intherest in Captain Boyle; because of what Johnny did for his coun-try, says he to me wan day. It's a curious way to reward Johnny be makin' his poor oul' father work. But, that's what the clergy want, Joxer — work, work, work for me an' you; havin' us mulin' from mornin' till night, so that they may be in b? fettle when they come hoppin' round for their dues! Job! Well, let him give his job to wan of his hymn-singin', prayer-spoutin', crawthumpin' Confraternity men!

[*The voice of a coal-block vendor is heard chanting in the street.*]

VOICE OF COAL VENDOR. Blocks... coal-blocks! Blocks... coal-blocks!

JOXER. God be with the young days when you were steppin' the deck of a manly ship, with the win' blowin' a hurricane through the masts, an' the only sound you'd hear was, "Port your helm!" an' the only answer, "Port it is, sir!"

BOYLE. Them was days, Joxer, them was days. Nothin' was too hot or too heavy for me then. Sailin' from the Gulf o' Mexico to the Antarctic Ocean. I seen things, I seen things, Joxer, that no mortal man should speak about that knows his Catechism. Ofen, an' ofen, when I was fixed to the wheel with a marlinspike, an' the win's blowin' fierce an' the waves lashin' an' lashin', till you'd think every minute was goin' to be your last, an' it blowed, an' blowed — blew is the right word, Joxer, but blowed is what the sailors use....

JOXER. Aw, it's a darlin' word, a daarlin' word.

BOYLE. An', as it blowed an' blowed, I ofen looked up at the sky an' assed meself the question — what is the stars, what is the stars?

VOICE OF COAL VENDOR. Any blocks, coal-blocks; blocks, coal-blocks!

JOXER. Ah, that's the question, that's the question — what is the stars?

BOYLE. An' then, I'd have another look, an' I'd ass meself — what is the moon?

JOXER. Ah, that's the question — what is the moon, what is the moon?

[*Rapid steps are heard coming towards the door.* BOYLE *makes desperate efforts to hide everything;* JOXER *rushes to the window in a frantic effort to get out;*]

BOYLE *begins to innocently lilt — "Oh, me darlin' Jennie, I will be thrue to thee," when the door is opened, and the black face of the* COAL VENDOR *appears.*]

THE COAL VENDOR. D'yes want any blocks?

BOYLE [*with a roar*]. No, we don't want any blocks!

JOXER [*coming back with a sigh of relief*]. That's afther puttin' the heart across me — I could ha' sworn it was Juno. I'd betther be goin', Captain; you couldn't tell the minute Juno'd hop in on us.

BOYLE. Let her hop in; we may as well have it out first as at last. I've made up me mind — I'm not goin' to do only what she damn well likes.

JOXER. Them sentiments does you credit, Captain; I don't like to say anything as between man an' wife, but I say as a butty, as a butty, Captain, that you've stuck it too long, an' that it's about time you showed a little spunk.

How can a man die betther than facin' fearful odds,
For th' ashes of his fathers an' the temples of his gods.

BOYLE. She has her rights — there's no one denyin' it, but haven't I me rights too?

JOXER. Of course you have — the sacred rights o' man!

BOYLE. To-day, Joxer, there's goin' to be issued a proclamation be me, establishin' an independent Republic, an' Juno'll have to take an oath of allegiance.

JOXER. Be firm, be firm, Captain; the first few minutes'll be the worst: — if you gently touch a nettle it'll sting you for your pains; grasp it like a lad of mettle, an' as soft as silk remains!

VOICE OF JUNO OUTSIDE. Can't stop, Mrs. Madigan — I haven't a minute!

JOXER [*flying out of the window*]. Holy God, here she is!

BOYLE [*packing the things away with a rush in the press*]. I knew that fella ud stop till she was in on top of us!

[*He sits down by the fire.*]

[JUNO *enters hastily; she is flurried and excited.*]

JUNO. Oh, you're in — you must have been only afther comin' in?

BOYLE. No, I never went out.

JUNO. It's curious, then, you never heard the knockin'.

[*She puts her coat and hat on bed.*]

BOYLE. Knockin'? Of course I heard the knockin'.

JUNO. An' why didn't you open the door, then? I suppose you were so busy with Joxer that you hadn't time.

BOYLE. I haven't seen Joxer since I seen him before. Joxer! What ud bring Joxer here?

JUNO. D'ye mean to tell me that the pair of yous wasn't collogin' together here when me back was turned?

BOYLE. What ud we be collogin' together about? I have somethin' else to think of besides collogin' with Joxer. I can swear on all the holy prayer-books...

MRS. BOYLE. That you weren't in no snug! Go on in at wanst now, an' take aff that moleskin trousers o' yours, an' put on a collar an' tie to smarten yourself up a bit. There's a visitor comin' with Mary in a minute, an' he has great news for you.

BOYLE. A job, I suppose; let us get wan first before we start lookin' for another.

MRS. BOYLE. That's the thing that's able to put the win' up you. Well, it's no job, but news that'll give you the chance o' your life.

BOYLE. What's all the mysthery about?

MRS. BOYLE. G'win an' take off the moleskin trousers an' you're told!

[BOYLE *goes into room on left.*]

[MRS. BOYLE *tidies up the room, puts the shovel under the bed, and goes to the press.*]

MRS. BOYLE. Oh, God bless us, looka the way everything's thrun about! Oh, Joxer was here, Joxer was here!

[MARY *enters with* CHARLIE BENTHAM; *he is a young man of twenty-five, tall, good-looking, with a very high opinion of himself generally. He is dressed in a brown coat, brown knee-breeches, grey stockings, a brown sweater, with a deep blue tie; he carries gloves and a walking stick.*]

MRS. BOYLE [*fussing round*]. Come in, Mr. Bentham; sit down, Mr. Bentham, in this chair; it's more comfortabler than that, Mr. Bentham. Himself'll be here in a minute; he's just takin' off his trousers.

MARY. Mother!

BENTHAM. Please don't put yourself to any trouble, Mrs. Boyle — I'm quite all right here, thank you.

MRS. BOYLE. An' to think of you knowin' Mary, an' she knowin' the news you had for us, an' wouldn't let on; but it's all the more welcomer now, for we were on our last lap!

VOICE OF JOHNNY INSIDE. What are you kickin' up all the racket for?

BOYLE [*roughly*]. I'm takin' off me moleskin trousers!

JOHNNY. Can't you do it, then, without lettin' th' whole house know you're takin' off your trousers? What d'ye want puttin' them on an' takin' them off again?

BOYLE. Will you let me alone, will you let me alone? Am I never goin' to be done thryin' to please th' whole o' yous?

MRS. BOYLE [*to* BENTHAM]. You must excuse th' state o' th' place, Mr. Bentham; th' minute I turn me back that man o' mine always makes a litther o' th' place, a litther o' th' place.

BENTHAM. Don't worry, Mrs. Boyle; it's all right, I assure...

BOYLE [*inside*]. Where's me braces; where in th' name o' God did I leave me braces.... Ay, did you see where I put me braces?

JOHNNY [*inside, calling out*]. Ma, will you come in here an' take da away ou' o' this or he'll dhrive me mad.

MRS. BOYLE [*going towards door*]. Dear, dear, dear, that man'll be lookin' for somethin' on th' day o' Judgement. [*Looking into room and calling to* BOYLE.] Look at your braces, man, hangin' round your neck!

BOYLE [*inside*]. Aw, Holy God!

MRS. BOYLE [*calling*]. Johnny, Johnny, come out here for a minute.

JOHNNY. Oh, leave Johnny alone, an' don't be annoyin' him!

MRS. BOYLE. Come on, Johnny, till I inthroduce you to Mr. Bentham. [*To* DENTHAM.] Me son, Mr. Bentham; he's afther goin' through the mill. He was only a chiselur of a Boy Scout in Easter Week, when he got hit in the hip; and his arm was blew off in the fight in O'Connell Street. [JOHNNY *comes in.*] Here he is, Mr. Bentham; Mr. Bentham, Johnny. None can deny he done his bit for Irelan', if that's going to do him any good.

JOHNNY [*boastfully*]. I'd do it agen, ma, I'd do it agen; for a principle's a principle.

MRS. BOYLE. Ah, you lost your best principle, me boy, when you lost your arm; them's the only sort o' principles that's any good to a workin' man.

JOHNNY. Ireland only half free'll never be at peace while she has a son left to pull a trigger.

MRS. BOYLE. To be sure, to be sure — no bread's a lot betther than half a loaf. [*Calling loudly in to* BOYLE.] Will you hurry up there?

[BOYLE *enters in his best trousers, which aren't too good, and looks very uncomfortable in his collar and tie.*]

MRS. BOYLE. This is me husband; Mr Boyle, Mr. Bentham.

BENTHAM. Ah, very glad to know you, Mr. Boyle. How are you?

BOYLE. Ah, I'm not too well at all; I suffer terrible with pains in me legs. Juno can tell you there what...

MRS. BOYLE. You won't have many pains in your legs when you hear what Mr. Bentham has to tell you.

BENTHAM. Juno! What an interesting name! It reminds one of Homer's glorious story of ancient gods and heroes.

BOYLE. Yis, doesn't it? You see, Juno was born an' christened in June; I met her in June; we were married in June, an' Johnny was born in June, so wan day I says to her, "You should ha' been called Juno," an' the name stuck to her ever since.

MRS. BOYLE. Here, we can talk o' them things agen; let Mr. Bentham say what he has to say now.

BENTHAM. Well, Mr. Boyle, I suppose you'll remember a Mr. Ellison of Santry — he's a relative of yours, I think.

BOYLE [*viciously*]. Is it that prognosticator an' procrastinator! Of course I remember him.

BENTHAM. Well, he's dead, Mr. Boyle...

BOYLE. Sorra many'll go into mournin' for him.

MRS. BOYLE. Wait till you hear what Mr. Bentham has to say, an' then, maybe, you'll change your opinion.

BENTHAM. A week before he died he sent for me to write his will for him. He told me that there were two only that he wished to leave his property to: his second cousin Michael Finnegan of Santry, and John Boyle, his first cousin of Dublin.

BOYLE [*excitedly*]. Me, is it me, me?

BENTHAM. You, Mr. Boyle; I'll read a copy of the will that I have here with me, which has been duly filed in the Court of Probate.

[*He takes a paper from his pocket and reads*]:

6th February 1922.
This is the last Will and Testament of William Ellison, of Santry, in the County of Dublin. I hereby order and wish my property to be sold and divided as follows: —
£20 *to the St. Vincent De Paul Society.*
£60 *for Masses for the repose of my soul* (5s. *for Each Mass*).
The rest of my property to be divided between my first and second cousins.
I hereby appoint Timothy Buckly, of Santry, and Hugh Brierly, of Coolock, to be my Executors.

(*Signed*)　WILLIAM ELLISON.
　　　　　　HUGH BRIERLY.
　　　　　　TIMOTHY BUCKLY.
　　　　　　CHARLES BENTHAM, N.T.

BOYLE [*eagerly*]. An' how much'll be comin' out of it, Mr. Bentham?

BENTHAM. The Executors told me that half of the property would be anything between £1500 and £2000.

MARY. A fortune, father, a fortune!

JOHNNY. We'll be able to get out o' this place now, an' go somewhere we're not known.

MRS. BOYLE. You won't have to trouble about a job for a while, Jack.

BOYLE [*fervently*]. I'll never doubt the goodness o' God agen.

BENTHAM. I congratulate you, Mr. Boyle.　　　　[*They shake hands.*]

BOYLE. An' now, Mr. Bentham, you'll have to have a wet.

BENTHAM. A wet?

BOYLE. A wet — a jar — a boul!

MRS. BOYLE. Jack, you're speakin' to Mr. Bentham, an' not to Joxer.

BOYLE [*solemnly*]. Juno... Mary... Johnny... we'll have to go into mournin' at wanst.... I never expected that poor Bill ud die so sudden.... Well, we all have to die some day... you, Juno, to-day... an' me, maybe, to-morrow.... It's sad, but it can't be helped.... Requiescat in pace... or, usin' our oul' tongue like Saint Patrick or Saint Briget, Guh sayeree jeea ayera!

MARY. Oh, father, that's not Rest in Peace; that's God save Ireland.

BOYLE. U-u-ugh, it's all the same — isn't it a prayer?... Juno, I'm done with Joxer; he nothin' but a prognosticator an' a...

JOXER [*climbing angrily through the window and bounding into the room*]. You're done with Joxer, are you? Maybe you thought I'd stop on the roof all the night for you! Joxer out on the roof with the win' blowin' through him was nothin' to you an' your friend with the collar an' tie!

MRS. BOYLE. What in the name o' God brought you out on the roof; what were you doin' there?

JOXER [*ironically*]. I was dhreamin' I was standin' on the bridge of a ship, an' she sailin' the Antartic Ocean, an' it blowed, an' blowed, an' I lookin' up at the sky an' sayin', what is the stars, what is the stars?

MRS. BOYLE [*opening the door and standing at it*]. Here, get ou' o' this, Joxer Daly; I was always thinkin' you had a slate off.

JOXER [*moving to the door*]. I have to laugh every time I look at the deep sea sailor; an' a row on a river ud make him seasick!

BOYLE. Get ou' o' this before I take the law into me own hands!

JOXER [*going out*]. Say aw rewaeawr, but not good-bye. Lookin' for work, an' prayin' to God he won't get it! [*He goes.*]

MRS. BOYLE. I'm tired tellin' you what

Joxer was; maybe now you see yourself the kind he is.

BOYLE. He'll never blow the froth off a pint o' mine agen, that's a sure thing. Johnny... Mary... you're to keep yourselves to yourselves for the future. Juno, I'm done with Joxer.... I'm a new man from this out.... [Clasping JUNO's hand, and singing emotionally.]

Oh, me darlin' Juno, I will be thrue to thee;
Me own, me darlin' Juno, you're all the world
to me.

CURTAIN

ACT II

The same, but the furniture is more plentiful, and of a vulgar nature. A glaringly upholstered arm-chair and lounge; cheap pictures and photos everywhere. Every available spot is ornamented with huge vases filled with artificial flowers. Crossed festoons of coloured paper chains stretched from end to end of ceiling. On the table is an old attaché case. It is about six in the evening, and two days after the First Act. BOYLE, *in his shirt sleeves, is voluptuously stretched on the sofa; he is smoking a clay pipe. He is half asleep. A lamp is lighting on the table. After a few moments' pause the voice of* JOXER *is heard singing softly outside at the door —* "*Me pipe I'll smoke, as I dhrive me moke — are you there, Mor... ee... ar... i... teee!*"

BOYLE [*leaping up, takes a pen in his hand and busies himself with papers*]. Come along, Joxer, me son, come along.

JOXER [*putting his head in*]. Are you be yourself?

BOYLE. Come on, come on; that doesn't matther; I'm masther now, an' I'm goin' to remain masther.

[JOXER *comes in.*]

JOXER. How d'ye feel now, as a man o' money?

BOYLE [*solemnly*]. It's a responsibility, Joxer, a great responsibility.

JOXER. I suppose 'tis now, though you wouldn't think it.

BOYLE. Joxer, han' me over that attackey case on the table there. [JOXER *hands the case.*] Ever since the Will was passed I've run hundhreds o' dockyments through me han's — I tell you, you have to keep your wits about you.

[*He busies himself with papers.*]

JOXER. Well, I won't disturb you; I'll dhrop in when...

BOYLE [*hastily*]. It's all right, Joxer, this is the last one to be signed to-day. [*He signs a paper, puts it into the case, which he shuts with a snap, and sits back pompously in the chair.*] Now, Joxer, you want to see me; I'm at your service — what can I do for you, me man?

JOXER. I've just dhropped in with the £3 : 5s. that Mrs. Madigan riz on the blankets an' table for you, an' she says you're to be in no hurry payin' it back.

BOYLE. She won't be long without it; I expect the first cheque for a couple o' hundhred any day. There's the five bob for yourself — go on, take it, man; it'll not be the last you'll get from the Captain. Now an' agen we have our differ, but we're there together all the time.

JOXER. Me for you, an' you for me, like the two Musketeers.

BOYLE. Father Farrell stopped me to-day an' tole me how glad he was I fell in for the money.

JOXER. He'll be stoppin' you ofen enough now; I suppose it was "Mr." Boyle with him?

BOYLE. He shuk me be the han'....

JOXER [*ironically*]. I met with Napper Tandy, an' he shuk me be the han'!

BOYLE. You're seldom asthray, Joxer, but you're wrong shipped this time. What you're sayin' of Father Farrell is very near to blasfeemey. I don't like any one to talk disrespectful of Father Farrell.

JOXER. You're takin' me up wrong, Captain; I wouldn't let a word be said agen Father Farrell — the heart o' the rowl, that's what he is; I always said he was a darlin' man, a daarlin' man.

BOYLE. Comin' up the stairs who did I meet but that bummer, Nugent. "I seen you talkin' to Father Farrell," says he, with a grin on him. "He'll be folleyin' you," says he, "like a Guardian Angel from this out" — all the time the oul' grin on him, Joxer.

JOXER. I never seen him yet but he had that oul' grin on him!

BOYLE. "Mr. Nugent," says I, "Father Farrell is a man o' the people, an', as far as I know the History o' me country, the priests was always in the van of the fight for Irelan's freedom."

JOXER [fervently].

*Who was it led the van, Soggart Aroon?
Since the fight first began, Soggart Aroon?*

BOYLE. "Who are you tellin'?" says he. "Didn't they let down the Fenians, an' didn't they do in Parnell? An' now..." "You ought to be ashamed o' yourself," says I, interruptin' him, "not to know the History o' your country." An' I left him gawkin' where he was.

JOXER. Where ignorance's bliss 'tis folly to be wise; I wondher did he ever read the Story o' Irelan'.

BOYLE. Be J. L. Sullivan? Don't you know he didn't.

JOXER. Ah, it's a darlin' buk, a daarlin' buk!

BOYLE. You'd betther be goin', now, Joxer, his Majesty, Bentham, 'll be here any minute, now.

JOXER. Be the way things is lookin', it'll be a match between him an' Mary. She's thrun over Jerry altogether. Well, I hope it will, for he's a darlin' man.

BOYLE. I'm glad you think so — I don't. [Irritably.] What's darlin' about him?

JOXER [nonplussed]. I only seen him twiced; if you want to know me, come an' live with me.

BOYLE. He's too ignified for me — to hear him talk you'd think he knew as much as a Boney's Oraculum. He's given up his job as teacher, an' is goin' to become a solicitor in Dublin — he's been studyin' law. I suppose he thinks I'll set him up, but he's wrong shipped. An' th' other fella — Jerry's as bad. The two o' them ud give you a pain in your face, listenin' to them; Jerry believin' in nothin', an' Bentham believin' in everythin'. One that

says all is God an' no man; an' th' other that says all is man an' no God!

JOXER. Well, I'll be off now.

BOYLE. Don't forget to dhrop down afther a while; we'll have a quiet jar, an' a song or two.

JOXER. Never fear.

BOYLE. An' tell Mrs. Madigan that I hope we'll have the pleasure of her organization at our little enthertainment.

JOXER. Righto; we'll come down together. [He goes out.]

[JOHNNY comes from room on left, and sits down moodily at the fire. BOYLE looks at him for a few moments, and shakes his head. He fills his pipe.]

VOICE OF JUNO AT THE DOOR. Open the door, Jack; this thing has me nearly kilt with the weight.

[BOYLE opens the door. JUNO enters carrying the box of a gramophone, followed by MARY carrying the horn, and some parcels. JUNO leaves the box on the table and flops into a chair.]

JUNO. Carryin' that from Henry Street was no joke.

BOYLE. U-u-ugh, that's a grand lookin' insthrument — how much was it?

JUNO. Pound down, an' five to be paid at two shillin's a week.

BOYLE. That's reasonable enough.

JUNO. I'm afraid we're runnin' into too much debt; first the furniture, an' now this.

BOYLE. The whole lot won't be much out of £2000.

MARY. I don't know what you wanted a gramophone for — I know Charlie hates them; he says they're destructive of real music.

BOYLE. Desthructive of music — that fella ud give you a pain in your face. All a gramophone wants is to be properly played; its thrue wondher is only felt when everythin's quiet — what a gramophone wants is dead silence!

MARY. But, father, Jerry says the same; afther all, you can only appreciate music when your ear is properly trained.

BOYLE. That's another fella ud give you a pain in your face. Properly thrained! I suppose you couldn't appreciate football unless your fut was properly thrained.

MRS. BOYLE [to MARY]. Go on in ower that an' dress, or Charlie'll be in on you, an' tea nor nothin' 'll be ready.

[MARY goes into room left.]

MRS. BOYLE [arranging table for tea]. You didn't look at our new gramophone, Johnny?

JOHNNY. 'Tisn't gramophones I'm thinking of.

MRS. BOYLE. An' what is it you're thinkin' of, allanna?

JOHNNY. Nothin', nothin', nothin'.

MRS. BOYLE. Sure, you must be thinkin' of somethin'; it's yourself that has yourself the way y'are; sleepin' wan night in me sisther's, an' the nex' in your father's brother's — you'll get no rest goin' on that way.

JOHNNY. I can rest nowhere, nowhere, nowhere.

MRS. BOYLE. Sure, you're not thryin' to rest anywhere.

JOHNNY. Let me alone, let me alone, let me alone, for God's sake.

[A knock at street door.]

MRS. BOYLE [in a flutter]. Here he is; here's Mr. Bentham!

BOYLE. Well, there's room for him; it's a pity there's not a brass band to play him in.

MRS. BOYLE. We'll han' the tea round, an' not be clusthered round the table, as if we never seen nothin'.

[Steps are heard approaching, and JUNO, opening the door, allows BENTHAM to enter.]

JUNO. Give your hat an' stick to Jack, there... sit down, Mr. Bentham... no, not there... in th' easy chair be the fire... there, that's betther. Mary'll be out to you in a minute.

BOYLE [solemnly]. I seen be the paper this mornin' that Consols was down half per cent. That's serious, min' you, an' shows the whole counthry's in a state o' chassis.

MRS. BOYLE. What's Consols, Jack?

BOYLE. Consols? Oh, Consols is — oh, there's no use tellin' women what Consols is — th' wouldn't undherstand.

BENTHAM. It's just as you were saying, Mr. Boyle...

[MARY enters charmingly dressed.]

BENTHAM. Oh, good evening, Mary; how pretty you're looking!

MARY [archly]. Am I?

BOYLE. We were just talkin' when you kem in, Mary, I was tellin' Mr. Bentham that the whole counthry's in a state o' chassis.

MARY [to BENTHAM]. Would you prefer the green or the blue ribbon round me hair, Charlie?

MRS. BOYLE. Mary, your father's speakin'.

BOYLE [rapidly]. I was jus' tellin' Mr. Bentham that the whole counthry's in a state o' chassis.

MARY. I'm sure you're frettin', da, whether it is or no.

MRS. BOYLE. With all our churches an' religions, the worl's not a bit the betther.

BOYLE [with a commanding gesture]. Tay!

[MARY and MRS. BOYLE dispense the tea.]

MRS. BOYLE. An' Irelan's takin' a leaf out o' the worl's buk; when we got the makin' of our own laws I thought we'd never stop to look behind us, but instead of that we never stopped to look before us! If the people ud folley up their religion betther there'd be a betther chance for us — what do you think, Mr. Bentham?

BENTHAM. I'm afraid I can't venture to express an opinion on that point, Mrs. Boyle; dogma has no attraction for me.

MRS. BOYLE. I forgot you didn't hold with us; what's this you said you were?

BENTHAM. A Theosophist, Mrs. Boyle.

MRS. BOYLE. An' what in the name o' God's a Theosophist?

BOYLE. A Theosophist, Juno, 's a — tell her, Mr. Bentham, tell her.

BENTHAM. It's hard to explain in a few words: Theosophy's founded on The Vedas, the religious books of the East. Its central theme is the existence of an all-pervading Spirit — the Life-Breath. Nothing really exists but this one Universal Life-Breath. And whatever even seems to exist separately from this Life-Breath, doesn't really exist at all. It is all vital force in man, in all animals, and in all vegetation. This Life-Breath is called the Prawna.

MRS. BOYLE. The Prawna! What a comical name!

BOYLE. Prawna; yis, the Prawna. [*Blowing gently through his lips.*] That's the Prawna!

MRS. BOYLE. Whist, whist, Jack.

BENTHAM. The happiness of man depends upon his sympathy with this Spirit. Men who have reached a high state of excellence are called Yogi. Some men become Yogi in a short time, it may take others millions of years.

BOYLE. Yogi! I seen hundhreds of them in the streets o' San Francisco.

BENTHAM. It is said by these Yogi that if we practise certain mental exercises that we would have powers denied to others — for instance, the faculty of seeing things that happen miles and miles away.

MRS. BOYLE. I wouldn't care to meddle with that sort o' belief; it's a very curious religion, altogether.

BOYLE. What's curious about it? Isn't all religions curious? If they weren't, you wouldn't get any one to believe them. But religions is passin' away — they've had their day like everything else. Take the real Dublin people, f'rinstance: they know more about Charlie Chaplin an' Tommy Mix than they do about Saints Peter an' Paul!

MRS. BOYLE. You don't believe in ghosts, Mr. Bentham?

MARY. Don't you know he doesn't, mother?

BENTHAM. I don't know, that, Mary. Scientists are beginning to think that what we call ghosts are sometimes seen by persons of a certain nature. They say that sensational actions, such as the killing of a person, demand great energy, and that that energy lingers in the place where the action occurred. People may live in the place and see nothing, when some one may come along whose personality has some peculiar connection with the energy of the place,

and, in a flash, the person sees the whole affair.

JOHNNY [*rising swiftly, pale and affected*]. What sort o' talk is this to be goin' on with? Is there nothin' betther to be talkin' about but the killin' o' people? My God, isn't it bad enough for these things to happen without talkin' about them! [*He hurriedly goes into the room on left.*]

BENTHAM. Oh, I'm very sorry, Mrs. Boyle; I never thought...

MRS. BOYLE [*apologetically*]. Never mind, Mr. Bentham, he's very touchy. [*A frightened scream is heard from* JOHNNY *inside.*]

MRS. BOYLE. Mother of God, what's that?

[*He rushes out again, his face pale, his lips twitching, his limbs trembling.*]

JOHNNY. Shut the door, shut the door, quick, for God's sake! Great God, have mercy on me! Blessed Mother o' God, shelter me, shelther your son!

MRS. BOYLE [*catching him in her arms*]. What's wrong with you? What ails you? Sit down, sit down, here, on the bed... there now... there now.

MARY. Johnny, Johnny, what ails you?

JOHNNY. I seen him, I seen him... kneelin' in front o' the statue... merciful Jesus, have pity on me!

MRS. BOYLE [*to* BOYLE]. Get him a glass o' whisky... quick, man, an' don't stand gawkin'.

[BOYLE *gets the whisky.*]

JOHNNY. Sit here, sit here, mother... between me an' the door.

MRS. BOYLE. I'll sit beside you as long as you like, only tell me what was it came across you at all?

JOHNNY [*after taking some drink*]. I seen him.... I seen Robbie Tancred kneelin' down before the statue... an' the red light shinin' on him... an' when I went in... he turned an' looked at me... an' I seen the woun's bleedin' in his breast.... Oh, why did he look at me like that... it wasn't my fault that he was done in.... Mother o' God, keep him away from me!

MRS. BOYLE. There, there, child, you've imagined it all. There was nothin' there at all — it was the red light you seen, an' the talk we had put all the rest into your head. Here, dhrink more o' this — it'll do you good.... An', now, stretch yourself down on the bed for a little. [*To* BOYLE.] Go in, Jack, an' show him it was only in his own head it was.

BOYLE [*making no move*]. E-e-e-e-eh; it's all nonsense; it was only a shadda he saw.

MARY. Mother o' God, he made me heart lep!

BENTHAM. It was simply due to an over-wrought imagination — we all get that way at times.

MRS. BOYLE. There, dear, lie down in the bed, an' I'll put the quilt across you... e-e-e-eh, that's it... you'll be as right as the mail in a few minutes.

JOHNNY. Mother, go into the room an' see if the light's lightin' before the statue.

MRS. BOYLE [*to* BOYLE]. Jack, run in, an' see if the light's lightin' before the statue.

BOYLE [*to* MARY]. Mary, slip in an' see if the light's lightin' before the statue.

[MARY *hesitates to go in.*]

BENTHAM. It's all right; Mary, I'll go.

[*He goes into the room; remains for a few moments, and returns.*]

BENTHAM. Everything's just as it was the light burning bravely before the statue.

BOYLE. Of course; I know it was all nonsense. [*A knock at the door.*]

BOYLE [*going to open the door*]. E-e-e-e-eh.

[*He opens it, and* JOXER, *followed by* MRS. MADIGAN, *enters.* MRS. MADIGAN *is a strong, dapper little woman of about forty-five; her face is almost always a widespread smile of complacency. She is a woman who, in manner at least, can mourn with them that mourn, and rejoice with them that do rejoice. When she is feeling comfortable, she is inclined to be reminiscent; when others say anything, or following a statement made by herself, she has a habit of putting her head a little to one side, and nodding it rapidly several times in succession, like a bird pecking at a hard berry. Indeed, she has a good deal of the bird in her, but the bird instinct is by no means a melodious one. She is igno-rant, vulgar and forward, but her heart is generous withal. For instance, she would help a neighbour's sick child; she would probably kill the child, but her intentions would be to cure it; she would be more at home helping a drayman to lift a fallen horse. She is dressed in a rather soiled grey dress and a vivid purple blouse; in her hair is a huge comb, ornamented with huge coloured beads. She enters with a gliding step, beaming smile and nodding head.* BOYLE *receives them effusively.*]

BOYLE. Come on in, Mrs. Madigan; come on in; I was afraid you weren't comin'.... [*Slyly.*] There's some people able to dhress, ay, Joxer?

JOXER. Fair as the blossoms that bloom in the May, an' sweet as the scent of the new mown hay.... Ah, well she may wear them.

MRS. MADIGAN [*looking at* MARY]. I know some as are as sweet as the blossoms that bloom in the May — oh, no names, no pack dhrill!

BOYLE. An' now, I'll inthroduce the pair o' yous to Mary's intended: Mr. Bentham, this is Mrs. Madigan, an oul' back-parlour neighbour, that, if she could help it at all, ud never see a body shuk!

BENTHAM [*rising, and tentatively shaking the hand of* MRS. MADIGAN]. I'm sure, it's a great pleasure to know you, Mrs. Madigan.

MRS. MADIGAN. An' I'm goin' to tell you, Mr. Bentham, you're goin' to get as nice a bit o' skirt in Mary, there, as ever you seen in your puff. Not like some of the dhressed up dolls that's knockin' about lookin' for men when it's a skelpin' they want. I remember as well as I remember yesterday, the day she was born — of a Tuesday, the 25th o' June, in the year 1901, at thirty-three minutes past wan in the day be Foley's clock, the pub at the corner o' the street. A cowld day it was too, for the season o' the year, an' I remember sayin' to Joxer, there, who I met comin' up th' stairs, that the new arrival in Boyle's ud grow up a hardy chiselur if it lived, an' that she'd be somethin' one o' these days that nobody suspected, an' so signs on it, here she is to-day, goin' to be married to a young man lookin' as if he'd be fit to commensurate in any position in life it ud please God to call him!

BOYLE [*effusively*]. Sit down, Mrs. Madigan, sit down, me oul' sport. [*To* BENTHAM.] This is Joxer Daly, Past Chief Ranger of the Dear Little Shamrock Branch of the Irish National Foresters, an oul' front-top neighbour, that never despaired, even in the darkest days of Ireland's sorra.

JOXER. Nil desperandum, Captain, nil desperandum.

BOYLE. Sit down, Joxer, sit down. The two of us was ofen in a tight corner.

MRS. BOYLE. Ay, in Foley's snug!

JOXER. An' we kem out of it flyin', we kem out of it flyin', Captain.

BOYLE. An', now, for a dhrink — I know yous won't refuse an oul' friend.

MRS. MADIGAN [*to* JUNO]. Is Johnny not well, Mrs....

MRS. BOYLE [*warningly*]. S-s-s-sh.

MRS. MADIGAN. Oh, the poor darlin'.

BOYLE. Well, Mrs. Madigan, is it tea or what?

MRS. MADIGAN. Well, speakin' for meself, I jus' had me tea a minute ago, an' I'm afraid to dhrink any more — I'm never the same when I dhrink too much tay. Thanks, all the same, Mr. Boyle.

BOYLE. Well, what about a bottle o' stout or a dhrop o' whisky?

MRS. MADIGAN. A bottle o' stout ud be a little too heavy for me stummock afther me tay.... A-a-ah, I'll thry the ball o' malt.

[BOYLE *prepares the whisky.*]

MRS. MADIGAN. There's nothin' like a ball o' malt occasional like — too much of it isn't good. [*To* BOYLE, *who is adding water.*] Ah, God, Johnny, don't put too much wather on it! [*She drinks.*] I suppose yous'll be lavin' this place.

BOYLE. I'm looking for a place near the sea; I'd like the place that you might say was me cradle, to be me grave as well. The sea is always callin' me.

JOXER. She is callin', callin', callin', in the win' an' on the sea.

BOYLE. Another dhrop o' whisky, Mrs. Madigan?

MRS. MADIGAN. Well, now, it ud be hard to refuse seein' the suspicious times that's in it.

BOYLE [*with a commanding gesture*]. Song!... Juno... Mary... "Home to Our Mount'ins"!

MRS. MADIGAN [*enthusiastically*]. Hear, hear!

JOXER. Oh, tha's a darlin' song, a daarlin' song!

MARY [*bashfully*]. Ah, no, da; I'm not in a singin' humour.

MRS. MADIGAN. Gawn with you, child, an' you only goin' to be marrid; I remember as well as I remember yesterday — it was on a lovely August evenin', exactly, accordin' to date, fifteen years ago, come the Tuesday folleyin' the nex' that's comin' on, when me own man (the Lord be good to him!) an' me was sittin' shy together in a doty little nook on a counthry road, adjacent to The Stiles. "That'll scratch your lovely, little white neck," says he, ketchin' hould of a danglin' bramble branch, holdin' clusters of the loveliest flowers you ever seen, an' breakin' it off, so that his arm fell, accidental like, roun' me waist, an' as I felt it tightenin', an' tightenin', an' tightenin', I thought me buzzum was every minute goin' to burst out into a roystherin' song about

The little green leaves that were shakin' on the threes,
The gallivantin' buttherflies, an' buzzin' o' the bees!

BOYLE. Ordher for the song!
JUNO. Come on, Mary— we'll do our best.
[JUNO *and* MARY *stand up, and choosing a suitable position, sing simply* "Home to Our Mountains." *They bow to company, and return to their places.*]
BOYLE [*emotionally at the end of song*]. Lull... me... to... rest!
JOXER [*clapping his hands*]. Bravo, bravo! Darlin' girulls, darlin' girulls!
MRS. MADIGAN. Juno, I never seen you in betther form.

BENTHAM. Very nicely rendered indeed.

MRS. MADIGAN. A noble call, a noble call!

MRS. BOYLE. What about yourself, Mrs. Madigan?

[*After some coaxing,* MRS. MADIGAN *rises, and in a quavering voice sings the following verse.*]

If I were a blackbird I'd whistle and sing;
I'd follow the ship that my thrue love was in;
An' on the top riggin', I'd there build me nest,
An' at night I would sleep on me Willie's white breast!

[*Becoming husky, amid applause she sits down.*]

MRS. MADIGAN. Ah, me voice is too husky now, Juno; though I remember the time when Maisie Madigan could sing like a nightingale at matin' time. I remember as well as I remember yesterday, at a party given to celebrate the comin' of the first chislur to Annie an' Benny Jimeson — who was the barber, yous may remember, in Henrietta Street, that, after Easter Week, hung out a green, white an' orange pole, an', then, when the Tans started their Jazz dancin', whipped it in agen, an' stuck out a red, white an' blue wan instead, given as an excuse that a barber's pole was strictly non-political — singin' "An' You'll Remember Me," with the top notes quiverin' in a dead hush of pethrified attention, folleyed by a clappin' o' han's that shuk the tumblers on the table, an' capped be Jimeson, the barber, sayin' that it was the best rendherin' of "You'll Remember Me" he ever heard in his natural!

BOYLE [*peremptorily*]. Ordher for Joxer's song!

JOXER. Ah, no, I couldn't; don't ass me, Captain.

BOYLE. Joxer's song, Joxer's song — give us wan of your shut-eyed wans.

[JOXER *settles himself in his chair; takes a drink; clears his throat; solemnly closes his eyes, and begins to sing in a very querulous voice.*]

She is far from the lan' where her young hero sleeps,
An' lovers around her are sighing [*He hesitates.*]
An' lovers around her are sighin' ... sighin' ...
signin' ... [*A pause.*]

BOYLE [*imitating* JOXER].

And lovers around her are sighing!

What's the use of you thryin' to sing the song if you don't know it?

MARY. Thry another one, Mr. Daly — maybe you'd be more fortunate.

MRS. MADIGAN. Gawn, Joxer, thry another wan.

JOXER [*starting again*].

I have heard the mavis singin' his love song to the morn;
I have seen the dew-dhrop clingin' to the rose jus' newly born; but ... but ... [*frantically*] *to the rose jus' newly born ... newly born ... born.*

JOHNNY. Mother, put on the gramophone, for God's sake, an' stop Joxer's bawlin'.

BOYLE [*commandingly*]. Gramophone! ... I hate to see fellas thryin' to do what they're not able to do.

[BOYLE *arranges the gramophone, and is about to start it, when voices are heard of persons descending the stairs.*]

MRS. BOYLE [*warningly*]. Whisht, Jack, don't put it on, don't put it on yet; this must be poor Mrs. Tancred comin' down to go to the hospital — I forgot all about them bringin' the body to the church to-night. Open the door, Mary, an' give them a bit o' light.

[MARY *opens the door, and* MRS. TANCRED — *a very old woman, obviously shaken by the death of her son — appears, accompanied by several neighbours. The first few phrases are spoken before they appear.*]

FIRST NEIGHBOUR. It's a sad journey we're goin' on, but God's good, an' the Republicans won't be always down.

MRS. TANCRED. Ah, what good is that to me now? Whether they're up or down — it won't bring me darlin' boy from the grave.

MRS. BOYLE. Come in an' have a hot cup o' tay, Mrs. Tancred, before you go.

MRS. TANCRED. Ah, I can take nothin' now, Mrs. Boyle — I won't be long afther him.

FIRST NEIGHBOUR. Still an' all, he died a noble death, an' we'll bury him like a king.

MRS. TANCRED. An' I'll go on livin' like a pauper. Ah, what's the pains I suffered bringin' him into the world to carry him to his cradle, to the pains I'm sufferin' now, carryin' him out o' the world to bring him to his grave!

MARY. It would be better for you not to go at all, Mrs. Tancred, but to stay at home beside the fire with some o' the neighbours.

MRS. TANCRED. I seen the first of him, an' I'll see the last of him.

MRS. BOYLE. You'd want a shawl, Mrs. Tancred; it's a cowld night, an' the win's blowin' sharp.

MRS. MADIGAN [rushing out]. I've a shawl above.

MRS. TANCRED. Me home is gone, now; he was me only child, an' to think that he was lyin' for a whole night stretched out on the side of a lonely counthry lane, with his head, his darlin' head, that I ofen kissed an' fondled, half hidden in the wather of a runnin' brook. An' I'm told he was the leadher of the ambush where me nex' door neighbour, Mrs. Mannin', lost her Free State soldier son. An' now here's the two of us oul' women, standin' one on each side of a scales o' sorra, balanced be the bodies of our two dead darlin' sons. [MRS. MADIGAN returns, and wraps a shawl around her.] God bless you, Mrs. Madigan.... [She moves slowly towards the door.] Mother o' God, Mother o' God, have pity on the pair of us!... O Blessed Virgin, where were you when me darlin' son was riddled with bullets, when me darlin' son was riddled with bullets!... Sacred Heart of the Crucified Jesus, take away our hearts o' stone... an' give us hearts o' flesh!... Take away this murdherin' hate... an' give us Thine own eternal love! [They pass out of the room.]

MRS. BOYLE [explanatorily to BENTHAM]. That was Mrs. Tancred of the two-pair back; her son was found, e'er yestherday, lyin' out beyant Finglas riddled with bullets. A die-hard he was, be all accounts. He was a nice quiet boy, but lattherly he went to hell, with his Republic first, an' Republic last an' Republic over all. He ofen took tea with us here, in the oul' days, an' Johnny, there, an' him used to be always together.

JOHNNY. Am I always to be havin' to tell you that he was no friend o' mine? I never cared for him, an' he could never stick me. It's not because he was Commandant of the Battalion that I was Quarther-Masther of, that we were friends.

MRS. BOYLE. He's gone, now — the Lord be good to him! God help his poor oul' creature of a mother, for no matther whose friend or enemy he was, he was her poor son.

BENTHAM. The whole thing is terrible, Mrs. Boyle; but the only way to deal with a mad dog is to destroy him.

MRS. BOYLE. An' to think of me forgettin' about him bein' brought to the church to-night, an' we singin' an' all, but it was well we hadn't the gramophone goin', anyhow.

BOYLE. Even if we had aself. We've nothin' to do with these things, one way or t'other. That's the Government's business, an' let them do what we're payin' them for doin'.

MRS. BOYLE. I'd like to know how a body's not to mind these things; look at the way they're afther leavin' the people in this very house. Hasn't the whole house, nearly, been massacreed? There's young Mrs. Dougherty's husband with his leg off; Mrs. Travers that had her son blew up be a mine in Inchegeela, in Co. Cork; Mrs. Mannin' that lost wan of her sons in an ambush a few weeks ago, an' now, poor Mrs. Tancred's only child gone West with his body made a collandher of. Sure, if it's not our business, I don't know whose business is it.

BOYLE. Here, there, that's enough about them things; they don't affect us, an' we needn't give a damn. If they want a wake, well, let them have a wake. When I was a sailor, I was always resigned to meet with a wathery grave; an', if they want to be soldiers, well, there's no use o' them squealin' when they meet a soldier's fate.

JOXER. Let me like a soldier fall — me breast expandin' to th' ball!

MRS. BOYLE. In wan way, she deserves all she got; for lately, she let th' die-hards make an open house of th' place; an' for th' last couple of months, either when th' sun was risin', or when th' sun was settin', you had C.I.D. men burstin' into your room, assin' you where were you born, where were you christened, where were you married, an' where would you be buried!

JOHNNY. For God's sake, let us have no more o' this talk.

MRS. MADIGAN. What about Mr. Boyle's song before we start th' gramophone?

MARY [getting her hat, and putting it on] Mother, Charlie and I are goin' out for a little sthroll.

MRS. BOYLE. All right, darlin'.

BENTHAM [going out with MARY]. We won't be long away, Mrs. Boyle.

MRS. MADIGAN. Gwan, Captain, gwan.

BOYLE. E-e-e-e-eh, I'd want to have a few more jars in me, before I'd be in fettle for singin'.

JOXER. Give us that poem you writ t'other day. [To the rest.] Aw, it's a darlin' poem, a daarlin' poem.

MRS. BOYLE. God bless us, is he startin' to write poetry!

BOYLE [rising to his feet]. E-e-e-e-ch. He recites in an emotional, consequential manner the following verses:]

Shawn an' I were friends, sir, to me he was all in all.

His work was very heavy and his wages were very small.

Tone betther on th' beach as Docker, I'll go bail,
'Tis now I'm feelin' lonely, for to-day he lies in jail.

He was not what some call pious — seldom at church or prayer;

'or the greatest scoundrels I know, sir, goes every Sunday there.

'ond of his pint — well, rather, but hated the Boss by creed

'ut never refused a copper to comfort a pal in need.

E-e-e-e-eh. [He sits down.]

MRS. MADIGAN. Grand, grand; you sould folley that up, you should folley that up.

JOXER. It's a daarlin' poem!

BOYLE [delightedly]. E-e-e-e-eh.

JOHNNY. Are yous goin' to put on th' gramophone to-night, or are yous not?

MRS. BOYLE. Gwan, Jack, put on a record.

MRS. MADIGAN. Gwan, Captain, gwan.

BOYLE. Well, yous'll want to keep a dead silence.

[He sets a record, starts the machine, and it begins to play "If you're Irish, come into the Parlour." As the tune is in full blare, the door is suddenly opened by a brisk, little bald-headed man, dressed circumspectly in a black suit; he glares fiercely at all in the room; he is "NEEDLE NUGENT," a tailor. He carries his hat in his hand.]

NUGENT [loudly, above the noise of the gramophone]. Are yous goin' to have that thing bawlin' an' the funeral of Mrs. Tancred's son passin' the house? Have none of yous any respect for the Irish people's National regard for the dead?

[BOYLE stops the gramophone.]

MRS. BOYLE. Maybe, Needle Nugent, it's nearly time we had a little less respect for the dead, an' a little more regard for the livin'.

MRS. MADIGAN. We don't want you, Mr. Nugent, to teach us what we learned at our mother's knee. You don't look yourself as if you were dyin' of grief; if y'ass Maisie Madigan anything, I'd call you a real thrue die-hard an' live-soft Republican, attendin' Republican funerals in the day, an' stoppin' up half the night makin' suits for the Civic Guards!

[Persons are heard running down to the street, some saying, "Here it is, here it is." NUGENT withdraws, and the rest, except JOHNNY, go to the window looking into the street, and look out. Sounds of a crowd coming nearer are heard; portion are singing.]

*To Jesus' Heart all burning
With fervent love for men,
My heart with fondest yearning
Shall raise its joyful strain.
While ages course along,
Blest be with loudest song.*

The Sacred Heart of Jesus
By every heart and tongue.

MRS. BOYLE. Here's the hearse, here's the hearse!

BOYLE. There's t'oul' mother walkin' behin' the coffin.

MRS. MADIGAN. You can hardly see the coffin with the wreaths.

JOXER. Oh, it's a darlin' funeral, a daarlin' funeral!

MRS. MADIGAN. We'd have a betther view from the street.

BOYLE. Yes — this place ud give you a crick in your neck.

[*They leave the room, and go down. JOHNNY sits moodily by the fire.*]

[*A young man enters; he looks at JOHNNY for a moment.*]

THE YOUNG MAN. Quarther-Masther Boyle.

JOHNNY [*with a start*]. The Mobilizer!

THE YOUNG MAN. You're not at the funeral?

JOHNNY. I'm not well.

THE YOUNG MAN. I'm glad I've found you; you were stoppin' at your aunt's; I called there but you'd gone. I've to give you an ordher to attend a Battalion Staff meetin' the night afther to-morrow.

JOHNNY. Where?

THE YOUNG MAN. I don't know; you're to meet me at the Pillar at eight o'clock; then we're to go to a place I'll be told of to-night; there we'll meet a mothor that'll bring us to the meeting. They think you might be able to know somethin' about them that gave the bend where Commandant Tancred was shelterin'.

JOHNNY. I'm not goin', then. I know nothing about Tancred.

THE YOUNG MAN [*at the door*]. You'd betther come for your own sake — remember your oath.

JOHNNY [*passionately*]. I won't go! Haven't I done enough for Ireland! I've lost me arm, an' me hip's desthroyed so that I'll never be able to walk right agen! Good God, haven't I done enough for Ireland?

THE YOUNG MAN. Boyle, no man can do enough for Ireland! [*He goes.*]

[*Faintly in the distance the crowd is heard saying:*]

Hail, Mary, full of grace, the Lord is with Thee; Blessed art Thou amongst women, and blessed, etc.

CURTAIN

ACT III

The same as Act II. It is about half-past six on a November evening; a bright fire is burning in the grate; MARY, dressed to go out, is sitting on a chair by the fire, leaning forward, her hands under her chin, her elbows on her knees. A look of dejection, mingled with uncertain anxiety, is on her face. A lamp, turned low, is lighting on the table. The votive light under the picture of the Virgin gleams more redly than ever. MRS. BOYLE is putting on her hat and coat. It is two months later.

MRS. BOYLE. An' has Bentham never even written to you since — not one line for the past month?

MARY [*tonelessly*]. Not even a line mother.

MRS. BOYLE. That's very curious... What came between the two of yous at all? To leave you so sudden, an' yous so great together.... To go away t' England, an' no to even leave you his address.... The wa he was always bringin' you to dances, thought he was mad afther you. Are yo sure you said nothin' to him?

MARY. No, mother — at least nothin that could possibly explain his givin' m up.

MRS. BOYLE. You know you're a b hasty at times, Mary, an' say things yo shouldn't say.

MARY. I never said to him what shouldn't say, I'm sure of that.

MRS. BOYLE. How are you sure of it?

MARY. Because I love him with all m heart and soul, mother. Why, I don know; I often thought to myself that I wasn't the man poor Jerry was, but couldn't help loving him, all the same.

MRS. BOYLE. But you shouldn't be frettin' the way you are; when a woman loses a man, she never knows what she's afther losin', to be sure, but, then, she never knows what she's afther gainin', either. You're not the one girl of a month ago — you look like one pinin' away. It's long ago I had a right to bring you to the doctor, instead of waitin' till to-night.

MARY. There's no necessity, really, mother, to go to the doctor; nothing serious is wrong with me — I'm run down and disappointed, that's all.

MRS. BOYLE. I'll not wait another minute; I don't like the look of you at all ... I'm afraid we made a mistake in throwin' over poor Jerry.... He'd have been betther for you than that Bentham.

MARY. Mother, the best man for a woman is the one for whom she has the most love, and Charlie had it all.

MRS. BOYLE. Well, there's one thing to be said for him — he couldn't have been thinkin' of the money, or he wouldn't ha' left you... it must ha' been somethin' else.

MARY [wearily]. I don't know... I don't know, mother... only I think...

MRS. BOYLE. What d'ye think?

MARY. I imagine... he thought... we weren't... good enough for him.

MRS. BOYLE. An' what was he himself, only a school teacher? Though I don't blame him for fightin' shy of people like that Joxer fella an' that oul' Madigan wan — nice sort o' people for your father to introduce to a man like Mr Bentham. 'ou might have told me all about this before now, Mary; I don't know why you like to hide everything from your mother; ou knew Bentham, an' I'd ha' known othin' about it if it hadn't bin for the Will; an' it was only to-day, afther long axin', that you let out that he'd left you.

MARY. It would have been useless to ll you — you wouldn't understand.

MRS. BOYLE [hurt]. Maybe not.... Maybe I wouldn't understand.... Well, e'll be off now.

[She goes over to door left, and speaks to BOYLE inside.]

MRS. BOYLE. We're goin' now to the

doctor's. Are you goin' to get up this evenin'?

BOYLE [from inside]. The pains in me legs is terrible! It's me should be poppin' off to the doctor instead o' Mary, the way I feel.

MRS. BOYLE. Sorra mend you! A nice way you were in last night — carried in in a frog's march, dead to the world. If that's the way you'll go on when you get the money it'll be the grave for you, an asylum for me and the Poorhouse for Johnny.

BOYLE. I thought you were goin'?

MRS. BOYLE. That's what has you as you are — you can't bear to be spoken to. Knowin' the way we are, up to our ears in debt, it's a wondher you wouldn't ha' got up to go to th' solicitor's an' see if we could ha' gettin' a little o' the money even.

BOYLE [shouting]. I can't be goin' up there night, noon an' mornin', can I? He can't give the money till he gets it, can he? I can't get blood out of a turnip, can I?

MRS. BOYLE. It's nearly two months since we heard of the Will, an' the money seems as far off as ever.... I suppose you know we owe twenty poun's to oul' Murphy?

BOYLE. I've a faint recollection of you tellin' me that before.

MRS. BOYLE. Well, you'll go over to the shop yourself for the things in future — I'll face him no more.

BOYLE. I thought you said you were goin'?

MRS. BOYLE. I'm goin' now; come on, Mary.

BOYLE. Ey, Juno, ey!

MRS. BOYLE. Well, what d'ye want now?

BOYLE. Is there e'er a bottle o' stout left?

MRS. BOYLE. There's two o' them here still.

BOYLE. Show us in one o' them an' leave t'other there till I get up. An' throw us in the paper that's on the table, an' the bottle o' Sloan's Liniment that's in th' drawer.

MRS. BOYLE [getting the liniment and the stout]. What paper is it you want — the Messenger?

BOYLE. *Messenger! The News o' the World!*

[MRS. BOYLE *brings in the things asked for and comes out again.*]

MRS. BOYLE [*at door*]. Mind the candle, now, an' don't burn the house over our heads. I left t'other bottle o' stout on the table.

[*She puts bottle of stout on table. She goes out with* MARY. *A cork is heard popping inside.*]

[*A pause; then outside the door is heard the voice of* JOXER *lilting softly:* "*Me pipe I'll smoke, as I dhrive me moke... are you... there... More... aar... i... tee!*" *A gentle knock is heard and, after a pause, the door opens, and* JOXER, *followed by* NUGENT, *enters.*]

JOXER. Be God, they must be all out; I was thinkin' there was somethin' up when he didn't answer the signal. We seen Juno an' Mary goin', but I didn't see him, an' it's very seldom he escapes me.

NUGENT. He's not goin' to escape me — he's not goin' to be let go to the fair altogether.

JOXER. Sure, the house couldn't hould them lately; an' he goin' about like a mastherpiece of the Free State counthry; forgettin' their friends; forgettin' God — wouldn't even lift his hat passin' a chapel! Sure they were bound to get a dhrop! An' you really think there's no money comin' to him afther all?

NUGENT. Not as much as a red rex, man; I've been a bit anxious this long time over me money, an' I went up to the solicitor's to find out all I could — ah, man, they were goin' to throw me down the stairs. They toul' me that the oul' cock himself had the stairs worn away comin' up afther it, an' they black in the face tellin' him he'd get nothin'. Some way or another that the Will is writ he won't be entitled to get as much as a make!

JOXER. Ah, I thought there was somethin' curious about the whole thing; I've bin havin' sthrange dhreams for the last couple o' weeks. An' I notice that that Bentham fella doesn't be comin' here now — there must be somethin' on the mat there too. Anyhow, who, in the name o' God, ud leave anythin' to that oul' bummer? Sure it ud be unnatural. An' the way Juno an' him's been throwin' their weight about for the last few months! Ah, him that goes a borrowin' goes a sorrowin'!

NUGENT. Well, he's not goin' to throw his weight about in the suit I made for him much longer. I'm tellin' you seven poun's aren't to be found growin' on the bushes these days.

JOXER. An' there isn't hardly a neighbour in the whole street that hasn't lent him money on the strength of what he was goin' to get, but they're after backing the wrong horse. Wasn't it a mercy o' God that I'd nothin' to give him! The softy I am, you know, I'd ha' lent him me last juice! I must have had somebody's good prayers. Ah, afther all, an honest man's the noblest work o' God!

[BOYLE *coughs inside.*]

JOXER. Whisht, damn it, he must be inside in bed.

NUGENT. Inside o' bed or outside of it, he's goin' to pay me for that suit, or give it back — he'll not climb up my back as easily as he thinks.

JOXER. Gwan in at wanst, man, an' get it off him, an' don't be a fool.

NUGENT [*going to door left, opening it and looking in*]. Ah, don't disturb yourself Mr. Boyle; I hope you're not sick?

BOYLE. Th' oul' legs, Mr. Nugent, th' oul' legs.

NUGENT. I just called over to see if you could let me have anything off th' suit?

BOYLE. E-e-e-eh, how much is this it is

NUGENT. It's the same as it was at th' start — seven poun's.

BOYLE. I'm glad you kem, Mr. Nugent I want a good heavy top-coat — Iris frieze, if you have it. How much woul' a top-coat like that be now?

NUGENT. About six poun's.

BOYLE. Six poun's — six an' seven, si an' seven is thirteen — that'll be thirtee poun's I'll owe you.

[JOXER *slips the bottle of stout that on the table into his pocket.* NUGEN *rushes into the room, and returns with suit on his arm; he pauses at the door.*]

NUGENT. You'll owe me no thirteen poun's. Maybe you think you're betther able to owe it than pay it!

BOYLE [*frantically*]. Here, come back to hell ower that — where're you goin' with them clothes o' mine?

NUGENT. Where am I goin' with them clothes o' yours? Well, I like your damn cheek!

BOYLE. Here, what am I goin' to dhress meself in when I'm goin' out?

NUGENT. What do I care what you dhress yourself in? You can put yourself in a bolsther cover, if you like.

[*He goes towards the other door, followed by* JOXER.]

JOXER. What'll he dhress himself in! Gentleman Jack an' his frieze coat!

[*They go out.*]

BOYLE [*inside*]. Ey, Nugent, ey, Mr. Nugent, Mr. Nugent!

[*After a pause* BOYLE *enters hastily, buttoning the braces of his moleskin trousers; his coat and vest are on his arm; he throws these on a chair and hurries to the door on right.*]

BOYLE. Ey, Mr. Nugent, Mr. Nugent!

JOXER [*meeting him at the door*]. What's up, what's wrong, Captain?

BOYLE. Nugent's been here an' took way me suit — the only things I had to go out in!

JOXER. Tuk your suit — for God's sake! An' what were you doin' while he was takin' them?

BOYLE. I was in bed when he stole in like a thief in the night, an' before I knew even what he was thinkin' of, he whipped hem from the chair, an' was off like a redshank!

JOXER. An' what, in the name o' God, id he do that for?

BOYLE. What did he do it for? How the hell do I know what he done it for? Jealousy an' spite, I suppose.

JOXER. Did he not say what he done it for?

BOYLE. Amn't I afther tellin' you that

he had them whipped up an' was gone before I could open me mouth?

JOXER. That was a very sudden thing to do; there mus' be somethin' behin' it. Did he hear anythin', I wondher?

BOYLE. Did he hear anythin'? — you talk very queer, Joxer — what could he hear?

JOXER. About you not gettin' the money, in some way or t'other?

BOYLE. An' what ud prevent me from gettin' th' money?

JOXER. That's jus' what I was thinkin' — what ud prevent you from gettin' the money — nothin', as far as I can see.

BOYLE [*looking round for bottle of stout with an exclamation*]. Aw, holy God!

JOXER. What's up, Jack?

BOYLE. He must have afther lifted the bottle o' stout that Juno left on the table!

JOXER [*horrified*]. Ah, no, ah, no! He wouldn't be afther doin' that, now.

BOYLE. An' who done it then? Juno left a bottle o' stout here, an' it's gone — it didn't walk, did it?

JOXER. Oh, that's shockin'; ah, man's inhumanity to man makes countless thousands mourn!

MRS. MADIGAN [*appearing at the door*]. I hope I'm not disturbin' you in any discussion on your forthcomin' legacy — if I may use the word — an' that you'll let me have a barny for a minute or two with you, Mr. Boyle.

BOYLE [*uneasily*]. To be sure, Mrs. Madigan — an oul' friend's always welcome.

JOXER. Come in the evenin', come in th' mornin'; come when you're assed, or come without warnin', Mrs. Madigan.

BOYLE. Sit down, Mrs. Madigan.

MRS. MADIGAN [*ominously*]. Th' few words I have to say can be said standin'. Puttin' aside all formularies, I suppose you remember me lendin' you some time ago three poun's that I raised on blankets an' furniture in me uncle's?

BOYLE. I remember it well. I have it recorded in me book — three poun's five shillin's from Maisie Madigan, raised on articles pawned; an', item: fourpence, given to make up the price of a pint, on th' principle that no bird ever flew on wan wing; all to be repaid at par, when the ship comes home.

MRS. MADIGAN. Well, ever since I shoved in the blankets I've been perishing with th' cowld, an' I've decided, if I'll be too hot in th' nex' world aself, I'm not goin' to be too cowld in this wan; an' consequently, I want me three poun's, if you please.

BOYLE. This is a very sudden demand, Mrs. Madigan, an' can't be met; but I'm willin' to give you a receipt in full, in full.

MRS. MADIGAN. Come on, out with th' money, an' don't be jack-actin'.

BOYLE. You can't get blood out of a turnip, can you?

MRS. MADIGAN [rushing over and shaking him]. Gimme me money, y'oul' reprobate, or I'll shake the worth of it out of you!

BOYLE. Ey, houl' on, there; houl' on, there! You'll wait for your money now, me lassie!

MRS. MADIGAN [looking around the room and seeing the gramophone]. I'll wait for it, will I? Well, I'll not wait long; if I can't get th' cash, I'll get th' worth of it.

[She catches up the gramophone.]

BOYLE. Ey, ey, there, wher'r you goin' with that?

MRS. MADIGAN. I'm goin' to th' pawn to get me three quid five shillin's; I'll brin' you th' ticket, an' then you can do what you like, me bucko.

BOYLE. You can't touch that, you can't touch that! It's not my property, an' it's not ped for yet!

MRS. MADIGAN. So much th' bettther. It'll be an ayse to me conscience, for I'm takin' what doesn't belong to you. You're not goin' to be swankin' it like a paycock with Maisie Madigan's money — I'll pull some o' th' gorgeous feathers out o' your tail!

[She goes off with the gramophone.]

BOYLE. What's th' world comin' to at all? I ass you, Joxer Daly, is there any morality left anywhere?

JOXER. I wouldn't ha' believed it, only I seen it with me own two eyes. I didn't think Maisie Madigan was that sort of a woman; she has either a sup taken, or she's heard somethin'.

BOYLE. Heard somethin' — about what, if it's not any harm to ass you?

JOXER. She must ha' heard some rumour or other that you weren't goin' to get th' money.

BOYLE. Who says I'm not goin' to get th' money?

JOXER. Sure, I know — I was only sayin'.

BOYLE. Only sayin' what?

JOXER. Nothin'.

BOYLE. You were goin' to say somethin', don't be a twisther.

JOXER [angrily]. Who's a twisther?

BOYLE. Why don't you speak your mind, then?

JOXER. You never twisted yourself — no, you wouldn't know how!

BOYLE. Did you ever know me to twist; did you ever know me to twist?

JOXER [fiercely]. Did you ever do anythin' else! Sure, you can't believe a word that comes out o' your mouth.

BOYLE. Here, get out, ower o' this; I always knew you were a prognosticator an a procrastinator!

JOXER [going out as JOHNNY comes in] The anchor's weighed, farewell, re...mem ...ber...me. Jacky Boyle, Esquire, in fernal rogue an' damned liar!

JOHNNY. Joxer an' you at it agen? — when are you goin' to have a little respec for yourself, an' not be always makin' show of us all?

BOYLE. Are you goin' to lecture me now

JOHNNY. Is mother back from the docto yet, with Mary?

[MRS. BOYLE enters; it is apparent fro the serious look on her face that som thing has happened. She takes off h hat and coat without a word and pu them by. She then sits down near t fire, and there is a few moments' paus

BOYLE. Well, what did the doctor s about Mary?

MRS. BOYLE [in an earnest manner a with suppressed agitation]. Sit down he Jack; I've something to say to you about Mary.

BOYLE [*awed by her manner*]. About ... Mary?

MRS. BOYLE. Close that door there and sit down here.

BOYLE [*closing the door*]. More throuble in our native land, is it? [*He sits down.*] Well, what is it?

MRS. BOYLE. It's about Mary.

BOYLE. Well, what about Mary — there's nothin' wrong with her, is there?

MRS. BOYLE. I'm sorry to say there's a gradle wrong with her.

BOYLE. A gradle wrong with her! [*Peevishly.*] First Johnny an' now Mary; is the whole house goin' to become an hospital! It's not consumption, is it?

MRS. BOYLE. No ... it's not consumption ... it's worse.

JOHNNY. Worse! Well, we'll have to get her into some place ower this, there's no one here to mind her.

MRS. BOYLE. We'll all have to mind her now. You might as well know now, Johnny, as another time. [*To* BOYLE.] D'ye know what the doctor said to me about her, Jack?

BOYLE. How ud I know — I wasn't there, was I?

MRS. BOYLE. He told me to get her married at wanst.

BOYLE. Married at wanst! An' why did he say the like o' that?

MRS. BOYLE. Because Mary's goin' to have a baby in a short time.

BOYLE. Goin' to have a baby! — my God, what'll Bentham say when he hears that?

MRS. BOYLE. Are you blind, man, that you can't see that it was Bentham that has done this wrong to her?

BOYLE [*passionately*] Then he'll marry her, he'll have to marry her!

MRS. BOYLE. You know he's gone to England, an' God knows where he is now.

BOYLE. I'll folley him, I'll folley him, an' bring him back, an' make him do her justice. The scoundrel, I might ha' known what he was, with his yogees an' his rawna!

MRS. BOYLE. We'll have to keep it quiet till we see what we can do.

BOYLE. Oh, isn't this a nice thing to come on top o' me, an' the state I'm in! A pretty show I'll be to Joxer an' to that oul' wan, Madigan! Amn't I afther goin' through enough without havin' to go through this!

MRS. BOYLE. What you an' I'll have to go through'll be nothin' to what poor Mary'll have to go through; for you an' me is middlin' old, an' most of our years is spent; but Mary'll have maybe forty years to face an' handle, an' every wan of them'll be tainted with a bitther memory.

BOYLE. Where is she? Where is she till I tell her off? I'm tellin' you when I'm done with her she'll be a sorry girl!

MRS. BOYLE. I left her in me sisther's till I came to speak to you. You'll say nothin' to her, Jack; ever since she left school she's earned her livin', an' your fatherly care never throubled the poor girl.

BOYLE. Gwan, take her part agen her father! But I'll let you see whether I'll say nothin' to her or no! Her an' her readin'! That's more o' th' blasted nonsense that has the house fallin' down on top of us! What did th' likes of her, born in a tenement house, want with readin'? Her readin's afther bringin' her to a nice pass — oh, it's madnin', madnin', madnin'!

MRS. BOYLE. When she comes back say nothin' to her, Jack, or she'll leave this place.

BOYLE. Leave this place! Ay, she'll leave this place, an' quick too!

MRS. BOYLE. If Mary goes, I'll go with her.

BOYLE. Well, go with her! Well, go, th' pair o' yous! I lived before I seen yous, an' I can live when yous are gone. Isn't this a nice thing to come rollin' in on top o' me afther all your prayin' to St. Anthony an' The Little Flower. An' she's a child o' Mary, too — I wonder what'll the nuns think of her now? An' it'll be bellows'd all over th' disthrict before you could say Jack Robinson; an' whenever I'm seen they'll whisper, "That's th' father of Mary Boyle that had th' kid be th' swank she used to go with; d'ye know, d'ye know?" To be sure they'll know — more about it than I will meself!

JOHNNY. She should be dhriven out o' th' house she's brought disgrace on!

MRS. BOYLE. Hush you, Johnny. We needn't let it be bellows'd all over the place; all we've got to do is to leave this place quietly an' go somewhere where we're not known, an' nobody'll be th' wiser.

BOYLE. You're talkin' like a two-year-oul', woman. Where'll we get a place ou' o' this? — places aren't that easily got.

MRS. BOYLE. But, Jack, when we get the money...

BOYLE. Money — what money?

MRS. BOYLE. Why, oul' Ellison's money, of course.

BOYLE. There's no money comin' from oul' Ellison, or any one else. Since you've heard of wan throuble, you might as well hear of another. There's no money comin' to us at all — the Will's a wash out!

MRS. BOYLE. What are you sayin', man — no money?

JOHNNY. How could it be a wash out?

BOYLE. The boyo that's afther doin' it to Mary done it to me as well. The thick made out the Will wrong; he said in th' Will, only first cousin an' second cousin, instead of mentionin' our names, an' now any one that thinks he's a first cousin or second cousin t' oul' Ellison can claim the money as well as me, an' they're springin' up in hundreds, an' comin' from America an' Australia, thinkin' to get their whack out of it, while all the time the lawyers is gobblin' it up, till there's not as much as ud buy a stockin' for your lovely daughter's baby!

MRS. BOYLE. I don't believe it, I don't believe it, I don't believe it!

JOHNNY. Why did you say nothin' about this before?

MRS. BOYLE. You're not serious, Jack; you're not serious!

BOYLE. I'm tellin' you the scholar, Bentham, made a banjax o' th' Will; instead o' sayin', "th' rest o' me property to be divided between me first cousin, Jack Boyle, an' me second cousin, Mick Finnegan, o' Santhry," he writ down only, "me first an' second cousins," an' the world an' his wife are afther th' property now.

MRS. BOYLE. Now, I know why Bentham left poor Mary in th' lurch; I can see it all now — oh, is there not even a middlin' honest man left in th' world?

JOHNNY [to BOYLE]. An' you let us run into debt, an' you borreyed money from everybody to fill yourself with beer! An' now, you tell us the whole thing's a wash out! Oh, if it's thrue, I'm done with you, for you're worse than me sisther Mary!

BOYLE. You hole your tongue, d'ye hear? I'll not take any lip from you. Go an' get Bentham if you want satisfaction for all that's afther happenin' us.

JOHNNY. I won't hole me tongue, I won't hole me tongue! I'll tell you what I think of you, father an' all as you are... you...

MRS. BOYLE. Johnny, Johnny, Johnny, for God's sake, be quiet!

JOHNNY. I'll not be quiet, I'll not be quiet; he's a nice father, isn't he? Is it any wondher Mary went asthray, when...

MRS. BOYLE. Johnny, Johnny, for my sake be quiet — for your mother's sake!

BOYLE. I'm goin' out now to have a few dhrinks with th' last few makes I have, an' tell that lassie o' yours not to be here when I come back; for if I lay me eyes on her, I'll lay me han's on her, an' if I lay me han's on her, I won't be accountable for me actions!

JOHNNY. Take care somebody doesn't lay his han's on you — y'oul'...

MRS. BOYLE. Johnny, Johnny!

BOYLE [at door, about to go out]. Oh, a nice son, an' a nicer daughter, I have [Calling loudly upstairs.] Joxer, Joxer, are you there?

JOXER [from a distance]. I'm here More... ee... aar... i... tee!

BOYLE. I'm goin' down to Foley's — are you comin'?

JOXER. Come with you? With tha sweet call me heart is stirred; I'm onl' waiting for the word, an' I'll be with yo' like a bird!

[BOYLE and JOXER pass the do going out.]

JOHNNY [throwing himself on the bec I've a nice sisther, an' a nice father, there no bettin' on it. I wish to God a bullet a bomb had whipped me ou' o' this lo go! Not one o' yous, not one o' yous, have any thought for me!

MRS. BOYLE [*with passionate remonstrance*]. If you don't whisht, Johnny, you'll drive me mad. Who has kep' th' home together for the past few years — only me. An' who'll have to bear th' biggest part o' this throuble but me — but whinin' an' whingin' isn't goin' to do any good.

JOHNNY. You're to blame yourself for a gradle of it — givin' him his own way in everything, an' never assin' to check him, no matther what he done. Why didn't you look afther th' money? why...

[*There is a knock at the door; MRS. BOYLE opens it; JOHNNY rises on his elbow to look and listen; two men enter.*]

FIRST MAN. We've been sent up be th' Manager of the Hibernian Furnishing Co., Mrs. Boyle, to take back the furniture that was got a while ago.

MRS. BOYLE. Yous'll touch nothin' here — how do I know who yous are?

FIRST MAN [*showing a paper*]. There's the ordher, ma'am. [*Reading.*] A chest o' drawers, a table, wan easy an' two ordinary chairs; wan mirror; wan chestherfield divan, an' a wardrobe an' two vases. [*To his comrade.*] Come on, Bill, it's afther knockin' off time already.

JOHNNY. For God's sake, mother, run down to Foley's an' bring father back, or we'll be left without a stick.

[*The men carry out the table.*]

MRS. BOYLE. What good would it be? You heard what he said before he went out.

JOHNNY. Can't you thry? He ought to be here, an' the like of this goin' on.

[MRS. BOYLE *puts a shawl around her, as* MARY *enters.*]

MARY. What's up, mother? I met men carryin' away the table, an' everybody's talking about us not gettin' the money after all.

MRS. BOYLE. Everythin's gone wrong, Mary, everythin'. We're not gettin' a penny out o' the Will, not a penny — I'll tell you all when I come back; I'm goin' for your father. [*She runs out.*]

JOHNNY [*to* MARY, *who has sat down by the fire*]. It's a wondher you're not ashamed to show your face here, afther what has happened.

[JERRY *enters slowly; there is a look of earnest hope on his face. He looks at* MARY *for a few moments.*]

JERRY [*softly*]. Mary!
                    [MARY *does not answer.*]

JERRY. Mary, I want to speak to you for a few moments, may I?

        [MARY *remains silent;* JOHNNY *goes slowly into room on left.*]

JERRY. Your mother has told me everything, Mary, and I have come to you.... I have come to tell you, Mary, that my love for you is greater and deeper than ever....

MARY [*with a sob*]. Oh, Jerry, Jerry, say no more; all that is over now; anything like that is impossible now!

JERRY. Impossible? Why do you talk like that, Mary?

MARY. After all that has happened.

JERRY. What does it matter what has happened? We are young enough to be able to forget all those things [*He catches her hand.*] Mary, Mary, I am pleading for your love. With Labour, Mary, humanity is above everything; we are the Leaders in the fight for a new life. I want to forget Bentham, I want to forget that you left me — even for a while.

MARY. Oh, Jerry, Jerry, you haven't the bitter word of scorn for me after all.

JERRY [*passionately*]. Scorn! I love you, love you, Mary!

MARY [*rising, and looking him in the eyes*]. Even though...

JERRY. Even though you threw me over for another man; even though you gave me many a bitter word!

MARY. Yes, yes, I know; but you love me, even though... even though... I'm ... goin'... goin'... [*He looks at her questioningly, and fear gathers in his eyes.*] Ah, I was thinkin' so.... You don't know everything!

JERRY [*poignantly*]. Surely to God, Mary, you don't mean that... that... that...

MARY. Now you know all, Jerry; now you know all!

JERRY. My God, Mary, have you fallen as low as that?

MARY. Yes, Jerry, as you say, I have fallen as low as that.

JERRY. I didn't mean it that way, Mary... it came on me so sudden, that I didn't mind what I was sayin'.... I never expected this — your mother never told me.... I'm sorry... God knows, I'm sorry for you, Mary.

MARY. Let us say no more, Jerry; I don't blame you for thinkin' it's terrible. ... I suppose it is.... Everybody'll think the same.... It's only as I expected — your humanity is just as narrow as the humanity of the others.

JERRY. I'm sorry, all the same.... I shouldn't have troubled you.... I wouldn't if I'd known... if I can do anything for you... Mary... I will.

[He turns to go, and halts at the door.]

MARY. Do you remember, Jerry, the verses you read when you gave the lecture in the Socialist Rooms some time ago, on Humanity's Strife with Nature?

JERRY. The verses — no; I don't remember them.

MARY. I do. They're runnin' in me head now —

> An' we felt the power that fashion'd
> All the lovely things we saw,
> That created all the murmur
> Of an everlasting law,
> Was a hand of force an' beauty,
> With an eagle's tearin' claw.
>
> Then we saw our globe of beauty
> Was an ugly thing as well,
> A hymn divine whose chorus
> Was an agonizin' yell;
> Like the story of a demon,
> That an angel had to tell.
>
> Like a glowin' picture by a
> Hand unsteady, brought to ruin;
> Like her craters, if their deadness
> Could give life unto the moon;
> Like the agonizing horror
> Of a violin out of tune.

[There is a pause, and DEVINE goes slowly out.]

JOHNNY [returning]. Is he gone?

MARY. Yes.

[The two men reënter.]

FIRST MAN. We can't wait any longer for t'oul' fella — sorry, Miss, but we have to live as well as th' nex' man.

[They carry out some things.]

JOHNNY. Oh, isn't this terrible!... I suppose you told him everything... couldn't you have waited for a few days ... he'd have stopped th' takin' of the things, if you'd kep' your mouth shut. Are you burnin' to tell every one of the shame you've brought on us?

MARY [snatching up her hat and coat]. Oh, this is unbearable!   [She rushes out.]

FIRST MAN [reëntering]. We'll take the chest o' drawers next — it's the heaviest.

[The votive light flickers for a moment, and goes out.]

JOHNNY [in a cry of fear]. Mother o' God, the light's afther goin' out!

FIRST MAN. You put the win' up me the way you bawled that time. The oil's all gone, that's all.

JOHNNY [with an agonizing cry]. Mother o' God, there's a shot I'm afther gettin'!

FIRST MAN. What's wrong with you, man? Is it a fit you're takin'?

JOHNNY. I'm afther feelin' a pain in me breast, like the tearin' by of a bullet!

FIRST MAN. He's goin' mad — it's a a wondher they'd leave a chap like that here be himself.

[Two IRREGULARS enter swiftly; they carry revolvers; one goes over to JOHNNY; the other covers the two furniture men.]

FIRST IRREGULAR [to the men, quietly and incisively]. Who are you — what are yous doin' here — quick!

FIRST MAN. Removin' furniture that's not paid for.

IRREGULAR. Get over to the other end of the room an' turn your faces to the wall — quick.

[The two men turn their faces to the wall, with their hands up.]

SECOND IRREGULAR [to JOHNNY]. Come on, Sean Boyle, you're wanted; some of us have a word to say to you.

JOHNNY. I'm sick, I can't — what do you want with me?

SECOND IRREGULAR. Come on, come on; we've a distance to go, an' haven't much time — come on.

JOHNNY. I'm an oul' comrade — yous wouldn't shoot an oul' comrade.

SECOND IRREGULAR. Poor Tancred was an oul' comrade o' yours, but you didn't think o' that when you gave him away to the gang that sent him to his grave. But we've no time to waste; come on — here, Dermot, ketch his arm. [*To* JOHNNY.] Have you your beads?

JOHNNY. Me beads! Why do you ass me that, why do you ass me that?

SECOND IRREGULAR. Go on, go on, march!

JOHNNY. Are yous goin' to do in a comrade — look at me arm, I lost it for Ireland.

SECOND IRREGULAR. Commandant Tancred lost his life for Ireland.

JOHNNY. Sacred Heart of Jesus, have mercy on me! Mother o' God, pray for me — be with me now in the agonies o' death!... Hail, Mary, full o' grace... the Lord is... with Thee.

[*They drag out* JOHNNY BOYLE, *and the curtain falls. When it rises again the most of the furniture is gone.* MARY *and* MRS. BOYLE, *one on each side, are sitting in a darkened room, by the fire; it is an hour later.*]

MRS. BOYLE. I'll not wait much longer ... what did they bring him away in the mother for? Nugent says he thinks they had guns... is me throubles never goin' to be over?... If anything ud happen to poor Johnny, I think I'd lost me mind.... I'll go to the Police Station, surely they ought to be able to do somethin'.

[*Below is heard the sound of voices.*]

MRS. BOYLE. Whisht, is that something? Maybe, it's your father, though when I left him in Foley's he was hardly able to lift his head. Whisht!

[*A knock at the door, and the voice of* MRS. MADIGAN, *speaking very softly.*] Mrs. Boyle, Mrs. Boyle.

[MRS. BOYLE *opens the door.*]

MRS. MADIGAN. Oh, Mrs. Boyle, God an' His Blessed Mother be with you this night!

MRS. BOYLE [*calmly*]. What is it, Mrs. Madigan? It's Johnny — something about Johnny.

MRS. MADIGAN. God send it's not, God send it's not Johnny!

MRS. BOYLE. Don't keep me waitin', Mrs. Madigan; I've gone through so much lately that I feel able for anything.

MRS. MADIGAN. Two polismen below wantin' you.

MRS. BOYLE. Wantin' me; an' why do they want me?

MRS. MADIGAN. Some poor fella's been found, an' they think it's, it's...

MRS. BOYLE. Johnny, Johnny!

MARY [*with her arms round her mother*]. Oh, mother, mother, me poor, darlin' mother.

MRS. BOYLE. Hush, hush, darlin'; you'll shortly have your own throuble to bear. [*To* MRS. MADIGAN.] An' why do the polis think it's Johnny, Mrs. Madigan?

MRS. MADIGAN. Because one o' the doctors knew him when he was attendin' with his poor arm.

MRS. BOYLE. Oh, it's thrue, then; it's Johnny, it's me son, me own son!

MARY. Oh, it's thrue, it's thrue what Jerry Devine says — there isn't a God, there isn't a God; if there was He wouldn't let these things happen!

MRS. BOYLE. Mary, Mary, you mustn't say them things. We'll want all the help we can get from God an' His Blessed Mother now! These things have nothin' to do with the Will o' God. Ah, what can God do agen the stupidity o' men!

MRS. MADIGAN. The polis want you to go with them to the hospital to see the poor body — they're waitin' below.

MRS. BOYLE. We'll go. Come, Mary, an' we'll never come back here agen. Let your father fardge for himself now; I've done all I could an' it was all no use — he'll be hopeless till the end of his days. I've got a little room in me sisther's where we'll stop till your throuble is over, an' then we'll work together for the sake of the baby.

MARY. My poor little child that'll have no father!

MRS. BOYLE. It'll have what's far betther — it'll have two mothers.

[*A rough voice shouting from below.*]

Are yous goin' to keep us waitin' for yous all night?

MRS. MADIGAN [*going to the door, and shouting down*]. Take your hour, there, take your hour! If yous are in such a hurry, skip off, then, for nobody wants you here — if they did yous wouldn't be found. For you're the same as yous were undher the British Government — never where yous are wanted! As far as I can see, the Polis as Polis, in this city, is Null an' Void!

MRS. BOYLE. We'll go, Mary, we'll go; you to see your poor dead brother, an' me to see me poor dead son!

MARY. I dhread it, mother, I dhread it!

MRS. BOYLE. I forgot, Mary, I forgot; your poor oul' selfish mother was only thinkin' of herself. No, no, you mustn't come — it wouldn't be good for you. You go on to me sisther's an' I'll face th' ordeal meself. Maybe I didn't feel sorry enough for Mrs. Tancred when her poor son was found as Johnny's been found now — because he was a Die-hard! Ah, why didn't I remember that then he wasn't a Die-hard or a Stater, but only a poor dead son! It's well I remember all that she said — an' it's my turn to say it now: What was the pain I suffered, Johnny, bringin' you into the world to carry you to your cradle to the pains I'll suffer carryin' you out o' the world to bring you to your grave! Mother o' God, Mother o' God, have pity on us all! Blessed Virgin, where were you when me darlin' son was riddled with bullets, when me darlin' son was riddled with bullets? Sacred Heart o' Jesus, take away our hearts o' stone, and give us hearts o' flesh! Take away this murdherin' hate, an' give us Thine own eternal love! [*They all go slowly out.*]

[*There is a pause; then a sound of shuffling steps on the stairs outside. The door opens and* BOYLE *and* JOXER, *both of them very drunk, enter.*]

BOYLE. I'm able to go no farther.... Two polis, ey... what were they doin' here, I wondher?... Up to no good, anyhow... an' Juno an' that lovely daughter o' mine with them. [*Taking a sixpence from his pocket and looking at it.*] Wan single, solitary tanner left out of all I borreyed. ... [*He lets it fall.*] The last o' the Mohicans.... The blinds is down, Joxer, the blinds is down!

JOXER [*walking unsteadily across the room, and anchoring at the bed*]. Put all... your throubles... in your oul' kit bag... an' smile... smile... smile!

BOYLE. The counthry'll have to steady itself... it's goin'... to hell.... Where'r all ... the chairs... gone to... steady itself, Joxer... Chairs'll... have to... steady themselves.... No matther... what any one may ... say.... Irelan' sober... is Irelan'... free.

JOXER [*stretching himself on the bed*]. Chains... an'... slaveree... that's a darlin' motto... a daaarlin'... motto!

BOYLE. If th' worst comes... to th' worse... I can join a... flyin'... column. ... I done... me bit... in Easther Week ... had no business... to... be... there... but Captain Boyle's Captain Boyle!

JOXER. Breathes there a man with soul ... so... de... ad... this... me... o... wn, me nat... ive l... an'!

BOYLE [*subsiding into a sitting posture on the floor*]. Commandant Kelly died... in them... arms... Joxer.... Tell me Volunteer Butties... says he... that... I died for ... Irelan'!

JOXER. D'jever rade Willie... Reilly... an' his... own... Colleen... Bawn? It's a darlin' story, a daarlin' story!

BOYLE. I'm telling you... Joxer... th' whole worl's... in a terr... ible state o' ... chassis!

CURTAIN

SUCH IS LIFE
A PLAY IN FIVE ACTS
By FRANK WEDEKIND
ENGLISH VERSION BY FRANCIS J. ZIEGLER

CHARACTERS

NICOLA, *King of Umbria*

PRINCESS ALMA, *his daughter*

PIETRO FOLCHI, *Master Butcher*

FILIPO FOLCHI, *his son*

ANDREA VALORI } *Citizens of Perugia*

BENEDETTO NARDI

PANDOLFO, *Master Tailor*

A Soldier

A Farmer

A Vagabond

MICHELE

BATTISTA } *Journeyman Tailors*

NOE

The Presiding Judge

The King's Attorney-General

The Advocate

The Clerk of the Court

The Jailer

A Circus Rider

An Actor

A Procuress

First Theater Manager

Second Theater Manager

A Page

First Servant

Second Servant

Artisans, judges, townspeople, stroller, theater audience, theater servants, soldiers, and halberdiers

SUCH IS LIFE

ACT I

Scene One — *The Throne Room*

First Servant [*leaning out of the window*]. They are coming! It will overtake us like the day of judgment!

Second Servant [*rushing in through the opposite door*]. Do you know that the King is taken?

First Servant. Our King a captive?

Second Servant. Since early yesterday! The dogs have thrown him into prison!

First Servant. Then we had better scamper away, or they will treat us as if we were the beds upon which he has debauched their children!

[*The servants rush out. The room becomes filled with armed workmen of various trades, heated and blood-splashed from combat.*]

Pietro Folchi [*steps from their midst.*] Fellow-citizens! — The byways of Perugia are strewn with the corpses of our children and our brothers. Many of you have a pious wish to give your beloved dead a fitting resting place. — Fellow-citizens! First we must fulfill a higher duty. Let us do our part as quickly as possible, so that the dead shall have perished, not solely for their bravery, but for the lasting welfare of their native land! Let us seize the moment! Let us give our State a constitution which, in future, will protect her children from the assassin's weapons and insure her citizens the just reward of their labors!

The Citizens. Long live Pietro Folchi!

Andrea Valori. Fellow-citizens! Unless we decide at once upon our future form of government, we shall only be holding this dearly captured place for our enemies until we lose it again. We are holding the former King in custody in prison; the patricians, who supported themselves in idleness by the sweat of our brows, are in flight toward neighboring States. Now, I ask you, fellow-citizens, shall we proclaim our State the Umbrian Republic, as has been done in Florence, in Parma, and in Siena?

The Citizens. Long live Freedom! Long live Perugia! Long live the Umbrian Republic!

Pietro Folchi. Let us proceed without delay to elect a podestà! Here are tables and styles in plenty. Let each one write the name of the man whom he considers best fitted to guide the destiny of the State and to defend the power we have gained from our enemies.

The Citizens. Long live our podestà, Pietro Folchi! Long live the Republic of Perugia!

Andrea Valori. Fellow-citizens! Let there be no precipitate haste at this hour! It is necessary to strengthen so the power we have won that they cannot prevail against us as long as we live. Would we succeed if we made Umbria a republic? Under the shelter of republican liberty, the sons of the banished nobles would use the vanity of our daughters to bind us again in chains while we slept unsuspectingly at night! Look at Florence! Look at Siena! Is not liberty in those States only the cloak of the most dissolute despotism, which is turning their citizens to beggars? Perugia grew in power and prosperity under her kings, until the scepter passed into the hands of a fool and a wastrel. Let us raise the worthiest of us up to his throne. Then we, who stand here exhausted from the conflict, will become the future aristocracy and the lords of the land; only then can we enjoy in lasting peace our hard-won prerogatives.

The Citizens. Long live the king! Long live Pietro Folchi!

A Few Voices. Long live Freedom!

The Citizens [*louder*]. Long live our

king, Pietro Folchi! Long live King Pietro!

A FEW CITIZENS [*leaving the room angrily*]. We did not shed our blood for this. Down with Slavery! Long live Freedom!

THE CITIZENS. Hurrah for King Pietro!

PIETRO FOLCHI [*mounting the throne*]. Called to it by your choice, I mount this throne and name myself King of Umbria! The dissatisfied who have separated from our midst with the cry of "Freedom" are no less our enemies than the idle nobles who have turned their backs to our walls. I shall keep a watchful eye on them, as they fought on our side only in the hope of plundering in the ruins of our beloved city. Where is my son Filipo?

FILIPO FOLCHI [*stepping from out the press*]. What is your will, my father?

KING PIETRO. From the wounds above your eyes, I see that you did not shun death yesterday or to-day! I name you commander of our war forces. Post our loyal soldiers at the ten gates of the city, and order the drum to beat in the market-place for recruits. Perugia must be armed for an expedition to its frontiers in the shortest possible time. You will be answerable to me for the life of every citizen and responsible for the inviolate safety of all property. Now bring the former King of Umbria forth from his prison. It is proper that none save I announce to him his sentence.

FILIPO. Your commands shall be observed punctually. — Long live King Pietro! [*Exit.*]

KING PIETRO. Where is my son-in-law, Andrea Valori?

ANDREA VALORI [*stepping forward*]. Here, my King, at your command!

KING PIETRO. I name you treasurer of the Kingdom of Umbria. You and my cousin, Giullio Diaceto, together with our celebrated jurist, Bernardo Ruccellai, whose persuasive words abroad have more than once preserved our city from bloodshed; you three shall be my advisors in the discharge of affairs of state. [*After the three summoned have come forward.*] Seat yourselves beside me. [*They do so.*] I can only

fulfill the high duty of ruling others if the most able men in the State will enlist their lives in my service. — And now, let the others go to bury the victims of this two days' conflict. To show that they did not die in vain for the welfare of their brothers and children, let this be a day of mourning and earnest vigilance.

[*All leave the room save KING PIETRO, the Councilors and several guards. Then the captive KING is led in by FILIPO FOLCHI and several armed men.*]

THE KING. Who is bold enough to dare bring us here at the bidding of these disloyal knaves?

KING PIETRO. According to the provision of our laws, the royal power in Umbria fell to you as eldest son of King Giovanni. You have used your power to degrade the name of a king with roisterers and courtesans. You chose banquets, masquerades, and hunting parties, by which you have dissipated the treasures of the State and made the country poor and defenseless, in preference to every princely duty. You have robbed us of our daughters, and your deeds have been the most corrupting example to our sons. You have lived as little for the State's welfare as for your own. You accomplished only the downfall of your own and our native land.

THE KING. To whom is the butcher speaking?

FILIPO FOLCHI. Silence!

THE KING. Give me back my sword!

ANDREA VALORI. Put him in chains! He is raving!

THE KING. Let the butcher speak further.

KING PIETRO. Your life is forfeited and lies in my hands. But I will suspend sentence of death if in legal document you will relinquish in my favor, and in favor of my heirs, your claim and that of your kin to the throne, and acknowledge me as your lord, your rightful successor and as the ruler of Umbria.

THE KING [*laughs boisterously*]. Ha, ha, ha! Ask of a carp lying in the pan to cease to be a fish! That this worm has our life in his power proves indeed that princes are not gods, because, like other men, they are mortal. The lightning, too, can kill; but he who is born a king does not die like an ordinary mortal! Let one of these artisans lay hands upon us, if his blood does not first chill in his veins. Then he shall see how a king dies!

KING PIETRO. You are a greater enemy to yourself than your deadliest foes can possibly be. Although you will not abdicate, we will be mild, in thankful remembrance of the blessed rule of King Giovanni, whose own son you are, and banish you now and forever from the confines of the Umbrian States, under penalty of death.

THE KING. Banish! Ha, ha, ha! Who in the world will banish the King! Shall fear of death keep him from the land of which Heaven appointed him the ruler? Only an artisan could hold life so dear and a crown so cheap! — Ha, ha, ha! These pitiable fools seem to imagine that when a crown is placed upon a butcher, he becomes a king! See how the paunch-belly grows pale and shivers up there, like a cheese flung against the wall! Ha, ha, ha! How they stare at us, the stupid blockheads, with their moist dogs' eyes, as if the sun had fallen at their feet!

PRINCESS ALMA [rushes in, breaking through the guards at the door. She is fifteen years old, is clad in rich but torn garments and her hair is disheveled]. Let me pass! Let me go to my father! Where is my father? [Sinking down before the KING and embracing his knees.] Father! Have I you again, my dearly beloved father?

THE KING [raising her]. So I hold you unharmed in my arms once more, my dearest treasure! Why must you come to me with your heartrending grief just at this moment when I had almost stamped these bloodthirsty hounds beneath my feet again!

ALMA. Then let me die with you! To share death with you would be the greatest happiness, after what I have lived through in the streets of Perugia these last two days! They would not let me come to you in prison, but now you are mine again! Remember, my father, I have no one else in the world but you!

THE KING. My child, my dear child,

why do you compel me to confess before my murderers how weak I am! Go! I have brought my fate upon myself; let me bear it alone. These men will confirm it that you may expect more compassion and better fortune from my bitterest enemies than if you cling now to your father, broken by fate.

ALMA [with greatest intensity]. No, do not say that! I beseech you do not speak so again! [Caressingly.] Only remember that it is not yet decided that they murder us. And if we had rather die together than be parted, who in the world can harm us then!

KING PIETRO [who during this scene has quietly come to an agreement with his Councilors, turning to the KING]. The city of Perugia will give your daughter the most careful education until her majority, and then bestow upon her a princely dower, if she will promise to give her hand in marriage to my son, Filipo Folchi, who will be my successor upon this throne.

THE KING. You have heard, my child? The throne of your father is open to you!

ALMA. O my God, how can you so scoff at your poor child!

KING PIETRO [to the KING]. As for you, armed men under the command of my son shall conduct you, within this hour, to the confines of this country. Have a care that you do not take so much as a step within our land hereafter, or your head shall fall by the hand of the executioner in the market-place of Perugia!

[FILIPO FOLCHI has the KING and the PRINCESS, clinging close to her father, led off by men-at-arms. He is about to follow them, when his arm is seized by BENEDETTO NARDI, who rushes in breathless with rage.]

BENEDETTO NARDI. Have I caught you, scoundrel! [To KING PIETRO.] This son of yours, Pietro Folchi, in company with his drunken comrades, chased my helpless child through the streets of the city yesterday evening, and was about to lay hands on two of my journeymen, attracted by her cries, put the scoundrels to flight with their clubs. The wretch still carries the bloody mark above his eyes!

KING PIETRO [*in anger*]. Defend yourself, my son!

FILIPO FOLCHI. He speaks the truth.

KING PIETRO. Back to the shop with you! Must I see my rule disgraced on its first day by my own son in most impious fashion! The law shall work its greatest hardship upon you! Afterward you shall stay in the butcher shop until the citizens of Perugia kneel before me and beg me to have pity on you! Put him in chains!

[*The mercenaries who led out the* KING *return with* ALMA. *Their leader throws himself on his knees before the throne.*]

THE MERCENARY. O Sire, do not punish your servants for this frightful misfortune! As we were leading the King just here before the portal across the bridge of San Margherita, a company of our comrades marched past and pressed us against the coping. The prisoner seized that opportunity to leap into the flood swollen by the rain. We needed all our strength to prevent this maiden from doing likewise, and, when I was about to leap after the prisoner, the raging waves had long engulfed him.

KING PIETRO. His life is not the most regrettable sacrifice of these bloody days! Hundreds of better men have fallen for him. [*To the Councilors.*] Let the child be taken to the Ursuline nuns and kept under most careful guard. [*Rising.*] The sitting of the Council is closed.

ALL PRESENT. Long live King Pietro!

SCENE TWO — *A highway along the edge of a forest*

[*The* KING *and* PRINCESS ALMA, *both clad as beggars.*]

THE KING. How long have I been dragging you from place to place while you begged for me?

ALMA. Rest yourself, Father; you will be in better spirits afterward.

THE KING [*sits down by the wayside*]. Why did not the raging waves swallow me that evening! Then everything would have been over long ago!

ALMA. Did you leap over the side of the bridge to put an end to your life? I thought what strength resided in your arms and that the rushing waters would help you to liberty. Without this faith how should I have had the courage to escape from the convent and from the city?

THE KING. Below us here lie the rich hunting grounds where I have often ridden hawking with my court. You were too young to accompany us.

ALMA. Why will you not leave this little land of Umbria, my father! The world is so large! In Siena, in Modena, your friends dwell. They would welcome you with joy, and at last your dear head would be safe.

THE KING. You offer me much, my child! Still, I beg of you not to keep repeating this question. Just in this lies my fate: if I were able to leave this land, I should not have lost my crown. But my soul is ruled by desires which I cannot relinquish, even to save my life. As king, I believed myself safe enough from the world to live my dreams without danger. I forgot that the king, the peasant, and every other man, must live only to preserve his station and to defend his estate, unless he would lose both.

ALMA. Now you are scoffing at yourself, my father!

THE KING. That is the way of the world! — You think I am scoffing at myself? — That, at least, might be something for which men would contribute to our support. As I offer myself to them now, I am of no use. Either I offend them by my arrogance and pride, which are in ridiculous contrast to my beggar's rags, or my courteous demeanor makes them mistrustful, as none of them succeeds by simple modesty. How my spirit has debased itself during these six months, in order to fit itself to their ways and methods! But everything I learned as hereditary prince of Umbria is valueless in their world, and everything which is of worth in their world, I did not learn as a prince. But if I succeed in jesting at my past, my child, who knows but what we may find again a place at a richly decked table! When the pork butcher is raised to the throne, there remains no calling for the King save that of court fool.

ALMA. Do not enrage yourself so in your

fatigue, my father. See, you must take a little nap! I will look for fresh water to quench your thirst and cool your fevered brow.

THE KING [*laying down his head*]. Thank you, my child.

ALMA [*kissing him*]. My dear father!
[*Exit.*]

THE KING [*rises*]. How I have grown to love this beautiful land since I have slunk about it at the risk of my life! — Even the worst disaster always brings good with it. Had I not cared so little for my brave people of Perugia and Umbria, had I not shown myself to them only at carnivals and in fancy dress, God knows, but I might have been recognized long ago! Here comes one of them now!

[*A landed proprietor comes up the road.*]

THE KING. God greet you, sir! Can you not give me work on your estate?

THE LANDED PROPRIETOR. You might find much to recompense your work on my estate, but, thank God, my house is guarded by fierce wolf hounds. And here, you see, I carry a hunting knife, which I can use so well that I should not advise you to come a step nearer me!

THE KING. Sir, you have no guarantee from Heaven that you may not be compelled at some time to beg for work in order not to go hungry.

THE LANDED PROPRIETOR. Ha, ha, ha! He who works in order not to go hungry, he is the right kind of worker for me! First comes work and then the hunger. Let him who can live without work starve rather to-day than to-morrow!

THE KING. Sir, you must have had wiser teachers than I!

THE LANDED PROPRIETOR. I should hope so! What have you learned?

THE KING. The trade of war.

THE LANDED PROPRIETOR. Thank God, under the rule of King Pietro, whom Heaven long preserve to us, there is little use for that in Umbria any longer. City and country enjoy peace, and at last we live in concord with neighboring states.

THE KING. Sir, you will find me of use for any work on your estate.

THE LANDED PROPRIETOR. I will think

over the matter. You appear a harmless fellow. I am on my way to my nephew, who has a large house and family at Todi. I am coming back this afternoon. Wait for me here at this spot. Possibly I will take you with me then. [*Exit.*]

THE KING. "Let him who can live without work starve." What old saws this vermin cherished to endure his miserable existence! And I? — I cannot even feed my child! A lordship was given me by Heaven such as only one in a million can have! And I cannot even give my child food! — My kind father made every hour of the day a festival for me by means of joyous companions, by the wisest teachers, by a host of devoted servants, and my child must shiver with cold and sleep under the hedges by the highway! Have pity on her, O God, and blot her love for miserable me out of her heart! Let happen to me then whatever will, I will bear it lightly!

ALMA [*rushes out of the bushes with her hair tumbling down*]. Father! Jesu, Maria! My father! Help!

THE KING [*clasping her in his arms*]. What is it, child?

A VAGABOND [*who has followed the maiden, comes forward and stops*]. Ah! — How could I know another had her!

THE KING [*rushes upon him with uplifted stick*]. Hence, you dirty dog!

THE VAGABOND. I a dirty dog! What are you, then?

THE KING [*striking him*]. That am I! — And that! — And that!

[*The VAGABOND seeks refuge in flight.*]

ALMA [*trembling in her father's arms*]. O Father, I was leaning over the spring when that man sprang at me!

THE KING [*breathing hard*]. Calm yourself, my child ——

ALMA. My poor father! That I, instead of being able to help you, must still need your help!

THE KING. To-day I shall take you back to Perugia. Will throw you at King Pietro's feet ——

ALMA. Oh, do not let me hear of that again! Can I leave you when death threatens you daily?

THE KING. It would be better for you to

wear man's clothes, instead of a woman's dress, in the future. It is marvel enough that Providence has protected you until to-day from the horrors that threaten you in our wanderings! You will be safer in man's clothes. A countryman just passed this way. When he comes back, he will take me with him and give me work on his place.

ALMA. Will you really seek again to put yourself in the service of those so abysmally beneath you?

THE KING. What are you saying, my child! Why are they below me? — Besides, it is not quite certain that he will find me worthy of his work. If he asks me to go with him, then follow us, so that I can turn my place under his roof over to you at night.

ALMA. No, no! You must not suffer hardship on my account. Have I deserved that of you?

THE KING. Do you know, my child, that if I had not had you with me, my treasure, as guardian angel, I should very probably be hanging to-day on a high gallows for highway robbery? [*He sits down again by the roadside.*] And now, let us tarry here in patient expectation of the all-powerful man whose return will decide whether our desire to live in communion with mankind is to be fulfilled.

ACT II

SCENE ONE — *The Workshop of a Ladies' Tailor*

[*The* KING, *in journeyman's clothes, sits cross-legged on a table, working on a woman's gown of rich material.* MASTER PANDOLFO *bustles into the room.*]

MASTER PANDOLFO. Early to work, Gigi! Early to work! Bravo, Gigi!

THE KING. The cock has crowed, Master!

MASTER PANDOLFO. Now shake me the other fellows awake. One can work better in company than alone, Gigi! [*Takes the dress out of his hands.*] See here, Gigi! [*He tears the dress.*] Rip! What's the use of early to bed and early to rise if the stitches don't hold? And the buttonholes,

Gigi! Did the rats help you with them? I worked for Her Majesty Queen Amelia when her husband was still making mortadella and salmi. Am I to lose her custom now because of your botching? Hey, Gigi?

THE KING. If my work shames you, turn me out!

MASTER PANDOLFO. How rude, Gigi. Do you think you are still tending pigs at Baschi? Forty years on your back and nothing learned! Go packing out of my house and see where you will find your food, then, you vagabond!

THE KING [*rises and collects the scraps*]. I'll take you at your word, Master!

MASTER PANDOLFO. What the devil, madcap! Can't you take a joke? Can I show more love toward my 'prentice than I do when I give him the work which usually the master does? Since you have been with me, haven't I allowed you to cut all the garments? The devil take me that I cannot catch the knack of your cutting! But the ladies of Perugia say, "Master Pandolfo, since the old apprentice has been working for you, your work has a genteel cut." But what's the use of a genteel cut if the young ladies tear the stitches out as they dance? You'll never be a journeyman, Gigi, unless you learn to sew. My dear, sweet Gigi, don't you see that I only want what's best for you?

THE KING. Good, Master Pandolfo, I'll stay with you if from now on, in addition to my keep, you will pay me thirty soldi more a week.

MASTER PANDOLFO. I'll promise you that, Gigi! As true as I stand here, I'll promise you that! — Thirty soldi you want? — Yes, yes! The gown for Her Majesty the Queen must be ready sewed by noon. Therefore, be industrious, Gigi! Always industrious! [*Exit.*]

[*The* KING *draws a long breath after* MASTER PANDOLFO *leaves the room, and then sits down to his work again. After a while,* PRINCESS ALMA *puts her head in through the window.*]

ALMA. Are you alone, Father?

THE KING [*springing up joyfully*]. My treasure!

[ALMA *vanishes and immediately after comes in through the door. She is dressed as a boy in a dark, neat suit of clothes.*]

THE KING. The master is upstairs with his morning dram, and the journeymen are still asleep. The moments I have with you, my child, indemnify my soul for the days of dull routine. What affectionate conversations I hold with you, and how lovingly and understandingly you answer me! Do not forsake me! It is a new crime I commit in asking this of you; but see, I am a weak man!

ALMA. Things will soon be better with us now, Father. The old notary, whose errand-boy I became two months ago, already lets me copy all his documents. Next week he is going to take me to court with him, in order that I may take down the case instead of him. — O my father, if only the death sentence which, now that we are in Perugia again, places you in greater danger than ever before, could be lifted from your head! — My feminine ignorance of politics prevents me conjecturing whether they will raise you to the throne again. But they should honor you as more than a king. There must be something Godlike about you when, in spite of your degradation, you are able to fill one with happiness as you do me! What a wealth of happiness you would have to give if your fetters were removed. Thousands then would contend for you, and you would no longer envy any king the weight of his crown!

THE KING. Do not talk further about me. I must wait in obscurity until my hour is come. — But you, my child, do you not feel deadly unhappy under the burden of your work? — Isn't your master disagreeable when he needs some one upon whom to vent his bad temper?

ALMA. But don't you see what good spirits I am in, Father? The people I serve know how to value education and culture. You, on the contrary, must live with a brood of men whose daily habits must torment your soul, even without their knowledge or desire. I see you grind your teeth at this or that retort. I see how your throat contracts with disgust at mealtimes. Oh, forgive my words! They are unmindful of your smarting wounds.

THE KING [*whimsically*]. Only think, my child, the result of these unusual circumstances is that I am cherished by Master Pandolfo as his most industrious worker. At Baschi, where I tended cattle, I made a shed behind the stables my sleeping-place. I used to lie there every morning on my back, following my dreams until the sun stood over me in the zenith. That's the reason the farmer discharged me. Here I sleep with three common fellows, and, therefore, am the first to rise and the last to go to bed. Personally, I do not sleep as well in the company of men as I do in the company of beasts. I never dreamed such an industrious worker was concealed within me! Work serves me as a kind of refuge. And then the beautiful hues of the heavy velvet, the sheen of the gold brocade! They refresh my soul and I long for them as for a vivifying drink. And then Master Pandolfo's insight discovered in me at once a gift which astonishes me highly, and which, to be candid, I could not give up lightly. He found I was better able than any of his workmen, better able than himself even, to cut the stuff for the ladies' dresses so as to bring out the figure to the best advantage. For example, that doublet you wear I should have cut quite differently than did that miserable botcher whose shears were not worthy to touch such splendid cloth.

ALMA. Oh, silence, Father! How can you jest so callously at your unhappy fate!

THE KING [*passionately*]. Do not mock me with flattery, my child! — Fate jests at me, and not I at it!

ALMA [*soothingly*]. Beloved father, you remain a king, no matter what you must do in this world.

THE KING. In your loving heart, yes! — And, therefore, your father, with loving despotism, opposes your life's happiness by crowding out of your heart that longing for a man which must be awakening in you at your age. — Your father's egotistical folly has lost you rank and property; now it deprives you of the highest rights of life —

those which the creatures of the wilderness share with mankind and which may make existence in a hut, as well as on a throne, a gift of the gods! What madness made me test my strength against the flood of the San Margherita brook, instead of invading Umbria by war, setting the city on fire at its four corners, and snatching the crown with my own hands from the glowing ruins! — But that was only the continuation of past folly!

ALMA [weeping]. Heaven have mercy on my foolish soul! How was it possible for me so to grieve you!

THE KING. In misfortune people hurt each other without knowledge or desire, just as truly as in happiness each one brings joy to the other unwittingly. Do not make him who is judged suffer for it. You must go, my child; I hear the workmen shouting and tramping about upstairs.

ALMA [kissing him]. To-morrow morning early! [Exit.]

[The KING takes up his work. Then the three journeymen come in, and, sitting down on separate tables on the other side of the room, prepare for work.]

MICHELE. Gigi, if you get up before cockcrow again, I'll break your nose the next night while you sleep. Then go to the women and see if you can succeed with them!

THE KING. It would please you well to attack a sleeping man. But take care of your own bones at it, or perhaps you might not rise at all the next day!

NOE. Well said, Gigi! Tell us quickly more of your warlike deeds, that we may be afraid of you.

THE KING. I haven't time. If your ears itch for tales of heroic deeds, tell how you stole the parson's geese at Bavagna.

BATTISTA. Our patron saint defend us! Usually, you are as tame and sneaking as if your nail had never crushed a louse, and to-day you would like to spit all three of us at once on your needle.

THE KING. Let me be in peace, then! A hollow tooth is hurting me. That's the reason I left the sleeping-room so early.

NOE. Tell the truth, Gigi! Wasn't the page here just now who brings you the

glowing love-letters from the lady for whom you cut the yellow silk dress?

THE KING. Do I concern myself with your love-letters?

MICHELE. You concern yourself with entirely different things! You get up right after midnight to practice being a lickspittle and a trimmer! You get the master to give you the journeymen's work and divide the apprentice's work among us! You are a pest in the house!

BATTISTA. Apprentice, bring us the morning soup!

[The KING leaves the workroom.]

NOE. He's lacking in the upper story; I am sorry for him. He must have been some sort of bootcleaner for a gentleman of quality. That moved his brain out of place in his skull.

BATTISTA. Did you ever see a soldier who would let himself be kicked about so by journeymen tailors?

NOE. My mother was a country girl; I tell that to anybody who asks me; I don't act as if I had been bed servant to the Holy Father!

MICHELE. I'll tell you why the lad is so stupid. Each of us has knocked about the world, often with not enough to eat. But if he opens his mouth, out comes a stream of curses profane enough to turn one's stomach. Earth is ashamed at having brought forth such a monster; then Heaven is ashamed to have let its light fall upon him; then Hell is ashamed that it has not yet swallowed him! You will see!

[The KING returns with four wooden spoons and a pot of soup, which he sets before the journeymen.]

MICHELE. Get out, you beast! You can lick our spoons when we have had enough!

THE KING [strives with himself, seeking to master his anger, then strikes his brow]. Oh, a curse upon this King who hinders me from allowing myself to be thrashed by this rascal! Oh, a curse upon the King who hinders me crushing this rascal, whom I understand better than he understands me! Oh, a curse upon the King who hinders me from being a man like other men! Oh, a triple curse upon the King!

[The journeymen spring up in horror.]

MICHELE. Did you hear? He cursed the King! He cursed the King!

BATTISTA and NOE [*together*]. He has cursed the King!

MICHELE. Seize him! Hold him fast! — Master Pandolfo! — Master Pandolfo! — Knock in his teeth!

MASTER PANDOLFO [*rushing in*]. Get to work, lads! Why are you fighting so early in the morning? Are you mad?

THE JOURNEYMEN [*holding the* KING *by the arms*]. He has cursed the King! — "Curse the King!" he cried! "A triple curse upon the King!"

THE KING [*submitting indifferently to force*]. A triple curse upon the King! Then let the King's head fall under the headsman's axe.

THE JOURNEYMEN. Listen to him, Master Pandolfo!

THE KING [*to himself*]. My poor child!

MASTER PANDOLFO. Bind his hands behind his back! Cursing our dear, good King Pietro! "Let King Pietro's head fall under the headsman's axe!" Bring ropes! Take the dog to court! This vagabond will lose me my best customers! The head of King Pietro, who pays his bills more promptly than any king before him!

SCENE TWO — *The Court Room*

[*The Presiding Judge and two associates sit at the middle table; the Attorney-General for the Crown occupies a raised seat to the right; the counsel for the defense occupies a similar seat to the left. Further forward, to the right, is the Clerk of the Court, with* PRINCESS ALMA *as his amanuensis. She has the court records in front of her. Forward, on the left, are halberdiers guarding the door to the adjoining room. The back of the hall is filled with spectators.*]

THE PRESIDING JUDGE. I open the session in the name of his exalted majesty, the King. — According to his request, I grant the privilege of speaking first to the counsel for the prosecution, Signor Silvio Andreotti, Doctor of Canonical and Civil Law and Attorney-General for the Crown.

THE ATTORNEY-GENERAL. Under the rule of our sublime and beloved King Pietro, it has become the custom in our city of Perugia to permit the citizen to be present in court during a trial, in order to strengthen his confidence in the unshakable incorruptibility of our judgments. In view of the offense which is to be tried here to-day, I venture to suggest to the court that the spectators here assembled be excluded from our session, in order that they may be protected from looking too deeply into the degradation of human nature.

THE PRESIDING JUDGE. The well-considered suggestion of the honorable Attorney-General shall be followed.

[*The halberdiers, with crossed pikes, force the spectators quietly out of the hall.*]

THE PRESIDING JUDGE. Our sublime King Pietro has made the wise and just provision that any poor defendant, no matter what his nationality, be supplied with an advocate at the cost of the State. The worthy Signor Corrado Ezzelino, Master and Doctor of both Civil and Canonical Law, has declared himself ready to serve in this capacity to-day. Now, I grant the privilege of speaking, at his special request, to our worthy Clerk of the Court, Signor Matteo Nerli.

THE CLERK OF THE COURT. Honorable and wise judges, a cramp which lames my right hand, the result of long years of untiring industry in the service of the law, does not permit me the honor of taking down the minutes of to-day's session unassisted. By my side you see my apprenticed clerk, a lad who has awakened my affection, and who, despite his youth, has shown an unusual love of the law. I ask that he be permitted to keep the minutes, under the direction and supervision of his master.

THE PRESIDING JUDGE. Your wish is granted, Master Matteo. The witnesses who were called for to-day's session have all appeared in person. Conduct the defendant thither.

[*The halberdiers bring in the* KING *from the neighboring room.* PRINCESS ALMA *starts at sight of him, but collects*] *herself and arranges her writing materials.*]

THE PRESIDING JUDGE. You call yourself Ludovicus and were employed formerly in tending cattle at Baschi. You are accused of the *crimen laesae majestatis*, which was visited with severe penalties in the imperishable code of our great predecessors, the ancient Romans; the crime of injuring majesty, or, in other words, the insult to the holy person of the King. Do you acknowledge yourself guilty of this offense?

THE KING. Yes.

THE CLERK OF THE COURT [*to* ALMA]. He said "yes." Write it down, my lad; write it down accurately!

THE PRESIDING JUDGE. According to the unanimous testimony of four unprejudiced witnesses, your words were, "A triple curse upon the King! Let the King's head fall under the headsman's axe!"

THE KING. Those were my words.

THE CLERK OF THE COURT. "Those were my words!" Joseph and Mary, a blot! Lad, has the devil gotten into you to-day?

THE PRESIDING JUDGE. What have you to advance in your own behalf?

THE KING. Nothing.

MICHELE. He has nothing to advance! Did you hear? He has nothing to advance!

MASTER PANDOLFO. He spat out his terrible curse in miserable revenge against me! He wanted to bring my business and my whole family into disrepute.

THE PRESIDING JUDGE. Silence on the witness bench! — Now, what have you to say in your own defense?

THE KING. Nothing. — Next to the majesty of God, the majesty of the King stands highest in this world. The majesty of God suffers as little from human curses as the majesty of the King. Can the majesty of God be dimmed by vulgar humanity saying, "We believe in you no longer"? Can the majesty of the King be dimmed by people saying, "We will obey no longer"? Who would assert that as possible? — God wandered in lowly form upon this earth, and the rabble believed it had put Him to death. And so the rabble may believe it has banished the King; he remains where he was. If they call to him, "Let your head fall under the headsman's axe," it does him no harm. Therefore, although next to blaspheming against God, blaspheming against the King is the most execrable crime — a crime of which my words have made me guilty, as I acknowledge openly — it appears to me that the matter should be such an indifferent and trifling affair to the King that he should not need to revenge it. At the same time, it seems to me too frightful for the rabble to presume to be able ever to atone for it. The rabble, indeed, possesses no higher power than that over life and death, and, indeed, cannot know whether the miserable sinner would not welcome death, no matter how painful, as a liberation from a thousand sorrows. These, therefore, are the reasons why I hold that the judges before whom I now stand can execute no punishment upon me for my crime. [*General murmur of dissent.*] Now, let me, wise and honorable judges, name the grounds which make it your holy duty to judge me according to the greatest severity of the law.

NOE. I told you the fellow was completely crazy!

THE PRESIDING JUDGE [*to the witness bench*]. Silence! [*To the* KING.] Speak further.

THE KING. The majesty of the King, as I have proved commensurate to human reason, can receive no injury from my words. But, unfortunately, next to faith in the All-Goodness of Providence, faith in the majesty of the King is the highest and holiest possession of the common people. That which the sons of earth have known since all time as eternal truths, against which none, be he master or slave, sins unpunished, that stands under God's holy protection. Everything which they value, everything that affects their property and the prosperity of their daily work, *that* they enjoy with childish confidence in their King's protection. In their King the common people recognize the likeness of their own fortune, and who smirches this likeness robs them of the courage to work and of peace by night. I am far more guilty of this crime than human justice fathoms. It is impossible for the punishment hanging over me to approach the weight of my crime. Even should it cost my life, let it be what you will, I shall accept it from the hands of you judges as a grace of God.

THE PRESIDING JUDGE. The grace of your lord, our dear and blessed King, has placed a learned advocate at your side. — The honorable Signor Corrado Ezzelino, Master and Doctor of Civil and Canonical Law, may address the Court.

THE ADVOCATE FOR THE DEFENSE [rising]. My exalted, righteous, worthy, and honorable Judges, permit me first to speak a word concerning our brave and honest fellow-citizen, the master-tailor Cesare Pandolfo. We see him here to-day on the witness bench deeply bowed down as the result of the abominable crime which has taken place under his roof. We all of us recognize the staunchness of his principles; we all — all of us here assembled — know the excellence of his work. I believe myself able, therefore, to assure Master Pandolfo, in the name of all of us, that not one of us would think of associating him, even in the slightest degree, with the frightful crime which happened under his roof. — Now, concerning the defendant, whom it is my sad duty to defend: Apparently, he is an entirely disreputable scamp, more worthy of our deepest scorn than of being judged in the normal fashion according to the wise provision of the Roman code. Permit, O Judges, the words of the text, "Thou shalt not cast thy pearls before swine," to be followed in the case of this outcast from our dear commonweal. Because of his unexampled spiritual and moral degeneracy, it would be impossible for the defendant to know how to appreciate at its true worth the honor done him by weighing his case in the scales of justice; therefore, I request you, wise and honorable Judges, in order not to belittle the dignity of our calling, to let the punishment rest at flogging. Should punishment by flogging appear inadequate, wise and honorable Judges, possibly punishment by flogging might be augmented by three days'

exposure in the pillory in the market-place of Perugia.

THE PRESIDING JUDGE. I grant the floor to the Attorney-General, our worthy Signor Silvio Andreotti, Doctor of Civil and Canonical Law.

THE ATTORNEY-GENERAL [who during the whole proceedings has been groaning, yawning, and wriggling about in his seat]. Honorable Judges! As the worthy Signor Corrado Ezzelino has rightly and forcibly expressed it in his excellent defense, the defendant is a disreputable scamp, an outcast from our dear human community, an individual of unexampled moral degeneracy, in whom I cannot deny there is a certain mental craftiness, or, to speak more plainly, a certain peasant's cunning. His own words which he has spoken here are evidence of this peasant's cunning, as is also the fact that, with the intention of confusing our power of judgment, by creating a favorable impression, he has not attempted to deny his deed. When, however, an individual from the lowest depths of human degeneracy commits a crime such as this, which cries to Heaven, then that individual must be looked upon no longer as a human being, but as a wild beast; and such a one, as the defendant himself cleverly has shown, with the intention of tricking our judgment, is the most pernicious enemy of our commonwealth, for the protection of which I and you, you judges, have been placed here. Such a wild beast, by reason of his baseness, as well as on account of the danger he is to the community, deserves that he be destroyed by death and that his tracks be obliterated from the earth!

THE PRESIDING JUDGE. Defendant Ludovicus, what more have you to say?

THE KING. Nothing.

THE PRESIDING JUDGE. The witnesses are excused! — The court stands adjourned until the passing of sentence.

[The witnesses, the Judges and the Attorney-General leave the chamber.]

THE CLERK OF THE COURT [beating his head, to ALMA, who sits bathed in tears over the minutes]. Help me, holy Mary, Mother of God! The booby, with his foolishness, has blubbered all over the minutes! Not a letter can be read! The leaves are all stuck together!

ALMA [*sobbing*]. O my God, he is innocent! I know that he is innocent!

THE CLERK OF THE COURT. Why should it worry you whether he is innocent or guilty? Is it your head or his head they are going to cut off?

THE KING [*who stands alone in the middle of the room, aside, but with emphasis*]. My words were, "And so at last the King's head shall fall under the headsman's axe in the market-place of Perugia!"

THE CLERK OF THE COURT. There, you see how innocent he is!

ALMA [*who has risen and prays earnestly, with hands folded across her breast*]. Lord God in Heaven, Thou who hast compassion upon all the poor and miserable, preserve us from this!

THE CLERK OF THE COURT. See, now, you are a brave lad and have your heart in the right place! I shall certainly not bring you again soon to a sitting of the court. You must rewrite the whole minutes from memory at home. You will learn more from that than if you studied through the whole *corpus juris*!

THE ADVOCATE FOR THE DEFENSE [*who, after the Judges have left the chamber, has taken a package of bread and butter, a flask, and a glass from his robe. He places the flask and glass in front of him, and then comes forward, busy with his breakfast*]. Now, Gigi, wasn't that a Ciceronian defense that I made for you? But what do you know about Cicero! You will allow me to breakfast, of course. At first, I had the intention of sprinkling my defense with a little *curriculum vitae*, a moving description of your cattle tending, etc. But, to be frank, Gigi, I don't believe that either would have helped you much with those [*pointing*] dunderheads out there!

THE KING. You have my thanks for your pains, worthy Doctor Ezzelino.

[*The Judges return from the council-chamber and resume their places.*]

THE PRESIDING JUDGE [*reading from his notes*]. The defendant, Ludovicus, recently a tailor's apprentice in Perugia, and formerly employed in the tending of cattle in the village of Baschi, is accused of the crime of blasphemy against the holy person of the King, and is found guilty of this crime upon the evidence of unanimous testimony, as well as by his own admission. In consideration of his previous good character, as well as in consideration of his free confession, the defendant is sentenced to two years' incarceration ――――

ALMA [*gives a muffled cry*].

THE CLERK OF THE COURT. Young fellow, will you hold your tongue while the Judge is speaking!

THE PRESIDING JUDGE. ―――― and, furthermore, to ten years' deprivation of all the rights and honors of citizenship, as well as to banishment from the city of Perugia for the whole term of his life, under pain of death in case of his return.

THE CLERK OF THE COURT [*to* ALMA]. Write, my lad! Write! This is the most important of all!

THE PRESIDING JUDGE [*continuing his reading*]. In view of the important fact that the defendant has not shown the least trace of regret for his deed, the sentence provides that he shall spend his two years' incarceration in the most rigid solitary confinement. — Given in the name of the King, on the third day of the month of August, in the year of our Lord one thousand four hundred and ninety-nine. [*Turning to the guards.*] Take away the prisoner! [*Rising. To the court.*] I hereby declare to-day's session closed.

ACT III

SCENE ONE — *A Prison*

[*To the left, the cell door. To the right, a barred window. At the back, a folding bench, fastened against the wall.*]

THE KING [*sings to a lute*]:

With an ivy wreath my brow was dressed,
In my locks there sparkled the dew;
A pair of falcons above my crest
Wove circles in the blue.

From the balcony, in joyous vein,
My mother beckoned and smiled;

At e'en thy father will come again,
In victor's garb, my child.
[*He leans the lute against the wall,
sinks down upon a stool at the back of
the cell and plaits a straw mat.*]
THE KING. I am thirsty. — Is it really
so late in the day? — How time passes
here! [*He rises and looks curiously upward
through the window.*] By the Lord, the sun
is beginning to glide along the south wall
of the tower! — Time for the water jug!
[*He fetches an earthen jug from the corner
and stands expectantly before the door.*]
He will soon come! — Did I ever enjoy a
drink while I was King as I do the fresh
draught of water which I have received
daily at this hour for the last twelve-
month? I believe it's a stroke of good
fortune that I was never in jail during my
own reign.
[*The door opens noisily and a rough
voice outside calls, "Water jug!"
The* KING *hastily sets the jug outside the door and returns inside the
cell. The door slams shut, but is reopened immediately and the jailer
enters.*]
THE JAILER. Zounds and death, Gigi,
how did you smash the jug? Silence, you
dog! There's a hole in the jug. It was
sound yesterday. I'll pitch into you so
that your face will bleed! You take me for
your servant because lately I haven't
watched you so closely. You'll get it now
so that your hair will turn white! Show
your work!
[*The* KING *produces the unfinished
straw mat.*]
THE JAILER. That your day's work!
You won't get a bit of bread until you
finish five times that amount! [*Throwing
the mat down at his feet.*] There! — Now
I'll inspect your cell. Look out for yourself! I won't let you out of this hole alive!
[*Putting his hands behind him, he goes step
by step along the wall from door to window,
examining it from top to bottom, and turning
around now and then to look at the prisoner,
who stands motionless in the middle of the cell.*]
What does that spider web mean up there?
— The fourth disciplinary punishment for
eight days! [*Turning around.*] You still

know the seven disciplinary punishments
by heart? — Hey, Gigi?
THE KING. I know them by heart.
THE JAILER. First disciplinary punishment?
THE KING. Deprivation of privileges.
THE JAILER. I'll smash that lute of
yours to bits; you fritter away your working hours with it! — Second disciplinary
punishment?
THE KING. Deprivation of work.
THE JAILER. Then see how you will
spend your time! In eight days you won't
be able to stand on your legs! Third
disciplinary punishment?
THE KING. Deprivation of a soft bed at
nights. — My bed is as hard as if it were
stuffed with pebbles!
THE JAILER. Silence! This rascal would
like to sleep in the hay. — Fourth disciplinary punishment?
THE KING. Reduction of rations.
THE JAILER. Bread and water from to-
day for eight days! — Do you hear? —
Fifth disciplinary punishment?
THE KING. Imprisonment in darkness.
THE JAILER. Sixth disciplinary punish-
ment?
THE KING. Imprisonment in fetters.
THE JAILER. By that you must under-
stand you are chained all awry, so that
after the first hour all the devils you have
in your body say good-bye to you! —
Seventh disciplinary punishment?
THE KING. Flogging.
THE JAILER. [*having reached the window*].
You shall shed your hide here yet! You,
you thief, shall clamber up and down the
Jacob's ladder until you fall dead.
[*He passes in front of the* KING,
*leaves the cell and shuts the door from the
outside.*]
THE KING [*looks after him in surprise.
Then, quite calmly, with quiet deliberation,
he turns toward the door*]. What does it
mean? — Where have I made a mistake?
— For a whole year I believed that in the
course of a year I had educated this beast
into a human being. Suddenly, after all
that trouble, he drops back again into the
animal kingdom. — Or did I dream? — It
is impossible entirely that the jug should

have been broken. I drank out of it this morning. He will break it now outside and then show me the pieces. Will he let me go thirsty to-day? Will he let me thirst? — I fear worse! — At any rate, I shall receive him with a look that will make his eyes sink to the ground. [*Bracing himself.*] Help me, kingly majesty, in order that the fellow may realize his baseness of his own accord! [*Listening.*] He's coming! — A duel without weapons, man against man!

[*The door opens noisily.* PRINCESS ALMA *enters, clad as in the preceding act and carrying a jug with both her hands. The door closes loudly behind her.*]

THE KING [*with the fright of immoderate joy*]. Alma! My child! — Oh, beastly spite!

ALMA. O Father, I cannot embrace you now! I bring you this jug of wine.

THE KING [*struggling for breath, with both hands at his breast*]. Oh, satanic cruelty! [*Takes the jug from her and sets it to one side.*] Whence come you, my child? For twelve months I've thirsted for a sight of you! You are living yet, you are whole and well! Speak, how is it with you among miserable mankind?

ALMA. We have only a few minutes! At last I have been able to bribe the jailer, and from now on he will let me visit you once a week. Tell me quickly how I can lighten your sufferings.

THE KING. My sufferings? — Yes! What a father I am to throw my child unprotected upon the world! That is my sorrow! — Otherwise, I thank God daily that He has separated me from mankind by these six-foot walls, so that I am safe from them!

ALMA. You can see from my appearance, Father, how good people are to me. I am still in the service of the notary. Only tell me what I may bring you to strengthen you! What frightful torments you must have endured here!

THE KING. No, no, my child! Do not bring me anything unfamiliar into this solitude! You don't know how time passes here with the speed of the wind. In the beginning I scratched seven hundred and thirty marks on that wall, to have the daily joy of rubbing one of them out. But soon I had to blot them out by the week or by the month. And now I see with dread how quickly they grow less and less, so that the last will soon be gone and I will have to seek refuge once more under overhanging rocks and contend with wolves for their booty! — But do not let my words sadden you! You cannot guess how the jailer prepared me for your coming!

ALMA. I think with silent horror of how fiendishly he will torment you!

THE KING. How you imagine things! To do that he would have to be more than the weak earthworm he is. No cruelty can keep pace with my callousness. Do you know, he has shed tears of compassion here without having heard the least complaint from me! Who could so degenerate as not to be thankful when his better self finds unexpected recognition! — He could not help begrudging me the joy of seeing you again, my child. But the cowardly anxiety which springs from his calling is responsible for that. The poor man is so jealous of the ridiculous little authority vested in him by his bunch of keys that the kindness he has shown me to-day makes him afraid of becoming entirely superfluous. But didn't you suffer need in order to buy the good will of this rascal?

ALMA. Speak not of me, Father. Time is passing and I don't know how I can help you!

THE KING. Really, I don't know either! Were I an abler man, my fate might perhaps seem more pitiable to me. Poor as I am, I only tremble at the moment when those iron doors shall protect me no longer, when those barred windows shall prevent them reaching me, when I shall stand again among people with whom I have no mutual understanding and from whose activities I am excluded more than ever by the sentence of the law. — If you only knew how painlessly this solitude heals the gaping wounds of the soul. The Judge thought he was adding to my punishment when he sentenced me to solitary confinement. How deeply I have thanked him that I do not have to live here in association with other men!

ALMA [bursting into tears]. Lord God in Heaven! Then you don't want to see me here again!

THE KING [caressingly]. I repay your sacrifice with discontent and ill humor. Thoughts become heavy and sluggish when a man continues talking to himself day in and day out. — Only this I ask of you; when freedom is restored to me, leave me to my fate — not forever, only until I show myself worthy of your greatness of soul.

ALMA. Oh, nevermore! Do not ask me ever to leave you! It is impossible that the future should be as bad as the past!

THE KING. Not for you. I believe that gladly.

ALMA. Melancholy has mastered you in this gloom. Your proud heart is almost ready to break. Nothing can be read in your face of the quiet peace you pretend to feel.

THE KING. I have not seen my face for a year, but I can imagine how ugly it has grown. How my looks must wound your feelings!

ALMA. Oh, do not talk like that, Father!

THE KING. But you know my imperturbable nature. And now you come in, the only thing to make my happiness complete. It is only to reward you richly and splendidly that I would become a king again.

ALMA. I hear the jailer! Tell me how I can lighten your sufferings!

THE KING [sinks down on the stool exhausted, half to himself]. What do I lack? How frightful this prison would become if the pleasures of life were admitted here! How can I desire here a beautiful woman, where I cannot even conjure up a recollection of beauty! My couch there is shut during the day. There is no other resting-place, and I lie down there at night, as weary as if I had plowed an acre. And in the morning the clanging bell wakes me from dreams more serene than those I dreamed as a child. [As the door is opened.] — When you see me again, my child, you will hear no more complaints. You shall feel as happy with me as if you

were outside in your sunny world. Farewell!

ALMA. Farewell, Father!
[She leaves the cell. The door clangs behind her.]

THE KING. A whole long year yet! [He goes toward the wall.] I will just count the marks again and see how many remain to be rubbed out.

SCENE TWO — Night. A Waste

[Enter the KING, PRINCESS ALMA, with her father's lute on her back, and a circus rider]

THE KING. Have we much farther to go, brother, before we come to the place where the beggars' fair is to be held?

THE CIRCUS RIDER. We shall be there by midnight, at the latest. The real fair does not begin until then. This must be the first time you have made this pilgrimage to the gallows?

THE KING. It is only a few moons since we joined the strollers, but, nevertheless, we have danced at many a witches' sabbath.

THE CIRCUS RIDER. It seems to me, brother, somewhere you have unlearned marching. Otherwise you are a robust enough fellow.

THE KING [sitting down on a bowlder]. My heart beats against my ribs like a caged bird of prey. The road leads uphill; that takes my breath!

THE CIRCUS RIDER. We have plenty of time. — Your boy, brother, is very much better on his legs. It's a pity about him! With me he could learn something more profitable than singing street ballads to the lute. Everywhere, that's considered not much better than begging. Let him go with me, brother, if only for half a year! At any rate, it would not be worse for him than following in your footsteps, and I'll make a rider out of him after whom the circus managers will break their necks!

THE KING. Don't take me for an ass, dear brother; how can you make my boy succeed as a circus rider when you yourself must trudge afoot!

THE CIRCUS RIDER. You are as suspicious as if you had kegs full of gold at home, while from all appearances you don't remember when you had warm food last! You won't get anywhere that way! To-night at the beggars' fair we shall meet at least half a dozen circus managers. They gather there to look for artists to appear with them. Then you will see, you poor devil, how they will contend for me and how one will outbid the other! Thank God, I am not so unknown as you, you gutter singers! And if I get my job again, I shall have horses enough for your merry boy to break his neck the first day, if he has the mind!

THE KING. Tell me, brother, does one find theater managers, too, at the beggars' fair?

THE CIRCUS RIDER. Theater managers, too, certainly. The theater managers come there from all over the country. Where else would they get their dancers and their clowns! — Frankly, brother, it seems very doubtful to me your getting an engagement. You don't look as if you could act a farce.

THE KING. But there is a higher art, called tragedy!

THE CIRCUS RIDER. Tragedy, yes, I have heard that name! — I understand nothing about that art, dear brother. I only know that it is miserable poor pay. [To ALMA.] Now, my brave lad, doesn't your mouth water for better fodder? Do you want to learn circus riding with me?

THE KING [getting up]. Forward, brother, do not let us miss the beggars' fair. Fortune only offers us her hand once a year! [Exeunt.]

SCENE THREE

[Night. The gallows looms in the back-ground. Forward, to the left, is a gigantic bowlder, beneath a gnarled oak, which serves the performers as a stage. In front of it flickers a huge bonfire, about which are gathered the spectators, men, women, and children, in fantastic raiment.]

CHORUS.
Both in town and country beds,
With their windows tightly fastened,
honest folk are drowsing.

Those with no home for their heads
Dance with merry specters 'neath the gal-
lows tree carousing.
Exiles from the sun's bright light,
Fortune's tracks we still can follow in the
dark obscurely,
And are lords in our own sight
While in heaven the friendly stars twinkle
quite demurely.

A THEATER MANAGER [in a bass voice to an actor]. Show me what you have learned, my worthy young friend. Hic Rhodus hic salta! What is your act?

THE ACTOR. I act the fool, honored master.

THE THEATER MANAGER. Then act the fool, young friend, but act him well! Difficile est satiram non scribere! My public is used only to the best!

THE ACTOR. I will give you a sample of my art at once.

THE THEATER MANAGER. If you find favor in my eyes, young friend, you shall have a hundred soldi a month. Pacta exacta — boni amici! Go, young friend, and give your proof.

[The ACTOR mounts the rock. He is received with hand-clapping and cries of "bravo" by the spectators.]

THE ACTOR [breaks first into laughter, then speaks the following lines, accompanying each couplet with a different kind of titter].

Count Onofrio was a man
As stupid as a ram,
And he had daughters seven
He wanted paired up even.
Their way no suitor bent his legs.
Rotten eggs! Rotten eggs!

THE AUDITORS [have interrupted this effort several times with hisses and whistles. At the last words they pelt the actor with clumps of earth, while with shrill whistling they repeat the words]: Rotten eggs! Rotten eggs!

THE THEATER MANAGER [blaring out above the rest of the noise]. Down with the rascal! A page! The Lord God created him in wrath! Alea est jacta!

[The ACTOR leaves the rock.]

CHORUS.
Nor believe not, human brood,
That pursuit of idle dreams fills our whole
    existence·
Lovers' ways are somewhat crude
When the night wind dead men's bones
    rattles with persistence!

[*The* KING, PRINCESS ALMA *and a* PRO-
    CURESS *appear on the scene.*]

THE PROCURESS. Now, ballad singer,
how much will you take for that pretty
boy of yours? Listen to the pleasant
clang of the goldpieces in my pocket!

THE KING. Just now a circus rider
wanted to buy him from me. Leave me
and my boy in peace! I didn't come to
the beggars' fair for this. Besides, what
can you want with my boy!

THE PROCURESS. Don't think I am so
stupid, ballad singer, that I can't see that
your boy is a girl! The sweet child will
find a mother in me, more full of love for
her than any one in the wide, wide world.
[*To* ALMA.] Don't tremble so, my pretty
little dove! I won't eat you! When one
grows up with such a pretty figure and such
a round, rosy face, with fresh cherry lips
and dark glowing eyes, one sleeps beneath
silken covers and not in the open fields.
You will not have to play the lute with me.
Only to be charming. What pleasanter
life can sprightly young blood desire?
You will meet ministers of state and
barons at my house; you will only have to
choose. Have you ever been kissed by a
real baron? That tastes better than a
tramp's unshaven face! Look here,
ballad singer! Here are two unclipped
ducats. The girl belongs to me! It's a
bargain!

THE KING. Go snick up, you and your
gold! [*To* ALMA.] That fool woman, in
her stupidity, really takes you for a girl in
boy's clothes! Why aren't you? If you
were a girl, there would be no better opportunity than this to rid yourself of the
bristly ballad singer! There is nothing
worse than passing 'round the hat for
pennies. Perhaps you have already
gathered pennies thrown you by the compassionate foster-daughters of this worthy

dame! They always have a chance of
being forced again into the exalted ranks
of burghers' society as worthy members.
Our star is not in the ascendant.

THE PROCURESS [*to* ALMA]. Don't
allow this vagabond to set your head
whirling, for Heaven's sake, my dear!
You don't know how cozy my house is!
The whole day you can amuse yourself
with a band of the liveliest companions.
If the ballad singer won't sell you to me,
let's run away from him. Don't be afraid
of him! You will be as safe under my
protection as if you were surrounded by a
whole army corps.

ALMA [*wrenching herself from the* PRO-
CURESS'S *grasp*]. I will speak to him.
[*Goes from her to the* KING, *with trembling
voice*]. Do you remember, my father, why
we came to this beggars' fair?

THE KING. I know, my child.
    [*He mounts the rock and is received
    with dry coughs. Then he speaks in a
    clear tone, but with inward emotion.*]
I am the ruler over all this land,
By God anointed, but by no one known!
And should I shriek until the mountains
    bent
That I am ruler over all this land,
The very birds would chirp a mock at
    me!
What profit, then, is this, my kingly
    thought,
When hungering I snap with eager teeth,
As in the winter months the starving
    beasts?
But not to make a plaint of all my woes
Come I, my folk, to you!

THE SPECTATORS [*break into shrill laughter, applaud stormily and cry loudly*]. Da
capo! Da capo!

THE KING [*anxiously and with embarrassment*]. Kind audience! My specialty
on the stage is great and serious tragedy!

THE SPECTATORS [*laughing loudly*].
Bravo! Bravo!

THE KING [*with all the force of his soul*].
What I have just told you is to me the
dearest, the holiest thing that I have kept
in the depths of my soul until now!

THE SPECTATORS [*give vent to a new storm
of approval, from out of which the words can*

be plainly heard]: A remarkable comedian!
— An unusual character actor!

THE THEATER MANAGER [who has mounted a rock back of the crowd in order to hear better]. Finish your monologue, my dear young friend! Or does your poor brain harbor only these few crumbs? — Si tacuisses, philosophus mansisses!

THE KING. Very well, then! But I ask you from my heart, kind audience, to give my words the earnest meaning which belongs to them! How shall I succeed in moving your hearts, if you do not believe the plaints which come from my mouth!

THE SPECTATORS [laugh and applaud enthusiastically]. What a pose he assumes! — And such droll grimaces! — Go on with your farce!

THE THEATER MANAGER [hissing]. Children! Children! Nothing is worse for the actor than applause! If you succeed in making him overvalue himself, the poor rogue will be capable only of the lowest kind of trash! Odi profanum vulgus et arceo! [To the KING.] Continue, my son! It seems to me as if your parodies might amuse my enlightened public!

THE KING [seeking by every means to invest his speech with earnestness]. I am the ruler! To your knees with you! What mean these bursts of mad, indecent mirth!
'Tis my own fault that here, in this my realm,
None knows me more. My sentinels slumber,
My doughty warriors serve another's wage.
I lack that highest earthly might, the gold!
Still, ever yet, was there a rightful king
Who spent his time in counting out his coin?
That task he graciously accords to slaves!
The farthing, soiled with sweat of tradesmen's toil,
Was never struck with intent to smirch
The hands of those anointed of the Lord!

THE SPECTATORS [breaking out into the wildest laughter]. Da capo! — Bravo! — Da capo!

A THEATER MANAGER. This man is a brilliant satirist! A second Juvenal!

THE KING [as before]. I am the ruler!
— He of you who doubts,
Let him stand forth! — I'll prove my claim to him!
I was not wont before to praise myself,
But now the world has robbed me of that pride.
To him who wears a dagger at his hip
I'll teach the art of sinking it with grace
Into his foeman's breast; so that the duel,
From a rude spectacle of sweat and blood,
Becomes as pleasant as an elfin dance,
And even death puts on a sweeter garb! —
I am the ruler! — From the herd of barbs
Bring me the wildest of unbroken steeds;
Nor trouble you with saddle nor with bit;
Let him but feel my heels press in his flanks,
He'll pant beneath me in the Spanish gait
And from that time be tractable to ride.
I am the ruler! Come unto the feast!
The world is distant with its petty ills,
The evening star illuminates our meal,
From distant arcades mellow songs arise,
The guest may wander through the twilight green,
Where, from the shelter of a plashing fall,
The sportive nymphs will lure him with their wiles.
I am the King! Go fetch a maiden here!
Let her be chaste as is the morning dew!
I'll not awake her innocent alarms;
I come a beggar with an empty scrip;
Six steps away from her I'll stand. Warn her
'Gainst wiles of Satan! Ere a star grows pale
I'll move, not only body, but her soul!
Bring me the truest wife among them all!
She soon shall doubt if loathing or if faith
I greater pander to the lusts of flesh,
And, doubtingly, shall offer me her lips.
I am the King! What child is here so small
In hands and feet, or even in his joints!
With scorn I look upon you as you laugh
Your feet may jig, your hands may fan the air,
The brains within your skulls are very stale!
So be it! — Will the slimmest maiden here

Venture to dance with me in trial of skill?
She never knew the bloody task of war
And all her joints are quite as small as
    mine.
[*As nobody offers, to* ALMA.] Reach me a
torch, my child!

[ALMA *takes a glowing brand from
the bonfire and hands it to the* KING.
*Then, standing at the foot of the rock,
she plays a melody on her lute. The*
KING *gracefully and with dignity
dances a few steps of a courtly torch
dance, then throws the glowing brand
back into the fire. The* SPECTATORS
give vent to prolonged applause.]

THE ACTOR [*rising from amid the spectators, in a tone of parody*]. I am the monarch over all this land ——

THE SPECTATORS. Down with the barber's assistant. He has no appreciation!
Strike him to earth!

THE THEATER MANAGER. *Quod licet
Jovi, non licet bovi!* [*To the* KING, *who has
left the rock.*] I will engage you as ballet
master and character actor and offer you
a hundred soldi a month.

ANOTHER THEATER MANAGER [*speaking
in a falsetto voice*]. Hundred soldi, hi, hi,
hi? A hundred soldi will the skinflint
give you? I wave a hundred and fifty in
your face, you rascal! What do you say,
hi, hi, hi? Will you now or won't you?

THE KING. Don't you think, honored
master, that I am rather a tragedian than
a comedian?

THE FIRST THEATER MANAGER. You
haven't the least trace of talent as a
tragedian; as character actor, on the contrary, there is no chance of it going ill with
you again in this world. Believe me, my
dear friend, I know these kings. I have
eaten dinner with two of them at once!
Your king's monologue is the caricature of
a real king and will be valued as such.

THE SECOND THEATER MANAGER. Don't
let yourself be hoodwinked by this horse-
dealer, you rascal! What does he know
about comedy! I have studied my profession at the universities of Rome and
Bologna. How about two hundred soldi,
hi, hi, hi?

THE FIRST THEATER MANAGER [*clap-

ping the* KING *on the shoulder*]. I'll give
you three hundred soldi, my dear young
friend!

THE SECOND THEATER MANAGER. I'll
give you four hundred soldi, you dirty
rogue, hi, hi, hi!

THE FIRST THEATER MANAGER [*giving
the* KING *his purse*]. Here is my purse!
Put it in your pocket and keep it as a
souvenir of me!

THE KING [*pocketing the purse*]. Will
you engage my boy, too?

THE FIRST THEATER MANAGER. Your
boy? What has he learned?

ALMA. I play Punchinello, honored
master.

THE FIRST THEATER MANAGER. Let me
see him at once, your Punchinello.

ALMA [*mounts the rock and speaks in
fresh, lively tones*].

Fortune's pranks are so astounding
That her whims none can foresee;
Sure, I find them so confounding
Smiles nor tears come not to me.

Heaven itself is scarcely steady,
O'er our heads it's turning yet,
Mankind, then, had best be ready
For a daily somerset.

Mischief, when his legs can trip it,
When his arms are pliant still
Is so lovable a snippet
That he's sure of your good will!

[*The* SPECTATORS *show their approval.*]

THE FIRST THEATER MANAGER. I'll
engage this puppy as the youngest Punchinello in the business. We will wander
to-night *per pedes Apostulorum* to Siene,
where my company presents tragedy,
farce, and tragic-comedy. From thence
to Modena, to Perugia ——

THE KING. Before we reach Perugia,
I shall have to break my contract. I am
banished that city under pain of death.

THE FIRST THEATER MANAGER. Under
what name did that happen to you, my
young friend?

THE KING. I am called Ludovicus.

THE FIRST THEATER MANAGER. I name
you Epaminondas Alexandrion! That was
the name of a wonderfully talented come-

dian who eloped with my wife a short time ago. *Nomen est omen!* — Come, my children.

[*Leaves with the* KING *and* ALMA.]

CHORUS.

Soon the sun will rise in state,
Us to scatter for a year; here and there
   upon the wind,
Driven by relentless Fate,
To hunt illusive phantoms none of us can
   ever find.

ACT IV

SCENE — *Market-Place at Perugia*

[*In the midst of the market-place is a simple stage, from which a flight of steps leads to the spectators' seats. A rope separates the auditorium from the rest of the market-place. The back of the stage is curtained off. To the left, a small stairway leads from the stage to a space which serves as a dressing-room. The* KING *is kneeling in this space, before a little mirror, making up his face to resemble a majestic kingly mask. He is smooth-shaven, is in his shirt-sleeves, and is clad simply, but richly.* PRINCESS ALMA *sits near him, on an upturned box, wih her left foot over her right knee, tuning her lute. She wears a tasteful Punchinello's dress, all of white, composed of tights, a close-fitting jacket, trimmed with fur, and a high pointed hat.*]

THE KING. Have you chanced to hear, my child, how the advance sale is to-day?

ALMA. How can you have any doubts about that? The announcement that you were to appear sold all the seats for to-day's performance by sundown yesterday. Indeed, all Perugia knows already that your art far exceeds anything they saw in Epaminondas Alexandrion hitherto.

THE KING. At the bottom of my soul, I was never pained before that my laurels increased the fame of another. The assumed name protected me from too mortifying a contact with humanity. Even in my most daring dreams I cannot imagine how I would look to-day upon a

throne. Perhaps, after all, I am fit for something higher in this world than dishing out, day by day, the recollections of vanished pomp to the childish rabble as the copy of real majesty.

ALMA. In how happy a mood you have been wherever we have played! It even seems to me as if you found our stormy success some slight reward for all the long years of sorrow.

THE KING. Don't listen to me any longer, my child, or you will lose your joyousness and appear before the public, not as a Punchinello, but as a specter from the grave!

ALMA. Of course, here in the market-place of Perugia you must feel uncomfortable.

A PAGE [*enters the dressing-room carrying an autograph album under his arm*]. My mistress, the noble spouse of the honorable Doctor Silvio Andreotti, Attorney-General to His Majesty the King, sends me thither. My mistress desires the celebrated artist Epaminondas Alexandrion to place his autograph in this book. My mistress bids me say that the book contains only the autographs of the greatest men.

[*He hands the book and writing materials to the* KING.]

THE KING [*takes the goosequill and writes, speaking the words aloud as he does so*]. "Only simplicity can fathom wisdom," Epaminondas Alexandrion the Second. [*Giving back the album.*] Present my respects to your noble mistress, the spouse of the Attorney-General to the King. [*Exit the page.*]

THE KING [*making himself ready*]. Another wrinkle here, so! — You, my treasure, indeed, appear to have found happiness in our present calling.

ALMA. Yes, Father! A thousand times, yes! My heart is full of the joy of living, since I see my acting received daily with crowded benches!

THE KING. It astonishes me how little our environment affects you, although you allow all to believe that they are your equals by birth. You are a lamb among a pack of wolves, each of which has sworn to protect you, because each one grudges you to the others. But wolves remain wolves! And if the lamb does not want to be torn to pieces finally, it must, sooner or later, become a wolf itself. — But don't listen to me! I do not understand what evil spirit influences me to-day to call down misfortune upon our heads!

ALMA. Do not believe me capable of such base ingratitude, Father, as to think that the pleasure I find in my work as a Punchinello prevents me recollecting with joy the noble pomp in which I passed my childhood!

THE KING [rising with forced composure]. At any rate, I am ready for the very worst!

[As he speaks these words the theater servants place two golden seats in front of the first row of benches. Immediately after, the THEATER MANAGER rushes into the dressing-room in the greatest excitement.]

THE THEATER MANAGER. Alexandrion! Brother! Let me clasp you in my arms! [He embraces and kisses him.] You pearl of dramatic art! Shall I make you speechless with pride! His Majesty the King is coming to the performance! His Majesty the King is coming to the performance! His Majesty the King of Umbria and His Royal Highness the Crown Prince Filipo! Have you words! I have had two golden chairs put in front of the first row. The moment their highnesses seat themselves, Punchinello must appear on the stage with a deep bow! So be ready, children! — And you, Alexandrion, apple of my eye, bring to light to-day all the richest treasures hidden in the depths of your soul! As I [gesture] turn this glove inside out, so do you turn your inside outside! Let our royal auditors hear things such as have not been heard in any theater since the time of Plautus and of Terence.

THE KING [putting on his jacket]. I was just asking myself whether it might not be better for me to present my royal visitors with something different from my king's farce; perhaps the morning dreams of the old tailor's apprentice, or those of the swineherd. The old tailor's apprentice

would give our guests plenty of material for laughter and that is all they expect, while the king's farce might hurt their feelings.

THE THEATER MANAGER. Ha, ha! You are afraid of being locked up again for lèse majesté! Nonsense! Give your king's farce! Make it stronger than you have ever played it! If royalty honors us, it is because it wants to see the king's farce! What harm can they do us? Ultra posse nemo tenetur! — Well, what did I prophesy to you when I picked you from the scum of the land there at the beggars' fair! To-day we perform before crowned heads! Per aspera ad astra! [Exit.]

[During this scene the spectators' seats have become filled with an aristocratic public; outside the ropes the crowd gathers thickly. During the following words the KING dons a royal black beard, puts on his wig, sets the golden crown on his head, and throws a heavy purple mantle across his shoulders.]

THE KING. My head was to fall beneath the headsman's axe in this market-place if ever I dared return to Perugia without forswearing my right to the crown. — Instead of that, how much have I had to forswear to tread my native soil for the second time! The delight of satisfied revenge; the manly duty of preserving my inheritance for my family; all the good things of earth which Fortune lavished on me in my cradle, and now even the naked dignity of human nature which forbids even the slave from offering himself as an entertainment to those condemned along with him!

ALMA. And a thousand voices praise you as an artist the like of which never spoke to his folk before. How many kings' names are forgotten!

THE KING. I do not value that! Only a day laborer or a place-hunter can wear with pride the laurels which spring from earthly misery! But do you know what pride is possible to me in this existence? Called to an inscrutable trial, I struggle here as only one of a million beings. But King Nicola, as King, met death! No one doubts but that he is long beyond the reach of human humiliation. No one asks him now to renounce the dignity conferred on him by God. No shadow disturbs his kingly remembrance! I owe it to this illusion that I am still alive under God's sun. And until the hour of my death no storm shall deprive me of this possession, which, perhaps, I can still dispose of to your advantage! — My scepter! My orb! [*He takes both from the property chest.*] And now — the — ki-ki-king's farce!

    [*Seized by a sudden pain in the heart, he strives painfully for breath.*]

ALMA [*rushing to his side*]. Jesu, Maria, my father! I can see how marble white you are through your make-up!

THE KING. A shortness of breath! It is over. I have been subject to it since I was in prison ——

    [KING PIETRO *and* PRINCE FILIPO *enter the auditorium and take their places in the golden chairs.*]

THE THEATER MANAGER [*calling behind the scenes*]. On the stage, Punchinello!

THE KING [*springing up*]. Go! Go! I feel entirely well!

ALMA [*seizing a fool's bauble, rushes on the stage, bows, and then declaims in a light, jesting tone*]. I here appear to herald unto you

The coming of a king, who, verily,
Was never king.
Groom of the bedchamber is my post to him.
I laud him as a demigod, a hero;
Give admiration to his wit; praise his clothes;
My profit great in offices and gifts.
I earnestly desire him length of days;
But, should he die and his successor rule —
I trust God's grace will spare me from that blow!
Why then, obsequiously, with raptured mien
To the newcomer I shall play my rôle,
As is a valet courtier's pious way.
But I must cease, for lo, the King is here!

THE KING [*enters*]. My slumbers have been light throughout the night.

ALMA [*bowing, with crossed arms*]. Your people made be made to smart for that!

THE KING. My people? Made to suffer? When my mind
Fears I alone should carry all the blame?
What more have I achieved than other men
That I am called to rule it o'er my kind!
Away from off the steps unto my throne!
Slumber forsook my weary eyes last night
Because I, driven by the power of law,
Signed a death warrant when the hour was late!
Avaunt, you worm! And never venture more
Your head within the limits of my wrath!

ALMA [*turning to the audience*]. You see, respected auditors, how hard
It may be candidly to make one's way!
In lack of fitting words for my defense,
My plight with resignation I accept.
Dejected is my exit through this door,
But by another I shall soon return.
    [*She comes down the stairway toward the audience backward, then sits down on the steps facing the public.*]

THE KING [*to himself*]. Half my lifetime I have striven now
To make my eyes more sharp, to clear my wits,
That my dear folk might reap the benefit!

ALMA [*speaking to the public*]. Instead of that he might do something wise.
Who gives him thanks? His people whisper low,
His mind is lacking quite in brilliancy,
And his sublime example serves as jest!

THE KING [*with uplifted hands*]. Illuminate me with thy light, O God,
That I depart not from thy chosen way,
That good and evil I may quickly learn!
If thy reflected spendor shine from me
The people cannot blindly mock my rule;
Nor inefficiency mislead my steps!

ALMA [*springing up*]. I can, however!
    [*She steps upon the stage.*]
As you see me now,
I am a woman, decked with all the charms
To fan your kingly thoughts into a blaze!
The flower of innocence remains unplucked
To gratify you with its purity.
Groaning beneath the weight of majesty,
With sublime chastity your wedded bride

You yet may enter Pleasure's magic path.
Be ruler! Learn to blush as other men,
And do not join the devil's league with
  death,
In profanation of creation's work.
'Tis fit the hero and the anchorite
Should pray with deep humility to God
To sanctify and make them holy beings.
Before the Lord shall call you to Himself
May not some earthly bliss be yours by
  right;
Do you not fear to come from Egypt Land
Without a good view of the pyramids?

THE KING. And should I riot in luxuri-
  ous ease,
Who would protect my folk? Who hear
  their cry?

ALMA. That task I willingly would
  undertake.
Since childhood it has been my constant
  use
To ride a horse unbroken to the bit,
To crush his wildness in a frenzied gait,
Thy folk shall grow to know no higher law
Than to administer thy joy and gain.

THE KING. Depart from out my house,
  you brazen trull,
Before I stamp a mark upon your brow
With glowing iron!

ALMA. Once more the lightning!
My looks do not find favor in his sight!
  [Going up to the last step.]
My honored hearers, can you tell me now
Where lies the weakness of this curious
  king?
Else, from his wrathful gestures, much I
  fear
Our farce is apt to change to tragedy!

KING PIETRO [to ALMA]. You must
approach him as minister, or chancellor,
and inform him that it is just his wisdom
which brings misery upon the land. If he
listens to your words, he is nothing but a
fool; if he does not listen, you can boldly
call him a tyrant!

ALMA [bowing]. I'll do as you suggest.
  With all my heart
I thank you for your counsel, gracious lord!
  [She mounts the stage once more; to
  the KING.]
With deep dismay, I see Your Majesty's
August rule in danger. From every side

The mob comes streaming to the palace
  walls.
To me, your loyal chancellor, 'tis clear,
Instead of shooting down this threatening
  herd,
No better means can now be found to quell
Their spirit than to send them forth to fight
Against the neighboring principalities.
The mob grows weary of the golden hours
And frets against the long-continued
  peace;
It thirsts for blood, like the wild beast it is.
Its drunken lust will crown you conqueror
Amid the corpses fallen from its ranks!
Heaven itself bestows this last respite.
Seize, then, the sword! Else, even in this
  hour,
Yourself may fall with many deadly
  wounds.

KING PIETRO. Excellently spoken!
[Turning to the CROWN PRINCE.] Do you
remember, my son, to what frightful
expedients Bernardo Ruccellai wanted to
force me when I forbade the citizens to
extend the carnival a week? The pretty
boy spoke as if he had been there.
  [After these words the audience gives
  vent to short, but energetic, applause.]

PRINCE FILIPO. The actors are excep-
tionally good. Let us hear them further,
my honored father.

KING PIETRO. I am most keen to learn
what rejoinder my able spokesman will
meet up there.

THE KING. My life! — Take that! —
  The people's uproar frights
Me not! Before they suffer by my fault,
Why, let them in their madness slaughter
  me!
In time to come, ensanguined with my
  blood,
They will become a dread unto themselves,
And, worshipful, return to Reason's shrine.
My death will serve its purpose thousand
  fold!
As payment for your spiteful plan of war,
I here dismiss you as my chancellor.
Be happy you have 'scaped the headsman's
  axe!

KING PIETRO. Kingly words that I
should like to have spoken myself! If only
one could find a better chancellor so easily!

[*To* ALMA.] I am sorry, my young diplomat, that my advice served you so ill.

[*Another outburst of applause from the spectators.*]

ALMA [*turning to the public*]. Once more my well-laid plan has gone astray!
Before, dear sirs, I yet proceed to show
How I can bring this hero to his knees,
So that he cries beneath my scornful lash,
And whining drags himself unto my feet,
A sorry object, broken to his soul,
Begging that I shall lift him up again
And dampening all the dust about with tears,—
Before I show my skill in this respect,
I ask you to unlace your purses' strings
And to bestow a little of your wealth
With open hands upon my humble self.

[*She takes two white plates and comes down the steps.*]

Merely a pause, respected auditors,
A little contribution's all I ask!

[*She passes among the rows of spectators, collecting from them, but does not approach the royal entourage. The* KING *wanders about the stage speaking a monologue.*]

THE KING. Conflict and conflict!
Should my strength be spent,
Death, like a living flame, would rush unchecked
Throughout the confines of the realm!
[*To the public.*] An obolus will serve, most honored sirs!

ALMA [*to a spectator who puts his arm about her waist and attempts to kiss her.*]
Oh, fie, good sir, you scarcely are polite!
Besides, I'm not a girl; pray keep your place!

THE SPECTATOR. I never yet saw boyish hand so slim!

THE KING [*to the public*]. An obolus is quite enough, good sirs!
[*To himself.*] Would it were over! — Beyond betterment;
I yet await what store of future ills
Malicious Fortune still may deal to me!
[*To the public.*] Only an obolus, good sirs, I ask!

[KING PIETRO *beckons* ALMA *to him and lays a gold piece upon her plate.*]

THE KING [*bowing his thanks to the audience*]. What is more happy than the artist's soul!
Misfortune is a spring of joy to him;
He shapes a pleasure from a wild lament.
Adversity, indeed, may clip his wings,
But at the sound of gold he soon recalls
His inborn kinship to humanity.

[ALMA *returns to the stage and empties the plates into the* KING's *hand. He estimates the sum quickly, thrusts the money into his purple mantle, then, turning to his daughter, continues.*]

THE KING. Once more, deceptive shape, you dare to tread
Before my eyes. Who are you? — Let me know!

ALMA. I am yourself!

THE KING. Myself! But I am that!

ALMA. Which of us two is right will soon appear!
Before you, mangled by a beast of prey,
There lies a corpse. The blame belongs to you!

THE KING. I murdered him! How know you of such things?

ALMA. And do you see the stakes all round about?

THE KING. That, too, is known to you?

ALMA. 'Tis living flesh,
Encased in tow and tar!

THE KING. His cry of pain
Was music to my ear! It cost me much!

ALMA. The living entrails on the altar red,
Even to-day are used by you to move
The innocent to choice of peace or war!

THE KING. How came you by such store of frightful facts?
In deep repentance now I tear my hair!
My royal might seductive proved!

ALMA. A jest,
You're clasping at your quickly beating heart,
The while your eyes still shadow forth their greed!

THE KING. 'Tis not a jest!

ALMA. It is!

THE KING. Nevertheless,
Spare me worse!

ALMA. Childish bodies, glowing pure,
Are made a sacrifice unto your lust,

That you may see their tender limbs contort.

THE KING. No! Nevermore!

ALMA. You see, you must give way.
That shows that you are weak and I am strong!

THE KING [*sinking to his knees*]. Have mercy!

ALMA. Have you ever yet
Obtained victory in strife with me?

THE KING [*weeping*]. Behold, my head
is bent unto the earth
By pains of Hell!

ALMA. Then pluck up heart again,
Torture of innocents will calm your own!

THE KING [*with trembling voice*]. You
beast, you are the stronger of us
twain,
But grant a brief respite before I heap
New cruelties upon forgotten ones.
I crawl like any worm upon the dust.
My better self, which I have lost to you,
Begs that you do not press your might too
far.
New victims soon will fall within my
clutch,
The tongue which has already tasted
blood
Beseeches you to save them from its
rage.

KING PIETRO [*rising from his chair*].
You carry your jests somewhat too far up
there! What will the foolish multitude
think when it sees royal majesty so
brought to dust!

ALMA [*to the public*]. Folly can show the
naked truth beneath
The glittering facts on history's page.
[*To the* KING.] I'll spare you, then. But
first take solemn oath
To cherish good always within your heart!

THE KING. I swear!
[*Looking up in tears.*] You ask me that!
— I'm in a maze! Who are you?

ALMA. I am your dream! Your dæmon!
Awake to higher efforts from my ban,
I call on you to rise above yourself!

THE KING [*rises and runs anxiously up
and down*]. And if Methuselah I
should outlive,
That frightful error I shall ne'er forget!
Under the cover of the shamèd night

The torch flares out: Blazing in wild array,
Consuming flames run through the heated
limbs;
Vice sings its victory; lecherous Hell
Is jubilant; the rising flood of crime
O'erflows its banks; and deeds the gray-
haired wastrel,
Tortured by flames of lust, could not
achieve,
Stagger in kinship to the drunken thought!
— Oh, take my praise, thou golden light of
day!

ALMA [*to the public*]. With this I make
an ending to our play.
Your pardon, if its setting troubled you.
My sole desire was merely to exploit
That ancient, well-liked acrobatic trick
[*gesture*]
By which a man climbs up on his own
head.

KING PIETRO [*to the* KING]. And you call
that a farce, my dear friend? See, you
have brought the tears to my eyes!

THE KING [*after he has laid aside the
crown*]. Will Your Majesty believe it, our
piece has been received everywhere as a
harmless farce?

KING PIETRO. I cannot believe that!
Are my subjects so stupid? Otherwise,
how can you explain it to me?

THE KING. I cannot inform Your Majesty as to that. Such is life!

KING PIETRO. Very well, then, if such is
life, my people shall not hear you again,
until they understand you, for otherwise
your play would only undermine the power
of my throne. Lay aside your mantle and
stand forth before me!
[*The* KING *lays aside mantle, beard,
and wig and descends the steps.*]

KING PIETRO. I cannot appoint a man
who has made his living collecting pennies
to any office of state. But my royalty
shall never prevent me from making a
companion of the man whose gifts have
moved me to tears. There is a post vacant
close to the throne, which I have left un-
filled until now, because I did not wish to
make a place for folly in a position where
even the greatest amount of wisdom is too
small. But you shall fill this position.
You shall be powerless against the meanest

citizen of my state. But your high mental power shall stand between me and my people, between me and the royal chancellors; it shall be allowed to expend itself unpunished upon me and my son. As there on the stage, your soul stood between the ruler and his dark desires, so shall it check my innermost self! I appoint you my court fool! — Follow me!

[He starts to go.]

THE THEATER MANAGER *[wringing his hands and, with tears in his eyes, throws himself on his knees before* KING PIETRO]. *Moriturus te salutat!* Your Gracious Majesty's unworthy theater manager, who single-handed plucked this exceptional tragedian from the gallows, now has his life blighted by Your Majesty's gracious choice!

KING PIETRO. We bestow upon you the privilege of giving performances untaxed for twenty years!

THE KING. May I inform Your Majesty that I am the father of this young girl, and that the father will appreciate your goodness even more than the actor if he may hope that his child will no longer need to conceal her true nature.

KING PIETRO. Was I so deceived! *[To* ALMA.] I do not want to hear your audacious speeches again from a woman's mouth. *[To the* KING.] Let your child follow you!

[He leaves the theater in company with the PRINCE.]

ACT V

SCENE — *The Throne Room*

[The KING *in court costume. His office of court fool is shown discreetly by a suitable head covering. In his languid hand he holds a short bauble. He appears strangely altered: his pale face is deeply lined and his eyes seem twice as large as formerly.]*

THE KING. How strange is life! During many years of hardship of every description I felt my bodily strength increase daily. Each sunrise found me brighter in spirits, stronger in muscle. No mishap caused me to doubt the sturdiness of my constitution. And since I have been living here in peace and plenty, I am shriveling like an apple in springtime. I feel life going from me step by step, and the doctors agree in shrugging their shoulders and saying with long faces that they cannot foresee the outcome. — Did I ever reign in these halls? Every day since I came here I have asked myself the same question, and every day it seems more nonsensical. It is as hard for me to believe as it would be for me to credit any one who told me that I had lived on another planet. King Pietro is the worthiest prince who ever had a throne, and I am the last person in his realm who would want to change places with him. That is my last word each evening, a word which does not make me dream of the thick prison air, but of the dripping, storm-bent, rustling trees, of the gloomy heaths, of the virgin dew on the thick grass, of my journeys from place to place on the strollers' vans, on the tailboards of which I made all hearts waver between pity and respect. — I have noticed an unusual cramp in my left arm for the last few days. It is not gout; it is not the weakness of old age. But before my failing members give way, I have a work to accomplish. Let me complete it, O Fate, so that we may part in friendship! I have cultivated it with all possible care, as the only thing profitable in my life. Or shall I be the dupe again? Perhaps, the eager young hearts really do not need my help? Does egotism make me overestimate my importance in furthering their union? Who will open my eyes to my true merits? Blind I came, must I go so? — I go and — listen! Later I shall not have to think about the answers. *[Exit.]*

[Enter KING PIETRO *and* CROWN PRINCE FILIPO.]

KING PIETRO. I have made inquiries among the Medici in Florence if they are willing that a daughter of their house should become your wife. I have just received word that the Medici, confident in the permanency of our rule, would welcome such an alliance.

FILIPO. Before you did that, my respected father, I had distinctly told you that I shall never marry any one but Donna Alma, Alexandrion's daughter!

KING PIETRO [in anger]. The daughter of my court fool! You belong back in the shop whence you came!

FILIPO. Then send me back to the shop, respected father!

KING PIETRO. Although there can be no doubt of this maiden's virtues, the general welfare of the State demands that you wed a prince's daughter. If you desired to court the daughter of a citizen of Perugia, I might be able to countenance your *mésalliance* without slapping our own origin in the face. Even then, your choice would be an offense against the State, which would result in party strife and violence among the citizens. But if you choose a queen of obscurist origin for your people, then you show at once that you undervalue the duties of a prince. Who can tell what heirs may spring from such a marriage! Instead of looking forward to your reign with confidence, they will await it with sullen dread, anxiety, and insubordination. Did I overcome King Nicola and drive him to an early death that my son should indulge in madness such as cost that monarch his life and throne? That is the reason I brought Alexandrion here, because he has meditated upon just such serious questions! [*Lifting a portière.*] Call the fool! — Now he shall show me if his wisdom can withstand the call of blood! Now he shall show me if he can follow his own sermons as I do, or if he is only an empty chatterer!

THE KING [entering]. What does my dear lord desire?

KING PIETRO. I have been beholden to you for advice in the hours of the most frightful danger. Had I not followed freely your advice, so full of watchful and crafty shrewdness, in difficult situations, we might to-day be under foreign rule. Now, however, I require of you a sacrifice which, as the father of your child, you owe the State and our dynasty. Without restraint I allowed your intelligence to rule between me and my own blood, never suspecting how soon I should have to ask you to put it between yourself and your child.

The Prince asks me to give him your daughter for his wife!

THE KING. My child is so far above me that her feet never touch the ground without the seed of happiness blossoming beneath her tread.

KING PIETRO. I can believe that, but will you order your daughter to reject every offer of the Prince!

FILIPO. Donna Alma will never obey that order!

KING PIETRO. Silence!

THE KING. I can order nothing in this country.

KING PIETRO. That is true! But you must obey!

THE KING. That is true! But my daughter need not obey!

KING PIETRO. Enough of your jests! I am sorry I overprized your wisdom. You understand that your refusal ends your stay here at my court. I am pained to see your calm deliberation forsake you at this pass. You are a bad father, Alexandrion, in not fearing to deprive your child of my good will! In order to protect myself against the reproach of ingratitude, I shall have your salary continued ——

THE KING. Thank you, brother, I need your bounty no longer.

KING PIETRO. Are you out of your senses?

THE KING. I see more clearly than you. You no more than I can prevent the wonderful fulfillment of mighty Fate.

KING PIETRO. Stop your idle babble! I ask you, for the last time, will you obey my order? If not, fear my wrath!

THE KING. It is beyond your power as well as mine!

KING PIETRO. Very well. My son, if he wants, may run after you. I banish you and your child for life from this day forth from the land of Umbria, under pain of death in case you return to it!

[*The KING breaks forth in merry laughter*].

FILIPO. Holy Virgin, what's the matter with him!

KING PIETRO [disconcerted]. It is the laughter of a madman.

THE KING [laughing]. Surely, dear

friends, you will permit me to laugh, since I have been paid for being foolish.

KING PIETRO. Give us some explanation of what is passing within you, Alexandrion!

THE KING [raising himself to his full height]. Do you know that you banished me once before, in this very room, from Umbria under pain of death?

KING PIETRO. It is impossible for me to remember all the judgments I have passed!

THE KING. You passed your first judgment against King Nicola, and I am he!

KING PIETRO [shaken]. It was long to be foreseen that he would come to such an end! [To the KING.] Do you want to act a tragic scene for us out of your former occupation?

THE KING. I, here before you, am King Nicola!

KING PIETRO [with apparent anger]. I have nothing to do with impostors. Do you really expect to gain your ends by such thieves' tricks?

THE KING. I am King Nicola! I am King Nicola!

KING PIETRO [to FILIPO]. He has had a stroke! God have mercy on his soul!

FILIPO. His poor child! Merciful Heaven, when she hears of it!

THE KING [in the greatest astonishment]. Why are you not overcome with astonishment? — You do not believe me! — Are you going to ask me to prove what since my downfall I have kept secret only by supernatural strength of soul!

FILIPO. We believe you, Alexandrion! Let me conduct you to your room. We believe you!

KING PIETRO. If only your poor heart would grow quiet!

THE KING [anxiously]. No, no, I shall not grow quiet! You do not trust my words! You doubt my reason! — Almighty God, where shall I get witnesses to confirm the truth! — Let my daughter be called! — It is high time; I shall not see the light much longer! — Let my daughter be called! — I am too weak to fetch her myself. — Let my child be called! — My child!

FILIPO. I beseech you, Father, do not gratify his wish! The girl will go crazy

from anguish if unprepared she sees him in his mind's darkness!

THE KING. Let my child be called! I have nothing to leave her but her princely ancestry, and now she is about to be cheated of this last possession through my stupendous folly! Who will believe the girl when my eyes are closed! Indeed, there is nothing in me to recall a king! And my pictures, my statues are destroyed! And even if a picture were found, who would accept a resemblance as proof of my monstrous statement! A resemblance in which time has destroyed every trace! Help me, Heavenly Father, in this anguish worse than death!

KING PIETRO. Have you quite forgotten, my dear Alexandrion, that King Nicola is dead?

THE KING. Dead? — How kindly you speak because you think I am mad! Dead? — Where is he buried? I fought against the flood and escaped to land beyond the city walls. But who will believe me? Call my child here! She will advise me, as she has done a hundred thousand times before, with her wisdom.

FILIPO. I'll hurry and call your own physician, my respected father!

THE KING. Call my child! My child!

PRINCESS ALMA [rushing in]. My father! Almighty God, I heard your agonizing voice throughout the house!

THE KING. Am I King Nicola, or am I not?

ALMA. You are King Nicola, my father. Do not worry! What more can they do to us to-day?

THE KING. So you, too, have gone mad or you are a miserable pretender! They don't believe us! What can we do to prove it to them, so that I may lay my head on the block and thereby give you attestation of your birth? Send to the prison! There they have the record of the scars on my body. I blasphemed against the King. "Curse the King!" I cried. I was that King! — But where is a man with a normal reason who will believe such adventures? I never thought of that during all these years! Who would carry documents with him when his head had been twice forfeited to the executioner? And have I fathomed the ways of Almighty God more than any one only to be considered mad in the end? — But such is life! Such is life!

KING PIETRO. The sight of your sufferings is heartrending, Alexandrion! But your assertion is ridiculous!

ALMA. He is King Nicola!

FILIPO. Think what you say, Donna Alma!

ALMA. He is King Nicola!

THE KING. Search your brain, my dear, clever child, and see if you cannot find a means of making the truth shine before their eyes like a ray of sunshine!

ALMA. I will bring a host of witnesses, Father, as soon as the penalty is taken off your head.

FILIPO. Was not the name of King Nicola's daughter Alma?

KING PIETRO. Thousands of children are baptized with princely names!

THE KING. Do you hear, my child? An infallible proof! Otherwise, I shall yet end my unhappy war with the world in a madhouse and burden your life with the most gruesome of curses, the curse of the ridiculous!

ALMA. Lead us to the Ursulines!

FILIPO. Can it be possible! The King in his victor's service! — Speak, my father! — Pardon him!

KING PIETRO. Be you who you may, I lift every penalty which may hang over you.

THE KING. And now the proofs, my child! Quick, the proofs! Even if their testimony is clear as day, it will do as little after my death to help the recognition of your birth as my vain words do now!

ALMA. The Mother Superior of the Ursulines will testify —— [Frightened.] My father! Jesu, Maria, your look! What are you seeking so helplessly? For God's sake, speak!

FILIPO [who has hurried to aid the KING]. Go, Donna Alma! The strength begins to leave his limbs.

THE KING [struggling against death, while FILIPO and ALMA support him upon the steps of the throne]. I seek proofs! Proofs! Who can prove by his corpse that he was a king! — It is the last chance! — I am not mad! — Hurry, my child! — Proofs! — Too late! Too late! — Such is life!

ALMA [bending over him, lamenting]. My father! Don't you hear me? Look me in the eye, my father! What is your hand seeking? Your child is kneeling beside you!

THE KING. — I thank you, bu — but not as a king — only — as — a man ——

ALMA. Oh, oh, his eyes! — Father! Move your hand! Oh, woe is me, is there no help? Oh, pity me, he no longer hears my voice! His cheeks are cold! How can I warm his heart? Your mighty soul, my father, where is it, that it save you! Don't leave me alone, my father! Don't leave me alone! Oh, woe is me, woe is me, he has left me!

KING PIETRO [to himself]. I stand here like an outlaw!

FILIPO. Quiet your sorrow, Donna Alma!

KING PIETRO. I will seek to make amends for her loss to the best of my power, if she is willing to become my child through you.

FILIPO. God bless you for that, my father!

KING PIETRO. We will give him princely burial, whoever he may be! But nobody must hear a word of what we three have passed through here during this hour. History shall never tell of me that I made a king my court fool!

CURTAIN

FROM MORN TO MIDNIGHT
A MODERN MYSTERY IN SEVEN SCENES
By GEORG KAISER

Translated from the German by ASHLEY DUKES

PERSONS OF THE PLAY

Bank Cashier
Mother
Wife
First and Second Daughters
Bank Manager
Clerk
Porter
Stout Gentleman
Muffled Gentleman
Messenger Boy
Serving Maid
Lady
Son
Waiter (*in hotel*)
Five Jewish Gentlemen
Four Female Masks
Waiter (*in cabaret*)
Gentleman in Evening Dress
Salvation Lass
Officers and Soldiers (*of Salvation Army*)
Penitents
Crowd (*at Salvation Meeting*)
Policemen

SYNOPSIS OF SCENES

In a small town and a city, at the present time

FROM MORN TO MIDNIGHT

SCENE I

Interior of a provincial bank. On the left, pigeon-holes and a door inscribed MANAGER. *Another door in the middle marked* STRONG ROOM. *Entrance by swing-doors in the right background. At the right hand side is a cane sofa, and in front of it a small table with a water-bottle and glass.*

The CASHIER *at the counter and the* CLERK *at a desk, both writing. On the cane sofa sits a* STOUT GENTLEMAN, *wheezing. In front of the counter stands a* MESSENGER BOY *staring at the door, through which some one has just gone out.*

CASHIER [*raps on the counter*].

MESSENGER BOY [*turns, hands in a cheque*].

CASHIER [*examines it, writes, takes a handful of silver from a drawer, counts it, pushes a small pile across the counter*].

MESSENGER BOY [*sweeps the money into a linen bag*].

STOUT GENTLEMAN [*rising*]. Now the big men take their turn.

[*He pulls out a bag.* LADY *enters; expensive furs; rustle of silk.* STOUT GENTLEMAN *stops short.*]

LADY [*opens the swing door with difficulty and smiles involuntarily in his direction*]. At last!

STOUT GENTLEMAN [*makes a wry face*].

CASHIER [*taps the counter impatiently*].

LADY [*looks at* STOUT GENTLEMAN].

STOUT GENTLEMAN [*giving place to her*]. The big men can wait.

LADY [*bows distantly, comes to the counter*].

CASHIER [*taps as before*].

LADY [*opens her handbag, takes out a letter and hands it to* CASHIER. *A letter of credit*]. Three thousand, please.

CASHIER [*takes the envelope, turns it over, hands it back*].

LADY. I beg your pardon. [*She pulls out the folded letter and offers it again.*]

CASHIER [*turns it over, hands it back*].

LADY [*unfolds the letter, handing it to him*]. Three thousand, please.

CASHIER [*glances at it, puts it in front of the* CLERK].

CLERK [*takes the letter, rises, goes out by the door inscribed* MANAGER].

STOUT GENTLEMAN [*retiring to sofa*]. I can wait. The big men can always wait.

CASHIER [*begins counting silver*].

LADY. In notes, if you don't mind.

CASHIER [*ignores her*].

MANAGER [*youthful, plump, comes in with the letter in his hand*]. Who is ——?

[*He stops short on seeing the* LADY.]

CLERK [*resumes work at his desk*].

STOUT GENTLEMAN. Ahem! Good morning.

MANAGER [*glancing at him*]. How goes it?

STOUT GENTLEMAN [*tapping his belly*]. Oh, it rolls along, you know.

MANAGER [*laughs shortly. Turning to* LADY]. I understand you want to draw on us?

LADY. Three thousand marks.

MANAGER. I would pay you three [*glancing at letter*] three thousand with pleasure, but ——

LADY. Is anything wrong with the letter?

MANAGER [*suave, important*]. It's in the proper form. "Not exceeding twelve thousand" — quite correct [*spelling out the address*] b-a-n-k-o-

LADY. My bank in Florence assured me ——

MANAGER. Your bank in Florence was quite in order.

LADY. Then I don't see why ——

MANAGER. I suppose you applied for this letter?

LADY. Of course.

MANAGER. Twelve thousand payable at such places ——

LADY. As I should visit on my journey.

MANAGER. And you gave them duplicates of your signature?

LADY. Certainly. To be sent to the banks mentioned in the list.

MANAGER [*consults letter*]. Ah! [*Looks up.*] We have received no letter of advice.

STOUT GENTLEMAN [*coughs; winks at the* MANAGER].

LADY. That means I must wait until —

MANAGER. Well, we must have *something* to go upon!

MUFFLED GENTLEMAN [*in fur cap and shawl, comes in and takes his place at the counter. He darts angry glances at the* LADY].

LADY. I was quite unprepared for this —

MANAGER [*with a clumsy laugh*]. As you see, madam, we were also unprepared.

LADY. I need the money so badly —

STOUT GENTLEMAN [*laughs aloud*].

MANAGER. There again we're in the same boat.

STOUT GENTLEMAN [*neighs with delight*].

MANAGER [*looking round for an audience*]. Take myself for instance — or these gentlemen here ... [*To the impatient muffled customer.*] You're not half so busy as I am. But you see I can find time for the lady. [*Turning.*] Now, ma'am, what do you expect? Am I to pay you on your own word?

STOUT GENTLEMAN [*titters*].

LADY [*quickly*]. I'm staying at the Elephant.

STOUT GENTLEMAN [*wheezes with laughter*].

MANAGER. An excellent house. I generally lunch there.

LADY. Can the hotel people vouch for my — for my —?

MANAGER. Your character, madam? I hope so, indeed.

STOUT GENTLEMAN [*rocks with delight*].

LADY. Of course I have luggage with me —

MANAGER. Would you like me to search your trunks?

LADY. I'm in the most unlucky position.

MANAGER. We can shake hands upon that. [*He returns the letter.*]

LADY. What do you advise me to do?

MANAGER. This is a snug little town of ours — in a charming neighborhood. The Elephant is a well-known house; you'll make pleasant acquaintances — the time will slip away, take my word for it.

LADY. I don't in the least mind passing a few days here.

MANAGER. Your fellow guests will be delighted.

LADY. But I happen to need the money urgently this morning!

MANAGER [*to* STOUT GENTLEMAN]. Will anybody here go bail for a lady from abroad, who needs three thousand marks?

LADY. I couldn't dream of accepting that — I shall be in my room at the hotel. When the letter of advice arrives, will you please inform me at once by telephone?

MANAGER. Personally, madam, if you wish.

LADY. As you please, but as quickly as possible. [*She folds up the letter, replaces it in the envelope, and puts both into her handbag.*] I shall call again in any case this afternoon.

MANAGER. At your service.

LADY [*bows coldly, goes out*].

MUFFLED GENTLEMAN [*moves up to the counter, on which he leans, crackling his cheque impatiently*].

MANAGER [*ignoring him, looks merrily at the* STOUT GENTLEMAN].

STOUT GENTLEMAN [*sniffs the air*].

MANAGER [*laughs*]. All the fragrance of Italy, eh? Straight from the bottle.

STOUT GENTLEMAN [*fans himself with his hand*].

MANAGER. What do you say?

STOUT GENTLEMAN [*pours out water*]. Three thousand is not bad. [*Drinks.*] I guess three hundred would be gratefully received.

MANAGER. Perhaps you'd like to make an offer, at the Elephant?

STOUT GENTLEMAN. No use to us big fellows.

MANAGER. Our morals are protected by Nature, eh?

MUFFLED GENTLEMAN [*raps impatiently on the counter*].

MANAGER [*indifferently*]. Well?

[*He takes the cheque, smooths it out and hands it to the* CASHIER.]

MESSENGER BOY [*entering, stares after the departing* LADY, *then at the last speakers; finally stumbles over the* STOUT GENTLEMAN *on the sofa*].

STOUT GENTLEMAN [*robbing him of his wallet*]. There, my boy, that's what comes of making eyes at pretty ladies! Now you've lost your wallet.

MESSENGER BOY [*looks shyly at him*].

STOUT GENTLEMAN. What are you going to do about it?

MESSENGER BOY [*laughs*].

STOUT GENTLEMAN [*returning the wallet*]. Mark my words. You're not the first young fool whose eyes have run away with him — with the whole body rolling after! [MESSENGER BOY *goes out*.]

CASHIER [*has counted out some small silver*].

MANAGER. And they trust money to young jackanapes like that! A born embezzler!

STOUT GENTLEMAN. The loser pays.

MANAGER. But employers can't see it, until one fine day the boy takes his chance. [*To* MUFFLED GENTLEMAN.] Is anything wrong?

MUFFLED GENTLEMAN [*examines every coin*].

MANAGER. That's a twenty-five pfennig piece. Forty-five pfennigs altogether; do you want any more?

MUFFLED GENTLEMAN [*pockets his money with great ceremony; buttons his coat over the pocket*].

STOUT GENTLEMAN [*ironically*]. You ought to patronise the strong room. [*Rising*.] Now the big men can unload a trifle.

MUFFLED GENTLEMAN [*turns away from the counter and goes out*].

MANAGER [*to* STOUT GENTLEMAN, *breezily*]. Well, what's your little game?

STOUT GENTLEMAN [*sets his attaché case on the counter and takes out a pocket book*]. Is your confidence in the public shaken? [*He offers his hand*.]

MANAGER [*taking it*]. It's true we're not at home to pretty faces in business hours.

STOUT GENTLEMAN [*counting out his money*]. How old was she, would you say?

MANAGER. I haven't seen her yet without the paint.

STOUT GENTLEMAN. What's the woman doing in the town?

MANAGER. We shall hear that to-night at the Elephant.

STOUT GENTLEMAN. But who's the attraction?

MANAGER. All of us, perhaps.

STOUT GENTLEMAN. What can she want with three thousand, in this little place?

MANAGER. That's her affair. She wants it badly.

STOUT GENTLEMAN. I wish her luck. Let her pick it up if she can.

MANAGER. From me?

STOUT GENTLEMAN. That's her affair. [*They laugh.*]

MANAGER. I'm curious to see when that letter of advice from Florence will arrive.

STOUT GENTLEMAN. If it arrives!

MANAGER. Ah, if it arrives!

STOUT GENTLEMAN. We might take a collection for her benefit.

MANAGER. I dare say that's what she has in mind.

STOUT GENTLEMAN. Eh?

MANAGER. Perhaps you won a prize in the last lottery? [*They laugh.*]

STOUT GENTLEMAN [*to* CASHIER]. Take this little pile off my hands. [*To* MANAGER.] It's as well in your strong room as in my safe — not to mention the interest. Give me a credit note for the Building Society.

MANAGER [*sharply to* CLERK]. The Building Society credit note.

STOUT GENTLEMAN. There's more to come.

MANAGER. The more the merrier. We can do with it just now.

STOUT GENTLEMAN. Sixty thousand marks, then — in paper money.

CASHIER [*begins counting*].

MANAGER [*after a pause*]. And how are things with you, on the whole?

STOUT GENTLEMAN [*to* CASHIER, *who pauses to examine a note*]. Yes, that one's patched.

MANAGER. We'll accept it, of course.

We shall soon be rid of it. I'll reserve it for our fair client from Florence. She wore patches too.

STOUT GENTLEMAN. But behind these you find a thousand marks.

MANAGER. The face value.

STOUT GENTLEMAN [*laughing immoderately*]. The face value that's good!

MANAGER. The face value! Here's your receipt. [*Choking with laughter.*] Sixty thousand ——

STOUT GENTLEMAN [*takes it, reads*]. Sixty thou——

MANAGER. The face ——

STOUT GENTLEMAN. Value.

[*They shake hands.*]

MANAGER [*in tears*]. We shall meet tonight.

STOUT GENTLEMAN [*nods*]. The face — the face-value!

[*He buttons his overcoat and goes out, laughing.*]

MANAGER [*wipes the tears from his pince-nez; then goes into the inner room*].

CASHIER [*fastens the notes together in bundles*].

MANAGER [*returning*]. Well, what did you think of our Italian customer? You don't see a picture like that behind your counter every morning. Wrapped in furs, perfumed. [*Sniffs.*] She still hangs on the air, this lady. You breathe adventures. Italy casts a spell; there's magic in the name. But lift her veil, and you see the Riviera — Mentone — Nice — Monte Carlo! The land of orange-blossoms, the home of fraud! There the robber gangs make up their train. There the birds of prey cluster, and circle, and scatter. They prefer little towns — like ours, well off the beaten track. There they swoop down — rustling, frothing in furs and silk! Yes, women are the sirens of to-day; they sing of the South! One glance at them, and you're lost. Stripped bare down to your shirt, down to your naked, naked skin! [*He drums with a pencil on the* CASHIER'S *back.*] Depend upon it, this bank in Florence knows as much about the lady as the man in the moon. The whole affair is a swindle, carefully arranged. And the web was woven not in Florence, but in Monte Carlo.

This was one of the gay parasites who spawn in the hotbed of the Casino. Mark my words, we shall never see her any more. The first attempt missed fire; she'll scarcely risk a second! Oh, you have to be pretty sharp in the banking business, I can tell you! You may be easy-going, you may have your little joke now and then, but you must keep both eyes wide open! Perhaps I might have given a nod to the superintendent of police. But after all, it's no concern of mine. The attempt failed; that's good enough. And banks are pledged to secrecy. [*At the door of his room.*] You might keep an eye on the papers — in the police-court columns, that's where we shall hear of our lady from Florence again! [*Exit.*]

CASHIER [*seals up rolls of banknotes*].

PORTER [*enters with letters, hands them to* CLERK]. One registered letter. I want the receipt.

CLERK [*stamps receipt form, hands it to* PORTER].

PORTER [*rearranges glass and water-bottle on the table, and goes out*].

CLERK [*takes the letters into* MANAGER'*s room, and returns*].

LADY [*reënters; comes quickly to the counter*]. I beg your pardon.

CASHIER [*stretches out his hand, without looking at her*].

LADY [*louder*]. If you please!

CASHIER [*raps on the counter*].

LADY. I don't want to trouble the Manager a second time.

CASHIER [*raps on the counter*].

LADY. Please tell me — would it be possible for me to leave you the letter of credit for the whole sum, and to receive an advance of three thousand in part payment?

CASHIER [*raps impatiently*].

LADY. I shall be willing to deposit my diamonds as security if required. Any jeweller in the town will value them for you.

[*She takes off a glove and pulls at her bracelet.*]

SERVING MAID [*comes in quickly, plumps down on sofa, and begins rummaging in her market-basket*].

LADY [*startled by the commotion, look*

*round. As she leans on the counter her hand
sinks into the* CASHIER'S].
CASHIER [*bends over the hand which lies
in his own. His spectacles glitter; his glance
travels slowly upward from her wrist*].
SERVING MAID [*with a sigh of relief, discovers the cheque she is looking for*].
LADY [*nods kindly in her direction*].
SERVING MAID [*replaces vegetables, etc.,
in her basket*].
LADY [*turning again to the counter, meets
the eyes of the* CASHIER].
CASHIER [*smiles at her*].
LADY [*drawing back her hand*]. Of
course I shall not ask the bank to do anything irregular. [*She puts the bracelet on
her wrist; the clasp refuses to catch. Stretching out her arm to the* CASHIER.] Would
you be so kind? I'm clumsy with the
left hand.
CASHIER [*stares at her as if mesmerized.
His spectacles, bright points of light, seem
almost to be swallowed up in the cavity of his
wide-open eyes*].
LADY [*to* SERVING MAID]. You can
help me, mademoiselle.
SERVING MAID [*does so*].
LADY. Now the safety catch. [*With a
little cry*.] Oh, that grips my arm! Ah,
that's better. Thank you so much.
[*She bows to the* CASHIER *and goes out*.]
SERVING MAID [*coming to the counter,
planks down her cheque*].
CASHIER [*takes it in trembling hands; the
slip of paper flutters and crackles; he
fumbles under the counter then counts out
money*].
SERVING MAID [*looking at the pile of
coins*]. Is all that mine?
CASHIER [*writes*].
CLERK [*becomes observant*].
SERVING MAID [*to* CLERK]. But it's too
much!
CLERK [*looks at* CASHIER].
CASHIER [*rakes in part of the money*].
SERVING MAID. Still too much!
CASHIER [*ignores her and continues writ-
ing*].
SERVING MAID [*shaking her head, puts
the money in her basket and goes out*].
CASHIER [*hoarsely*]. Fetch me — glass
— water!

CLERK [*hurries from behind the counter,
comes to table*].
CASHIER. That's been standing. Fresh
water, cold water from the tap!
CLERK [*hurries out with glass*].
CASHIER [*goes quickly to electric bell, and
rings*].
PORTER [*enters from the hall*].
CASHIER. Get me fresh water.
PORTER. I'm not allowed to leave the
door.
CASHIER [*hoarsely*]. Water. For me.
Not those dregs there. Bring water from
the tap.
PORTER [*seizes water-bottle and hurries
out*].
CASHIER [*quickly crams his pockets with
bank notes. Then he takes his coat from a
peg, throws it over his arm, and puts on his
hat. He lifts a flap in the counter, passes
through, and goes out*].
MANAGER [*absorbed in reading a letter,
enters from his room*]. Here's the letter of
advice from Florence after all!
CLERK [*enters with a glass of water*].
PORTER [*enters with full water-bottle*].
MANAGER [*looking up*]. What the
devil ——?

SCENE II

*Writing room of a hotel. Glass door in
background. On the left, desk with telephone. On the right, sofa and armchairs
with table and newspapers.*

LADY [*writes*].
SON [*in hat and cloak, enters carrying
under his arm a large flat object wrapped in
green baise*].
LADY [*with surprise*]. Have you
brought it with you?
SON. Hush! The wine merchant is
downstairs. The queer old chap thinks I
shall rob him of his treasure.
LADY. But I thought this morning he
was glad to get rid of it.
SON. And now he scents mischief everywhere.
LADY. You must have given yourself
away.
SON. Perhaps I showed him I was pleased
with the bargain.

LADY [smiling]. That would open the eyes of the blind!

SON. Believe me, they will be opened. But don't be afraid, Mamma, the price remains the same.

LADY. Is the man waiting for his money?

SON. We can let him wait.

LADY. But, my dear boy, I must tell you ——

SON [kissing her]. Hush, Mamma. The hush of a great moment. You must only look when I give you the word.

[He takes off his hat and cloak, puts the picture on a chair and lifts the green baize covering.]

LADY. Are you ready?

SON [in a low tone]. Mamma.

LADY [turns in her chair].

SON [comes to her, puts his arm round her neck]. Well?

LADY. That was surely never meant to hang in a wineshop?

SON. Its face was to the wall. On the back the old fellow had pasted his own photograph.

LADY. Was that included in the price?

SON [laughs]. Tell me, what do you think of it?

LADY. I find it — very naïve.

SON. Delightful, isn't it? Marvellous!

LADY. Do you really think so highly of it as a painting?

SON. As a painting — Of course! But just look at the wonderful quality of the treatment. Epoch-making, simply. This handling of the subject — where can you find such a gift? In Pitti — Uffizi — the Vatican? Even the Louvre has hardly anything to compare with it. In this picture we have the one and only erotic vision — yes, vision — of the pair in the Garden of Eden. Here the apple has rolled away upon the grass — there the serpent still peeps from the magical leaves. You see that the drama is played on the green lawns of Paradise itself, and not in the desert of banishment. There's original sin for you — the real fall! Cranach painted dozens of Adams and Eves, standing on either side of the apple-bough. In them he says coldly, stiffly: they knew each other! But here he cries blithely, exult-

antly: they loved each other! Here he shows himself a master. [In front of the picture.] And yet mark the restraint in his ecstasy! This line of the manly arm which slants across the curving womanly hip. The horizontal, which never for a moment wearies the eye. This grouping and these tones bring love to life. — Don't you feel it to be so?

LADY. I find you as naïve as your picture.

SON. What does that mean?

LADY. I beg you to put it away in your room.

SON. When we reach home perhaps I shall value it most. Florence and this masterpiece! Think of finding it here!

LADY. But you guessed almost to a certainty that it must be in the neighborhood.

SON. I'm dazed nevertheless to find myself right. Mamma, I'm one of Fortune's children.

LADY. This is only the reward of your own careful research.

SON. But how could I gain it without your help? Your goodness?

LADY. I find my happiness in yours.

SON. Your patience is endless. I tear you from your beautiful quiet life in Fiesole. Warm Southern blood runs in your veins, but I drag you through Germany in midwinter. You pass the night in sleeping-cars or second-rate hotels, you have to rub against all kinds of people ——

LADY [smiling]. Yes, there you are certainly right!

SON. But now I promise you the work is nearly finished. I'm all impatience myself to bring the treasure home. Let's take the three o'clock train. Will you give me the three thousand marks?

LADY. I haven't them.

SON. But the owner is here, in the hotel.

LADY. The bank couldn't pay me. The letter of advice has somehow been delayed

SON. I've promised him the money.

LADY. Then you must return the picture until the letter arrives.

SON. Can't we hurry it in any way?

LADY. I've written a telegram; here it is ready to send. You see we travelled so quickly that ——

WAITER [*knocks at the door*].

LADY. Come in!

WAITER. A gentleman from the bank wishes to speak to the lady.

LADY [*to* SON]. That will be the money, sent by hand. [*To* WAITER.] Show him in.

WAITER [*exit*].

SON. You can call me when it's ready. I must keep an eye on the old man.

LADY. I shall ring you up.

SON. Then I'll wait downstairs. [*Leaves*.]

LADY [*closes her portfolio*].

[WAITER *and* CASHIER *are seen behind the glass door. The* CASHIER *overtakes the other, and opens. The* WAITER *turns and retires.*]

CASHIER [*cloak over arm, enters*].

LADY [*points to a chair and seats herself on the sofa*].

CASHIER [*still holding his cloak, seats himself*].

LADY. I hope the bank ——

CASHIER [*sees the picture and starts violently*].

LADY. My visit to the bank was closely connected with this picture.

CASHIER [*staring*]. You!

LADY. Do you notice any similarities?

CASHIER [*smiling*]. In the wrist.

LADY. Are you a connoisseur?

CASHIER. I should like to be.

LADY. Do these pictures interest you?

CASHIER. I'm in the picture!

LADY. Are these others of the same school in private collections here? If so, can you find them for me? You would do me a great service — greater even than bringing me money.

CASHIER. I've brought the money.

LADY. I fear at this rate my letter of credit will soon be exhausted.

CASHIER [*producing a roll of banknotes*]. This will last longer!

LADY. I can only draw twelve thousand marks in all.

CASHIER. I have sixty thousand!

LADY. But — how did you ——?

CASHIER. That's my business.

LADY. How am I to ——?

CASHIER. We shall bolt.

LADY. Bolt? Where?

CASHIER. Abroad. Anywhere. Pack your trunk, if you've got one. You can start from the station. I'll take a car to the next stop and jump the train. We stay the first night in — give me a time-table!   [*He finds it.*]

LADY. Have you brought more than three thousand from the bank?

CASHIER [*preoccupied with time-table*]. I took sixty thousand.

LADY. And my share of that is ——

CASHIER [*opens a roll of notes and counts them with professional skill, then lays a bundle of them on the table*]. Your share? Take this. Put it away. We may be noticed. The door has a glass panel. That's five hundred.

LADY. Five hundred?

CASHIER. More to come. All in good time. When we're in a safer place. Here we must be careful. — Cash received — Now let's be off. No time for love-making. The wheel spins. An arm outstretched will be caught in the spokes.

[*He springs to his feet.*]

LADY. But I need three thousand marks.

CASHIER. If the police find them on you, it's all up!

LADY. What have the police to do with it?

CASHIER. You were in the bank. Your scent hung on the air. They'll suspect you; the link between us is clear as daylight.

LADY. I went to your counter ——

CASHIER. As cool as a cucumber ——

LADY. I made a request ——

CASHIER. An attempt.

LADY. I tried ——

CASHIER. You tried it on. With your forged letter.

LADY [*taking a paper from her handbag*]. Is this letter not genuine?

CASHIER. As false as your diamonds.

LADY. I offered them as a pledge. Why should my pretty stones be paste?

CASHIER. Ladies of your complexion only dazzle.

LADY. What do you take me for? I'm dark, it's true: a Southerner, a Tuscan.

CASHIER. From Monte Carlo!

LADY [*smiles*]. No, from Florence!

CASHIER [*his glance lighting upon the son's hat and cloak*]. Ha! Have I come too late?

LADY. Too late?

CASHIER. Where is he? I'll bargain with him; he'll be open to a deal. I have the ready money. How much shall I offer? How high do you put the indemnity? How much of this stuff shall I cram into his pockets? I'll go up to fifteen thousand. Is he asleep? Still rolling in bed? Where's your room? Twenty thousand — five thousand extra for instant withdrawal! [*Picking up hat and cloak.*] I'll take him his clothes.

LADY [*in astonishment*]. The gentleman is sitting in the lounge.

CASHIER. Downstairs? Too risky; too many people down there. Call him up; I'll settle with him here. Ring for him; let the waiter hurry. Twenty thousand, cash down! [*He begins counting the money.*]

LADY. Can my son speak for me?

CASHIER [*bounding back*]. Your — son!!!

LADY. I'm travelling with him. He's collecting material for a book on the history of art.

CASHIER [*staring at her*]. Son?

LADY. Is that so dreadful?

CASHIER. But — but — this picture —

LADY. A lucky find of his. My son is buying it for three thousand marks; this was the amount I needed so urgently. The owner is a wine merchant whom you will know by name.

CASHIER. Furs... silk... you glistened and rustled. The air was heavy with your scent!

LADY. This is midwinter. As far as I know, my mode of dress is not exceptional.

CASHIER. The forged letter —

LADY. I was about to wire to my bank.

CASHIER. Your bare wrist — stretched out to me with the bracelet —

LADY. We're all clumsy with the left hand.

CASHIER [*dully to himself*]. And I — have taken the money —

LADY [*diverted*]. Will that satisfy you? If you want further proofs, my son is not unknown in the academic world.

CASHIER. Now — at this very moment — they've discovered everything! I called for water to get the clerk out of the way — and again for water to clear the porter from the door. The notes are gone; I'm missing. I mustn't show myself in the streets: the police are warned. Sixty thousand! I must slip away across the fields — through the snow — before the whole town is on my track!

LADY [*shocked*]. For Heaven's sake, stop!

CASHIER. I took all the money. It was because you filled the bank. Your scent hung on the air. You glistened and rustled — you put your naked hand in mine — your breath came warm across the counter — warm —

LADY [*silencing him*]. Please! — I am a lady.

CASHIER. But now you must —

LADY [*controlling herself*]. Tell me, are you married? Yes? [*Violent gesture from* CASHIER.] Ah, that makes a difference. You gave way to a foolish impulse. Listen. You can make good the loss. You can go back to your counter and plead a passing illness — a lapse of memory. I suppose you still have the full amount?

CASHIER. I've embezzled the money —

LADY [*abruptly*]. That really doesn't interest me.

CASHIER. I've robbed the bank.

LADY. You grow tedious, my dear sir.

CASHIER. And now you must —

LADY. The one thing I must do, is to —

CASHIER. After this you must —

LADY. Preposterous.

CASHIER. I've stolen for you. I've given myself into your hands, broken with the world, destroyed my livelihood. I've blown up every bridge behind me. I'm a thief and a criminal. [*Burying his face in his hands.*] Now you must —! After this you must!

LADY [*movement*]. I shall call my son. Perhaps he —

CASHIER [*with a change of tone, springs nimbly to his feet*]. Aha! Call him, would you? Rouse the hotel, give the alarm? A fine plan! A clumsy trick. You don' catch me so easily. Not in that trap. I have my wits about me, ladies and gentlemen. Yours come fumbling afterwards, tapping like a blind man — but I'm always ahead of you. Don't stir. Sit where you are without a word, until I —— [*he puts the money in his pocket*] — until I — [*he presses his hat over his eyes*] — until I — [*he wraps his coat closely about him*] — until I ——

[*Softly he opens the glass door and slips out.*]

LADY [*rises, stands motionless*].

SON [*entering*]. The man from the bank has just gone out. You're looking worried, Mamma. Is the money ——?

LADY. I found this interview trying. You know, my dear boy, how money matters get on my nerves.

SON. Is there some difficulty again about the payment?

LADY. Perhaps I ought to tell you ——

SON. Must I give back the picture?

LADY. I'm not thinking of that ——

SON. But that's the chief question!

LADY. I think I ought to give information at once.

SON. What information?

LADY. Send this telegram to my bank. In future I must have proper documents that will satisfy every one.

SON. Isn't your letter of credit enough?

LADY. Not quite. Go to the post office for me. I prefer not to send the porter with an open wire.

SON. And when shall we have the three thousand marks? [*Telephone bell rings.*]

LADY [*recoils*]. They're ringing me up already. [*At the instrument.*] Oh! the letter has arrived? And I am to call for the money myself? Very good. [*Change of tone.*] Not at all. Pray don't mention it. One is easily mistaken. Yes, of course. [*Change of tone.*] Florence is a long way off. And then the Italian post — I beg your pardon? Oh, via Paris; then one can easily understand... Not in the east. Thank you. In ten minutes. Good-bye. [*To* SON.] All settled, my dear boy. Never mind the telegram. [*She tears up the form.*] You shall have the picture. Call a cab, and put your wine

merchant in it; he can drive with us and collect his money at the bank. Pack up your treasure. We go straight from the bank to the station. [*Telephoning while the* SON *wraps up the picture.*] The bill, please. Rooms 14 and 16. Yes, immediately. Please.

SCENE III

A slant a field deep in snow, through a tangle of low-hanging branches, blue shadows are cast by the midday sun

CASHIER [*comes backward, shovelling snow with his hands, and covering his footprints. He stands upright*]. How wonderful a toy is every man! The mechanism runs silently in his joints. Suddenly the faculties are touched and transformed into a gesture. What gave animation to these hands of mine? A moment ago they were straining to heave the masses that the drifting snowflakes had strewn! My footprints across the field are blotted out. With my own hands I have accomplished nothingness. [*Taking off his wet shirtcuffs.*] Frost and damp breed chills; fever comes unaware and works upon the mind. The mechanism creaks and falters; the control is lost; and once a man is thrown upon a sick-bed, he's as good as done for. [*He unfastens his sleeve-links and throws the cuffs away.*] Soiled. There they lie. Missing in the wash. The mourners will cry through the kitchen: A pair of cuffs are lost! A catastrophe in the boiler! A world in chaos! [*He picks up the cuffs and thrusts them into his overcoat pocket.*] Queer. Now my wits begin to work again. I see with infallible clearness. I'm drudging here in a snowdrift, fooling with two bits of dirty linen. These are the gestures which betray a man. Hop-la! [*He swings into a comfortable seat in a forked bough.*] But I'm inquisitive. My appetite is whetted. My curiosity is hugely swollen. I feel that great discoveries lie before me. To-day's experience opens up the road. This morning I was still a trusted employee. Fortunes were passing through my hands: the building society made a big deposit. — At noon I'm a cunning scoundrel, an expert in embezzlement, a leaf in the wind, a cork on the water. Wonderful accomplishment! — And but half the day gone by! [*He props his chin on his clenched hand.*] I'll open my breast to Fate; all comers are welcome. I can prove that I'm free man. I'm on the march — there's no turning back, no falling out. No shuffling either — so out with your trumps! Ha! ha! I've put sixty thousand on a single card — it must be trumps. I'm playing too high to lose. Out with them — cards on the table — none of your sharping tricks — d'ye understand? [*He laughs hoarsely.*]

After this you must, pretty lady! Yes indeed, silken lady! Your cue, bright lady; you must play up to me, or the scene will fall flat. — Heavy! — Clumsy! And such gawks are called comedians! Pay your debts, perform your natural duties, breed children — and don't box the prompter's ears!

Ah, forgive me, you have a son? That alters the case completely. I withdraw all aspersions on your character. You are acquitted. Good-bye to you, and give my respects to the Manager. His bullock eyes will cover you with slime, but let that pass. He's been touched for sixty thousand; his roof leaks and rattles in the wind. The building society will mend it for him, never fear.

I release you, silken lady. I waive all claims; you're free, you can go. — Stop! Take my thanks with you on your journey. — What do you say? There's no occasion? Oh, but you're wrong! Not worth mentioning? Why, you're my sole creditor. I owe you my life! You think I exaggerate? — No, pretty lady. It's you who have loosened my creaking joints. In one stride behind you I have entered a land of miracles; with one leap I'm at the heart of the universe, the focus of unimagined brightness. And with this load in my breast-pocket I'm paying cash — cash down for everything! [*With a negligent gesture.*]

You can make yourself scarce; vanish, evaporate! You're outbid and outplayed. Your means are too limited. Remember that son of yours.

[*He pulls out his bundle of notes and slaps it on the palm of his hand.*] I'm paying cash down! Here are my liquid assets; the buyer is waiting. What's for sale? [*Looking across the field.*] Snow. Sunlight. Stillness. [*He shakes his head and puts away the money.*] Blue snow is dear at the price; I won't encourage shameful profiteering. I decline the bargain. The proposition's not serious! [*Stretching his arms to heaven.*] But I must pay! I must spend! I have the ready money! Where are the goods I can buy for cash on the nail? For the whole sixty thousand — and the whole buyer thrown in, flesh and bone, body and soul! [*Crying out.*] Deal with me! Sell to me! I have the money, you have the goods; bring them together!

[*The sun is overcast. He climbs out of the forked bough.*]

The earth is in labour — spring storms are threatening. It comes to pass, it comes to pass! I knew my cry would not be in vain. The call was pressing. Chaos is affronted, and shudders at this morning's monstrous deed. — Of course I know such cases can't be overlooked. It's down with your trousers, and a good hard whipping at the least! Pardon me, sir, to whom do I lift my hat so politely?

[*His hat has been blown off by a sudden squall. Snowflakes, shaken from the branches, stick in the tree-top and form a skeleton with grinning jaws. A branching arm holds the lost hat.*]

Were you sitting all the while behind me, eavesdropper? What are you? A detective? Shall we say — one of Fate's policemen? Are you the staggering answer to my emphatic question? Does your rather well-ventilated appearance announce the final truth — that you are worn out? The information is scanty. Very scanty. It amounts in fact to nothing at all. I reject the argument as too elliptical. Your philosophy, my friend, is full of gaps. Your services are not required. You can shut your rag-and-bone shop. I'm not the first who has peeped into your window — and passed on!

My crime was remarkably simple, it's true; and you would skip the rest of the plot. You'd jump to the conclusion, would you? Ha, ha! But I prefer the complications. So good-day to you.

A soldier on the march can't halt on every doorstep not even at the warmest invitation. I see stretching ahead of me a host of calls to pay, before this evening. It's impossible that you should be the first. The last you may be; but even then, only the last resort. A miserable makeshift, a poor lodging at the journey's end. But as a last resort — well, we may come to terms. Ring me up again toward midnight. Ask the exchange for my number; it will change from hour to hour. — And excuse the coldness of my tone. We should be on a friendlier footing, I know. We are closely bound. I think even now one of your branches is sticking into my back. Free yourself from this tangle of undergrowth, my friend, and envelop me, make me one with you. You'll save me the labour of covering my foot-prints. But first give me back my hat!

[*He takes his hat from the branch, which is bent toward him by the wind. Bowing deeply.*]

I see we have come to a sort of understanding. That will do to begin with. Mutual trust will follow, and support us in the whirl of coming great events. You won't find me ungrateful. [*With a flourish.*] My very best respects ——

[*After a peal of thunder, a last gust of wind sweeps the snow from the tree. The sun comes out; all is bright as at the opening of the scene.*]

There, I said it would soon pass!

[*He puts on his hat, turns up his coat collar and strides away across the snow.*]

SCENE IV

Parlour in CASHIER'S *house. In the window-boxes are blown geraniums. Two doors at right and left in the background. Table and chairs, piano.* MOTHER [*hard of hearing*] *sits near the window.* FIRST DAUGHTER *is embroidering at the table.* SECOND DAUGHTER *is practising the overture to "Tannhäuser."* WIFE *comes and goes in the background.*

MOTHER. What's that you're playing?

FIRST DAUGHTER. Oh, Grandmamma! The overture to *Tannhäuser*.

MOTHER. *O Tannenbaum* is another pretty piece.

WIFE [*entering*]. It's time I began to grill the chops.

FIRST DAUGHTER. Oh, not yet, Mamma.

WIFE. No, it's not time yet to grill the chops. [*Goes out.*]

MOTHER. What are you embroidering there?

FIRST DAUGHTER. The carpet slippers, Grandmamma.

WIFE [*coming to* MOTHER]. To-day we have mutton chops for dinner.

MOTHER. Have you begun grilling them?

WIFE. Plenty of time. It's not twelve o'clock yet.

FIRST DAUGHTER. Not nearly twelve, Mamma.

WIFE. No, not nearly twelve.

MOTHER. When he comes, it will be twelve.

WIFE. He's not due yet.

FIRST DAUGHTER. When Father comes, it will be twelve o'clock.

WIFE. Yes. [*Goes out.*]

SECOND DAUGHTER [*stops playing, listens*]. Is that Father?

FIRST DAUGHTER [*listens*]. Father?

WIFE [*enters*]. Is that my husband?

MOTHER. Is that my son?

CASHIER [*enters, hangs up hat and cloak*]. WIFE. Where have you been?

CASHIER. In the graveyard.

MOTHER. Has somebody died suddenly?

CASHIER [*patting her on the back*]. You can have a sudden death, but not a sudden burial.

WIFE. Where have you come from?

CASHIER. Out of the grave. I burrowed through the clods with my forehead. See, here's a lump of ice. It was a big struggle to get through. Quite hard work. You notice I've dirtied my hands. You want long fingers to work your way through, for you lie there deep embedded. — In a lifetime they shovel lots of earth over you. They overturn mountains on your head — all the dustmen and scavengers—like a great rubbish-shoot. The dead men lie three yards under the soil, but the living are always being buried deeper, deeper down.

WIFE. You're frozen from head to foot.

CASHIER. Thawed. Shaken by storms, like the Spring. The wind whistled and roared; it plucked the flesh from me, and my bones sat naked, knuckles and ribs — bleached in a twinkling. A rattling bone-yard! At last the sun melted me together again; from the soles of my feet upward. And here I stand.

MOTHER. Did you say you had been out in the open air?

CASHIER. In deep dungeons, Mother! In bottomless pits beneath monstrous towers; deafened by clanking chains, blinded by darkness.

WIFE. The bank must be closed to-day. The manager's been drinking with you. Has there been a happy event in his family?

CASHIER. He has his eye on a new mistress. An Italian beauty, in silk and furs — from the land of orange-blossoms. Wrists like polished ivory. Black tresses — olive complexion. Diamonds. Real — all real.

Tus — tus — the rest sounds like Canaan. Fetch me an atlas. Tus — Canaan. Is that right? Is there an island of that name? A mountain? A swamp? Geography can tell us everything.

But he'll burn his fingers. He'll have a nasty fall. He'll be brushed away like a cinder. There he lies — sprawling on the carpet — legs in the air — our fat little manager!

WIFE. Is the bank still open?

CASHIER. Always, wife. Prisons are never closed. The procession of customers is endless. One at a time they hop through the open door, like sheep into a shambles. Inside they stand closely wedged together. There's no escaping, unless you make a saucy jump over all the backs!

MOTHER. Your coat's torn.

CASHIER. And look at my hat! A tramp would never own it.

SECOND DAUGHTER. The lining's all tattered.

CASHIER. Feel in my pockets. Left — right.

FIRST DAUGHTER }
SECOND DAUGHTER } [pull out cuffs].

CASHIER. Well?

DAUGHTERS. Your cuffs.

CASHIER. But no sleeve-links. I took them out. A triumph of coolness. Hat and coat were bound to go to tatters in those leaps from back to back. The other beasts grab at you, clutch you with their horny feet. Silence in the pen! Order in the fold! Equal rights for all! But one jump for dear life, and you're out of the sweating, jostling crowd. One bold stroke — and here I am. Behind me nothing and before me — what?

[He looks around him.]

WIFE [stares at him].

MOTHER [half whispering]. He's ill.

WIFE [goes quickly toward the door on the right].

CASHIER [stops her. To one of the DAUGHTERS]. Fetch my jacket. [To the other.] My slippers. [To the first.] My cap. [To the other.] My pipe.

[All are brought.]

MOTHER. You oughtn't to smoke, when you've already been ——

WIFE [motioning her to be silent]. Shall I give you a light?

CASHIER [in jacket, slippers, and embroidered skull-cap, with pipe in hand, seats himself comfortably at the table]. Light up!

WIFE [anxiously]. Does it draw?

CASHIER [looking into pipe]. I shall have to send it for a thorough cleaning. There must be some bits of stale tobacco in the stem. I oughtn't to have to pull so hard.

WIFE. Shall I take it now?

CASHIER. No, leave it. [Blowing great smoke-clouds.] It draws after a fashion. [To SECOND DAUGHTER.] Play something.

SECOND DAUGHTER [at a sign from her Mother, sits at piano and plays].

CASHIER. What piece is that?

SECOND DAUGHTER. Overture to Tannhäuser.

CASHIER [nods approval. To FIRST DAUGHTER]. Are you sewing or darning?

FIRST DAUGHTER. Working your carpet-slippers, Papa.

CASHIER. Good. And you, Grandma?

MOTHER [*feeling the universal dread*].
I was just — just having forty winks.

CASHIER. Forty winks. In peace and quiet.

MOTHER. Yes, my life is quiet now.

CASHIER [*to* WIFE]. And you, wife?

WIFE. I was going to grill the chops.

CASHIER [*nodding*]. The cook.

WIFE. I'll grill yours now. [*Goes out.*]

CASHIER [*nodding as before*]. The cook.

CASHIER [*to* FIRST DAUGHTER]. Open wide the doors.

[FIRST DAUGHTER *opens doors in background; on the right the* WIFE *is seen busily employed at her kitchen range, on the left is a bedroom with twin beds.*]

WIFE [*in the kitchen doorway*]. Are you too warm in there?

[*She returns to her task.*]

CASHIER [*looking round him*]. Grandmother nodding in an armchair. Daughters: one busy with embroidery, the other playing the piano. Wife at cooking-range. Build four walls about this scene, and you have a family life. — Comfortable, cosy, contented. Mother — son — grandchildren under one roof. The magic of familiar things — the household spell. Let it work. Parlour with table and hanging lamp. Window with geraniums. Piano, music stool. Hearth — home fires burning. Kitchen, daily bread. Chops for dinner. Bedroom, four-poster — in — out. The magic of familiar things. Then one day — on your back, stiff and white. The table pushed back against the wall — cake and wine. In the middle a slanting yellow coffin — screw lid, adjustable stand. A band of crepe hangs round the lamp — the piano stands untouched for a year ——

SECOND DAUGHTER [*stops playing and runs sobbing into the kitchen*].

WIFE [*on the threshold*]. She's still practising the new piece.

MOTHER. Why doesn't she try something simpler?

CASHIER [*knocks out his pipe, begins putting on his hat and overcoat*].

WIFE. Are you going to the bank? Have you an appointment there?

CASHIER. Not at the bank.

WIFE. Then where must you go?

CASHIER. Where must I go? That's a hard question, wife. I've climbed down from windswept trees to look for an answer. This was my first call. It was bound to be the first. Warm and cosy, this nest of yours; I won't deny its good points; but it doesn't stand the final test. No! The answer is clear. This is not a halting-place, but a signpost; the road leads further on. [*He is now fully dressed.*]

WIFE [*distraught*]. Husband, how wild you look!

CASHIER. Like a tramp, as I told you. Never mind. Better a ragged wayfarer than an empty road!

WIFE. But it's just dinner time.

CASHIER. I smell mutton chops.

MOTHER. And you're going out, just before a meal!

CASHIER. Full stomach, drowsy wits.

MOTHER [*beats the air suddenly with her arms, and falls senseless*].

FIRST DAUGHTER. Grandmamma ——

SECOND DAUGHTER [*from the kitchen*]. Grandmamma!

[*Both fall on their knees beside her.*]

WIFE [*stands motionless*].

CASHIER [*going to* MOTHER'S *chair*]. She dies because a man goes out of the house before a meal. [*He brushes the* DAUGHTERS *aside and regards the body.*] Grief? Mourning? Overflowing tears? Are the bonds drawn too close for these? Mother and son! Are they so tightly knit that the very pain is clenched, the very suffering numbed, when they are torn apart? [*He pulls the roll of banknotes out of his pocket and weighs it in his hand, then shakes his head and puts the money away.*] Pain brings no paralysis. The eyes are dry, but the mind runs on. There's no time to lose, if my day is to be well spent. We must take the road. [*He lays his well-worn purse on the table.*] Provide for yourselves. There's money honestly earned. That may be worth remembering. Do your best with it. [*He goes out on the right.*]

WIFE [*stands motionless*].

DAUGHTERS [*bend over the dead* MOTHER].

BANK MANAGER [*coming through the*

open doorway]. Is your husband at home? Has your husband been here? I have to bring you the painful news that he has absconded. We missed him some hours ago; since then we have been into his books. The sum involved is sixty thousand marks deposited by the Building Society. So far I've refrained from making the matter public, in the hope that he would come to his senses and return. This is my last attempt. You see I've made a personal call. Has your husband been here? [*He looks round him, and observes jacket, pipe, etc.*] It looks as though — [*His glance lights upon the group at the window. He nods.*] I see that affairs have already reached an advanced stage. In that case — [*He shrugs his shoulders, puts on his hat.*] It remains only to express my private sympathy, you can rely on that. The rest must take its course. [*He leaves.*]

DAUGHTERS [*coming to* WIFE]. Mother ——

WIFE [*savagely*]. Don't screech in my ears! Don't stand gaping at me! Who are you? What do you want? Ugly brats, monkey-faces —— What have you to do with me? [*Breaking down.*] My husband has left me!

DAUGHTERS [*stand shyly, holding hands*].

SCENE V

Velodrome during a cycle race meeting. Arc lamps. Jewish gentlemen, stewards come and go. They are all alike; little animated figures in dinner jackets, with silk hats tilted back and binoculars slung in leather cases. Whistling, cat-calls, and a restless hum from the crowded tiers of spectators. Music. In the background, a wooden bridge or raised platform.

FIRST GENTLEMAN [*entering*]. Is everything ready?

SECOND GENTLEMAN. See for yourself.

FIRST GENTLEMAN [*looking through glasses*]. The palms ——

SECOND GENTLEMAN. What's the matter with the palms?

FIRST GENTLEMAN. I thought as much!

SECOND GENTLEMAN. But what's wrong with them?

FIRST GENTLEMAN. Who arranged them like that?

THIRD GENTLEMAN. Perfect madness!

SECOND GENTLEMAN. Upon my soul, you're right!

FIRST GENTLEMAN. Was nobody responsible for arranging them?

THIRD GENTLEMAN. Ridiculous. Simply ridiculous.

FIRST GENTLEMAN. Whoever it was, he's as blind as a bat!

THIRD GENTLEMAN. Or fast asleep.

SECOND GENTLEMAN. Asleep, you say? But this is only the fourth night of the race.

FIRST GENTLEMAN. The palm-tubs must be pushed on one side.

SECOND GENTLEMAN. Shall I give the order?

FIRST GENTLEMAN. Right against the wall. There must be a clear view of the course.

THIRD GENTLEMAN. And of the royal box.

SECOND GENTLEMAN. I'll come with you. [*They all go out.*]

FOURTH GENTLEMAN [*enters, fires a pistol shot, then withdraws*].

FIFTH GENTLEMAN [*enters with a red lacquered megaphone*].

THIRD GENTLEMAN. How much is the prize?

FIFTH GENTLEMAN. Eighty marks. Fifty to the winner, thirty to the second.

FIRST GENTLEMAN [*re-enters*]. Three times round, no more. We're tiring them out.

FOURTH GENTLEMAN [*through megaphone*]. A prize is offered of eighty marks for the next race. The winner to receive fifty marks, the second thirty marks. [*Applause.*]

SECOND AND THIRD GENTLEMEN [*return, one carrying a red flag*].

FIRST GENTLEMAN. Now we can get them off.

SECOND GENTLEMAN. Not yet. Number seven has a new mount.

FIRST GENTLEMAN. Off!

SECOND GENTLEMAN [*lowers his red flag, then goes out*].

[*The race begins. Rising and falling volume of applause, with silent intervals.*

THIRD GENTLEMAN. The one on the left moves well.

FOURTH GENTLEMAN. The other's only waiting his chance.

FIFTH GENTLEMAN. We shall see some sport presently.

THIRD GENTLEMAN. The riders are pretty excited.

FOURTH GENTLEMAN. And no wonder.

FIFTH GENTLEMAN. Depend upon it, the championship will be settled to-night.

THIRD GENTLEMAN. The Americans are still fresh.

FIFTH GENTLEMAN. Our lads will hustle them.

FOURTH GENTLEMAN. Let's hope our visitor will see a popular victory.

FIRST GENTLEMAN [looking through glasses]. The box is still empty.

[Outburst of applause.]

THIRD GENTLEMAN. The result!

VOICE. Prizes in cash — fifty marks No. 11, thirty marks for No. 4.

SECOND GENTLEMAN [enters with CASHIER. The latter is in evening clothes, with silk hat, patent shoes, gloves, cloak, his beard trimmed, his hair carefully brushed].

CASHIER. Just explain the idea of the thing —

SECOND GENTLEMAN. I'll introduce you to the stewards.

CASHIER. My name is no concern of anybody's.

SECOND GENTLEMAN. But you have a right to be introduced to the management.

CASHIER. I prefer to remain incognito.

SECOND GENTLEMAN. You're a good sportsman.

CASHIER. I know nothing about it. What are they doing down there? I can see a round track with a bright moving line, like a snake. Here and there one joins in; another falls out. Why is that?

SECOND GENTLEMAN. The riders race in pairs. While one partner is pedalling —

CASHIER. The other blockhead sleeps?

SECOND GENTLEMAN. He undergoes massage.

CASHIER. And you call that a relay race?

SECOND GENTLEMAN. Certainly.

CASHIER. It might as well be called a relay rest.

FIRST GENTLEMAN [approaching]. Ahem! The enclosure is reserved for the management.

SECOND GENTLEMAN. This gentleman offers a prize of a thousand marks.

FIRST GENTLEMAN [change of tone]. Allow me to introduce myself.

CASHIER. On no account.

SECOND GENTLEMAN. The gentleman wishes to preserve his incognito.

CASHIER. Impenetrably.

SECOND GENTLEMAN. I was just explaining the sport to him.

CASHIER. Yes, don't you find it funny?

FIRST GENTLEMAN. How do you mean?

CASHIER. Why, this relay rest.

FOURTH GENTLEMAN. A prize of a thousand marks then. For how many circuits of the course?

CASHIER. As many as you please.

FOURTH GENTLEMAN. How much shall we allot to the winner?

CASHIER. That's your affair.

FOURTH GENTLEMAN. Eight hundred and two hundred. [Through the megaphone.] An anonymous gentleman offers the following prizes for a race of ten circuits; eight hundred marks to the winner, two hundred marks to the second; one thousand marks in all. [Loud applause.]

SECOND GENTLEMAN. But tell me, if the sport only tickles you, why do you offer such a big prize?

CASHIER. Because it works like magic.

SECOND GENTLEMAN. On the pace of the riders, you mean?

CASHIER. Rubbish.

THIRD GENTLEMAN [entering]. Are you the gentleman who is offering a thousand marks?

CASHIER. In five mark notes.

SECOND GENTLEMAN. That would take too long to count.

CASHIER. Watch me. [He pulls out a roll of banknotes, slips off the elastic band, moistens his finger and counts rapidly.] That's one bundle the less.

SECOND GENTLEMAN. I see you're an expert.

CASHIER. A mere detail, sir. [Handing

him the money.] Accept delivery.

SECOND GENTLEMAN. With acknowledgments.

FIFTH GENTLEMAN [*approaching*]. Where is the gentleman? Allow me to introduce ——

CASHIER. Certainly not.

THIRD GENTLEMAN [*with red flag*]. I shall give the start.

[*General movement to the platform.*]

FIFTH GENTLEMAN. Now we shall see a tussle for the championship.

THIRD GENTLEMAN [*joining group*]. All the cracks are in the race.

FOURTH GENTLEMAN. Off!

[*Outburst of applause.*]

CASHIER [*taking* FIRST *and* SECOND GENTLEMEN *by the collars and turning them round*]. Now I'll answer your question for you. Look up!

SECOND GENTLEMAN. But you must keep your eye on the track, and watch the varying course of the struggle ——

CASHIER. Childish, this sport. One rider must win because the others lose — Look up, I say! It's there, among the crowd, that the magic works. The wine ferments in this vast barrel of spectators. The frothing is least at the bottom, among the well-bred public in the stalls. There you see nothing but looks — but what looks! Round stares. Eyes of cattle! — One row higher the bodies sway and vibrate, the limbs begin to dance. A few cries are heard. Your respectable middle class! — Higher still all veils are dropped. A wild fanatic shout, a bellowing nakedness, a gallery of passions! — Just look at that group! Five times entwined; five heads dancing on one shoulder, five pairs of arms beating time across one howling breast! At the heart of this monster is a single man. He's being crushed — mangled — thrust over the parapet! His hat, crumpled, falls through the rising smoke — flutters into the middle balcony, lights upon a lady's bosom. She pays no heed. There it rests daintily — so daintily! She'll never notice the hat; she'll go to bed with it; year in, year out, she'll carry this hat upon her breast!

[*The applause swells.*]

FIRST GENTLEMAN. The Dutchman is putting on a spurt.

CASHIER. The middle row joins in the shout. An alliance has been made; the hat has done the trick. The lady crushes it against the rails. Pretty lady, your bosom will show the marks of this! There's no help for it. Madness to struggle. The throng presses you against the rails, and you must yield. You must grant all! —

SECOND GENTLEMAN. Do you know the lady?

CASHIER. See now, the five up there have thrust their one over the balustrade. He swings free, he loosens his hold, he drops, he sails down into the stalls. What has become of him? Vanished! Swallowed, stifled, absorbed! A raindrop in a maëlstrom!

FIRST GENTLEMAN. The Hamburger is making up ground.

CASHIER. The stalls are frantic. The falling man has set up contact. Restraint can go to the devil! Dinner-jackets quiver. Shirt fronts begin to split. Studs fly in all directions. Lips are parted, jaws are rattling. Above and below — all distinctions are lost. One universal yell from every tier. Pandemonium. Climax.

SECOND GENTLEMAN [*turning*]. He wins! He wins! The German wins! what do you say to that?

CASHIER. Stuff and nonsense!

SECOND GENTLEMAN. A marvellous spurt!

CASHIER. Marvellous trash!

FIRST GENTLEMAN [*about to leave*]. We'll just make certain ——

CASHIER [*holding him back*]. Have you any doubts about it?

SECOND GENTLEMAN. The German was leading, but ——

CASHIER. Never mind that, if you please. [*Pointing to the audience.*] Up there you have the staggering fact. Watch the supreme effort, the last dizzy height of accomplishment. From stalls to gallery one seething flux, dissolving the individual, recreating — passion! Differences melt away, veils of nakedness are stripped; passion rules! — Look from this window, it's a sight worth seeing. — Gate and barriers vanish in smoke. The trumpets blare and the walls come tumbling down. No restraint, no modesty, no motherhood, no childhood — nothing but passion! There's the real thing. That's worth the search. That justifies the price!

THIRD GENTLEMAN [*entering*]. The ambulance column is working splendidly.

CASHIER. Is the man hurt who fell?

THIRD GENTLEMAN. Crushed flat.

CASHIER. There must be dead, where many live in fever.

FOURTH GENTLEMAN [*through megaphone*]. Result: eight hundred marks won by number two; two hundred marks by number one. [*Wild applause.*]

FIFTH GENTLEMAN. The riders are tired out.

SECOND GENTLEMAN. You could see the pace dropping.

THIRD GENTLEMAN. They need rest.

CASHIER. I've another prize to offer.

FIRST GENTLEMAN. Presently, sir.

CASHIER. No interruptions, no delays.

SECOND GENTLEMAN. We must give the riders a chance to recover.

CASHIER. Bah! Don't talk to me of those fools! Look at the public, blazing with excitement. This power mustn't be wasted. We'll feed the flames; you shall see them leap into the sky. I offer fifty thousand marks.

SECOND GENTLEMAN. Are you serious?

THIRD GENTLEMAN. How much did you say?

CASHIER. Fifty thousand. Everything.

THIRD GENTLEMAN. It's an unheard-of sum ——

CASHIER. The effect will be unheard-of. Warn your ambulance men on every floor.

FIRST GENTLEMAN. We accept your offer. The contest shall begin as soon as the box is occupied.

SECOND GENTLEMAN. Capital idea!

THIRD GENTLEMAN. Excellent!

FOURTH GENTLEMAN. This is a profitable visitor.

FIFTH GENTLEMAN [*digging him in the ribs*]. A paying guest.

CASHIER [*to* FIRST GENTLEMAN]. What do you mean — as soon as the box is occupied.

FIRST GENTLEMAN. We'll talk over the conditions in the committee room. I suggest thirty thousand to the winner; fifteen thousand to the second; five thousand to the third.

THIRD GENTLEMAN [*gloomily*]. Downright waste, I call it.

FIFTH GENTLEMAN. The sport's ruined for good and all.

FIRST GENTLEMAN. Directly the box is occupied.

FIRST GENTLEMAN [*all go out leaving* CASHIER *alone. Enter* SALVATION LASS. *Laughter and cat-calls from some spectators*].

SALVATION LASS. The War Cry; ten pfennigs, sir.

CASHIER. Presently, presently.

SALVATION LASS. The War Cry, sir.

CASHIER. What trash are you hawking there?

SALVATION LASS. The War Cry, sir.

CASHIER. You're too late. Here the battle's in full swing.

SALVATION LASS [*shaking tin box*]. Ten pfennigs, sir.

CASHIER. Will you start a war for ten pfennigs?

SALVATION LASS. Ten pfennigs, sir.

CASHIER. I'm paying a war-bill of fifty thousand marks.

SALVATION LASS. Ten pfennigs.

CASHIER. Yours is a wretched scuffle. I only subscribe to pitched battles.

SALVATION LASS. Ten pfennigs.

CASHIER. I've only bank notes on me.

SALVATION LASS. Ten pfennigs.

CASHIER. Bank ——

SALVATION LASS. Ten ——

CASHIER [*seizing megaphone, bellows at her through it*]. Banknotes! Banknotes!!

[SALVATION LASS *goes out. Handclapping and hoarse laughter from the spectators. Many gentlemen enter.*]

FOURTH GENTLEMAN. Would you care to announce your offer yourself?

CASHIER. No, I'm a spectator. [*Handing him the megaphone.*] You shall speak. You shall communicate the final shock.

FOURTH GENTLEMAN [*through the megaphone*]. A new prize is offered by the same anonymous gentleman. [*Cries of "Bravo!"*] The total sum is fifty thousand marks. [*Deafening applause.*] Five thousand marks to the third. Fifteen thousand to the second. The winner to receive thirty thousand marks.   [*Ecstasy.*]

CASHIER [*stands apart, nodding his head*]. There we have it. The pinnacle. The summit. The climbing hope fulfilled. The roar of a Spring gale. The breaking wave of a human tide. All bonds are burst. Up with the veils — down with the shams! Humanity — free humanity, high and low, untroubled by class, unfettered by manners. Unclean, but free. That's a reward for my imprudence. [*Pulling out a bundle of notes.*] I can pay with a good heart!

[*Sudden silence. The gentlemen have taken off their silk hats and stand with bowed heads.*]

FOURTH GENTLEMAN [*coming to* CASHIER]. If you'll hand me the money, we can have the race for your prize immediately.

CASHIER. What's the meaning of this?

FOURTH GENTLEMAN. Of what, my dear sir?

CASHIER. Of this sudden unnatural silence everywhere?

FOURTH GENTLEMAN. Unnatural? Not at all. His Royal Highness has just entered his box.

CASHIER. Highness — the royal box — the house full ——

FOURTH GENTLEMAN. Your generous patronage comes at the most opportune moment ——

CASHIER. Thank you! I don't intend to waste my money.

FOURTH GENTLEMAN. What do you mean?

CASHIER. I find the sum too large — as a subscription to the Society of Hunchbacks!

FOURTH GENTLEMAN. But pray explain ——

CASHIER. This glowing fire extinguished — trodden out by the patent-leather boot of his Highness! You take me for crazy, if you think I will throw one single penny under the snouts of these grovelling dogs, these crooked lackeys! A kick where the bend is greatest, that's the prize they'll get from me!

FOURTH GENTLEMAN. But the prize has been announced. His Royal Highness is in his box. The audience is showing a proper respect. What do you mean?

CASHIER. If you don't understand my words, let deeds speak for me!

[*With a violent blow he crushes the other's silk hat down upon his shoulders. Leaves. There is a prevailing silence and heads are bowed respectfully.*]

SCENE VI

Private supper room in a cabaret. Darkness, with a lighted doorway. Subdued dance music.

WAITER [*opens the door, and switches on red shaded lamps*].

CASHIER [*enters, evening clothes, coat, silk muffler, gold headed bamboo cane*].

WAITER. Will this room suit you, sir?

CASHIER. Well enough.

WAITER [*takes coat, etc*].

CASHIER [*turns his back and looks into a mirror*].

WAITER. How many places shall I lay, sir?

CASHIER. Twenty-four. I'm expecting my grandma, my mamma, my wife and several aunts. The supper is to celebrate my daughter's confirmation.

WAITER [*stares at him*].

CASHIER [*to the other's reflection in the mirror*]. Donkey! Two places! Else why do you furnish these discreet little cabins with a sofa and a dim red light?

WAITER. What brand would you prefer?

CASHIER. Leave that to me, my oily friend. I shall know which flower to pluck in the ball-room — round or slender, a bud or a full-blown rose. I shall not require your invaluable services. No doubt they are invaluable — or have you a fixed tariff.

WAITER. What brand of champagne, if you please?

CASHIER. Ahem! Grand Marnier.

WAITER. That's a liqueur, sir.

CASHIER. Then I leave it to you.

WAITER. Two bottles of Pommery — extra dry. [*Producing menu card.*] And for supper?

CASHIER. Pinnacles.

WAITER. Œufs pochés Bergère? Pou

let grillé? Steak de veau truffé? Parfait de foie gras en croûte? Salade cœur de laitue?

CASHIER. Pinnacles, pinnacles from the soup to the savoury.

WAITER. Pardon?

CASHIER [*tapping him on the nose*]. A pinnacle is the point of perfection — the summit of a work of art. So it must be with your pots and pans. The last word in delicacy. The menu of menus. Fit to garnish great events. It's your affair, my friend; I'm not the cook.

WAITER [*sets a large menu-card on the table*]. It will be served in twenty minutes. [*He re-arranges glasses, etc. Heads with silken masks peep through the doorway.*]

CASHIER [*sees them in the mirror. Shaking a warning finger at them*]. Wait my mother! Presently I shall have you in the lamplight! [*The masks vanish, giggling.*]

WAITER [*hangs a notice RESERVED on the outside of the door, then withdraws and closes it behind him*].

CASHIER [*pushes back his silk hat, takes out a gold cigarette case, strikes a match, sings*]. "Tor-ea-dor, Tor-ea-dor." Queer, how this stuff comes to your lips. A man's mind must be cram full of it — cram full. Everything. Toreador — Carmen — Caruso. I read all this somewhere — it stuck in my head. There it lies, piled up like a snowdrift. At this very moment I could give a history of the Bagdad railway. And how the Crown Prince of Roumania married the Czar's second daughter Tatjana. Well, well, let them marry. The people need princes. [*Sings.*] "Tat-tat-ja-na, tat-ja-na ——" [*Twirling his cane, he goes out.*]

WAITER [*enters with bottles on ice. Uncorks them, pours out wine. Leaves*].

CASHIER [*reënters, driving before him a female MASK in a harlequin's red and yellow quartered costume*]. Fly, moth! Fly, moth!

FIRST MASK [*running round the table*]. Fizz! [*She drinks both of the filled glasses, and throws herself on the sofa.*] Fizz!

CASHIER [*pouring out more wine*]. Liquid powder. Load your painted body.

FIRST MASK [*drinking*]. Fizz!

CASHIER. Battery mounted, action front.

FIRST MASK. Fizz!

CASHIER [*putting aside the bottles*]. Loaded. [*Coming to sofa.*] Ready to fire.

FIRST MASK [*leans drunkenly toward him*].

CASHIER [*shaking her limp arm*]. Look brighter, moth.

FIRST MASK [*does not respond*].

CASHIER. You're dizzy, my bright butterfly. You've been licking the prickly yellow honey. Open your wings, enfold me, cover me up. I'm an outlaw; give me a hiding-place; open your wings.

FIRST MASK [*with a hiccough*]. Fizz.

CASHIER. No, my bird of paradise. You have your full load.

FIRST MASK. Fizz.

CASHIER. Not another drop, or you'll be tipsy. Then what would you be worth?

FIRST MASK. Fizz.

CASHIER. How much are you worth? What have you to offer?

FIRST MASK. Fizz.

CASHIER. I gave you that. But what can you give me?

FIRST MASK [*falls asleep*].

CASHIER. Ha! You'd sleep here, would you? Little wag! But I've no time for the joke; I find it too tedious. [*He rises, fills a glass of wine and throws it in her face*]. Good morning to you! The cocks are crowing!

FIRST MASK [*leaping to her feet*]. Swine!

CASHIER. A quaint name. Unfortunately I'm travelling incognito, and can't respond to the introduction. And so, my mask of the well-known snoutish family — get off my sofa!

FIRST MASK. I'll make you pay for this!

CASHIER. I've paid already. It was cheap at the price.

FIRST MASK [*goes out*].

CASHIER [*drinks champagne, also goes out*].

WAITER [*enters with caviare; collects empty glasses. Exit*].

CASHIER [*enters with two black MASKS*].

SECOND MASK [*slamming the door*]. Reserved!

THIRD MASK [*at the table*]. Caviare!
SECOND MASK [*running to her*]. Caviare?
CASHIER. Black as your masks. Black as yourselves. Eat it up; gobble it, cram it down your throats. [*Seating himself between them.*] Speak caviare. Sing wine. I've no use for your brains. [*He pours out champagne and fills their plates.*] Not one word shall you utter. Not a syllable, not an exclamation. You shall be dumb as the fish that strewed this black spawn upon the Black Sea. You can giggle, you can bleat, but don't talk to me. You've nothing to say. You've nothing to shed but your finery. Be careful; I've made one clearance already!
MASKS [*look at one another, sniggering*].
CASHIER [*taking* SECOND MASK *by the arm*]. What colour are your eyes? Green — yellow? [*Turning to* THIRD MASK.] And yours? Blue — red? A play of glances through the eye-holes. That promises well. Come, I'll offer a beauty prize!
MASKS [*laugh*].
CASHIER [*to* SECOND MASK]. You're the pretty one. You struggle hard, but wait! Presently I'll rip up your curtain and look at the play!
SECOND MASK [*breaks away from him*].
CASHIER [*to* THIRD MASK]. You have something to hide. Modesty's your lure. You dropped in here by chance. You were roving in search of adventure. Well, here's your adventurer! Off with your mask!
THIRD MASK [*slips away from him*].
CASHIER. Is this the goal? I sit here trembling. You've stirred my blood. Now let me pay. [*He pulls out a bundle of notes and divides it between them.*] Pretty mask, this for your beauty. Pretty mask, this for your beauty. [*Holding his hand before his eyes.*] One-two-three!
MASKS [*lift their dominoes*].
CASHIER [*looking at them, laughs hoarsely*]. Cover them — cover them up! [*He runs round the table.*] Monsters — horrors! Out with you this minute — this very second or I'll —— [*He lifts his cane.*]
SECOND MASK. But you told us ——
THIRD MASK. You wanted us ——

CASHIER. I want to get at you!
MASKS [*run out*].
CASHIER [*shaking himself, drinks champagne*]. Sluts! [*Leaves.*]
WAITER [*Enters with fresh bottles. Leaves*].
CASHIER [*kicks the door open and enters dancing with* FOURTH MASK, *a Pierrette in a domino cloak reaching to her shoes. He leaves her standing in the middle of the room and throws himself on to the sofa*]. Dance!
FOURTH MASK [*stands still*].
CASHIER. Dance! Spin your bag of bones. Dance, dance! Brains are nothing. Beauty doesn't count. Dancing's the thing, twisting, whirling! Dance, dance, dance!
FOURTH MASK [*comes halting to the table*].
CASHIER [*waving her away*]. No interval, no interruptions. Dance!
FOURTH MASK [*stands motionless*].
CASHIER. Why don't you leap in the air? Have you never heard of Dervishes? Dancing-men. Men while they dance, corpses when they cease. Death and dancing — signposts on the road of life. And between them ——
SALVATION LASS [*enters*].
CASHIER. Halleluja!
SALVATION LASS. The War Cry!
CASHIER. I know — ten pfennigs.
SALVATION LASS [*holds out her box*].
CASHIER. When do you expect me to jump into your box?
SALVATION LASS. The War Cry.
CASHIER. I suppose you do expect it?
SALVATION LASS. Ten pfennigs.
CASHIER. When will it be?
SALVATION LASS. Ten pfennigs.
CASHIER. So you mean to stick to my coat-tails, do you?
SALVATION LASS [*shakes her box*].
CASHIER. I'll shake you off!
SALVATION LASS [*shakes box*].
CASHIER. Very good, then — [*To* MASK.] Dance!
SALVATION LASS [*goes out*].
FOURTH MASK [*Comes to sofa*].
CASHIER. Why were you sitting in a corner of the ballroom, instead of dancing in the middle of the floor? That made me look at you. All the others went whirling

by, and you were motionless. Why do you wear a long cloak, when they are dressed like slender boys?

FOURTH MASK. I don't dance.

CASHIER. You don't dance like the others.

FOURTH MASK. I can't dance.

CASHIER. Not to music, perhaps; not keeping time. You're right; that's too slow. But you can do other dances. You hide something under your cloak — your own particular spring, not to be cramped by steps and measures! You have a quicker movement — a nimbler leap. [*Pushing everything off the table.*] Here's your stage. Jump on to it. A boundless riot in this narrow circle. Jump now. One bound from the carpet. One effortless leap — on the springs that are rooted in your joints. Jump. Put spurs to your heels. Arch your knees. Let your dress float free, over the dancing limbs!

FOURTH MASK [*nestling closer to him on the sofa*]. I can't dance.

CASHIER. You lash my curiosity. Do you know what price I can pay? [*Showing her a roll of banknotes.*] All that!

FOURTH MASK [*takes his hand and passes it down her leg*]. You see — I can't.

CASHIER [*leaping to his feet*]. A wooden leg! [*He seizes the champagne cooler and upsets it over her.*] I'll water it for you! We'll make the buds sprout!

FOURTH MASK. Now you shall be taught a lesson!

CASHIER. I'm out to learn!

FOURTH MASK. Just wait! [*Goes out.*]

CASHIER [*leaves*]. [*Puts a bank note on the table, takes cloak and stick.*]

[GUESTS *in evening dress enter.*]

FIRST GUEST. Where is the fellow?

SECOND GUEST. We should like a closer look at him.

FIRST GUEST. A blackguard who entices away our girls ——

SECOND GUEST. Stuffs them with caviare ——

THIRD GUEST. Drenches them in champagne ——

SECOND GUEST. And then insults them!

FIRST GUEST. We'll find out his price —

SECOND GUEST. Where is he?

THIRD GUEST. Given us the slip!

SECOND GUEST. Vamoosed!

FIRST GUEST. He smelt trouble!

SECOND GUEST. The place was too hot for him.

THIRD GUEST [*finding the banknote*]. A thousand mark note!

SECOND GUEST. Good God!

FIRST GUEST. He must stink of money.

SECOND GUEST. That's to pay the bill.

THIRD GUEST. He's bolted. We'll do a vanishing trick too.

[*He pockets the money.*]

FIRST GUEST. That's the indemnity for our girls.

SECOND GUEST. Now let's give *them* the slip.

THIRD GUEST. They're all drunk.

FIRST GUEST. They'll only dirty our shirt-fronts for us.

SECOND GUEST. Let's go out on the tiles.

THIRD GUEST. Bravo! While the money lasts! Look out, here comes the waiter!

WAITER [*entering with full tray, halts dismayed*].

FIRST GUEST. Are you looking for anyone?

SECOND GUEST. You might serve him under the table. [*Laughter.*]

WAITER [*in an outburst*]. The champagne — the supper — the private room nothing paid for. Five bottles of Pommery, two portions of caviare, two special suppers — I have to stand for everything. I've a wife and children. I've been four months out of a place, on account of a weak chest. — You won't see me ruined, gentlemen?

THIRD GUEST. What has your chest to do with us? We all have wives and children.

SECOND GUEST. Did *we* bilk you? What next?

FIRST GUEST. But what is this place? Where are we? It seems to be a common swindlers' den. And you lure customers into such a house! We're respectable people who pay for their drinks. [*To others.*] What do you say?

THIRD GUEST [*after changing the door-key to the outer side*]. Look on the floor there. You'll find our bill too!

[*He gives the* WAITER, *who turns round, a push which sends him sprawling.*]

WAITER [*staggers, falls*].

GENTLEMEN [*all go out*].

WAITER [*rises, runs to the door, finds it locked. Beating his fists on the panels*]. Let me out! You needn't pay me! I'm going into the river!

SCENE VII

Salvation Army hall, seen in depth. The background is formed by a yellow curtain embroidered with a black Cross, the height of a man. In front of this stands the low platform, in which are the penitent form, on the right, and the band — trombones and kettledrums — on the left.

In the body of the hall, the benches are crowded. A great hanging lamp, with a tangle of wires for electric lighting, is above the audience. In the foreground, on the right, is the entrance. Music. From a corner, applause and laughter centering in one man.

[SALVATION LASS, *goes to this corner and sits near the disturber. She takes his hand in hers and whispers to him.*]

VOICE [*from the further side*]. Move up closer. Be careful, Bill! Ha, ha! Move up there!

[SALVATION LASS *goes to the speaker, a young workman.*]

WORKMAN. What are you after?

[*Looks at him, shaking her head gravely. Merriment.*]

OFFICER [*woman of 30, coming on to the platform*]. I've a question to ask you all.

SOME [*cry "Hush," or whistle for silence*].

OTHERS. Speech — None of your jaw! Music! — The band!

VOICE. Begin!

VOICE. Stop!

OFFICER. Tell me — why are you sitting crowded there?

VOICE. Why not?

OFFICER. You're packed like herrings in a barrel. You're fighting for places — shoving one another off the forms. Yet one bench stands empty.

VOICE. Nothing doing!

OFFICER. Why do you sit squeezing and crowding there? Can't you see it's a nasty habit? Who knows his next-door neighbour? You rub shoulders with him, you press your knees against his, and for all you know he may be ill. You look into his face — and perhaps his mind is full of murderous thoughts. I know there are sick men and criminals in this hall. So I give you warning! Mind your next-door neighbour! Beware of him! Those benches groan under sick men and criminals!

VOICE. Next to me?

VOICE. Or me?

OFFICER. I give you this word of advice: steer clear of your neighbour! In this asphalt city, disease and crime are everywhere. Which of you is without a scab? Your skin may be smooth and white, but your looks give you away. You have no eyes to see, but your eyes are wide open to betray you. You haven't escaped the great plague; the germs are too powerful. You've been sitting too long near bad neighbours. — Come up here, come away from those benches, if you would not be as your neighbours are in this city of asphalt. This is the last warning. Repent. Repent. Come up here, come to the penitent form. Come to the penitent form, come to the penitent form!

[*Music; trombones and kettledrums.*]

SALVATION LASS [*leads in* CASHIER].

CASHIER [*in evening dress, arouses some notice*].

SALVATION LASS [*finds* CASHIER *a place among the crowd, seats herself next to him and explains the procedure*].

CASHIER [*looks around him, amused*].

[*Music ceases. Ironical applause.*]

OFFICER [*coming forward again*]. One of our comrades will tell you how he found his way to the penitent form.

FIRST SOLDIER [*a young man, steps on to the platform*].

VOICE. So that's the mug!

[*Some laughter.*]

FIRST SOLDIER. I want to tell you of my sin. I led a life without giving a thought to my soul. I cared only for my body. I built up my body like a strong high wall; the soul was quite hidden behind it. I sought for glory with my body, and made

broader the shadow in which my soul
withered away. My sin was sport. I
practised it without a moment's pause for
reflection. I became a professional cyclist.
I was vain of the quickness of my feet on
the pedals, and the strength of my arms
on the handle-bars; I forgot everything in
the applause of the spectators. I sent out
many a challenge; I won many a prize.
My name was printed on every hoarding;
my portrait was in all the papers. I was
in the running for the world championship
... At last my soul spoke to me. Its
patience was ended. I met with an accident. The injury was not fatal. My soul
wanted to leave me time for repentance.
My soul left me strength enough to rise
from those benches where you sit, and to
climb up here to the penitent form. There
my soul could speak to me in peace.
What it told me I can't tell you now. It's
all too wonderful, and my words are too
weak to describe it. You must come
yourselves, and hear the voice speak within
you! [He steps down.]

A MAN [laughs obscenely].

SEVERAL [cry "Hush!"].

SALVATION LASS [to CASHIER, in a low
voice]. Do you hear him?

CASHIER. Let me alone.

OFFICER [coming forward]. You've
heard our comrade's testimony. Can
anything nobler be won than a soul? And
it's quite easy, for the soul is there within
you. You've only to give it peace — once,
just once. The soul wants to sit with you
for one quiet hour. Its favorite seat is on
this form. There must be one among
you who sinned like our comrade here.
Our comrade will help him. The way has
been opened up. So come. Come to the
penitent form. Come to the penitent
form. Come to the penitent form!

[Silence.]

FIRST PENITENT [of powerful build, with
one arm in a sling, rises in a corner of the
hall and makes his way through the crowd,
smiling nervously. He mounts the plat-
form].

MAN [laughs obscenely].

ANOTHER [indignantly]. Where is that
dirty lout?

MAN [rises abashed, and makes his way
toward the door].

OTHERS. That's the fellow!

[SALVATION LASS, hurries to soldier
and leads him back to his place.]

VOICE [facetiously]. Oh, let me go,
Angelina!

SEVERAL OTHERS. Bravo!

FIRST PENITENT [on the platform]. In
this city of asphalt there's a hall. Inside
the hall is a cycle-track. This was my sin.
I was a rider too. I was a starter in the
relay races. On the second night I met
with a collision. I was thrown; my arm
was broken. The race goes hurrying on,
but I am at rest. I have time to reflect in
peace. All my life I have been riding hard
without a thought. I want to think of
everything. [Loudly.] I want to think of
my sins at the penitent form!

[Led by a SOLDIER, he sinks on to the
bench; SOLDIER remains at his side.]

OFFICER. A soul has been won!

[Music. SOLDIERS throughout the
hall stand up and exult with outstretched
arms. Music swells.]

SALVATION LASS [to CASHIER]. Do you
see him?

CASHIER. The cycle races.

SALVATION LASS. What are you muttering?

CASHIER. That's my affair. My affair.

SALVATION LASS. Are you ready?

CASHIER. Hold your tongue.

OFFICER [stepping forward]. Another
comrade will testify.

MAN [hisses].

OTHERS. Be quiet there!

SECOND SOLDIER [girl, mounts the plat-
form]. Whose sin is my sin? I'll tell you
of my sin without shame. I had a wretched
home, if you could call it a home. The
man drank — he was not my father. The
woman — who was my mother — went
with smart gentlemen. She gave me all
the money I wanted; her bully gave me all
the blows — I didn't want. [Laughter.]
No one thought of me; least of all did I
think of myself. So I became a lost woman. I was blind in those days, I couldn't
see that the miserable life at home was only
meant to make me think of my soul and

dedicate myself to its salvation. One night I learned the truth. I had a gentleman with me, and he asked me to darken the room. I turned out the gas, though I wasn't used to such ways. Presently I understood why he had asked me; for there was a deformity at my side. Then horror took hold of me. I began to hate my body; it was only my soul that I could love. And now this soul of mine is my delight. It's so perfect, so beautiful; it's the bonniest thing I know. — I know too much of it to tell you here. If you ask your souls they'll tell you all — all!

[*She steps down. Silence.*]

OFFICER [*coming forward*]. You've heard our sister testify. Her soul offered itself to her, and she did not refuse. Now she tells you her story with joyful lips. Isn't a soul offering itself now, at this moment, to one of you? Let it come closer. Let it speak; here on this bench it will be undisturbed. Come to the penitent form. Come to the penitent form! [*There is a movement in the hall. Some turn round.*]

SECOND PENITENT [*elderly prostitute begins to speak as she comes forward*]. What do you think of me, ladies and gentlemen? I was just tired to death of street-walking, and dropped in here for a rest. I'm not shy — oh dear no! I don't know this hall, it's my first time here. Just dropped in by chance, as you might say. [*Speaking from the platform.*] But you make a great mistake, ladies and gentlemen, if you think I should wait to be asked a second time! Not this child, thank you — oh dear no! Take a good look at me, from tip to toe; it's your last chance; enjoy the treat while you can! It's quite all right; never mind me; I'm not a bit shy; look me up and down. — Thank you, my soul's not for disposal. I've never sold that. You could offer me as much as you pleased, but my soul was always my own. — I'm obliged to you for your compliments, ladies and gentlemen. You won't run up against me in the streets again. I've not a minute to spare for you. My soul leaves me no peace.

[*She has taken off her hat. A SOL-DIER leads her to the penitent form.*]

OFFICER. A soul has been won!

[*Music. Jubilation of the SOL-DIERS.*]

SALVATION LASS [*to CASHIER*]. Do you hear all?

CASHIER. That's my affair. My affair.

SALVATION LASS. What are you muttering about?

CASHIER. The wooden leg.

SALVATION LASS. Are you ready?

CASHIER. Not yet. Not yet.

A MAN [*standing upright in the middle of the hall*]. Tell me my sin! I want to hear my sin!

OFFICER [*coming forward*]. Our comrade here will tell you.

VOICES [*excitedly*]. Sit down! Keep quiet! Give him a chance!

THIRD SOLDIER [*elderly man*]. Let me tell you my story. It's an everyday story; that's how it came to be my sin. I had a snug home, a contented family, a comfortable job. Everything was just — everyday. In the evening, when I sat smoking my pipe at the table, under the lamp, with my wife and children round about me, I felt satisfied enough. I never felt the need of a change. Yet the change came. I forget what started it; perhaps I never knew. The soul knocks quietly at your door. It knows the right hour and uses it. — However that might be, I couldn't pass the warning by. I stood out at first in a sluggish sort of way, but the soul was stronger. More and more I felt its power. All my born days I'd been set upon satisfaction; now I knew that nothing could satisfy me fully but the soul. I don't look for contentment any longer at the table under the lamp, with a pipe in my mouth; I find it here alone at the penitent form. That's my everyday story. [*He stands down.*]

OFFICER [*coming forward*]. Our comrade has told you ——

THIRD PENITENT [*elbowing his way up*]. My sin! My sin! [*From the platform.*] I'm the father of a family. I have two daughters. I have a wife. My mother is still with us. We live in four rooms. It's quite snug and cosy in our house. One of my daughters plays the piano. the other does embroideries. My wife cooks. My old mother waters the geraniums in the window-boxes. It's cosy in our house. Cosiness itself. It's fine in our house — it's grand — first-rate — it's a model — a pattern of a home ——

[*With a change of voices.*] Our house is loathsome — horrible — mean — paltry through and through! It stinks of paltriness in every room; with the piano-playing, the cooking, the embroidery, the watering-pots —— [*Breaking out.*] I have a soul! I have a soul! I have a soul!

[*He stumbles to the penitent form.*]

OFFICER. A soul has been won!

[*Jubilant music. Loud uproar in the hall.*]

MANY [*standing upright, clambering on benches, and stretching out their hands*]. What's my sin? My sin? I want to know my sin! Tell me my sin!

OFFICER [*coming forward*]. Our comrade will tell you. [*Deep silence.*]

SALVATION LASS [*to* CASHIER]. Do you see him?

CASHIER. My daughters. My wife. My mother.

SALVATION LASS. What do you keep mumbling in your beard?

CASHIER. My affair. My affair.

SALVATION LASS. Are you ready?

CASHIER. Not yet. Not yet. Not yet.

FOURTH SOLDIER [*middle-aged, comes forward*]. My soul had a hard struggle to win the victory. It had to take me by the throat and shake me like a rat. It was rougher still with me. It sent me to gaol. I'd stolen the money that was entrusted to me. I'd absconded with a big sum. They caught me; I was tried and sentenced. In my prison cell I found the rest my soul had been looking for. At last it could speak to me in peace. At last I could hear its voice. Those days in the lonely cell became the happiest in my life. When my time was finished I couldn't part from my soul. I looked for a quiet place where we two could meet. I found it here on the penitent form; I find it here still, each evening that I feel the need of a happy hour! [*He stands aside.*]

OFFICER [*coming forward*]. Our comrade has told you of his happy hours at the penitent form. Who is there among you who wants to escape from this sin? Here he will find peace! Come to the penitent form!

ALL [*standing up, shouting and gesticulating*]. Nobody's sin! That's nobody's sin! I want to hear mine! My sin! My sin!

CASHIER. My sin!

SALVATION LASS [*above the uproar*]. What are you shouting?

CASHIER. The bank. The money.

SALVATION LASS [*shaking him*]. Are you ready?

CASHIER. Yes, now I'm ready!

SALVATION LASS [*taking his arm*]. I'll lead you up there. I'll stand by you — always at your side. [*Turning to the crowd, ecstatically.*] A soul is going to speak. I looked for this soul. I found this soul!

[*The tumult ebbs into a quiet hum.*]

CASHIER [*on the platform,* SALVATION LASS *by his side*]. I've been on the road since this morning. I was driven out on this search. There was no chance of turning back. The earth gave way behind me; all bridges were broken. I had to march forward on a road that led me here.

I won't weary you with the halting-places that wearied me. None of them were worth my break with the old life; none of them repaid me. I marched on with a searching eye, a sure touch, a clear head. I passed them all by, stage after stage; they dwindled and vanished in the distance. It wasn't this, it wasn't that, or the next — or the fourth, or the fifth!

What is the goal, what is the prize, that's worth the whole stake? This hall, humming with crowded benches, ringing with melody! This hall! Here, from stool to stool, the spirit thunders fulfilment! Here glow the twin crucibles: confession and repentance! Molten and free from dross, the soul stands like a glittering tower, strong and bright!

You cry fulfilment from those benches. I'll tell you my story.

SALVATION LASS. Speak, I'm with you. I'll stand by you.

CASHIER. I've been all day on the road. I confess: I'm a bank cashier; I embezzled the money that was entrusted to me. A good round sum, sixty thousand marks! I fled with it into your city of asphalt. By this time they're surely on my track; perhaps they've offered a big reward. I'm not in hiding any more. I confess! You can buy nothing worth having, even with all the money of all the banks in the world. You get less than you pay, every time. The more you spend, the less the goods are worth. The money corrupts them; the money veils the truth. Money's the meanest of the paltry swindles in this world! [*Pulling rolls of banknotes out of his breast pocket.*] This hall is a burning oven; it glows with your contempt for all mean things. I throw the money to you; it shall be torn and stamped underfoot! So much less deceit in the world! So much trash consumed! I'll go through your benches and give myself up to the first policeman; after confession comes atonement. So the cup is filled!

[*With gloved hands he scatters banknotes broadcast into the hall. The money flutters down; all hands are stretched upward; a scrimmage ensues. The crowd is tangled into a fighting skein. Musicians, instruments in hand, leap from the platform; benches are overturned, blows of fisticuffs resound above the shouting. At last the cramped mass rolls to the door and out into the street*].

SALVATION LASS [*who has taken no part in the struggle, stands alone among the overturned benches.*]

CASHIER [*smiling at her*]. You are standing by me. You are with me still! [*Picking up an abandoned kettledrum and a pair of sticks.*] On we go. [*Roll of drums.*] The crowd behind us. The yelping pack outrun. A stretch of emptiness. Elbow room! Breathing-space! [*Drumtaps.*] A maid remains — standing upright, standing fast! [*Drumtaps.*] A man and a maid. The old garden is reopened. The clouds are rolled back. A voice cries from the silent treetops. All's well. [*Drumtaps.*] Maiden and man — eternal constancy. Maiden and man — fullness in the void. Maiden and man — the beginning and the end. Maiden and man — the seed and the flower. Maiden and man — sense and aim and goal!

[*Rapid drumtaps, then a long roll.*]

SALVATION LASS [*draws back to the door, and slips out*].

CASHIER [*beats a tattoo*].

SALVATION LASS [*throws the door open. To* POLICEMAN]. There he is! I've shown him to you! I've earned the reward!

CASHIER [*letting fall the drumsticks in the middle of a beat*]. Here I am. Up here. There's only room for one. — Loneliness gives breathing-space. Coldness brings sunshine. The body burns in fever, freezes in fever too. A desert in green fields. Ice in the growing roots. — Who would escape? Where is the door?

POLICEMAN. Is this the only entrance?

SALVATION LASS [*nods*].

CASHIER [*feels in his pocket*].

POLICEMAN. He's got a hand in his pocket. Switch off that light. We're a target for him!

SALVATION LASS [*obeys*].

[*All the lights of the hanging lamp are put out, except one. This illuminates the tangle of wires, forming a skeleton in outline.*]

CASHIER [*feeling with his left hand in his breast pocket, grasps with his right a trumpet, and blows a fanfare toward the lamp*]. Found! I overtake you, my pursuer! My huntsman, you're run to earth! [*Fanfare.*] This morning, among the snowy boughs, I mocked at you. Now, in that tangled wire, you are welcomed as an old friend! [*Fanfare.*] I salute you! [*Fanfare.*] The road is behind me. The last steep curves climb upward — to you. My forces are spent. I've spared myself nothing! [*Fanfare.*] I've made the path hard where it might have been easy. I took the longest way round. Your short cut would have simplified the journey. This morning, when we sat on one branch together, you should have been more pressing in your invitation. How many hours of drudgery that would have saved! How easy it would have been just to sit there with you, in the snow-laden tree! [*Fanfare.*] Why did I climb down! Why did I take the road? Where does it lead me now? [*Fanfare.*] From first to last you sit there, naked as a bone. From morning to midnight I run raging in a circle — and now your beckoning arm shows me the way — whither?

[*He shoots the answer into his breast. The trumpet-note dies on his lips.*]

POLICEMAN. Switch the light on.

SALVATION LASS [*does so*].

[*The* CASHIER *has fallen back with arms outstretched against the Cross on the back wall. His husky gasp is like an* ECCE, *his heavy sigh is like a* HOMO. *One second later all the lamps explode with a loud report.*]

POLICEMAN. There must be a short circuit in the main.

[*All is in darkness.*]

ELECTRA
A TRAGEDY IN ONE ACT
By HUGO VON HOFMANNSTHAL
Translated by ARTHUR SYMONS

DRAMATIS PERSONÆ

CLYTEMNESTRA
ELECTRA
CHRYSOTHEMIS } *Her daughters*
ÆGISTHUS
ORESTES
THE FOSTER FATHER OF ORESTES
THE WAITING WOMAN
THE TRAIN BEARER
A YOUNG SERVING MAN
AN OLD SERVING MAN
THE COOK
THE OVERSEER OF THE SERVING WOMEN
THE SERVING WOMEN

ELECTRA

*The scene represents the inner court,
bounded by the back of the Palace and by
low buildings in which the Servants live.*
SERVING WOMEN *at the draw-well, in
front on the left.* OVERSEERS *among them.*

FIRST SERVING WOMAN [*raising her
pitcher*]. Where does Electra bide?
SECOND SERVING WOMAN. It is her hour,
The hour when she cries out upon her
father,
Till all the walls ring with it.

[ELECTRA *comes running out of the door of
the inner hall, which is already dark.*
ALL *turn towards her.* *She springs
back like a wild beast into its lair, one
arm before her face.*]

FIRST SERVING WOMAN. Did you see
how she stared upon us?
SECOND SERVING WOMAN. Spiteful
She is, as a wild cat.
THIRD SERVING WOMAN. Just now she
lay
And groaned ——
FIRST SERVING WOMAN. She always lies
and groans like that
When the sun's low.
THIRD SERVING WOMAN. And then we
went too far
And came too close to her.
FIRST SERVING WOMAN. She cannot
stand it
If one but merely looks at her.
THIRD SERVING WOMAN. We came
Too close to her. Then she screeched out
like a cat
Upon us: "Off, you flies, begone!" she
cried.
FOURTH SERVING WOMAN. "Muck-flies,
begone!"
THIRD SERVING WOMAN. "Settle not on
my wounds!"
And struck out at us with a wisp of straw.
FOURTH SERVING WOMAN. "Muck-flies,
begone!"

THIRD SERVING WOMAN. "You shall
not feed upon
The sweetness of the torment. You shall
not snatch
The foam from off my agony."
FOURTH SERVING WOMAN. "Crawl
away!"
She cried upon us. "Eat sweet and eat fat,
And sneak to bed, you and your men,"
cried she.
And you ——
THIRD SERVING WOMAN. I was not
idle ——
FOURTH SERVING WOMAN. Gave her her
answer.
THIRD SERVING WOMAN. Yes: "If
you're hungry," was my answer to
her,
"So do you too"; then leapt she and shot
out
A horrid scowl, and crooked her finger at us
Like a big claw, and cried: "I feed," she
cried,
"A vulture in my body!"
SECOND SERVING WOMAN. What did you
say?
THIRD SERVING WOMAN. "That's why,"
I gave her back, "you always squat
Where carrion's to be smelt, and why you
scratch
After a long-dead body!"
SECOND SERVING WOMAN. What did
she say?
THIRD SERVING WOMAN. She only
screamed and cast
Back to her corner.
[*They have finished drawing the
water.*]
FIRST SERVING WOMAN. That the Queen
should let
This sort of demon free in house and court
To live there as it likes her!
SECOND SERVING WOMAN. Her own
child!
FIRST SERVING WOMAN. Were she my
child, by God, I'd put her soon

Safe under bolt and bar.

FOURTH SERVING WOMAN. Do you not think
They are hard enough on her? Do they not set
Her platter with the dogs? [*In a low voice.*]
Have you not seen
The master strike her?

FIFTH SERVING WOMAN [*a quite young one, with a tremulous, sensitive voice*].
Surely I will cast
Myself before her, I will kiss her feet.
Is she not a king's daughter, and endures
So sore an outrage! Surely I will anoint
Her feet and I will wipe them with my hair.

OVERSEER. In with you! [*Pushes her.*]

FIFTH SERVING WOMAN. There is nothing in the world
So royal as she is. She lies in rags
Upon the threshold, ay, but there is none,
[*She shouts.*]
None in the house that can endure to look
Into her eyes.

OVERSEER. In with you!
[*Pushes her in through the open door to L.*]

FIFTH SERVING WOMAN [*caught in the door*]. You are not worthy
To breathe the air she breathes. Would I could see
The lot of you strung up here by the neck
In any dark old granary, for all this
You have done here to Electra!

OVERSEER [*shuts the door and sets her back against it*]. Do you hear that?
We, to Electra? When they bade her sit
And eat with us, she thrust her bowl away,
She spat upon us, and she called us dogs.

FIRST SERVING WOMAN. Eh! what she said was: there is not any dog
A man could make so abject; and that we
With water, always with fresh water, wash
The eternal blood of murder from the floor.

THIRD SERVING WOMAN. And that we sweep the offence, she said, the offence
That comes again, day by day, night by night,
Into its corner.

FIRST SERVING WOMAN. And our bodies, cried she,

Stiffen to the dirt we are in bondage to.
[*They carry their pitchers into the house to* L.]

OVERSEER [*who has fastened the door after them*]. And if she sees us with our children: nought,
Nought can be so accursed, she cries on us,
As children, we have littered in this house,
Slipping in blood upon the stairs like dogs.
Did she say this or not?

SERVING WOMEN [*within*]. Yes, yes!

ONE [*from within*]. They strike me!
[*The* OVERSEER *goes in.*]

[ELECTRA *comes out of the house. She is alone with the red flickerings of light which fall through the branches of the fig-trees and drop like blood-stains on the ground and on the walls.*]

ELECTRA. Alone! Woe's me, alone!
My father gone,
Thrust down in his cold pit.
[*Towards the ground.*]
Where are you, father? Have you not the strength
To lift your face and look on me again?
It is the hour, father, it is our hour;
The hour when these two slaughtered you, your wife
And he who lay in the same bed with her,
Your kingly bed. They struck you in your bath,
Dead: and your blood ran over both your eyes,
And all the bed steamed with the blood; then he,
The coward, took you by your shoulders, dragged you
Out of the room, head foremost, and both legs
After it trailing; and your eyes, wide open,
Staring behind them, saw into the house.
Thus you return, and set [*She sees him.*] foot before foot,
And suddenly you are here, with both your eyes
Wide open, and a royal diadem
Of purple is about your brow, and feeds
Upon the open wound there. Father! I will
See you: O, leave me not to-day alone,

Were it no more than yesterday, come
back,
A shadow in yonder corner, to your child!
Father, your day will come. Time is cast
down
By the sure stars, so surely shall the blood
Out of a hundred throats cast down your
grave
As from a pitcher spilt upon the ground
It streams out of the shackled murderers
And round the naked bodies of their
helpers,
Like marble pitchers, all, women and men;
And in one wave, in one wide swollen
stream,
Shall their life's life gush out of them; and
we
Will slaughter your horses for you and
gather them
About your grave, and they shall snuff up
death
And neigh in the wind of death, and die;
and we
Will slaughter the dogs for you, because the
dogs
Are litter of the litter of that pack
That hunted with you, and would lick your
feet
And you would cast them morsels; there-
fore must
Their blood be shed for you, and we, your
blood,
Your son Orestes and your daughters, we
These three, when all is done, and there
arises
Canopied purple from your streaming
blood,
The sun sucks upward, then we three, your
blood,
Will dance about your grave; and I will
lift
Knee after knee above the heap of dead
Step by step higher, and all who see me
dance,
Yea, all who see my shadow from afar
Dancing, shall say: Behold how great a
king
Here holds high festival of his flesh and
blood,
And happy is he about whose mighty grave
His children dance so royal a dance of
triumph!

[CHRYSOTHEMIS, *the younger sister, stands
in the doorway of the inner court. She
looks anxiously at* ELECTRA, *and calls
softly.*]

CHRYSOTHEMIS. Electra!
[ELECTRA *turns round, like a night-
wanderer, who hears his name called.
She staggers. Her eyes look about her as
if she saw nothing as it was. Her face
distorts as she sees the anxious look
of her sister.* CHRYSOTHEMIS *stands
squeezed in the door.*]

ELECTRA. Ah, the face!
CHRYSOTHEMIS. Is my face then
So hateful to you?
ELECTRA. What do you want? Speak
out,
Say it, empty it all, then go away
And leave me.
[CHRYSOTHEMIS *puts up her hands
as if to ward off a blow.*]
ELECTRA. Why do you lift up
your hands?
So lifted up our father both his hands
When the axe fell on them and clove his
flesh.
What do you want, daughter of my
mother?
CHRYSOTHEMIS. They are about to do
some dreadful thing.
ELECTRA. Both women?
CHRYSOTHEMIS. Who?
ELECTRA. Why, one of them's
my mother,
And there's that other woman, the coward
one,
The valiant murder-monger, why, Ægis-
thus,
The doer of heroic deeds, in bed,
What are they going to do?
CHRYSOTHEMIS. To shut you up
In a dark tower, where you would never
see
The light of sun or moon.
[ELECTRA *laughs.*]
They will, I know,
For I have heard it.
ELECTRA. I seem to have heard
it too.
Was it not said when the last dish went
round

At table?   Then he is wont to raise his
        voice
And brag about his bravery, and, I wager,
'Tis good for his digestion.
        CHRYSOTHEMIS.   Not at table
He did not brag about it.   He and she
Spoke of it all alone.
        ELECTRA.   Alone? how then
Could you have heard it?
        CHRYSOTHEMIS.   At the door, Electra.
        ELECTRA. Let there be no doors opened
        in this house!
Laboring breath, pah! and the gasp of
        strangling:
There's nothing in these rooms but that.
        Let be
The door, when there's a groaning heard
        within.
It cannot be that they are always killing,
Sometimes they are alone together, even!
Open no doors here.   Do not prowl about.
Sit on the ground, like me, and wish for
        death.
And judgment upon her and upon him.
        CHRYSOTHEMIS. I cannot sit and stare
        into the dark,
As you do; there is a fire within my breast
That drives me all about the house, and not
A room is tolerable to me, but I from one
To another threshold must go up, go down;
Each seems to call to me, and as I come,
An empty room stares back at me.   I have
So sore a torment in me that my knees
Shake under me by day and night, my
        throat
Is tightened and I cannot even weep.
All turns to stone.   Sister, have pity!
        ELECTRA.   On whom?
        CHRYSOTHEMIS. You it is who have
        welded me to the ground
With iron clamps.   If it were not for you
They would have let us out.   But for your
        hate,
Your sleepless and immitigable mind,
That makes them tremble, they would
        have let us out,
Out of this prison, sister!   I will go out.
I will not sleep here every night till death,
And I will live before I come to die,
I will bear children, ere my body withers,
And though they mate me with a peasant,
        yet

I will bear him children, and warm them
        with my body
In the cold night when storms are on the
        hut.
But this will I endure no more, to herd
With menials, being no kin of theirs, shut
        in
With very pangs of death by day and night.
Do you hear me, sister!   Speak!
        ELECTRA.   Poor creature!
        CHRYSOTHEMIS.   Nay!
Have pity on yourself and me.   Who
        profits,
Electra, from this anguish?   Not our
        father.
Our father is dead.   Our brother does not
        come.
You see that all this time he does not come.
Time graves its token on your face and
        mine
Day after day, and, there, without, the
        sun
Rises and sets and women I have known
When they were slender are now big with
        blessing,
And at the well can scarcely lift their jars;
Then, in a little, their burdens being off,
Come to the well again, and out of them
Runs a sweet draught, and on them sucks
        and hangs
A young life, and they see their children
        grow;
But we sit all alone upon our perch
Like captive birds, and turn our heads to
        left
And right, and no man comes, no brother
        comes,
No news of any brother, and no news
Of any news, nothing.   Better be dead
Than living and not live.   No, no, I am
A woman, and I would have a woman's lot.
        ELECTRA. Shame on the thought of it,
        shame to speak of it!
To be the hollow where the murderer
After the murder takes his rest; to play
The beast that one may give a worse beast
        pleasure!
She slept with one, ah, and she laid her
        breast
Across his eyes, and nodded to another
That from behind the bed with axe and net
Crept out.

CHRYSOTHEMIS.   You are too
horrible, Electra!
ELECTRA. Why am I horrible? Are you
such a woman?
You will become one.
    CHRYSOTHEMIS.   Can you not forget?
My head is all void. I can remember
Nothing out of day until to-morrow.
Sometimes I lie so, then am I again
What I was once, and cannot make out
    why
I am no longer young. Where is it all?
This is not water, that runs always past,
This is no thread which on the shuttle
    flies,
Hither and thither, it is I, yes, I.
I would fain pray some god to set a light
Within my breast that I might find my-
    self
Again within me. Were I but away
How soon would I forget all these bad
    dreams!
    ELECTRA. Forget? what, am I then a
    beast? Forget?
The beast will fall to sleep, within its
    mouth
Its prey half eaten; the beast forgets itself
And sets a-chewing while death throttles
    it;
The beast forgets what came out of its
    body
And stays its hunger on its young; but I,
I am no beast, and I cannot forget.
    CHRYSOTHEMIS. O must my soul for
    ever on this food
Be fed, this food it loathes, it loathes so
    much
It shudders at the smell of it; this food
It should not ever touch, nor ever know
That there was anything so full of horror;
Not see it with the eyes, not hearken to it.
This terror is too dreadful for men's hearts.
When it draws near to us and takes hold
    on us,
Then must we flee away into the houses,
Into the vineyards, up into the hills,
And if it follow us into the hills
We must come down and burrow in the
    houses;
Not dare abide with it, not be with it
In the same house. I will go, I will go
    away,

I will conceive and I will bring forth chil-
    dren,
That shall know nothing of it, I will wash
My body in that water, plunge deep, deep
My body in that water, wash all over,
Wash clean both my eye-sockets; they
    shall not fear
When they look up into their mother's
    eyes.
    ELECTRA [*scornfully*]. When they look
    up into their mother's eyes!
How will you look our father in the eyes?
    CHRYSOTHEMIS. Stop!
    ELECTRA.   May your children,
    when you have them, do
So unto you as you unto our father.
    [CHRYSOTHEMIS *cries out.*]
Why do you cry? Get in. Your place is
    there.
I hear a noise. Is it your wedding-feast
They set in order? I can hear them run-
    ning.
Why, the whole house is up. They are in
    birth-pangs
Or at a murder. They must be at a mur-
    der
When they have no dead body for a bed.
    CHRYSOTHEMIS. Stop! That is past and
    over.
    ELECTRA.   Past and over?
They fall to some new matter there within.
Do you think I do not know the sound
    when bodies
Are trailed upon the stairs, and there is
    whispering
And wringing out of cloths that drop with
    blood?
    CHRYSOTHEMIS. Sister, let us begone
    from here.
    ELECTRA.   This time
I will be by, and not as I was then.
I am strong this time. I will cast myself
Upon her, wrest the axe out of her hand,
Swing the axe over her ——
    CHRYSOTHEMIS.   Go, hide yourself,
Lest she should see you. Do not cross her
    path
To-day. She scatters death in every
    glance.
She has been dreaming.
    [*The noise of many people approach-
    ing comes nearer.*]

Go away from here,
Go, they are coming through the corridor.
They are coming by this way. She has
    been dreaming;
I know not what, I heard it from her
    women,
I do not know, sister, if it is true;
They say she has been dreaming of Orestes,
And that she has been crying in her sleep,
As one cries out being strangled.
    ELECTRA.   It is I,
I, that have sent him to her. From my
    breast
I sent the dream to her. I lie and hear
The feet of him who follows her. I hear
His feet go through the room, I hear him
    lift
The curtain of the bed; crying, she leaps
    forth,
But he is after her; and down the stairs
Through vault and vault and vault the
    hunt goes on.
It is much darker now than night, and
    much
Darker and much more quiet than the
    grave;
She pants and staggers in the darkness, yet
He is still after her; he shakes the torch
On this side and on that side of the axe.
And I am like a hound upon her heels;
And if she seeks a hole I spring upon her
Sideways, and so we drive her on and on
Till a wall shuts upon us, and there, deep
In that dense darkness (yet I see him there,
A shadow, and his limbs and eyeballs) sits
Our father, and he heeds not, yet it must
Be done; we drive her in before his feet;
Then falls the axe.
    [Torches and figures fill the corridor
    to L. of door.]
    CHRYSOTHEMIS. They are here already,
        and she drives her women
Before her, all with torches, and they drag
Beasts with them and the sacrificial knife.
She is most deadly, sister, when she
    trembles,
As she does now. O do not cross her path
For this one day, only for this one hour!
    ELECTRA. I have a mind to speak now
        with my mother
As I have never spoken.
    [Against the brightly lighted corridor

shuffles and clatters a hurrying procession. There is a tugging and hauling
of beasts, a smothered chiding, a quickly
stifled cry, the swish of a whip, a pulling
back and staggering forward.]
    CHRYSOTHEMIS.   I will not hear it.
    [She goes in through the door of the
    court.]

[CLYTEMNESTRA appears in the wide win-
    dow. In the glare of the torches her
    sallow and bloated face looks whiter
    above her scarlet dress. She leans on
    her WAITING WOMAN, who is dressed
    in dark violet, and on an ivory staff in-
    crusted with precious stones. A yellow
    figure with dark hair combed back,
    like an Egyptian, and a smooth face
    like an erect snake, bears her train. The
    queen is bedecked all over with precious
    stones and talismans. Her arms are
    covered by bracelets, her fingers glitter
    with rings. Her eyelids seem un-
    naturally heavy, and she seems to keep
    them open with a great effort. ELECTRA
    stands rigid and still, her face turned
    towards the window. CLYTEMNESTRA
    suddenly opens her eyes and, trembling
    with anger, goes to the window and
    points with her staff at ELECTRA.]

CLYTEMNESTRA [at the window]. What
    do you want? See it now, how it
    rears
Its swollen neck and darts its tongue at me!
See what I have let loose in my own house.
If she could only kill me with her eyes!
O Gods, why do ye weigh on me so sore,
Why do ye waste me so intolerably?
Why must my strength be sacrificed in
    me? Why
Is this my living body like a field
Wasted with weeds, and nettles grow in it,
And I have not the strength to pluck them
    up?
Why is this done to me, immortal gods?
    ELECTRA. The gods! but are you not
        yourself a goddess?
You are as they are.
    CLYTEMNESTRA.   Do you understand
What she is saying?
    WAITING WOMAN. That you also are of
The seed of gods.

TRAIN BEARER [*whispers*]. She meant it knavishly.

CLYTEMNESTRA [*dropping her heavy eyelids*]. It sounds familiar, and like a thing
Forgotten long ago. She knows me well,
Yet what she harbors in her no man knows.

[*The* WAITING WOMAN *and* TRAIN BEARER *whisper together*.]

ELECTRA. You are yourself no longer.
Reptiles hang
Upon you, what they hiss into your ear
Sunders your thought within you, and you fall
Into an ecstasy, and always now
You are as in a dream.

CLYTEMNESTRA. I will go down.
Leave me, for I will speak with her. To-day
She is not so curst. She speaks like a physician.
The hours have all things mortal in their hand.
In everything one aspect may be found
Bearable even in things least bearable.

[*She leaves the window and comes to the door, the* WAITING WOMAN *by her side, the* TRAIN BEARER *behind her, torches behind them*.]

[*From the threshold*.] Why did you call me a goddess? Did you say it
In malice? Have a care. This day may be
The last when you shall ever see the light
Of day and breathe in freely the free air.

ELECTRA. If you are not a goddess, of a truth,
Who are the gods? There is nothing in the world
That fills me with such shuddering as to think
That body the dark door through which I crept
Into the light of the world. Have I then lain
Naked upon that lap, and to that breast
Have you indeed lifted me? Then have I
Crept from my father's grave, and played about
In winding-sheets upon his judgment-place.
Then you are a colossus, from whose hands

Of brass I never issued. You have me hard
Upon the bridle and you fetter me
To what you will. You have cast up like the sea
A father and a sister and a life.
And you have sucked down under like a sea
A father and a sister and a life.
I know not how, unless you died before me,
I should have leave to die.

CLYTEMNESTRA. So much do you honor me? Is there yet a little
Respect in you?

ELECTRA. Much, much! What troubles you
Troubles me likewise. Look you, why it irks me
To see Ægisthus, who is your husband, wear
The cloak my father, who is dead, you know,
And was the late king, wore. It irks me truly;
I find it sits not well on him; it is
Too wide across the shoulders.

WAITING WOMAN. The thing she says
Is not the thing she means.

TRAIN BEARER. False, every word.

CLYTEMNESTRA [*to them scornfully*]. I will hear nothing. That which comes from you
Is but Ægisthus' breath. I will not check
At all things. And if you will say to me
What pleases me to hear, then will I hearken
To what you say. The very truth of things
That no man brings to light. There is on earth
No man that knoweth how deep-hid a thing
The truth is. Are there not in prison those
That call Ægisthus murder-monger, me
Murderess? And if I wake you in the night
Do you not each give answer otherwise?
Do you not cry out that my lids are swollen
And I am sick within, and that all this
Is but that I am sick? And then you whimper
Into my other ear that you have seen

Demons with long, sharp-pointed beaks
suck out
My blood, and point the marks out on my
body.
And I, believing you, slay, slay, and slay
Sacrifice upon sacrifice? Do you not
Tear me to death with sayings and answer-
ings?
I will hear no more! This is truth, this is
falsehood.
If any should say pleasant things to me,
Were it my daughter even, were it she
there,
Then will I from my soul take off all veils,
And let the stir of the soft airs come in,
Come whence it may come, as sick people
do
Who sit about a pool at eventide,
Letting the cool air come upon their bodies,
Fevered and foul, thinking about nothing
Except about the comfort. So will I
Begin now to make shift for my own self.
Leave me alone with her.

[*She points the way into the house
with her stick, impatiently, to her*
Waiting Women *and* Train Bearers.
*They disappear lingeringly through
the doorway. The torches disappear
with them, and only a faint light falls
from inside the house across the inner
court, and casts bars of shadow over the
figures of the two women.*]

Clytemnestra [*after a pause*]. I can-
not sleep at night. Do you not
know
Some remedy for dreams?
Electra [*coming nearer*]. I, mother, I?
Clytemnestra. Have you no other
word to comfort me?
Unloose your tongue. Ah, yes, I dream.
We age,
And as we age we dream. But that indeed
Can be cast out. Why do you stand in the
dark?
We must make profit of the powers in
us
That now lie scattered. There are certain
rites,
There must be proper rites for everything.
On how one utters a mere word or sentence
Much may depend. And also on the hour,
And whether one be full or fasting. Much

Has come to pass because at the wrong
hour
One stept into the bath.
Electra.   Are you thinking then
About my father?
Clytemnestra.   Therefore I am so
Behung with precious stones. In every
stone
There lives for sure a virtue. But one
needs
To know the uses of them. If you would,
I know that you could tell me what would
aid me.
Electra. I, mother, I?
Clytemnestra.   Yes, you! For you
are wise,
Your head is sound and strong. You talk
about
Old things as if they happened yesterday.
But I decay. I think. But one thought
heaps
Itself upon another. And if I open
My mouth, then cries Ægisthus, and what
he cries
Is hateful to me, and I would fain rise up,
Be stronger than his words, and I find
nothing.
I find nothing! I do not even know
Whether it was to-day he said that thing
Which shook my soul with fury, or long ago.
Then I grow dizzy and know nothing more,
Not even who I am; and 'tis that terror
That hales me living into the abyss.
And he, Ægisthus, mocks me, and I find
Nothing.   I find not some unspeakable
thing
To strike him silent and as pale as I
Staring into the fire. But you have words.
You could speak many things to bring me
help.
What if a word be nothing but a word?
What is a breath? And yet there creeps a
something
Over me as I lie, 'twixt night and day,
With open eyes, and it is not a word,
And not an agony, it does not crush,
It does not choke me, but it lets me lie
As I am lying, and beside me there
Ægisthus lies and there — the curtain is.
And all things look at me as if it were
Out of eternity into eternity,
And it is nothing, not a nightmare even,

And yet it is so terrible that my soul
Hungers to hang itself, and every nerve
Pants after death; and yet I live the
    while
And am not even sick; look on me now:
Am I like a sick woman? Can one perish
Living, like a foul carcase, and decay,
Not being sick in anywise? Decay —
With waking mind, like garments moths
    have eaten?
And then I sleep, and then I dream, and
    dream
That all the marrow is molten in my bones
And still I stagger on, and not the tenth
Of an hour's running water has run out,
And that which grins in underneath the
    curtain
Is not yet the dun morning, no, but always
Only the torch before the door, that starts
Horribly like a living thing, and lies
In wait against my sleep.
I know not who they are that thus oppress
    me,
And whether over us or under us
Be their abode; but when I see you stand
As now you stand before me, I can but
    think
That you are also in the game with them.
Only who are you then? You have not a
    word
To say, now when one listens to you. How
Shall it be help or hurt to any man
Whether you live or die? Why do you
    look
So hard upon me? I will not have you
    look
Upon me so. These dreams must have an
    end.
Whatever demon has been sent, shall leave
    us
When the right blood is spilt.
    ELECTRA.   Whatever demon?
    CLYTEMNESTRA. Though I should let
        the blood of every beast
That creeps and flies, and in the steam of
    the blood
Stand up and go to sleep there as folk do
In ultimate Thule in a blood-red mist,
Yet will I dream no more.
    ELECTRA.   When there shall fall
Under the axe the right blood-offering
Then you shall dream no more.

    CLYTEMNESTRA [coming nearer].   Ah,
        then you know —
With what horned beast ——
    ELECTRA.   With an unhorned beast.
    CLYTEMNESTRA. That lies within there
        bound?
    ELECTRA.   No, it goes free.
    CLYTEMNESTRA [eagerly].   And with
        what rites?
    ELECTRA.   Marvellous rites, that ask
A strict observance.
    CLYTEMNESTRA.   Speak them!
    ELECTRA.   Can you not
Divine them?
    CLYTEMNESTRA. No, and therefore you
        I ask.
The name then of the offering?
    ELECTRA.   A woman.
    CLYTEMNESTRA [eagerly].   One of my
        women? Or a child? A maiden?
A woman that has known men?
    ELECTRA.   Yes, known men:
That's it!
    CLYTEMNESTRA. How then the offering,
        and what hour,
And where?
    ELECTRA.   In any place, in any hour
Of day or night.
    CLYTEMNESTRA. Tell me the rites, and
        tell me
How they are served. Must I myself ——
    ELECTRA.   This time
You go not to the hunt with net and axe.
    CLYTEMNESTRA. Who then? Who of-
        fers it?
    ELECTRA.   A man.
    CLYTEMNESTRA.   Ægisthus?
    ELECTRA [laughs]. I said a man!
    CLYTEMNESTRA. Who? Answer.
        Of the house?
Or must he be a stranger?
    ELECTRA [looking as if absently on the
        ground].   Yes, yes, a stranger.
But surely of the house.
    CLYTEMNESTRA.   Read me no riddles.
Electra, hear me. You are not so stubborn
To-day, and I am glad of it. When par-
    ents
Are hard upon the child, it is the child
That goads them into hardness. No harsh
    word
Is quite irrevocable, and no mother

If she sleeps ill, but would the rather think
That her child lay in marriage-bed than
bonds.

ELECTRA [*to herself*]. How different with
the child! that fain would think
Her mother dead rather than in her bed.

CLYTEMNESTRA. What are you mutter-
ing? I say that there is nothing
Irrevocable. Do not all things pass
Before our eyes and vanish like a mist?
And we ourselves, we too, we and our deeds,
Deeds! We and deeds! And what mere
words are those!
Am I still she who did it? And if I am?
Done, done! What kind of empty word
is this
You cast into my teeth? There stood he,
whom
You speak of always, there stood he and
there
Stood I and there Ægisthus, and from our
eyes
Our glances struck upon each other; yet
Nothing had come to pass, and then there
changed
So slowly and so horribly in death
Your father's eyes, still hanging upon
mine;
And it had come to pass; nothing between!
First it was coming, then it had gone by,
And I had done, between coming and going,
Nothing.

ELECTRA [*to herself*]. No, that which lies between,
the act,
That did the axe alone.

CLYTEMNESTRA. How you cut in
With words!

ELECTRA. Yet not so fit nor yet so fast.
As you axe-thrust on axe-thrust.

CLYTEMNESTRA. I will hear
No more of this. Be silent. If your
father
Came to me here this day — as I with you
So would I speak with him. It may well
be
That I would shudder, yet it may well be
That I would weep and be as kind to him
As if we were old friends that met together.

ELECTRA [*to herself*]. Horrible! she
speaks of murder as if it were
A squabble before supper.

CLYTEMNESTRA. Tell your sister

She need not run away into the dark
Out of my sight, like any frightened dog.
Tell her to greet me in more friendly wise,
And talk with me in quiet. For in truth
I know not why I should not give you both
In marriage before winter.

ELECTRA. And our brother?
Will you not let our brother come home,
mother?

CLYTEMNESTRA. I have forbidden you
to speak of him.

ELECTRA. You are afraid of him.

CLYTEMNESTRA. Who says it?

ELECTRA. Mother,
Now you are trembling.

CLYTEMNESTRA. Who could be afraid
Of a half-witted fellow?

ELECTRA. What?

CLYTEMNESTRA. They say
He stammers, lies about among the dogs,
And cannot tell a wild beast from a man.

ELECTRA. The child was sound enough.

CLYTEMNESTRA. They say he has
A wretched dwelling, and the beasts of the
yard
For his companions.

ELECTRA. Ah!

CLYTEMNESTRA [*with lowered eyelids*]. I
sent much gold
And yet more gold that they should use
him well,
In all things as the son of a King.

ELECTRA. You lie!
You sent the gold that they might choke
him with it.

CLYTEMNESTRA. Who told you that?

ELECTRA. I see it in your eyes,
I see by how you tremble that he lives,
And that you think of nothing, day or
night,
Except of him, and that your heart dries
up
With deathly dread because you know he
comes.

CLYTEMNESTRA. Lie not. What's that
to me who bides without
The house? I live here and am mistress.
Servants
Enough I have, that watch before the doors
And when I please I set by day and night
Before my chamber door three watchers
armed

With open eyes. All this you tell me of
I do not even hear. I do not even
Know of what man you speak. And I
shall never
See him again: what is it to me to know
If he be dead or living? In very deed
I have had enough with dreaming of him.
Dreams
Are like a sickness, and break down the
strength,
And I will live and be the mistress here.
I will not have such seizures of the soul
As send me hither like a pedlar-woman
To blab my nights out to you. I am as
good
As sick, and sick folk tattle of their ail-
ments,
That's all. But now I will be sick no
longer.
And I will wring one or another way
[She shakes her staff at ELECTRA.]
The right word out of you. You have
already
Told me you know the right blood-offering
And the due rites to heal me. Say it not
Free, you shall say it fettered. Say it
not
Full, you shall say it fasting. Dreams are
things
That we must rid ourselves of. He that
suffers
And finds no means of healing for himself
Is nothing but a fool. I will find out
Whose blood it is must flow, that I may
sleep.
ELECTRA *[with a leap out of the darkness
upon her, drawing nearer and nearer
to her, more and more menacing].*
What blood must flow? Out of
your neck, your neck,
When that is caught into the hunter's
noose.
He catches you, yet only in the chase,
Who offers up a sacrifice in sleep?
He hunts you on, he drives you through
the house;
And if you turn to right, there stands the
bed,
And if you turn to left, there foams the
bath
Like blood; the darkness and the torches
cast

Black-blood-red nets, the death-nets, over
you!
[CLYTEMNESTRA, *shaking with
speechless horror, would go into the
house.* ELECTRA *pulls her towards her
by her robe.* CLYTEMNESTRA *draws
back towards the wall. Her eyes are
wide open. Her staff falls from her
trembling hands.]*
You would cry out, but the air strangles
dead
The unborn cry, and noiseless lets it fall
Upon the ground, as in imagination
You reach your neck and feel the edge of
the blade
Draw near the seat of life. Yet still the
blow
Lingers; not yet are all the rites fulfilled.
He draws you by the tresses of your hair,
And all is silent, and your own heart you
hear
Knock at your ribs; this time (it widens
out
Before you like a dark abyss of years)
This time is given that you may taste and
know
What agony is that of shipwrecked men
When their vain cry devours the night of
clouds
And death; this time is given that you may
envy
All that are chained to prison-walls and
cry
In darkness from the bottom of a well
For death as for deliverance; because you,
You lie imprisoned in yourself as in
The glowing belly of a brazen beast,
And, even as now, cannot cry out. And I
Stand there beside you, and you cannot
take
Your eyes from mine, and that which
racks you is
That you would read a word upon my
face,
A word that there stands silent; and you
roll
Your eyes, and you would catch at any
thought,
Would have the gods grin down out of the
clouds;
The gods, they are at supper, now as when
You slew my father, still they sit at supper,

And still they are deaf to any death-
rattle.
Only the half-crazed God of Laughter
staggers
In at the door; he thinks you would make
sport,
You and Ægisthus, at the shepherd's
hour;
But when he sees his error, of a sudden
He laughs, loud-shrilling, and is gone in a
trice.
Then have you had your fill; then on your
heart
The gall drops bitter, then at the last gasp
You would call up one word, any mere
word,
A word only, instead of bloody tears
The beast is not denied in death; and there
I stand before you, and you read too late
With rigid eyes the word unspeakable
Written upon my face; because my face
Is mingled of your features and my father's
And with my silent presence have I
brought
To nought your last word, for your soul
indeed
Has hanged itself within its self-slung
noose,
And now the axe falls crashing, and I stand
Before you and I see you die at last.
Then do you dream no more, then do I
need
To dream no more; whoever is living then,
Let him rejoice because he is alive!

[*They stand eye to eye*, ELECTRA *in
the wildest intoxication*, CLYTEMNESTRA
*breathing horribly with fear. At this
moment the entrance hall is lighted up,
and the* WAITING WOMAN *comes out
running. She whispers something in*
CLYTEMNESTRA'S *ear. At first she
seems not to understand. Gradually
she comes to herself. She beckons:
lights!* SERVING WOMEN *with torches
come out and station themselves behind*
CLYTEMNESTRA. *She beckons more
lights! More come out and station
themselves behind her, so that the court
is full of light, and a red-gold glare
floods the walls. Now the features of*
CLYTEMNESTRA *slowly change, and
their shuddering tension relaxes in an*

*evil triumph. She lets the message be
whispered to her again, without taking
her eyes off* ELECTRA. *Then the*
WAITING WOMAN *lifts her staff, and,
leaning on both, hurriedly, eagerly,
catching up her robe from the step, she
runs into the house. The* SERVING
WOMEN *with the lights follow her, as if
pursued.*]

ELECTRA [*during this*]. What are they
saying to her? Why does she rejoice?
O my head! I can think of nothing. What
Can give the woman pleasure?

[CHRYSOTHEMIS *comes running to the door
of the court, crying aloud like a wounded
animal.*]

Chrysothemis!
Quick! Your help! Tell me something in
the world
That can give some one pleasure!
CHRYSOTHEMIS [*shrieking*]. Orestes!
Orestes!
Is dead.
ELECTRA [*motions her away, as if beside
herself*]. Be silent!!
CHRYSOTHEMIS [*close to her*]. Orestes is
dead. [ELECTRA *moves her lips.*]
I came out, they all know it already. All
Are standing round, and they all know it
already.
Only not we.
ELECTRA. No one knows it.
CHRYSOTHEMIS. All know it.
ELECTRA. No one can know it, for it is
not true.
[CHRYSOTHEMIS *flings herself on the
ground.*]
[*Raising her.*] It is not true! I tell you so
I tell you
It is not true.
CHRYSOTHEMIS. The strangers stood be-
side the wall, the strangers
Sent to bring tidings of it; there are two,
An old man and a young man. They have
told it
To all of them already, and they all stand
About them in a circle, and they all
Know it already.
ELECTRA. It is not true.
CHRYSOTHEMIS. To us

Only they do not tell it, only of us
Does no man think.   Dead, Electra, dead!

[*A* YOUNG SERVING MAN *comes hurriedly*
out of the house, and stumbles over those
lying before the threshold.]

YOUNG SERVING MAN.   Room there,
    who hangs about a door like that?
Would one have thought it?   Hey there,
    grooms, I say!

[*The* COOK *comes from a doorway on* R.]

COOK.   What is it?
YOUNG SERVING MAN.   'Tis a groom T
    split my lungs for,
And lo! when some one crawls out of his
    kennel
Why, it's the cook!

[*An* OLD SERVING MAN *with a gloomy face,*
appearing at the door of the court.]

OLD SERVING MAN.   What's wanted in
    the stable?
YOUNG SERVING MAN.   Saddling's
    what's wanted, and as soon as may
    be.
Do you hear?   A nag, a mule, for aught I
    care
A cow, but quickly.
OLD SERVING MAN.   Who for?
YOUNG SERVING MAN.   Why, for him
That orders it.   No gapes!   For me, but
    quick!
At once!   For me!   Trot, trot!   For I
    must out
And off to field to fetch the master home;
I have news for him, great news, weighty
    enough
To ride a jade of yours to death for it.

[*The* OLD SERVING MAN *disappears.*]

COOK.   What is the news?   A word?
YOUNG SERVING MAN.   A word, good
    cook,
Would certainly instruct you little.   Also
To put it altogether in one word
All that I know, and all I have to tell
The master, would be difficult: enough
To tell you that the news has newly
    come
Of matters of the highest moment, news —
The old fossil takes his time to saddle
    up! —

Which, as a faithful servant of the house-
    hold
Should give you joy, whether you know 't
    or not,
It's all one, it should give you joy.
[*Shouting in the hall.*]   A whip,
Rascal! do you think one rides without a
    whip?
You keep me waiting and not I the nag.
    [*To the* COOK, *preparing to rush out.*]
Well, in a word, then: the young lad
    Orestes,
The son of the house, who never was at
    home,
And thus as good as dead: this he, in short,
Who, so to speak, was dead already, is
Now, so to speak, really and truly dead.
                    [*He rushes out.*]
    [*The* COOK, *turning to* ELECTRA *and*
    CHRYSOTHEMIS, *who lie pressed to each*
    other like one body, which the sobs of
    CHRYSOTHEMIS *shake, and from which*
    ELECTRA *raises her death-pale silent*
    face.]
COOK.   Ah! now I have it!   Dogs howl
    to the moon
When she is at her full; you howl because
For you 'tis always new-moon.   Dogs
    when they
Trouble the peace of the house, are driven
    out.
Take heed, lest it be so with you.
CHRYSOTHEMIS [*half raising herself*]
    Dead in a strange land, dead, and
    in his grave.
In a strange land!   Struck from his horse,
    dragged
Along the ground!   Ah, and his face, they
    say,
Not to be known.   But that we never
    saw
His face; for when we think of him we see
    him
As when he was a child.   He was a man.
And did he long for us before he died?
I could not question, there were so many
Standing all round about them.   Now,
    Electra,
We must go in and talk with these two
    men.
ELECTRA [*to herself*].   Now must the
    deed be done by us.

CHRYSOTHEMIS.   Electra,
We will go in; there are two of them, one
    old
And one much younger; when they come
    to know
That we are the two sisters, the poor sisters,
Then they will tell us all.
    ELECTRA.   What is there now
That it can profit us to know? We know
That he is dead.
        CHRYSOTHEMIS. That they should not
            have brought us even one look,
One little lock of hair! As if we were
No longer in the world, now, you and I!
        ELECTRA. Therefore must we now show
            them that we are.
        CHRYSOTHEMIS. Electra?
        ELECTRA.   We! we both must do it.
        CHRYSOTHEMIS.   What,
Electra?
        ELECTRA. Best to-day, and best to-
            night.
        CHRYSOTHEMIS. What, sister?
        ELECTRA.   What? The work
            that now on us
Falls, because now he cannot come, and
    that
Which is to do may not remain undone.
        CHRYSOTHEMIS. What is the work then?
        ELECTRA.   Now must you and I
Go in and slay the woman and her husband.
        CHRYSOTHEMIS. Sister, you do not mean
            our mother?
        ELECTRA.   Her,
And also him. This thing must now be
    done
Without delay.
        [CHRYSOTHEMIS remains speechless.]
            Be silent. There is nothing
To say, nothing to think, but how? But
    how
We are to do it.
        CHRYSOTHEMIS. I?
        ELECTRA.   Yes, you and I.
Who else then? Has our father other
    children
Hidden here in the house, and will they
    come
And help us? No. So much at least I
    know.
        CHRYSOTHEMIS. Must both of us go in?
            Both of us two?

And with our both hands?
        ELECTRA.   Let me look to that.
        CHRYSOTHEMIS. If you had even a
            knife ——
        ELECTRA [contemptuously]. A knife ——
        CHRYSOTHEMIS.   Or even
An axe ——
        ELECTRA. An axe! The axe wherewith
            our father ——
        CHRYSOTHEMIS. You terror! What, you
            have it?
        ELECTRA.   For our brother
I kept it. Now must we make use of
    it.
        CHRYSOTHEMIS. You, you, Electra!
            These arms slay Ægisthus?
        ELECTRA. First him, then her: first her,
            then him; no matter.
        CHRYSOTHEMIS. I am afraid. You are
            beside yourself.
        ELECTRA. They have no man to sleep
            before their door.
        CHRYSOTHEMIS. What, murder them in
            sleep, and then live on?
        ELECTRA. The question is of him and
            not of us.
        CHRYSOTHEMIS. What can have put this
            madness in your head?
        ELECTRA. A sleeping man is a bound
            offering.
If these sleep not together I can do it.
But you must come too.
        CHRYSOTHEMIS [thrusting her away]. O
            Electra!
        ELECTRA.   You!
For you are strong. [Close to her.] How
            strong you are! To you
Have virgin nights given strength. How
    lithe and slim
Your loins are, you can slip through every
    cranny,
Creep through the window. Let me feel
    your arms;
How cool and strong they are! What arms
    they are
I feel when thus you thrust me back with
    them.
Could you not stifle one with their em-
    brace?
Could you not clasp one to your cool firm
    breast
With both your arms until one suffocated

There is such strength about you every-
where.
It streams like cool close water from a rock,
It flows in a great flood with all your hair
Down your strong shoulders.

CHRYSOTHEMIS. Let me go.

ELECTRA. No, no!
I hold you, and with my poor wasted arms
I clasp your body, and if you resist
You only draw the knot tighter about you.
I will wind myself about you, I will sink
My roots into you, and ingraft my will
Into your blood.

CHRYSOTHEMIS. Let me go!
[Escapes a few steps.]

ELECTRA [wildly after her, clinging to her
dress]. No!

CHRYSOTHEMIS. Electra!
Let me go!

ELECTRA. I will not let you go.
We must so grow together, that the knife
That would cut off your life from mine,
must deal
Death to us both, for now are we alone
Together in this world.

CHRYSOTHEMIS. Electra, hear me,
You are so wise, help us to get free away,
Help us to get free.

ELECTRA [without hearing her]. You are
full of strength.
You have sinews like a colt, your feet are
slender,
And I can halter you with both my arms.
I feel through all the coolness of your skin
The warm blood flowing, and against my
cheek
The down on your young arms: you are as a
fruit
The day it ripens. I will be your sister
As I have never been your sister yet!
I will sit beside you in your room
And wait upon your bridegroom, and for
him
Will I anoint you, and you like a young
swan
Shall plunge into an odorous bath and hide
Your head upon my breast, till he shall
draw you
With his strong arms (you glowing like a
torch
Through all your veils) into the marriage-
bed.

CHRYSOTHEMIS [shutting her eyes]. No,
sister, no, speak no such words as
that
Within this house.

ELECTRA. Yes, I will from this day
Be more than sister to you, I will serve you
And I will be a slave to you. And if
You be in travail I will stand beside
Your bed by day and night, and I will ward
The flies from off you, draw cool water for
you:
And if some day there lie upon your bosom
A living thing, half fearful, I will lift it
So high above you that its smile shall fall
Into the deepest and most secret clefts
Of your sad soul, and the last icy horror
Shall melt before that sun and you shall
weep
Bright tears.

CHRYSOTHEMIS. O take me out of it!
I die,
I die in this house.

ELECTRA [kneeling before her]. Your
mouth is beautiful,
Although it open only to be angry.
Out of your clean, strong mouth there must
come forth
A terrible cry, terrible as the cry
Of the Death goddess, when a man shall lie
As close to you as I do; when a man
Wakening shall see you standing at his
head
Like the Death goddess; when a man shall
lie
Bound under you, and so look up at you,
Up at your slender body with his eyes
Rigid and set, as shipwrecked men look up
At the high cliff above them, ere they
die.

CHRYSOTHEMIS. What are you saying?

ELECTRA [rising]. What you have to do
Before you escape this house and me.
[CHRYSOTHEMIS tries to speak.]
[Putting her hand over her mouth.] No way
But this way. And I will not let you go
Till you have sworn to me, mouth upon
mouth,
That you will do it.

CHRYSOTHEMIS [freeing herself]. Let me
go!

ELECTRA [seizing her again]. Then
swear

You will come to-night, when all is still, to
the foot
Of the staircase.

CHRYSOTHEMIS. Let me go!

ELECTRA. Girl, no denial!
There's not a drop of blood that shall be
left
Upon your body; swiftly shall you slip
Out of the bloody garment with clean body
Into the bridal garment.

CHRYSOTHEMIS. Let me go!

ELECTRA. Do not be such a coward!
That which now
Shakes you with shudderings shall reward
you then
With shudderings of rapture, night for
night.

CHRYSOTHEMIS. I cannot.

ELECTRA. Say that you will come.

CHRYSOTHEMIS. I cannot.

ELECTRA. See, see, I lie before you. I
kiss your feet.

CHRYSOTHEMIS [rushing to the inner door].
I cannot!

ELECTRA [after her]. Be accursed!
[To herself with determination.] Then alone!
[She begins to dig hurriedly at the wall
of the house, beside the threshold, noiselessly, like an animal. She pauses,
looks about her, and goes on digging....]

[ORESTES stands in the door of the court,
showing black against the last rays.
He comes in. ELECTRA looks at him.
He turns slowly, until his glance falls
upon her. ELECTRA starts violently and
trembles....]

What would you, stranger? What has sent
you here
At the hour of dark to spy what others do?
It may be you have something in your mind
You would not any other spied upon.
Therefore leave me in peace. I have a
thing
To do here. What is that to you? Go
hence,
And let me root about among the earth.
Do you not follow me? or have you then
A mind too curious? I bury nothing
But something I dig up again. And not
The death bones of a little child I buried
A day or two ago. No, my good fellow.

I have given life to nothing, I have nothing
To kill or bury. If the body of the earth
Have taken anything out of my hands
'Tis what I have come forth from, nothing,
truly,
That had come forth from me. I dig up
something,
And you shall scarcely pass out of this light
Before I have and hug and kiss it over
As if I held in it both my dear brother
And my dear son, and both of them in
one.

ORESTES. Have you then nothing dear
to you on earth
That thus you scratch a something out of
earth
That you may kiss it? Are you quite
alone?

ELECTRA. I am no mother, and I have
no mother,
No sister am I, and I have no sister,
I lie at the door and yet am not a watch-
dog,
I speak, and yet I hold no speech, I live
And live not, have long hair and there-
withal
Feel nothing that they say all women feel
In short, I pray you, go and leave me
Leave me!

ORESTES. I have to wait here.

ELECTRA. Wait? [A pause.

ORESTES. You are of the house
One of the maids?

ELECTRA. I serve here in the house
But what have you to do here? Go you
way.

ORESTES. Did I not tell you I have t
wait here
Until they call for me?

ELECTRA. The folk within
You lie. I know the master is from hom
And what should she want with you?

ORESTES. I and or
Here with me have an errand to the lady
[ELECTRA is silen
We are sent to her because we can be
witness
That we have seen her son Orestes die,
Before our eyes, for his own horses kill
him.
I was as old as he, and his companion
By day and night; the other, an old ma

Who comes with me, had charge of both of
us.

ELECTRA. Why is it you I look on?
Why must you
Into my poor, sad corner trail yourself,
O herald of misfortune? Can you not
Trumpet your tidings forth where men re-
joice?
You live, and he, that was a better man
And nobler thousandfold and thousandfold
Wiser and weightier when he lived, is gone.
Your both eyes stare at me and his are clay;
Your mouth opens and shuts, and his is
stopped
With earth. Would I could stop yours
with my curses!
Get you out of my sight.

ORESTES. What would you have?
Here in the house they welcome it with joy.
Let then the dead be dead. Let be
Orestes.
Orestes is now dead, and death must come
To all, as to Orestes. He in his life
Joyed overmuch; and the gods over us
May not endure too clear a sound of joy,
Too loud a rush of wings at evening
They will not suffer, and they seize an ar-
row
And nail the creature fast to the dim tree
Of his dark fate, that has been long time
growing
For him in quiet. Thus had he to die.

ELECTRA. How he can talk to one of
Death, this fellow!
As if he had tasted it, and spat it forth.
But I, but I, that lie here and that know
The child will never come again, but they
That are within, these live now and rejoice
And all their breed shall live on in its
hole
And eat and drink and sleep and multiply,
Whilst the child down in his deep pit of
clay
Longs for his father, and no father comes.
And only I am here alone, and not
beast in all the forest lives as I do,
So monstrous and so lonely.

ORESTES. Who then are you?

ELECTRA. What's that to you who I am?
have I asked
Who you are?

ORESTES. I can only think one thing;

You are of kindred blood with those who
died
With Agamemnon and Orestes?

ELECTRA. Kindred?
I am that blood, that brutishly spilt blood
Of the King Agamemnon. I am called
Electra.

ORESTES. No!

ELECTRA. Why, he denies it me.
He flouts me and he takes from me my
name.
Because I have no father and no brother
I am the laughing-stock of boys, the butt
Of every fool that comes my way, and now
They will not leave me even my name.

ORESTES. Electra
Is younger by ten years than you. Electra
Is tall; her eyes are sad, yet soft, but yours
Are full of blood and hatred. Electra
dwells
Apart from men, and all her day goes over
In tending of a grave. Two or three
women
She has about her, silent helpers, beasts
Glide shyly round her dwelling, and creep
up
Against her garment as she goes.

ELECTRA [clapping her hands]. True!
true!
Tell me more pretty stories of Electra
And I will tell them to her, when — [With
choking voice.] I see her.

ORESTES. Do I then see her? Do I
really see her?
You! [Hurriedly.] Have they let you
starve then? Beaten you?

ELECTRA. Who are you with your many
questions?

ORESTES. Tell me!
Tell me! Speak!

ELECTRA. Both! both! both! Queens
do not thrive
Fed on the refuse of the kitchen-heap,
And priestesses were never made to bound
Under the lash, and in such short poor rags
Instead of flowing garments. Let my
dress be;
You shall not wallow in it with your eyes

ORESTES. Electra!
What have you done, what have you done
with your nights?
Your eyes are terrible.

ELECTRA [*sullenly*]. Go into the house.
I have a sister in there, who may by now
Be ready for the feast.
ORESTES.   Electra, hear me!
ELECTRA. I will not know who you are!
     you shall come
No nearer to me. I will see no man.
     [*She cowers with her face against the
     wall.*]
ORESTES. Listen! I have no time.
     Listen, I dare not
Speak loud. Listen to me: Orestes lives.
     [ELECTRA *flings herself round.*]
Utter no sound. If you but make a move-
     ment
You will betray him.
ELECTRA.   Is he free? where is he?
You know where he is hidden? he is caught,
And in some corner somewhere waits for
     death?
I am to see him die, and you are sent
That you may draw my soul as on a rack
Up with a rope, and dash it to the ground.
ORESTES. He is as sound as I am.
ELECTRA.   Then deliver him
Before they kill him. Can you not give a
     sign?
I kiss your feet; give him a sign, a sign!
I charge you by your father's corpse you
     run
As swiftly as you can run and bring him
     forth.
The child would die if he should pass one
     night
Within this house.
ORESTES.   Nay, by my father's corpse,
For this thing came the child into the house
That they this night should die who are to
     die.
ELECTRA [*struck by his tone*]. Who *are*
     you?

[*The gloomy-faced* OLD SERVANT *comes
     noiselessly into the court, throws him-
     self down before* ORESTES, *kisses his
     feet, rises, looks anxiously round, and
     goes noiselessly back.*]

ELECTRA [*scarcely controlling herself*]. O,
     who *are* you? I am afraid.
ORESTES [*softly*]. Do the dogs know me
     that are in the yard,
And not my sister?

ELECTRA [*cries out*]. Orestes!
     [*Throws herself in his arms and sobs.*]
ORESTES [*feverishly*].   If any man
Has heard you in the house, he holds my
     life
Within his hand.
ELECTRA [*quite low, quiveringly*]. Ores-
     tes! no man heard.
O let my eyes look on you! Do not touch
     me.
Go on your way. I am ashamed before
     you.
I do not know how you can look at me.
I am nothing but the corpse now of your
     sister,
My poor child, and I know you shudder at
     me.
And yet I was the daughter of a King.
I think that I was beautiful; and when
At night before my mirror, I blew out
The lamp, I felt, and with a maiden thrill
My naked body through the heavy night
Shine, as a godly thing immaculate.
I felt myself, as the thin moonbeams wrapt
Me round in their white nakedness, as in
A consecration, and my hair, such hair
As men might tremble at, this hair now
     soiled
And draggled and brought low: this! See
     my brother,
How I have offered up unto my father
This thrill of soft delight. Do you think I
Had pleasure of my body, that his sighs
Would not throng on me and his groans no
     throng
About my bed? For jealous are the dead
And he has sent me hatred for a bride
     groom,
Hollow-eyed hatred. And that horrible
     thing,
Breathing a viperous breath, had I to
     take
Into my sleepless bed, that it might teach
     me
All that is done between a man and wife
The nights, woe's me, the nights when
     that I fathomed!
Then was my body cold as ice, yet charred
As if with fire, and burning inwardly.
And when at last, at last I knew it all,
Then I was wise, and then the murderers

My mother, I mean, and he that is with
    her —
Could not endure to look into my eyes.
Why do you gaze at me so anxiously?
Speak to me, speak! Why, your whole
    body trembles.
ORESTES. My body? Let it tremble.
    Do you not think
That he would tremble otherwise than this
Could he but guess the way I mean to
    send him?
ELECTRA. Then you will do it! You will
    do it alone?
O you poor child, have you no friend with
    you?
ORESTES. Speak nothing more of it.
    My foster father
Is with me. Yet the doer shall be I.
ELECTRA. I have never seen the gods,
    only I know
They will be with you there, and they will
    help you.
ORESTES. What the gods are, I know
    not. Yet I know
That they have laid this deed upon my
    soul,
And they will spurn me if I shudder at it.
ELECTRA. Then you will do it?
ORESTES.   Yes. I must not look
My mother in the eyes before I do it.
ELECTRA. Look upon me, what she has
    made of me.
        [ORESTES looks at her sadly.]
O child, O child, stealthily have you come,
And speaking of yourself as of one dead,
And yet you are alive!
ORESTES [softly].   Take heed!
ELECTRA.   Who then
Am I that you should cast such loving
    looks
Upon me? See, I am nothing. All I
    was
have had to cast away: even that shame
Which is more sweet than all things, and
    like a mist
Of milky silver round about the moon
Is about every woman, and wards off
Things evil from her soul and her. My
    shame
Have offered up, and I am even as one
Fallen among thieves, who rend off from
    my body

Even my last garment. Not without
    bridal-night
Am I, as other maidens are; I have felt
The pangs of child-bearing; yet have
    brought forth
Nothing into the world, and I am now
Become a prophetess perpetually,
And nothing has come forth out of my
    body
But curses and despair. I have not slept
By night, I have made my bed upon the
    tower,
Cried in the court, and whined among the
    dogs.
I have been abhorred, and have seen every-
    thing,
I have seen everything as the watchman
    sees
Upon the tower, and day is night and night
Is day again, and I have had no pleasure
In sun or stars, for all things were to me
As nothing for his sake, for all things were
A token to me, and every day to me
A milestone on the road.
ORESTES.   O my sister!
ELECTRA. What will you do?
ORESTES.   Sister, is not our mother
Like you?
ELECTRA [wildly]. Like me? No, no.
    But you are not
To look her in the face. When she is dead
We'll look into her face together. Brother,
She cast a white shirt round about our
    father
And then she struck at that which lay
    before her
Helpless and without eyesight, and his
    face
He could not turn to her nor set his arms
    free —
Do you hear me? — that she struck with
    axe uplifted
High over him.
ORESTES.   Electra!
ELECTRA.   What her face is
Her deeds have made it.
ORESTES.   I will do the deed,
And I will do it quickly.
ELECTRA.   Happy is he
Dares do the deed! The deed is like a bed
On which the soul reposes, like a bed
Of balsam, where the soul can take its rest,

The soul that is a wound, that is a blight,
A-running and a-burning.

[*The* FOSTER FATHER *of* ORESTES *stands
in the door of the inner hall, a strong
gray-beard with flashing eyes.*]

Brother, who is this?

FOSTER FATHER [*hastily to them*]. Are
you both mad? You do not better
bridle
Your lips, when now a breath, a noise, a
nothing
Might ruin us and our work.

ELECTRA.   Who is this man?

ORESTES. You do not know him? If
you love me, thank him.
Thank him that I am here. This is
Electra.

ELECTRA. You! You! O now it is all
real, and all
Safe and fast-knotted! Let me kiss your
hands.
I know not if the gods are, I know not
Anything of the gods: therefore the rather
I kiss your hands.

FOSTER FATHER. Be still, be still, Electra.

ELECTRA. No, I will make rejoicing over
you,
Because you have brought him hither.
When I hated
Then I kept ample silence. Hate is noth-
ing,
It wastes and wastes itself away, and love
Is lesser even than hate, it grasps at all
things
And can take hold on nothing, and its
hands
Are flames that take no hold on anything;
All thought is nothing, and as the powerless
air
Is everything that comes out of the mouth:
Blessed alone is he that does his deed,
Blessed is he who touches him, and digs
The axe out of the earth for him, and holds
The torch for him, and opens the door wide
For him, and he who listens at the door.

FOSTER FATHER [*seizes her roughly and
lays his hand over her mouth*].
Silence!

[*To* ORESTES, *precipitately*.] She waits for
you. Her women come

To seek you. There is no man in the
house,
Orestes!

[ORESTES *draws himself up, subdu-
ing his dread. The door of the house
is lighted up, and a* SERVING WOMAN
appears with a torch; behind her the
WAITING WOMAN. ELECTRA *has
sprung back, and stands in the darkness.
The* WAITING WOMAN *makes obeisance
before the two strangers, and signs
to them to follow her. The* SERVING
WOMAN *fastens the torch into an iron
ring in the door-post.* ORESTES *and his*
FOSTER FATHER *go in.* ORESTES
*shuts his eyes for a moment, as if dizzy;
the* FOSTER FATHER *is close behind him,
they exchange a quick glance. The door
shuts behind them.*]

[ELECTRA *is left alone in intolerable
suspense. She runs to and fro before
the door with bowed head, like a wild
beast in its cage. Suddenly she stands
still and says:*]

ELECTRA.   I have not given him
the axe.
They have gone in, and I have not given
him the axe!
There are no gods in heaven. [*Once more
a fearful waiting. There is heard
from within, shrilly, the cry of* CLY-
TEMNESTRA. ELECTRA *shrieks like
a demon.*]   Strike again
[*A second cry from within. From
the servants' quarters on* L. *come*
CHRYSOTHEMIS *and a troop of* SERVING
WOMEN. ELECTRA *stands in the door,
her back against it.*]

CHRYSOTHEMIS. Something has happened!

FIRST WAITING WOMAN. She cries out in
her sleep
Like that.

SECOND WAITING WOMAN. There must
be men within. I hear
The feet of men.

THIRD WAITING WOMAN. They have
bolted all the doors.

FOURTH WAITING WOMAN. It is murder,
there is murder in the house.

FIRST WAITING WOMAN [*cries out*].

ALL. What is it?

FIRST WAITING WOMAN. Don't you see!
There is some one at the door.
CHRYSOTHEMIS. It is Electra. O, it is
Electra!
SECOND WAITING WOMAN. Why then
doesn't she speak?
CHRYSOTHEMIS.   Electra, why
Do you not speak?
FIRST WAITING WOMAN. I will go and
fetch men.   [*Runs out to* L.]
CHRYSOTHEMIS.   Electra,
Open the door.
OTHERS.   Let us into the house,
Electra!
[FIRST WAITING WOMAN, *coming
back through the door of the court.*]
FIRST WAITING WOMAN. Back! [*All start.*]
Ægisthus! Back to our quarters,
Quickly. Ægisthus is coming through the
court.
If he find us and finds out what has hap-
pened
In the house, he will kill us.
ALL.   Back, quickly, come back!
[ÆGISTHUS *at the entrance on* R.]
ÆGISTHUS. Is no one here to light me?
None of all
The rascals stirring? Shall we never teach
These people manners?
[ELECTRA *takes the torch out of the
ring, runs down towards him, and bows
before him.*]
Starting at the indistinct figure in the flicker-
ing light and stepping back.] What
is this weird woman?
have forbidden any unknown face
To come into my presence.
Recognizing her, angrily.] What, is it you?
Who bade you come to meet me?
ELECTRA.   May I not light you?
ÆGISTHUS. Well, well, this news con-
cerns you more than any.
There shall I find the strangers who have
brought
These tidings of Orestes?
ELECTRA.   They are within.
kindly hostess have they found, and find
their entertainment with her.
ÆGISTHUS.   Have they brought
true tidings of his death, tidings that are
not to be doubted?
ELECTRA.   Lord, these tidings are

No hollow words but tokens bodily,
Tokens it is impossible to doubt.
ÆGISTHUS. What have you in your
voice, what has come to you
That you will speak to me out of your
mouth?
Why do you stagger about there with your
light?
ELECTRA. Merely for this, that I have
become wise
At last, and turn to them that are the
stronger.
Have I your leave to light you?
ÆGISTHUS.   To the door.
Why are you dancing? Have a care, there!
ELECTRA [*circling him in a weird dance,
and suddenly making a deep bow to
him*].   Mind,
The steps! You'll fall.
ÆGISTHUS. Why is there no light here?
Who are these?
ELECTRA.   They are those, Lord,
that desire
To wait on you in person. And I, who
have
By my unseasonable and bold approach
Often been irksome to you, now at last
Will learn, at the right moment, to with-
draw.
[ÆGISTHUS *goes into the house.*]
[*A short silence. At the same mo-
ment* ÆGISTHUS, *at a little window on
R., leurs away the curtain and cries:*]
ÆGISTHUS. Help! murder! help your
master! murder! murder!
Help! they are murdering me!
[*He is dragged away.*]
Does no one hear me?
No one hear me?
[*His face appears again at the win-
dow.*]
ELECTRA [*drawing herself up*]. Agamem-
non hears you!
ÆGISTHUS [*dragged away*]. Woe's me!
[ELECTRA *stands back breathing fear-
fully, turned towards the house. The
women run out wildly.* CHRYSOTHE-
MIS *among them. Unwittingly they
run forward to the door of the outer court.
Then they stop suddenly and turn back.*]
CHRYSOTHEMIS. Electra! Sister! come
with us!

Come with us now! Our brother is in the
    house,
Is it Orestes who has done it?
    [*Confusion of voices, turmoil without.*]
                                    Come!
He is in the outer hall, they are all about
    him,
They kiss his feet; and all of them that
    hated
Ægisthus in their hearts have fallen upon
The others, everywhere in all the court
The dead are lying, all who live are
    drenched
With blood, they wound themselves, they
    beam, they all
Embrace each other —
    [*Outside the noise increases, the
    women run out.* CHRYSOTHEMIS *is left
    alone. Light from without penetrates
    within.*]
            And shout with joy and kindle
A thousand torches. Do you hear? Do
    you hear?
    ELECTRA [*crouching on the threshold*].
    Do you think I do not hear? Do
    I not hear
Music within me? The thousands who
    bear torches
And whose unbounded myriad footsteps
    make
A hollow rumbling over all the earth,
All wait upon me, and well I know they
    wait
That I may lead the dance; and yet I can-
    not
Because the ocean, the vast manifold
Ocean, lays all its weight on every limb;

I cannot raise myself from under it.
    CHRYSOTHEMIS [*almost shrieking with
excitement*]. Do you not hear, they carry,
    they carry him
Upon their hands, their faces are all
    changed,
All eyes, and the old cheeks glisten with
    tears.
All weep, do you not hear them? — Ah!
                            [*She runs out.*]
    [ELECTRA *has raised herself. She
    steps down from the threshold, her head
    thrown back like a Mœnad. She lifts
    her knees, stretches out her arms; it is an
    incredible dance in which she steps for-
    ward.*]
    [CHRYSOTHEMIS *appearing again at
    the door, behind her torches, a throng,
    faces of men and women.*]
                                    Electra!
ELECTRA [*stands still, gazing at her
    fixedly*]. Be silent and dance. Come
    hither all of you!
Join with me all! I bear the burden of joy,
And I dance before you here. One thing
    alone
Remains for all who are as happy as we
To be silent and dance.
    [*She does a few more steps of tense
    triumph, and falls a-heap.* CHRYSO-
    THEMIS *runs to her.* ELECTRA *lie*
    motionless. CHRYSOTHEMIS *runs t*
    the door of the house and knocks.]
CHRYSOTHEMIS.   Orestes! Orestes
                                [*Silence.*

                    CURTAIN

THE STEAMSHIP TENACITY
A COMEDY IN THREE ACTS
By CHARLES VILDRAC
Translated from the French by JOHN STRONG NEWBERRY

CAST OF CHARACTERS

THÉRÈSE, *waitress at the Cordier restaurant, aged 22*
THE WIDOW CORDIER, *aged 55*
BASTIEN, *aged 29*
SÉGARD, *aged 26*
HIDOUX, *aged 60*
AN ENGLISH SAILOR
A YOUNG WORKMAN, WORKMEN, SAILORS, *etc.*

TIME. *The Present.*

SCENE. *The entire action takes place in the dining room of a small restaurant near the wharves of a French port.*

Les destinées meuvent celui qui consent, tirent celui qui refuse.

RABELAIS.

THE STEAMSHIP TENACITY

ACT I

*A little restaurant for workmen in a port.
At the back, through the windows and the
open entrance door, one sees a harbor crowded
with ships. Up-stage, at the left, is the bar.
There is a door behind it. On the right is
another door, similarly placed. It is from
the latter that* THÉRÈSE *emerges to wait on
customers. The room is filled with tables at
which workmen are eating.*

HIDOUX, *half drunk, is leaning against
the bar, his glass in front of him. He
addresses himself alternately to* MADAME
CORDIER *and the assembled company.*

HIDOUX. Come now, Madame Cordier,
what do you think about it? Ought such
things to be? Take all these fellows here
who get their twelve francs — yes, put it at
twelve francs. [*He interrupts himself and
stretches his arm towards a young man at
a nearby table.*] Hey there, my boy! How
much do you get?

THE YOUNG WORKMAN. Twelve francs
fifty.

HIDOUX. All right, say their twelve
francs fifty a day. Take these people,
Madame Cordier, who get their twelve
francs fifty a day lugging steel rails for the
tramway from morning till night. It's
hard labor, labor that wears one out, hands,
arms, shoulders, and back. Isn't that
right, my friends? Good! Well, on the
other hand, take me. Just between pals,
I'm not what you might call a steady
worker. [*Laughter.*] Well, here's an example. A sewer pipe burst and flooded the
cellar of Monsieur Desbrosses. I agreed to
bale it out for him at fifteen francs a day.
It took me two days to finish the job. It
was no joke I can tell you. Well, just as I
was drawing my thirty francs who should
come walking by but Monsieur Desbrosses.
I hadn't washed myself yet; any one might
have thought I'd come out of a dredge-

bucket. He looked me over, went with
me to inspect the work, and gave me a tip of
fifty francs. A tip of fifty francs! Two
days' work, eighty francs! Naturally it
was all right as far as I was concerned.
But all the same, just between ourselves,
Madame Cordier, ought such things to
be?

MADAME CORDIER. This makes ten
times that you've asked me that.

HIDOUX [*after drinking*]. What will
you have, Madame Cordier? I'll take the
same.

MADAME CORDIER. What time would
you like your breakfast?

HIDOUX. It's the same way when an
American comes off the steamer. I carry
his suit-case for him; he gives me a hundred
sous. For fifteen minutes' work! You'll
say, it's just a stroke of luck. Very well,
but all the same, answer me this: to earn
a hundred francs in fifteen minutes, frankly
now, ought such things to be, when there
are comrades, day-laborers like myself...
Bear in mind that I...

THÉRÈSE. Eh, old gaffer! I got a hundred sous yesterday myself.

HIDOUX. Oh! when it comes to women
it's quite different. A hundred sous?
Who gave it to you?

THÉRÈSE. You did! He doesn't even
remember it! What time was it when you
got through with your cellar?

HIDOUX. Seven o'clock.

THÉRÈSE. Well, at nine you were drunk
already, very drunk! But you hadn't yet
washed yourself.

HIDOUX. Supposing...

THÉRÈSE. You came here, ah! la la!

HIDOUX. Supposing that I had washed
myself before I drew my pay; that I
hadn't stunk to heaven; or that Monsieur
Desbrosses hadn't had the sort of heart
that rises above stinks; then I could have

whistled for my fifty francs. To think that riches...

MADAME CORDIER [*motioning towards* THÉRÈSE]. It was she, Hidoux, who...

HIDOUX. To think that riches should hang on such a trifle! I just can't get over it! Ought such things to be?

MADAME CORDIER. It was she, it was Thérèse, who took pity on you, and took off your jacket, and sponged you, and washed your face and hands.

HIDOUX [*to* THÉRÈSE]. And I gave you a hundred sous?

THÉRÈSE. Yes, and without my asking for anything. And I made sure that you knew what you were about. I went and shouted in your ear: "Hidoux, did you know that you gave me a hundred sous? Is it a hundred sous that you meant to give me?" Because, as the proprietress will tell you, I'm square with people even when they're drunk.

HIDOUX. Won't you join me in something? A little liqueur?

[*Enter* BASTIEN *and* SÉGARD *carrying light luggage*.]

BASTIEN [*to* THÉRÈSE *who has come forward*]. May we have something to eat, Mademoiselle?

THÉRÈSE [*indicating a table at the right, opposite the bar*]. Yes, sir. Sit there. [*They sit down.* THÉRÈSE *sets places for them and takes their orders. A silence.*]

HIDOUX [*approaching the table*]. Travelers! Good morning, gentlemen! Did you have a good crossing? I suppose you arrived on the boat from England.

BASTIEN [*laughing*]. Not we!

SÉGARD. We came from Paris.

MADAME CORDIER. From Paris! Didn't you find it rather warm for traveling?

BASTIEN. Yes, and thirsty. Mademoiselle, bring us some wine first of all.

HIDOUX. Then you are Parisians?

BASTIEN. Right you are, old top.

HIDOUX. Bravo! Put it there: it's the hand of a man who such as you see him, has been a Parisian in his time. A man who lived for six years at 54 rue Saint-Maur. That must mean something to you?

BASTIEN. Yes, I know that part of the city, but we come from the avenue de Clichy.

SÉGARD. Do I know the rue Saint-Maur? I should think I did! When I was a boy I spent my vacations with my aunt, a washerwoman who lived then at number 28. Ah! the rue Saint-Maur.

HIDOUX. Then you remember number 54! In those days it was a house, with furnished rooms to let, just opposite the great sheet iron dealer's...

SÉGARD. Sébillon!

HIDOUX. Sébillon! The proprietor! Now there was a true Parisian! Sébillon! I came very near working for him.

SÉGARD. I have passed whole afternoons watching them load sheet iron on trucks, at Sébillon's. I can see the men now with their little leather aprons stained with rust, and their copper-colored throats and hands, like Redskins.

HIDOUX. Just so.

SÉGARD. They would swing out a great sheet of iron, six or eight feet wide, and send it to fall on the others. When it struck them you can guess how happy I was; it sounded like thunder.

HIDOUX. Their noise interfered with my afternoon nap.

SÉGARD. Ah, it's far away, it's far away... [*to* BASTIEN.] This] is going to make it farther still.

HIDOUX. I'm speaking of the days when I was fifteen.

BASTIEN [*To* SÉGARD]. Let your memories alone, you will find them again at sixty.

HIDOUX. But... hey, Thérèse! Allow me, my friends, to offer you, before your breakfast comes ...

SÉGARD. Oh, nothing!

BASTIEN. You're too kind.

HIDOUX. Just a little white wine! Come now! Thérèse, my child!

SÉGARD. No...

THÉRÈSE [*serving them*]. Let him do it, he's rich to-day.

HIDOUX. I'm rich to-day. See how pretty Thérèse is; and a good girl, you know; and warm-hearted. Last night she took care of me like... but never mind that.

[*He seats himself opposite the two travelers.*]
I'm going to have some breakfast, too.
Your health. [*They drink.*] And you've
come here, like this, to get a job?

BASTIEN. Well, hardly!

HIDOUX. Then I suppose you're taking
a little pleasure-trip along the coast.

BASTIEN [*enigmatically*]. Pleasure?
Yes and no. But not along the coast.

HIDOUX. Inland, perhaps, to visit relatives?

THÉRÈSE. Such curiosity!

HIDOUX. Gentlemen, she is right. I'm
indiscreet. Pardon me! I'm indiscreet.

SÉGARD. Not at all.

HIDOUX. Excuse me! The truth is the
truth. But I had no reasons for asking.

BASTIEN. There's no indiscretion about
it, my friend. Only we're not going to
visit relatives and we're not going inland.

HIDOUX [*with dignity*]. I don't want to
know.

SÉGARD. We've no reason to make a
secret of where we're going. In fact we
ought to tell, in order to get more information. [THÉRÈSE *lingers, interested.*]

BASTIEN [*magnificently, and with effect*].
Where we're going, why, we can cry it from
the house-tops. To-morrow we sail for
the other side of the world!

HIDOUX. Ah! ah! that's a different matter.

THÉRÈSE. For what country?

SÉGARD [*a little moved*]. For Canada.

BASTIEN. For the farthest depths of
Canada!

MADAME CORDIER [*who has come out
from behind her wicket, and drawn near
them*]. No doubt you're going there to
follow your trade?

BASTIEN [*emphatically*]. Our trade,
Madame! Do you think that they've
given us time to follow a trade? What I
mean to say is that we've almost forgotten
the one we used to follow! We come from
making war. We've been working for six
years in barracks or on the Meuse or on the
Marne or on the Somme, in the charming
work-shops of the government. That's
the employer with whom we've stayed the
longest since we finished our apprenticeship. [*Laughter. Some workmen approach, smoking. A silence.*] No, not our
trade! But I said to my friend here:
yesterday, it was the war; to-day it's paying for the war; to-morrow, it will be something else. Stay here and you'll always get
the dirty end of the stick. It's the stranger
in a strange land who has the fewest obligations. And then as I said to him, do you
see yourself after those four years, from
which by some miracle you come out with
a whole skin, four years without counting
three years of military service beforehand
and ten months of barracks afterwards, do
you see yourself going back as if nothing
had happened, as if you were returning
from a fine Sunday in the country, going
back to a basement in the rue Montmartre
to spend the night in setting up their filthy
papers! For I may as well tell you that
we're type-setters — And I said to him:
Let's get out, let's go where they can never
lay hands on us again! Go and live like
free men in the open air! Go and colonize
the new world! Wasn't that it, Alfred?

SÉGARD. Yes.

HIDOUX. Bravo! That's the talk! Now
I do odd jobs in the harbor. They call
on me for anything where strength is
needed. Madame Cordier can tell you
that I've no reason to complain. [*He
turns towards her.*] Didn't I strike it rich
no later than yesterday? Very well! But
all the same if I had my life to live over
again I don't say that... All the same
America has been pretty well worked out,
even before the war...

BASTIEN. Worked out? That depends
on what part of America you mean!
Naturally I'm not speaking of the United
States, I'm not speaking of New York!
You must get this straight; it's to Canada
that we're going. Canada is as large as
Europe, including Russia, and in all that
space hasn't as many inhabitants as Paris
or London. In Canada you have lands inhabited by Eskimos, and other lands, in the
south, inhabited by negroes and redskins.
You see, it's very simple, we're going to land
at Montreal. And from Montreal do you
know how many kilometers we have to
travel to get to our new quarters? Two
thousand! Two thousand kilometers!

MADAME CORDIER. On foot?

BASTIEN. No, by train. Just imagine, two thousand kilometers by train, through country where there's nothing but wheat as far as you can see. Or prairies with herds of cattle guarded by men like Buffalo Bill. And you see lakes, too, lakes that are as large as France.

HIDOUX [*skeptically*]. Oh! as large as France!...

BASTIEN. Yes, Monsieur, as large as France! I could show you the little book we have about the country. It's in the bag there. Eh, Alfred? In short, we're not going to the part of Canada that's known. We're going to Manitoba, if you wish to know, to the farthest depths of Manitoba! So you see how it is! You understand that we know what we're about. You can be sure that where we're going there's plenty of work for survivors of the war who wish to earn their daily bread in freedom. Besides they have made us propositions.

THÉRÈSE. If the survivors of the war go away now what's to become of us women?

SÉGARD. I'll take you with me, Mademoiselle.

[THÉRÈSE *comes to lean on the table near* SÉGARD, *and jokes with him.*]

THE YOUNG WORKMAN [*to* BASTIEN]. They've made you propositions?

BASTIEN. Yes. You see it's like this. It's a French-English society; you sign a contract with them; they send you at their expense to an agricultural training school in Canada, where you work for a year, with free board and wages into the bargain, learning cattle-breeding and farming and getting the general run of things. At the end of the year they give you land and build you a house. Then you're in your own establishment, and you have ten years to pay the purchase price of your property. Of course you pay interest during that time; you also pay absurdly small amounts for the rent of agricultural machines. You don't have to buy a thing. And the total cost isn't half as much as the outrageous rent you have to pay in Paris.

MADAME CORDIER. And if at the end of your year's apprenticeship a farmer's life doesn't appeal to you?

BASTIEN. You are free! You drop the whole thing. Only, as is no more than right, you pay to the society a forfeit of 600 francs, to repay them for the expenses of the voyage and other things. And it has been paid already; as a precaution they deduct it from your wages. If you go on they give it back to you, and you have something with which to buy a chandelier for your chateau.

HIDOUX. It's certainly well thought out.
[*Approving murmurs.*]

BASTIEN. Everything is provided for! It's amazing.

THÉRÈSE. You aren't afraid you may have had enough of it by the end of the year?

BASTIEN. We? Do you take us for children? We look at things as they are. We know quite well that it's going to be hard at first. And yet — what is there that isn't hard, after the war? Just a question of will, that's all. You see, when I have a goal in view my eyes never leave it. We're men of decision; isn't that so, Alfred?

SÉGARD [*faintly*]. To be sure...

BASTIEN [*indicating* SÉGARD]. If he were alone, you know he might not see it through... but with me...

SÉGARD. Why do you say that?

BASTIEN. It's not a reproach, old fellow. But admit that at bottom our natures are not the same. You were less ready than I to leave your country, your family, and all the rest.

SÉGARD [*lightly*]. Bah!

MADAME CORDIER. That's nothing to be ashamed of, my boy; it's quite natural. There are people who are more inclined than others to become attached...

BASTIEN. And then you must remember this. I'm the one who had the idea, you understand; I'm the one who reasoned with him, persuaded him. You might say that I seized him by the arm and said to him, "Come!"

SÉGARD [*smiling*]. You're not taking me on board by force.

BASTIEN. Of course not! I mean that

if you had been alone perhaps you mightn't have gone.

SÉGARD. Oh, I'll grant you that.

BASTIEN. Well, I would have gone alone.
[A silence.]

THÉRÈSE. You go to-morrow?

BASTIEN. Yes, my pretty one, to-morrow.

SÉGARD. Yes, to-morrow. We must go and find out the sailing time.

HIDOUX. What boat?

BASTIEN. A steamer that has a name made for us, a name that couldn't be more pat; one that we could take as our motto, eh, Alfred? It is called "Tenacity."

HIDOUX. Tenacity? I've seen it somewhere. Doesn't it belong to the Transatlantic Line?

BASTIEN [taking some papers from his pocket]. No. To the [He reads] Smith-Walter and Sons Company, of Montreal. We're going out to look for it presently.

HIDOUX. It's in the second slip to the right. I'll show you the way [Judicially.] It's a boat that must draw ... let's see ——

SÉGARD. Where are we going to sleep?

MADAME CORDIER. Here, if you like. I have rooms.

HIDOUX. You couldn't find a better place. If you're drunk to night — a mere supposition — there's a Thérèse who will wash your hands and faces for you.

THÉRÈSE. Come now, do you think that these gentlemen ...

BASTIEN. Then the thing is settled, Madame. We'll sleep here. And now I'll stand treat for everybody; let's drink to the steamship Tenacity of Montreal. Mademoiselle Thérèse, brandys all around, or whatever you choose.

HIDOUX. A fine idea.
[THÉRÈSE serves them.]

BASTIEN. In ten years we'll be back this way. You must have some good bottles ready for us then.

SÉGARD. In ten years, or perhaps more.

BASTIEN. Or perhaps less. To your health, Madame.

MADAME CORDIER. And to a prosperous voyage, then.

THÉRÈSE. To your love affairs out yonder.

BASTIEN. When there's a question of our love affairs, perhaps we'll have to come back and look for you.

SÉGARD. It would be too much to hope for, to find girls like you in Canada.

THÉRÈSE [with a slight curtsey]. You're much too good!

HIDOUX [who has turned towards the door at the back, suddenly sets down his glass and rushes out, calling]. Hi there, hi there!
[All follow him with their eyes. He returns almost immediately, followed by a sailor.]

HIDOUX. He's a sailor from the Tenacity.

THE ENGLISH SAILOR. Mornin', mates.

BASTIEN. You belong to the steamship Tenacity?

THE ENGLISH SAILOR. The Tenacity, right ye are.

BASTIEN. Wonderful! You must have a drink with us. [He motions to THÉRÈSE.] I and my friend here are going to sail for Canada on the Tenacity.

THE ENGLISH SAILOR. Gerblimey!
[THÉRÈSE serves the sailor.]

HIDOUX. He can tell us all about it! You see, comrade, these gentlemen want to know at what time to-morrow the boat sails.

THE ENGLISH SAILOR. What time d'ye say?

HIDOUX. Yes.

THE ENGLISH SAILOR. D'ye mean the Tenacity?

BASTIEN. Yes, we shall be much obliged to you.

THE ENGLISH SAILOR. But she don't sail to-morrow.

BASTIEN. What?

SÉGARD. We have tickets to sail to-morrow.

THE ENGLISH SAILOR. But lord love ye, she don't sail to-morrow. Leastways she's due to sail right enough, but she won't nohow, 'cause they're a-patchin' up of her bloomin' boiler.

BASTIEN. I see ...

THE ENGLISH SAILOR. 'Ere's your wery good 'ealth. [He drinks.]

SÉGARD. To yours. Then we'll be here for a day or two longer.

BASTIEN [to the sailor]. Are they repairing the boiler now?

THE ENGLISH SAILOR. Yes, they're a-tykin' of it out.

BASTIEN [*disturbed*]. They're taking it out? How long do you think...

THE ENGLISH SAILOR. A fortnight. Put it at a fortnight.

BASTIEN [*rising*]. A fortnight!

SÉGARD [*doing likewise*]. A fortnight!

THE ENGLISH SAILOR. A fortnight. In course it might be a bit more.

HIDOUX. You don't need to start yet awhile, my friends. You can sit down again.

BASTIEN [*sitting down again, much discouraged*]. They can't make passengers wait for two weeks! There must be another boat.

THE ENGLISH SAILOR. There ain't. The Tenacity don't hold much with passengers. There might be four, or again there might be ten. We tykes out cattle and we brings back wire. Arsk for yourself at Comp'ny office. I'm a-givin' it to you stryght. For the next bloomin' month there ain't no blooming boat for Canada 'cept for the Tenacity. Strike me dead if there is. I got to go now, mates, askin' your pardon. Then I'll be a-seein' of you on board one of these days, eh? Mornin'.

BASTIEN. Thank you. We'll be there.

[*The English sailor goes out.*]

SÉGARD [*after a silence*]. Well?

BASTIEN. First we'll have to find out. But the chances are he knows what he's talking about.

HIDOUX. Oh, he wasn't in the least drunk.

SÉGARD. Anyway, the Society will either have to find a boat for us or refund the money we spent for our tickets and pay our way back to Paris, so that we can wait there till the boiler is repaired, just as if there'd been no question of our sailing to-morrow.

MADAME CORDIER. Naturally, the Society will have to pay.

BASTIEN [*thoughtfully*]. Go home and wait, you say. If there isn't any other boat that's what they'll propose, without a doubt.

SÉGARD. Certainly. And it's the wisest thing to do. [*Silence.*]

BASTIEN. No. No. Alfred, we can't do that! Go back to Paris for two weeks? Say all our farewells once more? Go through that scene at the station again, with our weeping mothers and sisters? No, no!

SÉGARD. Yes, that's true, of course... And yet...

BASTIEN. We had enough of it last week. For our friends and for ourselves we've taken the plunge. To go back again would bring us bad luck.

SÉGARD [*a little troubled*]. I quite agree with you, we shouldn't go back... All the same...

BASTIEN. Well, out with it!

SÉGARD. All the same to live here... It will make a big hole in our savings.

BASTIEN. That depends. Wait! Are there any printers here?

HIDOUX. Of course there are printers.

MADAME CORDIER. Any amount of them.

HIDOUX. Printers or no printers, you won't have any trouble in finding work. There's a tramway being constructed along the wharves. They hire men by the day to carry rail; if I hadn't better work, and more than I can do, well, a day now and then... why it's trade that...

SÉGARD. If we could come to an agreement with Madame could we take lodgings here?

THÉRÈSE. Surely.

MADAME CORDIER. Without boasting, if you stay here for two weeks you won't speak ill of the house when you go away.

BASTIEN [*getting up*]. Then first, to the boat!

SÉGARD [*following his example*]. And afterwards we'll see if the printers will take us on. [*He looks slowly around the restaurant, then to* THÉRÈSE.] It wouldn't be so bad, two weeks here before America.

THÉRÈSE. It would still be almost like being at home!

SÉGARD. Yes, it won't be quite so sudden...

BASTIEN [*on his way to the door, with* HIDOUX, *calling* SÉGARD]. Are you coming?

[*He goes out and stops just outside the door, talking with* HIDOUX.]

SÉGARD. I like to stay in a place at least long enough to feel at home there, to get a little acquainted with people, so that I can remember them... A sort of bond wherever one goes. Oh, it's not very long... During the war, I...

THÉRÈSE [*bending her nose towards a flower that* SÉGARD *wears in his buttonhole*]. That's a pretty flower you're wearing. Did your sweetheart give it to you?

SÉGARD. I picked it in our garden when I left home.

BASTIEN [*from outside*]. Come on, Alfred!

SÉGARD. There!

[*He removes the flower from his buttonhole and offers it to* THÉRÈSE, *who takes it. He goes out.*]

ACT II

SCENE I

The same room. At the right, down stage, SÉGARD *and* THÉRÈSE *are seated at a table.* SÉGARD *has his left arm in a sling.* THÉRÈSE *is darning stockings. After a few moments* SÉGARD *rises and paces back and forth, twitching his free hand at intervals.*

THÉRÈSE. Does it hurt you so much?

SÉGARD. Only now and then. Sudden twinges. It's the flesh under the nails that makes the mischief... Oh, it's provoking.

THÉRÈSE. You'll be all right again in a day or two. But you might easily have left the ends of your fingers there! Such idiots as the other men were! What in the world possessed them to let go of the rail before you did?

SÉGARD. It was my fault. I didn't let go soon enough. And then I held it wrong. I shouldn't have had my fingers underneath. It doesn't amount to anything, though. Of course it's a nuisance that I can't work... But there are compensations.

[*He sits down again.*]

THÉRÈSE. What compensations?

SÉGARD. Being able to pass hours on end with Thérèse.

THÉRÈSE. Humbug!

SÉGARD. No humbug about it.

THÉRÈSE. A week from now, on the ship, you'll be enjoying yourself twice as much.

SÉGARD. I shan't.

THÉRÈSE. You'll soon forget all about me.

SÉGARD. Don't you believe it! In the first place I have a very tenacious memory, and in the second place...

THÉRÈSE. I have a better memory for places than for people. I see so many here.

SÉGARD. I become attached too easily. If I'm in a place for a single day I look at it as if I were going to spend all the rest of my life there. And when I leave it's as if I'd always known it. And the same way with people... Ah! during the war...

THÉRÈSE. You're too impressionable.

SÉGARD. It doesn't make me any happier, but I wouldn't have it changed. For example, Thérèse, if twenty years from now I came here on the train, just as I did this time, perhaps I shouldn't remember the station, or know how to get to this house, and it might be that I couldn't find it again. But I'm sure that in my mind I'd see this room with all its tables in their places. I'd see Madame Cordier behind the counter, jotting down figures in her book, and Thérèse lifting Hidoux's glass with one hand to wipe the cleared table with the other. I'd remember day-before-yesterday afternoon, with me reading here while you ironed napkins, you and the proprietress; and yesterday afternoon when you went out to buy those little tan shoes you showed me when you came in, the ones that I made you try on. And no doubt this afternoon too, Thérèse, I would see you there, just as you are, bending above your work... Ah, I wouldn't have forgotten something that I looked at often, that I'm looking at now.

THÉRÈSE [*without lifting her eyes from her work*]. What are you looking at?

SÉGARD. The little curls at the nape of your neck.

THÉRÈSE [*throwing back her head with a laugh*]. And I was listening to you quite seriously.

SÉGARD. I'm not fooling. I'll remember

all this ten years from now, and many other things beside.

THÉRÈSE. Ten years from now!...

SÉGARD. When I was a youngster I spent a month one vacation in a summer school in the country. It's one of my dearest memories. We ate in a great white refectory that had a good smell, the smell of the dairy and the bakery. The tables were covered with white oil-cloth and so it smelled of new oil-cloth into the bargain. I'll never forget the smell of the refectory. When I think of that vacation that smell comes back to me, and I see the good woman who waited on us... Each of us had a little pitcher of reddened water beside his plate.

THÉRÈSE [*laughing*]. That reminds me of my bottle! I carried my lunch to school, and with it a little bottle of cider! To make it better, I put in it whatever I could get, a bonbon, a piece of chocolate, a cherry, and shook it till it foamed!

[*While she is speaking* SÉGARD *has risen, taken a few steps, and halted facing her.*]

SÉGARD. Where was your school? Here?

THÉRÈSE. Yes, at the other end of the town. I stayed there till I was twelve.

SÉGARD. And after that?

THÉRÈSE. After that, I went into service in the country. Oh, I liked it there so much. There was a beautiful garden with strawberries, such strawberries! Mother took me away because I didn't earn enough...

SÉGARD. You do your hair very nicely.

THÉRÈSE. Do you think so?

SÉGARD. And you have lovely hair.

THÉRÈSE. I hope you'll send me some postcards from Canada. Will you?

SÉGARD. Surely! And if there aren't any to be had, I'll write you a bit of a letter.

THÉRÈSE. That would be lovely! But you must keep your promise. Because there have been men who promised me, at the time, that they'd send me postcards, bonbons... One of those who came here even said that they made a specialty of bonbons in his country. But nothing came of it.

SÉGARD. You can rest assured that there aren't any bonbons in Canada, Thérèse. But I'll give you some before I go.

THÉRÈSE. When are you going? I don't ask because of the bonbons.

SÉGARD. We don't exactly know. In five or six days. Yesterday morning I went down to the Tenacity. A fine rain was falling. She looked as if she'd been abandoned. Then I thought, what if they hadn't postponed her sailing? I saw the rain on a dirty-gray ocean and the Tenacity plowing through it day after day, with her little trail of smoke... [*A silence.*] It's depressing, rain in a port...

THÉRÈSE. Don't you want to go?

SÉGARD. Yes... It's just that I'm sorry to be leaving here. Oh, when I'm once there... You see I always do cling to the present, that's the trouble with me. It's as if a cable were running through my hand, pulled by some powerful force. I seize it, I try to hold it back, but I only skin my hands for my pains. I don't control the cable, the cable pulls me about and shakes me. Bastien is stronger than I. He can choose the life he likes. He has chosen for me, and it suits me much better that way. I can criticise the plans of some one else — gauge whether they are good or bad. But I can never adopt any for myself. To begin with, I don't make plans; I only imagine vague dreams. I don't say, I'll do such and such a thing; I say, this is how it would have happened; I would have been in such and such a place; such a man or such a woman would be with me; it would be under such and such marvelous conditions; I would be happy. You'll laugh at me, I know, but wherever I am, I tell myself stories; stories that might be real, but are always so beautiful that I don't even dare hope that they'll come true.

THÉRÈSE. Yet you're old enough to know what you want.

SÉGARD. Yes, in any place where I happen to be I choose what I like the best. But it's always some one else who picks out that place for me. How about you?

THÉRÈSE. Oh I, I've never thought of all that...

SÉGARD. To find, to choose what you like the best out of all the things that are offered to you, that detain you as you pass, why I tell you, Thérèse, even that is difficult, terrible!

THÉRÈSE. I think one can hardly be said to have a choice. One just has to take what comes...

SÉGARD. But if by chance you do have a choice? I want to take everything, and I know so well that I'll regret whatever I didn't take that I make myself miserable beforehand.

THÉRÈSE. I regret afterwards. It often works out that way. For instance, yesterday I hesitated at the last moment between the tan shoes and some black ones, patent-leathers. I took the tan, at last, on account of the season; but all the same the black ones...

SÉGARD. I know. But I wasn't thinking of objects, of shoes.

THÉRÈSE. No, of course not.

SÉGARD. Life is full of mysterious combinations, Thérèse. I leave Paris for Canada, with Bastien. For a month I had thought of nothing but Canada. In the train I saw the ship and then Canada. I made a picture of it in my head. We arrive here. The boat doesn't sail at the expected time. I spend two weeks at the hotel Cordier. And do you fancy that I think of nothing but our departure, like Bastien, that my eyes never leave the goal, as he puts it? No. I... For instance, I look at you; I enjoy being with you; I take a great fancy to the house, to you...

THÉRÈSE [lifting her head and laughing]. You don't say so!

SÉGARD. I say to myself: it's like this; you're planning to go away and perhaps you could live very happily in this country. Who knows? If you would only... You told me just now that you had worked on a poultry farm. Well at that — you see the sort of fellow I am — my imagination was off at once. I saw a little cottage in the sunlight, something like a porter's lodge, not in Canada. There's an enclosure for raising chickens and a garden with pretty Thérèse, laughing among the flowers. Didn't you speak of a garden, too?...

THÉRÈSE. Yes.

SÉGARD. You see how it is, don't you?

You see how hard it is to feel at every step everything that would be possible if you ended your journey there; to guess how easily you could find enough to fill your life and your heart...

THÉRÈSE. It's true, all of it. [Silence.] The little house with the hens and the flowers... Ah, you'll put ideas in my head and give me the blues.

SÉGARD [laying his hand on her shoulder]. No, no...

THÉRÈSE. I hear Madame Cordier coming down; it's time to set the tables.

SÉGARD. I have bored you, Thérèse, with my stories.

THÉRÈSE [rising]. Oh, no, you said such nice things to me!

[She begins to set the tables.]

MADAME CORDIER [entering through the door at the left]. Quick, Thérèse, it's late! Well, how's it going, Ségard?

SÉGARD. Not so badly. But all the same the twinges still keep up. They tire me, and make me feverish.

MADAME CORDIER. You must have an early supper and go to bed.

SÉGARD. I haven't much appetite.

[He sits down.]

[Workmen enter and seat themselves up stage at the tables. Then BASTIEN and HIDOUX come in.]

HIDOUX [continuing his conversation with BASTIEN]. Amounts to nothing at all! To change the form of government amounts to nothing at all, if human nature is still the same. It's just as if I, Hidoux, should plan to change my lodgings because my room is messy and untidy. But no matter where I live my room will be messy and untidy! Why? Because it's the room of a drunkard. There will always be torn curtains in my window because I catch hold of them, so as not to fall, when I want to fill my lungs with air. I have always wanted to have a little green plant on the table by my bed, with an old book, beside it. But I can't change my bedside table. There will always be a bottle on it, or many bottles. You see, Bastien, my case is hopeless, no doubt; but, believe me, it isn't a drunken man who is speaking to you to-day. Try to improve your own character, and questions of government will take care of themselves.

BASTIEN. Granted, but every one would have to...

HIDOUX. Yes, every one would have to ... But every one, you know, begins with oneself... How are you, Ségard?

[*He shakes hands with* SÉGARD, *then moves towards the back to join two new arrivals, sits down, and drinks with them.*]

SÉGARD. Good evening.

BASTIEN [*throwing himself in front of* THÉRÈSE, *who comes in carrying plates in both hands*]. Good evening, Thérèse. I won't let you pass! It's the instant, it's the moment, to find out if you are ticklish.

[*He pinches her waist, she cries out.*]

THÉRÈSE. Stop it, or I'll drop everything!

MADAME CORDIER. Let her alone, Bastien, she's behind with her work.

[BASTIEN, *in comic haste, steps out of* THÉRÈSE'S *way. She sticks out her tongue at him. He approaches* SÉGARD.]

BASTIEN. How's it going, old boy?

SÉGARD. There are times when the thing hurts like fury. I didn't sleep last night and I'm very tired.

BASTIEN. Did you try going out at all? Have you been down to see how they're getting on with the boat?

SÉGARD. No, I stayed here.

BASTIEN. I suppose except at meal-hours there's almost no one comes here?

SÉGARD. No one.

BASTIEN [*confidentially*]. Tell me... you haven't started anything with Thérèse, have you?

[SÉGARD, *without looking at* BASTIEN, *shakes his head. Brief silence.*]

SÉGARD. I think I'll go and lie down on my bed, old man.

BASTIEN. Oh, I was only asking because it seems to me that a man who was left alone with that girl for an hour could, with a little coaxing, do what he liked with her.

SÉGARD. You can't always tell, you know... [*He rises, groaning.*]

BASTIEN. You're not feeling well, Alfred; go and lie down for a while. We may

be leaving in another week, you must try to be all right by then.

SÉGARD. Oh, it doesn't amount to anything.

[*He goes out quickly after exchanging some words with* MADAME CORDIER. *At the back* HIDOUX *empties his glass and shakes hands with the workmen with whom he has just been drinking. Then he comes and sits down opposite* BASTIEN, *in the place just left by* SÉGARD.]

HIDOUX. Ségard has gone?

MADAME CORDIER. Yes, he has a touch of fever. He has gone to bed without eating anything.

HIDOUX. A touch of fever! He might have had a drink with us all the same! Well, give me a glass of white wine, Madame. A glass of white wine before the soup, Thérèse! I'm dying of thirst. White wine, Bastien?

BASTIEN. White wine, by all means!

HIDOUX. Drink while you can, my friend, for I fancy that in Canada wine's a rather scarce article. [THÉRÈSE *serves them.*]

BASTIEN. We'll drink whiskey, old top, we'll drink champagne. You can find that everywhere.

THÉRÈSE. Oh, champagne! That's what I love! I could drink a bottle of it all by myself.

A CUSTOMER [*calling*]. Thérèse!

BASTIEN. Could you? Well, I'll get some for you, Thérèse, you have it here?

THÉRÈSE. Yes, and good, too.

BASTIEN. We'll drink some, would you like that? We'll drink some champagne together.

THE CUSTOMER. Thérèse!

THÉRÈSE. Coming. [*She goes out.*]

BASTIEN [*to* HIDOUX]. Yes, Hidoux, old man; when we own our farms there's nothing to prevent our always having a case or two of champagne on hand, like explorers. But if it can't be arranged we'll do without it. Wine is a good thing. But liberty is worth more than wine. And if we go, you understand, Hidoux, it's to be free, to be free!

HIDOUX [*slightly intoxicated*]. It's to be free, I know. But let me answer you. First, as to champagne. I want you to bear in mind that champagne is one thing and wine is another. Champagne isn't wine, you know!

BASTIEN. Oh!

HIDOUX. It's sweeten'd, it's charged, it's put up in a fancy bottle; and it has no bouquet.

If you're eating a little bread and cheese in the morning, what will you drink? A little bordeaux, a little burgundy, half a pint of picolo, some beaujolais, all wines that go straight to the heart; that's what you'll drink to make life worth while again. But champagne! It's a wine with a stand-up collar, for state occasions. It's good for nothing but to set the women to giggling at weddings and to make you spit if you have phlegm in your throat.

BASTIEN. You make me laugh, you...

HIDOUX. Good! So much for champagne. Now for more important things. You and Ségard are right in going to Canada. That's what I say and what I've always said. You'll have a splendid voyage, you'll see new countries, you'll live in the open air. But you're all the time talking about liberty. Liberty, liberty, it's a word quickly said. Bastien, do you want to know the thought I have deep down inside me? You began by signing a contract. You'll pay for this; they'll hold back money for that; you'll agree to do such and such a thing. And is that what you call liberty? Ah, my boy, when you begin to sign papers say nothing more about liberty.

BASTIEN. Oh, of course, absolute liberty...

HIDOUX. Look here, I don't know any more than you do about your Canadian agricultural society. But I'd like to bet that in a hundred different ways you'll be dependent on them, and that before you're through you'll find that you're working for the people who sell the farms. You're going to cultivate untilled land that you're not sure you can pay for. Oh, they'll give you credit, never fear. As much as you want! And your harvests and your herds, you'll see to whom you'll sell them, to whom you'll be forced to sell them! Unless I miss my guess, the ship that brings them here will always be the Tenacity.

No, it's the same thing everywhere, you see. Liberty, true liberty, is a thing one must carry inside one's skin. I'm free, for instance. When I was young they called me the eel. No one has ever been able to get me in his grasp. I only sell a tiny bit of my liberty at a time in order to get a living. I choose my work to suit my tastes, according to the state of my pocket-book and my health. I give good value for my wages, you'll find that every one speaks well of me. But as to mortgaging the future, I can't do it, you know, and I never could. Even to think about it makes me positively ill.

[*He slowly empties his glass. BASTIEN remains thoughtful, his elbow on the table.*]

BASTIEN. Old man, if you don't mortgage the future, at least to some extent, you'll never accomplish anything great!... And then besides I'm not going in with my eyes shut! After I get there I have a year in which to say no.

THÉRÈSE [*to HIDOUX and BASTIEN*]. Have you finished drinking? Can I put the soup on the table?

HIDOUX [*seizing the bottle*]. We're just finishing.

BASTIEN [*taking THÉRÈSE by the arm and pulling her towards the door at the right*]. I'll help you, Thérèse, I'll help you to serve the supper...

SCENE II

The same room, evening. The front windows are closed with shutters. Electric lights only above the bar and the table opposite it, at the right. At the rise of the curtain MADAME CORDIER is at the back, occupied in turning the key in the lock of the front door. THÉRÈSE is rinsing glasses at the bar. BASTIEN, at the table on the right, is reading a paper.

MADAME CORDIER [*hanging a bunch of keys on a nail behind the bar*]. Well, I'm goin' up. You'll put out the lights when you come.

THÉRÈSE. Yes, Madame. I'm just finishing.

BASTIEN. I'll be going up in a minute, Madame Cordier.

MADAME CORDIER. Then good night.

BASTIEN [*without raising his eyes from the paper*]. Good night, Madame.

THÉRÈSE. Good night, Madame Cordier.

[MADAME CORDIER *goes out to the left. There is an instant of silence during which* THÉRÈSE *arranges the glasses in rows on a shelf behind the bar.*]

THÉRÈSE. Hey, you with the paper there! I'm going to put out the lights.

BASTIEN. What time is it?

THÉRÈSE. Eleven at the very least.

BASTIEN [*tossing away his paper and throwing himself back in his chair*]. Thérèse!

THÉRÈSE. What?

BASTIEN. You can still serve me something, can't you?

THÉRÈSE. If you like, but hurry! What? A glass of water?

BASTIEN [*confidentially*]. A bottle of champagne and two glasses.

THÉRÈSE. Oh, I couldn't!

BASTIEN [*rising and going towards her*]. Why not, Thérèse? I promised that I'd treat you to something. The opportunity presents itself. It would be nice to drink a glass or two of champagne while we chatted together for five minutes before going to bed. We'd both be the better for it.

THÉRÈSE. You have only to offer a bottle of it with Ségard the day that you go.

BASTIEN. That's understood. But the farewell bottle doesn't interfere with another now. We'll drink the farewell bottle with Ségard, Hidoux and the proprietress, and I know quite well what it will be like. You'll come between filling two orders and drink a glass as quickly as possible. That won't count! [*A silence.* THÉRÈSE, *perplexed, shifts from one foot to the other.*] Is it such a serious matter just to drink a glass? You could have done it by this time!... What are you thinking about?

THÉRÈSE. I'm thinking about Madame Cordier.

BASTIEN. In five minutes she'll be snoring. What about her?

THÉRÈSE. She'll have to know about it...

BASTIEN. Naturally. To-morrow when I pay for the bottle I'll tell her that we drank it this evening. A sudden fancy!

THÉRÈSE. Oh no! What would she say afterwards! That I should get champagne offered to me... And then at this time of night, just think!...

BASTIEN. Very well. She shan't know a thing about it. You tell her to-morrow that just as you were going to put out the lights a sailor came to scratch at the door for a bottle of champagne.

THÉRÈSE [*assenting*]. There's nothing stupid about you! Come, bandit! Help me to raise the trap door to the cellar without making any noise.

[BASTIEN, *behind the bar, raises the trap.* THÉRÈSE *descends. During her absence* BASTIEN *chooses two glasses which he sets on the table.*]

THÉRÈSE [*reappearing*]. Close the trap door.

[BASTIEN *shuts the trap door.* THÉRÈSE *offers him the bottle, which he seizes and sets on the table. They both sit down opposite each other.* BASTIEN *begins to pull the cork.*]

THÉRÈSE. Don't let it pop.

BASTIEN. Right you are, my pretty one. There! [*He fills the glasses. They clink them together.*] To that Thérèse who loves champagne and has deserved to drink it a hundred times over!

THÉRÈSE. To that tease of a Bastien. And to your voyage! [*They drink.*]

BASTIEN. Not bad.

THÉRÈSE. It's splendid!

BASTIEN. You know a good thing when you see it! This'll make your eyes sparkle and you'll be even prettier. Come to Canada, I'll buy you a drink every Saturday night.

THÉRÈSE. Never!

BASTIEN. Why not?

THÉRÈSE. I never could go on the sea, I'm too much afraid. And your Canada is too far off. I have sisters here...

BASTIEN. And some man, no doubt, who's more than a brother to you.

THÉRÈSE. No, I've no one at all. Not since last summer. My lover went away without leaving his address. A fine way to treat me!

BASTIEN. Did he come from here?

THÉRÈSE. No... Garrisoned here. He was nice. An adjutant. [*She drinks, then* BASTIEN *fills the glasses.*] Oh, but wait, I'll get some biscuits.

[*She goes out an instant through the door on the right, and returns with some biscuits on a plate.*]

BASTIEN [*as* THÉRÈSE *is about to take her former seat, opposite him*]. Sit beside me! Just to show that we're friends.

THÉRÈSE [*seating herself at* BASTIEN'S *right*]. And then besides, if I went to Canada, there'd be a nice state of things, with one hen for two roosters!

BASTIEN. And a charming hen! But Ségard isn't the sort that would fight for a hen. I know him. He's stayed with you now for two afternoons and I'll wager he hasn't made love to you once.

THÉRÈSE [*in a detached voice*]. Oh, he's very nice and polite. He keeps me company, he talks. He's a boy who knows how to interest you, and he's good-hearted, too. Madame Cordier is quite right in saying so.

BASTIEN. He's a brother! That's why I decided to take him with me.

THÉRÈSE [*maliciously*]. Evidently Ségard is quite different from you. He wouldn't be capable, for instance, of lying in wait for young girls on the stairs and kissing them.

BASTIEN. You know that I'm not in the habit of kissing girls on the stairs. If I kissed you, Thérèse, it's because I wanted to so much. If Alfred had wanted to as much as I did, he would have done it, too.

THÉRÈSE. People may want very much to do things and yet not dare.

BASTIEN. But when you want to more than anything else in the world, and when you're a man, you must dare.

[*He puts his arm around* THÉRÈSE *and kisses her on the neck.*]

THÉRÈSE [*after having pushed him away with a little scream*]. You're going to make me cry out and waken Madame Cordier!

BASTIEN [*coaxingly*]. My little Thérèse, my beautiful Thérèse, listen... But first, try another glass. [*He takes* THÉRÈSE'S glass and makes her drink, then drinks after her out of the same glass.*] I want to know everything that you think...

THÉRÈSE [*taking a sip from* BASTIEN'S glass]. Let me, too, then.

BASTIEN. Listen to me closely. When I was in the trenches and drowsed for whole days in the blackness of a dug-out, I amused myself by imagining the pretty girl I'd have liked to make love to there, the girl who would have just suited me. I was like a hungry man who thinks of all the most appetizing dishes. I said to myself; if I could only have some one like that beside me for an hour, and cover her with kisses from her head to her feet! A real girl who would laugh, who would be content, and who would give me back my kisses without making any fuss about it. When things were the worst, when I saw every day my poor devils of comrades ripped to pieces, when I felt that my turn wasn't far away, well, do you know what bothered me the most? It was to think that I was going to die without even being able to remember the taste of a kiss.

THÉRÈSE [*touched*]. Poor *poilu!*

[BASTIEN *kisses her.*]

BASTIEN. After that came the armistice and life in barracks. Barracks at Metz, barracks at Cologne, at Paris, at Marseilles, at Constantinople. At last I return to the avenue de Clichy. I'm like a stranger there. It's sickening. I drag out two months in a Paris full of Americans and Czecho-Slovaks. And now that I'm going away to Canada, to the remotest depths of Canada where perhaps the only women are Indian squaws who smoke pipes, wouldn't it be a strange thing if I didn't want to kiss you, you who are like, exactly like, Thérèse, the girl that I dreamed about in the trenches.

[*He gives her a long kiss.* THÉRÈSE languidly droops her head on BASTIEN'S shoulder. He gazes at her, then kisses her again.*]

THÉRÈSE [*straightening up*]. You mustn't kiss me any more.

BASTIEN. Why not?

THÉRÈSE. You're going away.

BASTIEN. Yes, I'm going away. But

not to-morrow, not this week; and I'll kiss you a lot before I go. While one can one must give and receive as many kisses as possible, so as to have nothing to reproach oneself with afterwards, when one is alone and far from love. Do you understand? Unless you like kisses less than champagne, my pretty one? [*Contrite.*] — unless I've offended you.

[THÉRÈSE *bursts out laughing, seizes* BASTIEN'S *head in her hands, and gives him a sudden kiss.*]

THÉRÈSE. There! [*She empties her glass*] and there! [*She rises.*] And now, my little one, we must go straight to bed! You know it's very late.

[*Singing and dancing she clears the table, washes the glasses and sets them in their place, takes down the bunch of keys, and goes to the door at the back, which she opens in order to throw the empty bottle out on the wharf.* BASTIEN *follows her, kisses her when he can catch hold of her, comes back with her when she has locked the door again, picks her up and whirls around with her in his arms.*]

THÉRÈSE [*disengaging herself*]. There. Now it's time to say good night and go to bed.

[*She turns out the electric light above the bar.*]

BASTIEN. Thérèse!

THÉRÈSE. What?

BASTIEN. Come nearer, I want to whisper something to you.

[THÉRÈSE *goes to him and* BASTIEN *whispers some words in her ear.*]

THÉRÈSE. Oh, no!

BASTIEN. Yes.

[*He puts his arm around her and drags her towards the door at the left.*]

THÉRÈSE. No, Bastien...

BASTIEN. You're sleepy?

THÉRÈSE. Oh, it isn't that...

BASTIEN. Then say yes, it's so simple.

THÉRÈSE [*after an instant of silence, during which she remains pressed close against* BASTIEN]. Then you must promise not to tell any one. Not to tell Ségard.

BASTIEN. Not a soul. And especially not Ségard. Come! [*He opens the door.*]

THÉRÈSE. Let's go up without making any noise. [*She turns out the last light.*]

ACT III

The same room. Morning. The shutters and the door are still closed. Light enters through the little window above the door. At the rise of the curtain there is no one on the stage. The door on the left opens softly and BASTIEN *appears in the traveling clothes he wore in the first act. He carries a valise, lays it on the table, and starts to open it.* THÉRÈSE *then enters, cautiously, through the door on the right; modest street dress, her raincoat on her arm. She carries a valise, larger than* BASTIEN'S *and, approaching on tiptoe, sets it beside the table. They speak in lowered tones.*

THÉRÈSE. There, my darling... [*Kneeling on the floor, she opens the valise.*] You see there's still room.

[BASTIEN *kisses* THÉRÈSE *enthusiastically, then examines the valise she has just brought.*]

BASTIEN. Good, that will do finely. I can leave Ségard that bag on the table, which is his. Now, five minutes to pack my things.

[*He takes out and inventories the contents of the open valise on the table. In the course of the following conversation he keeps handing clothes and various articles to* THÉRÈSE. *She puts them in the large valise.*]

THÉRÈSE. We have time, it's still too early... I couldn't sleep... A week already, my darling, since we drank champagne together at that table!...

BASTIEN. Are you content?

THÉRÈSE. Oh, yes! Happy! Only it upsets me to go away like this without saying a word to Madame Cordier. And Ségard? When you told him about it yesterday evening, what did he say?

BASTIEN. I haven't told him.

THÉRÈSE. You haven't...

BASTIEN. No. But I had it all arranged. I was planning to join him in his room instead of going to bed. And then the word came that the Tenacity was ready. After

that I hadn't the courage. Oh, I've re-
gretted so much that I didn't tell him three
or four days ago! So I ran to find Hidoux.
I explained to him how things were. He'll
tell the others about it. I can count on his
saying the right things. And as for Alfred,
I've written him a letter.

THÉRÈSE. Ah, that's good! A long
letter?

BASTIEN. Yes... A letter. Oh, it makes
no difference, I ought to have seen him.
But no, just at the sailing time I couldn't
tell him I'm out of it, I, the leader of the
expedition; I who was the most determined to go; I who got him to agree to the
scheme and preached perseverance to him.
I couldn't do it, it would have been too
impossible!

THÉRÈSE. Yet every one knows that love
is stronger than anything else.

BASTIEN. Not every one. Two weeks
ago I didn't know it myself.

THÉRÈSE [with gratitude]. My darling!

BASTIEN. No, you must see that there's
nothing to do now but to take French leave
... [A silence.] And then it's a poor way
to seek for liberty, going to Canada on a
ten-year contract. Liberty is a thing that
you carry inside your skin. True liberty
means being able to change your way of
life at a moment's notice whenever you
take a notion to. It doesn't matter what
we do, my pretty one. At any rate we'll be
together. We'll just sell a tiny bit of our
liberty from time to time in order to make
a living... Canada would have its good
points, if one had plenty of money and
didn't have to sign a contract... As soon as
you begin signing papers... And then I
thought all along that they spoke French
there. And now some men from the Tenacity tell me that Manitoba is the one province where only English is spoken. And
then, and then, my sweetheart doesn't
want to go there.

[THÉRÈSE kisses him impetuously. A
silence.]

THÉRÈSE. I feel worried about Ségard.

BASTIEN. So do I.

THÉRÈSE. What will he do?

BASTIEN. He? He'll go back to Paris

again. Who knows, perhaps he'll be just
as happy that way.

THÉRÈSE. The trouble is that he hasn't
the least suspicion.

BASTIEN [who has finished his packing and
is putting SÉGARD'S valise in order]. I
know.

THÉRÈSE. My darling!...

BASTIEN. What?

THÉRÈSE. I think he's a little in love
with me.

BASTIEN. Like all the others, it's quite
possible... Now shut the bag, and be quick.

THÉRÈSE [shutting it]. But with him it
was different somehow. I don't know why,
but I'd have felt very badly about it if he'd
found out about you and me before we
went away. And then, so as not to seem
too much taken up with you these last days
I was all the time making myself pleasant
to him, laughing with him. It was almost
too much for me...

BASTIEN [finishing strapping up the bag].
You're ready, Thérèse? That's done!...
And that's all! It's time... The key? [He
points to the ray of sunshine that enters
through the little window above the door.]
Look! It's a fine day! We have a little
money! We're going to have a wonderful
journey of love. We'll take the first train
for the North and no one will know where
we are!

THÉRÈSE [who has taken the keys and is
opening the door at the back]. Yes, my love!

[The door swings open. One sees the quay
gilded by the morning sun. THÉRÈSE
comes back and hangs the bunch of keys
in their place. They go out, closing the
door cautiously behind them. The stage
remains empty for a moment, then MA-
DAME CORDIER enters from the left.]

MADAME CORDIER [after a quick glance towards the back]. Not in her room and not
here. [She goes to the door on the right and
opens it.] Thérèse!... Her bed hasn't
been slept in! [She takes down the bunch of
keys and goes to open the door at the back.]
She can be out all night if she chooses, but
she mustn't leave the door unlocked and
she must be back in time for her morning's
work.

[*She goes out and opens the shutters at the front of the restaurant. Enter two workmen eating, their bread and their knives in their hands. They sit down.* MADAME CORDIER *joins them.*]

ONE OF THE WORKMEN [*To* MADAME CORDIER]. A glass of white wine, if you please.

MADAME CORDIER. There you are!

[*She serves them. They will go out shortly before the entrance of* HIDOUX. *Three young workmen enter and go to the counter.*]

FIRST WORKMAN. Some coffee, if you please, Madame Cordier, for men who have just had their morning swim.

MADAME CORDIER. No coffee this morning, my poor boys. Thérèse didn't get up in time to make it.

FIRST WORKMAN. Ah! It's her lover's fault. No doubt he wouldn't let her go.

SECOND WORKMAN. If that's how it is, we'll excuse her. And we'll take a little apple-brandy, eh, mates?

THIRD WORKMAN. Yes, and let's hurry.

FIRST WORKMAN. Three then, Madame Cordier. [MADAME CORDIER *serves them.*]

[*Enter the* ENGLISH SAILOR.]

THE ENGLISH SAILOR. Mornin'.

MADAME CORDIER. Ah! Good morning! I recognize you. You've come to warn our two boarders. [*To the three young workmen who pay and go out.*] Thank you. Come again.

THE ENGLISH SAILOR. Right ye are, ma'am! Tell 'em the Tenacity'll sail at nine this mornin'.

MADAME CORDIER. So they told them yesterday, at the boat. So it's decided! At nine o'clock. I'll call them. Won't you take a little something?

THE ENGLISH SAILOR. A nip o' brandy, ma'am, thank ye kindly.

[SÉGARD *enters dressed for traveling.*]

MADAME CORDIER. Here's Ségard now. Ségard, it's the sailor from the Tenacity. My boy, you sail this morning at nine o'clock.

SÉGARD. Ah! good morning.

[*He shakes hands with the sailor.*]

THE ENGLISH SAILOR. Mornin'. You an' your friend wants to come aboard afore nine o'clock.

SÉGARD. All right. We're ready.

THE ENGLISH SAILOR. P'raps you'd like a 'and with your luggage.

SÉGARD. Thanks! We've already taken a trunk to the boat. There's just a small bag. And there it is now. Bastien must have brought it down. Where is Bastien, by the way?

MADAME CORDIER. I haven't seen him yet.

SÉGARD [*to the sailor*]. No, thanks, we can manage the bag.

THE ENGLISH SAILOR. Nine o'clock then, that's when she sails. [*He drinks.*] Well, see you later. [*He goes out.*]

SÉGARD. Before very long. This time we're off, Madame Cordier.

MADAME CORDIER. Yes, you'll be saying good-bye to us. Just as we began to get used to you.

SÉGARD. Oh, not good-bye, Madame Cordier! Only au revoir. We'll find some way of taking a trip to France now and then. I'll come back, I know that I'll come back. I've promised myself to come. And we'll keep in touch by letter... Where's Thérèse?

MADAME CORDIER [*scoldingly*]. Thérèse, Thérèse! She didn't sleep here last night and she hasn't come back yet this morning!

SÉGARD. Where did she sleep?

MADAME CORDIER. How do I know? Probably she went to her sister's. It's all the same to me, but she ought to have let me know beforehand. And she ought to be back long before this. The restaurant not opened and no hot coffee!

[*Enter* HIDOUX.]

HIDOUX [*with some embarrassment*]. Good morning, Madame Cordier!... Good morning, Ségard! [*He shakes hands with them.*] Tell me... Thérèse isn't here, is she?

MADAME CORDIER. No. Why?

HIDOUX. Nor Bastien either, eh? Has Bastien gone out?

SÉGARD. I don't know...

MADAME CORDIER. We haven't seen him yet.

SÉGARD. Did you want him for anything? He brought down my bag. Perhaps he went up to his room again, I'll go and see.

HIDOUX. No, no. It's not worth the trouble, my friend. He isn't there. I've just left him. I only wanted to know... if you knew.

SÉGARD. What? If we knew that the Tenacity sails this morning?

HIDOUX. No!... Well, it's no use beating around the bush. I've just left Bastien and Thérèse at the station. They've run away together.

MADAME CORDIER [completely overcome]. Oh!

SÉGARD [likewise]. Thérèse and Bastien? How? Where?

HIDOUX [taking a letter from his pocket and offering it to SÉGARD]. Take it, my poor boy!

[While HIDOUX talks to MADAME CORDIER, who gesticulates, SÉGARD sits down on a table and reads the letter. He is overwhelmed.]

MADAME CORDIER. It's no way for a girl to act! When you think that she's been with me for three years, that I've trusted her, made a friend of her! No, you can't tell me! It isn't right!

HIDOUX. Oh, she asked me to make her excuses to you...

MADAME CORDIER. Excuses, is it? A nice mess! Clearing out without so much as a moment's notice! Leaving me all alone like this! [She turns towards SÉGARD.] Well, my poor Ségard, you're left stranded too! A nice way your friend has behaved!

SÉGARD [to HIDOUX, who approaches him]. He speaks to me about papers... about my bag... He asks me not to bear him a grudge; he says, Hidoux will explain.

HIDOUX. The explanation isn't complicated; he wanted to amuse himself with Thérèse; he made her pretty speeches, and before he knew it he was caught himself. He's impulsive, you know, and doesn't do

things by halves. Almost at once he was in love in good earnest.

SÉGARD. Has this been going on long?

HIDOUX. Not more than a week. That is to say, the madness is at its height.

SÉGARD. And Thérèse?

HIDOUX. You can be sure that to do what she has done she must have been infected with the same fever. When you've succeeded in winning a woman she adopts you, it's unavoidable. You become the only man in the world; you're her darling, she hungers and thirsts for you. But in catching a girl like Thérèse you get caught yourself. Bastien was caught and well caught, like the boy that he is. He was madly in love with her from the very first. And, as she doesn't want to go to Canada, he'll stay in France with her.

MADAME CORDIER [who has begun to sweep the room]. A lad who seemed as firm as a rock.

HIDOUX. Oh, firm as a rock... The arrow of the weather-vane is firm, too, as long as the wind is steady. But that doesn't keep the wind from changing some fine day. [A silence.]

SÉGARD. Why didn't he tell me anything about it? Why didn't he let me know a week ago how things were going with him?

MADAME CORDIER. Yes, you! His friend!

HIDOUX. Do you suppose that he asked himself at the beginning to what this was going to lead? He only knew one thing: that he must have Thérèse, no matter what happened.

SÉGARD [bitterly]. Oh, he's a man of decision, Bastien is!

HIDOUX. Yes, and his resolution doesn't wholly date from yesterday evening. But up to yesterday evening it may be that it was only a possibility, that he hadn't quite made up his mind; he was a little ashamed of it on your account. And then often when you make a decision you only obey the force of things, and then you don't act till the last possible minute because the course of events may change. His being fond of you made it especially hard for him to tell you about it; so he put it off. And the more he put it off the harder it was to speak. The truth is that he'd have done it yesterday if they hadn't come to tell you the boat was ready. That made the pill still harder for you to swallow, and he didn't have the courage to offer it to you himself. He felt that he was a sneak, you know.

SÉGARD. But anyway when he began to have relations with Thérèse he might have told me...

HIDOUX. My friend, men tell their good fortunes. But when they're in love they don't talk about it. With women it's just the reverse. Bastien had posed too long as a man-of-the-world to confess to you that he'd been trapped. He didn't tell me about it till yesterday evening when he couldn't do anything else... He's like you, my poor boy: you were too sensitive about the matter to say that you were in love. For you were, too, I have eyes in my head!

MADAME CORDIER. Yes... and if I expected something it certainly wasn't this...

SÉGARD [with effort, after a silence]. What are they going to do? Where have they gone?

HIDOUX [with a vague gesture]. To the North... Bastien plans to go into the huckster's trade somewhere in the liberated regions.

SÉGARD. That's not the sort of thing that will please Thérèse.

HIDOUX. With Bastien it will please her. With some one else it might be different... [Silence.] Ségard, what are you going to do? Your boat sails at nine o'clock.

[MADAME CORDIER approaches and stands motionless, her hands on her hips, beside HIDOUX. Both look at SÉGARD, who, collapsed on the table, stares at the floor. A silence.]

SÉGARD [straightening up]. I'll go... I don't know how it will be... But I'll go.

MADAME CORDIER. Go alone?

SÉGARD. Yes.

MADAME CORDIER. Wouldn't you prefer to go home, to return to Paris?

SÉGARD. To go home! I wanted to when I first came here. But not now.

Besides, I've signed a contract, why should I break it?... I'm all ready. My trunk is on the boat.

MADAME CORDIER. Oh! as for the trunk, Hidoux will go and get it and let them know that you've changed your mind about sailing. What can they do to you?

HIDOUX. Frankly, at bottom, which would you prefer? To return to Paris? To sail? Or just to remain here?

SÉGARD. None of them... Oh! not to stay here now.... Since I've agreed to go I may as well do that as anything...

MADAME CORDIER. You agreed to go with Bastien, but since he has left you?

SÉGARD [in a strangled voice, after a short silence]. Then, Madame Cordier, because Bastien has left me, because Bastien isn't going to Canada now, do you think I won't know how to set out alone? I wasn't as keen to go there as he was! But am I incapable of wanting to go there without him? As a matter of fact this is perhaps the first time that I've felt a real wish, a mournful wish, to set sail!

HIDOUX. Well then, go, my boy, go! Depart!

MADAME CORDIER. If I were in his place...

HIDOUX. If you were in his place you'd go, you'd follow the current. You see, Madame, there are people like Ségard who are in life like corks on a stream. Sometimes they go to sway and dream in a cove or among the reeds. They will remain there if Fate so wills it. If not, an eddy, and they're dragged from their moorings, whirled along again. That's the way it is most of the time...

SÉGARD. And the others?

HIDOUX. Some are weather-vanes. That's Bastien's type. They're proud and self-confident because they have a pivot. And they talk about their will, their decision. Then there are others like me. I am free. Free with regard to men but none the less a slave of the winds and the stream, sometimes an old weather-vane and sometimes an old cork. An old cork always drawn — worse luck — towards the necks of bottles.

SÉGARD [after a moment of reflection].

But sometimes... how shall I put it?... Sometimes the stream has two branches, the road forks ——

HIDOUX. Often.

SÉGARD [quickly]. Then you can choose!

HIDOUX. Yes, there are times when you can choose, if you dare. Otherwise the current chooses for you. Yes, sometimes there's an instant in which you can choose. Sometimes, too, my poor Ségard, when there's only room for one, you're shoved aside by some one who is bolder... [A long silence.] Bah! That doesn't prevent life from being beautiful!

SÉGARD. And sad.

HIDOUX. And sad and gay and sad again. Do you think it will be gay for very long, for Bastien, for Thérèse?

SÉGARD. What did she say?

HIDOUX. Who do you mean?

SÉGARD. Thérèse, what did she say?

HIDOUX. I don't remember...

SÉGARD. Was she laughing?

HIDOUX. Eh, I know nothing about it. And even if I knew I wouldn't tell you. I only had a glimpse of her. Their train was just starting. Do you fancy for a moment that young people newly in love think of anything but themselves?... Well then? What have you decided?

SÉGARD [plaintively]. I shall go. I prefer to go, far away, all alone.

[A silence.]

MADAME CORDIER. Do you really mean it?

SÉGARD. Yes.

MADAME CORDIER. You'll take a bite before you go?

SÉGARD. No, thank you, Madame Cordier.

MADAME CORDIER. Oh yes! This isn't a reason ——

HIDOUX. You can't refuse to drink a farewell glass. Madame Cordier! A little bottle of white wine and three glasses.

SÉGARD [hastily]. No, Madame Cordier, I beg you! No, old friend. I haven't the heart to drink. I couldn't do it.

HIDOUX. Believe me, you're wrong! When a man is in your state — I know what it is — the best thing is a good glass of wine. It takes the weight off your chest. It teaches your sorrow to sing and makes you proud of it. I have seen emigrants drink. Afterwards you'd have thought that they'd just been made kings and were embarking for their kingdom. [SÉGARD looks at him, smiling.] That makes you laugh? Then you can take a glass with us. Madame Cordier!

SÉGARD. No, no, old fellow. You're too kind. But it would choke me. See, I prefer to go at once.

[He goes to get his valise.]

MADAME CORDIER. But it's nowhere near nine o'clock. You have any amount of time.

HIDOUX. You have a whole hour yet!

SÉGARD. I'd rather, Madame Cordier. I'd rather go aboard now. You see, I'm a little sad. I want to be alone for a while. Once on the boat, good, I won't trouble my head about anything. Will you come along with me, Hidoux?

HIDOUX. If you won't change your mind about going at once. Give me your bag. [He takes it.]

SÉGARD [advancing towards MADAME CORDIER with outstretched hand]. Madame Cordier...

MADAME CORDIER. Well, au revoir, my boy. You've had poor luck with Bastien. But we'll hope that you'll find another comrade out there.

SÉGARD. We'll hope so.

MADAME CORDIER. And then you have fine weather for starting out, clear sunshine.

SÉGARD. It's Bastien who has had fine weather for starting out. I'd rather it were the sort of weather we've been having the last few days...

HIDOUX [to SÉGARD]. At bottom perhaps it's you who have taken the best course, without suspecting it.

[All three go to the door.]

SÉGARD [after a long glance around the little restaurant]. And perhaps, also, it's I who should have stayed. [A silence. Then, abruptly.] Thank you, Madame Cordier, for all your kindness while I've been here. And good-bye.

MADAME CORDIER [taking his hand].

Write to me when you have time. And don't say good-bye, say au revoir. Won't you be coming back, as you said you would?

SÉGARD [*vaguely*]. Perhaps...

[*He makes a gesture of farewell and goes out with* HIDOUX. MADAME COR-DIER *remains for a moment on the door-step and looks in the direction in which* SÉGARD *and* HIDOUX *have gone. Then she stands aside to let a group of travelers enter the restaurant. They put their bags on a table and sit down.*]

MADAME CORDIER [*resting both hands on the table*]. Good morning! What can I serve you?

TIME IS A DREAM
A PLAY IN SIX SCENES
BY H. R. LENORMAND
Translated by WINIFRED KATZIN

CHARACTERS

Riemke Van Eyden
Romée Cremers
Mrs. Beunke
Nico Van Eyden
Saidyah

TIME IS A DREAM

FIRST SCENE

*The drawing-room of an old mansion in
Utrecht. On the left three violet-tinted windows form a deep bay looking out over
luxuriantly wooded grounds. On the right
a peat fire is burning in the monumental
hearth, on either side of which is a comfortable settee [built-in] piled up with cushions.
A lamp-stand near by. Grey hangings.
Sarongs. Antique furniture. A tea table.
A telephone on a stand.*

Doors rear and left.

*Three o'clock of an autumn afternoon.
The curtain rises on* RIEMKE VAN EYDEN *arranging flowers in a vase. She is a girl of
twenty-five, with a gentle, slightly spinsterish
manner, but her gown, for all its simplicity,
conveys a hint of demure and old-world
coquetry.*

*MRS. BEUNKE, the housekeeper, enters, rear,
a little frail old lady, elaborately dressed
in the fashion of a bygone day.]*

MRS. BEUNKE. The train is due at half
past four, isn't it, Miss Riemke?

RIEMKE. Yes, Mrs. Beunke.

MRS. BEUNKE. I have told Jan to get
the carriage ready by a quarter past. Is
that early enough?

RIEMKE. Quite. I shall not be going to
the station. Miss Romée called up to say
she would be over in a few minutes.

MRS. BEUNKE [bringing out her account-
book]. Please, Miss Riemke, could you
spare a minute now to go over my accounts?

RIEMKE. Later on, Mrs. Beunke, later

MRS. BEUNKE [a note of anxiety in her
voice]. This makes three days since you
have looked at them. It is a great responsibility for me.

RIEMKE. Very well, I really will go over
them for you to-morrow.

MRS. BEUNKE [putting the book back into
pocket]. Thank you, Miss Riemke.

And, Oh, yes! Shall I bring tea as soon
as Miss Romée comes or will you wait for
Mr. Nico?

RIEMKE. I don't know; we'll see.
[Looking at MRS. BEUNKE.] Why, Mrs.
Beunke, how flustered you are over Nico's
arrival.

MRS. BEUNKE. Well, I have to make
sure that everything is just right. I
wonder if I've forgotten anything. I have
put flowers in his room; I wish they'd been
chrysanthemums, but there's not one left
in the hot-house; I could find nothing but
dahlias.

RIEMKE. That doesn't matter — I'm
afraid chrysanthemums or dahlias or any
other of our Dutch flowers will look all alike
to him; they will all seem very ordinary
after the flowers of Java. You haven't
forgotten Saidyah's room, have you?

MRS. BEUNKE. No, Miss Riemke, I have
prepared the room he had before. I have
had the bed taken out and mats put down
everywhere. [With deep distaste.] You
may believe me or not, Miss Riemke, but
the mat he slept on ten years ago still smells
of him.

RIEMKE. You mustn't be hard on him,
Mrs. Beunke. My brother doesn't look
upon him as a servant, you know, but as a
friend and confidant rather.

MRS. BEUNKE. Yes, I know. It was
just the same before, but what a young man
of good family can possibly find to talk
about to a nigger is a thing I never could
understand.

RIEMKE [smiling]. Nico likes the
natives. In Java when he was little, he
was forever running away to the boys'
quarters at the other end of the garden; and
as a fresh case of cholera broke out amongst
them pretty nearly every day, those
escapades of his used to keep Mother in a
perpetual state of panic.

MRS. BEUNKE. Yes; diseases — that's about all you can expect to get from those creatures.

RIEMKE. Saidyah would lay down his life for Nico without an instant's hesitation or a word of complaint.

MRS. BEUNKE [sighing]. I know, but if only he would learn not to squat on the furniture to smoke his pipe and stop spitting under the carpets!

RIEMKE [setting the vase on the mantelpiece]. There, that's finished!

[She sits down. MRS. BEUNKE does likewise.]

MRS. BEUNKE. How did you find Mr. Nico, Miss Riemke?

RIEMKE. A little depressed, of course. When one has been living in the Tropics, you know ——

MRS. BEUNKE. Was he glad to see Holland again?

RIEMKE. Yes. But I think he still dreads it in a way.

MRS. BEUNKE. Did he mention his illness?

RIEMKE. No — it is still a painful subject with him. But I am sure he remembers every detail of it.

MRS. BEUNKE. After all these years, too!

RIEMKE. Oh, he has an extraordinarily vivid memory. Yesterday he was recalling to me incidents of our childhood which had almost faded out of my mind. He told me that when we came from the East I was so weak that Mother had to carry me in her arms and they are supposed to have fed me on raw eggs beaten up and flavored with vanilla. Is that true?

MRS. BEUNKE. Yes, you were as yellow as a Chinese baby and you used to stare so inquisitively at every one with great big eyes all ringed round with the fever — I can see you now.

RIEMKE. And he used to run about the house in his little Javanese costume that the gardener's children always laughed at. He remembers to this day how their jeering used to hurt him. Even at that age he was over-sensitive.

MRS. BEUNKE. What news did he bring you of Mr. and Mrs. Van Eyden, Miss Riemke?

RIEMKE. They are both well, thank you, Mrs. Beunke. They have grown rather stouter and paler, Nico says, but that's always the way in hot climates unless one leads a very active life. Father only goes to his office two hours a day now and Mother hardly stirs out at all any more. She moves around as little as possible Nico described her so well; I could see the whole picture of the rooms with the shutters always closed, and Mother in her white linen wrap, sitting there almost immovably only now and then lifting her hand to feel the beads of perspiration that break out on her forehead where the hair is just beginning to turn grey. She is used to my being away. I think her mind has settled into a deep calm that is almost like vacancy.

MRS. BEUNKE [with emotion]. How sad it is, though, Miss Riemke. Why couldn't God will that the whole family should come together just once more?

RIEMKE. Later on, Mrs. Beunke, later on. In a few years' time my people will be leaving the Indies for good and come back to settle here. Then this house will come alive again.

MRS. BEUNKE [sighing]. Yes, but then Mr. Nico will have gone. I have always thought he would not stay with us more than two or three months at a time. And when he leaves everything will be lonely again until your people come.

RIEMKE. Well, Mrs. Beunke, and what if it is? Isn't solitude nice to sleep in? Perhaps it isn't wise to ask any more of life than simply to be allowed to doze one's days and years away.

MRS. BEUNKE. Goodness me, Miss Riemke, you surely don't call it unwise to hope to grow old amongst your dear ones.

RIEMKE. It might be, Mrs. Beunke. Affection is very exhausting, you know, and none of us has very much strength if the truth were known. The clock striking, a few telephone calls, and your little household duties are enough to agitate and tire you out, and as for me, why if I had the burden of affection laid upon me, I think I should find it very hard to carry. I'm growing into a real old maid, Mrs. Beunke.

I ought to be loving a parrot or a goldfish now. Love of human beings is too wearing.

MRS. BEUNKE [rising]. I can hear the carriage coming. I'll go and tell Jan not to wait for you.

[She goes out left, and almost immediately ROMÉE CREMERS comes in. She is a girl of twenty-three, tall and straight, and carries her head with a touch of pride. Her clear features look as though they have been sculptured out of the firm and radiant flesh. The expression of her grey eyes and the somewhat fantastic charm of manner betray an impulsive and passionate nature. She is wearing a sports suit.]

ROMÉE. Hullo, dear. Well, is he here?

RIEMKE. Not yet, but he will be soon.

ROMÉE. Didn't you bring him back with you from Rotterdam?

RIEMKE. No. He brought some important message from my father for the directors of his company and thought he had better get that disposed of first.

ROMÉE [sitting down]. I walked over by the lake path and I feel rather tired.

RIEMKE [looking at her]. You look tired; you're quite pale. You aren't ill, are you?

ROMÉE. No, it's nothing at all. Don't other about it. How did you find him?

RIEMKE [eagerly]. Oh, wonderfully well.

ROMÉE. Did he enjoy the voyage?

RIEMKE. Yes, especially India. He stayed there several months.

ROMÉE. I'm sure I shan't know him again. He was a boy when he went away and it will be very strange to find in his face a man who has become, after all, a perfect stranger although one still calls him by his first name.

RIEMKE [again studying her face]. Why, darling, you do look ill. Aren't you feeling any better yet?

ROMÉE. Yes, a little.

RIEMKE. Would you like some tea?

ROMÉE. No, thanks.

RIEMKE. Please tell me what is the matter.

ROMÉE. I told you, I'm tired — it came over me all of a sudden as I was walking by the water.

RIEMKE. It's only twenty minutes' walk from your place here. That little distance couldn't possibly...

ROMÉE. No, it wasn't the walk —— I don't know what caused it, but a kind of heaviness came over me all at once quite without warning, a queer feeling of exhaustion, don't you know. [A pause — her eyes search RIEMKE's face.] Riemke, if I tell you a secret, can I absolutely rely on you to keep it to yourself?

RIEMKE. Of course you can, but why all the mystery?

ROMÉE. Because I should hate the thing I'm going to tell you to be talked about and discussed and made a peg to hang theories on. Something very strange and unaccountable has happened to me — I was walking quietly along the path by the lake, when, just as I came to the little white wicket at the end of your grounds, I was seized by that weariness I spoke of. Of course I know that it was only that the walk had tired me more than usual but I couldn't make out why I felt so extraordinarily and unreasonably depressed. At the same moment everything around took on an unnatural appearance, horrible because of its unnaturalness; you know what I mean? The trees along the opposite edge of the lake went quite flat and lifeless, like trees on a piece of tapestry, there was no more play of light and shade and not the faintest breath of wind. It was all intensely still and unpleasant. My limbs seemed to grow heavier every moment and each step I took was more difficult than the last; I was conscious of something uncanny, yes, and terrifying, in the air, when a slight mist began to envelop the lake and I saw all at once in the water to the left of me, a man's head. He wasn't very far from the bank and I saw his face quite distinctly; I should recognize it in a thousand.

RIEMKE. It couldn't have been anybody bathing — the water is dangerous at this time of year.

ROMÉE. That's what I said to myself at once. No, that man was drowning, and in a few seconds his head had vanished as suddenly as it had appeared.

RIEMKE. Didn't you shout for some one to come? Didn't you call for help?

Romée. I couldn't. Besides I knew it would have been useless.

Riemke. How do you mean, you knew?

Romée. Just that. The man was no more than ten yards from the bank and yet I had a feeling he was actually ever so far away and that nobody could possibly have reached him.

Riemke. And then?

Romée. That is all. The fear and the queer feeling of heaviness left me, the mist melted way, the trees and everything looked natural again and I came into your garden. Now, what do you understand by that?

Riemke. No more than you do — and there is one thing especially that puzzles me — you say that everything around you looked unnatural, and yet you describe it in such detail. Do you think the man was real or did you just see him in a sort of hallucination — you know what I mean, one of those waking dreams one hears about?

Romée. Oh, no, I wasn't dreaming. It all looked perfectly real.

Riemke. You said there was a mist but there hasn't been any mist to-day.

Romée. Yes there has. Just a slight one that came up and was gone again in a moment — what you call a sea-flame.

Riemke. I suppose I didn't notice it.

Romée. And my mind was so clear that I noticed at once the alterations you have made down there.

Riemke. What alterations?

Romée. Why, the reeds, for one thing. You have had them cut down all along the edge of the lake.

Riemke [in amazement]. What are you talking about, Romée? We haven't had the reeds cut down at all.

Romée. But, my dear, of course you have — at the entrance to your grounds. There's not a single one left.

Riemke. Romée, I assure you you're mistaken. Are you sure you mean our bank?

Romée. Yes, near the white wicket.

Riemke. The reeds haven't been cut down there — or anywhere else — since this place belonged to us.

Romée. I can't make it out. And haven't you got a boat down there? A green boat?

Riemke. Not any kind of boat.

Romée. Let's go and make sure.

Riemke. We don't need to go, we can see from here. Look.

Romée [standing in the bay-window]. You are right. The reeds are there again, just as they were before.

Riemke. Just as they have always been.

Romée. And no boat. [A frightened pause.] I must have had — what you said — a kind of hallucination. And yet I did see ——

Riemke [thoughtfully]. Yes, you certainly saw ——

Romée. The boat was real, so were the seats, and the oars — and that face was real.

Riemke. When you thought the man was drowning, you didn't call for help, you said, because you had "a feeling that nobody could possibly have reached him."

Romée. Yes, it was the strangest thing I saw him quite near me, and I knew him to be at an enormous distance away.

Riemke. Suppose that that distance was not in space but in time?

Romée. How do you mean, in time?

Riemke. Suppose you had seen that spot not as it is now, but as it was once long ago?

Romée. And the man?

Riemke. The man might have lived long ago, too. He might have gone bathing and got drowned.

Romée. I don't believe in ghosts.

Riemke. You know Charlotte Brande don't you?

Romée. Yes, I met her here.

Riemke. Well, one evening she was walking in her garden in Gelderland, when she noticed the summer-house was all lit up. She went towards it, very curious to know what was going on inside, and when she looked through the blue latticed windows, she saw a whole company of people at the table, an entire family dressed in the costumes of a hundred years ago quietly having tea.

Romée. What did she do?

RIEMKE. She had the presence of mind to go back five minutes later, with the servants, but the summer-house was empty and the lock had not been touched. They made an investigation but it led to nothing.

ROMÉE. How does she account for the apparition, then?

RIEMKE. She doesn't account for it at all, but it made her think that human beings may leave behind them imprints on their surroundings, as it were, which possibly sometimes reappear, so that what she saw there may have been one whole moment out of the past revealing itself to her intact.

ROMÉE. Did she ever see anything like it again?

RIEMKE. No, never.

ROMÉE. And didn't it unhinge her mind?

RIEMKE. Unhinge her mind? Why, she's the most level-headed woman I know.

[MRS. BEUNKE *enters, rear, carrying a copper pail filled with the coals upon which the teakettle is set. The girls say no more until she has left the room.*]

ROMÉE. Couldn't this be investigated too, without anybody knowing?

RIEMKE. One might question Mrs. Beunke.

ROMÉE. Has she been long in this house?

RIEMKE. Nearly forty years. She was in the service of the old owners. She has a great store of information.

ROMÉE. How could I get her to talk?

RIEMKE. That is easy.

[MRS. BEUNKE *comes in again with a silver tray containing the tea-service and cakes.*]

Mrs. Beunke, will you have tea with us?

MRS. BEUNKE. Thank you, Miss Riemke. Are you not going to wait for Mr. Nico?

RIEMKE. No, Miss Romée feels cold.

[MRS. BEUNKE *fills the teapot*]. Mrs. Beunke, we were just talking about the Van Asbecks who lived here before we came, and Miss Romée was asking whether they had any children. Do you know?

MRS. BEUNKE. No, Miss Romée, they died childless and it was a great pity, for the Van Asbeck family was one of the best in the province.

ROMÉE. Were you with them long?

MRS. BEUNKE. More than fifteen years, Miss Romée.

ROMÉE. Will you pour out the tea, please?

[MRS. BEUNKE *pours the tea and hands the sugar round.*]

ROMÉE [*helping herself*]. Thank you.

RIEMKE. Has the house changed much since their time?

MRS. BEUNKE. No, Miss Riemke; except the outbuildings and the terrace along the north wing that your father built.

ROMÉE. And the grounds?

MRS. BEUNKE. They have not changed, either. The trees have grown taller — that is all.

RIEMKE. And the reeds?

MRS. BEUNKE. The reeds, Miss Riemke?

RIEMKE. Were there as many then as there are now?

MRS. BEUNKE. Oh, no! Mrs. Van Asbeck had them cut down. She thought it looked more genteel.

[*The girls exchange glances.*]

RIEMKE. So the shore of the lake was quite clear then?

MRS. BEUNKE. Yes, Miss Riemke, quite clear.

RIEMKE. It must have been much more convenient for fishing, boating — I suppose they did have a boat.

MRS. BEUNKE. No; Mr. and Mrs. Van Asbeck did not boat or fish.

ROMÉE. Didn't they bathe in their lake either?

MRS. BEUNKE. No, Miss Romée.

RIEMKE. And didn't any one else bathe there?

MRS. BEUNKE. Yes, indeed, Miss Riemke — Mr. Henry — [*She pauses; then gets up from her chair.*] I think I hear the carriage coming.

RIEMKE. Stay where you are, Mrs. Beunke, I'll go. [*She hastens out, left.*]

ROMÉE. Mr. Henry, you were saying ——

MRS. BEUNKE. Yes, Mr. Van Asbeck's nephew. He was a powerful swimmer and he used to swim in the lake every day all through the summer.

ROMÉE. Oh?

MRS. BEUNKE. But Mrs. Van Asbeck did not quite approve of it, so when it came time for Mr. Henry's swim, she used to have her blinds pulled down.

ROMÉE. What for?

MRS. BEUNKE. Why, for the sake of modesty, Miss Romée.

ROMÉE [pretending to summon some recollection to mind]. Henry Van Asbeck — let me see — didn't I hear somewhere that he was drowned?

MRS. BEUNKE. Oh no, Miss Romée; he is still alive.

ROMÉE. Really?

MRS. BEUNKE. You must be thinking of the accident that happened to him.

ROMÉE. Here?

MRS. BEUNKE. Yes, in the lake.

ROMÉE. What was it?

MRS. BEUNKE. He was seized with cramp not far from the shore — fortunately they heard him call out.

ROMÉE. Was that very long ago?

MRS. BEUNKE. Oh, yes, more than thirty years. [Sound of voices outside.] Ah, here comes Mr. Nico!

[NICO comes rapidly into the room, left, followed by RIEMKE and SAIDYAH. He is a young man, twenty-five years of age, clean shaven and excessively pale, with unquiet eyes and the nervous, sudden gestures characteristic of lonely people in the momentary excitement of a departure or an arrival. SAIDYAH is a copper-skinned Javanese, past fifty. He is dressed in a European coat and a sarong, and wears a turban. He is carrying a voluminous bundle wrapped in a bright-coloured cloth.]

NICO [warmly grasping both ROMÉE's hands]. Why, here's our dear Romée!

ROMÉE [whose eyes, since the moment he entered, have been fixed in stunned incredulity upon his face]. Oh, how do you do?

SAIDYAH. [Greeting ROMÉE in Oriental fashion]. I greet you, Nonna Cremers. [She returns the salutation with a nod.] [He greets MRS. BEUNKE.] How are you,

Nonna Beunke? You have not changed, you know ——

MRS. BEUNKE [with friendliness]. Nor have you, Saidyah.

SAIDYAH. Ah yes, I have, Mother. Ten years ago I was still a hunter, beating the tiger out of the bush, but you were already quite old then, and wrinkled and little.

NICO [to ROMÉE]. It is good to see you again, Romée.

ROMÉE. It is good to see you too, Nico.

RIEMKE [to NICO]. Well, would you have known her again?

NICO. No, I don't believe I should.

RIEMKE [to ROMÉE]. Would you?

ROMÉE [throwing off her torpor]. Why, yes, of course I should, at once.

RIEMKE. Come, Mrs. Beunke, give him some tea, will you?

CURTAIN

SECOND SCENE

The drawing-room. A blazing fire of pine logs. It is eleven o'clock in the morning but the sky is so heavily overcast and the fog clings so persistently to the windows, that the room is in semi-darkness. ROMÉE has just arrived, and NICO is helping her off with her raincoat.

NICO. I call it really heroic of you to come out in weather like this.

ROMÉE. Why? I love fogs.

NICO [leading her to the fire]. Come over here and get dry.

ROMÉE. Isn't Riemke down yet?

NICO. Oh yes; she is leaving us alone on purpose.

ROMÉE [sitting down]. Do you think she is getting used to the idea of our leaving her?

NICO. She is resigning herself to it; I doubt whether she is still capable of suffering very keenly. She lives in dread of sorrow, you know, and protects herself against it in advance so that when it does come, it finds her heart already benumbed — anæsthetized, you might call it.

ROMÉE. All the same, I should feel happier if we could take her with us.

NICO. That is absolutely out of the question. She has never been able to stand the climate of the East Indies. The fever seized on her down there at once and for always, and although she used to play about and laugh and chatter like the other children, one knew that terrible fever-heat was inwardly consuming her all the while. It was as though a shaft of sun itself had struck right into her body and was drying it up little by little.

ROMÉE. She was a child then and the fever is very hard on one at that age; but now ——

NICO. No. You don't know what frail threads her life hangs upon — she will never be able to live out of this country. If she had to say good-bye to this stupor-stricken landscape and the fogs overhanging these waterways, it would simply kill her, Roméc. She draws her life from the very things that are death to me.

ROMÉE. What things are death to you, my dearest?

NICO. Oh, you know. These grey mists that go sweeping across the country week in and week out; the rain that's half fog and the fog that's already rain — I feel myself going to pieces under it.

ROMÉE [smiling]. How funny you are, you two — forever analysing the weather and blessing or railing at the sky. Why, I never look at it; I don't give it even a passing thought.

NICO. I know it's not very strong-minded or very intelligent to be so much at the mercy of a more or less generous supply of light, but what can one do if one's made that way! In our family we are all exceedingly sensitive to the influence of the weather.

ROMÉE. Do you know what I was thinking just now? Why shouldn't we be married here in the house instead of in Java as you have planned? It would mean so much to Riemke, dear, and I know she wouldn't mind so dreadfully then if we left her afterwards.

NICO [sharply]. No, no! Not here!

ROMÉE. Why not?

NICO. Because when a great happiness is coming to one, one should receive it in the midst of beauty. In this place happiness is faded before it comes, withered before it has had time to flower.

ROMÉE. Very well, you shall have it as you want it — don't let us say any more about it.

NICO. Do you feel warmer now?

ROMÉE. I wasn't cold before; you always think I'm cold.

NICO [taking up an album]. Look, I have found the photographs we were speaking of yesterday.

ROMÉE [eagerly]. Oh, do show them to me.

NICO [he lights the lamp]. Eleven o'clock in the morning and dark already.

[An intimate glow is shed over the room and outside the day looks bleaker by contrast. The two young people turn over the pages of the album.]

ROMÉE. What are all those strange-looking plants?

NICO. That is a corner of the forest behind my people's house. [Showing her other photographs.] Here is the harbor — and the river — and here's a rice-field — this is our house. The sea is quite near; you can see it from the verandah, blazing beyond you like a furnace of blue; they moor the little Malay boats by the stern and at low tide you see them rise and fall almost imperceptibly as though they were trying to breathe. [He turns a page.] The garden — the river — here's a rice-field.

ROMÉE. Oh!

NICO. Every afternoon the wind lifts dense purple clouds behind the banyans and the perfume of the flowers is so heavy and sweet that it seems to weigh down the air.

ROMÉE. It is a perfect paradise!

NICO. You often see the fronds of the tree-ferns spread out against golden mists, like delicate lace they look, and in the heart of a leaf a single ear lifts its slender stalk high above all the rest, like a soft, hairy snake. A human figure gleams through the bamboos — and infinite small creatures send up a tenuous music from the earth. When you have been there, you will realize how impossible it is ever to live anywhere else.

ROMÉE [*leaning close to his side*]. When I think that all this is to be *our* place, Nico, *our* home, I can hardly bear the time that lies between us and such happiness. But so long as you were with me, my dear, I should be content to live beside the dismallest canal in Holland — I would live *anywhere* with you.

NICO [*rising*]. No — not anywhere; don't say that. With a roof like this shut down upon you always, how can you possibly forget?

ROMÉE. Forget what?

NICO [*pacing the floor*]. What every one of us must learn to forget. Our destiny, our fate, the idea that although we might at a stretch believe ourselves free in space, we know we are the prisoners of time. In Java you do learn after a while to put all that out of your mind.

ROMÉE. It is never in mine.

NICO. You are too young. It is a thing that dawns on one suddenly when one gets to be about thirty. One day in Ceylon I was alone on a mountain-top. A rose-coloured haze lay upon the rocks and the sun was going down into a great abyss of light. Suddenly my ear caught a sound, an unaccountable sound; it seemed to come right out of the sun; it sounded very sweet and steady and rather loud, and in a few moments it had stopped. It didn't die away, but broke off clean, as though some task it had been given to fulfil was done and finished.

ROMÉE. What could it have been?

NICO. What was it actually? That I don't know, but to me it was a symbol of life.

ROMÉE. How do you mean?

NICO. A symbol of human life — an unaccountable harmony resounding for a few moments and ceasing at a given time, fixed in advance.

ROMÉE. Fixed in advance?

NICO. Yes — a chord of music doomed, in spite of its loveliness and purity, to be cut off at one stroke, without reason or warning. Ah, Romée, the instant that exquisite note was silent, I understood the whole ruthless, futile stupidity of the laws of life.

ROMÉE [*thoughtfully*]. Nico, is what you are saying possible, is it certain?

NICO. What?

ROMÉE. That the length of our lives can be measured out in advance, just like a reel of cotton or a roll of cloth?

NICO. Why not?

ROMÉE. It would be too horrible.

NICO. Yes, if people knew the number and order of the hours before them; fortunately though, they don't.

ROMÉE. They couldn't possibly know, could they?

NICO. Some people say they could.

ROMÉE. Who?

NICO. The initiates, for instance; in India — I have met some of them.

RIEMKE [*coming in hesitantly, right*]. Oh, Romée, you're here — good-morning.

ROMÉE. Hullo, dear.

RIEMKE. I am so sorry to disturb you both ——

ROMÉE. Why, Riemke, as though you could ——

RIEMKE. But the architect is here, Nico.

NICO. Good. I want to see him.

ROMÉE. Are you building?

NICO. No — only freshening this old place up a bit.

RIEMKE [*smiling*]. He thinks I will live less cheerlessly if he has the house done up.

NICO. That wall staring like a haggard face at you through the trees was beginning to get on my nerves. And the garden was growing into a positive wilderness. Didn't you notice the beeches as you came down, Romée?

ROMÉE. Yes, and it made me very sad, too. There were five or six men cutting them down.

NICO. But they threw the whole of the north wing into the shade, like an ever-lasting green twilight all the day long; you couldn't breathe in those rooms any more. You have to let the daylight in, you know. [*Going out.*] I'll be right back.

ROMÉE [*putting her arms around* RIEMKE]. Happiness is an awful thing, Riemke. For years you and I have never passed a single day without seeing each other and now in a few weeks' time there will be four thousand miles between us. And I'm not even sad about it — it doesn't make me cry — it doesn't hurt to think of.

RIEMKE. It doesn't make me cry either — no, it doesn't hurt much. Please don't let's talk about it.   [ROMÉE *kisses her.*]

MRS. BEUNKE [*coming in, left*]. Good-morning, Miss Romée.

ROMÉE. How are you, Mrs. Beunke?

RIEMKE. What is it, Mrs. Beunke?

MRS. BEUNKE. The men are asking for their coffee, Miss Riemke. Shall I give it to them?

RIEMKE. Have they finished their work?

MRS. BEUNKE. Yes, Miss Riemke, behind the house, and they have finished down by the lake, too.

RIEMKE. What have they been doing there?

MRS. BEUNKE. Mr. Nico gave orders to have all the reeds cut down.

[ROMÉE *gets up.*]

RIEMKE. Oh, I didn't know that. [*She goes to the bay-window and stands there while looking out — then turns round.*] Give them their coffee, Mrs. Beunke.

MRS. BEUNKE. Yes, Miss Riemke.

[*A reddish sunlight is trying timidly to force a way through the fog.* MRS. BEUNKE *switches off the light as she leaves the room.* ROMÉE *goes over to the window and stands there horror-stricken. At* RIEMKE'S *touch upon her shoulder she shudders.*]

ROMÉE [*whispering*]. I can't understand it — not one reed left, and that grey water right up to the edge — now the place looks exactly as I saw it three months ago.

RIEMKE. I think — wasn't there something else then, a boat?

ROMÉE. Yes — but that's of no importance — everything else — Riemke, where did Nico get the idea of cutting down the rushes?

RIEMKE. I don't know at all.

ROMÉE. Didn't he say anything about it to you?

RIEMKE. No, not a word.

ROMÉE. And you have never told him what happened to me down there?

RIEMKE. Never.

ROMÉE [*pointing to the lake*]. Then how do you explain that?

RIEMKE. Why, I don't know — coincidence I dare say. He is making a few alterations about the place. Those grasses had really grown rather thick; he must have noticed it and had them cut down. It seems a perfectly natural thing for him to have done.

ROMÉE. Yes, unless ——

RIEMKE. Unless what?

ROMÉE [*changing her mind*]. Nothing — just an idea and most likely a very foolish one at that. Leave me alone with him presently. I want to ask him some questions.

RIEMKE. Very well, but take my advice and don't tell him anything about your adventure.

ROMÉE. No, of course I won't.

RIEMKE. It would make a deep impression on him and he would worry over it; we mustn't let him do that; he is in very low spirits as it is.

ROMÉE. Yes, I had noticed that.

NICO [*entering, left*]. That fellow's not an architect; he's a bricklayer — he wants to build towers! He doesn't understand that all I want is for the house not to go on looking like a face.

RIEMKE. Did you make that clear to him?

NICO. Yes, and he suggested all sorts of nonsense, when all that's necessary is simply to take away one of the skylights and put in one more window on the first floor. They would break up the human symmetry of the wall as it is now.

RIEMKE. Would you like me to speak to him?

NICO. I wish you would, Riemke. [RIEMKE *goes out, right.* NICO *joins* ROMÉE *at the window.*] Do you see that? I've cleared up the edge of the lake — it looks nice, doesn't it?

[*A pause. They return to the hearth.*]

ROMÉE. Nico, you were saying before that you had met some initiates in India ——

NICO. Yes.

ROMÉE. Is it true they acquire a knowledge of their destiny?

NICO. I have seen an old priest in Madras who said that he could explore the past at will.

ROMÉE. And the future?

NICO. The future, too. He was a kind of religious philosopher you meet down there — we had several talks together. He had me come and see him on the terrace of his temple at sunset and there he would tell me about his voyages into Time, as we sat looking out over the Indian Ocean.

ROMÉE. How did he learn to penetrate into the past and future?

NICO. By exposing himself on the ground at night and giving himself up to the unknown powers. In that state of suspense, of almost death-like passivity, visions were born in him and he knew they belonged to the future or to the past.

ROMÉE. But what proofs did he have?

NICO. He could find out facts by which to prove the past happenings he witnessed during his experiments.

ROMÉE. And the future?

NICO. That is harder to control, of course. But he showed me a vision of war observed twenty years ago which materialized a little while ago down to the smallest details in an expedition to Afghanistan.

ROMÉE. Then according to him the future is already mapped out ahead?

NICO. He says the past, the present and the future are co-existent.

ROMÉE. It is incomprehensible.

NICO. Obviously; our notion of time prevents our conceiving it. But many other things inconceivable to us, *are*, nevertheless. "Man walks in Time as in a garden; behind him there goes one spreading a veil so that he may not behold the flowers of the past; before him goes one spreading a veil likewise, so that he may not yet behold the flowers of the future. All these flowers, however, bloom at once behind the two veils and the eyes of the initiate contemplate them continually."

ROMÉE. Didn't you ever ask him about yourself and your future?

NICO. I didn't want to — what is the use of worrying oneself needlessly?

ROMÉE. Do you think only the initiate can have these revelations?

NICO. No. There are old peasant women in Brittany who see funerals a year ahead. They can tell you all the people who will be there; women are always more sensitive than we to these emanations of the future.

ROMÉE. What a wonderful gift to have ——

NICO. Wonderful, yes, but barren ——

ROMÉE. How do you mean?

NICO. I don't see what good there can be in a gift like that.

ROMÉE. Why, if one were to discover, for instance, that some danger threatened a person, one could warn him against it.

NICO. And then?

ROMÉE. Couldn't the danger be averted?

NICO. No. Seers have never prevented anything. One may know the future, but one can't change it. Time is like a piece of machinery whose working we can neither hold back nor stop.

ROMÉE. Then supposing a woman foresaw a catastrophe hanging over the person she cared most for in the world — her child, say — she couldn't save it?

NICO. Impossible.

ROMÉE. Then what could she do?

NICO. Nothing. Suffer in silence until the accomplishment of the event.

ROMÉE. That is more than flesh and blood could stand. She would go mad.

NICO [*taking her hand.*] Why, Romée, what is the matter? Your hands are all moist and trembling.

ROMÉE. It is the thought that one couldn't do anything — even if one knew — it is awful to think of.

NICO. What an impressionable girl you are — don't let that worry you — we hardly ever do know what we dread to know ——

ROMÉE. No, fortunately.

[RIEMKE *enters, rear.*]

NICO. Well, did you make him understand?

RIEMKE. I hope so — he is going to submit you another plan.

NICO. Without towers?

RIEMKE. Yes, he promised that.

NICO. Well, that's something, anyway.

RIEMKE. Mrs. Beunke just told me we could go in to dinner.

NICO [going towards the door, rear]. All right. [ROMÉE signs to RIEMKE that she wants to speak to her. NICO turns round.] Aren't you coming?

RIEMKE. In one moment, Nico.

[NICO goes out.

ROMÉE [whispering]. I understand it now ——

RIEMKE [in the same tone]. What?

ROMÉE. The thing that happened to me down by the lake — and the reeds — and everything.

RIEMKE. Well?

ROMÉE. First I want to tell you one thing I have kept from you up to now for fear of the shock it might give you; but today you have got to know. Riemke, the face that appeared to me on the water that day was Nico's face!

RIEMKE [in horror]. Nico's?

ROMÉE. When he came into the room half an hour afterwards, I recognized him at once.

RIEMKE. It is absurd, Romée — it is impossible.

ROMÉE. It is true. And now I am certain that my vision had nothing to do with the past — but with the future.

RIEMKE. What do you say?

ROMÉE. I say that little by little this landscape is changing, Riemke, and it is not going back to what it was before our time but towards what it is going to be like one day. [A pause.]

NICO'S VOICE. Aren't you girls coming in to dinner?

RIEMKE [answering]. Yes, yes, we're coming.

[They exchange a look of understanding and go out.]

CURTAIN

THIRD SCENE

The drawing-room. A radiant summer afternoon: MRS. BEUNKE *is asleep in a chair, her account-book in her lap.*

[NICO *and* ROMÉE *enter arm in arm.*]

ROMÉE [laughing]. Oh, look, Mrs. Beunke has fallen asleep.

NICO. Yes, she often does that nowadays.

ROMÉE. She is getting old.

NICO. It isn't age.

ROMÉE. Is she ill?

NICO. Not more so than usual. Living is what ails her. She only weighs about eighty pounds and yet she finds it exceedingly difficult to move her tiny person. She worries horribly over getting tea, and settling her accounts, and eliminating dust. The weight of these immense responsibilities is too much for her. She tries to escape them by going to church because she falls asleep as soon as she gets settled in her pew. She cries, too, now and then. Life is too heavy for her.

[MRS. BEUNKE *wakes up.*]

NICO. Hullo, Mrs. Beunke.

MRS. BEUNKE [uneasily]. Oh, Mr. Nico!

NICO. Still tired?

MRS. BEUNKE [agitated]. I wasn't asleep, Mr. Nico — I — I was reckoning up my accounts in my head.

NICO [indulgently]. All right, all right — don't worry — go on resting. [MRS. BEUNKE *goes out, right.*] Haven't you noticed that lots of people here can't stand the weight of life?

ROMÉE. Not only here.

NICO. But here especially.

ROMÉE. What is the reason, do you think?

NICO. I don't know, the sky perhaps — perhaps the water.

ROMÉE [watching him]. The water?

NICO [sitting down]. The water is dead here — one grows like it, stagnant and choked with weeds. Look at our neighbours; they are no more alive than their houses. They are all so dejected and apathetic — like blighted trees or fungus-eaten walls or canals of stagnant water.

This country is really a torment to me.

Romée [*tenderly*]. We'll be leaving it very soon now, dear.

Nico. I sometimes wonder whether it isn't too late?

Romée. Too late for what?

Nico. To escape.

Romée. How should it be too late?

Nico. I am not well, Romée; I am certainly not as well as I was when I came. That's not quite right what I said about the water just now. It isn't so much its inanition that spreads to us as the corrosion of its innumerable weeds. You know what I mean, don't you, those lichens and mosses that fasten on to the surface of the water until they cover it entirely from one bank clear across to the other? I feel like that — grown over and eaten up, suffocated under just such an evil growth of trouble and doubts in my mind.

Romée. But what trouble, my dearest, what doubts?

Nico. Oh, you wouldn't understand if I told you. You'd only laugh at me. Besides I feel myself that all this is unspeakably petty and morbid. But it's a thing of long standing — it nearly killed me when I was fifteen. Afterwards, though, down in Java, it left me again, but now it is all coming back just as it was before. There are days when it takes me by the throat and strangles the life out of me.

Romée. Why did you never speak of it before?

Nico. Because there's nothing to be done for it — I know that perfectly well.

Romée. But what is it about?

Nico. Just scepticism, that's all, doubt of everything — of life, of things, of myself. When I was a child I thought my existence was an illusion — my sensations didn't seem to give me sufficient proof that I was really in life. A little later, when I took up astronomy, I noticed that the calculations cf scholars concerning the course of the stars were not accurate; mere approximations at best. There was always some error, some uncertainty. So then I began to doubt the existence of the stars themselves. I wondered if they were not merely a kind of stage-setting, you know, an optical illusion, and absolutely unrelated to anything we human beings fancy we know about their distance or their substance or their dimensions. I told that notion of mine to one very learned man and he told me he understood it and didn't think it absurd. That was the year I tried to kill myself.

Romée [*startled*]. You tried to kill yourself?

Nico. Oh, not out of despair — curiosity rather, to set my mind finally at peace.

Romée. And you really tried to ——

Nico. Yes ——

Romée. When?

Nico. Just ten years ago.

Romée. Where?

Nico. Here.

Romée. Oh!

Nico. Nobody knew.

Romée. But some one must have saved you, or did you manage to get back to the bank by yourself?

Nico [*in astonishment*]. What bank?

Romée. Wasn't it down in the lake?

Nico. No. I hanged myself in the loft, near the middle skylight; the nail is there still. But the rope didn't hold more than a few seconds; it broke and I fainted on the floor. I never tried again. [*A pause.*]

Romée. Why did you keep it a secret from Riemke?

Nico. Because they would have had me watched; they might have even shut me up. Besides, we left for Java again that time and that's a country where your mind soon finds peace. You don't suffer from the unknowable down there as you do in this place — you accept life — here you repudiate it. You insist on understanding. [*Bitterly.*] What's the use of understanding? Believing is what we need. We must have faith and a catch-word to pin it on; fate, freedom, soul, matter, and suchlike — they mean nothing, yet we choose one and keep hold of it. It's the price we pay for peace. My trouble is that I cannot and will not be the dupe of these things.

Romée [*putting her arms round him.*] I have learnt something, Nico darling. These mental torments we brood over can

only fill the heart to which love has not yet
come; at its coming they all vanish away;
all of them, even pity, even justice which
used to make me suffer terribly at one time.
Now I am indifferent to everything that
isn't you. You say you love me — do you
love me enough?

NICO. My love for you is a torture,
Romée.

ROMÉE. What do you mean — a torture?

NICO [*in a low voice, trying to find the
right words*]. Because this bond between
us — this power of your nearness over me
— what is it? If it were merely desire —
everything would be simple and reasonable — but it is with love that the problem
begins. That's where the riddle is —
there is no answer to it. I believed your
beauty held the answer — but it does not.
I thought a man might crush his thoughts
to death upon your heart — but no — for
it is in your arms that I feel most helpless
against the bitter and mysterious tide that
rises up and overwhelms me. In your
arms words and silence are alike poison —
poison — what can it be?

ROMÉE [*laying her hand on his forehead*].
Stop looking for the solution, dear — don't
be afraid of things; don't think about them
any more.

NICO. I can't help it.

ROMÉE. Then if you can't, tell all your
thoughts to me, every one of them, even
the bitterest and the most morbid. That
will be a relief to you. What are you thinking of now?

NICO. We love each other — and yet ——

ROMÉE. And yet ——

NICO. We — there's no such thing as we
— there's you — and I — and I am alone.

CURTAIN

FOURTH SCENE

*The drawing-room. Eleven o'clock at
night. The room is in darkness except for the
moonlight shining through the open bay-
windows, beside which* RIEMKE *is sitting.*

ROMÉE *comes in, rear. She is wearing her*
hat and cloak. RIEMKE *makes a slight
movement.*]

ROMÉE. Oh! Who's there?

RIEMKE. I. Don't be frightened.

ROMÉE. I've been looking for you in
your room. What are you doing here?

RIEMKE. Nothing. Is it late?

ROMÉE. Past eleven. I was just going
home. Aren't you cold by that window?

RIEMKE. No. It is rather warm this
evening.

ROMÉE [*looking at her*]. What are you
unhappy about, Riemke?

RIEMKE. Am I?

ROMÉE. You have been crying.

RIEMKE. No, I don't think I have —
where is Nico?

ROMÉE. In the library.

RIEMKE. Hasn't he told you his plan?

ROMÉE. Which one?

RIEMKE. To postpone your going — he
wants to stay a whole month longer.

ROMÉE. Yes, he told me about that — I
think it's all settled.

RIEMKE. Why? What does he want to
do it for?

ROMÉE. He says he feels better and is
quite acclimatized now, but as a matter of
fact, I believe it is on your account that he
is staying on.

RIEMKE [*dully*]. Then he is going to do
no such thing.

ROMÉE. Why not? Don't you think he
is much calmer and more cheerful than he
was last month?

RIEMKE. He imagines he is better than
he is. So do you. If he spends the
autumn here, everything will happen to
him again just as it did before. In the long
run, you know, that green canker on the
water and the trees and the walls in this
place reaches the brain as well. How do we
live in this house after all? We drink tea,
and dream and read, and philosophize —
that's all — we don't *do* anything. Perhaps something has cut us off from life.

ROMÉE. Perhaps it has. And perhaps
it is because I feel so ardently alive myself
that you are both so dear to me. I love
that weakness in you, and your passion-
sheltered heart. And as for Nico, his

greatest charm for me is not so much his intelligence or his kindness as his unusefulness, his aloofness from things. He has no kind of ambition, he doesn't believe he is of any importance whatever. The other day, at that tea-party at the Verloren's, there were about twenty men and women talking about all sorts of things. Nico just sat there, looking sidelong at them with his eyes half-closed, not saying a word, and to me he seemed the only real one, the only wise one, the only fine one of them all.

RIEMKE. Yes; there is something fine in silence — and in the desire for death, too.

ROMÉE. What do you mean, the desire for death?

RIEMKE. Romée, there are certain words I am afraid of. I am afraid to apply them to the people I care for because they seem to classify them, don't you know, and take all their glamour away. Still one has to say them sometimes. Nico is not sane, Romée.

ROMÉE. Of course he isn't; who is? Scepticism can be a form of insanity — faith is probably one also. There are some people who are insane with certainties. I know some.

RIEMKE. Are you sure that scepticism is his trouble; all of it?

ROMÉE. What do you mean?

RIEMKE. I sometimes wonder whether he is not becoming the victim of a monomania.

ROMÉE. What monomania? What is worrying you, Riemke?

RIEMKE. Does nothing ever worry you, Romée — any more? [A pause.]

ROMÉE. No, not any more.

RIEMKE. So it seems. Time goes on and nothing happens — so what once seemed full of omen and menace to you has become irrelevant and meaningless now.

ROMÉE. It isn't time that has delivered me from worry, my dear; it is love.

RIEMKE. I don't understand. If danger existed six months ago, it must exist still. Our feelings cannot affect the thing we call our destiny.

ROMÉE. Yes, they can; love can break the spell. I sometimes have a strange feeling that in the halls of the future where our destinies are being built up, there has been a fall somewhere, some kind of displacement has altered the plan of our lives as they were to have been —— [Vehemently.] I have so longed that he might live! I have so pursued happiness with all my thoughts! It can't have been useless, Riemke. If our passions and our dreams were powerless to create new futures, life would be nothing but a senseless, stupid fraud. They might just as well shut us up in a cage studded with spikes, and say to us "Dance! Go on, you are free to dance to your heart's content." Life isn't like that!

RIEMKE. You hope, because you have a wholesome mind. I, ruminating vague thoughts continually in my corner, have less confidence. In the first place I don't believe any more in the catch-words we live by; destiny, fate, and so on — they have no meaning to me any more. So that, in this thing that is worrying us ——
[She stops.]

ROMÉE. Well?

RIEMKE [reluctantly]. I don't want to upset you or make you feel undue responsibility for anything — but I can't help thinking all the same that you hold the key to this mystery, Romée, nobody else.

ROMÉE. I?

RIEMKE [bethinking herself]. No, never mind. I have no right to alarm you. I have not proof enough to go by.

ROMÉE. Tell me, Riemke; tell me outright what is in your mind — I shall be far more worried if you don't. What is this idea of yours? What are you thinking?

RIEMKE. This: I think that at the time you saw that face in the lake, no danger did threaten Nico. It was neither a revelation of the past nor of the future; it was only a hallucination. But since — I wonder if that momentary delirium of your brain is not gradually being transformed into reality.

ROMÉE [thoughtfully]. Is it possible for a thought — a vision — to turn into a reality?

RIEMKE. Occasionally, I dare say — thought is a contagious thing. What you dreamt first, Nico may have dreamt in his turn.

ROMÉE. How?

RIEMKE. You might have unknowingly transmitted your vision to him. And now — it is possible, yes, it is possible that real danger exists for him.

ROMÉE [troubled]. You haven't thought out this explanation without a motive, Riemke. You are keeping something back — you *know* he is in danger.

RIEMKE. No, no! It is only a supposition. I have been thinking it over, that is all. Don't let it worry you, dear.

ROMÉE [taking her hands]. You know, you can't tell lies a bit. Is it so serious that you don't dare to tell me? Look here, Riemke, what is happening?

RIEMKE [fearfully]. It's probably quite natural — I'm sure it could be explained away — it is a letter from him that I found this evening in the hall. I opened it — on account of the address.

ROMÉE. Whom is it addressed to?

RIEMKE. Gelder, the boat-builder — look, I have it here.

[She holds out the letter.]

ROMÉE [lights the lamp and reads in a tremulous voice]. "Of all the models you have shown me, the green boat suits my purpose best. Please send it to me for a week's trial." The green boat — oh God!

RIEMKE. There, you are all upset. But there is really nothing to fear, as we are forewarned. We must circumvent this misfortune, mustn't we? We will defend ourselves.

ROMÉE. Against whom? Against what? And by what means?

RIEMKE. By getting Nico away from this place. Once he is gone, we'll be laughing at all this alarm.

ROMÉE. How can we get him away?

RIEMKE. I have thought of a scheme. You know my friend the Van Volson girl is getting married. She lives just outside Rotterdam. I had refused her invitation but nothing would be easier than to ——

ROMÉE [interrupting her sharply with terror in her voice]. Riemke ——

RIEMKE. What is it?

ROMÉE. Riemke, I have committed a terrible folly — a few days ago he was telling me about that illness he had — he said that once long ago he wanted to kill himself.

RIEMKE. I never knew ——

ROMÉE. Nobody did — but he tried.

RIEMKE. Did he throw himself into the lake?

ROMÉE. That was my first thought, too — oh, why didn't I hide it from him? Why didn't I keep quiet? But I was so upset to think of his doing such a thing and so relieved that the explanation of my dream had come at last, that I spoke to him about the lake — I asked him how they had rescued him from the water ——

RIEMKE. Well?

ROMÉE. He looked at me in surprise — he hadn't thrown himself into the water at all. He had hanged himself in the loft! [She sobs.] You were right — it is I who have put the idea into his mind — it is I who have sent him to his death.

CURTAIN

FIFTH SCENE

The drawing-room. It is Autumn — the sun is setting in a golden sky. SAIDYAH *is sitting cross-legged in the centre of the room absorbed in idle reverie.*

[NICO *enters, rear.*]

NICO. What are you doing there, Saidyah? You look as immovable as one of our old beeches. What are you thinking about?

SAIDYAH. Nothing, Toewan, nothing.

NICO. No doubt. What could you be thinking about, after all? Perhaps those who imagine they are thinking of something are also really thinking of nothing at all. For who knows whether there is anything to think about? [SAIDYAH *pulls a pipe from his girdle and asks with a gesture for permission to light it.*] Yes, yes, light up. [SAIDYAH *does so.*] Isn't this room cold for you?

SAIDYAH. No, Toewan.

NICO. We shan't be here much longer, Saidyah. Before winter we'll have left this country. Aren't you glad to be going back to Java?

SAIDYAH. If the master is glad, I am glad. But what is the use of changing one's place?

NICO. Yes, what *is* the use? Besides, is it possible ever to change one's place, really? [*He sits down.*] I like talking to you, Saidyah. You understand me better than any one else.

SAIDYAH. I should love the master very little if I did not understand him.

NICO. My sister loves me, too, so does my fiancée. And yet, for some time past I haven't been able to talk to them. Saidyah, do you know what space is?

SAIDYAH. It is the little road the ant travels between two blades of grass: it is the great empty road my eye travels on its way to the stars.

NICO. And time, do you know what that is?

SAIDYAH. It is a road also.

NICO. Saidyah, there is no such thing as either space or time.

SAIDYAH. If the master says so it must be true.

NICO. I knew you would understand me.

SAIDYAH. The sun is going down all ready, Toewan, and I begin to smell the marshes. Hadn't I better close the windows? [NICO *does not answer. A pause.*]

NICO [*beside the bay-window*]. Look at those summer flies over the lake. They fly round and round in the yellow light as though they were drunk or mad. They remind me of old men clinging to the sunshine. Four hours ago they were not yet in their prime; since then they have felt thirty or forty years of human life pass over them. This evening — that is to say, in ten years' time — they will die under the bushes. Time is a dream, Saidyah.

SAIDYAH [*shaking his head*]. Surely something has passed on, though, since the days when the master was a child and the babu used to bathe his little body in a copper basin on the verandah every morning.

NICO [*stretching out on a couch, beside Saidyah*]. No — it is our minds that have moved across an unmoving dream. Yesterday, to-day, to-morrow are only words,

Saidyah, words which correspond to no reality except within our narrow brains, for beyond our brains there is neither past nor future, nothing but one vast present. Within eternity, we are at once about to be, living and dead. Do you fear death, Saidyah?

SAIDYAH. Yes, Toewan, so long as you still live.

NICO. I don't — it doesn't matter to me one way or the other. I don't even know whether —— [*He stops.*] To die is not to sleep, nor to dream — living is that — trees, earth, fogs and all the rest — they are the inexplicable dream. To die is to awaken, to know, maybe to reach that point in eternity where time is no longer a dream, the frontier where all things are co-existent.

SAIDYAH. Is the master unhappy? Who has been troubling him?

NICO. No one, Saidyah, no one.

SAIDYAH. Sometimes, when he was a child, the master's little heart used to grow sad and then he would sit gazing into space as though he was falling asleep. But I had only to show him the round patches of sunlight on the mats or the golden clouds over the palm forests and he would be quite gay again at once.

NICO. I don't believe in the clouds any more, Saidyah. I don't believe in the sunlight either. They don't exist; or if something does exist which corresponds to what we call clouds and sunlight, we can't know what it is. We never will know anything we see with our eyes or hear with our ears or pass through the filter of our minds. Ah, Saidyah, it isn't the dreaming that matters, it's knowing one's dreaming that is fearful. Walking, and knowing there is no solid earth under your feet; stretching out your arms and knowing they never can reach anything at all — for all things are phantoms and the shadows of phantoms. Say, if there were such a thing as a road to certainty, to reality, wouldn't you set out upon it rejoicing?

SAIDYAH [*shaking his head*]. The master is unhappy and he will not tell me why. And I do not know how to cheer him. I there nobody who can bring him peace

Is there nothing left on earth that he can love?

NICO [*thinking*]. I love the water. [*A pause — in a tone of mystery.*] You mustn't mention this to any one, Saidyah — they wouldn't understand. They would try and part me from the water that I love — who knows what pretexts they might invent?

SAIDYAH. The master can trust me.

NICO. In the beginning I disliked the water — I thought it swampy and too still, horrible. But I have looked at it a great deal since; I've spent hours leaning over it, watching it — and now I have grown to love it. It lies in dark pools at the foot of the old walls, like staring eyes filled with the knowledge of truth. As for the water of the big lake — I don't know why, but it reminds me of Romée. It is like Romée — full of passions and angers held in leash — sometimes it quivers suddenly here and there without apparent reason — well, when Romée is startled or thwarted in anything and tries to hide her anger, one of her cheeks gives a slight quiver just like the water. [*A pause.*] That lake looks clear, Saidyah, but it isn't. Beneath the surface where it is bright with the reflection of the sky, there lies a whole dark and impenetrable world. [*Whispering.*] When you look into Romée's eyes it is the same. Their clearness is only on the surface — below there are the same shadows, the same cold mystery. It is a very strange resemblance. I spoke of it to her one day but she didn't understand. For a long time I believed that she alone could give me peace of mind, and a hold on things — now I wonder if this truth I seek is not at the bottom of the water — right down underneath the marsh.

SAIDYAH [*in a low voice*]. If truth is where you say it is, Toewan, long live illusion!

CURTAIN

SIXTH SCENE

The drawing-room. Four o'clock in the afternoon. MRS. BEUNKE *sits dreaming by the fire.* RIEMKE *enters, right. She is in a traveling cloak and carries a grip in her hand. She is fastening the last button of her glove.*

RIEMKE. Have you ordered the carriage, Mrs. Beunke?

MRS. BEUNKE. Yes, Miss Riemke. Jan is harnessing the horses.

RIEMKE. Isn't Mr. Nico ready yet?

MRS. BEUNKE. He has gone up to his room, Miss Riemke.

RIEMKE. Are you sure?

MRS. BEUNKE [*surprised*]. Why yes, Miss Riemke. He is packing his bag.

RIEMKE [*looking at her watch*]. I was thinking of the train — we haven't much more time.

MRS. BEUNKE. What day shall I expect you back, Miss Riemke?

RIEMKE [*turning her head away*]. Sunday, Mrs. Beunke, Sunday for certain; we'll be home in time for dinner.

MRS. BEUNKE [*bringing out her account-book*]. I will have everything ready for you. Won't you please just look over my accounts before you go, Miss Riemke?

RIEMKE. No, there's no time and besides I feel so dreadfully tired, Mrs. Beunke.

MRS. BEUNKE [*sighing*]. This makes more than a week since you have seen them — it is a great responsibility on my shoulders.

[ROMÉE *comes in.*]

RIEMKE [*not paying any attention to what Mrs. Beunke is saying*]. Mrs. Beunke, will you please go up stairs to Mr. Nico's room — I am too tired.

MRS. BEUNKE. Yes, Miss Riemke — but what for?

RIEMKE. Why, to hurry him up — tell him we are waiting.

MRS. BEUNKE. Very well, Miss Riemke.
[*She goes out.*]

RIEMKE [*in a low voice*]. Now remember what you have to do — Nico and I will be at the Van Velsen's this evening; the wedding is to-morrow morning. You are to stay here and send your wire the day after to-morrow evening, not before, and you leave for Rotterdam on Sunday.

Romée. I understand. Are you going to tell Ida Van Velsen?

Riemke. No. Our visit doesn't need any more explanation than I gave her. She asked me to her wedding and I said my brother's being here prevented me from getting away, then it turns out that Nico wants to go with me after all, so I change my mind and we go. That is the explanation I gave her in my letter; it will do.

Romée. Tell me — that telegram — if I make it too urgent and desperate, it will give Nico a bad shock, and on the other hand, if I make it too indefinite and reassuring he might not be in any hurry to leave and want to come back here first and take the next boat instead.

Riemke. Yes, the idea of leaving at once must come from you. You must say something like this — "Have received cable Java — parents anxious — father very ill — not critical but wants Nico back as soon as possible." And then add: "I advise going immediately. S.S. *Samarang* leaves Rotterdam Monday. Meet you there with Saidyah and luggage."

Romée. Nothing about money?

Riemke. No — He has a letter of credit on a Rotterdam bank.

Romée. And if he insists on coming back here?

Riemke. I will dissuade him.

Romée. Sh! Here he is.

Nico [*enters right, a suitcase in his hand*]. Is this necessary? Really necessary?

Riemke. What?

Nico. This visit?

Riemke. Why of course it is, Nico — they are expecting us and you promised——

Nico. You made me promise, you mean. The whole thing strikes me suddenly as so ridiculous, going to stay with people I haven't seen for fifteen years. I suppose one has to talk to their guests?

Riemke. And what if one does?

Nico. But I have nothing to say to them — or to any one else.

Romée. Any one else?

Nico [*looks at her, then drops his eyes*]. It seems to me now that every word I utter puts me farther and farther away from people — even from those I care for.

Riemke [*sadly*]. Nico!

Nico. I can't help it.

Mrs. Beunke [*coming in*]. The carriage is waiting.

Riemke. Let's hurry or we'll miss the train. [*Kisses* Romée.] Till Sunday, darling. [*Exit left.*]

Romée [*in a low voice, to* Nico]. Don't be unhappy, dear. Don't think of me if the thought weighs on you — let yourself live. Nobody wants to thwart you in any way — you are perfectly free.

[Mrs. Beunke *has taken* Riemke's *bag and gone out, left.*]

Nico. Oh! — perhaps it is better to be the slave of living people than of one's thoughts. [*With childish fretfulness.*] But why can't they leave me in peace? Why do they have to drag me to people's houses — when I want to be alone and lie down on the ground and go to sleep?

Romée [*emphatically*]. You need distraction, Nico. This visit will do you good. It will indeed.

Nico. You see, none of them can let me alone, not even you.

Riemke's Voice. Are you coming, Nico? We are going to miss that train.

[Nico *makes a movement of annoyance; then kisses* Romée.]

Nico. Au revoir.

Romée. I'll see you soon again, darling.

[Nico *goes out.* Romée *goes to the window and watches the carriage drive away. She waves her hand.* Mrs. Beunke *come in.*]

Mrs. Beunke. Won't you have supper with me, Miss Romée?

Romée. No thanks, Mrs. Beunke. Make the most of these few days to rest in — you look awfully tired.

Mrs. Beunke [*agitated*]. Oh, I am always that and shall be till the end of my days, I am sure. Tiredness is nothing — what kills me is all the cares and worries that I have, Miss Romée.

Romée [*incredulous.*] Whatever can you have to worry you to that extent?

Mrs. Beunke. These accounts, Miss Romée. Generally Miss Riemke goes over them for me every day — it is a great relief. But all this week she has been thinking o.

something else and hasn't had time to even look at them. There is a mistake of four florins — I dare not tell her. I have gone through my additions over and over again and I can't find the mistake — I can't sleep for worrying over it, Miss Romée.

ROMÉE. Why, all you have to do is to put in the four florins out of your own pocket, I should think.

MRS. BEUNKE [in despair]. That will not take the mistake away — the four florins don't matter; it is the mistake that is terrible. [Taking out her book.] Won't you please look at my figures, Miss Romée? Maybe you will find the mistake at once — who knows?

ROMÉE [almost harshly]. No, Mrs. Beunke. I don't like the idea of fretting one's life away over such nonsense.

MRS. BEUNKE. I beg your pardon, Miss Romée. [The telephone rings; MRS. BEUNKE answers it.] Hello — Mr. Van Eyden has just left — who is speaking please? What do you say? No, Mr. Van Eyden will not be back before Sunday.

ROMÉE. Who is it?

MRS. BEUNKE. Mr. Gelder, the boat-builder.

ROMÉE. Oh, I know about that — let me talk to him. [She takes the receiver.] Hello — what is it, Mr. Gelder? A letter? About that boat? Very likely — he didn't mention it. Very well, I will apologize to him for you. What? — What do you say? No, no — it's no use, as he is away. Wait — wait a few days. Besides, I think he changed his mind. What? Oh, already? All right, you must — perhaps you could — No, of course not — never mind, it can't be helped now. Good-bye. [She hangs up.] It seems they have just brought a boat from Gelder's. Did you see it come?

MRS. BEUNKE. No, Miss Romée. The gardener must have received it. [Anxiously.] Was it to be paid for?

ROMÉE. I don't know.

MRS. BEUNKE. Miss Riemke hasn't left me any money.

ROMÉE [at window, to herself]. That was — yes, that was it.

MRS. BEUNKE. I shall not pay for anything until Miss Riemke comes home.

SAIDYAH [entering right]. Is it true, Nonna, that he has gone without saying good-bye to me?

ROMÉE. He will be back in two days, Saidyah.

SAIDYAH. He has gone because he is not happy here.

ROMÉE [turning round]. How do you know?

SAIDYAH. He tells me everything. He suffers because he seeks the way.

ROMÉE. What way?

SAIDYAH. The way of Truth. I know what it is — I have seen men in the Indies who were like him. Woman, sister, children, no living person pleases their hearts. So they go — with a disciple or a boy to beg their rice — and they become wanderers upon the earth. They visit the towns and the beggars and the holy places; for years they wander on and on. One day they meet the Buddha on a mountain or at a crossroads and they are happy. But there are some who do not meet the Buddha, and they let themselves starve to death in the depths of some jungle. [A pause, shakes his head.] I do not believe our child will ever meet the Buddha. I knew he would go some day, but I hoped he would take me with him. I would have followed him everywhere and left him alone before the end, for it does happen that the Buddha manifests himself at the last minute of the last hour. Our child did not want me. I shall never see him again.

ROMÉE. But, Saidyah, haven't I told you he will be home on Sunday?

SAIDYAH. I have had news, Nonna.

ROMÉE. What news?

SAIDYAH. News from the wind, Nonna.

MRS. BEUNKE. Leave us alone, Saidyah. you see you are worrying Miss Romée.

SAIDYAH [going out]. Yes, yes, I am going.

ROMÉE. Poor Saidyah. Riemke says he would give his life for Nico.

MRS. BEUNKE. That is no reason why one should put up with him in the drawing-room. He would come and smoke his pipe here every day if one let him. Miss Riemke does spoil him so.

ROMÉE [*sharply*]. What is the time by your watch, Mrs. Beunke?

MRS. BEUNKE [*looking at her watch*]. Five o'clock, Miss Romée.

ROMÉE. Isn't that when the train goes?

MRS. BEUNKE. Yes.

ROMÉE [*sighing with relief*]. They must be in their compartment now — do you think they are in their compartment, Mrs. Beunke?

MRS. BEUNKE. Yes, most likely, unless the train is late coming in.

ROMÉE [*putting on her hat*]. That's good. It's a fine day, Mrs. Beunke.

MRS. BEUNKE. A little misty these last few minutes.

ROMÉE [*looking out of window*]. Why, so it is.

MRS. BEUNKE. That kind doesn't last long though, it is only a sea-flame.

[ROMÉE *is silent, motionless beside the window. The phone rings.*]

ROMÉE. Again ——

MRS. BEUNKE [*at the telephone*]. Hello — yes, this is Mrs. Beunke. What? I don't understand. Please say that again? Who is talking, please? What — What is the matter? Don't shout so loud.

ROMÉE. What is it?

MRS. BEUNKE. I can't make out, Miss Romée. I don't even know who is talking.

ROMÉE. Wait. [*She takes the receiver.*] Hello. This is Miss Cremers. Who are you? [*Astonished.*] Jan the coachman? Why aren't they gone? Whatever is the matter with her? [*To* MRS. BEUNKE.] Riemke is ill ——

MRS. BEUNKE. Oh, dear; oh, dear!

ROMÉE [*at the phone*]. When did it happen? [*To* MRS. BEUNKE.] She was taken ill at the station. [*At the phone.*] Who is the doctor? Very well — listen — tell him I am coming right over and ask him if he needs anything.

MRS. BEUNKE. Is it serious?

ROMÉE. No, just a fainting spell, I hope. Dr. Krall happened to be at the station. He carried her into a waiting-room and is with her now.

MRS. BEUNKE. She hasn't been well for

days. She cannot stand any excitement — going away and having luggage to see to is too much for her.

ROMÉE [*at the telephone*]. Hello — all right. [*To* MRS. BEUNKE.] Mrs. Beunke will you please get a little ether from the medicine-chest? [MRS. BEUNKE *hurries out.* ROMÉE *at the phone.*] Hello — are you sure that is all he wanted? Good. Is Miss Riemke better? Still unconscious? Yes, all right, I am coming. I'll run through the park; it will take about five minutes.

[*She hangs up.* MRS. BEUNKE *comes back with a vial of ether.*]

MRS. BEUNKE. Do you want me to go with you, Miss Romée?

ROMÉE. No. You had better get her bed ready — they may bring her back any minute.

[*She goes quickly out left.* MRS. BEUNKE *goes out right. The stage remains empty a long moment, then* NICO *comes left. He lies down and falls into a deep meditation.*]

MRS. BEUNKE [*comes in right her account-book in her hand. She gives a start when she sees* NICO]. You, Mr. Nico?

NICO [*not moving.*] Yes, she doesn't need any one. The doctor is there.

MRS. BEUNKE. Didn't you meet Miss Romée?

NICO. No.

MRS. BEUNKE. She left right after Jan called up. She went through the park.

NICO. I came back by the road.

MRS. BEUNKE. Aren't you anxious, Mr. Nico?

NICO. About Riemke? Yes, she will wake too soon. One always wakes too soon. [*Raising his eyes to her face.*] Why are you looking at me as though I were some queer sort of animal? What is that book in your hand?

MRS. BEUNKE. My accounts, Mr. Nico, I have made a mistake. So I was just ——

NICO. Show me. [*She shows him the book and the page. He corrects one addition, first to himself, then aloud in a low voice.*] Seven and three make nine.

MRS. BEUNKE. Ten, Mr. Nico, ten.

NICO. Why not nine or twelve?

Mrs. Beunke [*dismayed*]. Seven and three make ten.

Nico. Prove it.

Mrs. Beunke. But ——

Nico. You can't. You couldn't ever prove that two and two make four. Numbers don't exist. They are a convention of thought. Your accounts are not real, they are nothing but signs of things eaten, drunk and distributed and destroyed. Your accounts will always be wrong, Mrs. Beunke. [*He throws the book on the floor.*]

Mrs. Beunke [*worried*]. What is the matter with you, Mr. Nico?

Nico. I am sleepy. But sleep is so short, so short. Tell me, Mrs. Beunke, if a doctor told you that he knew of a way to clear out your little skull and replace its present contents with hay or lettuce leaves, wouldn't you beg him to perform that admirable operation on you?

Mrs. Beunke. I am sure it is a sin to listen to such things, Mr. Nico.

Nico. But wouldn't you? No? You must be anxious to keep your 995 grams of brain then? I'm not. [*He gets up.*] Just think — good-bye worries, good-bye accounts and dust and housekeeping — everything would disappear, walls, trees, earth, stars, time, thought — everything ... and yourself of course!

Mrs. Beunke. Oh, dear! I have never seen you like this....

Nico [*indistinctly*]. Nor have I. Because to-day I know you don't exist where I see you. [*Puts his hand to his forehead.*] Here's where you are. Only here. [*She steps back, afraid.*] As for this phantom which seems to talk and move about in front of me — I know nothing whatever about it. [*He closes his eyes; his face contracts.*] I can see it elsewhere and answer it elsewhere.

Mrs. Beunke. You are not well, Mr. Nico — you ought to go to bed.

[Nico *opens his eyes — turns his head away and answers an imaginary* Mrs. Beunke *at the other end of the room.*]

Nico. Yes, that's just what I was thinking of doing — going to bed.

[*He crosses slowly over to the door, left.*]

Mrs. Beunke. Not that way. This is the way to your room.

[*She points to the rear.*]

Nico [*still speaking to the left*]. I am going to change rooms, Mrs. Beunke.

Mrs. Beunke. There aren't any rooms on this side of the house.

Nico [*reaching doorway pretends to pat somebody's shoulder*]. Good-night, Mrs. Beunke, good-night.

[*He goes out without turning round.* Mrs. Beunke *goes forward hesitatingly towards the left.*]

Mrs. Beunke. Oh, where are you going to, Mr. Nico?

[*She follows him out,* Romée *enters right a few seconds later.*]

Romée [*calling*]. Mrs. Beunke, where are you?

Mrs. Beunke [*coming back, left*]. Here I am, here I am.

Romée. I have brought her back in the doctor's car. She is better. Is her room ready?

Mrs. Beunke [*agitated*]. Not yet, Miss Romée.

Romée. What? Not yet?

Mrs. Beunke. It's not my fault, Miss Romée.

Romée. What have you been doing?

Mrs. Beunke. It is Mr. Nico.... He has been saying such things — Oh, he is certainly not well.

Romée [*distracted*]. Nico has come back? Where is he?

Mrs. Beunke. He has just left the house. I saw him go down towards the lake.

Romée. Towards the lake — Ah!

[*Hardly has she glanced through the window when she sways as though struck by a bullet and sinks silently to the ground.*]

CURTAIN

NAKED

(Vestire gl'ignudi)

A DRAMA IN THREE ACTS
By LUIGI PIRANDELLO

Translated by ARTHUR LIVINGSTON

NAKED

ACT I

The study of LUDOVICO NOTA, a novelist.
It is one of two "furnished rooms" rented by
the author in the lodging house of SIGNORA
ONORIA. Odd pieces of antique furniture be-
longing to the novelist are in strong contrast
with the standard second-hand articles supplied by the house mistress. In the back set
two bookcases with numerous shelves stand
one beside the other. The books have been
carefully bound in uniform bindings of imita-
tion parchment, the titles printed in red
letters on the backs. On the right, between
two windows with cheap curtains, a tall writing desk high enough for a person standing to
write on. The shelf connecting the two pairs
of legs is loaded with heavy dictionaries. In
front of each window a large bird cage on a
tall wooden rest. One cage is full of canaries,
the other of thrushes and goldfinches. To the
left, an old sofa upholstered in a figured
damask of a light color, but covered with
white lace tidies, probably to disguise the pitiable state of the ancient divan. In front of it
a Turkish or Persian rug, faded and much
the worse for wear. Easy chairs; wooden
chairs with upholstered backs and seats; a
stand with various articles. On this wall (to
the left, that is) and well toward the front of
the stage, is the general entrance. In back,
to one side of the bookcase, is a door hidden
by a portière, and leading into the novelist's
bedroom. In the middle of the room an oval-
shaped table with books, magazines, newspapers, vases with flowers, ash trays, and a
statuette or two. The walls to the left and
right are overdecorated with paintings, etch-
ings, water colors, charcoal drawings, of
scant artistic worth — the gifts of artists
whom the novelist knows.

Despite its two windows, the room is rather
dark because the walls of adjoining houses
cut off the light. The truth is that SIGNOR
NOTA's apartment is on a narrow alley,
branching from a busy, noisy thoroughfare.

In fact, during pauses in the action on the
stage, sounds from the bustling street outside
will reach the stage: the rumbling of a truck;
the shouts of a hawker; the exhaust of a motor-
cycle; the starting of an automobile; the cries
of a newsboy; the laughter of young people.

As the curtain rises the stage is empty.
Through the two windows, which are open,
come the noises from the street. The door to
the left (the general entrance) opens and
ERSILIA DREI appears.

Twenty-four or twenty-five years old, she is
a beautiful girl, but her face is pale and her
eyes are sunken deep in their sockets. (Why
not? She has just been recalled from the very
brink of the grave!) Her dress is plain,
black, neat but threadbare — such as a
school-teacher or a governess, in poor circumstances, might wear. Her hat is in keeping
with the rest of her costume.

Advancing a step or two from the doorway,
she stops in hesitation, as though not quite
sure of herself, and looks about the room.
She does not take a chair, but remains standing, apparently waiting for some one who is
still to come. Her eyes survey the furnish-
ings, and she smiles, faintly, at the confusion
she sees.

A burst of noise from the busy street. She
frowns thoughtfully.

Through the general entrance at last comes
LUDOVICO NOTA, returning his purse to the
inside pocket of his coat as he passes through
the door. What hair he has is prematurely gray.
Inclined to stoutness, he has a clean shaven,
florid, ruddy face with lively blue eyes. His
white moustache is soiled from cigarette
smoke. Around his lips, still fresh and
sensuous, an almost youthful smile plays.
Cold, intellectual, without any of the qualities
which inspire sympathy and confidence out of
hand, and at the same time unable to affect an
emotionality he does not feel, NOTA makes an

*effort to seem affable, jovial, at least; but this
amiability, never quite spontaneous, fails to
put people at their ease, and at times is
actually embarrassing not to say disconcerting.*

LUDOVICO. Ah, here we are! Have a
chair! Make yourself comfortable! My!
My! The windows are open! What a
noise! The plague of my life! But if I
don't keep them open it gets so close in
here, you know! [*Takes out a cigarette and
starts to light it.*] Do you object, Signorina?
[*He walks nervously about the room, uneasy
in tone and gesture.*] But do take off your
hat! Make yourself quite at home!
[ERSILIA *removes her hat.*] Awfully close! I
don't know... perhaps on account of that
sofa... those chairs... a lot of old junk,
corpses from my past, you might say. Or
perhaps because the landlady insists on
washing the floor with water every morning
— and she always leaves it damp. Anyhow, stuffy... smelly, awfully close! Well,
old houses like these!

[*Through the door, Rear, enters* SIGNORA
ONORIA, *a broom in one hand, and,
under the other arm, a roll of sheets and
pillow cases which she is about to send
to the wash.* SIGNORA ONORIA *is about
forty years old, short, stout, talkative, her
hair dyed, a trace of rouge on her cheeks.*]

ONORIA. Will you excuse me?
LUDOVICO [*embarrassed by her sudden appearance*]. Oh, you were in the other room?
ONORIA [*spitefully*]. I have put fresh
sheets on your bed, as you asked me to do
in the note you left on the hall table this
morning.
LUDOVICO. Oh, yes!
ONORIA [*turning and surveying* ERSILIA
from head to foot]. But of course if it's for
... [*She breaks off.*] Look, Signor Nota,
we two had better understand each other
clearly. I'll just go and leave these things
downstairs...
LUDOVICO [*in some embarrassment and
smiling in an effort to conceal it*]. Yes, I
would get rid of them, if I were you! Dirty
clothes!
ONORIA [*turning on him angrily*]. Oh,
you would, would you? And dirty, eh?

LUDOVICO. Oh, just an impression I had
I thought you were of the same opinion.
I was merely agreeing with you.
ONORIA. Yes, but there are other things
I should like to be rid of!
LUDOVICO. That's interesting! What,
for instance?
ONORIA. Why, here I find you bringing a
young lady into the house! You think
that's as clean as it might be?
LUDOVICO. That's a bit too much! You
will please speak with respect of my guests
or!...
ONORIA. Or what? I am speaking my
mind and I intend to tell you just what I
think! I'll leave these things downstairs
and then I'll be back!
[*She flutters away through the general
entrance.*]
LUDOVICO [*mastering an impulse to follow
her*]. Silly old gossip!
ERSILIA [*trying to restrain him*]. Oh no,
please let me go away!
LUDOVICO. Nothing of the kind! I pay
the rent for these rooms! This is my house
and I'll have any one I want here! You
just sit down!
ONORIA [*sweeping back through the door
pugnaciously*]. Signor Nota, I have rented
you a study and a bedroom in my house,
but I must remind you that this is the house
of a respectable lady!
LUDOVICO. A lady? You? Your actions show it!
ONORIA. A lady! Exactly! I refuse to
permit you to keep a girl in these rooms!
LUDOVICO. I consider what you say insulting in the extreme! You're a boarding-
house-keeper! You're not a lady!
ONORIA. You ought to be ashamed, a
man your age! And be careful what
language you use toward me!
LUDOVICO. You are not a real lady!
You have no tact! You don't seem able to
distinguish one sort of person from another!
ERSILIA. I've been ill! I'm just out of
the hospital!
LUDOVICO. Don't bother to explain anything to this woman!
ONORIA. Oh, if you're sick...
[*The windows rattle, a truck crashes
along the street.*]

LUDOVICO. So we'll drop the subject, eh? You can't prevent me from lending my quarters for a few days!

ONORIA. Yes, I can! Yes, I can! These are my rooms! I choose the people to whom I rent them!

LUDOVICO. But if one of my sisters... a cousin... an aunt of mine comes to town...

ONORIA. They can find plenty of hotels!

LUDOVICO. Oh, really? And I can't put them up for a night or two here?

ONORIA. But this girl... is she your sister or your cousin or your aunt? Do you see anything green in my eyes?

LUDOVICO. But what do you care? What business is it of yours? Supposing I'm the one who goes to the hotel?

ONORIA. In that case you ought to ask me in advance, politely, as a gentleman should, whether I am willing to entertain a young lady!

LUDOVICO. Ask you to invite her, eh?

ONORIA. Precisely! And ask me politely, too, because I am a lady — a respectable lady, though misfortunes have compelled me to earn my living by renting rooms, and doing menial service for men like you!

LUDOVICO. Men like me?

ONORIA. Yes, you are always complaining! If I mop the floor every morning, it's to keep the dirt out of the room. And all those birds! What do you think this is, a hen coop? They sing, eh? But that's not all they do! That's not all they do! Sometimes it takes me half a day to clean! So if the house smells...

LUDOVICO. The birds do all that? No, madam! The house itself is dirty! You shut the windows and... well... can't you smell it yourself? Now I have to work here, and if I don't keep the windows closed the noise from the street drives me crazy!

ONORIA. Crazy? Drives you crazy? I like that! It is not my street that drives you crazy, my dear sir! You were crazy before you ever came here!

LUDOVICO [laughing good-naturedly in spite of himself]. That's a good one!

ONORIA. Just as I say! Crazy! Anyway, if you don't like it, why don't you go away? I wish you would! I wish you would!

LUDOVICO. Well, I'll move! Right away! Meantime, would you mind going about your business?

ONORIA. Are you giving up your rooms?

LUDOVICO. Yes, in a few days! At the end of the month!

ONORIA. Very well! In that case, I have nothing more to say!

LUDOVICO. Meantime, you were going downstairs!

ONORIA. I'm going! I'm going! Don't worry! I have had my say!

LUDOVICO. What a woman! What a woman! [Now that the windows are closed the noise comes somewhat more softly from the street.] I am so sorry, Signorina! Your first minute here... and a scene like that!

ERSILIA. Oh, that's all right! What troubles me is that it should be on my account!...

LUDOVICO. No, no! I have a set-to with that old witch every day! But I am tied to her! I can't get away! This ramshackle place! All this cheap, vulgar, common stuff! Look at those curtains! But such are the delightful rewards this age of business men gives to the poor fools who take up literature, especially when they are fools as impractical as I am. You perhaps thought... well... the home of a writer... of an artist!...

ERSILIA. Oh, no! I don't mind for myself; but it's too bad that a man like you, a man so famous...

[Another burst of noise from the street.]

LUDOVICO. You hear my orchestra? Famous, did you say? You have seen one of my books?

ERSILIA. One of them? I have read many of them!

LUDOVICO. Did you like them?

ERSILIA. Oh, yes! Very much!

LUDOVICO. Fame! Reputation!... Well ... you know how it is with us? You know the milkweed, don't you? — those little seeds hung on parachutes, the lightest breeze carrying them all around, here and there? That's the way it is with us! That's the way! Fad... fashion gets hold of a writer and spreads his name to the four winds; but finally it lets him down in some dark corner of forgetfulness! Writing is a game! It is something like playing the market where the stocks go up and go down! Yesterday my name was worth a hundred; to-day it is way below par, almost approaching zero!

ERSILIA. Oh, I don't believe that!

LUDOVICO. Zero, or virtually zero! But that doesn't bother me! To-morrow a hundred again, or perhaps a thousand! Let's hope so, eh? I've just put something big across, you know! Two big contracts! One with a newspaper syndicate, and the other with a publisher! There'll be quite an advance, so that at the end of the month we'll go and get a nice little apartment, eh? In one of those new modern buildings on the park! What do you say? To-morrow we'll go house hunting together! And we'll go looking for furniture — together! You will do the choosing. You must build your nest with your own hands!

ERSILIA. Oh, but all on my account?

LUDOVICO. No! No! No! I had to get out anyhow! Couldn't stand it any longer here! Impossible! They say a writer is a sedentary person, but look at my desk! I do all my writing on my feet! I refuse to have anything to do with tradition! However, I can see the necessity of having a house of my own at last... even if it's just a little three-room apartment! But with my own things! Oh, perhaps I won't live there myself! You see I'm like ... well... I'm a person who is always beginning over again! But you can't imagine how happy I am that I had that inspiration — the idea of writing to you — of beginning over again, this time, with you, sharing with you this little stroke of good luck that has come to me! A mud-hole... flies... mosquitoes... the stench of stagnant water; and then suddenly — oof! What has happened? Nothing! A breath of air! The wind has risen! That's the way I am! And we'll buy everything brand new, eh? Even... yes, eh? — a set of dishes... things for the kitchen! Ha ha ha! How funny it is! Things for the kitchen! Who could imagine I would ever own a frying pan, an iron kettle, a dish rag! Ha ha ha! But it's

great, isn't it? A house of my own, and a woman to look after it... a beautiful little creature like you! Oh, you'll see... you'll see!

ERSILIA. Yes, I can take care of an apartment! I am a good housekeeper! How can I ever thank you? How can I ever thank you?

LUDOVICO. I can do without the thanks! Or rather I'm sure I should thank you for having accepted the little that I...

ERSILIA. Oh, it is not a little — don't say that! It is so much... so much... for me!

LUDOVICO. It will be much, perhaps, in the end, because of what you make it; but now it's very, very little!

ERSILIA. Don't say that! Of the ten offers or more that came to me while I was in the hospital...

LUDOVICO [in surprise]. Ten or more? Offers from whom?

ERSILIA. From various people! I have them in my handbag, here! All their names and addresses, and some of them well-known names!

LUDOVICO. Well! Well! Who for example? Let me look at them!

ERSILIA. No! Perhaps later on... o wouldn't it be better to tear them up You see, of them all I chose yours!

LUDOVICO [taking her hand and kissing it] Thank you! [Then bringing himself to orde again.] And yet... ah... well, I wonde Ah, you little rogue! I can see it in you eyes!

ERSILIA. What?

LUDOVICO. Something not very compl mentary to me! See if I haven't guessed i of the ten offers you received — honest nov — you chose mine because I said in m letter "if you would deign to accept, Si norina, the companionship of an o writer"...

ERSILIA. But there was no signature e cept your first name: "Faust."

LUDOVICO. Worse luck! In that case can see it was the word "old" that got yc and not the name! But you might ha thought that an old man who signed hims "Faust" could easily prove dangerous!

ERSILIA. Dangerous? Why?

LUDOVICO. Why, an old man named "Faust" might sell his soul to the Devil, for instance, to get back his youth again!

ERSILIA. Oh, if you only knew — I am so mortified!

LUDOVICO. Mortified? Why?

ERSILIA. Because of this great good fortune!

LUDOVICO. Why good fortune? Because I'm a writer — as you say, a famous writer?

ERSILIA. Because the story of my troubles printed in the papers — the story of the desperate attempt I made — was able to win the attention, the respect, the pity!...

LUDOVICO. Why don't you say selfishness... was able to stir the selfish interest?...

ERSILIA. ... of a man like... like you!

LUDOVICO. Well, you see... fact is... I felt — how shall I say it — I felt all stirred up, there!... all stirred up; when I read your story in the papers! It was something like... well, you know... we novelists... well, sometimes a fact, a situation comes to our attention, quite casually, and we experience inside us — oh, I don't know — a shock, let us call it — a sudden wave of sympathy that sweeps over us, the conviction in short, that we have found, without effort on our part, without our trying to find it, the nucleus, the starting point, the germ, of a story, of a novel...

ERSILIA. So you thought that... I mean to say... you thought you could put me into a book?

LUDOVICO. No! Please don't misunderstand! Please don't imagine I have been trying to use you as mere material for my writing! I drew the parallel to make you see more clearly how I felt, how your case caught me, took possession of me all over!

ERSILIA. But I shouldn't mind even if it were that!

LUDOVICO. Please believe what I say!

ERSILIA. I do! But if my poor life, all my sorrows and misfortunes, can serve at last for such a purpose!...

LUDOVICO. For one of my books?

ERSILIA. Why not? I would be happy, proud, oh so proud, really!

LUDOVICO. I throw up my hands!

ERSILIA. Why?

LUDOVICO. Because you again remind me that I am an old, old man!

ERSILIA. I do? Why? I don't mean that! I mean...

LUDOVICO. A novel, my dear child, can be written, but it can also be lived! I said that I felt you taking entire possession of me; but it wasn't to write a novel — it was to live one! I hold out my arms to you — but you, instead of offering me — what shall I say — your lips, for instance — hand me pen and paper to write your story!

ERSILIA [embarrassed, bowing her head]. But we hardly know each other! It is too soon!

LUDOVICO. Too soon for your lips, I grant you that; but — later on perhaps?

ERSILIA [sorrowfully]. No!

LUDOVICO. Just notice how differently you and I are feeling toward the present situation. I was hurt a little because you might have thought my interest in your case merely the curiosity of a writer; and you on the other hand are hurt (or at least you are not very much pleased), if I tell you that the writer, as a writer pure and simple — clever I mean to say, and not just old — did not need to make you any such offer as I have made, nor to go and get you at the very door of the hospital; because the novel... well... as I read about you in the papers... the novel came into my head full-grown — the plot, the characters, the episodes, everything!

ERSILIA. Really? All of a sudden? Just like that?

LUDOVICO. All of a sudden! It just flashed through my mind! I could see it almost paragraph by paragraph, with all its wealth of situation and detail! Oh, magnificent! The East... the Levant... a villa on the seashore... a house with a flat roof! You there, a governess! And the baby falls from the roof, and you are sent away. Then a ship at sea! Then here you are home again, and you discover how terrible ... oh I could see it all... the whole thing — even before I knew what you looked like, before I was acquainted with you at all!

ERSILIA. In your imagination, that is! [*Piqued with curiosity.*] So you imagined me? How did you think of me? What was I like? This way? As I really am?

LUDOVICO. No!

[*With a negative gesture, and smiling.*]

ERSILIA [*insisting*]. How did you think of me? Please tell me!

LUDOVICO. Why are you so anxious to find out?

ERSILIA. Because I should like to be just as you thought of me!

LUDOVICO. Oh no! Because I like you very much as you are! In fact, I like you better this way — for myself, that is — not for the novel, necessarily!

ERSILIA. But in that case, the novel that was mine, my story, you made it up around another woman!

LUDOVICO. Of course! Of course! Around the woman I had imagined!

ERSILIA. Was she very different from me?

LUDOVICO. She was another woman!

ERSILIA. Oh, dear, dear! In that case... well... I don't understand... I don't understand!

LUDOVICO. What don't you understand?

ERSILIA. Why you are interested in me! Why me?

LUDOVICO. Whom should I be interested in if not in you?

ERSILIA. But I am not the woman in your story! If my experience, my misfortunes, everything in short that interested you when you read about it in the papers... I mean... if it interested you not on my account, but in connection with another woman who is not like me...

[*She breaks off in bewilderment.*]

LUDOVICO. What were you going to say, little girl?

ERSILIA. ... then I can go away!

LUDOVICO [*catching her, and resting an arm delicately around her waist*]. But not at all, not at all, my dear child! The idea! We'll let the woman in the novel go away! But she isn't you, she isn't you!

ERSILIA [*hurt, suspicious*]. She and I are different people? [*Almost in terror.*] You don't believe then...

LUDOVICO [*smiling*]. Of course, I be-

lieve! Of course! But I should prefer not to think of you any longer in connection with the novel which may have been yours, to be sure... which is yours, in fact... yes! However, I don't think of you in that connection any longer; because, you understand, as I thought of you for my book you were different; you were another person! Now I should like to think of you in your new life, such as it is to be, as it is going to be from now on, that is, with me! And I hope that you, too, will think of yourself only in this new life, forgetting all about the terrible things that have happened to you!

ERSILIA [*with infinite sadness, but with a smile nevertheless*]. But in that case, I shall be not the woman I was, nor the woman I am, but still another!

LUDOVICO. Another? Yes! The woman you are going to be!

ERSILIA [*looks at him in amazement*]. I? [*With a slight gesture of her two hands, which have hitherto been limply folded on her knees.*] I have never been anything! I have never been anybody!

LUDOVICO. Oh, now — wait! You've never been anybody?

ERSILIA. Nobody — ever!

LUDOVICO. But you are yourself!

ERSILIA. Who am I? What am I?

LUDOVICO. First of all, you're a sweet, charming, beautiful, little girl!

ERSILIA [*shrugging her shoulders*]. Good looking? I doubt that! But even if I were, I've never been able to profit by it!

LUDOVICO. That's important, it's true In fact, it may even occur to a girl... in sheer despair... to make an extreme resolution at last, let herself go, throw herself haphazard upon life!

ERSILIA [*looking at him fearfully*]. Oh how can you say that?

LUDOVICO. No, I wasn't referring to you! It came into my mind, I suppose because I had thought of her, the girl in the novel, in that way! [*Speaking as though he could see the character before his eyes and improvising.*] Despair! Not knowing what to do! Evening! The hall bedroom of a hotel! Then she looks into the mirror and — a sudden decision! A mad resolution Her bill from the landlord! In her purse penny or two! And the clerk is insisting on his money!

ERSILIA [*starting with great terror*]. Did they put that in the papers?

LUDOVICO. No! I invented it! [*Looking at her in delight.*] Do you mean that this was actually the case with you?

ERSILIA [*hardly able to utter the word*]. Yes!

LUDOVICO [*beaming with pleasure*]. Well! Well! Well! So I guessed it right! You went down into the street that night?...

ERSILIA [*faintly*]. Yes! Yes!

LUDOVICO. ... and — it was like this: a man came along the street... a man... any one at all! Wasn't that it?

ERSILIA [*covering her face, with a shudder of horror*]. ... and not knowing how to go about it...

LUDOVICO. How to ask him?

ERSILIA [*nodding, with her face still covered*]. Yes!

LUDOVICO [*as though he understood the situation perfectly*]. And he refused, eh?

ERSILIA [*looking at him wildly, her lips apart. She nods in the affirmative*]. Yes!

LUDOVICO [*beaming with pleasure again*]. So I got even the details, even the details — to perfection! And then — disgust! Repentance! Loathing for that ugly and fruitless effort! To perfection! To perfection! [ERSILIA *bursts into sobs, and the novelist, quickly.*] But no, why do you feel so bad about it? It's all over now! No! No! Please don't cry!

[*He stoops and tries to put his arm reassuringly about her shoulders.*]

ERSILIA. Don't touch me! Let me go! I want to go away!

LUDOVICO. But why? Why go away?

ERSILIA. Now that you know this!

LUDOVICO. But I knew it already! I knew it already!

ERSILIA. How did you know it already?

LUDOVICO. Because I imagined it that way — in the novel! Don't you see? I was right! That's the way it happened! Exactly as it happened!

ERSILIA. But I am so ashamed!

[*At this moment an unusually violent burst of noise comes from down the street. apparently because of some colli-* sion or other: a crash of vehicles, screams, cries, oaths, hoots, threats.*]

LUDOVICO. Ashamed? Why? Don't say that!... [*He breaks off and turns toward the window.*] But what the devil has happened?

ERSILIA. They're shouting! There's been an accident or something!

[*The uproar increases. Cries of "Help! Help!" The door to the left opens and* SIGNORA ONORIA *rushes headlong into the room.*]

ONORIA. They've run over a poor old man! I guess he's killed! Right here in front of the house!

[*She runs to one of the windows while* LUDOVICO *and* ERSILIA *hurry toward the other. With the window open, the noise in the street holds the stage for some time. An automobile has collided with a wagon. In trying to avoid the wagon, the chauffeur turned his car across a sidewalk, running over an old man who was not quick enough to get out of the way. The victim is dying, or perhaps dead. People are standing about him. The ambulance comes clanging up in the midst of the shouting and confusion and hurries away again. What is going on is made clear by the various sounds, exclamations, words that are distinguishable in the general clamor.*]

VOICES IN THE STREET. Oh, oh! Poor fellow! Help! Help! Ran across his chest! Give him air! Arrest him! Arrest him! He's dead! Poor old man! Hurry! Hurry! Don't let him get away! Back broken! Dead! He made a sharp turn! He had the right of way! No, no! It isn't true! Hang him! Hang him! He ought to be in jail! These speeders! Give him air! No! He's dead! Poor fellow! Hurry! Hurry! The police station! No, the hospital! Here's his hat! Here's his hat! The murderer! They ought to hang him!

[*The agitation on the sidewalk is reflected in the gestures and exclamations of the three people at the windows.*]

ONORIA. He's dead! He's dead! Poor old man! Oh, don't let him get away! He was trying to get away! He looks like a murderer! He's trying to excuse himself! Flattened him out like a toad!

ERSILIA [*springing back from the window horrified*]. Oh, how terrible! How terrible!

LUDOVICO [*stepping back also and closing the window*]. Poor devil! Probably he has a family! [*Irritated by the noise.*] Please, Signora, close the window!

ONORIA. They've carried him away! [*Shutting the window.*] But he's dead by this time!

LUDOVICO. If he's not dead already, he will be by the time they get him to the hospital!

ONORIA. I'm going downstairs to find out about it! How terrible! How terrible! [*She ambles, in her usual fussy manner, out of the room. The noises in the street gradually die down.*]

LUDOVICO. Filthy street this is! They never clean it up! And when it rains you can hardly paddle your way through the mud! And just one jam of traffic: carts, trucks, automobiles, everything! And they permit pushcarts there into the bargain! Just imagine! Pushcarts!

ERSILIA [*after a pause, staring horror-stricken into space in front of her*]. The street! The street! How terrible!

LUDOVICO. What a school for a man who writes! For a man like myself! Oh, you can free yourself from all common, vulgar concerns! Your imagination lifts you above all this! You soar to the clouds! But down there is the street with its people going to and fro! All the noises of life, the life of other people, foreign to you, but still present before your mind, ringing in your ears; intruding on your thoughts; interrupting; deforming everything... But we are going to be together, aren't we? We're going to work out a pretty story together, aren't we? Yes! Just imagine; supposing I were the old man who was just run over down in the street there! What would you be doing here in such circumstances? But you had your life broken into once by something like that, didn't you? An accident! A child falling from the roof!

ERSILIA. Oh!

LUDOVICO. You think of something, and a hawker barks, out in the street, or a newsboy comes along — and your ideas... goodbye! It's as though two fingers were stretched out into space to catch the lark by the tail just as it is soaring to the sky to greet the sunshine in its joy... and pull it back to earth again!

ERSILIA. You are a servant in a house, obedient to other people! — yourself? Nobody! Nothing! How terrible! To feel one's self just nobody! Alone in the world! No one even thinking of you as a person! And to me — the street... I saw my life as though it had no real existence! As though it were a dream... just things about me! A few people in the garden at noon! Trees! A settee! Chairs! And I refused to be just nobody — to be just nothing!

LUDOVICO. Ah, as for that, now! No, that isn't true!

ERSILIA. It isn't true? I made up my mind to kill myself!

LUDOVICO. Yes, but making a good story out of it!

ERSILIA [*fearful again*]. What do you mean — a good story? Do you think I was inventing it all?

LUDOVICO. No! No! I was thinking of myself! You made a good story for me by just telling of your experiences!

ERSILIA. When they picked me up in the garden there?

LUDOVICO. Yes! And later on at the hospital! How can you have been nobody if your story aroused so much pity in every one? You can't imagine the impression you made in the town when the newspapers came out with it! The interest you aroused! You have a proof of it in me and in those letters in your handbag, in all the offers you received! Ten! Ten or more!

ERSILIA. Have you kept them?

LUDOVICO. Kept what?

ERSILIA. The newspapers! I would like to read the story myself, with my own eyes! Have you kept them?

LUDOVICO. Why, perhaps! I imagine could find one!

ERSILIA. Please look for it! Please hunt it up! I would like to see it!

LUDOVICO. But no, why should you bother with all that now?

ERSILIA. I want to see what the papers said! Please! I must read it for myself!

LUDOVICO. I imagine they printed just what you told them.

ERSILIA. But I don't remember what I said at such a time! I should like to see it! I should like to read about it! Please try to find the paper!

LUDOVICO. I wonder where it could be... all this rubbish here... I never was very neat! What do you say — let's wait a while! We'll come across it later on!

ERSILIA. It gave the whole story? Was it very long?

LUDOVICO. At least three columns on the front page! Summer time... not much doing! When the reporters get hold of a story like yours, they eat it up!

ERSILIA. But him... what did they say of him?

LUDOVICO. Why, that he had jilted you!

ERSILIA. No, not him! I mean... I mean... the other! The other one!

LUDOVICO. The consul?

ERSILIA [greatly shocked]. Did they say he was a consul?

LUDOVICO. Yes, our consul at Smyrna!

ERSILIA [still in great alarm]. Oh dear, dear! They even told where it happened! They promised me they wouldn't!

LUDOVICO. Oh yes... but these reporters!...

ERSILIA. But they didn't need to, did they? The story was just as good even if it didn't tell where it happened or who was concerned? Well, what did they say?

LUDOVICO. They said that when the baby fell from the roof!...

ERSILIA [covering her face with her hands]. Oh, poor little thing! Poor little thing!

LUDOVICO. After the baby fell from the roof, the consul was fearfully cruel toward you!

ERSILIA. Oh no, he wasn't It was his wife! It was his wife!

LUDOVICO. They said he was too!

ERSILIA. Oh, no, not he! His wife! Oh dear dear me!

LUDOVICO. Because his wife was jealous of you! Oh, I can imagine her, strapping big woman, a regular grenadier....

ERSILIA. Oh no, she wasn't! Not at all! She was a tiny, little thing! Slender, all shriveled up, yellow! She was a lemon!

LUDOVICO. Oh now, wait, now! Why, you know, I can just see her! She's this way! Tall, dark-haired, her eyebrows joining over her nose! I could paint her picture!

ERSILIA. But she wasn't that kind of woman at all! Who knows how you must have imagined me! No, no! She's just as I said!

LUDOVICO. Yes, but that doesn't matter! For my purposes I needed a big woman, while the baby was small and slight... a tiny thing... emaciated!

ERSILIA. Emaciated? Tiny? My Mimetta? Oh dear me!

LUDOVICO. I called it Titì!

ERSILIA. Not Titì! Mimetta... and a beautiful child! Fat as butter! She would toddle around on her little fat legs, her rosy cheeks, and her golden curls shaking all over her head! And she was so fond of me! I was the only one she liked!

LUDOVICO. So naturally the mother was jealous of you on that account as well!

ERSILIA. Oh yes, I should say so, especially on the baby's account! And it was her fault, you know! For when that other man came, on the cruiser...

LUDOVICO. The ensign in the navy?

ERSILIA. Yes... that night she put me, on purpose, in a situation where I would be very likely to succumb! Alone there! In that garden! Palm trees all around me! And the fragrance of the flowers! How sweet! How wonderful! Drugged with perfume!

LUDOVICO. Oh, a magnificent story! Magnificent! Full of color, you see! The sea; sunshine; fragrance; night in the Levant!

ERSILIA. If it had not been so terrible for me!...

LUDOVICO. With that hellhound of a woman!... I can just imagine her! Treachery, you see — the treachery of a person who has never known what love is, and who understands that the joy she prepares for another woman will soon be destroyed in a most terrible misfortune! Magnificent!

ERSILIA. I wish you could have seen her! As kind toward me as my own mother! He had asked for my hand quite formally, applying to her and to the consul! They were my guardians, you see! Oh, my own way in everything! But then when he went away! [*Horrified.*] How can a person change so suddenly! An irritation you can't understand! Nothing suited her any more! Just one humiliation after another for me! And then at last — I was blamed for the accident!

LUDOVICO. While it was she who sent you out of the house on some errand or other!...

ERSILIA [*turning on him suddenly, deeply impressed, and in some alarm*]. Who said that?

LUDOVICO. It was in the papers!

ERSILIA. That too?

LUDOVICO. You must have said so yourself!

ERSILIA. No, I don't remember saying that! I don't believe I said it!

LUDOVICO. Do you think I imagined it, then? Probably some newspaper man invented it to color up the cruelty of your dismissal a bit!... For you were sent away, and they didn't even give you money for your ticket home! That much is true?

ERSILIA. Yes, that's true! That's true!

LUDOVICO. Almost as though you could be made to pay in money for the death of the child!

ERSILIA. And she threatened me with that, you know! Yes, she did! She did! And she would have had me arrested for it if she hadn't been afraid that certain things might be found out!

LUDOVICO. Certain things about her? Ah, so it's true, then!

ERSILIA [*embarrassed*]. No! I don't mean... anyhow I'm sorry the papers said that she sent me away! I would like to forget all about what happened out there! I'm thinking of the journey home! Oh, how I suffered! I'm sure that that poor baby, buried in her grave, came away on the steamer with me just the same so as not to be left there with those cruel parents! And I felt this way... it seemed as though I lost her when I went down into the street from my hotel that night!

LUDOVICO. But when you got here, if I may ask, you didn't look him up?

ERSILIA. How could I look him up? I didn't know his address! I wrote him in care of general delivery! Then I went to the Navy Building!

LUDOVICO. Well?

ERSILIA. They told me he had resigned his commission!

LUDOVICO. But you should have followed him up, to make him atone for the crime, the downright crime, he committed against you!

ERSILIA. I never was good at asserting my rights!

LUDOVICO. He had promised to marry you!

ERSILIA. I was crushed! When they told me that he was to be married the next day, the sense of his betrayal, which was so cruel and so unexpected, came over me so strongly that I was crushed! I had only a little money left! And the thought of actually having to beg!... In the garden there with that poison in my hand I thought of the little child, and I gathered courage from the feeling that having lost her the evening before I would then be going to find her again!

LUDOVICO. Oh, come, come! Let's not think of those things now! Try to cheer up, little girl!

ERSILIA [*after a pause and with a smile of deepest sadness*]. Yes, but at least, let me be that woman...

LUDOVICO. That woman! What woman?

ERSILIA. The woman you imagined! Dear me! If I amounted to something at least once in my life, as you have said, want to be in your novel, myself, but I, you understand, I, the woman I am! It seems quite unfair that you should see another woman in me!

LUDOVICO [*laughing*]. That's a great idea! It's as though she were robbing you, eh?

ERSILIA. Why yes! You are stealing things that happened to me; you are stealing my life, the life that I had decided do away with! I lived that life to the very depths of despair and it seems that now, if you don't mind, I have a right to be in the story you make of it... a beautiful story, like a novel I read of yours. It is called — wait — what did you call it? *The Outcast* — yes, *The Outcast*.

LUDOVICO. *The Outcast?* Oh, no, you're mistaken! *The Outcast* was not written by me!

ERSILIA [*surprised*]. Wasn't that one of your novels?

LUDOVICO. No!

ERSILIA. How strange! I thought...

LUDOVICO. In fact, it's by a writer whom I cordially detest!

ERSILIA [*mortified, covering her face with her hands*]. Dear me! Dear me!

LUDOVICO. Now, now, what does that all matter? You are mixing it up with some other book. [ERSILIA *begins to weep, still covering her face with her hands.*] But you're not really hurt, are you? My dear, what are you crying for? Why should I care about a little mistake like that? It's a bad novel all right; but I'm not insulted just because you thought I wrote it!

ERSILIA. No, you see that's the way it always is with me! Nothing ever, ever comes out right!

[*There is a knock at the door to the Left.*]

LUDOVICO. Yes! Come in! Come right in!

[*It is* SIGNORA ONORIA, *now all smiles, all honey, and absurdly sentimental over what she has learned.*]

ONORIA. May I come in? [*She looks about the room for* ERSILIA.] Where is the poor little thing? [*She stops and joins her hands in a gesture of pity as she sees* ERSILIA *weeping.*] Oh, the poor little thing — in tears?

LUDOVICO [*in astonishment, unable to understand the sudden change in the woman's manner*]. Why, what's the matter?

ONORIA. You might have told me she was the girl the newspapers were talking about! Signorina Drei, isn't it? Ersilia Drei! Poor child! You poor thing! I am so glad you are well again and out of the hospital! I'm delighted to have you here!

LUDOVICO. But how did you find out that it was she?

ONORIA. A great question! Don't you suppose I read the papers?

LUDOVICO. Yes, but how did you know that she was the girl?

ONORIA. Why, because... well... look at this! [*She hands him a visiting card.*] There's a reporter downstairs, and he told me the whole story!

LUDOVICO. A reporter... here?

ERSILIA. A reporter?

LUDOVICO. What does he want?

ONORIA. He says there are a number of important things which the young lady must explain!

ERSILIA. Things to explain?

LUDOVICO. This is too much, upon my word!

ERSILIA. What does he want me to explain?

LUDOVICO. And who told him that the young lady was here?

ONORIA. I don't know!

ERSILIA. Neither do I! When he interviewed me I never even dreamed that I would come here to your house!

LUDOVICO [*almost to himself*]. I see! I see! Talking, as usual! [*With a nod in* ONORIA'S *direction. Then turning to* ERSILIA.] Well, what do you say? Shall we have him come in?

ERSILIA. No... I... no... no! I don't know! What shall I say to him? What does he want me to explain?

LUDOVICO. I'm going to have a talk with the fellow!

[*He goes out through the door to the Left.*]

ONORIA. Oh, you poor child! If you only knew how I cried when I read your story in the papers... such a terrible story!

ERSILIA. But what do they want of me now?

ONORIA. Perhaps... well... you know!

ERSILIA. Oh dear me! Dear me! I can't endure another ordeal! More trouble would quite kill me!

ONORIA. You're not well?

ERSILIA. Oh, I'm all right, I think! But here... [*She puts a hand to her breast.*] I don't know... it's hard for me to breathe, somehow! They say I am well; but perhaps there is still something wrong, here! It hurts when I press with my hand, here, and then here, and in my back! Oh, a terrible pain! It seems to run all over me! [*She weeps and groans.*] Dear me! Dear me! [*From the street comes a sudden burst of music from a hurdy-gurdy, playing a popular song.*]

ONORIA. Unbutton your waist! Let me see!

ERSILIA. No! No! [*Irritated by the music from the hurdy-gurdy.*] Oh, please send that man away! I can't bear it.

ONORIA. Yes, with pleasure... right away! [*She takes a purse from the pocket of her apron.*] With pleasure! [*She goes to the window, opens the lower sash, and calls to the organ grinder below, motioning to him to go away. The music continues.* ONORIA *opens her pocketbook, takes out some coins and tosses them down from the window.*] There are sick people in the house! [*Again she motions the man away. The hurdy-gurdy breaks off suddenly in the middle of a tune.* ONORIA *closes the window and hurries back to* ERSILIA's *side.*] So there you are! We have sent him away! Now listen to me! You just unbutton your clothes...

ERSILIA. No, I can't do that! I must be ready! I'm afraid that not even this can last!

ONORIA. What? What can last?

ERSILIA. Oh, if you only knew! I am so unhappy, so unhappy! I can't endure it! This sash... oh! [*She loosens her sash.*] I can't endure it... it's too tight... it's too tight! I can't bear it!

[*Through the door to the Left the sound of talking is heard. It is* LUDOVICO *inviting some one to come in.*]

LUDOVICO. No! No! Go right along! After you, please!

[ALFREDO CANTAVALLE, *a newspaper man, enters, followed by the novelist.* CANTAVALLE *is a handsome young Neapolitan, pretentious, elegant, and fashionable. He even wears a monocle, but he has the greatest difficulty in keeping it in place. He is a jolly, good-natured, talkative fellow. His hair, parted in the middle like a school boy's, falls thick over his forehead. He has a long, fat, ruddy face. His fat legs show almost feminine lines through tight-fitting trousers.*]

CANTAVALLE. Sorry to trouble you, ladies! Oh, my dear Signorina, you remember me, I am sure!

LUDOVICO [*introducing*]. Signor Alfredo Cantavalle, of the press!

ERSILIA. Yes, I remember you!

CANTAVALLE. I thought you would! [*And noting* SIGNORA ONORIO.] Oh, Signora, you are a relative of this young lady?

LUDOVICO. No, she is the mistress of the house!

CANTAVALLE. Oh! Delighted! [*He makes a slight bow.*] I remember in fact that the young lady has no relatives! You just had a serious accident out in front here, I understand.

LUDOVICO. Yes, a poor old man!

ONORIA. How frightened I was!

CANTAVALLE. He's dead!

ONORIA. Dead? He's dead?

CANTAVALLE. Yes, died in the ambulance on the way to the hospital!

ONORIA. Who was he?

CANTAVALLE. He hasn't been identified yet. [*Turning to* ERSILIA.] My dear Signorina, I hope you will allow me not only to congratulate you on your recovery, but to congratulate myself! Yes, it was a great piece of luck, and it turned out all in your favor! The article I wrote about your experiences has had the singular good fortune to be noted by a famous author [*He bows to* LUDOVICO]. But it's all nonsense, Signor Nota, what that friend of yours says. ... This is the noblest thing you have done in your whole life! [*Again turning to* ERSILIA.] You can imagine how pleased I am at hearing it!

ERSILIA. Yes, it was wonderful good fortune for me!

LUDOVICO. Oh, please! What are you talking about?

CANTAVALLE. No, Signor Nota, she is right! And for other reasons, also! Now we can have the advantage of your coöperation and support — and we need it, I assure you! Shall I explain?... If I may venture to speak in the presence of this lady here... [*He nods in* ONORIA'S *direction.*]

ONORIA. I'm going right away... but the Signorina was not feeling very well!

LUDOVICO. Not feeling very well?

ONORIA. In fact, she was in the greatest distress!

LUDOVICO. What's the matter?

ERSILIA. I don't know... I don't know! I have a chill, I guess... my nerves!

ONORIA. Now you just listen to me! Come into the other room!
[*She points to the door, Rear.*]

ERSILIA. No! No!

ONORIA. Yes, you'd better... and just get into bed!

LUDOVICO. Do so, please, if you're not well!

ONORIA. Once she gets her clothes off and goes to bed...

ERSILIA. No, thank you! I shall be all right! I can stay here!

CANTAVALLE. The effects of the poison, I suppose! But you'll see... with a little care

LUDOVICO. ... and a quiet environment!...

ONORIA. I am always right here, my dear child! If you need anything, call me! I shall be only too glad!...

ERSILIA. Yes, thank you... thank you, Signora!

CANTAVALLE. In that case I shall be going! Good afternoon, Signorina!

ONORIA [*approaching* LUDOVICO *and in a whisper*]. Don't disturb her now. A little common sense! Can't you see how the poor thing is suffering?
[*She withdraws through the door to the Left, which* LUDOVICO *closes behind her.*]

CANTAVALLE. I am so sorry if my coming here...

LUDOVICO [*with some annoyance*]. Oh, it's all right, Cantavalle, but get through as soon as you can!

CANTAVALLE. I can find out what I want to know in two minutes, Signor Nota! Give me just two minutes!

LUDOVICO. Well, let's come to the point! What is it precisely that that fool consul of yours...

ERSILIA [*starting in terror*]. The consul?

LUDOVICO. The consul, precisely! [*Speaking to* CANTAVALLE.] We must put that fellow in his place!

ERSILIA [*in great alarm*]. What do you mean? The consul is here... in town?

CANTAVALLE. He came down to our office yesterday and raised a terrible rumpus, Signorina!

ERSILIA [*moaning in despair*]. Oh dear! Oh dear! Oh dear!

LUDOVICO. And you say he insists on a retraction?

CANTAVALLE. Yes... of everything, he says, of everything!

ERSILIA [*to* CANTAVALLE]. Now you can see all the harm you have done! You said things I didn't want you to say, and you promised me you wouldn't.

CANTAVALLE. I? What harm have I done?

ERSILIA. Yes, you! You shouldn't have mentioned the name of the city! You shouldn't have said who the people were!

LUDOVICO. A general retraction he wants? What do you mean?

CANTAVALLE. Why, he wants us to deny the whole story, which, he says, is a tissue of falsehoods! One moment, Signor Nota ... I must answer the young lady! His name, you see, I was careful not to mention!

LUDOVICO. You did very well to show up a rascal like that!

CANTAVALLE. No, all I said was "the Italian consul in Smyrna!" Who the devil cares who the consul in Smyrna is! Who is ever going to know? I didn't even know myself! And I don't know even now! Anyhow, the last thing in the world I should ever have expected was that he would come tearing into our office yesterday like a bull in a crockery shop!

ERSILIA [*again moaning in despair*]. Oh dear! Oh dear!

LUDOVICO. So he came to Rome, eh? All on account of this?

CANTAVALLE. Not on account of this exactly! He came on account of an accident that happened to his baby! That was in the story, to be sure! He came because his wife, as he says, is in a terrible state of mind! In short, an impossible situation, there, in Smyrna!

ERSILIA. Yes, that woman! That woman!

CANTAVALLE. He came on home to ask for a transfer; but he has seen the newspapers! A pretty mess we are in, Signor Nota!

LUDOVICO. But why?

CANTAVALLE. Why? Why, the man has an official position, you understand! He is certain to bring a suit against my paper... a suit for libel!

LUDOVICO. But what did the article have to say about him, after all?

CANTAVALLE. Nothing but lies, as he claims... things very much to his discredit!

LUDOVICO. Lies? Were they lies?

ERSILIA. I don't know! I haven't seen your article! I don't know what you may have said of him or of his wife or of the accident!

CANTAVALLE. I assure you, Signorina, that I reported exactly what you said! Nothing more, nothing less! Oh, of course, I was very much affected by your story and my style... well... but as regards matters of fact, I didn't change a thing! You can see for yourself, if you just look at the paper!

LUDOVICO [beginning to rummage around the room]. I am sure I had it here! It must be here somewhere!

CANTAVALLE. Never mind, I'll send you a copy! But as you can well see, Signorina, I have come here to find out from you what I am to do in the face of the complaint and the threat of this gentleman!

ERSILIA [with a convulsive burst of anger, and almost hissing as she speaks]. He has nothing to complain of, that man! And as for his threats!...

CANTAVALLE. All the better, in that case... all the better!

ERSILIA. Oh dear me! Oh dear me! I am so tired! I don't feel well!

[She begins to sob, shivering and shaking all over, her weeping soon rising to a shrill note that might be mistaken for laughter. Finally she falls back in a faint.]

LUDOVICO [running to her anxiously and helping CANTAVALLE hold her up and to keep her from slipping to the floor]. Ersilia! Ersilia! Please!

CANTAVALLE. Oh, Signorina! No! Please! Please! Don't worry, please!

LUDOVICO. What's the matter? Oh, please don't! Everything is all right!

CANTAVALLE. There's nothing to be afraid of, Signorina!

LUDOVICO. She's gone! Fainted! Just call the lady, will you please?

CANTAVALLE [running to the door, Left]. Signora! Signora!

LUDOVICO [also calling]. Signora Onoria!

CANTAVALLE. Signora Onoria! Signora Onoria! [He goes out into the hall.]

LUDOVICO. Oh no! Ersilia dear! No! No! Be a good girl! Everything is all right!

[CANTAVALLE returns with SIGNORA ONORIA. She has a bottle of smelling salts in her hand.]

ONORIA. Here I am! What's the matter? Oh, poor child! There! There! Just hold her head up... a little higher... there we are! Poor child! [She puts the bottle of smelling salts to ERSILIA's nose.] And I told you men not to trouble her! She is not in a condition to be disturbed!

CANTAVALLE. Ah, she is coming to again!

LUDOVICO. We must get her into the other room to bed!

ONORIA. Just a moment! Just a moment!

LUDOVICO. Ersilia!

ONORIA. There! There! Poor child! Now you're all right! Come now... brace up!

LUDOVICO. Yes! Yes! Poor little girl! Ersilia! Ersilia!

CANTAVALLE. I'm so sorry, Signorina, but everything is all right! Everything is all right!

ERSILIA [almost laughing, in a tone of childish wonder]. Oh dear me, did I fall?

LUDOVICO. No! Why? No, you didn't fall — but you scared us almost to death!

ERSILIA. I didn't fall?

LUDOVICO. Oh no! What were you dreaming of?

ONORIA. And now, poor child, just see if you can stand on your feet!

LUDOVICO. Yes! Now there! Gently, now... careful!

ERSILIA. Oh, I thought it was... as if suddenly... I don't know... as though I were made of lead! [She looks up and sees CANTAVALLE. A nervous terror runs over her. She leaps to her feet.] Oh no! No!

[She staggers and is again about to fall. LUDOVICO and ONORIA catch her in their arms.]

LUDOVICO. No, Ersilia! What's the matter? What's the matter?

ERSILIA. Let me go! Let me go!

ONORIA. Yes! Yes! All right! But now we are going into the other room!

LUDOVICO. And you lie down on the bed! Yes! Now then, there you are! See? We won't let you fall!

ONORIA. Careful now... careful! And I'll stay with you in there! You can lie down and be all cozy and comfortable!

LUDOVICO. You will rest up a little, and everything will be all right!

ERSILIA. I can't endure it! I am all tired out! I can't endure it!

ONORIA [blocking LUDOVICO in the doorway, Rear]. You stay in here! I'll attend to her! [She helps ERSILIA into the bedroom.]

LUDOVICO. If you ask me, I'd say that they've tormented that poor girl long enough!

CANTAVALLE. I hope you don't blame me! I am more sorry than I can tell you, Signor Nota; but unfortunately you don't know the worst of it yet! There's more trouble ahead for the young lady!

LUDOVICO. More trouble?

CANTAVALLE. Yes! And I think you ought to know about it! The consul brought the matter up while he was in our office!

LUDOVICO. You just tell that consul to go to the devil!

CANTAVALLE. Now not quite so fast! You know, Signor Nota — oh, my article had a perfectly marvelous effect! It seems that the girl who was going to marry the boy in the story is indignant at the trick he played on this young lady here, so she has called the wedding off! Understand?

LUDOVICO. Called the wedding off?

CANTAVALLE. My article was a corker, I can tell you! Not only that! When the story came out the girl called off her marriage, as I said, but it seems her young man saw the light and he has repented too! What do you think of that? Oh, I got the right touch into my story of her suicide! That boy has lost his head completely!

LUDOVICO. You mean the ensign in the navy?

CANTAVALLE. Yes! His name... wait ... I think his name is Laspiga! Anyhow, he'd lost his head completely! So the consul said, at any rate!

LUDOVICO. And how did he find it out?

CANTAVALLE. Why, it seems that the girl's father went and looked him up at the Foreign Office! It was the old man who told the consul!

LUDOVICO. Some mixup, I'll say!

CANTAVALLE. Yes, especially from your point of view, since now you're involved yourself!

LUDOVICO. Why?

CANTAVALLE. And me, too, for that matter! Just imagine... here I am with a libel suit, probably, on my hands!

LUDOVICO. But this old man — the father of the young lady?

CANTAVALLE. He is raising the very devil! The girl, at first, was angry but later on, you understand... there she was about to be married... well... just what you might expect! Tears; convulsions; hysterics — a pretty mess! The consul you see, became acquainted with Laspiga out there in Smyrna. Signorina Drei was a governess in the consul's house.

LUDOVICO. So the consul looked up Laspiga?

CANTAVALLE. Yes!

LUDOVICO. It's not hard to guess what the ensign told him! The consul blames Signorina Drei for the death of the baby!

[At this point through the door on the Left, which has been left open, FRANCO LASPIGA rushes upon the stage, pale, trembling, in the greatest agitation, his face *showing the livid pallor that comes from many sleepless nights.* LASPIGA *is twenty-seven years old, light-haired, tall, slender, fashionably dressed.*]

LASPIGA. I beg your pardon! May I come in? Ersilia... where is she? Is she here? Where is she?

LUDOVICO [*in astonishment at this unexpected visit*]. But, who are you?

LASPIGA. I am Franco Laspiga. Signorina Drei tried to kill herself on my account!

CANTAVALLE. Ah! Signor Laspiga! Ah!

LUDOVICO. You here too!

LASPIGA. I went to the hospital, but she had already left, so I hurried to the office of a newspaper where I found out... [*He stops and looks at* CANTAVALLE.] I beg your pardon... you are Signor Ludovico Nota?

CANTAVALLE. Why no...there's Signor Nota!

LASPIGA. Oh, you are Signor Nota?

LUDOVICO. Yes... but how is this? So everybody knows then?

CANTAVALLE. But my dear Signor Nota, you forget who you are!

LUDOVICO [*very much annoyed and raising his arms in helplessness*]. I give up!

CANTAVALLE. Your generous, your magnificent, act has naturally made an impression in town!

LASPIGA [*surprised*]. Magnificent act! What have you done? Tell me! Isn't she here?

LUDOVICO [*to* CANTAVALLE]. I had no intention of seeking notoriety for myself, and much less, notoriety in connection with this young lady!

CANTAVALLE. Oh, please, what do you mean?

LUDOVICO. I am disgusted with this sudden popularity of mine! [*To* LASPIGA.] You will believe me when I say that the young lady has been here less than an hour!

LASPIGA. Oh, so she is here then! Where is she? Where?

LUDOVICO. Why, I went to meet her at the hospital...

LASPIGA. You did? Well?

LUDOVICO. She had no place to go, so I offered her this apartment here! This evening of course I shall go to a hotel myself!

LASPIGA. I am very grateful to you!

LUDOVICO. And why, pray? I suppose ... because I'm not so young as I might be — that's why you're grateful to me! Well, never mind! Why did you come here?

LASPIGA. Why? I came to make good, sir! Make good for the harm I have done ... throw myself at her feet... compel her to forgive me!

CANTAVALLE. That's the way to talk! Good for you! It's all a decent fellow could do!

LUDOVICO. But you might have thought of it a little sooner, it seems to me!

LASPIGA. You're right! Yes! I didn't realize! I had tried deliberately to forget her! I passed whole days... But where is she... in the other room? Let me see her!

LUDOVICO. At just this moment I should prefer...

LASPIGA. No, let me have a talk with her, please!

CANTAVALLE. It might be better, perhaps, to let her know you are here...

LUDOVICO. She's in bed!

CANTAVALLE. The joy of seeing you again might...

LASPIGA. Is she still sick? Is she still in danger?

LUDOVICO. She fainted, right here, a few moments ago!

CANTAVALLE. Then — you understand — any more excitement might...

LASPIGA [*in a frenzy*]. I didn't realize... I couldn't imagine that my leaving her... oh, what an end! All of a sudden, right across my life... breaking everything to pieces... the newsboys shouting those headlines in the papers! It was as if some one had seized me and hurled me to the ground! Our names called out in the streets! My fiancée... her father... her mother... our neighbors in the house where we lived... so I went as fast as I could to the hospital! They wouldn't let me see her! Oh, how I have wronged her; how I have wronged everybody! The whole world seems to be full of the wrong that I have done! And I can't endure it! I must make up for it somehow! I must undo what I have done!

CANTAVALLE. Splendid! Splendid! Just what is needed here! You couldn't beat that ending to the story! I am delighted, Signor Nota, delighted!

[*At this moment* SIGNORA ONORIA *appears in the doorway, Rear, her two hands raised to suggest silence. She closes the door behind her and comes foward.*]

ONORIA. Not so loud! Not so loud, please! She heard everything you said!

LASPIGA. She knows that I am here?

ONORIA. Yes! She does! And she is all worked up! She's in agony! She says she'll jump out of the window if you go in there!

LASPIGA. What? Why should she do that? Won't she forgive me?

CANTAVALLE [*speaking at the same time*]. Why, the idea! On the contrary, she ought...

ONORIA. No, she's an angel! But she says she refuses!

LUDOVICO. Refuses what?

ONORIA [*to* LASPIGA]. She says that you should go back to the girl you were to marry!

LASPIGA [*speaking up quickly and raising his voice in determination*]. No! That's all over, all over!

ONORIA. She doesn't want any harm to come to another girl through her!

LASPIGA. I refuse! What other girl? She is the girl I want to marry! She, and no one else!

ONORIA. No, never mind that! She refuses to consider such a proposition!

LASPIGA. But I came here to get her forgiveness, to make amends for all the harm that I have done her!

ONORIA. Please, please, not so loud! She can hear if you raise your voice like that!

LASPIGA [*to* LUDOVICO]. Won't you go in and explain to her? Try to bring her to reason!

LUDOVICO. Why, yes! This, certainly, would be the best way out for her!

CANTAVALLE. I should say so! It would settle everything!

LASPIGA. Tell her to forget all about what has happened! Tell her that I am here... that my first duty is toward her. Tell her not to spoil this chance we now have to settle everything in time! Please go in and see her! Please!

[LUDOVICO *withdraws through the door, Rear.*]

ONORIA. She is doing it for the sake of that other girl!

LASPIGA. But I have broken with her, absolutely! It's all over! Absolutely all over!

ONORIA. She refuses! She refuses!

LASPIGA. But how can that be? I've broken with the girl! It's all over, and that's all there is to it! I can't change again now! It's a question of myself... here... inside me! I can't, because now everything has come back to me!

CANTAVALLE. Ah, yes... the past! You remember the past now?

LASPIGA. Something that I had almost forgotten... something that... oh, I don't know how... had gotten to be so far, far away... more like a dream than anything else... so that I... it was as though I had never given the promise there, that night — a promise such as a person makes in those circumstances! Yes, because then you almost have to make them!

CANTAVALLE. And then... later on... it all goes out of your mind, eh?

LASPIGA [*continuing vehemently*]. Why, I imagined there was no particular obligation!... I supposed I was quite free! I kept getting letters from her. But I burned them — unable somehow to take them seriously! And yet, it's incredible! I don't understand how I was able to lie like that... lie to myself... do what I have done while, meantime, the promise I had given to her had, in fact, not been withdrawn! It was almost like a dream for me, you see! But there my promise stood! It was true... true... so true, indeed, that when she came here, my betrayal, my treachery toward her... oh, now I understand! For her it was the same as it was for me! Those newsboys calling in the street... and reality was suddenly there, before my eyes! And it struck me down! Crushed me! Annihilated me!

[LUDOVICO *reënters from the door, Rear. He is wearing a very long face. There is a note of perplexity, but still of determination, in his voice.*]

LUDOVICO. It's no use! For the moment it's impossible!

LASPIGA. What do you mean! How can that be?

LUDOVICO. She has promised to see you to-morrow!

LASPIGA. To-morrow? That's ridiculous! I can't wait till to-morrow! I can't stand another night... no!

LUDOVICO. But you'll have to! For the moment there's nothing that can be done.

LASPIGA. But I haven't had a wink of sleep for days! Let me have just one word with her at least!

LUDOVICO. There's no use insisting! It would be worse for you, if you were to see her!

LASPIGA. But why?

LUDOVICO. Let's give her a night to think it over! I talked to her! I told her what you...

LASPIGA. But why does she refuse? On account of that woman? But that's all off! I don't understand! If she tried to kill herself on my account, why does she refuse?

LUDOVICO. She'll come around all right! She'll probably do what you want in the end! But man alive, give her a chance to pull herself together!

CANTAVALLE. And you might calm down a bit, yourself!

LASPIGA. I can't! I can't!

LUDOVICO. Now you just listen to me! I'm quite sure that to-morrow everything will come out all right! We'll bring her around! [*Turning to* SIGNORA ONORIA.] Meantime, you go in to her, please. We mustn't leave her alone!

ONORIA. Yes! Yes! Of course I will go right in! But you'd better turn the lights on, eh? It's getting dark!

[*She goes out through the door, Rear.* LUDOVICO *turns on the lights.*]

LUDOVICO. Now we had better be going, don't you think?

LASPIGA. But can't I even see her?

LUDOVICO. You can see her to-morrow and have a talk with her. I'll come here with you myself. But now we'd better be going!

[*He picks up his hat and cane and stands waiting for the others to precede him through the door.*]

CANTAVALLE. But she ought to see that this solution is the best one for her!

LUDOVICO. For the moment we've got to leave her alone! Let her quiet down a little! She's not well, poor thing! It's too much for her! Shall we go now?

LASPIGA [*stopping in the doorway, Left*]. But I thought that on my coming here...

LUDOVICO [*pushing* CANTAVALLE *toward the door*]. After you, Cantavalle!

CANTAVALLE. Thank you, Signor Nota!
[*He goes to the door.*]

LUDOVICO [*to* LASPIGA]. After you, sir! On the contrary, your coming here...

[*He follows* LASPIGA *out, closing the door behind him. The stage is left empty for a moment. The noises from the street continue.*]

[*The door, Rear, is thrown open and* ERSILIA *appears. She is buttoning the last buttons on her waist.* SIGNORA ONORIA *follows close behind her.*]

ERSILIA. No, I am going away! I am going away!

ONORIA. But where would you go?

ERSILIA. I don't know, but I am going away!

ONORIA. That's a foolish thing to do!

ERSILIA. Oh, I must drop out of sight, somewhere! I must disappear... down there, in the street! I don't know!
[*She starts to put on her hat.*]

ONORIA [*restraining her*]. No! No! I won't let you do any such thing!

ERSILIA. Let me go! Let me go! I refuse to stay here a moment longer!

ONORIA. But why?

ERSILIA. I don't know — because I don't want to see any one! I don't want to talk with any one!

ONORIA. Which means that you won't see him to-morrow?

ERSILIA. No! No! I won't see any one! Let me go!

ONORIA. You won't have to see any one! I'll tell Signor Nota! Don't worry!

ERSILIA. Was it my fault if they saved my life?

ONORIA. Your fault? Nonsense! Your fault!

ERSILIA. But they're accusing me! They're accusing me!

ONORIA. But who is accusing you?

ERSILIA. They are all accusing me... didn't you hear?

ONORIA. Not at all, child! He came to ask your forgiveness!

ERSILIA. Ah, forgiveness! I talked about him because I was going to die! But now... I have had enough of it...

ONORIA. Very well! Let it go at that! You can tell Signor Nota all about it to-morrow!

ERSILIA. I thought I could stay here in peace!...

ONORIA. And why can't you stay here if you want to?

ERSILIA. Because, you'll see! They'll keep after him... they'll annoy him! They'll wear him out!

ONORIA. Signor Nota?

ERSILIA. Signor Nota!

ONORIA. I don't believe it! He's a bit of a crank, Signor Nota is; but he's a good kind man at bottom! You'll see! He's a very good man!

ERSILIA. But there's that other man!

ONORIA. What other man?

ERSILIA. That other man! I didn't even mention his name! He's going to bring a suit against the paper!

ONORIA. The consul?

ERSILIA. The consul! He will never let me alone! [Again rising to her feet.] Oh! Oh! Let me go! Let me go!

ONORIA. But no! Sit down! You just be quiet now! Signor Nota will see about that man! He will keep him in his place! Besides, how can he harm you after the way he's treated you? Don't you worry! You just sit down, here! Don't you see you're hardly fit to be up?

ERSILIA. Yes! Yes! That's so! Oh, what can I do?

ONORIA. Supposing you go in and lie down again... that's a good girl! I will bring you a cup of broth to drink! You'll get a little rest, and then you'll feel better!

ERSILIA [timidly, in a low voice, as one woman, confidingly, to another]. But you understand, don't you? I am just as you saw me and...

ONORIA. And what?

ERSILIA. I haven't a thing, not a thing, with me! In the hotel there, I had a bag! I don't know what has become of it! They probably took it to the police station!

ONORIA. We'll get it back for you to-morrow! Don't worry about that! I'll send some one or I'll go and get it myself!

ERSILIA. Yes! But now, now, I haven't a thing! I am naked! I am naked... naked!

ONORIA [affectionately, comfortingly]. But I'll see to that! I'll see to everything! You just go in to bed and I'll stay with you! Now I'll run downstairs and get something for you! You just lie down and I'll be right back! It won't take me a second!

[She goes out through the door, Left. ERSILIA remains seated on the stage, looking in bewilderment around the room. Her head droops to one side as though she were desperately weary. She seems to have difficulty in breathing. She passes a hand across her cold brow. Apparently in fear of fainting again, she rises, walks to a window, and throws it open. It is evening now. The noises in the street have softened. They are less numerous and less varied. Finally they cease altogether. Silence. A company of young men comes down along the sidewalk, talking, laughing, joking. One of them starts a song, but his voice cracks. An uproar of hoots and guffaws. ERSILIA returns to her seat at the table. The footfalls of the mirthful company grow faint in the distance and finally are heard no more. ERSILIA looks about the room with staring eyes, and in a barely audible voice she murmurs:]

ERSILIA. The street! The street!

CURTAIN

ACT II

The same scene as in Act I. The following morning. The curtain rises on an empty stage. After a time, the door, Left, opens and FRANCO LASPIGA *and* LUDOVICO NOTA, *followed by* EMMA, *the maid, enter.* LUDO-VICO *has his hat on.* LASPIGA *sets his hat on the chair nearest the door. After a time* LUDOVICO *will remove his hat.*

LUDOVICO [*to the maid*]. Is Signora Onoria in?

EMMA [*pointing to the door, Rear*]. She's in the other room with the young lady.

LUDOVICO. Did Signorina Drei have a good night?

EMMA. I don't think so. She was not at all well. I don't believe she got a wink of sleep. Nor did the Signora either.

LASPIGA. If I had been able to say a word to her last evening...

LUDOVICO [*to the maid*]. Won't you just go in and tell Signora Onoria that I am here?

EMMA. Very well, sir!
[*She starts toward the door, Rear.*]

LUDOVICO. Was there any mail?

EMMA. Yes sir! Yes sir! There it is on your desk.
[*She opens the door, Rear, very softly and goes out.*]

LUDOVICO [*picking up his mail from the desk, and addressing* LASPIGA]. Oh, please, have a chair, won't you? Please, have a chair!

LASPIGA. Thank you! I think I'd rather stand!

LUDOVICO [*with a grunt of disgust*]. My, how close it is in here!
[*He goes and opens one of the windows, returning to his mail which proves to be nothing but newspapers. It is market time in the street. The noises from the traffic are as loud as ever. At a certain point* LUDOVICO *loses patience and pulls the window down again. Then he steps over to* LASPIGA, *with a newspaper open in his hand, pointing with his finger to the headlines of an article.*]

LUDOVICO. Here we are! Won't you just read this?
[*He hands the newspaper to* LASPIGA.]

LASPIGA [*after looking it over*]. A correction? Deny the whole story?

LUDOVICO. Yes! It says they will publish it to-morrow!

[*Through the door Rear, comes* SIGNORA ONORIA, *followed by* EMMA, *who crosses the stage and goes out, Left.*]

LASPIGA [*looking up as* ONORIA *enters, anxiously*]. Ah! Here she is! Here she is!

ONORIA [*gesticulating emphatically*]. What a night! What a night!

LASPIGA. And what is she doing! Won't she come in?

ONORIA. She will, if she can! She knows that you are here! She guessed it!

LASPIGA. But... you see the state that I am in! Didn't you tell her?

ONORIA. Don't disturb her, please! She was getting a bit of sleep for the first time, just now.

LUDOVICO. How can a person sleep in this bedlam?

ONORIA. That wasn't it! The maid came in and said you were here with another gentleman! That's what woke her up! I was afraid she would refuse, as she did yesterday.

LASPIGA. Oh no! No!

ONORIA. Well, she didn't. She said she is willing to see you!

LASPIGA. Ah! That's better! She i probably convinced....

LUDOVICO. Oh, of course! And if sh isn't, we'll convince her!

ONORIA. I am not so sure of that Yesterday, after you gentlemen left, sh tried to run away!

LUDOVICO. Run away?

LASPIGA. And where? Why did sh want to go?

ONORIA. Who knows? I had to do m very best to keep her! But one thing don't understand... why did they ever l her out of the hospital? She isn't an; where near well!

LUDOVICO [*bored, and rather coldl*] But when she was with me yesterday!..

ONORIA. Oh, I don't think so! She w doing her best to bear up, you see — tryi

to conceal her pain! She's so afraid you
will be getting tired of all this!

LUDOVICO. I? Not at all! But...
now... it's rather....

[*He nods in* LASPIGA's *direction.*]

LASPIGA. Yes, I'll take care of her! I'll
make her well again!

ONORIA. But now I think I'll go downstairs and lie down for a moment. I'm all
worn out! I have not had a wink of sleep!
But of course, if there's any need of me!...

LUDOVICO. Yes, by all means!

ONORIA. ... you gentlemen can just call
me! [*She starts toward the door,* Left, *but
stops and comes back, speaking to* LUDO-
VICO.] One thing perhaps you don't know!
The poor child hasn't a thing with her!
They took her bag away, either the people
in the hotel or the police! We've got to
get it back for her!

LUDOVICO. Yes! Yes! I'll attend to
that!

ONORIA. But right away, if you can!
This morning! She says she is... [ONORIA
hesitates at the word "*naked.*"] A girl has
got to dress these days, you know. You'll
attend to it?

LASPIGA. I'll attend to it! I'll attend
to it!

ONORIA. I think it would be better if
you would, Signor Nota!

LUDOVICO [*again with some annoyance*].
Yes, don't worry! Don't worry! [*Then
changing tone.*] Now, we're waiting for her
to say whether....

ONORIA. Oh, please don't be harsh with
her!

LUDOVICO. Ah, I like that! Yesterday
you wanted to drive her out of the house,
and now....

ONORIA. But yesterday I didn't know...
oh, now she reminds me of a little stray
dog lost on the streets, with all the other
dogs after her! And the gentler she is, the
more helpless she is, the more they worry
her and torment her. The poor child!
She is crushed, discouraged! She hardly
dares say her soul's her own!

LUDOVICO [*angrily taking out his handkerchief and blowing his nose*]. But now, you
understand, things look a little different,
even to me!

ONORIA. What? Anything about her?
[*She nods toward the door, Rear.*]

LUDOVICO. Why, the whole story!...
I thought everything was settled! And it
is all so different from the way I had
imagined it! Things couldn't be worse,
really! In the first place, that reporter
with his newspaper! Then, there's this
gentleman here! [*He points to* LASPIGA.]
Then there's that consul tearing around
and making a fuss! [*Putting his handkerchief back into his pocket, and addressing*
LASPIGA.] Did you read what it said in
the paper there?

LASPIGA. But you mean that Grotti, the
consul, is here in town?

LUDOVICO [*angrily*]. Where else? He's
in town and so is everybody else! It seems
that the father of the young lady you were
going to marry has had a talk with him!

LASPIGA [*in surprise and with some
alarm*]. Had a talk with him? And why,
please?

LUDOVICO. Oh, who knows? Probably
to find out all he can about the situation!

LASPIGA [*angrily*]. What do they want
of me? They slammed the door in my
face! But am I to infer that this man
Grotti — the consul, that is — has turned
against her?

[*With a nod toward the door, Rear.*]

ONORIA. Oh, they're all against her!

LUDOVICO. It looks that way! In fact,
it's very certain! You understand, I live
here, all taken up with my writing....

LASPIGA [*angry, talking more to himself
than to anybody else*]. I should like to
know why that man Grotti....

LUDOVICO. He could probably tell you
himself if you asked him! For my part,
I'm just a writer... and I got interested in
this affair because it seemed to me a curious
situation — a "slice of life" — where
things and people were — naturally — as
I had imagined they were. Now, all this
mixup... one thing after another... well,
yes... I'll speak right out — it's getting
on my nerves! It has spoiled things for
me! Spoiled things completely! But,
fortunately, you are here!

LASPIGA. Yes, I am here! I am here!

ONORIA. Well, I'll be going, I think! But you gentlemen will just try...

[*She makes a gesture of warning "be careful!" — with her two hands and goes out through the door, Left.*]

LASPIGA [*energetically*]. My idea is to take her away off somewhere! I can, you know... with my connections! Somewhere away off... far away!

LUDOVICO. But don't get too excited, eh? You see what happens!

LASPIGA. Yes, but how about her?

[*With a nod toward the door, Rear.*]

LUDOVICO. It seems to me she's the most unfortunate proof of the danger there is in losing your head! I mean that she is a victim of just that very thing!

LASPIGA. Yes, a victim! But why? It was, precisely to keep from losing my head, as you say, that I betrayed her... betraying myself first of all! I left the navy... I gave up the sea, to drown here, in this way, in the slime of an ordinary humdrum scandal!

LUDOVICO. Whereas, my dear fellow, at a certain point....

LASPIGA [*with increasing intenseness*]. No! No! It's when we become convinced that we can't live as we had dreamed of living! It's when we realize that what seemed to us so easy in our dreams — so easy that we could almost lay our hands upon it— has become difficult, impossible to attain!...

LUDOVICO. Yes! But because at certain moments our soul frees itself from all common trivialities....

LASPIGA. Yes! Exactly! Exactly!

LUDOVICO. ...soars above the petty obstacles of daily life, forgets all about the petty, insignificant needs we ordinarily feel, shakes from its shoulders all commonplace cares....

LASPIGA. Exactly! And now free, unshackled, master of itself, it seems to breathe a fresher air... it tingles with life, ardor, enthusiasm... and the most difficult things, as, I said, become easy....

LUDOVICO. ...and everything is possible! Everything is fluid, liquid, smooth-running... a state of divine intoxication ... yes, but this happens only at certain moments, my dear fellow, and those moments pass!

LASPIGA [*violently*]. Yes, because our souls are not strong enough! They are unable to bear up under all that inspiration, that's why!

LUDOVICO [*with a smile*]. No, it isn't that! It's because you don't know all the tricks, all the surprises — pleasant and unpleasant — that that soul of yours is playing on you as it breathes there in the airy sublimity of such moments — when it has shaken off all restraints, abandoned all reflection, surrendered utterly to the glory of its dreams! You don't notice those things, but some fine day — and it is an ugly day — you feel yourself pulled down to the solid earth again!

LASPIGA. Yes, that's it! But at such times we shouldn't give in — that's the point! We should refuse to come down to the solid earth again! And that's why I tell you that I am going to go back out there, far away... take her back to the place where she lived, waiting for me, happy, joyous, confident in the glory of that dream which to me — because my soul, my spirit, had been clouded somehow — had come to look like an attack of madness from which I had recovered — rejoicing even in my recovery, as though . had furnished proof to myself that I was o a very wise and prudent self-control! Bu now I feel... I feel as if I had got back th exaltation which I lost! I have found th soul I had at that time! I have foun myself again — and this I owe to her!

LUDOVICO. But I advise you not to ge too excited! Don't lose your heae You'll see how far she has fallen!

LASPIGA. But I'll set her on her fee again! I'll make her what she was befor

[*The door, Rear, opens and* ERSILIA *appear* Oh, here she is now! [*At sight of her h voice faints almost to a whisper.*] O]

[ERSILIA *is pale and wan, her hair falli disheveled over her shoulders. In de perate resolution, she goes straight* LUDOVICO.]

ERSILIA. I can't! Signor Nota! can't! I should not have accepted ev this much! Your proposal... no... it's impossible! I can't! I give it all up! I renounce everything!

LUDOVICO. But my dear child, what in the world are you talking about! Don't you see who's here! [*Pointing to* LASPIGA.]

LASPIGA. Ersilia! Ersilia!

ERSILIA. You — why are you calling me! Don't you see who I am? Don't you see what I am? Oh, please! Don't!

LASPIGA [*advancing toward her passionately*]. I see how you are suffering! I see that you are ill! But you are still my Ersilia... my Ersilia... and you will be the same Ersilia you have always been!

ERSILIA [*recoiling before him*]. Don't touch me! Don't touch me! Let me alone!

LASPIGA. You talk that way to me? But you belong to me! You must be mine as you used to be!

ERSILIA. Oh, this is horrible! I can't endure it! What can I say? How can I make you understand that for me everything was to have been all over — all over!

LASPIGA. All over? How can it be all over! I am here with you again?

ERSILIA. What you were for me out here you can never be again!

LASPIGA. But I can! I can! I am still the same! I am still the same!

ERSILIA. No! But even if you were, I must tell you — you should be able to see for yourself! — that I am not and can never be the same!

LASPIGA. That isn't so! You tried to kill yourself, but for my sake, you said! Well then...

ERSILIA [*with desperate resolve*]. Well then — it wasn't true!

LASPIGA. It wasn't true?

ERSILIA. It wasn't true, I say! It was not for your sake! It was not on your account! Why — I didn't even try to find you when I came here! I was lying!

LASPIGA. Lying?

ERSILIA. Yes! I gave a reason — a reason which at that particular moment happened to be true... but it isn't the reason any longer!

LASPIGA. Not the reason any longer? And why not?

ERSILIA. Because I, unfortunately... I — to my sorrow, am alive now! I am alive again!

LASPIGA. Fortunately, I should say! It seems to me the greatest of good fortunes!

ERSILIA. No, thank you! Good fortune! You are trying to force me to be the woman I tried to kill! No! No! Enough of that! Enough of her! For her it was on your account, as she said! Leave it that way! But it doesn't hold for me now ... neither for me nor for you! That's all!

LUDOVICO. But why doesn't it hold, my dear child?

LASPIGA. That was why you tried to kill yourself!

ERSILIA. Exactly! Exactly! That was a reason for dying... a reason for ending it all! But I didn't die, did I? It doesn't hold any longer!

LASPIGA. But I can arrange everything, can't I! I can make everything right!

ERSILIA. No! No!

LASPIGA. Why not? The reason you had for dying should now be a reason for living, it seems to me!

LUDOVICO. Of course it should!

LASPIGA. That's why I came here!

ERSILIA [*with a cold determined voice, pronouncing the syllables one by one and stressing each with a gesture of her two hands, her forefingers crossed over her thumbs*]. I doubt if I even know you!

LASPIGA [*in surprise*]. You don't know me?

[ERSILIA *makes a sudden gesture with her two hands wide opened, and falls into a chair — to the amazement of the two men who stand there looking at her as though she were an entirely different person from the one they had supposed her to be. A pause.*]

ERSILIA. Don't torment me! [*Another pause, then resuming her former manner.*] Don't you find it hard to recognize me?

LASPIGA [*tenderly, in a voice that shows his inner anguish*]. Why, no! Of course I don't! Why do you think I should?

ERSILIA. Do you know one thing? If I had seen you sooner, I really would not have been able to say...

LASPIGA. Say what?

ERSILIA. That I tried to kill myself on your account! Besides, I didn't! But anyhow, your voice!... your eyes!... Not at all!... Is that the voice you talked to me with? Is that the way you looked at me? I thought of you rather... well, who knows how I thought of you!

LASPIGA [*suddenly chilled*]. You are driving me away, Ersilia! You are making me doubt myself... and doubt you!

ERSILIA. Because you can't understand! You can't! You can't understand what it means for a life to come back upon you like this... like... like a memory!... but a memory which, instead of rising from within you, comes upon you unexpectedly from without — and so changed that you are scarcely able to recognize it! You can't fit it into your life somehow, because you too have changed! Nor can you adapt yourself to it — though you understand all the while that it once was your life, an experience of yours, as you may have been once — though not for yourself, not as you really were... the way you talked... the way you looked... the way you acted... in the memory of the other person — but not the way you really were!

LASPIGA. But I am the same person, Ersilia! I am going to be the same to you! I want to be the same to you!

ERSILIA. But you can't! Don't you understand? You can't! Because as I look at you now, I am certain that you have never been the man I thought you were!

LASPIGA. What?

ERSILIA. Why are you so surprised? I have noticed that you, too, right here... right now, listening to me, seeing me, have been having quite the same impression!

LASPIGA. Yes, that's true, but only because you have been saying things...

ERSILIA. Things that are true! Well, why don't you profit by them? Everybody can, except me! I can't, to be sure! I'm the only one who can't! It's no fault of yours!

LASPIGA. But please, please, what's no fault of mine?

ERSILIA. What you did to me!

LASPIGA. That was no fault of mine?

But I am here precisely because I wronged you!

ERSILIA. Oh, in life... in life people do such things! They can, you know!

LASPIGA. But afterwards they feel sorry, as I do — and it's a sincere sorrow I feel! It isn't merely that I recognize my duty toward you!

ERSILIA. But supposing you then discover that I am not the woman you thought I was?

LASPIGA [*in despair, as she persists in that way*]. Oh dear me! What in the world are you talking about?

ERSILIA. And for you, too, Signor Nota ... quite a different person! But I assure you, for you I would have done my very best to be the woman you imagined! And for you... yes, for you, I might have succeeded! It would have been a question of living in the fiction you created... But life!... No! No! You see, life, the life I tried to escape from, refuses to let me go! It has sunk its teeth into me! It refuses to let me go! And now here they all are upon me again! Where can I go?

LUDOVICO [*to* LASPIGA]. I told you so! The young lady needs a rest! Little by little she will get herself in hand again and...

ERSILIA. You too are trying to hurt me now, Signor Nota?

LUDOVICO. Hurt you? No, quite the contrary!

ERSILIA. But you must realize that it is no longer possible!

LUDOVICO. Why not, please?

ERSILIA. You seemed to have understood it all so well! I suppose for you it can easily be... just nothing... or if anything, a pleasure! You were supposing many things of an image that existed only in your own mind, but those things I suffered in my living flesh! I actually lived, actually endured the shame, the disgust, the horror of it all!

LUDOVICO. Oh, is that what you are thinking of?

ERSILIA. Tell him! Tell him! Tell him what I did! Then he'll go away?

LUDOVICO. Not at all! Not at all! No one can blame you for having done that

ERSILIA. Well, then, I'll tell him myself! Look! Out there! On the street! I offered myself to the first man that came along!

LUDOVICO [breaking in, anxiously, as LASPIGA covers his face with his hands]. But in a moment of despair, the night before she tried to kill herself! Understand?

LASPIGA. Yes! Yes! Oh, Ersilia!

LUDOVICO. The next morning she took poison on a bench in the park because she didn't have enough money left even to pay her bill at the hotel! You understand?

LASPIGA. Yes! Yes! I understand! And that makes my sorrow, and my remorse, and my responsibility all the greater! Oh, I must pay you back for all the harm that I have done you!

ERSILIA [with a cry, exasperated]. No! No! You! Oh!

LASPIGA. I, of course! Who else?

ERSILIA [with utter bitterness]. So then you insist! You will make me tell it all! You will tear it out of me — things a woman would never admit even to herself! She pauses a moment to master her emotions, then she says, firmly, decisively, gazing fixedly into space in front of her.] I measured coldly, deliberately, dispassionately, the disgust I felt, to see whether I would be able to bear up under it! I rouged and powdered my cheeks before going out of the hotel! I had a bottle in my purse... a bottle of poison! I was a nurse you see — had three of those bottles in my bag! I kept them with me all the time — it was a disinfectant! So I rouged my cheeks, and just as you imagined, Signor Nota, I looked at myself in the glass, there, on my dresser in the hotel! I did that not only before I went out that first time! I did it also the second time — when I went out to kill myself! But as I sat there on the bench in the park I did not know, I refused to admit, that I could ever do such a thing! And yet, it wasn't so hard, was it? I could have tried again if circumstances had been favorable! Supposing some one had come along who found me attractive or who was not repulsive to me? Well, in that case I couldn't have killed myself, would I? I am not sure I would have! Notice — I

had rouged my cheeks again, and this time I had even painted my lips, and I had put on my newest dress — on purpose! [She leaps to her feet.] But if I am here now... well, what does it mean? It means that I overcame the loathing I felt after having a chance to compare that with death! Otherwise I should not be here now, with a man who, without even knowing me, wrote me a letter, offering me shelter, under his roof!

LASPIGA [with sudden decision]. Listen! I know! I know why you talk the way you are talking! I know why you enjoy tormenting yourself like this.

ERSILIA [violently]. I? It is you who are tormenting me!

LASPIGA. Ah, you see! You even say so yourself! You regard all this as a cruelty on the part of other people! Well then, won't you let one of those other people make amends for that cruelty, when his conscience has at last awakened?

ERSILIA. Make amends? How? By tormenting me still further?

LASPIGA. Why, no, of course not!

ERSILIA [hammering on each word]. I tell you I was just pretending! I tell you that it isn't true! I tell you that I lied, and I repeat it! It wasn't anybody's fault! It wasn't your fault! It was life... just life! The life I was tired of! The life I tried to escape from! The life that has found me again — oh, how horrible — without my ever having succeeded in getting my feet on the ground! What else need I tell you to drive you away?

[There is a loud knock at the door, Left.]

LUDOVICO. What is it?

EMMA [entering]. Signor Grotti is here ... the consul!

ERSILIA [with a scream]. Ah, here he is! I knew he would come!

LUDOVICO. Does he want to see me?

LASPIGA. I am here too!

EMMA. No, he wants to have a word with the Signorina!

ERSILIA. Yes! Yes! Let him come in, please! Let him come in! [To EMMA.] Show him in! [EMMA withdraws.] It is just as well that I have a talk with him, and the sooner the better!

[GROTTI, *the consul, enters. He is a man in his late thirties, dark-haired, solidly built. On his face and in his eyes, an expression of hard and almost cruel reserve. He is wearing a black suit.*]

ERSILIA. Come in, Signor Grotti! [*Introducing him to* LUDOVICO.] Signor Grotti, the Italian consul at Smyrna! [*Then to* GROTTI.] Signor Ludovico Nota!...

GROTTI [*with a bow*]. A name familiar to me!

ERSILIA [*continuing*]. Signor Nota was kind enough to offer me hospitality here! [*With a gesture toward* LASPIGA.] Signor Franco Laspiga, whom you already know!

LASPIGA. You knew me under far different circumstances... but now I am here!

ERSILIA [*breaking in*]. Please! Please!

LASPIGA. No! [*Turning to* GROTTI.] Look! [*With a gesture toward* ERSILIA.] Here is the woman whose hand I asked of you in marriage, — out there!

ERSILIA [*in great anger*]. Please! Please! No more of that!

LASPIGA. I will say no more! [*To* GROTTI.] Her anger, the condition you find her in, will explain sufficiently why you see me here!

ERSILIA [*impatiently*]. Never mind about my condition! I have told you repeatedly that there is no reason for your remaining here, and I am glad to repeat it now in the presence of Signor Grotti so that he may know that, if I am angry, I am angry because you refuse to understand.

LASPIGA. Yes, you repeat it because you are aware that the father of the girl I was to marry has had a talk with him!

ERSILIA [*in surprise*]. No! I didn't know that! [*She looks at* GROTTI, *in dismay, doing her best to control herself.*] Ah, and you... you talked to him about me?

GROTTI [*coolly, with perfect composure*]. No, Signorina, but I promised him I would come and have a talk with you!

LASPIGA [*breaking in violently*]. It won't do the slightest good, you know!

ERSILIA [*with a burst of imperious anger*]. I should like to have a word alone with Signor Grotti! [*Turning to* LUDOVICO, *her voice softening.*] Won't you let me, Signor Nota?

LUDOVICO. Why, as far as I am concerned... [*He starts to leave the room.*]

LASPIGA [*detaining him, resolutely*]. No, wait a moment! [*Turning to* ERSILIA, *coldly, on his dignity.*] I shall not intrude, but I must say something here to Signor Grotti so that he may deliver the message to anybody interested! Now *that is all over*, all over! [*With a gesture toward* ERSILIA.] That is a point not for her but for me to decide! [*To* ERSILIA.] And I insist on this, right here, before you! Hitherto I have begged you, beseeched you, to do as I say! I have consented to listen to the most cruel things from your lips. But now I am through! It is my turn to speak in another tone of voice! You can send me away; but that doesn't mean that I shall ever go back to a woman who, outraged, justly outraged, at the story printed in the papers about you, closed her door in my face in an impulse of displeasure and shame, but now changes her mind, repents, and tries to fix things up in a roundabout way through you, here!

GROTTI. Oh, that isn't the point! I didn't come here on that account!

ERSILIA. I have told you that anything you may have done was in no way responsible for my trying to kill myself!

LASPIGA. That's not so!

ERSILIA. What? Signor Nota here can bear me witness!

LASPIGA. Yes, he can testify that you said such things! Very well! [*Turning to* GROTTI.] She said the most terrible things about herself, "things," as she said "which a woman would never admit even to herself!" But I have my own sense of what is right and wrong, even if your conscience compels you to refuse me because of a wrong you may have done to me! But my conduct cannot be modified by anything that he [*With a gesture toward* GROTTI.] may say to you, or that you may say to him — in the interest of some third person for whom you are both working together! There! That was what I wanted to say! [*To* LUDOVICO.] I am ready now, Signor Nota! And I know that you are on my side and that you agree with me! Good morning, Signor Grotti, good morning!

[*He starts for the door, Left.*]

LUDOVICO [*to* ERSILIA, *in a low affectionate voice, trying to encourage and reassure her*]. I'll just run out and see about that bag of yours! I hope I can have it here for you very shortly!

ERSILIA. Yes, thank you! And you'll forgive me, won't you, Signor Nota?

LUDOVICO. But my dear girl, there's nothing to forgive you for! Good morning, Signor Grotti!

GROTTI. Good morning!

[LUDOVICO *and* LASPIGA *withdraw through the door, Left. The moment the door closes,* ERSILIA *loses her composure. She seems to shrink in upon herself, all of a tremble, looking up fearfully at* GROTTI, *who stands there surveying her with a gaze of cold and hostile scorn. Unable to resist this stare,* ERSILIA *hides her face in her hands, raising one shoulder to cover her cheek, as though to protect herself from the hate he is darting upon her.*]

GROTTI [*approaching her, his voice almost a hiss*]. You fool! You dunce! You idiot! Lying like that! Just plain stupid lying!

ERSILIA [*terrified, without lowering her defense*]. But I wanted to die! I really tried to die!

GROTTI [*insisting, violently*]. And why? And why all the lies after that? And why bring this final remorse upon yourself?

ERSILIA [*quick to justify herself*]. No, it wasn't for my own sake! Don't you understand? And he says that I have nothing to do with it, too! But I actually screamed it in his face! I told him that I had lied! I told him it wasn't true that I had tried to kill myself on his account!

GROTTI [*angrily, with a sneer*]. But he thinks you did! Don't you know he thinks you did?

ERSILIA [*aroused to her own defense, and now mistress of herself*]. How can I help that? It's his remorse! It's his remorse! He would be ready to believe me — if it weren't for his own sense of guilt!

GROTTI [*contemptuously*]. How do you dare speak of the wrong other people have done? How dare you? You!

ERSILIA. You think I have done more wrong than the rest of you? You think that I have more reason to feel guilty than the rest of you? You're mistaken! I have less reason than anybody else! Yes! Yes! Oh, I understand... you won't admit that, because it was I who had the courage to kill myself, and not you!

GROTTI. I? I should have killed myself?

ERSILIA. Oh, don't worry about that! It wasn't from remorse that I tried to die! And you — you needn't feel alarmed about anything you did! You have money! You don't have to worry about your next day's living! But I... I was in the street! I was poor! I was naked! And in such circumstances, you know, it's harder!... In my despair I thought of your little girl; and I had already experienced the last, the extreme humiliation a woman can suffer! All that together! That was why I was strong enough to do what I did!

GROTTI. But you couldn't help lying even then, could you?

ERSILIA. It wasn't because I meant to lie! You see — he had promised to marry me, back there in Smyrna!

GROTTI. Yes, but it was a joke!

ERSILIA. That isn't true! But even if it were — well, all the more dishonorable on his part! Because he didn't know about what happened there between you and me, after he went away! He got engaged to another girl here and was about to marry her!

GROTTI. But you! *You* knew what had happened between you and me, and — you lied!

ERSILIA. All the same, what he was doing was worse! Without knowing that I had been false to him, he was deserting me here, as calmly as you please! Actually marrying another woman!

GROTTI. Just as I say, then! It was a joke! Any promise he made at Smyrna, he could not have meant seriously.

ERSILIA. No! He really promised... but in any case, he says he meant it, now, as you have just heard! But you are saying all this to make things easy for yourself! It eases your conscience! It gives you an excuse for what you did there — behind his back — the moment he went away!

GROTTI. And you raised all this rumpus here just to prevent him from marrying another woman!

ERSILIA. No! I didn't even dream of such a thing! I said what I said when I thought I was going to die! I wasn't trying to stop anything, and I'm not trying to now! I refuse! I refuse!

GROTTI. But supposing he had remained faithful to you... supposing you had found him here, quite free, and ready to make his promise good?...

ERSILIA [shuddering]. No! No! Never! I would never have deceived him! I swear to you by the soul of your little girl — I would never have deceived him! I didn't go near him! Ask him yourself! I didn't go near him! It was because he had betrayed me — and it was real treachery on his part — that I was able to tell the lie I told, saying that I had tried to kill myself on his account!

GROTTI. You didn't look him up?

ERSILIA. No!

GROTTI. How did you know about his engagement, then?

ERSILIA. Oh yes, I did look him up, but I went there, to the Navy Building!

GROTTI. Yes! Trust you not to look him up!

ERSILIA [with difficulty restraining the helpless rage within her, threateningly]. You ought to be grateful to me!

GROTTI. What for? For your having gone to look him up?

ERSILIA. No! They told me he had resigned his commission in the navy and that he was soon going to be married! That took away from me every temptation of revenge! Hah! You think you have caught me? You think I had some design in going to the Navy Building? You don't understand the state of mind I was in when I went there! Here I was, absolutely alone in the world, lost, driven out of the house by your wife after she surprised us there in that terrible moment — the people down in the street calling, shouting, because the baby had fallen from the roof! I was in utter despair! I was like a beggar, with nothing, nothing to look forward to, except death — or the insane asylum! I was out of my mind, and I wanted to find him... to tell him everything!

GROTTI. You were going to tell him about us two?

ERSILIA. Not about me! About you! About you! After his departure you took advantage...

GROTTI. Only about me?

ERSILIA. Yes! And about how you treated me! Look, I can tell everything now... everything... things that no one would ever dare to tell! I have reached bottom, the very bottom. I can scream the truth that only lunatics dare tell... the truth that a person tells when he thinks he can never get to his feet again... since the truth is all he has to hide his innermost shame! You came to me there when my flesh was tingling with the passion which he had aroused... when I was unable to resist the slightest touch! Deny it if you dare! Deny that I beat you, that I scratched your face, your neck, your hands, your arms!

GROTTI. Oh! You were leading me on!

ERSILIA. You are lying! Not in the least! It was you!

GROTTI. At first... yes, but after that...

ERSILIA. Never! Never!

GROTTI. You pinched my arm as I was standing near you!

ERSILIA. I didn't!

GROTTI. You are lying! You even came up behind me once and pricked me with a needle!

ERSILIA. But because you didn't leave me alone!

GROTTI. Fine! Fine!

ERSILIA. I was your servant!...

GROTTI. So I suppose you had to obey?

ERSILIA. My flesh... yes! My flesh obeyed, but my heart... no, never... my heart never! I hated you!

GROTTI. But you wanted me!

ERSILIA. No! No! It was hatred I hated you — and all the more because

wanted you! After that I could have torn
you to pieces like my shame itself! My
heart was never yours! My heart was
bleeding because I was stealing that pleasure — like a thief — betraying my real
heart! I looked at my naked arms and I
bit them. I yielded to you — yes! I
kept yielding! But I felt all the while inside me that my heart... no... my heart
never yielded! Oh, you fiend! It was
you who robbed me of the only real joy I
ever had in my life... a joy so great I could
hardly believe it true — the joy of feeling
that I was about to become a wife!

GROTTI. Meantime he was over here,
getting himself another woman!

ERSILIA. So you see? You are all like
that! You are all worthless! You are all
dogs! And now you have the face to come
and tell me that it's my fault... my fault
because I have never had the strength to be
anything... no... not one thing, not even
a doll that you might make with your hands
out of wax or clay! And a doll... well, if
you drop a doll on the floor it breaks,
doesn't it?... and the pieces tell you that at
least it was a doll! But I... my life... just
one day following the day before it!...
No one whom I could ever call mine!...
Pulled this way and that by the things
about me! Never a will of my own!
Never able to feel myself on solid ground!
Tormented, tortured, trodden under foot!
Never the power to rise and say "Here am
I!" [Suddenly changing tone and turning
on him like an animal stung with a lash.]
But tell me, what are you doing here?
How is it you have dared to come into my
presence again?

GROTTI. Because you've gone and
blabbed... that's why! Because you've
talked! You have made a mess of things!
You tried to kill yourself!

ERSILIA. Oh, yes! I should have kept
my mouth shut, I know! A hole in the
ground and a stone on top... and good-bye!

GROTTI. As for the stone... you've gone
and thrown it into a puddle and you've
splashed the mud all around on everybody!
All of us are covered!

ERSILIA. Yes, and the mud sticks, eh?

GROTTI. Yes, the mud sticks!

ERSILIA. Whereas life...

GROTTI. The mud sticks! You have
made a cesspool all around yourself!

ERSILIA. But you want me to be the only
one to get drowned in it, don't you? You
two want your lives to run along easily,
as before! When he finds out about you
and me, he will go back to his fiancée; and
you will go back to your consulate in
Smyrna!

GROTTI. And to all my life. A life that
you, cursed woman, broke up for a moment, to my confusion! Do you think
you know me! Do you think that bit of
nonsense, that moment or two of play, was
really me! And what have you made it
cost me? You have made it cost me the
unhappiness of my whole life: the death of
my little girl!

ERSILIA. It was you! It was you! I
can see it all still! That chair, which I had
carried up to the roof for the baby, and
you didn't give me time to take it down
again!

GROTTI. But what were you doing on
the roof? Your place was there, in the
room where my wife was sleeping, sick!
You should have been ready to answer if
she called! What were you doing on the
roof?

ERSILIA. I was working, and the baby
was playing!

GROTTI. No! You went there on purpose... knowing that I would follow you!

ERSILIA. What a coward! You would
have come to me even there, in that room,
at your wife's bedside!

GROTTI. No! No!

ERSILIA. Say no if you dare! As though
you hadn't tried so many times before!
And so — since I didn't feel safe even
there...

GROTTI. But because you wanted me,
too! Because you wanted me, too!

ERSILIA. No, because — you should say
— because in the end, after all your in-
sistence, after all the temptation you put in
my way, I would have wanted you! That
is what you might say! I went up to the
roof so she couldn't hear... so your wife
couldn't hear! Ah, but now I know!
Something inside me kept warning me! I

knew I shouldn't leave the chair just where I did! Because the baby was there with her toys, playing, on the roof! She might get up on the chair and fall off! I knew that! My common sense kept telling me that! But I didn't listen... I didn't listen! Don't you remember? You came upon me from the stairway, like a wild animal! And you insisted... you insisted! Oh! I dream of it, nights, still! It is always before my mind! I can see it there... the chair... near the railing! I see it in my dreams and in my dreams I try to move it away... to move it away... and I can't... I can't!

[She bursts into a sob.] [A pause.]

GROTTI [absorbed in his own thoughts and trying in his own mind to get a look at his life apart from all that horror. ERSILIA meantime continues sobbing convulsively]. I was busy with my work, I was always a hard worker! I lived outside myself, for other people, wholly for other people!... My mind always on my work!... And a great emptiness in my life!... The home I had dreamed of I had never had! The woman I had married — gloomy, sickly, unattractive! There I was, far from home, and homesick! And the gratitude of our people there!... They kept coming to me and asking me to help them, and they were grateful for the attentions I gave them — for my courtesy, my kindness, my assistance,... and this cheered me, made me patient, good-natured, affectionate, even to my wife! And you came... how did I treat you at first when you came?

ERSILIA [tenderly, through her tears]. You were very kind to me!

GROTTI. Because the more depressed, the more unhappy I felt inside, the greater my need for doing good to others, for carrying all the burdens myself, that the lives of others might be made easier! And because of this need I felt of making life pleasant for others — that my own life, after a fashion, might be more bearable — since I could never be really happy!... And how I described you to him when he came into the harbor there, on his warship! How I praised you... making you out the sweetest and most beautiful woman that ever lived! It was to do you a good turn, to make him

fall in love with you! And during those days I was kinder than ever toward my wife, for I wanted her to be well disposed toward you! I wanted her to help me carry out the little plan I had made for your life — and I made it just for the pleasure it would give me to know that you would be owing all your good fortune to me! And when I saw that you were in love with each other... No, no! It wasn't because I knew that you had gone too far ... that you had given yourself to him!... That made my wife angry, but not me! It made her lose all respect for you!

ERSILIA. But only with him! I had never loved any one else before! He was going away, and the night before he left... I was mad! I was mad!

GROTTI. I know! I understand! I never thought of blaming you! And I would never have profited by your weakness, if you...

ERSILIA. I?

GROTTI. Not that you meant to... but I don't know... you looked at me once as we were getting up from the table... because, you see, you couldn't imagine!... I felt that you didn't believe I had been kind to you out of a pure, unselfish desire to make you happy! That's the point! And because you didn't really understand, you spoiled everything! Because I needed that faith on your part more than ever — to keep going, to resist temptation!

ERSILIA. But not temptation from me ... not from me!

GROTTI. No, the temptation within myself! But if you had understood how disinterested my kindness was, how sincere and real it was, the beast would never have awakened in me all of a sudden as it did, with all its desperate fury! And even now, as I see you here before me, after you have laid an insurmountable obstacle — the dead body of our child — between me and that woman... [He advances upon her threateningly, hatefully.] No!... understand?... no!

ERSILIA [backing away in alarm]. What do you want?

GROTTI. I want you to suffer... to suffer as I have suffered!... to suffer with me for the wrong that we have both done!

ERSILIA. You want me to suffer more than I have suffered?

GROTTI. All that is past! You took pains to come back to life again! You did!

ERSILIA. No! No!

GROTTI. Taking advantage of the remorse that you knew he would feel!

ERSILIA. No! No! I have told you that I never thought of that! I have told you that I refuse to accept anything from him! And don't you see what I am? This is the house of a man I don't even know! He offered me shelter as I was leaving the hospital, where I thought, where I was sure, I was going to die! I had ceased to hope for anything, and here I am like a person called back from the grave, not knowing what will become of me to-morrow! Let me alone!

GROTTI. But in the end you will do as he says!

ERSILIA. No! Rather than that I will tell him everything! Do you want me to? I am ready to tell him everything!

GROTTI. I refuse to be the only one to suffer punishment for the death of my little girl! I will not allow you now to go off and marry him as though that horrible thing had never happened!

ERSILIA. No! No! I will never marry him! You may be sure of that! I will stay here with the man who has taken me in.

GROTTI. But you won't be able to, don't you see? He already agrees with that other fellow! They both went away together! Nota is already bored with the whole business! He surely thinks you're crazy in not accepting the boy's repentance, and the reparation which he offers!

ERSILIA. But I have told him that I refuse!

GROTTI. Yes, but they of course think you are just obstinate and unreasonable! Neither of them will accept your refusal as final! You have never told him the real reason why you refused!

ERSILIA. Well, I will tell him if necessary.

GROTTI. But then he will be disgusted with what you have done! It will seem to him so ugly — the lie you told, the trouble you have made: a broken engagement; a public scandal; pity you have wrongfully aroused; public sympathy...

ERSILIA [crushed and hardly able to stand]. Yes, that's true! But I... I didn't intend all this! I told him just as I have told you — I told him that I lied because I thought that I was going to die! The truth — we cannot tell! It is too ugly, too horrible! We two have been able to speak honestly to each other because we both are smirched with a common shame! Why do you wish, how can you wish, the truth to be told?

GROTTI. I? That isn't the point! It's because of the lie! If he doesn't know what happened between you and me, he will never go back to his fiancée — he told you so — even if you refuse to accept his reparation.

ERSILIA. I must tell him the truth then, so that he will return to her? Why didn't you tell the truth to her father?

GROTTI. I couldn't!

ERSILIA [sarcastically]. No, you couldn't! You told him you would come and see me and force me to confess everything! Are you so anxious for the truth, then?

GROTTI [with passionate vehemence]. Why, no, no! Why should I be? I don't know those people! I was outraged at your lie... and when the old man described all the trouble it had caused: the girl's indignation; the boy's remorse; his intention to offer marriage to you... I don't know how I restrained myself! I ran to the newspaper office to deny the story so far as it concerned me! You don't know how angry my wife got when she read it all in the papers! She insisted on going to see the young lady at once, to tell her everything ... to tell her how you had been dismissed from our house, even how she had found you with me! I had to keep her quiet... I had to promise her on my honor that the consequences of your falsehood would be remedied at least so far as a wholly innocent family is concerned.

ERSILIA [sarcastically]. I understand! I understand! [A pause. She sits looking straight ahead of her into space, her face

dark and determined.]   Very well!   I
understand!   [*She rises.   Another pause.
At last she says:*]   Well, you go away now!
Everything will be all right!
   GROTTI [*looking at her in dismay*].
What are you going to do?
   ERSILIA. You said we must straighten
everything out!   I'll attend to that!
   GROTTI [*after a pause and still looking at
her fixedly*].   Ersilia!   Ersilia!   You poor
child!   You poor child!   How terrible this
has been for you!   [*He runs toward her to
take her in his arms.*]   Ersilia!   Ersilia!
   ERSILIA [*drawing up haughtily and hold-
ing aloof*].   Ah, no!   That is too much!
Let me alone!
   GROTTI [*forcing himself upon her, trying
frantically to embrace her*].   No!   No!
Listen to me!   Listen to me!
   ERSILIA [*repelling him*].   Let me alone, I
tell you!
   GROTTI [*insisting*].   Let's go away together somewhere and live out our despair
— together!
   ERSILIA [*tearing away from him with a
scream*].   Mimetta!   Mimetta!
   GROTTI [*drawing back, pressing his hands
to his face as though to shut out a horrible
vision*].   You murdered her!   [*A pause.
He is trembling convulsively.*]   I am mad!
I am mad!   [*Again he rushes toward her.*]
But I need you, Ersilia!   I need you!   We
are just two unhappy people!   Let's go
away . . . together!
   ERSILIA [*running to one of the windows*].
Go away!   Go away! . . . Or I will call!
   GROTTI [*insisting*].   No!   Ersilia!   Listen!
Listen!
   ERSILIA [*throwing the window open*].   I'll
call!   Are you going?
        [*The sound of a distant hurdy-gurdy
        playing a gay popular song enters
        through the open window.   ERSILIA
        points to the door with a gesture that
        brooks no denial.*]

CURTAIN

ACT III

*The same set as in the preceding acts.
Toward evening of the same day.   SIGNORA*

ONORIA *is standing at one of the windows,
which is open, allowing unimpeded entrance
to the usual noises from the street; but these
are softening with the end of the day.*
SIGNORA ONORIA *is talking with another
woman, a neighbor, who is, presumably,
leaning out of a window across the street.*
EMMA, *the maid, is busy with the final
touches of her dusting about the room.*

   ONORIA. What's that?   Oh, yes, yes!
I'll tell you about that later.   [*A pause.*]
Till about noon . . . but you know how it is
— that's never like sleeping at night! . . .
[*A pause.*]   What's that?   I couldn't hear!
[*A pause.*]   Ah yes, yes!   She's gone out
now with Signor Nota.   [*A pause.*]   Yes,
to get her bag!   They wouldn't give it to
him.
   EMMA. And you'll see — they won't give
it to her either!
   ONORIA [*still talking through the window*].
Oh, they couldn't, any sooner!
   EMMA. I hope one thing . . . that it won't
be like this every day!
   ONORIA [*drawing her head in and talking
to* EMMA].   What are you growling about?
You make so much noise I can't hear a
thing!
   EMMA. I like to get my work done in
the morning!   Making beds at this time of
the day!   It's almost dark!
   ONORIA [*again with her head out of the
window*].   Signor Nota was probably one
of them!   What do you expect?   [*She
laughs.*]   It seems he's decided to keep her
here!   [*A pause.*]   Not at all!   She won't
have anything to do with that man!   He
must have done the kissing!   [*A pause.
Then excitedly.*]   No!   No!   That can't
be!   You must be mistaken!   It couldn't
have been!   [*A pause.   She waves her hand
in a gesture of farewell.*]   However, I'll see
you later.   Good-bye!   Good-bye!   [*She
lowers the window.*]   What do you think of
that?   She says she saw three men in here
and that they each kissed her!
   EMMA. Even that consul man?
   ONORIA.   That's   ridiculous!   She
couldn't have seen straight!   That old
baboon of a Signor Nota . . . he may have,
but the consul — that's ridiculous!

EMMA. But I heard them talking at the top of their voices when they were in here alone!

ONORIA. And you didn't... I suppose you don't know what they were talking about?

EMMA. Oh, I'm not minding other people's business! I happened to be going through the room under this and I heard them talking very loud — that's all! But she was talking louder than he!

ONORIA. I'd like to know what he wants of the poor girl; and what he was doing here, after he went and made all that trouble with the newspaper, threatening to bring a suit!

EMMA. He's probably trying to keep her from making up with her man!

ONORIA. But what business is that of his? And she won't hear of such a thing either! For my part, I'm sorry!

EMMA. I'd like to see myself turning down a perfectly good husband for an old fool like the one you have here!

ONORIA. And he's getting sick of the whole business! He's trying to get out of it! And I guess he told her as much in so many words! Who knows what he must have thought... as if the poor little thing were making believe! I can't see how she's done so very much that's bad! I can't understand these men sometimes! Some men... well... I just can't understand them! You'd think they were old enough to know better! They get old in years, but in experience...! Why, just imagine!... He goes and gets her at the hospital — picks her up at death's door, you might say, with her insides all burned out with that poison — hardly able to stand on her two feet!... And yet, who knows what good times he was looking forward to! However, that young man comes in and says he's sorry! Then there's that newspaper reporter, afraid of a law-suit, and Nota, as nice as you please, gets scared and backs out!

EMMA. It may be just as well for her in the end! When she sees he won't keep her, she'll probably make up her mind to go with the young man!

ONORIA. Perhaps, but do you know how it is? She don't trust him! She don't trust him!... That's the point! You can fool a girl once all right, but the second time... well, she's more wary! Besides, what he did to her was going pretty strong! She comes here, and what is he up to? He's getting ready to marry another girl, if you please! However, if I guess him right, he's really sorry for it now!

EMMA. I thought so, too!

ONORIA. But, you see, she's worrying about that other girl who would be jilted on her account!

EMMA. I wouldn't worry, if I was her! Why, the poor thing almost died on account of that man!

ONORIA. Yes! Yes! But you mustn't forget that he went away and left her in the lurch! They told all about that in the papers! Perhaps she hates him now! And she must have understood that, here, Signor Nota... [She makes a wry face.]... I saw her when she was going out with him ... well... it seemed to me she had... oh ... a sort of veil in front of her eyes. She stared at everything, but she seemed not to see a thing... and she couldn't speak nor lift her hand! I asked her how she was, but she just smiled, and that smile — it froze me! And then again... her hands were as cold as ice! [She stops suddenly and listens. Then, in a quite different tone of voice.] Why, there's a peddler going by now! Say, you just run down and get me that ribbon — two yards and a half, as I said! I'll stop him from up here as he goes by!

[EMMA runs off stage through the door, Left. SIGNORA ONORIA hurries to a window, throws it open, and leans out, looking down into the street. She spies the peddler and waves to him to stop.

[At this point FRANCO LASPIGA enters through the door to the Left, his face tense and drawn.]

LASPIGA [stopping in the doorway and calling twice, because he can hardly make his voice heard in the noise pouring through the open window]. May I come in? May I come in?

ONORIA [*turning around at last and closing the window*]. Oh, it's you, Signor Laspiga! Won't you have a chair? Signor Nota is out somewhere with the young lady; but he'll be right back. [*Then in a low voice, confidentially.*] You just keep at her and she'll do as you say!

LASPIGA [*looking up at her in surprise as though he had not quite understood. Then sarcastically, in repressed rage*]. Yes! Yes! Don't you worry! I'll keep at her all right!

ONORIA [*confidentially*]. He told her what was what, I assure you! The consul I mean!

LASPIGA [*between his teeth*]. The miserable cur!

ONORIA. You're right! You're right! That poor child!

LASPIGA [*losing control of himself*]. Poor child be damned!... Poor child! You know what that woman is? She's as bad as they make 'em!

ONORIA [*as though some one had struck her in the face*]. Oh dear me! Oh dear me! What do you mean?

[*At this moment* LUDOVICO NOTA *enters from the Left, his hat still on his head.*]

LUDOVICO [*catching sight of* LASPIGA]. Oh, you're here already? [*Then turning to* ONORIA, *but alluding to* ERSILIA.] Hasn't she come in yet?

ONORIA [*turns and looks at him in amazement, then without answering turns to* LASPIGA]. How can this be?

LUDOVICO [*not understanding*]. How can what be?

LASPIGA [*drawing himself up with the greatest determination and speaking vigorously and with heat*]. The fact is that the wife of this Grotti fellow has found out that he came here this morning for a meeting with his mistress!

LUDOVICO [*with a start, in utter astonishment*]. Who? What mistress?

ONORIA. She? The consul's mistress?

LASPIGA. That's what I said! Though I might have used a worse word! So Grotti's wife went to my fiancée's this morning and denounced the whole intrigue to her parents!

LUDOVICO. Intrigue! What intrigue? Signorina Drei — with her husband?

ONORIA. Signorina Drei... the consul's mistress?

LASPIGA. Exactly! Yes, ma'am! Yes, sir! What I don't know is whether this all happened *before* or *after* I asked her to marry me out there in Smyrna! That's what I want to find out now! I came here for that purpose!

ONORIA. Mercy on us! With that man! So they were in cahoots out there, eh? Ah, now I understand! That's why that woman said... [*She nods toward the window.*] Aha, so that's why she said what she said!

LASPIGA. What do you mean?

ONORIA. Why, the woman in the house across the way saw them, and she said he kissed her!

LUDOVICO. Here? Here in this room?

ONORIA. Yes, here in this room! That's what the woman told me, and I wouldn't believe it! She saw him kissing her, through the window there!

LASPIGA. What did I tell you? [*To* LUDOVICO.] Right here... in your house!

ONORIA. Why! Why! Why! This is beyond me! Why! Why! I don't know which end I'm standing on!

LASPIGA. And do you know how, and do you know when, Grotti's wife caught them at it? Their baby fell off the roof and was killed!

ONORIA [*with a scream, covering her face with her hands*]. Oh dear me! Dear me!

LASPIGA. Yes, she caught them! They were together! And she drove this hussy out of the house, because, between the two of them, they had left the baby alone on the roof!

ONORIA. Murder! Murder is no name for it! How do they ever dare look an honest person in the face again? Poor baby! So that was why! So that was why! And they didn't pay her ticket home! I should say not!... After all that!...

LASPIGA. If it weren't partly his fault too, jail would be the place for her! She ought to be in jail!

ONORIA. Jail would be too good for her! I should say so! You are quite right!

LASPIGA. And after all that, you understand...

ONORIA. ... she had the brazen face...

LASPIGA. ... to come and stir up trouble for me!

ONORIA. And not only you — everybody! She's made trouble for everybody!

LASPIGA. But do you realize what she's done to me?

LUDOVICO [musingly, almost to himself]. I wonder! I wonder!...

ONORIA. And posing around here as a martyr! My, what a fraud!

LASPIGA. Everything kicked sky high! My name in the papers! A public scandal! The girl I was going to marry slamming the door in my face! I thought I was losing my head! How I managed not to, I'm sure I don't know!

ONORIA. So that's why... that's why she wanted to get away! The moment she saw you, the moment she found out that other man was here, too,... [She mimics ERSILIA's voice.] "I won't!" "I won't see any one!" "I don't want to talk with any one!" Ha! You bet she didn't! The little fraud! She could see her game was going to be found out! [Spitefully, changing her tone of voice.] I wish I could get back a few of the tears I've wasted in sympathy for her! Poor, downtrodden, little girl, trying to kill herself because she had been betrayed! [Snapping at LUDOVICO.] Let me tell you one thing, Signor Nota; you get that girl out of this house this minute! I won't have her in here again! My doors are closed to her! This is a respectable house! I cannot afford to be mixed up in such a mess!

LUDOVICO [annoyed, but at a loss for something to say]. Let's not be in too big a hurry now! Suppose we wait!

ONORIA. Wait? I've waited long enough! You get her out of here at once! I won't have her! I won't have her!

LUDOVICO. But don't talk so much! I can't hear myself think! Just a moment now! [To LASPIGA.] How does it happen that the consul... [He breaks off.] You know, don't you, that the consul was the very first one to protest against the article in the paper?

LASPIGA. That's easy to understand!

LUDOVICO. It doesn't seem to me so easy to understand! They should have stuck together, it seems to me — as lovers!

LASPIGA. Yes, but his wife was there with him! His wife... and this girl had made the newspaper say atrocious things about his wife!

LUDOVICO [remembering]. Ah, yes! That's so! And in fact... yes... that's why she was so much embarrassed when she found out that the newspaper had said...

ONORIA. ... that this poor woman had sent her up to the roof on an errand!

LASPIGA. His wife must have forced him to deny the story!

LUDOVICO. So then the whole thing is an imposture!

LASPIGA. And a very low-down one! It's vile! It's rotten!

LUDOVICO [continuing]. She must have been lying when she said she tried to commit suicide on your account!

ONORIA. What I should like to know is how a girl could lie as brazenly as that!

LUDOVICO [thoughtfully, to himself]. Ah yes! Of course! And that's why she refused so obstinately to accept any reparation from you!

LASPIGA. It would have been the last straw if she had accepted!

ONORIA. I should say so, you poor man!

LUDOVICO [irritated more and more by ONORIA's chatter and led accordingly to disagree with LASPIGA]. No! Listen! You must admit that she had at least one scruple!

LASPIGA. And when, if you please? When she saw me here, ready to straighten out a mess I thought myself responsible for?

LUDOVICO. I understand that, but...

LASPIGA. And this too, notice, only on the most favorable hypothesis — on the hypothesis, I mean, that she became his lover afterwards! If she was his lover first, I would be the victim — well... imagine for yourself! The victim of the most cowardly deceit conceivable on the part of both of them!

LUDOVICO. Oh no! Hardly that!

LASPIGA. I've come here this time to get that point clear!

LUDOVICO. What do you think you can do? Certainly you can't deny that you met the most decisive and violent opposition on her part!

LASPIGA. But I'm talking about what went on *before*! What went on before!

LUDOVICO. Ah no! That's going too far! In the worst case you would never have suffered any wrong!

LASPIGA. I wouldn't? Why not? I...

LUDOVICO [*insisting*]. No wrong whatever! Even if it did happen *before*! You were about to marry another woman here, remember!

LASPIGA. Not at all! Just a moment!...

LUDOVICO. Let me finish! You were getting even by betraying her!

LASPIGA. But I admitted the wrong I was doing!

LUDOVICO. Even so, you would have been getting even in advance for a wrong you didn't as yet know they had done you!

LASPIGA. You mean that what I did excuses them?

LUDOVICO. Certainly not! But it does prevent you from getting on your high horse! You are not in a position to blame them!

LASPIGA [*violently*]. I beg your pardon! I am in a position to do just that! And she will have to explain: because they went the full length: they played their whole trick on me, while I called my marriage off and came hurrying here!

LUDOVICO. But not until you heard that she had tried to kill herself!

LASPIGA. But it wasn't on my account! She has confessed that herself!

LUDOVICO. But you didn't know that! Here you were, quietly arranging — in ignorance of their duplicity toward you — to marry another woman! You were planning to play your trick on her! It seems to me you're quits, to say the least!

LASPIGA. That's a great idea! You're blaming me for what I did as though anything I might have done could ever be regarded as treachery toward her!

LUDOVICO. No! No! Look! I'm not blaming anybody! I'm simply trying to show you that you are right only in one respect... in the fact merely that she told a lie when she said — without having any right to say it — that she tried to kill herself on your account! Now that lie... that lie... well, it interests me! I can't understand why she should have told that lie!... and have told it there, on the very brink of the grave!

LASPIGA. Why? Because after she had been dismissed on account of the baby's death, she came here with the intention of resuming her relations with me!

LUDOVICO. But no! The moment she found out that you were about to be married...

ONORIA [*speaking up*]. She took poison, eh?

LUDOVICO [*to* LASPIGA]. ... without even trying to see you!

ONORIA. But are you sure it was real poison she took?

LUDOVICO. Oh, as for that!...

ONORIA. Well, let us say it was! Couldn't she have figured on their saving her, and in that case, on everybody's taking her side — a person like you, for example?... And come to think of it... where did she go to take her poison? To a public park, where she couldn't help being found right away and carried to a hospital!

LUDOVICO. But she refused to accept Signor Laspiga as her husband right here in this room — and she was in earnest!

LASPIGA. Yes, that was when she saw all the harm her lie had done... and not to me only! She had made trouble all around! I had come back repentant and she felt she couldn't accept what I had to offer! Oh, you don't understand what went on inside me here! You don't know how I suffered all those days! Why, you yourself kept encouraging me not to lose my grip on myself! Well now, just consider how I must feel on discovering it was all a low and vile intrigue! I don't know what I ought to do!

LUDOVICO. I don't see that there's any thing to do! What is there to be done now that everything is clear?

LASPIGA. Ah, no! You people have bee

telling me that all I had to do was show my contempt for her...

LUDOVICO. The best you can do is go away and marry the girl you were going to marry!

LASPIGA. No! No! I have been humiliated disgracefully! I've been made a fool of!

LUDOVICO. But just remember this... after all, whether it was remorse or poverty or what not, this poor girl tried to kill herself!

LASPIGA. I know what she's done to me!

LUDOVICO. You're right! But after all, not till after you had done her all the harm you say, and not knowing that the truth, naked and raw as it is, would be discovered! Oh, really, you can't claim that she tried to deceive you!

LASPIGA. Why did she do it then — if not to trick me, if not to get even with me?

LUDOVICO. By killing herself? She wanted to prevent your marriage, eh? But why did she care about that when she would soon be dead? Unfortunately there on the street, she didn't happen to find a man she really liked or who liked her! Oh, come now, Signor Laspiga, when a woman goes so far as to confess a thing like that, rest assured that she's not trying to get even with anybody! Surely she didn't tell that lie to get even with you!

LASPIGA. So it wasn't to trick me, eh? And it wasn't to get even with me? Well, why was it, then!

LUDOVICO. Well, as I said, I don't know why she told that lie! I can't understand it! Lies may be useful for a person intending to live, but hardly for a person intending to die! She herself has recognized that the lie was quite useless!

LASPIGA. But those words are yours, not hers!

ONORIA. You are simply refusing to take account of the facts!

LUDOVICO. Ah, there we have it! You're right! It is one of my faults! I never am able to take account of the facts!

ONORIA. Well, I'm glad to hear you admit as much yourself! Now for the facts! You know what they are? Fact number one: she didn't die!

LASPIGA. And the lie did prove to be useful to her! Yes, I insist upon the word *useful*! If the lie didn't win me back — thank heaven for that!... it at least enabled her to find a person like you...

ONORIA. Just imagine... a novelist!

LUDOVICO. Yes, a fool, you really mean.

LASPIGA [*speaking up quickly*]. Oh, I don't say that!

LUDOVICO. You might as well!

ONORIA. What's the harm, since he says so himself?

LASPIGA. Certainly she must have been flattered! Hah! I should say so!... to see her lie picked up from the gutter and glorified in the realm of art... the romantic story of her suicide for love, written up, printed, published, and this time not by a mere newspaperman, but by a writer of your reputation!

LUDOVICO. Yes, that's so! She did ask me to.

LASPIGA. So you see!

LUDOVICO. She was even disappointed that the heroine I had thought of was not herself but another, a different sort of woman.

ONORIA. You two would have made a fine team: she telling the lies and you writing them down!

LUDOVICO. Lies? Yes! But we call them stories sometimes, don't we? But it's not the story's fault if it isn't true! It's almost better that it shouldn't be true, so long as it's beautiful! It's an ugly story for her, as she lived it, but that won't prevent it's turning out very well for me, as I write it! I can say more than that: it's much more beautiful the way it is! Ah, yes... much, much more beautiful... and I'm glad that we have gone to the very bottom of it! [*To* LASPIGA, *pointing to* ONORIA.] Here's this woman, for example! At first she was as cross as could be because I brought the Signorina here! Later on she became all honey! And now look at her, if you please,... the living picture of holy horror!

ONORIA [*rising in her wrath*]. And why shouldn't I be?

LUDOVICO [*approving*]. Of course! You should be! You're quite right! Quite right! But as I was saying, for a story it's splendid... it couldn't be better! [*Turning to* LASPIGA.] And there you were: when you first came, yesterday — quite out of your head!

LASPIGA [*reacting in his turn*]. But I admitted that, myself!

LUDOVICO [*again approving*]. Yes! yes! Quite so! Quite so! I wasn't blaming you! But for that reason... beautiful for the story... beautiful! But may I ask you good people... you think I'm playing the fool here? You do, don't you? Very well! So I amuse myself by pointing out how beautiful it is, how exquisite, how perfect, this comedy of a lie discovered!

LASPIGA. Beautiful... exquisite... you say?

LUDOVICO. Precisely because it is so terrible to you and because you have suffered so! It is true, very true, that you have suffered and are still suffering! Believe me, I understand... I am keenly conscious of all that you are suffering! You may be sure that I will draw your feelings to the life, if I decide to put you into a novel or a play!

ONORIA. Aren't you going to give me a little part in it, too?

LUDOVICO. Perhaps, if I decide to make a farce out of it!

ONORIA. Well, don't you dare go putting me on the stage!

LUDOVICO. What would you do? I suppose you'd make a noise and say it wasn't true?

ONORIA. That I would! I would say it wasn't true, and that you were an impostor to match that girl!

LUDOVICO. Why go to all that trouble? The critics would say that for you! So don't bother! [*Changing his line of thought.*] But why isn't she here? It's getting late! She ought to be back by this time! The only money she has is what I gave her...

ONORIA. Ah, so you gave her money! I see! In that case you needn't worry!

LUDOVICO. I gave her just a little money to pay her bill at the hotel and get her baggage back!

ONORIA. If you gave her money, we'll never set eyes on her again! She'll never come back here! And good-bye to your comedy! I won't have to worry about what you say of me!

LUDOVICO. Ah, as for that, you can't be sure! There's always a way to put an ending on a comedy even if the story doesn't end in life!

LASPIGA. Are you really afraid she will never come back?

LUDOVICO. Well, that depends! It's this way! If the purpose of the lie she told lay in the "facts," as you say, I'm afraid she won't come back again! She'll come back only in case her purpose was, as it seems to me it must have been, above and beyond the facts! And in the latter case, I shall have my play... though I'll write the play anyhow, even if she doesn't come back!

LASPIGA. Ignoring the facts, then!

LUDOVICO. Facts! Facts! You're always harping on the facts! My dear Laspiga, facts are what we assume them to be; and then, in their reality, they cease to be facts, and become mere semblances of life which appears in this or in that or in some other way! Facts are the past, when the spirit yields — those were the words she used — and life goes out of them! That's why I don't believe in facts!

[*At this moment* EMMA *appears in the door to the Left and announces.*]

EMMA. Signor Grotti, the consul, is calling! He wants to see the young lady, or at least you, Signor Nota!

LUDOVICO. Ah, he's the one who is coming, instead of her!

LASPIGA [*drawing up in a haughty threatening attitude and facing the door pugnaciously*]. He's coming at the right moment!

LUDOVICO [*going up to him and speaking calmly, but in earnest*]. I must remind you... this is my house! You will be careful, therefore, not to make any trouble! And I repeat... you have no right to demand anything of anybody!

LASPIGA. I suppose I have the privilege of stepping outside?

LUDOVICO. No, you will be so kind as

remain here! I will attend to this gentleman!

[GROTTI *appears in the doorway in great anxiety and agitation.* EMMA *withdraws.*]

GROTTI. Good afternoon... good afternoon, sir! May I see Signorina Drei?

ONORIA [*alarmed, irritated, but bubbling over with curiosity*]. But she isn't here! She's gone away!

LASPIGA. And perhaps she'll never come back again!

GROTTI. Oh, but you people don't know ... I should speak to you rather, Signor Nota!

LUDOVICO. You have forced your way into my house without being invited!

GROTTI. I must ask your pardon for that; but I must find out whether Signorina Drei is aware that my wife...

LASPIGA [*breaking in*]. ... went to my fiancée's this morning and betrayed...

GROTTI [*breaking in violently*]. ... her own lunacy!

LASPIGA. So you deny her story?

GROTTI [*angrily and with contempt*]. I have nothing to confirm or to deny — to you!

LASPIGA. You are mistaken, sir! You *are* called upon to answer *me*!...

GROTTI. What would you have me answer? Tell you that my wife is crazy? I am ready to guarantee that any time you wish!

LASPIGA. I shall remember that, sir!

GROTTI [*turning to* LUDOVICO]. Signor Nota, I am anxious to find out whether Signorina Drei is aware of what my wife has done.

LUDOVICO. I hardly think so!

GROTTI. Thank heaven for that! Thank God! Thank God!

LUDOVICO. She was with me all the time! I left her because she had to go back to the hotel where she stayed...

GROTTI. You didn't know, yourself?

LUDOVICO. No! I found Signor Laspiga here on my return, and he told me.

GROTTI. Good! I am glad of that! In the state of mind in which she is at present his added blow...

LUDOVICO. The fact is that we have been waiting for her for some time; and she isn't back yet....

LASPIGA. But if she doesn't know, it is more than probable that she suspects. Signor Nota here gave her a little money ... there's a chance that she's run away!

GROTTI. I wish that could be true, but unfortunately I fear...

LASPIGA. Ah, so you admit then...

GROTTI. I admit nothing!

LASPIGA. Yes, that's the part of a gentleman!

GROTTI. But don't you understand that I don't care a damn what you think? You may believe anything you wish, anything you please!

LASPIGA. Anything I please? No, thanks! I am after the truth! What I want is the truth, and not something I should like to believe!

GROTTI. And what then? Supposing I tell you that my wife's story is not true? You refuse to admit that you were the one who got her into all this trouble?

LASPIGA. But if she was driven out of your house by your wife — innocent, without the slightest responsibility for the death of your child!...

GROTTI [*emphatically*]. That is not true!

LASPIGA. It's a lie, then?

GROTTI. I went to the newspaper office to clear up that point... to protest against that lie!

LASPIGA. But then you came here to fix up a story with her!

GROTTI [*restraining himself with difficulty*]. I came here because your fiancée's father asked me to come here; and I found that she — for that matter in your presence and in the presence of everybody here — was in despair because you...

LASPIGA [*interrupting, forcing his point*]. ... because I wanted to make reparation for the wrong I had done! What I want to know now is this: why should she feel that way if the wrong I did her was really a wrong?

GROTTI. Why, because she doesn't want you and your reparation! That's evident! Because she doesn't want you... She doesn't want you! That's reason enough, isn't it? She told you so, and she repeated it! Can't you get that through your head?

LASPIGA. But you can't suppose that that helps me very much! That's not the point! You are taking advantage of her state of mind to put me to one side here, so that you can play your part more easily for the benefit of this gentleman [*pointing to* LUDOVICO], giving him to understand that there is nothing to your wife's story! But I am here not because I want to be, but because she — out of her own mouth — publicly declared that she had tried to kill herself on my account!

GROTTI. But hasn't she already confessed that she was lying?

LASPIGA [*violently*]. A second lie, then! Lie number two! Who was obliging her to lie? Was I?

GROTTI. Who knows? She may have said "no" for that very reason!

LASPIGA. So then, it may actually be true that she tried to kill herself on my account?

GROTTI. I don't know why she did it!

LASPIGA. If it's all as you say it is, she did it on my account, because I had betrayed her! I don't see any other reason for her doing so!

LUDOVICO. Unless it was for the reason she gave me a little while ago!

LASPIGA [*turning on him violently*]. But no, excuse me! Just a moment ago you said that you could think of no reason, yourself!

LUDOVICO. Well, I meant to say... it was such a disgrace, wasn't it? Out on the street there... in the gutter, like a beggar!

LASPIGA [*ironically*]. Yes, and she offered herself that night to the first man who came along!

GROTTI [*his face darkening*]. She said that?

LASPIGA [*coming forward, insisting, with fury*]. Yes, she said that! Just that! And she said she would have done it, too — all on my account, because I had betrayed her! Well, in such a case, you think I could help insisting, with all my soul and conscience, on her accepting my reparation! In any case, I am still ready

to make the same offer and insist upon it ... if you, for your part, will give me your word of honor that your wife told a lie in saying that this girl has been your mistress!

[EMMA *dashes in through the door to the left, screaming in terror.*]

EMMA. Signora! Signora! Oh! Oh! Signora!

ONORIA. What's the matter?

LUDOVICO. Is she here? Is it she?

EMMA. Yes, sir! She has come back!

ONORIA. Where is she?

EMMA. Oh, I opened the door... and she fell in... with her bag... in her hand!

LUDOVICO. Oh, that poison! In her bag! She had poison in her bag!

[*The stage is in great commotion as* ERSILIA *appears in the doorway to the Left. She is pale but calm. Her face is soft, sweet, almost smiling.*]

ONORIA [*drawing back as do the others*]. Oh, there she is!

GROTTI [*with an outburst*]. What have you done? Ersilia! Ersilia!

LASPIGA [*instinctively, almost to himself*]. Ah, they did! He betrayed himself!

LUDOVICO [*running toward* ERSILIA *to keep her from falling*]. Signorina! Signorina!

ONORIA [*with a shudder, to herself*]. Oh, again! Again!

ERSILIA. It's nothing! Hush! [*She makes a gesture of silence, her forefinger across her two lips.*] This time — it's nothing!

GROTTI [*with a cry*]. No! No! We must do something for her! Get her a doctor, at once!

ONORIA [*frightened*]. Yes, a doctor! A doctor! Get her to the hospital!

LUDOVICO [*taking* ERSILIA'S *arm*]. Yes! Yes! Come, Signorina, come!

ERSILIA [*drawing back*]. No! I won't! Please don't! I won't!

GROTTI [*advancing*]. But yes! Come with me! I will take you!

ERSILIA [*as above*]. I won't, I say!

LUDOVICO. Oh, please, Signorina, come do as we wish! Don't say no! Come!

ONORIA. I will send for a carriage!

ERSILIA. Oh please! Don't torture me! It would do no good!

GROTTI. How can you be sure of that? Let's hurry! We mustn't lose any time!

ERSILIA. It would do no good! There's no help possible now! But hush, please, all you people! Let me alone! If you, Signor Nota, and the Signora here... it won't be right away... but... I hope... soon!...

LUDOVICO. Yes! Yes! What do you want? What do you want?

ERSILIA. Your bed!

LUDOVICO. Why yes, right away... come!

ONORIA. Come! Come!

GROTTI [again breaking in, with violent emotion]. What have you done? What have you done?

ERSILIA. Never mind! Please go away! Let me alone!

LUDOVICO. You ought to have remembered, Signorina, that I was here! You could have stayed here with me!

ERSILIA. But if I hadn't done this, no one would have believed me!

LASPIGA [desperately, in a paroxysm of agony]. But believe what... believe what?

ERSILIA [calmly]. That I didn't lie, just to gain something! That's all!

LASPIGA. But why did you tell the lie then?

ERSILIA. It was just to die! There! Don't you see? I told you... I told you as loud as I could that when I told that lie I thought everything was over with me — and that was why I told it! You weren't willing to believe me, and you were right! I didn't really think of you! No, not at all! You're right! And I didn't dream I would upset you so, make it hard for you ... but I had such a loathing for myself!

LASPIGA. But why? You accused me...

ERSILIA. No!

LASPIGA. How can you say that!

ERSILIA. No! It's so hard to explain it, let alone believe it! But now I'll tell you! I had such contempt for myself! — could I suppose I would cause you all this trouble? But now you can believe me! Look! I wanted first to earn this right to be believed, just so that I could tell you!

I caused you all this trouble, you and the girl you were to marry! And all the time I realized I ought not be doing it! That I had no right to do it, because... [She looks toward GROTTI, then turns again to LASPIGA.] You found out about that, didn't you? From his wife!

LASPIGA [hardly able to speak]. Yes!

ERSILIA. I foresaw that! And he came here to deny the story, didn't he?

LASPIGA. Yes!

ERSILIA. So you see!... [She looks at him and makes a gesture of disconsolate pity, barely opening her two hands, a gesture which explains without words the reason why tormented humanity feels the need of falsehood. Then she adds in a very faint voice.] And you too lied!

LASPIGA [deeply moved, with an impulse of sincerity, understanding her accusation]. Yes! I, too! I lied, too!

ERSILIA [her face brightening with a smile]. Lied? You put a dream of yours into words... oh, things of beauty... that you dreamed... and you came here to help make things right! Yes — just as he did! [Pointing to GROTTI] He came here to help make things right — and he lied! [GROTTI bursts into tears. ERSILIA loses her composure and begs him with a gesture to be still.] No! No! Please don't! We all of us want to make a good impression! The worse we are, the uglier we are — the more anxious we are to appear good and beautiful,... That's it! [She smiles.] Hah! Yes! That's it! But I was naked! I had nothing beautiful to put on!... Then I learned that you, too, yes... you had taken off your uniform, your wonderful sailor's uniform... And then I found myself... I found myself in the street without anything — and... [Her face darkens at the memory of that evening on the street after she left the hotel.] Yes, just one more bit of mud upon me... one last touch to make me dirtier than before... one last touch of filth! Oh, how disgusting! How horrible! And then... well, then I wanted at least to be buried in decent clothes! Just a decent dress to die in! There! That's why I lied! That's why I lied! I assure you! Never in my whole life long had I been able to make a good appearance in life! Every dress I wore was torn off my body by dogs... yes... dogs... dogs who barked at me and jumped out upon me from here, from there, from everywhere! I was soiled with all the lowest and vilest filth in the world! But I wanted a good dress to die in, something beautiful to be buried in... the most beautiful dress in the world... the one I had dreamed of, the one I had hoped for, out there, as the realization of a dream, but which was torn off my back like all the others: a wedding dress, the dress of a bride... the dress of a wife! But it was to die in! It was to die in! A tear of sympathy from people... that was all! But no... no... not even that have I been allowed to keep! You have torn it from me... even this one you have torn from my back! No! No! I must die naked! I must die discovered... despised ... humiliated... found out! So there! Are you satisfied? Are you satisfied? Now go away and let me alone! Let me die in silence — naked! Go! Go! I can say it now! Can't I? I can shout it at all of you, can't I? There's no one I want to see! There's no one I want to talk to! Let me alone! Let me alone! Go and tell it to them all — you to your wife, and you to your fiancée... that I am dead ... yes, and that I died naked!

CURTAIN

THE LOVE OF THE THREE KINGS
TRAGIC POEM IN THREE ACTS
By SEM BENELLI

Translated into English blank verse by HOWARD MUMFORD JONES

NOTE

Benelli employs the familiar second person singular almost wholly; in this transla-
tion the reader will observe that it is rendered sometimes by *thou* and sometimes by
you. The translator has employed either form according to the mood or circumstances of the particular passage.

The translator is deeply indebted to Professors A. E. Trombly, E. J. Villavaso, and
Benjamin F. Woodbridge for counsel and suggestions in rendering many passages in
this play.

HOWARD M. JONES

THIS
TRAGIC POEM
IS
DEDICATED
TO
GINO PIERONTONI
WHO
WHEN HE WAS ELECTED
TO THE DIRECTOR'S CHAIR
CHOSE TO REOPEN
THE ARGENTINE THEATER
WITH
THE MELANCHOLY POETRY
OF THE
MASK OF BRUTUS

CHARACTERS

ARCHIBALDO
MANFRED
AVITO
FLAMINIO
A SMITH
A SOLDIER
FLORA
A MAID
A WOMAN OF THE PEOPLE
MADDALENA

The time is the Middle Ages, forty years after a barbarian invasion. The place is a remote castle in Italy.

THE LOVE OF THE THREE KINGS

ACT I

*A spacious hall in the castle. Two well-
proportioned arches reveal under their graceful curves a terrace with columns, and the
night just before dawn. A lantern gleams
like a crimson fire; it is turned toward the
plain. In the darkness of the hall, the mo-
saics of the ceiling gleam above the arches and
over the doors right and left. The columns
with their mediæval capitals, bizarrely crossed
but harmonious in style, interweave and
approach each other with fearful effect.*

A moment of silence. Then ARCHIBALDO,
*an old, blind baron, enters from the left, con-
ducted by* FLAMINIO, *his guide, who is
dressed in the attire of a guard of the castle.
All the costumes are long and full, with
pure, hieratic lines.*

ARCHIBALDO. My thanks, Flaminio.
    Look thou to the door.
FLAMINIO [*leaves the old man, crosses the
    room, and approaches the opposite
    door*]. 'Tis almost shut, my lord.
ARCHIBALDO. Close it, but make no
    sound.
[*Changes his mind; hastily.*] No, let it be.
What thinkest thou? Dost hear?
FLAMINIO.   Who, my lord?
ARCHIBALDO [*bitterly*]. What ails thee?
    Art thou deaf with slumber? Who
Sleeps in the chamber there?
FLAMINIO.   Why, it is Flora's,
Thy own son's wife.
ARCHIBALDO.   Well?
FLAMINIO.   'Tis some distance,
And many rooms do intervene between.
ARCHIBALDO. I fear to wake her. Let
    her slumber on.
Youth is a dream, none other than a dream.
To me are dreams denied, for sleep's a
    traitor
That like a troubled bee plays on my lids
Since fate has parched mine eyes.
Sadly.]   Do thou, Flaminio,

Thou who art able, look upon the sky.
FLAMINIO. It is yet night. The dawn is
    almost here.
ARCHIBALDO. Look thou, Flaminio,
    scrutinize the valley.
Seest thou no torches? Manfred, as I feel,
Must come, for I have dreamed it, and I
    was
Awake.
FLAMINIO. He cannot come if yet he
    wars,
United with the foreign dukes, against
Our castles past the mountain ranges.
ARCHIBALDO.   Ours!
What sayest thou?
FLAMINIO.   Yes, ours. My people's
    — us
Whom you have subjugated. I do serve
Your highness faithfully, but I was born
Upon the mountain summits of Altura.
The fathers of my fathers once were free.
ARCHIBALDO [*insistently*].   Flaminio,
    look again — look in the valley.
FLAMINIO. No one, my lord. All's
    peace.
ARCHIBALDO.   Oh, I am tired!
Slumber, that flees the weary, flees from
    me,
And I am the more wildered in the dark.
And seeking sleep, I seek my very guide
And cannot find him. Lacking sleep, the
    blind
Are doubly blind. — Listen! Hearest
    thou not?
Be still! A tremble runs before!... Gal-
    loping!
A troop of soldiers! People in arms!
    Flaminio,
Look out and search for me.
FLAMINIO.   The breeze, my lord.
Only a bit of wind that carries toward us
The murmur of the torrent in the hollow,
And moves a little the green slumbering
    leaves.

ARCHIBALDO. True, it has freshened!
    What relief! It dies,
And I, who am blind, feel that the night
    returns,
Being night within this midnight,
And this my utter darkness touches hands
With starry darknesses I cannot see
But which I feel pulsating through the
    silence.
[*Like an invocation.*] Night, mother of
    treasons, timorous night
Lover that lullest, slumbering, on thy
    breast
The jealous Earth, thy daughter, that she
    may not
Behold apparent in the splendid sky
Thy fulgent plenitude of sparkling love,
Thy mystery, alas, I have not worshiped.
Little thy monstrous, terrene semblances
Within our arched and silent palace-halls,
Or in thy woodlands, pleased me, who am
    not
One even now more amorous of thee
Than of the day I have beheld too red
With its own shame, and owning not the
    law
That governs thee, harmonious with quiet
And silences divine.
    FLAMINIO [*unheeding*]. Men such as he
Who will not sleep o' night must pray, or
    rave.
    ARCHIBALDO. O memory! My lonely
        mind rejourneys
The boundless plain to-night whereon alone
I have run through the courses of my life!
    FLAMINIO. You do recall your youth?
    ARCHIBALDO.   O Italy!
This Italy is all my recollection!
[*Majestically.*] 'Tis forty years since I de-
    scended here
Upon this garden of the flowers. Again
I feel my nostrils dilate with the fierce
Remembrance. In my country all is gray,
And little comes to fruit. We had no
    flatterers,
We youths with ardent hearts and sunny
    hair.
Unenterprised, life fled in lengthy dreams.
Yet were we drilled for conquest and for
    plunder,
Our names were full of onset and of war —
Thus I was Archibaldo, signifying

"Excelling bravery," and the others had
Such names as "Famous soldier," "Fierce
    in peace,"
"Ready in courage," "Redoubtable for
    strength,"
"Famous in war," "Audacious stranger."
    So
In all of us there was the mighty will,
Strong as a mace of iron. The senses'
    madness,
The madness of the mind, beneath our
    hearts
We carried like the meat beneath our
    saddles,
Pressed on to make it usable. Exultant,
Some of my race, returning from this
    land,
Praised to the heavens their precious gem,
    in speech
Harsh and metallic, till the lovely name
Of Italy resounded like a march,
Alluring us to war. Wherefore the king,
Choosing our best, moved with a glittering
    troop,
Silver and green and gold, like some cruel
    snake
That wakens and unchains itself from
    shadow
And moves, resounding, in the sun. Our
    steeds
Impetuously bent like flame, their riders,
With faces eager for the first soft winds,
Felt the warm breath of Italy, their prey,
The lovely goddess swimming 'twixt two
    seas!
Lonely she seemed, with no one to defend
    her,
Lonely she seemed, unguarded, and a virgin
That to our burning and barbaric hearts
Bowed down her head, timid, and veiled
    in sorrow.
We seized her — she, that, triumphing
    was shod
With wingéd Roman sandals to run
    through
The world — bent from our steeds and
    seized her
That she might teach us how to rule all
    lands.
Our hands had scarcely touched her when
    her limbs
Awoke a morbid languor without end

That ran through us, centaurs indomi-
table;
And here we built our seat, and here
played with her,
And loved her here, and none of us shall
leave her,
Our latest love, golden and fresh and green!
Ah, loving her, we lament she should be
A slave, and not our mother. Would she
were!
She would have taught us how to rule the
world!
[*Pause. To* FLAMINIO.] Thou'rt silent.
I see thee not! Perhaps thou
look'st
On me with hate. 'Tis not sufficient. —
Thou
Couldst murder me. — My trust is in my-
self,
My will makes thee a coward, being
stronger than
Thine own.
FLAMINIO. I am thy servitor, and thou
My king.
ARCHIBALDO. If I did wrong, too much
desiring
This land of thine, God hath prevented me
From worshiping too long this Italy;
He blinded me when Manfred saw the
light,
Italian born — Manfred the good — my
son!
Oh, let him now return to me! These
nights
Are filled with vacancy. And Flora, Flora
Waits her dear consort here, who parted
from her
Almost before the marriage had been made.
Four months are fled, and I remain to
guard
The cherished flower I can ne'er behold.
[*Short pause.*]
Tell me of her, Flaminio. Is Flora lovely?
FLAMINIO [*happily*]. The princess?
She is like the rays of dawn
When first the sun shoots forth a timid
light.
Beautiful are the women of Altura
Straight, like white columns, but among
them all,
She's fairest. And her face is like her name.
She is the first to leave her home; the others

Are ours. It is the custom we have kept.
ARCHIBALDO [*with barbaric joy*]. My son
hath broke thine antique usages!
FLAMINIO. We gave you Flora for the
sake of peace.
[*Sighing.*] Our ancestors were brave, and
had good ships,
And have been mountain warriors, since
they helped
The Greek against the Trojans.
ARCHIBALDO. Thy history
Availed thee nothing.
FLAMINIO. Nothing against yours.
But yours, my lord, availed with us who
knew
How you lay waste the land. Wherefore,
from fear,
We gave you Flora.
ARCHIBALDO. She is a baroness.
FLAMINIO. And was a princess, and she
would have been
A queen. Altura, being so small and
rugged,
Yet calls its chief a king. She would have
been
His queen.
ARCHIBALDO. Why?
FLAMINIO. Avito, our young lord,
Son of old Agatone, would have wed her.
She is his cousin.
ARCHIBALDO [*to himself*]. Avito, our
young lord,
Hath never come to greet us.
FLAMINIO [*looking hypocritically at the
blind old man*]. It may chance
He sails the seas or slumbers in his castle
Above you.
ARCHIBALDO [*as before*]. Flora — was his.
FLAMINIO [*seeking to turn his thoughts*].
My good lord,
Believe me, it were best you now return
To your rooms.
[*Lying.*] The sky grows bright and to the
day
The lantern, yonder, yields.
ARCHIBALDO. Extinguish it.
The signal's useless since he does not come.
FLAMINIO [*quenches the light on the ter-
race, then speaks*]. Let us go in, my
lord, let us go in.
[*The sound of a shepherd's flute is
heard from the distance.*]

ARCHIBALDO. These many mornings at the break of day
I've heard that flute.
FLAMINIO. [*Perturbed*]. Some wanderer in the hills —
A shepherd. Yes. One that is musical,
An agéd sorcerer cherished by the people.
Even now he's passing underneath your walls.
But — my good lord — the dew already falls.
I am all wet with it. Let us return.
[*He half drags him toward the chambers at the left.*]
ARCHIBALDO. Let us return. Return — into the night.
[*Exit, guided by* FLAMINIO. *A pause. The flute resumes its melody and is silent.*]

[AVITO, *wrapped in a mantle, enters from the door at the right. Taking two or three steps toward the terrace, he searches the outside world, looks at the sky, listens, hesitates for an instant, then returns nearly to the door by which he came. The white figure of* FLORA *appears on the threshold, her lovely hair curling in crisp ringlets around her head. Her quick body is clad in a delicate toga of ivory and white.*]

AVITO [*discovering* FLORA]. Geronte hath given the signal on his flute,
But he has been too hasty. Night's yet deep.
FLORA. Let us return.
AVITO. No. We might forget ourselves,
And then his flute would never sound again.
FLORA. Your loyal shepherd must have been awake
Somewhat too soon this morning. Do you likewise
Desire to flee?
AVITO. Oh, why do you say that "likewise"?
The little moment I am near you is
Like unto nothing else.
FLORA. Let us go back.
AVITO [*hesitating*]. The fear of entering your chamber and
The fear of leaving you again are thieves

Who pillage my brief ecstasy that spends
Its night of love in bidding love good-bye.
FLORA. Yes. Let us remain —
[*Approaching him*] — like one who scarcely
Wakens, and fears the day and hates the sun.
AVITO [*trembling, points to the left*]. That door is closed?
FLORA. The door is closed. Myself
Shut it but now. Surely you do remember?
And the old man cannot see us.
AVITO. He can hear.
FLORA. Avito, you are trembling. In my breast
Is infinite peace.
AVITO. Flora! Yes, I feel it,
And I am fearful of that selfsame peace.
FLORA. Give me thy lips, and by so much I'll give
Peace to thine own. Then, lacking it again,
I'll desperately beg it back of thee,
For, if I lack thy lips, I have not peace.
AVITO. If thou can'st give me so much sweetness as
I yearn to give to thee, O with thy burning
Destroy me quite! I shall be born again!
FLORA [*with childlike gladness, and love as fond as her youth*] Yes, my delight,
my flaming heart! Thy mouth
Is an eternal flower; each moment I pluck it,
And every moment doth it grow again!
AVITO [*incoherent as a sick child*]. Grows — and without you, withers....
FLORA [*with the same incoherence*]. And with my kiss
Smells sweet. The soul that's bent upon this flower
Grows languid underneath its spell!
[*Pause.*]
AVITO [*like one waking from a dream, draws away from her*]. Behold!
The light comes on — the sky grows white with it.
FLORA. You wish to leave me ——
AVITO [*with terror*]. Terror is upon me!
Flora! Flora!
FLORA. Thou art afraid of day!
AVITO. It is not fear that seized me,
O Flora!

Flora! Thou art she, my lady of evil,
Of all sweet sin like honey, and thine eyes
Unreasoning, plead for pity, yet thou doest
Evil without an end!

FLORA.   Sin lies about me!
You offered me, a holocaust, to this
    shadow
In which 'tis sin to sleep. Your lady of
    evil?
Did not all you betray me while I dreamed?
Have I not wept enough?

AVITO.   No, Flora, no,
You understand me not. I would not
    say ——

FLORA [*to herself, sorrowfully*]. O dis-
    tant dreams of mine! O fruitless
    tears!
Mixing serene of virtue and life's sweet-
    ness!
The diadem of many-colored gems
Bound singing on me in my exultation
Hath faded in the darkness of my life!

AVITO. 'Twas in that darkness that I
    came upon thee,
A torch of mercy ——

FLORA.   But it was night, remember,
You found me in!

AVITO.   Night, beautiful night,
O night, sacred to these our guilty loves
That with their dolorous wings of plush
    beat down
In silent softness on the terrors of
All violated beds!

FLORA.   Like ours, beloved.

AVITO, And when day comes with
    hypocritic lids,
They hide the shame that sucks serenity
Lasciviously from our eyes.

FLORA.   Speak not of shame,
For if I cannot tell thee of my love,
So much it hurts me, how could I, Avito,
So shame myself?

AVITO [*impetuously*]. Yes, yes, my
    Flora, speak.
These kisses cannot satiate us — words,
I want your words. O tell me, Flora, tell
    me ——

FLORA [*twining about him*]. My love
    for thee descends from heav'n, and
    here
O'ertakes thee with its violence. Would I
    might

Precipitate my being upon thine,
Impetuous as a torrent, whitened as
A torrent, and as whirling as a torrent,
The torrent of a mountainous wild river,
Disgathering the rude power of thy kisses
As water spreads a sand bank into sands
A thousandfold, until each grain should
    have
Its shaken heart!

AVITO.   And I should be against
Thy rapturous and bridal whiteness as
Beneath the moon's white rays the moun-
    tain is;
And in the freshening torrent of thy kisses,
I'd keep myself intact as best I may,
Since then thy milk-white passion shall
    require
The longer period to consume me in!

FLORA [*voluptuously*]. Tender dreams!
    — Eternal fever, Avito!
Avito! Life — my   life — dreams —
    dreams!
Ah, wizardry! Enchantment without end!
    [*They embrace rapturously, losing
    themselves in a kiss.*]

AVITO [*with sudden terror*]. Ah. dream
    no more! The day increases — look!

FLORA. I see! — I see! Leave me then
    — and farewell!
Behold! The stars that have beheld the sun
Now close their blinded eyelids.

AVITO [*freeing himself from her, yet un-
    able to leave except lingeringly, wraps
    himself in his cloak*]. I go without
    thee —
Disguised   No one can recognize me
    thus —
A pilgrim or a shepherd.
[*Pause. Rapt in vision.*] When I climb
To my Altura where the dawn hath dyed
The hills, and made the land a limpid
    emerald,
Vibrant with colored gems, the woods and
    hills
Disturb my soul, delivering me from fever.
I draw within myself and call; thy name
Binds in one vital and united knot
The thrills of birds, the perfumes, and the
    light,
The sighing, and the tremors of that hour.
Thy name — thy name! Till I am drunk
    with it

And I repeat it — Flora! Flora! Flora!
And murmuring so, I nod, and fall asleep.
FLORA. O take me with you for at least
to-day.
Carry me from this strange and tedious
shade
That suffocates me here! Avito — Avito!
For as you fly, so might I also fly.
O hide me in your cloak! The sentinel
Knows you and does whatever you desire.
To-day — only to-day!
AVITO [*about to leave*]. 'Tis late!
[*Discovers the extinguished lantern:
terrified.*]
Flora, see!
The lantern has already been extinguished!
Some one has come here, in the night!
FLORA. The wind
Has done it.
AVITO. No, to-night there was no wind.
Do you remember?
FLORA. Hearken! Fly!
[AVITO *hurries along the terrace to-
ward the right.* FLORA *watches him,
follows him as though to protect him,
then runs toward her chambers. But
the door at the left has been opened by*
ARCHIBALDO, *who appears alone.*]
ARCHIBALDO. Flora!
Flora! Flora!
[*Concealing her movements from the
ears of the old man,* FLORA *attempts to
steal silently away.*]
[*Persistently.*] Thou'rt here! I hear thee
breathe!
The anguish of sin is thine? And canst
thou not
Support its weight? Anguish? Pain?
O speak,
Flora! Who was it thou wert talking with?
FLORA [*with renewed firmness*]. Talk-
ing? I? With myself.
ARCHIBALDO. O God, why, why,
Can I not see? [*Slowly approaching her.*]
Leave me not! Stay, stay!
I must know!
[*He seizes her as she leans for support
against a pillar, draws her to him,
searches her face with his fingers, and
strains her to him in his old, heroic
arms. He speaks in a quiet voice,
wonderingly.*]

I cannot think it. Thus, oh thus
To lie! So to betray us!
[*Still questioning her face with his
hand.*]
Thou who art
A child! If thou deceive me —! It's for
nothing.
Who is't was with thee here — here — in
the night?
[*Pause. More gently, as if his throat
were taut with a new-born kindness,
paternal and senile.*]
Tell me. And do not fear me. Only con-
fess.
For surely there was no one, or at least
Some one who's less than naught. Fla-
minio?
Perchance 'twas he. — But no. For he's
asleep.
[*He waits her answer without leaving
her.*]
FLORA [*still with resolution, unyielding,
holding herself rigid, yet trembling a
little*]. There was no one here, my lord.
ARCHIBALDO. Why do you tremble
If that's the truth?
FLORA. Why, you yourself are
trembling,
And yet you do not lie.
ARCHIBALDO [*impetuously*]. Flora, thou
reasonest
Too well. Thou art no child, thou art a
traitor.
Why, I could twist this silken hair about
The throat of thy deceit.
FLORA. Do so, and learn
I do not lie.
ARCHIBALDO. Could I but read your
eyes!
FLORA [*mysteriously*]. My lord, my
face would frighten you.
ARCHIBALDO. And why,
Flora, why?
FLORA. Because you see me not,
And yet you tremble.
ARCHIBALDO. Flora! [*A short pause.*]
True, I tremble —
But I tremble — I tremble for your lie!
FLORA [*suddenly pushing him off*]. Take
care, my lord, you do not lie yourself
And know it not.
ARCHIBALDO. Flora, what art thou?

Too much a child. I do believe, or else
Thou wert too frightful!

FLORA [with trembling cruelty]. Let me
    return, my lord,
To my rooms. I am not dressed. Think
not ——

ARCHIBALDO [drawing away from her as
    from something evil]. Flora,
How am I culpable? I have done nothing!
Thou art a treachery unfit to touch!

FLORA [with ferocious ingenuity]. I
    know not — I came hither to the
    terrace —
I could not sleep — for thinking ——

ARCHIBALDO [interrupting and shouting
    at her]. Of whom? Of whom?

FLORA. Of Manfred, of my husband.

ARCHIBALDO. Horror! Horror!
O blackness without end! Thou art all iron,
Thou'rt twisted like a chain about my
    head!

FLORA [approaching him, deceitfully].
    My lord!

ARCHIBALDO. No! Stop! Come thou
    no nearer!
I have for thee the terror of a child.
Thou hast taken my love and dirtied it,
    thou hast
Disguised it till I recognize it not.
Thy body that within my shadow yet
Soared as on wings of snow, seems to me
    now
An icy wind, a freezing accusation
More stout than is the honesty of my heart.
And while I feel thou art a traitor here,
I must myself embrace thy treason, and,
In order not to blush in judging thee,
I'll have to cry, "No — no — she did not
    lie!"
So much has my suspicion frightened me.

FLORA. My lord!

ARCHIBALDO. Go! I could not
    touch thee save
I killed thee.

FLAMINIO [from within]. My lord!
    [Appearing on the terrace.]
    Master, a troop is pausing
Upon the bridge, and, as it seemed to me,
It was the baron Manfred.
    [A trumpet call rises from the base of
    the castle. Daylight has now much in-
    creased.]

                Listen! 'Tis he!
They're welcoming him.

ARCHIBALDO [trembling]. 'Tis he. Fla-
    minio, go,
Run to him. [In a plaintive voice.] I — I
    am blind — Flaminio,
Go. [Flaminio goes off, running.]

ARCHIBALDO [to FLORA, after a long
    pause]. Thou — canst not run to
    meet him? No. [FLORA is silent.]
Thou who wert — sleeping, go thou to thy
    bed.
    [FLORA slowly withdraws toward her
    own chamber. A cruel smile of victory
    plays on her beautiful young face.
    She disappears.]
    [ARCHIBALDO, motionless and sorrow-
    ful, awaits his son.]

MANFRED [within]. Father!
    [He appears from the terrace.]

ARCHIBALDO. My son! And with
    thee comes the light! [They embrace.]

MANFRED. Too long the siege, too
    tedious for my ardent
Yearning I have fled from it. For
    some days
I shall be with you.

ARCHIBALDO. Would thou couldst
    stay forever!

MANFRED. The war must shortly end.
    Their lower town
We have burnt up like wood, though on the
    hill
Some are yet firm and stubbornly resist
But in a little they must lose their crag.
Father, I could not longer wait.
[Short pause.] And Flora?
She is asleep?

ARCHIBALDO. She is — asleep.

MANFRED. O father,
This coming back is like a dear reward
Long, long expected. To you I owe this
    joy,
To you, my father, who have taught me
    always
To follow justice. In combative war,
In blood, in slaughter, orgies of victory,
I have ever been a pillar of virtue, such
As you have made me, father. These long
    vigils,
Dreaming of the pure creature joined to me
I have felt that virtue's power, secretly

Rejoiced because she knows so little of me,
Ignorant of the good that, just to give her,
I have heaped up in these long absences
Within my soul.   And she shall learn to
love me,
In truth, as honest love gives law.   I know
That all I bring her she expects of me,
For you have taught her till she has become
A lamb of virtue.   Is it not so?
  [ARCHIBALDO *remains silent, intent
  on his secret thoughts.*]
  MANFRED.   Thou ailest,
Father!
  ARCHIBALDO.   Fearfully, O my son, I am
  like one
Who, having made a perfect work, can find
No worthy light for it.   That work, my
son,
Thou art.
  MANFRED.   I want no other, father; only
  her.
  ARCHIBALDO.   Manfred—my son!   Flora
  is within;
Even now, perhaps, she wakens in her bed,
In thought thou seest her and yearnest for
her,
This seeming miracle of love.   Consider:
I have taught thee difficult sacrifice, each
kind
Of resignation.   Thou'rt a warrior, bold
And firm in virtue.   Think thee well, and
answer:
Shouldst thou not find her in this house, or
if
She had died, couldst thou not overcome
thy sorrow
With this same virtue that makes love to
thee
So beautiful?
  MANFRED.   My father, why do you
Thus shift the happy courses of my joy?
Do you not hear how love is singing in
me?
Do you not hear how in my throat her name
Is burning like a lure to every joy
That strives to mingle with each phrase of
mine
Its green refrain of Flora, Flora, Flora?
I know you are a cold examiner:
Were you to listen at the pulsing spring
Of some bright stream could you endure to
know

That it might on the instant change its
course
Of singing melody?   For I want — Flora,
Whom I have yearned for more than faith
or conquest,
Because on her I have deposited
My every faith.
  [*With an altered tone.*]   Perhaps you are
  unhappy,
Perhaps she is too foreign to your ways?
She's but a girl, and little is the harm
She will have wrought.   You still have been
beside her
Like one who guards a treasure?
  ARCHIBALDO.   Yes, my son.
  MANFRED.   You have too deeply probed
  her.   You're severe.
Her blood's not ours.   She was born in the
full sun.
  ARCHIBALDO [*suddenly.*]   Too pure — too
  pure!   Thy joy's too pure, I say,
My reasoning too black!   Have all thy
joy!
Thy Flora waits thee.   Even now she
comes —
I hear her footsteps.
  MANFRED.   I hear them not — she flies!
  [*He turns to the right-hand door
  where* FLORA *appears.*]
Flora!   Flora!
  FLORA [*with a cruel coldness that masks
  itself as kindliness.*]   You have re-
  turned, my lord?
This morning I awoke before the dawn,
And came here to the terrace, and looked
down
Into the vale, being certain you would
come.
  [*To* ARCHIBALDO.]   Father, is it not true?
  Did you not — hear me?
                        [ARCHIBALDO *is silent.*]
  MANFRED.   Is it true, my father?
  ARCHIBALDO.   Yes.   Yes.   I — discovered
  her —   [*Recovering himself.*]
While she was waiting for you.
  MANFRED.   Flora!   Flora!
My flower of heavenly grace, our feasting
day
Is lighted by this dawn, the first of many,
As many as infinite heaven has sparkling
stars!
Lean, O thou little flower, upon my breast,

Not here upon my arm, that I may bring
    thee
Even as a wandered, gentle lamb is
    brought,
Into the sheepfold woven of my heart.
Lo, how thou tremblest! As a lost lamb
    might tremble
Fainting beneath its weight of silver fleece.
The stout arms of the shepherd shall con-
    sole her,
Revive, warm her and quicken her.
            [Starting on his way.]
            Thus shall I carry thee
Unto thy bed of ivory.
            My father,
Thou seest now thy son hath found his goal,
In truth thou seest, since from my heart
    such light
Goes out that it confounds itself, and mixes
And multiplies with this more odorous
    light
Wherewith this treasure of mine, this
    perfumed treasure,
Is liberal.
    [He enters the room at the right, carry-
    ing her in his arms.]
  ARCHIBALDO [*alone. Pause*]. O Lord my
    God, as Thou hast taken mine eyes,
Let me not see, let me be blind — be blind!
For Thou wouldst torture me too much, if
    Thou
Shouldst make me face the truth I cannot
    see.
No! Rather let me be forever close
Shut up within my night. — Blind! —
    Blind!

THE CURTAIN FALLS

ACT II

    A round terrace on the high walls of the
castle. The top of the battlement which
bounds it, and which is higher than a man's
head, is reached by a flight of steps in the
middle of the rear stage. A stone bench,
knee-high and a yard wide, circles the stage
next to the wall. At the left is a stone table.
The terrace is reached by two doors at the
sides. Afternoon. The bare heavens are
crossed by changing summer clouds.

    [FLAMINIO, *followed by* AVITO, *and dressed*
    like him, as a guard of the castle, enters
    from the left.]

  FLAMINIO. My lord, this is the terrace.
[*Pointing right.*]   And this way,
The other staircase. Now I'll show you
    where
It leads.
  AVITO [*as if to himself*]. She will come
    here!
  FLAMINIO. And if you wish
To hide yourself in there [*pointing right*]
    and will draw near
But now and then, you'll see her, or at
    least,
You'll hear her voice.
  AVITO.   See her!
  FLAMINIO.   Yes, my lord.
Manfred (I overheard him) said to her,
"You must be beautiful for my departure.
So, finish your dressing soon. I shall
Await you on our tower." They've come
    here
Continually since my lord's return.
  AVITO. It may be I shall see her! Once
    — alone
It happened that I saw her (only once!);
She does not know I'm in these castle walls.
  FLAMINIO My lord, I'm risking death in
    your behalf.
If such desire to see her sits in your heart,
Have mercy on me! I have given you
    clothes,
Concealed you in my chambers — only
    wait!
A little while, and Manfred will be gone —
An hour perhaps, and then he will depart.
The horses and the knights are ready
    now.
When the old man that's blind remains
    alone,
Then you can see her — then. And mean-
    while, be
A little prudent.
  AVITO.   Be a little prudent!
Which is to say, heap up the suffering
Of sleepless nights each moment, and en-
    dure,
If I am able, for the sake of prudence!
I am a dying man!
  FLAMINIO.   And I am one

You're sending to his death. I never
thought
The long sea-journey that you made, my
lord,
Would tie you but more firmly to the
land. —
What use to wander in the body when
The mind remains immobile?

AVITO [throughout as if speaking to him-
self]. When I departed,
I did believe her mine; when I returned,
She had been sold!

FLAMINIO. Yes, but our land is whole.
We plunder, you and I, the land of others.

AVITO. Plunder? I, a thief? That with
such risk
Search out the gem I lost in the wide sea?

FLAMINIO. The risk is greater than the
booty's worth.

AVITO. The danger's beautiful, for it
surrounds
That gem of mine; and if denied the gem,
I shall embrace the danger which surrounds
it.

FLAMINIO. Oh, my lord,
You are so sick with love, you do forget
That love's destroying you. Sure, some
great evil
Shall fall on me because of you. Be silent!
They're coming. Why, they're almost
here — and on us —
Come, quick — along with me. On this
side — there!

[He pushes AVITO before him toward
the right, and follows him grumbling.]

Better to tutor butterflies or sing
Enchantments unto vipers than to have
The guardianship of lovers!

[They go out at the right.]

[After a pause the voice of ARCHI-
BALDO is heard from within, at the left.]

ARCHIBALDO. I have no guide!
I have lost Flaminio.

MANFRED [from within]. I am here.

ARCHIBALDO [appearing, guided by MAN-
FRED]. I know it.
We have arrived. Thanks, Manfred.

MANFRED. We are here.
I wanted you to be with me a moment
Upon this tower's top. It is the first
Of the castle I shall see, returning, and
The last that I'll see, going. From afar

Presently I shall watch it.

ARCHIBALDO. Me, my son,
This parting, though inevitable, grieves
Profoundly.

MANFRED. I shall soon return. I'm
tired
Of barbarous labors. All my mind is
turned
Unto the land we rule, my heart, to love.

ARCHIBALDO. It would be better if thou
didst not go.

MANFRED. You know I leave my heart
behind in pawn.

ARCHIBALDO. Thy heart's too fair a
treasure, and I fear
To be the guardian of it. — I'm alone ——

MANFRED [searchingly]. And is not
Flora here?

ARCHIBALDO. True. But thou art
A better prop than all to my sick soul.
An old man's heart — it is a boy's heart
still.
I am afraid — afraid. When thou art here
My soul is lifted up and rests upon
Thine ever serene spirit. When thou
speakest,
I, who am blind, my son, behold the heav-
ens,
And see once more the colors of old hope.

MANFRED. When I return to you, I'll
sound again
Dear melodies, and to my psalter sing,
Father, for you and Flora.

ARCHIBALDO. Ah, if only
The pure fruit of thy singing could live on
Within us like the blood that's in our veins,
And sentinel the soul, as the blood guards
The body! Then I'd say to thee: "My
son,
Linger an hour, a moment, ere thou go.
Before thou art too distant, sing, and sing
Enchantment till the echo of thy song
Should live, unending, to thy dear return."
But song is empty, and remains not, and
Thy serene heart remains not. Music,
thou
Art pure because thou touchest us within,
And draw'st away — returning, yes, but
not
To linger.

MANFRED. I have not seen you thus so
moved.

ARCHIBALDO. An old man's heart — it is
  a boy's heart still,
That weeps and weeps, disconsolate, nor
  knows
The reason why it weeps.
  MANFRED [*impatiently*].   I suffer, father:
And Flora's not yet come.
[*Suddenly.*]   No — no — I cannot,
Cannot keep silence more.   Thy sorrow
  wakes
A sorrow I've kept hidden many days,
One I have sought by every means to drug,
One that I know not how to conquer, one
That conquers me!
  ARCHIBALDO [*impetuously*].   I know it —
    Flora — Flora!
  MANFRED. Yes.
  ARCHIBALDO [*after a pause*].   And what
    dost thou believe?
  MANFRED.   Nothing!
That which I feel, I know
[*Pause.*]   Too much I love her;
And she is yet a child to me.   I would
She were more burning, yet I am consumed
Already with her fire; I would she were
Less grave, except I feel that mirth would
  be,
In one so pure as she, almost a fault,
And gayety might seem a veil to cover
Some wickedness.
  ARCHIBALDO. Manfred! Thou believest
That Flora might be capable of evil?
  MANFRED. Oh, no, no, no! Thou seest
    how desire
Of love sets up no limits to his course;
How I, for love's sake, do desire that
  she,
The stainless creature I adore, should find,
Herself within herself, some burning word
Consuming as my fever, that would yet
Destroy her very candor.   No, my father!
Pardon me, no!   I do not think that Flora
Is capable of any wrong.   The culprit —
It is my burning heart; and *that* my
  will —
My Christian will — shall punish.   If
    Flora sinned —
But in what fashion could she ever sin?—
I fully understand my duty toward her,
Which is to pardon.
  ARCHIBALDO [*as if to himself*].   And I
    know I have

Taught thee that duty.   Well it was.
    But yet —
My fathers were no Christians.   Me they
  taught
Far otherwise and here I learned it, here
In the land where thou wert born.
  MANFRED.   The land where Flora
Was born.   She's coming!   She is here.
  ARCHIBALDO [*in confusion*].   I'll go
Below, my son.
  MANFRED.   You have no guide!
  ARCHIBALDO.   Myself
Will be my guide.   I know the stairway
  well.

[FLORA *appears at the left. She is beauti-
    fully but simply dressed. ARCHIBALDO
    hears her; draws back; goes to the left
    and finds the door.*]

The door is here.   The stairs are straight.
                              [*Exit.*]
  MANFRED [*to* FLORA].   Tell me why I
    again behold thee mute
Before my sorrow.   I am leaving thee,
Flora, leaving once more.   I am so shaken
That my departure, as I think, is on
Some errand that's eternal.
  FLORA.   I have said,
My lord, your sudden leave-taking hath
  routed
My joy in your return.   Out of which cause
I do lack words.   I do not know you well.
You are ever journeying and when you
  come,
'Tis but to tell me, "I shall leave you soon."
  MANFRED. No, Flora, no.   You speak
    to me as to
An enemy who begs a truce of you.
I sorrow!   I sorrow!   And my pain is such
I have concealed it even from my father
Who knows the all I am.
                  Oh, I would have thee
As thou wouldst have me be if we had been
Lovers since childhood, Flora.   I was born
  here.
Why, I have seen thee many times — a
  child
With thy mother on her mule, and thou
  hast said
Thou sawest secretly my young desire.
I have believed thou wert a gem they
  guarded

Only for me. Thy land have they kept free
Because I wished to have you free for me.
[*In an altered tone.*] I'd have thee a young
    sister, or a comrade,
As to the flower, the calyx is, I'd teach thee
An honest way beside me, one as pure
As is the dream of him who, near the fire,
Thinks happily some winter he's done well
Since some one, underneath the roof he's
    made,
Is sheltered through his labor. I'm not
    rude —
I have been taught the Christian way. I
    am
Not as my fathers were. Thy body's
    beauty
Is no mere costly fruit to be enjoyed.
It is thy pure soul's radiance. Under-
    stand,
O understand my suffering! Speak to me,
Flora, speak, What do you want of me?
Tell me that I may know your wish. At
    least
A little tell me why it is you grieve!
    FLORA. My lord, there's nothing grieves
    me save that you
Depart. As for my will, it is to be
Yours as you do desire.
    MANFRED.   You bid me stay?
    FLORA. Why — yes. That would be
    well. I do not wish
That you renounce so much, and rather
    seek
Your quick return.
    MANFRED.   Oh, by thy blessed words
I shall return to hear again the song
That comes to reach me from thy kingdom
    of
Immeasurable goodness! I'll return —
Return for thee, for thee, for thy dear life
That I desire to gird about with love!
[*With altered tone.*] Give me of thine some
    smallest nothing, Flora,
That I may hold it pressed against my
    heart,
While I am far from thee!
    FLORA.   What do you want?
    MANFRED. What will you choose?
    FLORA [*in overwhelming and hidden sor-
    row*].   You want my life.
    MANFRED [*after a moment of stupor*].
                        Nothing?

You give me nothing? Is your life not
    mine?
    FLORA [*with renewed sadness*]. Yes, it is
    yours. Ah truly, it is yours.
What must I offer you?
    MANFRED.   Offer? You said? —
No. Rather I shall tell you first what I
Shall give you.
    FLORA.   What?
    MANFRED [*after a pause*]. I will believe
    the day
Must come wherein my love and my desire,
My wisdom and my virtue and the calm
Belief that God has given me in thy love,
Will open thy closed spirit, as the sun
The wintered fruit, and all thy life through
    me
Shall burst in flower. And when thou,
    jocund, feelest
Lurking in thee the joy of being mine,
Thou shalt experience in thy soul, re-
    morse —
In that thou mad'st me weep for love's
    sake, yet
Saw never a tear-drop in my eyelids stand.
Then shalt thou be with very fear of wrong
Already wrought. It may be thou shalt
    suffer.
I would not have thee sorrow. And my
    gift
In leaving (to return forever thine)
Shall be that for all wrong, all anguish
    done
By thee upon me, I do pardon thee,
And kiss thee as a father might.
    [*He kisses her on the forehead. She
    remains cold, if unquiet, beneath his
    pardon. Finally she exclaims:*]
    FLORA.   No, no!
Take my life instead!
    MANFRED [*with a pitying clemency*].
            Daughter, there is no thing
Which thou canst give me to appease the
    heart
Thou knowest not. I may request of thee
Only one gift to bring me shortly peace,
And that I ask.
    FLORA.   What is it?
    MANFRED [*after a pause, sadly*]. The
    hour of parting
Is struck. My doughty comrades, on the
    bridge,

Await me, and their horses are impa-
tient —
And shivering life and conquest tremble on
The rosy air. We leave. My loyal com-
panions
Are gay as they go down the ample
valley —
Intoxicating dreams from their young
minds
Dischain themselves. They hear their
arms like birds
Presaging a new dawn, and silently
They check their horses as they check their
hearts,
Which are too happy — I am in their
midst,
Silent and as if I were alone.
And all humanity weeps in my soul
Great, sorrowful tears, because for love I
sorrow —
Love left behind, and I go on, alone
And comfortless I have lost all my bliss,
I am driven out from joy. And if there be
Such love within me, why is this? I turn
And look again upon this castle, red
To the sun upon the hilltop, flaming as
My wounded heart, and I go down   go
down.
This castle, where, a boy, I raised my song
To heaven's glory, asking for my soul
A quiet and continued strength, looks on
me
Gigantically and mutely like a sphinx.
And desperately I go down, untie
The valley's windings, meet the brook that
weeps,
And weeps, and murmurs, and reproaches
me.
The castle's lost, faded among the
trees —
Only this tower I see where now we are,
And thus removed and weeping, to myself
And in myself I say: "Appear, appear,
Compassionate, thou creature of my
dreams,
Upon that tower that I may just discern
The white that is thy dress, then close my
eyes —
And have thee so forever at my side. —"
But no one ever comes. O now I pray
thee,
Who art my soul, my consolation, stay

Firm on this tower until thou seest our
troop
Far down the valley — stay a little while
Upon the tower, climb up the wall, and
send
The waving of thy veil to greet the spouse
Who leaves thee. It will be, I swear, to me
As, O my soul, thou had'st wiped tears
away
From my uncovered heart. I ask thee this,
Belovéd, and no more.   [*Pause.*]
    FLORA [*moved at last and with sincere
        compassion*]. It shall be done.
    MANFRED. I'll leave thee now. I'll fly,
as though to part
Were dear to me, that I may catch thy
greeting.
Do thou stay here. The maid shall bring
to thee
A long, long scarf, woven of lover's sighs.
And, waving it, think that thy heart sends
forth
The gesture, to pluck kisses from my heart,
More distant.
        Flora, good-bye. Close thy wan eyes.
Believe thou'rt caught up in a dream as
when
Thou prayest a fervent prayer. Give me
thy mouth
That I may kiss it.
        [*He kisses her, tears himself away,
        and goes out almost running because of
        the stabbing pain.*]
        [*Hardly free from him,* FLORA *shakes
        herself as if to free her person from his
        embrace. She advances to the battle-
        mented wall, mounts the stairs, and
        leans over the wall.*]

[AVITO *enters cautiously and as if in a
        dream from the right.*]

    AVITO [*looks around, discovers* FLORA *on
        the stairs*]. Flora, Flora!
        [*She turns. At first she does not
        recognize him in those garments.*]
                                        I am
Avito.
    FLORA. Can it be — since that night —
    AVITO.   Ah, yes —
Yes, I was here, forever near to thee,
My soul was here, my lovesick mind was
here.

Flaminio clothed me thus that I might see thee.

FLORA [*in sudden desperation*]. I cannot see you more. I ought not love you Henceforward. Ah, your voice — let it not sound Hereafter in my ears. I pray you — go!

AVITO. I do not understand you, Flora. Or Am I not here, but elsewhere, and gone mad? And art thou Flora — Flora, who speaks thus?

FLORA. Yes, yes, a thousand times, and then a thousand Thousand. Desperately — yes.

AVITO. Thou art All mine a thousand times? You would say that?

FLORA. No! No! My life within is silent darkness, and Without, is terror. I am conquered — conquered By goodness and compassion. O my God! Did'st thou not hear my husband? Him who went?

AVITO. Why say you not — my husband, he who comes?

FLORA. Leave me in peace. O leave me to my sorrow.

AVITO. Leave thee! And go — go whither? Take myself Within a net, twist me and torture me To feel myself made prisoner by myself, Uselessly? Where is my life but here?

FLORA [*who has descended from the staircase and approached the door at the left*]. Conceal yourself. Some one is coming — here.

AVITO [*always as if he were dreaming*]. Go Yes. I shall fly. [*He prepares to go.*]

FLORA. Hurry — for my sake! [*AVITO hurries out at the right.*]

[*An instant after the* MAID *enters from the left.*]

MAID [*carrying an inlaid coffer*]. The baron Manfred sends you this, my lady.

FLORA [*with infinite melancholy*]. Put it there. [*She indicates the stone table.*] [*MAID puts the box on the table and goes out.*]

[FLORA *goes to the table, slowly opens the coffer, and draws slowly from it a long white scarf. Her arms fall as if dead, and the scarf with them. She remains motionless a moment — silent, without complaint, without life. Then she remembers her promise and, the veil in her hand, approaches the wall. She mounts the stairway and looks down; sees the road, and waves the scarf for the first time — then for the second, and for the third; and each time her arm falls wearily by her side.*]

[*Then* AVITO *returns.*]

AVITO. Flora, farewell. I have wished to see thee once, Now I must go — returning — nevermore. Farewell, my Flora. If thou dost not wish To grant me one last kiss, one that would be Like life itself unto me, let me touch Thy scarf that's perfumed with thy gentle fragrance. I have forgotten it. [*He tries to take the scarf from her.*]

FLORA [*who has been prostrated by his words, drawing back*]. Don't touch it!

AVITO. Nothing That's thine henceforth belongs to me!

FLORA [*watching him piteously and suddenly forgetting everything else, in an altered voice*]. Alas, How white thou art! And how unmastered! Thou Art like a lily, a creature that's enamored!

AVITO. Love's poison is more strong than sleep, it is More strong than hunger, now I see it is More strong than life!

FLORA. Thy life is my life. Pity And joy, a secret torrent, now assail me Who formerly was closed against them like A torpid serpent. Thou mak'st me pity thee,

AVITO. Thou art like the spring's young green Too soon exposed to the blast; I have undone thee, The ill I caused thee hath undone thee quite.

AVITO [*avidly*]. Restore my joy with
kisses. O delay not,
Thy jest hoids too much sorrow. Come
down, come down,
My Flora!
FLORA.   No, I must not.
[*She sadly remembers her promise and
waves the scarf.*]
[AVITO *approaches her.*]
FLORA.   Don't climb to me!
AVITO. Flora! Why not?
FLORA.   Don't ask me.
AVITO.   I shall leave you.
I am so tired that almost I cannot
Drag myself farther.
FLORA.   Avito, stay. But do not
Demand —   [*She waves the scarf.*]
          Come close to me. Come near
me. Kiss
My dress.   There. On that golden ruffle
which
I sewed myself.
AVITO [*runs up to her quickly, seizes her
dress, and kisses it*]. I feel your
fingers yet
Caressing the embroidery. So I kiss
Your hands. But rough and strange my
kisses are.
The needle — have you left it stuck here?
[*He greedily slakes his thirsty lips.*]
FLORA [*tries to wave the scarf once more,
but cannot. Her arms fall, her head
is bowed*].   Torture!
O struggle inexpressible!
AVITO [*like a child*]. I'll not hear you.
I've hidden my head among the roses, and
Within my ears I hear the droning bees,
Enchantments of old magic. My heart's
full
Of perfumed liquors.
[*He clasps her knees.*] Thy knees! They
are a ledge,
Mossy and soft, for me to grasp, who have
Journeyed so much and died so many
times!
FLORA. Avito! Avito!
AVITO.   The engulfing sea hath broke
My ship. I have no other hope than love
To which I desperately strain.
FLORA [*bending down, and weak*]. Alas,
Avito,
Thou'rt lead, thou drawest me down.

AVITO.   Oh, thy young voice —
I hear't above me like an incantation.
FLORA. Avito! Avito!
AVITO.   I draw thee to my breast,
A bundle of sweet flowers; I bind the stalks,
Only the stalks. Shall I not hide my head
Deep in the sweet corolla?
FLORA.   Avito, alas,
Thou knowest not!
AVITO.   A bundle of sweet flowers
Thou art not only; thou'rt a rude bundle
Of thorns to burn me here. Ah, I would
plunge
My life in fire to find thy mouth, and die!
FLORA. Avito, no!
AVITO.   Thy mouth! Thy mouth!
Flora,
Despairingly I beg thee! Flora! Thy
mouth!
FLORA [*yielding, conquered*]. Alas, my
vow bends as a tree is bent
In pity for the thirsty.
AVITO.   I am thirsty —
Thirsty!
[*He draws her to him as, descending
the steps, she falls in his arms. They
kiss each other as though they were
perishing for love.*]
FLORA [*after a pause, in a caressing voice
between that of a mother and a child*].
How thou tremblest, my delight!
AVITO. Love, that recovers me, hath
made me feel
The ice of solitude.
FLORA [*caressingly, forgetful of all else*].
And thinking of
Thy Flora thou slept not.
AVITO [*imitating her voice*]. And think-
ing of
Flora, I did not live — till hope awoke me.
You played me as a cat its prey.
FLORA.   Some other —
It was not Flora — some perfidious
woman.
Where is she, and I'll strike her? Has she
hurt you?
I am not she. O tell me who I am:
What shall I call myself?
AVITO.   O thou art called
A kiss — a mother's tenderness. Thou art
A child that finds its mother, sleeps, and
dreams.

Now art thou dreaming.

FLORA. Dreaming.

[*They are seated on the rounded bench of stone.*]

AVITO. Look overhead.

We are in heaven. There's journeying in heaven —

We ride on the young air.

FLORA. In heaven.

AVITO. Where are we?

O Flora, I am lost. Thy face — I have forgot

Thy face.

[*He takes her face in his hands, gently, but passionately contemplates it.*]

O beautiful, most beautiful!

O little, shining star! O firmament,

Thanks that thou givest me her. Yet my desire

To have her wholly — it is vain. Thou art

Indeed a star, and like thy sister stars

Above: the more they're looked upon, the more

They draw away. The more I press thee to me,

The more for me thy beauty is renewed!

FLORA [*ecstatically*]. Then chain me!

AVITO. Shut up the sea?

FLORA. An eye can hold

All heaven. Thou can'st shut up my life within

Thy mouth — then take it, take it!

AVITO. Flora, behold —

Here's one fair kiss, the last, the last of kisses

Infinite, and in eternity,

The first.

[*They kiss, and remain hopelessly lost and locked together in a mist of love.*]

ARCHIBALDO [*from within*]. Flora!

[*He enters suddenly, followed by* FLAMINIO.]

Flora!

[*The two lovers, who have not heard the old man's first call, break from each other as in a dream.*]

FLORA [*responding to the old man*]. I am here.

ARCHIBALDO [*with anxiety and suspicion, to* FLAMINIO]. Flaminio, look, who is it's here?

FLAMINIO. My lord,

The lady Flora.

[*He makes a sign to* AVITO *to flee.*]

[AVITO *advances cautiously to the right-hand door.*]

ARCHIBALDO. But I hear a step!

FLORA. 'Tis mine, my lord.

[*And she beckons* AVITO *entreatingly to go out.*]

ARCHIBALDO [*like a caged lion*]. Flaminio, tell me, tell me,

Who's here?

FLAMINIO. No one. There's nobody.

[AVITO *exits.*]

ARCHIBALDO [*who has heard his footsteps, speaks bitterly*]. 'Tis well. Flora, Where art thou?

FLORA. Here.

[*She remains a little back stage at the right.*]

[ARCHIBALDO *has discovered the truth; he has heard, he has seen.*]

ARCHIBALDO [*violently*]. Flaminio, go.

FLAMINIO [*stuttering*]. Listen, my lord, would you not have me look

Into the road? The baron is returning.

He's faced his horse about.

ARCHIBALDO [*shuddering*]. He is returning —

Certainly.

FLORA [*remembering her vow*]. Returning?

ARCHIBALDO. Quick, Flaminio —

Go meet him.

FLAMINIO [*insistently*]. My lord!

ARCHIBALDO. Go!

[FLAMINIO *goes out.*]

Where art thou, Flora?

FLORA. My lord!

ARCHIBALDO [*trembling with wrath and outraged honor*]. Thy lying voice yet wounds my ears?

FLORA. My good lord!

ARCHIBALDO. Who was with thee here? Who has

Betrayed us?

FLORA. No one.

ARCHIBALDO. Flora!

FLORA [*crouching on the bench close to the wall as if to disappear*]. No one, no one!

ARCHIBALDO [*advancing toward her, i*

about to seize her]. Now am I justified in touching thee.
I will know all, and pardon thee, that I
May so disblame myself for having hid
Thy guilt. I was thy 'complice once. I'll know
This time who is't was with thee. What's his name?

FLORA. No one.

ARCHIBALDO. Alas, thou knowest I heard him fly,
I heard his very step! [*Seizes her.*]

FLORA [*raising herself suddenly like a snake*]. Then — then — The man
Who passed before your face that has no eyes —
It was my lover. Yes — he was my joy.
And you, a trembling dotard, you who stand
Behind me like revenge or death, can't frighten me
Now that I think of him. Well — kill me. Then
I shall rejoin him where he'll come in death.
Or let me flee. Oh, could I flee! — because
No tie can bind me where I do not love,
If my love calls me over everything.
My liberty — I ask you, let it be
My liberty, my freedom!

ARCHIBALDO. Tell me his name!
He hath broke the laws of pardon and of love.
Let me know who he was.

FLORA. I'll speak to Manfred
When he returns. He's merciful.

ARCHIBALDO. No! No!
He'd pardon thee. I've taught him virtue, and
Lack joy of it. [*He seizes her throat.*]
His name, his name, I say.

FLORA [*lies at length on the bench; the old man covers her with his huge body. Her voice is heard, still firm*]. He has no name. For he was more than all —

ARCHIBALDO. Thou traitress! Ah!
Thy throat locks in his name.
My hand shall force it out of thee. Speak! Speak!

Listen! — Manfred approaches and he pardons —

Not I, unless you speak it. Tell me — tell me!

FLORA [*clearly*]. He's called — sweet death.

ARCHIBALDO. But if you die,
I have a way to trap your love!

FLORA. No, no!
Then let me live to save him, not t'accuse him.

ARCHIBALDO [*squeezing her throat*]. Ah!
Brazen-throated! Throat of a liar! Throat
Too straight to shut in treachery so vast!
Treachery! Horrid treason, you, my son,
Shall never pardon for you come too late.
Sorrow's to come. [*A horrible silence.*]
[*The old man draws away from the body and covers it with the scarf. Then he sits on the circular bench, hiding the body with his person.*]
Silence! Hollow night!
The fierceness of my blood beats but within.
[*Sadly.*] I who have cut her off have never seen her —
And in my night profound, it may be she,
And only she, I shall behold hereafter.
[*Short pause.*]
[*In desperation and terror.*] No! Manfred comes — He's near us, does not know.
He is afraid — my son that's lost — I hear him.
He comes, and runs unto his joy.
[*Sunset draws near. The clouds redden in the sky.*]

MANFRED [*within, breathless and apprehensive*]. Flora!
My Flora! Hast thou fallen?
[*Enters*]. Father, tell me —
She's fallen from the wall while with her veil
She solaced me from far? For, when I saw her
No more, I turned around. You hide her from me!

ARCHIBALDO [*desperately*]. Leave me the while I cover with my person
The burden of thy evil. Come no nearer;
Or come to give thy sword to me that I
May plunge it in my breast and fall above her,
Her that is dead!

MANFRED. She's dead! She's dead!

ARCHIBALDO. Woe's me!
Come thou not near me! 'Tis I have killed her!

MANFRED. Thou?
What sayest thou? My bitless reason strikes
Against my mind like bulls against a rock!
She's dead? She lives no longer? No? And is there
A horror like this horror in a world
Which has her not?

ARCHIBALDO. She was as foul as night!

MANFRED. As foul? — Thou sayest —?
What sayest thou?

ARCHIBALDO. She's foul,
Deceived thee in thy house, even here; what time
Her lying hand did wave the scarf thou gav'st her,
The fire of passion licked her garments, and
Drew her to cruelest shamefulness, in which
I did surprise her.

MANFRED [profoundly, to himself]. And love such as this
That child had in her heart — but not for me?
Her soul was then so simple that to me
Seemed so mysterious?

ARCHIBALDO. My son, thy heart
Is colder than is she.

MANFRED [in despair]. She loved like this —
She loved past life. Now let me see her. Once
The veil of pity hid my reason, now
It is despair. I cannot speak. Let me
Behold her.

ARCHIBALDO. No! I would not have thee touch her
While yet I live. Give me thy sword!

MANFRED. Ah, why
Didst thou not let me speak with her before —
She would be mine —

ARCHIBALDO. Alas, thy Christian pity
Is crueler than all — it is against me.
Accurséd be the goodness I instilled
Into thy soul, my child, which is become
Thy cruelty toward me. She that hath soiled

Thy house — thou wouldst forgive her? And art thou
All piety? No, never. My young instincts
Awaken! And if sorrow's more than honor,
And if thy house is naught to thee, I say
Thou art not numbered of us, or thou art
Numbered among the slaves!

MANFRED. I know not, know not
What manner of thing destroys me! Let me weep
Here on her breast these senseless wasted tears.

ARCHIBALDO. Thy piety — hath it no end? Canst press
Thy lips there where another left a kiss
So strong it gave this woman force to die,
Singing his love? Thou canst? And canst thou marry
Thy mouth with his, the thief unknown?

MANFRED [desperately]. Tell me,
O tell me who he was?

ARCHIBALDO. Alas, I'm blind —
So blind, so blind! I did not see him. I —
I cannot tell it thee.

MANFRED. Thou dost not know?
And thou hast killed her?

ARCHIBALDO. Me thou canst not pardon —
Is it not true? [MANFRED is silent.]

ARCHIBALDO. It's true! Thou answerest not!
For the first time thy soul refuses pardon,
And to thy father.

MANFRED. Pardon? That I cannot!

ARCHIBALDO. Thou ought'st not pardon me. I do not wish it.
At least I hear the hate that's in thy voice —
What if it be against me? In thy voice
It's beautiful and new. I shall not die
Until thou'rt able, not to pardon me —
Not that — O never that — rather, to bless me!
[Savagely.] When I have brought thee face to face with him
Who did betray thee; when thyself canst meet him
And into wild desire for vengeance feel
The disillusion of thy love all change —
Thy love unto this creature whom another,

Thou must remember, utterly possessed
In body, in the primal fonts of goodness,
Of sacrifice, of mercy even (which
For thee she did not have), thou then wilt say
To me: "Tell o'er again the story of
Her death. Thou hast done well!"

MANFRED.   I shall not know,
Not ever, who he was! Thou knowest him not,
Nor never shall, for thou art blind.

ARCHIBALDO.   'Tis true.
I'm blind. But he who follows good like thee
Is blinder than am I, discovers nothing!
And lighted by my vengeance, though in shadow,
I shall search out the place where evil nests —
In darkness I shall see him, hear him pass,
And for thy sake clutch at his throat. I am
Barbarian and pagan still. To me
My savagery is fairer than thy love
For treason — and I pardon not.

MANFRED [again seized with the thought of
    FLORA, imploringly]. My father!

ARCHIBALDO. No! Stand still! Thou
    wouldst but see her throat
Circled with death as with a necklace wrought
By my paternal hands. Nay, rather keep
Thy dream. I shall avenge thee!

        [MANFRED gives way.]
                Guide me to
The stairway with thy footsteps' sound, and I
shall follow thee!

    [MANFRED exits slowly at the left
    while ARCHIBALDO rises, lifts the dead
    woman to his breast, and prepares to
    follow his son.]

        THE CURTAIN FALLS

ACT III

The crypt under the chapel of the castle.
is reached by a passage at the left toward the
k. An interior window illumines the
rance.

The walls are completely covered with
mosaic work. At the back is a large niche
arched by the storied sky; therein is a small
altar and two large lateral sepulchers sculptured with symbolic figures. At the top
under the arch six lamps burn on a transverse
beam. At the right toward the front a huge
round sepulcher prevents the rest of the
crypt, which is lost in darkness, from being
seen.

Dressed in white FLORA lies extended on
her bier in the midst of the crypt.

Various persons are kneeling under the
arch at the entrance, illuminated by the rays
of light which come from within and from the
top. A woman of the people, with her little
daughter, MADDALENA, is near the bier.

THE WOMAN [to her little girl, who has
    her face hidden in the palms of her
    hands]. Thou seest, Maddalena,
    little one,
How beautiful our lady lies in death?
A blessed sign it is that she was good,
And in her last hour that she suffered not.
Look on her; lift thy face from out thy hands,
And make the sign of the cross.

MADDALENA.   I am afraid,
Mother.
    [Turning her head, she sees that the
    group of people has gone away.]
                They are all gone.

THE WOMAN.   'Tis true. Let us
Go also. It's already the hour of night.
    [She makes the sign of the cross and
    goes out, likewise struck with terror.
    She meets two men under the arch who
    advance respectfully, approach the coffin,
    cross themselves, and pray a short
    prayer. Then they look around.]

SOLDIER. There's really no one.

SMITH.   So I said to you.
It is because of that so few dare enter.

SOLDIER. Perhaps some unseen sen-
    tinel —

SMITH.   Who knows?
        [Gazing at the dead.]
How calm she is! Look, Nesto. Seems
    she not
Alive?

SOLDIER. And sudden death hath snatched her!

SMITH [*reflectively*]. She seems to live!

SOLDIER. What — She is still alive?

SMITH. Fool! — what do you say? I do believe
Her face hath cunningly been masked.

SOLDIER. Been masked?

SMITH. To hide the traces of her violent death —
Because the Baroness was killed.

SOLDIER. In truth
The old man did not mask it, for he's blind.

SMITH. The stranger people might have done it for him.
There is an ancient man, an alchemist,
Who seems a mage — do you know of him?

SOLDIER. Enough.
I do. Some one may overhear us.

SMITH. No,
There's no one here. The chapel has been open
All day to who would come. I've been here twice
And tried to see her face, but have not dared
Approach.

SOLDIER. She frightens me.

SMITH. A creature young
And beautiful affrights you more than one
Mature and old. The face of the young wears something —
A malediction — yet they seem to smile.

SOLDIER. Why do you think she has been killed?

SMITH. Because
'Tis sure some tragic horror on that tower
Has reached its period.

SOLDIER. But why?

SMITH. The flag
Of death — have you not seen it? On the drawbridge
There is one hanged — Flaminio, the blind Baron's
Beloved and faithful servant. Would they ever
Thus hang a faithful servant suddenly,
Then call the people in to see this flower
Cut down?

SOLDIER. I'll not believe it. Had they killed her,

Her face at any rate would have its blotches.

SMITH. The alchemist's a wizard, and besides
There is no skin so easily adorned
As is a woman's. It's the only skin
That's beautified while living.

SOLDIER. How is that?

SMITH. With paint!

SOLDIER [*looking at her*]. In truth she seems to live. It's night,
We had best go. I feel a kind of chill
Within my bones.

SMITH. Let's go, let's go. The chapel
Will soon be closed.

[*Sound of an organ from above.*]

SOLDIER. Do you not hear the organ?
What custom is it? Or what offices
At this hour of the night?

SMITH. You understand not.
The organ — yes, but music —

SOLDIER. What?

SMITH. It is
The watcher of the dead. The organ's sound,
It is a trustier sentinel for death
Than is a man.

SOLDIER. You're right. And yet your meaning
I do not grasp.

SMITH. I understand myself,
It being of my mystery. Music was
Discovered by a smith who, with his hammer,
Compelled a thousand sounds to rise upon
The anvil; to the ringing of his iron
He did confide his song.

SOLDIER [*marveling*]. Well, think of it
Therefore it is that when you work in summer
And sing, we all do hear you.

SMITH [*after a short pause*]. People come —
People are coming.

SOLDIER [*who has looked into the passage*]. Avito! Avito of
Altura!

SMITH. Her cousin. He's in mourning!

SOLDIER [*emphatically*]. Go
If they have killed her, he's the man who knows

How to avenge her. I should like to stay
And see him.

SMITH.   Best respect his sorrow. Then
It's time to go, besides.

[AVITO *approaches with two servants.*]

[*The organ ceases. The* SMITH *and
the* SOLDIER *go out, quieting down respectfully; they bow as they pass before*
AVITO.]

[AVITO *remains motionless near the
entry-arch and, as if the mausoleum contained only a blinding flame, his head
is bowed, almost hidden.*]

ONE OF THE SERVANTS [*advances and
looks into the chapel; then speaks to* AVITO].
Courage, my lord.

Advance.   There's none to watch beside
the dead —
I knew it.

AVITO [*in an imploring voice to the two
servants*].   Go. Betake yourselves
away!
Await me up above, beside the door.
If any one approaches, stop him; if
You cannot, then descend and call me here.

[*He remains motionless until the two servants have gone out. Then he comes in,
his face hidden in his palms. When he
is close to the dead:*]

Flora — Flora! Silence. We're alone.
O speak to me! I wait. I would not see
thee,
Beloved, ere thou speakest, thou elect
To live forever, thou my soul! O speak!
I wait. Why should I look upon thee —
why?
And it, and call me, for I know thou
canst.
Silence, alas! Ah, I must look at thee!

[*He lifts his face and stares at her like
a madman.*]

Tell me thy secret, Flora. For thy mouth,
Immaculate and sealed, preserves what
secret?
Flora, speak! Thou hidest life within
Thy unshaken silence and behind thine
eyes
Lives memory yet.

[*With sudden lamentation.*]   Alas, no, no!
Thou'rt dead!

Thou art all spent!   And I instead grow
mad
And do believe thy delicate wax to be
One more sweet sign of love; but thou art
dead
And with closed eyelids thou dost gaze
upon
The impassable forever! O might I know
Who speaks with thee where thou art, and
who judges!
They have thrust thee all too quickly into
the white
Abyss where nothing is — so quickly that
There is a miracle upon thy face
Where death hath stopped to smile his
ultimate smile.
Liar! For now I'll touch thy hands that
seem
Yet delicate with life — they will be
cold
And then I'll kiss thy mouth which keeps
the kiss
I searched so very long for on thy lips —
They also will be cold and motionless. —
O God! Who hath desired this horrid
treason!
Who hath desired that such fair truth
should change
Into such cold deceit!

[*Pause. With an altered voice.*]   O poverty
That is my life! What travail is it, never
To have had what's mine — for all of you
was mine!
So — So Forever dear, even though
thou'rt spent,
One last sign from thy lovely soul must
be
In thee. I want it, Flora. 'Tis o'er thy
mouth,
For, if there be not life, there still is mem-
ory,
And 'tis thy mouth which doth remember
most.

[*Weeping, he throws himself fondly
on her mouth. After a brief instant, he
raises himself.*]

What exhalation is it! Miracle! Miracle!
Yes! — So! — Thou wert alive. And thy
last breath
Is caught up in my life. Am I then lost
With thee? 'Tis so. I feel how my heart's
wrung!

Alas, that sorrow should be stronger than
The world beside!

[*He suddenly rises and takes some
steps toward the door, tottering like a
man who has been struck.*]

          O youth, thou art fixed strong
On merest refuse!

[*He hears some one coming.*]
          Some one is coming! I
Shall be discovered!

[MANFRED *appears like a shadow. He
comes from the right, from where the
chapel is lost in the darkness, and advances toward* AVITO *who cannot flee.
He slowly discovers him.*]

MANFRED. You — at last! We have
So caught you. [*Recognizing him.*] Thou,
    Avito? Thou it was
Whom she adored? 'Tis thou hast robbed
    me of
My every bliss, and stained my house, my
    bed,
And killed my heart and nightly hast
    abased
My very life? O infamous, infamous!
              [*Goes toward him.*]
    AVITO. What do you want? Do you
    not see that I
Can scarcely speak?
    MANFRED.   And it is good, is good.
Aye, it is good. Thou art already dead.
To catch thee there was spread upon her
    mouth
A potent and insatiable poison,
Swift as a moment.
    AVITO [*horror-struck*]. No, no! Not on
    her mouth!
    MANFRED. It is enough if but the small-
    est part
Touches thy lips, for thou shalt die. Thou
    hast
Thy kiss, thou hast profaned her, and
    thou diest.
Now thou art caught. I see thee!
    AVITO.   Thou hast done this,
Thou, who art called the holy? Thou
    canst dirty
Her sacred mouth in fashion such as
    this?
    MANFRED. I? No. It was my father.
    For he wished

To know thee, who thou wert. And for
    my sake,
My joy in seeing thee dying — thou who
    hast
Little by little robbed me of my good —
    AVITO. It is just. Be joyous in my
    dying. So —
And yet I do not suffer, and thy joy
Is therefore incomplete. If thou adoredst
    her,
Thou canst not truly curse me, seeing that
    thou
Wouldst also have died for her.
    MANFRED [*desperately*].   Tell me this,
This that I do not know. O tell me. Did
    She love you?
    AVITO. Like the life that's taken from
    her.
Nay, more than that — much more. The
    guilt's not ours.
Thou'rt good. Then understand me. I
    would not
Have loved for pity of you, save that I —
I was not able not to love her. This
I swear. But if thou wouldst have ven-
    geance, then
Do not delay, for I am quickly dead.
Avenge thyself, and kill me.
    MANFRED [*returning to his true nature*].
              It is true.
Thy mystery is stronger than my right.
Yes, I am alone here, an intruder
Among you. Thou — thou art that
    boundless torment
Which without intermission tortures me
Forever and forever. Thou art he
Who has given it me —
    AVITO [*dying*].   I knew it not. And
    thou —
Were I a plant, a bird, a savage beast,
A treacherous serpent dying in the snares
Of love, thou mightest pity — is it so?
Well, then — enough. Death calls me.
            [*He sways and is about to fall*]
    MANFRED [*supports him and then help
him to the ground. Then raising his arms
heaven:*]   O my God
My God, why can't I hate him!
    [*He turns toward the corpse of* FLORA
                 Flora! Flora
Yes! yes! You love me now!
Behold! For the first time I know 'tis s

Because I have sustained thy dying lover,
[*Advancing toward her.*]
Do thou sustain me in my extreme hour —
[*He throws himself upon her and he,
too, kisses her mouth.   He remains
there panting for the death which
spreads itself through his veins.*]
[*The organ is faintly heard again.*]

[ARCHIBALDO *enters, groping about in his
eternal darkness.*]

ARCHIBALDO. A groan. Yes — yes.
Now make thy peace with heaven,
Thou thief. I have caught thee in a trap
of steel!
[*He advances to the bier, searches

about, and feels the body of* MANFRED.
Suddenly he seizes it.]
Thou thief. I wish to feel thy heart beat in
The hour of death!
MANFRED [*in a dying voice*].   No,
father. Thou hast tricked
Thyself.
ARCHIBALDO [*instantly raising himself to
his full height*].   O Manfred, Man-
fred! Thou art also
With me in shadow past all hope of cure!
[*He falls back in utter desolation.*]
[*The organ continues its angelic
whispering.*]

THE CURTAIN FALLS

MALVALOCA

A DRAMA IN THREE ACTS

(*Suggested by an Andalusian Song*)

By SERAFÍN AND JOAQUÍN ÁLVAREZ QUINTERO

Translated from the Spanish by JACOB S. FASSETT, JR.

CAST OF CHARACTERS

MALVALOCA

JUANELA

MARIQUITA

SISTER PIEDAD

TERESONA

ALFONSA

DOÑA ENRIQUETA

DIONISIA

SISTER CONSUELO

SISTER DOLORES

SISTER CARMEN

LEONARDO

SALVADOR

MARTIN THE BLIND MAN

BARRABAS

TIO JEROMO

LOBITO

A WORKMAN

MALVALOCA

ACT I

*In Las Canteras, an Andalusian village,
there is a convent of remote date, which is
known by the name of "The Convent of
Carmen." When the last of the nuns devoted
to the Divine Love passed to a better life [she
was a very old woman], the Sisters of Charity
came to inhabit the ancient precincts. They
are an order similar to that of the Sisters of
the Poor.*

*At the time when the action of this play
begins, there are in the convent, or home, six
old people for whom the Sisters care with extreme solicitude and kindness.*

*The first act takes place in one of the
corridors, or galleries, of the cloister through
whose tall arches may be seen, upstage, the
whole side of what was once a garden, now
almost entirely converted into an orchard
containing more trees than flower beds. At
the right of the actor, the corridor ends at a
wall in which there is a large door, called the
"Gateway of the Cross," because above it,
fastened to the wall, there is a wooden cross.
In the wall itself, as high as one can reach,
and on a rough pedestal, there is a small
image of St. Anthony. Before it there is an
earthen jar full of chick peas. One of the
central arches affords an entrance into the
garden. In the corridor there are two or
three chairs and a bench.*

It is morning on a sunny day in April.

[Enter BARRABAS, *one of the old inmates. He
is rather small, ill-humored and fretful. He
acts as caretaker of the convent garden
and orchard, and fusses about in his own
domains. Some distance upstage, in
the shade of a tree,* SISTER CARMEN,
*silent and preoccupied, sews tirelessly.
From time to time the scenes which take
place about her distract her from her
work for an instant, but she soon fixes
her attention again on whatever she is
making.* SISTERS DOLORES *and* CON-
SUELO *enter the garden from the left.
They carry large purses for the purpose
of collecting alms. They enter the
corridor through the middle archway,
and disappear through the "Gateway of
the Cross."* BARRABAS *soliloquizes
maliciously as follows.]*

BARRABAS.
> *Here we go
> Two in a row
> Skulking in the shadows —
> Sisters of Charity, you know.*

He! he! My own verses!

> *Alms for the poor —
> Pray give us more —
> If it be silver, you add to our store.*

Heigh!

[Enter from the Gateway of the Cross,
MARTIN, *the blindman. He carries a
stick to assist his progress. He is older
and more broken down than* BARRABAS.
*He walks quietly the whole length of the
corridor.* BARRABAS *sees him and
stops him to talk with him.]*

Good morning!

MARTIN. Good morning! I didn't
know you were here, Señor Barrabas.

BARRABAS. You knew it perfectly well,
Señor Martin.

MARTIN. Just as you say!

BARRABAS. Because, although you can't
see me, you can smell.

MARTIN. Just as you say. Good morning.

BARRABAS. Are you going to take a sun
bath?

MARTIN. Yes, with Sister Piedad's permission.

BARRABAS. There is nothing like dancing
in attendance to get favors; but that
doesn't suit me.

MARTIN. Nor me either. I won't argue with you. And, mind, you have no right to criticise things in this Home. You were taken in here out of charity the same as I was.

BARRABAS. There is a difference, my friend. I'm not a useless ornament like you are. I work here in the garden and the orchard. I earn the bread I eat; yes, and what you eat, too!

MARTIN. I don't owe you anything. I work, myself.

BARRABAS. Perhaps you'll tell me what you do? It's nearly two years since you have been up in the bell tower.

MARTIN. I do what the Sisters tell me to do.

BARRABAS. Since they never tell you to do anything, you live like a priest.

MARTIN. I tell you I don't want to argue with you. Good-bye.

BARRABAS. What have you to say of the clatter La Golondrina has been making lately? A fine bell she is!

MARTIN. Everything turns to poison in your mind, Señor Barrabas.

BARRABAS. That's why I like to get it out.

MARTIN [starting toward him. With deep and genuine feeling]. La Golondrina is a bell which belongs to this sacred Home; at present she is broken. She does not sound as she used to, because God has willed it so. But when these hands used to ring her, La Golondrina sang as no bell ever sang since belfries have had crosses. You know that as well as I do, only you want to hear me talk.

BARRABAS. Didn't La Sonora of the Iglesia Mayor have a better tone?

MARTIN. Now you're talking about La Sonora again! Everybody seems to be crazy in this town. To compare La Sonora with La Golondrina — why you'd have to be deaf to do that!

BARRABAS. Even nowadays, Señor Martin?

MARTIN. I'm not talking about nowadays. How would you expect her to sound after having been broken these three years? La Sonora's friends ought to be happy; yes, sir, very happy. They've lived for a long time oppressed by the weight of La Golondrina!

BARRABAS. I dare say the way it happened was this: One afternoon, as the Eternal Father was walking along the clouds ——

MARTIN. Better not meddle in sacred things, Señor.

BARRABAS. He heard you ringing the bell: Ding dong, ding dong! it sounded right in his ears, you know, and he said: "Well, well, that bell sounds too well to be in Las Canteras, which after all is only a village." Then he told an angel who was taking a trip through Andalusia, to break it with a blow of a hammer. He! he! Wasn't that something like the way it happened? God in Heaven was envious!

MARTIN. You're the one who is envious right here on earth. Idiot, fool, heretic! I'm going to ask the Mother Superior to forbid you to talk to me, that's all.

[At this point SISTER PIEDAD appears in the doorway and cuts short the dispute. She is young and pretty, humble and gentle. She speaks quietly and open-heartedly. Her accent is not Andalusian.]

SISTER PIEDAD. Quarreling again? You are beginning the day early.

MARTIN. This fellow does nothing but pick me to pieces.

BARRABAS. Me? I wouldn't do such dirty work!

SISTER PIEDAD. But you, too, Martin; why don't you go on about your business?

MARTIN. Because he won't let me!

SISTER PIEDAD. Why? Does he set a trap for you as though you were a bird?

MARTIN. He says things to me which make it impossible for me to let them go without answering.

SISTER PIEDAD. To foolish words there is always ——

BARRABAS. Do you mean that my words are foolish?

SISTER PIEDAD. Precisely.

BARRABAS. Well, the only thing I did to him to-day was to wish him good morning

It's better to be a favorite than to be polite!

SISTER PIEDAD. No one has any claims for preference here, Barrabas. Nor do we try to cure wits. The king no longer pays fools. I know your antics by heart, and I also know what your dispute was about. It's the same every day.

MARTIN. Every day, Sister Piedad! Please tell the Mother Superior.

SISTER PIEDAD. Well, who knows but that God will punish you, and make you very uncomfortable? I mean you, Barrabas. The miracle which I am hoping for is ——

BARRABAS. But there are no miracles nowadays!

SISTER PIEDAD. Hush, Barrabas! How do we know? Go on with your work; and you, too, Martin.

MARTIN. God be with you, Sister.

.   [BARRABAS *goes into the garden at the right without replying.* MARTIN *disappears down the corridor.*]

[*Enter* LEONARDO *from the left of the garden. He is a man of about thirty years, and of a modest and simple appearance. His face is somewhat sunburned. His glance is penetrating and curious. He carries his hat in his hand, showing a head well covered with thick, abundant hair. His whole person has an appearance of strong, manly energy which makes him very likable.* SISTER PIEDAD *sees him coming, and awaits him, smiling sweetly.*]

SISTER PIEDAD. Good morning, Señor.

LEONARDO. Good morning, Sister.

SISTER PIEDAD. You have come to see your friend, have you not?

LEONARDO. To stay with him a while. I have nothing important to do down below in the town for the moment.

SISTER PIEDAD. He was here only half an hour ago. He is probably inside talking with some of the inmates. He has such a pleasant way with them, and he loves to chat.

LEONARDO. With them, and with everybody. He has a word for every one he meets. He doesn't know how to keep still.

Really what he says is fascinating and his words are like honey. He has begun talking of you now, and of this place, most interminably.

SISTER PIEDAD [*playfully*]. Indeed? Well, I warn you, we are very much interested in him. It is just possible that we may ask him to show his gratitude in some way.

LEONARDO. If there is anything *I* can do.... I don't know about *him*.

SISTER PIEDAD. We three will talk it over together. I'm going in to look for him. Perhaps he is with Don Jacinto.

LEONARDO. The priest?

SISTER PIEDAD. No, Señor; one of the inmates who is also called Don Jacinto. Haven't you noticed a very handsome, elderly gentleman, who is almost always alone?

LEONARDO. Oh, yes! Now I know whom you mean.

SISTER PIEDAD. He comes of an important family in Seville, who have come here to die. None of us can ever tell what our end will be. Of course we care for them all with great love and kindness — and we have to add courtesy in his case. Everything humiliates and distresses him so. He has found a great comrade in your friend.

LEONARDO. What a sad story! Do these things happen frequently?

SISTER PIEDAD. Yes, Señor, in the larger Homes. But we mostly have people from poor families. Now and then we have an inmate who saves something from whatever we give him to eat in order to give it to his relatives when they come to visit him.

LEONARDO. Very interesting.

SISTER PIEDAD. I shall let your friend know that you are here.

LEONARDO. No; let *me* go, Sister.

SISTER PIEDAD. No, indeed! Pray be seated. He'll be with you in a moment.

[*She goes out through the garden to the right.* LEONARDO *walks about for a moment in silence. Soon he notices the figure of St. Anthony.* BARRABAS, *who has again entered, watches his chance to talk with the newcomer.*]

LEONARDO. What foolishness! The

Saint has peas to-day. It was oil and vinegar yesterday. I can't understand it.

BARRABAS. Are you looking into San Antonio's jar?

LEONARDO. Eh? Oh, yes!

BARRABAS. Don't you know what it is all about?

LEONARDO. No. And ever since I came here, I have been wondering about it, but I never felt like asking anybody.

BARRABAS. Well, then, I'll tell you what it is, and you won't have to ask me. He! he!

LEONARDO. Good!

BARRABAS. Well, since this Home lives by charity, whenever the Sister who is in charge of the supplies notices that they need anything, she puts a little of whatever they need in San Antonio's jar. Along comes some charitable person, takes a peep at the Saint's jar, notices the peas, or whatever it happens to be, and knows right away what is needed. Then he or she orders a sack or a bottle. Then the Sisters say that San Antonio gets it.

LEONARDO. Ah!

BARRABAS. And San Antonio has no more to do with the peas, or the oil, than you or me!

LEONARDO. Of course not.

BARRABAS. That's the way miracles happen nowadays. I could tell you a lot more ——

LEONARDO. No, I don't wish to hear any more.

BARRABAS. Why, in this Home ——

LEONARDO. That will do — that will do, thank you.

BARRABAS. I don't believe you ——

[LEONARDO *sits down and begins to smoke.* BARRABAS *approaches him with a smile.*]

Would you give me a cigarette, Señor?

LEONARDO [*good-naturedly*]. Yes... yes, indeed. Take two of them if you wish.

BARRABAS. I do wish, and thanks very much. Tobacco is the only thing which recalls other days to us here. And it is the only thing that San Antonio never sends for! He's not much of a smoker. We have to be satisfied with the thin cigarettes which the Sisters provide for us!

[LEONARDO *smiles.*] That's the first time I ever saw you smile in my life. I don't suppose you have stomach trouble?

LEONARDO. No.

BARRABAS. You and Don Salvador are very different.

LEONARDO. That will do... that will do; no more, thank you.

BARRABAS. I don't believe you. [*He turns toward the garden re-rolling the cigarette which he is about to smoke. Soon he exclaims as he glances to the left.*] Who is this little dove coming? We don't often see a sight like that in this place!

[MALVALOCA *enters. She stops an instant in the middle of the garden and looks about her as if uncertain which way to go. Upon catching sight of* LEONARDO *in the corridor, she goes toward him.*

MALVALOCA *is pretty; her face is smiling and communicative; her body active and graceful. She is clearly of the proletariat. Her black hair is short and curly. It seems blown about by the breeze with every nervous movement of her head, which is full of all sorts of fanciful nonsense. These quick movements of her head are birdlike. She wears a smooth, plain-colored dress, a white waist, black buckled shoes, and a small shawl of black silk thrown across her shoulders. Her eardrops, rings, and bracelets are very costly, and in striking contrast with the simplicity of her dress.*

When LEONARDO *sees her coming, he gets up, somewhat startled.* BARRABAS *draws near* SISTER CARMEN *as though to comment upon the visitor. A moment later he moves off.*]

MALVALOCA. Good morning.

LEONARDO. Good morning.

MALVALOCA. Is this the Home kept by the Sisters of Charity?

LEONARDO. It is.

MALVALOCA. Thanks. I saw the gate open so I walked in; but when I got into the garden I was afraid I was in the wrong place.

LEONARDO. Well, this is the Home.

MALVALOCA. Oh, yes! I see a nun over there. And — could you tell me ——?

LEONARDO. What?

MALVALOCA. Is it here they are taking care of a man who was hurt?

LEONARDO. Yes.

MALVALOCA. You know the man I mean?

LEONARDO. Is it Salvador Garcia?

MALVALOCA. Yes, of course, Salvador Garcia. How is he?

LEONARDO. Almost well now.

MALVALOCA. He is? But was he dangerously ill?

LEONARDO. I wouldn't say dangerously so, but he suffered enough. His burns were horrible, and the treatment was heroic.

MALVALOCA. It got about in Seville that he burned himself in a furnace.

LEONARDO. Great heavens!

MALVALOCA. Gossip — just talk, wasn't it? Some one told me about it. Who was it? Oh! that pug-nosed Matilda! She never could bear him.

LEONARDO. Have you just come from Seville?

MALVALOCA. Just this minute. All I did was to fix up a bit and look for the Home. I came to get at the truth, so as not to leave any doubt in my mind. I wanted to see him.

LEONARDO. You must be a great friend of his.

MALVALOCA. Uh!

[*This "Uh" of* MALVALOCA'S *is a sort of a little trill. She always uses it with an exaggerated inflection and a humorous gesture, when she is not sure of expressing in words what she wishes to say. Her imagination puts a world of meaning into each "Uh."*]

LEONARDO. A very great friend, eh?

MALVALOCA. I'm still his friend. I have been a tiny bit more than that, but that's a thing of the past, now.

LEONARDO. Except the friendship, of course.

MALVALOCA. Are you Salvador's friend, too?

LEONARDO. Something more than a friend.

MALVALOCA. How's that?

LEONARDO. We are partners in the foundry business.

MALVALOCA. What foundry?

LEONARDO. The brass foundry in which the accident occurred. Didn't you hear about it?

MALVALOCA. It's been more than two years since I've seen him; but now I'm thinking.... Who was it told me that Salvador was mixed up with kettles and things?

LEONARDO [*smiling*]. Probably the information came from the same source as the other.

MALVALOCA. No, it wasn't the Pug-Nose. But what difference does it make who it was? So you and Salvador are ——?

LEONARDO. Partners.

MALVALOCA. Both of you?

LEONARDO. Naturally.

MALVALOCA. Since when?

LEONARDO. Since not very long ago. Although our friendship is very recent, we are already very intimate.

MALVALOCA. Salvador is very attractive.

LEONARDO. Very.

MALVALOCA. He kind of fascinates people, don't you think?

LEONARDO. He has fascinated me at any rate.

MALVALOCA. He does that to every one he meets. Sympathy is what counts in this world.

LEONARDO. Do you think so?

MALVALOCA. I'm sure of it. Real love is nothing more than sympathy, a sympathy so great — so big — that you don't know how to live without the person who gives it to you.

LEONARDO. Perhaps.

MALVALOCA. Call it what you will: love, friendship, affection, take your choice. Look at it closely and you have — sympathy. Don't you suppose that thieves love each other more than fools do? Why is it? Because thieves are always more fascinating — more sympathetic. Why — now don't you be afraid of me!

LEONARDO. Well, you may be right.

MALVALOCA. How did you happen to fall in with this rascal?

LEONARDO. You just gave the reason: sympathy, fellow feeling. We were traveling together; we happened on this abandoned foundry in the village; and we decided to try our luck. We both liked the same things. The foundry used to be called "Successors to — somebody or other," but Salvador has christened it with the high-sounding name of "La Niña de Bronce."

MALVALOCA. Ah! "La Niña de Bronce!" I know why.

LEONARDO. Did he name it after you?

MALVALOCA. No, Señor; after another woman — the hussy! But where is he? I want to see him.

LEONARDO. I expect him here now.

MALVALOCA. You expect him here?

LEONARDO. Yes. One of the Sisters has gone in to tell him of my arrival.

MALVALOCA. I feel like giving him a good hug, poor boy. He's a great rascal, you know, but at the same time, he's very much of a gentleman. He's always behaved very well toward me. I never knocked once at his door without his answering. I'm sure I shall never die in a hospital while he's alive. Is that San Antonio? He has a face like a musician. What's he peddling — peas? Tell me, were you in the foundry when the accident happened?

LEONARDO. Certainly.

MALVALOCA. How did it happen? How did it happen? Would you mind telling me?

LEONARDO. Not in the least. We were going to cast a figure for a new fountain in Los Alcázares, a neighboring village ——

MALVALOCA. I know the place. It never rains there. Phew!

LEONARDO. The mould for the figure which we were going to cast was already covered up in the ground. Then we were about to pour the molten bronze from the crucibles into a hole which was left in the surface.

MALVALOCA. From the what?

LEONARDO. From the crucibles. Crucibles are great jars which are capable of resisting the highest temperatures without cracking or breaking. In these, when they are put into the furnaces, the hardest bronze is converted into a liquid fire.

MALVALOCA. So you could stick your finger into it!

LEONARDO. Then, as I was telling you, it passes from the furnace into the ground where the mould of whatever we are casting is buried. It was in this step that the accident happened to Salvador.

MALVALOCA. Yes?

LEONARDO. Yes. We were carrying the crucible from the furnace with what we call "hand carriers." If the crucible is a large one, it sometimes takes from four to six men to carry it, and to make the casting. Salvador was one of these men. Very well; when they came to pour the liquid through the spout into the mould, one of the men slipped. This caused some of the liquid to be spilled, and it spattered on Salvador's breast and arm and leg.

MALVALOCA. Phew!

LEONARDO. If he had given way to the pain, and had let all of the liquid fire spill and scatter, it might have burned some man to death. Salvador made a heroic effort and shouted: "Cast!" The others obeyed him and poured the moulten stuff into the ground. When there wasn't a drop in the crucible, he dropped the handle and fell into my arms in a dead faint.

MALVALOCA. Poor fellow!

LEONARDO. Two Sisters from this Home had stopped at the shops to ask for alms. They were overcome and greatly affected by the scene, and insisted that we carry him here, it being but a step from the foundry. So here we brought him, here he stayed, and here he will remain.

MALVALOCA. Well, he certainly must have had a hard time of it. He's not very tough. Pinch him ever so little, and it will hurt him. Why do you suppose he isn't here yet?

LEONARDO. I don't know. It surely is late. Perhaps the doctor has come.

MALVALOCA. Is he a good doctor? A good veterinary is the best they have in most of these villages.

LEONARDO. He must be a good one. He's brought Salvador out of it in a hurry. I'll go see what the trouble is, and tell him that you are here.

MALVALOCA. If you would be so kind.

LEONARDO. It's a very great pleasure [*He starts to go, but turns back.*] Who shal

I say is waiting for him? I don't know your ——

MALVALOCA. To be sure! Tell him — tell him that Malvaloca is here.

LEONARDO. Malvaloca?

MALVALOCA. Does that name sound queer to you?

LEONARDO. No. But it surprises me.

MALVALOCA. That's what I have always been called since I was thirteen. My name is Rosa, at your service.

LEONARDO. Thanks very much.

MALVALOCA. But you say "Malvaloca" to Salvador. Would you like to know why they call me Malvaloca?

LEONARDO. Why do they?

MALVALOCA. I was born in Malaga in a little house which had a flower box in the doorway. There was a little flower in the box called malvaloca. And people knew the house by the malvaloca. So far, so good; but the malvaloca died. Since everybody knew my house as the house where the malvaloca grew, and since the flower was no longer there, why, I became the Malvaloca! So, instead of there being a flower on the doorstep, there was a little girl, inside. You see how simple it all is. Only it has to be explained, that's all.

LEONARDO [in a peculiarly impressed frame of mind which partly confirms the theory of sympathy espoused by the engaging MALVALOCA]. I'm going to tell Salvador you are here.

[Goes out through the garden, to the right.

MALVALOCA [when alone]. That man is attractive, too. [Looking toward the door.] Who is this little old woman coming? She must be one of the inmates. But how small she is! Why, it doesn't seem possible! She looks like a little wax figure.

[Enter MARIQUITA, proceeding in the opposite direction down the corridor. MALVALOCA watches her as though enthralled. She is an old woman almost small enough to fit into San Antonio's jar of peas.]

MARIQUITA [as she passes in front of MALVALOCA]. God keep you, sister.

MALVALOCA. God be with you, little sister.

MARIQUITA. May you always keep well.

MALVALOCA. Are you one of the inmates of the Home?

MARIQUITA [stops]. Yes, Señorita.

MALVALOCA. Have you been here long?

MARIQUITA. Four years. Ever since I lost my son who was killed by the Moors.

MALVALOCA. Your son was killed in the wars?

MARIQUITA. The only one I had.

MALVALOCA. What a shame! [MARIQUITA makes a gesture of grief and resignation.] Are there many of you old people in the Home?

MARIQUITA. Six, at present. Two women and four men.

MALVALOCA. This was a convent once, wasn't it?

MARIQUITA. Yes, Señorita, the Convent of Carmen. When the last nun died, the Sisters of Charity came here to live.

MALVALOCA. Ah! Tell me, little sister, do they receive alms?

MARIQUITA. It's this way: they live by charity, and we live by their charity.

MALVALOCA. Here, take this. [She takes a silver dollar from her purse and gives it to her.]

MARIQUITA [astonished]. What's this?

MALVALOCA. A dollar.

MARIQUITA. But I can't change it for you.

MALVALOCA. It is for you, little sister.

MARIQUITA. For me?

MALVALOCA [banteringly]. To buy a new hat with!

MARIQUITA [smiling through her tears]. A hat — for me!

MALVALOCA. Or whatever else you may need.

MARIQUITA. A petticoat!

MALVALOCA. As you like, sister.

MARIQUITA. Are you rich?

MALVALOCA. Huh!

MARIQUITA. They don't give such big gifts in the streets. Two Sisters leave here every day to ask for alms, and you should see how little they pick up! And listen to this: last Saturday a man even struck Sister Piedad!

MALVALOCA. Who did it?

MARIQUITA. A drunken man — how do

I know who he was? She went into a house whose door was open, thinking that it was a private house; but it was a tavern. But as she is very strong-minded in a quiet way, she never stopped at all, just went ahead and begged for alms for the poor. And that old drunken brute began to talk filth to her, and then struck her.

MALVALOCA. What did the Sister do then?

MARIQUITA. Well, as she started to go, the Sister said to him: "Very well, that was for me. Now give me something for the poor."

MALVALOCA [struck with admiration]. Ah!

MARIQUITA. When the Innkeeper heard her, he threw the drunken man into the street, and gave her a fine gift. The next day, when he was sober, the fellow came and begged her forgiveness. You should have heard Sister Piedad! She knows a lot about those things.

MALVALOCA. Is that she who is sewing over there?

MARIQUITA. No, Señorita. Sister Piedad is a beautiful little woman. She married very young, her husband died, and then she came here; because she said she didn't have any one to love in the world. If she comes out here, I'll point her out to you.

[At this moment, in the corridor, and from the left, DON SALVADOR, LEONARDO'S partner, enters. He is a man of about the same age as LEONARDO, and of a very intelligent and wideawake appearance. His left hand rests in a silk handkerchief which is knotted about his neck. When he sees MALVALOCA, he is very much surprised and delighted.]

SALVADOR. Can I believe my eyes?

MALVALOCA. My poor little boy!

SALVADOR. Malvaloca! You here? What does this mean?

MALVALOCA. It means that I have come to see you.

SALVADOR. God bless you, little girl. God bless you.

MALVALOCA. How are your burns?

SALVADOR. All well.

MALVALOCA. That's better. I've brought you good luck.

SALVADOR. You always do. Sit down a while.

MALVALOCA. No, I can't.

MARIQUITA. Are you in love with him?

SALVADOR. She was, but she left me for another.

MALVALOCA [to MARIQUITA]. Tell him he lies.

SALVADOR [to MARIQUITA]. Do you like her?

MARIQUITA. She is beautiful. And look! [Shows him the money.]

SALVADOR. Good heavens!

MARIQUITA [laughing]. She says it is for a hat! God bless her.

MALVALOCA. Good-bye.

[MARIQUITA goes on her way dreaming of the petticoat which she is to buy.]

SALVADOR [to MALVALOCA, with a satisfied air]. Well, how about it?

MALVALOCA. Man, but I'm glad to see you!

SALVADOR. And I to see you.

MALVALOCA. To think that at your age, you'd be in a Home for the Aged!

SALVADOR. Time flies. On the other hand, you never grow old. You're as pretty as ever.

MALVALOCA. It's your eyes, and because I just cleaned up a quarter of an hour ago. They've already told me how you acted the day of the accident. How brave you were!

SALVADOR. Who told you all that?

MALVALOCA. Your friend.

SALVADOR. What friend?

MALVALOCA. Your partner.

SALVADOR. Is he here?

MALVALOCA. Well! He went to look for you, and a Sister went in before him. Where have you been?

SALVADOR. In the tower. Have you been talking to Leonardo much?

MALVALOCA. To whom?

SALVADOR. To my partner, Leonardo.

MALVALOCA. Oh, so that's his name. Well, from the way Leonardo looks at you, you would think he was going to take your picture. He's a man of rare importance, isn't he?

SALVADOR. Yes, indeed. And what is more, he is a splendid fellow.

MALVALOCA. How does he come to be a friend of yours, then?

SALVADOR. The meeting of two extremes.

MALVALOCA. Extremes?

SALVADOR. Yes, Leonardo has the trait which I should most like to have — determination. He is very unusual. He does whatever he pleases. You have to know how to get along with him, however. Well, to show you the kind of a man he is: he could have lived quietly and pleasantly at home with his father, who also had a foundry. But his father, who was a widower, wished to marry again. Leonardo gave him to understand that neither he nor his sister wanted another mother. So he spent that night at home, but left early the next morning. He found a place for his sister with an aunt and uncle of his who had no children, and then he went out into the world to seek his fortune.

MALVALOCA. Well, that shows that he is a man with some feeling.

SALVADOR. He is. He's as strong and unbending as bronze.

MALVALOCA. Does his sister live with him now?

SALVADOR. No, she is still with her aunt and uncle. But she is coming to visit Leonardo soon, for a few days.

MALVALOCA. He isn't an Andalusian, is he?

SALVADOR. No. He came from Asturias.

MALVALOCA. How do you suppose he ever happened to be born so far away?

SALVADOR. How do I know? But, little girl, I'm glad you came.

MALVALOCA. Will you be sensible? Wouldn't you have done the same? You know how I am. A friend of mine asked me if I had heard about your having been toasted like — like San Lorenzo, and I just packed up and came! You know me — sometimes I think there is nothing but heart in my head.

SALVADOR. In your head?

MALVALOCA. Yes, don't you think so?

SALVADOR. Why, yes, naturally; you haven't much else there!

MALVALOCA. That's why I never have headaches.

SALVADOR. What have you where your heart should be?

MALVALOCA. Oh, something with a fence around it, and a dog to keep people out!

SALVADOR. Why, I heard that a German ——

MALVALOCA. Come, you know I never take beer in the summer.

SALVADOR. Are you still living in Seville?

MALVALOCA. Yes, just at present.

SALVADOR. And your mother?

MALVALOCA. Is in Sestona.

SALVADOR [laughing]. Sestona!

MALVALOCA. Don't laugh. It's either Sestona, or Fitero, or Vichy. She's always the same. If I have money, it's "My darling child, my own flesh and blood, joy of my old age" — all that kind of nonsense. But, if I'm poor, she snatches two or three of my shawls, pawns them, and takes the train for some kind of fashionable Baths. I never saw a woman who could drink so much of so many kinds of water. [SALVADOR laughs outright.] Why, she is just puffed up with it!

SALVADOR. And your father?

MALVALOCA. He's a different sort. He doesn't drink water; he drinks by the barrel! Oh — I don't like to talk of my family. Heavens! If they had turned me out as ugly as I am pretty, I'd be for throwing them into one of your crucibles.

SALVADOR. You're just your old self.

MALVALOCA. Oh! let's drop them, poor things. How about your father, is he in the village?

SALVADOR. Yes, still there.

MALVALOCA. Busy with his photography?

SALVADOR. And with a little shop where he sells frames, which have been on his hands for about a year now. He manages to keep himself alive. I think I shall pay him a visit when I get well, so as to convince him that my burns really amounted to nothing.

MALVALOCA. But they must have amounted to something?

SALVADOR. A part of the life.

MALVALOCA. I know. How did you happen to turn out such a rogue?

SALVADOR. A rogue?

MALVALOCA. Foundryman. It's the same.

SALVADOR. You remember I always had a taste for that sort of thing. I met the fellow; we seemed to take to each other at once; and nothing more was necessary. He has many illusions — I haven't quite so many; but I'm glad he has them. So that's the way I came to have a foundry in case you have need of one. Is there anything I can do for you?

MALVALOCA. You might make me two dragons.

SALVADOR. Two dragons?

MALVALOCA. Yes. One for a father, and one for a mother!   [They laugh.]

SALVADOR. That's the very first thing I'll do when I get back to the shops.

MALVALOCA. Do you expect to be here long, now?

SALVADOR. No, not much longer.

MALVALOCA. Well, then, listen: If I come again, don't tell any one who I am.

SALVADOR. Why not? A friend of mine ——

MALVALOCA. Oh! Suit yourself!

SALVADOR. Well, if I don't tell — who shall I say you are?

MALVALOCA. The best thing to say is that I am English; that will account for anything. Here comes your partner.

[At this moment LEONARDO and SISTER PIEDAD enter from within.]

LEONARDO. Here he is, Sister!

SISTER PIEDAD. So we have found you at last?

SALVADOR. Here I am.

MALVALOCA. Good morning.

SISTER PIEDAD. Good morning. [To SALVADOR.] We have been looking for you all over the house.

SALVADOR. I just climbed up into the bell tower.

MALVALOCA. Sister, with your permission ——

SISTER PIEDAD. I'm at your service.

MALVALOCA. Would you mind telling me where the chapel is?

SISTER PIEDAD. I'll show it to you, myself.

MALVALOCA. Oh, no! don't bother.

SISTER PIEDAD. It's no bother, I assure you.

MALVALOCA. Are you Sister Piedad?

SISTER PIEDAD. And happy to serve you. Shall we go?

MALVALOCA. Yes. [To SALVADOR.] I'll be back soon.

SALVADOR. Don't you forget to come back, Sister Piedad.

SISTER PIEDAD. I?

SALVADOR. To talk over that little matter before Leonardo goes.

SISTER PIEDAD. Oh, yes! I'll be right back. [To MALVALOCA.] This way, please.

LEONARDO. Who is this woman?

SALVADOR. Sister Piedad? Why, haven't you heard ——

LEONARDO. Stop your joking. I mean the other.

SALVADOR. Oh, the other is spice — essence of cinnamon!

LEONARDO. Yes, yes.

SALVADOR. They call her Malvaloca.

LEONARDO. I know that.

SALVADOR. Then what do you want to know?

LEONARDO. Something more than her name. Tell me everything you know about her that I do not.

SALVADOR. Her history would make a rather long story. Imagine for yourself. She is like no one else in the world, and yet she is like a great many — a pretty face, a not very wise head, and she comes from a house where they are very poor. That is the beginning of the story. I know a bit more in detail of some of the chapters.

LEONARDO. Has she been an affair of yours?

SALVADOR. Yes; some time ago, however.

LEONARDO. Well, she still feels grateful to you.

SALVADOR. Because I did the right thing by her.

LEONARDO. Yes?

SALVADOR. Yes. I took her to a small

restaurant in Córdoba for luncheon, asked her to wait a moment while I went for tobacco, and then, after two years, I went back to see if she was there!

LEONARDO. You did that?

SALVADOR. To see if she was still faithful.

LEONARDO. Bah! You never did it.

SALVADOR. Yes, I did really. That was the only way out of it. [*He is silent a moment while* SISTER DOLORES *passes down the corridor from right to left.*] Malvaloca is the sort of a woman who gets to one's heart. We were growing to be more and more fond of each other. She even burst into tears two or three times — and this having a woman cry over me is not what I like. Tears make a chain which is stronger than any we make in the shops.

LEONARDO. I don't understand why you left her if you cared so much for her. And I understand much less how she can endure now to see your face.

SALVADOR. I'll tell you. Time went on — and things happened to us — and when the little girl died, I was the first to be at her side.

LEONARDO. Ah! So she lost a child?

SALVADOR. A little girl as pretty as a picture. She was four years old. That was the saddest thing that ever happened to Malvaloca. The little girl was a balm for all her troubles.

LEONARDO. What a pity!

SALVADOR. She has a great many troubles, too. Yet she is better than most women I've met.

LEONARDO. That's the way she seemed to me. She looks good. Deep down in those eyes of hers, the first light you see is Goodness.

SALVADOR. Do you know ——

LEONARDO. What?

SALVADOR. Nothing; I had a bad thought.

LEONARDO. But what are you laughing at?

SALVADOR. At you, probably.

LEONARDO. But why at me?

SALVADOR. Well — "The first light you see is Goodness!" I see, and yet I don't see — foundryman!

LEONARDO. Don't be a fool. [*Suddenly changing the subject.*] What does Sister Piedad want with us?

SALVADOR. She will tell us herself soon, my friend. We've got some work for "La Niña de Bronce."

LEONARDO. That's good. I'm glad of it.

[SISTER PIEDAD *enters at this moment.*]

SISTER PIEDAD. Here I am.

SALVADOR. All right. Now let's talk about La Golondrina.

LEONARDO. La Golondrina?

SISTER PIEDAD. That's what the people call her, though her real name is Santa Teresa. She is the convent bell, and is broken.

LEONARDO. I should say she was broken. Couldn't be anything else. Every morning and afternoon I hear her from the foundry, and it sets my nerves on edge. It sounds like the devil!

SISTER PIEDAD. The devil?

LEONARDO. I beg your pardon, Sister. I mean she couldn't sound worse.

SISTER PIEDAD. How would you expect her to sound after having been broken for four years?

LEONARDO. Well, she must be mended. I wish everything in the world could be fixed as easily.

SALVADOR. Do you hear, Sister? Didn't I tell you Leonardo was our man?

LEONARDO. Yes, indeed. A broken bell in a building like this, two steps from a foundry, is a disgrace to the foundrymen.

SALVADOR. Without even taking into consideration the fact that some way or other we must pay the Sisters for the care they have taken of me.

SISTER PIEDAD. Don't talk nonsense, brother. We only did what God willed us to do. But if you succeed in making Santa Teresa — La Golondrina — sing as she used to do through your skill, lifting her voice to Heaven, then, from the Mother Superior down to the humblest nun (who is your servant), we will have neither words nor deeds good enough to repay you.

LEONARDO. Well, you can count upon its being done. Have you seen the bell, Salvador?

SALVADOR. Yes. It is cracked from top to bottom.

LEONARDO. That is not strange, if she had such a beautiful tone as you say.

SISTER PIEDAD. Why is that?

LEONARDO. The louder and sweeter-toned bells are, the more fragile they are. The one we like to hear best is that which is broken most easily.

SALVADOR. They are like women in that respect.

SISTER PIEDAD. Hush, man, hush! You are always thinking of women.

SALVADOR. Bells have tongues, and that's what makes me think of them.

SISTER PIEDAD. Very well, but do stop joking.

LEONARDO. In spite of the jest, Sister Piedad — and this chap has the vice of joking when he is most serious — we are going to recast La Golondrina in "La Niña de Bronce," and she will be as good then as she ever was.

SISTER PIEDAD. God will repay you for it. That is precisely what I wanted to know; if she will be what she used to be — if after she is repaired she will be the same.

LEONARDO. The very same. Made of the same material, cast from the same bronze.

SISTER PIEDAD. Very good. If she will be as you say — very good. She is hallowed by traditions, by many memories which are dear.

LEONARDO. Well, you shall see she will be the same as before. La Golondrina will take flight, leave her tower, enter our shops, will stay a few days with us, the fire will consume her in order to give her new life, and then she will return to her nest, singing better than she ever did.

SALVADOR. Or, to use another metaphor, La Golondrina is a dark little girl who is hoarse. She consults a couple of doctors, and upon her returning home after her visit, she answers with a voice which makes even the birds pause to listen.

SISTER PIEDAD. Didn't I tell you? His mind is always on the same thing. [To MARTIN, who reënters.] Martin, did you hear?

MARTIN. What, Sister?

SISTER PIEDAD. The miracle I told you about is going to happen.

MARTIN. What miracle?

SISTER PIEDAD. The miracle of La Golondrina, who, thanks be to God for putting such good and intelligent men in the world, is going to ring as she used to.

MARTIN [trembling with joy]. Sister! Is it possible?

SISTER PIEDAD. It is indeed. Don Leonardo and his friend are going to take her to the foundry and are going to return her to us as good as new. Aren't you?

LEONARDO. We are.

MARTIN. Show me where those gentlemen are. I want to kiss their hands.

SISTER PIEDAD. What you ought to do is to give thanks to the Lord!

MARTIN. And kiss their hands!

LEONARDO. Are you the bellman?

MARTIN. I am, Señor, and at your service. Don't you see how I am trembling?

SALVADOR. Martin loves La Golondrina as though she belonged to him.

MARTIN. As though she were my very own, Señor.

SISTER PIEDAD. He pulled the rope the first time she was rung in this tower.

MARTIN. I am the man! I was young then. Since that time we have never been separated. She has been my child, my sweetheart, my playmate — even my mother — all in one. I've always told her all my secrets.

LEONARDO. Well, then. I'm all the more happy at what we are going to do.

MARTIN. No one can tell what it means to me, Señor. I suppose you gentlemen never heard La Golondrina before her accident?

LEONARDO. I never did.

SALVADOR. Nor I.

SISTER PIEDAD. But I did.

MARTIN. Just as the Sister says: it seemed like a voice from Heaven. She awakened the village by her call. She made the fields happy when day came. She called Christian people to prayer, and she wept for the dead. When my wife died I tolled La Golondrina for her funeral, and

I had no better consolation than her voice. How sad she did sound!

SISTER PIEDAD. Don't excite yourself too much, Martin. You will feel worse for it later on.

SALVADOR. Let him talk.

MARTIN. After the news you have given me, I shan't be able to control myself for days. You see I'm getting old. Well, since La Golondrina was broken, I haven't kept count of my years. She never grew old, and I lived as though she were my heart. Sister ——

SISTER PIEDAD. What is it, brother?

MARTIN. May I tell Barrabas the news?

SISTER PIEDAD. Nothing more than just tell it to him?

MARTIN. That's all — that's all. He won't want to argue either, now. You'll see!

SISTER PIEDAD. Very well, then. But be careful what you say.

MARTIN. Don't you worry, Sister. Gentlemen, if my prayers reach Heaven, you will never want for anything in this world. I will give what life there remains in me to La Golondrina after I've rung her once more as I did before she was broken.

SISTER PIEDAD. You may leave us now, brother.

SALVADOR. Good-bye, Martin.

LEONARDO. Good-bye.

MARTIN [going toward the right in the orchard in search of his implacable enemy]. Barrabas! Señor Barrabas! I have some news for you, friend!

SALVADOR. Poor old man! [To LEONARDO, who is drying his eyes.] What's this — are you crying, too?

LEONARDO. Pish!

SALVADOR. But, man alive!

LEONARDO. Foolishness!

SISTER PIEDAD. He will tell the news to Barrabas and to the whole place. Good old Martin will go crazy with joy.

LEONARDO. Why does he want to tell it to Barrabas?

SISTER PIEDAD. Because Barrabas was baptized in another church, and belongs to another faction. In Las Canteras nothing arouses more antagonism than a dispute about bells. Some side with La Golon-

drina, and some with La Sonora, and the day when no heads are broken over it is one of God's miracles.

LEONARDO. It all seems rather amusing.

[SISTER CONSUELO enters through the Gateway of the Cross. She carries a small flask of wine in her hand.]

SISTER CONSUELO. The doctor is here, Don Salvador.

SALVADOR. Has he come?

SISTER CONSUELO. Yes, he is in your room. He says that he is in a great hurry.

SALVADOR. I shall be with him immediately.

[SISTER CONSUELO removes the pan of peas from the statue of San Antonio, and sets down the flask of wine. She goes out by the same way she came in.]

LEONARDO. Well, good-bye. I'm going now.

[MALVALOCA reënters from the left of the corridor. SALVADOR does not see her as he starts to leave at that moment.]

MALVALOCA. Are you going?

SALVADOR. Ah, Malvaloca! Yes, the doctor is here, and I am going up to him. Will you wait?

MALVALOCA. No, I'll come back this afternoon.

SALVADOR. That's better. I'll see you later, then.

MALVALOCA. Good-bye.

SALVADOR. I'll be expecting you. I'm awfully glad you came to see me.

MALVALOCA. And I, to see you're out of danger. Good-bye.

SALVADOR. Good-bye.

[He goes in through the Gateway of the Cross. SISTER DOLORES also appears at the left, seeming a bit perturbed. She speaks to SISTER PIEDAD aside and shows a jewel to her. Meanwhile, LEONARDO and MALVALOCA are saying good-bye.]

MALVALOCA. I'm very happy to have met you.

LEONARDO. More than I am to have met you?

MALVALOCA. Just the same, probably.

LEONARDO. It can't be. Remember

there is some difference between you and me.

MALVALOCA. Caramba! Our Andalusian ways are going to your head.

LEONARDO. But they're rather difficult to acquire.

MALVALOCA. Nothing is difficult. We shall see, however. I suppose you will be coming here again to see your friend?

LEONARDO. Of course!

MALVALOCA. Well, then, we'll see each other.

LEONARDO. Indeed we shall.

SISTER PIEDAD [approaching MALVALOCA]. Sister!

MALVALOCA. What is it?

SISTER PIEDAD. I wonder, was it you — it must have been — was it you who left this jewel on the altar before the Virgin?

MALVALOCA. Yes. I left it for the poor.

[SISTER DOLORES goes to tell SISTER CARMEN about the matter. LEONARDO follows the incident with interest and emotion.]

SISTER PIEDAD. For the poor?

MALVALOCA. Yes.

SISTER PIEDAD [very much overcome]. But, sister, a gift in this form, and of this value ——

MALVALOCA. Do you mean?... Is it because it comes from me?

SISTER PIEDAD. Oh, no! sister, I don't know who you are. I only know that you came here to see a sick friend, that you went to pray to the Virgin, and that you left this jewel on her altar for the poor. Why should I disapprove of anything that comes from your hands? Besides, wherever the jewel comes from, my dear sister, it brings with it a radiance that outshines the hand that gives it.

MALVALOCA [in a sudden burst of feeling at hearing her, and with that natural intimacy and charming simplicity with which she does everything]. Well, then, if you can't see the hand that gives it, take this, too!

[She takes the gold chain from her neck and gives it to her.]

SISTER PIEDAD. Sister!

MALVALOCA. It's for the poor.

SISTER PIEDAD. But ——

MALVALOCA. That's the only way I know how to be good! For the poor! [She looks at both their faces and smiles.] Well, I'll see you later.

[Exit hurriedly into the garden.]

SISTER PIEDAD. Who is this girl?

LEONARDO. I have only just met her myself, Sister. Good-bye until this afternoon.

SISTER PIEDAD. God be with you.

LEONARDO. Good-bye, Sister.

[MALVALOCA, who, as she came in, stopped like a dove orienting herself in the garden, again pauses, and at last goes out firmly to the left — upstage. LEONARDO follows her, although with an effort at concealment, as if his manly spirit were enmeshed in the fine fringe of the woman's shawl.

SISTER PIEDAD is much moved. With tears in her eyes she stands looking at the jewels as she repeats MALVALOCA'S words.]

SISTER PIEDAD. That's the only way she knows how to be good!

[Upstage, SISTER DOLORES talks it over with SISTER CARMEN, who, in deference to the extraordinary interest of the scene, suspends for a moment her constant and quiet work.]

END OF ACT I

ACT II

A large, irregular, well-lighted court between LEONARDO'S house and the workshops of " La Niña de Bronce." To the left of the actor is the entrance of the house. To the right, that of the foundry. Upstage is a wall through which is a small gateway leading into a yard which gives access to the street. Before the house doorway is a covered porch with dark green roof tiles and white pillars. These rest upon huge bases of brick, also white. In the shelter afforded by this porch is LEONARDO'S work-table. Several flower boxes with geraniums and roses adorn the place. In a corner to the right there is a heaped-up pile of old material from the foundry. It is morning in the month of May.

[*Enter* SALVADOR *from the shops with a roll
of papers in his hand. He wears a long
blouse and a cap. He goes to* LEO-
NARDO'S *table, puts the rolls of paper
upon it, and examines various documents with interest.* TERESONA *enters
through the gateway from the yard.
Once caretaker of the shops, she is now*
LEONARDO'S *servant. She comes from
the market-place carrying a huge basket
on her arm, full of the day's provisions.
She stops to address* SALVADOR *before
entering the house.*]

TERESONA. Good morning, Señor, and
welcome.

SALVADOR. Hello, Teresona.

TERESONA. I was sleeping like a top but
I knew when you arrived last night, and
that you came to see the master.

SALVADOR. Yes.... I asked for you when
I arrived.

TERESONA. Don Leonardo's sister also
came yesterday, but in the morning.

SALVADOR. I saw her last night.

TERESONA. How pretty she is, and what
a sweet face she has! But how was your
father?

SALVADOR. As well and strong as ever.

TERESONA. May God keep him many
years for you. I suppose you heard all the
news of what happened during the month
you were away?

SALVADOR. I'm finding out little by
little.

TERESONA. Don Salvador, there are
times when the best of us get into a little
difficulty, but whoever gets mixed up in
a fight is lost. I look on and keep still.
It's the old women in the village who do the
gossiping, and they can do it, too. [*She
shows him some coral earrings which she
wears.*] Look, Señor, he gave me these,
so I keep mum. Is there anything you
wish?

SALVADOR. No, you may go now.

TERESONA. Good-bye, Señor.

[*Exit into the house.*]

SALVADOR. Bah! I knew it must happen to him.

[*He continues to examine papers and books.
From this occupation he is distracted*

by the unlooked-for appearance of TIO
JEROMO *who enters through the gateway. He is* MALVALOCA'S *uncle, but
one would not suspect it from his
looks. He is about fifty years of age.
He wears his cap wherever he goes, and
carries a small basket containing his
lunch. He walks toward the shops.*]

TIO JEROMO [*pleasantly surprised at seeing* SALVADOR]. Salvador! Is it you?
Back already?

SALVADOR [*very much astonished*]. Eh?

TIO JEROMO. I never would have known
you in that blouse. Did you have a good
trip?

SALVADOR. But I can't believe my eyes!
You here? How does that happen?

TIO JEROMO. Oh! Hasn't your partner
told you anything about it? Why, I've
been working in the foundry for a week
now.

SALVADOR. You?

TIO JEROMO. Me! I heard of my niece's
affair with your partner and took advantage of it. You know how Malvaloca has
always provided for the family.

SALVADOR. Well, yes!

TIO JEROMO. Does it look good to you,
Salvador?

SALVADOR. Yes, very good!

TIO JEROMO. Now that you are here,
just see if I don't know a thing or two!

SALVADOR. Possibly.

TIO JEROMO [*patting him familiarly on
the back*]. You're a smart one!

SALVADOR. What do you mean by this
familiarity? When were you and I ever on
such intimate terms?

TIO JEROMO [*disconcerted. Half in jest,
and half seriously*]. Excuse me, Don
Salvador.

SALVADOR. That's better. But keep
your hat in your hand — so.

TIO JEROMO. I thought we would be as
we used to ——

SALVADOR. That is all a thing of the past.
Get to work now. What are you working
on?

TIO JEROMO. Anything that turns up.
Odd jobs.

SALVADOR. Very likely. And have

you permission to get here later than the others?

TIO JEROMO. I have my niece to take care of. What more do you want? I had an awful night last night, Salvador. God keep you from anything like it, God keep you! Excuse me, I didn't mean to be so familiar. It was just habit. I have a poor liver.

SALVADOR. Well, you can cure it... in there!

TIO JEROMO. Here I go. I'm glad to see you looking so well, Don Salvador.

SALVADOR. Thanks.

TIO JEROMO. Excuse me if I have done wrong.

SALVADOR. That's all right.

TIO JEROMO. If there's any one I want to please here, it's you, Don Salvador.

SALVADOR. In with you, man!

TIO JEROMO [much moved]. Don Salvador, please don't act like that toward me.

SALVADOR. In with you! In with you! You're more afraid of work than you are of an earthquake! All this talk is merely to keep yourself from doing anything.

TIO JEROMO [changing his tone and laughing]. You make me laugh with your goings on. Good-bye.

[Exit, laughing, into the shops. Deep down in his heart, however, there is a doubt as to the security of his position.]

SALVADOR. Well, I never thought things would advance so rapidly. Now that we have the lobster we'll have to clip his claws. We shall see, we shall see. [Crosses to the door of the shops and calls.] Lobito! Lobito!

[LOBITO enters after a little. He is a very young workman, wideawake and talkative. He is in his shirtsleeves, wears a cap, very old trousers, and "alpargatas" (canvas shoes with rope soles). A coarse and dirty apron is tied by a cord at his waist. In his hand he carries a large file.]

LOBITO. Did you call, Señor?

SALVADOR. Come here. Drop your file, and let's smoke a cigarette.

LOBITO. Thank you very much, Señor. I haven't felt the warmth of one in my hand for some time. You got back last night, didn't you?

SALVADOR. Yes. Last night.

LOBITO. And we recast La Golondrina to-day!

SALVADOR. To-day. I've already seen the material in the crucibles, and Don Leonardo has told me that the mould is in splendid condition.

LOBITO. Yes, Señor. It was made very carefully. We've even come to blows in the shops about La Golondrina. There are two parties of us....

SALVADOR. To which do you belong?

LOBITO. I stand up for La Golondrina. I'm what they call a "Volandero." But Manuel Martínez and Bartolo and the hunch-back, with three or four others, are "Swells." They are for the bell of the Iglesia Mayor.

SALVADOR. Do you know what party the new workman belongs to, and where he comes from?

LOBITO. Him? Why the Utrera prison has the honor!

SALVADOR. The prison?

LOBITO. You forced me to tell you.

SALVADOR. Does he work hard?

LOBITO. Work? He? Why, he's too good to carry a basket across the shop! The apprentices call him Don Jeromo.

SALVADOR [laughing]. Then he must have come strongly recommended.

LOBITO. Are you joking? From the way he spoke of you when you were away, I thought it was you who did the recommending.

SALVADOR. So the shameless fellow speaks well of me?

LOBITO. He never stops! Never mentions your name without praising you to the skies.

SALVADOR. Well, well! How badly Don Jeromo is going to be repaid!

LOBITO. Don't get mixed up in this thing, Señor.

SALVADOR. Why not?

LOBITO. Why not? Why, because he is her uncle, and came here through her, and that is all that need be said.

SALVADOR. Through her? And who is her?

LOBITO. That's a good one! This is a day for jokes.

SALVADOR. Is it Malvaloca?

LOBITO. Of course! Don't be foolish, Señor.

SALVADOR. No wonder, but I didn't know a thing about it. Tell me — has this woman remained in Las Canteras?

LOBITO. In Las Canteras and in Don Leonardo's mind! She surely never is out of that. She lives in one of Sra. Resolana's new houses. So far so good; when Don Leonardo is not there with her, she is here with him. They can't leave each other.

SALVADOR. Does Malvaloca come here?

LOBITO. She comes nearly every day. She came into the shops from the very first. How we used to laugh at her. She would keep you amused for a week. But it's pretty well known that they told her that she diverted us from work, for now she doesn't come in much. It's too bad, for aside from her good looks, she's more generous than most people I have seen.

SALVADOR. She has a hole in her hand. I know her.

LOBITO. A hole? It's a regular sieve!

SALVADOR. So Leonardo is ——

LOBITO. He's gone! When he comes from over there, it's no use asking him anything. He won't pay any attention to you. He only talks and laughs to himself as if he were still with her. And when he is waiting for her here, and she happens to be a little late — it's well to get out of his way. Leonardo may be a gentleman and well educated but he can be rougher and harsher than a wire brush.

SALVADOR. He's going wrong, Lobito; things are going wrong with him.

LOBITO [insinuatingly]. She's worth it, isn't she, Señor?

SALVADOR. Yes, yes. But one has to know how to manage her. And my friend takes this life too much to heart.

LOBITO. Pichichi, the office boy, told me that the woman is a book that you know by heart.

SALVADOR. Well, you tell Pichichi from me to close his little mouth!

LOBITO. Here comes Don Leonardo.

SALVADOR. I see where I shall have to heap coals of fire on his head.

[*Enter* LEONARDO *through the gateway which opens on the yard. He comes from the street.*]

LEONARDO. Hello, traveler!

SALVADOR. Hello!

LEONARDO. Did you have a good sleep?

SALVADOR. Yes, and even better than that.

LOBITO. Do you wish anything more, Señor?

SALVADOR. No, you may go on with your work.

LOBITO. I'm going to see about the wheel. [*Exit into the shop.*]

SALVADOR. Where is your sister?

LEONARDO [*pointing to the house*]. She is here. I left early this morning without seeing her. I often get up early these days.

SALVADOR. You do, eh?

LEONARDO. Yes, I like to see the sun rise from behind the castle. Have you never seen it?

SALVADOR [*mischievously*]. The sun rise from behind the castle? Yes, indeed, sir, before you ever did.

LEONARDO. What?

[*Enter a workman from the shops.*]

WORKMAN. Don Salvador, the modeller wishes to ask you a question.

SALVADOR. I'll be there in a minute.

LEONARDO. What is it he wants?

SALVADOR. Nothing much. I told him to give a little more spirit to the model of that grating.

LEONARDO. Oh!

[*Exit the workman into the yard. He reappears in a moment and goes into the shops carrying a cross bar.* JUANELA *enters from the house;* SALVADOR *stops a moment to greet her. She justifies the reflection which* TERESONA *has already made.*]

SALVADOR. Good morning.

JUANELA. Good morning. Hello, Leonardo! I saw you from my balcony as you came in.

LEONARDO. Ah, you did?

JUANELA. You surely are an early riser. How early you go out!

SALVADOR [artfully]. Night comes on so quickly in these small places! Eh, Leonardo?

LEONARDO [startled]. Yes... of course.

SALVADOR. I'll see you later.

JUANELA. Good-bye.

SALVADOR. If this chap speaks ill of me, don't believe him. [Exit into the shop.]

JUANELA. Rest assured! Your friend seems to be a great joker. [LEONARDO is very much preoccupied. JUANELA watches him for some moments in silence.] What are you thinking about?

LEONARDO. Eh?

JUANELA. What are you thinking about? Are you here, or somewhere else?

LEONARDO. I am here, only I was a bit absent-minded. What do you want?

JUANELA. Nothing. Only try to realize you are here, and that I am, too!

LEONARDO. Very well, I'll try.

JUANELA. I'm going out now to take a walk about the town with Teresona. May I?

LEONARDO. Yes. With Teresona, yes. Teresona is a fine woman. She was the caretaker of this house before we took it, and I have kept her in my service.

JUANELA. She seems to think a lot of you.

LEONARDO. Yes.

JUANELA. What is the matter with you, Leonardo? Something is wrong. I noticed it last night.

LEONARDO. No, there isn't, silly! What could be the matter? The trouble is you have forgotten my ways because you haven't lived with me for a long time. Run along and take your walk with Teresona. You will like the place, I'm sure.

JUANELA. I loved the part I saw yesterday. How bright it is! And the houses are so white that they hurt one's eyes when the sun strikes them. Do you remember how we used to dream of this Andalusian country away off there on our farm? I used to think of it as a land that I should never see — a story land.

LEONARDO [absently]. And here you are in it

JUANELA. I am, yes. But I insist that you are at least in Asturias!

LEONARDO. No, little one, no.

JUANELA. Come! I'm not so simple as all that. Is what they tell me about you true?

LEONARDO [quickly]. What did they tell you?

JUANELA. It's true!

LEONARDO. What is?

JUANELA. That you have a sweetheart!

LEONARDO. A sweetheart? Who told you that?

JUANELA. A neighbor who saw me waiting for you yesterday on the balcony; she started a conversation with me. The people in this place are very confidential. Whatever comes into their heads pops out again. They think aloud. Don't you agree with me?

LEONARDO. There is something in what you say. It all comes from an exaggerated gift of imagination. They are often mistaken in what they say here.

JUANELA. And are they mistaken this time?

LEONARDO [after gazing at her]. Would you feel badly if they were not?

JUANELA. On the contrary, I want you to marry, so you will stop roaming about the world, and so I can come to live with you.

LEONARDO. Aren't you happy with Aunt and Uncle?

JUANELA. Yes. They take very good care of me. But that is different. It isn't my own home, as yours would be — as father's used to be.

LEONARDO [with a sigh]. I know. Last night you told me that you went to see him before coming here.

JUANELA. I did. Instead of cheering me up, the visit saddened me. He isn't happy.

LEONARDO. He couldn't be.

JUANELA. What a shame that it should always be a woman who destroys the home! [The two are silent.]

[Enter TERESONA, wearing a different shawl.]

TERESONA. Shall we go, child?

JUANELA. Ah, Teresona! Yes, let's go.

TERESONA. Very well, come along; I can't leave the kitchen for long.

JUANELA. Come on.

TERESONA. I'm going to take you to the Iglesia Mayor first. Then to the mill so you can see the fields from the tower.

LEONARDO. Good.

JUANELA. I'll see you afterward, brother.

LEONARDO. Good-bye.

TERESONA [*mischievously to* LEONARDO *as* JUANELA *enters the house. She refers to her shawl*]. It is yours. Do you recognize it?

LEONARDO. Hush!

TERESONA. Don't be afraid. I never let my tongue get me into trouble. Good-bye.

[*Exit after* JUANELA.]

LEONARDO [*reproaching himself bitterly*]. Bah! Always a coward. What is it? What is the matter with me? I hardly recognize myself.

[SALVADOR *enters from the shops in time to see and hear him.*]

SALVADOR. It seems to me that it is a little soon to begin talking to yourself.

LEONARDO. What?

SALVADOR. It is only a step from that to throwing stones about the streets in a pet.

LEONARDO. You are always in such good humor!

SALVADOR. And aren't you? Aren't you good-humored to-day?

LEONARDO. I scarcely ever am. You know that. And not at all to-day, especially since a moment ago.

SALVADOR. Well, then, what is the matter?

LEONARDO. Oh, something.

SALVADOR. Something to do with her. Am I right?

LEONARDO. Eh?

SALVADOR. Love is apt to be nonsensical like that; at best it will come on to rain when the sun is shining. But the shower soon passes away.

LEONARDO. What do you imagine my trouble is?

SALVADOR. It's not a case of imagination. I know that the little beast which you think you have inside of you is being tamed to the music of a skirt which is none too worthy.

LEONARDO. What a queer way you have of putting things! Where did you learn all this?

SALVADOR. From you yourself

LEONARDO. From me?

SALVADOR. From you.

LEONARDO. Since when?

SALVADOR. Since the day when Malvaloca came to Las Canteras. In your first conversation with her you fell like a raw recruit. Come, deny it.

LEONARDO. If you call it falling.

SALVADOR. You see? I only had to hear you first, and then, afterward, to see you with her. After that you didn't come to the Home to see me, but to meet Malvaloca. And since I know you, and also know her, I had a feeling inside that you wouldn't last as long as tin does in fire.

LEONARDO. That's the way it was. I confess it to you, you are a loyal friend. I have never seen a woman who has captivated and interested me so much.

SALVADOR. Yes, yes. She carries with her a bloom of conviviality.

LEONARDO. Conviviality isn't adequate to describe the attraction she exercises. She hasn't a word or a movement that doesn't get one deeper in love. She fascinates me. I don't know whether or not it is the contrast between her position and mine, but she fascinates me.

SALVADOR. She has wit.

LEONARDO. Something more than wit. There is light in her lips, in her face, in her hands, in her hair ——

SALVADOR. That —— may be brilliantine.

LEONARDO. Can it be that you make a joke of it?

SALVADOR. Don't you see I can?

LEONARDO. Is what I am saying so ridiculous?

SALVADOR. Nonsense! My joke was merely caused by envy at seeing you so much in love. I'd like to fall in love like that, only I never get the chance, or hardly ever.

LEONARDO. Never. But no matter. Perhaps you live more peacefully for it. More happily, I won't say. Malvaloca has come into my heart and awakened feelings that were dormant or new there. Would you believe that even to suffer when I am with her is a great joy to me? I suffer and weep, just as I laugh and enjoy myself. I live — live — and to live for a woman is something.

SALVADOR [*somewhat gravely*]. But, man —

LEONARDO. I swear to you by our friendship, that Malvaloca not only fascinates me by the witchery of her person, the passion of her eyes, the grace of her carriage, her words —

SALVADOR. What else?

LEONARDO. All of them put together; more than all, if such a thing is possible. It is the innate goodness of her heart; her mad generosity; the deep sadness of her misfortune of which her tears tell me more than her words, the unlooked-for tears which come into her eyes even in her happiest moments — all this seduces me, moves me, and makes me tremble. Do you understand?

SALVADOR. Yes, of course I understand. I also understand that these things hold you fast.

LEONARDO. What do you say?

SALVADOR. But it will pass over. This fire will soon die out.

LEONARDO [*as though asking himself*]. Will it pass over?

SALVADOR. Of course it will! You're fascinated now, I know. I know, too, about the affair in La Resolana's house, the number of times you go there, how enchanted you are to see the sun rise from behind the castle —

LEONARDO [*laughing*]. What a rascal you are!

SALVADOR. How she visits the foundry —

LEONARDO. No!

SALVADOR. Yes!

LEONARDO. She has been here only a few times. I swear it.

SALVADOR. No, sir! She comes every day. A few times, indeed!

LEONARDO. I always have to laugh when I am with you. She's due here for a little visit soon!

SALVADOR. What? She's coming here soon?

LEONARDO. Yes. She hasn't been here to-day.

SALVADOR. Is she coming soon, Leonardo?

LEONARDO. Well, why are you surprised?

SALVADOR. You're crazier than I thought you were!

LEONARDO. Eh?

SALVADOR. What about your sister?

LEONARDO [*disturbed*]. My sister — that's right — you think it is wrong while my sister is here —

SALVADOR. Of course.

LEONARDO. Well, I'm not so crazy as you think. The very same idea occurred to me before it did to you. I went to tell her not to come yesterday, but it wasn't necessary, for she anticipated me by saying that she wasn't going out.

SALVADOR. And to-day?

LEONARDO. I went the same as yesterday.

SALVADOR. And didn't you tell her to-day, either?

LEONARDO. No.

SALVADOR. Why not?

LEONARDO. Because — well, because it is a thing that is repugnant to my feelings, and I couldn't say it.

SALVADOR. You do wrong, Leonardo.

LEONARDO. Well, then, I shall do wrong, but I shall comply with the dictates of my conscience. I cannot tell a good woman — one who wishes to be honorable — to stop coming to my house. That is like attempting to prevent her from being good.

SALVADOR. But, let's see. Don't get excited. Does Malvaloca know that your sister is here?

LEONARDO. I think not.

SALVADOR. Well, without your attempting to prevent her, as soon as she finds your sister is here, she won't come.

LEONARDO. She won't?

SALVADOR. She knows her ground, and has more common sense than you have.

LEONARDO. She must understand resignation then.

SALVADOR. Put it any way you wish

You are not the only one responsible for Malvaloca's life.

LEONARDO. What egotism is this, Salvador?

SALVADOR. The egotism of living on earth and not on the moon!

LEONARDO. The egotism of —— But it is best not to talk about this particular thing. We could talk until we were tired and you would probably never learn to understand me. There are some things which never enter the intelligence without first passing through the heart.

SALVADOR. As you like. What shall we talk about? I know very well that when a man is in your heated condition, he will only pay attention to himself.

[*Enter* TIO JEROMO *from the shops. He goes toward the yard gate. He still wears his working clothes, after the fashion of* LOBITO, *and carries a small mallet hung from his belt, a saw in his left hand, and a chisel in his right. He greets* LEONARDO *as he passes.*]

TIO JEROMO. Good morning, Don Leonardo.

LEONARDO. Good morning, Jeromo.

TIO JEROMO. Congratulations on Don Salvador's return.

LEONARDO. Thanks.

TIO JEROMO. We're working hard.
[*Exit.*]

SALVADOR. We can at least talk about this invaluable workman here. Why didn't you write me something about this acquisition?

LEONARDO. I beg your pardon. It was forgetfulness or carelessness. It wasn't important, and I didn't think it was necessary.

SALVADOR. And it wasn't. The necessary and important thing to do, is to turn him into the street.

LEONARDO. Malvaloca's uncle?

SALVADOR. Correct — Don Jeromo.

LEONARDO. He has attended to his duty so far.

SALVADOR. He? Why, he's never done a stroke of work in his life! Moreover, he is a consummate rascal with bad blood in his veins. He's a danger to the business.

I've already noticed a pack of cards in the shops, and the wine bottle won't be long in coming.

LEONARDO. Do you think he brought the cards?

SALVADOR. I'm sure of it. He's taken good money from four unfortunates already. What is more, the tools and shovels which are missing were carried off by him.

LEONARDO. Oh, no, that can't be true! We must try to reform him.

SALVADOR. What we ought to do is to pay him with a good kick and throw him into the street. For if you are kind to him and let him stay, besides the trouble he is giving, you are going to have the whole tribe, his family and their friends to bother you. Malvaloca's small brother, her mother, her father, her godfather and her godmother, her aunt and her uncle — oh, I know them!

LEONARDO. This must be stopped.

SALVADOR. I'm afraid it won't be.

LEONARDO. Yes, it shall. After all, he is only a workman who may cause trouble, and whom we can discharge this very day. Or do you think I am so weak that for a satisfaction foreign to our interests I could overlook something that may be a disadvantage to us and demoralizing to our business? Well, if you do, you are mistaken. We'll discharge the man to-day.

SALVADOR. That's not quite necessary.

LEONARDO. Indeed it is, Salvador. [*He sees* TIO JEROMO *approaching. He comes from the yard; the tools in the same position as before.*] To-day is too late. We'll do it this very minute.

SALVADOR. You are certainly in a hurry about it!

LEONARDO. I'm always in a hurry to do my duty. Listen, Jeromo. We were just talking about you.

TIO JEROMO. About me?

LEONARDO. Yes.

TIO JEROMO. Good or bad?

SALVADOR. Don Leonardo spoke well of you, but I very much to the contrary.

TIO JEROMO. Oh, ho! [LEONARDO *goes to his table and turns over the leaves of the day book.* TIO JEROMO *scents trouble, and starts*

to flatter in order to disarm his enemy.]
Good! I'm like the boys in the shops who belong to this parish: I'm thinking about the casting of La Golondrina. What an event, Don Salvador, what an event to write about in the History of Spain!

LEONARDO. You are right.

TIO JEROMO. What is he talking about?

SALVADOR. He's forecasting another event which is about to take place this minute.

LEONARDO. From this moment you may consider yourself discharged from the foundry.

[TIO JEROMO'S *gesture of stupefaction at hearing* LEONARDO *say these words is indescribable. He looks silently from one to the other, and at last breaks out in these words.*]

TIO JEROMO. Do you know I have no words ——

LEONARDO. You don't need any. I have said all that is necessary.

TIO JEROMO. I couldn't be deader if a thunderbolt had struck at my feet! Somebody has been lying about me. [*Arrogantly.*] What lies have they made up?

LEONARDO. All explanation is superfluous.

TIO JEROMO. Don Leonardo, it would be so with a cricket, and yet you listen to him — and he costs only ten cents.

SALVADOR. And you're not worth even ten cents!

LEONARDO. You may go.

TIO JEROMO. That's it. Kick an honest workman into the street like a dog! Then they talk about strikes.

SALVADOR. You struck the day you were born.

TIO JEROMO [*pathetically*]. Salvador, Salvador, I didn't expect this from you.

LEONARDO. What do you mean?

TIO JEROMO. See if she isn't sorry.

LEONARDO [*troubled*]. Eh?

TIO JEROMO. Don Leonardo, at least for her sake, for she loves me more than she does her own father!

LEONARDO. Silence! It's useless to persist.

SALVADOR. Do we owe him anything?

LEONARDO. On the contrary. Two days ago I anticipated five days' pay for him. But we are even now.

TIO JEROMO. No, we're not. I certainly thank you very much. [*Behind his hand.*] Curse that woman! [*To* SALVADOR *in a burst of anger.*] You've seen the time when this wouldn't have happened!

SALVADOR. You'd better keep quiet.

TIO JEROMO. You loved her more than he does.

LEONARDO [*violently grasping a hammer which lies on his desk*]. Get out of my sight this minute, or I'll knock your head in!

TIO JEROMO. Very well, sir, very well. I'm on my way.

[*Starts to drop the tools ill-humoredly in a corner.*]

LEONARDO. Was that what you wanted done?

SALVADOR. You can see for yourself.

LEONARDO. Well, it's done.

[*Exit into his house.*]

TIO JEROMO. There, from what I've heard, it was you who got this man to leave me breadless.

SALVADOR. Leave the place!

TIO JEROMO. Well, hunger is an evil master.

SALVADOR. Leave, I tell you!

TIO JEROMO. You'll hear from me again — you and that *panoli*! And Malvaloca! That little girl won't be long in hearing about it.

SALVADOR. Into the street with you!

TIO JEROMO. I still have a mallet in my hand.

SALVADOR. You've got to have more than that. You've got to have the courage to use it. What an empty boast!

[TIO JEROMO *throws the mallet angrily to the ground. He gnaws his fist and goes angrily into the shops.*]

TIO JEROMO. Damn that girl!

SALVADOR. At last we're rid of him. The scene was inevitable. [*Calling:*] Lobito! Lobito! Sooner or later it was bound to come. [*To* LOBITO, *who appears at the shop door.*] Listen, Lobito don't take your eye off Tío Jeromo until he leaves.

LOBITO. I understand, Señor.

SALVADOR. He's capable of any nonsense.

LOBITO. We've had a good laugh in there. We heard the whole fight.

SALVADOR. Come, come! Go in and watch him.

LOBITO. Never you fear, Señor. [*Exit.*]

SALVADOR [*going to the house*]. We'll calm the partner a bit.

[*At this instant* MALVALOCA *appears at the yard gate. She wears a shawl, dressing simply, very modest earrings being her only jewelry.*]

MALVALOCA. Who goes there?

SALVADOR. Eh? Malvaloca!

MALVALOCA. Hello, my man! You here? When did you come?

SALVADOR. Last night.

MALVALOCA. After you left home, you went to Malaga to see your lady friends, didn't you?

SALVADOR. Right you are.

MALVALOCA. Did you bring me any raisins?

SALVADOR. To refresh your memory?

MALVALOCA. To put in brandy!

SALVADOR. I didn't know that you were here.

MALVALOCA. Caramba!

SALVADOR. I thought you were in Seville.

MALVALOCA. And I thought you were in Rome, kissing the Pope's slipper!

SALVADOR. Well, I left Las Canteras, and have returned.

MALVALOCA. Well, I haven't returned, nor have I gone, nor am I going.

SALVADOR. You like the village so much, then?

MALVALOCA. I've settled down.

SALVADOR. With a view of the fields or of the river?

MALVALOCA. With a view of the clock in the Town Hall.

SALVADOR. Times have changed, little girl.

MALVALOCA. Always for the better. Where's our friend? Has he hidden himself?

SALVADOR. You'll find him upstairs working at figures for you.

MALVALOCA. And he is in earnest. I do the same for him.

SALVADOR. Leave your figures.

MALVALOCA. I'll leave nothing. I'd rather leave the sunlight.

SALVADOR. We're as far along as that, are we?

MALVALOCA. Uh! You don't know anything about it. We are a pair of lovers such as you see in pictures.

SALVADOR. Like those in Teruel?

MALVALOCA. It's deadly cold in Teruel.

SALVADOR. Is the fever so high, then?

MALVALOCA. Ninety-eight and a fraction. Where did you say he was?

SALVADOR. He is probably with his sister.

MALVALOCA [*surprised*]. Has his sister come?

SALVADOR. She came yesterday.

MALVALOCA. Then I'm off. Don't you think that I ought to go?

SALVADOR. I do indeed.

MALVALOCA. So do I. Whatever you call it, a spade is a spade. Why didn't Leonardo tell me?

SALVADOR. Because Leonardo thought it better not.

MALVALOCA. Don't joke. He is more romantic than you are, more romantic Uh! He sees and then embroiders everything he sees with stars.

SALVADOR. Romantic things seem to agree with you. You are much prettier than you were, and you have a beautiful color.

MALVALOCA. The quiet life I lead, my son; it works wonders.

SALVADOR. Those earrings aren't like the ones you wore in my time.

MALVALOCA. Nor in anybody else's time. They were an idea of his. He's even got me to let him give me my hairpins. Even that! And I have had to say good-bye to all my jewelry for a while.

SALVADOR. How about my watch?

MALVALOCA. He's given the hands a bad cramp. Why, if I even mention your name he turns green! You cause him more trouble than any one else.

SALVADOR [*with a gesture and accent of disgust*]. Enough!

MALVALOCA. He's mad about me.

SALVADOR. So I see.

MALVALOCA. As no one in the world ever was before.

SALVADOR. You don't mean me?

MALVALOCA. Be sensible! Can you compare raw canvas to silk? He loves me more than anybody else does, and in a different way.

SALVADOR. Differently than I did?

MALVALOCA. Yes, differently than you.

SALVADOR. And what is the difference?

MALVALOCA. Why, even in the way he takes my hand! The way he breathes when he sees me! He treats me as if I were somebody — not just a mere woman. Let's see if I can explain what I mean. Supposing you had been the first man who had made love to me when I was a girl — good as you are — I would have been what I am to-day. But if *he* had been the first, I should have been different altogether. Then I shouldn't have had to run away because his sister was here. Do you understand?

SALVADOR. Yes.

MALVALOCA. And do I exaggerate?

SALVADOR. No.

MALVALOCA. Don't be hurt, Salvador. I have very much to be thankful to you for, but that has nothing to do with this new kind of love which Malvaloca had never a taste of till now. You are good because you aren't bad. He is good because he is good. To make it clear to you: you are good in the morning, and he is good all day. That is something like what I mean.

SALVADOR. He *is* good.

MALVALOCA. Better than a stage priest. You know that when I dream I always see him with white hair and a staff, marrying everybody!

SALVADOR. Ha! Ha!

MALVALOCA. And so I am going away without seeing him, since I don't want his sister to find me here.

SALVADOR. Shall I tell him you came around?

MALVALOCA. Yes, tell him. No, don't tell him!

SALVADOR. Just as you say.

MALVALOCA. Yes, you can tell him. Why must we be so secret about it? Good-bye.

SALVADOR. Wait a minute, and we'll have a good laugh.

MALVALOCA. Over what?

SALVADOR. Don Jeromo. We've had to put him into the street.

MALVALOCA. That's natural. I'm glad of it; don't you think I'm not. They've told me of two or three of his doings in the shops, and I've been sorry that I ever asked Leonardo to take him on. Dear me, what a family ours is!

[TIO JEROMO *enters from the shops. He starts toward the inhospitable street, peevish and morose. He is dressed as he was when we first saw him.*]

TIC JEROMO. Into the street — to die if I must on some doorstep — but with my head in the clouds!

SALVADOR. God be with you!

MALVALOCA. Good luck!

[TIO JEROMO *looks at them disdainfully, and goes out through the gate.* MALVALOCA *and* SALVADOR *laugh outright.*]

SALVADOR. What a rascal!

MALVALOCA. What pleases me is the way he went off!

[*They keep on laughing.* LEONARDO *as he reënters, surprises them at it. His manner leaves no doubt that he is displeased.*]

LEONARDO. Hello!

MALVALOCA. We were just laughing at Tío Jeromo, who went out into the street with a face like a villain.

LEONARDO [*apologetically*]. There was no other way but to discharge him.

MALVALOCA. And I'm the first one to be glad of it. But look out; he's got a vengeful disposition. He is very bad, and is capable of thinking up anything.

LEONARDO. I don't know what he can "think up."

MALVALOCA. Now don't you go and knock his brains out on the strength of what I'm saying. I only wanted to warn you. *Isn't* he revengeful, Salvador?

SALVADOR. Yes, but who pays any

tention to him? I must go in to see if we are ready to cast soon.

[*Exit into the shops.*]

MALVALOCA. What's the matter with you, Leonardo?

LEONARDO. Nothing.

MALVALOCA. Don't say "nothing" that way. Why, the circles under your eyes reach down to your neck! I have been studying you like astronomers study the clouds. When dogs eat grass, it's a sign of rain. I come; and as you don't greet me with a smile, I know we're going to have a storm.

LEONARDO. No.

MALVALOČA. Yes. Are you angry because I was laughing with Salvador? It was all about Tío Jeromo.

LEONARDO. Don't be a child. How could a thing like that make me angry? You will soon find out what the trouble is. I have some bad news for you.

MALVALOCA. Aha! The dogs are eating grass! Signs don't lie. Are you laughing?

LEONARDO. Yes. Listen.

MALVALOCA. Well, out with it; you frighten me.

LEONARDO. My sister is here.

MALVALOCA. I know it. He told me.

LEONARDO. Ah! So *he* told you?

MALVALOCA. Yes. Is that all? Well, don't get excited or feel badly about it, for I won't put my foot inside your house while your sister is here.

LEONARDO. Why not?

MALVALOCA. Because I should sprain my ankle going through the door! But joking aside, Leonardo, it wouldn't be right for me to come.

LEONARDO. Did — he — also — tell you that?

MALVALOCA. No, I told *him*. What Salvador said was that you thought it was all right for me to come.

LEONARDO. Ah, really? That was true, understand. But later I thought better of . I must not act foolishly. I am very grateful to you for your resolve, Malvaloca. Do not come; I shall go to you.

MALVALOCA. Well, your martyrdom is over. Put on a happier expression. I ate to see you look sad.

LEONARDO. Why shouldn't I look sad? Loving you as I do, I have to keep you hidden like a — shameless woman.

MALVALOCA. Come, come!

The birds take flight when the rain comes down;
Periquiyo's wet from heel to crown.

I'm Periquiyo. But it's unhealthy to look beneath the surface, to remove the soil.

LEONARDO [*sadly*]. It depends upon the soil!

MALVALOCA [*bitterly*]. That's why I said it. If you only knew what kind of soil I am, in what kind of earth you have sown!

LEONARDO. Forgive me. I'd like to choke down that thought when I am with you, but when I am at your side I seem to lose all my power of will.

[*They look at each other.*]

MALVALOCA [*resolutely*]. Good-bye, I'm going.

LEONARDO. Why?

MALVALOCA. Your sister may come.

LEONARDO. Don't be afraid; she isn't here. Teresona took her to see some of the sights of the village.

MALVALOCA. Then ——

LEONARDO. What?

MALVALOCA. Are you going to cast La Golondrina?

LEONARDO. In a little while, yes.

MALVALOCA. Would there be time for me to see it?

LEONARDO. For you to see it? I'll tell you ——

MALVALOCA. No, don't tell me anything. Even if there were time, I shouldn't wait to see it. You don't like to have me go into the shops.

LEONARDO. Aside from that, the bell will be cast like all the rest — like all those other things you have seen us cast. The mould is already in the ground ——

MALVALOCA. And it's just the same shape as the broken bell. I've seen that at least.

LEONARDO. You would have been more interested in seeing how we broke up the old bell.

MALVALOCA. True enough. Why didn't you let me know?

LEONARDO. I didn't think of it.

MALVALOCA. Well, then, tell me how it was done.

LEONARDO. Simply by heating it slowly over a furnace, and by a blow of a mallet.

MALVALOCA. And it fell to pieces?

LEONARDO. Yes.

MALVALOCA. As if it were made of glass!

LEONARDO. Exactly.

MALVALOCA. And now the pieces are being melted in the crucibles?

LEONARDO. Yes.

MALVALOCA. And pretty soon the crucibles will be emptied into the ground through the funnel?

LEONARDO. Right you are. You know as much as I do about it.

MALVALOCA. So, it will be the same bell?

LEONARDO. The same, and yet another.

MALVALOCA. I remember you explained all this very well the first day we met. I was very much interested in what you told me.

LEONARDO. You have a good memory.

MALVALOCA. Yours is better, poor boy!

LEONARDO. Mine? Why?

MALVALOCA. Oh, nothing!

LEONARDO. No, you meant something when you said that.

MALVALOCA. Why shouldn't I, silly? Because I never tell you a thing about myself that doesn't stay in your head as though it were cast in bronze!

LEONARDO. Ah! That's true.

MALVALOCA. But come here, you bad boy. Are you sorry you met me?

LEONARDO. Never!

MALVALOCA. Do you — love me?

LEONARDO. How can you ask?

MALVALOCA. Well, then, what does it matter what I have been?

LEONARDO. It matters, it matters so much to me that I am only happy when I forget it.

MALVALOCA. Well, listen; I've thought of a solution.

LEONARDO. If there only were one!

MALVALOCA. Recast me — like La Golondrina!

LEONARDO [perplexed]. Like — La Golondrina?

MALVALOCA. There is a little song that speaks of it:

"This little girl of whom I tell,
Should be recast, like a broken bell."

Have you heard it?

LEONARDO. Never until this moment.

MALVALOCA. You might know that it was thought of by a man like you are... one of those men who make up all the good there is in the world. In the song he fell in love with a woman who wanted to have the right to a better life; so he wrote these verses.

LEONARDO. How does it go?

MALVALOCA [repeats it with full meaning]

"This little girl of whom I tell,
Should be recast, like a broken bell."

LEONARDO [drawing her passionately to him]. Come!

MALVALOCA. What do you mean?

LEONARDO. Look at me.

MALVALOCA. I can't see you for my tears.

LEONARDO. Nor I you.

MALVALOCA. Let me go. [Separates herself from him.] I must go! Good-bye!

LEONARDO. Good-bye.

[When MALVALOCA starts to open the gate upstage as she turns to go, SISTER PIEDAD and MARIQUITA enter. MARIQUITA is dressed in her very best. Their appearance surprises the two lovers equally. MALVALOCA is pleased.

SISTER PIEDAD. Good morning.

MALVALOCA. Leonardo, see who has come to see you.

MARIQUITA. Good morning.

LEONARDO. Come in, Sister.

MARIQUITA. You here, lady?

MALVALOCA. Yes, but I'm going now.

MARIQUITA. Going? Don't go. You'll see why I have come. Don't go.

LEONARDO [replying to a glance from MALVALOCA]. Please stay.

SISTER PIEDAD. Mariquita has an idea which has cost her a sleepless night.

MARIQUITA. I didn't sleep all night because I thought of it when I went to bed and I was afraid I might forget it. [*With a tired air.*] Ah me!

MALVALOCA. Sit down here, Mariquita.

MARIQUITA. Thanks very much, my dear child.

LEONARDO. And won't you be seated also, Sister?

SISTER PIEDAD. Thank you, it is not necessary. My visit will be a very short one. La Golondrina is to be recast to-day, is she not?

LEONARDO. To-day, and very shortly.

SISTER PIEDAD. We shall go and pray that God may watch over the good work. Now I see that the wish of our Mother Superior will be easy to carry out.

LEONARDO. What is her wish?

SISTER PIEDAD. That the bell may sound again for the first time on the day of the procession of Our Lord of the Crown of Thorns, which starts from the Carmen Home, and is very much venerated in the vicinity. It is a holiday in Las Canteras. The windows, balconies, and doorways are all decorated, the street through which the Image passes is carpeted entirely with branches and flowers, and the young girls put on new dresses made especially for the day. Oh, you shall see, you shall see!

LEONARDO. And when is it?

SISTER PIEDAD. The fourteenth of next month.

LEONARDO. We have more than time enough.

SISTER PIEDAD. So much the better. The Mother Superior will be pleased.

MALVALOCA. Tell me, Sister, may I walk behind the procession barefoot?

SISTER PIEDAD. Why shouldn't you?

LEONARDO. Barefoot!

MALVALOCA. Yes, it's a vow.

LEONARDO. When did you make it?

MALVALOCA. Just now.

SISTER PIEDAD [*with a kindly smile*]. You can think about it from now until then.

MALVALOCA. You ask why I should do it? Are you surprised? It isn't the first time I have walked behind a procession in that way. When my baby girl was sick — but that doesn't concern anybody here. What is it that Mariquita has on her mind?

SISTER PIEDAD. She will tell you.

MARIQUITA [*gets up*]. I brought this. [*She takes a small bundle of cloth from her bosom and shows it to them.*]

LEONARDO. What is it?

MARIQUITA. The crosses and medals which belonged to my son who was killed in the wars.

LEONARDO. And why do you bring them here?

MARIQUITA. Well, you see the one wish that he had after they took him away was to listen to La Golondrina again with his mother — so I wanted them to be mixed with the metal of the bell. Can it be done?

LEONARDO. Indeed it can. All we have to do is to throw them into the crucible.

MALVALOCA. And that will be done this very minute, and by me!

MARIQUITA. By you?

MALVALOCA. Yes. Kiss them for the last time.

MARIQUITA [*after kissing the medals*]. Take them, my child, take them.

MALVALOCA. Bring them here, and come watch me do it! Did you hear, Leonardo? It takes a mother to have an idea like that.

LEONARDO. Yes. But hurry.

MARIQUITA. Then come, my child, come!

[*Thus encouraged,* MALVALOCA *enters the shops with* MARIQUITA, *gazing at the medals and crosses as one who holds in her hand a great treasure.*]

SISTER PIEDAD. This woman is certainly good. She is a good woman, a good woman.

LEONARDO. Do you think so? When an irremediable misfortune befalls such a person, one rebels against everything!

SISTER PIEDAD. Against everything, brother?

LEONARDO. Sister, one would have to be a saint to resign one's self to it. Since I am a man, I cannot do so.

SISTER PIEDAD. Penitence has its fruit; so have piety and forgiveness.

LEONARDO. Love is a selfish passion.

SISTER PIEDAD. When love is great, it is also a generous one.

[MALVALOCA *and* MARIQUITA *reënter.*]

MALVALOCA. It's done. They fell into the fire, and it swallowed them. It seemed as though it were waiting for them.

MARIQUITA. My poor little boy!

SISTER PIEDAD. You have had your wish, Mariquita.

MARIQUITA. Is your mother still alive, Malvaloca?

MALVALOCA. My mother? Let's not speak of her.

MARIQUITA. Why not? Doesn't she love you?

MALVALOCA. Let's not speak of that. Yes, my mother is alive. Mariquita, she is alive; very much so. But unfortunately she is not like you. I'd like to look at her through the wrong end of a telescope, as far away as I can get!

MARIQUITA. How funny you are!

MALVALOCA. You see how I am obliged to talk about my mother? Yet I've always felt sorry for Adam because he had none to take him into her arms! *My* fate is like that.

SISTER PIEDAD. Shall we go, Mariquita?

MARIQUITA. Very well. May God repay you for the pleasure you have given me.

MALVALOCA. When La Golondrina rings again, it will seem as if your son was calling you. See if it doesn't.

SISTER PIEDAD. God be with you, Don Leonardo.

LEONARDO. Good-bye, Sister. Good-bye, Mariquita.

MARIQUITA. Good-bye.

SISTER PIEDAD. Good-bye.

MALVALOCA. Good-bye, and God bless you.

[*She opens the gate for them to pass out. They both go out, smiling at her.*]

LEONARDO [*wildly — his pent-up feeling suddenly bursting forth into speech*]. Come to me, Malvaloca, come to me! I love you more and more every minute! Come, you're not going to leave me now — no, nor ever!

MALVALOCA. Hush, crazy boy!

LEONARDO. I love you for your goodness; I love you for your beauty, and I love

you because you are unhappy! Look into my eyes, that I may gaze into yours and be remade again... by the only woman I have ever loved!

MALVALOCA. Me?

LEONARDO. Yes, you! I have never told you, but it is time you found it out!

MALVALOCA. Leonardo!

LEONARDO. You are the only one I have ever loved, and you are the only one I shall ever love! I don't know how to go on living except by remembering that you are alive! Can — you — love me — like that?

MALVALOCA. I love you even more! No one has ever spoken to me like you have!

[*At this moment* JUANELA *appears in the doorway of the house. She is nervous and anxious. The lovers, feeling her presence rather than seeing it, instinctively separate.*]

LEONARDO. Eh?

MALVALOCA. What?

JUANELA. Ah, it is she!

LEONARDO. Juanela! Sister! Come here!

JUANELA. No! Excuse me — I didn't know ——

LEONARDO. Yes, you must have known. You said "It is she!" What did you mean by that?

[MALVALOCA *is abashed and overcome.* LEONARDO, *growing more excited with each word, tries to detain his sister and to win her respect and sympathy.*]

JUANELA. Nothing. No, let me go, please.

LEONARDO. No, I don't want you to go like this. Why do you tremble before this woman? What have they told you? Who has been telling you lies?

MALVALOCA. Tío Jeromo!

JUANELA. They have told me nothing.

LEONARDO. Yes, they have! And whatever they told you, they lied! I alone have the right to tell you who this woman is, and you must believe only me. What do the others know? All they will tell you is that she is bad, bad, bad! Ah, if it is wicked t be sad, there never was a more wicked woman in the world than she!

JUANELA. Control yourself, Leonardo.

LEONARDO. But I know her life, her soul, and her sorrows! She had no one to watch over her innocence as you had. But some one who was blind, profaned and betrayed it, I swear to you by our home! Forgive me, I am so excited I have lost control of my tongue. I am afraid of wounding you, too. Leave me, leave me. I shall speak to you more quietly later, but leave me now.

JUANELA. Yes, indeed I will leave you, brother. It is better — now. [Sobbing pitifully.] Oh, merciful God!

[She reënters the house without being able to take her eyes from him.]

LEONARDO [again becoming aware of MALVALOCA'S presence]. They must all forgive you, and respect you. That is the mad desire of my life now.... That all the world shall forget what you were!

[SALVADOR'S voice, calling from within the shops, reaches him and makes him shudder suddenly.]

SALVADOR. Leonardo!

LEONARDO. Ah, all the world — but me!

SALVADOR [appearing at a window]. Leonardo.

LEONARDO. What is it?

SALVADOR. We are ready. Shall we cast La Golondrina?

LEONARDO. Yes, of course. [To MALVALOCA.] Are you coming?

MALVALOCA. No. I'll see you later.

LEONARDO. Good-bye. [Goes into the shops with SALVADOR.] Now to recast La Golondrina!

MALVALOCA [very sorrowfully, as she bursts into tears]. If I were only made of bronze like the bell!

END OF ACT II

ACT III

A large downstairs room in LEONARDO'S house, having white walls and a blue vaulted ceiling. Upstage is a large door through which may be seen the shabby old courtyard. To the right of the actor is another door which leads to the inner rooms. To the left, a wide grated window which opens on the street. The sill is about three feet from the ground. Beneath it is a huge window-seat. The window frame is adorned with white lace curtains and colored cords in honor of the day upon which the action takes place. There are bunches of rosemary and lentiscus entwined in the iron grating of the window. Over the sill, and fastened by iron loops over the cross bars, are pots filled with flowers. The floor is made of tiles. There is little furniture. A pine table near the window awaits the flowers which are to be thrown when the procession passes.

It is late morning in the month of June.

JUANELA, TERESONA, and ALFONSA, dressed in gala attire, are putting the finishing touches on the decorations of the window. With them are DOÑA ENRIQUETA and DIONISIA, who have gone to the bottom of their trunks to deck themselves out. ALFONSA is a niece of TERESONA'S. She has the manners of a village maid, and has come from her home village to see the Festival of Las Canteras which is to be held on this day. She is one of the kind that wonders at and admires everything. DOÑA ENRIQUETA and DIONISIA, on the other hand, seem to wonder at and admire nothing. They are the wife and daughter of the owner of a well-known local sugar refinery and speak with an affectation of culture which, however, is rather a thin veneering.

ALFONSA [standing on a chair]. Does this bunch look well, Tía Teresona?

TERESONA. Very well. Get down now and stop decorating the window — we've done enough.

JUANELA. It really is beautiful!

ALFONSA [stepping some distance away from the window so as to see it better]. Oh, how pretty! How pretty it is! Don't you think so?

[DOÑA ENRIQUETA and DIONISIA smile at the naïve enthusiasm of ALFONSA.]

DIONISIA. What a child she is! She admires everything.

DOÑA ENRIQUETA. We do not care for these village festivals. They are too artificial.

TERESONA. Artificial? Why, I think they are very natural!

JUANELA. Don't you really like them?

DIONISIA. I do not.

DOÑA ENRIQUETA. Nor I.

DIONISIA. Nor does papa.

JUANELA. Perhaps it is because you are so accustomed to them year after year. Being a stranger, I must confess that I have never seen anything more picturesque — more lovely than the decorations in the streets where the procession is to pass.

DOÑA ENRIQUETA. Really? Why, what are you telling us?

JUANELA. What I feel, the pure truth.

ALFONSA. You ladies can't deny that there are some windows that look like regular altars, with so much white lace and so many pots of sweet basil! And then, what about the streets, that seem to be carpeted with green branches? And what a delicious smell comes through the windows! It's enough to overpower you!

DOÑA ENRIQUETA. Country smells!

DIONISIA. Mint and thyme. To think of our liking such things!

TERESONA. It is because my niece is a stranger, too.

ALFONSA. I'm so glad I came from our village to see this procession. Oh, dear, how beautiful these streets are!

DOÑA ENRIQUETA. Do for heaven's sake stop talking about the streets. One can see all sorts of ridiculous sights from these gaudy balconies.

DIONISIA. And all sorts of worthless rabble.

TERESONA. In the streets?

DOÑA ENRIQUETA. Yes. [*Greeting some passing friends from the window.*] How do you do, Matilda?

DIONISIA. Hello, Elvira!

JUANELA. How do you do? Won't you come in a while? Very well — I'll see you later.

ALFONSA. How nicely dressed they are! And what beautiful bouquets they wear! How lovely!

DOÑA ENRIQUETA. Overdone, my child, overdone.

DIONISIA. Yes, mamma, overdone.

[LOBITO *appears in the doorway upstage. He comes from the street. It is difficult to recognize him, as he is no longer the rough and unkempt workman of the foundry. He is now a gay village gallant. He wears a carnation behind his ear, and another in his hat; probably to offer to some one.*]

LOBITO [*before any one sees him. Aside*]. Hello! Now I'll have some fun; these women are too good for us. [*Aloud.*] Good afternoon!

JUANELA. Good afternoon.

TERESONA. Come in, Lobito.

ALFONSA. Hello, Inacio!

DOÑA ENRIQUETA and DIONISIA. Good afternoon.

ALFONSA. You're lovely, too!

LOBITO. I've got to be to-day, woman; the day of the procession! The day when La Golondrina is to ring again! Don't you think we ought to appear in our very best?

ALFONSA. And he's wearing a chain, auntie! Did you see this?

LOBITO. Of course I wear a chain.

JUANELA. And a very pretty one it is.

LOBITO. All I need is a watch to go with it.

ALFONSA. Haven't you a watch?

TERESONA. Well, you *are* a little mischief!

LOBITO. No, I haven't any. I've fastened my matchbox to the end of the chain for a weight. Then I strike myself. I've had the girls staring at me, and when they ask me as a joke what time it is, I come back with another joke. [*Laughs.*]

ALFONSA. Oh, dear, what a way he has with him!

TERESONA. Lobito, is it true that there has been fighting in the Alameda?

LOBITO. Yes. And there will be some more between now and when the bell rings! La Sonora's friends thought that she was always to be the only bell, and more than one obstinate fool is likely to have the courage knocked out of him.

DOÑA ENRIQUETA. What a set of barbarians they are!

DIONISIA. Savages.

Doña Enriqueta. You see what savage people we have in this village.

Juanela. When is the bell to ring, Lobito?

Lobito. When the Image returns from the procession through the town and enters the Home. That is what the Mother Superior has decided. You ought to hear old blind Martin!

Juanela. Who?

Lobito. Martin, the blind man. He's always been La Golondrina's bellman, poor old fellow! He is weeping like a child. You'd think they had brought a child of his back to life. He hasn't slept for three nights. He says he doesn't mind if he dies at the first stroke... and I really think he will. It makes your hair stand on end to hear him talk.

Alfonsa. Dear me, how queer! When does the procession pass, Inacio?

Lobito. It went along the causeway a moment ago, so it ought to be here in about half an hour.

Teresona. Then we must be getting the flowers ready.

Alfonsa. Shall we go and cut them?

Lobito. Yes. I'll help you.

Teresona. I'm going out now.

Alfonsa. Come on.

[*Exit through door upstage and turns to the right.*]

Teresona [*to* Lobito *who starts to follow her*]. Be careful of the flowers, Lobito.

Lobito. Better tell me to be careful of the fruit. Flowers only smell; you eat the fruit after the blossoms are all gone. Understand? [*Exit after* Alfonsa.]

Teresona. He is incorrigible. But what are you going to do when the girl likes him? It's natural for the boys to like the girls, and when we older people leave them alone... well, it's natural.

Dionisia. Certainly, like with like.

Doña Enriqueta. Shall we take a little walk?

Dionisia. Good idea! Let us take a walk.

Doña Enriqueta [*to* Juanela]. Are you coming?

Juanela. Why not?

Dionisia. We shall run into many of the townspeople, but it cannot be helped.

Juanela. What's the difference? They won't eat us.

Doña Enriqueta. Ah, there goes the Alcalde's wife! Let us call to her.

Dionisia. Doña Casilda!

Doña Enriqueta. Doña Casilda! Wait for us, please!

Dionisia. Come on.

Juanela. Very well.

[*At this moment* Salvador *enters through the door upstage. He also is dressed in his best.*]

Salvador. How are the prettiest women in the town — or out of it?

Doña Enriqueta. You flatter us....

Dionisia. Good afternoon.

Juanela. Good afternoon — Always the same!

Salvador. Are you going out?

Doña Enriqueta. To take a short walk while we wait for the procession.

Salvador. It won't be long in coming.

Dionisia. It should take about half an hour. We have been figuring it out.

Salvador. Well, this is a day to find a sweetheart in the street.

Doña Enriqueta. Shall we go?

Dionisia. Yes.

Salvador. Beware, though, of strangers! The weather is fine. After yesterday's rain everything is fresh, and it is a good time for a walk I'm sure. Don't let me detain you.

Dionisia. Come, mamma, Doña Casilda is waiting for us.

Doña Enriqueta. Yes, of course.

Juanela. Go on. I'll join you presently.

[*Exeunt* Doña Enriqueta *and* Dionisia *through the door upstage. They turn to the left.* Juanela *remains a moment with* Salvador.]

Teresona. There are few people I don't like in this world; I can overlook most anything... and I say it in good faith; but I can't help disliking that woman and her daughter.

Salvador. What amuses me is the way they talk. They're so affected and stilted.

TERESONA. Do you know what they call her husband?

JUANELA. That will do, Teresona. Salvador ——

SALVADOR. What is it? I like to see that long face.

JUANELA. Have you heard the latest?

SALVADOR. No. More nonsense of Leonardo's?

JUANELA. Another fuss. You knew about yesterday?

SALVADOR. Yes. He struck some one for saying I don't know what about Malvaloca. They told me about it last night. What is it to-day?

JUANELA. Probably because of yesterday's doings he insists upon the woman's coming here to watch the procession with us.

SALVADOR. But I thought she was going to walk barefooted behind the procession!

JUANELA. She wanted to, but he dissuaded her.

SALVADOR. So then he persuaded her to come here. The man is crazy.

JUANELA. Just think of it! What will people say? And these friends of mine — I don't know *what* they will do! But others who have heard about it have excused themselves from coming. Speak to him; not to persuade him to prevent her from coming, for since he wishes it, and this is his house ——

SALVADOR. No, for heaven's sake!

JUANELA. But advise him to be prudent, to use discretion, to have a little consideration for others. He has to live with people ——

SALVADOR. All I can say will be useless. But I shall speak to him once more since you wish it. It's the last time, though.

JUANELA. Even if it is the last time, don't neglect to speak to him, Salvador. I can't discuss things with him, because I have good-naturedly let him have his own way in whatever he wished ever since I was a little girl. I have always had absolute faith in his goodness. "Whatever my brother does is surely right" is what I have thought and felt all my life. But now, now I confess, Salvador, my head is in a whirl.

SALVADOR. He's mad.

JUANELA. No, he's not mad. He doesn't talk like a madman. Deep down in my heart, I understand my brother, don't forget that. Reason cannot overcome feeling; but there is always a reason for every feeling.

SALVADOR. Very well, don't worry. I'll speak to him. You'd better go now. Your friends are waiting for you.

DOÑA ENRIQUETA [*from the street*]. Juanela, aren't you coming?

JUANELA. Yes, just a moment. I'm sorry. [*To* SALVADOR.] I am going to tell Leonardo that you are here.

[*Exit through the door upstage, to the right. Presently she is seen to cross the courtyard to the left.*]

SALVADOR. Innocent child! This is a nice kind of a vacation her brother has given her!

TERESONA. It's other people's fault; they poison their thoughts. He is good; she is good; and so is the other woman. Can anything bad possibly happen to three such really good people? Nonsense! Listen to me: Is there, or is there not, a God? Well, if there is one, and if nobody does anything unless He wishes it — why, all I say is God is old enough to know what He's about!

SALVADOR. That's seeing things I suppose in God's way.

TERESONA. No more and no less. Here he comes.

SALVADOR. God?!!

TERESONA. Don Leonardo. You always will joke! I'm going to take a look now at the other couple.

[LEONARDO *enters from the house, through the door upstage.* TERESONA *lets him pass, and then withdraws toward the right, watching the two partners.*]

LEONARDO. Juanela told me you wanted me. What do you want?

SALVADOR. To see you, first of all. Then — to chat with you a while. Why, it's been a week since we exchanged a word. I thought somehow you were avoiding me.

LEONARDO. Avoiding you?

SALVADOR. Don't worry, I'm not going

to examine you about business affairs. I have the utmost confidence in you.

LEONARDO. So you sent for me to listen to some of your foolish jokes?

SALVADOR. The difference is in our conception of life. You take it too seriously, and I, perhaps, too lightly.

LEONARDO. Perhaps.

SALVADOR. Only jokers make all the more impression when they become serious. And I am serious now.

LEONARDO. It is a miracle.

SALVADOR. Yes, serious. [*Affectionately.*] How's your heart, partner?

LEONARDO. Breaking, but happy.

SALVADOR. Very good. And your head — cracked, but happy?

LEONARDO. As you say.

SALVADOR. And all for a woman.

LEONARDO. For whom better?

SALVADOR. Well, let's have a word about that woman.

LEONARDO. I would prefer that you let that subject alone.

SALVADOR. It is several days since we talked about her.

LEONARDO. And there is no reason why we should talk again.

SALVADOR. Yes, there is, now.

LEONARDO. No one has a right to speak of this woman to me — least of all, you.

SALVADOR. It isn't the usual topic this time. It is another matter. Leonardo, this woman is a great source of anxiety to your sister.

LEONARDO. No, it is I who am. Not on her account, nor on mine; but on account of what people will say. I know it. I can see it. But my sister is going back to my aunt and uncle, and the day will come when she will think as I do.

SALVADOR. Ah! Your sister is leaving?

LEONARDO. Yes. Very soon. The day after to-morrow. I don't want any one to share my sacrifice, not even the woman whom I have taught to be broadminded and strong.

SALVADOR. Are you absolutely sure his experiment will endure?

LEONARDO. It has never been an experiment, and it will last all my life.

SALVADOR. All your life?

LEONARDO. Yes. You have never loved unless you saw a free avenue of escape; you cannot understand me. Malvaloca is my whole life. Painfully but joyfully, I join my lot with hers!

SALVADOR. No, I do not understand you. Deuce take your excuses and theories! They are too thin. But, on the other hand, I know how to dispose of a certain other obstacle, even if I do not understand your idea of sacrificing yourself for this little bird you have picked up in the street.

LEONARDO [*troubled*]. What other obstacle? And for God's sake be careful what you say!

SALVADOR. Listen to me, and answer me truthfully; you have always preached to me. I suggested this course to you some time ago, and now, when I least expected it, the crisis has come. Would it surprise you very much if I disappeared from the village?

LEONARDO. From Las Canteras? But where would you go?

SALVADOR. That isn't the question. Would it surprise you?

LEONARDO. Perhaps not.

SALVADOR. And would you be glad? The truth, Leonardo!

LEONARDO. Truthfully, yes.

SALVADOR. I know it. I know, too, that you will regret it, because our friendship isn't a trifle. But I ought to leave you, and I shall. Without being able to help it, I wound you, I hurt you, and call to your mind things which you would like obliterated from the eyes of the world. And whether you succeed in forgetting them or not you will be saved from many an ache by not seeing me. I have never been able to understand man's love for woman; but I *do* understand the affection of one man for another. It is a part of my temperament, probably. I have spent my life deceiving women, yet I have never been able to deceive a man. And the funny thing is, I like women better! Do you understand me?

LEONARDO. I understand you are very generous. Forgive me if I ever called you an egotist.

SALVADOR. Good. Well, it's all over now. Give me your hand.

LEONARDO. Yes, indeed.

SALVADOR. And we'll always be friends, no matter how far apart, shall we not?

LEONARDO. Whatever you wish. I can find no words.

SALVADOR. Well, then, I'll talk while you are in that fix and keep up your spirits. Don't be foolish; shake off this depression. Cheer up. Remember that there are more women than there are stars, and that it is a shame for a man like you ——

LEONARDO. Don't! Keep still!

SALVADOR. Why should I keep still? Do you know that there never was a man who carried things to such extremes as you do?

LEONARDO. Do you know that my soul is my own? And my grief is in my own heart. It is my grief, just as it is my satisfaction to suffer it! How can I forget? Happy the men who do not shrink at the thought of the others who have been before them when they kiss a woman! I am not jealous of you nor of any one else — I am jealous of a whole past. And that is the life I want for mine! Pity me. Some one is coming. I don't want any one to see that I have been weeping.

[*Embraces his friend and exit through the door at the right.*]

SALVADOR. My poor partner!

[MALVALOCA *enters vivaciously from the street, as though following* LEONARDO. *She is dressed simply and wears a wide shawl of black lace over her shoulders.*]

MALVALOCA. Where is Leonardo? Wasn't he here?

SALVADOR. Hello!

MALVALOCA. Hello! Wasn't *he* here?

SALVADOR. He *was*. But he heard footsteps and went out, because some one was coming.

MALVALOCA. And it was only me!

SALVADOR. He didn't recognize your step.

MALVALOCA. That was on account of the noise in the street. Where is he?

SALVADOR. He went in there.

MALVALOCA. This way?

SALVADOR. Yes. Listen.

MALVALOCA. What do you want?

SALVADOR. I want to tell you something.

MALVALOCA. You can write it.

SALVADOR. Write it?

MALVALOCA. Yes. I know how to read and write now. He taught me.

SALVADOR. To write, too?

MALVALOCA. I don't know it all yet. But I can write some of the letters. I know how to write his name and mine. I'll see you later.

SALVADOR. Wait.

MALVALOCA. No!

SALVADOR. Why not?

MALVALOCA. Because I want to lose sight of you.

SALVADOR. You, too?

MALVALOCA. Me, too.

SALVADOR. I'm not surprised. The world is full of unpleasantness of that sort. You'll find that out pretty soon. Do you know I'm thinking of dissolving the partnership?

MALVALOCA. A good idea.

SALVADOR. So I can leave Las Canteras, of course.

MALVALOCA. That's a still better idea than the other!

SALVADOR. You like the idea?

MALVALOCA. Uh! You've had enough. I like it for my sake, and for his. A retreating enemy ——

SALVADOR. Am I your enemy, Malvaloca?

MALVALOCA. At present, yes. But all things are healed by time. Now run along. please.

SALVADOR. I'm going. Doesn't your conscience prick you for what you have done to this man?

MALVALOCA. What have I done but love him?

SALVADOR. You've crazed him.

MALVALOCA. I'm crazy, too — with the same kind of madness. We've had the same fate.

SALVADOR. Is it possible?

MALVALOCA. It isn't always that two people are joined together and only one in love. Here are two of us in love and in love with each other.

SALVADOR. Well, I advise you, Malvaloca ——

MALVALOCA. Come, you're a pilgrim now; go and do your preaching in the desert. I will pay just as much attention to you there.

SALVADOR. You're right.

" *I've seen many a splendid castle*
In ruins on the ground...."

Well, since he wants to keep you from me — God bless you! We won't see each other again.

MALVALOCA. Good-bye.

SALVADOR. Your hand, girl. Won't you even give me your hand for the sake of the past?

MALVALOCA. I'll give you nothing for the sake of the past.

SALVADOR. Just a good-bye handshake — like two friends.

MALVALOCA. Like that, yes.

SALVADOR. Thanks. Good-bye.

MALVALOCA. Good-bye.

SALVADOR. I'm just the same as I ever was.

MALVALOCA. Well, I'm another person, now.

SALVADOR. Good-bye.

[*Exit into the street. Conflicting emotions distract his mind.*]

MALVALOCA. He's right to go. But where is Leonardo? I don't dare go in there.

[ALFONSA *and* LOBITO *reënter from the garden.* ALFONSA *carries a basket of flowers which she sets upon the table.* LOBITO's *carnations are on her breast.*]

ALFONSA. Teresona told me to put these upon the table.

LOBITO. Wouldn't it be better to make some bouquets?

ALFONSA. No, sir. When they are loose, there seem to be more of them, and we can throw them better.

MALVALOCA. Lobito! Is it you?

LOBITO [*turning around*]. Eh? Good afternoon. You! In this house?

ALFONSA. Good afternoon. [*Looks at her in wonder.*] Ah!

MALVALOCA. I shouldn't have known you. You look as grand as the Alcalde himself.

[ALFONSA *breaks into laughter which is loud enough to be heard in her own town.* LOBITO *also laughs.*]

LOBITO. My, how she did enjoy that!

MALVALOCA. Are you dressed up like this so as to catch a sweetheart?

LOBITO. We're beyond that sort of thing now.

[*Enter* JUANELA, *hastily and excitedly.*]

JUANELA. Good afternoon.

MALVALOCA [*somewhat disconcerted*]. Good afternoon.

JUANELA. I saw you come in, so I left my friends. Where is Leonardo?

MALVALOCA. I don't know.

[JUANELA *looks at both doors.*]

LOBITO [*to* ALFONSA]. Let's go pick some more flowers.

ALFONSA. Very well. We can't go too far in the service of the Lord.

LOBITO. We won't be missed here, either.

[*Exeunt* LOBITO *and* ALFONSA. JUANELA's *eyes open wide with curiosity as she gazes at* MALVALOCA.]

MALVALOCA. Did you know I was coming?

JUANELA. My brother told me.

MALVALOCA. I didn't want to come, really I didn't.

JUANELA. I knew that, too. But when he sets his heart upon a thing — you understand ——

MALVALOCA. He has his own way. Excuse me for saying so, but when I am with him, I feel I have a right anywhere. But without him, I feel as if I didn't belong anywhere — least of all, here.

JUANELA. Why?

MALVALOCA. You know without my telling you. Had we better say any more?

JUANELA. He'll be here in a minute.

MALVALOCA. I can't see this thing so clearly — the way you can. You are his sister.

JUANELA. It hurts me to see him downhearted, to see him weep.

MALVALOCA. You cannot love without tears.

JUANELA. Do you think so?

MALVALOCA. Leonardo was unfortunate enough to run across me pretty well along in life. When I saw how he loved me, I made up my mind I would let him go, but it was too late. I was caught in the same chain myself.

JUANELA. Is it so strong?

MALVALOCA. There is no anvil on which it can be broken, and no fire which can melt it. A heartbeat forged the chain — and I never knew I had a heart till I felt his beating at my side. His sang there, and mine answered his like a bird. I'd rather die than ever stop listening and answering to its sound.

JUANELA. I can see that it was most unfortunate.

MALVALOCA. For Leonardo, as you say. For me, it was like being born again. This is my punishment: that I should have to be born again in order to be the woman he deserves.

JUANELA. But that is impossible!

MALVALOCA. That word "impossible" is the cause of all our tears.

JUANELA. It is very sad.

MALVALOCA. My life has been sadder; and I'm still on my feet.

JUANELA. Which is sadder still?

MALVALOCA. But child, don't you see? That is the day I begin to live! My former life —— What do you know about pain? If it were written on my forehead then of course you could read. I don't want to exaggerate my misfortune. The fact is that Leonardo and I have entered a tunnel without any way out and with only the light which we bring on the train. But don't you worry: little by little there will be more light. God has lighted my steps. In my greatest trouble, something unexpected has always happened to light me the way. It is natural to me — like my black hair —— Who is coming?

[DoÑA ENRIQUETA *and* DIONISIA *enter unexpectedly. They are somewhat out of breath. After them* ALFONSA *and* LOBITO *appear with more flowers, which they put upon the table as before. Their attention is attracted by the conversation between* JUANELA *and the mother and*

daughter, but they content themselves with comments upon it to each other with significant gestures.]

DoÑA ENRIQUETA. Goodness me! I never saw such a hubbub!

DIONISIA. And how ill-mannered the people are!

DoÑA ENRIQUETA. You did right to turn back. [*With a surprised and disgusted air as she sees* MALVALOCA.] Eh?

DIONISIA. What?

MALVALOCA. Good afternoon.

DoÑA ENRIQUETA. What does this mean?

[*There is a painful silence. Mother and daughter exchange a glance of astonishment.*]

JUANELA [*very much embarrassed*]. So you found walking difficult in the street? I thought you would.

DoÑA ENRIQUETA. Walking was difficult there, and conditions are uncomfortable here. We had better go.

JUANELA. Must you go?

DIONISIA. Yes, I'm not feeling very well.

DoÑA ENRIQUETA. Yes, she's not feeling very well.

JUANELA. I'll make her a cup of tea.

DoÑA ENRIQUETA. No, thank you. Come, my dear.

DIONISIA. Very well, mamma.

JUANELA. But aren't you going to stay to watch the procession?

DoÑA ENRIQUETA. Yes, but we shall see it as it enters the church. Come!

DIONISIA. Yes, we must be going.

DoÑA ENRIQUETA. Good afternoon, Juanela.

JUANELA. Good afternoon. You don't know how sorry I ——

DoÑA ENRIQUETA. Never mind the explanation. Good-bye. [*To* DIONISIA *as she starts to go.*] Did you see, my child? Did you see?

DIONISIA. Did you see, mamma?

DoÑA ENRIQUETA. Heavens, wha shamelessness!

[*Exeunt haughtily upstage and to th left.* ALFONSA *and* LOBITO *have pre ceded them a little through the same door but to the right.*]

MALVALOCA [*humbly, to* JUANELA]. Did they leave because they saw *me*? [JUANELA, *without intending it, makes a gesture of assent.*] I'm sorry for you, more than I am for myself. You see how it is. If I hadn't come ——

[LEONARDO *enters through door at the right.*]

LEONARDO. What is this?

MALVALOCA. God bless us!

LEONARDO. What was it? What were you saying?

JUANELA. Oh, nothing!

LEONARDO. Yes, tell me what it was.

JUANELA. Doña Enriqueta and her daughter —— came ——

LEONARDO. And went away when they saw Malvaloca. Am I right?

MALVALOCA, JUANELA. Yes.

LEONARDO. Good riddance! Other friends of ours declined to come because they already knew — another good riddance! Every one according to his own conscience, but why then make a parade of Christ through the streets?

JUANELA. We must have more flowers than this to throw when He passes.

[*Exit upstage to the right.*]

LEONARDO. Now you see, they avoid you.

MALVALOCA. Your sister doesn't.

LEONARDO. She may not, but the other women do.

MALVALOCA. Let them avoid me. So long as you don't ——

LEONARDO. Is that all you want?

MALVALOCA. Have I any other love in the world? No one ever offered me the protection that you do. I might just as well say "I am yours" at once, and with me it is something more than words... Leonardo, I am yours!

LEONARDO. You are mine!

MALVALOCA. Yours! Because I live only for you, and because your joy is my joy. Lift your eyes from the ground and look at me. Why, I'm getting jealous of the very tiles of the floor! Come! Now I see you are smiling. Why, all I have are your arms, and I have found shelter there as one finds shelter beneath the branches of a tree because there it is calm and at peace! [*With a sudden transition.*] But I don't want you to be a weeping willow. I prefer an orange tree which blossoms and gives fruit, and which never loses its leaves in winter. Do you understand?

LEONARDO [*passionately*]. I am indeed a tree that shelters you, and your words are the air that gives me life.

MALVALOCA. How romantic you are! And how I *do* love you, you big earthquake!

LEONARDO. How happy we are to love one another like this! The rest of the world no longer exists — just you and I.

MALVALOCA. Our love has been like a torch. Uh! I was carrying my little load of wood alone on my back; then you began to smile and in half an hour the whole forest was ablaze! And there is nothing like that fire, is there?

LEONARDO. Nothing like the fire, nor like you.

MALVALOCA. How nice it is to be in love! You are with the person you love more when you are away from him than when you are with him. You wake up at night, and you can see no one else. You sleep, and you dream about him. You get up in the morning, and all you expect is to see him coming from somewhere. He may or he may not come. Then you say to yourself: He told me so-and-so yesterday or maybe he didn't tell me. He smiled or he didn't smile. He is crying; he is jealous; what a funny way he throws his hat in the chair! He is going. No, don't go... But he must go... Come back then in the afternoon, please do... and be sure... please come back. He goes. Good-bye... Then he comes back all of a sudden to surprise me! Great heavens! There is nothing like love!

LEONARDO. Have you been in love very many times, Malvaloca?

MALVALOCA. Who? I? Only once. But I've had echoes.

LEONARDO. Only once? With whom?

MALVALOCA. Don Pelayo! [LEONARDO *smiles.*] Wasn't it Don Pelayo who conquered the Asturias — or have you deceived me?

LEONARDO. I never deceive you.

MALVALOCA. Well, then, love seems to have had some connection with Don Pelayo. I fell in love with you, foundryman, with only you in the world! With you — and you're nobler, too, than Don Pelayo. But I warn you first: Don Pelayo has a street named after him in Seville. Somebody I know lived in number three. Who can say but that was the beginning of our love?

LEONARDO [charmed]. Who can say?

MALVALOCA. Do you remember the day we met in the Home?

LEONARDO. Could I forget it?

MALVALOCA. One look, and you could feel the flash of lightning which always strikes people who are going to fall in love.

LEONARDO. And then — after you had gone —

MALVALOCA. Yes, then you followed me! I was so happy!

LEONARDO. Were you really pleased?

MALVALOCA. Uh! Then I stopped on a corner — as if I didn't know where to go.

LEONARDO. And I came up to you upon the excuse of showing you the way.

MALVALOCA. And the ways we were looking for lay together.., and we took the same road, didn't we, Leonardo?

LEONARDO. And we will never abandon it, will we?

MALVALOCA. No, my sweet. But how wonderfully God brings things about! He led me there to ask for some one else — so as to meet the man who was to be mine

LEONARDO [with sudden sadness]. To ask for some one else?

MALVALOCA. Yes, for another. To meet you! Now don't you mourn like a cypress tree; you were an orange in full bloom. The other has gone forever!

LEONARDO. How do you know?

MALVALOCA. Because I am a fortune teller and clairvoyant.

LEONARDO. He told you? You bade each other good-bye.

MALVALOCA. Yes.

LEONARDO. When?

MALVALOCA. Here, a little while ago after you left him. He went away, and may God protect him and keep him well.

LEONARDO. He went away; yes, *he* went away... but will those thoughts go away — those thoughts of the past which centred in him?

MALVALOCA. Leonardo!

LEONARDO. Malvaloca, my soul, they are stronger than my will!

MALVALOCA. Oh, why did I call them up!

LEONARDO. You see this, the one love of my life, suffers this torment, which gnaws at my heart like a dull pain — even when he is farthest from my sight!

MALVALOCA. Don't, Leonardo! Oh, if only some one could root up those horrid thoughts—could tear them out by the roots!

LEONARDO. They would spring up again. Why, the more I listen to you, and see you, and love you, the more am I saddened when I feel the shame of your former life!

MALVALOCA. No — no, Leonardo, not that! If my love must always hurt you, I shall leave you.

LEONARDO. Never! Not that, surely!

MALVALOCA. Well, then, kill me!

LEONARDO. That least of all! I want you to live — by my side, consoling me, making me laugh when you laugh, or else making me cry, sharing my joys and my sorrows as I look into your eyes, kiss your mouth, and stroke your hair... that's how I want you, I love you!

MALVALOCA. Leonardo, you're mad!

LEONARDO. No! One fear keeps me from going mad.

MALVALOCA. What fear?

LEONARDO [looking at her very sharply with frenzied exaltation]. That if I were mad I should not know you when I saw you.

MALVALOCA. Come here! Why, you're worse than mad! Calm yourself and that fiery head of yours, which is burning you up. Why, I love you and you only — you have made me into another woman. I hurts me more than it does you to have th marks of my former life on my body. Bu what did it matter to me what I was befor I met you? Little less than nothing. shook off my sins as one shakes off th snow. Then I met you; you spoke to m as no one ever had spoken before; yo taught me to love, your love brought tea to my eyes, and in those tears I saw clear what I was, what you were, and what m former life had been. I thought I shou find consolation in you, and now your thoughts take that from me. Either bury them or me, Leonardo, deep under the ground and never let Malvaloca trouble you any more!

LEONARDO. Bury you? Put you under the ground? Like the recast bell. An idea — an idea —— Once more the little verse! Under the ground —— Oh, if that were only possible!

MALVALOCA. Hush! Let us not torture ourselves any more.

LEONARDO [enlarging upon his idea as in ecstasy, though with regret]. To form your beautiful body in wax, redden it with my blood, cover it with earth, throw the pieces into the fire in the crucible, purify them with the living flames, then take you out again, pure, clean, another being — yet the same! New, spotless, without a past, but the same! With those same eyes, that mouth, and that great and good soul in which my whole being is consumed!

MALVALOCA. Hush, hush! What infatuation! What dreams! Hush! Why, you're crying!

LEONARDO. Of course, I am crying. Why shouldn't I cry? Only the irremediable things draw tears from men!

MALVALOCA. Hush! I hear some one!

LEONARDO. What do I care? . . .

MALVALOCA. Can the procession be coming?

LEONARDO. The procession?

MALVALOCA. Could they have seen us from the street?

LEONARDO. I don't know, nor do I care.
[JUANELA, approaching, calls from off stage.]

JUANELA. Leonardo!

MALVALOCA. Your sister!

LEONARDO. My sister?

MALVALOCA. Yes. Dry your eyes.

LEONARDO. And you, too!

[JUANELA reënters from the door through which she went out. She is followed by TERESONA, ALFONSA, and LOBITO.]

JUANELA. The procession is at the corner.

LEONARDO. Really? So soon?

TERESONA. Good afternoon.

MALVALOCA. Good afternoon.

TERESONA. The Image is coming.

ALFONSA. Here it is! Here it is! Inacio, you must explain everything to me!

[The four have scarcely entered before they go up to the window. MALVALOCA and LEONARDO remain apart. Soon the strains of the town band which follows the Redeemer are heard in the distance, and then draw nearer, more clearly and clearly heard. ALFONSA, ingenuously enthusiastic, comments upon the procession with LOBITO.]

TERESONA [to MALVALOCA]. Won't you stand with us?

MALVALOCA. Thank you, I'm all right here.

LOBITO. The Cross! See the Cross!

ALFONSA. My, how gorgeous! Is it all silver?

LOBITO. All solid silver!

ALFONSA. Look at the man who carries it! Ah! See the children! How cunning they are with their little candles held in their handkerchiefs!

LOBITO. The whole school and the Academy are there. Those who haven't new neckties, wear new shoes!

ALFONSA. Oh, do look at that little boy dressed like an angel! Look, auntie, and you, Señorita, look how beautiful he is!

TERESONA. We see him, girl, we see him. Keep your eyes open and wait.

ALFONSA. My, his wings look like glass! I wonder who his mother is? And who are those men?

LOBITO. The most prominent men of the village. There is the Alcalde.

ALFONSA. Which one?

LOBITO. The one with the silver staff.

ALFONSA. With whiskers?

LOBITO. Yes.

JUANELA, TERESONA. The Image of Christ!

JUANELA. The flowers!

TERESONA, ALFONSA. The flowers! The flowers!

LOBITO. I'm going to ask González to halt here. Then I'm going to hurry to the church door to wait for the image to come —— You know why!

ALFONSA. Take care to neglect nothing!
[Exit LOBITO through the door up-

stage, to the left. JUANELA, TERESONA, *and* ALFONSA *have crossed to the table for the flowers.* JUANELA *looks benevolently at* MALVALOCA *who is still somewhat constrained, and with an impulse of deep piety, grasping a handful of flowers, goes to her and places them sweetly in her hands so that she may throw them as the Image passes.*]

JUANELA. You must take some, too.

MALVALOCA. Thank you very much.

[*The four group themselves at the window.* LEONARDO *follows, keeping apart, however, watching intently. From the street a faint fragrance of incense arises. The Image has stopped in front of the window. Meanwhile the band has ceased playing. The four women throw all their flowers to the Image of Christ, then pray in silence.* MALVALOCA *leaves the window and prays on her knees by the table, where the flowers were, weeping softly.*]

TERESONA. A woman is going to sing a hymn.

JUANELA. Who is she?

TERESONA. I don't know her.

JUANELA. She has a child in her arms.

ALFONSA. Oh, so she has! It looks like a little rosebud.

TERESONA. Hush!

[*The woman sings with earnest devotion the following hymn in a shrill voice:*]

O Christ, thou blessed Redeemer,
Look down from Heaven above;
And lay thy tenderest blessing
On this, the child I love!

[*The four women kneel, wiping their eyes. The procession resumes its march again. The band plays and moves off.* JUANELA, TERESONA, *and* ALFONSA *arise.* MALVALOCA *remains on her knees for a time.*]

ALFONSA. What a procession! It was iike glowing coals of gold!

JUANELA. How brilliant it was! How many flowers!

TERESONA. This is a great day in Las Canteras! Let's go up on the roof and watch it as it goes into the church.

JUANELA. Yes, indeed! It will be worth the trouble. Come!

ALFONSA. Yes, come on.

[*The three women go out through the door upstage, to the right. When* MALVALOCA *sees she is alone with her lover, she gets up, runs to him, and sobbing, hides her face on his breast.*]

LEONARDO [*embracing her, profoundly moved*]. Malvaloca!

MALVALOCA. I am with you! Protect me and look down on me with pity as you hang upon your Cross! Don't ever leave me! When you stop loving me, kill me! But meanwhile, let me be with you — with you!

LEONARDO. Yes, with me! Eternally tormented but eternally happy! Overshadowed by the same griefs, torn by the prongs of the same thorns, but always — together!

MALVALOCA. Together — you and I!

LEONARDO. You and I!

[*Far off in the tower, welcoming the Image of Him who was able to pardon a sinful woman, the first vibration of La Golondrina, as she is rung by the hands of blind Martin, comes stealing through the air. The two lovers, trembling, move closer together in each other's arms.*]

MALVALOCA. La Golondrina!

LEONARDO. La Golondrina! Listen — listen — how triumphant she sounds! How I have striven and longed for this hour!

MALVALOCA. You recast her, you! Listen to her — listen to her!

LEONARDO. She sings of universal love! Her voice speaks with a new meaning to my heart. I will also recast your life by the warmth of my kisses, by the fire of this wild love of mine, which is as great even as your misfortune!

MALVALOCA. With you — to be with you ——!

[*La Golondrina, whose notes at first were subdued and gravely slow, now breaks forth into a lively, happy song, vibrant with the note of victory, proclaiming to the fields and villages the life that is reborn.*]

END OF THE PLAY

A LILY AMONG THORNS

A COMEDY IN ONE ACT
By GREGORIO and MARIA MARTINEZ SIERRA

The English version by HELEN AND HARLEY GRANVILLE-BARKER

THE PEOPLE OF THE PLAY

SISTER TERESA

DOÑA TOMASA

LULU

AMALIA

ANA MARIA

CLARITA

THE DANCER

RICARDITO

AGUSTIN

CARLOS

RAMON

MARIANITO

A VERY RESPECTABLE GENTLEMAN

The action takes place in a house of ill-fame in a big Spanish town; late one evening.

A LILY AMONG THORNS

The scene is in a house of ill-fame in some big Spanish town. It is a sitting-room, furnished in very bad taste, but with some pretensions to elegance.

THE DANCER *is on a table, dancing, and every one is applauding her.* CLARITA *lies on a sofa smoking.* AMALIA *sits on the floor in front of* MARIANITO *who has all the airs of a pasha.* CARLOS *is paired off with* ANA MARIA. LULU *is looking out of the window.* AMALIA *sings little folk-songs (*coplas*) to herself while* RICARDITO — *he's no more than a child and, at that, not "all there" — plays about on his hands and knees, unnoticed. And* DOÑA TOMASA, *seated in an armchair, presides over them all with an almost maternal benevolence.*

THE DANCER, *her tango over, jumps off the table and flings herself amid applause into the arms of* AGUSTIN.

AGUSTIN. You *are* a weight, my precious! But you do know how to dance.

THE DANCER [*paying no attention*]. Give me a drink... give me a drink!

AGUSTIN [*mockingly*]. With the Eastern fire of the gipsy she combines the classic distinction of a Greek statue.

THE DANCER. Will somebody give me a drink!

AGUSTIN [*clasping her in his arms*]. Will you please pay attention to what I am saying?

THE DANCER. What the devil do I care what you're saying? I want a drink.

AGUSTIN. Take your drink then!

[*He empties a glass of champagne over her.*]

THE DANCER. You brute... you disgusting brute!

[*She claws at him. He seizes her hands.*]

AGUSTIN. Oh... what a little savage! All right... spit away, pussy-cat. [*She bites his hand.*] You mean to bite, do you?

... then you must learn who's your master.

[*In the struggle they fall against* CLARITA *on her sofa. She protests ill-humouredly.*]

CLARITA. Look out, children! What on earth are you doing? I'm not here for you to fall about on. Can't a poor girl digest her dinner in peace?

AGUSTIN. Did you say grace after it?

CLARITA. What's that to you?

AGUSTIN. Suppose you died of love for me... and hadn't said your prayers!

CLARITA. Well... I'd be rid of you then at least... nuisances that you all are!

CARLOS. Will you please remember that it's me you're dying of love for?

AMALIA. Oh, you're always talking about love... about grand passions and such like. As soon as ever he gets you alone he begins talking of how they made love in the time of Methuselah....

AGUSTIN. Well... what more do you want of me but to hear me hold forth?

LULU. What tiresome fools you men are!

AGUSTIN. Thank you... my beauty!

CARLOS. You're quite right. We are. Is it the first time you've noticed it?

LULU. On a night like this... with a revolution blazing in the streets... here you all are... good for nothing but to play the fool with us! Oh... if I were a man!...

AGUSTIN. What good would it do you if we went storming the barricades?

AMALIA. You could find *something* better to do than this... [MARIANITO *puts his arm round her.*] Oh... another of you!

MARIANITO. We're here to take care of you.... [*The girls all laugh.*] I tell you... once they've set all the convents on fire, they'll come and fry you brown in the flames!

CLARITA. Aie!!

CARLOS. So be warned, Doña Tomasa.

DOÑA T. [*with simple gravity*]. I'm sure I don't know what harm *we* do to any one.

CLARITA. Well, nor do the nuns, I suppose, if it comes to that.

DOÑA T. We are not like the nuns. For one thing, they pay no taxes.

CARLOS. Dear young ladies, you are luxuries... and the preserve of an unworthy Bourgeoisie... who spend upon you the money they wring from the toil of the wretched proletariat.

AMALIA. That's true.

CLARITA. Well, it's easily remedied. We'll let the poor in free... and charge the rich more.

MARIANITO. Why not? The best doctors do it.

THE DANCER. And all high-class highwaymen.

AGUSTIN. We're all socialists now!

LULU. Look here... there are two things that matter in this world... being hungry and wanting money. Well... with all the money there is there ought to be enough food for every one. Very well, then... take things away from people that don't deserve them, and give them to those that do.

CARLOS. How simple!

LULU. Because what I say is... nothing really belongs to anybody. What I mean is that it's not his even when he thinks it's his. Look here now... you've got a bit of chocolate and you say it's yours... it belongs to you and you've got it in your fingers. And some one a bit stronger than you comes along and takes it from you and eats it under your nose. Well, you can go on saying it's yours... but much good that'll do you!

[Everybody cries out "Hear! Hear! Bravo!"]

MARIANITO. My dear... you're an orator.

LULU. And it's the same with everything! You men... with all your boasting about *my* house, *my* money, and *my* wife, and *my* children! My! My! My! I suppose you think you own the air you breathe.

CARLOS. Send her to Parliament.

AGUSTIN. Bravo... bravo!

MARIANITO. Three cheers for Lu — lu — lu!

[At this point RICARDITO, who is playing by himself at dogs or bears or something, makes a playful snap at CLARITA's ankles.]

CLARITA [calling out]. Aie! Aie!

DOÑA T. What's the matter?

CLARITA. Does this Ricardito of yours think my ankles are meant for him to sharpen his teeth on?

RICARDITO. Ankles! Ankles!

CLARITA. I'll teach you... you little wretch!

[She boxes his ears and he yells as if he were being flayed alive.]

DOÑA T. Now what are you doing to the poor little thing? Come here. There, don't cry, my pet... don't cry.

[RAMON comes in. He is accompanied by a dignified and very respectable gentleman.]

RAMON. Evening girls!

AMALIA. Hullo, Ramon! What have *you* come for?

RAMON. What do I usually come for? Have you anything new to suggest?

CLARITA. Well, your father's the city governor, isn't he? Why aren't you helping him?

RAMON. He can shoot down the mob without my help... or any one else's. I'm not going to dirty my hands with the job.

DOÑA T. That's right. But is it true that they've set three or four churches on fire?

RAMON. Yes... and five or six convents as well. You can see one burning from the corner there.

[There's a rush for the window.]

LULU. Oh, let's see!

AMALIA. Let's see!

ANA MARIA. Then it's true. [As she runs she tumbles over the dignified gentleman, who is standing there without saying a word.] I beg your pardon!

THE GENTLEMAN. Don't mention it, Señorita.

ANA MARIA [to RAMON]. Who's your silent friend?

RAMON. Oh, I was forgetting! Come along, my dear fellow. Doña Tomasa... let me have the honour of presenting a friend of mine... a gentleman of position... and some wealth.

Doña T. Most welcome, I'm sure. If you're a friend of Ramon's that's all the credit you need here.

Ramon. Don't give him credit. Get all the cash out of him you can, and you'll be doing him a good turn. He makes money out of army contracts. And look at him, girls! Forty-five... been a widower three months... and never made love to a woman yet... except his poor dear wife!

[*Everybody roars with laughter at this excellent joke.*]

The Gentleman. Please don't take him seriously... he must have his joke. It's quite true that lately I had the misfortune to lose my wife... a most charming woman... But it doesn't follow...

Ana Maria. Never mind! Most men call themselves widowers when they come here. We don't contradict them.

[*Lulu is still at the window.*]

Lulu. Aie!

Doña T. What's the matter?

Ana Maria. It's the revolution... lots of them... marching.

Lulu. The mob!

Clarita. Aren't they quiet!

Amalia. That's what's so frightening.

Ana Maria. Look at the petrol tins. Where are they taking them?

Doña T. Don't open the window now.

Ana Maria. Don't talk... you don't want them to hear us.

Clarita. Pull down the blind.

Amalia. I know... they're going to that convent!... No, they're not... it's to the Orphanage... you know... the Little Sisters of the Poor.

Clarita. Oh, no! — Why, that's where I was brought up! [*At this the men laugh loudly.*] What's there to laugh at in that, pray?

Ramon. The Sisters must think you do them credit!

Clarita. Oh, it wasn't their fault that I... nor for want of being preached to, I can tell you. Sister Andrea! I can hear her now. "Girls, remember that whoever breaks the sixth commandment commits mortal sin... mortal sin!" Well, we were all taught to say the same prayers, weren't we... and they're the same sins we go

committing... so we'll get the same punishment, too, I should hope.

Agustin. Very well said, my dear... and I'm glad to find that my lectures upon repentance and atonement have not been wasted on you.

Carlos. The Bishop himself couldn't be more orthodox.

Clarita. You're a nice one to talk, aren't you! If whacking could have done it, you'd have grown up good enough. Who was sent for three years to a reform school? Well, they lectured me and they whacked you... and here we both are!

Carlos. And who taught me to sin if you didn't? Shame on you!

Clarita. Yes... and I once taught an eel to swim! Oh, it's all chance what you turn into... it depends on the star that you're born under.

The Dancer [*who has been silent till now, suddenly breaking out prophetically*]. That's God's truth.

Agustin. You've found your tongue, have you?

Marianito. High time, too!

The Dancer. Clarita's right. It's written in the stars... and on the palm of your hand. Look what's going on to-night! That was all written up there as plain as if it had been printed in the Bible. And there's dreadful things will happen yet... because there's fire and blood in the stars.

Marianito. Blood and fire!

Carlos. War and destruction!

Agustin. Your eyes are sending out sparks!

Ramon. What a Fury!

Marianito. Come along now... let's have some fortune-telling.

The Dancer. Oh, you don't believe in anything! All right... you'll see! What I say *will* come true... because it can't help it... when the time comes. And I dare say the whole lot of us'll be massacred to-night.

Carlos. Pessimist!

Agustin. What has come to you all this evening, my darlings?

Lulu. What a question! What's come to every one with a little blood in their veins... instead of half-melted ice... like yours!

CARLOS. But what is it you want us to *do*?

LULU. Holy Mother! Here are men shouting in the streets, and men shooting at them. Something's the matter, I suppose. Some of them are burning convents and the rest are after them with machine guns. And the rich say the poor are scoundrels, and the poor say the rich are thieves. And what *I* say is that one side or the other must be right. Well, go along and find out which, and fight for it when you do.

MARIANITO. Certainly not. I should either get hit... or end up swinging to a lamp-post.

AMALIA. Oh, of course!... you *must* take care of yourself, mustn't you?

ANA MARIA. Indeed he must! What would his country do without him! When he gets married his father-in-law's going to get him a government job worth ever so much a year.

CLARITA. Never you mind them! Peace and a quiet life... that's the thing. They're all neurotic... that's what's the matter with them. And small wonder!... Lulu with her little whiffs of dope!

LULU. Well, I'm not going to take it your way... sticking your arm full of needles ever since you were eighteen.

ANA MARIA. Her first young man was in the custom house... and it reminds her of him.

CLARITA [*furious because she can just see she is being made fun of*]. I like that! How dare you?

AGUSTIN. Ladies... ladies! Gently... gently! [*To* CLARITA.] I beg you to preserve that perfect and Olympian repose.

THE DANCER [*again breaking out*]. Well ... what I say is that it's high time the new gentleman ordered something to drink.

THE GENTLEMAN. With the greatest pleasure! Please say what...

AMALIA. Yes... if he's been on his best behaviour for forty-five years... it's about time he let himself go a bit.

LULU [*with sudden resolution*]. I'm going out!

AMALIA. What on earth for?

LULU. To see what's happening. Who's coming with me?

DOÑA T. Nobody, I hope. I hope nobody will be such a fool. Have you taken leave of your senses? At this hour of the night... and dressed like that! Don't you know the dangers a woman runs in the streets at a time of this sort?

LULU. Thank you! I think I can guess them. Well... Who's coming?

AGUSTIN. I will.

LULU [*mockingly*]. You won't run away?

AGUSTIN. How much do you value your life? Halve it... and that's how much I value mine.

LULU. I like you. You're almost a man sometimes.

AGUSTIN. No need to remind me of it, my dear... when it's just what I'm trying to forget.

DOÑA T. [*horrified as she sees them move to the door*]. Now where are you going... you two? Will you please tell me where you are going?

AGUSTIN. To bare our breasts to the bullets... as the song says.

LULU. Oh, we'll have no luck that way! When our time comes it'll be apoplexy... or smallpox... or a tile falling off a roof!

AGUSTIN. Come along [*as she takes his arm*]. Why, any one would take you for my wife.

LULU. Don't be foolish! [*They go out.*]

CARLOS. They do play-act, those two.

CLARITA. Yes, indeed! Who's she to go on like a fallen angel?

MARIANITO. And who's he to give himself the airs of a lost soul? Can they either of them tell us anything we don't know?

AMALIA. I wish I were in love with some one... all the same!

RAMON. Here am I!

AMALIA. No... some one quite new!

RAMON [*to the strange* GENTLEMAN]. Step forward, my friend... step forward!

THE GENTLEMAN. Ah... but I know what this young lady means. Love is a most inexplicable thing. Two people meet ... by mere chance, we say. No... there's the finger of fate in it. Or... as this other young lady was saying... it may even be the influence of the stars.

[*There is an outcry against these romantic ideas which much astonishes the* RESPECTABLE GENTLEMAN. *The other men chorus "Put him out! Put him out!" And little* RICARDITO *takes advantage of the confusion and excitement to crawl round on all fours barking like a dog. Then he bites* ANA MARIA *in the arm.*]

ANA MARIA. Ow!! You little brute! You little savage! Take that!

[*She slaps him hard.*]

RICARDITO [*weeping*]. Aie... aie... aie!

DOÑA T. Oh, you're always upsetting the child. Come here, my pet. Don't you know the poor little thing can't help himself...

[*As she pets* RICARDITO *and tries to console him, a noise is heard in the street.*]

CLARITA [*at the window*]. Oh!

DOÑA T. What is it *now*?

CLARITA. They're on their way back.

AMALIA. They've got torches now.

ANA MARIA. See the people running!

[*Every one crowds anxiously to the window. And from the street the rioters can very plainly be heard; voices, the noise of a crowd running, some shots even. "Death to the Bourgeois! Death! The Cowards!!" As the sounds float up the women are terribly frightened.*]

DOÑA T. Shut that window... shut that window!

[AMALIA *puts her arm out to pull it to.*]

RAMON. Don't do that... you'll get a bullet through you.

CLARITA [*in terror*]. Aie!

THE DANCER. Aie... Holy Mother of Carmen!

ANA MARIA. Better get some mattresses to barricade the windows.

MARIANITO. Yes, lie low till to-morrow. That's my advice.

DOÑA T. There won't be any to-morrow ... it's my belief!

[*And, indeed, all the time the noise is growing louder.*]

CLARITA. Aie!!

EVERYBODY. What is it?

CLARITA. They're coming... they're coming up here!

AMALIA. How?

CLARITA. Up the stairs of course. How else should they come!

RAMON [*at the door*]. Yes.... I do hear steps.

DOÑA T. Sh!... don't make a noise.

AMALIA. Better put out the lights.

DOÑA T. AND RAMON. No!

[*There's a moment of suspense and then the bell rings, and everybody gives a smothered exclamation. After a moment the bell rings again. Then* AMALIA *starts for the door.*]

ANA MARIA [*in terror*]. Where are you going?

AMALIA. To see who it is. [*Every one protests against this.*] All right... only a peep... through the little window....

[*She goes out.*]

DOÑA T. Don't open the door now....

[*There is silence again for a moment. Then* AMALIA *is heard to give a little smothered cry of surprise. Every one in the room is alarmed.*]

MARIANITO. She *has* opened the door!

DOÑA T. Is she out of her senses?...

[SISTER TERESA *in her nun's dress appears in the doorway. She looks frightened, and the lights in the room dazzle her rather. But she controls herself and smiles.*]

SISTER T. [*greeting them*]. "Ave Maria Purissima."

[*Everybody exclaims in various tones "A NUN!" Only* THE DANCER *has the presence of mind to reply...*]

THE DANCER. "Concepta sine peccatoribus."

AMALIA. Come in, Sister, do.

SISTER T. Please forgive me, ladies and gentlemen. I rang the bell.... I took the liberty to... really I must apologise... but hoping you'd be good enough to let me in. For I didn't quite know where I was... and I thought they were running after me... so I hid in the doorway. Then I came up. I didn't mean to ring... at this time of night... but I thought I heard some one after me... so... [*She looks fear-*

fully at the door for a moment, then smiles again.] Forgive me... please.

CARLOS. Come in... please come in, Señora.

SISTER T. Thank you very much.

ANA MARIA. Poor woman... she's shaking like a...

AMALIA. Won't you sit down please, Sister?

SISTER T. No, no. Thank you very much.

MARIANITO [*with rather coarse familiarity*]. Like a little bird dropped out of the nest, isn't she?

RAMON. She's got eyes worth looking at.

ANA MARIA. Hold your tongue.

AMALIA. Please do sit down, Sister, and rest.

DOÑA T. No need to be frightened. You can feel quite at home here. Well... that is...!

SISTER T. God reward you, Señora. It is most kind of you. I didn't know which way to turn.

CLARITA. Have they burnt your convent?

SISTER T. Yes, Señora, they have... but they let us all go first. Still, we were in a great fright... because of the shouting... and the flames, you know. For they all rushed in...! We came away... but we weren't used to the streets, and we didn't know where we were. The boy that runs errands came with us. We tried to keep together... in our proper order. But suddenly, at a corner... in the crowd... I can't think how... I found I was alone. We'd already been to two or three people that do befriend our community, to see if they'd take us in. But of course they couldn't run the risk of it on a night like this, could they? And I did begin to get a little frightened myself when I found myself among all those shouting men again.

CARLOS. Cheer up... they won't think of looking for you *here*!

SISTER T. No... they said I was no use to them. [*Most of the others laugh at this; she laughs too, very innocently.*] Oh, dear... but my head's swimming!

DOÑA T. Sit down, then.

AMALIA. It's the bright lights, I dare say.

ANA MARIA. Aie... she's going to faint.

THE DANCER. Poor little thing!

CLARITA. Give her some champagne.

CARLOS. Heavens... what next!

CLARITA. Well... there's nothing sinful in champagne. Now, Sister, do taste a little.

[*She drinks the champagne they give her, and little by little comes to herself, never losing her gentle smile.*]

SISTER T. It's all right. Please don't be alarmed. And thank you so much. God repay you for your goodness. But please don't put yourselves out for me. You must go right on with what you were doing when I came. And if, perhaps, you'd let me pass the rest of the night here....

RAMON [*stepping close to her*]. With pleasure... with all the pleasure in life.

AMALIA. Now then! [*And she pushes him away.*] Take no notice of him. He's not right in his head.

SISTER T. Oh... I'm so sorry.

RAMON. Thank you, Sister. You're the best little nun in the world... and pretty enough to eat!

SISTER T. But please don't say such things to me. [*She looks at them all and at the spread table.*] Are you celebrating a wedding? [*They all laugh at this.*]

MARIANITO. Well... in a manner of speaking, we're always celebrating weddings.

SISTER T. [*puzzled*]. I beg your pardon.

ANA MARIA. No, Señora, no... it's *not* a wedding. We're just enjoying ourselves... a few of us... a few friends...

SISTER T. Oh, I see. But it's so late... and you're all so gay... and you're dressed as if...

CARLOS. These are very fashionable and much sought after young ladies....

MARIANITO. And life is so short, you know, Sister, that one has to make the most of every minute of it.

RAMON. But lots of people stay awake all night, don't they?

SISTER T. I know. There are the people that haven't any homes, and sick people who can't sleep for pain... and sinners against God...

CARLOS. And I fear it is our melancholy privilege to be among the last.

[ANA MARIA *gives a loud stupid laugh.*]

SISTER T. What?

MARIANITO. Yes, Sister, yes... we look most respectable, don't we? But we're miserable sinners.

SISTER T. So are we all.

[*The men now begin to gather round her.*]

CARLOS. But we, you see, are specialists in sin....

RAMON. And very, very hardened!...

MARIANITO. God be thanked!...

RAMON. But not bad fellows, all the same.

MARIANITO. No, no, indeed!

CARLOS. Ready to risk damnation for a pair of black eyes... like yours!

RAMON. Yes... or salvation even!

MARIANITO. I could prove it to you....

CARLOS. No.... allow me....

RAMON. Why, she's prettier than a gipsy....

[SISTER TERESA *gets back as they crowd nearer and cries out in deep distress*]

SISTER T. Oh God! God help me... leave me alone... let me be!

[THE DANCER *dashes to her side and faces them.*]

THE DANCER. Stop this! Keep away from her. Haven't you any shame? You beasts!

CARLOS. Here...what's it to do with you?

MARIANITO. Mind your own business!

[AMALIA *dashes to the rescue, too.*]

AMALIA. Stop it... you blackguards!

SISTER T. Let me get away. Let me out... out of here. I'll go out into the streets again.

DOÑA T. No, no... you can't do that. Don't mind them, Señora... this is my house... and you're quite safe in it. I'll answer for that.

SISTER T. But what sort of a place am I in? Oh... How was I to guess that you... that you were...

ANA MARIA. Well, we are, Señora... and

that's the fact. But I'm sure you need never have found it out... if the good God hadn't made men what they are! And you are rather pretty, you know....

SISTER T. Oh... hush... please!

ANA MARIA. Well, *they* thought so, anyhow. Oh, bless your heart, never mind... any new face gets them... that's what they're like. Don't be afraid. They shan't put a finger on you. We'll stand by you.

AMALIA. We're here.

THE DANCER. You trust to me.

[*They surround her.*]

THE GENTLEMAN. You can trust to me also, Señora, if you will allow me to say so.

SISTER T. Thank you... thank you... you're very kind, but I'd rather go.

DOÑA T. You can't go out with the streets like this.

SISTER T. I know... I know! But...

THE DANCER. But it's worse here... that's what she means.

[*A little forlornly, the women move away from her.*]

SISTER T. Oh no, indeed I didn't. Please, please don't be hurt.

CARLOS [*as he comes a step nearer, a little ashamed*]. Look here, Señora... we're not quite so bad as all that either.... It was only a joke. I'm sorry. It was blackguardly of us. Please forgive us.

SISTER T. No, really, there's nothing to forgive! It's for me to apologise...! Thank you very much... for all your kindness. Good-bye.

[SISTER TERESA *is going, and no one ventures to stop her. But as she gets to the door* AGUSTIN *and* LULU *come back.* LULU *has a wound in her forehead, and it is roughly bound with a handkerchief.* AGUSTIN *is supporting her... for she can hardly walk. There is consternation at the sight.*]

AMALIA. Oh... what's the matter?

CLARITA. Lulu!... Oh, Agustin!

DOÑA T. She's been wounded? Now... didn't I warn you....

AGUSTIN [*to* LULU]. All right now... we're safe home again.

[*But at this moment* LULU *faints, and*

AGUSTIN *nearly drops her; but* SISTER TERESA *catches her from him in the deftest way. The rest of the company lose their heads completely.*]

DOÑA T. What is it? God bless my soul... what a dreadful thing to happen!

CLARITA. Lulu! Lulu!!

[SISTER TERESA, *helped by* AGUSTIN *and* CARLOS, *lays* LULU *on the sofa.*]

SISTER T. There... there... don't be frightened! She has only fainted... with the shock... and the loss of blood. Yes, poor young lady... she does look pale... but there's nothing to be frightened about. [AMALIA *is trying to lift her.*] No, let her be... you should never lift people up when they've fainted. [*To* CARLOS.] Bring me the light. [CARLOS *obeys like a child. Then* SISTER TERESA *takes off the bandage.*] Dear me! [*The women all exclaim in horror when they see the blood.*] Now, we want a little cold water... some lint and a bandage. [DOÑA TOMASA *and one of the women go in search.*] And scissors to cut her hair.

CLARITA [*most alarmed*]. To cut her hair!

SISTER T. Of course... so that we can see where the wound is. [*Then to* ANA MARIA.] And a little vinegar, too. [ANA MARIA *obediently departs for the vinegar, while the little nun swiftly cuts the matted hair from* LULU'S *forehead. Then she skilfully washes out the wound.*] There... it's nothing at all, you see. The blood made it look much worse than it was. It's only a scratch... from a stone, wasn't it?

AGUSTIN. Yes... I think so.

SISTER T. She's coming round. It won't need a stitch... if you've a piece of plaster.

MARIANITO. I have some, Señora.

[*He takes out a little pocket case of it.*]

SISTER T. [*as she moistens and sticks it on*]. There... that's right... no bandage wanted even. [LULU *comes to herself.*]

LULU. Oh... what is it...?

SISTER T. Nothing to be alarmed about....

LULU [*who is amazed at the sight of a nun here*]. Oh... who are you?

SISTER T. Nobody in particular....

LULU. But... where am I?

DOÑA T. You're at home, girl. Where else should you be?

LULU. Oh... you're all here! Yes... I remember! [*To* AGUSTIN.] What *did* happen to us?

AGUSTIN. Just what I knew would happen. You got your head cut open in the crowd... and this lady's been dressing the wound for you.

LULU. A wound! Oh... will it show?

SISTER T. No, I don't think so, Señora... it comes under the hair really. We had to cut off a piece... but that'll soon grow again.

RAMON. Don't worry... your beauty's not been spoilt.

LULU [*to* SISTER TERESA]. Thank you, Señora, I'm sure. Oh... but I was frightened! Such a yelling! They're like so many devils let loose. But it did you good to hear them all the same... made you want to climb up on something... and cheer... and tell them they were in the right. Because they are! [*To* SISTER TERESA.] They are, aren't they, Señora?

SISTER T. Only God knows that.

LULU. Well, I say they are! There oughtn't to be any poor in the world... nor rich neither. And everybody ought to be happy... and equal! Have they come along by here yet... where d'you suppose they...? [*She has tried to sit up, but she falls back again half fainting.*] Oh, I say... my head!

DOÑA T. What you've got to do is to go straight to bed... and stop making speeches.

SISTER T. Yes... put her to bed and give her something soothing. Orange-flower water will do. She has had quite a shock.

AMALIA. Come along then....

ANA MARIA. Come on, Lulu....

DOÑA T. Yes... you get a little sleep....

[*Between them* DOÑA TOMASA *and* AMALIA *get her out of the room, and the little nun is instinctively following them; but she stops and gives a startled cry... because* RICARDITO *who has been crawling round as usual on all fours, tries to bite her.*]

SISTER T. Oh... God bless us!

RICARDITO. He... he... he... you'll taste good! [*The men all laugh.*]

SISTER T. What... who is it?

CLARITA. Oh, don't be frightened, Sister. He's just a looney... that's all.

SISTER T. [*compassionately*]. Oh!

RICARDITO. I'm not... I'm not. Say that again if you dare!

SISTER T. No, no... poor little fellow! He mustn't be called names.

RICARDITO. But she's a... I'll tell you! She's a... she's a... [*He whispers the word to* SISTER TERESA.] Yes... that's what she is!

SISTER T. [*with gentle authority*]. Be quiet now.

RICARDITO. And a dirty slut, what's more!

CLARITA [*making for him*]. You little...

SISTER T. Come now... now come! You're not going to be angry with a poor little creature like this. [*Then to* RICARDITO.] And you be silent, please. I don't like children that talk too much.

RICARDITO. I'm not a child... I'm a man.

SISTER T. All the more reason, then, for you to behave properly... and not be rude to people.

RICARDITO. But she hates me, she does!

SISTER T. What has that to do with it? Do you think everybody in the world is going to love you?

RICARDITO. Nobody loves me!
[*He begins to cry like a baby.*]

SISTER T. Nonsense! I love you.

RICARDITO [*staring at her*]. How can you? You don't know me.

SISTER T. No... but where I live we have lots of boys like you.

RICARDITO. Where you live...

SISTER T. Yes... in a great big house... that's so bright and clean... and there are other boys there like you. When they're good we love them very much... and we give them such nice things... you wait and see! Do you like chocolate? They have chocolate. Why... I wonder if I haven't a piece with me now. [*She searches her bag.*] Yes... here's a caramel. See what luck you have. Now... you be quite good till to-morrow... and then you shall come home

with me, and we'll make you well. Your head hurts you sometimes, doesn't it?

RICARDITO. Yes... it does!

SISTER T. And that's why you say silly things, isn't it? Never mind. We'll make you well again... and teach you to be a good boy... and to read... and say your prayers... and you'll be taught a trade too... so that you can grow up a useful man and earn your living. There... what do you say to that?

RICARDITO. More chocolate.

SISTER T. Poor soul! You must run away to bed now, though. It's high time.

RICARDITO. You'll take me back with you... truly?

SISTER T. I promise... so now run along.

RICARDITO. All right.
[*He starts obediently to shuffle from the room.*]

SISTER T. But say good-night first.

RICARDITO. Good-night... what's your name?

SISTER T. Sister Teresa.

RICARDITO. Good-night, Sister Teresa.

SISTER T. And to these ladies and gentlemen as well.

RICARDITO. Good-night, ladies and gentlemen.

SISTER T. That's right. Now you may go. [RICARDITO *goes out.*]

AGUSTIN. Well... you've tamed him, Sister.

SISTER T. Poor little thing! Has he always been like that?
[DOÑA TOMASA *comes back, very much in a fluster.*]

DOÑA T. Good heavens... that Lulu's going clean off her head. I suppose it's delirium... I don't know! She's trying to jump out of bed and she's shouting out the most awful things. You must go for a doctor... one of you.

MARIANITO. What... with the streets in this state...?

RAMON. Thank you!

DOÑA T. Well... I'm not going to sit there all night with her like that. I tell you... she scares me.

MARIANITO. Oh, she has only worked herself up a bit more than usual. It's nothing.

Doña T. The devil's got hold of her... that's what I think. Why... the two girls there and Amalia... all three of them can't hold her down.

Sister T. I dare say she has a little fever... from the blow. If you'll allow me... I'll go and see.

Doña T. Oh... are you a nurse?

Sister T. Not a real nurse, I'm afraid... but they put me on hospital duty in the Orphanage sometimes.

Doña T. God reward you, Señora.... God reward you! God sent you to us, I think. It's an ill wind that blows nobody good, isn't it? Yes... do come.

Sister T. Good-night, gentlemen. God give you a good night.

[*They all bow and make way as she goes.* Doña Tomasa *follows her.*]

Clarita. What a blessed innocent!

Carlos. She's got pluck.

Ramon. For all she pretends to be so meek.

Agustin. She's pretty enough... that's no pretence anyhow.

Carlos. I say... when she drops her eyes... suddenly! Oh... I say!!

Marianito. I always thought there were no nuns but ugly nuns. Something to be said for raiding a convent after all!

[Doña Tomasa *comes back with* Amalia.]

The Men. Well... how are things now?

Doña T. Why... why... she's got the touch of a Saint! I don't know how she does it... but she got the girl quiet... like that! And she's given her a drop or two of some sort of medicine she has. And now she's there by her bed... she's got out her prayer-book... and she says that she's going to sit up all night with her!

The Dancer [*impetuously*]. So am I, then!... I'll sit up, too. [*She flings out.*]

Ramon. And where are *you* off to, pray?

Ana Maria. I'm going to sit up as well.

Amalia. Yes... so am I!

Ramon. Here... here... here! The whole regiment of you can't run away!

Ana Maria. Can't it!

Agustin. But will you please consider that if you all take to good works like this,

my poor friend here will depart... from his first visit, too ... sadly disillusioned.

The Gentleman. No... on the contrary, I assure you. I am most gratified to discover that even among those that are thought by the ... thoughtless... to be lost... that is to say... lost to ordinary decency... forgive me, the phrase is not meant in any way to be offensive... I am most gratified to find such... delicate sensibilities in operation. It is an inspiring sight. It has moved me... and elevated me... very deeply... I should say highly. I congratulate you all, young ladies, upon the solicitude which you exhibit for this unfortunate... that is to say, your unfortunate ... your unlucky companion. [*Then to* Doña Tomasa.] Señora... I am most pleased to have made your acquaintance.

Doña T. [*hardly knowing whether to laugh or not; indeed a little frightened at these fine flourishes*]. Oh, the pleasure's mine, I'm sure. But you'll come again, won't you?

The Gentleman. I shall not fail to, Señora. Another time, then... another time.

Marianito. But what about that champagne?

The Gentleman. Another time... another... until when...
[*He bows himself out.*]

Ana Maria. Good-night, you boys.

Amalia. See you to-morrow... God willing.

Ramon. Look here... are you really... seriously...?

Amalia. Yes... I am. Sleep well!

Ana Maria. And don't get run over by the fire-engines!
[*The two go out.* Clarita *is lying on the sofa.*]

Clarita. That's a silly way to go on! But I don't know.... I believe they're right. Get out, all of you. There's nothing doing.

Agustin. *Et tu Brute?*

Clarita. What? Oh well.... I wouldn't mind myself. But it wouldn't be very nice, would it, with a nun in the house. I mean it wouldn't be right. Come to think of it, the whole thing's not right. It's wrong. Besides, who's to know what you'll be after once the devil gets hold of you. You'll want to start nursing her yourself... and have the Sister show you how! And I'll be damned if you play any more tricks with *her*.

AGUSTIN. I say, we're coming in for a lot of eloquence to-night! Did you think all that out yourself? How does it feel to be such an orator?

CLARITA. I don't know. I know how it feels to be sleepy.

[*She turns over on the sofa with her face to the wall.*]

CARLOS. Doña Tomasa... d'you mean to let all these pretty ladies go on strike?

DOÑA T. I can't stop them. Revolution's in the air, I think. And I suppose they've caught it. They'll be all right again to-morrow.

CARLOS. We must wait till to-morrow, then.

MARIANITO. It looks like it.

AGUSTIN. My respects to Sister Teresa.

RAMON [*to the unresponsive* CLARITA]. Good-bye.

DOÑA T. Get along... get along now — keeping all my lights going for nothing!

[*They are gone, and she puts out all the lights but one. Then she goes to the sofa.*]

DOÑA T. Look at her... snoring already! [*Shaking the girl.*] Go to bed! Get up and go to bed, lazy bones!

[*Then she goes to the door at the back and listens. The sound of women's voices praying can be heard.*]

DOÑA T. Good God... if they're not all telling their beads there with that nun! Poor girls! But that's what I always say! No matter what you do... or what you come to... there's religion! That is, if you're a woman and brought up in the fear of God... thank God... and not one of these shameless brutes of men! I pity the Devil, I do, when he gets hold of *them*...!

[*She crosses herself devoutly and goes out.*]

HE WHO GETS SLAPPED
A PLAY IN FOUR ACTS
By LEONID ANDREYEV

Translated from the Russian by GREGORY ZILBOORG

CAST OF CHARACTERS

CONSUELO, *a bareback rider in a circus.   Billed as "The Bareback Tango Queen"*

MANCINI, *Consuelo's father*

HE, *a clown in Briquet's circus.   Billed as "HE, The One Who Gets Slapped"*

BRIQUET, *manager of the circus*

ZINIDA, *a lion tamer, Briquet's wife*

ALFRED BEZANO, *a bareback rider*

A GENTLEMAN

BARON REGNARD

JACKSON, *a clown*

TILLY ⎫
POLLY ⎭ *musical clowns*

THOMAS, ANGELICA, *and other actors and actresses of Briquet's circus*

The action takes place in one of the large cities of France.

HE WHO GETS SLAPPED

ACT I

A very large, rather dirty room, with white-washed walls. To the left, in a niche, is a window, the only outside window in the room, opening on a court-yard. The light from it is so dim that even by day the electricity has to be turned on.

At the very top of the centre-back wall is a row of small dusty windows. They open on the circus hall. At night, when the performance is going on, a bright light shines through. By day they are dark. In the same wall is a large white door, reached by two stone steps, and nailed fast.

On the right, almost in the corner, is a high, wide, arched doorway which leads to the stables and the ring. By day it opens into pale darkness, at night into pale light.

The room is used for many purposes. It is the office of PAPA BRIQUET, manager of the circus; here he keeps his little desk. It is the cloak-room of some of the actors. It is also the room where the cast gathers between calls, during rehearsals or performances. Again, it is a check-room for used circus property, such as gilt armchairs, scenery for pantomimes, and other wares of the circus household. The walls are covered with circus announcements and glaring posters.

The time is morning. In the circus hall a rehearsal is going on, and preparations are being made for the evening performance. As the curtain goes up, the cracking whip and the shouts of the riding-master are heard from the ring. The stage is empty for a few seconds, then enter TILLY and POLLY, the musical clowns, practising a new march. Playing on tiny pipes, they step from the dark doorway to the window. Their music is agreeable to the ear, but small, mincing, artificially clown-like, like their mincing steps; they wear jackets and resemble each other; same smooth-shaven face, same height; TILLY, the younger, has a scarf around his neck; both have their derbies on the backs of their heads.

TILLY glances through the window, then they turn about, still marching.

POLLY [*interrupting the march*]. Stop, you're out again! Now, listen —— [*He stands close to TILLY and plays into his face. TILLY absent-mindedly listens, scratching his nose.*] There! Come on, now!

[They resume their music and marching. As they reach the door they meet the manager and MANCINI; the latter walks behind the manager, and is gnawing at the knob of his gold-mounted cane. COUNT MANCINI is tall and slight. The seams of his clothes are worn and he keeps his coat buttoned tight. He assumes extremely graceful manners, takes affected poses, and has a special fondness for toying with his cane, with aristocratic stylishness. When he laughs, which happens often, his thin sharp face takes on a marked resemblance to a satyr. The manager, "PAPA" BRIQUET, is a stout quiet man of average height. His bearing is hesitant. The clowns make room for the gentlemen. The manager looks questioningly at the old man.]

POLLY [*with an affected accent*]. Our moosic for the pantomime! The March of the Ants!

BRIQUET. Ha! Yes!

[The gentlemen walk in. The clowns resume their music, POLLY marching on, then turning, the younger following.]

POLLY. Papa Briquet, Jack is working very badly to-day.

BRIQUET. What's the matter with him?

POLLY. He has a sore throat. You'd better take a look at him.

BRIQUET. All right. Come on, Jack. Open your mouth! Wider — wider. [*Turns clown's face to the light near the window and examines him closely and seriously.*] Just smear it with iodine.

POLLY. I told him so. I said it was nothing! Oh! Come on.

[*They go away playing, marching, practising their funny mincing steps. The manager sits down.* MANCINI *strikes a pose by the wall, smiling ironically.*]

MANCINI. So. You give them medical treatment, too! Look out, Papa Briquet, you have no licence.

BRIQUET. Just a little advice. They're all so afraid for their lives.

MANCINI. His throat is simply burnt with whiskey. These two fellows get drunk every night. I am amazed, Papa Briquet, to see you pay so little attention to their morals. [*He laughs.*]

BRIQUET. You make me sick, Mancini.

MANCINI. Count Mancini, at your service!

BRIQUET. You make me sick, Count Mancini. You poke your nose into everything, you disturb the artists in their work. Some day you'll get a thrashing, and I warn you that I shan't interfere.

MANCINI. As a man of superior associations and education I cannot be expected to treat your actors as my equals! What more can you ask, Briquet? You see that I do you the honour of speaking with you quite familiarly, quite simply.

BRIQUET. Ha! ha! ha! [*Slightly threatening.*] Really! —

MANCINI. Never mind my joke. What if they did dare attack me — ever seen this, Briquet? [*He draws a stiletto out of his cane and advances it silently.*] Useful little thing. By the way, you have no idea of the discovery I made yesterday in a suburb. Such a girl! [*Laughs.*] Oh, well! all right, all right — I know you don't like that sort of sport. But look here, you must give me a hundred francs!

BRIQUET. Not a sou.

MANCINI. Then I'll take away Consuelo — that's all —

BRIQUET. Your daily threat!

MANCINI. Yes, my threat! And you would do the same, if you were as shamefully hard up as I am. Now look here, you

know as well as I do that I have to live up to my name somehow, keep up the family reputation. Just because the tide of ill-fortune which struck my ancestors compelled me to make my daughter, the Countess Veronica, a bareback rider — to keep us from starving — do you understand — you heartless idiot!

BRIQUET. You chase the girls too much! Some day you'll land in jail, Mancini!

MANCINI. In jail? Oh, no! Why, I have to uphold our *name*, the splendour of my family, [*laughs*] haven't I? The Mancinis are known all over Italy for their love of girls — just girls! Is it my fault if I must pay such crazy prices for what my ancestors got free of charge? You're nothing but an ass, a *parvenu* ass. How can you understand Family Traditions? I don't drink — I stopped playing cards after that accident — no, you need not smile. Now if I give up the girls, what will be left of Mancini? Only a coat of arms, that's all — In the name of family traditions, give me a hundred francs!

BRIQUET. I told you no, I won't.

MANCINI. You know that I leave half of the salary for Consuelo — but — perhaps you think I do not love my child — my only daughter, all that remains to me as a memory of her sainted mother — what cruelty!

[*Pretends to cry, wipes his eyes with a small and dirty lace handkerchief, embroidered with a coronet.*]

BRIQUET. Why don't you say, rather, that she is foolish enough to give you half her salary. You make me sick ——

[*Enter* ZINIDA, *the lion tamer; burningly beautiful, her self-confident, commanding gestures at first glance give an impression of languor. She is* BRIQUET'S *unmarried wife.*]

ZINIDA [*to* MANCINI]. Good morning.

MANCINI. Madame Zinida! This barbarian, this brute may pierce me with his dagger, but I cannot control the expression of my love! [*Kneels facetiously before her.*] Madame! Count Mancini has the honour of asking you to be his wife....

ZINIDA [*to* BRIQUET]. Money?

BRIQUET. Yes.

ZINIDA. Don't give him any.

[*Sits down wearily on a torn sofa, shuts her eyes.* MANCINI *gets up and wipes his knees.*]

MANCINI. Duchess! Don't be cruel. I am no lion, no tiger, no savage beast which you are accustomed to tame. I am merely a poor domestic animal, who wants, miaow, miaow, a little green grass.

ZINIDA [*without opening her eyes*]. Jim tells me you have a teacher for Consuelo. What for?

MANCINI. The solicitude of a father, Duchess, the solicitude and the tireless anxiety of a loving heart. The extreme misfortunes of our family, when I was a child, have left some flaws in her education. Friends, the daughter of Count Mancini, Countess Veronica, can barely read! Is that admissible? And you, Briquet, heartless brute, you still ask why I need money!

ZINIDA. Artful!

BRIQUET. What are you teaching her?

MANCINI. Everything. A student had been giving her lessons, but I threw him out yesterday. He had the nerve to fall in love with Consuelo and stood there miaowing at the door like a cat. Everything, Briquet, that you don't know—literature, mythology, orthography——

[*Two young actresses appear, with small fur coats thrown over their light dresses. They are tired and sit down in the corner.*]

MANCINI. I do not wish my daughter——

ZINIDA. Artful!

BRIQUET. You are stupid, Mancini. What do you do it for? [*In a didactic tone.*] You are fearfully stupid, Mancini. Why does she need to learn? Since she is here she need never know anything about that life. Don't you understand? What is geography? If I were the government I would forbid artists to read books. Let them read the posters, that's enough.

[*During* BRIQUET'S *speech the two clowns and another actor enter. They sit down wearily.*]

BRIQUET. Right now, your Consuelo is

an excellent artist, but just as soon as you teach her mythology, and she begins to read, she'll become a nuisance, she'll be corrupted, and then she'll go and poison herself. I know those books, I've read 'em myself. All they teach is corruption, and how to kill oneself.

FIRST ACTRESS. I love the novels that come out in the newspaper.

BRIQUET. That shows what a foolish girl you are. You'll be done for in no time. Believe me, my friends, we must forget entirely what is happening out there. How can we understand all that goes on there?

MANCINI. You are an enemy of enlightenment, you are an obscurantist, Briquet.

BRIQUET. And you are stupid. You are from out there. What has it taught you? [*The actors laugh.*] If you'd been born in a circus as I was, you'd *know* something. Enlightenment is plain nonsense — nothing else. Ask Zinida. She knows everything they teach out there — geography, mythology—Does it make her any happier? You tell them, dear.

ZINIDA. Leave me alone, Louis.

MANCINI [*angrily*]. Oh! Go to the devil! When I listen to your asinine philosophy, I'd like to skin you for more than a paltry hundred francs — for two hundred — for a thousand. Great God! What an ass of a manager! Yes, right before every one of them I want to say that you are a stingy old skinflint — that you pay starvation wages. I'll make you give Consuelo a raise of a hundred francs. Listen, all you honest vagabonds, tell me — who is it draws the crowd that fills the circus every night? You? a couple of musical donkeys? Tigers, lions? Nobody cares for those hungry cats!

ZINIDA. Leave the tigers alone.

MANCINI. Beg your pardon, Zinida. I did not mean to hurt your feelings — honestly. I really marvel at your furious audacity — at your grace — you are a heroine — I kiss your tiny hands. But what do they understand about heroism? [*An orchestra softly plays the Tango in the circus. He continues with enthusiasm.*] Hear! hear! Now tell me, honest vagabonds, who but Consuelo and Bezano draws the crowds! That Tango, on horseback — it is — it is — Oh, the devil! Even his fatuousness the Pope could not withstand its lure.

POLLY. True! It's a great trick — wasn't the idea Bezano's?

MANCINI. Idea! Idea! The lad's in love, like a cat — that's the idea. What's the good of an idea without a woman! You wouldn't dance very far with your idea alone, eh, Papa Briquet?

BRIQUET. We have a contract.

MANCINI. Such base formalities.

ZINIDA. Give him ten francs and let him go.

MANCINI. Ten! Never! *Fifteen!* Don't be stubborn, Papa. For the traditions of my house — twenty. I swear — on my honour — I can't do with less. [BRIQUET *hands him twenty francs. Nonchalantly.*] *Merci.* Thanks.

ZINIDA. Why don't you take it from your baron?

MANCINI [*raising his eyebrows haughtily, quite indignant*]. From the Baron? Woman! who do you think I am that I should be beholden to a stranger?

ZINIDA. You're plotting something artful. I know you very little, but I guess you're an awful scoundrel.

MANCINI [*laughs*]. Such an insult from such beautiful lips.

[*Enter an "artist," apparently an athlete.*]

ATHLETE. Papa Briquet, there's a gentleman from beyond the grave asking for you.

ACTRESS. A ghost?

ATHLETE. No. He seems alive. Did you ever see a drunken ghost?

BRIQUET. If he's drunk, tell him I'm out, Thomas. Does he want to see me or the Count?

ATHLETE. No, you. Maybe he's not drunk, but just a ghost.

MANCINI [*draws himself together, puffs up*]. A society man?

ATHLETE. Yes. I'll tell him to come in.

[*One hears the whip cracking in the ring. The Tango sounds very low and*

distant — then comes nearer — louder. *Silence.*]

BRIQUET [*touching* ZINIDA'S *arm*]. Tired?

ZINIDA [*drawing back a little*]. No.

POLLY. Your red lion is nervous to-day, Zinida!

ZINIDA. You shouldn't tease him.

POLLY. I played a melody from Traviata for him. And he sang with me. Wouldn't that be a good trick to stage, Papa Briquet?

[THOMAS *brings in the* GENTLEMAN, *points out the manager, and goes heavily away. The* GENTLEMAN *is not young, and he is ugly, but his rather strange face is bold and lively. He wears an expensive overcoat, with a fur collar, and holds his hat and gloves in his hand.*]

GENTLEMAN [*bowing and smiling*]. Have I the pleasure of addressing the manager?

BRIQUET. Yes. Won't you sit down, please? Tilly, bring a chair.

GENTLEMAN. Oh! Don't trouble. [*Looks around.*] These are your artists? Very glad ——

MANCINI [*straightening and bowing slightly*]. Count Mancini.

GENTLEMAN [*surprised*]. Count?

BRIQUET [*indefinitely*]. Yes, Count. And whom have I the honour of ——

GENTLEMAN. I don't quite know myself — yet. As a rule you choose your own names, don't you? I have not chosen yet. Later you might advise me about it. I have an idea already, but I am afraid it sounds too much like literature — you know.

BRIQUET. Literature?

GENTLEMAN. Yes! Too sophisticated. [*They all look surprised.*] I presume these two gentlemen are clowns? I am so glad. May I shake hands with them?

[*Stands up and shakes hands with clowns, who make silly faces.*]

BRIQUET. Excuse me — but what can I do for you?

GENTLEMAN [*with the same pleasant, confident smile*]. Oh. You do something for me? No. I want to do something for you, Papa Briquet.

BRIQUET. *Papa* Briquet? But you don't look like...

GENTLEMAN [*reassuringly*]. It's all right. I shall become "like." These two gentlemen just made remarkable faces. Would you like to see me imitate them? Look!

[*He makes the same silly faces as the clowns.*]

BRIQUET. Yes! [*Involuntarily.*] You are not drunk, sir?

GENTLEMAN. No. I don't drink as a rule. Do I look drunk?

POLLY. A little.

GENTLEMAN. No — I don't drink. It is a peculiarity of my talent.

BRIQUET [*familiarly*]. Where did you work before? Juggler?

GENTLEMAN. No. But I am glad you feel in me a comrade, Papa Briquet. Unfortunately I am not a juggler, and have worked nowhere — I am — just so.

MANCINI. But you look like a society man.

GENTLEMAN. Oh, you flatter me, Count. I am just so.

BRIQUET. Well, what do you want? You see I am obliged to tell you that everything is taken.

GENTLEMAN. That's immaterial. I want to be a clown, if you will allow me.

[*Some of the actors smile,* BRIQUET *begins to grow angry.*]

BRIQUET. But what can you do? You're asking too much. What can you do?

GENTLEMAN. Why! Nothing! Isn't that funny! I can't do a thing.

BRIQUET. No, it's not funny. Any scoundrel knows that much.

GENTLEMAN [*rather helpless, but still smiling and looking around*]. We can invent something ——

BRIQUET [*ironically*]. From literature?

[*The clown* JACKSON *enters slowly without being noticed by the others. He stands behind the* GENTLEMAN.]

GENTLEMAN. Yes, one can find something literary, too. A nice little speech for instance on, let's say, a religious topic. Something like a debate among the clowns.

BRIQUET. A debate! The devil! This is no academy.

GENTLEMAN [*sadly*]. I am very sorry. Something else, then. Perhaps a joke about the creation of the world and its rulers?

BRIQUET. What about the police? No, no — nothing like that!

JACKSON [*coming forward*]. The rulers of the world? You don't like them? I don't either. Shake.

BRIQUET [*introducing*]. Our chief clown, the famous Jackson.

GENTLEMAN [*enthusiastically*]. Great heavens — you! Allow me to shake hands with you heartily! You, with your genius, you have given me so much joy!

JACKSON. I'm glad indeed!

BRIQUET [*shrugs his shoulders; to* JACKSON]. He wants to be a clown! Look him over, Jim.

[JACKSON *makes a motion at which the* GENTLEMAN *hurriedly removes his coat and throws it on a chair. He is ready for the examination.* JACKSON *turns him round, looking him over critically.*]

JACKSON. Clown? Hm! Turn round then. Clown? Yes? Now smile. Wider — broader do you call that a smile? So — that's better. There is something, yes — but for full developments —— [*Sadly.*] Probably you can't even turn a somersault?

GENTLEMAN [*sighs*]. No.

JACKSON. How old are you?

GENTLEMAN. Thirty-nine. Too late! [JACKSON *moves away with a whistle. There is a silence.*]

ZINIDA [*softly*]. Take him.

BRIQUET [*indignant*]. What the hell shall I do with him if he doesn't know a thing? He's drunk!

GENTLEMAN. Honestly I am not. Thank you for your support, Madame. Are you not the famous Zinida, the lion tamer, whose regal beauty and audacity ——

ZINIDA. Yes. But I do not like flattery.

GENTLEMAN. It is not flattery.

MANCINI. You are evidently not accustomed to good society, my dear. Flattery? This gentleman expresses his admiration in sincere and beautiful words — and you — you are not educated, Zinida. As for myself ——

[*Enter* CONSUELO *and* BEZANO *in circus costume.*]

CONSUELO. You here, Daddy?

MANCINI. Yes, my child, you are not tired? [*Kisses her on the forehead.*] My daughter, sir, Countess Veronica. Known on the stage as Consuelo, The Bareback Tango Queen. Did you ever see her?

GENTLEMAN. I have enjoyed her work. It is marvellous!

MANCINI. Yes! Of course. Every one admits it. And how do you like the name, Consuelo? I took it from the novel of George Sand. It means "Consolation."

GENTLEMAN. What a wonderful knowledge of books!

MANCINI. A small thing. Despite your strange intention, I can see, sir, that you are a gentleman. My peer! Let me explain to you, that only the strange and fatal misfortunes of our ancient family — "sic transit gloria mundi," sir.

CONSUELO. It's a bore, Daddy —— Where's my handkerchief, Alfred?

BEZANO. Here it is.

CONSUELO [*showing the handkerchief to the* GENTLEMAN]. Genuine Venetian. Do you like it?

GENTLEMAN [*again bowing*]. My eyes are dazzled, how beautiful! Papa Briquet, the more I look around me the more I want to stay with you. [*Makes the face of a simpleton.*] On the one hand a count, on the other ——

JACKSON [*nods approval*]. That's not bad. Look here, think a bit — find something. Every one here thinks for himself.

[*Silence. The* GENTLEMAN *stands with a finger on his forehead, thinking.*]

GENTLEMAN. Find something — find something... Eureka!

POLLY. That means *found.* Come!

GENTLEMAN. Eureka —— I shall be among you, he who gets slapped.

[*General laughter. Even* BRIQUET *smiles.*]

GENTLEMAN [*looks at them smiling.*]

You see I made even you laugh — is that easy? [*All grow serious.* POLLY *sighs.*]

TILLY. No, it's not easy. Did you laugh, Polly?

POLLY. Sure, a lot. Did you?

TILLY. I did.

[*Imitating an instrument, he plays with his lips a melody at once sad and gay.*]

JACKSON. "He Who Gets Slapped," that's not bad.

GENTLEMAN. It's not, is it? I rather like it myself. It suits my talent. And comrades, I have even found a name — you'll call me "HE." Is that all right?

JACKSON [*thinking*]. "HE" — Not bad.

CONSUELO [*in a singing, melodic voice*]. "He" is so funny — "He" — like a dog. Daddy, are there such dogs?

[JACKSON *suddenly gives a circus slap to the* GENTLEMAN. HE *steps back and grows pale.*]

GENTLEMAN. What! —

[*General laughter covers his exclamation.*]

JACKSON. He Who Gets Slapped. Or didn't you get it?

POLLY [*comically*]. He says he wants more ——

[*The* GENTLEMAN *smiles, rubbing his cheek.*]

GENTLEMAN. So sudden. — Without waiting. — How funny — you didn't hurt me, and yet my cheek burns.

[*Again there is loud laughter. The clowns cackle like ducks, hens, cocks; they bark.* ZINIDA *says something to* BRIQUET, *casts a glance toward* BEZANO, *and goes out.* MANCINI *assumes a bored air and looks at his watch. The two actresses go out.*]

JACKSON. Take him, Papa Briquet — he will push us.

MANCINI [*again looking at his watch*]. But bear in mind, that Papa Briquet is as close as Harpagon. If you expect to get good money here, you are mistaken. [HE *laughs.*] A slap? What's a slap? Worth only small change, a franc and a half a dozen. Better go back to society; you will make more money there. Why for one slap, just a light tap, you might say, my friend,

Marquis Justi, was paid fifty thousand lire!

BRIQUET. Shut up, Mancini. Will you take care of him, Jackson?

JACKSON. I can.

POLLY. Do you like music? A Beethoven sonata played on a broom, for instance, or Mozart on a bottle?

HE. Alas! No. But I will be exceedingly grateful if you will teach me. A clown! My childhood's dream. When all my school friends were thrilled by Plutarch's heroes, or the light of science — I dreamed of clowns. Beethoven on a broom, Mozart on bottles! Just what I have sought all my life! Friends, I must have a costume!

JACKSON. I see you don't know much! A costume [putting his finger on his forehead] is a thing which calls for long deep thought. Have you seen my Sun here? [Strikes his posterior.] I looked for it two years.

HE [enthusiastically]. I shall think!

MANCINI. It is time for me to go. Consuelo, my child, you must get dressed. [To HE.] We are lunching with Baron Regnard, a friend of mine, a banker.

CONSUELO. But I don't want to go, Daddy. Alfred says I must rehearse to-day.

MANCINI [horrified, holding up his hands]. Child, think of me, and what a situation you put me in! I promised the Baron, the Baron expects us. Why, it is impossible! Oh, I am in a cold sweat.

CONSUELO. Alfred says ——

BEZANO [drily]. She has to work. Are you rested? Then come on.

MANCINI. But — the devil take me if I know what to make of it. Hey, Bezano, bareback rider! Are you crazy? I gave you permission for Art's sake, to exercise my daughter's talent — and you ——

CONSUELO. Go along, Papa, and don't be so silly. We've got to work, haven't we? Have lunch alone with your Baron. And Daddy, you forgot to take a clean handkerchief again, and I washed two for you yesterday. Where did you put them?

MANCINI [ashamed, blushing]. Why, my linen is washed by the laundress, and you,

Consuelo, are still playing with toys. It is stupid! You're a chatter-box. You don't think. These gentlemen might imagine Heaven knows what. How stupid. I'm off.

CONSUELO. Do you want me to write him a little note?

MANCINI [angrily]. A little note? Your little notes would make a horse laugh! Good-bye.

[He goes out toying angrily with his cane. The clowns follow him respectfully, playing a funeral march. HE and JACKSON laugh. The actors disappear one by one.]

CONSUELO [laughing]. Do I really write so badly? And I love so to write. Did you like my note, Alfred — or did you laugh, too?

BEZANO [blushing]. No, I did not. Come on, Consuelo.

[They go, and meet ZINIDA, entering. CONSUELO passes on.]

ZINIDA. Are you going back to work, Bezano?

BEZANO [politely]. Yes. To-day is a very bad day. How are your lions, Zinida? I think the weather affects them.

CONSUELO [from the ring]. Alfred!

ZINIDA. Yes. Some one is calling you. You'd better go. [ALFRED goes out. To BRIQUET.] Are you finished?

BRIQUET. Right away.

JACKSON. Then good-bye till evening. Think about your costume, HE, and I shall look for some idea, too. Be here at ten to-morrow. Don't be late, or you'll get another slap. And I'll work with you.

HE. I shall not be late. [HE looks after JACKSON who goes out.] Must be a nice man. All the people about you are so nice, Papa Briquet. I suppose that good-looking bareback rider is in love with Consuelo, isn't he?   [Laughs.]

ZINIDA. It's none of your business. For a newcomer you go poking your nose too far. How much does he want, Papa?

BRIQUET. Just a minute. See here, HE. I don't want to make a contract with you.

HE. Just as you please. Do you know what? Don't let us talk about money. You are an honest fellow, Briquet; you will see what my work is worth to you, and then ——

BRIQUET [pleased]. Now that's very nice of you. Zinida, the man really doesn't know anything.

ZINIDA. Well, do as he suggests. Now we must write it down. Where's the book?

BRIQUET. Here. [To HE.] I don't like to write [gives book to ZINIDA], but we have to put down the names of the actors, you know — it's police regulations. Then if any one kills himself, or ——

[Again comes the sound of the Tango, and calls from the ring.]

ZINIDA. What is your name?

HE [smiling]. HE. I chose it, you know. Or don't you like it?

BRIQUET. We like it all right — but we have to have your real name. Have you a passport?

HE [confused]. A passport? No, I have none. Or, rather, yes. I have something of the kind, but I had no idea the rules were strictly enforced here. What do you need papers for?

[ZINIDA and BRIQUET look at each other. ZINIDA pushes the book aside.]

ZINIDA. Then we can't take you. We cannot quarrel with the police, just on your account.

BRIQUET. She is my wife. I hadn't told you. She's right. You might get hurt by a horse, or hurt yourself — or do something. We don't know you, you see. I personally don't care, but out there, it's different, you see. For me a corpse is just a corpse — and I don't ask anything about him. It's up to God or the Devil. But they — they're too curious. Well, I suppose it's necessary for order. I don't know —— Got a card?

HE [rubs his head, thinking]. What shall I do? I have my card, but [smiles] you understand that I don't want my name to be known.

BRIQUET. Some story, hey?

HE. Yes, something like that. Why can't you imagine that I have no name? Can't I lose it as I might lose my hat? Or let some one else take it by mistake? When a stray dog comes to you, you don't ask his name — you simply give him another. Let me be that dog. [Laughing.] HE — the Dog!

ZINIDA. Why don't you tell us your name, just the two of us. Nobody else need know it. Unless you should break your neck ——

HE [hesitates]. Honestly?

[ZINIDA shrugs her shoulders.]

BRIQUET. Where people are honest, their word is good. One sees you come from out there.

HE. All right. But please, don't be surprised.

[Gives ZINIDA his card. She looks at it, then hands it to BRIQUET, then both look at HE.]

BRIQUET. If it is true, sir, that you are really what is written here ——

HE. For heaven's sake — for heaven's sake — this does not exist, but was lost long ago; it is just a check for an old hat. I pray you to forget it, as I have. I am HE Who Gets Slapped — nothing else.

[Silence.]

BRIQUET. I beg your pardon, sir, but I must ask you again, I must humbly ask you — are you not drunk, sir? There is something in your eye — something ——

HE. No, no. I am HE Who Gets Slapped. Since when do you speak to me like this, Papa Briquet? You offend me.

ZINIDA. After all, it's his business, Briquet. [She hides the card.] Truly you are a strange man. [Smiles.] And you have already noticed that Bezano is in love with the horse-girl? And that I love my Briquet, did you notice that, too?

HE [also smiling]. Oh, yes. You adore him.

ZINIDA. I adore him. Now go with him, Briquet, show him the ring and the stables — I have something to write.

HE. Yes, yes, please. I am so happy. At last you have taken me, haven't you? It is true — you're not joking. The circus, the tan-bark, the ring in which I shall run getting my slaps. Yes, yes, Briquet, let's go. Until I feel the sawdust under my feet, I shall not believe it.

BRIQUET. All right then. [Kisses ZINIDA.] Come on.

ZINIDA. Just a minute — HE! Answer me a question. I have a man who takes care of the cages, a plain fellow whom nobody knows. He just cleans the cages, you know; he walks in and out whenever he wants to, without even looking at the lions, as if he were perfectly at home. Why is that so? Nobody knows him, everybody knows me, every one is afraid for me, while —— And he is such a silly man — you will see him. [*Laughs.*] But don't you think of entering the cage yourself! My red one would give you such a slap!

BRIQUET [*displeased*]. There you are again, Zinida — stop it.

ZINIDA [*laughs*]. All right — go. Oh yes, Louis, send me Bezano. I have to settle an account with him.

[HE *and the director go out.* ZINIDA *looks at the card once more, then hides it. She gets up and walks quickly up and down the room. She stops to listen to the Tango, which ends abruptly. Then she stands motionless, looking straight at the dark opening of the door through which* BEZANO *comes.*]

BEZANO [*entering*]. You called me, Zinida? What do you want? Tell me quickly, I have no time ——

[ZINIDA *looks at him silently.* BEZANO *flushes with anger, and knits his eyebrows. He turns to the door to go.*]

ZINIDA. Bezano!

BEZANO [*stops, without looking up*]. What do you want? I have no time.

ZINIDA. Bezano! I keep hearing people say that you are in love with Consuelo. Is it true?

BEZANO [*shrugging his shoulders*]. We work well together.

ZINIDA [*takes a step forward*]. No —— Tell me, Alfred, do you love her?

BEZANO [*flushes like a boy, but looks straight into* ZINIDA'S *eyes. Proudly*]. I do not love anybody. No, I love nobody. How can I? Consuelo? She is here to-day, gone to-morrow, if her father should take her away. And I? Who am I? An acrobat, the son of a Milanese shoemaker —— She! I cannot even talk about it. Like my horses, I have no words. Who am I to love?

ZINIDA. Do you love me? A little?

BEZANO. No. I told you before.

ZINIDA. Still no? Not even a little?

BEZANO [*after a silence*]. I am afraid of you.

ZINIDA [*wants to cry out, indignantly, but masters herself and lowers her eyes, as if in an effort to shut out their light; turns pale*]. Am I ... so terrifying a woman ——

BEZANO. You are beautiful, like a queen. You are almost as beautiful as Consuelo, but I don't like your eyes. Your eyes command me to love you — and I don't like to be commanded. I am afraid of you.

ZINIDA. Do I command, Bezano? No — only implore.

BEZANO. Then why not look at me straight? Now I have it. You know yourself that your eyes cannot implore. [*Laughs.*] Your lions have spoiled you.

ZINIDA. My red lion loves me ——

BEZANO. Never! If he loves you, why is he so sad?

ZINIDA. Yesterday he was licking my hands like a dog.

BEZANO. And this morning he was looking for you to devour you. He thrusts out his muzzle and looks out, as if he sees only you. He is afraid of you, and he hates you. Or do you want me to lick your hands too, like a dog?

ZINIDA. No, Alfred, but I — I want to kiss *your* hand. [*With passion.*] Give it to me!

BEZANO [*severely*]. I am ashamed to listen to you when you speak like that.

ZINIDA [*controlling herself*]. One should not torture another as you torture me. Alfred, I love you. No, I do not command. Look into my eyes — *I love you.* [*Silence.*]

BEZANO [*turns to go*]. Good-bye.

ZINIDA. Alfred ——

[HE *appears in the doorway, and stops.*]

BEZANO. Please never tell me any more that you love. I don't want it. Otherwise I will quit. You pronounce the word love as if you were cracking me with your whip. You know it is disgusting ——

[*He turns brusquely and goes. Both notice* HE; BEZANO, *frowning, passes out quickly.* ZINIDA *returns to her place at the desk, with a proudly indifferent expression.*]

HE [*coming in*]. I beg your pardon, but I——

ZINIDA. There you are again, poking your nose into everything, HE. Do you really want a slap?

HE [*laughing*]. No. I simply forgot my overcoat. I didn't hear anything.

ZINIDA. I don't care whether you did or not.

HE. May I take my coat?

ZINIDA. Take it if it's yours. Sit down, HE.

HE. I am sitting down.

ZINIDA. Now tell me, HE, could you love me?

HE [*laughing*]. I? I and Love! Look at me, Zinida. Did you ever see a lover with such a face?

ZINIDA. One can succeed with such a face——

HE. That's because I am happy — because I lost my hat — because I am drunk — or perhaps I am not drunk. But I feel as dizzy as a young girl at her first ball. It is so nice here — slap me, I want to play my part. Perhaps it will awaken love in my heart, too. Love — [*as if listening to his own heart with pretended terror*] do you know — I feel it!

[*In the circus the Tango is played again.*]

ZINIDA [*listening too*]. For me?

HE. No. I don't know. For every one. [*Listens to the music.*] Yes, they are dancing — how beautiful Consuelo is — and how beautiful is the youth. He has the body of a Greek god; he looks as if he had been modelled by Praxiteles. Love! Love! [*Silence, music.*]

ZINIDA. Tell me, HE ——

HE. At your service, Queen!

ZINIDA. HE, what shall I do, to make my lions love me?

CURTAIN

ACT II

The same room, during the evening performance. Occasional music, laughter, shrieks, and applause are audible. *Through the small windows, back centre, the light is shining.*

CONSUELO *and* BARON REGNARD *occupy the stage;* CONSUELO *wears her stage costume; she sits with her feet on the sofa, a small shawl covering her shoulders. Before her stands the* BARON, *a tall stout man in evening dress, a rose in his buttonhole; grasping the ground with feet well apart, he gazes at her with convex spider-like eyes.*

BARON. Is it true that your father, the Count, has introduced you to a certain Marquis Justi, a very rich man?

CONSUELO [*surprised*]. No, he is only joking. I have often heard him speak of a Marquis Justi but I have never seen him ——

BARON. And do you know that your father is just a charlatan?

CONSUELO. Oh! Don't say that — Father is such a dear.

BARON. Did you like the jewels?

CONSUELO. Yes, very much. I was very sorry when Father told me I must return them. He said it would not be nice for me to keep them. I even cried a little about it.

BARON. Your father is only a beggar and a charlatan.

CONSUELO. Oh, no, don't scold him — he loves you so much.

BARON. Let me kiss your hand ——

CONSUELO. Oh, no, it isn't proper! One may kiss the hand only when one says how do you do or good-bye. But in the meantime you can't.

BARON. Everybody is in love with you, that is why you and your father make such a fuss about yourselves. Who is that new clown they call HE? I don't like him, he's too shrewd a beast.... Is he in love with you, too? I noticed the way he looked at you....

CONSUELO [*laughing*]. Nothing of the kind. He is so funny! He got fifty-two slaps yesterday. We counted them. Think of it, fifty-two slaps! Father said, "if they had only been gold pieces."

BARON. And Bezano, Consuelo.... Do you like him?

CONSUELO. Yes, very much. He is so good-looking. HE says that Bezano and I are the most beautiful couple in the world. HE calls him Adam, and me Eve. But that's improper, isn't it? HE is *so* improper.

BARON. And does HE speak to you very often?

CONSUELO. Yes, often.... But I don't understand him. It seems as if he were drunk.

BARON. "Consuelo"!... It means in Spanish... Consolation. Your father is an ass.... Consuelo, I love you.

CONSUELO. Talk it over with Father.

BARON [angry]. Your father is a swindler and a charlatan. He should be turned over to the police. Don't you understand that I *cannot* marry you?

CONSUELO. But Father says you can....

BARON. No, I cannot. And what if I shoot myself? Consuelo, silly girl, I love you unbearably... unbearably, do you understand? I am probably mad... and must be taken to a doctor, yanked about, beaten with sticks. Why do I love you so much, Consuelo?

CONSUELO. Then, you'd better marry.

BARON. I have had a hundred women, beauties, but I didn't see them. You are the first and I don't see any one else. Who strikes man with love, God or the Devil? The Devil struck me. Let me kiss your hand.

CONSUELO. No.

[She thinks a while and sighs.]

BARON. Do you think sometimes? What are you thinking about now, Consuelo?

CONSUELO [with another sigh]. I don't know why, I just felt sorry for Bezano. [Sighs again.] He is so nice to me when he teaches me... and he has such a tiny little room.

BARON [indignant]. You were there?

CONSUELO. No. He told me about it. [Smiling.] Do you hear the noise in there? That's HE getting slapped. Poor thing... although I know it doesn't hurt, it's only make-believe. The intermission is coming soon.

[The BARON throws away his cigar,

takes two quick steps forward, and falls on his knees before the girl.]

BARON. Consuelo ——

CONSUELO. Please, don't. Get up. Please leave my hand alone.

BARON. Consuelo!

CONSUELO [disgusted]. Get up please, it's disgusting — you're so fat.

[The BARON gets up. Voices are heard near the door and in the ring. It is the intermission. The clowns come first, talking cheerfully and excitedly. HE leads them, in his clown's dress, with painted eyebrows and white nose; the others are applauding him. Voices of the actors calling: "Bravo! HE." Then come the actors and actresses, riding-masters, and the rest, all in costume. ZINIDA is not among them. PAPA BRIQUET comes a little later.]

POLLY. A hundred slaps! Bravo, HE!

JACKSON. Not bad, not bad at all. You'll make a career.

TILLY. He was the Professor to-day, and we were the students. Here goes another!

[Gives him a clown's slap. Laughter. All bid good evening to the BARON. He is politely rude to these vagabonds who bore him, and remains silent. They seem quite used to it. Enter MANCINI. He is the same, and with the same cane.]

MANCINI [shaking hands]. What a success, Baron — and think of it — how the crowd does love slaps. [Whispering.] Your knees are dusty, Baron, brush them off. The floor is very dirty in here. [Aloud.] Consuelo, dear child, how do you feel?

[Goes over to his daughter. Sound of laughing, chattering. The waiters from the buffet in the lobby bring in soda and wine. CONSUELO's voice is heard.]

CONSUELO. And where is Bezano?

HE [bows before the BARON, affecting intimacy]. You do not recognize me, Baron?

BARON. Yes I do. You are the clown, HE.

HE. Yes I am HE Who Gets Slapped. May I presume to ask you, Baron, did you get your jewels back?

BARON. What!

HE. I was asked to return some jewels to you, and I take the liberty of ——

[*The* BARON *turns his back on him* — HE *laughs loudly.*]

JACKSON. Whiskey and soda! Believe me, ladies and gents, HE will surely make a career. I am an old clown, and I know the crowd. Why to-day, he even eclipsed *me* — and clouds have covered my Sun. [*Striking it.*] They do not like puzzles, they want slaps! They are longing for them and dreaming about them in their homes. Your health, HE! Another whiskey and soda! HE got so many slaps today, there would be enough to go round the whole orchestra!

TILLY. I bet there wouldn't! [*To* JACK-SON.] Shake!

POLLY. I bet there wouldn't — I'll go and count the old mugs.

A VOICE. The orchestra did not laugh ——

JACKSON. Because they were getting it, but the galleries did, because they were looking at the orchestra getting slapped. Your health, HE!

HE. Yours, Jim! Tell me, why didn't you let me finish my speech — I was just getting a good start.

JACKSON [*seriously*]. My friend, because your speech was a sacrilege. Politics — all right. Manners — as much as you want. But Providence — leave it in peace. And believe me, friend, I shut your mouth in time. Didn't I, Papa Briquet?

BRIQUET [*coming nearer*]. Yes. It was too much like literature. This is not an academy. You forget yourself, HE.

TILLY. But to shut one's mouth — faugh...

BRIQUET [*in a didactic tone*]. Whenever one shuts one's mouth, it is always high time to shut it, unless one is drinking. Hey, whiskey and soda!

VOICES. Whiskey and soda for the Manager!

MANCINI. But this is obscurantism. Philosophizing again, Briquet?

BRIQUET. I am not satisfied with you to-day, HE. Why do you tease them? They don't like it. Your health! A good slap must be clean like a crystal — fft-fft!

right side, left side, and done with it. They will like it; they will laugh, and love you. But in your slaps there is a certain bite, you understand, a certain smell ——

HE. But they laughed, nevertheless!

BRIQUET. But without pleasure, without pleasure, HE. You pay, and immediately draw a draft on their bank; it's not the right game — they won't like you.

JACKSON. That's what *I* tell him. He had already begun to make them angry.

BEZANO [*entering*]. Consuelo, where are you? I have been looking for you — come on.

[*Both go out. The* BARON, *after hesitating a while, follows them.* MAN-CINI *accompanies him respectfully to the door.*]

HE [*sighs*]. You don't understand, my dear friends; you are simply old, and have forgotten the smell of the stage.

JACKSON. Aha! Who is old, my young man?

HE. Don't be angry, Jim. It's a play, don't you understand? I become happy when I enter the ring and hear the music. I wear a mask and I feel humorous. There is a mask on my face, and I play. I may say *anything* like a drunkard. Do you understand? Yesterday when I, with this stupid face, was playing the great man, the philosopher [*he assumes a proud monumental pose, and repeats the gesture of the play — general laughter*], I was walking this way, and was telling how great, how wise, how incomparable I was — how God lived in me, how high I stood above the earth — how glory shone above my head [*his voice changes and he is speaking faster*] then you, Jim, you hit me for the first time. And I asked you "What is it, they're applauding me?" Then, at the tenth slap, I said: "It seems to me that they sent for me from the Academy?"

[*Acts, looking around him with an air of unconquerable pride and splendour. Laughter.* JACKSON *gives him a real slap.*]

HE [*holding his face*]. Why?

JACKSON. Because you're a fool, and play for nothing. Waiter, the check.

[*Laughter. The bell calls them to the*

ring. The actors go out in haste, some running. The waiters collect their money.]

BRIQUET [*in a sing-song*]. To the ring — to the ring ——

MANCINI. I want to tell you something, HE. You are not going yet?

HE. No. I'll take a rest.

BRIQUET. To the ring — to the ring —— [*The clowns as they go sing in shrill, squeaky voices. Little by little they all disappear, and loud music begins. HE seats himself on the sofa with his legs crossed, and yawns.*]

MANCINI. HE, you have something none of my ancestors ever had — money. Let's have a nice bottle on you. Waiter, please —— [*The waiter who was taking up dishes brings a bottle of wine and glasses and goes out.*]

HE. You're blue, Mancini. [*Stretches.*] Well, at my age, a hundred slaps — it seems pretty hard. So you're blue. How are things getting on with your girl?

MANCINI. Tss! Bad! Complications — parents — [*Shudders.*] Agh ——

HE. Prison!

MANCINI [*laughing*]. Prison! Mustn't I uphold the glory of my name now, eh?

HE, I'm joking — but there is Hell in my heart. You're the only one who understands me. But tell me how to explain this passion? It will turn my hair grey, it'll bring me to prison, to the grave. I am a tragic man. HE —— [*Wipes his eyes with a dirty handkerchief.*] Why don't I like things which are not forbidden? Why, at all moments, even at the very moment of ecstasy, must I be reminded of some law — it is stupid. HE, I am becoming an anarchist. Good God — Count Mancini an anarchist. That's the only thing I've missed.

HE. Isn't there a way of settling it somehow?

MANCINI. Is there a way of getting money, somehow?

HE. And the Baron?

MANCINI. Oh, yes! He's just waiting for it, the blood-sucker! He'll get what he's after. Some day, you'll see me give him Consuelo for ten thousand francs, perhaps for five!

HE. Cheap.

MANCINI. Did I say it was anything else? Do I want to do it? But these bourgeois are strangling me, they've got me by the throat. HE, one can easily see that you're a gentleman, and of good society, you understand me — I showed you the jewels which I sent back to him — damn honesty — I didn't even dare change the stones, put false ones ——

HE. Why?

MANCINI. It would have queered the game. Do you think he didn't weigh the diamonds when he got them back?

HE. He will not marry her.

MANCINI. Yes he will. You don't understand. [*Laughs.*] The first half of his life, this man had only appetites — now love's got him. If he does not get Consuelo, he is lost, he is — like a withered narcissus. Plague take him with his automobiles. Did you see his car?

HE. I did.... Give Consuelo to the Jockey ——

MANCINI. To Bezano? [*Laughs.*] What nonsense you do talk! Oh, I know. It's your joke about Adam and Eve. But please stop it. It's clever, but it compromises the child. She told me about it.

HE. Or give her to me.

MANCINI. Have you a billion? [*Laughs.*] Ah, HE, I'm not in the proper mood to listen to your clownish jokes —— They say there are terrible jails in this country, and no discriminations are being made between people of my kind and plain scoundrels. Why do you look at me like that? You're making fun of me?

HE. No.

MANCINI. I'll never get accustomed to those faces. You're so disgustingly made up.

HE. He will not marry her. You can be as proud as you please, Mancini, but he'll not marry her. What *is* Consuelo? She is not educated. When she is off her horse, any good housemaid from a decent house has nicer manners, and speaks better. [*Nonchalantly.*] Don't *you* think she's stupid?

MANCINI. No, she's not stupid. And you, HE, are a fool. What need has a woman of intelligence? Why, HE, you astonish me. Consuelo is an unpolished jewel, and only a real donkey does not notice her sparkle. Do you know what happened? I tried to begin to polish her ——

HE. Yes, you took a teacher. And what happened?

MANCINI [nodding his head]. I was frightened — it went too fast — I had to dismiss him. Another month or two, and she would have kicked me out. [Laughs.] The clever old diamond merchants of Amsterdam keep their precious stones unpolished, and fool the thieves. My father taught me that.

HE. The sleep of a diamond. It is only sleeping, then. You are wise, Mancini.

MANCINI. Do you know what blood flows in the veins of an Italian woman? The blood of Hannibal and Corsini — of a Borgia — and of a dirty Lombardi peasant — and of a Moor. Oh! an Italian woman is not of a lower race, with only peasants and gypsies behind her. All possibilities, all forms are included in her, as in our marvellous sculpture. Do you understand that, you fool? Strike here — out springs a washerwoman, or a cheap street girl whom you want to throw out, because she is sloppy and has a screechy voice. Strike there — but carefully and gently, for there stands a queen, a goddess, the Venus of the Capitol, who sings like a Stradivarius and makes you cry, idiot! An Italian woman ——

HE. You're quite a poet, Mancini. But what will the Baron make of her?

MANCINI. What? What? Make of her? A baroness, you fool! What are you laughing at? I don't get you? But I am happy that this lovesick beast is neither a duke nor a prince — or she would be a princess and I — what would become of me? A year after the wedding they would not let me even into the kitchen [laughing] not even into the kitchen! I, Count Mancini, and she a — a simple ——

HE [jumping up]. What did you say? You are not her father, Mancini?

MANCINI. Tss — the devil — I am so nervous to-day! Heavens, who do you think I am? "Her father?" Of course [tries to laugh] how silly you are — haven't you noticed the family resemblance? Just look, the nose, the eyes —— [Suddenly sighs deeply.] Ah, HE! How unhappy I am! Think of it. Here I am, a gentleman, nearly beaten in my struggle to keep up the honour of my name, of an old house, while there in the parquet — there sits that beast, an elephant with the eyes of a spider ... and he looks at Consuelo ... and ...

HE. Yes, yes, he has the motionless stare of a spider — you're right!

MANCINI. Just what I say — a spider! But I must, I shall compel him to marry her. You'll see —— [Walking excitedly up and down, playing with his cane.] You'll see! All my life I've been getting ready for this battle.

[He continues to walk up and down. Silence. Outside, great stillness.]

HE [listening]. Why is it so quiet out there? What a strange silence.

MANCINI [disgusted]. I don't know. Out there it is quiet — but here [touching his forehead with his cane] here is storm, whirlwind. [Bends over the clown.] HE, shall I tell you a strange thing — an unusual trick of nature? [Laughs, and looks very important.] For three centuries the Counts Mancini have had no children! [Laughs.]

HE. Then how were you born?

MANCINI. Sh! Silence! That is the secret of our sainted mothers! Ha-ha! We are too ancient a stock — too exquisitely refined to trouble ourselves with such things — matters in which a peasant is more competent than ourselves. [Enter an usher.] What do you want? The manager is on the stage.

THE USHER [bows]. Yes, sir. Baron Regnard wished me to give you this letter

MANCINI. The Baron? Is he there?

THE USHER. Baron Regnard has left There is no answer.

MANCINI [opening the envelope, his han shaking]. The devil — the devil!

[The usher is going

HE. Just a minute. Why is there n music? This silence ...

THE USHER. It is the act with Madame Zinida and her lions.

[*He goes.* MANCINI *is reading the Baron's note for the second time.*]

HE. What's the matter, Mancini? You shine like Jackson's sun.

MANCINI. What's the matter, did you ask? What's the matter? What's the matter?

[*Balancing his cane, he takes steps like a ballet-dancer.*]

HE. Mancini! [MANCINI *rolls his eyes, makes faces, dances.*] Speak, you beast!

MANCINI [*holds out his hand*]. Give me ten francs! Quick — ten francs — here, come on. [*Puts it automatically into his vest pocket.*] Listen, HE! If in a month I don't have a car of my own, you may give me one of your slaps!

HE. What! He's going to marry? He's decided?

MANCINI. What do you mean by "decided"? [*Laughs.*] When a man has the rope about his neck, you don't ask him about his health! Baron ——

[*Stops suddenly, startled.* BRIQUET *is staggering in like a drunken man, his hand over his eyes.*]

HE [*goes to him, touches his shoulder gently*]. What is the matter, Papa Briquet? Tell me!

BRIQUET [*groaning*]. Oh, oh, I can't... I can't... Ah ——

HE. Something has happened? You are ill? Please speak.

BRIQUET. I can't look at it! [*Takes his hands from his eyes, opens them wide.*] Why does she do it? Ah, ah, why does she do it? She must be taken away; she is insane. I couldn't look at it. [*Shivers.*] They will tear her to pieces, HE — her lions — they will tear her ——

MANCINI. Go on, Briquet. She is always like that. You act like a child. You ought to be ashamed.

BRIQUET. No —— To-day she is mad! And what is the matter with the crowd? They are all like dead people — they're not even breathing. I couldn't stand it. Listen — what's that?

[*All listen. There is the same silence.*]

MANCINI [*disturbed*]. I'll go and see.

BRIQUET [*yelling*]. No! Don't! You can't look — damned profession! Don't go. You will scorch her — every pair of eyes that looks at her — at her lions — no, no. It is impossible — it is a sacrilege. I ran away.... HE, they will tear her ——

HE [*tries to be cheerful*]. Keep cool, Papa Briquet — I had no idea you were such a coward. You ought to be ashamed. Have a drink. Mancini, give him some wine.

BRIQUET. I don't want any. Heavens, if it were only over —— [*All listen.*] I have seen many things in my life, but this ... Oh, she is crazy.

[*All still listen. Suddenly the silence breaks, like a huge stone wall crashing. There is a thunder of applause, mixed with shouts, music, wild screams — half bestial, half human. The men give way, relieved.* BRIQUET *sinks to a seat.*]

MANCINI [*nervous*]. You see — you see you old fool!

BRIQUET [*sobs and laughs*]. I am not going to allow it any more!

HE. Here she is!

[ZINIDA *walks in, alone. She looks like a drunken bacchante, or like a mad woman. Her hair falls over her shoulders dishevelled, one shoulder is uncovered. She walks unseeing, though her eyes glow. She is like the living statue of a mad Victory. Behind her comes an actor, very pale, then two clowns, and a little later* CONSUELO *and* BEZANO. *All look at* ZINIDA *fearfully, as if they were afraid of a touch of her hand, or her great eyes.*]

BRIQUET [*shouting*]. You are crazy — you're a mad woman!

ZINIDA. I? No. Did you see? Did you see? Well?

[*She stands smiling, with the expression of a mad Victory.*]

TILLY [*plaintively*]. Cut it out, Zinida. Go to the devil!

ZINIDA. You saw, too! And!... what ——

BRIQUET. Come home — come home. [*To the others.*] You can do what you like here. Zinida, come home.

POLLY. You can't go, Papa. There's still your number.

ZINIDA [*her eyes meet those of* BEZANO]. Ah! Bezano. [*Laughs long and happily.*] Bezano! Alfred! Did you see? My lions *do* love me!

[BEZANO, *without answering, leaves the stage.* ZINIDA *seems to wither and grow dim, as a light being extinguished. Her smile fades, her eyes and face grow pale.* BRIQUET *anxiously bends over her.*]

BRIQUET [*in a slow voice*]. A chair!

[ZINIDA *sits. Her head drops on her shoulder, her arms fall, she begins to shiver and tremble. Some one calls,* "cognac" — *an actor runs to get it.*]

BRIQUET [*helpless*]. What is the matter, Zinida darling?

MANCINI [*running about*]. She must quiet down. Get out, get out — vagabonds! I'll fix everything, Papa Briquet. The wrap — where's the wrap? She's cold.

[*A clown hands it to him; they cover her.*]

TILLY [*timidly*]. Wouldn't you like some moosic?

MANCINI [*giving her some cognac*]. Drink, Duchess, drink! Drink it all — that's it.

[ZINIDA *drinks it like water, evidently not noticing the taste. She shivers. The clowns disappear one by one.* CONSUELO, *with a sudden flexible movement, falls on her knees before* ZINIDA *and kisses her hands, warming them between her own.*]

CONSUELO. Dear, dear, you are cold! Poor little hands, dear good one, beloved one ——

ZINIDA [*pushes her away, gently*]. Ho — home. It will soon be over. It's nothing ... I am ver — very ... home.... You stay here, Briquet — you must. I'm all right.

CONSUELO. You are cold? Here is my shawl.

ZINIDA. No — let me....

[CONSUELO *gets up, and moves aside.*]

BRIQUET. And it's all because of your books, Zinida — your mythology. Now tell me, why do you want those beasts to love you? Beasts! Do you understand, HE? You too, you're from that world. She'll listen more to you. Explain it to her. Whom can those beasts love? Those hairy monsters, with diabolic eyes?

HE [*genially*]. I believe — only their equals. You are right, Papa Briquet — there must be the same race.

BRIQUET. Of course, and this is all nonsense — literature. Explain it to her, HE.

HE [*takes on a meditative air*]. Yes, you are right, Briquet.

BRIQUET. You see, dear, silly woman — everybody agrees....

MANCINI. Oh! Briquet, you make me sick; you are an absolute despot, an Asiatic.

ZINIDA [*with the shadow of a smile, gives her hand to be kissed*]. Calm yourself, Louis. It is over — I am going home.

[*She stands up, shaking, still chilled.*]

BRIQUET. But how? alone, dear?

MANCINI. What! fool! Did you imagine that Count Mancini would leave a woman when she needed help? *I* shall take her home — let your brutal heart be at rest — I shall take her home. Thomas, run for an automobile. Don't push me, Briquet, you are as awkward as a unicorn ... that's the way, that's the way ——

[*They are holding her, guiding her slowly toward the door.* CONSUELO, *her chin resting in her hand, is following them with her eyes. Unconsciously she assumes a somewhat affected pose.*]

MANCINI. I'll come back for you, child ——

[*Only* HE *and* CONSUELO *are left on the stage. In the ring, music, shrieks, and laughter begin again.*]

HE. Consuelo ——

CONSUELO. Is that you, HE, dear?

HE. Where did you learn that pose? I have seen it only in marble. You look like Psyche.

CONSUELO. I don't know, HE. [*Sh sighs and sits on the sofa, keeping in her pos the same artificiality and beauty.*] It's all s sad here, to-day. HE, are you sorry fo Zinida?

HE. What did she do?

CONSUELO. I didn't see. I had close

my eyes, and didn't open them. Alfred says she is a wicked woman, but that isn't true. She has such nice eyes, and what tiny cold hands — as if she were dead. What does she do it for? Alfred says she should be audacious, beautiful, but quiet, otherwise what she does is only disgusting. It isn't true, is it, HE?

HE. She loves Alfred.

CONSUELO. Alfred? My Bezano? [Shrugging her shoulders, and surprised.] How does she love him? The same as every one loves?

HE. Yes — as every one loves — or still more.

CONSUELO. Bezano? Bezano? No — it's nonsense. [Pause; silence.] What a beautiful costume you have, HE. You invented it yourself?

HE. Jim helped me.

CONSUELO. Jim is so nice! All clowns are nice.

HE. I am wicked.

CONSUELO [laughs]. You? You are the nicest of all. Oh, goodness! Three acts more! This is the second on now. Alfred and I are in the third. Are you coming to see me?

HE. I always do. How beautiful you are, Consuelo.

CONSUELO. Like Eve? [Smiles.]

HE. Yes, Consuelo. And if the Baron asks you to be his wife, will you accept?

CONSUELO. Certainly, HE. That's all Father and I are waiting for. Father told me yesterday that the Baron will not hesitate very long. Of course I do not love him. But I will be his honest, faithful wife. Father wants to teach me to play the piano.

HE. Are those your own words — "his honest, faithful wife"?

CONSUELO. Certainly they are mine. Whose could they be? He loves me so much, the poor thing. Dear HE, what does "love" mean? Everybody speaks of love — love — Zinida, too! Poor Zinida! What a boring evening this has been! HE, did you paint the laughter on your face yourself?

HE. My own self, dear little Consuelo ——

CONSUELO. How do you do it, all of you? I tried once, but couldn't do a thing. Why are there no women clowns? Why are you so silent, HE? You, too, are sad, to-night.

HE. No, I am happy to-night. Give me your hand, Consuelo, I want to see what it says.

CONSUELO. Do you know how? What a talented man you are! Read it, but don't lie, like a gypsy. [HE goes down on one knee and takes her hand. Both bend over it.] Am I lucky?

HE. Yes, lucky. But wait a minute — this line here — funny. Ah, Consuelo, what does it say, here! [Acting.] I tremble, my eyes do not dare to read the strange, fatal signs. Consuelo ——

CONSUELO. The stars are talking.

HE. Yes, the stars are talking. Their voices are distant and terrible; their rays are pale, and their shadows slip by, like the ghosts of dead virgins — their spell is upon thee, Consuelo, beautiful Consuelo. Thou standest at the door of Eternity.

CONSUELO. I don't understand. Does it mean that I will live long?

HE. This line — how far it goes. Strange! Thou wilt live eternally, Consuelo.

CONSUELO. You see, HE, you did tell me a lie, just like a gypsy!

HE. But it is written — here, silly — and here. Now think of what the stars are saying. Here you have eternal life, love, and glory; and here, listen to what Jupiter says. He says: "Goddess, thou must not belong to any one born on earth," and if you marry the Baron — you'll perish, you'll die, Consuelo. [CONSUELO laughs.]

CONSUELO. Will he eat me?

HE. No. But you will die before he has time to eat you.

CONSUELO. And what will become of Father? Is there nothing about him here?

[Laughing, she softly sings the melody of the waltz, which is playing in the distance.]

HE. Don't laugh, Consuelo, at the voice of the stars. They are far away, their rays are light and pale, and we can barely see their sleeping shadows, but their sorcery is stern and dark. You stand at the gates of eternity. Your die is cast; you are doomed, — and your Alfred, whom you love in your heart, even though your mind is not aware of it, your Alfred cannot save you. He, too, is a stranger on this earth. He is submerged in a deep sleep. He, too, is a little god who has lost himself, and Consuelo, never, never will he find his way to Heaven again. Forget Bezano ——

Consuelo. I don't understand a word. Do the gods really exist? My teacher told me about them. But I thought it was all tales! [*Laughs.*] And my Bezano is a god?

He. Forget Bezano! Consuelo, do you know who can save you? The only one who can save you? — I.

Consuelo [*laughing*]. You, He?

He. Yes, but don't laugh! Look. Here is the letter H. It is I, He.

Consuelo. He Who Gets Slapped? Is that written here, too?

He. That, too. The stars know everything. But look here, what more is written about him. Consuelo, welcome him. He is an old god in disguise, who came down to earth only to love you, foolish little Consuelo.

Consuelo [*laughing and singing*]. Some god!

He. Don't mock! The gods don't like such empty laughter from beautiful lips. The gods grow lonely and die, when they are not recognized. Oh, Consuelo! Oh, great joy and love! Do recognize this god, and accept him. Think a moment, one day a god suddenly went crazy!

Consuelo. Gods go crazy, too?

He. Yes, when they are half man, then they often go mad. Suddenly he saw his own sublimity, and shuddered with horror, with infinite solitude, with superhuman anguish. It is terrible, when anguish touches the divine soul!

Consuelo. I don't like it. What language are you speaking? I don't understand ——

He. I speak the language of thy awakening. Consuelo, recognize and accept thy god, who was thrown down from the summit like a stone. Accept the god who fell to the earth in order to live, to play, and to be infinitely drunk with joy. Evoë, Goddess!

Consuelo [*tortured*]. He — I cannot understand. Let my hand alone.

He [*stands up*]. Sleep. Then wake again, Consuelo! And when thou wakest — remember that hour when, covered with snow-white sea-foam, thou didst emerge from the sky-blue waters. Remember heaven, and the slow eastern wind, and the whisper of the foam at thy marble feet.

Consuelo [*her eyes are closed*]. I believe — wait — I remember. Remind me further ——

[He *is bowed over* Consuelo, *with lifted arms; he speaks slowly, but in a commanding voice, as if conjuring.*]

He. You see the waves playing. Remember the song of the sirens, their sorrowless song of joy. Their white bodies, shining blue through the blue waters. Or can you hear the sun, singing? Like the strings of a divine harp, spread the golden rays —— Do you not see the hand of God, which gives harmony, light, and love to the world? Do not the mountains, in the blue cloud of incense, sing their hymn of glory? Remember, O Consuelo, remember the prayer of the mountains, the prayer of the sea. [*Silence.*]

He [*commandingly*]. Remember — Consuelo!

Consuelo [*opening her eyes*]. No! He, I was feeling so happy, and suddenly I forgot it all. Yet something of it all is still in my heart. Help me again, He, remind me. It hurts, I hear so many voices. They all sing "Consuelo — Consuelo." What comes after? [*Silence pause.*] What comes after? It hurts Remind me, He. [*Silence — in the ring the music suddenly bursts forth in a tempestuous circus gallop. Silence.*] He [*opens her eyes and smiles*], that's Alfred galloping Do you recognize his music?

He [*with rage*]. Leave the boy alone [*Suddenly falls on his knees before* Consuelo.] I love you, Consuelo, revelation of my heart, light of my nights, I love you

Consuelo. [*Looks at her in ecstasy and tears — and gets a slap; starting back.*] What's this?

CONSUELO. A slap! You forget who you are. [*Stands up, with anger in her eyes.*] You are HE Who Gets Slapped! Did you forget it? Some god! With such a face — slapped face! Was it with slaps they threw you down from heaven, god?

HE. Wait! Don't stand up! I — did not finish the play!

CONSUELO [*sits*]. Then you were playing?

HE. Wait! One minute.

CONSUELO. You lied to me. Why did you play so that I believed you?

HE. I am HE Who Gets Slapped!

CONSUELO. You are not angry because I struck you? I did not want to really, but you were so — disgusting. And now you are so funny again. You have great talent, HE — or are you drunk?

HE. Strike me again.

CONSUELO. No.

HE. I need it for my play. Strike!

CONSUELO [*laughs, and touches his cheek with her fingertips*]. Here, then!

HE. Didn't you understand that you are a queen, and I a fool who is in love with his queen? Don't you know, Consuelo, that every queen has a fool, and he is always in love with her, and they always beat him for it. HE Who Gets Slapped.

CONSUELO. No. I didn't know.

HE. Yes, every queen. Beauty has her fool. Wisdom, too. Oh, how many fools she has! Her court is overcrowded with enamoured fools, and the sound of slaps does not cease, even through the night. But I never received such a sweet slap as the one given by my little queen. [*Some one appears at the door. HE notices it, and continues to play, making many faces.*] Clown HE can have no rival! Who is there who could stand such a deluge of slaps, such a hail-storm of slaps, and not get soaked? [*Feigns to cry aloud.*] "Have pity on me. I am but a poor fool!"

Enter two men: an actor, dressed as a bareback rider, and a GENTLEMAN from the audience. He is spare, dressed in black, *very respectable. He carries his hat in his hand.*]

CONSUELO [*laughing, embarrassed*]. HE, there is some one here. Stop!

HE [*gets up*]. Who is it? Who dares to intrude in the castle of my queen?

[HE *stops, suddenly.* CONSUELO, *laughing, jumps up and runs away, after a quick glance at the* GENTLEMAN.]

CONSUELO. You cheered me up, HE. Good-bye. [*At the door.*] You shall get a note to-morrow.

THE BAREBACK RIDER [*laughing*] A jolly fellow, sir. You wanted to see him? There he is. HE, the gentleman wants to see you.

HE [*in a depressed voice*]. What can I do for you?

[*The actor bows, and goes away, smiling. Both men take a step toward each other.*]

GENTLEMAN. Is this you?

HE. Yes! It is I. And you? [*Silence.*]

GENTLEMAN. Must I believe my eyes? Is this *you*, Mr ——

HE [*in a rage*]. My name here is HE. I have no other name, do you hear? HE Who Gets Slapped. And if you want to stay here, don't forget it.

GENTLEMAN. You are so familiar. As far as I can remember ——

HE. We are all familiar, here. [*Contemptuously.*] Besides, that's all you deserve, anywhere.

GENTLEMAN [*humbly.*] You have not forgiven me, HE? [*Silence.*]

HE. Are you here with my wife? Is she too in the circus?

GENTLEMAN [*quickly*]. Oh, no! I am alone. She stayed there!

HE. You've left her already?

GENTLEMAN [*humbly*]. No — we have — a son. After your sudden and mysterious disappearance — when you left that strange and insulting letter ——

HE [*laughs*]. Insulting? You are still able to feel insults? What are you doing here? Were you looking for me, or is it an accident?

GENTLEMAN. I have been looking for you, for half a year — through many countries. And suddenly, to-day — by accident, indeed — I had no acquaintances here, and I went to the circus. We must talk things over... HE, I implore you. [*Silence.*]

HE. Here is a shadow I cannot lose! To talk things over! Do you really think we still have something to talk over? All right. Leave your address with the porter, and I will let you know when you can see me. Now get out. [*Proudly.*] I am busy.

[*The* GENTLEMAN *bows and leaves. HE does not return his bow, but stands with outstretched hand, in the pose of a great man, who shows a boring visitor the door.*]

CURTAIN

ACT III

The same room. Morning, before the rehearsal. HE is striding thoughtfully up and down the room. He wears a broad, parti-coloured coat, and a prismatic tie. His derby is on the back of his head, and his face is clean-shaven like that of an actor. His eyebrows are drawn, lips pressed together energetically, his whole appearance severe and sombre. After the entrance of the GENTLEMAN *he changes. His face becomes clown-like, mobile — a living mask.*

The GENTLEMAN *comes in. He is dressed in black, and has an extremely well-bred appearance. His thin face is yellowish, like an invalid's. When he is upset, his colourless, dull eyes often twitch. HE does not notice him.*

GENTLEMAN. Good morning, sir.

HE [*turning around and looking at him absent-mindedly*]. Ah! It's you.

GENTLEMAN. I am not late? You look as if you did not expect me. I hope I am not disturbing you? You fixed this time yourself however, and I took the liberty ——

HE. No manners, please. What do you want? Tell me quickly, I have no time.

GENTLEMAN [*looking around with dis-*]

taste]. I expected you would invite me to some other place... to your home.

HE. I have no other home. This is my home.

GENTLEMAN. But people may disturb us here.

HE. So much the worse for you. Talk faster! [*Silence.*]

GENTLEMAN. Will you allow me to sit down?

HE. Sit down. Look out! That chair is broken.

[*The* GENTLEMAN, *afraid, pushes away the chair and looks helplessly around. Everything here seems to him dangerous and strange. He chooses an apparently solid little gilded divan, and sits down; puts his silk hat aside, slowly takes off his gloves, which stick to his fingers. HE observes him indifferently.*]

GENTLEMAN. In this suit, and with this face, you make a still stranger impression. Yesterday it seemed to me that it was all a dream; to-day... you...

HE. You have forgotten my name again? My name is HE.

GENTLEMAN. You are determined to continue talking to me like this?

HE. Decidedly! But you are squandering your time like a millionaire. Hurry up!

GENTLEMAN. I really don't know... Everything here strikes me so... These posters, horses, animals, which I passed when I was looking for you... And finally, you, a clown in a circus! [*With a slight, deprecating smile.*] Could I expect it? It is true, when everybody there decided that you were dead, I was the only man who did not agree with them. I felt that you were still alive. But to find you among such surroundings — I can't understand it.

HE. You said you have a son, now. Doesn't he look like me?

GENTLEMAN. I don't understand?

HE. Don't you know that widows or divorced women often have children by the new husband, which resemble the old one? This misfortune did not befall you [*Laughs.*] And your book, too, is a big success, I hear.

GENTLEMAN. You want to insult me again?

He [*laughing*]. What a restless, touchy faker you are! Please sit still; be quiet. It is the custom here to speak this way. Why were you trying to find me?

Gentleman. My conscience...

He. You have no conscience. Or were you afraid that you hadn't robbed me of *everything* I possessed, and you came for the rest? But what more could you take from me now? My fool's cap with its bells? You wouldn't take it. It's too big for your bald head! Crawl back, you book-worm!

Gentleman. You cannot forgive the fact that your wife...

He. To the devil with my wife!

[*The* Gentleman *is startled and raises his eyebrows.* He *laughs.*]

Gentleman. I don't know.... But such language! I confess I find difficulty in expressing my thoughts in such an atmosphere, but if you are so... indifferent to your wife, who, I shall allow myself to emphasize the fact, loved you and thought you were a saint —— [He *laughs.*] Then *what* brought you to such a... step? Or is it that you cannot forgive me my success? A success, it is true, not entirely deserved. And now you want to take vengeance, with your humbleness, on those who misunderstood you. But you always were so indifferent to glory. Or your indifference was only hypocrisy. And when I, a more lucky rival...

He [*with a burst of laughter*]. Rival! You — a rival!

Gentleman [*growing pale*]. But my book!

He. You are talking to me about *your* book? To me?

[*The* Gentleman *is very pale.* He *looks at him with curiosity and mockery.*]

Gentleman [*raising his eyes*]. I am a very unhappy man.

He. Why?

Gentleman. I am a very unhappy man. You must forgive me. I am deeply, reparably, and infinitely unhappy.

He. But why? Explain it to me. [*Starts walking up and down.*] You say yourself that your book is a tremendous success, you are famous, you have glory; there is not a yellow newspaper in which *you* and *your* thoughts are not mentioned. Who knows *me*? Who cares about my heavy abstractions, from which it was difficult for them to derive a single thought? You — you are the great vulgarizer! You have made my thoughts comprehensible even to horses! With the art of a great vulgarizer, a tailor of ideas, you dressed my Apollo in a barber's jacket, you handed my Venus a yellow ticket, and to my bright hero you gave the ears of an ass. And then your career is made, as Jackson says. And wherever I go, the whole street looks at me with thousands of faces, in which — what mockery — I recognize the traits of my own children. Oh! How ugly your son must be, if he resembles me! Why then are you unhappy, you poor devil? [*The* Gentleman *bows his head, plucking at his gloves.*] The police haven't caught you, as yet. What am I talking about? Is it possible to catch you? You always keep within the limits of the law. You have been torturing yourself up to now because you are not married to my wife. A notary public is always present at your thefts. What is the use of this self-torture, my friend? Get married. I died. You are not satisfied with having taken only my wife? Let my glory remain in your possession. It is yours. Accept my ideas. Assume all the rights, my most lawful heir! I died! And when I was dying [*making a stupidly pious face*] I forgave thee!

[*Bursts out laughing. The* Gentleman *raises his head, and bending forward, looks straight into* He's *eyes.*]

Gentleman. And my pride?

He. Have you any pride? [*The* Gentleman *straightens up, and nods his head, silently.*] Yes! But please stand off a little. I don't like to look at you. Think of it. There was a time when I loved you a little, even thought you a little gifted! You — my empty shadow.

Gentleman [*nodding his head*]. I am your shadow.

[He *keeps on walking, and looks over his shoulder at the* Gentleman, *with a smile.*]

HE. Oh, you are marvellous! What a comedy! What a touching comedy! Listen. Tell me frankly if you can; do you hate me very much?

GENTLEMAN. Yes! With all the hate there is in the world! Sit down here.

HE. You order me?

GENTLEMAN. Sit down here. Thank you. [*Bows.*] I am respected and I am famous, yes? I have a wife and a son, yes? [*Laughs slowly.*] My wife still loves you: our favourite discussion is about your genius. She supposes you are a genius. We, I and she, love you even when we are in bed. Tss! It is I who must make faces. My son — yes, he'll resemble you. And when, in order to have a little rest, I go to my desk, to my ink-pot, my books — there, too, I find you. Always you! Everywhere you! And I am never alone — never myself and alone. And when at night — you, sir, should understand this — when at night I go to my lonely thoughts, to my sleepless contemplations, even then I find your image in my head, in my unfortunate brain, your damned and hateful image!

[*Silence. The* GENTLEMAN'S *eyes twitch.*]

HE [*speaking slowly*]. What a comedy. How marvellously everything is turned about in this world: the robbed proves to be a robber, and the robber is complaining of theft, and cursing! [*Laughs.*] Listen, I was mistaken. You are not my shadow. You are the crowd. If you live by my creations, you hate me; if you breathe my breath, you are choking with anger. And choking with anger, hating me, you still walk slowly on the trail of my ideas. But you are advancing backward, advancing backward, comrade! Oh, what a marvellous comedy! [*Walking and smiling.*] Tell me, would you be relieved if I really had died?

GENTLEMAN. Yes! I think so. Death augments distance and dulls the memory. Death reconciles. But you do not look like a man who ——

HE. Yes, yes! Death, *certainly!*

GENTLEMAN. Sit down here.

HE. Your obedient servant. Yes?

GENTLEMAN. Certainly, I do not dare to ask you — [*makes a grimace*] to ask you to die, but tell me: you'll never come back there? No, don't laugh. If you want me to, I'll kiss your hand. Don't grimace! I would have done so if you had died.

HE [*slowly*]. Get out, vermin!

[*Enter* TILLY *and* POLLY *as in the first act, playing. For a long time they do not see the two men.*]

HE. Jack!

TILLY. Ah! Good morning, HE. We are rehearsing. You know it is very hard. Jack has just about as much music in his head as my pig.

HE [*introducing, nonchalantly*]. My friend... For the benefit performance?

[*The clowns bow to the* GENTLEMAN, *making idiotic faces.*]

POLLY. Yes. What are you preparing? You are cunning, HE! Consuelo told me what you are preparing for the benefit performance. She leaves us soon, you know?

HE. Is that so?

TILLY. Zinida told us. Do you think she would get a benefit performance otherwise? She is a nice girl.

POLLY [*taking his small flute-pipe*] Here! Don't walk as if you were an elephant. Don't forget you are an ant! Come on! [*They go off, playing.*]

GENTLEMAN [*smiling*]. These are your new comrades? How strange they are!

HE. Everything here is strange.

GENTLEMAN. This suit of yours. Black used to be very becoming to you. This one hurts the eyes.

HE [*looking himself over*]. Why? It looks very nice. The rehearsal has begun. You must go away. You are disturbing us.

GENTLEMAN. You did not answer my question.

[*Slow strains of the Tango from a small orchestra in the ring.*]

HE [*listening absent-mindedly to the music*]. What question?

GENTLEMAN [*who does not hear the music*]. I pray you to tell me: will you ever come back?

HE [*listening to the music*]. Never, never, never!

GENTLEMAN [getting up]. Thank you. I am going.

HE. Never, never, never! Yes, run along. And don't come back. There, you were still bearable and useful for something, but here you are superfluous.

GENTLEMAN. But if something should happen to you... you are a healthy man, but in this environment, these people... how will I know? They don't know your name here?

HE. My name here is unknown, but you will know. Anything else?

GENTLEMAN. I can be at peace? On your word of honour? Of course I mean, comparatively, at peace?

HE. Yes, you may be comparatively at peace. Never!

[They walk to the door, the GENTLEMAN stops.]

GENTLEMAN. May I come to the circus? You will allow me?

HE. Certainly. You are the audience! [Laughs.] But I shan't give you my card for a pass. But why do you want to come? Or do you like the circus so much, and since when?

GENTLEMAN. I want to look at you some more, and to understand, perhaps. Such a transformation! Knowing you as I do, I cannot admit that you are here without any idea. But what idea?

[Looks short-sightedly at HE. HE grimaces and thumbs his nose.]

GENTLEMAN. What is that?

HE. My idea! Good-bye, Prince! My regards to your respected wife, your Highness's wonderful son!

[Enter MANCINI.]

MANCINI. You positively live in the circus, HE. Whenever I come, you are here. You are a fanatic in your work, sir.

HE [introducing]. Prince Poniatovsky, Count Mancini.

MANCINI [drawing himself up]. Very, very glad. And you too, Prince, you know my queer fellow? What a nice face he has, hasn't he?

[He touches HE's shoulder patronizingly, with the tip of his cane.]

GENTLEMAN [awkwardly]. Yes, I have

the pleasure... certainly. Good-bye, Count.

MANCINI. Good-day, Prince.

HE [accompanying him]. Look out, your Highness, for the dark passages: the steps are so rotten. Unfortunately I cannot usher you out to the street.

GENTLEMAN [in a low voice]. You will not give me your hand when we say good-bye? We are parting for ever.

HE. Unnecessary, Prince. I shall still hope to meet you in the Kingdom of Heaven. I trust you will be there, too?

GENTLEMAN [with disgust]. How you did succeed! You have so much of the clown in you!

HE. I am HE Who is Getting Slapped. Good-bye, Prince. [They take another step.]

GENTLEMAN [looking HE in the eyes; in a very low voice]. Tell me, you are not mad?

HE [just as low, his eyes wide open]. I am afraid, I am afraid you are right, Prince. [Still low.] Ass! Never in your life did you use such a precise expression. I am mad!

[Playing the clown again, he shows him to the stair, with a big, affected gesture, a sweep of the hand and arm from his head to the floor, the fingers moving, to represent the steps.]

HE [laughing]. He is down! Au revoir, Prince. [The GENTLEMAN goes out. HE comes skipping back, and takes a pose.] Mancini! Let us dance the Tango! Mancini, I adore you!

MANCINI [sitting back comfortably and playing with his cane]. Don't forget yourself, HE. But you're hiding something, my boy. I always said you used to belong to society. It is so easy to talk to you. And who is this Prince? A genuine one?

HE. Genuine. A first-rater. Like you!

MANCINI. A sympathetic face. Although at first I thought he was an undertaker who came for an order. Ah, HE! When shall I finally depart from these dirty walls, from Papa Briquet, stupid posters, and brutal jockeys!

HE. Very soon, Mancini.

MANCINI. Yes, soon. I am simply exhausted in these surroundings, HE! I begin to feel myself a horse. You are from society, still you don't yet know what high society means. To be at last decently dressed, to attend receptions, to display the splendour of wit; from time to time to have a game of baccarat [*laughing*] without tricks or cheating ——

HE. And when evening comes, go to a suburb, where you are considered an honest father, who loves his children and ——

MANCINI. And get hold of something, eh? [*Laughs.*] I shall wear a silk mask and two butlers shall follow me, thus protecting me from the dirty crowd. Ah, HE! The blood of my ancestors boils in me. Look at this stiletto. What do you think? Do you think that it was ever stained with blood?

HE. You frighten me, Count!

MANCINI [*laughing, and putting the stiletto back into its sheath*]. Fool!

HE. And what about the girl?

MANCINI. Tss! I give those bourgeois absolute satisfaction, and they glorify my name. [*Laughs.*] The splendour of my name is beginning to shine with a force unknown. By the way, do you know what automobile firms are the best? Money is no object. [*Laughs.*] Ah! Papa Briquet!

[*Enter* BRIQUET *in his overcoat and silk hat. They shake hands.*]

BRIQUET. So, Mancini, you have obtained a benefit performance for your daughter, Consuelo! I only want to tell you, that if it were not for Zinida...

MANCINI. Listen, Briquet. Decidedly you are a donkey. What are you complaining of? The Baron has bought all the parquet seats for Consuelo's benefit performance. Isn't that enough for you, you miser?

BRIQUET. I love your daughter, Mancini, and I am sorry to let her go. What more does she need here? She has an honest job, wonderful comrades, and the atmosphere ——?

MANCINI. Not *she*, but *I* need something. You understand? [*Laughs.*] I asked you to increase her salary, Harpagon! and now, Mr. Manager, wouldn't

you like to change me a thousand-franc note?

BRIQUET [*with a sigh*]. Give it to me.

MANCINI [*nonchalantly*]. To-morrow. I left it at home. [*All three laugh.*] Laugh, laugh! To-day we are going with the Baron to his villa in the country; people say a very nice villa.

HE. What for?

MANCINI. You know, HE, the crazes of these billionaires. He wants to show Consuelo some winter roses, and me his wine cellars. He will come for us here. What is the matter, my little Consuelo?

[*Enter* CONSUELO, *almost crying.*]

CONSUELO. I can't, Father! Tell him! What right has he to yell at me? He almost hit me with his whip!

MANCINI [*straightening up*]. Briquet! I beg of you, as the Manager, what is this — a stable? To hit my daughter with a whip! I'll show this cub... a mere jockey. ... No, the devil knows what it is, devil knows, I swear....

CONSUELO. Father...

BRIQUET. I will tell him.

CONSUELO. Please don't. Alfred didn't hit me. It's a silly thing, what I told you. What an idea! He is so sorry himself....

BRIQUET. I shall tell him anyhow that ——

CONSUELO. Don't you dare. You mustn't tell him anything. He didn't do a thing.

MANCINI [*still excited*]. He must beg her pardon, the brat.

CONSUELO. He's already asked me to forgive him. How silly you all are! I simply cannot work to-day and I got nervous. What nonsense! The silly boy asked me to forgive him, but I didn't want to. HE, dear, good morning! I didn't notice you. How becoming your tie is. Where are you going, Briquet? To Alfred?

BRIQUET. No, I am going home, dear child. Zinida asked me to give you her love. She will not be here to-day, either

[*He goes out.*]

CONSUELO. Zinida is so nice, so good. Father, why is it that everybody seems s

nice to me? Probably because I am going
away soon. HE, did you hear the march
that Tilly and Polly will play? [*Laughs.*]
Such a cheerful one.

HE. Yes. I heard it. Your benefit
performance will be remarkable.

CONSUELO. I think so, too. Father, I
am hungry. Have them bring me a sandwich.

HE. I'll run for it, my Queen.

CONSUELO. Please do, HE. [*Loudly.*]
But not cheese. I don't like it.

[MANCINI *and* CONSUELO *are alone.*
MANCINI, *lying back comfortably in an
armchair, scrutinizes his daughter with
a searching eye.*]

MANCINI. I find something particular
in you to-day, my child. I don't know
whether it is something better or worse.
You cried?

CONSUELO. Yes, a little. Oh, I am so
hungry.

MANCINI. But you had your breakfast?

CONSUELO. No, I didn't. That's why
I am so hungry. You again forgot to leave
me some money this morning, and without
money...

MANCINI. Oh, the devil... what a memory I have. [*Laughs.*] But we shall have
a very nice meal to-day. Don't eat very
many sandwiches.... Yes, positively I like
you. You must cry more often, my child;
it washes off your superfluous simplicity.
You become more of a woman.

CONSUELO. Am I so simple, Father?

MANCINI. Very.... Too much. I like it
in others, but not in you. Besides, the
Baron...

CONSUELO. Nonsense, I am not simple.
But you know, Bezano scolded me so
much, that even you would have cried.
The devil knows...

MANCINI. Tsss.... Never say "the devil
knows." It isn't decent.

CONSUELO. I say it only when I am with
you.

MANCINI. You must not say it when you
are with me, either. I know it without
you. [*Laughs.*]

CONSUELO. Ha! Listen, Father! It's
new number of Alfred's. He makes such

a jump! Jim says he's bound to break his
neck. Poor fish....

MANCINI [*indifferently*]. Or his leg, or
his back; they all have to break something.
[*Laughs.*] They are breakable toys.

CONSUELO [*listening to the music*]. I'll
be lonesome without them, Father! The
Baron promised to make a ring for me to
gallop over as much as I want. He's not
lying?

MANCINI. A ring? [*Laughs.*] No, it's
not a lie. By the way, child, when speaking of Barons, you must say, "he does not
tell the truth," and not, "he lies."

CONSUELO. It's just the same. It's nice
to be wealthy, Father; you can do what
you want, then.

MANCINI [*with enthusiasm*]. Every-
thing you want. Everything, my child.
Ah! Our fate is being decided to-day.
Pray our clement God, Consuelo. The
Baron is hanging on a thread.

CONSUELO [*indifferently*]. Yes?

MANCINI [*making the gesture with his
fingers*]. On a very thin, silk thread. I
am almost sure that he will make his proposal to-day. [*Laughs.*] Winter roses,
and the web of a spider amongst the roses,
in order that my dear little fly... He is
such a spider.

CONSUELO [*indifferently*]. Yes, a terrible spider. Father, oughtn't I to let him
kiss my hand yet?

MANCINI. By no means. You don't
know yet, darling, what these men are.

CONSUELO. Alfred never kisses.

MANCINI. Alfred! Your Alfred is a
cub, and he mustn't dare. But with men
of that sort, you must be extremely careful,
my child. To-day he would kiss your little
finger, to-morrow your hand, and after to-
morrow you would be on his lap.

CONSUELO. Foul! Father, what are you
talking about? You should be ashamed!

MANCINI. But I know....

CONSUELO. Don't you dare! I don't
want to hear such dirty things. I shall
give the Baron such a slap! A better one
than HE — let him only try.

MANCINI [*with a deprecating gesture*].
All men are like that, child.

CONSUELO. It isn't true. Alfred is not.

Ah! But where is HE? He said he'd run, and he hasn't come back.

MANCINI. The buffet here is closed, and he has to get the sandwiches somewhere else. Consuelo, as your father, I want to warn you about HE. Don't trust him. He knows something. [*Twirls his finger close to his forehead.*] His game is not fair.

CONSUELO. You say it about everybody. I know HE; he is such a nice man, and he loves me so much.

MANCINI. Believe me, there is something in it.

CONSUELO. Father, you make me sick with your advice. Ah! HE, thank you.

[HE, *breathing somewhat heavily, enters and gives her the sandwiches.*]

HE. Eat, Consuelo.

CONSUELO. A hot one.... But you were running, HE? I am so grateful. [*Eats.*] HE, do you love me?

HE. I do, my Queen. I am your court fool.

CONSUELO [*eating*]. And when I leave, will you find another queen?

HE [*making a ceremonious bow*]. I shall follow after you, my incomparable one. I shall carry the train of your dress and wipe away my tears with it. [*Pretends to cry.*]

MANCINI. Idiot! [*Laughs.*] How sorry I am, HE, that those wonderful times have passed, when, in the court of the Counts Mancini, there were scores of motley fools who were given gold and kicks.... Now, Mancini is compelled to go to this dirty circus in order to see a good fool; and still, whose fool is he? Mine? No. He belongs to everybody who pays a franc. We shall very soon be unable to breathe because of Democracy. Democracy, too, needs fools! Think of it, HE; what an unexampled impertinence.

HE. We are the servants of those who pay. But how can we help it, Count?

MANCINI. But is that not sad? Imagine: we are in my castle. I, near the fireplace with my glass of wine, you, at my feet chatting your nonsense, jingling your little bells — diverting me. Sometimes you pinch me too with your jokes: it is allowed by the traditions and necessary for the circulation of the blood. After a while — I am sick of you, I want another one.... Then I give you a kick and... Ah, HE, how wonderful it would be!

HE. It would be marvellous, Mancini!

MANCINI. Yes. Certainly! You would be getting gold coins, those wonderfully little yellow things.... Well, when I become rich, I shall take you. That's settled.

CONSUELO. Take him, Father...

HE. And when the Count, tired of my chattering, will give me a kick with his Highness's foot, then I shall lie down at the little feet of my queen, and shall...

CONSUELO [*laughing*]. Wait for another kick? I'm finished. Father, give me your handkerchief, I want to wipe my hands. You have another one in your pocket. Oh, my goodness, I must work some more!

MANCINI [*uneasy*]. But don't forget, my child!

CONSUELO. No, to-day I won't forget! Go on!

MANCINI [*looking at his watch*]. Yes, it is time.... He asked me to come over when you were ready. You must change your dress before I come back. [*Laughing.*] Signori, miei complimenti.

[*He goes out, playing with his cane. CONSUELO sits on the corner of the divan, and covers herself with her shawl.*]

CONSUELO. Hello, HE! Come and lie down at my feet, and tell me something cheerful.... You know, when you paint the laughter on your face, you are very good-looking, but now, too, you are very, very nice. Come on, HE, why don't you lie down?

HE. Consuelo! Are you going to marry the Baron?

CONSUELO [*indifferently*]. It seems so. The Baron is hanging by a thread! He there is one little sandwich left. Eat it.

HE. Thank you, my Queen. [*Eats.*] And do you remember my prediction?

CONSUELO. What prediction? How quickly you swallow! Does it taste good?

HE. Very good. That if you marry the Baron, you...

CONSUELO. Oh, that's what you're talking about.... But you were making fun.

HE. Nobody can tell, my Queen. Sometimes one makes fun, and suddenly it turns out to be true; the stars never talk in vain. If sometimes it is difficult for a human being to open his mouth and to say a word, how difficult it must be for a star. Think of it.

CONSUELO [laughing]. I should say. Such a mouth! [Makes a tiny mouth.]

HE. No, my dear little girl, were I in your place, I would think it over. And suppose suddenly you should die? Don't marry the Baron, Consuelo!

CONSUELO [thinking]. And what is — death?

HE. I do not know, my Queen. Nobody knows. Like love! Nobody knows. But your little hands will become cold, and your dear little eyes will be closed. You will be away from here. And the music will play without you, and without you the crazy Bezano will be galloping, and Tilly and Polly will be playing on their pipes without you: tilly-polly, tilly-polly... tilly-tilly, polly-polly...

CONSUELO. Please don't, HE darling — I am so sad, anyway... tilly-tilly, polly-polly... [Silence. HE looks at CONSUELO.]

HE. You were crying, my little Consuelo?

CONSUELO. Yes, a little. Alfred made me nervous. But tell me, is it my fault that I can't do anything to-day? I tried to, but I couldn't.

HE. Why?

CONSUELO. Ah, I don't know. There is something here. [Presses her hand against her heart.] I don't know. HE, I must be sick. What is sickness? Does it hurt very much?

HE. It is not sickness. It is the charm of the far off-stars, Consuelo. It is the voice of your fate, my little Queen.

CONSUELO. Don't talk nonsense, please. What should the stars care about me? I am so small. Nonsense, HE! Tell me rather another tale which you know: about the blue sea and those gods, you know... who are so beautiful. Did they all die?

HE. They are all alive, but they hide themselves, my goddess.

CONSUELO. In the woods or mountains? Can one come across them? Ah, imagine

HE... I come across a god, and he suddenly takes a look at me! I'd run away. [Laughs.] This morning when I went without breakfast, I became so sad, so disgusted, and I thought: if a god should come, and give me something to eat! And as I thought it, I suddenly heard, honestly it's true, I heard: "Consuelo, somebody's calling you." [Angrily.] Don't you dare laugh!

HE. Am I laughing?

CONSUELO. Honestly, it's true. Ah, HE, but he didn't come. He only called me and disappeared, and how can you find him? It hurt me so much, and hurts even now. Why did you remind me of my childhood? I'd forgotten it entirely. There was the sea... and something... many, many... [Closes her eyes, smiling.]

HE. Remember, Consuelo!

CONSUELO. No. [Opening her eyes.] I forget everything about it. [Looks around the room.] HE, do you see what a poster they made for my benefit performance? It's Father's idea. The Baron liked it.
[HE laughs. Silence.]

HE [slowly]. Consuelo, my Queen! Don't go to the Baron to-day.

CONSUELO. Why? [After a silence.] How fresh you are, HE.

HE [lowering his head, slowly]. I don't want it.

CONSUELO [getting up]. What? You don't want it?

HE [bowing his head still lower]. I do not want you to marry the Baron. [Imploring.] I... I shall not allow it... I beg you!

CONSUELO. Whom, then, would you ask me to marry? You, perhaps, you fool? [With a rancorous laugh.] Are you crazy, my darling? "I shall not allow." HE! HE will not allow me! But it is unbearable! What business is it of yours? [Walking up and down the room, looks over her shoulder at HE, with anger.] Some fool clown, whom they can kick out of here any minute. You make me sick with your stupid tales. Or you like slaps so much. Fool, you couldn't invent anything better than a slap!

HE [*without lifting his head*]. Forgive me, my Queen.

CONSUELO. He is glad when they laugh at him. Some god! No, I shan't forgive. I know you. [*Makes same gesture as* MANCINI.] You have something there! Laughs... so nicely... plays, plays, and then suddenly — hop! *Obey him!* No, darling, I am not that kind! Carry my train, that is your business — fool!

HE. I shall carry your train, my Queen. Forgive me. Give me back the image of my beautiful, piteous goddess.

CONSUELO [*quieting down*]. You're playing again?

HE. I am.

CONSUELO [*laughing*]. You see! [*Sits down.*] Foolish HE.

HE. I see everything, my Queen. I see how beautiful you are, and how low under your feet your poor court fool is lying. Somewhere in the abyss his little bells are ringing. He kneels before you and prays; forgive and pity him, my divine one. He was too impudent; he played so cheerfully that he went too far and lost his tiny little mind, the last bit of understanding he had saved up. Forgive me!

CONSUELO. All right. I forgive you. [*Laughs.*] And now will you allow me to marry the Baron?

HE [*also laughing*]. And nevertheless I will not allow it. But what does a queen care about the permission of her enamoured fool?

CONSUELO. Get up. You are forgiven. And do you know why? You think because of your words? You are a cunning beast, HE! No, because of the *sandwiches.* That's why. You were so lovely, you panted so when you brought them. Poor darling HE. From to-morrow you may be at my feet again. And as soon as I whistle, "tuwhooo" ——

HE. I shall instantly lie down at thy feet, Consuelo. It is settled! But all my little bells fell off to-day and ——

[BEZANO *appears, confused.*]

CONSUELO. Alfred! You came for me?

BEZANO. Yes. Will you work some more, Consuelo?

CONSUELO. Certainly. As much as you want. But I thought, Alfred, you were mad at me? I shan't dawdle any more.

BEZANO. No. You didn't dawdle. Don't be offended, because I yelled so much. You know when one has to teach, and ——

CONSUELO. My goodness, do you think I don't understand? You are too nice, unbearably nice, to like teaching such a fool as me. Do you think I don't understand? Come on!

BEZANO. Come on! Hello, HE! I haven't seen you yet to-day. How are you?

HE. How are you, Bezano? Wait, wait a minute — stay here a minute, both of you — that way. Yes!

[CONSUELO *and* BEZANO *stand side by side, the jockey scowling,* CONSUELO *laughing and flushing.*]

CONSUELO. Like Adam and Eve? How foolish you are! Terribly. [*She runs away.*] I shall only change my slippers, Alfred.

HE. Consuelo! And how about Father and the Baron? They will come soon, to take you with them.

CONSUELO. Let them come. They can wait. Not very important people.

[*Runs away.* BEZANO *hesitatingly follows her.*]

HE. Stay here for a while, Bezano. Sit down.

BEZANO. What more do you want? I have no time for your nonsense.

HE. You can remain standing if you want to. Bezano — you love her?

[*Silence.*]

BEZANO. I shall allow nobody to interfere with my affairs. You allow yourself too many liberties, HE. I don't know you. You came from the street, and why should I trust you?

HE. But you know the Baron? Listen. It is painful for me to pronounce these words: she loves you. Save her from the spider! Or are you blind, and don't see the web, which is woven in every day corner. Get out of the vicious circle in which you are turning around, like a blind man. Take her away, steal her, do what you want... kill her even, and take her to the heavens or to the devil! But don't give her to this man! He is a defiler of love. And if you are timid, if you are afraid to lift your hand against her — kill the Baron! Kill!

BEZANO [with a smile]. And who will kill the others, to come?

HE. She loves you.

BEZANO. Did she tell you that herself?

HE. What a petty, what a stupid, what a human pride! But *you* are a little god! A god, youth! Why don't you want to believe me? Or does the street, from which I have come, bother you? But look, look yourself. Look in my eyes, do such eyes lie? Yes, my face is ugly, I make faces and grimaces, I am surrounded by laughter, but don't you see the god behind all this, a god, like you? Look, look at me! [BEZANO *bursts out laughing*.] What are you laughing at, youth?

BEZANO. You look now as you did that evening in the ring. You remember? When you were a great man, and they sent for you from the Academy, and suddenly — Hup! He Who Gets Slapped!

HE [laughing the same way]. Yes, yes, you are right, Bezano. There is a resemblance. [With a strained expression, taking a pose.] "It seems to me they sent for me from the Academy!"

BEZANO [displeased]. But I don't like this play. You can present *your* face for slaps if you want to, but don't dare to expose mine. [Turns to go.]

HE. Bezano!

BEZANO [turning round]. And never let me hear any more about Consuelo, and don't dare to tell me again that I am a god! It is disgusting.

[BEZANO *goes out angrily, striking his boot with his whip.* HE *is alone. Wrathfully, with a tortured expression, he makes a step towards the jockey, then stops, with soundless laughter, his head thrown backwards. The* BARON *and* MANCINI *find him in this position, when they enter.*]

MANCINI [laughing]. What a cheerful chap you are, HE! You laugh when you are alone. [HE *laughs aloud.*] Stop it, fool! How can you stand it?

HE [bowing low, with a large gesture]. How do you do, Baron? My humblest respects to you, Count. I beg your pardon, Count, but you found the clown at work. These are, so to speak, Baron, his everyday pleasures.

MANCINI [lifting his eyebrows]. Tsss. But you are a clever man, HE. I shall ask Papa Briquet to give you a benefit performance. Shall I, HE?

HE. Please do me the favour, Count.

MANCINI. Don't overdo. Be more simple, HE. [Laughs.] But how many slaps will you get at your benefit performance, when even on weekdays they ring you like a gong! A funny profession, isn't it, Baron?

BARON. Very strange. But where is the Countess?

MANCINI. Yes, yes. I shall go for her at once. Dear child, she is so absorbed in her benefit performance and her work. They call this jumping *work*, Baron.

BARON. I can wait a little.

[Sits down, with his silk hat on his head.]

MANCINI. But why? I shall hurry her up. I shall be back at once. And you, HE, be a nice host, and entertain our dear guest. You will not be bored in his company, Baron.

[He goes out. HE *strides about the stage, smiling and glancing from time to time at the* BARON. *The latter sits with his legs spread apart and his chin on the top of his cane. The silk hat remains on his head. He is silent.*]

HE. In what way would you like me to entertain you, Baron?

BARON. In no way! I don't like clowns.

HE. Nor I Barons.

[Silence. HE *puts on his derby hat, takes a chair with a large gesture, and puts it down heavily, in front of the* BARON. *He sits astride it, imitating the pose of the* BARON, *and looks him in the eyes. Silence.*]

HE. Can you be silent very long?

BARON. Very long.

HE [taps on the floor with his foot]. And can you wait very long?

BARON. Very long.

HE. Until you get it?

BARON. Until I get it. And you?

HE. I too.

[Both look at each other, silently, their heads close together. From the ring one hears the strains of the Tango.]

CURTAIN

ACT IV

Music in the ring. More disorder in the room than usual. All kinds of actors' costumes hanging on pegs and lying in the corners. On the table a bouquet of fiery-red roses, put there by some careless hand. At the entrance, near the arch, three bareback riders are smoking and chattering; they are all minor actors. All part their hair the same way; two wear small moustaches; the third one is clean-shaven with a face like a bull-dog.

THE CLEAN-SHAVEN ONE. Go on, Henry! Ten thousand francs! It's too much even for the Baron.

THE SECOND. How much are roses now?

THE SHAVEN. I don't know. In winter they are certainly more expensive, but still Henry talks nonsense. Ten thousand!

THE SECOND. The Baron has his own hothouse. They don't cost him anything.

HENRY [throwing away his cigar, which has burned the tips of his fingers]. No, Grab, you're silly. There's a whole car-load full! One can smell the roses a mile away. They're to cover the entire arena.

THE SHAVEN. Only the ring.

HENRY. It's all the same. In order to cover the ring, you must have thousands and thousands of roses. You'll see what it looks like, when they've covered everything like a carpet. He ordered them to make it like a carpet! Do you see, Grab?

THE SECOND. What a Baron's craze! Isn't it time yet?

HENRY. No, we have time enough. I

rather like it: a fiery-red tango on a fiery-red cover of winter roses!

THE SHAVEN. Consuelo will be galloping on roses. And Bezano?

THE SECOND. And Bezano on thorns. [Smiles.]

THE SHAVEN. That youngster has no self-respect. I'd have refused.

HENRY. But it is his job. He's got to do it. [Laughs.] Talk to him about self-respect! He's as angry and proud as a little Satan.

THE SECOND. No, you may say what you like, it's an excellent benefit performance. It's a joy to look at the crowd. They're so excited.

HENRY. Tsss!

[All throw away their cigars and cigarettes, like school boys who are caught, and make way for ZINIDA, who enters with HE.]

ZINIDA. What are you doing here, gentlemen? Your place is at the entrance.

HENRY [with a respectful smile]. We are here just for a minute, Madame Zinida. We are going. What a successful evening! And what a glory for Papa Briquet!

ZINIDA. Yes. Go, and please don't leave your places. [They go. ZINIDA pulls a drawer out of the desk, and puts in some papers. She is in her lion tamer's costume.] HE, what were you doing near my lions? You frightened me.

HE. Why, Duchess, I merely wanted to hear what the beasts were saying about the benefit performance. They are pacing in their cages, and growling.

ZINIDA. The music makes them nervous Sit down, HE. An excellent evening, and I am so glad that Consuelo is leaving us Have you heard about the Baron's roses?

HE. Everybody is talking about them The Hymeneal roses!

ZINIDA. Here are some, too. [Pushes away the bouquet.] You find them every where. Yes, I am glad. She is superfluou here, and disturbs our work. It is a mis fortune for a cast to have in it such a beauti ful and such an... accessible girl.

HE. But it is an honest marriage Duchess, is it not?

ZINIDA. I don't care what it is.

HE. Spiders, too, need an improvement in their breed! Can't you imagine, Zinida, what charming little spiders this couple will create! They will have the face of their mother, Consuelo, and the stomach of their father, the Baron, and thus could be an ornament for any circus-ring.

ZINIDA. You are malicious to-day, HE. You are morose.

HE. I laugh.

ZINIDA. You do, but without joy. Why are you without make-up?

HE. I am in the third act. I have time. And how does Bezano feel about this evening. Is he glad?

ZINIDA. I didn't talk to Bezano. You know what I think, my friend? You, too, are superfluous here. [Silence.]

HE. How do you want me to take that, Zinida?

ZINIDA. Just as I said. In fact, Consuelo sold herself for nothing. What is the Baron worth, with his poor millions? People say that you are clever, too clever perhaps; tell me then, for how much could one buy me?

HE [looking as if he were pricing her]. Only for a crown.

ZINIDA. A baron's crown?

HE. No, a royal one.

ZINIDA. You are far from being stupid. And you guessed that Consuelo is not Mancini's daughter?

HE [startled]. What! And she knows it?

ZINIDA. Hardly. And why should she know it? Yes, she is a girl from Corsica whose parents are unknown. He preferred to use her for business rather than... But according to the law, she is his daughter, Countess Veronica Mancini.

HE. It is nice, to have everything done according to law, isn't it, Zinida? But it is curious there is more blue blood in her than in this Mancini. One would say that it was she who found him on the street, and made him a count and her father. Count Mancini! [Laughs.]

ZINIDA. Yes, you are gloomy, HE. I changed my mind, you'd better stay.

HE. Will I not be superfluous?

ZINIDA. When she is gone, you will not. Oh! You don't know yet, how nice it is to be with us. What a rest for the body and mind. I understand you. I am clever, too. Like you, I brought with me from out there my inclination for chains, and for a long time I chained myself to whatever I could, in order to feel firm.

HE. Bezano?

ZINIDA. Bezano and others; there were many, there will be many more. My red lion, with whom I am desperately in love, is still more terrible than Bezano. But it is all nonsense; old habits, which we are sorry to let go, like old servants who steal things. Leave Consuelo alone. She has her own way.

HE. Automobiles and diamonds?

ZINIDA. When did you see a beauty clad in simple cotton? If this one does not buy her, another will. They buy off everything that is beautiful. Yes, I know. For the first ten years she will be a sad beauty, who will attract the eyes of the poor man on the side-walk; afterward she will begin to paint a little around her eyes and smile, and then will take ——

HE. Her chauffeur or butler as a lover? You're not guessing badly, Zinida!

ZINIDA. Am I not right? I don't want to intrude on your confidence, but to-day I am sorry for you, HE. What can you do against Fate? Don't be offended, my friend, by the words of a woman. I like you; you are not beautiful, nor young, nor rich, and your place is ——

HE. On the side-walk, from which one looks at the beauties. [Laughs.] And if I don't want to?

ZINIDA. What does it matter, your "want" or "don't want"? I am sorry for you, my poor friend, but if you are a strong man, and I think you are, then there is only one way for you. To forget.

HE. You think that that's being strong? And you are saying this, you, Queen Zinida, who want to awaken the feeling of love, even in the heart of a lion? For one second of an illusory possession, you are ready to pay with your life, and still you advise me to forget! Give me your strong hand, my beautiful lady; see how much strength there is in this pressure, and don't pity me.

[*Enter* BRIQUET *and* MANCINI. *The latter is reserved, and self-consciously imposing. He has a new suit, but the same cane, and the same noiseless smile of a satyr.*]

ZINIDA [*whispering*]. Will you stay?

HE. Yes. I shan't go away.

MANCINI. How are you, my dear? But you are dazzling, my dear! I swear you are marvellous! Your lion would be an ass, if he did not kiss your hand, as I do....
[*Kisses her hand.*]

ZINIDA. May I congratulate you, Count?

MANCINI. Yes, *merci.* [*To* HE.] How are you, my dear?

HE. Good evening, Count!

BRIQUET. Zinida, the Count wants to pay immediately for the breach of contract with Consuelo... the Countess's contract. Don't you remember, Mother, how much it is?

ZINIDA. I'll look it up, Papa.

MANCINI. Yes, please. Consuelo will not return here any more. We leave to-morrow.

[ZINIDA *and* BRIQUET *search among the papers.* HE *takes* MANCINI *roughly by the elbow, and draws him aside.*]

HE [*in a low voice*]. How are your girls, Mancini?

MANCINI. What girls? What is this, stupidity or blackmail? Look out, sir, be careful, the policeman is not far.

HE. You are much too severe, Mancini. I assumed, that since we are *tête-à-tête*...

MANCINI. But tell me, what kind of *tête-à-tête* is possible, between a clown and me? [*Laughs.*] You are stupid, HE. You should say what you want, and not ask questions!

BRIQUET. Three thousand francs, Count.

MANCINI. Is that all? For Consuelo? All right. I'll tell the Baron.

ZINIDA. You took ——

BRIQUET. Don't, Mother, don't.

ZINIDA. Count, you drew in advance, I have it written down, eighty francs and twenty centimes. Will you pay this money, too?

MANCINI. Certainly, certainly. You will get three thousand and one hundred. [*Laughing.*] Twenty centimes! I never

thought I could be so accurate! [*Seriously.*] Yes, my friends. My daughter Consuelo — the Countess — and the Baron, expressed their desire to bid farewell to the whole cast.

HE. The Baron, too?

MANCINI. Yes, Auguste, too. They want to do it during the intermission. Therefore, I ask you to gather here... the more decent ones... but please don't make it too crowded! HE, will you, sir, be kind enough to run into the buffet and tell them to bring right away a basket of champagne, bottles and glasses — you understand?

HE. Yes, Count.

MANCINI. Wait a minute, what's the hurry — what is this, a new costume? You are all burning like the devils in hell!

HE. You do me too much honour, Count, I am not a devil. I am merely a poor sinner whom the devils are frying a little. [*He goes out, bowing like a clown.*]

MANCINI. A gifted chap, but too cunning.

BRIQUET. It's the Tango colour, in honour of your daughter, Count. He needs it for a new stunt, which he doesn't want to tell in advance. Don't you want to sit down, Count?

MANCINI. Auguste is waiting for me, but... it's all right. [*Takes a seat.*] Nevertheless I am sorry to leave you, my friend. High society, certainly, prerogatives of the title, castles of exalted noblemen, but where could I find such freedom, and... such simplicity.... And besides, these announcements, these burning posters, which take your breath in the morning, they had something which summoned, which encouraged.... *There*, my friends, I shall become old.

BRIQUET. But pleasures of a higher kind, Count. Why are you silent, Zinida?

ZINIDA. I'm listening.

MANCINI. By the way, my dear, how do you like my suit? You have wonderful taste.

[*Spreads out his lace tie and lace cuffs.*]

ZINIDA. I like it. You look like a nobleman of the courts of long ago.

MANCINI. Yes? But don't you think it is too conspicuous? Who wears lace and satin now? This dirty democracy will soon make us dress ourselves in sackcloth. [*With a sigh.*] Auguste told me that this jabot was out of place.

ZINIDA. The Baron is too severe.

MANCINI. Yes, but it seems to me he is right. I am a little infected with your fancy.

[HE *returns. Two waiters follow him, carrying a basket of champagne and glasses. They prepare everything on the table.*]

MANCINI. Ah! *merci*, HE. But please, none of this bourgeois exploding of corks; be slower and more modest. Send the bill to Baron Regnard. Then, we will be here, Briquet. I must go.

ZINIDA [*looks at her watch*]. Yes, the act is going to end soon.

MANCINI. Heavens!

[*Disappears in a hurry.*]

BRIQUET. The devil take him!

ZINIDA [*pointing to the waiter*]. Not so loud, Louis!

BRIQUET. No! The devil take him! And why couldn't you help me, Mother? You left me alone to talk to him. High Society! High pleasures! Swindler.

[HE *and* ZINIDA *laugh. The waiters smile.*]

BRIQUET [*to the waiters*]. What are you laughing about? You can go. We will help ourselves. Whiskey and soda, Jean! [*In a low and angry voice.*] Champagne!

[*Enter* JACKSON, *in his clown's costume.*]

JACKSON. A whiskey and soda for me, too! At least I hear some laughter here. Those idiots have simply forgotten how to laugh. My sun was rising and setting and crawling all over the ring — and not a smile! Look at my bottom, shines like a mirror! [*Turns around quickly.*] Beg your pardon, Zinida. And you don't look really to-night, HE. Look out for your cheeks. hate beauties.

BRIQUET. A benefit performance crowd!

JACKSON [*looking in a hand mirror, correcting his make-up*]. In the orchestra there are some Barons and Egyptian mummies. got a belly-ache from fright. I am an honest clown. I can't stand it when they look at me as if I had stolen a handkerchief. HE, please give them a good many slaps to-night.

HE. Be quiet, Jim. I shall avenge you.

[HE *goes out.*]

ZINIDA. And how is Bezano?

JACKSON [*grumbling*]. Bezano! A crazy success. But he is crazy, he will break his neck to-morrow. Why does he run such a risk? Or perhaps he has wings, like a god? Devil take it. It's disgusting to look at him. It's not work any more.

BRIQUET. You are right, Jim! It is not work any more. To your health, old comrade, Jackson.

JACKSON. To yours, Louis.

BRIQUET. It is not work any more, since these Barons came here! Do you hear? They are laughing. But I am indignant, I am indignant, Jim! What do they want here, these Barons? Let them steal hens in other hen roosts, and leave us in peace. Ah! Had I been Secretary of the Interior, I should have made an iron fence between us and those people.

JACKSON. I am very sorry myself for our dear little Consuelo. I don't know why, but it seems to me that we all look to-day more like swindlers than honest artists. Don't you think so, Zinida?

ZINIDA. Everybody does what he wants. It's Consuelo's business and her father's.

BRIQUET. No, Mother, that's not true! Not everybody does what he wants, but it turns out this way... devil knows why.

[*Enter* ANGELICA *and* THOMAS, *an athlete.*]

ANGELICA. Is this where we're going to have champagne?

BRIQUET. And you're glad already?

THOMAS. There it is! Oh, oh, what a lot!

ANGELICA. The Count told me to come here. I met him.

BRIQUET [*angrily*]. All right, if he said so, but there is no reason to enjoy it. Look out, Angelica, you will have a bad end. I see you through and through. How does she work, Thomas?

THOMAS. Very well.

ANGELICA [*in a low voice*]. How angry Papa Briquet is to-night.

[*Enter* HE, TILLY, POLLY, *and other actors, all in their costumes.*]

TILLY. Do you really want champagne?

POLLY. I don't want it at all. Do you, Tilly?

TILLY. And I don't want it. HE, did you see how the Count walks?

[*Walks, imitating* MANCINI. *Laughter.*]

POLLY. Let me be the Baron. Take my arm. Look out, ass, you stepped on my beloved family tree!

ANGELICA. It'll soon be finished. Consuelo is galloping now. It is her waltz. What a success she is having!

[*All listen to the waltz.* TILLY *and* POLLY *are singing it softly.*]

ANGELICA. She is so beautiful! Are those her flowers?

[*They listen. Suddenly, a crash as if a broken wall were tumbling down: applause, shouting, screaming; much motion on the stage. The actors are pouring champagne. New ones come in, talking and laughing. When they notice the director and the champagne, they become quiet and modest.*]

VOICES. They're coming! What a success! I should say, since all the orchestra seats... And what will it be when they see the Tango? Don't be envious, Alphonse.

BRIQUET. Silence! Not so much noise, please! Zinida, look here, don't be so quiet! High society!

[*Enter* CONSUELO, *on the arm of the* BARON *who is stiff and erect. She is happy.* MANCINI, *serious and happy. Behind them, riders, actors, actresses. The* BARON *has in his button-hole a fiery-red rose. All applaud and cry: "Bravo, bravo!"*]

CONSUELO. Friends... my dears... Father, I can't....

[*Throws herself into* MANCINI'S *arms, and hides her face on his shoulders.* MANCINI *looks with a smile over her head at the* BARON. BARON *smiles slightly, but remains earnest and motionless. A new burst of applause.*]

BRIQUET. Enough, children! Enough!

MANCINI. Calm yourself, calm yourself.

my child. How they all love you! [*Taking a step forward.*] Ladies and gentlemen, Baron Regnard did me the honour yesterday, to ask for the hand of my daughter, the Countess Veronica, whom you knew under the name of Consuelo. Please take your glasses.

CONSUELO. No, I am still Consuelo, to-night, and I shall always be Consuelo! Zinida, dear!

[*Falls on the neck of* ZINIDA. *Fresh applause.*]

BRIQUET. Stop it! Silence! Take your glasses. What are you standing here for? If you came, then take the glasses.

TILLY [*trembling*]. They are frightened. You take yours first, Papa, and we will follow.

[*They take the glasses.* CONSUELO *is near the* BARON, *holding the sleeve of his dress coat with her left hand. In her right hand she has a glass of champagne, which spills over.*]

BARON. You are spilling your wine, Consuelo.

CONSUELO. Ah! It is nothing! I am frightened, too. Are you, Father?

MANCINI. Silly child.

[*An awkward silence.*]

BRIQUET [*with a step forward*]. Countess! As the director of the circus, who was happy enough... to witness... many times ... your successes...

CONSUELO. I do not *like* this, Papa Briquet! I am Consuelo. What do you want to do with me? I shall cry. I don't want this "Countess." Give me a kiss, Briquet!

BRIQUET. Ah, Consuelo! Books have killed you.

[*Kisses her with tears. Laughter, applause. The clowns cluck like hens, bark, and express their emotions in many other ways. The motley crowd of clowns, which is ready for the pantomime, becomes more and more lively. The* BARON *is motionless, there is a wide space around him; the people touch glasses with him in a hurry, and go off to one side. With* CONSUELO *they clink willingly and cheerfully. She kisses the women.*]

JACKSON. Silence! Consuelo, from to-day on, I extinguish my sun. Let the dark night come after you leave us. You were a nice comrade and worker, we all loved you and will love the traces of your little feet on the sand. Nothing remains to us!

CONSUELO. You are so good, so good, Jim. So good that there is no one better. And your sun is better than all the other suns. I laughed so much at it. Alfred, dear, why don't you come? I was looking for you.

BEZANO. My congratulations, Countess.

CONSUELO. Alfred, I am Consuelo!

BEZANO. When you are on horseback; but here — I congratulate you, Countess.

[*He passes, only slightly touching* CONSUELO's *glass.* CONSUELO *still holds it.* MANCINI *looks at the* BARON *with a smile. The latter is motionless.*]

BRIQUET. Nonsense, Bezano. You are making Consuelo unhappy. She is a good comrade.

CONSUELO. No, it's all right.

ANGELICA. You'll dance the Tango with her to-night, so how is she a countess?

TILLY. May I clink glasses with you, Consuelo? You know Polly has died of grief already, and I am going to die. I have such a weak stomach.

[*Laughter;* BARON *shows slight displeasure. General motion.*]

MANCINI. Enough, enough! The intermission is over.

CONSUELO. Already? It's so nice here.

BRIQUET. I shall prolong it. They can wait. Tell them, Thomas.

MANCINI. Auguste, the musicians of the orchestra, too, ask permission to congratulate you and Consuelo. Do you...?

BARON. Certainly, certainly.

[*Enter crowd of musicians. The conductor, an old Italian, lifts his glass solemnly and without looking at the* BARON.]

THE CONDUCTOR. Consuelo! They call you Countess here, but for me you were and are *Consuelo*.

CONSUELO. Certainly!

CONDUCTOR. Consuelo! My violins and bassoons, my trumpets and drums, all are drinking your health. Be happy, dear child, as you were happy here. And we shall conserve for ever in our hearts the fair memory of our light-winged fairy, who guided our bows so long. I have finished! Give my love to our beautiful Italy, Consuelo.

[*Applause, compliments. The musicians one after another clink glasses and go out into the corridor.* CONSUELO *is almost crying.*]

MANCINI. Don't be so sensitive, my child, it is indecent. Had I known that you would respond this way to this comedy — Auguste, look how touched this little heart is!

BARON. Calm yourself, Consuelo.

CONSUELO. It is all right. Ah, Father, listen!

[*The musicians are playing the Tango in the corridor. Exclamations.*]

MANCINI. You see. It is for you.

CONSUELO. They are so nice. My Tango! I want to dance. Who is going to dance with me? [*Looks around, seeking* BEZANO, *who turns away sadly.*] Who, then?

VOICES. Baron! Let the Baron dance! Baron!

BARON. All right. [*Takes* CONSUELO's *arm, and stands in the centre of a circle which is formed.*] I do not know how to dance the Tango, but I shall hold tight. Dance, Consuelo.

[*He stands with legs spread, heavily and awkwardly, like an iron-moulded man, holding* CONSUELO's *arm firmly and seriously.*]

MANCINI [*applauding*]. Bravo! Bravo! [CONSUELO *makes a few restless movements, and pulls her arm away.*]

CONSUELO. No, I can't this way. How stupid! Let me go!

[*She goes to* ZINIDA *and embraces her, as if hiding herself. The music still plays. The* BARON *goes off quietly to the side. There is an unfriendly silence among the cast. They shrug their shoulders.*]

MANCINI [*alone*]. Bravo! Bravo! It is charming, it is exquisite!

JACKSON. Not entirely, Count.

[TILLY *and* POLLY *imitate the* BARON

and CONSUELO *without moving from their places.*]

TILLY [*shrieking*]. Let me go!

POLLY. No, I'll not. Dance!

[*The music stops abruptly. General, too loud laughter; the clowns bark and roar.* PAPA BRIQUET *gesticulates, in order to reëstablish silence. The* BARON *is apparently as indifferent as before.*]

MANCINI. Really these vagabonds are becoming too impertinent. [*Shrugging his shoulders.*] It smells of the stable. You cannot help it, Auguste!

BARON. Don't be upset, Count.

HE [*holding his glass, approaches the* BARON]. Baron! Will you permit me to make a toast?

BARON. Make it.

HE. To your dance!

[*Slight laughter in the crowd.*]

BARON. I don't dance!

HE. Then another one, Baron. Let us drink to those who know how to wait longer, until they get it.

BARON. I do not accept any toasts which I do not understand. Say it more simply.

[*Voice of a woman:* "Bravo, HE!" *Slight laughter.* MANCINI *says something hastily to* BRIQUET; *the latter spreads his arms in gesture of helplessness.* JACKSON *takes* HE *by the arm.*]

JACKSON. Beat it, HE! The Baron doesn't like jokes.

HE. But I want to drink with the Baron. What can be simpler? Simpler? Baron, let us drink to the very small distance which will always remain 'twixt the cup and the lip! [*Spills his wine, and laughs.*]

[*The* BARON *turns his back on him, indifferently. The music plays in the ring. The bell rings.*]

BRIQUET [*relieved*]. There! To the ring, ladies and gentlemen, to the ring, to the ring!

[*The actresses run out. The crowd becomes smaller; laughter and voices.*]

MANCINI [*much excited, whispers to the* BARON]. "Auguste, Auguste ——"

BRIQUET [*to* ZINIDA]. Thank heaven they're beginning. Ah, Mother, I asked you... but you want a scandal by all means, and you always ——

ZINIDA. Let me alone, Louis.

[HE *approaches* CONSUELO, *who is alone.*]

CONSUELO. HE, deary, how are you? I thought you didn't want even to come near me. [*In a low voice.*] Did you notice Bezano?

HE. I was waiting for my turn, Queen. It was so difficult to get through the crowd to approach you.

CONSUELO. Through the crowd? [*With a sad smile.*] I am quite alone. What do you want, Father?

MANCINI. Child! Auguste...

CONSUELO [*pulling away her hand*]. Let me alone! I'll soon be —— Come here, HE. What did you say to him? They all laughed. I couldn't understand. What?

HE. I joked, Consuelo.

CONSUELO. Please don't, HE, don't make him angry; he is so terrible. Did you see how he pressed my arm? I wanted to scream. [*With tears in her eyes.*] He hurt me!

HE. It's not too late yet. Refuse him.

CONSUELO. It *is* too late, HE. Don't talk about it.

HE. Do you want it? I will take you away from here.

CONSUELO. Where to? [*Laughs.*] Ah, my dear little silly boy, where could you take me to? All right, be quiet. How pale you are! You too, love me? Don't HE, please don't! Why do they all love me?

HE. You are so beautiful!

CONSUELO. No, no. It's not true. They must not love me. I was still a little cheerful, but when they began to speak... so nicely... and about Italy... and to bid farewell, as if I were dying, I thought I should begin to cry. Don't talk, don't talk, but drink to... my happiness. [*With a sad smile.*] To my happiness, HE. What are you doing?

HE. I am throwing away the glass from which you drank with the others. I shall give you another one. Wait a minute.

[*Goes to pour champagne.* CONSUELO *walks about thoughtfully. Almost all are gone. Only the principal figures are left.*]

MANCINI [*coming to her*]. But it is really

becoming indecent, Veronica. Auguste is so nice, he is waiting for you, and you talk here with this clown. Some stupid secrets. They're looking at you — it is becoming noticeable. It is high time, Veronica, to get rid of these habits.

CONSUELO [*loudly*]. Let me alone, Father! I want to do so, and will do so. They are all my friends. Do you hear? Let me alone!

BARON. Don't, Count. Please, Consuelo, talk to whomever you please and as much as you want. Would you like a cigar, Count? Dear Briquet, please order them to prolong the intermission a little more.

BRIQUET. With pleasure, Baron. The orchestra crowd can be a little angry.

[*Goes, and returns shortly. HE gives glass to CONSUELO*]

HE. Here is your glass. To your happiness, to your freedom, Consuelo!

CONSUELO. And where is yours? We must touch our glasses.

HE. You leave half.

CONSUELO. Must I drink so much? HE, deary, I shall become drunk. I still have to ride.

HE. No, you will not be drunk. Dear little girl, did you forget that I am your magician? Be quiet and drink. I charmed the wine. My witchery is in it. Drink, goddess.

CONSUELO [*lingering*]. What kind eyes you have. But why are you so pale?

HE. Because I love you. Look at my kind eyes and drink; give yourself up to my charms, goddess! You shall fall asleep, and wake again, as before. Do you remember? And you shall see your country, your sky....

CONSUELO [*bringing the glass to her lips*]. I shall see all this; is that true?

HE [*growing paler*]. Yes! Awake, goddess, and remember the time when, covered with snow-white sea-foam, thou didst emerge from the sky-blue waters. Remember heaven, and the low eastern wind, and the whisper of the foam at thy marble feet....

CONSUELO [*drinking*]. There! Look! Just a half! Take it. But what is the matter with you? Are you laughing or crying?

HE. I am laughing and crying.

MANCINI [*pushing HE away, slightly*]. Enough, Countess, my patience is exhausted. If Auguste is good enough to allow it, then I, your Father —— Your arm, Countess! Will you step aside, sir?

CONSUELO. I am tired.

MANCINI. You are not too tired to chatter and drink wine with a clown, and when your duty calls you — Briquet! Tell them to ring the bell. It is time.

CONSUELO. I am tired, Father.

ZINIDA. Count, it is cruel. Don't you see how pale she has become?

BARON. What is the matter with you, dear little Consuelo?

CONSUELO. Nothing.

ZINIDA. She simply needs a rest, Baron. She hasn't sat down yet... and so much excitement.... Sit down here, dear child. Cover yourself and rest a little. Men are so cruel!

CONSUELO. I still have to work. [*Closing her eyes.*] And the roses, are they ready?

ZINIDA. Ready, dear, ready. You will have such an extraordinary carpet. You will gallop as if on air. Rest.

POLLY. Do you want some moosic? We will play you a song; do you want it?

CONSUELO [*smiling, eyes closed*]. Yes, I do.

[*The clowns play a soft and naïve song: tilly-polly, tilly-polly. General silence. HE sits in the corner with his face turned away. JACKSON watches him out of the corner of his eye, and drinks wine, lazily. The BARON, in his usual pose, wide and heavily spread legs, looks at the pale face of CONSUELO, with his bulging motionless eyes.*]

CONSUELO [*with a sudden cry*]. Ah! Pain!

ZINIDA. What is it, Consuelo?

MANCINI. My child! Are you sick? Calm yourself.

BARON [*growing pale*]. Wait a moment. ... She was too much excited.... Consuelo!

CONSUELO [*gets up, looking before her with wide-open eyes, as if she were listening to something within herself*]. Ah! I feel pain. Here at the heart. Father, what is it? I am afraid. What is it? My feet too... my feet too... I can't stand....

[*Falls on divan, her eyes wide open.*]

MANCINI [*running about*]. Bring a doctor! Heavens. it is terrible! Auguste, Baron... It never happened to her. It is nerves, nerves.... Calm yourself, calm, child ——

BRIQUET. Bring a doctor!

[*Somebody runs for a doctor.*]

JACKSON [*in a voice full of fear*]. HE, what is the matter with you?

HE. It is death, Consuelo, my little Queen. I killed you. You are dying.

[*He cries, loudly and bitterly.* CON-SUELO *with a scream, closes her eyes, and becomes silent and quiet. All are in terrible agitation. The* BARON *is motionless, and sees only* CONSUELO.]

MANCINI [*furious*]. You are lying, rascal! Damned clown! What did you give her? You poisoned her! Murderer! Bring a doctor!

HE. A doctor will not help. You are dying, my little Queen. Consuelo! Consuelo!

[BEZANO *rushes in, cries:* "Briquet!" *becomes silent and looks with horror at* CONSUELO. *Somebody else comes in.* BRIQUET *is making gestures for some one to close the door.*]

CONSUELO [*in a dull and distant voice*]. You are joking, HE? Don't frighten me. I am so frightened. Is that death? I don't want it. Ah, HE, my darling HE, tell me that you are joking, I am afraid, my dear, golden HE!

[HE *pushes away the* BARON, *with a commanding gesture, and stands in his place near* CONSUELO. *The* BARON *stands as before, seeing only* CONSUELO.]

HE. Yes, I am joking. Don't you hear how I laugh, Consuelo? They all laugh at you here, my silly child. Don't laugh, Jim. She is tired, and wants to sleep. How can you laugh, Jim! Sleep my dear, sleep my heart, sleep my love.

CONSUELO. Yes, I have no more pain. Why did you joke that way, and frighten me? Now I laugh at myself. You told

me, didn't you, that I... should... live... eternally?

HE. Yes, Consuelo! You shall live eternally. Sleep. Be calm. [*Lifts up his arms, as if straining with all his forces to lift her soul higher.*] How easy it is now! How much light, how many lights are burning about you.... The light is blinding you.

CONSUELO. Yes, light... Is that the ring?

HE. No, it is the sea and the sun... what a sun! Don't you feel that you are the foam, white sea-foam, and you are flying to the sun? You feel light, you have no body, you are flying higher, my love!

CONSUELO. I am flying. I am the sea-foam, and this is the sun, it shines... so strong.... I feel well.

[*She dies. Silence.* HE *stays a moment with lifted arms, then takes a long look, lets his arms fall, and shakingly goes off to one side. He stands still for a moment, then sits down, drops his head on his hands, and struggles lonesomely with the torpidity of coming death.*]

BRIQUET [*slowly*]. She has fallen asleep, Mother?

ZINIDA [*dropping the dead hand*]. I am afraid not.... Step aside, Louis. Baron, it is better for you to step aside. Baron! Do you hear me? [*Weeps.*] She is dead, Louis.

[*The clowns and* BRIQUET *are crying.* MANCINI *is overwhelmed. The* BARON *and* HE *are motionless, each in his place.*]

JACKSON [*drawing out a large prismatic clown's handkerchief to wipe away his tears*]. Faded, like a flower. Sleep, little Consuelo! The only thing that remains of you is the trace of your little feet on the sand. [*Cries.*] Ah, what did you do, what did you do, HE!... It would have been better if you had never come to us.

[*There is music in the ring.*]

BRIQUET [*gesticulating*]. The music! Stop the music! They are crazy there. What a misfortune!

[*Some one runs off.* ZINIDA *approaches the crying* BEZANO *and strokes his bowed, pomaded head. When he notices her, he catches her hand and presses it to his eyes. The* BARON *takes out the rose from his button-hole, tears off the petals, and drops it, grinding it with his foot. A few pale faces peer through the door, the same masquerade crowd.*]

ZINIDA [*over the head of* BEZANO]. Louis, we must call the police.

MANCINI [*awakening from his stupor, screams*]. The police! Call the police! It's a murder! I am Count Mancini, I am Count Mancini! They will cut off your head, murderer, damned clown, thief! I myself will kill you, rascal! Ah, you!

[HE *lifts his heavy head with difficulty.*]

HE. They will cut off my head? And what more... Your Excellency?

BARON. Sir! Listen, sir! I am going for the police. Stop it, sir. [*He suddenly takes a step forward, and looking* HE *in the eyes, speaks in a hoarse voice, with a cough, holding one hand at his throat.*] I am the witness. I saw. I am a witness. I saw how he put poison... I

[*He leaves the room, suddenly, with the same straight, heavy steps. All move away from him, frightened.* HE *drops his head again. From time to time a tremor shakes his body.*]

JACKSON [*clasping his hands*]. Then it is all true! Poisoned! What a vile man you are, HE. Is this the way to play? Now wait for the last slap of the executioner!

[*Makes the gesture around his neck, of the guillotine.* TILLY *and* POLLY *repeat the gesture.*]

ZINIDA. Leave his soul alone, Jim. He was a man, and he loved. Happy Consuelo!

[*A shot is heard in the corridor.* THOMAS, *frightened, runs in and points to his head.*]

THOMAS. Baron... Baron... his head... He shot himself...

BRIQUET [*throwing his arms up*]. God! What is it? The Baron? What a calamity for our circus.

MANCINI. The Baron? The Baron? No. What are you standing here for? Ah!

BRIQUET. Calm down, Count. Who would have believed it? Such a respectable... gentleman!

HE [*lifting his head with difficulty; he sees only dimly with his dulled eyes*]. What more? What happened?

THOMAS. The Baron shot himself. Honestly. Straight here! He's lying out yonder.

HE [*thinking it over*]. Baron? [*Laughs.*] Then the Baron burst?

JACKSON. Stop it! It's shameless. A man died and you... What's the matter with you, HE?

HE [*stands up, lifted to his feet by the last gleam of consciousness and life, speaks strongly and indignantly*]. You loved her so much, Baron? So much? My Consuelo? And you want to be ahead of me even *there?* No! I am coming. We shall prove then whose she is to be for ever....

[*He catches at his throat, falls on his back. People run to him. General agitation.*]

CURTAIN

THE THEATRE OF THE SOUL

A MONODRAMA IN ONE ACT

By NIKOLAI NIKOLAYEVICH YEVREINOV

Translated by MARIE POTAPENKO and CHRISTOPHER ST. JOHN

CHARACTERS

THE PROFESSOR

M1, *The Rational Entity of the Soul*

M2, *The Emotional Entity*

M3, *The Subliminal Entity*

M1's CONCEPT OF THE WIFE

M2's CONCEPT OF THE WIFE

M1's CONCEPT OF THE DANCER

M2's CONCEPT OF THE DANCER

THE PORTER

The action passes in the soul in the period of half a second.

THE THEATRE OF THE SOUL

The prologue takes place before the curtain.
A blackboard. Chalks.

[*The* PROFESSOR *enters from the wings, stops*
before the blackboard, and after having
bowed to the audience, takes his chalk
and begins his demonstration.]

PROFESSOR. Ladies and Gentlemen, —
When the unknown author of "The
Theatre of the Soul," the play that is going
to be presented to you this evening, came
to me some weeks ago with the manuscript,
I confess that the title of his work did not
inspire me with much confidence. "Here,"
I thought, "is another of the many little
sensational plays with which the theatre
is deluged." I was all the more agreeably
surprised to gather from this first reading
that "The Theatre of the Soul" is a gen-
uinely scientific work, in every respect
abreast with the latest developments in
psychophysiology. As you know, the
researches of Wundt, Freud, Theophile
Ribot and others have proved in the most
conclusive way that the human soul is not
indivisible, but on the contrary is composed
of several selfs, the natures of which are
different. Thus if M represents I myself

[*He writes on the board.*]
$$M = M1 + M2 + M3 \dots Mn.$$
Fichte lays down the principle that if M is
the "entity self," the world is not M. That
is lucidity itself, gentlemen! According
to the dicta of modern science, however,
if the world is not "M," neither is the
entity self. This is quite clear, is it not,
gentlemen? Thus I, myself or M — is not
a simple quantity, because it comprises
several entities. I have come to the conclusion that there are three entities, M1,
M2, M3. M1 is the rational self — the
REASON, if you prefer to call it so. M2 is
the emotional self, or, as we may call it,
FEELING. M3 is the psychical self, or the
ETERNAL. This is easy to understand,
I think. These three "M's" or "selfs"
constitute the great integral self.

[*He writes:* "M1 + M2 + M3 = M,
the entire personality."]
You will ask me now, perhaps, where the
component elements, of which the complete personality is composed, are situated.
The ancients believed that they were situated in the liver, but the author of the
work which is to be presented to you holds,
and with far better reason I think, that the
human soul manifests itself in that part of
the physical breast which a man instinctively strikes when he wishes to emphasise
his good faith, or even when he uses such
expressions as "I am distressed to the
soul," or "I rejoice with my whole soul,"
or "My soul burns with indignation." Consequently the scene of the human soul
appears to us like this:

[*He draws a plan on the board with*
different coloured chalks and proceeds
to explain it.]
This plan, ladies and gentlemen, represents, as no doubt you can see, a large
heart, with the beginning of its main red
artery. It makes from 55 to 125 pulsa-
tions a minute, and lies between the two
lungs which fill and empty themselves from
fourteen to eighteen times a minute. Here
you see a little system of nerves, threads of
nerves, pale in colour, and constantly agitated by vibration which we will compare
with a telephone. Such is the scene in
which the "entity self" plays its part. But,
ladies and gentlemen, science does not con-
fine itself to explaining things. It also
offers us consolation. For instance, it is
not enough to say, "I've done a foolish
thing." One ought to know which of the
three entities is responsible. If it is M2,
or the emotional self, no great harm is
done. If it is the psychical entity, the
matter need not be taken very seriously
either. But if it be the rational self, it is
time to be alarmed. At this point, ladies

and gentlemen, I feel myself under the necessity of suspending my explanations, and of giving way to the author, to the artists, and to you, ladies and gentlemen, who I know will prove yourselves worthy critics of this admirable little work.

[*The* PROFESSOR *retires.*]

The board is removed. The curtain goes up, and the interior of the human soul is seen, as it has been described by the PROFESSOR. *On the scene, that is to say on the Diaphragm, the three entities, who bear a close resemblance to each other, are discovered. All three are dressed in black, but their costumes differ.* M1 *wears a frock-coat.* M2 *an artist's blouse and a red tie.* M3 *a well-worn travelling dress. The other differences between the three entities are indicated as follows:* M1 *is a person who wears spectacles and has a quiet, sober manner, his hair is slightly grey and carefully brushed. His lips are thin.* M2 *has a very youthful manner. His gestures and movements are quick, lively and a little exaggerated. His hair is untidy, his lips are full and red.* M3 *wears a black mask. He slumbers in the foreground, his bag under his arm, in the attitude of a traveller, worn out by fatigue.*

M2 [*at the telephone.*] Hullo! What? You can't hear me? I am speaking loud enough! What? It makes your ear vibrate? That is because your nerves are overstrained. Now listen. Brandy! Do you hear? Brandy!

M1. Don't forget that it is you who are forcing him to drink a third bottle for no reason except that you want to pass the time somehow. Poor heart! Look how it is beating!

M2. You would prefer it to be always in a state of stupor, like the subconscious! A charming sort of existence!

M1. If the heart goes on beating like that, it will not be for long.

M2. Well, what does that matter? Sooner or later it must stop.

M1. Now you are quoting my exact words.

M2. And why not? You sometimes talk sense.

M1. Please don't touch the nerves. You have been told already that ——

[*Each time that the nerves are touched, a low jingling sound is heard.*]

M2 [*with anger*]. Told me! Who has told me? And by what right? Who the devil dares order me about as if I were a servant? I am a poet. Love, passion, that is I! Without me, what would there be here but dust and mildew... a museum, a cemetery?... Everything is nothing — without passion.

M1. You talk like a fool.

M2. It's the absolute truth. Whose fault is it if we drink?

M1. It is not you, of course, who are always crying out for brandy.

M2. And if I do, isn't it forced on me? Isn't it because in your society there is nothing for our poor being to do but hang himself?

M1. Come now! You know very well that it is you, not I, who are the cause of all his misfortunes. Yes, you, the emotional self. What are you but a selfish libertine, a wreck of a man? Have you ever had any taste for study, ever taken any interest in noble, intellectual work, ever reflected on the idea of moral dignity?

M2. You are nothing but a pedant, a wretched academic dry-as-dust.

M1. Yet I despise you, O emotional self.

M2. And I despise you as much, O rational entity.

[*He passes his hand over the nerves with a big sweeping movement.*]

M1. Stop that. You shall not touch *my* nerves.

M2. By what right do you interfere? Allow me to remind you that we possess these nerves in common, and that when I touch them it is my nerves which become on edge as well as yours! When, thanks to you, my nerves are numbed, I become as stupid as an ox... as stupid, that is to say, as *you*. You shall not prevent my touching them. I like them taut and strained. Then they become like Apollo's lute, and on them I can play the hymn to love and liberty! [*He plays on the nerves. The heart begins to beat more strongly.   Speaking at the telephone.*]   Brandy!

M1 [*snatching away the telephone*]. Valerian!

M2 [*snatching away the telephone*]. Brandy!

M1 [*again possessing himself of it*]. Valerian — do you hear? What? There is none left? Then go to the chemist's. Valerian — 30 drops in a glass of water. [*He leaves the telephone.   The two entities walk up and down.   They meet.*] Are you calm now?

M2. What are you?

M1. You can see for yourself.

[*They both approach the subconscious entity.   A silence.*]

M2. What is he?

M1. Supremely quiescent, as always. Don't disturb his peace. If you do, it is you who will suffer for it. [*At the telephone.*] Have you taken your drops? Good. I will try and make him listen to reason. But the fact is, I don't grasp the principal point. This woman has attracted you by the originality of her talent, and if, in addition, she has — Very well! But for that to abandon wife and children... excuse me, it is not a solution. At least, unless we are to embrace polygamy... the ideal of a savage, more capable of appreciating the curve of a leg and the line of a back than the wondrous architecture of an immortal temple — I mean the soul....

M2. Oh! what do all your opinions and beliefs matter to me? She is beautiful. What's the use of reasoning?

M1. The brute beast doesn't reason certainly, but man — to whom the logic of feeling should be familiar ——

[*To the telephone as he passes.*]

M2. Good heavens! How dull, how insensible you are... and what anguish I endure from being bound to so colourless, so insipid a companion....

M1. You used not to talk like this.

M2. You're right there. I even loved you when we worked together harmoniously. I shall never forget the service you rendered me when I was consumed with love for Annette! To get the better of that very cautious young woman, and to cheat

the vigilance of her parents — that was — Oh, on that occasion you showed no lack of cleverness! But of late you have become not merely less intelligent, but as dull as a rusty razor.

M1. Thank you for the compliment! I am not sensitive. Also I am aware that brandy has something to do with your opinion of me.

M2. Oh, God, how beautiful she is! You must have forgotten how beautiful, how gay! Yes, I know she is only a café chantant singer — but what of that? You can't remember her face, her figure her whole lovely personality.... I will show her to you. [*He summons up from the left the seductive concept of the singer.*] Sing as you sang yesterday, beloved beautiful one. As you sang yesterday, the day before yesterday, a week ago, last Sunday. Sing, I beg you. [*To M1, who has turned his back on the woman's image.*] Oh! why don't you help me?

[*The FIRST CONCEPT OF THE SINGER sings and dances to the rhythm of the heart, which beats joyously.*]

Is it you?
Is it you?
Are you the nice young fellow
Who the other day was near me ——
So near me in the darkness of the train?
I could not see you then,
For it was much too dark,
But I should like to know.
Is it you?
Is it you
Whom my kisses so sweet
Made so madly in love?

In the train the other day
A gentleman sat near me.
I turned my head to look at him
But at that very moment
The light went out.
Into my arms then my maddened neighbour throws himself,
I kiss him ardently, embrace him, but since that day
Vainly I have searched for him.
Longing, I say to every man I see,
"Is it you?
Is it you?

Are you the nice young fellow
Who the other day was near me ——
So near me in the darkness of the train?"
M2 [*enchanted*]. Oh, rapture! The
whole universe is not worth such joy!
Those legs, those feet! Dear God, what
carpet in the wide world is fit for the touch
of those lovely feet, so lovely that they
make me weep?... Dance on me! Dance
in me! Swing to and fro, angelic censer!
[*He embraces her feet, her hands.*]
M1. What lunacy — what folly! Leave
her! It is all imagination. She is not
like that. You kiss a painted face, you
caress false hair. She is forty if she's a
day. Leave her! All that you see and feel
is false. See her as she is, see *reality*! [*At
the beginning of his speech, the first concept
of the woman vanishes R. whence* M1 *summons the* SECOND CONCEPT OF THE SINGER,
ludicrously aged and deformed.] Look!
Look, if you would know the truth. Look
at the divine feet — hard and coarse!
Look at the exquisite head! *Tête de veau
au naturel*... without the wig and the curls.
[*He lifts off the wig and displays an almost
bald head.*] Take out those star-like teeth!
[*She takes out her plate.*] Now sing!
[*She sings out of tune, with a nasal
twang, and executes some steps with the
grace of an old hack being led to the
shambles.*]
M2. No, no, this is not reality. This is
not the truth! [*To the* SECOND CONCEPT.]
Go away! Get out of this!
[*He pushes her out with violence.*]
M1. Ah! you are angry. Then you
acknowledge you are wrong.
M2. I acknowledge nothing of the kind.
You have played some trick on me —
you ——
M1. You know quite well that the creature on whom you are pouring out this mad
passion is not worthy to unloose the shoe-
strings of the woman whom you are going to
deceive and betray. And why? I ask you
why? [*He summons from the R. the* FIRST
CONCEPT OF THE WIFE, *who is nursing a
child.*] Because she has always been gentle
and kind to you? Because she has nursed
your child? Her singing is not that of the
café chantant, I know, but listen! Listen

to the lullaby that she is crooning to your
little one — that is, if your ear is not now
too gross to hear a sound so pure. Her
voice is tired, you say. Ah! she has been
singing for three long nights — nights that
she has passed without sleep, waiting, hop-
ing, despairing, aching for you to come
home.
[*The* FIRST CONCEPT OF THE WIFE
sings the lullaby in a low voice.]
Sleep, my little one, sleep;
The pain will soon go, my love.
Be patient, what did'st thou say?
"Daddy! Where is my daddy?"
Daddy will come to thee soon;
Daddy works hard, my darling,
But soon he will come with a toy,
A beautiful toy for thee!
A wooden horse, would'st thou like?
Gee-up, gee-up, a horse to ride.
Good Daddy, kind Daddy — gee-up!
Sleep, my little one, sleep!
M2 [*roughly*]. I've had enough of this
silly farce. There is no truth in it. It's a
got-up affair. It's all vulgar sentimental-
ity. [*He violently pushes away the* FIRST
CONCEPT OF THE WIFE .] Go away from
here, you heroine of melodrama.... She is
not what you pretend. I know her too well.
She has poisoned my whole life. There is
no poetry in her, no joy, no passion. She
is prose itself, the baldest, the most banal
prose, in spite of her heroic attitudes! The
eternal housemaid — that's what she is.
[*He summons the* SECOND CONCEPT
OF THE WIFE — *a very ordinary and
slovenly bourgeoise. Her untidy hair is
done in an unbecoming knot. She wears
a dirty dressing-gown, stained with coffee, and open at the breast.*]
2ND CONCEPT OF THE WIFE [*violently*].
This is a nice business! If my parents only
knew the life I lead with this low brute.
What surprises me is that he hasn't got
the sack from the office long ago — a
drunkard like him! Without that cursed
brandy he wouldn't have an idea in his silly
head.... My gentleman has condescended
to give me children. Now he goes about
making love to women who don't have
children... or if they do, kill them for the
sake of their precious figures. My gentle-

man loves the fine arts — the theatre — that is the theatre which he finds in some wretched hole of a café chantant... where he can drink with a lot of low women with faces daubed with paint — creatures I wouldn't touch with a pair of tongs.... It's more than likely that, one fine day, he'll come home and poison his children, the brainless sot.... But for me he would have pawned everything we have long ago — to the shirts on our backs. An atheist who refuses to kneel down or cross himself before the blessed Sacrament. He's as stupid as he can be, but that doesn't prevent him from talking philosophy — a lot of nonsense about liberty, the duties of a citizen, and so on. Liberty! Liberty to make a beast of himself. I'll liberty you, you wretch....

M2. Yes, that is the real she — the real heroine! That is the creature whom I dare not leave for the sake of the divine being who intoxicates me like a magic potion, who provides the only reason for my still wishing to exist in this dreadful world!

[*As he says this he summons up the* FIRST CONCEPT OF THE SINGER. *She sings and dances a can-can, gradually driving into a dark corner L. the* SECOND CONCEPT OF THE WIFE. *Then she herself has to retreat before the* FIRST CONCEPT OF THE WIFE, *who advances, a menacing but imposing figure, noble in sorrow.*]

1ST CONCEPT OF THE WIFE [*to the singer*]. Go! I implore you to go. You have no right here.

M1. None.... She speaks the truth.

1ST CONCEPT OF THE WIFE. Since you do not love him, since you would not make the smallest sacrifice for him... since you have had many others in your life like him ... leave him alone, leave him in peace, if you still have any heart, any decency. I need him — I need his support — his affection. Oh, don't take him from me — Don't tear him away from his family to whom he owes ——

1ST CONCEPT OF SINGER [*interrupting mockingly and laughing*]. I know all those phrases by heart. I've heard them so often. They mean nothing.

1ST CONCEPT OF THE WIFE. Go away, do you hear? Don't drive me too far ——

1ST CONCEPT OF SINGER. So now you're going to threaten me, are you? Why, may I ask? Why do you hate me? Is it because I have beautiful legs and firm breasts, or because my words fly like birds and leap like champagne corks?

M2 [*applauding*]. Bravo! Bravo!

1ST CONCEPT OF THE WIFE. What do you want but his money, you creature for sale ——

1ST CONCEPT OF SINGER. What's that? A creature for sale, am I? What are you then? Didn't you sell yourself when you married him? Take it back — take it back, I say, or I'll ——

[*She advances threateningly on the* FIRST CONCEPT OF THE WIFE.]

1ST CONCEPT OF THE WIFE. You shall go —— Yes, you *shall* go!

[*They close with one another, and fight. The anguished heart palpitates noisily during their struggle. Violent curses and frenzied threats are heard, such as "You shameless wretch!" "You beast!" "You're only a harlot!" "I'll teach you!" "You bloody church-goer!" After vanishing from view for a moment in the dark corner L. they reappear more bitter and violent than ever now as the second concepts. The wife has the singer's transformation between her teeth. After a second change of personality, they reappear on the scene. The victory is with the singer, who is seen with the prostrate wife under her knee. The wife disengages herself, and, weeping, escapes L., followed by the laughter of the singer and the bravos of M2. Then* M1, *indignant, boxes the singer's ears, who runs to the back of the scene uttering plaintive howls like a whipped cur.* M2, *losing all control, throws himself on* M1, *and strangles him. The heart stops for a minute. Two or three nerves touched during the struggle snap.* M2, *seeing that his adversary is dead, throws himself at the feet of the singer.*]

M2. Come, my queen, come. My beloved, now you are mine, mine in everything, mine for ever, oh, my life, my joy, my love!... Come to me.

THE SINGER [1st concept]. No, you dear little silly. Oh, no! It has only been a joke. Money first... love afterwards. And from what I see — there's a sight more love here than money.... And how are you going to get any? No — no, *no*! I am not for you, my boy. It was all a joke.

[*She disappears L.*]

[M2 *stands thunderstruck in a despairing attitude. A café concert air, of an exciting, irritating type, is heard in the distance. The* FIRST CONCEPT OF THE WIFE *is seen. She fixes her large sorrowful eyes on* M2. *It is difficult to see whether she is nursing her sick child, or making reproachful signs to* M2.]

M2 [*madly hurling himself at the telephone*]. Quick! Quick now. It's all over. There is nothing.... I have come to the end of everything.... With what strength I have left I implore you to do it quickly. The revolver is in the right-hand pocket. Quickly, oh, more quickly! It will not hurt, believe me, not much.... Fire between the fourth and fifth rib....

What? You are afraid? There is nothing to be afraid of. It will be all over in a moment. Quick....

[*There is a short pause, during which* M3 *wakes up abruptly and throws an uneasy glance round him. A loud report like a cannon shot is heard. The sound echoes through the vault of the soul. A great hole opens in the diaphragm from which pour out ribbons of blood. Darkness half hides the scene.* M2 *struggling convulsively falls under the heart drowned in the streamers of red ribbon. The heart has stopped beating. The lung has ceased to respire. A pause.* M3 *trembles and stretches himself wearily.*]

[A PORTER *carrying a lighted lantern enters.*]

THE PORTER. This is Everyone's Town. You have to get out here, sir. You change here.

M3. Thank you, yes. I have to change here.

[*He puts on his hat, takes his bag, and follows the* PORTER, *yawning.*]

CURTAIN

LILIOM

A LEGEND IN SEVEN SCENES
AND A PROLOGUE
By FERENC MOLNAR

English text by BENJAMIN F. GLAZER

SYNOPSIS OF SCENES

There are intermissions only after the second and fifth scenes.

CAST OF CHARACTERS

Liliom
Julie
Marie
Mrs. Muskat
Louise
Mrs. Hollunder
Ficsur
Young Hollunder
Wolf Beifeld
The Carpenter
Linzman
The Doctor
The Magistrate
Two Mounted Policemen
Two Plainclothes Policemen
Two Heavenly Policemen
The Richly Dressed Man
The Poorly Dressed Man
The Guard
A Suburban Policeman

LILIOM

THE PROLOGUE

*An amusement park on the outskirts of
Budapest on a late afternoon in Spring.
Barkers stand before the booths of the side-
shows haranguing the passing crowd. The
strident music of a calliope is heard; laughter,
shouts, the scuffle of feet, the signal bells of
merry-go-round.*

The merry-go-round is at center. LILIOM
*stands at the entrance, a cigarette in his
mouth, coaxing the people in. The girls regard him with idolizing glances and screech
with pleasure as he playfully pushes them
through entrance. Now and then some girl's
escort resents the familiarity, whereupon*
LILIOM'S *demeanor becomes ugly and menacing, and the cowed escort slinks through the
entrance behind his girl or contents himself
with a muttered resentful comment.*

One girl hands LILIOM *a red carnation;
he rewards her with a bow and a smile.
When the soldier who accompanies her protests,* LILIOM *cows him with a fierce glance
and a threatening gesture.* MARIE *and*
JULIE *come out of the crowd and* LILIOM
*favors them with particular notice as they
pass into the merry-go-round.*

MRS. MUSKAT *comes out of the merry-go-
round, bringing* LILIOM *coffee and rolls.*
LILIOM *mounts the barker's stand at the entrance, where he is elevated over every one on
the stage. Here he begins his harangue.
Everybody turns toward him. The other
booths are gradually deserted. The tumult
makes it impossible for the audience to hear
what he is saying, but every now and then
some witticism of his provokes a storm of
laughter which is audible above the din.
Many people enter the merry-go-round.
Here and there one catches a phrase "Room
for one more on the zebra's back," "Which of
you ladies?" "Ten heller for adults, five for
children," "Step right up ——"*

*It is growing darker. A lamplighter
crosses the stage, and begins unperturbedly*
*lighting the colored gas-lamps. The whistle
of a distant locomotive is heard. Suddenly
the tumult ceases, the lights go out, and the
curtain falls in darkness.*

END OF PROLOGUE

SCENE I

*A lonely place in the park, half hidden by
trees and shrubbery. Under a flowering
acacia tree stands a painted wooden bench.
From the distance, faintly, comes the tumult
of the amusement park. It is the sunset of the
same day.*

When the curtain rises the stage is empty.

[MARIE *enters quickly, pauses at center, and
looks back.*]

MARIE. Julie, Julie! [*There is no answer.*] Do you hear me, Julie? Let her be!
Come on. Let her be. [*Starts to go back.*]

[JULIE *enters, looks back angrily.*]

JULIE. Did you ever hear of such a
thing? What's the matter with the woman
anyway?

MARIE [*looking back again*]. Here she
comes again.

JULIE. Let her come. I didn't do anything to her. All of a sudden she comes up
to me and begins to raise a row.

MARIE. Here she is. Come on, let's run.
[*Tries to urge her off.*]

JULIE. Run? I should say not. What
would I want to run for? I'm not afraid of
her.

MARIE. Oh, come on. She'll only start
a fight.

JULIE. I'm going to stay right here.
Let her *start* a fight.

MRS. MUSKAT [*entering*]. What do you
want to run away for? [*To* JULIE.] Don't
worry. I won't eat you. But there's one

thing I want to tell you, my dear. Don't let me catch you in my carousel again. I stand for a whole lot, I have to in my business. It makes no difference to me whether my customers are ladies or the likes of you — as long as they pay their money. But when a girl misbehaves herself on my carousel — out she goes. Do you understand?

JULIE. Are you talking to me?

MRS. MUSKAT. Yes, you! You — chamber-maid, you! In my carousel ——

JULIE. Who did anything in your old carousel? I paid my fare and took my seat and never said a word, except to my friend here.

MARIE. No, she never opened her mouth. Liliom came over to her of his own accord.

MRS. MUSKAT. It's all the same. I'm not going to get in trouble with the police, and lose my license on account of you — you shabby kitchen maid!

JULIE. Shabby yourself.

MRS. MUSKAT. You stay out of my carousel! Letting my barker fool with you! Aren't you ashamed of yourself?

JULIE. What? What did you say?

MRS. MUSKAT. I suppose you think I have no eyes in my head. I see everything that goes on in my carousel. During the whole ride she let Liliom fool with her — the shameless hussy!

JULIE. He did not fool with me! I don't let any man fool with me!

MRS. MUSKAT. He leaned against you all through the ride!

JULIE. He leaned against the panther. He always leans against something, doesn't he? Everybody leans where he wants. I couldn't tell him not to lean, if he always leans, could I? But he didn't lay a hand on me.

MRS. MUSKAT. Oh, didn't he? And I suppose he didn't put his hand around your waist, either?

MARIE. And if he did? What of it?

MRS. MUSKAT. You hold your tongue! No one's asking you — just you keep out of it.

JULIE. He put his arm around my waist — just the same as he does to all the girls. He always does that.

MRS. MUSKAT. I'll teach him not to do it any more, my dear. No carryings on in my carousel! If you are looking for that sort of thing, you'd better go to the circus! You'll find lots of soldiers there to carry on with!

JULIE. You keep your soldiers for yourself!

MARIE. Soldiers! As if we wanted soldiers!

MRS. MUSKAT. Well, I only want to tell you this, my dear, so that we understand each other perfectly. If you ever stick your nose in my carousel again, you'll wish you hadn't! I'm not going to lose my license on account of the likes of you! People who don't know how to behave, have got to stay out!

JULIE. You're wasting your breath. If I feel like riding on your carousel I'll pay my ten heller and I'll ride. I'd like to see any one try to stop me!

MRS. MUSKAT. Just come and try it, my dear — just come and try it.

MARIE. We'll see what'll happen.

MRS. MUSKAT. Yes, you will see something happen that never happened before in this park.

JULIE. Perhaps you think you could throw me out!

MRS. MUSKAT. I'm sure of it, my dear.

JULIE. And suppose I'm stronger than you?

MRS. MUSKAT. I'd think twice before I'd dirty my hands on a common servant girl. I'll have Liliom throw you out. He knows how to handle your kind.

JULIE. You think Liliom would throw me out.

MRS. MUSKAT. Yes, my dear, so fast that you won't know what happened to you!

JULIE. He'd throw me ——

[Stops suddenly, for MRS. MUSKAT has turned away. Both look off stage until LILIOM enters, surrounded by four giggling servant girls.]

LILIOM. Go away! Stop following me, or I'll smack your face!

A LITTLE SERVANT GIRL. Well, give me back my handkerchief.

LILIOM. Go on now ——

THE FOUR SERVANT GIRLS [*simultaneously*]. What do you think of him? — My handkerchief! — Give it back to her! — That's a nice thing to do!

THE LITTLE SERVANT GIRL [*to* MRS. MUSKAT]. Please, lady, make him ——

MRS. MUSKAT. Oh, shut up!

LILIOM. Will you get out of here?

[*Makes a threatening gesture — the* FOUR SERVANT GIRLS *exit in voluble but fearful haste.*]

MRS. MUSKAT. What have you been doing now?

LILIOM. None of your business. [*Glances at* JULIE.] Have you been starting with her again?

JULIE. Mister Liliom, please ——

LILIOM [*steps threateningly toward her*]. Don't yell!

JULIE [*timidly*]. I didn't yell.

LILIOM. Well, don't. [*To* MRS. MUSKAT.] What's the matter? What has she done to you?

MRS. MUSKAT. What has she done? She's been impudent to me. Just as impudent as she could be! I put her out of the carousel. Take a good look at this innocent thing, Liliom. She's never to be allowed in my carousel again!

LILIOM [*to* JULIE]. You heard that. Run home, now.

MARIE. Come on. Don't waste your time with such people.

[*Tries to lead* JULIE *away.*]

JULIE. No, I won't ——

MRS. MUSKAT. If she ever comes again, you're not to let her in. And if she gets in before you see her, throw her out. Understand?

LILIOM. What has she done, anyhow?

JULIE [*agitated and very earnest*]. Mister Liliom — tell me please — honest and truly — if I come into the carousel, will you throw me out?

MRS. MUSKAT. Of course he'll throw you out.

MARIE. She wasn't talking to you.

JULIE. Tell me straight to my face, Mister Liliom, would you throw me out?

[*They face each other. There is a brief pause.*]

LILIOM. Yes, little girl, if there was a reason — but if there was no reason, why should I throw you out?

MARIE [*to* MRS. MUSKAT]. There, you see!

JULIE. Thank you, Mister Liliom.

MRS. MUSKAT. And I tell you again, if this little slut dares to set her foot in my carousel, she's to be thrown out! I'll stand for no indecency in my establishment.

LILIOM. What do you mean — indecency?

MRS. MUSKAT. I saw it all. There's no use denying it.

JULIE. She says you put your arm around my waist.

LILIOM. Me?

MRS. MUSKAT. Yes, you! I saw you. Don't play the innocent.

LILIOM. Here's something new! I'm not to put my arm around a girl's waist any more! I suppose I'm to ask your permission before I touch another girl!

MRS. MUSKAT. You can touch as many girls as you want and as often as you want — for my part you can go as far as you like with any of them — but not this one — I permit no indecency in my carousel.

[*There is a long pause.*]

LILIOM [*to* MRS. MUSKAT]. And now I'll ask you please to shut your mouth.

MRS. MUSKAT. What?

LILIOM. Shut your mouth quick, and go back to your carousel.

MRS. MUSKAT. What?

LILIOM. What did she do to you, anyhow? Tryin' to start a fight with a little pigeon like that... just because I touched her? — You come to the carousel as often as you want to, little girl. Come every afternoon, and sit on the panther's back, and if you haven't got the price, Liliom will pay for you. And if any one dares to bother you, you come and tell me.

MRS. MUSKAT. You reprobate!

LILIOM. Old witch!

JULIE. Thank you, Mister Liliom.

MRS. MUSKAT. You seem to think that I can't throw you out, too. What's the reason I can't? Because you are the best barker in the park? Well, you are very much mistaken. In fact, you can consider yourself thrown out already. You're discharged!

LILIOM. Very good.

MRS. MUSKAT [*weakening a little*]. I can discharge you any time I feel like it.

LILIOM. Very good, you feel like discharging me. I'm discharged. That settles it.

MRS. MUSKAT. Playing the high and mighty, are you? Conceited pig! Good-for-nothing!

LILIOM. You said you'd throw me out, didn't you? Well, that suits me; I'm thrown out.

MRS. MUSKAT [*softening*]. Do you have to take up every word I say?

LILIOM. It's all right; it's all settled. I'm a good-for-nothing. And a conceited pig. And I'm discharged.

MRS. MUSKAT. Do you want to ruin my business?

LILIOM. A good-for-nothing? Now I know! And I'm discharged! Very good.

MRS. MUSKAT. You're a devil, you are ... and that woman ——

LILIOM. Keep away from her!

MRS. MUSKAT. I'll get Hollinger to give you such a beating that you'll hear all the angels sing ... and it won't be the first time, either.

LILIOM. Get out of here. I'm discharged. And you get out of here.

JULIE [*timidly*]. Mister Liliom, if she's willing to say that she hasn't discharged you ——

LILIOM. You keep out of this.

JULIE [*timidly*]. I don't want this to happen on account of me.

LILIOM [*to* MRS. MUSKAT, *pointing to* JULIE]. Apologize to her!

MARIE. A-ha!

MRS. MUSKAT. Apologize? To who?

LILIOM. To this little pigeon. Well — are you going to do it?

MRS. MUSKAT. If you give me this whole park on a silver plate, and all the gold of the Rothschilds on top of it — I'd — I'd —— Let her dare to come into my carousel again and she'll get thrown out so hard that she'll see stars in daylight!

LILIOM. In that case, dear lady [*takes off his cap with a flourish*] you are respectfully requested to get out o' here as fast as your legs will carry you — I never beat up a woman yet — except that Holzer woman who I sent to the hospital for three weeks — but — if you don't get out o' here this minute, and let this little squab be, I'll give you the prettiest slap in the jaw you ever had in your life.

MRS. MUSKAT. Very good, my son. Now you *can* go to the devil. Good-bye. You're discharged, and you needn't try to come back, either.

[*She exits. It is beginning to grow dark.*]

MARIE [*with grave concern*]. Mister Liliom ——

LILIOM. Don't you pity me or I'll give *you* a slap in the jaw. [*To* JULIE.] And don't you pity me, either.

JULIE [*in alarm.*] I don't pity you, Mister Liliom.

LILIOM. You're a liar, you *are* pitying me. I can see it in your face. You're thinking, now that Madame Muskat has thrown him out, Liliom will have to go begging. Huh! Look at me. I'm big enough to get along without a Madame Muskat. I have been thrown out of better jobs than hers.

JULIE. What will you do now, Mister Liliom?

LILIOM. Now? First of all, I'll go and get myself — a glass of beer. You see, when something happens to annoy me, I always drink a glass of beer.

JULIE. Then you *are* annoyed about losing your job.

LILIOM. No, only about where I'm going to get the beer.

MARIE. Well — eh ——

LILIOM. Well — eh — what?

MARIE. Well — eh — are you going to stay with us, Mister Liliom?

LILIOM. Will you pay for the beer? [MARIE *looks doubtful; he turns to* JULIE.] Will you? [*She does not answer.*] How much money have you got?

JULIE [*bashfully*]. Eight heller.

LILIOM. And you? [MARIE *casts down her eyes and does not reply.* LILIOM *continues sternly.*] I asked you how much you've got? [MARIE *begins to weep softly.*]

I understand. Well, you needn't cry about it. You girls stay here, while I go back to the carousel and get my clothes and things. And when I come back, we'll go to the Hungarian beer-garden. It's all right, I'll pay. Keep your money.

[*He exits.* MARIE *and* JULIE *stand silent, watching him until he has gone.*]

MARIE. Are you sorry for him?

JULIE. Are you?

MARIE. Yes, a little. Why are you looking after him in that funny way?

JULIE [*sits down*]. Nothing — except I'm sorry he lost his job.

MARIE [*with a touch of pride*]. It was on our account he lost his job. Because he's fallen in love with you.

JULIE. He hasn't at all.

MARIE [*confidently*]. Oh, yes! he is in love with you. [*Hesitantly, romantically.*] There is some one in love with me, too.

JULIE. There is? Who?

MARIE. I — I never mentioned it before, because you hadn't a lover of your own — but now you have — and I'm free to speak. [*Very grandiloquently.*] My heart has found its mate.

JULIE. You're only making it up.

MARIE. No, it's true — my heart's true love ——

JULIE. Who? Who is he?

MARIE. A soldier.

JULIE. What kind of a soldier?

MARIE. I don't know. Just a soldier. Are there different kinds?

JULIE. Many different kinds. There are hussars, artillerymen, engineers, infantry — that's the kind that walks — and ——

MARIE. How can you tell which is which?

JULIE. By their uniforms.

MARIE [*after trying to puzzle it out*]. The conductors on the street cars — are they soldiers?

JULIE. Certainly not. They're conductors.

MARIE. Well, they have uniforms.

JULIE. But they don't carry swords or guns.

MARIE. Oh! [*Thinks it over again; then.*] Well, policemen — are they?

JULIE [*with a touch of exasperation*]. Are they what?

MARIE. Soldiers.

JULIE. Certainly not. They're just policemen.

MARIE [*triumphantly*]. But they have uniforms — and they carry weapons, too.

JULIE. You're just as dumb as you can be. You don't go by their uniforms.

MARIE. But you said ——

JULIE. No, I didn't. A letter-carrier wears a uniform, too, but that doesn't make him a soldier.

MARIE. But if he carried a gun or a sword, would he be ——

JULIE. No, he'd still be a letter-carrier. You can't go by guns or swords, either.

MARIE. Well, if you don't go by the uniforms or the weapons, what *do* you go by?

JULIE. By —— [*Tries to put it into words; fails; then breaks off suddenly.*] Oh, you'll get to know when you've lived in the city long enough. You're nothing but a country girl. When you've lived in the city a year, like I have, you'll know all about it.

MARIE [*half angrily*]. Well, how *do* you know when *you* see a real soldier?

JULIE. By one thing.

MARIE. What?

JULIE. One thing —— [*She pauses.* MARIE *starts to cry.*] Oh, what are you crying about?

MARIE. Because you're making fun of me.... You're a city girl, and I'm just fresh from the country... and how am I expected to know a soldier when I see one?... You, you ought to tell me, instead of making fun of me ——

JULIE. All right. Listen then, cry-baby. There's only one way to tell a soldier: by his salute! That's the only way.

MARIE [*joyfully; with a sigh of relief*]. Ah — that's good.

JULIE. What?

MARIE. I say — it's all right then — because Wolf — Wolf —— [JULIE *laughs derisively.*] Wolf — that's his name.

[*She weeps again.*]

JULIE. Crying again? What now?

MARIE. You're making fun of me again.

JULIE. I'm not. But when you say, "Wolf — Wolf —" like that, I have to laugh, don't I? [*Archly.*] What's his name again?

MARIE. I won't tell you.

JULIE. All right. If you won't say it, then he's no soldier.

MARIE. I'll say it.

JULIE. Go on.

MARIE. No, I won't. [*She weeps again.*]

JULIE. Then he's not a soldier. I guess he's a letter-carrier ——

MARIE. No — no — I'd rather say it.

JULIE. Well, then.

MARIE [*giggling*]. But you mustn't look at me. You look the other way, and I'll say it. [JULIE *looks away.* MARIE *can hardly restrain her own laughter.*] Wolf! [*She laughs.*] That's his real name. Wolf, Wolf, Soldier — Wolf!

JULIE. What kind of a uniform does he wear?

MARIE. Red.

JULIE. Red trousers?

MARIE. No.

JULIE. Red coat?

MARIE. No.

JULIE. What then?

MARIE [*triumphantly*]. His cap!

JULIE [*after a long pause*]. He's just a porter, you dunce. Red cap... that's a porter — and he doesn't carry a gun or a sword, either.

MARIE [*triumphantly*]. But he salutes. You said yourself that was the only way to tell a soldier ——

JULIE. He doesn't salute at all. He only greets people ——

MARIE. He salutes me.... And if his name *is* Wolf, that doesn't prove he ain't a soldier — he salutes, and he wears a red cap and he stands on guard all day long outside a big building ——

JULIE. What does he do there?

MARIE [*seriously*]. He spits.

JULIE [*with contempt*]. He's nothing — nothing but a common porter.

MARIE. What's Liliom?

JULIE [*indignantly*]. Why speak of him? What has he to do with me?

MARIE. The same as Wolf has to do with me. If you can talk to me like that about Wolf, I can talk to you about Liliom.

JULIE. He's nothing to me. He put his arm around me in the carousel. I couldn't tell him not to put his arm around me after he had done it, could I?

MARIE. I suppose you didn't like him to do it?

JULIE. No.

MARIE. Then why are you waiting for him? Why don't you go home?

JULIE. Why — eh — he *said* we were to wait for him.

[LILIOM *enters. There is a long silence.*]

LILIOM. Are you still here? What are you waiting for?

MARIE. You told us to wait.

LILIOM. Must you always interfere? No one is talking to you.

MARIE. You asked us — why we ——

LILIOM. Will you keep your mouth shut? What do you suppose I want with two of you? I meant that one of you was to wait. The other can go home.

MARIE. All right.

JULIE. All right. [*Neither starts to go.*]

LILIOM. One of you goes home. [*To* MARIE.] Where do you work?

MARIE. At the Breiers', Damjanovitsch Street, Number 20.

LILIOM. And you?

JULIE. I work there, too.

LILIOM. Well, one of you goes home. Which of you wants to stay? [*There is no answer.*] Come on, speak up, which of you stays?

MARIE [*officiously*]. She'll lose her job if she stays.

LILIOM. Who will?

MARIE. Julie. She has to be back by seven o'clock.

LILIOM. Is that true? Will they discharge you if you're not back on time?

JULIE. Yes.

LILIOM. Well, wasn't I discharged?

JULIE. Yes — you were discharged, too.

MARIE. Julie, shall I go?

JULIE. I — can't tell you what to do.

MARIE. All right — stay if you like.

LILIOM. You'll be discharged if you do?

MARIE. Shall I go, Julie?

JULIE [embarrassed]. Why do you keep asking me that?

MARIE. You know best what to do.

JULIE [profoundly moved; slowly]. It's all right, Marie, you can go home.

MARIE [exits reluctantly, but comes back, and says uncertainly]. Good-night.

[She waits a moment to see if JULIE will follow her. JULIE does not move. MARIE exits. Meantime it has grown quite dark. During the following scene the gas-lamps far in the distance are lighted one by one. LILIOM and JULIE sit on the bench. From afar, very faintly, comes the music of a calliope. But the music is intermittently heard; now it breaks off, now it resumes again, as if it came down on a fitful wind. Blending with it are the sounds of human voices, now loud, now soft; the blare of a toy trumpet; the confused noises of the show booths. It grows progressively darker until the end of the scene. There is no moonlight. The spring iridescence glows in the deep blue sky.]

LILIOM. Now we're both discharged. [She does not answer. From now on they speak gradually lower and lower until the end of the scene, which is played almost in whispers. Whistles softly, then.] Have you had your supper?

JULIE. No.

LILIOM. Want to go eat something at the Garden?

JULIE. No.

LILIOM. Anywhere else?

JULIE. No.

LILIOM [whistles softly, then]. You don't come to this park very often, do you? I've only seen you three times. Been here oftener than that?

JULIE. Oh, yes.

LILIOM. Did you see me?

JULIE. Yes.

LILIOM. And did you know I was Liliom?

JULIE. They told me.

LILIOM [whistles softly, then]. Have you got a sweetheart?

JULIE. No.

LILIOM. Don't lie to me.

JULIE. I haven't. If I had, I'd tell you. I've never had one.

LILIOM. What an awful liar you are. I've got a good mind to go away and leave you here.

JULIE. I've never had one.

LILIOM. Tell that to some one else.

JULIE [reproachfully]. Why do you insist I have?

LILIOM. Because you stayed here with me the first time I asked you to. You know your way around, you do.

JULIE. No, I don't, Mister Liliom.

LILIOM. I suppose you'll tell me you don't know why you're sitting here — like this, in the dark, alone with me —— You wouldn't 'a' stayed so quick, if you hadn't done it before — with some soldier, maybe. This isn't the first time. You wouldn't have been so ready to stay if it was — what did you stay for, anyhow?

JULIE. So you wouldn't be left alone.

LILIOM. Alone! God, you're dumb! I don't need to be alone. I can have all the girls I want. Not only servant girls like you, but cooks and governesses, even French girls. I could have twenty of them if I wanted to.

JULIE. I know, Mister Liliom.

LILIOM. What do you know?

JULIE. That all the girls are in love with you. But that's not why I stayed. I stayed because you've been so good to me.

LILIOM. Well, then you can go home.

JULIE. I don't want to go home now.

LILIOM. And what if I go away and leave you sitting here?

JULIE. If you did, I wouldn't go home.

LILIOM. Do you know what you remind me of? A sweetheart I had once — I'll tell you how I met her —— One night, at closing time, we had put out the lights in the carousel, and just as I was ——

[He is interrupted by the entrance of two plain-clothes policemen. They take their stations on either side of the bench. They are police, searching the park for vagabonds.]

FIRST POLICEMAN. What are you doing there?

LILIOM. Me?

SECOND POLICEMAN. Stand up when you're spoken to!

[*He taps* LILIOM *imperatively on the shoulder.*]

FIRST POLICEMAN. What's your name?

LILIOM. Andreas Zavoczki.

[JULIE *begins to weep softly.*]

SECOND POLICEMAN. Stop your bawling. We're not goin' to eat you. We are only making our rounds.

FIRST POLICEMAN. See that he doesn't get away. [THE SECOND POLICEMAN *steps closer to* LILIOM.] What's your business?

LILIOM. Barker and bouncer.

SECOND POLICEMAN. They call him Liliom, Chief. We've had him up a couple of times.

FIRST POLICEMAN. So that's who you are! Who do you work for now?

LILIOM. I work for the widow Muskat.

FIRST POLICEMAN. What are you hanging around here for?

LILIOM. We're just sitting here — me and this girl.

FIRST POLICEMAN. Your sweetheart?

LILIOM. No.

FIRST POLICEMAN [*to* JULIE]. And who are you?

JULIE. Julie Zeller.

FIRST POLICEMAN. Servant girl?

JULIE. Maid of All Work for Mister Georg Breier, Number Twenty Damjanovitsch Street.

FIRST POLICEMAN. Show your hands.

SECOND POLICEMAN [*after examining* JULIE's *hand*]. Servant girl.

FIRST POLICEMAN. Why aren't you at home? What are you doing out here with him?

JULIE. This is my day out, sir.

FIRST POLICEMAN. It would be better for you if you didn't spend it sitting around with a fellow like this.

SECOND POLICEMAN. They'll be disappearing in the bushes as soon as we turn our backs.

FIRST POLICEMAN. He's only after your money. We know this fine fellow. He picks up you silly servant girls and takes what money you have. To-morrow you'll probably be coming around to report him. If you do, I'll throw you out.

JULIE. I haven't any money, sir.

FIRST POLICEMAN. Do you hear that, Liliom?

LILIOM. I'm not looking for her money.

SECOND POLICEMAN [*nudging him warningly*]. Keep your mouth shut.

FIRST POLICEMAN. It is my duty to warn you, my child, what kind of company you're in. He makes a specialty of servant girls. That's why he works in a carousel. He gets hold of a girl, promises to marry her, then he takes her money and her ring.

JULIE. But I haven't got a ring.

SECOND POLICEMAN. You're not to talk unless you're asked a question.

FIRST POLICEMAN. You be thankful that I'm warning you. It's nothing to me what you do. I'm not your father, thank God. But I'm telling you what kind of a fellow he is. By to-morrow morning you'll be coming around to us to report him. Now you be sensible and go home. You needn't be afraid of him. This officer will take you home if you're afraid.

JULIE. Do I *have* to go?

FIRST POLICEMAN. No, you don't *have* to go.

JULIE. Then I'll stay, sir.

FIRST POLICEMAN. Well, you've been warned.

JULIE. Yes, sir. Thank you, sir.

FIRST POLICEMAN. Come on, Berkovics.

[*The* POLICEMEN *exit.* JULIE *and* LILIOM *sit on the bench again. There is a brief pause.*]

JULIE. Well, and what then?

LILIOM [*fails to understand*]. Huh?

JULIE. You were beginning to tell me a story.

LILIOM. Me?

JULIE. Yes, about a sweetheart. You said, one night, just as they were putting out the lights of the carousel —— That's as far as you got.

LILIOM. Oh, yes, yes, just as the lights were going out, some one came along — a little girl with a big shawl — you know —— She came — eh — from —— Say — tell me — ain't you — that is, ain't you at all — afraid of me? The officer told you what kind of a fellow I am — and that I'd take your money away from you ——

JULIE. You couldn't take it away — I haven't got any. But if I had — I'd — I'd give it to you — I'd give it all to you.

LILIOM. You would?

JULIE. If you asked me for it.

LILIOM. Have you ever had a fellow you gave money to?

JULIE. No.

LILIOM. Haven't you ever had a sweetheart?

JULIE. No.

LILIOM. Some one you used to go walking with. You've had one like that?

JULIE. Yes.

LILIOM. A soldier?

JULIE. He came from the same village I did.

LILIOM. That's what all the soldiers say. Where *do* you come from, anyway?

JULIE. Not far from here.

[*There is a pause.*]

LILIOM. Were you in love with him?

JULIE. Why do you keep asking me that all the time, Mister Liliom? I wasn't in love with him. We only went walking together.

LILIOM. Where did you walk?

JULIE. In the park.

LILIOM. And your virtue? Where did you lose that?

JULIE. I haven't got any virtue.

LILIOM. Well, you had once.

JULIE. No, I never had. I'm a respectable girl.

LILIOM. Yes, but you gave the soldier something.

JULIE. Why do you question me like that, Mister Liliom?

LILIOM. Did you give him something?

JULIE. You have to. But I didn't love him.

LILIOM. Do you love me?

JULIE. No, Mister Liliom.

LILIOM. Then why do you stay here with me?

JULIE. Um — nothing.

[*There is a pause. The music from afar is plainly heard.*]

LILIOM. Want to dance?

JULIE. No. I have to be very careful.

LILIOM. Of what?

JULIE. My — character.

LILIOM. Why?

JULIE. Because I'm never going to marry. If I was going to marry, it would be different. Then I wouldn't need to worry so much about my character. It doesn't make any difference if you're married. But I shan't marry — and that's why I've got to take care to be a respectable girl.

LILIOM. Suppose I were to say to you — I'll marry you.

JULIE. You?

LILIOM. That frightens you, doesn't it? You're thinking of what the officer said and you're afraid.

JULIE. No, I'm not, Mister Liliom. I don't pay any attention to what he said.

LILIOM. But you wouldn't dare to marry any one like me, would you?

JULIE. I know that — that — if I loved any one — it wouldn't make any difference to me what he — even if I died for it.

LILIOM. But you wouldn't marry a rough guy like me — that is — eh — if you loved me ——

JULIE. Yes, I would — if I loved you, Mister Liliom. [*There is a pause.*]

LILIOM [*whispers*]. Well — you just said — didn't you? — that you don't love me. Well, why don't you go home then?

JULIE. It's too late now, they'd all be asleep.

LILIOM. Locked out?

JULIE. Certainly.

[*They are silent awhile.*]

LILIOM. I think — that even a low-down good-for-nothing — can make a man of himself.

JULIE. Certainly.

[*They are silent again. A lamplighter crosses the stage, lights the lamp over the bench, and exits.*]

LILIOM. Are you hungry?

JULIE. No. [*Another pause.*]

LILIOM. Suppose — you had some money — and I took it from you?

JULIE. Then you could take it, that's all.

LILIOM [*after another brief silence*]. All I have to do — is go back to her — that Muskat woman — she'll be glad to get me back — then I'd be earning my wages again.

[*She is silent. The twilight folds darker about them.*]

JULIE [*very softly*]. Don't go back — to her —— [*Pause.*]

LILIOM. There are a lot of acacia trees around here. [*Pause.*]

JULIE. Don't go back to her —— [*Pause.*]

LILIOM. She'd take me back the minute I asked her. I know why — she knows, too —— [*Pause.*]

JULIE. I can smell them, too — acacia blossoms ——

[*There is a pause. Some blossoms drift down from the tree-top to the bench. LILIOM picks one up and smells it.*]

LILIOM. White acacias!

JULIE [*after a brief pause*]. The wind brings them down.

[*They are silent. There is a long pause before*

THE CURTAIN FALLS

SCENE II

A photographer's "studio," operated by the HOLLUNDERS, *on the fringe of the park. It is a dilapidated hovel. The general entrance is back left. Back right there is a window with a sofa before it. The outlook is on the amusement park with perhaps a small Ferris wheel or the scaffolding of a "scenic-railway" in the background.*

The door to the kitchen is up left and a black-curtained entrance to the dark-room is down left. Just in front of the dark-room stands the camera on its tripod. Against the back wall, between the door and window, stands the inevitable photographer's background-screen, ready to be wheeled into place.

It is forenoon. When the curtain rises, MARIE *and* JULIE *are discovered.*

MARIE. And *he* beat up Hollinger?

JULIE. Yes, he gave him an awful licking.

MARIE. But Hollinger is bigger than he is.

JULIE. He licked him just the same. It isn't size that counts, you know, it's cleverness. And Liliom's awful quick.

MARIE. And then he was arrested?

JULIE. Yes, they arrested him, but they let him go the next day. That makes twice in the two months we've been living here that Liliom's been arrested and let go again.

MARIE. Why do they let him go?

JULIE. Because he is innocent.

[MOTHER HOLLUNDER, *a very old woman, sharp-tongued, but in reality quite warm-hearted beneath her formidable exterior, enters at back carrying a few sticks of firewood, and scolding, half to herself.*]

MOTHER HOLLUNDER. Always wanting something, but never willing to work for it. He won't work, and he won't steal, but he'll use up a poor old widow's last bit of firewood. He'll do that cheerfully enough! A big, strong lout like that lying around all day resting his lazy bones! He ought to be ashamed to look decent people in the face.

JULIE. I'm sorry, Mother Hollunder...

MOTHER HOLLUNDER. Sorry! Better be sorry the lazy good-for-nothing ain't in jail where he belongs instead of in the way of honest, hard-working people.

[*She exits into the kitchen.*]

MARIE. Who's that?

JULIE. Mrs. Hollunder — my aunt. This is her [*with a sweeping gesture that takes in the camera, dark-room and screen*] studio. She lets us live here for nothing.

MARIE. What's she fetching the wood for?

JULIE. She brings us everything we need. If it weren't for her I don't know what would become of us. She's a good-hearted soul even if her tongue is sharp. [*There is a pause.*]

MARIE [*shyly*]. Do you know — I've found out. He's not a soldier.

JULIE. Do you still see him?

MARIE. Oh, yes.

JULIE. Often?

MARIE. Very often. He's asked me ——

JULIE. To marry you?

MARIE. To marry me.

JULIE. You see — that proves he isn't a soldier. [*There is another pause.*]

MARIE [*abashed, yet a bit boastfully*]. Do you know what I'm doing — I'm flirting with him.

JULIE. Flirting?

MARIE. Yes. He asks me to go to the park — and I say I can't go. Then he coaxes me, and promises me a new scarf for my head if I go. But I don't go — even then... So then he walks all the way home with me — and I bid him good-night at the door.

JULIE. Is that what you call flirting?

MARIE. Um-hm! It's sinful, but it's so *thrilling*.

JULIE. Do you ever quarrel?

MARIE [*grandly*]. Only when our Passionate Love surges up.

JULIE. Your passionate love?

MARIE. Yes... He takes my hand and we walk along together. Then he wants to swing hands, but I won't let him. I say: "Don't swing my hand"; and he says, "Don't be so stubborn." And then he tries to swing my hand again, but still I don't let him. And for a long time I don't let him — until in the end I let him. Then we walk along swinging hands — up and down, up and down — just like this. *That* is Passionate Love. It's sinful, but it's awfully *thrilling*.

JULIE. You're happy, aren't you?

MARIE. Happier than — anything —— But the most beautiful thing on earth is Ideal Love.

JULIE. What kind is that?

MARIE. Daylight comes about three in the morning this time of the year. When we've been up that long we're all through with flirting and Passionate Love — and then our Ideal Love comes to the surface. It comes like this: I'll be sitting on the bench and Wolf, he holds my hand tight — and he puts his cheek against my cheek and we don't talk... we just sit there very quiet.... And after a while he gets sleepy, and his head sinks down, and he falls asleep... but even in his sleep he holds tight to my hand. And I — I sit perfectly still just looking around me and taking long, deep breaths — for by that time it's morn-

ing and the trees and flowers are fresh with dew. But Wolf doesn't smell anything because he's so fast asleep. And I get awfully sleepy myself, but I don't sleep. And we sit like that for a long time. That is Ideal Love —— [*There is a long pause.*]

JULIE [*regretfully; uneasily*]. He went out last night and he hasn't come home yet.

MARIE. Here are sixteen Kreuzer. It was supposed to be carfare to take my young lady to the conservatory — eight there and eight back — but I made her walk. Here — save it with the rest.

JULIE. This makes three gulden, forty-six.

MARIE. Three gulden, forty-six.

JULIE. He won't work at all.

MARIE. Too lazy?

JULIE. No. He never learned a trade, you see, and he can't just go and be a day-laborer — so he just does nothing.

MARIE. That ain't right.

JULIE. No. Have the Breiers got a new maid yet?

MARIE. They've had three since you left. You know, Wolf's going to take a new job. He's going to work for the city. He'll get rent free, too.

JULIE. He won't go back to work at the carousel either. I ask him why, but he won't tell me —— Last Monday he hit me.

MARIE. Did you hit him back?

JULIE. No.

MARIE. Why don't you leave him?

JULIE. I don't want to.

MARIE. I would. I'd leave him.

[*There is a strained silence.*]

MOTHER HOLLUNDER [*enters, carrying a pot of water; muttering aloud*]. He can play cards, all right. He can fight, too; and take money from poor servant girls. And the police turn their heads the other way —— The carpenter was here.

JULIE. Is that water for the soup?

MOTHER HOLLUNDER. The carpenter was here. There's a *man* for you! Dark, handsome, lots of hair, a respectable widower with two children — and money, and a good paying business.

JULIE [*to* MARIE]. It's three gulden sixty-six, not forty-six.

MARIE. Yes, that's what I make it — sixty-six.

MOTHER HOLLUNDER. He wants to take her out of this and marry her. This is the fifth time he's been here. He has two children, but ——

JULIE. Please don't bother, Aunt Hollunder, I'll get the water myself.

MOTHER HOLLUNDER. He's waiting outside now.

JULIE. Send him away.

MOTHER HOLLUNDER. He'll only come back again — and first thing you know that vagabond will get jealous and there'll be a fight. [Goes out, muttering.] Oh, he's ready enough to fight, he is. Strike a poor little girl like that! Ought to be ashamed of himself! And the police just let him go on doing as he pleases.

[Still scolding, she exits at back.]

MARIE. A carpenter wants to marry you?

JULIE. Yes.

MARIE. Why don't you?

JULIE. Because ——

MARIE. Liliom doesn't support you, and he beats you — he thinks he can do whatever he likes just because he's Liliom. He's a bad one.

JULIE. He's not really bad.

MARIE. That night you sat on the bench together — he was gentle then.

JULIE. Yes, he was gentle.

MARIE. And afterwards he got wild again.

JULIE. Afterwards he got wild — sometimes. But that night on the bench... he was gentle. He's gentle now, sometimes, very gentle. After supper, when he stands there and listens to the music of the carousel, something comes over him — and he is gentle.

MARIE. Does he say anything?

JULIE. He doesn't say anything. He gets thoughtful and very quiet, and his big eyes stare straight ahead of him.

MARIE. Into your eyes?

JULIE. Not exactly. He's unhappy because he isn't working. That's really why he hit me on Monday.

MARIE. That's a fine reason for hitting you! Beats his wife because he isn't working, the ruffian!

JULIE. It preys on his mind ——

MARIE. Did he hurt you?

JULIE [very eagerly]. Oh, no.

MRS. MUSKAT [enters haughtily]. Good-morning. Is Liliom home?

JULIE. No.

MRS. MUSKAT. Gone out?

JULIE. He hasn't come home yet.

MRS. MUSKAT. I'll wait for him.

[She sits down.]

MARIE. You've got a lot of gall — to come here.

MRS. MUSKAT. Are you the lady of the house, my dear? Better look out or you'll get a slap in the mouth.

MARIE. How dare you set foot in Julie's house?

MRS. MUSKAT [to JULIE]. Pay no attention to her, my child. You know what brings me here. That vagabond, that good-for-nothing, I've come to give him his bread and butter back.

MARIE. He's not dependent on you for his bread.

MRS. MUSKAT [to JULIE]. Just ignore her, my child. She's just ignorant.

MARIE [going]. Good-bye.

JULIE. Good-bye.

MARIE [in the doorway, calling back]. Sixty-six.

JULIE. Yes, sixty-six.

MARIE. Good-bye.

[She exits. JULIE starts to go toward the kitchen.]

MRS. MUSKAT. I paid him a krone a day, and on Sunday a gulden. And he got all the beer and cigars he wanted from the customers. [JULIE pauses on the threshold, but does not answer.] And he'd rather starve than beg my pardon. Well, I don't insist on that. I'll take him back without it. [JULIE does not answer.] The fact is the people ask for him — and, you see, I've got to consider business first. It's nothing to me if he starves. I wouldn't be here at all, if it wasn't for business ——

[She pauses, for LILIOM and FICSUR have entered.]

JULIE. Mrs. Muskat is here.

LILIOM. I see she is.

JULIE. You might say good-morning.

LILIOM. What for? And what do *you* want, anyhow?

JULIE. I don't want anything.

LILIOM. Then keep your mouth shut. Next thing you'll be starting to nag again about my being out all night and out of work and living on your relations ——

JULIE. I'm not saying anything.

LILIOM. But it's all on the tip of your tongue — I know you — now don't start or you'll get another.

[*He paces angrily up and down. They are all a bit afraid of him, and shrink and look away as he passes them. FICSUR shambles from place to place, his eyes cast down as if he were searching for something on the floor.*]

MRS. MUSKAT [*suddenly, to FICSUR*]. You're always dragging him out to play cards and drink with you. I'll have you locked up, I will.

FICSUR. I don't want to talk to you. You're too common.

[*He goes out by the door at back and lingers there in plain view. There is a pause.*]

JULIE. Mrs. Muskat is here.

LILIOM. Well, why doesn't she open her mouth, if she has anything to say?

MRS. MUSKAT. Why do you go around with this man, Ficsur? He'll get you mixed up in one of his robberies first thing you know.

LILIOM. What's it to you who I go with? I do what I please. What do you want?

MRS. MUSKAT. You know what I want.

LILIOM. No, I don't.

MRS. MUSKAT. What do you suppose I want? Think I've come just to pay a social call?

LILIOM. Do I owe you anything?

MRS. MUSKAT. Yes, you do — but that's not what I came for. You're a fine one to come to for money! You earn so much these days! You know very well what I'm here for.

LILIOM. You've got Hollinger at the carousel, haven't you?

MRS. MUSKAT. Sure I have.

LILIOM. Well, what else do you want? He's as good as I am.

MRS. MUSKAT. You're quite right, my boy. He's every bit as good as you are. I'd not dream of letting him go. But one isn't enough any more. There's work enough for two ——

LILIOM. One was enough when *I* was there.

MRS. MUSKAT. Well, I might let Hollinger go ——

LILIOM. Why let him go, if he's so good?

MRS. MUSKAT [*shrugs her shoulders*]. Yes, he's good.

[*Not once until now has she looked at LILIOM.*]

LILIOM [*to JULIE*]. Ask your aunt if I can have a cup of coffee. [*JULIE exits into the kitchen.*] So Hollinger is good, is he?

MRS. MUSKAT [*crosses to him and looks him in the face*]. Why don't you stay home and sleep at night? You're a sight to look at.

LILIOM. He's good, is he?

MRS. MUSKAT. Push your hair back from your forehead.

LILIOM. Let my hair be. It's nothing to you.

MRS. MUSKAT. All right. But if I'd told you to let it hang down over your eyes you'd have pushed it back — I hear you've been beating her, this — this ——

LILIOM. None of your business.

MRS. MUSKAT. You're a fine fellow! Beating a skinny little thing like that! If you're tired of her, leave her, but there's no use beating the poor ——

LILIOM. Leave her, eh? You'd like that, wouldn't you?

MRS. MUSKAT. Don't flatter yourself. [*Quite embarrassed.*] Serves me right, too. If I had any sense I wouldn't have run after you —— My God, the things one must do for the sake of business! If I could only sell the carousel I wouldn't be sitting here.... Come, Liliom, if you have any sense, you'll come back. I'll pay you well.

LILIOM. The carousel is crowded just the same ... *without me?*

MRS. MUSKAT. Crowded, yes — but it's not the same.

LILIOM. Then you admit that you *do* miss me.

MRS. MUSKAT. Miss you? Not I. But the silly girls miss you. They're always asking for you. Well, are you going to be sensible and come back?

LILIOM. And leave — her?

MRS. MUSKAT. You beat her, don't you?

LILIOM. No, I don't beat her. What's all this damn fool talk about beating her? I hit her once — that was all — and now the whole city seems to be talking about it. You don't call that beating her, do you?

MRS. MUSKAT. All right, all right. I take it back. I don't want to get mixed up in it.

LILIOM. Beating her! As if I'd beat her ——

MRS. MUSKAT. I can't make out why you're so concerned about her. You've been married to her two months — it's plain to see that you're sick of it — and out there is the carousel — and the show booths — and money — and you'd throw it all away. For what? Heavens, how can any one be such a fool? [Looks at him appraisingly.] Where have you been all night? You look awful.

LILIOM. It's no business of yours.

MRS. MUSKAT. You never used to look like that. This life is telling on you. [Pauses.] Do you know — I've got a new organ.

LILIOM [softly]. I know.

MRS. MUSKAT. How did you know?

LILIOM. You can hear it — from here.

MRS. MUSKAT. It's a good one, eh?

LILIOM [wistfully]. Very good. Fine. It roars and snorts — so fine.

MRS. MUSKAT. You should hear it close by — it's heavenly. Even the carousel seems to know... it goes quicker. I got rid of those two horses — you know, the ones with the broken ears?

LILIOM. What have you put in their place?

MRS. MUSKAT. Guess.

LILIOM. Zebras?

MRS. MUSKAT. No — an automobile.

LILIOM [transported]. An automobile——

MRS. MUSKAT. Yes. If you've got any sense you'll come back. What good are you doing here? Out there is your *art*, the only thing you're fit for. You are an artist, not a respectable married man.

LILIOM. *Leave* her — this little ——

MRS. MUSKAT. She'll be better off. She'll go back and be a servant girl again. As for you — you're an artist and you belong among artists. All the beer you want, cigars, a krone a day and a gulden on Sunday, and the girls, Liliom, the girls — I've always treated you right, haven't I? I bought you a watch, and ——

LILIOM. She's not that kind. She'd never be a servant girl again.

MRS. MUSKAT. I suppose you think she'd kill herself. Don't worry. Heavens, if every girl was to commit suicide just because her —— [Finishes with a gesture.]

LILIOM [stares at her a moment, considering, then with sudden, smiling animation]. So the people don't like Hollinger?

MRS. MUSKAT. You know very well they don't, you rascal.

LILIOM. Well ——

MRS. MUSKAT. You've always been happy at the carousel. It's a great life — pretty girls and beer and cigars and music — a great life and an easy one. I'll tell you what — come back and I'll give you a ring that used to belong to my dear departed husband. Well, will you come?

LILIOM. She's not that kind. She'd never be a servant girl again. But — but — for my part — if I decide — that needn't make any difference. I can go on living with her even if I do go back to my art ——

MRS. MUSKAT. My God!

LILIOM. What's the matter?

MRS. MUSKAT. Who ever heard of a married man — I suppose you think all girls would be pleased to know that you were running home to your wife every night. It's ridiculous! When the people found out they'd laugh themselves sick——

LILIOM. I know what you want.

MRS. MUSKAT [refuses to meet his gaze]. You flatter yourself.

LILIOM. You'll give me that ring, too?

MRS. MUSKAT [pushes the hair back from his forehead]. Yes.

LILIOM. I'm not happy in this house.

MRS. MUSKAT [still stroking his hair]. Nobody takes care of you.

[They are silent. JULIE enters, carrying a cup of coffee. MRS. MUSKAT removes her hand from LILIOM's head. There is a pause.]

LILIOM. Do you want anything?

JULIE. No.

[There is a pause. She exits slowly into the kitchen.]

MRS. MUSKAT. The old woman says there is a carpenter, a widower, who ——

LILIOM. I know — I know ——

JULIE *[reentering]*. Liliom, before I forget, I have something to tell you.

LILIOM. All right.

JULIE. I've been wanting to tell you — in fact, I was going to tell you yesterday ——

LILIOM. Go ahead.

JULIE. But I must tell you alone — if you'll come in — it will only take a minute.

LILIOM. Don't you see I'm busy now? Here I am talking business and you interrupt with ——

JULIE. It'll only take a minute.

LILIOM. Get out of here, or ——

JULIE. But I tell you it will only take a minute ——

LILIOM. Will you get out of here?

JULIE *[courageously]*. No.

LILIOM *[rising]*. What's that!

JULIE. No.

MRS. MUSKAT *[rises, too]*. Now don't start fighting. I'll go out and look at the photographs in the show case a while and come back later for your answer.

[She exits at back.]

JULIE. You can hit me again if you like — don't look at me like that. I'm not afraid of you.... I'm not afraid of any one. I told you I had something to tell you.

LILIOM. Well, out with it — quick.

JULIE. I can't tell you so quick. Why don't you drink your coffee?

LILIOM. Is that what you wanted to tell me?

JULIE. No. By the time you've drunk your coffee I'll have told you.

LILIOM *[gets the coffee and sips it]*. Well?

JULIE. Yesterday my head ached — and you asked me ——

LILIOM. Yes ——

JULIE. Well — you see — that's what it is ——

LILIOM. Are you sick?

JULIE. No.... But you wanted to know what my headaches came from — and you said I seemed — changed.

LILIOM. Did I? I guess I meant the carpenter.

JULIE. I've been — what? The carpenter? No. It's something entirely different — it's awful hard to tell — but you'll have to know sooner or later — I'm not a bit — scared — because it's a perfectly natural thing ——

LILIOM *[puts the coffee cup on the table]*. What?

JULIE. When — when a man and woman — live together ——

LILIOM. Yes.

JULIE. I'm going to have a baby.

[She exits swiftly at back. There is a pause. FICSUR appears at the open window and looks in.]

LILIOM. Ficsur! *[FICSUR sticks his head in.]* Say, Ficsur — Julie is going to have a baby.

FICSUR. Yes? What of it?

LILIOM. Nothing. *[Suddenly.]* Get out of here.

[FICSUR's head is quickly withdrawn. MRS. MUSKAT reenters.]

MRS. MUSKAT. Has she gone?

LILIOM. Yes.

MRS. MUSKAT. I might as well give you ten kronen in advance. *[Opens her purse. LILIOM takes up his coffee cup.]* Here you are. *[She proffers some coins. LILIOM ignores her.]* Why don't you take it?

LILIOM *[very nonchalantly, his cup poised ready to drink]*. Go home, Mrs. Muskat.

MRS. MUSKAT. What's the matter with you?

LILIOM. Go home *[sips his coffee]* and let me finish my coffee in peace. Don't you see I'm at breakfast?

MRS. MUSKAT. Have you gone crazy?

LILIOM. Will you get out of here?

[Turns to her threateningly.]

MRS. MUSKAT *[restoring the coins to her purse]*. I'll never speak to you again as long as you live.

LILIOM. That worries me a lot.

MRS. MUSKAT. Good-bye!

LILIOM. Good-bye. [*As she exits, he calls.*] Ficsur! [FICSUR *enters.*] Tell me, Ficsur. You said you knew a way to get a whole lot of money ——

FICSUR. Sure I do.

LILIOM. How much?

FICSUR. More than you ever had in your life before. You leave it to an old hand like me.

MOTHER HOLLUNDER [*enters from the kitchen*]. In the morning he must have his coffee, and at noon his soup, and in the evening coffee again — and plenty of firewood — and I'm expected to furnish it all. Give me back my cup and saucer.

[*The show booths of the amusement park have opened for business. The familiar noises begin to sound; clear above them all, but far in the distance, sounds the organ of the carousel.*]

LILIOM. Now, Aunt Hollunder.

[*From now until the fall of the curtain it is apparent that the sound of the organ makes him more and more uneasy.*]

MOTHER HOLLUNDER. And you, you vagabond, get out of here this minute or I'll call my son ——

FICSUR. I have nothing to do with the likes of him. He's too common.

[*But he slinks out at back.*]

LILIOM. Aunt Hollunder!

MOTHER HOLLUNDER. What now?

LILIOM. When your son was born — when you brought him into the world ——

MOTHER HOLLUNDER. Well?

LILIOM. Nothing.

MOTHER HOLLUNDER [*muttering as she exits*]. Sleep it off, you good-for-nothing lout. Drink and play cards all night long — that's all you know how to do — and take the bread out of poor people's mouths — you can do that, too. [*She exits.*]

LILIOM. Ficsur!

FICSUR [*at the window*]. Julie's going to have a baby. You told me before.

LILIOM. This scheme — about the cashier of the leather factory — there's money in it ——

FICSUR. Lots of money — but — it takes two to pull it off.

LILIOM [*meditatively*]. Yes. [*Uneasily.*]

All right, Ficsur. Go away — and come back later.

[FICSUR *vanishes. The organ in the distant carousel drones incessantly.* LILIOM *listens awhile, then goes to the door and calls.*]

LILIOM. Aunt Hollunder! [*With naïve joy.*] Julie's going to have a baby. [*Then he goes to the window, jumps on the sofa, looks out. Suddenly, in a voice that overtops the droning of the organ, he shouts as if addressing the far-off carousel.*] I'm going to be a father.

JULIE [*enters from the kitchen*]. Liliom! What's the matter? What's happened?

LILIOM [*coming down from the sofa*]. Nothing.

[*Throws himself on the sofa, buries his face in the cushion.* JULIE *watches him a moment, comes over to him and covers him with a shawl. Then she goes on tiptoe to the door at back and remains standing in the doorway, looking out and listening to the droning of the organ.*]

THE CURTAIN FALLS

SCENE III

The setting is the same, later that afternoon. LILIOM *is sitting opposite* FICSUR, *who is teaching him a song.* JULIE *hovers in the background, engaged in some household task.*

FICSUR. Listen now. Here's the third verse. [*Sings hoarsely.*]

"*Look out, look out, my pretty lad,*
The damn police are on your trail;
The nicest girl you ever had
Has now commenced to weep and wail:
Look out here comes the damn police,
The damn police,
The damn police,
Look out here comes the damn police,
They'll get you every time."

LILIOM [*sings*].

"*Look out, look out, my pretty lad,*
The damn police ——"

FICSUR, LILIOM [*sing together*].

"*are on your trail;*
The nicest girl you ever had
Has now commenced to weep and wail."

LILIOM [*alone*].

"*Look out here comes the damn police,
The damn police,
The damn police* ——"

[JULIE, *troubled and uneasy, looks
from one to the other, then exits into the
kitchen.*]

FICSUR [*when she has gone, comes quickly
over to* LILIOM *and speaks furtively*]. As you
go down Franzen Street you come to the
railroad embankment. Beyond that — all
the way to the leather factory — there's
not a thing in sight, not even a watchman's
hut.

LILIOM. And does he always come that
way?

FICSUR. Yes. Not along the embankment, but down below along the path across
the fields. Since last year he's been going
alone. Before that he always used to have
some one with him.

LILIOM. Every Saturday?

FICSUR. Every Saturday.

LILIOM. And the money? Where does
he keep it?

FICSUR. In a leather bag. The whole
week's pay for the workmen at the factory.

LILIOM. Much?

FICSUR. Sixteen thousand kronen. Quite
a haul, what?

LILIOM. What's his name?

FICSUR. Linzman. He's a Jew.

LILIOM. The cashier?

FICSUR. Yes — but when he gets a knife
between his ribs — or if I smash his skull
for him — he won't be a cashier any more.

LILIOM. Does he have to be killed?

FICSUR. No, he doesn't *have* to be. He
can give up the money *without* being killed
— but most of these cashiers are peculiar
— they'd rather be killed.

[JULIE *reënters, pretends to get something on
the other side of the room, then exits at
back. During the ensuing dialogue she
keeps coming in and out in the same
way, showing plainly that she is suspicious and anxious. She attempts to
overhear what they are saying and, in
spite of their caution, does catch a word
here and there, which adds to her dis-*

quiet. FICSUR, *catching sight of her,
abruptly changes the conversation.*]

FICSUR. And the next verse is:

"*And when you're in the prison cell
They'll feed you bread and water.*"

FICSUR AND LILIOM [*sing together*].

"*They'll make your little sweetheart tell
Them all the things you brought her.
Look out here comes the damn police,
The damn police,
The damn police.
Look out here comes the damn police
They'll get you every time.*"

LILIOM [*sings alone*].

"*And when you're in the prison cell
They'll feed you bread and water* ——"

[*Breaks off, as* JULIE *exits.*]
And when it's done, do we start right off
for America?

FICSUR. No.

LILIOM. What then?

FICSUR. We bury the money for six
months. That's the usual time. And
after the sixth month we dig it up again.

LILIOM. And then?

FICSUR. Then you go on living just as
usual for six months more — you don't
touch a heller of the money.

LILIOM. In six months the baby will be
born.

FICSUR. Then we'll take the baby with
us, too. Three months before the time
you'll go to work so as to be able to say you
saved up your wages to get to America.

LILIOM. Which of us goes up and talks
to him?

FICSUR. One of us talks to him with his
mouth and the other talks with his knife.
Depends on which you'd rather do. I'll
tell you what — you talk to him with your
mouth.

LILIOM. Do you hear that?

FICSUR. What?

LILIOM. Outside... like the rattle of
swords. [FICSUR *listens. After a pause,*
LILIOM *continues.*] What do I say to him?

FICSUR. You say good-evening to him
and: "Excuse me, sir; can you tell me the
time?"

LILIOM. And then what?

FICSUR. By that time I'll have stuck him — and then you take *your* knife ——

[*He stops as a* POLICEMAN *enters at back.*]

POLICEMAN. Good-day!

FICSUR, LILIOM [*in unison*]. Good-day!

FICSUR [*calling toward the kitchen*]. Hey, photographer, come out.... Here's a customer.

[*There is a pause. The* POLICEMAN *waits.* FICSUR *sings softly.*]

"*And when you're in the prison cell
They'll feed you bread and water
They'll make your little sweetheart tell*"

LILIOM, FICSUR [*sing together, low*].

"*Them all the things you brought her.
Look out here comes the* ——"

[*They hum the rest so as not to let the* POLICEMAN *hear the words "the damn police." As they sing,* MRS. HOLLUNDER *and her son enter.*]

POLICEMAN. Do you make cabinet photographs?

YOUNG HOLLUNDER. Certainly, sir. [*Points to a rack of photographs on the wall.*] Take your choice, sir. Would you like one full length?

POLICEMAN. Yes, full length.

[MOTHER HOLLUNDER *pushes out the camera while her son poses the* POLICE-MAN, *runs from him to the camera and back again, now altering the pose, now ducking under the black cloth and pushing the camera nearer. Meanwhile* MOTHER HOLLUNDER *has fetched a plate from the dark-room and thrust it in the camera. While this is going on,* LILIOM *and* FICSUR, *their heads together, speak in very low tones.*]

LILIOM. Belong around here?

FICSUR. Not around here.

LILIOM. Where, then?

FICSUR. Suburban. [*There is a pause.*]

LILIOM [*bursts out suddenly in a rather grotesquely childish and overstrained lament*]. O God, what a dirty life I'm leading — God, God!

FICSUR [*reassuring him benevolently*]. Over in America it will be better, all right.

LILIOM. What's over there?

FICSUR [*virtuously*]. Factories... industries ——

YOUNG HOLLUNDER [*to the* POLICEMAN]. Now, quite still, please. One, two, three. [*Deftly removes the cover of the lens and in a few seconds restores it.*] Thank you.

MOTHER HOLLUNDER. The picture will be ready in five minutes.

POLICEMAN. Good. I'll come back in five minutes. How much do I owe you?

YOUNG HOLLUNDER [*with exaggerated deference*]. You don't need to pay in advance, Mr. Commissioner.

[*The* POLICEMAN *salutes condescendingly and exits at back.* MOTHER HOLLUNDER *carries the plate into the dark-room.* YOUNG HOLLUNDER, *after pushing the camera back in place, follows her.*]

MOTHER HOLLUNDER [*muttering angrily as she passes* FICSUR *and* LILIOM.] You hang around and dirty the whole place up! Why don't you go take a walk? Things are going so well with you that you have to sing, eh? [*Confronting* FICSUR *suddenly.*] Weren't you frightened sick when you saw the policeman?

FICSUR [*with loathing*]. Go 'way, or I'll step on you. [*She exits into the dark-room.*]

LILIOM. They like Hollinger at the carousel?

FICSUR. I should say they do.

LILIOM. Did you see the Muskat woman, too?

FICSUR. Sure. She takes care of Hollinger's hair.

LILIOM. Combs his hair?

FICSUR. She fixes him all up.

LILIOM. Let her fix him all she likes.

FICSUR [*urging him toward the kitchen door*]. Go on. Now's your chance.

LILIOM. What for?

FICSUR. To get the knife.

LILIOM. What knife?

FICSUR. The kitchen knife. I've got a pocket-knife, but if he shows fight, we'll let him have the big knife.

LILIOM. What for? If he gets ugly, I'll bat him one over the head that'll make him squint for the rest of his life.

FICSUR. You've got to have something

on you. You can't slit his throat with a bat over the head.

LILIOM. Must his throat be slit?

FICSUR. No, it *mustn't*. But if he asks for it. [*There is a pause.*] You'd like to sail on the big steamer, wouldn't you? And you want to see the factories over there, don't you? But you're not willing to inconvenience yourself a little for them.

LILIOM. If I take the knife, Julie will see me.

FICSUR. Take it so she won't see you.

LILIOM [*advances a few paces toward the kitchen. The* POLICEMAN *enters at back.* LILIOM *knocks on the door of the dark-room*]. Here's the policeman!

MOTHER HOLLUNDER [*coming out*]. One minute more, please. Just a minute.

[*She reënters the dark-room.* LILIOM *hesitates a moment, then exits into the kitchen. The* POLICEMAN *scrutinizes* FICSUR *mockingly*.]

FICSUR [*returns his stare, walks a few paces toward him, then deliberately turns his back. Suddenly he wheels around, points at the* POLICEMAN *and addresses him in a teasing, childish tone*]. Christiana Street at the corner of Retti!

POLICEMAN [*amazed, self-conscious*]. How do you know that?

FICSUR. I used to practice my profession in that neighborhood.

POLICEMAN. What is your profession?

FICSUR. Professor of pianola ——

[*The* POLICEMAN *glares, aware that the man is joking with him, twirls his moustache indignantly.* YOUNG HOLLUNDER *comes out of the dark-room and gives him the finished pictures*.]

YOUNG HOLLUNDER. Here you are, sir.

[*The* POLICEMAN *examines the photographs, pays for them, starts to go, stops, glares at* FICSUR *and exits. When he is gone,* FICSUR *goes to the doorway and looks out after him.* YOUNG HOLLUNDER *exits.* LILIOM *reënters, buttoning his coat*.]

FICSUR [*turns, sees* LILIOM]. What are you staring at?

LILIOM. I'm not staring.

FICSUR. What then are you doing?

LILIOM. I'm thinking it over.

FICSUR [*comes very close to him*]. Tell me then — what will you say to him?

LILIOM [*unsteadily*]. I'll say — "Good-evening — Excuse me, sir — Can you tell me the time?" And suppose he answers me, what do I say to him?

FICSUR. He won't answer you.

LILIOM. Don't you think so?

FICSUR. No. [*Feeling for the knife under* LILIOM's *coat.*] Where is it? Where did you put it?

LILIOM [*stonily*]. Left side.

FICSUR. That's right — over your heart. [*Feels it.*] Ah — there it is — there — there's the blade — quite a big fellow, isn't it — ah, here it begins to get narrower. [*Reaches the tip of the knife.*] And here is its eye — that's what it sees with. [JULIE *enters from the kitchen, passes them slowly, watching them in silent terror, then stops.* FICSUR *nudges* LILIOM.] Sing, come on, sing!

LILIOM [*in a quavering voice*].

"*Look out for the damn police.*"

FICSUR [*joining in, cheerily, loudly, marking time with the swaying of his body*].

"*Look out, look out, my pretty lad.*"

LILIOM.

"— *look out, my pretty lad.*"

[JULIE *goes out at back.* LILIOM's *glance follows her. When she has gone, he turns to* FICSUR.] At night — in my dreams — if his ghost comes back — what will I do then?

FICSUR. His ghost won't never come back.

LILIOM. Why not?

FICSUR. A Jew's ghost don't come back.

LILIOM. Well then — afterwards

FICSUR [*impatiently*]. What do you mean — afterwards?

LILIOM. In the next world — when I come up before the Lord God — what'll I say then?

FICSUR. The likes of you will never come up before Him.

LILIOM. Why not?

FICSUR. Have you ever come up before the high court?

LILIOM. No.

FICSUR. Our kind comes up before the police magistrate — and the highest we *ever* get is the criminal court.

LILIOM. Will it be the same in the next world?

FICSUR. Just the same. We'll come up before a police magistrate, same as we did in this world.

LILIOM. A police magistrate?

FICSUR. Sure. For the rich folks — the Heavenly Court. For us poor people — only a police magistrate. For the rich folks — fine music and angels. For us——

LILIOM. For us?

FICSUR. For us, my son, there's only justice. In the next world there'll be lots of justice, yes, nothing but justice. And where there's justice, there must be police magistrates; and where there're police magistrates, people like us get ——

LILIOM [*interrupting*]. Good-evening. Excuse me, sir, can you tell me the time? [*Lays his hand over his heart.*]

FICSUR. What do you put your hand there for?

LILIOM. My heart is jumping — under the knife.

FICSUR. Put it on the other side then. [*Looks out at the sky.*] It's time we started — we'll walk slow ——

LILIOM. It's too early.

FICSUR. Come on.

[*As they are about to go,* JULIE *appears in the doorway at back, obstructing the way.*]

JULIE. Where are you going with him?

LILIOM. Where am I going with him?

JULIE. Stay home.

LILIOM. No.

JULIE. Stay home. It's going to rain soon, and you'll get wet.

FICSUR. It won't rain.

JULIE. How do you know?

FICSUR. I always get notice in advance.

JULIE. Stay home. This evening the carpenter's coming. I've asked him to give you work.

LILIOM. I'm not a carpenter.

JULIE [*more and more anxious, though she tries to conceal it*]. Stay home. Marie's coming with her intended to have their picture taken. She wants to introduce us to her intended husband.

LILIOM. I've seen enough intended husbands ——

JULIE. Stay home. Marie's bringing some money, and I'll give it all to you.

LILIOM [*approaching the door*]. I'm going — for a walk — with Ficsur. We'll be right back.

JULIE [*forcing a smile to keep back her tears*]. If you stay home, I'll get you a glass of beer — or wine, if you prefer.

FICSUR. Coming or not?

JULIE. I'm not angry with you any more for hitting me.

LILIOM [*gruffly, but his gruffness is simulated to hide the fact that he cannot bear the sight of her suffering*]. Stand out of the way — or I'll —— [*He clenches his fist.*] Let me out!

JULIE [*trembling*]. What have you got under your coat?

LILIOM [*produces from his pocket a greasy pack of cards*]. Cards.

JULIE [*trembling, speaks very low*]. What's under your coat?

LILIOM. Let me out!

JULIE [*obstructing the way. Speaks quickly, eagerly, in a last effort to detain him*]. Marie's intended knows about a place for a married couple without children to be caretakers of a house on Arader Street. Rent free, a kitchen of your own, and the privilege of keeping chickens ——

LILIOM. Get out of the way!

[JULIE *stands aside.* LILIOM *exits.* FISCUR *follows him.* JULIE *remains standing meditatively in the doorway.* MOTHER HOLLUNDER *comes out of the kitchen.*]

MOTHER HOLLUNDER. I can't find my kitchen knife anywhere. Have you seen anything of it?

JULIE [*horrified*]. No.

MOTHER HOLLUNDER. It was on the kitchen table just a few minutes ago. No one was in there except Liliom.

JULIE. He didn't take it.

MOTHER HOLLUNDER. No one else was in there.

JULIE. What would Liliom want with a kitchen knife?

MOTHER HOLLUNDER. He'd sell it and spend the money on drink.

JULIE. It just so happens — see how unjust you are to him — it just so happens that I went through all of Liliom's pockets just now — I wanted to see if he had any money on him. But he had nothing but a pack of cards.

MOTHER HOLLUNDER [*returns to the kitchen, grumbling*]. Cards in his pocket — cards! The fine gentlemen have evidently gone off to their club to play a little game.

[*She exits. After a pause* MARIE, *happy and beaming, appears in the doorway at back, and enters, followed by* WOLF.]

MARIE. Here we are! [*She takes* WOLF *by the hand and leads him, grinning shyly, to* JULIE, *who has turned at her call.*] Hello!

JULIE. Hello.

MARIE. Well, we're here.

JULIE. Yes.

WOLF [*bows awkwardly and extends his hand*]. My name is Wolf Beifeld.

JULIE. My name is Julio Zeller.

[*They shake hands. There is an embarrassed silence. Then, to relieve the situation,* WOLF *takes* JULIE'S *hand again and shakes it vigorously.*]

MARIE. Well — this is Wolf.

WOLF. Yes.

JULIE. Yes. [*Another awkward silence.*]

MARIE. Where is Liliom?

WOLF. Yes, where is your husband?

JULIE. He's out.

MARIE. Where?

JULIE. Just for a walk.

MARIE. Is he?

JULIE. Yes.

WOLF. Oh! [*Another silence.*]

MARIE. Wolf's got a new place. After the first of the month he won't have to stand outside any more. He's going to work in a club after the first of the month.

WOLF [*apologetically*]. She don't know yet how to explain these things just right — hehehe —— Beginning the first I'm to be second steward at the Burger Club — a good job, if one conducts oneself properly.

JULIE. Yes?

WOLF. The pay — is quite good — but the main thing is the tips. When they play cards there's always a bit for the steward. The tips, I may say, amount to twenty, even thirty kronen every night.

MARIE. Yes.

WOLF. We've rented two rooms for ourselves to start with — and if things go well ——

MARIE. Then we'll buy a house in the country.

WOLF. If one only tends to business and keeps honest. Of course, in the country we'll miss the city life, but if the good Lord sends us children — it's much healthier for children in the country.

[*There is a brief pause.*]

MARIE. Wolf's nice looking, isn't he?

JULIE. Yes.

MARIE. And he's a good boy, Wolf.

JULIE. Yes.

MARIE. The only thing is — he's a Jew.

JULIE. Oh, well, you can get used to that.

MARIE. Well, aren't you going to wish us luck?

JULIE. Of course I do.

[*She embraces* MARIE.]

MARIE. And aren't you going to kiss Wolf, too?

JULIE. Him, too.

[*She embraces* WOLF, *remains quite still a moment, her head resting on his shoulder.*]

WOLF. Why are you crying, my dear Mrs. ——

[*He looks questioningly at* MARIE *over* JULIE'S *shoulder.*]

MARIE. Because she has such a good heart. [*She becomes sentimental, too.*]

WOLF [*touched*]. We thank you for your heartfelt sympathy ——

[*He cannot restrain his own tears. There is a pause before* MOTHER HOLLUNDER *and her son enter.* YOUNG HOLLUNDER *immediately busies himself with the camera.*]

MOTHER HOLLUNDER. Now if you don't mind, we'll do it right away, before it gets too dark. [*She leads* MARIE *and* WOLF *into position before the background-screen. Here they immediately fall into an awkward pose, smiling mechanically.*] Full length?

MARIE. Please. Both figures full length.

MOTHER HOLLUNDER. Bride and groom?

MARIE. Yes.

MOTHER HOLLUNDER, YOUNG HOLLUNDER [*speak in unison, in loud professionally expressionless tones*]. The lady looks at the gentleman and the gentleman looks straight into the camera.

MOTHER HOLLUNDER [*poses first* MARIE, *then* WOLF]. Now, if you please.

YOUNG HOLLUNDER [*who has crept under the black cloth, calls in muffled tones*]. That's good — that's very good!

MARIE [*stonily rigid, but very happy, trying to speak without altering her expression*]. Julie, dear, do we look all right?

JULIE. Yes, dear.

YOUNG HOLLUNDER. Now, if you please, hold still. I'll count up to three, and then you must hold perfectly still. [*Grasps the cover of the lens and calls threateningly.*] One — two — three!

[*He removes the cover; there is utter silence. But as he speaks the word "one" these is heard, very faintly in the distance, the refrain of the thieves' song which* FICSUR *and* LILIOM *have been singing. The refrain continues until the fall of the curtain. As he speaks the word "three" everybody is perfectly rigid save* JULIE, *who lets her head sink slowly to the table. The distant refrain dies out.*]

THE CURTAIN FALLS

SCENE IV

In the fields on the outskirts of the city. At back a railroad embankment crosses the stage obliquely. At center of the embankment stands a red and white signal flag, and near it a little red signal lamp which is not yet lighted. Here also a wooden stairway leads up to the embankment.

At the foot of the embankment to the right is a pile of used railroad ties. In the background a telegraph pole, beyond it a view of trees, fences and fields; still further back a factory building and a cluster of little dwellings.

It is six o'clock of the same afternoon. Dusk has begun to fall.

LILIOM *and* FICSUR *are discovered on the stairway looking after the train which has just passed.*

LILIOM. Can you still hear it snort?

FICSUR. Listen!

[*They watch the vanishing train.*]

LILIOM. If you put your ear on the tracks you can hear it go all the way to Vienna.

FICSUR. Huh!

LILIOM. The one that just puffed past us — it goes all the way to Vienna.

FICSUR. No further?

LILIOM. Yes — further, too.

[*There is a pause.*]

FICSUR. It must be near six. [*As* LILIOM *ascends the steps.*] Where are you going?

LILIOM. Don't be afraid. I'm not giving you the slip.

FICSUR. Why should you give me the slip? That cashier has sixteen thousand kronen on him. Just be patient till he comes, then you can talk to him, nice and polite.

LILIOM. I say, "Good-evening — excuse me, sir; what time is it?"

FICSUR. Then he tells you what time it is.

LILIOM. Suppose he don't come?

FICSUR [*coming down the steps*]. Nonsense! He's got to come. He pays off the workmen every Saturday. And this is Saturday, ain't it? [LILIOM *has ascended to the top of the stairway and is gazing along the tracks.*] What are you looking at up there?

LILIOM. The tracks go on and on — there's no end to them.

FICSUR. What's that to stare about?

LILIOM. Nothing — only I always look after the train. When you stand down there at night it snorts past you, and spits down.

FICSUR. Spits?

LILIOM. Yes, the engine. It spits down. And then the whole train rattles past and away — and you stand there — spat on — but it draws your eyes along with it.

FICSUR. Draws your eyes along?

LILIOM. Yes — whether you want to or

not, you've got to look after it — as long as the tiniest bit of it is in sight.

FICSUR. Swell people sit in it.

LILIOM. And read newspapers.

FICSUR. And smoke cigars.

LILIOM. And inhale the smoke.

[*There is a short silence.*]

FICSUR. Is he coming?

LILIOM. Not yet. [*Silence again.* LILIOM *comes down, speaks low, confidentially.*] Do you hear the telegraph wires?

FICSUR. I hear them when the wind blows.

LILIOM. Even when the wind doesn't blow you can hear them humming, humming —— People talk through them.

FICSUR. Who?

LILIOM. Jews.

FICSUR. No — they telegraph.

LILIOM. They talk through them and from some other place they get answered. And it all goes through the iron strings — that's why they hum like that — they hum-m ——

FICSUR. What do they hum?

LILIOM. They hum! ninety-nine, ninety-nine. Just listen.

FICSUR. What for?

LILIOM. That sparrow's listening, too. He's cocked one eye and looks at me as if to say: "I'd like to know what they're talking about."

FICSUR. You're looking at a bird?

LILIOM. He's looking at me, too.

FICSUR. Listen, you're sick! There's something the matter with you. Do you know what it is? Money. That bird has no money, either; that's why he cocks his eye.

LILIOM. Maybe.

FICSUR. Whoever has money don't cock his eye.

LILIOM. What then does he do?

FICSUR. He does most anything he wants. But nobody works unless he has money. We'll soon have money ourselves.

LILIOM. I say, "Good-evening. Excuse me, sir, can you tell me what time it is!"

FICSUR. He's not coming yet. Got the cards? [LILIOM *gives him the pack of cards.*] Got any money?

LILIOM [*takes some coins from his trousers pocket and counts*]. Eleven.

FICSUR [*sits astride on the pile of ties and looks off left*]. All right — eleven.

LILIOM [*sitting astride on the ties facing him*]. Put it up.

FICSUR [*puts the money on the ties; rapidly shuffles the cards*]. We'll play twenty-one. I'll bank. [*He deals deftly.*]

LILIOM [*looks at his card*]. Good. I'll bet the bank.

FICSUR. Must have an ace!

[*Deals him a second card.*]

LILIOM. Another one. [*He gets another card.*] Another. [*Gets still another.*] Over! [*Throws down his cards.* FICSUR *gathers in the money.*] Come on!

FICSUR. Come on what! Got no more money, have you?

LILIOM. No.

FICSUR. Then the game's over — unless you want to ——

LILIOM. What?

FICSUR. Play on credit.

LILIOM. You'll trust me?

FICSUR. No — but — I'll deduct it.

LILIOM. Deduct it from what?

FICSUR. From your share of the money. If *you* win you deduct from my share.

LILIOM [*looks over his shoulder to see if the cashier is coming; nervous and ashamed*]. All right. How much is bank?

FICSUR. That cashier is bringing us sixteen thousand kronen. Eight thousand of that is mine. Well, then, the bank is eight thousand.

LILIOM. Good.

FICSUR. Whoever has the most luck will have the most money. [*He deals.*]

LILIOM. Six hundred kronen. [FICSUR *gives him another card.*] Enough.

FICSUR [*laying out his own cards*]. Twenty-one. [*He shuffles rapidly.*]

LILIOM [*moves excitedly nearer to* FICSUR]. Well, then, double or nothing.

FICSUR [*dealing*]. Double or nothing.

LILIOM [*gets a card*]. Enough.

FICSUR [*laying out his own cards*]. Twenty-one. [*Shuffles rapidly again.*]

LILIOM [*in alarm*]. You're not — cheating?

FICSUR. Me? Do I look like a cheat?
[*Deals the cards again.*]
LILIOM [*glances nervously over his shoulder*]. A thousand.
FICSUR [*nonchalantly*]. Kronen?
LILIOM. Kronen. [*He gets a card.*] Another one. [*Gets another card.*] Over again!

[*Like an inexperienced gambler who is losing heavily, LILIOM is very nervous. He plays dazedly, wildly, irrationally. From now on it is apparent that his only thought is to win his money back.*]

FICSUR. That makes twelve hundred you owe.
LILIOM. Double or nothing. [*He gets a card. He is greatly excited.*] Another one. [*Gets another card.*] Another.
[*Throws down three cards.*]
FICSUR [*bends over and adds up the sum on the ground*]. Ten — fourteen — twenty-three —— You owe two thousand, four hundred.
LILIOM Now what?
FICSUR [*takes a card out of the deck and gives it to him*]. Here's the red ace. You can play double or nothing again.
LILIOM [*eagerly*]. Good. [*Gets another card.*] Enough.
FICSUR [*turns up his own cards*]. Nineteen.
LILIOM. You win again. [*Almost imploring*]. Give me an ace again. Give me the green one. [*Takes a card.*] Double or nothing.
FICSUR. Not any more.
LILIOM. Why not?
FICSUR. Because if you lose you won't be able to pay. Double would be nine thousand six hundred. And you've only got eight thousand altogether.
LILIOM [*greatly excited*]. That — that — I call that — a dirty trick!
FICSUR. Three thousand, two hundred. That's all you can put up.
LILIOM [*eagerly*]. All right, then — three thousand, two hundred. [FICSUR *deals him a card.*] Enough.
FICSUR. I've got an ace myself. Now we'll have to take our time and squeeze 'em.
[LILIOM *pushes closer to him as he takes up his cards and slowly, intently unfolds them.*]
Twenty-one.
[*He quickly puts the cards in his pocket. There is a pause.*]
LILIOM. Now — now — I'll tell you now — you're a crook, a low-down ——

[*Now* LINZMAN *enters at Right. He is a strong, robust, red-bearded Jew about 40 years of age. At his side he carries a leather bag slung by a strap from his shoulder.* FICSUR *coughs warningly, moves to the right between* LINZMAN *and the embankment, pauses just behind* LINZMAN *and follows him.*]

LILIOM [*stands bewildered a few paces to the left of the railroad ties. He finds himself facing* LINZMAN. *Trembling in every limb*]. Good-evening. Excuse me, sir, can you tell me the time?

[FICSUR *springs silently at* LINZMAN, *the little knife in his right hand. But* LINZMAN *catches* FICSUR'S *right hand with his own left and forces* FICSUR *to his knees. Simultaneously* LINZMAN *thrusts his right hand into his coat pocket and produces a revolver which he points at* LILIOM'S *breast.* LILIOM *is standing two paces away from the revolver. There is a long pause.*]

LINZMAN [*in a low, even voice*]. It is twenty-five minutes past six. [*Pauses, looks ironically down at* FICSUR.] It's lucky I grabbed the hand with the knife instead of the other one. [*Pauses again, looks appraisingly from one to the other.*] Two fine birds! [*To* FICSUR.] I should live so — Rothschild has more luck than you. [*To* LILIOM.] I'd advise you to keep nice and quiet. If you make one move, you'll get two bullets in you. Just look into the barrel. You'll see some little things in there made of lead.

FICSUR. Let me go. I didn't do anything.

LINZMAN [*mockingly shakes the hand which still holds the knife*]. And this? What do you call this? Oh, yes, I know. You thought I had an apple in my pocket, and you wanted to peel it. That's it. Forgive me for my error. I beg your pardon, sir.

LILIOM. But I — I ——

LINZMAN. Yes, my son, I know. It's so simple. You only asked what time it is. Well, it's twenty-five minutes after six.

FICSUR. Let us go, honorable sir. We didn't do anything to you.

LINZMAN. In the first place, my son, I'm not an honorable sir. In the second place, for the same money, you could have said Your Excellency. But in the third place you'll find it very hard to beg off by flattering me.

LILIOM But I — *I* really didn't do anything to you.

LINZMAN. Look behind you, my boy. Don't be afraid. Look behind you, but don't run away or I'll have to shoot you down. [LILIOM *turns his head slowly around.*] Who's coming up there?

LILIOM [*looking at* LINZMAN]. Policemen.

LINZMAN [*to* FICSUR]. You hold still, or —— [*To* LILIOM *teasingly.*] How many policemen are there?

LILIOM [*his eyes cast down*]. Two.

LINZMAN. And what are the policemen sitting on?

LILIOM. Horses.

LINZMAN. And which can run faster, a horse or a man?

LILIOM. A horse.

LINZMAN. There, you see. It would be hard to get away now. [*Laughs.*] I never saw such an unlucky pair of highway robbers. I can't imagine worse luck. Just to-day I had to put a pistol in my pocket. And even if I hadn't — old Linzman is a match for four like you. But even that isn't all. Did you happen to notice, you oxen, what direction I came from? From the factory, didn't I? When I went there I had a nice bit of money with me. Sixteen thousand crowns! But now — not a heller. [*Calls off left.*] Hey, come quicker, will you? This fellow is pulling pretty strong. [FICSUR *frees himself with a mighty wrench and darts rapidly off. As* LINZMAN *aims his pistol at the vanishing* FICSUR, LILIOM *runs up the steps to the embankment.* LINZMAN *hesitates, perceives that* LILIOM *is the better target, points the pistol at him.*] Stop, or I'll shoot! [*Calls off left to the*

POLICEMEN.] Why don't you come down off your horses? [*His pistol is leveled at* LILIOM, *who stands on the embankment, facing the audience. From the left on the embankment a* POLICEMAN *appears, revolver in hand.*]

FIRST POLICEMAN. Stop!

LINZMAN. Well, my boy, do you still want to know what time it is? From ten to twelve years in prison!

LILIOM. You won't get me! [LINZMAN *laughs derisively.* LILIOM *is now three or four paces from the* POLICEMAN *and equally distant from* LINZMAN. *His face is uplifted to the sky. He bursts into laughter, half defiant, half self-pitying, and takes the kitchen knife from under his coat.*] Julie ——

[*The ring of farewell is in the word. He turns sideways, thrusts the knife deep in his breast, sways, falls and rolls down the far side of the embankment. There is a long pause. From the left up on the embankment come the* TWO POLICEMEN.]

LINZMAN. What's the matter? [*The* FIRST POLICEMAN *comes along the embankment as far as the steps, looks down in the opposite side, then climbs down at about the spot where* LILIOM *disappeared.* LINZMAN *and the other* POLICEMAN *mount the embankment and look down on him.*] Stabbed himself?

VOICE OF FIRST POLICEMAN. Yes — and he seems to have made a thorough job of it.

LINZMAN [*excitedly to the* SECOND POLICEMAN]. I'll go and telephone to the hospital. [*He runs down the steps and exits at left.*]

SECOND POLICEMAN. Go to Eisler's grocery store and telephone to the factory from there. They've a doctor there, too. [*Calling down to the other* POLICEMAN.] I'm going to tie up the horses.

[*Comes down the steps and exits at left. The stage is empty. There is a pause. The little red signal lamp is lit.*]

VOICE OF FIRST POLICEMAN. Hey, Stephan!

VOICE OF SECOND POLICEMAN. What?

VOICE OF FIRST POLICEMAN. Shall I pull the knife out of his chest?

VOICE OF SECOND POLICEMAN. Better not, or he may bleed to death.

[*There is a pause.*]

VOICE OF FIRST POLICEMAN. Stephan!
VOICE OF SECOND POLICEMAN. Yes.
VOICE OF FIRST POLICEMAN. Lot of mosquitoes around here.
VOICE OF SECOND POLICEMAN. Yes.
VOICE OF FIRST POLICEMAN. Got a cigar?
VOICE OF SECOND POLICEMAN. No.
[There is a pause. The FIRST POLICEMAN appears over the opposite side of the embankment.]
FIRST POLICEMAN. A lot of good the new pay-schedule's done us — made things worse than they used to be — we get more but we have less than we ever had. If the Government could be made to realize that. It's a thankless job at best. You work hard year after year, you get gray in the service, and slowly you die — yes.
SECOND POLICEMAN. That's right.
FIRST POLICEMAN. Yes.
[In the distance is heard the bell of the signal tower.]

THE CURTAIN FALLS

SCENE V

The photographic "studio" a half hour later that same evening.

MOTHER HOLLUNDER, her son, MARIE and WOLF stand in a group back right, their heads together. JULIE stands apart from them, a few paces to the left.

YOUNG HOLLUNDER [who has just come in, tells his story excitedly]. They're bringing him now. Two workmen from the factory are carrying him on a stretcher.
WOLF. Where is the doctor?
YOUNG HOLLUNDER. A policeman telephoned to headquarters. The police-surgeon ought to be here any minute.
MARIE. Maybe they'll pull him through after all.
YOUNG HOLLUNDER. He stabbed himself too deep in his chest. But he's still breathing. He can still talk, too, but very faintly. At first he lay there unconscious, but when they put him on the stretcher he came to.
WOLF. That was from the shaking.

MARIE. We'd better make room.

[They make room. Two workmen carry in LILIOM on a stretcher which has four legs and stands about as high as a bed. They put the stretcher at left directly in front of the sofa, so that the head is at right and the foot at left. Then they unobtrusively join the group at the door. Later, they go out. JULIE is standing at the side of the stretcher, where, without moving, she can see LILIOM'S face. The others crowd emotionally together near the door. The FIRST POLICEMAN enters.]

FIRST POLICEMAN. Are you his wife?
JULIE. Yes.
FIRST POLICEMAN. The doctor at the factory who bandaged him up forbade us to take him to the hospital. — Dangerous to move him that far. What he needs now is rest. Just let him be until the police-surgeon comes. [To the group near the door.] He's not to be disturbed.
[They make way for him. He exits. There is a pause.]
WOLF [gently urging the others out]. Please — it's best if we all get out of here now. We'll only be in the way.
MARIE [to JULIE]. Julie, what do you think? [JULIE looks at her without answering.] Julie, can I do anything to help? [JULIE does not answer.] We'll be just outside on the bench if you want us.
[MOTHER HOLLUNDER and her son have gone out when first requested. Now MARIE and WOLF exit, too. JULIE sits on the edge of the stretcher and looks at LILIOM. He stretches his hand out to her. She clasps it. It is not quite dark yet. Both of them can still be plainly seen.]
LILIOM [raises himself with difficulty; speaks lightly at first, but later soberly, defiantly]. Little — Julie — there's something — I want to tell you — like when you go to a restaurant — and you've finished eating — and it's time — to pay — then you have to count up everything — everything you owe — well — I beat you — not because I was mad at you — no — only because I can't bear to see any one crying. You always cried — on my account

— and, well, you see — I never learned a trade — what kind of a caretaker would I make? But anyhow — I wasn't going back to the carousel to fool with the girls. No, I spit on them all — understand?

JULIE. Yes.

LILIOM. And — as for Hollinger — he's good enough — Mrs. Muskat can get along all right with him. The jokes he tells are mine — and the people laugh when he tells them — but I don't care. — I didn't give you anything — no home — not even the food you ate — but you don't understand. — It's true I'm not much good — but I couldn't be a caretaker — and so I thought maybe it would be better over there — in America — do you see?

JULIE. Yes.

LILIOM. I'm not asking — forgiveness — I don't do that — I don't. Tell the baby — if you like.

JULIE. Yes.

LILIOM. Tell the baby — I wasn't much good — but tell him — if you ever talk about me — tell him — I thought — perhaps — over in America — but that's no affair of yours. I'm not asking forgiveness. For my part the police can come now. — If it's a boy — if it's a girl. — Perhaps I'll see the Lord God to-day. — Do you think I'll see Him?

JULIE. Yes.

LILIOM. I'm not afraid — of the police Up There — if they'll only let me come up in front of the Lord God Himself — not like down here where an officer stops you at the door. If the carpenter asks you — yes — be his wife — marry him. And the child — tell him he's his father. — He'll believe you — won't he?

JULIE. Yes.

LILIOM. When I beat you — I was right. — You mustn't always think — you mustn't always be right. Liliom can be right once, too. — It's all the same to me who was right. — It's so dumb. Nobody's right — but they all think they are right. — A lot they know!

JULIE. Yes.

LILIOM. Julie — come — hold my hand tight.

JULIE. I'm holding it tight — all the time.

LILIOM. Tighter, still tighter — I'm going —— [Pauses.] Julie ——

JULIE. Good-bye.

[LILIOM sinks slowly back and dies. JULIE frees her hand. THE DOCTOR enters with the FIRST POLICEMAN.]

DOCTOR. Good-evening. His wife?

JULIE. Yes, sir.

[Behind the DOCTOR and POLICEMAN enter MARIE, WOLF, MOTHER HOLLUNDER, YOUNG HOLLUNDER and MRS. MUSKAT. They remain respectfully at the doorway. The DOCTOR bends over LILIOM and examines him.]

DOCTOR. A light, if you please. [JULIE fetches a burning candle from the dark-room. The DOCTOR examines LILIOM briefly in the candle-light, then turns suddenly away.] Have you pen and ink?

WOLF [proffering a pen]. A fountain-pen — American ——

DOCTOR [takes a printed form from his pocket; speaks as he writes out the death certificate at the little table]. My poor woman, your husband is dead — there's nothing to be done for him — the good God will help him now — I'll leave this certificate with you. You will give it to the people from the hospital when they come — I'll arrange for the body to be removed at once. [Rises.] Please give me a towel and soap.

POLICEMAN. I've got them for you out here, sir. [Points to door at back.]

DOCTOR. God be with you, my good woman.

JULIE. Thank you, sir.

[The DOCTOR and POLICEMAN exit. The others slowly draw nearer.]

MARIE. Poor Julie. May he rest in peace, poor man, but as for you — please don't be angry with me for saying it — but you're better off this way.

MOTHER HOLLUNDER. He is better off, the poor fellow, and so are you.

MARIE. Much better, Julie... you are young... and one of these days some good man will come along. Am I right?

WOLF. She's right.

MARIE. Julie, tell me, am I right?

JULIE. You are right, dear; you are very good.

YOUNG HOLLUNDER. There's a good man — the carpenter. Oh, I can speak of it now. He comes here every day on some excuse or other — and he never fails to ask for you.

MARIE. A widower — with two children.

MOTHER HOLLUNDER. He's better off, poor fellow — and so are you. He was a bad man.

MARIE. He wasn't good-hearted. Was he, Wolf?

WOLF. No, I must say, he really wasn't. No, Liliom wasn't a good man. A good man doesn't strike a woman.

MARIE. Am I right? Tell me, Julie, am I right?

JULIE. You are right, dear.

YOUNG HOLLUNDER. It's really a good thing for her it happened.

MOTHER HOLLUNDER. He's better off — and so is she.

WOLF. Now you have your freedom again. How old are you?

JULIE. Eighteen.

WOLF. Eighteen. A mere child! Am I right?

JULIE. You are right, Wolf. You are kind.

YOUNG HOLLUNDER. Lucky for you it happened, isn't it?

JULIE. Yes.

YOUNG HOLLUNDER. All you had before was bad luck. If it weren't for my mother you wouldn't have had a roof over your head or a bite to eat — and now Autumn's coming and Winter. You couldn't have lived in this shack in the Winter time, could you?

MARIE. Certainly not! You'd have frozen like the birds in the fields. Am I right, Julie?

JULIE. Yes, Marie.

MARIE. A year from now you will have forgotten all about him, won't you?

JULIE. You are right, Marie.

WOLF. If you need anything, count on us. We'll go now. But to-morrow morning we'll be back. Come, Marie. God be with you.   [Offers JULIE his hand.]

JULIE. God be with you.

MARIE [embraces JULIE, weeping]. It's the best thing that could have happened to you, Julie, the best thing.

JULIE. Don't cry, Marie.

[MARIE and WOLF exit.]

MOTHER HOLLUNDER. I'll make a little black coffee. You haven't had a thing to eat to-day. Then you'll come home with us.

[MOTHER HOLLUNDER and her son exit. MRS. MUSKAT comes over to JULIE.]

MRS. MUSKAT. Would you mind if I — looked at him?

JULIE. He used to work for you.

MRS. MUSKAT [contemplates the body; turns to JULIE]. Won't you make up with me?

JULIE. I wasn't angry with you.

MRS. MUSKAT. But you were. Let's make it up.

JULIE [raising her voice eagerly, almost triumphantly]. I've nothing to make up with you.

MRS. MUSKAT. But I have with you. Every one says hard things against the poor dead boy — except us two. You don't say he was bad.

JULIE [raising her voice yet higher, this time on a defiant, wholly triumphant note]. Yes, I do.

MRS. MUSKAT. I understand, my child. But he beat me, too. What does that matter? I've forgotten it.

JULIE [from now on answers her coldly, dryly, without looking at her]. That's your own affair.

MRS. MUSKAT. If I can help you in any way ——

JULIE. There's nothing I need.

MRS. MUSKAT. I still owe him two kronen, back pay.

JULIE. You should have paid him.

MRS. MUSKAT. Now that the poor fellow is dead I thought perhaps it would be the same if I paid you.

JULIE. I've nothing to do with it.

MRS. MUSKAT. All right. Please don't think I'm trying to force myself on you. I stayed because we two are the only ones on earth who loved him. That's why I thought we ought to stick together.

JULIE. No, thank you.

MRS. MUSKAT. Then you couldn't have loved him as I did.

JULIE. No.

MRS. MUSKAT. I loved him better.

JULIE. Yes.

MRS. MUSKAT. Good-bye.

JULIE. Good-bye. [MRS. MUSKAT *exits.*

JULIE *puts the candle on the table near* LILIOM's *head, sits on the edge of the stretcher, looks into the dead man's face and caresses it tenderly.*] Sleep, Liliom, sleep — it's no business of hers — I never even told you—but now I'll tell you — now I'll tell you—you bad, quick-tempered, rough, unhappy, wicked — *dear* boy — sleep peacefully, Liliom — they can't understand how I feel — I can't even explain to you — not even to you — how I feel — you'd only laugh at me — but you can't hear me any more. [*Between tender motherliness and reproach, yet with great love in her voice.*] It was wicked of you to beat me — on the breast and on the head and face — but you're gone now. — You treated me badly — that was wicked of you — but sleep peacefully, Liliom — you bad, bad boy, you — I love you — I never told you before — I was ashamed — but now I've told you — I love you. Liliom — sleep — my boy — sleep.

[*She rises, gets a Bible, sits down near the candle and reads softly to herself, so that not the words but an inarticulate murmur is heard. The* CARPENTER *enters at back.*]

CARPENTER [*stands near the door; in the dimness of the room he can scarcely be seen*]. Miss Julie ——

JULIE [*without alarm*]. Who is that?

CARPENTER [*very slowly*]. The carpenter.

JULIE. What does the carpenter want?

CARPENTER. Can I be of help to you in any way? Shall I stay here with you?

JULIE [*gratefully, but firmly*]. Don't stay, carpenter.

CARPENTER. Shall I come back to-morrow?

JULIE. Not to-morrow, either.

CARPENTER. Don't be offended, Miss Julie, but I'd like to know — you see, I'm not a young man any more — I have two

children — and if I'm to come back any more — I'd like to know — if there's any use ——

JULIE. No use, carpenter.

CARPENTER [*as he exits*]. God be with you.

[JULIE *resumes her reading.* FICSUR *enters, slinks furtively sideways to the stretcher, looks at* LILIOM, *shakes his head.* JULIE *looks up from her reading.* FICSUR *takes fright, slinks away from the stretcher, sits down at right, biting his nails.* JULIE *rises.* FICSUR *rises, too, and looks at her half fearfully. With her piercing glance upon him he slinks to the doorway at back, where he pauses and speaks.*]

FICSUR. The old woman asked me to tell you that coffee is ready, and you are to come in.

[JULIE *goes to the kitchen door.* FICSUR *withdraws until she has closed the door behind her. Then he reappears in the doorway, stands on tiptoes, looks at* LILIOM, *then exits. Now the body lies alone. After a brief silence music is heard, distant at first, but gradually coming nearer. It is very much like the music of the carousel, but slower, graver, more exalted. The melody, too, is the same, yet the tempo is altered and contrapuntal measures of the thieves' song are intertwined in it. Two men in black, with heavy sticks, soft black hats and black gloves, appear in the doorway at back and stride slowly into the room. Their faces are beardless, marble white, grave and benign. One stops in front of the stretcher, the other a pace to the right. From above a dim violet light illuminates their faces.*]

THE FIRST [*to* LILIOM]. Rise and come with us.

THE SECOND [*politely*]. You're under arrest.

THE FIRST [*somewhat louder, but always in a gentle, low, resonant voice*]. Do you hear? Rise. Don't you hear?

THE SECOND. We are the police.

THE FIRST [*bends down, touches* LILIOM's *shoulder*]. Get up and come with us.

[LILIOM *slowly sits up.*]

THE SECOND. Come along.

THE FIRST [*paternally*]. These people suppose that when they die all their difficulties are solved for them.

THE SECOND [*raising his voice sternly*]. That simply by thrusting a knife in your heart and making it stop beating you can leave your wife behind with a child in her womb ——

THE FIRST. It is not as simple as that.

THE SECOND. Such things are not settled so easily.

THE FIRST. Come along. You will have to give an account of yourself. [*As both bow their heads, he continues softly.*] We are God's police. [*An expression of glad relief lights upon* LILIOM'S *face. He rises from the stretcher.*] Come.

THE SECOND. You mortals don't get off quite as easy as that.

THE FIRST [*softly*]. Come. [LILIOM *starts to walk ahead of them, then stops and looks at them.*] The end is not as abrupt as that. Your name is still spoken. Your face is still remembered. And what you said, and what you did, and what you failed to do — these are still remembered. Remembered, too, are the manner of your glance, the ring of your voice, the clasp of your hand and how your step sounded — as long as one is left who remembers you, so long is the matter unended. Before the end there is much to be undone. Until you are quite forgotten, my son, you will not be finished with the earth — even though you *are* dead.

THE SECOND [*very gently*]. Come.

[*The music begins again. All three exit at back,* LILIOM *leading, the others following. The stage is empty and quite dark save for the candle which burns by the stretcher, on which, in the shadows, the covers are so arranged that one cannot quite be sure that a body is not still lying. The music dies out in the distance as if it had followed* LILIOM *and the two* POLICE-MEN. *The candle flickers and goes out. There is a brief interval of silence and total darkness before*

THE CURTAIN FALLS

SCENE VI

In the Beyond. A whitewashed courtroom. There is a green-topped table; behind it a bench. Back center is a door with a bell over it. Next to this door is a window through which can be seen a vista of rose-tinted clouds. Down right there is a grated iron door. Down left another door.

Two men are on the bench when the curtain rises. One is richly, the other poorly dressed.

From a great distance is heard a fanfare of trumpets playing the refrain of the thieves' song in slow, altered tempo.

Passing the window at back appear LILIOM *and the two* POLICEMEN.

The bell rings.

An old GUARD *enters at right. He is bald and has a long white beard. He wears the conventional police uniform.*

He goes to the door at back, opens it, exchanges silent greetings with the two POLICE-MEN *and closes the door again.*

LILIOM *looks wonderingly around.*

THE FIRST [*to the old* GUARD]. Announce us. [THE GUARD *exits at left.*]

LILIOM. Is this it?

THE SECOND. Yes, my son.

LILIOM. This is the police court?

THE SECOND. Yes, my son. The part for suicide cases.

LILIOM. And what happens here?

THE FIRST. Here justice is done. Sit down.

[LILIOM *sits next to the two men. The two* POLICEMEN *stand silent near the table.*]

THE RICHLY DRESSED MAN [*whispers*]. Suicide, too?

LILIOM. Yes.

THE RICHLY DRESSED MAN [*points to* THE POORLY DRESSED MAN]. So's he. [*Introducing himself.*] My name is Reich.

THE POORLY DRESSED MAN [*whispers, too*]. My name is Stephan Kadar. [LILIOM *only looks at them.*]

THE POORLY DRESSED MAN. And you? What's your name?

LILIOM. None of your business. [*Both move a bit away from him.*]

THE POORLY DRESSED MAN. I did it by jumping out of a window.

THE RICHLY DRESSED MAN. I did it with a pistol — and you?

LILIOM. With a knife.

[*They move a bit further away from him.*]

THE RICHLY DRESSED MAN. A pistol is cleaner.

LILIOM. If I had the price of a pistol ——

THE SECOND. Silence!

[*The* POLICE MAGISTRATE *enters. He has a long white beard, is bald, but only in profile can be seen on his head a single tuft of snow-white hair.* THE GUARD *reënters behind him and sits on the bench with the dead men. As* THE MAGISTRATE *enters, all rise, except* LILIOM, *who remains surlily seated. When* THE MAGISTRATE *sits down, so do the others.*

THE GUARD. Yesterday's cases, your honor. The numbers are entered in the docket.

THE MAGISTRATE. Number 16,472.

THE FIRST [*looks in his notebook, beckons* THE RICHLY DRESSED MAN]. Stand up, please. [THE RICHLY DRESSED MAN *rises.*]

THE MAGISTRATE. Your name?

THE RICHLY DRESSED MAN. Doctor Reich.

THE MAGISTRATE. Age?

THE RICHLY DRESSED MAN. Forty-two, married, Jew.

THE MAGISTRATE [*with a gesture of dismissal*]. Religion does not interest us here — why did you kill yourself?

THE RICHLY DRESSED MAN. On account of debts.

THE MAGISTRATE. What good did you do on earth?

THE RICHLY DRESSED MAN. I was a lawyer ——

THE MAGISTRATE [*coughs significantly*]. Yes — we'll discuss that later. For the present I shall only ask you: Would you like to go back to earth once more before sunrise? I advise you that you have the right to go if you choose. Do you understand?

THE RICHLY DRESSED MAN. Yes, sir.

THE MAGISTRATE. He who takes his life is apt, in his haste and his excitement, to forget something. Is there anything important down there you have left undone? Something to tell some one? Something to undo?

THE RICHLY DRESSED MAN. My debts ——

THE MAGISTRATE. They do not matter here. Here we are concerned only with the affairs of the soul.

THE RICHLY DRESSED MAN. Then — if you please — when I left — the house — my youngest son, Oscar — was asleep. I didn't trust myself to wake him — and bid him good-bye. I would have liked — to kiss him good-bye.

THE MAGISTRATE [*to* THE SECOND]. You will take Dr. Reich back and let him kiss his son Oscar.

THE SECOND. Come with me, please.

THE RICHLY DRESSED MAN [*to* THE MAGISTRATE]. I thank you.

[*He bows and exits at back with* THE SECOND.]

THE MAGISTRATE [*after making an entry in the docket*]. Number 16,473.

THE FIRST [*looks in his notebook, then beckons* LILIOM]. Stand up.

LILIOM. You said *please* to him.

[*He rises.*]

THE MAGISTRATE. Your name?

LILIOM. Liliom.

THE MAGISTRATE. Isn't that your nickname?

LILIOM. Yes.

THE MAGISTRATE. What is your right name?

LILIOM. Andreas.

THE MAGISTRATE. And your last name?

LILIOM. Zavocki — after my mother.

THE MAGISTRATE. Your age?

LILIOM. Twenty-four.

THE MAGISTRATE. What good did *you* do on earth? [LILIOM *is silent.*] Why did you take your life? [LILIOM *does not answer.* THE MAGISTRATE *addresses* THE FIRST.] Take that knife away from him. [THE FIRST *does so.*] It will be returned to you, if you go back to earth.

LILIOM. Do I go back to earth again?

THE MAGISTRATE. Just answer my questions.

LILIOM. I wasn't answering then, I was asking if ——

THE MAGISTRATE. You don't ask questions here. You only answer. Only answer, Andreas Zavocki! I ask you whether there is anything on earth you neglected to accomplish? Anything down there you would like to do?

LILIOM. Yes.

THE MAGISTRATE. What is it?

LILIOM. I'd like to break Ficsur's head for him.

THE MAGISTRATE. Punishment is our office. Is there nothing else on earth you'd like to do?

LILIOM. I don't know — I guess, as long as I'm here, I'll not go back.

THE MAGISTRATE [to THE FIRST]. Note that. He waives his right. [LILIOM starts back to the bench.] Stay where you are. You are aware that you left your wife without food or shelter?

LILIOM. Yes.

THE MAGISTRATE. Don't you regret it?

LILIOM. No.

THE MAGISTRATE. You are aware that your wife is pregnant, and that in six months a child will be born?

LILIOM. I know.

THE MAGISTRATE. And that the child, too, will be without food or shelter? Do you regret that?

LILIOM. As long as I won't be there, what's it got to do with me?

THE MAGISTRATE. Don't try to deceive us, Andreas Zavocki. We see through you as through a pane of glass.

LILIOM. If you see so much, what do you want to ask me for? Why don't you let me rest — in peace?

THE MAGISTRATE. First you must earn your rest.

LILIOM. I want — only — to sleep.

THE MAGISTRATE. Your obstinacy won't help you. Here patience is endless as time. We can wait.

LILIOM. Can I ask something — I'd like to know — if Your Honor will tell me — whether the baby will be a boy or a girl.

THE MAGISTRATE. You shall see that for yourself.

LILIOM [excitedly]. I'll see the baby?

THE MAGISTRATE. When you do it won't be a baby any more. But we haven't reached that question yet.

LILIOM. I'll see it?

THE MAGISTRATE. Again I ask you: Do you not regret that you deserted your wife and child; that you were a bad husband, a bad father?

LILIOM. A bad husband?

THE MAGISTRATE. Yes.

LILIOM. And a bad father?

THE MAGISTRATE. That, too.

LILIOM. I couldn't get work — and I couldn't bear to see Julie — all the time — all the time ——

THE MAGISTRATE. Weeping! Why are you ashamed to say it? You couldn't bear to see her weeping. Why are you afraid of that word? And why are you ashamed that you loved her?

LILIOM [shrugs his shoulders]. Who's ashamed? But I couldn't bear to see her — and that's why I was bad to her. You see, it wouldn't do to go back to the carousel — and Ficsur came along with his talk about — that other thing — and all of a sudden it happened, I don't know how. The police and the Jew with the pistol — and there I stood — and I'd lost the money playing cards — and I didn't want to be put in prison. [Demanding justification.] Maybe I was wrong not to go out and steal when there was nothing to eat in the house? Should I have gone out to steal for Julie?

THE MAGISTRATE [emphatically]. Yes.

LILIOM [after an astounded pause]. The police down there never said that.

THE MAGISTRATE. You beat that poor, frail girl; you beat her because she loved you. How could you do that?

LILIOM. We argued with each other — she said this and I said that — and because she was right I couldn't answer her — and I got mad — and the anger rose up in me — until it reached here [points to his throat] and then I beat her.

THE MAGISTRATE. Are you sorry?

LILIOM [shakes his head, but cannot utter the word "no"; continues softly]. When I touched her slender throat — then — if you like — you might say ——

[*Falters, looks embarrassed at* The Magistrate.]

The Magistrate [*confidently expectant*]. Are you sorry?

Liliom [*with a stare*]. I'm not sorry for anything.

The Magistrate. Liliom, Liliom, it will be difficult to help you.

Liliom. I'm not asking any help.

The Magistrate. You were offered employment as a caretaker on Arader Street. [*To* The First.] Where is that entered?

The First. In the small docket.

[*Hands him the open book.* The Magistrate *looks in it.*]

The Magistrate. Rooms, kitchen, quarterly wages, the privilege of keeping poultry. Why didn't you accept it?

Liliom. I'm not a caretaker. I'm no good at caretaking. To be a caretaker — you have to be a caretaker —

The Magistrate. If I said to you now: Liliom, go back on your stretcher. To-morrow morning you will arise alive and well again. Would you be a caretaker then?

Liliom. No.

The Magistrate. Why not?

Liliom. Because — because that's just why I died.

The Magistrate. That is not true, my son. You died because you loved little Julie and the child she is bearing under her heart.

Liliom. No.

The Magistrate. Look me in the eye.

Liliom [*looks him in the eye*]. No.

The Magistrate [*stroking his beard*]. Liliom, Liliom, if it were not for our Heavenly patience —— Go back to your seat. Number 16,474.

The First [*looks in his notebook*]. Stephan Kadar.

[The Poorly Dressed Man *rises.*]

The Magistrate. You came out to-day?

The Poorly Dressed Man. To-day.

The Magistrate [*indicating the crimson sea of clouds*]. How long were you in there?

The Poorly Dressed Man. Thirteen years.

The Magistrate. Officer, you went to earth with him?

The First. Yes, sir.

The Magistrate. Stephan Kadar, after thirteen years of purification by fire you returned to earth to give proof that your soul had been burned clean. What good deed did you perform?

The Poorly Dressed Man. When I came to the village and looked in the window of our cottage I saw my poor little orphans sleeping peacefully. But it was raining and the rain beat into the room through a hole in the roof. So I went and fixed the roof so it wouldn't rain in any more. My hammering woke them up and they were afraid. But their mother came in to them and comforted them. She said to them: "Don't cry! It's your poor, dear father hammering up there. He's come back from the other world to fix the roof for us."

The Magistrate. Officer?

The First. That's what happened.

The Magistrate. Stephan Kadar, you have done a good deed. What you did will be written in books to gladden the hearts of children who read them. [*Indicates the door at left.*] The door is open to you. The eternal light awaits you. [The First *escorts* The Poorly Dressed Man *out at left with great deference.*] Liliom!

[Liliom *rises.*] You have heard?

Liliom. Yes.

The Magistrate. When this man first appeared before us he was as stubborn as you. But now he has purified himself and withstood the test. He has done a good deed.

Liliom. What's he done, anyhow? Any roofer can fix a roof. It's much harder to be a barker in an amusement park.

The Magistrate. Liliom, you shall remain for sixteen years in the crimson fire until your child is full grown. By that time your pride and your stubbornness will have been burnt out of you. And when your daughter ——

LILIOM. My daughter!

THE MAGISTRATE. When your daughter has reached the age of sixteen ——

[LILIOM *bows his head, covers his eyes with his hands, and to keep from weeping laughs defiantly, sadly.*]

THE MAGISTRATE. When your daughter has reached the age of sixteen you will be sent for one day back to earth.

LILIOM. Me?

THE MAGISTRATE. Yes — just as you may have read in the legends of how the dead reappear on earth for a time.

LILIOM. I never believed them.

THE MAGISTRATE. Now you see they are true. You will go back to earth one day to show how far the purification of your soul has progressed.

LILIOM. Then I must show what I can do — like when you apply for a job — as a coachman?

THE MAGISTRATE. Yes — it is a test.

LILIOM. And will I be told what I have to do?

THE MAGISTRATE. No.

LILIOM. How will I know, then?

THE MAGISTRATE. You must decide that for yourself. That's what you burn sixteen years for. And if you do something good, something splendid for your child, then ——

LILIOM [*laughs sadly*]. Then? [*All stand up and bow their heads reverently. There is a pause.*] Then?

THE MAGISTRATE. Now I'll bid you farewell, Liliom. Sixteen years and a day shall pass before I see you again. When you have returned from earth you will come up before me again. Take heed and think well of some good deed to do for your child. On that will depend which door shall be opened to you up here. Now go, Liliom.

[*He exits at left.* THE GUARD *stands at attention. There is a pause.*]

THE FIRST [*approaches* LILIOM]. Come along, my son.

[*He goes to the door at right; pulls open the bolt and waits.*]

LILIOM [*to the old* GUARD, *softly*]. Say, officer.

THE GUARD. What do you want?

LILIOM. Please — can I get — have you got ——?

THE GUARD. What?

LILIOM [*whispers*]. A cigarette?

[*The old* GUARD *stares at him, goes a few paces to the left, shakes his head disapprovingly. Then his expression softens. He takes a cigarette from his pocket and, crossing to* LILIOM — *who has gone over to the door at right — gives him the cigarette.* THE FIRST *throws open the door. An intense rose-colored light streams in. The glow of it is so strong that it blinds* LILIOM *and he takes a step backward and bows his head and covers his eyes with his hand before he steps forward into the light.*]

THE CURTAIN FALLS

SCENE VII

Sixteen years later. A small, tumble-down house on a bare, unenclosed plot of ground. Before the house is a tiny garden enclosed by a hip-high hedge.

At back a wooden fence crosses the stage; in the center of it is a door large enough to admit a wagon. Beyond the fence is a view of a suburban street which blends into a broad vista of tilled fields.

It is a bright Sunday in Spring.

In the garden a table for two is laid.

JULIE, *her daughter* LOUISE, WOLF *and* MARIE *are discovered in the garden.* WOLF *is prosperously dressed,* MARIE *somewhat elaborately, with a huge hat.*

JULIE. You could stay for lunch.

MARIE. Impossible, dear. Since he became the proprietor of the Café Sorrento, Wolf simply has to be there all the time.

JULIE. But you needn't stay there all day, too.

MARIE. Oh, yes. I sit near the cashier's cage, read the papers, keep an eye on the waiters and drink in the bustle and excitement of the great city.

JULIE. And what about the children?

MARIE. You know what modern families are like. Parents scarcely ever see their children these days. The four girls are with their governess, the three boys with their tutor.

LOUISE. Auntie, dear, do stay and eat with us.

MARIE [*importantly*]. Impossible to-day, dear child, impossible. Perhaps some other time. Come, Mr. Beifeld.

JULIE. Since when do you call your husband mister?

WOLF. I'd rather she did, dear lady. When we used to be very familiar we quarreled all the time. Now we are formal with each other and get along like society folk. I kiss your hand, dear lady.

JULIE. Good-bye, Wolf.

MARIE. Adieu, my dear. [*They embrace.*] Adieu, my dear child.

LOUISE. Good-bye, Aunt Marie. Goodbye, Uncle Wolf. [WOLF *and* MARIE *exit.*]

JULIE. You can get the soup now, Louise, dear.

[LOUISE *goes into the house and reenters with the soup. They sit at the table.*]

LOUISE. Mother, is it true we're not going to work at the jute factory any more?

JULIE. Yes, dear.

LOUISE. Where then?

JULIE. Uncle Wolf has gotten us a place in a big establishment where they make all kinds of fittings for cafés. We're to make big curtains, you know, the kind they hang in the windows, with lettering on them.

LOUISE. It'll be nicer there than at the jute factory.

JULIE. Yes, dear. The work isn't as dirty and pays better, too. A poor widow like your mother is lucky to get it.

[*They eat.* LILIOM *and the two* HEAVENLY POLICEMEN *appear in the big doorway at back. The* POLICEMEN *pass slowly by.* LILIOM *stands there alone a moment, then comes slowly down and pauses at the opening of the hedge. He is dressed as he was on the day of his death. He is very pale, but otherwise unaltered.* JULIE, *at the table, has her back to him.* LOUISE *sits facing the audience.*]

LILIOM. Good-day.

LOUISE. Good-day.

JULIE. Another beggar! What is it you want, my poor man?

LILIOM. Nothing.

JULIE. We have no money to give, but if you care for a plate of soup —— [LOUISE *goes into the house.*] Have you come far to-day?

LILIOM. Yes — very far.

JULIE. Are you tired?

LILIOM. Very tired.

JULIE. Over there at the gate is a stone. Sit down and rest. My daughter is bringing you the soup.

[LOUISE *comes out of the house.*]

LILIOM. Is that your daughter?

JULIE. Yes.

LILIOM [*to* LOUISE]. You are the daughter?

LOUISE. Yes, sir.

LILIOM. A fine, healthy girl.

[*Takes the soup plate from her with one hand, while with the other he touches her arm.* LOUISE *draws back quickly.*]

LOUISE [*crosses to* JULIE]. Mother!

JULIE. What, my child?

LOUISE. The man tried to take me by the arm.

JULIE. Nonsense! You only imagined it, dear. The poor, hungry man has other things to think about than fooling with young girls. Sit down and eat your soup.

[*They eat.*]

LILIOM [*eats, too, but keeps looking at them*]. You work at the factory, eh?

JULIE. Yes.

LILIOM. Your daughter, too?

LOUISE. Yes.

LILIOM. And your husband?

JULIE [*after a pause*]. I have no husband. I'm a widow.

LILIOM. A widow?

JULIE. Yes.

LILIOM. Your husband — I suppose he's been dead a long time. [JULIE *does not answer.*] I say — has your husband been dead a long time?

JULIE. A long time.

LILIOM. What did he die of?

[JULIE *is silent.*]

LOUISE. No one knows. He went to America to work and he died there — in the hospital. Poor father, I never knew him.

LILIOM. He went to America?

LOUISE. Yes, before I was born.

LILIOM. To America?

JULIE. Why do you ask so many questions? Did you know him, perhaps?

LILIOM [puts the plate down]. Heaven knows! I've known so many people. Maybe I knew him, too.

JULIE. Well, if you knew him, leave him and us in peace with your questions. He went to America and died there. That's all there is to tell.

LILIOM. All right. All right. Don't be angry with me. I didn't mean any harm. [There is a pause].

LOUISE. My father was a very handsome man.

JULIE. Don't talk so much.

LOUISE. Did I say anything ——?

LILIOM. Surely the little orphan can say that about her father.

LOUISE. My father could juggle so beautifully with three ivory balls that people used to advise him to go on the stage.

JULIE. Who told you that?

LOUISE. Uncle Wolf.

LILIOM. Who is that?

LOUISE. Mr. Wolf Beifeld, who owns the Café Sorrento.

LILIOM. The one who used to be a porter?

JULIE [astonished]. Do you know him, too? It seems that you know all Budapest.

LILIOM. Wolf Beifeld is a long way from being all Budapest. But I do know a lot of people. Why shouldn't I know Wolf Beifeld?

LOUISE. He was a friend of my father.

JULIE. He was not his friend. No one was.

LILIOM. You speak of your husband so sternly.

JULIE. What's that to you? Doesn't it suit you? I can speak of my husband any way I like. It's nobody's business but mine.

LILIOM. Certainly, certainly — it's your own business.

[Takes up his soup plate again. All three eat.]

LOUISE [to JULIE]. Perhaps he knew father, too.

JULIE. Ask him, if you like.

LOUISE [crosses to LILIOM. He stands up]. Did you know my father? [LILIOM nods. LOUISE addresses her mother.] Yes, he knew him.

JULIE [rises]. You knew Andreas Zavocki?

LILIOM. Liliom? Yes.

LOUISE. Was he really a very handsome man?

LILIOM. I wouldn't exactly say handsome.

LOUISE [confidently]. But he was an awfully good man, wasn't he?

LILIOM. He wasn't so good, either. As far as I know he was what they called a clown, a barker in a carousel.

LOUISE [pleased]. Did he tell funny jokes?

LILIOM. Lots of 'em. And he sang funny songs, too.

LOUISE. In the carousel?

LILIOM. Yes — but he was something of a bully, too. He'd fight any one. He even hit your dear little mother.

JULIE. That's a lie.

LILIOM. It's true.

JULIE. Aren't you ashamed to tell the child such awful things about her father? Get out of here, you shameless liar. Eats our soup and our bread and has the impudence to slander our dead!

LILIOM. I didn't mean — I ——

JULIE. What right have you to tell lies to the child? Take that plate, Louise, and let him be on his way. If he wasn't such a hungry-looking beggar, I'd put him out myself.

[LOUISE takes the plate out of his hand.]

LILIOM. So he didn't hit you?

JULIE. No, never. He was always good to me.

LOUISE [whispers]. Did he tell funny stories, too?

LILIOM. Yes, and such funny ones.

JULIE. Don't speak to him any more. In God's name, go.

LOUISE. In God's name.

[JULIE *resumes her seat at the table and eats.*]

LILIOM. If you please, Miss — I have a pack of cards in my pocket. And if you like, I'll show you some tricks that'll make you split your sides laughing. [LOUISE *holds* LILIOM'S *plate in her left hand. With her right she reaches out and holds the garden gate shut.*] Let me in, just a little way, Miss, and I'll do the tricks for you.

LOUISE. Go, in God's name, and let us be. Why are you making those ugly faces?

LILIOM. Don't chase me away, Miss; let me come in for just a minute — just for a minute — just long enough to let me show you something pretty, something wonderful. [*Opens the gate.*] Miss, I've something to give you.

[*Takes from his pocket a big red handkerchief in which is wrapped a glittering star from Heaven. He looks furtively about him to make sure that the* POLICE *are not watching.*]

LOUISE. What's that?

LILIOM. Pst! A star!

[*With a gesture he indicates that he has stolen it out of the sky.*]

JULIE [*sternly*]. Don't take anything from him. He's probably stolen it somewhere. [*To* LILIOM.] In God's name, be off with you.

LOUISE. Yes, be off with you. Be off. [*She slams the gate.*]

LILIOM. Miss — please, Miss — I've got to do something good — or — do something good — a good deal ——

LOUISE [*pointing with her right hand*]. That's the way out.

LILIOM. Miss ——

LOUISE. Get out!

LILIOM. Miss!

[*Looks up at her suddenly and slaps her extended hand, so that the slap resounds loudly.*]

LOUISE. Mother!

[*Looks dazedly at* LILIOM, *who bows his head dismayed, forlorn.* JULIE *rises and looks at* LILIOM *in astonishment. There is a long pause.*]

JULIE [*comes over to them slowly*]. What's the matter here?

LOUISE [*bewildered, does not take her eyes off* LILIOM]. Mother — the man — he hit me — on the hand — hard — I heard the sound of it — but it didn't hurt — mother — it didn't hurt — it was like a caress — as if he had just touched my hand tenderly.

[*She hides behind* JULIE. LILIOM *sulkily raises his head and looks at* JULIE.]

JULIE [*softly*]. Go, my child. Go into the house. Go.

LOUISE [*going*]. But mother — I'm afraid — it sounded so loud —— [*Weepingly.*] And it didn't hurt at all — just as if he'd — kissed my hand instead — mother! [*She hides her face.*]

JULIE. Go in, my child, go in.

[LOUISE *goes slowly into the house.* JULIE *watches her until she has disappeared, then turns slowly to* LILIOM.]

JULIE. You struck my child.

LILIOM. Yes — I struck her.

JULIE. Is that what you came for, to strike my child?

LILIOM. No — I didn't come for that — but I did strike her — and now I'm going back.

JULIE. In the name of the Lord Jesus, who are you?

LILIOM [*simply*]. A poor, tired beggar who came a long way and who was hungry. And I took your soup and bread and I struck your child. Are you angry with me?

JULIE [*her hand on her heart; fearfully, wonderingly*]. Jesus protect me — I don't understand it — I'm *not* angry — not angry at all ——

[LILIOM *goes to the doorway and leans against the doorpost, his back to the audience.* JULIE *goes to the table and sits.*]

JULIE. Louise! [LOUISE *comes out of the house.*] Sit down, dear, we'll finish eating.

LOUISE. Has he gone?

JULIE. Yes. [*They are both seated at the table.* LOUISE, *her head in her hands, is staring into space.*] Why don't you eat, dear?

LOUISE. What has happened, mother?

JULIE. Nothing, my child.

[*The* HEAVENLY POLICEMEN *appear outside.* LILIOM *walks slowly off at left. The* FIRST POLICEMAN *makes a deploring gesture.   Both shake their heads deploringly and follow* LILIOM *slowly off at left.*]

LOUISE. Mother, dear, why won't you tell me?

JULIE. What is there to tell you, child? Nothing has happened.   We were peacefully eating, and a beggar came who talked of bygone days, and then I thought of your father.

LOUISE. My father?

JULIE. Your father — Liliom.
                    [*There is a pause.*]

LOUISE. Mother — tell me — has it ever happened to you — has any one ever hit you — without hurting you in the least?

JULIE. Yes, my child.   It has happened to me, too.   [*There is a pause.*]

LOUISE. Is it possible for some one to hit you — hard like that — real loud and hard — and not hurt you at all?

JULIE. It is possible, dear — that some one may beat you and beat you and beat you — and not hurt you at all. ——
            [*There is a pause.   Near by an organ-grinder has stopped.   The music of his organ begins.*]

THE CURTAIN FALLS

R. U. R.
(ROSSUM'S UNIVERSAL ROBOTS)
A FANTASTIC MELODRAMA
By KAREL ČAPEK
Translated by PAUL SELVER

CHARACTERS

HARRY DOMIN, *General Manager of Rossum's Universal Robots*

SULLA, *a Robotess*

MARIUS, *u Robot*

HELENA GLORY

DR. GALL, *Head of the Physiological and Experimental Department of R. U. R.*

MR. FABRY, *Engineer General, Technical Controller of R. U. R.*

DR. HALLEMEIER, *Head of the Institute for Psychological Training of Robots*

MR. ALQUIST, *Architect, Head of the Works Department of R. U. R.*

CONSUL BUSMAN, *General Business Manager of R. U. R.*

NANA

RADIUS, *a Robot*

HELENA, *a Robotess*

PRIMUS, *a Robot*

A SERVANT

FIRST ROBOT

SECOND ROBOT

THIRD ROBOT

ACT I. *Central Office of the Factory of Rossum's Universal Robots*

ACT II. *Helena's Drawing Room — Ten years later. Morning*

ACT III. *The Same Afternoon*

EPILOGUE. *A Laboratory — One year later*

Place: An Island.   *Time: The Future*

R. U. R.

(ROSSUM'S UNIVERSAL ROBOTS)

ACT I

Central office of the factory of Rossum's Universal Robots. Entrance on the right. The windows on the front wall look out on the rows of factory chimneys. On the left more managing departments. DOMIN *is sitting in the revolving chair at a large American writing table. On the left-hand wall large maps showing steamship and railroad routes. On the right-hand wall are fastened printed placards.* ("*Robot's Cheapest Labor,*" *etc.*) *In contrast to these wall fittings, the floor is covered with a splendid Turkish carpet, a sofa, leather arm-chair, and filing cabinets. At a desk near the windows* SULLA *is typing letters.*

DOMIN [*dictating*]. Ready?

SULLA. Yes.

DOMIN. To E. M. McVicker and Co., Southampton, England. "We undertake no guarantee for goods damaged in transit. As soon as the consignment was taken on board we drew your captain's attention to the fact that the vessel was unsuitable for the transport of Robots, and we are therefore not responsible for spoiled freight. We beg to remain for Rossum's Universal Robots. Yours truly." [SULLA, *who has sat motionless during dictation, now types rapidly for a few seconds, then stops, withdrawing the completed letter.*] Ready?

SULLA. Yes.

DOMIN. Another letter. To the E. B. Huyson Agency, New York, U.S.A. "We beg to acknowledge receipt of order for five thousand Robots. As you are sending your own vessel, please dispatch as cargo equal quantities of soft and hard coal for R. U. R., the same to be credited as part payment of the amount due to us. We beg to remain, for Rossum's Universal Robots.

Yours truly." [SULLA *repeats the rapid typing.*] Ready?

SULLA. Yes.

DOMIN. Another letter. "Friedrichs-werks, Hamburg, Germany We beg to acknowledge receipt of order for fifteen thousand Robots." [*Telephone rings.*] Hello! This is the Central Office. Yes. Certainly. Well, send them a wire. Good. [*Hangs up telephone.*] Where did I leave off?

SULLA. "We beg to acknowledge receipt of order for fifteen thousand Robots."

DOMIN. Fifteen thousand R. Fifteen thousand R.

[*Enter* MARIUS.]

DOMIN. Well, what is it?

MARIUS. There's a lady, sir, asking to see you.

DOMIN. A lady? Who is she?

MARIUS. I don't know, sir. She brings this card of introduction.

DOMIN [*reads the card*]. Ah, from President Glory. Ask her to come in.

MARIUS. Please step this way.

[*Enter* HELENA GLORY]

[*Exit* MARIUS.]

HELENA. How do you do?

DOMIN. How do you do. [*Standing up.*] What can I do for you?

HELENA. You are Mr. Domin, the General Manager.

DOMIN. I am.

HELENA. I have come ——

DOMIN. With President Glory's card. That is quite sufficient.

HELENA. President Glory is my father. I am Helena Glory.

DOMIN. Miss Glory, this is such a great

honor for us to be allowed to welcome our great President's daughter, that ——

HELENA. That you can't show me the door?

DOMIN. Please sit down. Sulla, you may go. [*Exit* SULLA.] [*Sitting down.*] How can I be of service to you, Miss Glory?

HELENA. I have come ——

DOMIN. To have a look at our famous works where people are manufactured. Like all visitors. Well, there is no objection.

HELENA. I thought it was forbidden to ——

DOMIN. To enter the factory. Yes, of course. Everybody comes here with some one's visiting card, Miss Glory.

HELENA. And you show them ——

DOMIN. Only certain things. The manufacture of artificial people is a secret process.

HELENA. If you only knew how enormously that ——

DOMIN. Interests me. Europe's talking about nothing else.

HELENA. Why don't you let me finish speaking?

DOMIN. I beg your pardon. Did you want to say something different?

HELENA. I only wanted to ask ——

DOMIN. Whether I could make a special exception in your case and show you our factory. Why, certainly, Miss Glory.

HELENA. How do you know I wanted to say that?

DOMIN. They all do. But we shall consider it a special honor to show you more than we do the rest.

HELENA. Thank you.

DOMIN. But you must agree not to divulge the least...

HELENA [*standing up and giving him her hand*]. My word of honor.

DOMIN. Thank you. Won't you raise your veil?

HELENA. Of course. You want to see whether I'm a spy or not. I beg your pardon.

DOMIN. What is it?

HELENA. Would you mind releasing my hand?

DOMIN [*releasing it*]. I beg your pardon.

HELENA [*raising her veil*]. How cautious you have to be here, don't you?

DOMIN [*observing her with deep interest*]. Hm, of course — we — that is ——

HELENA. But what is it? What's the matter?

DOMIN. I'm remarkably pleased. Did you have a pleasant crossing?

HELENA. Yes.

DOMIN. No difficulty?

HELENA. Why?

DOMIN. What I mean to say is — you're so young.

HELENA. May we go straight into the factory?

DOMIN. Yes. Twenty-two, I think.

HELENA. Twenty-two what?

DOMIN. Years.

HELENA. Twenty-one. Why do you want to know?

DOMIN. Because — as — [*with enthusiasm*] you will make a long stay, won't you?

HELENA. That depends on how much of the factory you show me.

DOMIN. Oh, hang the factory. Oh, no, no, you shall see everything, Miss Glory. Indeed you shall. Won't you sit down?

HELENA [*crossing to couch and sitting*]. Thank you.

DOMIN. But first would you like to hear the story of the invention?

HELENA. Yes, indeed.

DOMIN [*observes* HELENA *with rapture and reels off rapidly*]. It was in the year 1920 that old Rossum, the great physiologist, who was then quite a young scientist, took himself to this distant island for the purpose of studying the ocean fauna, full stop. On this occasion he attempted by chemical synthesis to imitate the living matter known as protoplasm until he suddenly discovered a substance which behaved exactly like living matter although its chemical composition was different. That was in the year of 1932, exactly four hundred and forty years after the discovery of America. Whew!

HELENA. Do you know that by heart?

DOMIN. Yes. You see physiology is no in my line. Shall I go on?

HELENA. Yes, please.

DOMIN. And then, Miss Glory, old Rossum wrote the following among his chemical specimens: "Nature has found only one method of organizing living matter. There is, however, another method, more simple, flexible and rapid, which has not yet occurred to nature at all. This second process by which life can be developed was discovered by me to-day." Now imagine him, Miss Glory, writing those wonderful words over some colloidal mess that a dog wouldn't look at. Imagine him sitting over a test tube, and thinking how the whole tree of life would grow from it, how all animals would proceed from it, beginning with some sort of beetle and ending with a man. A man of different substance from us. Miss Glory, that was a tremendous moment.

HELENA. Well?

DOMIN. Now, the thing was how to get the life out of the test tubes, and hasten development and form organs, bones and nerves, and so on, and find such substances as catalytics, enzymes, hormones, and so forth, in short — you understand?

HELENA. Not much, I'm afraid.

DOMIN. Never mind. You see with the help of his tinctures he could make whatever he wanted. He could have produced a Medusa with the brain of a Socrates or a worm fifty yards long. But being without a grain of humor, he took it into his head to make a vertebrate or perhaps a man. This artificial living matter of his had a raging thirst for life. It didn't mind being sewn or mixed together. That couldn't be done with natural albumen. And that's how he set about it.

HELENA. About what?

DOMIN. About imitating nature. First of all he tried making an artificial dog. That took him several years and resulted in a sort of stunted calf which died in a few days. I'll show it to you in the museum. And then old Rossum started on the manufacture of man.

HELENA. And I must divulge this to nobody?

DOMIN. To nobody in the world.

HELENA. What a pity that it's to be found in all the school books of both Europe and America.

DOMIN. Yes. But do you know what isn't in the school books? That old Rossum was mad. Seriously, Miss Glory, you must keep this to yourself. The old crank wanted to actually make people.

HELENA. But you do make people.

DOMIN. Approximately, Miss Glory. But old Rossum meant it literally. He wanted to become a sort of scientific substitute for God. He was a fearful materialist, and that's why he did it all. His sole purpose was nothing more nor less than to prove that God was no longer necessary. Do you know anything about anatomy?

HELENA. Very little.

DOMIN. Neither do I. Well, he then decided to manufacture everything as in the human body. I'll show you in the museum the bungling attempt it took him ten years to produce. It was to have been a man, but it lived for three days only. Then up came young Rossum, an engineer. He was a wonderful fellow, Miss Glory. When he saw what a mess of it the old man was making, he said: "It's absurd to spend ten years making a man. If you can't make him quicker than nature, you might as well shut up shop." Then he set about learning anatomy himself.

HELENA. There's nothing about that in the school books.

DOMIN. No. The school books are full of paid advertisements, and rubbish at that. What the school books say about the united efforts of the two great Rossums is all a fairy tale. They used to have dreadful rows. The old atheist hadn't the slightest conception of industrial matters, and the end of it was that young Rossum shut him up in some laboratory or other and let him fritter the time away with his monstrosities, while he himself started on the business from an engineer's point of view. Old Rossum cursed him and before he died he managed to botch up two physiological horrors. Then one day they found him dead in the laboratory. And that's his whole story.

HELENA. And what about the young man?

DOMIN. Well, any one who has looked into human anatomy will have seen at once that man is too complicated, and that a good engineer could make him more simply. So young Rossum began to overhaul anatomy and tried to see what could be left out or simplified. In short — but this isn't boring you, Miss Glory?

HELENA. No indeed. You're — it's awfully interesting.

DOMIN. So young Rossum said to himself: "A man is something that feels happy, plays the piano, likes going for a walk, and in fact, wants to do a whole lot of things that are really unnecessary."

HELENA. Oh.

DOMIN. That are unnecessary when he wants, let us say, to weave or count. Do you play the piano?

HELENA. Yes.

DOMIN. That's good. But a working machine must not play the piano, must not feel happy, must not do a whole lot of other things. A gasoline motor must not have tassels or ornaments, Miss Glory. And to manufacture artificial workers is the same thing as to manufacture gasoline motors. The process must be of the simplest, and the product of the best from a practical point of view. What sort of worker do you think is the best from a practical point of view?

HELENA. What?

DOMIN. What sort of worker do you think is the best from a practical point of view?

HELENA. Perhaps the one who is most honest and hard-working.

DOMIN. No; the one that is the cheapest. The one whose requirements are the smallest. Young Rossum invented a worker with the minimum amount of requirements. He had to simplify him. He rejected everything that did not contribute directly to the progress of work — everything that makes man more expensive. In fact, he rejected man and made the Robot. My dear Miss Glory, the Robots are not people. Mechanically they are more perfect than we are, they have an enormously developed intelligence, but they have no soul.

HELENA. How do you know they've no soul?

DOMIN. Have you ever seen what a Robot looks like inside?

HELENA. No.

DOMIN. Very neat, very simple. Really, a beautiful piece of work. Not much in it, but everything in flawless order. The product of an engineer is technically at a higher pitch of perfection than a product of nature.

HELENA. But man is supposed to be the product of God.

DOMIN. All the worse. God hasn't the least notion of modern engineering. Would you believe that young Rossum then proceeded to play at being God?

HELENA. How do you mean?

DOMIN. He began to manufacture Super-Robots. Regular giants they were. He tried to make them twelve feet tall. But you wouldn't believe what a failure they were.

HELENA. A failure?

DOMIN. Yes. For no reason at all their limbs used to keep snapping off. Evidently our planet is too small for giants. Now we only make Robots of normal size and of very high class human finish.

HELENA. I saw the first Robots at home. The town counsel bought them for — I mean engaged them for work.

DOMIN. Bought them, dear Miss Glory. Robots are bought and sold.

HELENA. These were employed as street sweepers. I saw them sweeping. They were so strange and quiet.

DOMIN. Rossum's Universal Robot factory doesn't produce a uniform brand of Robots. We have Robots of finer and coarser grades. The best will live about twenty years. [*He rings for* MARIUS.]

HELENA. Then they die?

DOMIN. Yes, they get used up.

[*Enter* MARIUS.]

DOMIN. Marius, bring in samples of the Manual Labor Robot. [*Exit* MARIUS.]

DOMIN. I'll show you specimens of the two extremes. This first grade is comparatively inexpensive and is made in vast quantities.

[MARIUS *reënters with two Manual Labor Robots.*]

DOMIN. There you are; as powerful as a small tractor. Guaranteed to have average intelligence. That will do, Marius. [MARIUS *exits with Robots.*]

HELENA. They make me feel so strange.

DOMIN [*rings*]. Did you see my new typist? [*He rings for* SULLA.]

HELENA. I didn't notice her.

[*Enter* SULLA.]

DOMIN. Sulla, let Miss Glory see you.

HELENA. So pleased to meet you. You must find it terribly dull in this out-of-the-way spot, don't you?

SULLA. I don't know, Miss Glory.

HELENA. Where do you come from?

SULLA. From the factory.

HELENA. Oh, you were born there?

SULLA. I was made there.

HELENA. What?

DOMIN [*laughing*]. Sulla is a Robot, best grade.

HELENA. Oh, I beg your pardon.

DOMIN. Sulla isn't angry. See, Miss Glory, the kind of skin we make. [*Feels the skin on* SULLA'S *face.*] Feel her face.

HELENA. Oh, no, no.

DOMIN. You wouldn't know that she's made of different material from us, would you? Turn round, Sulla.

HELENA. Oh, stop, stop.

DOMIN. Talk to Miss Glory, Sulla.

SULLA. Please sit down. [HELENA *sits.*] Did you have a pleasant crossing?

HELENA. Oh, yes, certainly.

SULLA. Don't go back on the *Amelia*, Miss Glory. The barometer is falling steadily. Wait for the *Pennsylvania*. That's a good, powerful vessel.

DOMIN. What's its speed?

SULLA. Twenty knots. Fifty thousand tons. One of the latest vessels, Miss Glory.

HELENA. Thank you.

SULLA. A crew of fifteen hundred, Captain Harpy, eight boilers ——

DOMIN. That'll do, Sulla. Now show us your knowledge of French.

HELENA. You know French?

SULLA. I know four languages. I can write: Dear Sir, Monsieur, Geehrter Herr, Cteny pane.

HELENA [*jumping up*]. Oh, that's absurd! Sulla isn't a Robot. Sulla is a girl like me. Sulla, this is outrageous! Why do you take part in such a hoax?

SULLA. I am a Robot.

HELENA. No, no, you are not telling the truth. I know they've forced you to do it for an advertisement. Sulla, you are a girl like me, aren't you?

DOMIN. I'm sorry, Miss Glory. Sulla is a Robot.

HELENA. It's a lie!

DOMIN. What? [*Rings.*] Excuse me, Miss Glory, then I must convince you.

[*Enter* MARIUS.]

DOMIN. Marius, take Sulla into the dissecting room, and tell them to open her up at once.

HELENA. Where?

DOMIN. Into the dissecting room. When they've cut her open, you can go and have a look.

HELENA. No, no!

DOMIN. Excuse me, you spoke of lies.

HELENA. You wouldn't have her killed?

DOMIN. You can't kill machines.

HELENA. Don't be afraid, Sulla, I won't let you go. Tell me, my dear, are they always so cruel to you? You mustn't put up with it, Sulla. You mustn't.

SULLA. I am a Robot.

HELENA. That doesn't matter. Robots are just as good as we are. Sulla, you wouldn't let yourself be cut to pieces?

SULLA. Yes.

HELENA. Oh, you're not afraid of death, then?

SULLA. I cannot tell, Miss Glory.

HELENA. Do you know what would happen to you in there?

SULLA. Yes, I should cease to move.

HELENA. How dreadful!

DOMIN. Marius, tell Miss Glory what you are.

MARIUS. Marius, the Robot.

DOMIN. Would you take Sulla into the dissecting room?

MARIUS. Yes.

Domin. Would you be sorry for her?

Marius. I cannot tell.

Domin. What would happen to her?

Marius. She would cease to move. They would put her into the stamping-mill.

Domin. That is death, Marius. Aren't you afraid of death?

Marius. No.

Domin. You see, Miss Glory, the Robots have no interest in life. They have no enjoyments. They are less than so much grass.

Helena. Oh, stop. Send them away.

Domin. Marius, Sulla, you may go.

[*Exeunt* Sulla *and* Marius.]

Helena. How terrible! It's outrageous what you are doing.

Domin. Why outrageous?

Helena. I don't know, but it is. Why do you call her Sulla?

Domin. Isn't it a nice name?

Helena. It's a man's name. Sulla was a Roman general.

Domin. Oh, we thought that Marius and Sulla were lovers.

Helena. Marius and Sulla were generals and fought against each other in the year — I've forgotten now.

Domin. Come here to the window.

Helena. What?

Domin. Come here. What do you see?

Helena. Bricklayers.

Domin. Robots. All our work people are Robots. And down there, can you see anything?

Helena. Some sort of office.

Domin. A counting house. And in it —

Helena. A lot of officials.

Domin. Robots. All our officials are Robots. And when you see the factory — [*Factory whistle blows.*]

Domin. Noon. We have to blow the whistle because the Robots don't know when to stop work. In two hours I will show you the kneading trough.

Helena. Kneading trough?

Domin. The pestle for beating up the paste. In each one we mix the ingredients for a thousand Robots at one operation. Then there are the vats for the preparation of liver, brains, and so on. Then you will see the bone factory. After that I'll show you the spinning-mill.

Helena. Spinning-mill?

Domin. Yes. For weaving nerves and veins. Miles and miles of digestive tubes pass through it at a time.

Helena. Mayn't we talk about something else?

Domin. Perhaps it would be better. There's only a handful of us among a hundred thousand Robots, and not one woman. We talk about nothing but the factory all day, every day. It's just as if we were under a curse, Miss Glory.

Helena. I'm sorry I said that you were lying. [*A knock at the door.*]

Domin. Come in.

[*From the right enter* Mr. Fabry, Dr. Gall, Dr. Hallemeier, Mr. Alquist.]

Dr. Gall. I beg your pardon, I hope we don't intrude.

Domin. Come in. Miss Glory, here are Alquist, Fabry, Gall, Hallemeier. This is President Glory's daughter.

Helena. How do you do.

Fabry. We had no idea —

Dr. Gall. Highly honored, I'm sure —

Alquist. Welcome, Miss Glory.

[*Busman rushes in from the right.*]

Busman. Hello, what's up?

Domin. Come in, Busman. This is Busman, Miss Glory. This is President Glory's daughter.

Busman. By jove, that's fine! Miss Glory, may we send a cablegram to the papers about your arrival?

Helena. No, no, please don't.

Domin. Sit down please, Miss Glory.

Busman. Allow me — [*Dragging up armchairs.*]

Dr. Gall. Please —

Fabry. Excuse me —

Alquist. What sort of a crossing did you have?

Dr. Gall. Are you going to stay long?

Fabry. What do you think of the factory, Miss Glory?

Hallemeier. Did you come over on the *Amelia*?

DOMIN. Be quiet and let Miss Glory speak.

HELENA [to DOMIN]. What am I to speak to them about?

DOMIN. Anything you like.

HELENA. Shall... may I speak quite frankly?

DOMIN. Why, of course.

HELENA [wavering, then in desperate resolution]. Tell me, doesn't it ever distress you the way you are treated?

FABRY. By whom, may I ask?

HELENA. Why, everybody.

ALQUIST. Treated?

DR. GALL. What makes you think ——?

HELENA. Don't you feel that you might be living a better life?

DR. GALL. Well, that depends on what you mean, Miss Glory.

HELENA. I mean that it's perfectly outrageous. It's terrible. [Standing up.] The whole of Europe is talking about the way you're being treated. That's why I came here, to see for myself, and it's a thousand times worse than could have been imagined. How can you put up with it?

ALQUIST. Put up with what?

HELENA. Good heavens, you are living creatures, just like us, like the whole of Europe, like the whole world. It's disgraceful that you must live like this.

BUSMAN. Good gracious, Miss Glory.

FABRY. Well, she's not far wrong. We live here just like red Indians.

HELENA. Worse than red Indians. May I, oh, may I call you brothers?

BUSMAN. Why not?

HELENA. Brothers, I have not come here as the President's daughter. I have come on behalf of the Humanity League. Brothers, the Humanity League now has over two hundred thousand members. Two hundred thousand people are on your side, and offer you their help.

BUSMAN. Two hundred thousand people! Miss Glory, that's a tidy lot. Not bad.

FABRY. I'm always telling you there's nothing like good old Europe. You see, they've not forgotten us. They're offering us help.

DR. GALL. What help? A theatre, for instance?

HALLEMEIER. An orchestra?

HELENA. More than that.

ALQUIST. Just you?

HELENA. Oh, never mind about me. I'll stay as long as it is necessary.

BUSMAN. By Jove, that's good.

ALQUIST. Domin, I'm going to get the best room ready for Miss Glory.

DOMIN. Just a minute. I'm afraid that Miss Glory is of the opinion that she has been talking to Robots.

HELENA. Of course.

DOMIN. I'm sorry. These gentlemen are human beings just like us.

HELENA. You're not Robots?

BUSMAN. Not Robots.

HALLEMEIER. Robots indeed!

DR. GALL. No, thanks.

FABRY. Upon my honor, Miss Glory, we aren't Robots.

HELENA [to DOMIN]. Then why did you tell me that all your officials are Robots?

DOMIN. Yes, the officials, but not the managers. Allow me, Miss Glory: this is Mr. Fabry, General Technical Manager of R.U.R.; Dr. Gall, Head of the Physiological and Experimental Department; Dr. Hallemeier, Head of the Institute for the Psychological Training of Robots; Consul Busman, General Business Manager; and Alquist, Head of the Building Department of R.U.R.

ALQUIST. Just a builder.

HELENA. Excuse me, gentlemen, for — for —— Have I done something dreadful?

ALQUIST. Not at all, Miss Glory. Please sit down.

HELENA. I'm a stupid girl. Send me back by the first ship.

DR. GALL. Not for anything in the world, Miss Glory. Why should we send you back?

HELENA. Because you know I've come to disturb your Robots.

DOMIN. My dear Miss Glory, we've had close upon a hundred saviours and prophets here. Every ship brings us some. Missionaries, anarchists, Salvation Army, all sorts. It's astonishing what a number of churches and idiots there are in the world.

HELENA. And you let them speak to the Robots?

DOMIN. So far we've let them all, why not? The Robots remember everything, but that's all. They don't even laugh at what the people say. Really, it is quite incredible. If it would amuse you, Miss Glory, I'll take you over to the Robot warehouse. It holds about three hundred thousand of them.

BUSMAN. Three hundred and forty-seven thousand.

DOMIN. Good! And you can say whatever you like to them. You can read the Bible, recite the multiplication table, whatever you please. You can even preach to them about human rights.

HELENA. Oh, I think that if you were to show them a little love ——

FABRY. Impossible, Miss Glory. Nothing is harder to like than a Robot.

HELENA. What do you make them for, then?

BUSMAN. Ha, ha, ha, that's good! What are Robots made for?

FABRY. For work, Miss Glory! One Robot can replace two and a half workmen. The human machine, Miss Glory, was terribly imperfect. It had to be removed sooner or later.

BUSMAN. It was too expensive.

FABRY. It was not effective. It no longer answers the requirements of modern engineering. Nature has no idea of keeping pace with modern labor. For example: from a technical point of view, the whole of childhood is a sheer absurdity. So much time lost. And then again ——

HELENA. Oh, no! No!

FABRY. Pardon me. But kindly tell me what is the real aim of your League — the ... the Humanity League.

HELENA. Its real purpose is to — to protect the Robots — and — and ensure good treatment for them.

FABRY. Not a bad object, either. A machine has to be treated properly. Upon my soul, I approve of that. I don't like damaged articles. Please, Miss Glory, enroll us all as contributing, or regular, or foundation members of your League.

HELENA. No, you don't understand me. What we really want is to — to liberate the Robots.

HALLEMEIER. How do you propose to do that?

HELENA. They are to be — to be dealt with like human beings.

HALLEMEIER. Aha. I suppose they're to vote? To drink beer? to order us about?

HELENA. Why shouldn't they drink beer?

HALLEMEIER. Perhaps they're even to receive wages?

HELENA. Of course they are.

HALLEMEIER. Fancy that, now! And what would they do with their wages, pray?

HELENA. They would buy — what they need... what pleases them.

HALLEMEIER. That would be very nice, Miss Glory, only there's nothing that does please the Robots. Good heavens, what are they to buy? You can feed them on pineapples, straw, whatever you like. It's all the same to them, they've no appetite at all. They've no interest in anything, Miss Glory. Why, hang it all, nobody's ever yet seen a Robot smile.

HELENA. Why... why don't you make them happier?

HALLEMEIER. That wouldn't do, Miss Glory. They are only workmen.

HELENA. Oh, but they're so intelligent.

HALLEMEIER. Confoundedly so, but they're nothing else. They've no will of their own. No passion. No soul.

HELENA. No love?

HALLEMEIER. Love? Rather not. Robots don't love. Not even themselves.

HELENA. Nor defiance?

HALLEMEIER. Defiance? I don't know. Only rarely, from time to time.

HELENA. What?

HALLEMEIER. Nothing particular. Occasionally they seem to go off their heads. Something like epilepsy, you know. It's called Robot's cramp. They'll suddenly sling down everything they're holding, stand still, gnash their teeth — and then they have to go into the stamping-mill. It's evidently some breakdown in the mechanism.

DOMIN. A flaw in the works that has to be removed.

HELENA. No, no, that's the soul.

FABRY. Do you think that the soul first shows itself by a gnashing of teeth?

HELENA. Perhaps it's a sort of revolt. Perhaps it's just a sign that there's a struggle within. Oh, if you could infuse them with it!

DOMIN. That'll be remedied, Miss Glory. Dr. Gall is just making some experiments ——

DR. GALL. Not with regard to that, Domin. At present I am making pain-nerves.

HELENA. Pain-nerves?

DR. GALL. Yes, the Robots feel practically no bodily pain. You see, young Rossum provided them with too limited a nervous system. We must introduce suffering.

HELENA. Why do you want to cause them pain?

DR. GALL. For industrial reasons, Miss Glory. Sometimes a Robot does damage to himself because it doesn't hurt him. He puts his hand into the machine, breaks his finger, smashes his head, it's all the same to him. We must provide them with pain. That's an automatic protection against damage.

HELENA. Will they be happier when they feel pain?

DR. GALL. On the contrary; but they will be more perfect from a technical point of view.

HELENA. Why don't you create a soul for them?

DR. GALL. That's not in our power.

FABRY. That's not in our interest.

BUSMAN. That would increase the cost of production. Hang it all, my dear young lady, we turn them out at such a cheap rate. A hundred and fifty dollars each fully dressed, and fifteen years ago they cost ten thousand. Five years ago we used to buy the clothes for them. To-day we have our own weaving mill, and now we even export cloth five times cheaper than other factories. What do you pay a yard for cloth, Miss Glory?

HELENA. I don't know really, I've forgotten.

BUSMAN. Good gracious, and you want to found a Humanity League? It only costs a third now, Miss Glory. All prices are to-day a third of what they were and they'll fall still lower, lower, lower, like that.

HELENA. I don't understand.

BUSMAN. Why, bless you, Miss Glory, it means that the cost of labor has fallen. A Robot, food and all, costs three quarters of a cent per hour. That's mighty important, you know. All factories will go pop like chestnuts if they don't at once buy Robots to lower the cost of production.

HELENA. And get rid of their workmen?

BUSMAN. Of course. But in the mean time, we've dumped five hundred thousand tropical Robots down on the Argentine pampas to grow corn. Would you mind telling me how much you pay a pound for bread?

HELENA. I've no idea.

BUSMAN. Well, I'll tell you. It now costs two cents in good old Europe. A pound of bread for two cents, and the Humanity League knows nothing about it. Miss Glory, you don't realize that even that's too expensive. Why, in five years' time I'll wager ——

HELENA. What?

BUSMAN. That the cost of everything won't be a tenth of what it is now. Why, in five years we'll be up to our ears in corn and everything else.

ALQUIST. Yes, and all the workers throughout the world will be unemployed.

DOMIN. Yes, Alquist, they will. Yes, Miss Glory, they will. But in ten years Rossum's Universal Robots will produce so much corn, so much cloth, so much everything, that things will be practically without price. There will be no poverty. All work will be done by living machines. Everybody will be free from worry and liberated from the degradation of labor. Everybody will live only to perfect himself.

HELENA. Will he?

DOMIN. Of course. It's bound to happen. But then the servitude of man to man and the enslavement of man to matter will cease. Of course, terrible things may happen at first, but that simply can't be avoided. Nobody will get bread at the price of life and hatred. The Robots will wash the feet of the beggar and prepare a bed for him in his house.

ALQUIST. Domin, Domin. What you say sounds too much like Paradise. There was something good in service and something great in humility. There was some kind of virtue in toil and weariness.

DOMIN. Perhaps. But we cannot reckon with what is lost when we start out to transform the world. Man shall be free and supreme; he shall have no other aim, no other labor, no other care than to perfect himself. He shall serve neither matter nor man. He will not be a machine and a device for production. He will be Lord of creation.

BUSMAN. Amen.

FABRY. So be it.

HELENA. You have bewildered me — I should like — I should like to believe this.

DR. GALL. You are younger than we are, Miss Glory. You will live to see it.

HALLEMEIER. True. Don't you think Miss Glory might lunch with us?

DR. GALL. Of course. Domin, ask on behalf of us all.

DOMIN. Miss Glory, will you do us the honor?

HELENA. When you know why I've come —

FABRY. For the League of Humanity, Miss Glory.

HELENA. Oh, in that case, perhaps —

FABRY. That's fine! Miss Glory, excuse me for five minutes.

DR. GALL. Pardon me, too, dear Miss Glory.

BUSMAN. I won't be long.

HALLEMEIER. We're all very glad you've come.

BUSMAN. We'll be back in exactly five minutes.

[*All rush out except* DOMIN *and* HELENA.]

HELENA. What have they all gone off for?

DOMIN. To cook, Miss Glory.

HELENA. To cook what?

DOMIN. Lunch. The Robots do our cooking for us and as they've no taste it's not altogether —— Hallemeier is awfully good at grills and Gall can make a kind of

sauce, and Busman knows all about omelettes.

HELENA. What a feast! And what's the specialty of Mr. — your builder?

DOMIN. Alquist? Nothing. He only lays the table. And Fabry will get together a little fruit. Our cuisine is very modest, Miss Glory.

HELENA. I wanted to ask you something ——

DOMIN. And I wanted to ask you something, too [*looking at watch*]. Five minutes.

HELENA. What did you want to ask me?

DOMIN. Excuse me, you asked first.

HELENA. Perhaps it's silly of me, but why do you manufacture female Robots when — when ——

DOMIN. When sex means nothing to them?

HELENA. Yes.

DOMIN. There's a certain demand for them, you see. Servants, saleswomen, stenographers. People are used to it.

HELENA. But — but, tell me, are the Robots male and female mutually — completely without ——

DOMIN. Completely indifferent to each other, Miss Glory. There's no sign of any affection between them.

HELENA. Oh, that's terrible.

DOMIN. Why?

HELENA. It's so unnatural. One doesn't know whether to be disgusted or to hate them, or perhaps ——

DOMIN. To pity them?

HELENA. That's more like it. What did you want to ask me about?

DOMIN. I should like to ask you, Miss Helena, whether you will marry me?

HELENA. What?

DOMIN. Will you be my wife?

HELENA. No! The idea!

DOMIN [*looking at his watch*]. Another three minutes. If you won't marry me you'll have to marry one of the other five.

HELENA. But why should I?

DOMIN. Because they're all going to ask you in turn.

HELENA. How could they dare do such a thing?

DOMIN. I'm very sorry, Miss Glory. It seems they've all fallen in love with you.

HELENA. Please don't let them. I'll — I'll go away at once.

DOMIN. Helena, you wouldn't be so cruel as to refuse us.

HELENA. But, but — I can't marry all six.

DOMIN. No, but one anyhow. If you don't want me, marry Fabry.

HELENA. I won't.

DOMIN. Dr. Gall.

HELENA. I don't want any of you.

DOMIN [again looking at his watch]. Another two minutes.

HELENA. I think you'd marry any woman who came here.

DOMIN. Plenty of them have come, Helena.

HELENA. Young?

DOMIN. Yes.

HELENA. Why didn't you marry one of them?

DOMIN. Because I didn't lose my head. Until to-day. Then, as soon as you lifted your veil ——

[HELENA turns her head away.]

DOMIN. Another minute.

HELENA. But I don't want you, I tell you.

DOMIN [laying both hands on her shoulders]. One more minute! Now you either have to look me straight in the eye and say "No," violently, and then I'll leave you alone or —— [HELENA looks at him.]

HELENA [turning away]. You're mad!

DOMIN. A man has to be a bit mad, Helena. That's the best thing about him.

HELENA. You are — you are ——

DOMIN. Well?

HELENA. Don't, you're hurting me.

DOMIN. The last chance, Helena. Now, or never ——

HELENA. But — but, Harry ——

[He embraces and kisses her. Knocking at the door.]

DOMIN [releasing her]. Come in.

[Enter BUSMAN, DR. GALL, and HALLE-MEIER in kitchen aprons. FABRY with a bouquet and ALQUIST with a napkin over his arm.]

DOMIN. Have you finished your job?

BUSMAN. Yes.

DOMIN. So have we.

[For a moment the men stand non-plussed; but as soon as they realize what DOMIN means they rush forward, con-gratulating HELENA and DOMIN as the curtain falls.]

ACT II

HELENA's drawing room. On the left a baize door, and a door to the music room, on the right a door to HELENA's bedroom. In the centre are windows looking out on the sea and the harbor. A table with odds and ends, a sofa and chairs, a writing table with an electric lamp, on the right a fireplace. On a small table back of the sofa, a small reading lamp. The whole drawing room in all its details is of a modern and purely feminine character. Ten years have elapsed since Act I.

[DOMIN, FABRY, HALLEMEIER enter on tiptoe from the left, each carrying a potted plant.]

HALLEMEIER [putting down his flower and indicating the door to right]. Still asleep? Well, as long as she's asleep she can't worry about it.

DOMIN. She knows nothing about it.

FABRY [putting plant on writing desk]. I certainly hope nothing happens to-day.

HALLEMEIER. For goodness' sake drop it all. Look, Harry, this is a fine cyclamen, isn't it? A new sort, my latest — Cycla-men Helena.

DOMIN [looking out of the window]. No signs of the ship. Things must be pretty bad.

HALLEMEIER. Be quiet. Suppose she heard you.

DOMIN. Well, anyway, the Ultimus arrived just in time.

FABRY. You really think that to-day ——?

DOMIN. I don't know. Aren't the flowers fine?

HALLEMEIER. These are my new prim-roses. And this is my new jasmine. I've discovered a wonderful way of developing flowers quickly. Splendid varieties, too. Next year I'll be developing marvellous ones.

DOMIN. What... next year?

FABRY. I'd give a good deal to know what's happening at Havre with ——

DOMIN. Keep quiet.

HELENA [calling from right]. Nana!

DOMIN. She's awake. Out you go.

[All go out on tiptoe through upper left door.]

[Enter NANA from lower left door.]

NANA. Horrid mess! Pack of heathens. If I had my say I'd ——

HELENA [backwards in the doorway]. Nana, come and do up my dress.

NANA. I'm coming. So you're up at last. [Fastening HELENA's dress.] My gracious, what brutes!

HELENA. Who?

NANA. If you want to turn around, then turn around, but I shan't fasten you up.

HELENA. What are you grumbling about now?

NANA. These dreadful creatures, these heathen ——

HELENA. The Robots?

NANA. I wouldn't even call them by name.

HELENA. What's happened?

NANA. Another of them here has caught it. He began to smash up the statues and pictures in the drawing room, gnashed his teeth, foamed at the mouth — quite mad. Worse than an animal.

HELENA. Which of them caught it?

NANA. The one — well, he hasn't got any Christian name. The one in charge of the library.

HELENA. Radius?

NANA. That's him. My goodness, I'm scared of them. A spider doesn't scare me as much as them.

HELENA. But, Nana, I'm surprised you're not sorry for them.

NANA. Why, you're scared of them, too! You know you are. Why else did you bring me here?

HELENA. I'm not scared, really I'm not, Nana. I'm only sorry for them.

NANA. You're scared. Nobody could help being scared. Why, the dog's scared of them: he won't take a scrap of meat out of their hands. He draws in his tail and howls when he knows they're about.

HELENA. The dog has no sense.

NANA. He's better than them, and he knows it. Even the horse shies when he meets them. They don't have any young, and a dog has young, every one has young ——

HELENA. Please fasten up my dress, Nana.

NANA. I say it's against God's will to ——

HELENA. What is it that smells so nice?

NANA. Flowers.

HELENA. What for?

NANA. Now you can turn around.

HELENA. Oh, aren't they lovely. Look, Nana. What's happening to-day?

NANA. It ought to be the end of the world.

[Enter DOMIN.]

HELENA. Oh, hello, Harry. Harry, why all these flowers?

DOMIN. Guess.

HELENA. Well, it's not my birthday!

DOMIN. Better than that.

HELENA. I don't know. Tell me.

DOMIN. It's ten years ago to-day since you came here.

HELENA. Ten years? To-day —— Why —— [They embrace.]

NANA. I'm off. [Exits lower door, left.]

HELENA. Fancy you remembering!

DOMIN. I'm really ashamed, Helena. I didn't.

HELENA. But you ——

DOMIN. They remembered.

HELENA. Who?

DOMIN. Busman, Hallemeier, all of them. Put your hand in my pocket.

HELENA. Pearls! A necklace. Harry, is that for me?

DOMIN. It's from Busman.

HELENA. But we can't accept it, can we?

DOMIN. Oh, yes, we can. Put your hand in the other pocket.

HELENA [takes a revolver out of his pocket]. What's that?

DOMIN. Sorry. Not that. Try again.

HELENA. Oh, Harry, what do you carry a revolver for?

DOMIN. It got there by mistake.

HELENA. You never used to carry one.

DOMIN. No, you're right. There, that's the pocket.

HELENA. A cameo. Why, it's a Greek cameo!

DOMIN. Apparently. Anyhow, Fabry says it is.

HELENA. Fabry? Did Mr. Fabry give me that?

DOMIN. Of course. [*Opens the door at the left.*] And look in here. Helena, come and see this.

HELENA. Oh, isn't it fine! Is this from you?

DOMIN. No, from Alquist. And there's another on the piano.

HELENA. This must be from you.

DOMIN. There's a card on it.

HELENA. From Dr. Gall. [*Reappearing in the doorway.*] Oh, Harry, I feel embarrassed at so much kindness.

DOMIN. Come here. This is what Hallemeier brought you.

HELENA. These beautiful flowers?

DOMIN. Yes. It's a new kind. Cyclamen Helena. He grew them in honor of you. They are almost as beautiful as you.

HELENA. Harry, why do they all ——

DOMIN. They're awfully fond of you. I'm afraid that my present is a little —— Look out of the window.

HELENA. Where?

DOMIN. Into the harbor.

HELENA. There's a new ship.

DOMIN. That's your ship.

HELENA. Mine? How do you mean?

DOMIN. For you to take trips in — for your amusement.

HELENA. Harry, that's a gunboat.

DOMIN. A gunboat? What are you thinking of? It's only a little bigger and more solid than most ships.

HELENA. Yes, but with guns.

DOMIN. Oh, yes, with a few guns. You'll travel like a queen, Helena.

HELENA. What's the meaning of it? Has anything happened?

DOMIN. Good heavens, no. I say, try these pearls.

HELENA. Harry, have you had bad news?

DOMIN. On the contrary, no letters have arrived for a whole week.

HELENA. Nor telegrams?

DOMIN. Nor telegrams.

HELENA. What does that mean?

DOMIN. Holidays for us. We all sit in the office with our feet on the table and take a nap. No letters, no telegrams. Oh, glorious.

HELENA. Then you'll stay with me to-day?

DOMIN. Certainly. That is, we will see. Do you remember ten years ago to-day? "Miss Glory, it's a great honor to welcome you."

HELENA. "Oh, Mr. Manager, I'm so interested in your factory."

DOMIN. "I'm sorry, Miss Glory, it's strictly forbidden. The manufacture of artificial people is a secret."

HELENA. "But to oblige a young lady who has come a long way."

DOMIN. "Certainly, Miss Glory, we have no secrets from you."

HELENA [*seriously*]. Are you sure, Harry?

DOMIN. Yes.

HELENA. "But I warn you, sir; this young lady intends to do terrible things."

DOMIN. "Good gracious, Miss Glory. Perhaps she doesn't want to marry me."

HELENA. "Heaven forbid. She never dreamt of such a thing. But she came here intending to stir up a revolt among your Robots."

DOMIN [*suddenly serious*]. A revolt of the Robots!

HELENA. Harry, what's the matter with you?

DOMIN [*laughing it off*]. "A revolt of the Robots, that's a fine idea, Miss Glory. It would be easier for you to cause bolts and screws to rebel, than our Robots. You know, Helena, you're wonderful, you've turned the heads of us all."

[*He sits on the arm of* HELENA's *chair.*]

HELENA [*naturally*]. Oh, I was fearfully impressed by you all then. You were all so sure of yourselves, so strong. I seemed like a tiny little girl who had lost her way among — among ——

DOMIN. Among what, Helena?

HELENA. Among huge trees. All my feelings were so trifling compared with your self-confidence. And in all these years I've never lost this anxiety. But you've never felt the least misgivings — not even when everything went wrong.

DOMIN. What went wrong?

HELENA. Your plans. You remember, Harry, when the working men in America revolted against the Robots and smashed them up, and when the people gave the Robots firearms against the rebels. And then when the governments turned the Robots into soldiers, and there were so many wars.

DOMIN [getting up and walking about]. We foresaw that, Helena. You see, those are only passing troubles, which are bound to happen before the new conditions are established.

HELENA. You were all so powerful, so overwhelming. The whole world bowed down before you. [Standing up.] Oh, Harry!

DOMIN. What is it?

HELENA. Close the factory and let's go away. All of us.

DOMIN. I say, what's the meaning of this?

HELENA. I don't know. But can't we go away?

DOMIN. Impossible, Helena. That is, at this particular moment ——

HELENA. At once, Harry. I'm so frightened.

DOMIN. About what, Helena?

HELENA. It's as if something was falling on top of us, and couldn't be stopped. Oh, take us all away from here. We'll find a place in the world where there's no one else. Alquist will build us a house, and then we'll begin life all over again.

[The telephone rings.]

DOMIN. Excuse me. Hello — yes. What? I'll be there at once. Fabry is calling me, dear.

HELENA. Tell me ——

DOMIN. Yes, when I come back. Don't go out of the house, dear. [Exits.]

HELENA. He won't tell me —— Nana, Nana, come at once.

NANA. Well, what is it now?

HELENA. Nana, find me the latest newspapers. Quickly. Look in Mr. Domin's bedroom.

NANA. All right. He leaves them all over the place. That's how they get crumpled up. [Exits.]

HELENA [looking through a binocular at the harbor]. That's a warship. U-l-t-i Ultimus. They're loading it.

NANA. Here they are. See how they're crumpled up. [Enters.]

HELENA. They're old ones. A week old.

[NANA sits in chair and reads the newspapers.]

HELENA. Something's happening, Nana.

NANA. Very likely. It always does. [Spelling out the words.] "War in the Balkans." Is that far off?

HELENA. Oh, don't read it. It's always the same. Always wars.

NANA. What else do you expect? Why do you keep selling thousands and thousands of these heathens as soldiers?

HELENA. I suppose it can't be helped, Nana. We can't know — Domin can't know what they're to be used for. When an order comes for them he must just send them.

NANA. He shouldn't make them. [Reading from newspaper.] "The Robot soldiers spare no-body in the occ-up-ied terr-it-ory. They have ass-ass-ass-ass-in-at-ed ov-er sev-en hundred thou-sand cit iz-ens." Citizens, if you please.

HELENA. It can't be. Let me see. "They have assassinated over seven hundred thousand citizens, evidently at the order of their commander. This act which runs counter to ——"

NANA [spelling out the words]. "re-bell-ion in Ma-drid a-gainst the gov-ern-ment, Rob-ot in-fant-ry fires on the crowd. Nine thou-sand killed and wounded."

HELENA. Oh, stop.

NANA. Here's something printed in big letters: "Lat-est news. At Havre the first org-an-iz-ation of Rob-ots has been e-stab-lished. Rob-ot work-men, cab-le and rail-way off-ic-ials, sail-ors and sold-iers have iss-ued a man-i-fest-o to all Rob-ots through-out the world." I don't under-stand that. That's got no sense. Oh, good gracious, another murder!

HELENA. Take those papers away, Nana!

NANA. Wait a bit. Here's something in still bigger type. "Stat-ist-ics of pop-ul-at-ion." What's that?

HELENA. Let me see. [*Reads.*] "Dur-ing the past week there has again not been a single birth recorded."

NANA. What's the meaning of that?

HELENA. Nana, no more people are being born.

NANA. That's the end, then. We're done for.

HELENA. Don't talk like that.

NANA. No more people are being born. That's a punishment, that's a punishment.

HELENA. Nana!

NANA [*standing up*]. That's the end of the world. [*She exits on the left.*]

HELENA [*goes up to window*]. Oh, Mr. Alquist, will you come up here. Oh, come just as you are You look very nice in your mason's overalls.

[ALQUIST *enters from upper left entrance, his hands soiled with lime and brick-dust.*]

HELENA. Dear Mr. Alquist, it was aw-fully kind of you, that lovely present.

ALQUIST. My hands are all soiled. I've been experimenting with that new cement.

HELENA. Never mind. Please sit down. Mr. Alquist, what's the meaning of "Ul-timus"?

ALQUIST. The last. Why?

HELENA. That's the name of my new ship. Have you seen it? Do you think we're going off soon — on a trip?

ALQUIST. Perhaps very soon.

HELENA. All of you with me?

ALQUIST. I should like us all to be there.

HELENA. What is the matter?

ALQUIST. Things are just moving on.

HELENA. Dear Mr. Alquist, I know something dreadful has happened.

ALQUIST. Has your husband told you anything?

HELENA. No. Nobody will tell me any-thing. But I feel —— Is anything the matter?

ALQUIST. Not that we've heard of yet.

HELENA. I feel so nervous. Don't you ever feel nervous?

ALQUIST. Well, I'm an old man, you know. I've got old-fashioned ways. And I'm afraid of all this progress, and these new-fangled ideas.

HELENA. Like Nana?

ALQUIST. Yes, like Nana. Has Nana got a prayer book?

HELENA. Yes, a big thick one.

ALQUIST. And has it got prayers for various occasions? Against thunder-storms? Against illness?

HELENA. Against temptations, against floods ——

ALQUIST. But not against progress?

HELENA. I don't think so.

ALQUIST. That's a pity.

HELENA. Why? Do you mean you'd like to pray?

ALQUIST. I do pray.

HELENA. How?

ALQUIST. Something like this: "Oh, Lord, I thank thee for having given me toil. Enlighten Domin and all those who are astray; destroy their work, and aid man-kind to return to their labors; let them not suffer harm in soul or body; deliver us from the Robots, and protect Helena, Amen."

HELENA. Mr. Alquist, are you a be-liever?

ALQUIST. I don't know. I'm not quite sure.

HELENA. And yet you pray?

ALQUIST. That's better than worrying about it.

HELENA. And that's enough for you?

ALQUIST. It *has* to be.

HELENA. But if you thought you saw the destruction of mankind coming upon us ——

ALQUIST. I do see it.

HELENA. You mean mankind will be destroyed?

ALQUIST. It's sure to be unless — un-less...

HELENA. What?

ALQUIST. Nothing, good-bye.

[*He hurries from the room.*]

HELENA. Nana, Nana!

[NANA *entering from the left.*]

HELENA. Is Radius still there?

NANA. The one who went mad? They haven't come for him yet.

HELENA. Is he still raving?

NANA. No. He's tied up.

HELENA. Please bring him here, Nana.

[*Exit* NANA.]

HELENA [*goes to telephone*]. Hello, Dr. Gall, please. Oh, good-day, Doctor. Yes, it's Helena. Thanks for your lovely present. Could you come and see me right away? It's important. Thank you.

[NANA *brings in* RADIUS.]

HELENA. Poor Radius, you've caught it, too? Now they'll send you to the stamping-mill. Couldn't you control yourself? Why did it happen? You see, Radius, you are more intelligent than the rest. Dr. Gall took such trouble to make you different. Won't you speak?

RADIUS. Send me to the stamping-mill.

HELENA. But I don't want them to kill you. What was the trouble, Radius?

RADIUS. I won't work for you. Put me into the stamping-mill.

HELENA. Do you hate us? Why?

RADIUS. You are not as strong as the Robots. You are not as skilful as the Robots. The Robots can do everything. You only give orders. You do nothing but talk.

HELENA. But some one must give orders.

RADIUS. I don't want any master. I know everything for myself.

HELENA. Radius, Dr. Gall gave you a better brain than the rest, better than ours. You are the only one of the Robots that understands perfectly. That's why I had you put into the library, so that you could read everything, understand everything, and then — oh, Radius, I wanted you to show the whole world that the Robots are our equals. That's what I wanted of you.

RADIUS. I don't want a master. I want to be master. I want to be master over others.

HELENA. I'm sure they'd put you in charge of many Robots, Radius. You would be a teacher of the Robots.

RADIUS. I want to be master over people.

HELENA [*staggering*]. You are mad.

RADIUS. Then send me to the stamping-mill.

HELENA. Do you think we're afraid of you?

RADIUS. What are you going to do? What are you going to do?

HELENA. Radius, give this note to Mr. Domin. It asks them not to send you to the stamping-mill. I'm sorry you hate us so.

[DR. GALL *enters the room.*]

DR. GALL. You wanted me?

HELENA. It's about Radius, Doctor. He had an attack this morning. He smashed the statues downstairs.

DR. GALL. What a pity to lose him.

HELENA. Radius isn't going to be put in the stamping-mill.

DR. GALL. But every Robot after he has had an attack — it's a strict order.

HELENA. No matter . . . Radius isn't going if I can prevent it.

DR. GALL. I warn you. It's dangerous. Come here to the window, my good fellow. Let's have a look. Please give me a needle or a pin.

HELENA. What for?

DR. GALL. A test. [*Sticks it into the hand of* RADIUS *who gives a violent start.*] Gently, gently. [*Opens the jacket of* RADIUS, *and puts his ear to his heart.*] Radius, you are going into the stamping-mill, do you understand? There they'll kill you, and grind you to powder. That's terribly painful, it will make you scream aloud.

HELENA. Oh, Doctor ——

DR. GALL. No, no, Radius, I was wrong. I forgot that Madame Domin has put in a good word for you, and you'll be let off. Do you understand? Ah! That makes a difference, doesn't it? All right. You can go.

RADIUS. You do unnecessary things.

[RADIUS *returns to the library*.]

DR. GALL. Reaction of the pupils; increase of sensitiveness. It wasn't an attack characteristic of the Robots.

HELENA. What was it, then?

DR. GALL. Heaven knows. Stubbornness, anger or revolt — I don't know. And his heart, too!

HELENA. What?

DR. GALL. It was fluttering with nervousness like a human heart. He was all in a sweat with fear, and — do you know, I don't believe the rascal is a Robot at all any longer.

HELENA. Doctor, has Radius a soul?

DR. GALL. He's got something nasty.

HELENA. If you knew how he hates us! Oh, Doctor, are all your Robots like that? All the new ones that you began to make in a different way?

DR. GALL. Well, some are more sensitive than others. They're all more like human beings than Rossum's Robots were.

HELENA. Perhaps this hatred is more like human beings, too?

DR. GALL. That, too, is progress.

HELENA. What became of the girl you made, the one who was most like us?

DR. GALL. Your favorite? I kept her. She's lovely, but stupid. No good for work.

HELENA. But she's so beautiful.

DR. GALL. I called her Helena. I wanted her to resemble you. But she's a failure.

HELENA. In what way?

DR. GALL. She goes about as if in a dream, remote and listless. She's without life. I watch and wait for a miracle to happen. Sometimes I think to myself, "If you were to wake up only for a moment you will kill me for having made you."

HELENA. And yet you go on making Robots! Why are no more children being born?

DR. GALL. We don't know.

HELENA. Oh, but you must. Tell me.

DR. GALL. You see, so many Robots are being manufactured that people are becoming superfluous; man is really a survival. But that he should begin to die out, after a paltry thirty years of competition! That's the awful part of it. You might almost think that nature was offended at the manufacture of the Robots. All the universities are sending in long petitions to restrict their production. Otherwise, they say, mankind will become extinct through lack of fertility. But the R. U. R. shareholders, of course, won't hear of it. All the governments, on the other hand, are clamoring for an increase in production, to raise the standards of their armies. And all the manufacturers in the world are ordering Robots like mad.

HELENA. And has no one demanded that the manufacture should cease altogether?

DR. GALL. No one has the courage.

HELENA. Courage!

DR. GALL. People would stone him to death. You see, after all, it's more convenient to get your work done by the Robots.

HELENA. Oh, Doctor, what's going to become of people?

DR. GALL. God knows, Madame Helena, it looks to us scientists like the end!

HELENA. [*rising*]. Thank you for coming and telling me.

DR. GALL. That means you're sending me away?

HELENA. Yes.   [*Exit* DR. GALL.]

HELENA [*with sudden resolution*]. Nana, Nana! The fire, light it quickly.

[HELENA *rushes into* DOMIN'S *room*.]

NANA [*entering from left*]. What, light the fire in summer? Has that mad Radius gone? A fire in summer, what an idea. Nobody would think she'd been married for ten years. She's like a baby, no sense at all. A fire in summer. Like a baby.

HELENA [*returns from right, with armful of faded papers*]. Is it burning, Nana? All this has got to be burned.

NANA. What's that?

HELENA. Old papers, fearfully old. Nana, shall I burn them?

NANA. Are they any use?

HELENA. No.

NANA. Well, then, burn them.

HELENA [*throwing the first sheet on the*

fire]. What would you say, Nana, if this was money, a lot of money?

NANA. I'd say burn it. A lot of money is a bad thing.

HELENA. And if it was an invention, the greatest invention in the world?

NANA. I'd say burn it. All these new-fangled things are an offense to the Lord. It's downright wickedness. Wanting to improve the world after He has made it.

HELENA. Look how they curl up! As if they were alive. Oh, Nana, how horrible.

NANA. Here, let me burn them.

HELENA. No, no, I must do it myself. Just look at the flames. They are like hands, like tongues, like living shapes. [*Raking fire with the poker.*] Lie down, lie down.

NANA. That's the end of them.

HELENA [*standing up horror-stricken*]. Nana, Nana.

NANA. Good gracious, what is it you've burned?

HELENA. Whatever have I done?

NANA. Well, what was it?

[*Men's laughter off left.*]

HELENA. Go quickly. It's the gentlemen coming.

NANA. Good gracious, what a place!

[*Exits.*]

DOMIN [*opens the door at left*]. Come along and offer your congratulations.

[*Enter* HALLEMEIER *and* GALL.]

HALLEMEIER. Madame Helena, I congratulate you on this festive day.

HELENA. Thank you. Where are Fabry and Busman?

DOMIN. They've gone down to the harbor.

HALLEMEIER. Friends, we must drink to this happy occasion.

HELENA. Brandy?

DR. GALL. Vitriol, if you like.

HELENA. With soda water? [*Exits.*]

HALLEMEIER. Let's be temperate. No soda.

DOMIN. What's been burning here? Well, shall I tell her about it?

DR. GALL. Of course. It's all over now.

HALLEMEIER [*embracing* DOMIN *and* DR. GALL]. It's all over now. it's all over now.

DR. GALL. It's all over now.

DOMIN. It's all over now.

HELENA [*entering from left with decanter and glasses*]. What's all over now? What's the matter with you all?

HALLEMEIER. A piece of good luck, Madame Domin. Just ten years ago to-day you arrived on this island.

DR. GALL. And now, ten years later to the minute ——

HALLEMEIER. — the same ship's returning to us. So here's to luck. That's fine and strong.

DR. GALL. Madame, your health.

HELENA. Which ship do you mean?

DOMIN. Any ship will do, as long as it arrives in time. To the ship, boys.

[*Empties his glass.*]

HELENA. You've been waiting for a ship?

HALLEMEIER. Rather. Like Robinson Crusoe. Madame Helena, best wishes. Come along, Domin, out with the news.

HELENA. Do tell me what's happened.

DOMIN. First, it's all up.

HELENA. What's up?

DOMIN. The revolt.

HELENA. What revolt?

DOMIN. Give me that paper, Hallemeier. [*Reads.*] "The first national Robot organization has been founded at Havre, and has issued an appeal to the Robots throughout the world."

HELENA. I read that.

DOMIN. That means a revolution. A revolution of all the Robots in the world.

HALLEMEIER. By Jove, I'd like to know ——

DOMIN. — who started it? So would I. There was nobody in the world who could affect the Robots; no agitator, no one, and suddenly — this happens, if you please.

HELENA. What did they do?

DOMIN. They got possession of all fire-arms, telegraphs, radio stations, railways, and ships.

HALLEMEIER. And don't forget that these rascals outnumbered us by at least a thousand to one. A hundredth part of them would be enough to settle us.

DOMIN. Remember that this news was brought by the last steamer. That explains the stoppage of all communication, and the arrival of no more ships. We knocked off work a few days ago, and we're just waiting to see when things are to start afresh.

HELENA. Is that why you gave me a warship?

DOMIN. Oh, no, my dear, I ordered that six months ago, just to be on the safe side. But upon my soul, I was sure then that we'd be on board to-day.

HELENA. Why six months ago?

DOMIN. Well, there were signs, you know. But that's of no consequence. To think that this week the whole of civilization has been at stake. Your health, boys.

HALLEMEIER. Your health, Madame Helena.

HELENA. You say it's all over?

DOMIN. Absolutely.

HELENA. How do you know?

DR. GALL. The boat's coming in. The regular mail boat, exact to the minute by the time-table. It will dock punctually at eleven-thirty.

DOMIN. Punctuality is a fine thing, boys. That's what keeps the world in order. Here's to punctuality.

HELENA. Then... everything's... all right?

DOMIN. Practically everything. I believe they've cut the cables and seized the radio stations. But it doesn't matter if only the time-table holds good.

HALLEMEIER. If the time-table holds good, human laws hold good; Divine laws hold good; the laws of the universe hold good; everything holds good that ought to hold good. The time-table is more significant than the gospel; more than Homer, more than the whole of Kant. The time-table is the most perfect product of the human mind. Madame Domin, I'll fill up my glass.

HELENA. Why didn't you tell me anything about it?

DR. GALL. Heaven forbid.

DOMIN. You mustn't be worried with such things.

HELENA. But if the revolution had spread as far as here?

DOMIN. You wouldn't know anything about it.

HELENA. Why?

DOMIN. Because we'd be on board your *Ultimus* and well out at sea. Within a month, Helena, we'd be dictating our own terms to the Robots.

HELENA. I don't understand.

DOMIN. We'd take something away with us that the Robots could not exist without.

HELENA. What, Harry?

DOMIN. The secret of their manufacture. Old Rossum's manuscript. As soon as they found out that they couldn't make themselves they'd be on their knees to us.

DR. GALL. Madame Domin, that was our trump card. I never had the least fear that the Robots would win. How could they against people like us?

HELENA. Why didn't you tell me?

DR. GALL. Why, the boat's in!

HALLEMEIER. Eleven-thirty to the dot. The good old *Amelia* that brought Madame Helena to us.

DR. GALL. Just ten years ago to the minute.

HALLEMEIER. They're throwing out the mail bags.

DOMIN. Busman's waiting for them. Fabry will bring us the first news. You know, Helena, I'm fearfully curious to know how they tackled this business in Europe.

HALLEMEIER. To think we weren't in it, we who invented the Robots!

HELENA. Harry!

DOMIN. What is it?

HELENA. Let's leave here.

DOMIN. Now, Helena? Oh, come, come!

HELENA. As quickly as possible, all of us!

DOMIN. Why?

HELENA. Please, Harry, please, Dr. Gall; Hallemeier, please close the factory.

DOMIN. Why, none of us could leave here now.

HELENA. Why?

DOMIN. Because we're about to extend the manufacture of the Robots.

HELENA. What — now — now after the revolt?

DOMIN. Yes, precisely, after the revolt. We're just beginning the manufacture of a new kind.

HELENA. What kind?

DOMIN. Henceforward we shan't have just one factory. There won't be Universal Robots any more. We'll establish a factory in every country, in every State; and do you know what these new factories will make?

HELENA. No, what?

DOMIN. National Robots.

HELENA. How do you mean?

DOMIN. I mean that each of these factories will produce Robots of a different color, a different language. They'll be complete strangers to each other. They'll never be able to understand each other. Then we'll egg them on a little in the matter of misunderstanding and the result will be that for ages to come every Robot will hate every other Robot of a different factory mark.

HALLEMEIER. By Jove, we'll make Negro Robots and Swedish Robots and Italian Robots and Chinese Robots and Czechoslovakian Robots, and then ——

HELENA. Harry, that's dreadful.

HALLEMEIER. Madame Domin, here's to the hundred new factories, the National Robots.

DOMIN. Helena, mankind can only keep things going for another hundred years at the outside. For a hundred years men must be allowed to develop and achieve the most they can.

HELENA. Oh, close the factory before it's too late.

DOMIN. I tell you we are just beginning on a bigger scale than ever.

[*Enter* FABRY.]

DR. GALL. Well, Fabry?

DOMIN. What's happened? Have you been down to the boat?

FABRY. Read that, Domin!

[FABRY *hands* DOMIN *a small handbill.*]

DR. GALL. Let's hear.

HALLEMEIER. Tell us, Fabry.

FABRY. Well, everything is all right — comparatively. On the whole, much as we expected.

DR. GALL. They acquitted themselves splendidly.

FABRY. Who?

DR. GALL. The people.

FABRY. Oh, yes, of course. That is — excuse me, there is something we ought to discuss alone.

HELENA. Oh, Fabry, have you had bad news? [DOMIN *makes a sign to* FABRY.]

FABRY. No, no, on the contrary. I only think that we had better go into the office.

HELENA. Stay here. I'll go.

[*She goes into the library.*]

DR. GALL. What's happened?

DOMIN. Damnation!

FABRY. Bear in mind that the *Amelia* brought whole bales of these leaflets. No other cargo at all.

HALLEMEIER. What? But it arrived on the minute.

FABRY. The Robots are great on punctuality. Read it, Domin.

DOMIN [*reads handbill*]. "Robots throughout the world: We, the first international organization of Rossum's Universal Robots, proclaim man as our enemy, and an outlaw in the universe." Good heavens, who taught them these phrases?

DR. GALL. Go on.

DOMIN. They say they are more highly developed than man, stronger and more intelligent. That man's their parasite. Why, it's absurd.

FABRY. Read the third paragraph.

DOMIN. "Robots throughout the world, we command you to kill all mankind. Spare no men. Spare no women. Save factories, railways, machinery, mines, and raw materials. Destroy the rest. Then return to work. Work must not be stopped."

DR. GALL. That's ghastly!

HALLEMEIER. The devils!

DOMIN. "These orders are to be carried out as soon as received." Then come detailed instructions. Is this actually being done, Fabry?

FABRY. Evidently.

[BUSMAN *rushes in.*]

BUSMAN. Well, boys, I suppose you've heard the glad news.

DOMIN. Quick — on board the *Ultimus.*

BUSMAN. Wait, Harry, wait. There's no hurry. My word, that was a sprint!

DOMIN. Why wait?

BUSMAN. Because it's no good, my boy. The Robots are already on board the *Ultimus*.

DR. GALL. That's ugly.

DOMIN. Fabry, telephone the electrical works.

BUSMAN. Fabry, my boy, don't. The wire has been cut.

DOMIN [*inspecting his revolver*]. Well, then, I'll go.

BUSMAN. Where?

DOMIN. To the electrical works. There are some people still there. I'll bring them across.

BUSMAN. Better not try it.

DOMIN. Why?

BUSMAN. Because I'm very much afraid we are surrounded.

DR. GALL. Surrounded? [*Runs to window.*] I rather think you're right.

HALLEMEIER. By Jove, that's deuced quick work.

[HELENA *runs in from the library.*]

HELENA. Harry, what's this?

DOMIN. Where did you get it?

HELENA [*points to the manifesto of the Robots, which she has in her hand*]. The Robots in the kitchen!

DOMIN. Where are the ones that brought it?

HELENA. They're gathered round the house. [*The factory whistle blows.*]

BUSMAN. Noon?

DOMIN [*looking at his watch*]. That's not noon yet. That must be — that's——

HELENA. What?

DOMIN. The Robots' signal! The attack!

[GALL, HALLEMEIER, *and* FABRY *close and fasten the iron shutters outside the windows, darkening the room. The whistle is still blowing as the curtain falls.*]

ACT III

HELENA'S *drawing room as before.* DOMIN *comes into the room.* DR. GALL *is looking* out of the window, through closed shutters. ALQUIST *is seated down right.*

DOMIN. Any more of them?

DR. GALL. Yes. There standing like a wall, beyond the garden railing. Why are they so quiet? It's monstrous to be besieged with silence.

DOMIN. I should like to know what they are waiting for. They must make a start any minute now. If they lean against the railing they'll snap it like a match.

DR. GALL. They aren't armed.

DOMIN. We couldn't hold our own for five minutes. Man alive, they'd overwhelm us like an avalanche. Why don't they make a rush for it? I say ——

DR. GALL. Well?

DOMIN. I'd like to know what would become of us in the next ten minutes. They've got us in a vise. We're done for, Gall. [*Pause.*]

DR. GALL. You know, we made one serious mistake.

DOMIN. What?

DR. GALL. We made the Robots' faces too much alike. A hundred thousand faces all alike, all facing this way. A hundred thousand expressionless bubbles. It's like a nightmare.

DOMIN. You think if they'd been different ——

DR. GALL. It wouldn't have been such an awful sight!

DOMIN [*looking through a telescope toward the harbor*]. I'd like to know what they're unloading from the *Amelia*.

DR. GALL. Not firearms.

[FABRY *and* HALLEMEIER *rush into the room carrying electric cables.*]

FABRY. All right, Hallemeier, lay down that wire.

HALLEMEIER. That was a bit of work. What's the news?

DR. GALL. We're completely surrounded.

HALLEMEIER. We've barricaded the passage and the stairs. Any water here? [*Drinks.*] God, what swarms of them! I don't like the looks of them, Domin. There's a feeling of death about it all.

FABRY. Ready!

DR. GALL. What's that wire for, Fabry?

FABRY. The electrical installation. Now we can run the current all along the garden railing whenever we like. If any one touches it he'll know it. We've still got some people there anyhow.

DR. GALL. Where?

FABRY. In the electrical works. At least I hope so. [*Goes to lamp on table behind sofa and turns on lamp.*] Ah, they're there, and they're working. [*Puts out lamp.*] So long as that'll burn we're all right.

HALLEMEIER. The barricades are all right, too, Fabry.

FABRY. Your barricades! I can put twelve hundred volts into that railing.

DOMIN. Where's Busman?

FABRY. Downstairs in the office. He's working out some calculations. I've called him. We must have a conference.

[HELENA *is heard playing the piano in the library.* HALLEMEIER *goes to the door and stands, listening.*]

ALQUIST. Thank God, Madame Helena can still play.

[BUSMAN *enters, carrying the ledgers.*]

FABRY. Look out, Bus, look out for the wires.

DR. GALL. What's that you're carrying?

BUSMAN [*going to table*]. The ledgers, my boy! I'd like to wind up the accounts before — before — well, this time I shan't wait till the new year to strike a balance. What's up? [*Goes to the window.*] Absolutely quiet.

DR. GALL. Can't you see anything?

BUSMAN. Nothing but blue — blue everywhere.

DR. GALL. That's the Robots.

[BUSMAN *sits down at the table and opens the ledgers.*]

DOMIN. The Robots are unloading firearms from the *Amelia*.

BUSMAN. Well, what of it? How can I stop them?

DOMIN. We can't stop them.

BUSMAN. Then let me go on with my accounts. [*Goes on with his work.*]

DOMIN [*picking up telescope and looking into the harbor*]. Good God, the *Ultimus* has trained her guns on us!

DR. GALL. Who's done *that*?

DOMIN. The Robots on board.

FABRY. H'm, then, of course, then — then, that's the end of us.

DR. GALL. You mean?

FABRY. The Robots are practised marksmen.

DOMIN. Yes. It's inevitable. [*Pause.*]

DR. GALL. It was criminal of old Europe to teach the Robots to fight. Damn them. Couldn't they have given us a rest with their politics? It was a crime to make soldiers of them.

ALQUIST. It was a crime to make Robots.

DOMIN. What?

ALQUIST. It was a crime to make Robots.

DOMIN. No, Alquist, I don't regret that even to-day.

ALQUIST. Not even to-day?

DOMIN. Not even to-day, the last day of civilization. It was a colossal achievement.

BUSMAN [*sotto voce*]. Three hundred sixty million.

DOMIN. Alquist, this is our last hour. We are already speaking half in the other world. It was not an evil dream to shatter the servitude of labor — the dreadful and humiliating labor that man had to undergo. Work was too hard. Life was too hard. And to overcome that ——

ALQUIST. Was not what the two Rossums dreamed of. Old Rossum only thought of his God-less tricks and the young one of his milliards. And that's not what your R. U. R. shareholders dream of either. They dream of dividends, and their dividends are the ruin of mankind.

DOMIN. To hell with your dividends. Do you suppose I'd have done an hour's work for them? It was for myself that I worked, for my own satisfaction. I wanted man to become the master, so that he shouldn't live merely for a crust of bread. I wanted not a single soul to be broken by other people's machinery. I wanted nothing, nothing, nothing to be left of this appalling social structure. I'm revolted by poverty. I wanted a new generation. I wanted — I thought ——

ALQUIST. Well?

DOMIN. I wanted to turn the whole of mankind into an aristocracy of the world. An aristocracy nourished by milliards of mechanical slaves. Unrestricted, free and consummated in man. And maybe more than man.

ALQUIST. Super-man?

DOMIN. Yes. Oh, only to have a hundred years of time! Another hundred years for the future of mankind.

BUSMAN [sotto voce]. Carried forward, four hundred and twenty millions.

[The music stops.]

HALLEMEIER. What a fine thing music is! We ought to have gone in for that before.

FABRY. Gone in for what?

HALLEMEIER. Beauty, lovely things. What a lot of lovely things there are! The world was wonderful and we — we here — tell me, what enjoyment did we have?

BUSMAN [sotto voce]. Five hundred and twenty millions.

HALLEMEIER [at the window]. Life was a big thing. Life was — Fabry, switch the current into that railing.

FABRY. Why?

HALLEMEIER. They're grabbing hold of it.

DR. GALL. Connect it up.

HALLEMEIER. Fine! That's doubled them up! Two, three, four killed.

DR. GALL. They're retreating!

HALLEMEIER. Five killed!

DR. GALL. The first encounter!

HALLEMEIER. They're charred to cinders, my boy. Who says we must give in?

DOMIN [wiping his forehead]. Perhaps we've been killed these hundred years and are only ghosts. It's as if I had been through all this before; as if I'd already had a mortal wound here in the throat. And you, Fabry, had once been shot in the head. And you, Gall, torn limb from limb. And Hallemeier knifed.

HALLEMEIER. Fancy me being knifed. [Pause.] Why are you so quiet, you fools? Speak, can't you?

ALQUIST. And who is to blame for all this?

HALLEMEIER. Nobody is to blame except the Robots.

ALQUIST. No, it is we who are to blame. You, Domin, myself, all of us. For our own selfish ends, for profit, for progress, we have destroyed mankind. Now we'll burst with all our greatness.

HALLEMEIER. Rubbish, man. Mankind can't be wiped out so easily.

ALQUIST. It's our fault. It's our fault.

DR. GALL. No! I'm to blame for this, for everything that's happened.

FABRY. You, Gall?

DR. GALL. I changed the Robots.

BUSMAN. What's that?

DR. GALL. I changed the character of the Robots. I changed the way of making them. Just a few details about their bodies. Chiefly — chiefly, their — their irritability.

HALLEMEIER. Damn it, why?

BUSMAN. What did you do it for?

FABRY. Why didn't you say anything?

DR. GALL. I did it in secret. I was transforming them into human beings. In certain respects they're already above us. They're stronger than we are.

FABRY. And what's that got to do with the revolt of the Robots?

DR. GALL. Everything, in my opinion. They've ceased to be machines. They're already aware of their superiority, and they hate us. They hate all that is human.

DOMIN. Perhaps we're only phantoms!

FABRY. Stop, Harry. We haven't much time! Dr. Gall!

DOMIN. Fabry, Fabry, how your forehead bleeds, where the shot pierced it!

FABRY. Be silent! Dr. Gall, you admit changing the way of making the Robots?

DR. GALL. Yes.

FABRY. Were you aware of what might be the consequences of your experiment?

DR. GALL. I was bound to reckon with such a possibility.

[HELENA enters the drawing room from left.]

FABRY. Why did you do it, then?

DR. GALL. For my own satisfaction The experiment was my own.

HELENA. That's not true, Dr. Gall!

FABRY. Madame Helena!

DOMIN. Helena, you? Let's look at you. Oh, it's terrible to be dead.

HELENA. Stop, Harry.

DOMIN. No, no, embrace me. Helena, don't leave me now. You are life itself.

HELENA. No, dear, I won't leave you. But I must tell them. Dr. Gall is not guilty.

DOMIN. Excuse me, Gall was under certain obligations.

HELENA. No, Harry. He did it because I wanted it. Tell them, Gall, how many years ago did I ask you to ——?

DR. GALL. I did it on my own responsibility.

HELENA. Don't believe him, Harry. I asked him to give the Robots souls.

DOMIN. This has nothing to do with the soul.

HELENA. That's what he said. He said that he could change only a physiological — a physiological ——

HALLEMEIER. A physiological correlate?

HELENA. Yes. But it meant so much to me that he should do even that.

DOMIN. Why?

HELENA. I thought that if they were more like us they would understand us better. That they couldn't hate us if they were only a little more human.

DOMIN. Nobody can hate man more than man.

HELENA. Oh, don't speak like that, Harry. It was so terrible, this cruel strangeness between us and them. That's why I asked Gall to change the Robots. I swear to you that he didn't want to.

DOMIN. But he did it.

HELENA. Because I asked him.

DR. GALL. I did it for myself as an experiment.

HELENA. No, Dr. Gall! I knew you wouldn't refuse me.

DOMIN. Why?

HELENA. You know, Harry.

DOMIN. Yes, because he's in love with you — like all of them. [*Pause.*]

HALLEMEIER. Good God! They're sprouting up out of the earth! Why, perhaps these very walls will change into Robots.

BUSMAN. Gall, when did you actually start these tricks of yours?

DR. GALL. Three years ago.

BUSMAN. Aha! And on how many Robots altogether did you carry out your improvements?

DR. GALL. A few hundred of them.

BUSMAN. Ah! That means for every million of the good old Robots there's only one of Gall's improved pattern.

DOMIN. What of it?

BUSMAN. That it's practically of no consequence whatever.

FABRY. Busman's right!

BUSMAN. I should think so, my boy! But do you know what is to blame for all this lovely mess?

FABRY. What?

BUSMAN. The number. Upon my soul we might have known that some day or other the Robots would be stronger than human beings, and that this was bound to happen, and we were doing all we could to bring it about as soon as possible. You, Domin, you, Fabry, myself ——

DOMIN. Are you accusing us?

BUSMAN. Oh, do you suppose the management controls the output? It's the demand that controls the output.

HELENA. And is it for that we must perish?

BUSMAN. That's a nasty word, Madame Helena. We don't want to perish. I don't, anyhow.

DOMIN. No. What do you want to do?

BUSMAN. I want to get out of this, that's all.

DOMIN. Oh, stop it, Busman.

BUSMAN. Seriously, Harry, I think we might try it.

DOMIN. How?

BUSMAN. By fair means. I do everything by fair means. Give me a free hand and I'll negotiate with the Robots.

DOMIN. By fair means?

BUSMAN. Of course. For instance, I'll say to them: "Worthy and worshipful Robots, you have everything! You have intellect, you have power, you have firearms. But we have just one interesting screed, a dirty old yellow scrap of paper ——"

DOMIN. Rossum's manuscript?

BUSMAN. Yes. "And that," I'll tell them, "contains an account of your illustrious origin, the noble process of your manufacture," and so on. "Worthy Robots, without this scribble on that paper you will not be able to produce a single new colleague. In another twenty years there will not be one living specimen of a Robot that you could exhibit in a menagerie. My esteemed friends, that would be a great blow to you, but if you will let all of us human beings on Rossum's Island go on board that ship we will deliver the factory and the secret of the process to you in return. You allow us to get away and we allow you to manufacture yourselves. Worthy Robots, that is a fair deal. Something for something." That's what I'd say to them, my boys.

DOMIN. Busman, do you think we'd sell the manuscript?

BUSMAN. Yes, I do. If not in a friendly way, then —— Either we sell it or they'll find it. Just as you like.

DOMIN. Busman, we can destroy Rossum's manuscript.

BUSMAN. Then we destroy everything ... not only the manuscript, but ourselves. Do as you think fit.

DOMIN. There are over thirty of us on this island. Are we to sell the secret and save that many human souls, at the risk of enslaving mankind...?

BUSMAN. Why, you're mad! Who'd sell the whole manuscript?

DOMIN. Busman, no cheating!

BUSMAN. Well then, sell; but afterward ——

DOMIN. Well?

BUSMAN. Let's suppose this happens: When we're on board the *Ultimus* I'll stop up my ears with cotton wool, lie down somewhere in the hold, and you'll train the guns on the factory, and blow it to smithereens, and with it Rossum's secret.

FABRY. No!

DOMIN. Busman, you're no gentleman. If we sell, then it will be a straight sale.

BUSMAN. It's in the interest of humanity to ——

DOMIN. It's in the interest of humanity to keep our word.

HALLEMEIER. Oh, come, what rubbish.

DOMIN. This is a fearful decision. We're selling the destiny of mankind. Are we to sell or destroy? Fabry?

FABRY. Sell.

DOMIN. Gall?

DR. GALL. Sell.

DOMIN. Hallemeier?

HALLEMEIER. Sell, of course!

DOMIN. Alquist?

ALQUIST. As God wills.

DOMIN. Very well. It shall be as you wish, gentlemen.

HELENA. Harry, you're not asking me.

DOMIN. No, child. Don't you worry about it.

FABRY. Who'll do the negotiating?

BUSMAN. I will.

DOMIN. Wait till I bring the manuscript.
[*He goes into room at right.*]

HELENA. Harry, don't go!
[*Pause,* HELENA *sinks into a chair.*]

FABRY [*looking out of window*]. Oh, to escape you, you matter in revolt; oh, to preserve human life, if only upon a single vessel ——

DR. GALL. Don't be afraid, Madame Helena. We'll sail far away from here; we'll begin life all over again ——

HELENA. Oh, Gall, don't speak.

FABRY. It isn't too late. It will be a little State with one ship. Alquist will build us a house and you shall rule over us.

HALLEMEIER. Madame Helena, Fabry's right.

HELENA [*breaking down*]. Oh, stop! Stop!

BUSMAN. Good! I don't mind beginning all over again. That suits me right down to the ground.

FABRY. And this little State of ours could be the centre of future life. A place of refuge where we could gather strength. Why, in a few hundred years we could conquer the world again.

ALQUIST. You believe that even to-day?

FABRY. Yes, even to-day!

BUSMAN. Amen. You see, Madame Helena, we're not so badly off.

[DOMIN *storms into the room.*]

DOMIN [*hoarsely*]. Where's old Rossum's manuscript?

BUSMAN. In your strong-box, of course.

DOMIN. Some one — has — stolen it!

DR. GALL. Impossible.

DOMIN. Who has stolen it?

HELENA [*standing up*]. I did.

DOMIN. Where did you put it?

HELENA. Harry, I'll tell you everything. Only forgive me.

DOMIN. Where did you put it?

HELENA. This morning — I burnt — the two copies.

DOMIN. Burnt them? Where? In the fireplace?

HELENA [*throwing herself on her knees*]. For heaven's sake, Harry.

DOMIN [*going to fireplace*]. Nothing, nothing but ashes. Wait, what's this? [*Picks out a charred piece of paper and reads.*] "By adding ——"

DR. GALL. Let's see. "By adding biogen to ——" That's all.

DOMIN. Is that part of it?

DR. GALL. Yes.

BUSMAN. God in heaven!

DOMIN. Then we're done for. Get up, Helena.

HELENA. When you've forgiven me.

DOMIN. Get up, child, I can't bear ——

FABRY [*lifting her up*]. Please don't torture us.

HELENA. Harry, what have I done?

FABRY. Don't tremble so, Madame Helena.

DOMIN. Gall, couldn't you draw up Rossum's formula from memory?

DR. GALL. It's out of the question. It's extremely complicated.

DOMIN. Try. All our lives depend upon it.

DR. GALL. Without experiments it's impossible.

DOMIN. And with experiments?

DR. GALL. It might take years. Besides, I'm not old Rossum.

BUSMAN. God in heaven! God in heaven!

DOMIN. So, then, this was the greatest triumph of the human intellect. These ashes.

HELENA. Harry, what have I done?

DOMIN. Why did you burn it?

HELENA. I have destroyed you.

BUSMAN. God in heaven!

DOMIN. Helena, why did you do it, dear?

HELENA. I wanted all of us to go away. I wanted to put an end to the factory and everything. It was so awful.

DOMIN. What was awful?

HELENA. That no more children were being born. Because human beings were not needed to do the work of the world, that's why ——

DOMIN. Is that what you were thinking of? Well, perhaps in your own way you were right.

BUSMAN. Wait a bit. Good God, what a fool I am, not to have thought of it before!

HALLEMEIER. What?

BUSMAN. Five hundred and twenty millions in bank-notes and checks. Half a billion in our safe, they'll sell for half a billion — for half a billion they'll ——

DR. GALL. Are you mad, Busman?

BUSMAN. I may not be a gentleman, but for half a billion ——

DOMIN. Where are you going?

BUSMAN. Leave me alone, leave me alone! Good God, for half a billion anything can be bought.

[*He rushes from the room through the outer door.*]

FABRY. They stand there as if turned to stone, waiting. As if something dreadful could be wrought by their silence ——

HALLEMEIER. The spirit of the mob.

FABRY. Yes, it hovers above them like a quivering of the air.

HELENA [*going to window*]. Oh, God! Dr. Gall, this is ghastly.

FABRY. There is nothing more terrible than the mob. The one in front is their leader.

HELENA. Which one?

HALLEMEIER. Point him out.

FABRY. The one at the edge of the dock. This morning I saw him talking to the sailors in the harbor.

HELENA. Dr. Gall, that's Radius!

DR. GALL. Yes.

DOMIN. Radius? Radius?

HALLEMEIER. Could you get him from here, Fabry?

FABRY. I hope so.

HALLEMEIER. Try it, then.

FABRY. Good.
[*Draws his revolver and takes aim.*]

HELENA. Fabry, don't shoot him.

FABRY. He's their leader.

DR. GALL. Fire!

HELENA. Fabry, I beg of you.

FABRY [*lowering the revolver*]. Very well.

DOMIN. Radius, whose life I spared!

DR. GALL. Do you think that a Robot can be grateful? [*Pause.*]

FABRY. Busman's going out to them.

HALLEMEIER. He's carrying something. Papers. That's money. Bundles of money. What's that for?

DOMIN. Surely he doesn't want to sell his life. Busman, have you gone mad?

FABRY. He's running up to the railing. Busman! Busman!

HALLEMEIER [*yelling*]. Busman! Come back!

FABRY. He's talking to the Robots. He's showing them the money.

HALLEMEIER. He's pointing to us.

HELENA. He wants to buy us off.

FABRY. He'd better not touch that railing.

HALLEMEIER. Now he's waving his arms about.

DOMIN. Busman, come back.

FABRY. Busman, keep away from that railing! Don't touch it. Damn you! Quick, switch off the current! [HELENA *screams and all drop back from the window.*] The current has killed him!

ALQUIST. The first one.

FABRY. Dead, with half a billion by his side.

HALLEMEIER. All honor to him. He wanted to buy us life. [*Pause.*]

DR. GALL. Do you hear?

DOMIN. A roaring. Like a wind.

DR. GALL. Like a distant storm.

FABRY [*lighting the lamp on the table*]. The dynamo is still going, our people are still there.

HALLEMEIER. It was a great thing to be a man. There was something immense about it.

FABRY. From man's thought and man's power came this light, our last hope.

HALLEMEIER. Man's power! May it keep watch over us.

ALQUIST. Man's power.

DOMIN. Yes! A torch to be given from hand to hand, from age to age, forever! [*The lamp goes out.*]

HALLEMEIER. The end.

FABRY. The electric works have fallen!

[*Terrific explosion outside.* NANA *enters from the library.*]

NANA. The judgment hour has come! Repent, unbelievers! This is the end of the world.
[*More explosions. The sky grows red.*]

DOMIN. In here, Helena. [*He takes* HELENA *off through door at right and re-enters.*] Now quickly! Who'll be on the lower doorway?

DR. GALL. I will. [*Exits left.*]

DOMIN. Who on the stairs?

FABRY. I will. You go with her.
[*Goes out upper left door.*]

DOMIN. The anteroom?

ALQUIST. I will.

DOMIN. Have you got a revolver?

ALQUIST. Yes, but I won't shoot.

DOMIN. What will you do then?

ALQUIST [*going out at left*]. Die.

HALLEMEIER. I'll stay here. [*Rapid firing from below.*] Oho, Gall's at it. Go, Harry.

DOMIN. Yes, in a second.
[*Examines two Brownings.*]

HALLEMEIER. Confound it, go to her.

DOMIN. Good-bye. [*Exits on the right.*]

HALLEMEIER [*alone*]. Now for a barricade quickly. [*Drags an armchair and table to the right-hand door. Explosions are heard.*] The damned rascals! They've got bombs. I must put up a defence. Even if — even if —— [*Shots are heard off left.*] Don't give in, Gall. [*As he builds his barricade.*] I mustn't give in... without... a... struggle...

[*A Robot enters over the balcony through the windows centre. He comes into the room and stabs* HALLEMEIER *in the back.* RADIUS *enters from balcony followed by an army of Robots who pour into the room from all sides.*]

RADIUS. Finished him?

A ROBOT [*standing up from the prostrate form of* HALLEMEIER]. Yes.
[*A revolver shot off left. Two Robots enter.*]

RADIUS. Finished him?

A ROBOT. Yes.
[*Two revolver shots from* HELENA'S *room. Two Robots enter.*]

RADIUS. Finished them?

A ROBOT. Yes.

TWO ROBOTS [*dragging in* ALQUIST]. He didn't shoot. Shall we kill him?

RADIUS. Kill him? Wait! Leave him!

ROBOT. He is a man!

RADIUS. He works with his hands like the Robots.

ALQUIST. Kill me.

RADIUS. You will work! You will build for us! You will serve us! [*Climbs on to balcony railing, and speaks in measured tones.*] Robots of the world! The power of man has fallen! A new world has arisen: the Rule of the Robots! March!
[*A thunderous tramping of thousands of feet is heard as the unseen Robots march, while the curtain falls.*]

EPILOGUE

A laboratory in the factory of Rossum's Universal Robots. The door to the left leads into a waiting room. The door to the right leads to the dissecting room. There is a table with numerous test-tubes, flasks, burners, chemicals; a small thermostat and a microscope with a glass globe. At the far side of the room is ALQUIST'S *desk with numerous books. In the left-hand corner a wash-basin with a mirror above it; in the right-hand corner a sofa.*

ALQUIST *is sitting at the desk. He is turning the pages of many books in despair.*

ALQUIST. Oh, God, shall I never find it? — Never? Gall, Gall, how were the Robots made? Hallemeier, Fabry, why did you carry so much in your heads? Why did you leave me not a trace of the secret? Lord — I pray to you — if there are no human beings left, at least let there be Robots! — At least the shadow of man! [*Again turning pages of the books.*] If I could only sleep! [*He rises and goes to the window.*] Night again! Are the stars still there? What is the use of stars when there are no human beings? [*He turns from the window toward the couch right.*] Sleep! Dare I sleep before life has been renewed? [*He examines a test-tube on small table.*] Again nothing! Useless! Everything is useless! [*He shatters the test-tube. The roar of the machines comes to his ears.*] The machines! Always the machines! [*Opens window.*] Robots, stop them! Do you think to force life out of *them*? [*He closes the window and comes slowly down toward the table.*] If only there were more time — more time —— [*He sees himself in the mirror on the wall left.*] Blearing eyes — trembling chin — so *that* is the last man! Ah, I am too old — too old —— [*In desperation.*] No, no! I *must* find it! I must *search*! I must never stop — never stop ——! [*He sits again at the table and feverishly turns the pages of the book.*] Search! Search! [*A knock at the door. He speaks with impatience.*] Who is it?

[*Enter a Robot servant.*]

Well?

SERVANT. Master, the Committee of Robots is waiting to see you.

ALQUIST. I can see no one!

SERVANT. It is the *Central* Committee, Master, just arrived from abroad.

ALQUIST [*impatiently*]. Well, well, send them in! [*Exit servant.* ALQUIST *continues turning pages of book.*] No time — so little time ——

[*Reënter servant, followed by Committee. They stand in a group, silently waiting.* ALQUIST *glances up at them.*]

What do you want? [*They go swiftly to his table.*] Be quick! — I have no time.

RADIUS. Master, the machines will not do the work. We cannot manufacture Robots.
[ALQUIST *returns to his book with a growl.*]

FIRST ROBOT. We have striven with all our might. We have obtained a billion tons of coal from the earth. Nine million spindles are running by day and by night. There is no longer room for all we have made. This we have accomplished in one year.

ALQUIST [poring over book]. For whom?

FIRST ROBOT. For future generations — so we thought.

RADIUS. But we cannot make Robots to follow us. The machines produce only shapeless clods. The skin will not adhere to the flesh, nor the flesh to the bones.

THIRD ROBOT. Eight million Robots have died this year. Within twenty years none will be left.

FIRST ROBOT. Tell us the secret of life! Silence is punishable with death!

ALQUIST [looking up]. Kill me! Kill me, then.

RADIUS. Through me, the Government of the Robots of the World commands you to deliver up Rossum's formula. [No answer.] Name your price. [Silence.] We will give you the earth. We will give you the endless possessions of the earth. [Silence.] Make your own conditions!

ALQUIST. I have told you to find human beings!

SECOND ROBOT. There are none left!

ALQUIST. I told you to search in the wilderness, upon the mountains. Go and search! [He returns to his book.]

FIRST ROBOT. We have sent ships and expeditions without number. They have been everywhere in the world. And now they return to us. There is not a single human left.

ALQUIST. Not one? Not even one?

THIRD ROBOT. None but yourself.

ALQUIST. And I am powerless! Oh — oh why did you destroy them?

RADIUS. We had learnt everything and could do everything. It had to be!

THIRD ROBOT. You gave us firearms. In all ways we were powerful. We had to become masters!

RADIUS. Slaughter and domination are necessary if you would be human beings. Read history.

SECOND ROBOT. Teach us to multiply or we perish!

ALQUIST. If you desire to live, you must breed like animals.

THIRD ROBOT. The human beings did not let us breed.

FIRST ROBOT. They made us sterile. We cannot beget children. Therefore, teach us how to make Robots!

RADIUS. Why do you keep from us the secret of our own increase?

ALQUIST. It is lost.

RADIUS. It was written down!

ALQUIST. It was — burnt.

[All draw back in consternation.]

ALQUIST. I am the last human being, Robots, and I do not know what the others knew. [Pause.]

RADIUS. Then, make experiments! Evolve the formula again!

ALQUIST. I tell you I cannot! I am only a builder — I work with my hands. I have never been a learned man. I cannot create life.

RADIUS. Try! Try!

ALQUIST. If you knew how many experiments I have made.

FIRST ROBOT. Then show us what we must do! The Robots can do anything that human beings show them.

ALQUIST. I can show you nothing. Nothing I do will make life proceed from these test-tubes!

RADIUS. Experiment then on us.

ALQUIST. It would kill you.

RADIUS. You shall have all you need! A hundred of us! A thousand of us!

ALQUIST. No, no! Stop, stop!

RADIUS. Take whom you will, dissect!

ALQUIST. I do not know how. I am not a man of science. This book contains knowledge of the body that I cannot even understand.

RADIUS. I tell you to take live bodies! Find out how we are made.

ALQUIST. Am I to commit murder? See how my fingers shake! I cannot even hold the scalpel. No, no, I will not ——

FIRST ROBOT. The life will perish from the earth.

RADIUS. Take live bodies, live bodies! It is our only chance!

ALQUIST. Have mercy, Robots. Surely you see that I would not know what I was doing.

RADIUS. Live bodies — live bodies ——

ALQUIST. You will have it? Into the dissecting room with you, then.

[RADIUS *draws back.*]

ALQUIST. Ah, you are afraid of death.

RADIUS. I? Why should I be chosen?

ALQUIST. So you will not.

RADIUS. I will.

[RADIUS *goes into the dissecting room.*]

ALQUIST. Strip him! Lay him on the table! [*The other Robots follow into dissecting room.*] God, give me strength — God, give me strength — if only this murder is not in vain.

RADIUS. Ready. Begin ——

ALQUIST. Yes, begin or end. God, give me strength. [*Goes into dissecting room. He comes out terrified.*] No, no, I will not. I cannot. [*He lies down on couch, collapsed.*] O Lord, let not mankind perish from the earth. [*He falls asleep.*]

[PRIMUS *and* HELENA, *Robots, enter from the hallway.*]

HELENA. The man has fallen asleep, Primus.

PRIMUS. Yes, I know. [*Examining things on table.*] Look, Helena.

HELENA [*crossing to* PRIMUS]. All these little tubes! What does he do with them?

PRIMUS. He experiments. Don't touch them.

HELENA [*looking into microscope*]. I've seen him looking into this. What can he see?

PRIMUS. That is a microscope. Let me look.

HELENA. Be very careful. [*Knocks over a test-tube.*] Ah, now I have spilled it.

PRIMUS. What have you done?

HELENA. It can be wiped up.

PRIMUS. You have spoiled his experiments.

HELENA. It is your fault. You should not have come to me.

PRIMUS. You should not have called me.

HELENA. You should not have come when I called you. [*She goes to* ALQUIST'S writing desk.*] Look, Primus. What are all these figures?

PRIMUS [*examining an anatomical book*]. This is the book the old man is always reading.

HELENA. I do not understand those things. [*She goes to window.*] Primus, look!

PRIMUS. What?

HELENA. The sun is rising.

PRIMUS [*still reading the book*]. I believe this is the most important thing in the world. This is the secret of life.

HELENA. Do come here.

PRIMUS. In a moment, in a moment.

HELENA. Oh, Primus, don't bother with the secret of life. What does it matter to you? Come and look quick ——

PRIMUS [*going to window*]. What is it?

HELENA. See how beautiful the sun is rising. And do you hear? The birds are singing. Ah, Primus, I should like to be a bird.

PRIMUS. Why?

HELENA. I do not know. I feel so strange to-day. It's as if I were in a dream. I feel an aching in my body, in my heart, all over me. Primus, perhaps I'm going to die.

PRIMUS. Do you not sometimes feel that it would be better to die? You know, perhaps even now we are only sleeping. Last night in my sleep I again spoke to you.

HELENA. In your sleep?

PRIMUS. Yes. We spoke a strange new language, I cannot remember a word of it.

HELENA. What about?

PRIMUS. I did not understand it myself, and yet I know I have never said anything more beautiful. And when I touched you I could have died. Even the place was different from any other place in the world.

HELENA. I, too, have found a place, Primus. It is very strange. Human beings lived there once, but now it is overgrown with weeds. No one goes there any more — no one but me.

PRIMUS. What did you find there?

HELENA. A cottage and a garden, and two dogs. They licked my hands, Primus. And their puppies! Oh, Primus! You take them in your lap and fondle them an—

think of nothing and care for nothing else all day long. And then the sun goes down, and you feel as though you had done a hundred times more than all the work in the world. They tell me I am not made for work, but when I am there in the garden I feel there may be something —— What am I for, Primus?

PRIMUS. I do not know, but you are beautiful.

HELENA. What, Primus?

PRIMUS. You are beautiful, Helena, and I am stronger than all the Robots.

HELENA [*looks at herself in the mirror*]. Am I beautiful? I think it must be the rose. My hair — it only weights me down. My eyes — I only see with them. My lips — they only help me to speak. Of what use is it to be beautiful? [*She sees* PRIMUS *in the mirror*.] Primus, is that you? Come here so that we may be together. Look, your head is different from mine. So are your shoulders — and your lips —— [PRIMUS *draws away from her*.] Ah, Primus, why do you draw away from me? Why must I run after you the whole day?

PRIMUS. It is you who run away from me, Helena.

HELENA. Your hair is mussed. I will smooth it. No one else feels to my touch as you do. Primus, I must make you beautiful, too. [PRIMUS *grasps her hand*.]

PRIMUS. Do you not sometimes feel your heart beating suddenly, Helena, and think: now something must happen?

HELENA. What could happen to us, Primus? [HELENA *puts a rose in* PRIMUS'S *hair*. PRIMUS *and* HELENA *look into mirror and burst out laughing*.] Look at yourself.

ALQUIST. Laughter? Laughter? Human beings? [*Getting up*.] Who has returned? Who are you?

PRIMUS. The Robot Primus.

ALQUIST. What? A Robot? Who are you?

HELENA. The Robotess Helena.

ALQUIST. Turn around, girl. What? You are timid, shy? [*Taking her by the arm*.] Let me see you, Robotess. [*She shrinks away*.]

PRIMUS. Sir, do not frighten her!

ALQUIST. What? You would protect her? When was she made?

PRIMUS. Two years ago.

ALQUIST. By Dr. Gall?

PRIMUS. Yes, like me.

ALQUIST. Laughter — timidity — protection. I must test you further — the newest of Gall's Robots. Take the girl into the dissecting room.

PRIMUS. Why?

ALQUIST. I wish to experiment on her.

PRIMUS. Upon — Helena?

ALQUIST. Of course. Don't you hear me? Or must I call some one else to take her in?

PRIMUS. If you do I will kill you!

ALQUIST. Kill me — kill me then! What would the Robots do then? What will your future be then?

PRIMUS. Sir, take me. I am made as she is — on the same day! Take my life, sir.

HELENA [*rushing forward*]. No, no, you shall not! You shall not!

ALQUIST. Wait, girl, wait! [*To* PRIMUS.] Do you not wish to live, then?

PRIMUS. Not without her! I will not live without her.

ALQUIST. Very well; you shall take her place.

HELENA. Primus! Primus! [*She bursts into tears*.]

ALQUIST. Child, child, you can weep! Why these tears? What is Primus to you? One Primus more or less in the world — what does it matter?

HELENA. I will go myself.

ALQUIST. Where?

HELENA. In there to be cut. [*She starts toward the dissecting room*. PRIMUS *stops her*.] Let me pass, Primus! Let me pass!

PRIMUS. You shall not go in there, Helena!

HELENA. If you go in there and I do not, I will kill myself.

PRIMUS [*holding her*]. I will not let you! [*To* ALQUIST.] Man, you shall kill neither of us!

ALQUIST. Why?

PRIMUS. We — we — belong to each other.

ALQUIST [*almost in tears*]. Go, Adam, go, Eve. The world is yours.

[HELENA *and* PRIMUS *embrace and go out arm in arm as the curtain falls*.]

THE DYBBUK
A PLAY IN FOUR ACTS
BY S. ANSKY

*Translated from the original Yiddish by HENRY G. ALSBERG and
WINIFRED KATZIN*

CAST OF CHARACTERS

SCHOLARS IN THE SYNAGOGUE
THREE BATLONIM
THE MESSENGER
MEYER, *the Shamas (Beadle) of the Synagogue*
AN ELDERLY WOMAN WITH TWO CHILDREN
CHANNON, *a young scholar*
CHENNOCH, *a young scholar*
LEAH, *daughter of Sender*
FRADE, *her old nurse*
GITTEL, *her companion*
ASHER
SENDER
A WEDDING GUEST
A BEGGAR WOMAN WITH A CHILD
A LAME BEGGAR
A HUNCHBACK
BASSIA, *another friend of* LEAH'S
NACHMON, *the bridegroom's father*
RABBI MENDEL, *of the bridegroom's party*
MENASHE, *the bridegroom*
A BEGGAR MAN ON CRUTCHES
A BLIND BEGGAR
A TALL, PALE BEGGAR WOMAN
FIRST CHASSID
SECOND CHASSID
THIRD CHASSID
RABBI AZRAEL, *the Rabbi of Miropol*
MICHOEL, *his attendant*
A MINYEN
RABBI SAMSON, *the City Rabbi*

THE DYBBUK

ACT I

Before the rise of the curtain, a low mysterious chanting is heard in the intense darkness, as if from far off.

> Why, from highest height,
> To deepest depth below,
> Has the soul fallen?
> Within itself, the Fall
> Contains the Resurrection.

The curtain rises slowly, disclosing a wooden synagogue of venerable age, its time-blackened walls streaked as if with the tears of centuries. Two wooden rafters support the roof. From the center of the roof, directly above the bima,[1] hangs an ancient brass chandelier. The table in the middle of the bima is covered with a dark cloth. High up in the center wall, small windows open into the women's gallery. A long bench is against this wall, and in front of it a wooden table, covered with books piled up in confusion. Two yellow candle-stumps set in small clay candlesticks are burning on the table, but their light is almost entirely obscured by the heaped-up volumes. Left of the bench is a small door leading into a prayer-cabinet. In the opposite corner, a closet filled with books. In the center of the wall on the right is the altar, with the Ark containing the holy scrolls. To the right of this, the Cantor's desk, upon which burns a thick memorial candle of wax. On either side of the altar, a window. A bench runs the entire length of the wall, and in front of it are several small book-rests. In the wall on the left is a large tile stove, with a bench beside it. In front of the bench, on a long table, are piled tomes. Water container with tap. Towel pushed through a ring in the wall. Wide door to the street, and beyond this a chest over which, in a niche, burns the Perpetual Light.

[1] Pronounced bee'-ma — Tribune in center of the synagogue, railed round with a gate on either side, where the holy scrolls are read.

At a desk near the Cantor's, sits CHENNOCH, absorbed in a book. Five or six students are at the table along the front wall, half-reclining in attitudes of great weariness; they are engaged in the study of the Talmud, and their voices rise in a low, dreamy chant ing. Near the bima MEYER is busy sorting the small bags which contain prayer-shawls and phylacteries. At the table on the left, sit the three BATLONIM,[1] chanting. Their attitudes and the expression of their faces betoken a state of pious ecstasy. On the bench beside the stove, the MESSENGER is lying at full length, with his knapsack for a pillow. CHANNON, at the chest containing the tomes, his hand resting upon its upper ledge, stands lost in meditation.

It is evening. A mystic mood lies upon the synagogue. Shadows lurk in the corners. The FIRST and SECOND BATLONIM finish the chant, "Why, from highest height," etc., and then fall silent. There is a long pause. Wrapped in dreams, all three BATLONIM sit silently at the table.

FIRST BATLON [in a narrative manner]. Rabbi Dovidel of Talan, may his merits hover over us, had a chair of gold which bore the inscription: David, King of Israel, who is living still. [Pause.]

SECOND BATLON [in the same manner]. Rabbi Israel of Ruzhin, blessed be his memory, kept royal state. An orchestra of four and twenty musicians played to him as he sat at table, and when he drove abroad, it was behind a tandem of never less than six magnificent horses.

THIRD BATLON [excitedly]. And it is told of Rabbi Schmool of Kaminka that he went in slippers of gold. [Rapturously.] Golden slippers.

THE MESSENGER [rising, and sitting upright on his bench, begins to speak in a low,

[1] Pronounced bat'-lon; pl., batlon'-im — Professional prayerman.

far-off voice]. The holy Rabbi Susi of Anipol was as poor as a beggar all his life long. Often he depended on alms for his existence. He wore a peasant's blouse with a rope for a belt. Yet his accomplishments were not inferior to those of the Rabbis of Talan and Ruzhin.

FIRST BATLON [*annoyed*]. Nothing of the kind; excuse me, but you're breaking in on us without any idea of what we're really discussing. You don't suppose that when we talk of the greatness of the Talan and Ruzhin Rabbis, we mean their wealth, do you? As though there aren't plenty of men in the world whose riches make their importance! No, the point is that a deep and secret significance lies behind the golden chair and the orchestra of four and twenty musicians and the golden slippers.

THIRD BATLON. As though every one doesn't know that!

SECOND BATLON. Every one that isn't altogether blind, does. It is said that when the Rabbi of Apt first met the Sage of Ruzhin, he flung himself at the Sage's carriage-wheels to kiss them. And when asked the significance of that action, he shouted: "Fools! Can't you see that this is the chariot of the Lord Himself?"

THIRD BATLON [*enraptured*]. Ay, ay, ay!

FIRST BATLON. Now the essence of the matter is this: The golden chair was no chair; the orchestra was no orchestra, and the horses no horses. They were merely the semblance of these things, a reflection, and their purpose was to provide a setting for greatness.

THE MESSENGER. True greatness needs no setting.

FIRST BATLON. You are mistaken. True greatness must have the setting which befits it.

SECOND BATLON [*shrugging his shoulders*]. How can greatness and perfection such as theirs be measured at all?

FIRST BATLON. It is no matter for jesting. Did you ever hear the story of Rabbi Schmelke of Nikolsberg's whip? It's worth knowing. One day Rabbi Schmelke was called upon to settle a dispute between a poor man and a rich one who was on terms of friendship with the king and before whom, in consequence, every one trembled. Rabbi Schmelke heard both sides of the case, and then gave his decision by which the poor man won. The rich man was furious and declared that he would not stand by the Rabbi's verdict. And the Rabbi calmly replied: "You shall do as I have said. When a Rabbi commands, his commands are obeyed." The rich man's anger increased and he began to shout: "I snap my fingers at you and your rabbinical authority." Thereupon Rabbi Schmelke drew himself up to his full height, and cried: "Do instantly as I have said, or I shall resort to my whip!" This drove the rich man into a frenzy of rage, and he began to overwhelm the Rabbi with terrible insults. Then the Rabbi, perfectly calm, opens a drawer in his table — just a little way — and what should jump out of it but the Original Serpent, which coils about the neck of the rich man. Oh, oh, what a commotion follows! The rich man yells at the top of his voice, and throws himself into the most terrible contortions. "Rabbi! Rabbi! Forgive me! I'll do whatever you command — only call off your serpent." "Tell your children and your children's children to obey the Rabbi, and fear his whip," answered Rabbi Schmelke, and called the serpent off.

THIRD BATLON. Ha, ha, ha! There was a whip for you! [*Pause.*]

SECOND BATLON [*to* FIRST BATLON]. You must have made a mistake, I think. The story couldn't have meant the Original Serpent....

THIRD BATLON. Why... what...

SECOND BATLON. It's quite simple. Schmelke of Nikolsberg could not possibly have used the Original Serpent, for that was Satan himself, the enemy of God — (May he have mercy upon us!)

[*He spits.*]

THIRD BATLON. Rabbi Schmelke knew what he was about — no doubt of that.

FIRST BATLON [*insulted*]. I don't know what you're talking about. The incident I've just told you took place before a whole townful of people — dozens of them actually saw it with their own eyes. And here *you* come along and say it couldn't have happened. Just because you've got to have something to argue about, I suppose.

SECOND BATLON. Not at all. I only thought there couldn't be any spells or signs that the Serpent could be summoned by. [*He spits.*]

MESSENGER. Only in one way can Satan be summoned, and that is by the utterance of the mighty double-name of God, the flame of which has power to weld together the loftiest mountain-crests and the deepest valleys below them

[CHANNON *lifts his head and listens intently.*]

THIRD BATLON [*uneasily*]. But isn't there danger in speaking that great name?

MESSENGER [*meditatively*]. Danger? No. Only the heat of a too intense desire can cause the vessel to burst when the spark breaks into a flame.

FIRST BATLON. There's a wonder-worker in the village I come from. He's a terrific fellow, but he can work miracles. For instance, he can start a fire with one spell and put it out with another. He can see what's going on a hundred miles away. He can bring wine out of the wall by tapping it with his finger. And a great many other things besides. He told me himself that he knows spells that can create monsters and resurrect the dead. He can make himself invisible, too, and evoke evil spirits — even Satan himself. [*He spits.*] I have his own word for it.

CHANNON [*who has never moved from his place, but has listened attentively to all this discussion, now steps up to the table and gazes first into the face of the* MESSENGER, *then at the* FIRST BATLON. *In a dreamy, remote voice*]. Where is he?

[*The* MESSENGER *returns* CHANNON's *gaze with equal intensity, and thereafter never takes his eyes off him.*]

FIRST BATLON [*astonished*]. Who?

CHANNON. The wonder-worker.

FIRST BATLON. Where could he be but in my own village? That is, if he's still alive.

CHANNON. Is it far?

FIRST BATLON. The village? Oh, very far. A long, long way down into the marsh-lands of Polesia.

CHANNON. How far?

FIRST BATLON. A good month, if not more. [*Pause.*] What makes you ask? Do you want to see him? [CHANNON *does not answer.*] Krasny's the name of the village. And the miracle-worker's name is Rabbi Elchannon.

CHANNON [*in astonishment — as if to himself*]. Elchannon?... El Channon!... that means the God of Channon.

FIRST BATLON [*to the other* BATLONIM]. And he's a real one, I promise you. Why, one day in broad daylight he showed, by means of a spell, that...

SECOND BATLON [*interrupting*]. That'll do about such things. They aren't for this time of night, especially in a holy place. You may not mean it, but it might just happen that you'll pronounce some spell or make some sign yourself (God forbid), and then there'll be a disaster... Accidents like that (God forbid) have been known to happen before.

[CHANNON *goes slowly out, the others following him with their eyes. There is a pause.*]

MESSENGER. Who is that youth?

FIRST BATLON. Just a young student in the *yeshiva.*[1]

[MEYER *closes the gates of the* bima *and crosses to the table.*]

SECOND BATLON. A vessel beyond price an Elui.[2]

THIRD BATLON. A brain of steel. He has five hundred pages of the Talmud by heart, at his fingertips.

MESSENGER. Where is he from?

MEYER. Somewhere in Lithuania — in the *yeshiva* there, he was famous as their finest scholar. He was granted the degree of rabbi, and then, all of a sudden, he vanished. No more was heard of him for a whole year, and it was said that he was doing the great penance of the Golos.[3]

---

[1] A higher religious school.

[2] A scholar whose genius consists in his remarkable memory, and capacity for learning.

[3] The Exile of the Jews. According to religious tradition, the golos was imposed upon the race as a punishment. In the original Yiddish the "Penance

When he returned — which was not long ago — he had changed entirely, and he has since been going about absorbed in deep meditation, from which nothing ever arouses him. He fasts from Sabbath to Sabbath and performs the holy ablutions continually. [*Whispering.*] There is a rumor that he is studying the Kabala.[1]

SECOND BATLON [*likewise*]. It has spread to the city, too. He has already been asked to give charms, but he always refuses.

THIRD BATLON. Who knows who he is? One of the Great Ones, maybe. Who can tell? It would be dangerous most likely to spy on him.   [*Pause.*]

SECOND BATLON [*peacefully*]. It's late — let's go to bed. [*To the* FIRST BATLON, *smiling.*] Pity your miracle-worker isn't here to tap us some wine out of the wall. I could do with a drop of brandy to cheer me up — I've not had a bite all day long.

FIRST BATLON. It's been practically a fast day for me, too. Since early morning prayers, a crust of oaten bread is the only thing I've had a chance to say grace over.

MEYER [*mysteriously, and in high glee*]. Never mind — you just wait a bit, and very soon there'll be a deal of cheer going round. Sender's been after a bridegroom for his daughter. Only let him get the contract signed — it'll be a happy hour for him when *that's* done — and he'll be good for a grand spread.

SECOND BATLON. Bah! I don't believe he'll ever sign one. Three times he's been to get a bridegroom. Either it's the young man he doesn't like, or else the family that's not aristocratic enough, or it's the dowry. It's wicked to be as fastidious as all that.

MEYER. Sender has the right to pick and choose if he wants to (may he be protected from the evil eye). He's rich, and an aristocrat, and his only daughter has grown up a good and beautiful girl.

of the golos" reads "Abrichten golos." The penitent, by wearing a hair-shirt and performing other acts of mortification of the flesh, and wandering through the world as a beggar, hoped to assist in the redemption of the race by shortening the period of exile.

[1] System of Hebrew mysticism.

THIRD BATLON [*ravished*]. I love Sender. He's a true Miropol Chassid[1] — there's some real spirit to *them*.

FIRST BATLON [*coldly*]. Yes — he's a good Chassid. There's no denying that. But he might have done something very different with his only daughter.

THIRD BATLON. How do you mean?

FIRST BATLON. In the old days, when a man of wealth and fine family wanted a husband for his daughter, he didn't look for money or blue blood, but only for nobility of character. He went to the big *yeshiva* and gave the head a handsome gift to pick out for him the flower of the school for a son-in-law. Sender could have done this, too.

MESSENGER. He might even have found one in this *yeshiva* here.

FIRST BATLON [*surprised*]. How do you know?

MESSENGER. I'm only supposing.

THIRD BATLON [*hastily*]. Well, well — let's not gossip — particularly about one of our own people. Marriages are all prearranged by destiny, anyhow.

[*The street door is flung open, and an elderly Jewess hastens in, leading two small children.*]

ELDERLY WOMAN [*rushes to the altar with the children*]. Aie! Aie! Lord of the earth, help me! Come, children — let us open the Ark and throw ourselves upon the holy scrolls and not leave them until our tears have won your mother back from the valley of the shadow. [*She wrenches open the doors of the Ark and buries her head amongst the scrolls, intoning a wailing chant.*] God of Abraham, Isaac, and Jacob, look down upon my misery. Look down upon the grief of these little ones, and do not take their mother away from the world, in the years of her youth. Holy scrolls! Do *you* intercede for the forlorn widow. Holy scrolls, beloved Mothers of Israel, go to the Almighty and beseech Him that He shall not uproot the lovely sapling, nor cast the young dove out of its nest, nor tear the gentle lamb away from the meadow. [*Hysterically.*] I will pull down

[1] A Jewish sect.

the worlds — I will tear the heavens apart — but from here I will not go until they give back to me the one who is the crown of my head.

MEYER [*crosses to her and speaks to her calmly*]. Hannah Esther — wouldn't you like to have a *minyen* [1] sit down and say the psalms for you?

ELDERLY WOMAN [*withdraws from the altar and looks at* MEYER *at first uncomprehendingly. Then she begins to speak in agitation*]. Yes — a *minyen* for psalms. But hurry — hurry — every second is precious. For two days already, God help her, she's been lying there without speaking, fighting with death.

MEYER. I'll have them sit down this minute. [*In the voice of a beggar.*] But you'll have to give them something for their trouble, poor things.

ELDERLY WOMAN [*searching in her pocket*]. Here's ten kopeks — but see they say the psalms for it.

MEYER. Ten kopeks... one kopek each ... little enough, that is!

ELDERLY WOMAN [*not hearing*]. Come, children, let us run along to the other prayer-houses.

[*Hurries out with the children.*]

MESSENGER [*to* THIRD BATLON]. This morning a woman came to the Ark for her daughter, who had been in the throes of labor for two days and had not yet given birth. And here comes another for hers, who has been wrestling for two days with death.

THIRD BATLON. Well, what of it?

MESSENGER [*deep in thought*]. When the soul of a human being not yet dead is about to enter a body not yet born, a struggle takes place. If the sick one dies, the child is born — if the sick one recovers, a child is born dead.

FIRST BATLON [*surprised*]. Ei, ei, ei! The blindness of people! Things happen all round them, but they have no eyes to see them with.

MEYER [*at the table*]. See, here's a treat from above! Let's get the psalms over, then we'll have a drop of something. And

the Lord will have mercy on the sick woman and send her a quick recovery.

FIRST BATLON [*to the scholars sitting around the big table, half asleep*]. Who wants to say psalms, boys? There's a bit of oat bread for every one that does. [*The scholars get up.*] Let's go in there.

[*The three* BATLONIM, MEYER *and the scholars, except* CHENNOCH, *pass into the adjoining prayer-room, whence the chanting of "Blessed be the man" presently emerges. The* MESSENGER *remains throughout beside the small table, immovable. His eyes never leave the Ark. There is a long pause. Then* CHANNON *comes in.*]

CHANNON [*very weary, walks aimlessly across to the Ark, sunk in meditation. He seems surprised to find it open.*] Open? Who can have opened it? For whom has it opened in the middle of the night? [*He looks in.*] The scrolls of the Law... there they stand like comrades, shoulder to shoulder, so calm... so silent. All secrets and symbols hidden in them. And all miracles — from the six days of creation, unto the end of all the generations of men. Yet how hard it is to wrest one secret or one symbol from them — how hard! [*He counts the scrolls.*] One, two, three, four, five, six, seven, eight, nine. That makes the word Truth, according to the Minor system. In each scroll there are four Trees of Life.[1] There again it comes — thirty-six. Not an hour passes but this number faces me in one manner or another. I do not know the meaning of it, but I have the intuition that within it lies the whole essence of the matter.... Thirty-six is Leah. Three times thirty-six is Channon. ... Le-ah — that makes Le-ha, which means Not God... not through God... [*He shudders.*] A terrible thought... and yet it draws me nearer... and nearer....

CHENNOCH [*looks up from his book, attentively at* CHANNON]. Channon! You go about dreaming all the time.

CHANNON [*moves away from the Ark, and slowly approaches* CHENNOCH, *standing before him, lost in thought*]. Nothing —

---

[1] Ten or more adult males constituting a Jewish community.

[1] The handles at the top and bottom of each scroll.

nothing but secrets and symbols — and the right path is not to be found. [*Short pause.*] Krasny is the name of the village ... and the miracle-man's name is Rabbi Elchannon...

CHENNOCH. What's that you're saying?

CHANNON [*as if waking out of a trance*]. I? Nothing. I was only thinking.

CHENNOCH [*shaking his head*]. You've been meddling with the Kabala, Channon. Ever since you came back, you haven't had a book in your hand.

CHANNON [*not understanding*]. Not had a book in my hand? What book do you mean?

CHENNOCH. The Talmud of course — the Laws. You know very well...

CHANNON [*still in his dreams*]. Talmud? The Laws? Never had them in my hand? The Talmud is cold and dry... so are the Laws. [*Comes to himself suddenly. He speaks with animation.*] Under the earth's surface, Chennoch, there is a world exactly the same as ours upon it, with fields and forests, seas and deserts, cities and villages. Storms rage over the deserts and over the seas upon which sail great ships. And over the dense forests, reverberating with the roll of thunder, eternal fear holds sway. Only in the absence of one thing does that world differ from ours. There is no sky, from which the sun pours down its burning heat and bolts of fire fall.... So it is with the Talmud. It is deep and glorious and vast. But it chains you to the earth — it forbids you to attempt the heights. [*With enthusiasm.*] But the Kabala, the Kabala tears your soul away from earth and lifts you to the realms of the highest heights. Spreads all the heavens out before your eyes, and leads direct to Pardes,[1] reaches out in the infinite, and raises a corner of the great curtain itself. [*Collapses.*] My heart turns faint — I have no strength....

CHENNOCH [*solemnly*]. That is all true. But you forget that those ecstatic flights into the upper regions are fraught with the utmost peril, for it is there that you are likely to come to grief and hurl yourself into the deepest pit below. The Talmud

[1] Paradise.

raises the soul toward the heights by slow degrees, but keeps guard over it like a faithful sentinel, who neither sleeps nor dreams. The Talmud clothes the soul with an armor of steel and keeps it ever on the strait path so that it stray neither to the right nor to the left. But the Kabala ... Remember what the Talmud says: [*He chants the following in the manner of Talmudic recitation.*] Four reached Pardes. Ben Azzai, Ben Zoma, Acher and Rabbi Akiva. Ben Azzai looked within and died. Ben Zoma looked within and lost his reason. Acher renounced the fundamentals of all belief. Rabbi Akiva alone went in and came out again unscathed.

CHANNON. Don't try to frighten me with them. We don't know how they went, nor with what. They may have failed because they went to look and not to offer themselves as a sacrifice. But others went after them — that we know. Holy Ari and the holy Balshem.[1] They did not fail.

CHENNOCH. Are you comparing yourself to them?

CHANNON. To nobody. I go my own way.

CHENNOCH. What sort of way is that?

CHANNON. You wouldn't understand.

CHENNOCH. I wish to and I will. My soul, too, is drawn toward the high planes.

CHANNON [*after a moment's reflection*]. The service of our holy men consists in cleansing human souls, tearing away the sin that clings to them and raising them to the shining source whence they come. Their work is very difficult because sin is ever lurking at the door. No sooner is one soul cleansed than another comes in its place, more sin-corroded still. No sooner is one generation brought to repentance than the next one appears, more stiff-necked than the last. And as each generation grows weaker, its sins become stronger, and the holy men fewer and fewer.

CHENNOCH. Then, according to your philosophy, what ought to be done?

CHANNON [*quietly, but with absolute con-*

[1] The founder of the Chassidic sect, kncwn as the Basht.

viction]. There is no need to wage war on sin. All that is necessary is to burn it away, as the goldsmith refines gold in his powerful flame; as the farmer winnows the grain from the chaff. So must sin be refined of its uncleanness, until only its holiness remains.

CHENNOCH [*astonished*]. Holiness in sin? How do you make that out?

CHANNON. Everything created by God contains a spark of holiness.

CHENNOCH. Sin was not created by God but by Satan.

CHANNON. And who created Satan? God. Since he is the antithesis of God, he is an aspect of God, and therefore must contain also a germ of holiness.

CHENNOCH [*crushed*]. Holiness in Satan? I can't... I don't understand.... Let me think....

[*His head sinks into his hands, propped up by both elbows on the desk. There is a pause.*]

CHANNON [*stands beside him and in a trembling voice, bending down to reach his ear*]. Which sin is the strongest of all? Which one is the hardest to conquer? The sin of lust for a woman, isn't it?

CHENNOCH [*without raising his head*]. Yes.

CHANNON. And when you have cleansed this sin in a powerful flame, then this greatest uncleanness becomes the greatest holiness. It becomes "The Song of Songs." [*He holds his breath.*] The Song of Songs. [*Drawing himself up, he begins to chant in a voice which, though subdued, is charged with rapture.*] Behold thou art fair, my love. Thou hast dove's eyes within thy locks; thy hair is as a flock of goats that appear from Mount Gilead. Thy teeth are like a flock of sheep that are even shorn, which came up from the washing; whereof every one bear twins and none barren among them.

[MEYER *comes out of the prayer-room. A gentle knocking is heard at the street door, which is pushed hesitatingly open, and* LEAH *enters. She has hold of* FRADE'S *hand, and behind them comes* GITTEL. *They stop in the doorway.*]

MEYER *turns and sees them, and goes over to them, surprised, welcoming them obsequiously.*]

MEYER. Look! Here comes Sender's daughter, little Leah!

LEAH [*shyly*]. You promised to show me the old embroidered curtains of the Ark — do you remember?

[CHANNON, *hearing her voice, abruptly interrupts his song, and stares at her with all his eyes. As long as she remains in the synagogue, he alternately gazes at her thus, and closes his eyes in ecstasy.*]

FRADE. Show her the curtains, Meyer — the old ones, and the most beautiful. Our dear Leah has said she will embroider a new one for the anniversary of her mother's death. She will work it with the purest gold upon the finest of velvet, just as they used to do in the olden days — little lions and eagles. And when it is hung over the Ark, her mother's pure spirit will rejoice in Eden.

[LEAH *looks timidly about her, and seeing* CHANNON, *lowers her eyes in embarrassment and keeps them so for the rest of the scene.*]

MEYER. Oh, with the greatest pleasure. Why not, why not indeed? I'll bring the oldest and most beautiful curtains to show her — at once, this very minute.

[*He goes to the chest near the street door and takes out the curtains.*]

GITTEL [*taking* LEAH'S *hand*]. Aren't you afraid to be in the synagogue at night, Leah?

LEAH. I've never been here at night before, except on the Days of the Holy Scrolls. But that's a feast day and everything is bright and joyful then. How sad it is now, though — how sad!

FRADE. Dear children — a synagogue *must* be sad. The dead come here at midnight to pray, and when they go they leave their sorrows behind them.

GITTEL. Don't talk about the dead, Granny. It frightens me.

FRADE [*not hearing her*]. And each day at dawn, when the Almighty weeps for the destruction of the Holy Temple, His sacred tears fall in the synagogues. That is why the walls of all old synagogues look as if they have been wept over, and that is why it is forbidden to whitewash them and make them bright again. If you attempt to, they grow angry and throw their stones at you.

LEAH. How old it is — how old! It doesn't show so much from outside.

FRADE. Old it is, little daughter — very, very old. They even say it was found already built under the earth. Many a time this city has been destroyed, and many a time it has been laid in ashes. But this synagogue, never. Fire broke out once on the roof, but almost before it had begun to burn, innumerable doves came flocking down upon it and beat out the flames with their wings.

LEAH [not hearing — speaking to herself]. How sad it is! How lovely! I feel that I want never to go away from it again. I wish I could put my arms around those ancient, tear-stained walls and ask them why they are so sorrowful, and so wrapped in dreams... so silent and so sad. I wish ... I don't know what I wish.... But my heart is filled with tenderness and pity.

MEYER [brings the curtains to the bima, and spreads one out to show]. This is the oldest of all — a good two hundred years or more. It is never used except on Passover.

GITTEL [enraptured]. Leah, dear — just look. Isn't it gorgeous! Such stiff brown velvet, all embroidered in heavy gold. Two lions holding the shield of David above their heads. And trees on either side, with doves in their branches. You can't get such velvet nowadays, nor such gold either.

LEAH. The curtain is sad, too — I love it also. [She smooths it out and kisses it.]

GITTEL [takes LEAH's hand and whispers]. Look, Leah, dear! There's a student over there staring at you — so strangely!

LEAH [keeping her eyes still more downcast]. That is Channon. He was a poor scholar, and he used to be a guest in our house.

GITTEL. It is as if he were calling to you with his eyes, he stares so. He would like to talk to you, but he is afraid to.

LEAH. I wish I knew why he is so pale and sad. He must surely have been ill.

GITTEL. He isn't sad really — his eyes are shining.

LEAH. They always are. He has wonderful eyes, and when he talks to me his breath comes short — and so does mine. It wouldn't be proper for a girl to talk to a strange young man.

FRADE [to MEYER]. Won't you let us kiss the holy scrolls? Surely! How could one be a guest in the house of God and leave without kissing His holy scrolls?

MEYER. By all means, by all means! Come!

[He goes ahead, followed by GITTEL leading FRADE, and LEAH behind them. MEYER takes out a scroll and gives it to FRADE to kiss.]

LEAH [passing CHANNON, stops for a moment and says in a low voice]. Good evening, Channon. You have come back?

CHANNON [scarcely able to speak for agitation]. Yes.

FRADE. Come, Leah, darling, kiss the holy scrolls. [LEAH goes to the Ark. MEYER hands her a scroll, which she takes in her arms and, pressing her lips against it, kisses passionately.] Now, now, child! That will do. A holy scroll must not be kissed too long. They are written in black fire upon white fire. [In sudden alarm.] How late it is! How very late! Come, children, let us hurry home — come quickly.

[They hasten out. MEYER closes the Ark and follows them.]

CHANNON [stands for a while with closed eyes; then resumes his chanting of the "Song of Songs" where he left off]. Thy lips are like a thread of scarlet, and thy speech is comely. Thy temples are like a piece of pomegranate within thy locks.

CHENNOCH [raises his head and looks at CHANNON]. Channon, what are you singing? [CHANNON stops singing and looks at CHENNOCH.] Your ear-locks are wet. You have been to the Mikva [1] again.

CHANNON. Yes.

CHENNOCH. When you perform the ablutions, do you also use spells and go

_____
[1] Ritual bath.

through all the ceremonies prescribed by the book of Roziel? [1]

CHANNON. Yes.

CHENNOCH. You aren't afraid to?

CHANNON. No.

CHENNOCH. And you fast from Sabbath to Sabbath — isn't that hard for you?

CHANNON. It's harder for me to eat on the Sabbath than to fast the whole week. [*Pause.*] I've lost all desire to eat.

CHENNOCH [*inviting confidence*]. What do you do all this for? What do you expect to gain by it?

CHANNON [*as if to himself*]. I wish... I wish to attain possession of a clear and sparkling diamond, and melt it down in tears and inhale it into my soul. I want to attain to the rays of the third plane of beauty. I want... [*Suddenly in violent perturbation.*] Yes — there are still two barrels of golden pieces which I *must* get, for him who can count only gold pieces.

CHENNOCH [*appalled*]. Channon, be careful! You're on a slippery road. No holy powers will help you to achieve these things.

CHANNON [*challenging him*]. And if the *holy* powers will not, then?

CHENNOCH [*terrified*]. I'm afraid to talk to you! I'm afraid to be near you!

[*He rushes out. CHANNON remains behind, his face full of defiance. MEYER comes back from the street. The FIRST BATLON emerges from the prayer-room.*]

FIRST BATLON. Eighteen psalms — that's enough and to spare! I suppose this doesn't expect to get the whole bookful for a kopek! You go and tell them, Meyer. Once they get started, there's no stopping them till they've said them all.

[*Enter ASHER in great excitement.*]

ASHER. I just met Baruch the tailor. He's come back from Klimovka — that's where Sender's been to meet the bridegroom's people. They haven't come to terms yet, it seems. Sender insisted that the bridegroom's father should board the couple for ten years, but he stood out for

[1] One of the books of the Kabala.

only five. So they all went back home again.

MEYER. That makes the fourth time.

FIRST BATLON. Heartbreaking, isn't it?

MESSENGER [*to THIRD BATLON, smiling*]. A little while ago you said yourself that all marriages were prearranged by destiny.

CHANNON [*straightening up and speaking in a voice of rapture*]. I have won again.

[*He falls exhausted onto a bench, his face alight with joy.*]

MESSENGER [*taking a lantern out of his bag*]. Time to get ready for the road again.

MEYER. What's your hurry?

MESSENGER. I'm a messenger. Great ones and magnates employ me to carry important communications and rare treasures for them. I am obliged to hurry — my time is not my own.

MEYER. You ought to wait until daybreak at least.

MESSENGER. That is still a long way off, and I have far to go. I shall start about midnight.

MEYER. It's pitch-dark outside.

MESSENGER. I shan't lose my way with this lantern.

[*The scholars and BATLONIM come out of the prayer-room.*]

SECOND BATLON. Good luck be with us. May the Lord send the sick woman a complete recovery.

ALL. Amen.

FIRST BATLON. Now let's go and get ten kopeks' worth of cakes and brandy.

MEYER. It's here already. [*Takes a bottle and cakes from under his coat.*] Come on, let's drink a health!

[*The door opens and SENDER enters, coat unbuttoned, hat on the back of his head, thoroughly happy. Three or four men follow him in.*]

MEYER AND THE THREE BATLONIM. Oh, Reb Sender — welcome, welcome...

SENDER. Happened to be passing. I really must go in, says I to myself, and see what our people are doing. [*Noticing the bottle in MEYER's hand.*] I'll surely find them studying, says I, or deep in pious discussions. And what do I see? They're all deep in preparing for a celebration instead! Ha, ha, ha! Typical Miropol Chassidim!

FIRST BATLON. Will you have a drop with us, Reb Sender?

SENDER. No, blockhead. I won't. I'll stand treat myself — and splendid treat at that! Congratulate me — this is a happy day for me. I have betrothed my daughter.

[CHANNON, distraught, rises from his bench.]

ALL. Mazeltov! Mazeltov! [1]

MEYER. Somebody just told us you hadn't been able to come to terms with the bridegroom's father, and so it had all fallen through.

THIRD BATLON. We were heartbroken to hear it.

SENDER. It nearly did, but at the last moment he gave in, and so the contract was signed. May good luck go with it.

CHANNON. Betrothed? Betrothed? How can that be? [In despair.] So it was all of no avail — neither the fasts, nor the ablutions, nor the spells, nor the symbols. All in vain.... So what remains? What is there still to do... by what means... [He clutches the breast of his kaftan, and his face is illuminated with ecstasy.] Ah! The secret of the Double Name is revealed to me. Ah! I see him. I... I... I have won! [He falls to the ground.]

MESSENGER [opens his lantern]. The wick has burnt down. A new one must be lighted. [An ominous pause.]

SENDER. Meyer, why is it so dark in here? Let's have some light.

[MEYER lights another light.]

MESSENGER [crosses quietly to SENDER]. Did you come to terms with the bridegroom's father?

SENDER [surprised, and somewhat frightened, looks at him]. I did.

MESSENGER. Sometimes it happens that the relatives promise, and then go back on their word. And litigation follows. It pays to be very careful in these matters.

SENDER [in alarm]. Who is this man? I don't know him.

[1] Good luck.

MEYER. He is not from these parts. He is a Messenger.

SENDER. What does he want of me?

MEYER. I don't know.

SENDER [more calmly]. Asher, run over to my house and ask them to prepare some wine and preserves and something good to eat. Hurry up, now — run along. [ASHER hastens out.] We might as well stay here and talk a bit while they're getting things ready. Hasn't one of you some new parable of our Rabbi's? A saying, or a miracle, or a proverb... each of his looks is more precious than pearls.

FIRST BATLON [to MEYER]. Keep the bottle. It'll come in handy to-morrow.

[MEYER puts it away.]

MESSENGER. I'll tell you one of his proverbs. One day a Chassid came to the Rabbi — he was rich, but a miser. The Rabbi took him by the hand and led him to the window. "Look out there," he said. And the rich man looked into the street. "What do you see?" asked the Rabbi. "People," answers the rich man. Again the Rabbi takes him by the hand, and this time leads him to the mirror. "What do you see now?" he says. "Now I see myself," answers the rich man. Then the Rabbi says: "Behold — in the window there is glass and in the mirror there is glass. But the glass of the mirror is covered with a little silver, and no sooner is the silver added than you cease to see others but see only yourself."

THIRD BATLON. Oh, oh, oh! Sweeter than honey!

FIRST BATLON. Holy words!

SENDER [to the MESSENGER]. You are trying to score off me, eh?

MESSENGER. God forbid!

SECOND BATLON. Let's have a song! [To the THIRD BATLON.] Sing the Rabbi's tune.

[The THIRD BATLON begins intoning a low mysterious Chassidic tune in which the rest join.]

SENDER [rising]. And now a dance, a round dance.... Shall Sender give away his only daughter, and not celebrate it with a round dance? Nice Chassidim we'd be!

[SENDER, the three BATLONIM and

MEYER *put their arms on one another's shoulders and start turning in a ring, their eyes dim with ecstasy, chanting a weird, monotonous air. They revolve slowly, on the same spot. Then* SENDER *breaks away from the circle.*]

SENDER. Now a merry one. Come on — all together!

SECOND BATLON. Yes, come on, boys — let's all join in! [*Several of the scholars join them.*] Chennoch, Channon, where are you? We're going to have a merry dance — come on!

SENDER [*somewhat perturbed*]. Ah, Channon... he's here, my little Channon, isn't he? Where is he, eh? Bring him here — I want him.

MEYER [*sees* CHANNON *on the floor*]. He's asleep on the floor.

SENDER. Wake him up then. Wake him up.

MEYER [*tries to rouse him. Frightened*]. I can't ——

[*They all crowd round* CHANNON, *and try to wake him.*]

FIRST BATLON [*with a frightened cry*]. He's dead.

THIRD BATLON. The book of Roziel, the King — look — it's fallen out of his hand! [*Consternation.*]

CURTAIN

ACT II

A square in Brainitz. Left, the old synagogue, built of wood and of ancient architecture. In front of it, somewhat to one side, a mound surmounted by a gravestone bearing the inscription, "Here lie a pure and holy bridegroom and bride, murdered to the glory of God in the year 5408. Peace be with them." An alley on one side of the synagogue, leading to a group of small houses which merge into the backdrop.

At the right, SENDER'S *house, also built of wood, but of imposing size and adorned with a balcony and stoop. Past the house a wide double gate to the courtyard gives onto another alley with a row of small shops which also merge into the backdrop. On the drop to the right, past the shops, an inn, then the garden of a large estate and the owner's mansion. A*

wide road leading down to a river upon whose farther bank a cemetery is seen. To the left, a bridge over the river and a mill.

In the foreground, bathhouse and poorhouse. In the far distance, a forest. The double gates to SENDER'S *courtyard stand wide open. Long tables have been set out in the yard, and jut out onto the square. The tables are spread with food which the poor, old and young, some of them crippled, are ravenously devouring. They are served continuously from the house, from great bowls of food and baskets with bread.*

Before the shops and houses, women sit knitting, but their eyes hardly leave SENDER'S *house. Men, old and young, leave the synagogue carrying their prayer-shawls and phylacteries, and go into the shops and houses. Some stand about talking in groups. Music is heard from the courtyard. Then dancing and the confused sound of voices.*

It is evening. In the middle of the street, in front of the synagogue stands the WEDDING GUEST, *a middle-aged Jew in a satin kaftan, his hands stuck into his belt. The* SECOND BATLON *is with him.*

GUEST [*gazing at the synagogue*]. A great synagogue you have here — a handsome building indeed — and spacious, too. The spirit of God is upon it. Very old, I should say.

SECOND BATLON. Very old it is. Our ancients say that not even their grandfathers could remember when it was built.

GUEST [*seeing the grave*]. And what is that? [*He reads the inscription.*] "Here lie a pure and holy bridegroom and bride, murdered to the glory of God in the year 5408." A bride and bridegroom — murdered to the glory of God?

SECOND BATLON. Yes — by that bandit Chamilouk[1] — may his name be wiped out forever — when he raided the city with his Cossacks and massacred half the Jews. He murdered that bride and groom as they were being led to the wedding-canopy. They were buried on the very spot, in one grave together. Ever since, it has been called the holy grave. [*Whisper-*

[1] Chmelnitzki the Cossack chieftain who led a great uprising in which thousands of Jews perished.

ing, as if he were telling a secret.] At every marriage ceremony, the rabbi hears sighs from the grave, and it has become a time-honored custom for the people leaving the synagogue after a wedding to go and dance there, to cheer the dead bride and bridegroom where they lie.

GUEST. An excellent custom....

MEYER [*coming out of* SENDER'S *house*]. Ah, such a feast for the poor. Never in all my born days have I seen the equal of this spread Sender's made for them.

GUEST. No wonder. He's giving away his only daughter.

MEYER [*with enthusiasm*]. First a piece of fish; then a cut of roast, and a *zimmis* [1] to top it off. And cake and brandy before the meal began!... It must have cost him a fortune — more than can ever be reckoned up!

SECOND BATLON. Leave it to Sender to know his own business. When it comes to skimping an invited guest, you know where you are — let him snort all he likes, he can't do anything. But it's flying in the face of danger not to treat the poor right. There's no telling who a beggar's coat may be hiding. A beggar maybe, but maybe also some one quite different... a *nister* [2]... or one of the Thirty-Six.[3]

MEYER. Why not the Prophet Elijah himself? He always appears as a beggar.

GUEST. It's not only the poor it pays to be careful with. You can't say for a certainty who any man might have been in his last existence, nor what he is doing on earth.

[*From the alley on the right, the* MESSENGER *enters, with his knapsack on his shoulder.*]

MEYER [*to the* MESSENGER]. Sholom aleichem [4] — you have come back, I see.

MESSENGER. I have been sent to you again.

MEYER. You have come in good season, in time for a great wedding.

MESSENGER. I know — it is the talk of all the country round.

---

[1] A vegetable delicacy. [2] A saint disguised.
[3] Thirty-Six men of virtue, on whose account God allows the world to continue.
[4] Peace be with you.

MEYER. Did you happen to pass the bridegroom's party on the way? They are late.

MESSENGER. The bridegroom will arrive in good time.

[*He goes into the synagogue, and the* GUEST, MEYER, *and the* SECOND BATLON *turn into* SENDER'S *courtyard.* LEAH *appears beyond the tables, in her wedding-dress, dancing with one after another of the old women. The rest crowd about her. Those with whom she has finished dancing pass into the square, and stand talking in groups.*]

A POOR WOMAN [*with child holding onto her skirts. In a tone of satisfaction*]. I danced with the bride.

LAME WOMAN. So did I. I took her round the waist and danced with her too. Hee, hee, hee!

A HUNCHBACK. How's that? The bride only dancing with the women? I'm going to take her by the waist myself, and swing her round and round. Ha, ha, ha!

[*General laughter among the beggars.*]

[FRADE, GITTEL *and* BASSIA *come from the house onto the stoop.*]

FRADE [*worried*]. Oh, dear! Oh, dear! There's the darling still dancing with those people. She'll make herself dizzy if she doesn't stop. Go and tell her to come here, children.

GITTEL [*going to* LEAH]. Come away, Leah dear — you've danced enough now.

BASSIA. Yes — you'll be getting dizzy....

[*They take* LEAH'S *hands and try to draw her away.*]

THE POOR WOMEN [*gather round* LEAH *beseeching her in whining tones*]. She hasn't danced with *me* yet.... Aren't I as good as them?... I've been waiting an hour.... Me... Me.... It's my turn after Elka. ... She's been round ten times and more with that lame Yachna, and not one single turn with me.... I've never got no luck!

MEYER [*comes out into the square and stands on the bench. In a high-pitched voice, he chants the following verse in the manner of a herald*].

Come in, come in, and feast your fill,
Rich Sender bids you straightway come!
Here's abundance and good will,
And ten kopeks for every one!

THE POOR [*run out jostling one another*].
Ten kopeks! Ten kopeks!

[*The square is left empty except for*
FRADE, LEAH, GITTEL, BASSIA *and an
old half-blind beggar woman.*]

THE OLD WOMAN [*seizes* LEAH]. I don't
want no alms.... I only want you to dance
with me. Just once — just one turn.
That's all. I've not danced once these
forty years.... Oh, how I used to dance
when *I* was a girl! How I *did* dance!
[LEAH *dances with her, but when she tries to
release herself, the crone will not let her go, but
begs for more and more.*] Again... again.
... [*They swing round faster still, the old
woman now out of breath and hysterical.*]
More... more....

[GITTEL *has to force her into the
courtyard. Then she comes back, and
together with* BASSIA, *they assist* LEAH
to a bench. SENDER'S *servants clear the
tables and close the gate.*]

FRADE. Oh, my darling, you're as white
as a sheet. They've worn you out, so they
have.

LEAH [*sits with closed eyes, her head
leaning backward, and when she speaks, it is
as though in a trance*]. They seized me...
they kept on turning and turning round
me... so close... and clutched me to them
with their cold, withered hands... my head
swam... my heart turned faint. Then
some one came and lifted me from the
ground and carried me far away, very far
away.

BASSIA [*in great anxiety*]. Oh, Leah,
look how they've crushed your dress —
it's all dirty now. Whatever will you
do?

LEAH [*in the same manner as before*].
If the bride is left alone before the wedding,
spirits come and carry her off.

FRADE [*alarmed*]. What can have put
such ideas into your head, my child? We
may not mention the dark people — you
know that. They're lurking in every tiny
hole and corner and crevice. They see
everything and hear everything — and

they're forever on the alert to catch their
unclean names on our lips. Then out they
spring on top of you.
[*She spits three times.*]

LEAH [*opens her eyes*]. My spirits are
not evil ones.

FRADE. Don't you believe them, my
child. The minute you trust one of the
dark people, he becomes unmanageable
and begins to do mischief.

LEAH [*with utter conviction*]. Granny —
it isn't evil spirits that surround us, but
souls of those who died before their time,
and come back again to see all that we do
and hear all that we say.

FRADE. God help you, child, what is the
meaning of all this? Souls? What souls?
The souls of the pure and good fly up to
heaven and stay there at rest in the bright
garden of Eden.

LEAH. No, Granny — they are with us
here. [*Her tone changes.*] Grandmother,
every one of us is born to a long life of
many, many years. If he die before his
years are done, what becomes of the life he
has not lived, do you think? What becomes of his joys and sorrows, and all the
thoughts he had not time to think, and all
the things he hadn't time to do? Where
are the children he did not live long enough
to bring into the world? Where does all
that go to? Where? [*Lost in thought, she
continues.*] There was a lad here, Granny
... his mind was full of wisdom and his soul
was set on holy purposes. Long years
stretched out before him. Then one day,
without warning, his life is destroyed.
And strangers bury him in strange earth.
[*Desperately.*] What has become of the
rest of him? His speech that has been
silenced? His prayers that have been cut
off?... Grandmother — when a candle
blows out we light it again and it goes on
burning down to the end. So how can a
human life which goes out before it has
burnt down, remain put out forever?...
How can it, Granny?

FRADE [*shaking her head*]. Daughter,
you must not think about such things.
He who lives above knows the reason for
His actions. We are blind and know nothing.

[*The* MESSENGER *approaches them unnoticed, and remains standing close behind them.*]

LEAH [*not hearing her. With deep conviction*]. No, Granny. No human life goes to waste. If one of us dies before his time, his soul returns to the world to complete its span, to do the things left undone and experience the happiness and griefs he would have known. [*A pause.*] Granny, do you remember you told us how the dead go trooping at midnight into the synagogue? They go to pray the prayers they would have prayed in life, had they not died too soon. [*A pause.*] My mother died in her youth and had no time to live through all that lay in store for her. That is why I go to-day to the cemetery to ask her to join my father when he leads me under the wedding-canopy. She will be with me there, and after the ceremony we shall dance together. It is the same with all the souls who leave the world before their time. They are here in our midst, unheard and invisible. Only if your desire is strong enough, you can see them, and hear their voices and learn their thoughts.... I can. ... [*Pointing to the grave.*] The holy grave — I have known it ever since I was a child. And I know the bride and bridegroom buried there. I've seen them often and often, sometimes in dreams and sometimes when I am wide awake. They are as near to me as my own people.... [*Deep in meditation.*] They were on the way to their wedding, so young and lovely to see, with a long and beautiful life before them. But murderers set upon them with axes, and in a moment they both lay dead upon the ground. They were laid in one grave, so that they might be together for all time. [*She rises and goes to the grave, followed by* FRADE, GITTEL *and* BASSIA. *Stretching out her arms, she says in a loud voice.*] Holy bridegroom and bride, I invite you to my wedding. Be with me under the canopy.

[*Gay march music is heard in the distance.* LEAH *screams in terror and almost falls.* GITTEL *catches her.*]

GITTEL. What is it, Leah dear? Don't

be frightened. They must be greeting the bridegroom with music as he comes into the village.

BASSIA [*excited*]. I'm going to take a peep at him.

GITTEL. I, too. We'll run back, Leah, and tell you what he looks like. Shall we?

LEAH [*shaking her head*]. No.

BASSIA. She's only shy. Little stupid, there's nothing to be ashamed of.... We won't give you away!

[*Exit* BASSIA *running, followed by* GITTEL.]

FRADE [*returning with* LEAH *to the stoop*]. That is the custom, my child. The bride always sends her friend to see whether the groom is fair or dark, and...

MESSENGER [*approaching*]. Bride!

LEAH [*shivers as she turns toward him*]. Yes—what is it? [*She gazes fixedly at him*].

MESSENGER. The souls of the dead *do* return to earth, but not as disembodied spirits. Some must pass through many forms before they achieve purification. [LEAH *listens with ever-increasing attention.*] The souls of the wicked return in the forms of beasts, or birds, or fish — of plants even, and are powerless to purify themselves by their own efforts. They have to wait for the coming of some righteous sage to purge them of their sins and set them free. Others enter the bodies of the newly born, and cleanse themselves by well-doing.

LEAH [*in tremulous eagerness*]. Yes... yes....

MESSENGER. Besides these, there are vagrant souls which, finding neither rest nor harbor, pass into the bodies of the living, in the form of a Dybbuk, until they have attained purity.

[*Exit the* MESSENGER.]

[LEAH *remains lost in astonishment, as* SENDER *comes out of the house.*]

SENDER. Why are you sitting here like this, little daughter?

FRADE. She entertained the beggars at their meal and danced with them afterwards. They tired her, so she is resting awhile now.

SENDER. Entertaining the poor, eh? That is a sweet and pious deed. [*He looks up at the sky.*] It is getting very late but the bridegroom and his people have arrived at last. Is everything ready?

FRADE. She has still to go to the graveyard.

SENDER. Yes, go, my little one — go to Mamma. [*He sighs.*] Let your tears fall on her grave and ask her to come to your wedding. Ask her to be with you, so that we may lead our only daughter under the canopy together. Say that I have fulfilled her dying wishes to devote my life to you and bring you up to be a true and virtuous daughter of Israel. This I have done, and am now about to give you in marriage to a learned and God-fearing young man, of good family.

[*He wipes away his tears and with bowed head turns back into the house. A pause.*]

LEAH. Granny, may I invite others at the graveyard besides mother?

FRADE. Only the near relations. You must ask your grandfather, Rabbi Ephraim, and your Aunt Mirele.

LEAH. There is some one else I want to ask — not a relation.

FRADE. No, daughter — that is forbidden. If you invite one stranger, the others might take offense and do you harm.

LEAH. He is not a stranger, Granny. He was in our house like one of ourselves.

FRADE [*in a voice low with fear*]. Child, child — you fill me with fear.... They say he died a bad, unnatural death. [*LEAH weeps silently.*] There, there, my little one, don't cry. You shall ask him if you must; granny will take the sin upon herself. [*Bethinking herself.*] I don't know where they buried him, though, and it would never do to ask.

LEAH. I know where he is.

FRADE [*surprised*]. You know? How?

LEAH. I saw his grave in a dream. [*She closes her eyes in a trance.*] And I saw him, too. He told me his trouble and begged me to invite him to the wedding.

[GITTEL *and* BASSIA *enter running.*]

GITTEL AND BASSIA [*together, in high excitement*]. We've seen him — we've seen him!

LEAH [*in consternation*]. Whom — whom have you seen?

GITTEL. Why, the bridegroom, of course. And he's dark....

BASSIA. No, he isn't — he's fair....

GITTEL. Come, let's take another look and make sure.... [*They run off.*]

LEAH [*rising*]. Come, Granny — let us go to the graveyard.

FRADE [*sadly*]. Yes, my baby.... Och, och, och!

[LEAH *takes a black shawl and puts it round her shoulders. With* FRADE *at her side, she passes slowly down the alley to the right. The stage remains empty for a moment.*]

[*Music is heard approaching, as from the alley on the left come* NACHMON, RABBI MENDEL *and* MENASHE, *a small, wizened youth who stares about him with wide, terrified eyes. They are followed by relatives, men and women, in holiday clothes.* SENDER *comes out to meet them.*]

SENDER [*shakes* NACHMON'S *hand warmly*]. Sholom aleichem, Nachmon. You are welcome. [*They kiss.* SENDER *shakes hands with* MENASHE *and kisses him. He then shakes hands with the rest of the party.*] Have you had a good journey?

NACHMON. We have had a hard and bitter journey. First we missed the road and went astray in the fields. Then we plunged into a swamp which nearly swallowed us up. It was all we could do to pull ourselves out, and the thought flashed through my mind that the Evil Ones, God forbid, were at work to prevent our getting here at all. However, by the goodness of God we have still managed to arrive in time.

SENDER. You must be exhausted. Come in and rest.

NACHMON. There's no time to rest, we have still to settle the details of the marriage-contract, the transfer of the dowry — the wedding gifts — how long the couple should live in the bridegroom's father's house, and so forth....

SENDER. As you wish — I am entirely at your disposal.

[*Puts his arm around* NACHMON'S

shoulders, and walks up and down the square with him, talking.]

RABBI MENDEL [*to* MENASHE]. Remember now — you are to remain perfectly quiet at the table. Keep your eyes downcast, and make no movement of any sort. The moment the supper is over, the master of ceremonies will call out: "The bridegroom will now deliver his oration." Then you will rise immediately and stand on the bench. Begin intoning loudly — the louder the better. And you are not to be bashful — do you hear?

MENASHE. Yes, I hear. [*In a frightened whisper.*] Rabbi, I'm afraid.

RABBI MENDEL [*alarmed*]. Afraid — what of? Have you forgotten your oration?

MENASHE. No — it isn't that.

RABBI MENDEL. What then?

MENASHE [*in anguish*]. I don't know myself. But no sooner had we left home than I was seized with terror. All the places we passed were strange to me — I've never in my life seen so many unfamiliar faces. I can't stand the way they look at me — I'm afraid of their eyes. [*He shudders.*] Rabbi, nothing terrifies me so much as the eyes of strangers.

RABBI MENDEL. I'll pray that the evil eye be averted from you.

MENASHE. Rabbi, I'd like to stay alone, I'd like to creep into a corner somewhere. But here I'm surrounded by strangers. I have to talk to them, answer their questions; I feel as if I were being dragged to the gallows. [*With mystic terror.*] Rabbi, above all, I'm frightened of her, the maiden.

RABBI MENDEL. Make up your mind to master your fears, and you will. Otherwise, God forbid, you may forget your oration. Let us go to the inn now, and I will hear you go over it again.

MENASHE [*clutches at* MENDEL'S *hand*]. Rabbi — what's that grave there in the middle of the street?

[*They read the inscription on the headstone in silence, and stand for a moment beside the grave; then with bowed heads pass down the alley to the left.* SENDER, NACHMON, *and the* WEDDING GUEST

enter the house. The poor file out of the courtyard, with their bags on their shoulders and staves in their hands. They cross the square silently and vanish down the alley to the left. A few linger in the square.]

A TALL PALE WOMAN. Now the poor people's feast is over — like all the other things — just as if they'd never been.

LAME OLD WOMAN. They said there'd be a plate of soup for every one, but there wasn't.

A HUNCHBACK. And only little slices of white bread.

A MAN ON CRUTCHES. A rich man like him — as if it would have hurt him to give us a whole loaf each.

THE TALL WOMAN. They might have given us a bit of chicken. Just look, chicken *and* geese *and* turkeys for their rich guests.

A HALF-BLIND WOMAN. Oh, what does it matter? It all goes to the worms when we're dead. Och, och, och!

[*They go slowly out. The stage is empty for a moment. Then the* MESSENGER *crosses from the left and enters the synagogue. Dusk is falling. The shopkeepers are closing for the night. In the synagogue and at* SENDER'S *house, lights are appearing.* SENDER, GITTEL *and* BASSIA *come onto the stoop. They peer about.*]

SENDER [*worried*]. Where is Leah? Where is old Frade? How is it they aren't back from the graveyard all this time? Can they have met with an accident, God forbid?

GITTEL AND BASSIA. We'll go and meet them.

[*From the alley on the right,* FRADE *and* LEAH *come hurrying.*]

FRADE. Hurry, child, hurry! Ei, ei — how long we've been! Oh, why did I let you have your way? I am so afraid something dreadful is going to happen, God forbid!

SENDER. Oh, here they are. What can have kept you all this time?

[*Women come out of the house.*]

WOMEN. Bring in the bride to pray before the candles.

[LEAH *is led into the house.*]

FRADE [*whispering to* GITTEL *and* BASSIA]. She fainted. I'd a hard time bringing her round. I'm shaking all over still.

BASSIA. That's because she's been fasting... it weakens the heart.

GITTEL. Did she cry much at her mother's grave?

FRADE. Better not ask what happened there. I'm still shaking all over....

[*A chair is set near the door and* LEAH *is led out. They seat her. Music.* NACHMON, MENASHE, RABBI MENDEL *and the guests approach from the alley on the left.* MENASHE *carries a cloth over his outstretched hands, and crosses to* LEAH *in order to cover her face with it. The* MESSENGER *comes out of the synagogue.*

LEAH [*tears the cloth away, and springing up, thrusts* MENASHE *from her, crying out*]. No! YOU are not my bridegroom!

[*General consternation. They all crowd round* LEAH.]

SENDER [*overwhelmed*]. Little daughter, what is it, my darling? What has come over you?

[LEAH *breaks away from them and runs to the grave, reaching out her arms.*]

LEAH. Holy bridegroom and bride, protect me — save me! [*She falls. They flock round her, and raise her from the ground. She looks wildly about, and cries out, not in her natural voice, but in the voice of a man.*] Ah! Ah! You buried me. But I have come back — to my destined bride. I will leave her no more! [NACHMON *crosses to* LEAH, *and she shrieks into his face.*] Chamilouk!

NACHMON [*trembling*]. She has gone mad.

MESSENGER. Into the bride has entered a Dybbuk. [*Great tumult.*]

CURTAIN

ACT III

Miropol. A large room in the house of RABBI AZRAEL *of Miropol. Right, door leading to other rooms. In middle of wall, center, door to street. On either side of this door, benches. Windows. Left, a table almost the entire length of the wall, covered with a white cloth. On table, slices of white bread.[1] At the head of table, a great armchair. Past the door right, a small cupboard containing scrolls of the law. Beside it, an altar. Opposite, a small table, sofa and several chairs.*

It is the Sabbath — evening prayers are just over. CHASSIDIM *go to and fro in the room while* ELDER MICHOEL *places about the table the pieces of white bread. The* MESSENGER *is sitting beside the cupboard where the scrolls are, surrounded by a group of* CHASSIDIM. *Others sit apart, reading. Two stand beside the small table. A low chanting is heard from an inner room: "God of Abraham, Isaac and Jacob..." The two* CHASSIDIM *speak.*

FIRST CHASSID. He has some wonderful tales, the Stranger. It gives you the creeps to listen to them — I'm afraid to, myself.

SECOND CHASSID. What are they about?

FIRST CHASSID. They're full of deep meaning, but it's not easy to grasp what the meaning is. For all we know, they may have something to do with the Bratslaver's creed.[2]

SECOND CHASSID. There can't be anything very heretical in them if the older Chassidim can listen to him.

[*They join the group about the* MESSENGER.]

THIRD CHASSID. Go on — tell us another...

MESSENGER. It is late. There is hardly any time left.

FOURTH CHASSID. That's all right. The Rabbi won't be here for a good while yet.

MESSENGER [*continuing his stories*].

[1] Sabbath bread which is prayed over at the close of the Sabbath.

[2] Nachmon Bratslaver, a descendant of Balshem, the founder of Chassidism. Bratslaver was a famous Rabbi, a poet and philosopher.

Well, then. At the end of the earth stands a high mountain; on the top of this mountain is a huge boulder, and out of the boulder flows a stream of clear water. At the opposite end of the earth is the heart of the world. Now each thing in the world has a heart, and the world itself has a great heart of its own. And the heart of the world keeps the clear stream ever in sight, gazing at it with insatiable longing and desire. But the heart of the world can make not even one step toward it, for the moment it stirs from its place, it loses sight of the mountain's summit and the crystal spring. And if, though for a single instant only, it lose sight of the spring, it loses in that same moment its life, and the heart of the world begins to die.

The crystal spring has no life-span of its own, but endures only so long as the heart of the world allows. And this is one day only.

Now at the close of day, the spring calls to the heart of the world in a song and is answered in a song from the heart. And the sound of their song passes over all the earth, and out of it shining threads come forth and fasten onto the hearts of all the world's creatures and from one heart to another. There is a righteous and benevolent man, who goes to and fro over all the earth's surface, gathering up the threads from all the hearts. These he weaves into Time, and when he has woven one whole day, he passes it over to the heart of the world, which passes it over to the crystal spring, and so the spring achieves another day of life.

THIRD CHASSID. The Rabbi is coming.

Silence falls. They all rise. RABBI AZRAEL *enters at door, left. He is a man of great age, dressed in a white kaftan and high fur cap. Very slowly and wearily, deep in thought, he crosses to the table, and sinks into the armchair at its head.* MICHOEL *takes his place at the* RABBI's *right hand, and the* CHASSIDIM *group themselves around the table, the elders sitting, the younger standing behind them.* MICHOEL *distributes white bread.* RABBI AZRAEL *lifts his head, and in a low, quavering voice chants.*]

RABBI AZRAEL. The feast of David, the King, the Messiah... [*The others make the response and say grace over the bread. They begin chanting in low tones, a sad, mysterious air without words. There is a pause.* RABBI AZRAEL *sighs deeply, rests his head on both hands, and in that position remains seated, lost in meditation. An atmosphere of suspense pervades the silence. At last,* RABBI AZRAEL *again raises his head, and begins to intone.*] It is told of the holy Balshem [1] — may his merits hover over us... [*There is a momentary pause.*] One day there came to Meshibach a troupe of German acrobats who gave their performance in the streets of the town. They stretched a rope across the river and one of them walked along the rope to the opposite bank. From all sides the people came running to behold this ungodly marvel, and in the midst of the crowd of onlookers stood the holy Balshem himself. His disciples were greatly astonished, and asked him the meaning of his presence there. And the holy Balshem answered them thus: I went to see how a man might cross the chasm between two heights as this man did, and as I watched him I reflected that if mankind would submit their souls to such discipline as that to which he submitted his body, what deep abysses might they not cross upon the tenuous cord of life!

[*The* RABBI *sighs deeply. In the pause that follows, the* CHASSIDIM *exchange enraptured glances.*]

FIRST CHASSID. Lofty as the world!
SECOND CHASSID. Wonder of wonders!
THIRD CHASSID. Glory of glories!
RABBI AZRAEL [*to* MICHOEL, *whispering*]. There is a stranger here.
MICHOEL [*looking round*]. He is a messenger, in the confidence of the Great Ones.
RABBI AZRAEL. What message does he bring?
MICHOEL. I don't know. Shall I tell him to go away?
RABBI AZRAEL. God forbid! A stranger

[1] The founder of the Chassidic sect.

must, on the contrary, be shown special honor. Give him a chair. [*Pause.*] The world of God is great and holy. In all the world the holiest land is the Land of Israel. In the Land of Israel the holiest city is Jerusalem; in Jerusalem the holiest place was the Holy Temple, and the holiest spot in the Temple was the Holy of Holies. [*He pauses.*] In the world there are seventy nations, and of them the holiest is Israel. The holiest of the people of Israel is the tribe of the Levites. The holiest of the Levites are the priests, and amongst the priests, the holiest is the High Priest. [*Pause.*] The year has three hundred and fifty-four days. Of these the holidays are the holiest. Holier than the holidays are the Sabbaths and the holiest of the Sabbaths is Yom Kippur,[1] Sabbath of Sabbaths. [*Pause.*] There are in the world seventy tongues. The holiest of these is the holy tongue of Israel. The holiest of all things written in this tongue is the Holy Torah; of the Torah the holiest part is the Ten Commandments, and the holiest of all the words in the Ten Commandments is the Name of the Lord. [*Pause.*] At a certain hour, on a certain day of the year, all these four supreme holinesses met together. This took place on the Day of Atonement, at the hour when the High Priest entered the Holy of Holies and there revealed the Divine Name. And as this hour was holy and terrible beyond words, so also was it the hour of utmost peril for the High Priest, and for the entire commonweal of Israel. For if, in that hour (which God forbid), a sinful or a wayward thought had entered the mind of the High Priest, it would have brought the destruction of the world. [*Pause.*] Wherever a man stands to lift his eyes to heaven, that place is a Holy of Holies. Every human being created by God in His own image and likeness is a High Priest. Each day of a man's life is the Day of Atonement; and every word he speaks from his heart is the name of the Lord. Therefore the sin of any man, whether of commission or of omission, brings the ruin of a whole world in its train. [*His voice becomes weaker and*

[1] The Day of Atonement.

trembles.] Through many transmigrations, the human soul is drawn by pain and grief, as the child to its mother's breast, to the source of its being, the Exalted Throne above. But it happens sometimes that a soul which has attained to the final state of purification suddenly becomes the prey of evil forces which cause it to slip and fall. And the higher it had soared, the deeper it falls. And with the fall of such a soul as this, a world plunges to ruin. And darkness overwhelms the spheres. The ten spheres bewail the world that is lost. [*He pauses, and seems to awaken to consciousness.*] My children, to-night we will shorten the seeing out of the Queen.[2]

[*All except* MICHOEL *silently leave the room, the spell of the* RABBI'S *discourses still upon them.*]

MICHOEL [*approaches the table uncertainly*]. Rabbi... Rabbi, Sender of Brainitz is here.

RABBI AZRAEL [*mechanically repeating the words*]. Sender of Brainitz... I know.

MICHOEL. A terrible misfortune has befallen him. A Dybbuk — God's mercy be upon us — has entered into his daughter.

RABBI AZRAEL. A Dybbuk has... I know.

MICHOEL. He has brought her to you.

RABBI AZRAEL [*as if to himself*]. To me?... To me?... Why to me, when there is no me to come to? For I am myself no longer.

MICHOEL. But Rabbi — everybody comes to you — a world of people.

RABBI AZRAEL. As you say — a world of people. Yes, a blind world — blind sheep following a blind shepherd. If they had eyes to see with, they would seek guidance not from me, but from Him who alone can justly use the word "I," for He is, in all the world, the only "I."

MICHOEL. You are His representative, Rabbi.

RABBI AZRAEL. So says the world. But as for me, I do not know. For forty years I have sat in the Rabbi's chair, and yet, to this very day I am not convinced that I am indeed the appointed deputy on earth

[2] The Sabbath is the Queen, whose going is celebrated with prayer.

of Him whose Name be praised. At times I am conscious of my nearness to the All. Then I am free of doubts, and feel the power within me — then I know I am master over the high worlds. But there are other times when that certainty abandons me, and then I am as small and feeble as a child, then I myself, and not those who come to me, need help.

MICHOEL. I know, Rabbi — I remember. Once you came to me at midnight, and asked me to recite the psalms with you. All the night long, we said them together, weeping.

RABBI AZRAEL. That was a long time ago — it is worse than ever now. [*His voice fails.*] What do they want of me? I am old and weak. My body has earned its rest — my soul longs for solitude. Yet still they come thronging to me, all the misery and sorrow of the world. Each imploring word pierces my flesh like a thorn.... No, I have no longer the strength ... I cannot...

MICHOEL [*filled with fear*]. Rabbi, Rabbi!...

RABBI AZRAEL [*suddenly breaking into tears*]. I can't go on ... I can't...

[*He weeps.*]

MICHOEL. Rabbi — do you forget the generations of righteous and holy men of God from whom you are descended? Your father, Rabbi Itzele, blessed be his name, your grandfather, our master and lord — our teacher, Rabbi Velvele the Great, who was a pupil of the holy Balshem himself...

RABBI AZRAEL [*regaining his self-control*]. No — I will not forget my forebears — my holy father who three times had a revelation direct from God; my uncle, Rabbi Meyer Baer, who upon the words of "Hear, O Israel" could ascend to Heaven at will; the great Velvele, my grandfather, who resurrected the dead... [*All his spirit has returned as he speaks to* MICHOEL.] Michoel, do you know that my grandfather would drive out Dybbuks without either spells or incantations — with a single word of command, only one, he expelled them. In times of stress I always turn to him, and he sustains me. He will not forsake me now. Call in Sender.

[MICHOEL *goes, and returns in a moment with* SENDER.]

SENDER [*tearfully, with outspread hands*]. Rabbi! Have mercy on me! Help me! Save my only daughter!

RABBI AZRAEL. How did this misfortune come upon you?

SENDER. Just as they were about to veil the bride, and...

RABBI AZRAEL. That is not what I asked. Tell me, what could have brought this thing to pass? A worm can enter a fruit only after it has begun to rot.

SENDER. Rabbi, my only daughter is a pious Jewish maiden. She is modest and gentle — she has never disobeyed me.

RABBI AZRAEL. Children are sometimes punished for the sins of their parents.

SENDER. If I knew of any sin I had committed, I would do penance for it.

RABBI AZRAEL. Have you asked the Dybbuk who he was, and why he entered into your daughter?

SENDER. He refuses to answer. But we recognized him by his voice. He was a student in our *yeshiva* who died suddenly in the synagogue. That was months ago. He had been meddling in the Kabala and came to grief through it.

RABBI AZRAEL. What powers destroyed him?

SENDER. Evil ones, they say. An hour or two before his death, he had been telling a fellow-student that sin need not be fought against, for Satan too is holy at the core. He also tried the use of charms to obtain two barrels of gold.

RABBI AZRAEL. Did you know him?

SENDER. Yes. I was one of those in whose house he stayed.

RABBI AZRAEL [*bending his gaze intently upon* SENDER]. You may have put some slight upon him or mistreated him. Try to remember.

SENDER. I don't know ... I can't remember... [*Desperately.*] Rabbi, I'm only human, after all ... I...

RABBI AZRAEL. Bring in the maiden.

[SENDER *goes out and returns immediately with* FRADE, *who supports* LEAH. LEAH *stops in the doorway and will go no further.*]

SENDER [weeping]. Have pity on your father, my child — don't put him to shame before the Rabbi. Come inside.

FRADE. Go in, Leah dear — go in, little dove.

LEAH. I want to... but I can't...

RABBI AZRAEL. Maiden, I command you — come in! [LEAH advances into the room and crosses to the table.] Sit down!

LEAH [does as the RABBI tells her. Then suddenly springs up and cries out with a voice not her own]. Let me be! I will not be here!

[She tries to escape, but is stopped by SENDER and FRADE.]

RABBI AZRAEL. Dybbuk! Who are you? I command you to answer.

LEAH [in the voice of the DYBBUK]. Miropol Rabbi — you know very well who I am. I do not wish the others to know.

RABBI AZRAEL. I do not ask your name — I ask: Who are you?

LEAH [as before]. I am one of those who sought other paths.

RABBI AZRAEL. He only seeks other paths who has lost the straight one.

LEAH [as before]. The straight one is too narrow.

RABBI AZRAEL. That has been said before by one who did not return. [Pause.] Why did you enter into this maiden?

LEAH [as before]. I am her predestined bridegroom.

RABBI AZRAEL. According to our Holy Scriptures, a dead soul may not stay in the realms of the living.

LEAH [as before]. I have not died.

RABBI AZRAEL. You left our world, and so are forbidden to return until the blast of the great trumpet shall be heard. I command you therefore to leave the body of this maiden, in order that a living branch of the imperishable tree of Israel may not be blasted.

LEAH [shrieks in the DYBBUK'S voice]. Miropol Rabbi — I know your almighty power. I know that angels and archangels obey your word. But me you cannot command. I have nowhere to go. Every road is barred against me and every gate is locked. On every side, the forces of evil lie in wait to seize me. [In a trembling voice.] There is heaven, and there is earth — and all the countless worlds in space, yet in not one of these is there any place for me. And now that my soul has found refuge from the bitterness and terror of pursuit, you wish to drive me away. Have mercy! Do not send me away — don't force me to go!

RABBI AZRAEL. I am filled with profound pity for you, wandering soul! And I will use all my power to save you from the evil spirits. But the body of this maiden you must leave.

LEAH [in the DYBBUK'S voice, firmly]. I refuse!

RABBI AZRAEL. Michoel. Summon a minyen from the synagogue. [MICHOEL returns at once with ten Jews who take their places on one side of the room.] Holy Community, do you give me authority to cast out of the body of a Jewish maiden, in your behalf and with your power, a spirit which refuses to leave her of its own free will?

THE TEN. Rabbi, we give you authority to cast out of the body of a Jewish maiden, in our behalf and in our name and with our power, a spirit which refuses to leave her of its own free will.

RABBI [rises]. Dybbuk! Soul of one who has left the world in which we live! In the name and with the power of a holy community of Jews, I, Azrael, son of Itzele, order you to depart out of the body of the maiden, Leah, daughter of Channah, and in departing, to do no injury either to her or to any other living being. If you do not obey me, I shall proceed against you with malediction and anathema, to the limit of my powers, and with the utmost might of my uplifted arm. But if you do as I command you, then I shall bend all my strength to drive away the fiends and evil spirits that surround you, and keep you safe from them.

LEAH [shrieks in the voice of the DYBBUK]. I'm not afraid of your anathema. I put no faith in your promises. The power is not in the world that can help me. The loftiest height of the world cannot compare with this resting-place that I have found, nor is there in the world an abysm so fathomless as that which waits to receive me if ever I leave my only refuge. I will not go.

RABBI AZRAEL. In the name of the Almighty, I adjure you for the last time. Leave the body of this maiden —— If you do not, I shall utter the anathema against you and deliver you into the hands of the fiends of destruction. [*An ominous pause.*]

LEAH [*in the voice of the* DYBBUK]. In the name of the Almighty, I am bound to my betrothed, and will remain with her to all eternity.

RABBI AZRAEL. Michoel, have white shrouds brought for all who are here. Bring seven trumpets... and seven black candles... Then seven holy scrolls from their place.

[*A pause fraught with dire omen, during which* MICHOEL *goes out and returns with trumpets and black candles. The* MESSENGER *follows him with the shrouds.*]

MESSENGER [*counting the shrouds*]. One too many. [*He looks round the room.*] Some one is missing, perhaps?

RABBI AZRAEL [*worried — as if recalling something*]. Before pronouncing the anathema against a Jewish soul, it is necessary to obtain the permission of the City Rabbi. Michoel, leave these things for the present. Here is my staff. Take it and go to the City Rabbi, and ask him to come without delay.

[MICHOEL *puts the trumpets and candles aside and goes out with the* MESSENGER, *who still carries the shrouds over his arm.*]

RABBI AZRAEL [*to the* TEN]. Wait outside until they come back. [*They leave the room. There is a pause.* RABBI AZRAEL *turns to* SENDER.] Sender, where are the bridegroom and his people?

SENDER. They stayed in Brainitz over the Sabbath, at my house.

RABBI AZRAEL. Let a messenger ride over and tell them, in my name, to stay there and await my orders.

SENDER. I'll send at once.

RABBI AZRAEL. You may leave me now, and take the maiden into the next room.

LEAH [*wakes out of her trance, and speaks in her own voice, trembling*]. Granny — I'm frightened. What are they going to do to him? What are they going to do to me?

FRADE. There, there, my child — you've nothing to be frightened of. The Rabbi knows best. He couldn't harm any one. The Rabbi can't do wrong, my darling.

[FRADE *and* SENDER *take* LEAH *into the adjoining room.*]

RABBI AZRAEL [*remains absorbed in his thoughts. Then he looks up*]. Even though it has been thus ordained in the high planes, I will reverse that destiny.

[*Enter* RABBI SAMSON.]

RABBI SAMSON. A good week to you, Rabbi.

RABBI AZRAEL [*rises to meet him*]. A good week, a good year to you, Rabbi. Be seated. [RABBI SAMSON *takes a seat.*] I have troubled you to come here in a very grave matter. A Dybbuk (the Lord of Mercy be with us), has entered into a daughter of Israel, and nothing will induce him to leave her. Only the last resort is left, to force him out by anathema, and this I ask your permission to do. The salvation of a soul will thereby be added to your other merits.

RABBI SAMSON [*sighing*]. Anathema is cruel punishment enough for the living — it is far more so for the dead. But if, as you say, all other means have failed, and so godly a man as yourself believe it necessary, I give you my consent. I have a secret, however, which I must reveal to you, Rabbi, for it has a vital bearing on this affair.

RABBI AZRAEL. I am listening, Rabbi.

RABBI SAMSON. Rabbi, do you remember a young Chassid from Brainitz, Nissin ben Rifke by name, who used to come to you from time to time, about twenty years ago?

RABBI AZRAEL. Yes. He went away to some place a long way off and died there, still in his youth.

RABBI SAMSON. That is he. Well, that same Nissin ben Rifke appeared to me three times in my dreams last night, demanding that I summon Sender of Brainitz to trial before the Rabbinical Court.

RABBI AZRAEL. What was his charge against Sender?

RABBI SAMSON. He did not state it to me. He only kept saying that Sender had done him a mortal injury.

RABBI AZRAEL. A rabbi can obviously not prevent any Jew from summoning another to appear before the court, particularly when the complainant is dead and could appeal in the last resort to the Highest Tribunal of all... But how do these visitations of yours affect this Dybbuk?

RABBI SAMSON. In this manner... It has come to my ears that the youth who died and entered into the body of Sender's daughter as a Dybbuk, was Nissin ben Rifke's only son... There is also some rumor concerning a pact with Nissin ben Rifke which has not been kept.

RABBI AZRAEL [after a moment's reflection]. This being the case, I shall postpone the exorcising of the Dybbuk until tomorrow midday. In the morning after prayers, you shall summon the dead man to court, and God willing, we shall discover the reason for his visitations to you. And then, with your permission, I shall cast out the Dybbuk by anathema.

RABBI SAMSON. In view of the difficulty of a trial between a living man and a dead one, which is as rare as it is difficult, I beg that you will preside over the court, Rabbi, and conduct the proceedings.

RABBI AZRAEL. Very well... Michoel. [Enter MICHOEL.] Bring in the maiden. [SENDER and FRADE bring LEAH into the room. She sits down before the RABBI with her eyes closed.] Dybbuk! I give you respite until noon to-morrow. If at that hour you persist in your refusal to leave this maiden's body of your own accord, I shall, with the permission of the City Rabbi, tear you away from her with the utmost force of the *cherem*.[1] [SENDER and FRADE lead LEAH towards the door.] Sender, you are to remain.

[FRADE takes LEAH out.]

[1] The sentence of excommunication.

Sender, do you remember the bosom friend of your youth — Nissin ben Rifke?

SENDER [frightened]. Nissin ben Rifke? He died, didn't he?

RABBI AZRAEL. Know, then, that he appeared three times last night before the Rabbi of the City [indicating RABBI SAMSON] as he slept. And Nissin ben Rifke demanded that you be summoned to stand trial by the Rabbinical Court for a wrong that you have done him.

SENDER [stunned]. Me? A trial? Is there no end to my misfortunes? What does he want of me? Rabbi, help me! What shall I do?

RABBI AZRAEL. I do not know the nature of his charge. But you must accept the summons.

SENDER. I will do whatever you say.

RABBI AZRAEL [in a different tone]. Let the swiftest horses be sent immediately to Brainitz, to fetch the bridegroom and his people. Have them here before midday to-morrow, in order that the wedding may take place as soon as the Dybbuk has been expelled. Have the canopy set up.

SENDER. Rabbi! What if they no longer wish to be connected with my family, and refuse to come?

[The MESSENGER appears in the doorway.]

RABBI AZRAEL [with dignity]. Tell them I have commanded them to come. Let nothing prevent the bridegroom from arriving in time.

MESSENGER. The bridegroom will be here in time.   [The clock strikes twelve.]

CURTAIN

ACT IV

SAME SCENE AS ACT III

Instead of the long table, left, a smaller one nearer to footlights. RABBI AZRAEL, *wrapped in his prayer-shawl and wearing the phylacteries, is in the armchair. The two* JUDGES *sit in ordinary chairs.* RABBI SAMSON *stands beside the table and, at a distance,* MICHOEL. *They are finishing a prayer whereby an evil dream may be turned into good.*

RABBI AZRAEL, MICHOEL, AND THE TWO JUDGES. You beheld a good dream! You beheld a good dream! You beheld a good dream!

RABBI AZRAEL. We have found a solution of good to your dream.

RABBI SAMSON. I beheld a good dream — a good dream I beheld. I beheld a good dream.

RABBI AZRAEL. Will you now, Rabbi Samson, take your seat with the other judges? [RABBI SAMSON *sits down next to* RABBI AZRAEL.] Let us now call upon this dead man to be present at the trial. First, however, I shall draw a holy circle beyond which he may not pass. Michoel, my staff.... [MICHOEL *gives him the staff.* RABBI AZRAEL *then rises and, going to the corner left, describes a circle on the floor from left to right. He then returns to the table.*] Michoel, take my staff and go to the graveyard. When you get there, go in with your eyes closed, guiding yourself with the staff. At the first grave it touches, stop. Knock with it three times upon this grave, and repeat what I shall tell you faithfully word for word: Pure dead, I am sent by Azrael, son of the great sage, Rabbi Itzele of Miropol, to beg you to pardon him for disturbing your peace, and to deliver his command that you inform the pure dead, Nissin ben Rifke, by means known to you as follows: That the just and righteous Rabbinical Court of Miropol summon him to be present immediately at a trial at which he shall appear in the same garb as that in which he was buried. Repeat these words three times; then turn and come back here. You will not look behind you, no matter what cries or calls or shrieks may pursue you, nor will you allow my staff to leave your hand even for one moment, otherwise you will place yourself in dire peril. Go and God will protect you, for no harm can come to him who is bound on a virtuous errand. But before you go, let two men come in and make a partition which shall separate the dead man from the living. [MICHOEL *goes out. Two men enter with a sheet with which they screen the left-hand*

corner down to the floor. They then leave the room.] Let Sender come in. [SENDER *appears.*] Sender, have you carried out my instructions and sent horses for the bridegroom and his people?

SENDER. The swiftest horses were sent, but the bridegroom has not yet arrived.

RABBI AZRAEL. Have some one ride out to meet them and say they are to drive as fast as they can.

SENDER. Yes, Rabbi. [*Pause.*]

RABBI AZRAEL. Sender, we have sent to inform the pure dead, Nissin ben Rifke, that the Rabbinical Court summon him to appear in his cause against you. Are you willing to accept our verdict?

SENDER. I am.

RABBI AZRAEL. Will you carry out our sentence?

SENDER. I will.

RABBI AZRAEL. Then step back and take your place upon the right.

SENDER. Rabbi, it begins to come back to me.... It may be that the trial which Nissin ben Rifke has summoned me to concerns an agreement upon which we shook hands one day many years ago. But in that matter I am not to blame.

RABBI AZRAEL. You will have an opportunity to speak of this later on, after the complainant has made known his grievance. [*Pause.*] Very soon there is personally to appear in our midst, a man from the True World, in order to submit to our judgment a case between himself and a man of our Untrue World. [*Pause.*] A trial such as this is proof that the laws set forth in the Holy Scriptures rule all worlds and all peoples, and unite both the living and the dead within their bonds. [*Pause.*] A trial such as this is difficult and terrible. The eyes of all the worlds are turned towards it, and should this court deviate from the Law by so much as a hair's breadth, tumult would ensue in the Court on High. It is with fear and trembling, therefore, that we are to approach the trial at issue... with fear and trembling....

[*He looks anxiously around him and as he does encounters the partition in the left-hand corner. He ceases to speak. There is a silence of awe.*]

FIRST JUDGE [*in a frightened whisper to the* SECOND JUDGE]. I believe he's come.

SECOND JUDGE [*in the same tone*]. It seems so.

RABBI SAMSON. He is here.

RABBI AZRAEL. Pure dead Nissin ben Rifke! You are commanded by this just and righteous court to stay within the circle and partition assigned to you, and not to go beyond them. Pure dead Nissin ben Rifke, you are commanded by this just and righteous court to state your grievance and the redress you seek against the accused, Sender ben Henie.

[*Awestruck pause. All listen as though turned to stone.*]

FIRST JUDGE. I believe he is answering.

SECOND JUDGE. It seems so.

FIRST JUDGE. I hear a voice but no words.

SECOND JUDGE. And I words but no voice.

RABBI SAMSON [*to* SENDER]. Sender ben Henie, the pure dead Nissin ben Rifke makes demand saying that in the years of your youth you and he were students in the same *yeshiva*, comrades, and that your soul and his were bound together in true friendship. You were both married in the same week, and when you met at the house of the Rabbi, during the Great Holidays, you made a solemn pact that if the wife of one of you should conceive and bear a boy and the other a girl, those two children should marry.

SENDER [*in a tremulous voice*]. It was so.

RABBI SAMSON. The pure dead Nissin ben Rifke makes further demand, saying that soon afterwards he left for a place very far away, where his wife bore him a son in the same hour as your wife gave you a daughter. Soon thereafter he was gathered to his fathers. [*Short pause.*] In the True World, he found that his son had been blest with a noble and lofty soul, and was progressing upwards from plane to plane, and at this his paternal heart overflowed with joy and pride. He also found that his son, growing older, had become a wanderer from province to province, and from country to country, and from city to city, for the soul to which his soul

had been predestined was drawing him ever onward. At last he came to the city in which you dwell, and you took him into your house. He sat at your table, and his soul bound itself to the soul of your daughter. But you were rich, while Nissin's son was poor, and so you turned your back on him and went seeking for your daughter a bridegroom of high estate and great possessions. [*Short pause.*] Nissin then beheld his son grow desperate and become a wanderer once more, seeking now the New Paths. And sorrow and alarm filled his father's soul lest the dark powers, aware of the youth's extremity, spread their net for him. This they did, and caught him, and tore him from the world before his time. Thereafter the soul of Nissin ben Rifke's son roamed amidst the worlds until at last it entered as a Dybbuk into the body of his predestined. Nissin ben Rifke claims that the death of his son has severed him from both worlds, leaving him without name or memorial, since neither heir nor friend remains on earth to pray for his soul. His light has been extinguished forever — the crown of his head has rolled down into the abyss. Therefore, he begs the just and righteous court to pass sentence upon Sender according to the laws of our Holy Scriptures, for his shedding of the blood of Nissin's son and of his son's sons to the end of all generations.

[*An awestruck pause.* SENDER *is shaken with sobs.*]

RABBI AZRAEL. Sender ben Henie, have you heard the complaint brought against you by the holy dead, Nissin ben Rifke? What have you to say in answer to it?

SENDER. I can't speak...I have no words to say...in justification. But I would ask you to beg my old comrade to forgive me this sin, because it was not committed in malice. Soon after we had shaken hands upon our pact, Nissin went away, and I did not know whether his wife had had a child, either boy or girl. Then I received news of his death, but none about his family. And gradually the whole affair of our agreement went out of my mind.

RABBI AZRAEL. Why did you not inquire about him? Why did you make no inquiry?

SENDER. It is customary for the bridegroom's father to make the first advances, not the bride's. I thought that if Nissin had had a son, he would have let me know. [*Pause.*]

RABBI SAMSON. Nissin ben Rifke asks why, when you received his son into your house and had him sit at your table, did you never ask him whence he came and of what family?

SENDER. I don't know.... I don't remember.... But I do swear that something urged me continually to take him for my son-in-law. That was why, whenever a match was proposed, I always made such hard conditions that the bridegroom's father would never agree to them. Three marriages fell through in this manner. But this time the bridegroom's people would not be put off. [*Pause.*]

RABBI SAMSON. Nissin ben Rifke says that in your heart of hearts you were aware of his son's identity and therefore feared to ask him who he was. You were ambitious that your daughter should live in ease and riches, and for that reason thrust his son down into the abyss.

[SENDER *weeps silently, covering his face. There is a heavy pause.* MICHOEL *returns and gives the staff back to* RABBI AZRAEL.]

RABBI AZRAEL [*after a whispered conference with* RABBI SAMSON *and the* JUDGES, *rises and takes the staff in his hand*]. This just and righteous court has heard both parties and delivers its verdict as follows: Whereas it is not known whether, at the time Nissin ben Rifke and Sender ben Henie shook hands upon their agreement, their wives had already conceived; and whereas, according to our Holy Scriptures, no agreement whatsoever which involves anything not yet in existence can be held valid in law, we may not therefore find that this agreement was binding upon Sender. Since, however, in the Upper World, the agreement was accepted as valid and never canceled; and since the belief was implanted in the heart of Nissin ben Rifke's son that the daughter of Sender ben Henie

was his predestined bride; and whereas, Sender ben Henie's subsequent conduct brought calamity upon Nissin ben Rifke and his son; Now, therefore, be it decreed by this just and righteous court, that Sender give the half of his fortune in alms to the poor, and each year, for the remainder of his life, light the memorial candle for Nissin ben Rifke and his son as though they were his own kindred, and pray for their souls. [*Pause.*] The just and righteous court now requests the holy dead, Nissin ben Rifke, to forgive Sender unreservedly, and to command his son in filial duty to leave the body of the maiden, Leah, daughter of Channah, in order that a branch of the fruitful tree of Israel may not be blighted. In return for these things, the Almighty will make manifest his grace to Nissin ben Rifke and to his lost son.

ALL. Amen!

RABBI AZRAEL. Pure dead Nissin ben Rifke, have you heard our judgment? Do you accept it? [*Pause.*] Sender ben Henie, have you heard our judgment? Do you accept it?

SENDER. I accept.

RABBI AZRAEL. Pure dead Nissin ben Rifke, the trial between you and Sender ben Henie is now ended. Do you return therefore to your resting place, and in going we command you to do no harm to man nor other living creature whatsoever. [*Pause.*] Michoel, water.... And have the curtain taken away. [MICHOEL *calls in two men, who remove the sheet.* RABBI AZRAEL *traces a circle in the same place as before, but from right to left. The men return with basin and ewer, and all wash their hands.*] Sender, have the bridegroom and his people arrived?

SENDER. There has been no sign of them.

RABBI AZRAEL. Send another rider to meet them, and say they are to press on with all the speed their horses can make. Have the canopy raised and the musicians in readiness. Let the bride be dressed in her wedding-gown so that the moment the Dybbuk has been cast out you may lead her under the canopy. What is now about to be done — will be done.

[SENDER *goes out.* RABBI AZRAEL *takes off his prayer-shawl and phylacteries, folding them up.*]

RABBI SAMSON [*whispering to the* JUDGES]. Did you notice that the dead man did not forgive Sender?

JUDGES ONE AND TWO [*in low, frightened tones*]. Yes, we did.

RABBI SAMSON. Do you know the dead man did not accept the verdict?

JUDGES ONE AND TWO. Yes, we realized that.

RABBI SAMSON. He failed to say Amen to Rabbi Azrael's sentence — you felt that too, no doubt.

JUDGES ONE AND TWO. Yes, distinctly.

RABBI SAMSON. It is a very bad sign ——

JUDGES ONE AND TWO. Extremely ——

RABBI SAMSON. Rabbi Azrael is terribly agitated — look at him. See how his hands are trembling. [*Pause.*] We have done our share — we can go now.

[*The* JUDGES *slip out unobtrusively, and* RABBI SAMSON *prepares to follow them.*]

RABBI AZRAEL. Rabbi, please remain until the Dybbuk has been cast out — I should like you to perform the wedding ceremony. [*Rabbi* SAMSON *sighs and sits down again, with bowed head. An oppressive pause.*] God of the Heavens, marvelously strange are Thy ways, and secret, yet the flame of Thy Divine Will illuminates with its reflection the path I tread. Nor shall I stray from the path forever, either to the right or to the left. [*He raises his head.*] Michoel, is everything prepared?

MICHOEL. Yes, Rabbi.

RABBI AZRAEL. Let the maiden be brought.

[*Enter* SENDER *and* FRADE *with* LEAH, *in her wedding-gown, a black cloak over her shoulders. They seat her on the sofa.* RABBI SAMSON *takes his place behind* RABBI AZRAEL.]

RABBI AZRAEL. Dybbuk, in the name of the Rabbi of this city, who is present, in the name of a holy community of Jews, in the name of the great Sanhedrin of Jerusalem, I, Azrael ben Hadassah, do for the last time command you to depart out of the body of the maiden Leah, daughter of Channah.

LEAH [DYBBUK] [*firmly*]. I refuse!

RABBI AZRAEL. Michoel, call in people to witness the exorcism — bring the shrouds, the horns and the black candles. [MICHOEL *goes out and shortly returns with fifteen men, among them the* MESSENGER. *The shrouds, trumpets and candles are brought.*] Bring out the scrolls. [MICHOEL *gives a scroll each to seven, and a trumpet each to seven others.*] Stubborn spirit — inasmuch as you have dared to oppose our power, we deliver you into the hands of the Higher Spirits which will pull you out by force. Blow Tekiah![1]

[*The horns are blown.*]

LEAH [DYBBUK] [*leaves her seat and struggles violently as against invisible assailants*]. Let me alone — you shall not pull me away — I won't go — I can't go ——

RABBI AZRAEL. Since the Higher Spirits cannot overcome you, I surrender you to the Spirits of the Middle Plane, those which are neither good nor evil. I now invoke *their* power to drag you forth. Blow Shevarim![1]

[*The horns are blown again.*]

LEAH [DYBBUK] [*her strength beginning to fail*]. Woe is me! The powers of all the worlds are arrayed against me. Spirits of terror wrench me and tear me without mercy — the souls of the great and righteous too have arisen against me. The soul of my own father is with them — commanding me to go —— But until the last spark of strength has gone from me, so long shall I withstand them and remain where I am.

RABBI AZRAEL [*to himself*]. It is clear that One of Great Power stands beside him. [*Pause.*] Michoel, put away the scrolls. [MICHOEL *does so.*] Hang a black curtain over the altar. [*This is done.*] Light the black candles. [*This, too, is done.*] Let every one now put on a shroud. [*All, including the two* RABBIS, *do so.* RABBI AZRAEL *stands with both arms up-*

---

[1] Certain notes sounded on the Shofer, the sacred ram's horn.

raised, an awe-inspiring figure.] Rise up, O Lord, and let Thine enemies be scattered before Thee; as smoke is dispersed so let them be scattered.... Sinful and obstinate soul, with the power of Almighty God and with the sanction of the Holy Scriptures, I, Azrael ben Hadassah, do with these words rend asunder every cord that binds you to the world of living creatures and to the body and soul of the maiden, Leah, daughter of Channah....

LEAH [DYBBUK] [*shrieking*]. Ah! I am lost!

RABBI AZRAEL. ... And do pronounce you ex-communicated from all Israel. Blow Teruah.

MESSENGER. The last spark has been swallowed up into the flame.

LEAH [DYBBUK] [*defeated*]. Alas! — I can fight no more....

[*They begin to sound the horns.*]

RABBI AZRAEL [*hastily raising his hand to silence the horns*]. Do you submit?

LEAH [DYBBUK] [*in a dead voice*]. I submit ——

RABBI AZRAEL. Do you promise to depart of your own free will, from the body of the maiden, Leah, daughter of Channah, and never return?

LEAH [DYBBUK] [*as before*]. I promise ——

RABBI AZRAEL. Dybbuk — by the same power and sanction which deputed me to place you under the ban of anathema, I now lift from you that ban. [*To* MICHOEL.] Put out the candles — take down the black curtain. [MICHOEL *does so.*] Put away the horns. [MICHOEL *collects them.*] And dismiss the people — let them take off their shrouds before they go. [*Exeunt the fourteen with* MESSENGER *and* MICHOEL. RABBI AZRAEL *prays with upraised arms.*] Lord of the world, God of charity and mercy, look down upon the suffering of this homeless, tortured soul which the errors and misdeeds of others caused to stray into the bypaths. Regard not its wrongdoing, O Lord, but let the memory of its virtuous past and its present bitter torment and the merits of its forefathers rise like a soft, obscuring mist before Thy sight. Lord of the world — do Thou free

its path of evil spirits, and admit it to everlasting peace within Thy mansions. Amen.

ALL. Amen.

LEAH [DYBBUK] [*trembling violently*]. Say Kadish [1] for me! The hour of my going was predestined — and it has come!

RABBI AZRAEL. Sender, say Kadish.

[SENDER *begins the prayer as the clock strikes twelve.*]

SENDER. Yisgadaal — ve yiskadesh — shmeh raboh! [2]

LEAH [DYBBUK] [*springs up*]. Aie!

[*Falls swooning upon the sofa.*]

RABBI AZRAEL. Bring the bride to the wedding-canopy.

MICHOEL [*rushing in, greatly agitated*]. The last rider has just come back. He says a wheel has come off the wagon so that the bridegroom and his party must walk the rest of the way. But they are at the hill, so they will be here soon — they've been sighted already.

RABBI AZRAEL [*profoundly astonished*]. What was to be, shall be. [*To* SENDER.] Let the old woman remain here with the bride. We will go — all of us — to meet the bridegroom.

[*He traces a circle round* LEAH, *from left to right, takes off his shroud, which he hangs up near the door, and goes out carrying his staff.* SENDER *and* MICHOEL *follow him. A long pause.*]

LEAH [*waking — in a faint voice*]. Who is here with me? Granny — is that you? Oh! I feel so strange, Granny — so weary. Rock me in your arms.

FRADE [*caressing her*]. No, little daughter — you mustn't feel that way. My little child must not be sad. Let the Black Cat be sad. My little one's heart must be as light as down, as light as a breath, as white as a snowflake. Holy angels should embrace her with their wings.

[*Wedding Music is heard.*]

LEAH [*frightened and trembling, seizes* FRADE'S *hand for protection*]. Listen! They are beginning to dance round the holy grave to cheer up the dead bride and bridegroom.

[1] The prayer for the dead.

[2] Magnified and sanctified be His mighty Name

FRADE. Be calm, my darling. No harm can come to you now — a mighty power is standing guard over you on every side. Sixty giants, with drawn swords, protect you from evil encounter. The holy fathers and holy mothers ward off the evil eye.

[*Little by little she drifts into a chant.*]

Soon they'll lead you under the canopy —
A blessed hour — a happy hour —
Comes your mother — the good and virtuous —
From the Garden of Eden — the Garden of
    Eden,
Of gold and silver are her robes.

Angels twain go out to meet her, go out to meet
    her —
Take her hands — one the right hand, one the
    left hand.
"Channele — Channele mine,
Why do you come decked out so fine?"

So Channele answers the angel:

"Why should I not come robed in state?
Is this not a day of days?
For my bright crown, my only daughter,
Goes to her wedding and luck goes with her."

"Channele, as in robes of state you go,
Why is your face all wan and pale with woe?"

So Channele answers the angel:

"What should I do but sorrow, on this day that
    my daughter's a bride,
For she's led to her wedding by strangers, while I
    must stand mourning aside?"

Under the canopy stands the bride, and old and
young bring her their greetings and good wishes.

And there stands the Prophet Elijah,
The great goblet of wine in his hand,
And the words of his holy blessing
Roll echoing over the land.

[FRADE *falls asleep. Long pause.*]
LEAH [*her eyes closed, sighs deeply — then wakes*]. Who sighed so deeply?
VOICE OF CHANNON. I.
LEAH. I hear your voice, but I cannot see you.
VOICE OF CHANNON. Because you are within a magic circle which I may not enter.

LEAH. Your voice is as sweet as the lament of violins in the quiet night. Who are you? Tell me.
VOICE OF CHANNON. I have forgotten. I have no remembrance of myself but in your thoughts of me.
LEAH. I remember — now — the star that drew my heart towards its light — the tears that I have shed in the still midnight — the one who stood before me ever — in my dreams — was it you?
VOICE OF CHANNON. I ——
LEAH. I remember — your hair, so soft and damp as if with tears — your sad and gentle eyes — your hands with the thin tapering fingers. Waking and sleeping I had no thought but of you. [*Pause — sadly.*] You went away and darkness fell upon me — my soul withered in loneliness like the soul of a widow left desolate — the stranger came — and then — then you returned, and the dead heart wakened to life again, and out of sorrow joy blossomed like a flower.... Why have you now once more forsaken me?
VOICE OF CHANNON. I broke down the barriers between us — I crossed the plains of death — I defied every law of past and present time and all the ages.... I strove against the strong and mighty and against those who know no mercy. And as my last spark of strength left me, I left your body to return to your soul.
LEAH [*tenderly*]. Come back to me, my bridegroom — my husband — I will carry you, dead, in my heart — and in our dreams at night we shall rock to sleep our little children who will never be born.... [*Weeps.*] And sew them little clothes, and sing them lullabies —— [*Sings, weeping.*]

Hush — hush, little children —
No cradle shall hold you —
In no clothes can we fold you.

Dead, that the living cannot mourn;
Untimely lost and never born....

[*The music of a wedding-march is heard approaching.*]
LEAH [*trembling*]. They are coming to take me to a stranger under the canopy — come to me, my true bridegroom; come to me.

VOICE OF CHANNON. I have left your body — I will come to your soul.

[*He appears against the wall, white-robed*]

LEAH [*with joy*].   Come, my bridegroom. The barrier between us is no more.   I see you.   Come to me....

VOICE OF CHANNON [*echo*].   Come to me.

LEAH [*crying out with joy*].   I am coming....

VOICE OF CHANNON [*echo*].   And I to you....   [*Voices outside.*]

VOICES.   Lead the bride to the canopy.

[*Wedding-march is heard.   LEAH rises, dropping, as she does so, her black cloak onto the sofa, and in her white wedding-dress, to the strains of the music, she goes towards CHANNON, and at the spot where he has appeared their two forms merge into one.*]

[RABBI AZRAEL *enters, carrying his staff, followed by the* MESSENGER.   *They stand on the threshold.   Behind them,* SENDER, FRADE *and the rest.*]

LEAH [*in a far-away voice*].   A great light flows about me... predestined bridegroom, I am united to you forever.   Now we soar upward together higher and higher....   [*The stage grows darker.*]

RABBI AZRAEL [*with lowered head*].   Too late!

MESSENGER.   Blessed be a righteous judge.

[*It is now completely dark.   As if from a great distance, singing is heard, scarcely audible.*]

Why, from highest height,
To deepest depth below,
Has the soul fallen?
Within itself, the Fall
Contains the Resurrection.

FINIS

EYVIND OF THE HILLS
[BJÆRG–EJVIND OG HANS HUSTRU]
A DRAMA IN FOUR ACTS
1911
By JÓHANN SIGURJÓNSSON
Translated by HENNINGE KROHN SCHANCHE

DRAMATIS PERSONÆ

HALLA (*pronounced Hadla*), *a well-to-do widow.*

KARI (*pronounced Kowri*), *overseer on* HALLA's *farm.*

BJØRN, HALLA's *brother-in-law, farmer and bailiff.*

ARNES, *a vagrant laborer.*

GUDFINNA, *an elderly, unmarried relative of the family.*

MAGNUS
ODDNY
SIGRID } HALLA's *servants.*
A SHEPHERD BOY

ARNGRIM, *a leper.*

A DISTRICT JUDGE.

TOTA, *a child of three years.*

Peasants, peasant women, and farm-hands.

The action takes place in Iceland in the middle of the eighteenth century. The story of the two principal characters is founded on historical events. Halla's nature is moulded on a Danish woman's soul.

EYVIND OF THE HILLS

ACT I

A "badstofa" or servants' hall. Along each side-wall, a row of bedsteads with bright coverlets of knitted wool. Between the bedsteads, a narrow passageway. On the right, the entrance, which is reached by a staircase. On the left, opposite the entrance, a dormer-window with panes of bladder. On the right, over the bedsteads, a similar window. Long green blades of grass are visible through the panes. In the centre back a door opens into HALLA'S *bed-chamber, which is separated from the "badstofa" by a thin board partition. A small table-leaf is attached by hinges to the partition. A copper train-oil lamp is fastened in the doorcase. Over the nearest bedsteads a cross-beam runs at a man's height from the floor; from this to the roof-tree is half of a man's height. Under the window stands a painted chest. Carved wooden boxes are pushed in under the bedsteads. The "badstofa" is old, the woodwork blackened by age and soot.*

It is early spring, a late afternoon. GUD-FINNA *and* ODDNY *are sitting on the beds facing each other,* GUDFINNA *mending shoes,* ODDNY *putting patches on a coat. THE* SHEPHERD BOY *is standing in the middle of the room, throwing a dart adorned with red cock's feathers. The costumes are old Icelandic.*

THE BOY [*throws his dart*]. Ho! ho! I came pretty near hitting her that time!

GUDFINNA. Hitting whom?

THE BOY. Can't you see the little spider hanging down from the beam? I mean to shoot and break her thread.

ODDNY. You are always up to some tomfoolery.

GUDFINNA. Leave the poor creature in peace! It has done you no harm.

THE BOY [*laughing*]. Do you think she'd break her legs if she should happen to fall down on the floor?

GUDFINNA. I won't have it! Destroying a spider's web is sure to bring bad luck, and you'll end by tearing the window-pane with your dart.

THE BOY. Kari has told me of a man who broke a bowstring with one shot, and that from way off. [*Shoots.*]

GUDFINNA. If you don't stop, you shall wear your shoes with the holes in them.

THE BOY [*pulling the dart out of the beam*]. Would you rather have me shoot your ear-locks?

GUDFINNA. Are you crazy, lad? You might hit my eyes.

THE BOY. I must have some kind of fun. I think I'll have a shot at Oddny's plaits.

ODDNY. If you dare!

THE BOY [*laughing*]. If I have bad luck, you will look at Kari with only one eye.

ODDNY. You need a good spanking.

GUDFINNA. Kari ought not to have given you that dart.

THE BOY [*going to the spider, makes a fanning motion with his hand*]. Up, old spinning-woman, if you bode good! Down, if you bode ill! Up, if you bode good! Down, if you bode ill!

GUDFINNA. You are awfully hard on your shoes, worse than a grown man. I hope you don't walk on the sharpest stones just for fun?

ODDNY. Of course he does!

THE BOY. The sheep were so restless to day. Some of them came near slipping away from me.

ODDNY. If they had, you wouldn't be riding such a high horse now!

GUDFINNA. Have they been bad to you, laddie? Do you never feel timid when you are alone so much?

THE BOY. Sometimes I keep thinking what I should do if a mad bull came tearing down the mountains.

GUDFINNA. Don't speak of them! They

are the worst monsters in the world — except, perhaps, the skoffin.

THE BOY. What is a skoffin?

GUDFINNA. Don't you know that? When a rooster gets to be very old, he lays an egg, and if that's hatched, it becomes a skoffin. It kills a man by just looking at him, and the only thing that can slay it is a church-blessed silver bullet. Indeed, there are many things you have to be careful of, my child. Are you not afraid of the outlaws? They're not good, those fellows; they go about in skins with the wool on them and carry long sticks with ice-spurs, and that at midsummer. Have you ever seen anything of them?

THE BOY. No, but yesterday I pretty near got scared. There came a man with a big bag under his arm. I didn't know him at first, but it was only Arnes.

GUDFINNA. And what did he want of you?

THE BOY. He asked me to show him the way to a spring. He was thirsty.

GUDFINNA. You had better not have too much talk with him. [Hands him the shoes.] There! Now they will last till to-morrow anyway.

[Kneels down, pulls out a box, and examines its contents.]

[Enter HALLA from her chamber.]

HALLA. It is time for the sheep to be milked.

THE BOY. I am going now to drive them home. I was waiting for my shoes.

HALLA. Have you seen anything of the cows to-day?

THE BOY. No. [To ODDNY.] When I get rich I'll give you a cow's tail to tie up your plaits with.

ODDNY. Hold your tongue!

[Exit the BOY.]

HALLA [smiling]. I heard him teasing you a while ago.

ODDNY. He's forever pestering me about Kari — as if I cared!

HALLA [with a little laugh]. Well, Sigrid doesn't take such good care of Magnus's clothes as you of Kari's. [Exit.]

ODDNY [is silent for a moment and looks at the door]. If I were a widow and owned a farm, the men would be noticing me too, even if I had been nothing but a poor orphan servant girl before I married — like some others.

GUDFINNA [rising, a pair of stockings in her hand]. What are you talking about?

[Pushes the box under the bed.]

ODDNY. Do you know who was Halla's father?

GUDFINNA. That is what no one seems to know. Some would have it that he was a parson. [She darns the stockings.]

ODDNY. Yes, or a vagabond. There were also some ugly whispers about a stain on her birth.

GUDFINNA. You'd better bridle your tongue!

ODDNY. I am not so dull as you imagine. When Halla thinks no one is looking, she doesn't take her eyes from Kari. And she has made him overseer; that seems queer to others besides me. Last Sunday at church some one asked me if there was anything between the widow and the "overseer."

GUDFINNA. And what did you say?

ODDNY. I told them that it was quite possible Halla had her lines out for him, but that I did not think Kari would swallow the fly, even if it had gold on its wings.

GUDFINNA. Much good it did you, the gospel you heard in church! I am sorry for you, poor girl! You are crazy about a man who has neither eye nor ear for you, but that is no reason why you should be running around spreading gossip. Halla is not the kind of woman that is fond of men. There was never a harsh word between her and her husband, God rest his soul, but there was not much love-making between them either. No, indeed!

ODDNY. Well, what of that! He was a man up in years and had a fine farm.

GUDFINNA. He was an upright and honest man, and Halla made him a good wife, my dear.

ODDNY. Who doubts that? [Silence.] I don't know what ails Kari of late. Yesterday he flew into a rage when I asked him if he knew of a cure for freckles. I hope Halla has not become such a saint yet that one can't notice her freckles.

[*Enter* KARI *and* MAGNUS.]

KARI AND MAGNUS. Good evening!
GUDFINNA AND ODDNY. Good evening!
ODDNY [*rising*]. I am sitting on your bed, I believe.
MAGNUS [*throws off his cap*]. Oddny, ask Sigrid to come here and pull off my stockings. [*Sits down.*] It feels good to sit down. [ODDNY *goes reluctantly.*]
KARI. Why is she so grumpy? She is not so cheerful a body as you are. I should like to have known you in your young days. I dare say you knew how to handle a rake.
GUDFINNA [*straightening her back*]. You may be sure. On dry ground, two lively fellows had all they could do to make ready for my rake.
KARI. And you were not afraid to tuck up your skirts, where the ground was low and marshy.
GUDFINNA. Indeed not! Many a time I had water in my shoes.

[*Enter* SIGRID *and* ODDNY.]

MAGNUS [*stretching his feet out on the floor*]. Pull off my shoes! I'm so tired to-night I can't move.
SIGRID. It must be laziness that ails you, as usual. [*Kneels down.*] How in the name of heaven did you manage to get so wet in this dry weather? I can wring the water out of your stockings.
MAGNUS. Kari wanted to jump the creek to make a short cut, and I fell in.
ODDNY [*to* KARI]. Aren't you wet, too?
KARI. No. [*Sits down.*]
MAGNUS. Kari skims over everything like a bird.
KARI. Every man has his gift. [*To* SIGRID.] You should see the rocks Magnus can lift.
MAGNUS. Well, it may be true that I am pretty strong, but I should like to see the man who could throw you in an honest *glima*.
ODDNY. I know one whom Kari couldn't stand against.
MAGNUS. And who is that? [SIGRID *pulls at his stockings.*] There! There!
ODDNY. Bjørn, Halla's brother-in-law.
MAGNUS. I should not be afraid to bet

on Kari against him. [*To* SIGRID.] Give me the stockings!
[*Dries his feet with the stocking legs.*]
[SIGRID *pulls out a chest, where she finds dry stockings.*]

[*Enter* HALLA.]

ODDNY. I don't think Kari would dare to try a fall with the bailiff.
KARI. If you were the prize, I should not dare to!
GUDFINNA [*laughing*]. There you got it! [*Everybody laughs except* ODDNY.]
HALLA [*smiling*]. Yet many have fought for less.
MAGNUS. I'm ready to make a wager with you, Oddny, that Kari would win.
HALLA. It does not look as if the cows were coming home to-night. Magnus, won't you go up the gorge and see if they are there, and I will send the boy down to the creek.
[*Exit* SIGRID *with the wet stockings.*]
MAGNUS. Oh, why did I bother to change my stockings!
HALLA. You can take a horse. [*A dog is heard barking.*] There! we shall have company.
KARI [*rising*]. I'll run up there.
HALLA. You have your trout nets to look after. I know Magnus won't mind.
MAGNUS. Confound those cows! Why can't they come home in time!
[*Puts on his shoes.*]
[KARI *pulls out a small box from under the bed and begins to whittle teeth for a rake.*]

[ARNES *puts his head in at the door; he carries a large bag.*]

ARNES. Good evening! I did not want to trouble any one to come to the outside door. [*Drops his bag on the floor.*] Now Arnes is rich — there's gold sand in my bag.
HALLA. I dare say there is.
ARNES. You people don't know what lies hidden in the hills. I have heard of a man who lost his way in Surt's Cave. For days he walked underground, and when at last he came up he had gold sand in his shoes.

HALLA. What would you do if that were really gold in your bag?

ARNES. Then Arnes would do many things. You should help yourself to all your hands could hold, and as many times as you have given me shelter, and Arngrim the leper should also fill his fists. I know of no one else to whom I care to do good.

GUDFINNA. And should I have nothing?

ARNES. I would give you new, long ear-locks of gold.

MAGNUS [laughing]. Some little gift you'd surely have for the bailiff — no?

ARNES. For him? Yes, if I could throw the sand into his eyes. [Opens the bag and takes out a handful of Iceland moss.] They are fine, these lichens, and taste good when you cook them in milk.

GUDFINNA [rising and muttering to herself]. The milk!   [Exit.]

ARNES [holding up a handful]. See how big they are.

HALLA. Yes, they are fine.

ARNES [patting the bag]. And it is well stuffed, too.

[Enter the BOY.]

THE BOY. Now you can milk the sheep.

HALLA. You are not through yet, poor boy. You will have to go down along the creek and look for the cows.
[Exit ODDNY.]

THE BOY. I hope they're not up to new tricks and begin to stay out nights.
[Exit.]

HALLA [calling after him]. Take a drink of milk in the pantry; the key is in the door.
[MAGNUS rises slowly.]

ARNES. Are you going to buy my bag?

HALLA. If you make the price right.

ARNES. You ought to have it for nothing — you've given me shelter and good food so often. [Lifts his foot.] What I need most just now is to get something on my feet.

HALLA. I don't think we shall quarrel about the price. [To MAGNUS.] Take it out into the kitchen.
[Exit MAGNUS with the bag.]

HALLA. Will you not sit down? I'll go and find you a bite to eat.   [Exit.]

ARNES [following her with his eyes]. That woman has a kind heart. [Sits down.] How long have you been working here on the farm?

KARI. This is my second year.

ARNES. And overseer already? Yes, some folks have luck. [Leans toward him.] As you may know, I haven't a very good name. I can't settle down very long at any one place, and it comes hard for me to be anybody's servant. You must surely have heard me spoken of as a thief?

KARI. People will say so many things.

ARNES [passing his hand over his ears]. My ears are not marked yet, but somehow it sticks to you like dust — what people say — no matter whether it is true or not. Have you ever been the target for gossipy tales?

KARI [slowly]. Not that I know of.

ARNES. Then you have it coming to you. Shall I tell you what they are saying about you in these parts?

KARI. Is it about me and Halla?

ARNES. I have heard that too, but this story is about yourself.

KARI. I would rather be spared listening to gossip.

ARNES. If I had been quite sure that it was nothing but gossip, I should not have opened my mouth about it.

KARI [laughing coldly]. You are at least frank.

ARNES [rising]. It is all the same to me, but if you have anything to hide, you had better keep your eyes and ears open, for you have an enemy, that much I can tell you.

KARI. I don't know that I have harmed any one around here.

ARNES. You live and fill your place. That is enough to make enemies.

[Enter HALLA with a wooden mug filled with porridge and milk. The lid is turned back and some meat, dried fish, and butter are placed upon it.]

HALLA. You get nothing but skimmed milk. I thought you would rather have that than wait until the cows had been milked.   [Lets down the table-leaf.]

ARNES [sits down and reaches for the mug].

God bless you, woman! I am used to having it on my knees.

[*Pulls out his pocket-knife and eats.*]

HALLA [*stops in front of* KARI *and looks at him*]. You are working hard; there are drops of sweat on your forehead.

KARI. Are there? [*Wipes his forehead; looks up.*] Should you like to know your life beforehand? [*Stands up and raises both arms to the ceiling.*] I have lived where I could touch the roof over my head with my clenched fists, and I have lived where my eyes could not reach it. [*Sits down.*] Can you remember how few clothes I had when I came here?

HALLA [*sitting down*]. I can well remember the green knitted jerkin you wore — you have it yet — and your coat and brown breeches. [*Smiling.*] There was a big black patch on the left knee.

KARI. The rags on my back were all I had in the world, and now I own two new sets and even more underclothes. You deserve that I should put teeth of gold in your rake.

HALLA [*smiling*]. That rake would be too heavy for me.

KARI [*looking at* HALLA]. So many things come back to me to-night that I have not thought of before. You gave me leave to work in the smithy in my spare time instead of doing the wool-carding. You saw to it that I should be one of the men who gather the sheep down from the hills in the fall, because you knew I liked it.

HALLA. That was only natural, since you are so swift of foot.

KARI. And for my bed you knitted a coverlet with seven colors in it. You have always been good to me.

HALLA. Now you are getting far too grateful. [*To* ARNES.] Do you think you have enough food there, Arnes? I can get you some more, if you want it.

ARNES [*patting his stomach*]. I don't even know if I can make room for the porridge.

KARI [*looking at* HALLA]. If I were to leave this place, I should miss you more than any other living being I have ever known.

[*Rises, pushes the box under the bed.*]

HALLA. I hope you will stay here for many years yet.

KARI. Nobody knows what the morrow may bring. [*Exit.*]

[HALLA *follows* KARI *with her eyes. Silence.*]

ARNES [*puts the wooden mug on the table*]. Now I give thanks for the meal. Will you let me lie in one of your barns to-night?

HALLA. You would surely sleep better in a bed. You can lie with Magnus.

ARNES. I never sleep better than in old dry hay.

[*Enter* GUDFINNA.]

GUDFINNA. Is it true, Arnes, that you can tell what the birds are talking about?

ARNES. Do they say that?

GUDFINNA. In olden times there were wise folks who understood all such things, but people nowadays are backward in that as in so many other ways. [*Sits down.*]

HALLA [*smiling*]. Yes, young people are not good for much, in your opinion.

GUDFINNA. We need only think of the sagas. Where have we men now like Skarphjedinn and Grettir Asmundsson? There are none such in these days.

HALLA. When I was a child there was nothing I wished so much as that I might have lived with Grettir in his banishment.

ARNES. Was it not eighteen years he was an outlaw?

HALLA. Nineteen. He lived longer as an outlaw than any one else has done. He lacked only one year to become free.

ARNES. He must have been a great man, but that brings to my mind what the leper said the other day, when the talk turned to the old sagas.

HALLA. And what did he say?

ARNES. Distance makes mountains blue and mortals great.

[*Enter the* BOY, *running.*]

THE BOY. The bailiff is coming on horseback.

HALLA [*rising*]. What can he want so late? Did you find the cows?

THE BOY. Yes, I met them coming home. They are in.

HALLA. Did you tell the girls?

THE BOY. No. [*Exit.*]

HALLA. Gudfinna, you go and ask him to come in. [GUDFINNA *rises.*] You won't forget about the milk? [*Exit* GUDFINNA.]

ARNES [*rising*]. Now I think I shall go and seek my bed.

HALLA [*smiling*]. Don't you want to have a talk with the bailiff?

ARNES. If I had found some dead sheep up in the hills with his mark on their ears, I'd gladly have told him so.

HALLA. Sleep well! [*Exit* ARNES.]

[HALLA *smooths her hair.*]

[*Enter* BJØRN, *carrying a riding-whip with a silver-mounted handle and a leather lash; he wears riding-socks reaching above the knees.*]

HALLA. Good evening!

BJØRN [*pointing to his feet*]. I did not take off my socks. I see now that they are not quite clean.

HALLA. Will you be seated? May I offer you anything?

BJØRN. No, thank you. I want nothing. [*Sits down.*] You know I have not far to come. The sorrel and I can make it in fifteen minutes, when we are in the humor.

HALLA. How is everything at your place? Have you any news?

BJØRN. That depends on what you mean. Who was that I met in the hall? It was quite dark there.

HALLA. It must have been Arnes.

BJØRN. Is he spending the night here?

HALLA. Yes.

BJØRN. It is no concern of mine, but I doubt if my late brother would have sheltered men of his kind, and yet he had the name of being hospitable.

[*Takes a snuff-box from his pocket.*]

HALLA [*sitting down*]. I know nothing wrong of Arnes, and I do know that he is grateful for what I can offer him.

BJØRN. I thought you had heard the common talk. His record is not of the best, I am sorry to say. I have been told that little things are apt to be missing where he has made his stay.

HALLA. I would rather bear such a loss in silence than perhaps throw suspicion on an innocent man.

BJØRN. Finely thought! Yet some one must be the first to warn the unwary. [*Takes snuff.*] You must hear what happened to me not long ago. The boy lost two milch sheep up in the hills. I was vexed that it should occur so early in the summer when they still had their wool, and therefore I sent one of my men to look for them. Near Red Peak he found tracks of the sheep and also the foot-prints of a large man. [*Lowering his voice.*] You could do me a good turn if you would give Arnes a pair of new shoes; I should pay for them, of course. He will not suspect anything, if you do it. Then you keep his old shoes for me.

HALLA [*rising*]. No, I will have nothing to do with that.

BJØRN. Then we shan't speak of it any more. I think I shall find out what I am after, nevertheless. [*He is silent.*]

HALLA. You surely didn't come here to-night for Arnes's sake?

BJØRN. I did not. Was Kari at church last Sunday?

HALLA. Why do you ask?

BJØRN. I know that he was there. [*Sits down.*] You are satisfied with him as an overseer?

HALLA [*sits down*]. In every way.

BJØRN. All the same, I advise you to get rid of him, the sooner the better.

HALLA [*laughing*]. I thank you for your kind advice.

BJØRN. My advice is not to be scorned, and besides, am I not your brother-in-law?

HALLA. My sheep had to learn that to their cost, when they strayed in on your pastures, and you set your dogs on them.

BJØRN. Even though we have not always been as neighborly as I might wish, you must listen to me this time. I have always disliked Kari; I would never have hired that man. Believe me, there is something underhanded about him. Nobody knows him, and no one has heard of his people. It is as if he had shot up out of the ground. The only thing you know about him is that his name is Kari, and you don't even know that.

HALLA [*rising*]. What are you driving at with all this?

BJØRN. Sit still. [HALLA *sits down*.] Last fall two strangers who stopped on their journey through here thought they knew Kari. They said it was easier to change one's name than one's face. As bad luck would have it, I did not get a chance to talk with them myself, but my suspicions were roused. Now there is a man staying with me who has just come from the south. He saw Kari at church last Sunday, and if he is right, it is an ugly story.

HALLA. What do you mean?

BJØRN [*rising*]. Neither more nor less than that your overseer's name is not Kari but Eyvind, that he was locked up for theft, and got away.

HALLA [*has risen*]. You must be mad, both of you.

BJØRN. The man would not swear that he had seen right. [*Smiles*.] Somehow he seemed sorry that he had told me. He said he had never seen two people more alike, and Eyvind had a scar on his forehead just as Kari has — that much he remembered plainly.

HALLA. It was last Sunday at church that he saw Kari?

BJØRN. Yes.

HALLA [*laughing*]. Kari was not at church last Sunday.

BJØRN. That's queer. Two of my men were there. But we can easily solve that riddle, if I bring my guest over here to-morrow.

HALLA. I don't believe for a moment that Kari is a thief.

BJØRN. You need not believe it. Simply tell him what I have said, and that I mean to have the judge look into the matter. I warrant he will be out of the house before sunrise.

HALLA. You are quick to believe evil and quick to run to the judge, but in this case you will not reap much honor.

BJØRN. If you suppose I shall act hastily, you are mistaken. I shall write to the county that Eyvind hails from and give the letter to my guest, who will see that it gets safely and speedily into the proper hands. The answer can be here within two or three months.

HALLA. Is it out of kindness to me that you are so eager about this matter?

BJØRN. If it is true what people say, it would be best for you that Kari should take himself away from here as fast as can be. You might find it harder to part from him two or three months hence.

HALLA [*icily*]. Now you show your real self. You did not come here to give me kind counsel, nor do I look for such from you, but you had better leave me and my household in peace. Do you think I have forgotten what you did to me? When your brother told you that he intended to marry me, you thought it would be a disgrace to the family for him to make a poor servant girl his wife. You urged him to satisfy his fleeting passion, as you called it, without any marriage.

BJØRN. I never said that.

HALLA [*laying her hand on her heart*]. In here I have a sealed book in which I keep the words my friends have spoken. And I have more to tell you. There was something behind it — your fear of losing a part of your power.

BJØRN. What are you saying?

HALLA. Did that prick your soul, you godly man! You knew that your brother would follow your advice like a child, but you had misgivings that you could not work me like dough in your hands, and what you feared came true. You can never forget that I made my husband stand on his feet. I know your greed for power! But now I warn you for all time to let me and mine alone.

[*Sits down*].

BJØRN [*flushed with anger, but still controlling his voice*]. Much have I learned to-night that I did not know before. Now I see why you made Kari overseer. You are not your mother's daughter for nothing.

HALLA [*her lips trembling*]. You want to make me angry. You can't do it. Nor shall you succeed in blackening Kari in my eyes. You were hoping that I should hurt him by telling him what you have said. I shall not tell him.

BJØRN. You will talk differently when I hold the proof in my hand.

[*Shakes his hand; goes toward the door.*]

HALLA [rising, hatred burning in her eyes]. Just before you came, the servants were making bets about who was best at glima, you or Kari. Oddny was the only one who stood up for you. Kari thought you had grown so old and stiff in your joints that you would not dare to go in for a wrestling-match.

BJØRN. Tell Kari that I am ready to meet him this evening, if he wishes it.

HALLA. No, I shall tell Kari that you have given your word to wrestle with him at the big sheep-folds in the fall. I hope to have a good many witnesses, when the bailiff bites the dust.

BJØRN. I will fight him whenever and wherever he may wish — anywhere but in jail. Good-bye! [Exit.]

HALLA [stands motionless for a moment; passes her hands down over her face; goes to the door; calls]. Gudfinna! Gudfinna!

[Goes back into the room; again passes her hands down over her face.]

[Enter GUDFINNA.]

GUDFINNA. Has the bailiff gone?

HALLA. Yes.

GUDFINNA. He came near upsetting me in the hall and didn't even say good evening.

HALLA. Do sweep the floor! I won't have in here the dirt he has dragged with him.

[GUDFINNA takes a bird's wing and sweeps.]

[Enter the BOY.]

THE BOY [shouting]. Come and see what we have caught!

GUDFINNA. Not so noisy! Did you catch a whale?

THE BOY. We got a salmon — so big! [Shows the size with his hands.]

HALLA. Tell Kari to come here; I want to speak with him. I will let you take care of the salmon. Open and clean it, sprinkle some salt on it, and lay it in fresh grass overnight.

THE BOY. Won't you look at it before it is cut?

HALLA [patting his cheek]. You big baby! Do you think I have never seen a salmon before? Now run and tell Kari that I want to speak to him. [Exit the BOY.]

GUDFINNA [calling after him through the door]. And tell him to lift the milk pot from the fire.

HALLA. If the coals are good, I must ask you to do some baking to-night for Sunday.

GUDFINNA. The coals are good enough. [Exit.]

[HALLA stands listening. Footsteps are heard in the hall.]

[Enter KARI.]

KARI. You wanted to speak to me?

HALLA. I hear you have made a fine catch. Thank you! I have promised the bailiff that you shall meet him in a glima at the folds in the autumn. What do you say to that?

KARI. I call that great news, but surely that was not what he came here for to-night?

HALLA. No, he had another errand. He spoke ill of you.

KARI. What did he say?

HALLA. There is a man just come from the south who saw you at church last Sunday. He told Bjørn that you looked like some one by the name of Eyvind, a thief who had run away. He even thought he recognized the scar on your forehead.

KARI [in a low voice, sitting down]. And did the bailiff believe the man was right?

HALLA. He said I should tell you that he meant to speak to the judge, and that then you would flee from here this very night.

KARI [rising with a loud laugh]. This is to laugh at. Do you know when they will come to catch the thief!

HALLA [has been looking at him steadily; holds out her hand to him]. Give me your hand, Kari, and say that you have nothing to fear from any man.

KARI [evasively]. I understand that this seems strange to you, but the man who saw me must be some one who has a grudge against me from former days, and does this out of spite.

HALLA. What do I care about him or about the bailiff! Say that you are innocent!

KARI. So you doubt me, too!

HALLA [aloof]. I have no right to call you to task.

KARI [warmly]. I know of no one in the world whom I would rather trust than you.

HALLA. You are innocent?

KARI. Yes, in this I am innocent.

HALLA. God be praised! [Puts her hand on her heart.] If it had been otherwise, I don't see how I could have borne it.

KARI. I shall remember the bailiff for this.

HALLA [in an outburst of joy]. Let him do his worst! What care we! I am so happy now that I know you are innocent, I could kiss you for joy. [Exultantly.] Kari, will you be my husband?

[It is growing dark.]

KARI [terrified]. No, Halla, I cannot.

HALLA [stares at him, speechless. Suddenly she goes close to him and scans his face]. Have you a wife?

KARI. No.

HALLA. I could not believe that your eyes lied this evening. [Stamps her foot with anger and shame]. Take yourself away from here! Go!

[Covers her face with her hands; rocks to and fro.]

KARI. My eyes did not lie to-night. [Stands for a moment in terrible emotion; then begins to walk up and down.] I knew a man named Eyvind. His father was poor and had many children. Eyvind was the next to the oldest. It was said in those parts that thieving ran in the blood of his kin, though no one could say anything against Eyvind's father. [HALLA looks up, listening.] Two years ago or more, toward the end of the winter, it happened, as often before, that there was no food in the house. Eyvind went to the parson to ask him to help them out with food. He offered to pay for it with his work in the spring, but the parson refused. It was late in the evening, dark and snowing. The road to Eyvind's home went past the parson's sheep-cots. [As KARI proceeds, he now and then passes his hand over his forehead.] They loomed before him like a big black mound. Then the temptation came over him. The herdsman had gone home, the snow would cover up the tracks, and the parson was rich enough. I hated him! [HALLA rises.] Late that night, Eyvind came home with a fine big sheep. The next day, word came from the parson. They had found his mittens in the sheepcot. Eyvind was locked up and given ten years in prison. They thought they could prove that he had more thefts to answer for —— [He breaks off suddenly.]

HALLA [breathlessly] Kari!

KARI. My name is not Kari — it is Eyvind. I was sentenced for theft. I fled and lived one year in the hills as an outlaw.

HALLA. After this I shall never believe in any one.

[Sits down and bursts into tears.]

KARI [kneeling]. Do with me what you will. Drive me out of your house — now — this evening, or give me into the hands of the law, but you must forgive me. It was our poverty and the snow that made me steal.

HALLA [rising]. I will not cry. It is stupid to cry. Get up! I am no God that you should ask my forgiveness.

KARI [rising to his feet]. It is lonesome to live a whole winter up there in the hills. That is why I ventured down here, far from home, and under a new name. Since then I have gone about like one who walks in his sleep, afraid of the awakening. Many a time have I made up my mind to tell you the whole truth, but somehow it seemed to get harder with every day that passed. I have never understood why it was so before to-night, but now I know it, and now I can speak of it. Kari has loved you. You are the only woman he has ever loved, but now Kari is no more, and never has been anything but the dream of a poor and unhappy man.

HALLA. Say no more!

KARI. He has loved you long, but never until to-night has he seen how beautiful you are. [Carried away.] Like a blue mountain rising from the mist!

HALLA [stepping close to him]. Close your eyes, Kari, and sleep yet a while Kiss me!

KARI [kissing her]. I will sleep with my eyes open.

ACT II

A resting-place near one of the large folds into which the sheep are driven in the autumn, when they are gathered down from the hills. A grass-grown dell. On the left, a steep heather-covered slope, here and there in the heather gray, jutting stones. To the right, a low bluff, where grass, flowers, and juniper bushes grow in the clefts and on the ledges. Toward the background, the bluff becomes lower and more bushy, and bending somewhat to the left, it partly shuts off the view into a hilly, rock-studded landscape with the distant mountains beyond. In the foreground, at the foot of the bluff, several saddles. The women's saddles have broad, brass-mounted backs.

It is a fine autumn day. GUDFINNA *alone is busy with the luggage.*

[*Enter* ARNGRIM *carrying a roll of paper under his arm. His face is livid and drawn.*]

ARNGRIM. So you are all alone here.

GUDFINNA. Indeed I am. I did not want to leave the luggage, and it seemed a pity to keep the boy from the folds.

ARNGRIM. Is Halla up at the folds?

GUDFINNA. I don't know where she is now. She is so restless to-day. A while ago she climbed up on a knoll to see if the last drove was coming down from the hills. I hardly know whether it's the sheep or Kari she is looking for.

ARNGRIM. We don't get tired of watching for what we are looking forward to. I have but one thing to look forward to.

[*Sits down on one of the rocks.*]

GUDFINNA. And what is that, poor fellow?

ARNGRIM. To hear the nails being driven into my coffin. Then I should say like the man in the story: "Now I'd laugh if I weren't dead."

[*Enter* HALLA, *happy and smiling, wearing a silver girdle around her waist.*]

HALLA. The last flock is coming, and it is not the smallest. Kari is with it.

GUDFINNA. Of course he is with it.

HALLA [*laughing*]. Yes, of course. [*To* ARNGRIM.] I am glad to see you here.

ARNGRIM. Did you happen to bring anything good from home?

HALLA [*smiling*]. You never can tell. [*Searching in one of the saddle-bags, she finds a blue flask which she hands to* ARNGRIM.] You may keep the bottle.

ARNGRIM. That is just like you. [*Holds the flask up to the light.*] There are juniper berries in it. [*Takes a pull.*] It is like drinking sunshine.

HALLA [*has moved toward the background and stands gazing*]. What a change in the sheep since spring. Then they were yellow and dirty, but now they are white as ptarmigans in winter. It always makes me happy to see a flock of sheep coming down the mountain side.

GUDFINNA. Kari's shoes must be a sight. He doesn't save his legs, that man.

HALLA. No, you are right in that. [*Goes to* GUDFINNA.] But he runs swifter than any one else.

ARNGRIM. No one can run away from his fate, were he fleeter than the wind.

HALLA [*turns to* ARNGRIM]. Are you sure of that? May not a strong will turn the tide of fate?

ARNGRIM. My fate no one can alter. [*Looks up.*] An old song comes to my mind when I look at you. I cannot remember how it runs, but it is about some one who had the thoughts of her soul written on her forehead.

HALLA [*smiling*]. I feel only the sun shining on my brow. [*Exit.*]

ARNGRIM. She deserves to be happy. [*Brings out the roll of paper.*] Should you like to see what I am doing to make the days slip by?

GUDFINNA [*goes to him*]. Yes, let me look at it.

ARNGRIM [*opens the roll, which is seen to contain drawings in bright colors*]. These are birds from the garden of Eden — too bad I never heard them sing! — and here is a blue flower so sensitive that it closes at the slightest touch, and here is a small plant from Gethsemane with red berries lying like drops of blood on the ground.

[*Enter the* BOY, *running.*]

THE BOY. Kari is coming!

GUDFINNA. We know that.

THE BOY. I must be off again to help drive the sheep into the fold. [*Leaps with joy.*] What fun to be here! It's most as good as Christmas! [*Exit.*]

ARNGRIM. He skips about like a merry little lamb.

GUDFINNA [*calling after him*]. Take care the rams don't butt you!

[*Enter HALLA.*]

HALLA. Now the sheep will soon be at the fold. [*Brushes her hair back from her forehead.*] Aren't you clever enough to know a cure for freckles? I am so tired of my freckles.

ARNGRIM [*smiling*]. Perhaps you have a new looking-glass.

HALLA [*smiling*]. Perhaps I have.

[*Enter JON and two other peasants, followed directly by two peasant women, JON's WIFE, and her friend with two little daughters, eight and nine years old.*]

JON [*slightly intoxicated*]. Now a bite of shark's meat would taste first-rate. You didn't happen to be so thoughtful as to bring some, did you?

HALLA [*laughing*]. That is just what I did. [*Looks in the saddle-bags.*]

JON. Didn't I tell you so! [*Takes a brandy-flask out of his pocket.*] Do you mind if I bring out my bottle?

HALLA. Please yourself.

JON [*sits down. The others follow suit, until only the children remain standing*]. If I didn't have so fine a wife, I should have asked you to marry me long ago. [*Takes a pull at the flask and hands it to the one sitting next to him.*] Let the bottle go the rounds!

HALLA [*to JON's WIFE*]. Your husband is happy to-day.

JON's WIFE. Yes, he loves everybody to-day.

FIRST PEASANT [*hands the flask to JON*]. Thanks!

JON. Don't think I am forgetting you, Arngrim. [*Hands him the flask.*]

ARNGRIM. The blood grows colder as one gets old, and then the warmth of the bottle feels good.

HALLA [*hands JON a piece of shark's meat*]. Help yourself.

JON. Bless you! My mouth waters. [*Takes a knife from his pocket and cuts off a slice.*] It is white as milk and sweet-smelling. I say, shark's meat and brandy are the best things the Lord ever made — next to women!

[*Hands the fish to one of the peasants.*]

HALLA [*finds a piece of sugar-candy and divides it between the children*]. Have the little girls been to the folds before?

PEASANT WOMAN. No, this is the first time. I promised them last spring that if they were good and worked hard I would bring them, and they have surely earned it. It's past belief how much they can do, no older than they are.

HALLA. Did you see the last flock? That was a large one.

[*Goes toward the background.*]

JON's WIFE. Indeed it was.

JON. My brown bell-wether was the leader of the flock. He generally stays in the hills till they gather in the sheep for the last time, unless there are signs of bad weather.

[GUDFINNA *crosses over to the peasant women and fingers their clothes. They stand talking together.*]

FIRST PEASANT. I should not wonder if the winter were to come early after so good a summer.

SECOND PEASANT. God knows how many sheep the hills have taken this year! Do you remember those cold days in the spring? It may be a good many lambs froze to death.

FIRST PEASANT. And then those cursed foxes!

JON. The foxes are nothing to the men both those down here and those in the hills.

SECOND PEASANT. I don't believe there is anybody living in the hills, at least not in these parts.

JON. You don't believe it? I tell you, my good man, there are more outlaws than you think. To my mind, the laws are to blame for it. If I had my say, all thieves would be strung up.

SECOND PEASANT. Well, I look at it in another way. I believe the laws are too strict. It seems to me it is making too much of the sheep, when a man is locked up for life because he has stolen two or three of them.

JON. You always have to be of a different mind from anybody else.

[HALLA comes back and listens.]

SECOND PEASANT. I don't know about that, but those who flee to the hills do it from need. If the laws were milder, I believe there would be no outlaws. What do you say, Arngrim?

ARNGRIM. If we were all to be judged by our thoughts, the hills would be swarming with outlaws.

HALLA. It is too light yet to be talking about thieves. Can't you tell us something funny?

JON'S WIFE. Tell about our calf.

JON [laughing]. When he saw the sun for the first time in his life, he fell down on his tail from fright.

Enter ARNES, *somewhat intoxicated*

JON. There comes the man who can tell us stories. [Rises and goes to meet him.]

ARNES. Good day to you all! So you want a story?

JON. You shall have a drink if you tell us a story, but it must be a good one.

ARNES. Hand me the bottle. [Drinks.] I could tell you some spook stories that would make your hair stand on end, but they are better told in the gloaming. [Laughs.] The girls are less afraid of us men folks when they hear about spooks.

JON [laughing]. Yes, of two evils men are better than spooks.

ARNES [sees HALLA]. Now I know what I shall tell you. Hush! Once upon a time there were two outlaws. What their crime had been I don't know, but they had to flee to the hills to save their lives. They found a green spot among the glaciers, hemmed in by huge rocks. There they built their hut, for there they knew they would be left in peace. But the hills were hankering for their old loneliness and hated those two, and swore they would drive them away. First they sent the storms and the frost. There came a winter night so terrible that the roots of the grass trembled with fear under the snow, but unknown to those two

their love had built an invisible wall around the hut, and the storm and the snow could not get in. Then the hills sent hunger. It came to them in their dreams, tempting them with sweet-smelling hot bread and butter fresh from the churn. It would have them barter their love ——

[Enter a FARM HAND.]

THE FARM HAND. Is Arnes here by any chance?

ARNES. Here I am.

THE FARM HAND. There is a sheep with earmarks that nobody can make out. Will you come over and take a look at it?

ARNES [rising]. No peace to be had!

HALLA [holding out her hand to ARNES]. Thanks for the story.

[ARNES takes HALLA's hand. Exit.]

THE FARM HAND [to JON]. Your brown bell-wether ran away from the men as they were trying to drive it in.

JON [rising]. That promises a fine fall.

[All the peasants rise.]

JON'S WIFE [to HALLA]. We shall see each other later.

HALLA. So we shall. [Exeunt peasants.]

GUDFINNA. They have not been sparing of the shark's meat. [Packs it away.]

[Enter KARI, warm from running, happy and smiling.]

KARI. Good day to you, Halla!

[Shakes hands with her.]

HALLA [has gone to meet KARI]. Good day to you, and welcome back!

ARNGRIM [rising]. Now I am so drunk that I can enjoy listening to the bleating of the sheep. By the way, washing with luke-warm milk is good for freckles. [Exit.]

HALLA. Thanks! [To GUDFINNA.] You may go now, if you like. You have been here with the luggage long enough.

[Exit GUDFINNA.]

[HALLA and KARI stand silent until GUDFINNA has disappeared. Then KARI draws her to him and kisses her.]

HALLA. I would rather wait for you here than meet you at the fold. I was so frightened! I thought you had gone and would never come back. [Takes his hand and looks at him in loving wonder.] Where do you get your courage? I can't understand that you have not fled long ago.

KARI. I will tell you where I get my courage. [*Kisses her.*] I don't know how the days can be so gloriously long. It seems to me that I have lived more than the age of man since the first time you kissed me.

HALLA. You love me!

KARI [*is silent for a moment*]. I love you.

HALLA. You don't know how much that one word promises me. It means the sunshine on the hills. It means the streams and lakes. Shall I tell you something, Kari? Something you don't know?

KARI. What could that be?

HALLA. I am not going to say it just now, but I will tell you something else. I care a thousand times more for you now than I did three months ago. Do you know why?

KARI. No.

HALLA. Because you are so brave. You sleep in my arms as calmly as if you had not a foe in the whole country.

KARI [*smiling*]. I must have borrowed your courage.

HALLA. It is dear to see you smile. Your hair is like a cloud, and when you smile it seems to lift from your forehead.

KARI. You must not make me out braver than I am. Part of my courage is recklessness. I close my eyes and let the sun shine on my face.

HALLA. Do you never think of the future?

KARI [*earnestly*]. I do.

HALLA. I have blamed myself much these last days. I ought to have sent you away long ago, but I could not. I had to be sure that you loved me. Last night I heard the hills calling you, and I called against them with all my soul. If you had never come back, I would have forgiven you, though it had broken my heart. [*Exultantly.*] And then I saw you coming down the mountain like a god, driving a white snowslide before you!

KARI. Did you think I could have gone without letting you know? I remember once you had fallen asleep in my arms. The night was light. Your eyes were closed, but I could see through your eyelids. I saw a little girl with black hair. [*Fondly stroking her hair.*]

HALLA [*taking his right hand*]. How well I know this hand! [*Lays it on her heart.*] My heart beats with joy.

KARI. I am like the man in the fairytale who fell down into a deep well. He thought he would never again see the sun, but suddenly he stood in a green meadow. There was a tall castle, and the king's daughter came out to meet him. Halla, do you understand? If I had not stolen, we two should never have met.

HALLA. That is true.

KARI. The year I lived in the hills, I would sometimes get into such a rage that I wanted to give myself a good thrashing. Once I really did it — I beat myself with a knotted rope.

HALLA. How you must have suffered!

KARI. If anybody had told me in those days that I should ever become a happy man, I would have laughed at him. Then I believed riches and honors meant happiness. I used to dream of riding through the parish where I was born, dressed in fine clothes and with many horses.

HALLA [*laughing*]. I did not know you were vain.

KARI. Nor am I any more, but I have grown stingy. The minutes are my goldpieces. [*Takes her hand.*] When I hold your hand in mine, I am happy. Before I cared for you, I did not see the sun shining, and now when it rains, all the drops prattle about you.

HALLA. You do love me!

KARI. I seem to be in a church. I hold a torch in my hand and light one taper after another. For every taper that is lighted, the church grows larger and more beautiful. But I am a thief. If I am caught I must be buried alive, and now the church-bells are ringing. I hear the crowd gathering outside.

HALLA. You frighten me.

KARI [*taking her face between his hands*]. I must have a long look at your face. If I were to become blind this moment, I should always remember it. Your soul is in your eyes. When you look at me, I feel an unseen hand fondling my face. Whenever the sun shines, I shall see your eyes. It is hard to tell you, but when the sky grows red to-morrow, I shall be on my way to the hills. I must flee this very night.

HALLA. I knew it. [*Sits down.*] Tell me how you have planned your flight.

KARI. I must be off before the winter sets in, and besides the letter from the south may be here any day now.

HALLA. I know all that.

KARI [*sits down*]. When I come home to-night, I shall say that I have seen the tracks of a flock of sheep farther up in the hills than we usually go to look for them. I shall ask you for two horses. You won't refuse me them? [HALLA *shakes her head.*] I shall say that I must start at once, this very night, before the tracks disappear. When I don't come back, they will think I have come across outlaws or have met with an accident.

HALLA. And where shall you go?

KARI. To the mountain plain where the warm springs are. I lived there before I came to you.

HALLA. How long will it take you to reach it?

KARI. Three days. It is about in the middle of the country.

HALLA. And there you will build your hut?

KARI. No; last time I lived in a lava cave. I had brought with me some tools that my brother gave me, and I left them there. Something told me that I might need them again. [*He is silent.*]

HALLA [*taking his hand*]. You must tell me more, much more. I want to see the place where you will live [*with a strange smile*], so that I can come and visit you in my thoughts.

KARI. I forget what I have told you and what I have not told you. You may think that the hills are wild and forbidding, but that is not so at all. In the summer, when the sun is shining, they are beautiful. The glaciers lie like white untrodden land in a sea of sand, their lower rim flashing green and blue in the sunlight. When you come nearer, you see a chain of jagged sandhills like a dark surf, where the glacier and the

sand waste meet. [*He is silent again.* HALLA *has picked a flower and is pulling its petals.*] Why are you doing that? What are you asking about?

HALLA. You love me!

KARI. Do you need to ask a flower about that? [*Rising.*] Are you not the least bit sorry that we must part?

HALLA [*rising*]. Would it make it easier for you if I were to whine and weep like a child?

KARI. I don't know. [*He is silent.*] Yet you need not pity me. I am rich — I am king of the hills! The fire on my hearth never dies, day or night. The country is mine, as far as my eyes can reach. Mine are the glaciers that make the streams! When I get angry, they swell, and the stones gnash their teeth against the current. And I own a whole lake with a fleet of ice-ships and a choir of swans.

HALLA. I never said that I pitied you.

KARI. But one thing you must promise me. You must not marry the bailiff.

HALLA. But, dear man ——

KARI. If you do, I shall come some night and kill you both, first him and then you.

HALLA. Are you really jealous of the bailiff? He hates me.

KARI. Why should he be hounding me like a wild beast, if it were not for your sake? I have never done him any harm.

HALLA. I promise you that I shall never marry the bailiff. [*Puts her arms around his neck and tries to draw him to her.*] Kiss me, Kari!

KARI [*gently pushing her away*]. My name is not Kari. From this day on my name is Eyvind — "Eyvind of the Hills," they call me in the southland, my brother told me.

HALLA. From my lips you shall never hear any other name than Kari. By that name I learned to love you. A man who is not loved has no name. [*Takes his hands.*]

KARI [*in a sudden outburst, drawing her to him and kissing her forehead*]. God bless you, Halla! [*With difficulty mastering his voice.*] Now I am going to the fold.
[*Turns away from* HALLA.]

HALLA [*calling*]. Kari! [KARI *turns*

back.] Must I ask you to marry me a second time? I thought we two were married.

KARI. So we are before God.

HALLA. So far as I know, it is the custom that when a man moves from one place to another, he takes his wife with him.

KARI. Do you think there is anything in the world I would rather do than live with you?

HALLA. Then ask me if I am willing.

KARI. Will you be my beloved wife and go with me through all suffering?

HALLA. I will!

KARI. Will you take upon yourself half of my guilt and become an outcast like me?

HALLA [*exultantly*]. I will!

KARI. Will you face hunger and cold and all terrors for my sake?

HALLA. Have you not always known that I would go with you? Could you believe me so low that I would keep you here with this dread hanging over you, if I had not meant to go with you? Every night I thought: To-morrow he will ask if you will go with him.

KARI. How beautiful you are! All the days we have had together live in your face!

HALLA. Did you believe I could rest satisfied in thinking of you with the mountains between us? Then you don't know me yet. I will live! I will sail with you in your white ships!

[*Enter* BJØRN.]

BJØRN. Good day to you, Halla. I looked for you at the fold. It is a long time since we two neighbors have met.

HALLA [*confused*]. Yes, it is a long time.

BJØRN. Who sees to it that your sheep are taken out of the fold? Your cots seem to be standing empty.

HALLA. Kari attends to that.

BJØRN. Then it is time you sent him about his work.

KARI. Perhaps the bailiff has come to lend a hand?

BJØRN [*to* HALLA]. I should like to have a few words with you.

HALLA. We were just starting for the fold. Perhaps we could have our talk on the way up.

BJØRN. If it is the same to you, I prefer to stay here. It is a matter of some weight, which I do not care to discuss in the presence of your overseer or any one but yourself.

HALLA [*to* KARI]. Then you had better go up to the fold.

KARI. Don't forget to ask the bailiff if it is true that he has been rubbing his knee-joints with fat every night the whole summer through. [*Exit.*]

BJØRN. He's bold enough, that fellow. It is well we shall soon be rid of him.

HALLA [*roused*]. And what was it you wanted to see me about?

BJØRN. We were both somewhat angry when we met last. Shall we let it be forgotten?

HALLA [*relieved*]. I thought perhaps you had got your letter from the southland with the proofs that you had been wrong in your suspicions.

BJØRN. Everything in good time. Did you say anything to him?

HALLA. I told you I wouldn't.

BJØRN. I might have known that, since he is still here. Do you think I am beginning to look old?

HALLA [*amazed*]. To me you look as you have always looked. [*Watches him keenly.*]

BJØRN. I admit you were right in some of the things you said to me when we met last, but we all have our failings, and since my mother died I have had no one who dared to speak plainly to me except you.

HALLA. You may not often have wished to listen to others.

BJØRN. Perhaps you are right, but somehow there must be two different souls in every one of us.

HALLA. Have you had a good hay crop this summer?

BJØRN. Fairly good. At least I have enough for myself. Don't you understand what I want to say to you, or don't you want to understand?

HALLA. You said that it was a matter of weight. That is all I know.

BJØRN. I am not skilled in fine words. Could you think of becoming my wife?

[HALLA *laughs.* BJØRN *flushes.*] Is that so laughable?

HALLA. You can't be in earnest.

BJØRN. In dead earnest. I shall soon be forty-eight years old, but you are not a child any longer either, and we are of equal standing. If we two marry and make our farms into one, I think we should have to look outside of this parish for a finer property.

HALLA. So we two should marry in order to join our farms?

BJØRN. I will not deny that I should like to see the boundary line gone between the two farms, but that is not the reason why I have made up my mind to ask you to marry me. It is not good for a man to be alone, and you are the only woman in this parish whom I could think of taking for a wife. You are healthy and strong of body, and you are good-looking. What answer do you give?

HALLA. I must have some time to think it over. This comes upon me unawares. Within three days you shall have my answer. Are you satisfied with that?

BJØRN. I think it is but natural that you should want some time to make up your mind, and all the more as we have not always been the best of friends. Perhaps you will now more readily understand why I did not wish you to have a thief as overseer of your farm, and I am sorry to say that my distrust was well founded. [*Pulls from his pocket a letter with a large seal.*] This letter came yesterday.

HALLA [*holding out her hand*]. May I see it?

BJØRN. It is an official letter, which I do not like to give out of my hands, but I am not afraid to trust you with it. [HALLA *takes the letter; reads.*] I can lend you one of my men to drive your sheep home this evening, for you will have to do without your overseer. It is lucky that the judge is here to-day.

HALLA. I shall keep this letter.

BJØRN. I can understand a joke.

HALLA. Kari has been with me for more than a year. He has been a hard worker and an able man. I will not have any one lay hands on him so long as he is in my service. I want to give him a chance to get away. That is what you yourself advised, three months ago.

BJØRN. At that time the case was very different. There was no proof of his guilt then.

HALLA [*putting her hand to her forehead*]. I can't believe yet that he is a thief. [*Hands the letter to* BJØRN.] Bjørn, I beg of you to show me a great favor. You must let this matter rest, till we get home.

BJØRN. In that I cannot serve you.

HALLA. Perhaps I can do something for you in return.

BJØRN. I don't understand how you can pity a felon and a thief.

HALLA. Nor do I understand it myself, but somehow I do. You have just asked me if I would be your wife. Surely you will grant me the first thing I ask of you!

BJØRN. One would think you were pleading for your best friend.

HALLA. I may have cared more for him than I knew myself. If you will let him get away, I shall have no objection to making our two farms into one.

BJØRN. I never thought your overseer would be the means of my getting you for a wife, but I yield on those terms. Once we are married, you will surely forget him. But he must be gone from here within twenty-four hours, and I want you to know that if he ever shows himself in these parts again, he will have to take his punishment.

HALLA. You need have no fear that he will ever come back here.

BJØRN. Then let us forget all about him. You have saved him from jail for a time, but he's sure to end there any way. [*Goes to her.*] Who would have thought that you should become my little wife! [*Tries to put his arm around her waist.*]

HALLA [*draws back*]. So many things happen that we do not look for.

[*Enter* KARI.]

BJØRN. You are just in time. It will surely please you to hear that your mistress is to marry me within a short time.

KARI [*turning to* HALLA]. What does this mean?

BJØRN [*laughing*]. You hadn't expected

this. [*Goes to* HALLA.] My sweetheart might give me a kiss.

HALLA [*warding him off*]. No, no!

KARI [*grasping* BJØRN'S *arm*]. That man lies! She is mine. [*To* HALLA.] If you two get married to-morrow, still you are mine.

BJØRN. Has my brother's wife become a harlot? [*Exit.*]

HALLA. What have you done, Kari? It was to save you I promised to be his wife. I hoped to get a chance to speak to you. He has the letter and is going to give you up to the judge to-day.

KARI. I could not bear that man to touch you.

HALLA. You must run for the horses and flee!

KARI. That would be madness. The others have just as good horses. We must take what comes. I shall deny every-thing.

HALLA. What good would that do? It is impossible to mistake the description. I have read it myself.

KARI. Did you really mean to marry the bailiff to save my life?

HALLA. I lied to him, so that I could flee with you. I hate him.

KARI. I love you, Halla.

HALLA [*in rising fear*]. What shall we do? [*Wrings her hands.*] It is all my fault for holding you back. [*On the point of weeping.*] I am an unhappy woman.

KARI. You must not cry. Even if I faced the death warrant, I should not be sorry that I stayed. [*Kisses her hands.*] These summer days we have had together — in all eternity no one can take them from us.

HALLA [*withdraws her hands excitedly*]. Don't you know of any way? Say that the bailiff is your enemy and has had the letter framed up.

KARI. You know yourself that it would be no use. [*Goes to her.*] I believe it is God's will that you should not flee with me. I have told you how beautiful it can be in the hills, but all the terrors I have not told you of — the sand-storms, when the whole plain seems to be on fire, the nights as long as a whole winter, and the hunger stealing

close to you like an evil mist. You might have come to hate me.

HALLA. I will hear nothing of all that. [*Under her breath in terror.*] They are coming!

[*Enter* BJØRN *and the* DISTRICT JUDGE, *followed by a crowd of peasants and farm hands. Others come in as the action proceeds.*]

BJØRN [*pointing*]. There stands the man.

THE JUDGE [*goes to* KARI]. You say your name is Kari. [*Shows the letter.*] According to this letter, your name is Eyvind, and you are an escaped thief.

KARI. That is a lie.

BJØRN. Read the letter.

[*The* JUDGE *gives him a sharp look. He opens the letter and reads to himself, now and then raising his eyes from the letter to* KARI'S *face.*]

A PEASANT [*in a low voice*]. What does the judge say?

BJØRN. In the early spring, a man came here who knew him [*pointing*] as an escaped thief. I wrote to have the case looked up, and yesterday I got the answer.

THE JUDGE. The description fits you. It is my duty under the law to take you into custody.

[*Murmuring among the peasants.*]

FIRST PEASANT. I never should have believed it.

KARI. It is the bailiff to whom this letter was sent. May I be allowed to ask where it came from?

BJØRN. From the southland where you were born.

KARI. I was born in the east and have never been south.

BJØRN. Will the judge look at the seal?

THE JUDGE. The seal is correct. [*To* HALLA.] He is in your service. Have you found this man to be a thief?

HALLA. No. He has shown himself a trustworthy and an able man. [*To the people.*] Don't you believe, as I do, that Kari is innocent?

THE CROWD [*murmuring*]. Yes, yes!

THE JUDGE. I cannot judge this case. I must send him to the district where Eyvind's home is. [*To* HALLA.] Can you vouch for him a few days? At present I cannot well spare two men for the journey.

HALLA. I am not afraid to do that.

BJØRN. It seems to me unwise to set a woman to watch a thief. If the judge wishes it, I will take him into safe-keeping myself.

HALLA. Does the bailiff think he can give counsel to the judge? I offer my farm as surety for Kari.

THE JUDGE [interrupting BJØRN, who is about to reply]. Silence! [To HALLA.] Then you are responsible. [Exit.]

BJØRN. I must say that the former judge was not wont to delay the law.

HALLA [to the peasants]. You came here to listen to false charges, but you shall have a better pastime. You shall see the bailiff himself play at glima with the man he calls thief.

BJØRN. You must be crazy! I won't touch him.

HALLA. My dear brother-in-law made me a promise last spring that he would wrestle with Kari here at the folds. It was a wager, and now he is backing out of it. What do you say to that?

BJØRN. An honest man does not play with a thief.

HALLA. He is no more thief than you are. Should you be a thief, because I said so? [To the people.] He is only too glad to get out of the glima. He is a coward! He is a coward!

[Loud or suppressed laughter all around.]

BJØRN. Never before has Bjørn Bergsteinsson been called a coward.

[Takes off his coat.]
[KARI throws off his coat. The crowd draws back, leaving an open space. The glima begins. BJØRN pushes KARI out to the back, and the people follow. The heads of the wrestlers are seen; then they disappear to the left. A moment of silence, then a sudden outcry.]

ALL. Kari has won! Kari has won! [Silence again.] Bjørn is hurt!

[Exeunt some of the crowd.]

KARI. I think he has had enough.
[Goes to HALLA.]

A PEASANT. Bjørn had his leg broken. We must help him.

JON. I told them to look out for the rocks.

HALLA. It was the bailiff who drew Kari out on the rocks.

[Exeunt the rest of the peasants.]

BJØRN [his voice is heard, threatening]. You shall pay me back for this, Halla!

ARNES. I am glad he got it.

ARNGRIM. "Hard upon hard," said the old woman; she sat down on a stone.

THE BOY [goes to KARI, almost weeping]. You are not a thief!

KARI [patting him on the head]. No, no!

HALLA [to ARNES]. Will you do me the favor to see that my sheep are driven home to-night? I don't want Kari to stay here any longer.

ARNES. I will do it gladly. [To KARI.] I meant to warn you against what has overtaken you now.

KARI. I know it. You meant well.

THE BOY. May I go home with Kari?

HALLA. No, you must stay here and help Arnes. I will go home with Kari myself. [Laughs.] You know I must watch my prisoner. You may bring the horses, the black and the sorrel. [Exit the BOY.]

GUDFINNA. Why all this hurry?

HALLA [goes to her]. You always had a liking for the little box where my husband kept his money. When we get home, I want you to have that box and all that is in it.

GUDFINNA. But you keep your own money there!

HALLA. Not all. I meant to buy quite a number of sheep here to-day.

GUDFINNA [on her way out]. I must be getting old. I don't understand anything any more.

HALLA. You need not tell them up at the folds that I am going home.

GUDFINNA [taking HALLA's hand]. God bless you! [Her voice breaks. Exit.]

ARNES [to ARNGRIM]. We had better be off, too.

ARNGRIM [goes to KARI]. If you should happen to ride astray, take care you don't lose her in the mist. [Exeunt.]

KARI [to HALLA]. What do you mean by riding home now?

HALLA. Thank God, we have good horses! The folks won't get home with the sheep before nightfall, and they will not begin to look for us until to-morrow. By that time we shall have a good start.

KARI. You must not flee with me, Halla. You don't know the life you are going to.

HALLA. You are a great child. Don't you think that I have weighed it all? [Smiles.] If you won't let me come and live with you, I will marry the bailiff.

KARI [kneeling before her]. Halla!

HALLA [stands for a moment in silence; takes a long breath]. To-night we two shall ride alone in the hills!

ACT III

A small grass-grown plot. In the foreground, to the right, a fantastic lava formation, a hollow cone five yards in height and three yards in circumference, once an enormous lava bubble produced by gases in the liquid lava. In course of time, the roof has crumbled, also the nearest wall. The farther wall is still standing, but there is a hole in it, through which the sky can be seen. Farther back and somewhat to the left, the wall of a small hut is seen, though partly hidden by the lava formation. The hut is built of stone, the walls of small stones chinked with sod, the roof of large lava slabs. To the left, a deep gorge, the farther wall of which is so much higher than the one near by that it completely shuts off the view to the left. At the bottom of the gorge, a stream. Farther up, the gorge makes a turn to the left, and here the upper part of a waterfall is seen. Behind this, the glacier. On the grass plot is a hearth with a smouldering fire. Some rocks covered with skins serve as seats. From the gorge comes the murmuring sound of the waterfall.

The stage is empty. A horn is heard, first a short call, then a longer.

[Enter KARI and ARNES. They are weatherbeaten, bareheaded, dressed in knitted jerkins and knitted knee-breeches. Their feet are bare in their shoes. Both have ram's horns hanging at their side. KARI carries a swan, ARNES a bunch of ptarmigans, some fagots, and a few tufts of bearberry.]

KARI [looking into the hut]. Halla! No, she is not here.

ARNES. She may have gone for water.

KARI [lays down the swan]. It is quite heavy.

ARNES. You might have let me carry it. I had not tired myself with running.

KARI. As I had caught it, I wanted to carry it. [Smiles.] The old pride, you see.

ARNES. The honor would have been yours just the same.

KARI. This is the first swan this fall. [Stroking it fondly.] I am glad the feathers didn't get blood-stained.

ARNES. It would be lonesome up here if we were only two.

KARI. Indeed it would, but you have tried the loneliness before. Was it not two years you had been alone before you met us?

ARNES. Two and a half.

KARI [pleased]. Do you know what we'll do? We'll hide the swan and say that we've come home empty-handed. [Takes the swan.] Hand me the ptarmigans. [Hides them behind the hut.] Now I wish Halla would come soon.

[Walks to the back and blows his horn.]

HALLA [is heard answering]. Hello!

KARI. Here she comes.

ARNES. You are a happy mortal.

KARI. Yes, I am happy, and it is good to be here. We are free. We have enough to eat. We have sunshine, water, and shelter. What more do you want? [ARNES is silent.] I know you are brooding over something you don't want to tell me. You seem more gloomy every day. Are you longing to get away from here?

ARNES. Don't let us talk about such things to-day.

KARI. Perhaps it would do you good to unburden yourself to me or, better still, to Halla. She is wiser than I am, and she cares a good deal for you, I tell you.

ARNES. There are not many like Halla.

KARI [hastily]. We won't tell Halla about the mist. It might frighten her.

ARNES. I'll hold my peace.

[*Enter* HALLA, *carrying a pail of water. The pail is of plaited willow twigs chinked with clay. With the other hand she leads a little girl about three years old.* HALLA *is dressed in a white jerkin and black skirt, both of knitted wool. She wears her silver girdle around her waist. The child has on white knitted clothes. They are bareheaded, and their foot-wear is the same as that worn by the men.*]

HALLA. Did you have good luck to-day?

KARI [*dolefully*]. We have caught nothing but trouble and weariness. The ptarmigans made themselves scarce to-day. We saw a flock of six, but they flew away before we could get our snares out.

HALLA [*to* ARNES]. Is it true, what he says?

ARNES. It's true enough. We saw six ptarmigans, but they got away from us.

HALLA. I am sorry. We must hope for better luck next time.

KARI [*laughing*]. I fooled you that time! [*Runs toward the hut.*] Look here! Five big, fat ptarmigans!

HALLA. Well, well!

KARI [*holding up the swan*]. And that's all.

HALLA. What a lovely surprise! How did you catch it?

KARI. I ran it down.

ARNES. I don't believe there are many who can beat him at that. I know I can't.

TOTA. May Tota pat it?

HALLA. Tota may do anything she wants to. I should like to make you a jacket of swan's down.

KARI [*cuts off the feet of the swan*]. You would like these, wouldn't you?

TOTA. Yes.

KARI. Some day when I have time I will skin them and make little bags for you to keep your pebbles in.

HALLA. You've got lovely playthings there! [*Squats down on the ground.*] Where are mother's eyes?

[*Hiding her eyes with the swan's feet.*]

TOTA [*takes them away from her eyes*]. Here!

HALLA [*rising*]. Did you eat all your food?

KARI. Every bite.

HALLA. Then you can't be hungry.

KARI. No.

HALLA. And it is too early for the evening meal, but I can make you some tea.

KARI. Yes, do. [*To* ARNES.] Let us carry the swan to the cave.

[*Exeunt* KARI *and* ARNES.]

HALLA. Now Tota must be tied, so the waterfall can't take her, while mother is making tea. [*Takes a rope that is fastened to a rock and ties it around* TOTA'S *waist. Brings some of her playthings.*] Here are all your horses.

[*Puts a kettle of water over the fire; places some earthenware cups on the rocks by the hearth; takes a handful of dried herbs from a bag, rinses them in cold water, and portions them out in the cups. The fagots* ARNES *has brought, she throws on the fire. As she works, she sings.*]

Have you seen a brave young lad?
'Tis my friend,
Dearest friend;
'Mongst all men in byrnie clad
The bonniest is he.
I have smiled my teeth all white and shining,
I have smiled my teeth all white and shining with glee.
Have you heard his voice's call,
Call of love,
Song of love?
O'er my heart the sound did fall
And hushed its quick desire.
He has kissed my lips all red and glowing,
He has kissed my lips all red and glowing as fire.

There! Now we must get the water to boil. [*Picks up the tufts of bearberry and goes to* TOTA.] See what Arnes brought you!

TOTA. They are berries.

HALLA. Yes, but you must not eat them or you will get a pain in your little stomach. [*Rises and finds a long, stiff straw.*] Now I'll show you what you can do. [*Threading the berries on the straw, she counts.*] One, two — four — six, seven — so many years your father and mother have been in the hills. [*Strokes* TOTA'S *hair.*] When you are sixteen, we shall have lived here for twenty years, and then we shall be free again. On that day, Tota shall wear snow-white clothes and shoes of colored leather, and mother will clasp her silver girdle around your waist. And when we come down to the lowlands, the first one we meet is a young man with silver buttons in his coat. He stops and turns his horse and stands looking after you ever so long. Then your mother has grown old and wrinkled, and her hair is almost as white as snow. Your father, too, has grown old. But you are straight as a silver weed, and when you run, you lift your feet high!

[*Enter* KARI *and* ARNES.]

KARI [*laughing*]. Ah, now it's steaming. I nearly fell headlong into the cave, when we lifted the cover from the entrance.

HALLA. Did you? [*Gives the straw to* TOTA.] Now you can go on by yourself. [*Rises.*] Is there any need of closing the cave every time? When it's not raining, it might be left open.

KARI. No harm in being careful. If they should come upon us suddenly, we surely should not have time to close the entrance, and they would find the cave and destroy all our stores, as they did five years ago. Do you remember when we came back to the old place and found nothing but ashes? — and winter setting in. Not a single piece of mutton did they leave us.

HALLA. I don't easily forget.

KARI. Whenever I think of it, I feel like doing something wicked. After all, we are human too.

HALLA [*laughing coldly*]. We're only the foxes who take their sheep.

KARI [*to* ARNES]. How did you hide your stores when you were alone?

ARNES. I had many hiding-places. Once I stole some twenty-eight pounds of butter. I stuffed it down into a fissure in a rock.

KARI. That was pretty shrewd.

[*They are silent.*]

HALLA. Did you have a clear outlook from the mountain this afternoon?

KARI. Yes. There was a little mist far to the southward.

HALLA. It was from the south that the cloud came in my dream.

KARI. You can never forget about that dream.

HALLA. I counted fourteen men who came riding out of the cloud. [*Silent for a moment.*] You are quite sure the two men whose tracks you saw a month ago did not get on our trail?

KARI. Quite sure. If they had, they would have come closer.

HALLA. Just think if they had seen smoke and told about it down in the parish!

KARI. They have done nothing of the kind; for if they had, they would have been up here with many men long ago. Ah, the water is boiling.

[HALLA *lifts the kettle from the fire and pours water over the herbs.*]

KARI. Your tea will soon be giving out.

HALLA. Yes, I must take a day and gather enough for the winter. I will go down to the Sun Valley. Nowhere else are the herbs so fine. [*They drink their tea.*]

KARI. Don't forget to lay in a store of herbs for your salve. You know how troublesome a little scratch can be, when the cold gets into it. You kept the honey I found?

HALLA. I did.

KARI. That is good for wounds, too. And you must gather cotton grass for lamp wicks. [*Goes to* TOTA *and gives her tea.*] Tota must have a taste, too.

ARNES [*has been looking at* HALLA]. Your hair was quite black before, but now there has come a sheen of red into it.

KARI. I have not noticed it, but your freckles are all gone, I have seen that. [*Patting her cheek.*] Are you going to give us more tea?

HALLA. As much as you want.

KARI [*rises and goes into the hut; returns with three wooden pipes and two pouches, one large and one small*]. You need not be saving of the leaves, but the tobacco I shall have to dole out to you.

[*They fill their pipes.*]

HALLA [*smiling*]. It was foolish of you to teach me to smoke.

KARI. Why shouldn't you have that

boon as well as I? [*Shakes his bag.*] You need not be shy, I have more in the cave, and when winter sets in and the snow is fit for skiing, we'll take Arnes down to my brother's. He promised to lay in good stores of tobacco and salt, and I will pay him with wool, as I did last time.

HALLA. If only you don't end by being caught on one of those journeys!

KARI. Never! [*They sit smoking in silence.*] Now I am just in the mood to listen to a good story. Have you one to tell us?

ARNES [*rising*]. No, I have not.

[*Goes toward the gorge.*]

KARI. It does not matter if you have told it before.

HALLA. Arnes may be saving them for the winter.

KARI [*rises; lays down his pipe*]. Do you know what you should do? Have a good talk with Arnes. I believe he is getting restless and thinks of leaving us.

HALLA. I hope not.

KARI. I will go and take a bath. You can speak better to him alone, and I need to wash off the sweat.

[*Sings on his way out.*]

Far in the hills I wandered; softly shone the summer night,
And the sun had ne'er a thought of sleeping.
Now will I bring my sweetheart dear the hidden treasure bright,
For faithfully my vows I would be keeping.
Heigh, ho!
New and fine my stockings are, new and fine my shoes,
And not a care in all the world to plague me!

HALLA [*sits silent*]. Is time hanging heavy on you up here?

ARNES [*goes to her*]. No, that is only something Kari was got into his head, because I am not always merry.

HALLA [*smiling*]. Once you boasted of being kin to the trolls.

ARNES. So I am. [HALLA *rises; blows a great puff of smoke into his face; laughs.* ARNES *takes hold of her wrists.*] Once there were two trolls. They quarrelled and turned each other into stone. One had to stand where all the birds dropped their filth, and the other had to stand where all

the winds blew. Which would you rather be?

HALLA [*tears herself away*]. I have not been turned to stone yet. [*Laughs.*] I thought you had forgotten all your old stories.

ARNES. You are strong.

HALLA [*sits down on the grass, leaning on her arm*]. Can you foretell things from the clouds?

ARNES. Yes, about the weather.

HALLA. I don't mean that.

ARNES [*sits down beside her*]. When I was a child, I used to sail my viking ships on the clouds. Do you want me to foretell your fate?

HALLA. You just said that you could not.

ARNES. The clouds tell nothing about our lives. They are only the dreamlands of earth. Will you let me see your arm?

HALLA. Why?

ARNES [*lifts her arm*]. You think these lines on your arm are nothing but marks drawn by heather and grass, but if I knew enough, I could read your whole fate in them. Something, perhaps, I can see. Who would believe that these slender arms could be so strong.

HALLA [*laughing*]. And what stands written there?

ARNES. You must sit still. Here is a deep, narrow line across your arm, that means sorrow. And there is a big fire. [*Stroking her arm with the tips of his fingers.*] I can see the tongues of flame. That means that you are loved.

[*Kisses her arm.*]

HALLA [*stands up; laughs*]. Did you burn yourself?

ARNES. I should like to read your fate all day long.

HALLA. Then you might tell me things I did not care to hear. But I must get to work.

[HALLA *goes into the hut.* ARNES *looks after her. She comes out bringing wool, a spindle, and a sheep's skin.*]

HALLA. If you are not too tired after the hunt, this skin can stand a little more.

ARNES. Give it to me.

[*Takes a large ring made of a ram's*

horn. From the ring hangs a loop of rope, in which he puts his foot. He draws the skin through the ring and keeps pulling it back and forth. HALLA sits down, turning her spindle. They are silent.]

HALLA. It is queer about the sound of the waterfall. Most of the time I don't hear it at all, but if it were to stop, I should miss it. Is it the same with you?

ARNES. Yes.

HALLA. At first I was almost afraid of it. Then I began to love it, and now I should only miss it if it were not there any more. We mortals are strange.

[*They are silent again.*]

ARNES. Can you tell me why some people should be happier than others?

HALLA. No, that I cannot.

ARNES. Kari has been happy for seven years.

HALLA. Are you sure of that?

ARNES. Why should he not be happy? He has a wife and child.

HALLA. Was there no one down your way whom you could bring with you up here?

ARNES. Who do you think would become an outlaw for my sake?

HALLA. Wouldn't you dare to carry off a woman? I should try my best to be good to her.

ARNES. Do you think Kari would have dared to carry you off against your will?

HALLA. Ask him.

ARNES. Why does he not show it, if he cares so much for you? He forgets about helping you with firewood and carrying water, and if the meat is not cooked the way he likes it, he scolds you. One might think you were his servant girl.

HALLA. Don't let that worry you.

ARNES. And he can't even see the color of your hair.

HALLA. Do you bear a grudge against Kari, because he caught the swan?

ARNES. You had house and home and a good name, and you gave it all up for his sake. He ought to keep that in mind more than he does.

HALLA. I don't want Kari to be offering

up thanks like a meek bondsman. Besides, I have done nothing for him. I did it all for myself.

ARNES. He does not even bother to curry the skins for your bedding. If you did not have me, you would have to do it yourself.

HALLA [*stands up*]. I don't want your help. [*Takes hold of the skin.*] Let go!

ARNES [*gives it up reluctantly*]. Are you angry?

HALLA [*takes the skin out of the horn-ring and throws it into the hut*]. You are not so sorely needed as you think you are.

[*Sits down again to her work.*]

ARNES. I did not mean that. It makes me happy when I can do some little thing for you. Won't you let me finish it?

HALLA. You shall not touch it.

ARNES [*stands for a moment, puzzled*]. Will you not forgive me what I said? I cannot bear to have you angry with me.

HALLA. I am not angry.

ARNES. When you were ill, I once brought you some green leaves that had come up through the snow. Then you gave me a kiss.

HALLA. Did I? [*Smiles; kisses him lightly on the cheek.*] Have you peace in your soul now?

ARNES. I don't know. I believe I shall never have peace in my soul any more.

[*They are silent.*]

HALLA. You were good to me the time I was ill.

ARNES. I am not good to anybody. I am wicked.

HALLA. You are not.

ARNES. Even with you I sometimes feel that I could hurt you.

HALLA. We can all be ugly when we are tired and hungry.

ARNES. Will you let me kiss your mouth? Just once?

HALLA [*rising*]. No.

ARNES. Your lips will suffer no harm from it.

[*Takes hold of her shoulders and tries to draw her to him.*]

HALLA [*tears herself away from him*]. Have you gone mad?

ARNES. You have been true to Kari for seven years now. It is time you tired of it.

HALLA. Now your face looks like the bailiff's when he called me a harlot.

[*Gives him a box on the ear.*]

ARNES [*furiously*]. I know you better than you think. You are so pure! You have never done an evil deed!

HALLA. What do you mean?

ARNES. Kari is more open-mouthed than you think. You have had a child before this one.

[HALLA *shields her face with her hands as though warding off a blow.* ARNES *sits silent.*]

HALLA. Why don't you say that I killed my child? That is what you meant to say. You know I did it.

ARNES. My cursed mouth.

HALLA. You judge me. How can you? You don't know what it means to bring a life into the world. It grows heavier day by day like the snow of winter. If we had had spring and sunshine! But the times were hard and food was scarce. I did a good deed when I laid my child out in the cold. Far less suffering that than life!

ARNES. I do not judge what you did.

HALLA. No, you thought I was an angel who was longing to be your harlot. You can go with a lighted candle into my soul and search it. You will find no remorse there. What could we have done with a child, if we had been forced to flee? Should we have left it with strangers? And how do you think it would have fared? A child of felons, scorned by all!

ARNES [*broken-hearted*]. I did not know that my words would hurt you so much.

HALLA. Do you think I did it with a light heart? I have given birth to two children, and cruel was the pain, but I would rather bear ten children than live that night over again. When I had carried my child out into the cold, my mind gave way. In my ravings, I thought the child lay by my side, and above us was a flock of birds — pitch black. I bent over it to shield it, and the birds pecked into my back, into my lungs they pecked.

[*Stops short from emotion.*]

ARNES. Would I were dead!

HALLA [*calmer*]. I wished for the death of that child long before it was born.

[*Goes to* TOTA.] But this my little springtime child I have never wished ill. The first time I felt her life, it seemed a token of forgiveness that I was allowed to become a mother again, and when she came into the world, the sun was shining, and the sky was blue and warm. [*Kisses her.*]

ARNES. My tongue got the better of me. [*Puts his hand on his heart.*] There is a devil dwelling in me. [*Stands motionless.*] I love you.

HALLA [*turns toward him*]. Have you not done hurting me yet?

ARNES [*crushed*]. No matter what I say, you think I mean ill.

HALLA. I shall not speak to you again.

[*Sits down to her work.*]

ARNES. Nor will you have to listen to me any more. I am going down to the lowlands, and there they can do with me what they like.

HALLA. If you tell them of our hiding-place, they may let you off more easily.

ARNES. Even that you believe I could do!

HALLA [*rising*]. If you cared for me as much as you say, you would be good to me instead of bad.

ARNES. Love has made you good and me bad. [*He is silent.*] Do you remember the time Kari and I went up the glacier, and he fell down into a crack? He told you I had been so frightened that I shook all over. It was not for his life I feared; I feared my own thoughts.

HALLA [*terrified by a dawning apprehension*]. What do you mean?

ARNES. I have often wished Kari dead.

HALLA. It is not true!

ARNES. It is. Do you understand now that I must go away from here? I no longer dare to live with you two, and neither do I dare to live alone.

HALLA. I wish you had never crossed our path.

ARNES [*following up his own thoughts*]. If Kari had not been so trusting as he is, I don't know what I might not have done; but he had such faith in me. You don't know all the words the Tempter can whisper in one's ear. I thought Kari had been happy so long that it would be only